Tort

Other Titles in the Textbook Series

Cretney's Family Law
Employment Law
Environment Law
Equity & Trust
Criminal Law
Land Law
Public Law
Contract

BPP Professional Education
32-34 Colmore Circus
Birmingham B4 6BN
Phone: 0121 345 9843

D1388734

BPP University

133355

Tort

SEVENTH EDITION

by
Paula Giliker, M.A. (Oxon.), B.C.L., Ph.D. (Cantab.)
Barrister, Professor of Law, University of Bristol

SWEET & MAXWELL
LONDON • 2020

First edition   (2000)
Second edition   (2004)
Third edition   (2008)
Fourth edition   (2011)
Fifth edition   (2014)
Sixth edition   (2017)
Seventh edition   (2020)

Published in 2020 by
Thomson Reuters,
trading as Sweet & Maxwell.
Registered in England & Wales, Company No.1679046.
Registered Office and address for service:
5 Canada Square, Canary Wharf, London, E14 5AQ.

Typeset by Servis Filmsetting Ltd, Stockport, Cheshire
Printed and bound by CPI Group (UK) Ltd, Croydon, CR0 4YY
For further information on our products and services,
visit www.sweetandmaxwell.co.uk

No natural forests were destroyed to make this product;
only farmed timber was used and re-planted.
A CIP catalogue record for this book is available from the British Library.

ISBN (print): 978-0-414-07775-1
ISBN (proview): 978-0-414-07779-9
ISBN (print and proview): 978-0-414-07777-5
ISBN (e-book): 978-0-414-07778-2

Dedication

To my family

Guide to the Book

Table of Contents

The Table of Contents provides you with an at a glance overview of the coverage for each chapter.

Table of Cases

The Table of Cases provides you with a handy list of all cases referred to througout this book.

Table of Statutes

The Table of Statutes provides you a handy list of all statutes referred to throughout this book.

Key Cases

All cases are highlighted making your research of the subject easier.

The Common Law Position

9–003 Prior to *Donoghue v Stevenson*, tort law provided little assistance to persons injured by a defective product. Most claimants were forced to rely on contract law, provided, of course, that they could establish the necessary contractual relationship. There are a number of benefits in bringing a contractual claim. First, the claimant is not required to show the fault of the seller, but simply that the seller is in breach of a term of the contract. The seller is therefore strictly liable for his or her breach. Secondly, contract law has no problem in awarding compensation for personal injury and property damage caused by the supply of a defective product[2] and will also award compensation for the cost of replacing the defective product itself. The buyer's position is further improved by the existence of implied terms. For example, under the Sale of Goods Act 1979, it is implied that, where the seller sells the goods in the course of a business, the goods must be of satisfactory quality[3] and be fit for their purpose.[4] On this basis, the buyer can sue for breach of contract if the goods fail to satisfy these terms.

There are, however, a number of disadvantages in bringing a claim in contract law. First, there must be a term (express or implied) in the contract which provides that the product should not be defective. Secondly, subject to the provisions of the Contract (Rights of Third Parties) Act 1999,[5] the rules of privity of contract only allow the parties to the contract to take

---

Note to Sweet & Maxwell: The Guide to the Book section in this and other titles has, as far as we aware, always been on a spread due to its nature, i.e. verso and recto — Servis (we can change if you want)

Key Extracts

Key extracts are boxed throughout to make them easily identifiable.

the manufacturer and the buyer will ultimately pass liability back up the chain to the manufacturer, this chain is easily broken, for example, by exclusion clauses or the insolvency of one of the parties. Liability may therefore fall arbitrarily on one party in the chain, regardless of the fact that the fault is solely that of the manufacturer.

As stated earlier, prior to 1932, tort law had a very limited application to defective products. A manufacturer would only be liable in tort if the product was classified as "dangerous" (for example, dynamite) or was actually known to the manufacturer to be dangerous, in which case he or she would then be obliged to warn the product's recipient of the danger. The distinction between "dangerous" and "non-dangerous" products was not particularly helpful and indeed made little sense. As Scrutton L.J. famously commented:

> "Personally, I do not understand the difference between a thing dangerous in itself, as poison, and a thing not dangerous as a class, but by negligent construction dangerous as a particular thing. The latter, if anything, seems the more dangerous of the two; it is a wolf in sheep's clothing instead of an obvious wolf".[7]

The courts' reluctance to adopt a general principle of negligence liability and their adherence to the "privity of contract fallacy" (by which the contract between the manufacturer and the retailer was deemed to obstruct any other form of liability in favour of third parties)[8] prevented the emergence of a general defective product action in tort.

In *Donoghue v Stevenson*,[9] the majority of the House of Lords overturned the questionable distinction between dangerous and non-dangerous chattels and discarded the "privity of contract fallacy". The court saw no reason why the same set of facts should not give one person a right in contract and another a concurrent right to sue in tort.[10] It will be recalled that the

---

the goods to reach the consumer intact. A reasonable possibility of intermediate examination would appear to exclude liability. Thirdly, the case deals with the manufacture of products and not with design. Design defects in products are of particular concern. Whereas a problem with manufacture may be limited to a particular batch, a design defect will affect many more products, thereby increasing the possibility of harm. We shall have to consider how *Donoghue v Stevenson*[13] applies to defects in design and what protection it gives to potential claimants.

The scope of *Donoghue v Stevenson*

9-004 The burden will be on the claimant to satisfy the ordinary rules of negligence, i.e. to establish a duty of care, breach, causation and remoteness. Their application to defective product claims will be discussed below.

The duty of care

9-005 This is the ordinary common law duty of care, discussed in Ch.2. It is not confined to the relationship between manufacturers and ultimate consumers. Makers of component parts, repairers, fitters, erectors, assemblers and even distributors may find themselves liable to the consumer for their failure to exercise reasonable care in dealing with a product. Equally, the range of claimants has extended beyond the ultimate consumer to parties coming into contact with the product. In *Stennett v Hancock and Peters*,[14] for example, a decision which followed shortly after *Donoghue*, the plaintiff suffered injury when part of a wheel from a passing lorry flew off and struck her on the leg. The lorry had recently been repaired by the second defend

Paragraph Numbering

Paragraph numbering helps you move between sections and references with ease.

Footnotes

Footnotes help minimise text distractions while providing access to relevant supplementary material.

The courts' reluctance to adopt a general principle of negligence liability and their adherence to the "privity of contract fallacy" (by which the contract between the manufacturer and the retailer was deemed to obstruct any other form of liability in favour of third parties)[8] prevented the emergence of a general defective product action in tort.

In *Donoghue v Stevenson*,[9] the majority of the House of Lords overturned the questionable distinction between dangerous and non-dangerous chattels and discarded the "privity of contract fallacy". The court saw no reason why the same set of facts should not give one person a right in contract and another a concurrent right to sue in tort.[10] It will be recalled that the case concerned the decomposed remains of snail, alleged to have been found in an opaque bottle of ginger beer that had been bought by Mrs Donoghue's friend. The existing rules of tort law seemed to preclude Mrs Donoghue's claim. A ginger beer bottle is not dangerous in itself and it was not known to contain a noxious substance. Mrs Donoghue had no contractual

answering a particular description s.1(1). These requirements will limit the number of possible claims under the Act.

6   Unless, of course, the purchaser sues for his or her own loss, which includes that arising from the injury of a third party. For example, in *Frost v Aylesbury Dairy* [1905] 1 K.B. 608, the purchaser sued to recover the expenses to which he had been put by the illness and death of his wife due to typhoid fever caught from the milk supplied by the defendants.

7   *Hodge & Sons v Anglo-American Oil Co* [1922] 12 Lloyd's Rep. 183 at 187.

8   See *Winterbottom v Wright* [1842] 10 M. & W. 109, 152 E.R. 402, discussed in Ch.2.

9   [1932] A.C. 562.

10 [1932] A.C. 562 per Lord Macmillan at 610.

Preface

This book is designed for readers approaching tort law for the first time. I have sought to set out clearly and succinctly the rules applicable to each tort and illustrate how they work in practice by reference to case law. Whilst the discussion of case law can by no means replace reading the cases themselves, I have set out the salient points to serve as an *aide mémoire* and to enable the reader to consider the law in a factual context. Similarly, I have outlined the main statutory provisions in this area of law and have sought to help the reader understand the wording and impact of these provisions.

The book has a traditional structure. The first chapter gives an overview of tort liability and considers its aims and objectives, the interests it seeks to protect, and its role in modern society. Chapters 2–6 examine the tort of negligence. Negligence is the most commonly used tort and forms an essential part of any tort law course. It is therefore considered in some detail and is divided into a number of issues which tend to be studied separately. Chapter 6 examines the law relating to causation. This is dealt with in the context of negligence, although it is relevant to all torts. The second half of the book deals with negligence-related liability, strict liability, and other torts. Chapter 7 explores tort liability arising in an employment relationship, whilst Ch.8 examines tort liability arising from occupation of premises. Chapter 9 considers two examples of strict liability statutes—the Consumer Protection Act 1987 and the Animals Act 1971—and their role within the law of tort. The book then deals with other torts, namely nuisance (and associated liability under the rule in *Rylands v Fletcher*), trespass, economic torts, defamation and privacy law. The final two chapters deal with the important subjects of defences and remedies.

No understanding of the law would be complete without an appreciation of the impact of government reforms and recent case law in the law of tort. This new edition examines the impact of the Civil Liability Act 2018 and key recent cases in the fields of negligence, notably in relation to duty of care where the Supreme Court has been very active (*Robinson v Chief Constable of West Yorkshire Police*,[1] *Darnley v Croydon Health Services NHS Trust*,[2] *James-Bowen v Commissioner of Police of the Metropolis*[3] and *Poole BC v GN*[4]), and pure economic loss (*Dryden v Johnson Matthey Plc*,[5] *Playboy Club London Ltd v Banca Nazionale del Lavoro SpA*[6] and *Steel v*

---

1 [2018] UKSC 4; [2018] A.C. 736.
2 [2018] UKSC 50; [2019] A.C. 831.
3 [2018] UKSC 40; [2018] 1 W.L.R. 4021.
4 [2019] UKSC 25; [2019] 2 W.L.R. 1478.
5 [2018] UKSC 18; [2019] A.C. 403.
6 [2018] UKSC 43; [2018] 1 W.L.R. 4041.

NRAM Ltd[7]). It also considers significant developments in the field of vicarious liability (*Armes v Nottinghamshire CC*,[8] *Barclays Bank Plc v Various Claimants*[9] and *WM Morrison Supermarkets Plc v Various Claimants*[10]), false imprisonment (*R. (Jalloh (formerly Jollah) v Secretary of State for the Home Department*[11]), defamation (*Lachaux v Independent Print Ltd*,[12] *Stocker v Stocker*[13] and *Economou v de Freitas*[14]), privacy (*Richard v BBC*[15]), defences (*Henderson v Dorset Healthcare University NHS Foundation Trust*[16]) and damages (*Whittington Hospital NHS Trust v XX*[17]).

In writing this book, I have received considerable support from my colleagues, friends and family, to whom I would like to express my thanks. I have also benefited from teaching students over a number of years at the University of Bristol. I would also like to thank all at Sweet and Maxwell, in particular Nicola Thurlow for her ongoing support and Keith and Jasper Syrett for their help and encouragement. I have attempted to state the law as it stood in April 2020.

Two final points on terminology. The Civil Procedure Rules came into force on 26 April 1999. Their aim is to speed up and simplify civil litigation. Accordingly, in an effort to demystify the law, the term "plaintiff" was replaced in 1999 by the term "claimant". The latter term is thus used when discussing principles of law and recent cases. The term "plaintiff", however, will be used when discussing cases decided prior to the date of the change. More recently in October 2009, the Supreme Court replaced the Appellate Committee of the House of Lords as the highest court in the UK. For cases decided after this date, the term "Supreme Court" will be used; prior to that date the text will refer to "the House of Lords". Both signify the highest court in the UK.

Paula Giliker
Bristol, April 2020.

---

7   [2018] UKSC 13; [2018] 1 W.L.R. 1190.
8   [2017] UKSC 60; [2018] A.C. 355.
9   [2020] UKSC 13; [2020] 2 W.L.R. 960, overturning [2018] EWCA Civ 1670.
10   [2020] UKSC 12; [2020] 2 W.L.R. 941, overturning [2018] EWCA Civ 2339.
11   [2020] UKSC 4; [2020] 2 W.LR. 418.
12   [2019] UKSC 27; [2020] A.C. 612.
13   [2019] UKSC 17; [2019] 2 W.L.R. 1033.
14   [2018] EWCA Civ 2591; [2019] E.M.L.R. 7.
15   [2018] EWHC 1837 (Ch); [2019] Ch 169.
16   [2018] EWCA Civ 1841; [2018] 3 W.L.R. 1651.
17   [2020] UKSC 14; [2020] 2 W.L.R. 972.

Acknowledgments

Grateful acknowledgment is made to the following authors and publishers for permission to quote from their works:

THE INCORPORATED COUNCIL OF LAW REPORTING FOR ENGLAND AND WALES: Law Reports and Weekly Law Reports.

We have also quoted from the following sources:

Published by Appellate Press:
  Lord Hoffmann, "Constitutionalism and private law" (2014–15) 6 UKSCY 177.

Published by Bloomsbury Professional, an imprint of Bloomsbury Publishing:
  M. A. Jones, (2007) 23 P.N. 238.
  P. Case, "Limitation periods and sexual abuse" (2009) 25 P.N. 22.

Published by Hart Publishing, an imprint of Bloomsbury Publishing:
  J. Wright, *Tort Law and Human Rights*, 2nd edn (Hart, 2017).

Published by *The Guardian*:
  J. Rozenberg, "The Supreme Court's ruling will be greeted with dismay at the MoD" *The Guardian*, 19 June 2013.

Published by Reed Elsevier (UK) Limited, trading as LexisNexis:
  Daborn v Bath Tramways Motor Co Ltd [1946] 2 All E.R. 333.
  A v National Blood Authority [2001] 3 All E.R. 289.

Published by Thomson Reuters, trading as Sweet & Maxwell:
  McHale v Watson (1966) 115 C.L.R. 119.
  Khatun v United Kingdom (38387/97) (1998) 26 E.H.R.R. CD 212.
  Osman v United Kingdom (1998) 29 E.H.R.R. 245.
  Von Hannover v Germany (59320/00) (2005) 40 E.H.R.R. 1.
  Kaye v Robertson [1991] F.S.R. 62.
  P. H. Winfield, "The history of negligence in the law of torts" (1926) 42 L.Q.R. 184.

Table of Contents

2   Negligence: The Duty of Care

3 Negligence: Economic Loss

4   Negligence: Psychiatric Illness

5 Negligence: Breach of Duty

6   Causation and Remoteness

7   Employers' Liability

8   Occupiers' Liability

9 Strict Liability Statutes

10 Nuisance and the Rule in *Rylands v Fletcher*

11   Trespass

12   The Economic Torts

13 Defamation

14 Defences to Defamation

15   Privacy (or Misuse of Private Information)

16   General Defences and Extinction of Liability

17   Remedies

Table of Cases

Table of Statutes

Table of Statutory Instruments

Table of European and International Legislation

1

The Nature of Tortious Liability

1–001

Liability in tort can be imposed for a diverse range of conduct, extending from negligent behaviour to attacking a person's reputation or limiting a person's freedom of movement. This book aims to provide an understanding of the nature of tortious liability by explaining how and why a defendant can be liable in these and other situations. This chapter provides a starting point. Here, we shall examine what is meant by "tort", the aims and objectives of the current system of tort law, and the factors that seem to influence tortious liability. We shall also consider how tort law fits in with other forms of civil liability, namely contract and restitution. The second part of this chapter addresses some different questions: How well does tort law fulfil its role in English law? Are there any alternatives to tort law which could or should be adopted? By gaining a basic understanding of the scope and nature of tort, the reader will be better able to understand the law in following chapters.

What is tort?

1–002

Tort takes many forms. It includes, for example, negligence, nuisance, libel, slander, trespass, assault and battery. It is therefore more accurate to speak of a "Law of Torts", rather than a "Law of Tort". To provide a definition which encompasses the whole of this area of law is impossible. Each tort has its own particular characteristics. Some torts, such as negligence, require proof of damage, whilst others, such as trespass and libel, are actionable without proof of damage. Whilst the tort of negligence obviously requires "negligent" behaviour, other torts, such as trespass, require intentional behaviour or at least recklessness. It is best, therefore, to confine ourselves to a statement that the law of tort is the law of *civil wrongs*[1] that is to say, it is concerned with behaviour which is legally classified as "wrong" or "tortious", so as to entitle the claimant to a remedy.

---

1   The word "tort" is in fact Norman-French for "harm" or "wrong". It dates from the times when Norman-French was used within the English judicial system.

It must be conceded that this definition is somewhat circular, but it is the only one that will suffice. More precise definitions, such as that of the great tort lawyer Professor Winfield, have been widely criticised. Winfield defined tort as arising "from the breach of a duty primarily fixed by law; this duty is towards persons generally and its breach is redressible by an action for unliquidated damages".[2] This definition has been criticised because it ignores the fact that some tortious duties arise by consent,[3] some are owed only to specific individuals,[4] and a breach of duty does not automatically make the defendant liable.

Whilst it may not be possible to provide a precise definition of "tort", it is certainly possible to identify a number of principles that determine when liability in tort will arise. It is to these that we now turn.

Principles of Liability

1–003 Tort law determines who bears the loss that results from the defendant's actions. For example, driver A knocks down pedestrian B in the street. B suffers personal injury. Tort law will determine who bears the loss suffered by B. If A is not liable, B bears the loss. If A is liable, A (or rather his or her insurance company) will bear the loss. The aim of shifting loss does not tell us, however, what makes a court choose between A and B. A number of principles seem to underlie the decision whether or not to impose liability on A, and it is important to note that no one principle predominates. These principles may be broadly summarised as:

- compensation;
- fault;
- retributive justice (punishment);
- deterrence;
- economic efficiency (market deterrence); and
- loss distribution (spreading losses in a socially fair way).

We examine each principle below.

2 P.H. Winfield, *The Province of the Law of Tort* (1931), p.32.
3 e.g. if you invite someone into your home (see Occupiers' Liability, discussed in Ch.8).
4 e.g. duties owed to employees (see Employers' Liability, discussed in Ch.7).

(1) Compensation

Perhaps the most obvious objective of tort law is to award compensation for loss. In doing so, the courts are guided by the principle known as restitutio in integrum. Lord Blackburn, in *Livingstone v Rawyards Coal Co*,[5] explained the meaning of this principle when he said that compensation in tort should take the form of:

"the sum of money which will put the party who has been injured, or who has suffered, in the same position as he would have been in if he had not sustained the wrong for which he is now getting his compensation or reparation."

The goal of compensation, of course, is subject to practical constraints. For example, where the claimant has lost an arm, the best tort law can do is to provide a sum of money which represents that loss. Tort law has also recognised that liability must be subject to certain rules that limit the availability of compensation. Fears of indeterminate liability (the so-called "floodgates of litigation") and of disproportionate liability (or "crushing liability") have dictated that tort law must set limits to the types of loss it will compensate. Thus, for example, compensation for mental distress is rarely awarded, and a restrictive approach is adopted towards liability for "pure economic loss" and psychiatric illness. The idea of full compensation, therefore, translates into "compensation within reason".

Tort law has been supported in its compensatory goal by the growth of the insurance industry.[6] Statistically, most tort claims for personal injury arise from road traffic accidents or accidents in the workplace. In both cases, it is compulsory for the defendant to insure against liability.[7] The Road Traffic Act 1988 makes liability insurance compulsory for motorists[8] and its objectives are underpinned by the existence of the Motor Insurers' Bureau, which administers schemes to compensate victims of uninsured drivers and hit-and-run incidents where the driver is untraceable.[9] Similarly, the Employers' Liability (Compulsory Insurance) Act 1969 provides that employers must be insured against accidents in the workplace. In these areas, then, legislation and the law of tort work in tandem. The legislation ensures that deserving claimants

1-004

---

5 (1880) 5 App. Cas. 25 at 39 per Lord Blackburn.

6 See M. Davies, "The End of the Affair: Duty of Care and Liability Insurance" (1989) 9 L.S. 67 and R. Merkin and J. Steele, *Insurance and the Law of Obligations* (OUP, 2013) who argue that tort law and insurance are symbiotic, both playing vital roles in allocating risks of harm.

7 See R. Lewis and A. Morris, "Challenging views of tort" [2013] J.P.I. Law 69, who note that insurers are the paymasters of the tort system and are responsible for 94% of tort compensation for personal injury. See also R. Lewis, "Insurers and Personal Injury Litigation: Acknowledging 'The Elephant in the Living Room'" [2005] J.P.I. Law 1. A YouGov report on Personal Injuries in 2015 reported that personal injury and accident legal work primarily comes from claims for injuries sustained at work, in public places and on someone else's property. The largest number of claims come from road traffic accidents.

8 See Road Traffic Act 1988 ss.143 and 145.

9 See *https://www.mib.org.uk/making-a-claim/* [Accessed 1 August 2020].

are guaranteed compensation (rather than being at the mercy of the defendant's resources), whilst the law of tort provides the mechanism through which they can obtain it.

Of course, compensating misfortune is not an objective peculiar to the law of tort. Tort operates in the context of a wider regime which includes statutory compensation schemes such as the Criminal Injuries Compensation Scheme and, ultimately, the cushion of social security payments. The law's efforts to reconcile the relationship between these different ways of providing compensation are examined in Ch.17. What should be noted here, however, is that the existence of tort law means that society applies the principle of full compensation selectively. In the absence of a universal system of compensation for all accident injuries, successful tort claimants are likely to receive substantial compensation, whilst victims of naturally occurring accidents (unless they are privately insured) receive no compensation, except possibly low-level social security payments.

(2) Fault

Fault is the idea most commonly used to *justify* an award of compensation. Fault-based liability embodies the idea of taking personal responsibility for one's own conduct. It may also serve as a deterrent or even satisfy a retributive purpose in that a claimant's anger at being the victim of a wrong is more likely to be placated if he or she receives compensation from the person who has been at fault. Here liability can be justified as a form of inter-personal justice seeking to reverse a wrong committeed against the innocent victim by requiring the person who has acted without justification to compensate the other (sometimes known as corrective justice).

Liability for fault has become particularly significant because of the growth of the tort of negligence. As we shall see in Ch.2, liability for negligence was opposed by most of the judges in the nineteenth century, because it ran contrary to the ideas of individualism and laissez-faire that dominated the political philosophy of the age. But this philosophy gradually changed, so that in 1932, Lord Atkin in *Donoghue v Stevenson*[10] was able to justify fault-based liability by saying that members of society ought to take reasonable care to avoid harming their "neighbours". The idea of fault nowadays pervades many areas of tort law, but it is not to be thought that all torts are fault-based. In libel, for example, a defendant who writes a defamatory article in a newspaper may be liable even if he or she has taken all due care in researching the article.

It should be noted that the context in which tort law operates in modern society means that, whilst the notion of "fault" is used to justify imposing liability, often, legal "fault" does not equate with moral blame. In relation to driving accidents, for example, the administrative advantages for the law in being able to settle claims easily have triumphed over moral considerations. Thus, as we shall see in Ch.5, a driver can be held legally at "fault" for a mistake that by the standards of society is morally excusable. Moreover, in many areas of tort law, the wide-

---

10 [1932] A.C. 562 at 580. See also *Sedleigh-Denfield v O'Callaghan* [1940] A.C. 880 (expanding the tort of nuisance on the basis of fault).

spread practice of insuring against liability means that, in reality, it is an insurer rather than a morally guilty defendant who foots the bill for compensation. The fault principle is similarly undermined by the doctrine of vicarious liability.[11] Vicarious liability renders one person responsible for the torts committed by another. The most common example is that of employer and employee. If an employee commits a tort in the course of employment, the claimant is perfectly entitled to sue the employer for damages in tort. In these circumstances, then, the burden of the wrong done may be shouldered by the innocent employer, rather than by the employee who is to blame. Insurance and vicarious liability subordinate the fault principle to the overriding need to compensate victims of accidents. In the light of this, fault can be only *one* possible explanation of how the tort system works.[12]

(3) Retributive justice

Vengeance or retribution is the most ancient justification for imposing liability on a defendant who has committed a wrong. It was to fulfil the objective of preventing "blood feuds" that the law developed an action for compensating harm, which eventually became the law of torts. In modern times, perhaps, this objective is less relevant. Even today, though, it should be recognised, for example, that a person is less likely to commit an act of "road rage" against a driver who has dented his or her bumper if a tort claim (settled by insurers) will pay for a new one.

1-006

Nowadays, the idea of retribution as an objective of tort sits very uneasily with the existence of the criminal law. It is the function of the criminal law to punish the wrongdoer and see that he gets his "just deserts". It is hard to justify importing the concept of punishment into civil proceedings for two reasons. First, in a civil trial, the punishment may be meted out in the absence of the evidential and procedural safeguards to which a defendant is entitled in criminal proceedings. Secondly, because tort law and criminal law operate concurrently, the defendant may receive "double punishment" for a single wrong. Nevertheless, in the modern law of tort there are certain circumstances where the courts may punish a defendant by an award of "punitive" damages. Such damages are justified on the basis of their deterrent effect. This is discussed below.

(4) Deterrence

In its basic form, the concept of tort liability acting as a deterrent is a simple one: if I cause harm through my actions or inaction and have to pay compensation, I will try to behave differently next time. We can see the deterrence principle at work in various contexts. Publishers, for

1-007

---

11   See Ch.7.
12   For a more detailed critique of the fault principle, see P. Cane and J. Goudkamp, *Atiyah's Accidents, Compensation and the Law*, 9th edn (2018), Ch.7.

example, aware of the high cost of compensation if they publish defamatory material, often employ lawyers to screen publications so as to avoid liability. Equally, professionals such as doctors and lawyers may be encouraged to take care in their work because they fear the consequences of liability—not just in terms of financial cost, but in terms of the harm litigation may cause to their professional reputations.

The objective of deterrence is supported by the courts' power to award "exemplary" or "punitive" damages in tort.[13] These are damages which seek not to compensate the claimant, but to punish a defendant for acting deliberately with a view to profiting from his or her tort, or to punish the executive arm of government for acting in an arbitrary, oppressive or unconstitutional manner.[14] Their goal is to show that tort does not pay and thereby deter the defendant from contemplating such conduct in future.[15] A good example is the classic US case of *Grimshaw v Ford Motor Co*[16] concerning the Ford Pinto. Here, Ford was alleged to have discovered a defect in the car which rendered it susceptible to explosion when struck from the rear. Nevertheless, it continued to market the car on the basis that it would be cheaper to pay compensation to victims of the defect than to redesign the car. Such cynical disregard for human safety led a jury[17] to award exemplary damages of $125 million, reduced to $3.5 million on appeal.

In the tort of negligence, however, deterrence theory has limited application. This is because, in a case where A has injured B by simple *inadvertence* (which the law may call "negligence"), it is difficult to see how making A liable can alter the behaviour of a person in A's position. A is liable because he or she has failed to meet the standard of behaviour expected of the "reasonable person". As we shall see in Ch.5, this is an *objective* standard—which means that in applying it the court takes little account of the personal characteristics of the defendant. What this means is that a defendant can be held liable even though he or she is already taking all the care which he or she could possibly take in pursuing a particular activity. The point is well illustrated by the decision of the Court of Appeal in *Nettleship v Weston*[18] (discussed further in Ch.5). Here, a learner driver on her third lesson was held liable in negligence for driving below the standard of the "reasonable driver"—which was set at the standard of an ordinary, competent, qualified driver. No concession was made to the fact that she was a learner (or even that she was being sued by her instructor—arguably the very person whose skill was supposed to prevent the accident!).

There are further objections to regarding deterrence as an important aim of tort law—a deterrent can only work if the people whose actions or inaction cause damage are the same people who have to pay for that damage. We have seen that the doctrine of vicarious liability

---

13   Discussed more fully in Ch.17.
14   See *Rookes v Barnard (No.1)* [1964] A.C. 1129.
15   [1964] A.C. 1129 at 1228 per Lord Devlin.
16   119 Cal. App. 3d 757 (1981).
17   Juries are still used in tort cases in the US, but are rarely used in English courts, save for torts such as fraud and false imprisonment: see Senior Courts Act 1981 s.69.
18   [1971] 2 Q.B. 691.

means that the employer pays for the damage, rather than the negligent employee. In such circumstances, it cannot be said that the prospect of having to pay compensation has an effect on the amount of care taken by the employee in his or her work. Similarly, the existence of liability insurance removes the sting of arguments based on deterrence. When a motorist gets in a car, it is rather far-fetched to say that his or her mind is concentrated by the prospect of civil liability for careless driving, because that is a prospect against which he or she is insured. To the careless motorist, the cost of a car crash is likely to be no more than the loss of a "no-claims bonus", entailing a small increase in premiums (against which, nowadays, it is even possible to insure). In the context of employers' liability to their employees, whilst it is true that the threat of liability may provide an incentive for employers to adopt safer working practices, in a commercial world, these will only be adopted where they are cost effective. Moreover, because of the way the insurance industry works—spreading the cost of accidents amongst all policyholders—the full force of the incentive is seldom brought to bear on employers.[19]

All of the problems with deterrence theory we have examined, then, are really part of the same problem: the objective of deterrence is accorded less importance in tort law than the objective of compensation. This is so for two reasons. First, by social consensus, vicarious liability and insurance make compensation available at the expense of deterrence. Secondly, there are limits to the extent to which deterrence arguments can be considered in the context of a tort trial. If a court seeks to deter a whole class of potential defendants from wrongful conduct by imposing liability on the particular defendant in the case (or by awarding punitive damages), then the result of the case may be unjust—the particular defendant is singled out to pay the price for wrongful conduct that may be the common practice of his or her peers, and (in the case of punitive damages) the particular claimant receives a windfall in addition to compensation.[20] Similarly, effective deterrence requires that potential defendants be given guidance about how to avoid liability. Whilst the courts occasionally provide such guidance, constraints of time and resources prevent them from going into details. Moreover, because the guidance is given in the context of a particular case, it may be difficult to interpret in terms of general application. In the light of these factors, such guidance is better provided by statute (for example, health and safety legislation) than by ad hoc decisions in tort.

(5) Economic efficiency (market deterrence)

If, through the operation of law, a manufacturer of products (for example) is forced to bear the cost of harm caused by those products, and to pass that cost on to consumers, he or she will seek to maximise the safety of the products in order to obtain the best price in the marketplace. Logically, therefore, as a result of this process the safest products will become

1–008

---

19   For a defence of the deterrence argument even in the face of liability insurance and vicarious liability, see J. Morgan, "Abolishing personal injuries law?" (2018) 34 P.N. 122, 127–133.

20   But note that the Law Commission in its report No.247 "Aggravated, Exemplary and Restitutionary Damages" (1997) recommended a more generous approach to punitive damages, which will be discussed in Ch.17.

the cheapest, and market competition should operate to reduce the *total amount* of harm caused in society by all products on the market. This idea is known as the principle of "market deterrence".

Once we start to explore such arguments, we venture into the difficult realm of economic analysis of law. To use the language of economists, every product (or activity) has the potential to produce "externalities" ("extra costs" not reflected in the price) when either it causes harm, or necessitates precautions to prevent harm from arising. Economic analysis of law seeks to discover how these "externalities" are paid for. Economists argue that the framework of any legal system should be such as to ensure that externalities are paid for in a way that maximises "efficiency". In economic language, the most "efficient" way of doing things is the way that produces the least cost to society as a whole. What all this means for the law of tort is that the courts should seek to develop rules under which the risk of harm in any given situation is borne by the person who will expend the least amount of society's resources in taking precautions against it. This person is sometimes known as the "best cost-avoider".

We can see that this principle already operates in the law to some extent by considering a simple example. Suppose that a number of televisions are sold with wrongly wired mains plugs, presenting risks of fire and electric shock. It is likely that tort law will make the manufacturer of the televisions liable if these risks materialise. Whilst this result will accord with the principles of compensation and fault, it will also fulfil the objective of efficiency. This is because, whilst it will be relatively inexpensive for the manufacturer to change his or her production methods so that the wires are put in the plug the right way round, it would be relatively expensive (in terms of missed opportunities to create wealth) if all of the individuals affected by the problem had to rewire a plug themselves.

Whilst it is clear that tort law can be analysed in terms of economics, economic concepts are seldom referred to by English judges.[21] This might be explained by the fact that the "economics and law" debate is largely a US one,[22] and reflects the political trends of that country, namely right-of-centre market economics. It is sometimes also suggested that much of the academic commentary on the subject may be rather impenetrable to non-economist judges—yet it should be remembered that the Supreme Court includes judges with a commercial law background who are undoubtedly familiar with economic concepts. Perhaps the true explanation for the lack of judicial enthusiasm in this area is that economic analysis of tort law cannot in many cases be reconciled with more pressing objectives of the tort system. Economic analysis takes as its starting point the assumption that in most, if not all cases, the potential human cost of the defendant's actions can be given a monetary value. Whilst, arguably, this is just a cold fact of life, it is one which society and the judiciary are understandably reluctant to face. Society may not be prepared to quantify in monetary terms the cost of a young child being

---

21 But see, e.g. the analysis of Lord Hoffmann in *Stovin v Wise* [1996] 1 A.C. 923 at 944 in the context of liability for omissions.

22 Most of the relevant academic commentary is American. See, e.g. R.A. Posner, *Economic Analysis of Law*, 9th edn (Wolters Kluwer, 2014); R.B. Cooter Jr and T. Ulen, *Law and Economics*, 6th edn (Pearson, 2014) Chs 5 and 6.

hideously disfigured, so as to weigh it against the purely financial cost of preventing such an occurrence. Equally, whilst an economic perspective can be instructive in explaining decisions in negligence and nuisance[23] cases, it is less helpful in explaining torts like trespass and defamation, whose primary aim is to protect the integrity of the individual.

(6) Loss distribution

As stated earlier, tort law shifts loss from the victim to the tortfeasor by imposing liability. In a broader context, however, it can be seen that tort law operates to shift losses so that they are borne by the whole (or large sections) of society. This function of tort law is known as "loss spreading" or simply "loss distribution". It is fulfilled mainly through vicarious liability—part of tort law itself—and through liability insurance—part of the context in which it operates.

1–009

Vicarious liability makes employers liable for accidents caused by their employees, but employers cover themselves by insurance and pass the cost of the premiums on to consumers in the prices of their goods and services. In this way, the cost of compensating accident victims is spread throughout the community, in much the same way that social security payments, funded by taxation, spread the cost of compensating social need. Similarly, because the legislature has imposed compulsory liability insurance for road traffic accidents, the cost of accidents will be met first by insurance companies, who will then pass on this cost in the form of premiums paid by their clients. The cost of accidents is thereby spread amongst the (insured) driving community.

Clearly, "loss distribution" can be criticised for a number of reasons. It can be criticised for ignoring the importance of fault and undermining the objective of deterrence. It can also be criticised as unjust: why should a careful driver or employer subsidise the cost of accidents caused by the tortious activities of others? It can only be justified by acceptance of its underlying rationale—that a certain amount of "distributive justice" is desirable in a civilised society.[24]

Conclusions

Tort law is an amalgam of all six of the concepts considered above.[25] Its mixed aims are the inevitable result of the common law system of justice where law is developed on a case-by-case

1–010

---

23   The role of economic deterrence in the tort of nuisance is discussed in the influential article of A. Ogus and G. Richardson, "Economics and the Environment: A Study of Private Nuisance" [1977] C.L.J. 284.

24   The concept of "distributive justice" is referred to in a number of negligence cases, most notably *McFarlane v Tayside Health Board* [2000] 2 A.C. 59 (discussed in Ch.2) and *White v Chief Constable of South Yorkshire* [1999] 2 A.C. 455 (discussed in Ch.4).

25   Glanville Williams has commented that "Where possible the law seems to like to ride two or three horses at once": G. Williams, "The aims of the law of tort" [1951] C.L.P. 137. See also recently J. Morgan, "Abolishing personal injuries law?" (2018) 34 P.N. 122 on the different functions of tort law.

basis. Lord Steyn in *McFarlane v Tayside Health Board* commented on the tension which exists between the principles of compensation, fault and loss distribution:

> "It is possible to view the case simply from the perspective of corrective justice [which] requires somebody who has harmed another without justification to indemnify the other . . . But one may also approach the case from the vantage point of distributive justice. It requires a focus on the just distribution of burdens and losses among members of a society."[26]

Although compensation is the most common reason for bringing a tort action, claimants may have a number of other reasons, including deterrence and retribution. In *Hill v Chief Constable of West Yorkshire*,[27] for example, the mother of the last victim of Peter Sutcliffe (a serial killer known as the "Yorkshire Ripper") sued the police for negligence, mainly in order to criticise their carelessness in failing to apprehend the murderer soon enough, and to make the point that police practices should be improved. In Lord Templeman's view, the action was misconceived. His Lordship pointed out that:

> "an action for damages for alleged acts of negligence by individual police officers in 1980 could not determine whether and in what respects the West Yorkshire police force can be improved in 1988."

Lord Templeman's remarks emphasise that an adversarial system is ill-suited to a proper consideration of broad questions of social and economic policy. The focus of the courts' attention is whether compensation should be awarded to do justice in the particular cases before them. This does not prevent courts using their skill and experience to address broader concerns, but it is important to recognise that there are constraints on their ability to do so.

The Interests Protected by Tort

1–011

Tort law aims to protect the individual from actual or threatened harm to certain specific interests. In this section, we examine the degree of protection afforded to each interest. Tort law does not protect *all* interests from harm, and certain interests, such as personal safety, receive

---

26 [2000] 2 A.C. 59 at 82. See also Lord Steyn, "Perspectives of corrective and distributive justice in tort law" (2002) 37 Irish Jurist 1. The division between corrective and distributive justice comes from Aristotle: see *The Nichomachaean Ethics*, revised edn (Penguin Classics, 2004).
27 [1989] A.C. 53.

better protection than others. As tort law has developed, the nature of protection offered to each interest has reflected the importance of that interest to society at the relevant period in history. Thus, whilst in feudal times trespass to land was the most sophisticated and important tort, in the modern industrial age protection against personal injury has dominated the agenda.

(1) Personal harm

1–012

The industrial revolution brought with it new threats to the safety of individuals with the introduction of heavy machinery, motor vehicles and railways. Tort law responded by developing the tort of negligence. This supplemented the existing protection provided by trespass to the person, where the torts of assault, battery and false imprisonment serve to protect individuals from intentional interference with their personal freedom and bodily integrity.[28] Yet, whilst tort law has clearly offered protection against physical injury, the judiciary has been reluctant to offer protection against other forms of personal harm, such as psychiatric illness and distress. Considerable scepticism was expressed in the nineteenth century towards claims for "nervous shock", on the basis that they would leave "a wide field open for imaginary claims".[29] Although claims for psychiatric illness may now be brought, the law still adopts a restrictive regime of recovery, as will be seen in Ch.4. Claims for mental distress still cannot be brought in their own right,[30] although this is a developing area of the law. The problem of harassment has become more significant in recent times and developments in tort law have now been replaced by a statutory tort under the Protection from Harassment Act 1997. We shall see in Ch.2 also the debate whether the Human Rights Act 1998 has had any effect on the scope of negligence liability. In Ch.15, we consider the extent to which the law now provides a remedy for invasion of privacy.

(2) Harm to property

1–013

Protection against harm to property remains important, but no longer has the primacy accorded to it during feudal times. "Property" here is used to signify both personal property and land (real property). Personal property is protected by the torts of trespass to goods and conversion (civil theft). Real property is protected by a number of torts, including trespass to land, nuisance, and the rule in *Rylands v Fletcher*, which are discussed in Chs 10 and 11. Property loss is also recoverable in other torts such as negligence.

---

28   See Ch.11.
29   See *Victorian Railway Commissioners v Coultas* (1888) 13 App. Cas. 222 at 226.
30   On claims for mental distress in tort generally, see P. Giliker, "A 'new' head of damages: damages for mental distress in the English law of torts" (2000) 20 L.S. 19; E. Descheemaeker, "Rationalising Recovery for Emotional Harm in Tort Law" (2018) 134 L.Q.R. 602.

(3) Harm to reputation

1-014

Reputation is protected by the tort of defamation, which creates liability for untrue statements which diminish the claimant's reputation in the eyes of right-thinking members of society. Defamation is examined in Chs 13 and 14 of this book. It should be noted that defamation protects the claimant's *reputation* and not his or her *feelings*, so that there will be no action for defamation if the claimant is insulted in private or if the statement fails to diminish his or her reputation. As will be discussed, protection of reputation must be weighed against the public interest in free speech and a free press. In practice, this balance is far from easy to achieve.

(4) Harm to financial interests

1-015

Tort law gives limited protection to financial interests. Such interests are usually protected outside tort law, for example by contract law or by legislation such as the Competition Act 1998 and the Enterprise Act 2002. In this area, tort law is particularly conscious of the potential number of claims and the threat of "liability in an indeterminate amount for an indeterminate time to an indeterminate class".[31] Whereas the cost of compensating physical injury tends to be limited, the potential for "crushing liability", resulting from a flood of claims for financial loss, presents a problem for the law. Courts are therefore reluctant to impose liability for *negligent* infliction of financial loss, save in the specific situations where the defendant has voluntarily assumed responsibility for the claimant's interests, or where the loss is consequential on physical damage.[32]

However, tort law does offer some protection where the defendant has *intentionally* interfered with the claimant's economic and trading interests. The tort of deceit (fraud) imposes liability where the defendant has made a false statement[33] to the claimant in the knowledge that it is false, or reckless as to its truth, with the intention that the claimant will act on it.[34] The claimant may recover damages for economic loss suffered by acting on the statement.[35] Likewise, the "economic torts", which we examine in Ch.12, impose liability in a limited number of situations for intentional interference with business interests.

---

31   See Cardozo CJ in *Ultramares Corp v Touche* 255 N.Y. Rep. 170 at 179 (1931); 174 N.E. Rep. 441 at 444 (1931).

32   See Ch.3.

33   Which must be of an existing fact: *Edgington v Fitzmaurice* (1885) 29 Ch. D. 459.

34   See *Derry v Peek* (1889) 14 App. Cas. 337.

35   The claimant can recover for all the losses directly flowing from the fraudulent misstatement: *Doyle v Olby (Ironmongers) Ltd* [1969] 2 Q.B. 158. Deceit or fraud generally appears in the context of contract law and reference should be made to works on contract law.

(5) Harm to the due process of law

1–016

This will be dealt with briefly. Certain torts seek to protect the claimant against misuse of the legal system. In this book, we refer specifically to one such tort: malicious prosecution.[36] In a system where the criminal law permits individuals to instigate prosecutions, this tort affords the claimant valuable protection against prosecutions which are brought maliciously without reasonable and probable cause. In the leading case of *Martin v Watson*[37] the tort was used to protect the plaintiff where the defendant had maliciously made a groundless accusation of indecent exposure against the plaintiff, leading to his prosecution. Although it is a difficult tort to prove, it demonstrates the willingness of the English legal system to intervene to prevent abuse of the law.

The Role of Tort in the Law of Obligations

1–017

In this section, we compare the role of tort with two other aspects of civil law, namely the law of contract and the law of restitution (or unjust enrichment). Together with tort, these heads of liability are sometimes referred to as the "Law of Obligations". In English law, the same defendant may be liable under more than one of these heads of liability. This is known as "concurrent liability". A claimant is not obliged to choose between bringing an action in contract, tort or restitution[38] and may plead all three. Nevertheless, the three causes of action perform different roles in English law, which are examined below.

The distinction between tort and contract

1–018

The role of contract law is, put simply, the enforcement of promises.[39] Liability is therefore centred around the contract itself: Has it been formed? What are its terms? Have they been breached? Contractual remedies seek to place the claimant in the position, so far as money can do it, that he or she would have been in had the contract been performed.[40] By contrast, tort

---

36   See Ch.11.

37   [1996] 1 A.C. 74.

38   See *Henderson v Merrett Syndicates Ltd (No.1)* [1995] 2 A.C. 145, overturning the doubts experienced following Lord Scarman's equivocal judgment in *Tai Hing Cotton Mill Ltd v Liu Chong Hing Bank Ltd* [1986] A.C. 80 at 107. This is not the case in all jurisdictions. The position is different, e.g. in France where there is a rule against accumulation of actions (*non-cumul*).

39   Although it has been argued that its real role is in the protection of detrimental reliance: see, e.g. P.S. Atiyah, "Contract, Promises and the Law of Obligations" (1978) 94 L.Q.R 193 and in P.S. Atiyah, *Essays on Contract* (OUP, 1990).

40   *Robinson v Harman* (1848) 1 Ex. 850 at 855 per Parke B.

is concerned with compensating the victim who has suffered injury as a result of conduct classified as a civil wrong by law. The aim here is not to enforce a bargain, but to compensate the victim for his or her out-of-pocket expenses, thereby placing the victim in the same position as he or she would have been in had the victim not sustained the wrong for which compensation is being awarded.[41]

Readers should be wary of attempts to distinguish contract and tort on the basis that contract consists of obligations imposed by consent and tort consists of obligations imposed by law. Contract law is subject to considerable legislative and judicial intervention and terms may be imposed by statute[42] or by the courts. Equally, the defendant in tort law may, in a sense, agree to undertake certain tortious responsibilities, for example by inviting a guest into his or her household[43] or by undertaking to advise the claimant on the merits of a particular business transaction.[44] Such a theory, therefore, is really too general to be of much use. In practice, the distinction between contract and tort is determined simply by asking the question: "Have the rules of contract law been complied with?" If the answer is "no", the obligation or wrong in question cannot be classified as contractual, but may be classified as tortious.

The distinction between tort and restitution

1–019

Restitution is a growing area of civil liability, the proper scope of which remains unclear. The law of restitution intervenes where the defendant has been unjustly enriched at the expense of the claimant. Rather than compensating the claimant, it seeks to restore to the claimant the amount by which the defendant has been wrongfully enriched. Whilst its goal is therefore distinct from that of tort, it is clear that restitutionary damages may be awarded as an alternative to tort in certain limited circumstances. These are discussed in Ch.17.[45]

---

41   Lord Blackburn in *Livingstone v Rawyards Coal Co* (1880) 5 App. Cas. 25 at 39.

42   e.g. under the Sale of Goods Act 1979 or Consumer Rights Act 2015.

43   See Ch.8.

44   See Ch.3.

45   For a more detailed discussion, see leading texts on the law of restitution. Helpful academic discussion may be found in I.M. Jackman, "Restitution for wrongs" [1989] C.L.J. 302; C. Rotherham, "The conceptual structure of restitution for wrongs" [2007] C.L.J. 172 and J. Edelman, who controversially argues that restitutionary damages should be available for all wrongs: *Gain-based damages* (Hart, 2002), 81.

The Impact of European and Human Rights Law

1–020

In examining the English law of torts, it is worth recognising that, regardless of the UK leaving the EU ("Brexit"), European law and policy has had some impact on tort law over the years. For example, in Ch.9, we examine liability for defective products, which is now largely dealt with under the Consumer Protection Act 1987 Pt 1. This was introduced to comply with EU Directive 85/374 on liability for defective products (the Product Liability directive).[46] As we will see in Ch.9, the UK Government's introduction of the Product Liability directive into UK law led not only to a legal action against the UK by the European Commission, but ongoing controversy as to how the relevant law should be interpreted and applied in UK law.[47] The government intends to retain the provisions of the Consumer Protection Act 1987 Pt 1, after Brexit, although the Court of Justice of the European Union (CJEU) will no longer have authority over UK law. In future, also, legislative changes to EU law after Brexit will no longer be binding. It remains to be seen precisely what will be the new relationship between the EU and the UK after Brexit.

One casualty of Brexit, however, will be State liability for breach of EU law. Following the European Court's decision in *Francovich v Italy*,[48] liability would arise in tort where a Member State was found to have breached EU law, for example, by failing to implement a directive within the stipulated time period. This was actionable in the national court. The English courts classified such claims as a type of breach of statutory duty, but, as will be discussed in Ch.7, this cause of action proved to be distinct from the tort of breach of statutory duty in a number of ways.[49] *Francovich* liability does not survive the UK leaving the EU.

However, Brexit should not distract us from the fact that human rights remain relevant to the law of tort and can also raise matters of political controversy. In October 2000, the Human Rights Act 1998 (the HRA 1998) came into force in the UK. The HRA 1998 permits claimants to bring claims against public authorities acting in breach of the rights protected by the European Convention on Human Rights (ECHR). Litigants are no longer required to pursue their case before the European Court of Human Rights in Strasbourg. Section 7 of the Act permits claims against public authorities which act (or propose to act) in a way which is incompatible with a Convention right. Section 6(3) of the Act provides that the term "public authority" includes the courts,[50] and this means that the courts must also take account of the rights established in

---

46 Directive 85/374 on the approximation of the laws, regulations and administrative provisions of the Member States concerning liability for defective products [1985] OJ L210/29.

47 Treaty of the Functioning of the European Union (TFEU) art.288(3) provides that directives are binding on all European Member States, but leaves it to each State to determine how they are introduced into national law.

48 (C6/9) [1991] E.C.R. I-5357.

49 In *Brasserie du Pêcheur v Germany; R. v Secretary of State for Transport Ex p. Factortame (No.4)* (C46/93 and C48/93) [1996] Q.B. 404, the CJEU established the conditions for *Francovich* liability (see Ch.7).

50 On the definition of "public authority", see *Aston Cantlow v Wallbank* [2003] UKHL 37; [2004] 1 A.C. 546 and

the Convention and the case law of the Strasbourg court when relevant.[51] Section 8 of the Act allows the court to grant such relief or remedy as it considers just and appropriate, which may, at the court's discretion, include an award of damages.

The 1998 Act also introduced changes where legislation is concerned. Section 3(1) of the Act provides that, "so far as it is possible to do so, primary legislation and subordinate legislation must be read and given effect in a way which is compatible with the Convention rights". While the Act does not affect the validity of any incompatible primary legislation,[52] a court may make a declaration of incompatibility.[53] In practice, the courts have generally sought under s.3(1) to interpret legislation in a Convention-compliant manner and avoid any confrontation with the legislator under s.4.[54]

The question for us to consider in this book is the impact of the Human Rights Act 1998 on the law of torts. The Act remains in force, despite its lack of popularity with the Conservative party. The s.3 interpretative duty will have a potential impact on statutory defences in tort. We shall see also in Ch.2 how far arts 2 and 3 (right to life and right not to be subject to inhuman or degrading treatment) have influenced negligence claims by victims against public authorities. We also discuss the effect of the 1998 Act on other torts, for example nuisance (in Ch.10). In Ch.14 we specifically consider the effect art.10 (the right to freedom of expression) on the tort of defamation and in Ch.15 whether the 1998 Act has triggered the introduction of a right to privacy into English law. While the impact of the 1998 Act has not been as significant as many predicted, it continues to be used to challenge restrictions on the claimant's right to sue.[55]

Tort in Modern Society

1-021

Detailed study of tort law sometimes tends to obscure the fact that, especially in personal injury cases, there are often other means by which a claimant may be compensated for his or her loss. It is appropriate, therefore, to say something about tort law in its wider social context, to give the reader a clearer view of where it fits in modern society. In this section, we explore the role of tort in providing compensation and consider proposals for its reform, focusing par-

---

YL v Birmingham City Council [2007] UKHL 27; [2008] 1 A.C. 95. See D. Oliver [2004] P.L. 329 and J. Landau [2007] P.L. 630.

51 See HRA 1998 s.2.

52 HRA 1998 s.3(2). It also does not affect the validity, continuing operation or enforcement of any incompatible subordinate legislation if (disregarding any possibility of revocation) primary legislation prevents removal of the incompatibility.

53 HRA 1998 s.4(2). See, e.g. *Smith v Lancashire Teaching Hospitals NHS Trust* [2017] EWCA Civ 1916; [2018] Q.B. 804.

54 See, e.g. *Ghaidan v Godin-Mendoza* [2004] UKHL 30; [2004] 2 A.C. 557.

55 See, e.g. *Smith v Ministry of Defence* [2013] UKSC 41; [2014] A.C. 52 on combat immunity and J. Wright, *Tort Law and Human Rights*, 2nd edn (Hart, 2017).

ticularly on the New Zealand experience of replacing tort with a no-fault system of accident compensation.

Tort and other compensation systems

It is important to realise that in practice tort law plays a minor role in compensating accident victims. The Pearson Commission,[56] which undertook a survey of accident compensation in England and Wales in the 1970s, reported that only 6.5% of accident victims received any form of tort damages.[57] This means that the bulk of compensation comes from sources outside the tort system. These include payments from employers, from insurance, from schemes such as the Criminal Injuries Compensation Scheme and the Industrial Injuries Scheme, and social security payments. Whilst the level of such payments is usually well below that of tort damages, which are unique in seeking to provide full compensation for the victim, in practice they provide financial assistance for the majority of accident victims. This assistance is supplemented by the provision of publicly funded health care under the National Health Service. As we shall see in Ch.17, there are sometimes problems involving "double-counting" where a claimant has received tort damages and also benefits from insurance, or perhaps a charitable donation. The courts (with the help of legislation) have evolved a number of complicated rules which govern the relationship between different sources of compensation.

The importance of these alternative sources of compensation varies. Social security payments are obviously significant, particularly for those on low incomes. However, the amounts are relatively small. As at April 2020, income support for a single person over 25 was set at £74.35 per week.[58] Insurance is also important, particularly in respect of property damage, where tort actions are rarely brought.[59] Health insurance, critical or terminal illness cover, and unemployment insurance are also significant, as are payments from the accident victim's employer, such as occupational sick pay and pensions. The Criminal Injuries Compensation Scheme makes provision for victims of crimes of violence and those sustaining injuries in the course of apprehending an offender, although a tariff system is adopted and compensation in respect of a single injury is capped at £500,000.[60] Criminal courts also have the power to make compensation

---

56   Royal Commission on Civil Liability and Compensation for Personal Injury (Cmnd.7054 1978).
57   Royal Commission on Civil Liability and Compensation for Personal Injury (Cmnd.7054), Vol.1 Table 5(i).
58   See *https://www.gov.uk/income-support/what-youll-get* [Accessed 1 August 2020].
59   See P. Cane and J. Goudkamp, *Atiyah's Accidents, Compensation and the Law*, 9th edn (2018), 18.5.
60   See Criminal Injuries Compensation Act 1995. See generally P. Cane and J. Goudkamp, *Atiyah's Accidents, Compensation and the Law*, 9th edn (2018), Ch.12 and S. Macleod, "Criminal Injuries Compensation Scheme" in S. Macleod and C. Hodges, *Redress Schemes for Personal Injuries* (Hart, 2017). For a critical perspective, see D. Miers, "Compensating deserving victims of violent crime: the Criminal Injuries Compensation Scheme 2012" (2014) 34 L.S. 242.

orders when sentencing in a criminal court,[61] but the amounts awarded tend to be low and the awards have limited impact if the convicted defendant does not have the means to pay.

Why not tort?

1–023

Given that tort compensation tends to be paid at a higher level than the other forms of compensation, why is it that the majority of claimants do not bring an action in tort? One reason is that, in many circumstances, the rules of tort are well established. This means that whilst a tort *claim* may be made (perhaps on a very informal basis) and quickly settled, it is unnecessary to bring a tort *action*. The Pearson Commission found that 86% of tort claims were disposed of without the issue of writ or summons, and that, of the total number of claims made (including those where no legal proceedings were commenced) only 1% actually reached the courts. There are, however, a number of additional reasons why tort litigation is seldom used.

Cost

1–024

Litigation is extremely expensive. A claimant must be able to fund litigation and take the risk that if he or she loses, the court is likely to order the claimant to pay not only his or her own costs, but also those of the defendant. Publicly funded legal aid is generally unavailable for personal injury claims. The burden of cost has to some extent been alleviated by the introduction of conditional fees. Under the original form of conditional fee agreements (CFAs), a solicitor agreed to take on a client's case on the basis that no fee would be charged if the client lost, but a larger fee (the "success fee") would be charged if the client succeeded in his or her action which would normally be recoverable in whole or part from the losing party.[62] Such agreements are commonly known as "no win no fee" agreements. Conditional fee agreements mark an attempt to increase access to justice but cannot be considered a universal panacea in that a solicitor is only likely to take on cases with reasonable prospects of success, and may be reluctant to take on complicated and time-consuming cases. Further, the original idea that the losing party would now be forced to pay the success fee agreed by the claimant to fund the action (which could amount to a doubling of the fee in question) was challenged in the House of Lords' case of *Campbell v Mirror Group Newspapers Ltd (Costs)*.[63] Here, the *Mirror* newspaper argued that it should not be liable to pay the success fee of the successful claimant, here supermodel Naomi Campbell, on the basis that the amount payable was disproportionate and infringed its rights under ECHR art.10 (freedom

---

61   Powers of Criminal Courts (Sentencing) Act 2000 s.130.
62   Courts and Legal Services Act 1990 s.58.
63   [2005] UKHL 61; [2005] 1 W.L.R. 3394. Comment: R. Caddell [2006] C.L.J. 45. See also *Coventry v Lawrence* [2015] UKSC 50; [2015] 1 W.L.R. 3485 (regime compatible with ECHR art.6 and Protocol 1 art.1) and *Times Newspapers Ltd v Flood* [2017] UKSC 33; [2017] 1 W.L.R. 1415.

of expression). Campbell had brought a claim against the *Mirror* for breach of her right to privacy and had funded her action at the highest level with the assistance of a CFA. Her CFA had provided that if she won the case, solicitors and counsel would be entitled to success fees of 95% and 100% respectively. The threat of having to pay out such a large amount of money would, the newspaper argued, discourage defendants from publishing in future for fear of defamation or privacy actions. In the privacy case, Ms Campbell had been awarded damages of just £3,500, but, as the losing party, the Mirror Group had been found liable for its own costs and the claimant's bill of costs which amounted to over £1 million. The House of Lords rejected the claim. Nevertheless, it did express some reservations as to the wisdom or justice of the CFA system as it was then constituted. The European Court of Human Rights in January 2011[64] found unanimously that the success fees in *Campbell* had been disproportionate and violated the art.10 right to freedom of expression. The Strasbourg court noted, however, that the question of success fees was being reviewed at governmental level.

In 2008, the Government set up an inquiry in response to concerns about the rising costs of civil justice. This led to a report, in 2010, by Jackson LJ.[65] In the forward to the report, his Lordship states:

> **"In some areas of civil litigation costs are disproportionate and impede access to justice. I therefore propose a coherent package of interlocking reforms, designed to control costs and promote access to justice."**

The Government introduced reforms under the Legal Aid, Sentencing and Punishment of Offenders Act 2012 (the LASPO Act) Pt 2. This came into effect on 1 April 2013 and via secondary legislation including the Civil Procedure Rules.[66] The Government recognised that the reforms would have the most impact on personal injury cases, where "no win no fee" conditional fee agreements (CFAs) are used significantly. While CFAs will remain available to cover the costs of litigation, additional costs involved (success fees and insurance premiums) are no longer payable by the losing side (thereby resolving the situation in *Campbell* above).[67] The Act also introduced for the first time contingency fees which it terms "damages-based agreements" (DBAs). Under a DBA, no fee is paid if the case is lost, but if successful the lawyers may take a percentage of the damages recovered as their fee.[68] Equally, in an attempt to curb the

---

64   *MGN Ltd v United Kingdom* (39401/04) (2011) 53 E.H.R.R. 5. Comment: D. Howarth, "The cost of libel actions: a sceptical note" [2011] C.L.J. 397.

65   *Review of Civil Litigation Costs Final Report* (HMSO, 2010), also known as the Jackson Review.

66   See, generally, *https://www.gov.uk/government/policies/civil-justice-reform* [Accessed 1 August 2020]. See, generally, S. Sime (2012) 31(4) C.J.Q. 413. For a critical response, see J. Ayling [2013] J.P.I. Law 127.

67   LASPO Act 2012 ss.44 and 46, which amend the Courts and Legal Services Act 1990 (see ss.58 58A and 58C) in line with recommendations made by the Jackson Review.

68   LASPO Act 2012 s.45 (see now Courts and Legal Services Act 1990 s.58AA), Damages-Based Agreements Regulations 2013/609. See J. Peysner, "Tail wags dog: contingency fees (and Pt 36 and third party funding)"

"compensation culture", referral fees (that is fees payable for introducing potential clients to solicitors) are now banned in personal injury cases.[69] The Government has reassured litigants that the claimants' damages will be protected. Although the claimant will now have to pay the "success fee", it will be capped at 25% of the damages awarded in personal injury cases as general damages and for past losses (and will not apply to damages for future care and loss), and up to 50% of damages in other cases.[70] General damages have also been increased by 10% from 1 April 2013 in order to compensate successful claimants as a class for being deprived of the right enjoyed since 2000 to recover success fees from defendants.[71] The hope is that claimants will appreciate that they now have a financial stake in keeping their lawyers' costs down. The Act also further restricts legal aid, which is now effectively replaced by CFAs and DBAs in most civil litigation.[72] The Law Society (which represents solicitors in England and Wales) has been less than enthusiastic about the reforms:

> **"Government reforms to civil litigation costs and funding will reduce access to justice, increase costs to business and result in a windfall for insurers. Many claimants will lose a substantial proportion of their damages under the reforms and solicitors may not be in a position to take on higher-risk or lower-value claims."[73]**

A 2019 Ministry of Justice review found that on balance the Pt 2 reforms had met their objectives and that costs had been reduced, fewer unmeritorious cases had been taken forward and that access to justice at a proportionate cost was generally being achieved.[74] Lord Jackson, writing in 2018,[75] agreed that the abolition of recoverable success fees has substantially reduced litigation costs and that the ban on referral fees has (despite some circumventions) significantly reduced the cost of PI litigation. He accepted that DBAs had been a failure as few people used them. Nevertheless, he concluded that: "Despite all the criticisms which I have received over the last 10 years, the blunt and inescapable fact is that the Jackson reforms have achieved significant reductions in the costs of litigation."

(2013) 32 C.J.Q. 231. DBAs have been used very sparingly by the legal profession since the Jackson reforms took effect in 2013: note the 2015 report of the Civil Justice Council (CJC), *The Damages-Based Agreements Reform Project: Drafting and Policy Issues.*

69 LASPO Act 2012 ss.56–60. Enforcement is through the relevant regulator.

70 A recent case has condemned the practice of automatically setting the success fee at 25% of the damages without first carrying out an assessment of the risk: *Herbert v HH Law Ltd* [2018] EWHC 580 (QB), affirmed on appeal [2019] EWCA Civ 527; [2019] 1 W.L.R. 4253.

71 *Simmons v Castle* [2012] EWCA Civ 1288; [2013] 1 W.L.R. 1239, amending earlier judgment: [2012] EWCA Civ 1039.

72 See LASPO Act 2012 s.9 and Sch.1. Part 1 of Sch.1 describes the civil legal services that can generally be made available under the arrangements for civil legal aid.

73 For its current view, see *https://www.lawsociety.org.uk/topics/civil-litigation/* [Accessed 1 August 2020].

74 See *https://www.gov.uk/government/publications/post-implementation-review-of-part-2-of-laspo* (Published February 2019) [Accessed 1 August 2020].

75 R. Jackson, "Was it worth it?" (2018) 34 P.N. 61.

Time

Litigation moves very slowly (which of course adds to its cost). Despite the attempts of the Woolf reforms to speed up litigation[76] and despite time limits (set under the Limitation Act 1980) within which actions must be brought, it remains the fact that many cases take years to get to court, during which the claimant will generally have to wait to receive any compensation.

1–025

Risk

The adversarial system makes litigation a risky option. Indeed, the risk of litigation is often used by defendants to force the claimant to settle, rather than face the possibility of losing every-thing in a court of law. Lewis commented recently that the outcome of a personal injury action is not simply a matter of the rules of tort law, but that, in reality, factors such as the skills of the lawyers, the resources available to establish evidence and the ability of the parties to bear the threat of legal costs make a difference. In his view, bearing in mind that the majority of claims are settled, one should not underestimate also how far the strategies and tactics adopted by lawyers make a difference.[77]

1–026

Difficulty

Despite the intervention of Lord Woolf, going to law is often a complicated process. The workings of the law seem impenetrable to many lay people. Few would attempt a claim in tort without the assistance of qualified lawyers, and getting this assistance may be expensive, time-consuming and often alienating to an individual who simply wishes to be compensated for his or her injury.

1–027

Absence of litigation consciousness

Traditionally, there has been a lack of litigation awareness in England and Wales. Accident victims have been far more likely to contact their insurers, or blame bad luck, than seek a possible defendant on whom to transfer their loss.[78] This, however, seems to have changed in recent years with the introduction of conditional fees. Few can have missed the aggressive advertising of numerous firms offering to take on personal injury claims. Such advertising has raised litigation awareness, but its effect must, of course, be balanced against the other

1–028

---

76 See the final report of Lord Woolf, *Access to Justice* (1996).

77 R. Lewis, "Strategies and tactics in litigating personal injury claims: Tort law in action" [2018] J.P.I. Law 113.

78 A survey conducted by researchers at the Centre for Socio-Legal Studies in Oxford in 1976 found that only 14% of personal injury victims consulted a lawyer: D. Harris, *Compensation and Support for Illness and Injury* (Clarendon Press, 1984).

problems with litigation which we have considered. Datamonitor, an organisation which tracks personal injury litigation, found only a gradual increase in the number of personal injury claims in recent years, with claims rising by 8.3% in 2006–07 and 10.9% in 2008–09. Although it estimated that the personal injury market increased by 17.1% between 2010 and 2011, Global Data in 2016 noted a small decline in litigation following the government reforms discussed in para.1–024.[79] Lewis and Morris argue that, in fact, the majority of injured people still do not go on to claim compensation despite being encouraged to do so through widespread "no-win no-fee" advertising. An exception arises in the context of road traffic accidents where there is a strong culture of claiming and it is these figures which serve to inflate the relevant statistics.[80] For example, there was a rise in motor claims of 1.6% between 2017/18 and 2018/19, while clinical negligence claims dropped by 3.4% during this period.[81]

Whilst the statistical reality, therefore, is that there is no alarming growth of a "compensation culture" in the UK,[82] the Government has felt the need to address a *perception* to the contrary—this perception was apparently held by some local authorities, who had acted defensively to protect themselves from the prospect of litigation, in one case, for example, by closing down a popular public beach to avoid any risk of drowning.[83] The Compensation Act 2006 puts on a statutory footing what has always been the position at common law, namely that the courts, in deciding whether to impose liability in negligence, can take into account the question of whether such liability might be adverse to the public interest by preventing "desirable activities" from taking place.[84] The Act also provides that "an apology, an offer of treatment or other redress, shall not of itself amount to an admission of negligence"[85] and makes provision for the regulation of the claims management industry.[86] The Social Action, Responsibility and Heroism Act 2015 (SARAH) further states that a court, which is determining whether a defendant has met the standard of care in a specific case, should have regard to the matters mentioned in ss.2 to 4 of the Act, namely[87]:

79   UK Personal Injury Litigation 2016 (Global Data, 2016)

80   R. Lewis and A. Morris, "Challenging views of tort" [2013] J.P.I. Law 69. See also R. Lewis, "Compensation culture reviewed: incentives to claim and damages levels" [2014] J.P.I. Law 209. Note also the introduction of Part 1 of the Civil Liability Act 2018 which seeks to reduce the number of whiplash personal injury claims in road traffic accidents and thereby lead to a reduction in motor insurance premiums (not yet in force).

81   Employer claims do also seem to be on the rise with a further increase of 29% between 2017/18 and 2018/19. See statistics from the government's Compensation Recovery Unit, available at *https://www.gov.uk/government/ publications/compensation-recovery-unit-performance-data/compensation-recovery-unit-performance-data* [Accessed 1 August 2020].

82   See, e.g. A. Morris, "Spiralling or stabilising? The compensation culture and our propensity to claim damages for personal injury" (2007) 70 M.L.R. 349 and "'Common sense common safety': the compensation culture perspective" (2011) 27 P.N. 82. Note also E. Quill and R.J. Friel (eds), *Damages and Compensation Culture: Comparative Perspectives* (Hart, 2016).

83   *Tomlinson v Congleton BC* [2004] 1 A.C. 46, discussed in Ch.8.

84   See Compensation Act 2006 s.1.

85   Compensation Act 2006 s.2.

86   Compensation Act 2006 Pt II. For further discussion, see R. Herbert, "The Compensation Act 2006" [2006] 4 J.P.I. Law 337.

87   See Partington, who comments on the ambiguous and opaque meaning of the terms "for the benefit of society"

- whether the alleged negligence or breach of statutory duty occurred when the person was acting for the benefit of society or any of its members (s.2);

- whether the person, in carrying out the activity giving rise to the claim, demonstrated a predominantly responsible approach towards protecting the safety or other interests of others (s.3);

- whether the alleged negligence or breach of statutory duty occurred when the person was acting heroically by intervening in an emergency to assist an individual in danger (s.4).

Again, the aim is not to change the law but to emphasise to judges that it is necessary to consider all relevant circumstances in the case.[88] The underlying message, however, is to reassure defendants that they should not desist from acts of heroism for fear of being sued.

Proposals for reform

It is clear that tort law is far from perfect. A number of suggestions for reform have been made, which we consider below. These suggestions are not without problems and all require the legislature to take tough political decisions about the aims of any reformed compensation system. On current thinking, the possibilities for reform are threefold:

1–029

(1) A mixed system

The Pearson Commission made a number of recommendations about reforming the system of compensation in England and Wales.[89] Its main proposal was that a mixed system of tort law and social security should be retained, but with greater emphasis on the role of social security payments.[90] Greater attention would also be paid to how tort and social security worked together. For certain accidents, such as road traffic accidents[91] (which represent a large proportion of total accident claims) special provision would be made. The Commission proposed a

1–030

---

and "a predominantly responsible approach" in the Act: N. Partington, "'It's just not cricket'. Or is it?" (2016) 32 P.N. 77. For further criticism, see R. Mulheron, "Legislating dangerously: Bad samaritans, good society and the Heroism Act 2015" (2017) 80 M.L.R. 88.

88   The Act applies to England and Wales only and came into force on 13 April 2015.

89   See J. Fleming, "The Pearson report: its 'strategy'" (1979) 42 M.L.R. 249.

90   Vol.1 para.275, on the basis that social security payments were quick, certain and inexpensive to administer and already covered the majority of accident victims.

91   Specific proposals were also suggested for airline and vaccination accidents, defective products and extraordinary risks.

no-fault system for road traffic accidents funded by a 1p tariff per gallon of petrol.[92] This would spread the cost of such accidents, whilst placing the greatest burden on those who consume the most petrol. This was justified on the basis that drivers who use the most petrol—either by driving long distances or by driving vehicles with high petrol consumption—are those most likely to cause an accident.

The proposals were criticised for singling out road traffic accident victims and giving them preferential treatment over victims of other types of accident.[93] They can also be criticised, of course, for ignoring the functions of tort law in terms of deterrence and retribution (although the Commission felt that these ends could be adequately served if tort law were retained concurrently with a no-fault scheme). Delivered in 1978, immediately prior to the election of the new Thatcher Conservative Government, a plan of reform based on increasing state involvement in individual welfare stood little chance of success. In the event, of the Commission's 188 recommendations, only a handful have been implemented.[94] It is most unlikely that this situation will change.

(2) No-fault liability

1–031

This is a more radical proposal. It is based on the proposition that if tort law primarily aims to compensate victims, it achieves this in an inefficient and often arbitrary way. Tort law is inefficient because of the sheer costs of administering the system. The Pearson Commission reported that the operating costs of the tort system amounted to a figure representing about 85% of the money paid out in compensation. In other words, for every £100 paid out, it costs about £85 (in insurers' handling fees, lawyers' fees etc) just to make the payment. Clearly this can be seen as a waste of society's resources. The costs of running a no-fault scheme may be much lower.

Tort is arbitrary in the sense that only those victims who can point to a tortfeasor can recover full compensation. All other accident victims must fall back on other forms of compensation which are likely to be paid at a lower level. By contrast, no-fault liability seeks to compensate all accident victims on the basis of need.

Although the Pearson Commission felt that the adoption of a comprehensive no-fault scheme to the exclusion of tort was beyond their terms of reference,[95] a different view was taken by the Woodhouse Commission in New Zealand, which in 1967 recommended that such

---

92   Vol.1 Ch.18.

93   See, e.g. A. L. Ogus, P. Corfield and D. R. Harris, "Pearson: Principled Reform or Political Compromise?" (1978) 7 I.L.J. 143.

94   e.g. special treatment for vaccine-damaged children was implemented in the Vaccine Damage Payments Act 1979, which provides for a tax-free lump-sum payment of £120,000 where serious mental or physical damage has been caused by the administration of specified vaccines: Vaccine Damage Payments Act 1979 Statutory Sum Order 2007 (SI 2007/1931) art.2.

95   Vol.1 para.274, although it may be questioned whether this was an excuse to avoid discussion due to the obvious disagreement within the Commission as to the relationship between tort and no-fault liability.

a scheme should be adopted in that country.[96] A comprehensive system of state-run compensation for all "accidents" causing personal injury and death was brought in by the New Zealand Labour Government in 1974 and tort actions for personal injury were abolished. The term "accident" has been extended to cover medical misadventure and intentional acts such as battery and rape. With its five aims of community responsibility, comprehensive entitlement, real compensation, complete rehabilitation and administrative efficiency, the system provides a dramatic contrast to our own system of tort law. Under the scheme, everyone in New Zealand is eligible for comprehensive injury cover no matter whether the victim is driving, playing sport, at home, at work, no matter how the injury happened, even if the victim was contributory negligent, and no matter whether the victim is retired, a child, on benefit or studying. The scheme is funded by citizens paying premiums into relevant funds. Accordingly, employers and the self-employed pay to cover work-related injuries, and drivers to cover road traffic accidents.[97] Accidents which occur outside of these contexts are funded by general taxation.

The New Zealand scheme has run for over 40 years, and the New Zealand experience is useful in evaluating our own system.[98] A number of conclusions can be drawn. First, a comprehensive system which seeks to replace tort law damages in every respect is inevitably expensive. The escalating cost of the New Zealand scheme led to the passing of legislation to curtail the scheme and reduce the level of benefits available to accident victims. Generally speaking, the scheme now compensates only lost earnings, although additional lump-sum payments for victims with permanent disability have been re-introduced, in response to criticism from claimants that the scheme was unfair by comparison to a tort action. Compensation for non-financial loss (such as pain and suffering), however, is not available. The scheme is administered by the Accident Compensation Corporation, whose tasks now include the promotion of accident-prevention measures (such as speed limits) and the promotion of rehabilitation of accident victims.[99] Secondly, it is clear that the success of a no-fault scheme depends on the political mood of the country. This, of course, may change over time. In the early 1970s, many contemplated that the New Zealand scheme would expand, but in fact it has contracted. In the UK, the political mood is not in favour of the no-fault option, which requires a dominant philosophy of state intervention and responsibility. Thirdly, deterrence theorists have questioned

---

96   See *Report of the Royal Commission of Inquiry on Compensation for Personal Injury in New Zealand* (1967).

97   By means of part of the motor vehicle licensing fee and a percentage of petrol sales.

98   Information can be gathered from the website of the Accident Compensation Corporation which administers the scheme at *http://www.acc.co.nz* [Accessed 1 August 2020]. See, further, K. Oliphant, "Beyond misadventure: compensation for medical injuries in New Zealand" (2007) 15 Med. L. Rev. 357, P. Blake; "Medical mishap: no fault compensation as an alternative to civil litigation—a review of 30 years' experience with the New Zealand Accident Compensation Corporation system" (2010) 78 Med. Leg. J. 126, J.M. Manning, "Plus ca change, plus c'est la meme chose: Negligence and treatment injury in New Zealand's accident compensation scheme" (2014) 14 Med. L. Int. 22 and C. Hodges and S. Macleod, "New Zealand: The Accident Compensation Scheme" in S. Macleod and C. Hodges, *Redress Schemes for Personal Injuries* (Hart, 2017).

99   For the history of the New Zealand scheme, see *https://www.acc.co.nz/about-us/who-we-are/our-history/* [Accessed 1 August 2020].

whether no-fault liability removes incentives to avoid accidents[100] and current statistics from New Zealand indicate ongoing concern at the level of accidents in this country.[101]

In 2003, the Chief Medical Officer, Sir Liam Donaldson, rejected the option of a comprehensive no-fault compensation scheme for treatment under the NHS, when faced with an estimated cost of £4 billion a year.[102] Instead, a fault-based scheme was proposed under the NHS Redress Act 2006. This scheme (which would permit claims only where there is "qualifying liability in tort") aimed to supplement tort law by providing victims of medical negligence with up to £20,000 in compensation, together with an apology or remedial care, as appropriate. Patients would have been able to withdraw from the scheme if they decided that they would rather take their claim to court. The idea behind the scheme was to settle claims in a non-adversarial way. This is in the interests of patient welfare, since it avoids the stress and delay associated with litigation. It is also in the interests of the medical profession—it was hoped that, free from the prospect of court action, medical professionals might be more willing to admit their mistakes and treat them as opportunities for learning. The scheme was not without its critics, however, who feared that it would deprive claimants of their right to have claims decided by a judge, that it was too narrow in scope and that, by permitting both fact- and fault-finding to be managed and controlled by the NHS, it would enable the NHS to act as judge and jury of its own (negligent) mistakes.[103] As Quick noted in 2012, such criticisms now seem redundant given that the scheme has yet to be implemented in England (and this remains the case in 2020),[104] although the Welsh Government has taken forward the reforms in the NHS Redress Act 2006 by passing regulations as part of its "Putting Things Right" project.[105] It remains to be seen whether, if the scheme in Wales proves effective,[106] the Government will look again at introducing a no-fault scheme for clinical negligence.

---

100 See J.H. Arlen, "Compensation systems and efficient deterrence" (1993) 52 Md. L. Rev. 1093; R. Posner, "A theory of negligence" (1972) 1 J. Legal Stud. 29.

101 Statistics, for example, on New Zealand motor vehicle accident claims may be found at *https://catalogue.data.govt.nz/dataset/motor-vehicle-accident-claims* [Accessed 1 August 2020]. An Independent Taskforce on Workplace Health and Safety in 2013 found that New Zealand's health and safety system was not fit for purpose and commented on a lack of adequate 'motivation' for employers.

102 See Chief Medical Officer, *Making Amends: A consultation paper setting out proposals for reforming the approach to clinical negligence in the NHS* (Department of Health, 2003).

103 See P. Gooderham, "Special Treatment?" (2007) 157 N.L.J. 694. See, generally, E. Cave, "Redress in the NHS" (2011) 27 P.N. 138.

104 O. Quick, "Patient safety and the problem and potential of law" (2012) 28 P.N. 78, 87.

105 The National Health Service (Concerns, Complaints and Redress Arrangements) (Wales) Regulations 2011 (SI 2011/704). See A.L. Ferguson and E. Braithwaite, "Putting Things Right in Wales" (2012) 18 *Clinical Risk* 6–8. See, generally at *http://www.wales.nhs.uk/governance-emanual/putting-things-right* [Accessed 1 August 2020].

106 See A. L. Ferguson, G. Cooper and G. Rees, "Putting things right in NHS Wales" [2018] J.P.I. Law 182 which concludes that it promotes a welcome culture of transparency, efficiency and learning. Others are, however, more critical: S. Davies and H. James, "Are the Welsh NHS redress arrangements 'putting things right' for patients in Wales" [2018] J.P.I. Law 190.

(3) Insurance

This proposal is perhaps more consistent with current political views on free market economics. It is primarily advanced by Professor Atiyah, who explains it in his book *The Damages Lottery*.[107] Insurance, as we have seen, is an important adjunct to the law of tort, yet the influence of insurance on the law of tort is a matter of some dispute.[108] Whilst the orthodox position is that the courts should ignore the presence of insurance cover,[109] judges such as Lord Denning have used the presence of insurance cover to justify developments in the law aimed at achieving the principle of loss distribution.[110] Professor Atiyah's approach is more radical. Put simply, he argues that the tort system should be replaced by a system of first party insurance. By purchasing "first party" insurance, a person insures himself or herself against suffering harm. (It should be distinguished from "third party" insurance, where a person insures against liability for harm suffered by others.) The argument runs that, if everyone were covered by first party insurance, there would be no need for an inefficient system of tort law. Accident compensation and prevention could be dealt with through the more efficient medium of the market. There are a number of objections to this suggestion,[111] the strongest of which is that not everyone in society has the means to pay for first party insurance. One must also have doubts about the morality and the wisdom of placing all accident compensation in the hands of insurers. At present, tort law provides the benchmark against which the appropriate levels of compensation for personal injuries are assessed. It is questionable whether justice would be seen to be done if this function were removed from the judiciary and placed in the hands of insurance companies.

Tortious liability: conclusion

Tort law is a stimulating, if sometimes complicated and often frustrating subject to study. It faces a number of challenges, some of which are of quite recent origin. The effects of the Human Rights Act 1998, and the Woolf reforms on civil litigation continue to shape the contours of tortious liability. Despite its failings, tort law continues to offer a humane and pragmatic response to the problems of Twenty-first century life.

---

107 P.S. Atiyah, *The Damages Lottery* (Hart, 1997).

108 See J. Stapleton, "Tort, Insurance and Liability" (1995) 58 M.L.R. 820; criticised by J. Morgan, "Tort, insurance and incoherence" (2004) 67 M.L.R. 384 and, more recently, R. Merkin, "Tort, insurance and ideology: Further thoughts" (2012) 75 M.L.R. 301, who argues that Stapleton's argument that neither insurance nor insurability are relevant to the construction of tort liability underplays the role of insurance in the law of obligations, particularly when legislation requires compulsory insurance.

109 See Lord Bridge in *Hunt v Severs* [1994] 2 A.C. 350 at 363 who held that at common law the fact that the defendant is insured can have no relevance in assessing damages. See also Viscount Simonds in *Lister v Romford Ice and Cold Storage Co Ltd* [1957] A.C. 555 at 576–577.

110 See, e.g. *Nettleship v Weston* [1971] 2 Q.B. 691 at 700.

111 See the excellent review of Professor Atiyah's book by J. Conaghan and W. Mansell, "From the Permissive to the Dismissive Society" (1998) 25 J.L.S. 284.

2

Negligence: The Duty of care

Introduction

2–001

The tort of negligence is the most frequently used of all the torts and is therefore perhaps the most important. It flourished in the latter part of the Twentieth century, rising to a dominant position because of the flexible nature of its rules, which have allowed the judges to expand the tort to protect many claimants who would otherwise have been left unprotected by the law. Unfortunately for the law student, however, this broadness of judicial approach can make the principles of the tort seem frustratingly vague.

This book explores negligence over five chapters, taking each ingredient of the tort in turn. This chapter introduces these ingredients and then, from a general perspective, discusses the first of them, namely the duty of care. The next two chapters explore some of the special difficulties the courts have encountered in deciding whether a duty of care should exist in relation to economic loss and psychiatric illness. The last two chapters on negligence deal with the remaining ingredients of the tort, namely breach of duty and causation.

This chapter begins with a basic definition. There then follows a short section describing the correct approach to be taken when studying negligence and a section giving a brief overview of the tort. These sections introduce certain important ideas which, once grasped, will help dispel some of the frustration often experienced by those who approach the subject for the first time.

Definition of "Negligence"

The tort of negligence has been usefully defined as:

> **". . . a breach of a legal duty to take care which results in damage to the claimant."[1]**

The tort is not usually concerned with harm inflicted *intentionally*. Rather, it is concerned with harm inflicted "accidentally" or through want of care. We shall see, however, that establishing negligence involves much more than simply showing that the defendant behaved "carelessly"—careless behaviour is only one ingredient of the tort.

To establish the tort of negligence, the claimant must prove three things:

- the defendant owes the claimant a duty of care;

- the defendant has acted in breach of that duty, and

- as a result, the claimant has suffered damage which is not too remote a consequence of the defendant's breach.

For the purpose of learning the law, it is convenient to consider each element of the tort in turn. Rarely in practice, however, will disputes ever involve all three elements. Moreover, the courts have a tendency to blur the distinctions between each of the separate elements of negligence. Quite often, therefore, a judgment may indicate that the defendant is not liable but may not make it clear which of the three separate requirements of the tort has not been fulfilled.[2] This difficulty stems from the fact that, as we shall see, the concept of "reasonable foreseeability" is used by the courts in establishing all three elements of the tort.

Studying Negligence

The tort of negligence covers such a wide range of factual situations that the search for a single "set of rules", applicable to all types of negligence case, will be fruitless. The correct approach, then, is to focus on the *type of interest* which the claimant is trying to use the tort to protect (physical safety, the safety of property, financial well-being, or psychological well-being), and

---

1 W.H.V. Rogers, *Winfield and Jolowicz on Tort*, 18th edn (Sweet & Maxwell, 2010), p.150.
2 This is not necessarily to be regarded as a failing. See *Sam (aka Al-Sam) v Atkins* [2005] EWCA Civ 1452, *Calvert v William Hill* [2008] EWCA Civ 1427; [2009] Ch.330.

then to think about why the courts have felt either able or unable to extend the scope of negligence to protect that interest in particular situations. The language of the judges, and the pattern of their decision-making, will only begin to make real sense when considered alongside the political and economic forces which motivate decisions in negligence cases.

When one looks at what negligence is trying to achieve within society—the redistribution of certain risks associated with day-to-day activities—it becomes clear why the judges have had such difficulty in formulating workable rules for the tort. The point to grasp is that negligence is essentially concerned with a conflict of values within society. The driver of a car, for example, wishes to go fast to reach his destination, but the pedestrian crossing the road wishes the driver were going more slowly so as to lessen the likelihood of being knocked down. In essence, therefore, in order to decide the question of negligence, the judge must make a *political and moral value-judgment* as to the relative merits of fast driving and road safety in society. Making this sort of judgment, however, is not a task with which judges feel very comfortable, because it is one for which the British Constitution does not equip them. As Lord Scarman put it in *McLoughlin v O'Brian*[3]:

> **". . . the policy issue where to draw the line is not justiciable. The problem is one of social, economic and financial policy. The considerations relevant to a decision are not such as to be capable of being handled within the limits of the forensic process."**

Clearly, his Lordship is referring to the fact that, in constitutional theory, the role of the judge is not to make law, but only to interpret it. Much of the interest in studying negligence, however, comes from exploring the way in which the judges have managed to make new law, usually without explicitly stating that they have done so. For constitutional reasons, the judges are not able to use the explicit language of politicians or economists in their judgments. This means that where the relevant political and economic reasoning is present in cases, it is often encoded in "judicial", rather than "political" language. A proper understanding of the tort of negligence, then, requires a good deal of "reading between the lines".

An Overview of Negligence

2–004

In 1932, Lord Atkin, in the landmark case of *Donoghue v Stevenson*,[4] formulated a general principle (known as the "neighbour principle") by which the existence of a legal duty to take care could be determined, thus effectively inventing the modern tort of negligence. The problem

---

3   [1983] 1 A.C. 410 at 431.
4   [1932] A.C. 562.

with Lord Atkin's general principle, however, was that it contained too little by which, on the basis of logic, the limits of the tort could ever be confined.

As the tort of negligence developed, the courts sought to qualify Lord Atkin's general principle with a number of complex, inherently vague and sometimes rather arbitrary rules. These rules were necessary in order to keep the scope of negligence within acceptable bounds. In particular, the courts felt it important to avoid being overrun with a multiplicity of negligence claims (they were afraid to open the so-called "floodgates of litigation") because, as was noted in Ch.1, the tort system is very costly to administer. The courts were also afraid of allowing what is sometimes called "crushing liability". Crushing liability would occur if one particular defendant were made liable for a very large amount of loss, of which the defendant's actions were the logical cause, but for which it would be unfair or economically inefficient to make the defendant responsible in law.

In studying negligence, we shall see how, during the period from 1963 until the mid–1980s, the House of Lords was willing to apply Lord Atkin's "neighbour principle" fairly broadly, so that it came to be applied to factual situations which were far removed from the facts of *Donoghue v Stevenson*. During this period, the tort of negligence grew from a tort protecting only property and physical well-being into one which, to a limited extent, now protects the financial and psychological well-being of claimants. We shall then see how, in recent years, faced with the problems of indeterminate and crushing liability, their Lordships have retraced their steps, diminishing the scope of the tort.

To some extent, it can be seen that the expansion of negligence, and its subsequent contraction, have mirrored certain changes in political thought. This period saw a gradual change away from a philosophy of welfarism and state control towards a philosophy of individualism and contraction of state responsibility. The long rule of a Conservative Government, from 1979 to 1997, brought arguments about economic efficiency into tighter focus than ever before. Subsequent governments have done little to change this focus. It is likely that these arguments have influenced the courts, resulting in their reluctance to make people responsible for certain types of loss particularly when, under a contract, the risk of that loss (and the reward for taking that risk) has been allocated to someone else. This point is further explored in Ch.3.

The Duty of Care

An overview

As the courts have struggled to determine the proper scope of negligence, they have used each of its three ingredients—duty, breach and causation—as a *control mechanism* to set limits to the tort. This multi-faceted approach can sometimes be rather confusing. What is clear, however, is that in recent times there has been a marked tendency to deal with the question of

2–005

liability by reference to the scope of the duty of care. Logically, establishing the existence of a duty of care is the first hurdle a claimant must overcome. It therefore makes sense for a court to deal with this first, because it simplifies the decision-making process.

In many situations, it will be obvious from established case law that the defendant owes the claimant a duty of care. The real problem for the courts has been to decide whether a duty of care should be owed in *novel* factual situations which are not covered by authority. This point was made clearly by the UK Supreme Court in its recent decision in *Robinson v Chief Constable of West Yorkshire Police*.[5] *Robinson* stated that English law adopts an approach based on precedent, developing the law incrementally and by analogy with established authorities. In many situations it will be clearly established by case-law that a duty of care is owed e.g. that motorists owe a duty of care to other road users, manufacturers to consumers, employers to their employees, doctors to their patients, and so on. Only where this case-law does not exist and established principles do not provide an answer—that is, in *novel* cases—will the courts need to go beyond those principles to decide whether a duty of care should be recognised However, formulating a test for novel cases has not proven to be straightforward exercise. In *Caparo v Dickman*,[6] Lord Roskill concluded:

> "It has now to be accepted that there is no simple formula or touchstone to which recourse can be had in order to provide in every case a ready answer."

With this in mind, we can now examine more closely the historical development of the duty of care, and the modern approach to deciding whether it exists.

The historical background

2–006

Until the late Nineteenth century, negligence was not regarded as a tort in its own right. The traditional system of writs, under which claims would not be recognised unless they had been made in the prescribed form, did not include a specific writ for negligence. Early case law, however, did suggest that in certain situations liability based on carelessness could arise. For example, it was established from early times that innkeepers and common carriers could be liable for the careless performance of a specific task. Later, in the seventeenth century, it became established that a surgeon or an attorney would be liable if his conduct was less than that expected of a reasonably skilled professional. Although, at the time, such cases were not considered in terms of a separate tort of negligence, with hindsight they show us how the courts came gradually to accept that liability could arise where a defendant had merely been careless, as opposed to having committed an intentional act of wrongdoing.

---

5   [2018] UKSC 4; [2018] A.C. 736 at [21] and [27] per Lord Reed. See also *Michael v Chief Constable of South Wales Police* [2015] UKSC 2; [2015] A.C. 1732 at [106].
6   [1990] 2 A.C. 605 at 628.

In the Nineteenth century, the technology of the industrial revolution brought with it great potential for personal injury. In addition, as urban areas became more densely populated, congestion on city streets led to an increase in the number of "running down" cases. These factors brought about a change in judicial attitudes. As Professor Winfield observes:

> **"Early railway trains, in particular, were notable neither for speed nor for safety. They killed any object from a Minister of State to a wandering cow, and this naturally reacted on the law."[7]**

The stage was set for the emergence of a new tort which could meet the needs of claimants in an increasingly dangerous age.

The first step: identifying a general principle

Whilst, in the nineteenth century, the courts came to recognise that liability could be based on careless conduct, there was no general principle of law applicable to these situations. Instead, a body of case law emerged consisting of a collection of isolated instances where such liability had been imposed. The major obstacle to the development of a general principle seems to have been the Victorian belief that individuals should bear all responsibility for their own welfare and that they could not be expected to look out for the welfare of others unless they were being paid to do so. The concept of "collectivism"—the idea that every member of society can benefit if each member takes some responsibility for the well-being of others—whilst central to our modern way of thinking, was alien to Victorian political culture. Thus, whilst the courts were happy to make defendants liable where they had *assumed* responsibility for the care of another by entering into a contract with that other for reward, they were less happy about *imposing* on defendants a gratuitous duty to look after others.

This attitude was apparent in the decision in *Winterbottom v Wright*.[8] The plaintiff was a coach driver, employed by the Postmaster-General, who suffered serious injuries when he fell from a coach that had been defectively built by the defendants. It was held that the driver could not recover compensation from the builders of the coach because he was not a party to the contract with the Postmaster-General, under which the defendants had supplied the coach. It was decided that while the defendants had assumed responsibility under a contract for the quality of a thing supplied, they would not also be liable for damage suffered by a third party who was not privy to the contract. This idea later became known as the "privity of contract fallacy". It persisted in the law until it was overturned by the decision in *Donoghue v Stevenson*[9] in 1932.

2-007

---

7 P.H. Winfield, "The history of negligence in the law of torts" (1926) 42 L.Q.R. 184, 195.
8 (1842) 10 M. & W. 109.
9 [1932] A.C. 562.

The first real suggestion that there could be a general principle of law governing the existence of the duty of care came in 1883. Brett MR, in *Heaven v Pender*,[10] observed that the following proposition appeared to cover all of the recognised cases of liability for careless conduct:

> "... whenever one person is by circumstances placed in such a position with regard to another that everyone of ordinary sense who did think would at once recognise that if he did not use ordinary care and skill in his own conduct with regard to those circumstances he would cause danger of injury to the person or property of the other, a duty arises to use ordinary care and skill to avoid such danger."

The majority of the Court of Appeal, however, were unwilling to adopt such a broad principle of liability,[11] and in his later decision in *Le Lievre v Gould*,[12] Brett MR (now Lord Esher MR), declined to apply the principle to a case involving purely financial loss. In a sense, Brett MR's formulation of a general principle came before its time. It was not until 1932 that a change in judicial attitudes, which mirrored the political and economic changes that had taken place in society, allowed for a unified approach to cases of careless conduct.

A further problem with Brett MR's formulation of the principle was that, although it referred to the "position" of one person "with regard to another" as giving rise to a duty of care, it did not go very far in describing the nature of the relationship which had to exist between the claimant and the defendant. This meant that, on the face of it, Brett MR's general principle would have given rise to liability in any case where a person should have foreseen that his conduct might cause harm to another. We shall see that Lord Atkin's reformulation of the principle in *Donoghue v Stevenson*[13] makes it much clearer that foreseeability of harm alone should not be sufficient to establish the existence of a duty of care.

Lord Atkin's "neighbour principle"

2–008

In 1932, the House of Lords decided the famous case of *Donoghue v Stevenson*.[14] The facts of the case have become legendary,[15] although it should be noted that, because the case was decided by the House of Lords on a point of law and was then settled before going to trial,

---

10   (1883) 11 Q.B.D. 503 at 509.
11   (1883) 11 Q.B.D. 503 at 516 per Cotton and Bowen LJJ.
12   [1893] 1 Q.B. 491 at 497.
13   [1932] A.C. 562.
14   [1932] A.C. 562.
15   For an entertaining review of the case, see A. Rodger QC (who became a Supreme Court justice), "Mrs Donoghue and Alfenus Varus" (1988) 41 C.L.P. 1.

these facts were never actually proved. It was alleged that Mrs Donoghue and her friend visited Minchella's Wellmeadow Café, in Paisley.[16] At the café, the friend bought for Mrs Donoghue a "ginger beer float", consisting of ginger beer, supplied in an opaque bottle, and ice-cream. Mrs Donoghue drank some of the mixture, and when her friend topped up the drink, out of the ginger beer bottle floated the decomposed remains of a snail. Mrs Donoghue claimed that the sight of the snail, together with the ginger beer she had already drunk, made her ill.

Mrs Donoghue had no claim in contract law because the contract for the ginger beer had been made between the retailer and her friend. She therefore brought an action in tort against the *manufacturer* of the ginger beer (the *retailer* had not been at fault in that the ginger beer had been supplied to him in a sealed opaque bottle, so that he could not have looked inside the bottle to check that its contents were wholesome). There was no possibility that the snail could have entered the bottle at any stage after it had been supplied by the manufacturer.

Mrs Donoghue's position, however, was very similar to that of the coach driver in *Winterbottom v Wright*. She had been the victim of a defective product that had been supplied to another person under a contract to which she was not a party. According to *Winterbottom v Wright*, it appeared that the manufacturer would only be liable under his contract with the retailer. Yet Mrs Donoghue succeeded in her claim. A majority of the House of Lords distinguished *Winterbottom v Wright*, holding that a manufacturer of products, which he sells in such a form as to show that he intends them to reach the ultimate consumer in the form in which they left him, with no reasonable possibility of intermediate examination before the products are consumed, would be liable to the consumer in tort if he failed to take reasonable care to ensure that the products were safe. Their Lordships rejected the so-called "privity of contract fallacy" of *Winterbottom*—privity of contract did not prevent a third party bringing an action in tort.

At first sight, it seemed that the decision in *Donoghue v Stevenson* had simply added yet another category to the separate instances of negligence recognised by the law. What has become significant about the case, however, is Lord Atkin's analysis of the law and his subsequent formulation of a general principle for determining the existence of a duty of care. This is what Lord Atkin said[17]:

> "... in English law there must be, and is, some general conception of relations giving rise to a duty of care, of which the particular cases found in the books are but instances ... The rule that you are to love your neighbour becomes, in law, you must not injure your neighbour; and the lawyer's question who is my neighbour? receives a restricted reply. You must take reasonable care to avoid acts or

---

16 Paisley is in Scotland and the case was therefore brought in Scots law. The House of Lords (now Supreme Court) is the highest appeal court in private law matters for England and Wales, Scotland and Northern Ireland. The House of Lords in this case accepted that no difference existed between English and Scots law in this instance.

17 [1932] A.C. 562 at 580.

> omissions which you can reasonably foresee would be likely to injure your neighbour. Who then, in law is my neighbour? The answer seems to be—persons who are so closely and directly affected by my act that I ought reasonably to have them in contemplation as being so affected when I am directing my mind to the acts or omissions which are called in question."

Lord Atkin's general principle contained two elements. First, there was the element of "reasonable foreseeability". Thus, a duty of care would be owed where the defendant ought reasonably to foresee that his failure to take care may cause injury to another. (This, of course, is consistent with Brett MR in *Heaven v Pender*.) The second element was the test of "neighbourhood"—a duty of care would be owed only where the claimant was "closely and directly" affected by the defendant's conduct. Brett MR's simple test of foreseeability of harm, therefore, became qualified by the additional need to show, as Lord Atkin put it, a degree of "proximity"[18] between the claimant and the defendant, not in the sense of physical proximity, but in the sense of "close and direct relations".

Lord Atkin's general test of foreseeability plus "proximity", then, gave the courts a basis on which the existence of a duty of care could be decided in all cases. It allowed them to view negligence as a tort in its own right, capable of being developed to meet any new factual situation which arose.

It is important, however, not to overestimate the significance of Lord Atkin's general principle which has a number of flaws. First, although Lord Atkin speaks of "acts or omissions", we shall see that the law treats liability for acts very differently from liability for omissions. Secondly, as the law has developed, it has become clear that, besides identifying the defendant's "neighbour", it is also necessary to identify the *type of loss* which the "neighbour" is likely to suffer (or, in other words, the *type of interest* which the claimant is seeking to use the law to protect) before any decision can be made about whether to impose a duty of care. Lord Atkin's words, spoken in the context of personal injury caused by a defective product, gave little indication of the degree of "proximity" which would be required in other factual situations. We shall see that, especially where other types of harm are in issue, the courts, for policy reasons, have had to say that a far greater degree of "proximity" is required in some situations than in others. In *Donoghue v Stevenson*, Lord Atkin observed:

> "There will no doubt arise cases where it will be difficult to determine whether the contemplated relationship is so close that the duty arises."[19]

Such prescience, it will be seen, was all too accurate.

---

18   Interestingly, the term "proximity" was first used by Brett MR in *Thomas v Quartermaine* (1887) 18 Q.B.D. 685 at 688.
19   [1932] A.C. 562 at 582.

The second step: applying the neighbour principle

Without Lord Atkin's "neighbour principle", the decision in *Donoghue v Stevenson* would simply have been another isolated example of negligence liability. (The case did indeed establish liability in English law for defective products, which is discussed in Ch.9.) It should be noted that Lord Atkin's principle did not form part of the ratio of the case, because the two other majority judges in the case refrained from adopting it. As might be expected, then, the first response of the courts was to treat the case as a narrow example of liability. The judges were particularly reluctant to apply the principle in situations where there was clear authority which excluded liability in negligence, such as where the claimant suffered financial loss because of a carelessly made statement. And so things might have remained, but for a number of radical decisions in the 1960s and 1970s, in which the House of Lords was prepared to overturn previous authority to extend the scope of the duty of care.

2–009

The decision in *Hedley Byrne*

The first of these cases came in 1963. The decision in *Hedley Byrne v Heller and Partners*[20] established, contrary to previous authority, that there could be liability in English law in respect of financial loss caused by negligent misstatement. The case is examined more fully in Ch.3, but it will be convenient to state the facts here.

2–010

Hedley Byrne, who were advertising agents, were about to enter into certain contracts on behalf of one of their clients—a company called Easipower—on terms which meant that, if Easipower failed to honour its obligations under the contracts, Hedley Byrne would become liable to pay Easipower's debts. Hedley Byrne therefore wished to find out whether Easipower was creditworthy, so, through their own bankers, they sought a reference from Easipower's bankers, Heller and Partners. Heller and Partners wrote saying that although the amounts in question were larger than they were accustomed to see, they considered Easipower to be good for the ordinary course of business. But they made it clear that they were providing this advice "without responsibility" on their part. In other words, they included a disclaimer of liability.[21]

On the basis of the favourable credit reference, Hedley Byrne went ahead with the advertising contracts. It turned out, however, that Heller and Partners had carelessly failed to realise that, at the time they gave the reference, Easipower was in a very bad way financially. Easipower went into liquidation shortly after the contracts had been made, so that Hedley Byrne became liable to pay Easipower's debts. Hedley Byrne therefore brought an action against Heller and Partners for the negligently given advice.

Two major problems faced Hedley Byrne. First, their action concerned a statement which had been made carelessly, but previous authority had decided that there could only be liability

---

20 [1964] A.C. 465. For an insightful review of *Hedley Byrne v Heller* and its law-making effect, see R. Buxton, "How the Common Law Gets Made: *Hedley Byrne* and other cautionary tales" (2009) 125 L.Q.R. 60.

21 The validity (or otherwise) of disclaimers of tort liability will be examined at para.16–011.

where a statement had been made fraudulently.[22] Secondly, their action was for financial loss, rather than for personal injury or damage to property—the areas where the courts had so far been willing to impose negligence liability.

Nevertheless, the House of Lords was prepared to hold that, but for the disclaimer of liability, Heller and Partners would have been liable for their negligent statement. Whilst their Lordships were prepared to use Lord Atkin's "neighbour principle" as a starting point in establishing liability, they were not prepared to decide the case purely by analogy to the facts of *Donoghue v Stevenson*. Their Lordships made it clear that there were important differences between negligently made statements causing financial loss and negligently manufactured products causing personal injury. These differences meant that Lord Atkin's principle could not be applied without qualification in negligent misstatement cases. The reasoning in *Hedley Byrne v Heller and Partners* is considered more fully in Ch.3. For present purposes, however, it is sufficient to note that, in order to avoid the problems of indeterminate and "crushing" liability, their Lordships held that in negligent misstatement cases a high degree of "proximity", or closeness of relationship, would be required. It was held that for liability to arise, a "special relationship" had to be shown between the maker of the statement and the person who subsequently relied on it.

The decision in *Dorset Yacht*

2–011

The next landmark case was *Home Office v Dorset Yacht*.[23] This case was important because it imposed a duty of care on the defendant to prevent damage being caused by the actions of others. Liability for the acts of third parties has proved to be a difficult area for the courts and is further discussed later in this chapter.

In *Home Office v Dorset Yacht*, the Home Office had established a Borstal (a prison training camp for young male offenders) on an island off the Dorset coast. One night, because of the carelessness of the guards, a number of the prisoners escaped and caused damage to some yachts moored in the harbour. The House of Lords was prepared to impose liability for the damage on the guards (for whom the Home Office was responsible in law), holding that there were "special relations" between the Home Office and Borstal boys, so that the Home Office could be liable for its failure to prevent the boys from causing damage. This, together with a high degree of foreseeability—escaping and causing the damage was the "very kind of thing" the boys were likely to do—made the Home Office liable.

Lord Reid made the following observation:

> *"Donoghue v Stevenson* **may be regarded as a milestone, and the well-known passage in Lord Atkin's speech should, I think, be regarded as a statement of principle. It is not to be treated as if it**

---

22 See *Derry v Peek* (1889) 14 App. Cas. 337 and *Candler v Crane Christmas & Co* [1951] K.B. 164 (discussed in Ch.3).
23 [1970] A.C. 1004.

> were a statutory definition. It will require qualification in new cir-
> cumstances. But I think the time has come when we can and should
> say that it ought to apply unless there is some justification or valid
> explanation for its exclusion."[24]

Lord Wilberforce's "two stage test"

This positive affirmation of Lord Atkin's principle was approved by the House of Lords in the next important case—the now discredited case of *Anns v Merton LBC*.[25] Here, a local authority had failed to notice that the foundations of a new block of maisonettes had not been dug to an adequate depth. The plaintiffs, who had taken long leases of the maisonettes, found that cracks appeared in the walls. They sued the local authority for the cost of rebuilding. (Nowadays, this case is regarded as one of pure economic loss. It was overruled in 1990 by the decision in *Murphy v Brentwood DC*,[26] discussed in Ch.3.)

2-012

In *Anns*,[27] Lord Wilberforce reformulated the test for determining the existence of a duty of care. According to his Lordship, the judges should ask themselves two questions, one after the other. This became known as Lord Wilberforce's "two stage test" and can be summarised as follows:

> "*Stage one*: is there, between the claimant and defendant, a suf-
> ficient relationship of 'proximity or neighbourhood' such that the
> defendant can reasonably foresee that carelessness on his or her
> part would be likely to cause damage to the claimant? If the answer
> to this question is 'yes', then a prima facie duty of care arises.
> *Stage two*: are there any considerations which should nevertheless
> lead the court to deny a duty of care, or to limit its scope, in these
> particular circumstances?"

This straightforward test had the appeal of simplicity, but unfortunately was flawed. Essentially, the problem was that it was unclear what Lord Wilberforce meant by the word "proximity" in stage one of the test. We have seen that Lord Atkin thought that "foreseeability" and "proximity" were two separate things. Foreseeability of harm alone would not give rise to a duty of care—there had also to be "close and direct relations" between the claimant and the defendant. Lord Wilberforce, on the other hand, now appeared to say that foreseeability *was* the test for proximity. This meant that, in applying the two stage test, if a judge felt that,

---

24 [1970] A.C. 1004 at 1027. Contrast the more reserved approach of Lord Diplock at 1060.
25 [1978] A.C. 728.
26 [1991] A.C. 398.
27 [1978] A.C. 728 at 751.

although harm was foreseeable, liability should not be imposed because the relationship between the claimant and the defendant was not sufficiently close, the judge would have to find some way of expressing this idea by answering Lord Wilberforce's second question, i.e. by explicitly stating a policy reason for denying the existence of a duty of care.

Lord Wilberforce's approach proved difficult, and was eventually abandoned, because, on this interpretation, it did not truly reflect the way the courts decide the existence of the duty of care. The courts do not assume a duty of care and then consider, as a matter of policy, whether in the circumstances the type of damage in question should be compensated. Rather, the policy question of whether certain types of damage should be recoverable in certain circumstances goes to the central question of whether, in each case, a duty should exist in the first place. Reading between the lines, we might observe that the problem with Lord Wilberforce's formulation was that it made it difficult for judges to avoid explicit reference to *political* and *economic* considerations when answering the second question in the two stage test.

Lord Wilberforce's two stage test, then, embodied a more generous approach to the duty of care issue—a *presumption* that a duty of care would exist unless clear policy objections could be found. This approach was adopted in *Junior Books Ltd v Veitchi & Co Ltd*[28] (discussed in Ch.3), where the majority of the House of Lords supported a claim brought by factory-owners against specialist sub-contractors who had negligently installed a floor in their factory.

After *Junior Books*, however, the courts began to express concern about the way in which the duty of care was expanding. Insufficient attention seemed to be given to the problems of indeterminate and crushing liability. Moreover, if tort were prepared to intervene and upset the delicate contractual allocation of risk between a main contractor and a sub-contractor, this would have implications for the prices charged by sub-contractors.

In *Donoghue v Stevenson*, Lord Atkin had recognised these problems when he said:

> **". . . it is of particular importance to guard against the danger of stating propositions of law in wider terms than is necessary, lest essential factors be omitted in the wider survey."[29]**

From the mid-1980s, then, the courts began to examine these "essential factors" more closely and to stress their importance in limiting the scope of the duty of care.

The third step: the retreat from *Anns*

2-013

In a series of decisions, from 1985 onwards, the House of Lords began to reject Lord Wilberforce's broad approach to the duty of care. Lord Keith in *Governors of the Peabody Donation Fund v*

---

28 [1983] 1 A.C. 520.
29 [1932] A.C. 562 at 583.

Sir Lindsay Parkinson & Co Ltd[30] criticised the tendency to treat Lord Wilberforce's simple two stage test as a definitive formula, saying that the temptation to do so should be resisted. In *Leigh & Sillivan Ltd v Aliakmon Shipping Co Ltd (The Aliakmon)*,[31] Lord Brandon stated that Lord Wilberforce's two stage test should only be applied in novel factual situations where the courts had not previously ruled on the existence of a duty of care. Where a precedent existed (either directly or by analogy), the court should follow it, rather than apply the test. In *The Aliakmon*, this approach allowed the House of Lords to reject a claim by a buyer for damage caused by the negligent stowage of goods on board a ship. Whilst the claim may well have satisfied Lord Wilberforce's criteria, their Lordships preferred to follow previous authority which excluded such claims where the buyer had not yet acquired a proprietary interest in the goods.[32]

In 1988, the Privy Council, deciding *Yuen Kun Yeu v Att-Gen of Hong Kong*,[33] was openly critical of the approach adopted in *Anns*. Lord Keith commented that the two stage test appeared to have been elevated to a degree of importance that it did not deserve and that it should not in all circumstances be regarded as a suitable guide to determining the existence of a duty of care. In particular, his Lordship highlighted the danger of misinterpreting stage one of the Wilberforce test as a simple test of foreseeability.

In the light of their Lordships' growing reservations about Lord Wilberforce's approach, it was perhaps unsurprising that in 1990, a seven-member House of Lords took the unusual step of using the 1966 Practice Statement[34] to overturn its own decision in *Anns*. In *Murphy v Brentwood DC*,[35] their Lordships expressed their concerns about the potentially extensive liability permitted under the two stage test, and asserted that *Anns* should no longer be regarded as good law.[36] Instead, the courts should favour the approach suggested by Brennan J, an Australian judge, in *Sutherland Shire Council v Heyman*,[37] that is to say, novel categories of negligence should be developed incrementally and by analogy with established categories, rather than under a general principle which permits a massive extension of a prima facie duty of care, restrained only by indefinable policy considerations. This "incremental" approach is now the accepted means of finding a duty of care in English law.

---

30 [1985] A.C. 210 at 240. See also Lord Bridge in *Curran v Northern Ireland Co-ownership Housing Assoc Ltd* [1987] A.C. 718.
31 [1986] A.C. 785 at 815.
32 Note that the Carriage of Goods by Sea Act 1992 introduced certain amendments to the law which would nowadays enable the claimants to recover.
33 [1988] A.C. 175. Applied in *Davis v Radcliffe* [1990] 1 W.L.R. 821 at 826.
34 Practice Statement (HL: Judicial Precedent) [1966] 1 W.L.R. 1234.
35 [1991] 1 A.C. 398.
36 Contrast the position in Canada, where the Supreme Court retained the *Anns* test and declined to follow *Murphy*, although its reformulation of the *Anns* test in *Cooper v Hobart* (2002) 206 D.L.R. (4th) 193 has brought it closer to the position in English law. See L.N.Klar, "Is Lord Atkin's neighbour principle still relevant to Canadian negligence law?" [2013] Jur. Rev 357.
37 (1985) 60 A.L.R. 1 at 43; (1985) 157 C.L.R. 424 at 480.

The modern approach: *Robinson and Caparo*

2–014

In *Robinson v Chief Constable of West Yorkshire Police*,[38] the claimant (aged 76) had been knocked over by two police officers who were attempting to arrest a drug dealer in a shopping street. The officers had not noticed that she was nearby. The Court of Appeal treated the question as a novel case and applied the *Caparo* test (outlined below) finding that it would not be fair, just and reasonable to impose a duty of care on the police when apprehending offenders. This approach was rejected by the Supreme Court at [29]:

> **In the ordinary run of cases, courts consider what has been decided previously and follow the precedents (unless it is necessary to consider whether the precedents should be departed from). In cases where the question whether a duty of care arises has not previously been decided, the courts will consider the closest analogies in the existing law, with a view to maintaining the coherence of the law and the avoidance of inappropriate distinctions. They will also weigh up the reasons for and against imposing liability, in order to decide whether the existence of a duty of care would be just and reasonable. In the present case, however, . . . all that is required is the application to particular circumstances of established principles governing liability for personal injuries.**

Where, therefore, previous case-law indicated that a duty of care to avoid causing reasonably foreseeable injury to persons and property existed when police were engaged in their core operational activities,[39] the question for the Supreme Court was simply whether to follow the precedent or overturn previous authority. It chose the former.

Equally in *Darnley v Croydon Health Services NHS Trust*,[40] the Supreme Court regarded the question whether the Accident & Emergency hospital receptionist owed a duty of care to the defendant who had wrongly been told there was a four to five hour wait before seeing a doctor as covered by pre-existing authority. This was a recognised situation where a duty of care existed between patient and health provider; it was long established that a duty of care is owed by those who provide and run a casualty department to persons presenting themselves complaining of illness or injury before they are treated or received into care in the hospital's wards.[41]

In contrast, in *James-Bowen v Commissioner of Police of the Metropolis*[42] police officers sought to establish their employer owed them a duty of care to protect them from economic

---

38   [2018] UKSC 4; [2018] A.C. 736 at [21] and [27] per Lord Reed. See also *Michael v Chief Constable of South Wales Police* [2015] UKSC 2; [2015] A.C. 1732 at [106].

39   See para.2–045.

40   [2018] UKSC 50; [2019] A.C. 831.

41   *Barnett v Chelsea and Kensington Hospital Management Committee* [1969] 1 Q.B. 428, per Nield J at 435–436.

42   [2018] UKSC 40; [2018] 1 W.L.R. 4021.

and reputational harm in the conduct of proceedings against the Commissioner based on their alleged misconduct. There was no decided case-law on this point. It was very clearly one in which the claimant sought to extend a duty of care to a new situation. Here, in determining whether a duty should be recognised, the law proceeds incrementally and by analogy with previous decisions. The task for the court is to test the proposed duty against considerations of legal policy and judgement to achieve both justice in the particular case and the coherent development of the law. Here, the Supreme Court took the view that the underlying policy considerations precluded the imposition of a duty of care.

The *Caparo* criteria for novel cases

In the absence of case-law authority, then, we need to go back to core principle. In *Caparo v Dickman*,[43] the House of Lords gave guidance as to how to decide whether a duty of care should exist. Rejecting as impractical the task of articulating a *single* general principle for the existence of a duty of care, the Court concluded that where the claimant cannot point to a direct or closely analogous precedent, the court should apply three criteria to determine whether there is a duty of care. All of the following three criteria must be satisfied before a court should be willing to impose a duty of care:

2–015

- the damage must be foreseeable;

- there must be a sufficiently proximate relationship between the parties; and

- it must be "fair, just and reasonable" for the court to impose a duty of care in the light of policy considerations with which the court is concerned.

The application of the three *Caparo* criteria is sometimes referred to as a "threefold test". It should be noted that, unlike the "two stage test" put forward by Lord Wilberforce in *Anns*, the *Caparo* criteria are designed to be considered all at once, not one after the other. This follows from the fact that the criteria cannot be precisely defined or evaluated in isolation from one another. As Lord Oliver noted in *Caparo* itself, the three criteria are, in most cases, "facets of the same thing".[44] On this basis, then, it might be said that the more foreseeable the harm suffered by the claimant, the closer the proximity of the parties, and vice versa. Equally, the closer the proximity, or the more foreseeable the damage, the more likely it is that the third criterion will be satisfied.

In *Customs & Excise Commissioners v Barclays Bank*[45] (discussed in more detail in Ch.3), the House of Lords concluded that the *Caparo* criteria provide (in the words of Lord Mance)

43 [1990] 2 A.C. 605.
44 [1990] 2 A.C. 605 at 633.
45 [2006] UKHL 28; [2007] 1 A.C. 181.

"a convenient general framework"[46] for determining the existence of a duty of care. However, they can only give the courts limited help. It is therefore necessary for the courts to consider the detailed factual circumstances of each particular case, and especially the nature of the relationship between the parties. As Lord Walker put it, the courts, since *Caparo*, have shown an:

> **"increasingly clear recognition that the threefold test . . . does not provide an easy answer to all our problems, but only a set of fairly blunt tools."**[47]

It will be appreciated, then, that the *Caparo* criteria are somewhat vague.[48] On one view, though, it is this very vagueness which makes them so useful. We have seen that the problem with the approach in *Anns* was that it required the judges openly to refer to policy considerations in their judgments. Their reluctance to rule on policy meant that the expansion of the duty of care was inevitable. Under the modern approach, however, judges are no longer forced to confront policy issues so directly. Of course, they continue to make decisions based on policy, but they are now able to frame those decisions in appropriate judicial language by finding that there is insufficient proximity between the parties, or by declaring that the imposition of a duty would not be "fair, just and reasonable".

The problem with an approach considering what is "fair, just and reasonable" is that it can lead to uncertainty in the law—in the *Barclays Bank* case, for example, different weight placed on various different policy factors meant that a unanimous Court of Appeal decision ended up being overruled by a unanimous House of Lords. In these circumstances, it is very difficult for potential litigants to know whether their cases stand any chance of success.[49] The Supreme Court in *Robinson* sought to reduce this uncertainty by emphasising that the *Caparo* test would only apply to novel cases, and that, in most cases, guidance could be obtained from existing case-law.

Although each of the *Caparo* criteria is a "facet of the same thing", it is nevertheless possible to say something about each criterion in turn.

▶ (1) Foreseeability

2–016

It should be remembered that the relevant question is not what the defendant *actually did foresee*, but what a "reasonable person" in the circumstances of the defendant *ought to have foreseen*. The duty of care can only be owed in respect of preventing loss if the type of loss in

---

46 *Customs & Excise Commissioners v Barclays Bank* [2006] UKHL 28 at [93].
47 *Customs & Excise Commissioners v Barclays Bank* [2006] UKHL 28 at [71].
48 The *Caparo* test has been rejected by the High Court of Australia in favour of a multi-faceted approach which addresses the policy issues arising in the case itself: see *Perre v Apand Pty Ltd* (1999) 198 C.L.R. 108, and *Sullivan v Moody* (2001) 207 C.L.R. 562.
49 See J. Morgan, "The rise and fall of the general duty of care" (2006) 22 P.N. 206.

question is "reasonably foreseeable". Implicit in this idea is that it must be reasonably foreseeable that the conduct of the defendant will affect the *particular claimant* in the case. This point is examined below:

The foreseeable claimant

2–017

In English law, it is said that negligence cannot exist "in the air". This is simply another way of saying that the particular claimant in the case must be, as Lord Atkin put it, someone who is "closely and directly affected" by the defendant's conduct. Thus, it is not sufficient to say that the defendant breached a duty of care owed to person A and the claimant (person B) was affected because he or she happened to be in the general area of the negligence.

This principle is illustrated by the House of Lords' decision in *Bourhill v Young*.[50] A heavily pregnant woman was descending from a tram when she heard a road traffic accident some 50 feet away from her, caused by the defendant's negligence. She arrived at the scene of the accident and saw blood on the road where a motorist had been killed (although his body had been removed) and subsequently suffered a miscarriage and psychiatric illness. Their Lordships were unsympathetic. Whilst the defendant would be liable for damage suffered by other road-users, the claimant was too far removed from the scene of the accident to be a reasonably foreseeable victim.

A more graphic illustration is the well-known US case of *Palsgraf v Long Island Railroad*,[51] where the negligence of railway employees caused a passenger to drop a box of fireworks as he was boarding a moving train. The fireworks exploded and knocked over some heavy metal scales several feet away, which struck the plaintiff. The New York Court of Appeals rejected her claim for damages, holding that if any wrong had been committed, it had not been committed against *her*, because she was not a foreseeable victim of the railway company's negligence.

Is an unborn child a "foreseeable claimant"?

2–018

Obviously, the "no negligence in the air" principle serves to prevent indeterminate liability by restricting the range of claims that can result from a single negligent act. Its distinguishing feature is that it will not allow a claimant to base his or her claim on a wrong done to someone else. A difficult question of policy has arisen, however, in determining how far this principle should be applied in respect of children who are born disabled because of a wrong done to one of their parents before they are born.

For people born on or after 22 July 1976, the sort of claim that can be made is determined by the provisions of the Congenital Disabilities (Civil Liability) Act 1976.[52] In summary, this

---

50   [1943] A.C. 92.
51   248 N.Y. 339 (1928); 162 N.E. 99.
52   As amended by the Human Fertilisation and Embryology Act 1990 and the Human Fertilisation and Embryology

states that if a child is born disabled as a result of an injury to either parent which affects that parent's ability to have a normal child, or which affects the mother during pregnancy, or affects the mother or child during birth, the child may sue for his or her resulting disability.[53] It is not necessary to show that the parent has suffered personal injury of a type which would enable the parent to maintain an action in his or her own right.[54] However, any defences which would apply if the parent were suing for injuries to himself or herself will be available to the defendant in fighting the child's claim.[55] Equally it must be established that the negligence caused the child's injury on the balance of probabilities, which will not always be easy.[56] It should be remembered that the Act not only covers injury to the foetus, it extends to cover situations where, before a child is conceived, a wrong is done to either of the parents which prevents them from conceiving a normal baby.

For policy reasons, the Act does not allow children to bring claims against their mothers, except in one particular situation, namely where the mother injures the child by negligently driving a motor vehicle when she knows (or ought to know) that she is pregnant.[57] The moral objections against children suing their mothers are overcome in this situation because the mother is, by law, obliged to be insured.[58] In such cases, the insurance company will meet or defend the child's claim. It should be noted that the general immunity granted to mothers does not extend to fathers.[59]

Moral objections have prevented the courts from holding that an unborn child is a fore-seeable claimant in so-called "wrongful life" cases. These are cases in which disabled claimants argue, in effect, that they should never have been born, and were only born because of the defendant's negligence. The defendant may, for example, have failed to recommend an abortion to the mother, in circumstances where it was likely that the claimant would be born disabled. In *McKay v Essex AHA*,[60] the court struck out such a claim as contrary to public policy.

Act 2008. Note that in 1992, *Burton v Islington Health Authority* [1993] Q.B. 204 finally established that a duty of care could be owed at common law to an unborn child, even though a foetus has no independent legal personality. It was held that the wrong done to the parent would "crystallise" into a cause of action, maintainable at the suit of the child, once the child was born.

53 Congenital Disabilities (Civil Liability) Act 1976 s.1. See also Consumer Protection Act 1987 s.6(3) (specific application of the 1976 Act to situations where the parent is affected by a defect in a product, e.g. a drug).

54 Congenital Disabilities (Civil Liability) Act s.1(3).

55 Congenital Disabilities (Civil Liability) Act ss.1(4), 1(6), and 1(7). Note, however, that contractual exclusions or limitations cannot be relied on where the case concerns the supply of a defective product: Consumer Protection Act 1987 s.6(3).

56 *McCoy v East Midlands SHA* [2011] EWHC 38 (QB); [2011] Med. L.R. 103 (insufficient evidence to show that a negligently performed cardiotocograph scan, and the failure to perform a second or continued scan, caused the claimant to be born suffering from diplegic cerebral palsy).

57 Congenital Disabilities (Civil Liability) Act s.2.

58 Road Traffic Act 1988 s.143.

59 Although the Pearson Commission thought that it should (see Cmnd.7034, Vol.1 para.1471).

60 [1982] Q.B. 1166 at 1180. The court, obiter, also ruled out any claim under the 1976 Act. See also C. R. Symmons, "Policy factors in actions for wrongful birth" (1987) 50 M.L.R. 269 and R. Scott, "Reconsidering 'wrongful life' in England after thirty years: Legislative mistakes and unjustifiable anomalies" [2013] C.L.J. 115.

It was not prepared to state that in law a disabled life was to be regarded as less valuable than that of an able-bodied person. Equally, the court was reluctant to set a precedent under which an action might be maintained by a child against a mother who, knowing of the risk of the child's disability, refused to have an abortion.[61]

Although children themselves have not been allowed to sue for "wrongful life", the courts have in the past been prepared to allow *parents* to sue for the cost of bringing up "unintended children" where the negligence of the defendant has prevented them from choosing not to conceive, or choosing to terminate the pregnancy. In recent times, however, the House of Lords has declined, for public policy reasons, to allow such claims to succeed. The relevant cases are considered later in this chapter, in the context of the liability of the NHS.

(2) Proximity

2–019

It is impossible to define the concept of "proximity" in concrete terms. What can be said, however, is that it refers to the *closeness of the relationship* between the defendant and the claimant. The degree of closeness which the law will require before imposing a duty of care differs according to the *type of damage* for which the claimant is seeking redress. Therefore, as we shall see, in cases of economic loss and psychiatric illness, the courts require a very close relationship between the parties, whilst in cases of physical injury, the requirement of proximity is more easily satisfied.[62] Thus, if I negligently make a statement causing you financial loss, I must (generally speaking) know who you are and that you are likely to rely on that statement before I can be made liable, but if I negligently drive my car, causing you personal injury, I will be liable to you without knowing who you are or that you, in particular, were relying on me to drive carefully.

The fact that the courts' insistence on "proximity" appears to be confined to certain types of situation, then, indicates that questions of *policy* are relevant to the question of whether or not, in a given situation, the required degree of proximity exists. As Lord Oliver put it, in *Alcock v Chief Constable of South Yorkshire*[63]:

> "... no doubt 'policy', if that is the right word, or perhaps more properly, the impracticability or unreasonableness of entertaining claims to the ultimate limits of the consequences of human activity, necessarily plays a part in the court's perception of what is sufficiently proximate ... in the end, it has to be accepted that the concept of

---

61   The difficulty of assessing the level of damages also concerned the court.

62   See Lord Oliver in *Murphy v Brentwood DC* [1991] 1 A.C. 398 at 487; *Perrett v Collins* [1998] 2 Lloyd's Rep. 255. Note, however, that in *Sutradhar v Natural Environment Research Council* [2006] UKHL 33; [2006] 4 All E.R. 490 the HL also stressed the necessity of showing proximity in claims for personal injury caused by negligent statements.

63   [1992] 1 A.C. 310 at 410.

> 'proximity' is an artificial one which depends more upon the court's perception of what is the reasonable area for the imposition of liability than upon any logical process of analogical deduction."

In determining "what is the reasonable area for the imposition of liability", the courts will often have to ask themselves how the relationship between the parties (i.e. what actually happened in their dealings with one another) should define the *scope* of the defendant's duty of care. Thus, in some cases, although a certain duty is owed, the relationship (degree of proximity) between the parties may indicate that the defendant has not assumed responsibility for safeguarding the claimant against the actual loss suffered. So, for example, in *Calvert v William Hill*,[64] the bookmakers, William Hill, which operated a telephone betting service, had entered into a "self-exclusion" arrangement with Mr Calvert for problem gamblers whereby they would refuse his telephone bets for six months. Unfortunately, through carelessness on their part, this arrangement was never implemented and Mr Calvert continued placing telephone bets, ultimately losing £1.8 million. The Court of Appeal held that William Hill had not assumed a responsibility to enable Mr Calvert to gamble free from all risk. The scope of their duty of care to Mr Calvert was limited to the arrangement between them and, as a matter of causation, even if the "self-exclusion" arrangement had been implemented, other forms of gambling would have brought about his financial ruin (Mr Calvert was a compulsive gambler). The court cited with approval the observations of Lord Oliver in *Murphy v Brentwood DC*[65]:

> "The essential question which has to be asked in every case, given that damage which is the essential ingredient of the action has occurred, is whether the relationship between the plaintiff and the defendant is such . . . that it imposes upon the latter a duty to take care to avoid or prevent that loss which has in fact been sustained."

▶ (3) "Fair, just and reasonable"

2–020

Because, as shown above, policy concerns are relevant to the degree of proximity required, it is often unclear how to divide the questions of proximity and whether a duty of care would be fair, just and reasonable in the circumstances. Commentators have asked what useful purpose is served by an additional consideration of whether the imposition of a duty of care is "fair, just and reasonable" or, alternatively, whether the fair, just and reasonable test renders the test of proximity unnecessary. Does proximity simply obscure the real reasons for a decision, reasons

---

64 [2008] EWCA Civ 1427; [2009] Ch.330. Comment: J. Morgan [2009] C.L.J. 268.
65 [1991] 1 A.C. 398 at 486, cited by Sir Anthony May P in *Calvert v William Hill* [2008] EWCA Civ 1427 at [45].

the court should have had the courage to explain openly and at length?[66] Or is, as Lord Kerr suggested in *Michael v Chief Constable of South Wales,*[67] the question of whether it is fair, just and reasonable better considered against the background of whether a sufficiently proximity relationship exists? In *Marc Rich & Co AG v Bishop Rock Marine Company (The Nicholas H),*[68] Balcombe LJ doubted whether the criterion added anything to the requirement of proximity. There may be exceptional cases, however (such as the old cases of advocates' immunity, discussed elsewhere in this chapter) where the courts wish to deny the existence of a duty of care, but where it will be a nonsense for them to speak in terms of an insufficiently close relationship between the parties. In such cases, the "fair, just and reasonable" criterion provides a "long stop", enabling the courts to determine liability on the basis of policy.

Further factors relevant to the imposition of a duty of care

To understand when a duty of care arises in English law, three factors should be borne in mind. First, *as* already noted, the *type of harm* the claimant has suffered (physical, financial, or psychiatric) has a profound effect on whether a duty of care will be owed. This factor is further considered in Chs 3 and 4. In the following sections of this chapter, we examine two further factors which have influenced the courts in deciding whether a duty of care should be owed:

2–021

- whether the damage in question is caused by a positive act, or by an omission (non-feasance);

- the *type of defendant* who is being sued.

Liability for omissions?

Lord Atkin, in *Donoghue v Stevenson*, spoke of a duty of care arising in respect of "acts or omissions", yet, as Lord Goff notes in *Smith v Littlewoods Organisation Ltd*[69]:

2–022

---

66   See Howarth commenting on the decision in *Sutradhar v Natural Environmental Research Council*: D. Howarth [2005] C.L.J. 23, 26.
67   [2015] UKSC 2 at [156]. He argued that what is "fair, just and reasonable" tends to blend with the concept of "proximity": see [158].
68   [1994] 1 W.L.R. 1071.
69   [1987] A.C. 241 at 271.

> "... the common law does not impose liability for what are called pure omissions."

The law draws a distinction between a positive act which causes harm (misfeasance) and a mere failure to prevent harm from arising (non-feasance), there being no liability for the latter. Lord Keith in *Yuen Kun Yeu v Att-Gen of Hong Kong*[70] gave a classic example of this—there is, he stated, no liability "on the part of one who sees another about to walk over a cliff with his head in the air, and forbears to shout a warning".[71] In the absence, then, of a special relationship e.g. the defendant was the carer of the person walking over the cliff, there is no duty to go to the rescue of another.

The distinction between acts and omissions is sometimes very difficult to draw and has given rise to problems. A motorist who causes an accident by failing to stop at a red light is technically guilty of an omission, but the law says that he or she is liable because this omission cannot be considered in isolation from the positive act of driving. The key question, therefore, is whether the "omission" in question can be seen as having been made *in the course of doing some positive act*. If so, it will be treated as misfeasance and not treated as a pure omission. In contrast, in *Sutradhar v Natural Environment Research Council*,[72] the House of Lords denied the existence of a duty of care on the part of a scientific advisory body which had reported on the quality of water in Bangladesh. The defendants' failure to test the water for arsenic was regarded as a case of mere non-feasance, because they had not assumed any positive obligation to do so.[73]

In *Stovin v Wise*,[74] Lord Hoffmann made the following important observations about liability for omissions[75]:

> "There are sound reasons why omissions require different treatment from positive conduct. It is one thing for the law to say that a person who undertakes some activity shall take reasonable care not to cause damage to others. It is another thing for the law to require that a person who is doing nothing in particular shall take steps to prevent another from suffering harm ... One can put the matter in political, moral or economic terms. In political terms it is less of an invasion of freedom for the law to require him to consider the safety of others in his actions than to impose upon him a duty to rescue or protect. A moral version of this point may be called the 'why pick on me?' argument. A duty to prevent harm to others or to render

---

70   [1988] A.C. 175.
71   [1988] A.C. 175 at 192.
72   [2006] UKHL 33; [2006] 4 All E.R. 490.
73   See Lord Hoffmann in *Sutradhar v Natural Environment Research Council* [2006] UKHL 33 at [27].
74   [1996] A.C. 923.
75   [1996] A.C. 923 at 943.

> assistance to a person in danger or distress may apply to a large and indeterminate class of people who happen to be able to do something. Why should one be held liable rather than another? In economic terms, the efficient allocation of resources usually requires an activity should bear its own costs. If it benefits from being able to impose all or some of its costs on other people (what economists call 'externalities') the market is distorted because the activity appears cheaper than it really is. So liability to pay compensation for loss caused by negligent conduct acts as a deterrent against increasing the cost of the activity to the community and reduces externalities. But there is no similar justification for requiring a person who is not doing anything to spend money on behalf of someone else."

It can be seen from the reasoning in these cases that whether a case is one of misfeasance or a pure omission depends essentially on the *nature of the relationship* between the claimant and the defendant. The issue therefore overlaps with the idea of "proximity". This is illustrated by the decision in *Michael v Chief Constable of South Wales*.[76] In this case (discussed in more detail later), a young woman had been murdered by her ex-boyfriend after the police had failed to respond promptly to an urgent 999 call. The Supreme Court found that the police did not owe her a duty of care. The common law does not generally impose liability for pure omissions. Here the police had failed to act promptly, but while the law might require a person who embarks upon conduct which may harm others to exercise care, it was another matter to impose a duty of care on the police to prevent harm caused by someone else. It was not a case where the police could be said to have undertaken responsibilities giving rise to a duty of care towards an individual member of the public.

The rule against liability for pure omissions, then, gives rise to two important propositions:

- in English law, in contrast to civil law jurisdictions,[77] there is no general duty to rescue another;

- there is no *general* duty to prevent other people from causing damage.

These matters are considered below.

---

76 [2015] UKSC 2; [2015] A.C. 1732.
77 See, e.g. French Criminal Code art.223–6, which punishes (with corresponding tortious liability) anyone who wilfully refrains from assisting a person in danger, when he or she could have done so without risk to himself or herself or to third parties. Equally, German Criminal Code para.323c provides that "Whosoever does not render assistance during accidents or a common danger or emergency although it is necessary and can be expected of him under the circumstances, particularly if it is possible without substantial danger to himself and without violation of other important duties shall be liable to imprisonment not exceeding one year or a fine".

No duty to rescue

2-023

In *Smith v Littlewoods Organisation Ltd*,[78] Lord Goff stated that the refusal of English law to impose liability for mere omissions might one day need to be reconsidered, in the light of the "affirmative duties of good neighbourliness" imposed in other countries.[79] It seems, however, that that day is still some way off. In order for a duty to rescue to arise in English law, a prior relationship of care must exist between the defendant and the person who needs rescuing. Thus, whilst parents (who have a duty to care for their children) may be liable in negligence if they stand by and let their children drown in shallow water, the same cannot be said of a mere bystander at a swimming pool.[80] There is a related point that should be noted here in terms of the potential *liability* of rescuers for flawed rescue attempts: because there is no duty to rescue, it follows that in cases where a rescuer chooses to intervene, he or she cannot be liable in negligence unless it can be said that the intervention has made the claimant's position *worse* than if it had not taken place.[81]

No general duty to prevent others from causing damage

2-024

In the same way that there is no duty to save others from natural perils, there is, generally speaking, no duty to save them from perils arising from the actions of others. This was affirmed by Lord Goff in *Smith v Littlewoods Organisation Ltd*. The defendants had acquired a disused cinema, intending to develop the land where it stood. Shortly after they had taken possession of the cinema, vagrants occupied the building. On two occasions, small fires had been started using rubbish that had been left lying outside the cinema, but these fires had not been reported to the defendants or to the police. Then, one evening, the cinema was set on fire, damaging the plaintiffs' neighbouring property. The plaintiffs argued that the defendants ought to have prevented the vagrants from starting the fire. It was held that whilst the defendants were under a duty to prevent their property from becoming a source of danger to neighbouring property, on the facts, this duty did not extend to controlling the activities of the vagrants. Because the defendants had not known about the previous fires, it was not reasonably foreseeable that a fire would be started that would damage neighbouring property.

The decision in *Smith v Littlewoods* represented the culmination of a number of judicial attempts to identify the legal basis on which a defendant should be absolved from liability for the consequences of a wrong committed by a third party. Previously, there had been three Court of Appeal decisions on similar facts to *Smith v Littlewoods*, each of which had used a dif-

---

78   [1987] A.C. 241 at 271.
79   Citing J. Fleming, *The Law of Torts*, 6th edn (1983), 138.
80   per Lord Nicholls in *Stovin v Wise* [1996] A.C. 923 at 931.
81   *Horsley v MacLaren (The Ogopogo)* [1971] 2 Lloyd's Rep. 410, applied in *Capital & Counties v Hampshire CC* [1997] Q.B. 1004.

ferent element of the tort of negligence to deny liability. In *Lamb v Camden LBC*[82] it had been held that the third party's actions were too remote a consequence of the defendant's breach, whilst in *P.Perl (Exporters) Ltd v Camden LBC*[83] it had been held that, because the defendant could not be expected to control the third party, no duty of care was owed. In *King v Liverpool CC*,[84] it had been held that although a duty was owed, the defendants were not in breach of their duty because there was nothing they could reasonably have done to prevent the third parties from causing the damage.

Lord Goff's approach in *Smith v Littlewoods*, however, centred firmly on the absence of a duty of care as the appropriate legal mechanism for confining liability for wrongs committed by other people. Although this approach was not adopted by the other Law Lords in the case (who spoke in terms of breach of duty) it has met with subsequent approval by the House of Lords in the case of *Mitchell v Glasgow City Council*[85] and by the Supreme Court in *Michael v Chief Constable of South Wales*.[86] In both cases, the complaint had been raised that the public authority in question had failed to protect the lives of, in *Mitchell*, one of its council tenants when it took no steps to give a warning about the possible actions of a violent neighbour who was facing eviction following a complaint by Mitchell and, in *Michael*, a young mother when the police had failed to respond promptly to an urgent 999 call in which Ms Michael had expressed her fear that her ex-partner was coming back to kill her.[87]

In the first case, Mitchell, a council tenant aged 72, had informed the council about the violent and abusive behaviour of his next-door neighbour, Drummond. The council summoned Drummond to a meeting, where he was told that he might be evicted if his behaviour did not improve. Shortly after the meeting, Drummond assaulted Mitchell with a stick or an iron bar, which led to Mitchell's death. Mitchell's widow and daughter brought an action claiming that the council had owed a duty to warn Mitchell that the meeting was taking place, so that he could take steps to avoid the danger posed by Drummond.

The House of Lords rejected the claim. Whilst landlords owed some duties to their tenants, these did not extend to warning tenants of steps taken to evict other tenants. Nor could the council be liable for a wrong committed by a third party (Drummond) unless the case had some extraordinary "feature" going beyond mere foreseeability of harm (such as clear evidence that they had assumed responsibility for Mitchell's safety).

In *Michael*, the majority of the Supreme Court stated that imposing a duty of care to individual members of the public who made 999 calls would be contrary to the ordinary prin-

2-025

---

82 [1981] Q.B. 625.

83 [1984] Q.B. 342.

84 [1986] 3 All E.R. 544.

85 [2009] UKHL 11; [2009] 2 W.L.R. 481. Comment: J. O'Sullivan, "Liability for criminal acts of third parties" [2009] C.L.J. 270. See also *Poole BC v GN* [2019] UKSC 25; [2019] 2 W.L.R. 1478.

86 [2015] UKSC 2; [2015] A.C. 1732.

87 In both cases, claims were brought in negligence and also under the Human Rights Act 1998, for breach of art.2 (right to life). In *Mitchell* [2009] UKHL 11, the HRA claim failed because it did not satisfy the "real and immediate risk" test for art.2 liability. The Supreme Court in *Michael* [2015] UKSC 2, however, allowed the art.2 claim to proceed. This aspect of the cases will be discussed later in this chapter.

ciple of common law that the law does not generally impose liability for pure omissions. There was no reason why this rule should not apply equally to private litigants and public bodies.[88] While exceptions existed to this rule: (see exceptions below), none applied on the facts of the case. The 999 call operator had not assumed any responsibility to safeguard Ms Michael and the police did not control her attacker. While the police owed a duty to the public at large, Lord Toulson (speaking for the majority) took the view that:

> **"If it is thought that there should be public compensation for victims . . . in cases of pure omission by the police to perform their duty for the prevention of violence, it should be for Parliament to determine whether there should be such a scheme and, if so, what should be its scope as to the types of crime, types of loss and any financial limits."**[89]

The liability of the police to members of the public in negligence will be examined in more detail later in this chapter. In both cases, the courts endorsed the approach taken by Lord Goff in *Smith v Littlewoods*. This approach takes as a starting point the proposition that, as a general rule, there is no duty of care owed to prevent third parties from causing damage, but acknowledges that there appear to be certain exceptions to this rule in cases which have extraordinary features. There are four particular situations where liability for the acts of third parties can arise. These can be summarised as follows:

(1) Special relationship between the defendant and the claimant

2–026

The first situation is where the defendant has assumed responsibility to look after the claimant's property. In *Stansbie v Troman*,[90] the plaintiff had employed a decorator who went out and left the premises unsecured. The decorator was held liable for losses caused by a thief who entered the premises and stole some of the plaintiff's property. The contractual relationship between the plaintiff and the decorator justified the imposition of liability—the decorator had agreed to look after the premises. In contrast, in *Michael*,[91] the 999 call handler did not assume responsibility to Ms Michael, but simply told her that she would pass on the call to the South Wales police.

---

88   For criticism of this view, see S. Tofaris and S. Steel, "Negligence liability for omissions and the police" [2016] C.LJ. 128.
89   [2015] UKSC 2 at [130].
90   [1948] 2 K.B. 48.
91   [2015] UKSC 2 at [138].

(2) Special relationship between the defendant and the third party

In *Home Office v Dorset Yacht* (discussed above), the defendants were liable because they had a relationship of control over the third parties (the young male offenders) who had caused the damage.

2–027

(3) Creating a source of danger which is "sparked off" by a third party

The defendant may be liable for creating a dangerous situation which is subsequently "sparked off" by the foreseeable actions of third parties. This principle may apply, for example, to a defendant who keeps an unsecured shed full of fireworks that are subsequently ignited by mischievous children.[92] The principle was applied in *Haynes v Harwood*,[93] where the defendants left their horses unattended in the street and a boy threw a stone at them and caused them to bolt. The defendants were liable when the plaintiff was injured trying to save people from being injured by the horses.

2–028

(4) Failing to take reasonable steps to abate a danger created by a third party

Where the defendant knows, or reasonably ought to know, that third parties are creating a danger on his or her premises, the defendant is under a duty to take reasonable steps to abate that danger. Thus, in *Clark Fixing Ltd v Dudley MBC*,[94] where known trespassers on a vacant development site started a fire which burned down neighbouring property, the Court of Appeal, distinguishing *Smith v Littlewoods*, held the defendant council liable for failing to remove combustible material from the site, so as to prevent the spread of fire. If, in *Smith v Littlewoods*, the previous fires had been reported to the defendants, they too may have been held liable on this principle.

2–029

The Type of Defendant

In novel cases, before imposing liability on a particular defendant, the court will consider both the individual case and, more broadly, the consequences of creating a precedent which establishes

2–030

---

92 per Lord Goff in *Smith v Littlewoods* [1987] A.C. 241 at 273.
93 [1935] 1 K.B. 146.
94 [2001] EWCA Civ 1898.

that a duty of care is owed by this type of defendant. If the defendant is a member of a particular profession or group, any precedent will have the effect of fixing all members of that profession or group with the duty in question. Decisions on liability can have far-reaching implications about the allocation of financial resources by potential defendants. This is of particular concern where the defendant in question is providing a public service. For example, if Doctor X is held liable to Patient Y in undertaking a certain procedure, then in future, all doctors will be liable in similar circumstances. This may increase the insurance costs of the hospitals employing the doctors and may even lead to doctors becoming reluctant to undertake the procedure in question, or to their insisting that excessive safeguards be taken. The cost of the precautions will increase the cost of the procedure and may reduce its availability in a financially constrained health service.

The problem of increasing the scope of negligence liability affects a number of different professions and groups. In relation to each of these, the courts have adopted a slightly different approach. In relation to NHS medical services, for example, the usual mechanism for limiting negligence liability is not to restrict the scope of the duty of care. Rather, it is to hold that a doctor (or other medical professional) will not be in *breach* of the duty of care if his or her behaviour lives up to the standard of other responsible medical professionals.[95] In relation to some other public services, however, the courts are at times prepared to hold that, for policy reasons, no duty of care is owed. This discrepancy in approach between different types of defendant has attracted judicial comment,[96] but it remains the case that certain types of defendant may escape negligence liability because they owe no duty, whilst others are judged by the standard of their profession.

For the sake of convenience, we deal with different types of defendant under four headings:

- local authorities;

- other public servants;

- regulators and advisory bodies; and

- lawyers.

(1) Local authorities

2–031

Actions against local authorities are common. Often, a claimant will seek to show that he or she is owed a duty of care by a local authority, even though its contribution to the damage has been minor, because the authority has the funds to pay compensation. To succeed, however, a claimant must overcome a number of hurdles. In exploring these hurdles, it is helpful to appreciate that, in essence, the courts are here faced with the difficult task of determining the terms

---

95 *Bolam v Friern Barnet Hospital Management Committee* [1957] 1 W.L.R. 582 (discussed in Ch.5).
96 See *Capital and Counties Plc v Hampshire CC* [1997] Q.B. 1004 per Stuart-Smith LJ at 1040.

of the "social contract" under which taxpayers pay for the services the authorities provide. The fundamental question in most local authority cases is simply this: how far is it appropriate to provide a remedy in negligence where the state fails to confer a benefit on an individual?

Policy arguments

There are a number of policy objections that have been traditionally raised to the imposition of a duty of care on local authorities.[97] A common objection is that the threat of liability may lead to the local authority adopting overly cautious practices at the public expense. Another objection is that allowing liability in tort will undermine or distort the framework of public protection provided by statute[98] or available in another area of the common law. In many cases, the claimant will have an alternative means of redress. He or she may be able to seek judicial review, for example, or take advantage of a remedy provided by the statute under which the local authority has acted. Moreover, it is argued that making a local authority pay compensation is contrary to the general public interest, because it forces the authority to divert scarce financial resources away from general public welfare, reallocating them to a small number of litigants.

2–032

In recent years, the courts have placed more emphasis on the fact that tort law should not be used to impose a duty to *confer a benefit* on others, as opposed to a duty to refrain from causing harm.[99] These reasons were cogently enunciated by Lord Hoffmann in *Stovin v Wise* (the relevant passage is set out earlier in this chapter). The question arises, however, whether it is appropriate to maintain this sharp distinction in the context of the welfare state, when to do so may create an unacceptable social divide between those who rely on the state for their welfare and those who look after themselves privately. In the context of the NHS (discussed later), the courts have clearly found such a divide unacceptable—therefore an NHS patient has substantially the same remedy in tort as a private patient would have for breach of contract.

Similarly, in the context of state education, the House of Lords has held in *Phelps v Hillingdon LBC*[100] that a local authority can owe a duty of care when providing educational services. This mirrors the legal position which would arise if the pupil (or his or her parents) had contracted privately for educational services. In relation to other state services, however, such as the provision of safe roads (*Stovin v Wise*), the courts have been reluctant to hold that a local authority owes a duty of care. Arguably, the courts have only been able to deny a duty of care in these cases because this does not create an obvious contrast with services provided in the private sector.

---

97 In line with the courts' general opposition to claims for pure economic loss, such claims against local authorities will normally be disallowed: see *Murphy v Brentwood DC* [1991] 1 A.C. 398. The policy reasons preventing economic loss claims are considered in Ch.3.

98 See *X v Bedfordshire CC* [1995] 2 A.C. 633 at 750; *Yuen Kun-Yeu v Att-Gen of Hong Kong* [1988] A.C. 175 at 198.

99 For a critical appraisal, see D. Nolan, "The liability of public authorities for failing to confer benefits" (2011) 127 L.Q.R. 260.

100 [2001] 2 A.C. 619. See also, in the context of non-delegable duties discussed in Ch.7, *Woodland v Essex CC* [2013] UKSC 66; [2014] A.C. 537 at [30]–[32] per Baroness Hale.

With this in mind, we can now examine some of the reasoning the courts have employed to determine liability. Following the introduction of the Human Rights Act 1998, some difficult cases have arisen where claimants have argued that the exercise of (or failure to exercise) a statutory function has resulted in a violation of their human rights. These cases have forced the courts to re-evaluate their traditional approach to public authority negligence liability and address a difficult question: should the scope of the duty of care be widened to accommodate the demands of human rights law, or should a restrictive approach remain? As this issue has unfolded, some early cases suggested that negligence liability should expand to encompass human rights law. Later cases, however, have made it clear that negligence liability and liability under the 1998 Act should be treated separately. It is therefore possible to find cases where a duty of care is denied but a human rights claim based on the same facts might succeed.

Statutory functions and the intention of Parliament

2–033

One important question in all of these cases is whether, on a proper construction of the statute, Parliament intended that a failure to carry out the statutory function in question should give rise to claims for compensation from individuals affected by that failure. Where this *is* the case (and provided the statute imposes a *duty* rather than grants a mere *power* to act), there may be a claim for breach of statutory duty (a separate tort, considered in Ch.7), but the courts may disallow negligence liability, so as not to create an overlap with another cause of action. Where Parliament did *not* intend to create a right to compensation, there can be no claim under the tort of breach of statutory duty. In these circumstances the courts will not normally disturb the intention of Parliament by imposing liability in negligence. As Lord Hoffmann put it, in *Stovin v Wise*:

> **"Whether a statutory duty gives rise to a private cause of action is a question of construction . . . if the policy of the Act is not to create a statutory liability to pay compensation, the same policy should ordinarily exclude the existence of a common law duty of care."**[101]

"Policy matters" and "operational matters"

2–034

Further, where the public authority has exercised its discretion under a statutory power or duty, the courts have drawn a distinction between activities involving matters of "pure policy" (which are not justiciable) and activities which can be regarded as "operational" (i.e. activities which *implement* policy). This was explored at some length in *Anns v Merton LBC*. On the basis of the policy/

---

101 [1996] A.C. 923 at 952. The same view is expressed in *Gorringe v Calderdale MBC* [2004] 1 W.L.R. 1057 by Lord Hoffmann (at [23]) and Lord Scott (at [71]).

operational distinction, so the argument ran, it could be said that the way in which buildings were inspected was an "operational" activity, to which negligence liability might attach, whilst a decision to allocate financial resources which resulted in too few building inspectors being appointed would be immune from a negligence suit, because such policy decisions are not justiciable.

The problem with the policy/operational distinction, however, is that it is difficult logically to identify "operational" activities which do not involve any element of "policy". This is because, whenever a person exercises *discretion* in the performance of a task, some element of "policy" will be involved. Is this task to be done quickly or slowly? How much money will be spent in performing this task? Logically, these matters are just as much matters of "policy" as resolutions passed in committee meetings. As Lord Slynn noted in *Barrett v Enfield LBC*,[102] "even knocking a nail into a piece of wood involves the exercise of some choice or discretion".

The attempt in *Anns v Merton LBC*[103] to assert the relevance of a policy/operational distinction met with considerable criticism. In *Rowling v Takaro Properties*,[104] Lord Keith observed:

> ". . . this distinction does not provide a touchstone of liability, but rather is expressive of the need to exclude altogether those cases in which the decision under attack is of such a kind that a question whether it has been made negligently is unsuitable for judicial resolution, of which notable examples are discretionary decisions on the allocation of scarce resources or the distribution of risks."

Lord Hoffmann in *Stovin v Wise* concluded that it had become clear that "the distinction between policy and operations is an inadequate tool with which to discover whether it is appropriate to impose a duty of care or not".[105] On this basis whilst the distinction is attractive, because it enables the court to wash its hands of political matters by declaring them not justiciable, the distinction provides only guidance. We can say nevertheless that the courts will be reluctant to find a duty of care in relation to matters of "high policy", while more likely to find liability in relation to "operational" matters.

When does a local authority "assume responsibility" for a claimant's welfare?

2–035

In most cases against local authorities, the claimant will allege that he or she has been harmed due to the way in which a local authority has exercised (or failed to exercise) a statutory function. In deciding the question of liability, the court will examine the wording of the statute

---

102 [2001] 2 A.C. 550 at 571.
103 [1978] A.C. 728 at 754.
104 [1988] A.C. 473 at 501.
105 [1996] A.C. 923, 951. But contrast the view of Laws LJ in *Connor v Surrey CC* [2010] EWCA Civ 286; [2011] Q.B. 429.

under which the local authority has acted and determine whether the function in question has been given for the benefit of individuals, or whether it serves only a general governmental purpose.[106] In the latter case, there may be no liability, because it cannot be said that the authority has assumed responsibility to the aggrieved individual.

Whether or not the statute in question confers on the local authority a *power* or a *duty*, the key issue is whether, in the light of the statutory framework and other relevant policy concerns, the local authority can be said to have assumed responsibility for preventing specific losses to individual claimants. In the classic case of *Gorringe v Calderdale MBC*,[107] the claimant, Mrs Gorringe had been severely injured when she had driven her car head-on into a bus. The bus had been concealed from view on the other side of a steep hill. She argued that the council had caused the accident by failing to give her proper warning of the danger of driving fast over the hill when she could not see what was coming. In particular, she argued that the council should have painted "SLOW" on the road. Their Lordships were unsympathetic, and Mrs Gorringe lost her case. They pointed out that drivers were expected to look after themselves by driving at an appropriate speed, and that the law did not impose a duty to give warnings about obvious dangers.[108] Moreover, Parliament, in giving local authorities statutory obligations in respect of signs and road markings, had not intended compensation to be payable to individuals injured by a breach of those obligations. Such a breach, therefore, could not give rise to a duty of care. Similar reasoning was employed by the Court of Appeal in *Sandhar v Department of Transport, Environment and the Regions*[109] to deny liability when a driver was injured after a failure to salt a road so as to prevent the formation of ice.

It is clear that an omission to exercise a *power* will render liability less likely. In *Stovin v Wise*,[110] the plaintiff had been involved in a road traffic accident at a dangerous junction. The question arose whether the local authority, which had resolved to carry out improvements to the junction, could be liable for its *failure* to do so. By a 3:2 majority, the House of Lords held that the local authority was not liable for its omission to act. The local authority had a statutory *power* to improve the junction, but not a *duty* to do so. Thus, its omission to improve the junction could not be seen as having occurred in the context of any positive obligation to protect the plaintiff from harm.[111] In *Sumner v Colborne*,[112] the Court of Appeal re-iterated that a failure by the local authority to cut back the vegetation at a road junction

---

106　See, e.g. *Governors of the Peabody Donation Fund v Sir Lindsay Parkinson & Co Ltd* [1985] A.C. 210, *Yuen Kun-Yeu v Attorney General of Hong Kong* [1988] A.C. 175.

107　[2004] UKHL 15; [2004] 1 W.L.R. 1057. Comment: D. Howarth, "Public authority non-liability: spinning out of control?" [2004] C.L.J. 546.

108　Their Lordships cited *Tomlinson v Congleton BC* [2003] UKHL 47; [2004] 1 A.C. 46 (discussed in Ch.8).

109　[2004] EWCA Civ 1440; [2005] 1 W.L.R. 1632.

110　[1996] A.C. 923.

111　Contrast *Kane v New Forest DC* [2001] EWCA Civ 878; [2002] 1 W.L.R. 312. It has been pointed out that this decision places a very onerous burden on planning authorities to monitor and enforce planning conditions where a source of danger may have been created.

112　[2018] EWCA Civ 1006; [2019] Q.B. 430.

to prevent it from obstructing visibility did not give rise to liability in the absence of a positive act.

Despite the courts' reluctance to find a duty of care where local authorities have failed to exercise statutory functions, there remains the possibility of liability in exceptional circumstances. This question was examined recently by the Supreme Court in *Poole BC v GN*.[113] The local authority in this case had housed a family which, included a disabled child, next door to a family known for anti-social behaviour. The family were harassed by their neighbours, and measures by the local authority to halt this were unsuccessful. One of the children became suicidal and ran away from home. In an action against the local authority, the children (assessed as children in need under the Children Act 1989) claimed that in failing to rehouse them, the local authority had been negligent in the exercise of its functions under the 1989 Act. The Supreme Court disagreed. Local authorities do not owe a duty of care at common law merely because they have statutory powers or duties, even if, by exercising their statutory functions, they can prevent a person from suffering harm. The principles applicable to private individuals or bodies would apply in the same way to local authorities. On that basis, unless the local authority had created the source of danger or had assumed a responsibility to protect the claimant from harm, a duty of care would not arise.

Here, the local authority had not created the danger in that the claim did not relate to the exercise of the council's function under housing legislation. In any event, it was already established in *Mitchell v Glasgow City Council*[114] that the council would not owe a duty to protect its tenants from violent assaults by their neighbours. Nor had it assumed responsibility to protect them from third parties by undertaking to monitor their welfare under the Act. Only if it had taken the children into care, would such an assumption arise.

Any assumption of responsibility for the claimants' welfare must therefore arise *independently* of the mere exercise of statutory functions. Thus (as Lord Hoffmann had explained in *Gorringe*) an NHS doctor might provide care to patients pursuant to statutory duties in the National Health Service Act 1977, but it is not the exercise of this public law function which creates a duty of care towards the patient. Rather, the duty of care arises from an *independent* assumption of responsibility, namely the acceptance by the doctor of a professional relationship with the patient no different from that which would be accepted by a doctor in private practice.[115]

The Supreme Court also added another qualification. A duty of care would, in any event, not arise against a local authority if it was inconsistent with the relevant legislation.[116] The employers' liability case of *Connor v Surrey CC*[117] provides a good example of this. Here, the claimant was a headteacher who suffered psychiatric illness after she had been subjected to

---

113   [2019] UKSC 25; [2019] 2 W.L.R. 1478.

114   [2009] UKHL 11; [2009] 2 W.L.R. 481 (statutory functions in managing social housing).

115   per Lord Hoffmann in *Gorringe v Calderdale MBC* [2004] 1 W.L.R. 1057 at [38].

116   *Poole BC v GN* [2019] UKSC 25; [2019] 2 W.L.R. 1478 at [65] per Lord Reed.

117   [2010] EWCA Civ 286; [2011] Q.B. 429. Comment: S. Tofaris, "Negligence liability of public bodies: Locating the interface between public and private law" [2011] C.L.J. 294.

criticism and inappropriate behaviour by school governors. She argued that her illness had been caused by the local authority's failure to intervene and replace the board of governors with an interim executive board. The Court of Appeal held that the local authority owed the claimant a duty of care. This did not arise because of its statutory functions in managing schools, but because the claimant was the authority's employee (and so there was a pre-existing duty of care). In the circumstances, its duty of care as employer had been breached by its failure to exercise a statutory discretion to intervene. The court made it clear, however, that the local authority would only be liable for its failure to provide appropriate protection for its employee if it would be consistent with the statutory powers in question.

Human rights issues

2–037 There are certain cases where, although the claimant is denied a remedy in negligence for poor performance of statutory functions, he or she might instead have a remedy for breach of human rights.[118] Below, we consider the question of whether or not human rights law should be accommodated within negligence by expanding the duty of care. The most recent court decisions indicate that negligence will not generally be modified to accommodate human rights law. The current view, therefore, is that claims in tort law and for breach of human rights under the ECHR may arise on the same facts, but, following the introduction of the Human Rights Act 1998, have, as du Bois put it, "separate spheres of operation".[119]

The decision in *Z v United Kingdom*

2–038 *Z v United Kingdom*[120] was an appeal to the European Court of Human Rights (the Human Rights Act 1998 not being in force at the time) which alleged breach of art.3 (inhuman and degrading treatment) when the House of Lords had in *X v Bedfordshire CC*[121] rejected claims:

- (in the first group of cases), that a local authority had owed a duty of care to children it had negligently failed to take into care and, conversely, to those it had wrongly decided to take into care; and

---

118   See M. Arden, "Human rights and civil wrongs: Tort law in the spotlight" [2010] P.L. 140, now republished in M. Arden, *Human Rights and European Law: Building New Legal Orders* (OUP, 2015), Ch.14.

119   F. du Bois, "Human rights and the tort liability of public authorities" (2011) 127 L.Q.R. 589, 598.

120   (2002) 34 E.H.R.R. 3.

121   [1995] 2 A.C. 633. This decision must now be read subject to the ruling of the Supreme Court that the extent to which the Court had ruled out the possibility that a duty of care might be owed by local authorities or their staff towards children with whom they came into contact *on the grounds of public policy* is no longer good law: *Poole BC v GN* [2019] UKSC 25; [2019] 2 W.L.R. 1478 at [74].

- (in the second group of cases), that a local authority owed a duty of care to provide adequate education for children with special needs.

For example, the claimants in *Z* had suffered terrible abuse at the hands of their mother—they had, for example, been locked in filthy unlit bedrooms, which they had been forced to use as toilets, and had been left so hungry that they had had to scavenge for food in dustbins. The local authority had repeatedly decided not to appoint a social worker for the children and had declined to place them on the Child Protection Register.

The ECtHR was prepared to award the claimants compensation, to be paid by the UK Government, on the basis that the UK had breached two of its obligations under the Convention—it had allowed the claimants to be subjected to "inhuman and degrading treatment" (contrary to art.3) when it failed to act to ensure their welfare, and it had denied them a right to an effective remedy in respect of that treatment (contrary to art.13). The ECtHR made it clear, however, that the "effective remedy" which must be provided for breach of Convention rights did not *necessarily* have to be a remedy in the tort of negligence—another form of remedy would suffice. This left open the possibility that, in future cases, where claimants could show a breach of the Human Rights Act 1998,[122] UK courts might decide to grant a remedy under the Act, despite a finding that no duty of care was owed in the tort of negligence. The Act creates statutory rights that individuals can enforce directly against local authorities, without needing to invoke the tort of negligence. Under the Act, it is "unlawful for a public authority [e.g. a local authority] to act in a way which is incompatible with a Convention right": s.6(1). An "act" includes a "failure to act": s.6(6).

The Impact of the Human Rights Act 1998

2–039

The Human Rights Act 1998 came into force in October 2000. For injuries after that date, claimants could sue local authorities both in the tort of negligence and under s.7 of the Act for damages. Initially there was some support for changes to the tort of negligence. Lord Bingham in his dissenting speech in *D v East Berkshire NHS Trust*[123] observed that:

> "... the question does arise whether the law of tort should evolve, analogically and incrementally, so as to fashion appropriate remedies to contemporary problems or whether it should remain essentially static, making only such changes as are forced upon it, leaving difficult and, in human terms, very important problems to be swept up by the Convention. I prefer evolution."

---

122 Damages under the Act are discussed in Ch.17.
123 [2005] UKHL 23; [2005] 2 A.C. 373 at [50].

However other judges, including Lord Brown in *Van Colle v Chief Constable of Hertfordshire*,[124] pointed out that there were good reasons for maintaining the separation: negligence claims and human rights claims serve different purposes. The main purpose of negligence claims is to compensate losses, whilst the purpose of human rights claims is to uphold standards of behaviour and vindicate rights.

Lord Bingham's view, if it had been followed, would have required a wholesale re-evaluation of public bodies' negligence liability.[125] Recent case law suggests that this is not something the courts are prepared to entertain.

Jain, Rabone and DSD: Keeping negligence and human rights separate[126]

2-040 The current approach of the courts is to view negligence and human rights liability as separate entities, each requiring separate consideration. This approach is exemplified by reasoning of the House of Lords in *Jain v Trent Strategic Health Authority*[127] and the Supreme Court in *Rabone v Pennine Care NHS Foundation Trust*[128] and *DSD v Commissioner of Police of the Metropolis*.[129]

Jain was a case in which Mr and Mrs Jain had their nursing home business destroyed by executive action taken against them by a regulatory authority. The home had been closed down following an application to magistrates made by the Health Authority that the registration needed to operate the nursing home should be cancelled. This application was made without notice and ex parte (that is, without allowing the Jains to be present in court). As a result, the residents, most of them elderly, were moved out. The Jains successfully appealed against the decision (which had been made in the absence of sufficient evidence, and on the basis of irrelevant and prejudicial information) but the four-month delay in hearing the appeal was sufficient to cause them financial ruin. Their Lordships declined to impose liability in negligence. Despite sympathy for the Jains' plight, they were not prepared to hold that a local authority should owe a duty of care to nursing homeowners when exercising its statutory power to regulate homes. The purpose of the power was to protect vulnerable residents. The potential for conflict—between a duty to protect the vulnerable and a duty to others affected by actions designed to do so—dictated that a duty of care would be inappropriate.

What is interesting, for present purposes, is that their Lordships went on to consider whether the Jains might have had an alternative claim under the Human Rights Act 1998. The

---

124 [2008] UKHL 50 at [138]. See also *DSD v Commissioner of Police of the Metropolis* [2015] EWCA Civ 646; [2016] Q.B. 161 at [64]–[67] per Laws LJ who commented at [67]: "the focus of the human rights claim is not on loss to the individual, but on the maintenance of a proper standard of protection". *Van Colle* is discussed later in this chapter.

125 See D. Nolan, "Negligence and human rights law: the case for separate development" (2013) 76 M.L.R. 286.

126 See, generally, J. Wright, *Tort and Human Rights*, 2nd edn (Hart, 2017).

127 *Jain v Trent Strategic Health Authority* [2009] UKHL 4; [2009] 1 A.C. 853.

128 [2012] UKSC 2; [2012] 2 A.C. 72.

129 [2018] UKSC 11; [2019] A.C. 196.

issue was academic, because the Act had not been in force when the order to close the home had been made. Nevertheless, Lord Scott justified considering the issue as having a bearing on whether the courts should, in light of the Act, now develop the common law so as to provide a remedy in cases such as this. On the facts, had the Act been in place, the Court found it difficult to see how the Health Authority could avoid being found in breach of the right to enjoy possessions (art.1 of the First Protocol to the Convention)[130] and the right to a fair and public hearing (art.6.1). The draconian approach of ruining the Jains' business by means of an application made ex parte and without notice amounted to breach of these rights.[131] It was made clear, however, that the fact that the Jains might have a good case for violation of their human rights did not necessarily mean that a duty of care should be imposed. Lord Scott endorsed the view that Lord Brown had expressed in *Van Colle v Chief Constable of Hertfordshire*, namely, that when the Human Rights Act 1998 is in force, "it is quite simply unnecessary now to develop the common law to provide a parallel cause of action".[132]

This position was followed by the Supreme Court in *Rabone v Pennine Care NHS Foundation Trust*.[133] Against the wishes of her parents, the hospital had allowed a 24-year-old patient, who had been admitted to the hospital following a suicide attempt, two days' home leave during which she committed suicide. A negligence claim had been settled, but the parents brought a claim under the Human Rights Act 1998, claiming that the hospital had breached ECHR art.2 (right to life) by failing to take reasonable steps to protect their mentally ill daughter from the risk of suicide. Despite the fact that the parents' claim was one of bereavement, which, as discussed in Ch.17, is not available to parents of an adult child, the Supreme Court saw no reason for this to obstruct a claim for damages for distress under the Act. As Baroness Hale commented, "We are here because the ordinary law of tort does not recognise or compensate the anguish suffered by parents who are deprived of the life of their adult child".[134] Here, the division operated for the benefit of the claimants, who were able to outflank the limitations of negligence law, but reflects the same position: the decision by the courts not to amend tort law, but to apply tort and human rights law side-by-side.

A similar position was reached in *DSD v Commissioner of Police of the Metropolis*.[135] Here it was argued that where the claimants could not establish that they were owed a duty of care in negligence, it would be inappropriate to award damages under the Human Rights Act 1998 for failings in the course of a police investigation. The Supreme Court disagreed. It took the view that English law now makes a clear distinction between tort law and Convention claims. A Convention-based duty is not aimed at compensation,

---

130 The legal right to run a nursing home would qualify as a "possession": see *Van Marle v Netherlands* (1986) 8 E.H.R.R. 483.

131 The Jains appealed to the European Court of Human Rights and the case was ultimately settled for £733,500: *Jain v United Kingdom* (39598/09) [2010] E.C.H.R. 411.

132 *Van Colle v Chief Constable of Hertfordshire Police* [2009] 1 A.C. 225 at [136].

133 [2012] UKSC 2; [2012] 2 A.C. 72.

134 [2012] UKSC 2; [2012] 2 A.C. 72 at [92]. For criticism that this, in fact, undermines the law of tort, see A. Tettenborn, "Wrongful death, human rights, and the Fatal Accidents Act" (2012) 128 L.Q.R. 327.

135 [2018] UKSC 11; [2019] A.C. 196. For criticism of the majority decision, see J. Morgan [2018] C.L.J. 244.

but at upholding and vindicating minimum human rights standards. On that basis, the position under the tort of negligence should not prevent the court finding liability under art.3.

Any remaining influence: *D v East Berkshire NHS Trust?*

2-041 Nevertheless, some earlier cases had made a partial accommodation of human rights law within negligence. This was apparent from the decision of the House of Lords in *D v East Berkshire NHS Trust*.[136] The claimants in *D* were a mixture of children and parents who alleged that they had suffered psychiatric harm because various health authorities (and in one case a local authority) had wrongly diagnosed that the children had been suffering from abuse at the hands of the parents. As a result, the claimants' family life had been disrupted in various ways—either the child had been removed from the parents, or the child had been placed on an "at risk" register with the parents under a cloud of suspicion, or limitations had been placed on the parents' contact with the child.

The House of Lords held that in relation to the wrongly suspected *parents*, there were cogent reasons for denying a duty of care, namely that to allow such a duty would conflict with the duty owed to the child, and would constrain the public body's ability to discharge its statutory duties properly. The welfare of the child was paramount, and to impose on health professionals a duty towards parents would compromise their ability to investigate suspicions of child abuse effectively. However, no issue was taken with the view of the Court of Appeal that a duty of care was owed to *children* by public bodies when exercising their child welfare functions.

This position was, however, reviewed by the Supreme Court in *Poole BC v GN*.[137] While it agreed that a duty of care could be owed to children by public bodies, it sought to apply the same rules of tort law that would apply to any private individual. A duty of care would arise, then, not for reasons of public policy (or human rights), but because either the doctors or the social workers had harmed the child, or they had created a source of danger or assumed responsibility towards the minor. On this basis, the division between negligence and human rights law could be maintained.

The education cases

2-042 The Supreme Court in *Poole* also re-examined the decision of the House of Lords in *Phelps v Hillingdon LBC*.[138] This held that, in certain circumstances, a local authority could owe a duty of care in respect of the provision of educational services.

In *Phelps*, the claimant had suffered from dyslexia as a child, causing her severe learning

---

136 [2005] UKHL 23; [2005] 2 A.C. 373.
137 [2019] UKSC 25; [2019] 2 W.L.R. 1478.
138 [2001] 2 A.C. 619. *Phelps* was applied in *Carty v Croydon LBC* [2005] EWCA Civ 19; [2005] 1 W.L.R. 2312.

difficulties when she was at school. She had been referred to an educational psychologist when she was 11, but the psychologist failed to notice her dyslexia. She subsequently left school with no qualifications, and later sued the local authority for negligence in having failed to provide her with an appropriate education. The appeal in *Phelps* was consolidated with three other cases in which it was alleged that local authorities had been negligent in their provision of education for children with special needs. The House of Lords found in favour of all the claimants. While again *Phelps* was decided in the shadow of the Human Rights Act 1998, the Supreme Court explained that, in modern law, it should be viewed as an assumption of responsibility case—the psychologist advising in relation to a specific child, knowing that the child, through her parents, would rely on the advice in question. Liability therefore arose because the educational psychologist assumed responsibility for the professional advice that he provided about a child in circumstances where it was reasonably foreseeable that the child's parents would rely on that advice.

(2) Other public servants

In this section, we consider the duty of care in relation to the following types of defendant:

2–043

- the police;

- the fire brigade;

- the coastguard;

- the ambulance service;

- the NHS; and

- the armed forces.

The police

To understand the courts' approach to police liability, it is necessary to distinguish two different types of case. In the first type of case, the courts have little problem in holding that the police owe a duty of care. In the second type of case, however, the courts deny that the police are liable in respect of their general public functions of investigating and suppressing crime. We consider each type of case below.

2–044

1. CASES WHERE THE POLICE OWE A DUTY OF CARE

Some of these cases are examples of so-called "operational negligence", where the police cause damage by negligent performance of their day-to-day activities, in much the same way

2–045

that any other defendant might do. A good example would be where a pedestrian is hit by a negligently driven police car. These cases are treated in the same way as any other negligence claim. Thus, in *Rigby v Chief Constable of Northamptonshire*,[139] the plaintiff's gun shop had been under siege and the police had negligently fired a canister of CS gas into the shop without taking adequate precautions against the high risk of fire. When a fire occurred, the plaintiff was successful in his negligence claim. In *Robinson v Chief Constable of West Yorkshire Police*,[140] police were equally under a duty of care towards pedestrians in a busy shopping centre when seeking to arrest a suspect. The reasonably foreseeable risk of injury in attempting an arrest when members of the public were close-by was enough to create a duty of care.

Also in this category are cases where the police assume a very specific responsibility to safe-guard particular individuals against harm. This might be because the individuals in question are police employees, suspects in custody, or police informants. In *Mullaney v Chief Constable of West Midlands*,[141] for example, the police authority was liable when a probationary constable suffered serious injury whilst attempting an arrest, in circumstances where fellow officers had failed to respond to his calls for assistance. In *Reeves v Metropolitan Police Commissioner*,[142] the police were liable for failing to safeguard the welfare of a suspect, a known suicide risk, who hanged himself in his cell, and in *Swinney v Chief Constable of Northumbria Police*,[143] a duty of care was owed to an informant who had received threats from a violent suspect after her con-tact details had been stolen from an unattended police car. The facts of the case suggested that the police had assumed responsibility for the informant's safety.[144] In contrast, in *Michael v Chief Constable of South Wales Police*,[145] the emergency services, which had taken a call from a woman stating that her former partner had attacked her and was returning to hit kill her, were not found liable in negligence when she was later found stabbed to death. The Supreme Court held that they had not assumed responsibility for her welfare when the operator had reassured her that the South Wales police would call her and that she should keep her phone free. In the

---

139 [1985] 1 W.L.R. 1242. See also *Knightley v Johns* [1982] 1 W.L.R. 349 (negligent traffic management decision).
140 [2018] UKSC 4; [2018] A.C. 736.
141 [2001] EWCA Civ 700. See also *Costello v Chief Constable of Northumbria Police* [1999] 1 All E.R. 550; *Waters v Commissioner of Police of the Metropolis* [2000] 1 W.L.R. 1607 HL. Compare *Leach v Chief Constable of Gloucestershire Constabulary* [1999] 1 All E.R. 215 where, by a majority, the Court of Appeal struck out a claim by the appropriate adult who had sat with Frederick West (a serial killer) in police interviews. The police had not assumed responsibility for her psychological well-being. Their only obligation was to provide counselling during or within a short time of the interviews.
142 [2000] 1 A.C. 360. Compare *Orange v Chief Constable of West Yorkshire* [2002] Q.B. 347 and *Vellino v Chief Constable of Greater Manchester* [2002] 1 W.L.R. 218.
143 [1997] Q.B. 464. The court was conscious of the strong public policy argument in favour of allowing liability in such cases, so that informants would be encouraged to give information vital to the suppression of crime. At the full hearing, however, it was held that the police had not been in breach of their duty of care. See *Swinney v Chief Constable of Northumbria Police (No.2)* (1999) 11 Admin. L.R. 811.
144 Per Lord Brown in *Van Colle v Chief Constable of Hertfordshire* [2008] UKHL 50; [2009] 1 A.C. 255 at [120]. See also *An Informer v Chief Constable* [2012] EWCA Civ 197; [2013] Q.B. 579 (police under duty of care for safety and well-being of informer but this did not extend to a duty to protect the informer against pure economic loss).
145 [2015] UKSC 2; [2015] A.C. 1732. Comment: J. Goudkamp (2015) 131 L.Q.R. 131.

words of Lord Toulson, "the only assurance which the call handler gave to Ms Michael was that she would pass on the call to the South Wales Police. She gave no promise how quickly they would respond".[146]

2. CASES WHERE THE POLICE DO NOT OWE A DUTY OF CARE

2-046

The courts have persistently refused to allow negligence liability where the claimant has suffered loss because the police made an error in the course of fulfilling their general public functions of investigating and preventing crime. As we shall see, the position is complicated by the fact that, although no common law duty of care is owed, in many cases claimants may have a parallel claim under the Human Rights Act 1998.

The "core principle" of no liability was established in *Hill v Chief Constable of West Yorkshire*.[147] The mother of the last victim killed by Peter Sutcliffe (a serial killer known as the "Yorkshire Ripper") sued the police authority for negligence, alleging that it had failed to use reasonable care in apprehending him. Sutcliffe had been interviewed by the police and subsequently released. It was argued that the police had carelessly failed to realise, at an earlier stage in their investigations, that Sutcliffe was the murderer. Had they done so, his last victim, Jacqueline Hill, would not have been killed.

The House of Lords refused to impose a duty of care. Lord Keith held that, since it could not be shown that there was any exceptional risk to Jacqueline Hill personally, there was insufficient proximity between her, as the potential victim of a crime, and the police.[148] His Lordship also objected to liability on policy grounds, identifying some important reasons why the police should owe no duty of care in this type of case. The two reasons[149] which have proved most enduring in the light of later cases might be summarised as follows:

> The prospect of liability would lead to defensive practices e.g. excessive record-keeping or a preoccupation with "closing the loop" by following up all lines of enquiry, however apparently unhelpful. These practices would be likely to impede the progress of investigations.[150]

---

146   [2015] UKSC 2; [2015] A.C. 1732 at [138]. See also *Alexandrou v Oxford* [1993] 4 All E.R. 328 CA (police owed no duty to owners of business premises who had a burglar alarm connected to a police station).

147   [1989] A.C. 53. The application of the *Hill* principle was subsequently challenged before the ECtHR in *Osman v United Kingdom* (1998) 29 E.H.R.R. 245 as being contrary to the European Convention on Human Rights art.6.1 (right of access to a court). The ECtHR later retreated from this position in *Z v United Kingdom* (2002) 34 E.H.R.R. 3.

148   *Hill v Chief Constable of West Yorkshire* [1989] A.C. 53 at 62.

149   Lord Keith also opined (at 63) that: (1) the police did not need the threat of liability as an incentive for maintaining high standards. (This is no longer accepted as a justification for the *Hill* principle—see the reasoning of the House of Lords in *Brooks v Commissioner of Police* [2005] UKHL 24); and (2) it would be undesirable to conduct the "elaborate investigation of the facts" needed in many cases to determine whether discretionary and policy decisions were such as could be called into question by the courts.

150   For criticism, see C. McIvor, "Getting defensive about police negligence: The *Hill* principle, the Human Rights Act 1998 and the House of Lords" [2010] C.L.J. 133.

> ■ Defending this type of claim would involve much time, trouble and expense. It would involve police officers in (amongst other things) preparing documents and attending court as witnesses. This would cause the police to divert considerable time and resources from their most important function—the suppression of crime.

The reasoning in *Hill* has been applied in subsequent cases, in a variety of different factual contexts.[151]

2-047

The conjoined appeals in *Van Colle v Chief Constable of Hertfordshire* and *Smith v Chief Constable of Sussex*[152] have proven particularly instructive in that they confirm the application of the *Hill* principle, but also throw light on the relationship between the tort of negligence and the Human Rights Act 1998 in claims against the police (the police being a public authority that could be sued under the 1998 Act). The cases were heard together because they concerned, as Lord Bingham put it, a common underlying problem: if the police are alerted to a threat that D may kill or inflict violence on V, and the police take no action to prevent that occurrence, and D does kill or inflict violence on V, may V or his relatives obtain civil redress against the police, and if so, how and in what circumstances?[153]

In the *Van Colle* case, Van Colle was shot dead by Brougham shortly before he was due to give evidence for the prosecution at Brougham's trial on charges of theft. In the weeks preceding the trial Brougham had approached witnesses, including Van Colle, and attempted to dissuade them from giving evidence. Despite all this, the police officer dealing with the matter had taken no action to protect Van Colle, and a police disciplinary tribunal subsequently found him guilty of failing to perform his duties properly.

The claimants, Van Colle's parents, brought an action under the Human Rights Act 1998, alleging a breach of art.2 (the right to life) by the police. A concurrent claim in common law negligence was considered by the High Court, but rejected in the Court of Appeal, who were content to assume that the *Hill* principle would preclude the existence of a duty of care.[154] The Court of Appeal's finding of liability under the Human Rights Act 1998 was challenged in the House of Lords.

In dismissing the appeal, their Lordships applied *Osman v United Kingdom*,[155] in which the European Court of Human Rights had held that the duty of a state to protect the lives of

---

151 See *Brooks v Commissioner of Police* [2005] UKHL 24; [2005] 1 W.L.R. 1495. Applied by analogy to the Crown Prosecution Service in *Elguzouli-Daf v Commissioner of Police of the Metropolis* [1995] Q.B. 335 (but compare *Welsh v Chief Constable of the Merseyside Police* [1993] 1 All E.R. 692).

152 [2008] UKHL 50; [2009] 1 A.C. 225. A subsequent challenge by Van Colle's parents to the European Court of Human Rights was rejected: *Van Colle v United Kingdom* (7678/09) (2013) 56 E.H.R.R. 23.

153 *Van Colle v Chief Constable of Hertfordshire* [2008] UKHL 50 per Lord Bingham at [1].

154 *Van Colle v Chief Constable of Hertfordshire* [2007] 1 W.L.R. 1821 CA per Sir Anthony Clarke MR at [95].

155 (1998) 29 E.H.R.R. 245.

its citizens under art.2 involved not only putting in place effective criminal law provisions, but, in appropriate cases, taking positive steps to protect individuals whose lives were at risk from criminal actions. According to *Osman*, however, the threshold of state liability was a high one. Liability could only arise where:

> **". . . the authorities knew or ought to have known *at the time* of the existence of a *real and immediate* risk to the life of an identified individual or individuals from the criminal acts of a third party and . . . failed to take measures within the scope of their powers which, judged reasonably, might have been expected to avoid that risk."[156]**

Their Lordships held unanimously that, on the facts of *Van Colle*, this threshold had not been met. Brougham's criminal record was that of a petty offender not given to extreme violence, and the phone calls he had made were unpleasant, but did not contain explicit death threats. In these circumstances, it would have been unrealistic for the police to conclude that there was a real and immediate risk to Van Colle's life.

The appeal in *Smith v Chief Constable of Sussex* concerned a claim for common law negligence. No human rights claim was brought.[157] The claimant, Smith, reported to the police that he had received persistent and threatening telephone, text and internet messages from his former partner, Gareth Jeffrey, following the break-up of their relationship. The messages were extremely abusive and contained explicit death threats. The police, however, declined to look at or record the messages, took no statement from Smith and completed no crime form. Shortly thereafter, Jeffrey attacked Smith with a claw-hammer in such a way that, had Smith been killed, it would have been a clear case of murder. Unsurprisingly, perhaps, Smith brought an action in negligence.

The House of Lords (Lord Bingham dissenting) refused to impose liability. The "core principle" of no liability established in *Hill* operated in the interests of the whole community, by ensuring that police resources were well-used. It should not, therefore, be abandoned, even in extreme cases such as this, where it might produce injustice for the individual claimant. As Lord Hope put it, "We must be careful not to allow ourselves to be persuaded by the shortcomings of the police in individual cases to undermine that principle".[158]

Their Lordships were not, of course, directly concerned with whether a human rights claim for breach of art.2 might have succeeded, had one been brought by Smith. Nevertheless, Lord Brown commented that:

> **". . . the apparent strength of this case might well have brought it within the *Osman* principle so as to make a Human Rights Act claim here irresistible."**

---

156 *Osman v United Kingdom* (1998) 29 E.H.R.R. 245 at [116]. Emphasis added.
157 Mr Smith had failed to meet the one year limitation period under the Human Rights Act 1998 s.7(5).
158 *Van Colle v Chief Constable of Hertfordshire* and *Smith v Chief Constable of Sussex* [2008] UKHL 50 at [75].

His Lordship was clear, however, that this did not mean that it was desirable to enlarge the scope of the duty of care in negligence so as to accommodate human rights concerns. On the contrary, the very existence of the Act made it ". . . quite simply unnecessary now to develop the common law to provide a parallel cause of action". His Lordship saw no great difficulty in allowing the principle to co-exist with the state's duty to protect human rights. As stated earlier in this chapter, negligence claims and human rights claims serve different purposes—the main purpose of negligence claims is to compensate losses, whilst the purpose of human rights claims is to uphold standards of behaviour and vindicate rights.[159]

Lord Bingham dissented in the *Smith* appeal, proposing that a common law duty of care should be found in cases where the police were aware of apparently credible evidence that an identified individual was presenting a specific and imminent threat to life or safety. The adoption of this narrow "liability principle" would not, in his Lordship's view, distract the police from their primary function of suppressing crime and catching criminals—it would simply require reasonable performance of that function. This approach, however, was rejected by the majority, who thought that it would prove unworkable in practice. (When is evidence "credible"? When is a threat "imminent"?)[160]

2-048

In *Michael v Chief Constable of South Wales*,[161] Lord Toulson (for the majority) affirmed the ruling in *Van Colle/Smith* and rejected the arguments that the police would owe a duty of care in negligence where (i) they are aware or ought reasonably to be aware of a threat to the life or physical safety of an identifiable person, or member of an identifiable small group (the argument of the Interveners) or (ii) a member of the public gives the police apparently credible evidence that a third party, whose identity and whereabouts are known, presents a specific and imminent threat to his life or physical safety (Lord Bingham's Liability Principle stated above). The majority also rejected the test based on proximity proposed by the dissenting judge, Lord Kerr.[162]

The majority's argument was simple: according to the rules relating to omissions (discussed at para.2–024), there is no general duty on the police to prevent others from causing harm in the absence of any assumption of responsibility or control over the offender. It allowed, however, the claim based on art.2 ECHR to proceed. Lord Reed in *Robinson* clarified that the decision in *Hill* now has to be understood in the light of later case-law.[163] We should therefore treat the *Hill*, *Smith* and *Michael* cases as concerned with omissions—in each case the claimant

---

159 *Van Colle v Chief Constable of Hertfordshire* and *Smith v Chief Constable of Sussex* [2008] UKHL 50 at [138]. Lord Brown also pointed out that, in human rights cases, the courts appear to adopt a looser approach to causation—claimants need only establish some lost chance of (e.g.) being kept safe by the police. They do not need to prove that police action would probably have kept them safe.

160 *Van Colle v Chief Constable of Hertfordshire* and *Smith v Chief Constable of Sussex* [2008] UKHL 50. See Lords Hope, Carwell and Brown at [77], [109] and [129].

161 [2015] UKSC 2; [2015] A.C. 1732.

162 [2015] UKSC 2 at [144].

163 [2018] UKSC 4 at [54]. He explained that the policy reasoning of Lord Keith reflects the period during which the case was decided when the two-stage *Anns* case continued to be influential and so his Lordship was applying the second policy limb.

sought to have the police held liable for failing to prevent death or personal injury caused by a third party. While Lord Keith in *Hill* was happy to rely on policy reasons, the courts would now rely on the law relating to omissions to justify not imposing a duty of care.

The combined result of the *Van Colle*, *Smith*, *Michael* and *Robinson* appeals, then, is:

- The police continue to be protected from negligence claims arising from poor performance of their general public functions of investigating and preventing crime. This is because, generally, the police are not liable for failing to prevent a third party committing a crime. Liability will only arise if they assume responsibility to an individual or create a danger.

- In appropriate cases, art.2 human rights claims may be brought instead, but these will only succeed if the claimant can satisfy the stringent test for liability set out in *Osman v United Kingdom*.[164]

The fire brigade

2-049

In *Capital & Counties Plc v Hampshire CC*,[165] the liability of the fire brigade was examined by the Court of Appeal. The case was consolidated with three other appeals in which it was alleged that the fire brigade had been negligent in tackling fires. In the first two cases (*Capital & Counties* and *Digital Equipment*), the alleged negligence consisted of ordering that a sprinkler system, which had been operating at the location of the fire, be turned off. In the third case (*John Munroe*), it was alleged that, after fighting a fire on adjacent premises, the fire brigade left the scene without ensuring that the fire was properly extinguished, with the result that it re-ignited, damaging the plaintiff's premises. In the fourth case (*Church of Jesus Christ of Latter-Day Saints*), it was alleged that the fire brigade had negligently failed to take proper steps to ensure that an adequate supply of water was available at the scene of the fire.

The plaintiffs faced objections that were similar to those advanced in the police cases—the fire brigade undertakes a duty to the public and the complaints related to what it failed to do (the omissions argument). Stuart-Smith LJ, giving the judgment of the Court of Appeal, held that the fire brigade's attendance at the scene of a fire did not, of itself, give rise to the requisite

---

164 See, generally, J. Wright, "The operational obligation under article 2 of the European Convention on Human Rights and challenges for coherence—Views from the English Supreme Court and Strasbourg" (2016) 7 J.E.T.L. 58.

165 [1997] Q.B. 1004. Consolidated with *Digital Equipment Co Ltd v Hampshire CC, John Munroe (Acrylics) Ltd v London Fire and Civil Defence Authority* and *Church of Jesus Christ of Latter-Day Saints (Great Britain) v West Yorkshire Fire and Civil Defence Authority*. For the limits of this immunity, see *Wembridge Claimants v Winter* [2013] EWHC 2331 (QB), which applied the guidance of the Supreme Court in *Smith v Ministry of Defence* [2013] UKSC 41 (discussed below) that any immunity should be narrowly construed and based on specific findings of fact.

degree of proximity. In the court's view, this followed from the fact that the fire brigade was under no duty to attend the fire in the first place. As Stuart-Smith LJ put it:

> "... the fire brigade are not under a common law duty to answer the call for help, and are not under a duty to take care to do so. If, therefore, they fail to turn up, or fail to turn up in time, because they have carelessly misunderstood the message, get lost on the way or run into a tree, they are not liable."[166]

The fire brigade's statutory powers to act, then, would not be converted into a common law duty and a brigade was not under a duty to answer a call for assistance nor to take care to do so. However, consistent with the law relating to omissions discussed above, where the fire brigade, by its own negligence, created the danger which caused the claimant's injury, he or she could recover damages for negligence. Accordingly, the plaintiffs in *John Munroe* and *Church of Jesus Christ of Latter Day Saints* could not succeed because, although the fire brigade had intervened, its actions had not caused any damage that would not have occurred had it failed to attend the fire. In the first two cases, however, the position was different. Here, it could be said that the incompetence of the fire brigade in ordering the sprinklers to be turned off had created a fresh source of danger, making the plaintiffs' position worse. So, their claims succeeded.

The coastguard

2–050

The coastguard, a non-statutory public authority, has equally been held not to owe a duty of care in respect of its watching, search and rescue functions. In *OLL v Secretary of State for the Home Department*,[167] it was alleged that the coastguard, by misdirecting a rescue operation, had substantially increased the risk of injury to those in peril and that it should therefore be liable on the same basis that the fire brigade had been liable in *Capital & Counties*. It was held, somewhat questionably perhaps, that on the facts this had not been the case. The coastguard had not directly inflicted physical injury on those who were lost at sea, and May J declined to draw an arbitrary distinction between situations where the coastguard had misdirected itself (for which, in the light of *Capital & Counties*, it would not be liable) and situations where it had misdirected other organisations such as the Royal Navy. Clearly, though, his Lordship's decision reflected sympathy for a publicly funded service partly staffed by volunteers.[168]

---

166 *Capital and Counties Plc v Hampshire CC* [1997] Q.B. 1004 at 1030. See also *Alexandrou v Oxford* [1993] 4 All E.R. 328 (police).
167 [1997] 3 All E.R. 897. See also *Skinner v Secretary of State for Transport, The Times* 3 January 1995.
168 *OLL v Secretary of State for the Home Department* [1997] 3 All E.R. 897 at 907.

The ambulance service

In *Kent v Griffiths*,[169] the Court of Appeal held that the arguments applicable to the police, fire brigade and coastguard had no general application to the ambulance service. The ambulance service was to be regarded as part of the health service rather than as a "rescue" service (see below). The claimant suffered an asthma attack, and her doctor called an ambulance which took 40 minutes to arrive. Whilst waiting for the ambulance, she suffered a respiratory arrest, which would probably have been prevented if the ambulance had arrived within a reasonable time. Lord Woolf MR, giving the judgment of the court, stated that the acceptance of the 999 call established a duty of care. Although cases might arise where policy considerations could exclude a duty of care—such as where the ambulance service had properly exercised its discretion to deal with a more pressing emergency before attending the claimant, or where it had made a choice about the allocation of resources—this was not such a case.

The decision in *Kent v Griffiths*, then, illustrates the idea that the courts are unwilling to deny a duty of care where this would create a divide between the standards to be expected from public and private sector service providers. Had Mrs Kent contracted privately for health care services including emergency ambulance provision, she would have been able to claim for breach of contract. It would be socially unacceptable if she were placed in a worse position because of her reliance on the National Health Service. In relation to firefighting and the suppression of crime, however, such arguments do not arise, because people do not commonly contract privately for those services.

The National Health Service

The normal way for a claimant to proceed in a medical negligence case is to allege that a medical professional has been negligent and that an NHS provider (e.g. an NHS Foundation Trust) is vicariously liable.[170] In most cases, the duty of care owed by such professionals is well established, although, as seen in *Rabone* above, there may be situations where a claim under the Human Rights Act 1998 has practical advantages, for example, in permitting parents to claim for distress damages not usually available in the law of tort.[171] Generally, however, the courts confine the scope of negligence liability by reference to the concept of breach of duty. This was seen recently in the Supreme Court decision in *Darnley v Croydon Health Services NHS Trust*.[172] The Court held the Trust vicariously liable for the negligence of a receptionist who had wrongly told a man attending Accident & Emergency with a head injury that there was a four to five hour wait before seeing a doctor. This had led him to go home where his condition deteriorated. In fact, he could have been seen by a triage nurse within 30 minutes. Bearing in

---

169 [2001] Q.B. 36. Compare *King v Sussex Ambulance NHS Trust* [2002] EWCA Civ 953; [2002] I.C.R. 1413.
170 Vicarious liability is discussed in Ch.7.
171 See also *Reynolds v United Kingdom (2694/08)* (2012) 55 E.H.R.R. 35.
172 [2018] UKSC 50; [2019] A.C. 831.

mind that there is a well established duty of care owed by those who provide and run a casualty department to persons presenting themselves complaining of illness or injury before they are treated or received into care in the hospital's wards, the question for the court was one of breach.[173] Breach of duty will be discussed in Ch.5.

There is one group of cases, however, in which the courts have been willing to limit NHS negligence liability by using the scope of the duty of care as a control mechanism—the "unintended children" cases.

2-053

The "unintended children" cases. Until 1999, the courts had been prepared to entertain claims against the NHS for the cost of bringing up children born as a result of negligent advice or treatment having been given to the parents.[174] Then, in *McFarlane v Tayside Health Board*,[175] the House of Lords decided that, in the case of healthy, able-bodied children, the law would no longer entertain such claims. In rejecting a claim in respect of a healthy baby girl, who was conceived as a result of wrong advice that a vasectomy had been successful, Lord Millett said that "the law must take the birth of a normal, healthy baby to be a blessing, not a detriment".[176] Their Lordships declined to compensate the claimant for the cost of bringing up the child—damages were to be confined to compensating the pain and suffering endured as a result of the pregnancy. Various reasons were advanced by their Lordships for reaching this conclusion. In particular, their Lordships were unwilling to accept that the law might regard a baby as being "more trouble than it was worth"[177]—parenthood had its burdens but also its rewards, and since the rewards of parenthood were incalculable, they could not sensibly be weighed up against the burdens, so it was impossible to quantify what the parents had lost by having a child. Their Lordships were also conscious of the fact that awarding compensation to the parents of a healthy child, at the expense of a financially constrained NHS, might offend against ordinary people's views of how public money should be spent. More recently the Court of Appeal has clarified that at the core of the legal policy denying recovery in *McFarlane* was the impossibility of calculating the loss, given the benefits and burdens of bringing up a healthy child.[178]

---

173 *Darnley* is notable in refusing to distinguish between medical and non-medical staff in imposing a duty of care in relation to the provision of misleading information as to the time within which medical attention might be available, although the Court conceded that this distinction might be relevant in determining whether there was a negligent breach of duty (at [17]).

174 See, e.g. *Emeh v Kensington & Chelsea AHA* [1985] Q.B. 1012; *Thake v Maurice* [1986] Q.B. 644.

175 [2000] 2 A.C. 59. Compare the approach of the High Court of Australia in *Cattanach v Melchior* [2003] HCA 38. The legal policy behind the decision is equally applicable to breach of contract claims, e.g. where an IVF clinic had implanted an embryo into the claimant's former partner without his consent: *ARB v IVF Hammersmith* [2018] EWCA Civ 2803; [2018] 2 W.L.R. 1094.

176 [2000] 2 A.C. 59 at 113–114.

177 [2000] 2 A.C. 59 at 82 (per Lord Steyn) and 114 (per Lord Millett).

178 *ARB v IVF Hammersmith* [2018] EWCA Civ 2803; [2020] Q.B. 93 at [33]. For the view that this is a red herring and that the real policy underlying *McFarlane/Rees* is the moralistic idea that a healthy child should always be viewed as a blessing, see K. Amirthalingam (2019) 35 P.N. 112.

The decision in *McFarlane* did not resolve the question of whether compensation should be available for the costs of bringing up a *disabled* child. In *Parkinson v St James NHS Trust*[179] the claimant, who already had four children, underwent a sterilisation operation. The operation was carelessly performed and she subsequently became pregnant. She eventually gave birth to a child with significant disabilities. The Court of Appeal, mindful of *McFarlane*, could not award the claimant the normal costs associated with bringing up a child. Nevertheless, it felt able to award damages in respect of the *additional costs* associated with providing for a disabled child's special needs. This was so, even though the negligence of the doctors in performing the sterilisation operation had not been the cause of the child's disabilities.

Hale LJ justified a departure from the approach taken in *McFarlane* by saying that, whatever ordinary people might think about the NHS having to pay the costs of bringing up a normal, able-bodied child, they would not regard it as unfair that where the NHS had undertaken to prevent the birth of further children, and had negligently failed to do so, it should meet the additional costs of bringing up a disabled child.[180] A departure from the *McFarlane* principle in such circumstances did not entail a suggestion that a disabled child was any less valued by its parents than an able-bodied one. It simply reflected the reality of the situation, which was that significant extra expenses were incurred by parents of disabled children in seeking to provide them with an upbringing comparable with that of an able-bodied child.[181]

In *Rees v Darlington Memorial Hospital NHS Trust*,[182] the House of Lords was faced with a new factual variation. Here, a healthy, able-bodied child was born to a blind mother, as a result of a negligently performed sterilisation. The mother claimed the additional costs of bringing up the child that would be attributable to *her* disability. By a 4:3 majority, a seven-member House of Lords held that no exception to the principle in *McFarlane* was justified in such circumstances—the task of bringing up a normal, healthy baby could not be regarded as a loss that deserved compensation. In reaffirming this principle, however, their Lordships held that the law set out in *McFarlane* should be changed to a limited extent—there should be an award of a modest sum in all cases where negligence had caused an unintended pregnancy. The purpose of this award—which their Lordships called a "conventional award"—was to mark the courts' recognition of the fact that a legal wrong had been done, and to compensate the parents for having lost their right to limit the size of their family. The level of the award was fixed at £15,000.

In the light of *Rees*, the status of the decision in *Parkinson* is uncertain. Three of their Lordships broadly endorsed the decision,[183] whilst three doubted its correctness.[184] The remaining Law Lord, Lord Millett, expressly stated that the question whether *Parkinson* was correct

---

179 [2002] Q.B. 266.
180 *Parkinson v St James NHS Trust* [2002] Q.B. 266 at 295.
181 [2002] Q.B. 266 at 293.
182 [2004] 1 A.C. 309. Comment: P. Cane, "Another failed sterilisation" (2004) 120 L.Q.R. 189 and A. Pedain, "Unconventional justice in the House of Lords" [2004] C.L.J. 19.
183 Lords Steyn, Hope and Hutton.
184 Lords Bingham and Nicholls were in favour of a conventional award in all cases, whilst Lord Scott thought that the additional costs of bringing up a disabled child might be recoverable where the reason for seeking

should be left open. Thus, the decision in *Rees* did not overrule *Parkinson*, so future claims for the additional costs of bringing up a disabled child remain a possibility.

The armed forces

2-054

The armed forces have never been treated as ordinary employers. Thus, in *Mulcahy v Ministry of Defence*,[185] the Court of Appeal held that, in battle conditions, common sense and sound policy dictated that the army could not owe a duty of care to its members. The plaintiff had been injured during the Gulf War, his injury being due to the negligence of his sergeant in causing a gun to fire whilst he was in front of it fetching water, rather than to active enemy involvement. The court accepted the argument that a duty of care would lead to defensive practices and undue caution, which would be wholly inappropriate to battle conditions. Whilst the immunity is likely to apply to all war-time activities, it is unlikely to apply to activities in peace-time. Thus, in *Jebson v Ministry of Defence*,[186] where the claimant was injured as a result of drunken horse-play in the back of an army truck, on the way back from an organised social event, the Court of Appeal held that the defendants were in breach of their duty to provide suitable transport and supervision for soldiers in high spirits.

Some cases, however, will be less clear-cut. The Supreme Court in 2013 in *Smith v Ministry of Defence*[187] considered again the scope of "combat immunity", this time in relation to injuries sustained by soldiers in Iraq. The claimants alleged that the MoD had breached its duty of care in failing properly to equip and train soldiers which led to an incident in which soldiers had been killed and injured by so-called "friendly fire" between two British Challenger tanks. The majority of the court[188] took the view that the scope of the immunity should be construed narrowly. Lord Hope, giving the majority judgment, argued that the extension of combat immunity to the planning of and preparation for operations in which the injury was sustained would be too generous and would involve an unjustifiable extension to include steps taken far away in place and time from the actual combat operations.[189] In this case, the complaints had related to failures in training and the provision of technology and equipment, that is, matters which should have been dealt with long before the commencement of hostilities. The question, therefore, was not whether there was a duty of care, but whether, bearing in mind the nature and circumstances of the activities in question, this duty had been breached. The majority thus

---

the advice or treatment was precisely to avoid having a disabled child (e.g. where there was a likelihood of congenital abnormalities).

185 [1996] Q.B. 732. The idea of granting the armed forces "combat immunity" may be traced back to *Shaw Savill & Albion Co Ltd v Commonwealth* (1940) 66 C.L.R. 344.

186 [2000] 1 W.L.R. 2055. See also *Barrett v Ministry of Defence* [1995] 1 W.L.R. 1217 and *Bici v Ministry of Defence* [2004] EWHC 786 (QB) (peacekeeping and policing functions in Kosovo). Note that in respect of incidents occurring before 1987, Crown Proceedings Act 1947 s.10 confers immunity.

187 [2013] UKSC 41; [2014] 1 A.C. 52. The majority also refused to strike out a claim based on breach of ECHR art.2.

188 Lords Mance, Wilson and Carnwath JJSC dissenting.

189 [2013] UKSC 41 at [89].

adopted a narrow definition of combat immunity, confining it to operations or acts of war where the parties are subject to the pressures and risks of an active operation. The ruling predictably received considerable criticism from the Ministry of Defence. Some other commentators have been more positive:

> **"With goodwill on all sides—and adequate resources—it should surely be possible to reach a compromise that allows troops to do their duty without exposing them to avoidable risks. That must be good for morale. This judgment requires troops to be properly equipped for combat. It does not require commanders to go to war with one hand behind their backs."**[190]

(3) Advisory bodies and regulators

In this section, we consider the liability of a number of advisory and regulatory bodies. Although in some cases these bodies receive government funding, they cannot be regarded as "public authorities" (like local authorities or NHS Trusts) because they do not act on behalf of the state. They are essentially "clubs" formed for the promotion or protection of certain interests. In some cases, however, they perform a public service role that would otherwise have to be performed by a government organisation.

2–055

Ship classification societies

A ship classification society is an independent and non-profit-making entity, created and operating for the sole purpose of promoting the safety of lives and ships at sea. In this way, it fulfils a role akin to a public service which would otherwise have to be fulfilled by individual states. In this light, the question arises whether such societies should be treated in the same manner as the coastguard or the fire brigade (see above).[191] In *Marc Rich & Co v Bishop Rock Marine Co Ltd (The Nicholas H)*,[192] a classification society had issued a certificate which indicated the seaworthiness of a ship. The ship subsequently sank. The House of Lords asserted that despite the presence of physical loss resulting from the carelessly made report of the society's surveyor, and despite the fact that the loss was clearly foreseeable, no duty of care was owed to the owner of the cargo that was lost.

There are suggestions, however, that the courts may be willing to overcome traditional

2–056

---

190 J. Rozenberg, "The Supreme Court's ruling will be greeted with dismay at the MoD" *The Guardian* 19 June 2013.

191 See, generally, J. de Bruyne, "Tort law and the regulation of classification societies" (2019) 27 E.R.P.L. 429.

192 [1996] A.C. 211. See also *Reeman v Department of Transport* [1997] 2 Lloyd's Rep. 648 (Department of Transport surveyor causing economic loss).

objections to liability where a classification society inflicts physical loss in a more direct way. Lord Steyn commented in *The Nicholas H*[193] that if the surveyor had caused an explosion by carelessly dropping a lighted cigarette into a hold known to contain combustible cargo, he would have been more willing to find that the society owed a duty of care. This approach was followed by the Court of Appeal in *Perrett v Collins*[194] where an inspector's role in certifying the airworthiness of light aircraft was critical, and, as a direct result of his negligence, the plaintiff suffered personal injury. The court saw no reason why the inspector should not owe the plaintiff a duty of care. Although the inspector worked for the Popular Flying Association, whose aim was to facilitate the construction and flying of light aircraft by amateurs, the imposition of a duty of care was not inconsistent with this aim.

Scientific advisory bodies

2-057

Similar arguments arise in relation to scientific advisory bodies. In *Sutradhar v Natural Environment Research Council*[195] the defendants were a UK government-funded agency, established under Royal Charter, whose purpose was to undertake research, disseminate knowledge, and provide advice relating to the earth sciences and ecology. As part of a project to assist development in Bangladesh, they undertook a hydrological survey in that country which aimed to provide an understanding of how water might be used for irrigation and fish farming. They therefore conducted a number of tests on samples of groundwater to identify the presence of harmful chemicals. Unfortunately, they did not test the water for the presence of arsenic, having no reason to believe that arsenic was likely to be present.

The claimant was one of 700 Bangladeshi residents who had suffered from arsenical poisoning by drinking contaminated water from the sources which had been tested. He argued that the defendants were negligent in having issued a report which gave the impression that the water was safe to drink. In dismissing his claim, the House of Lords pointed to the lack of proximity between the claimant and the defendants and noted that the purpose of the report had not been to protect the claimant from harm. The decisions in *Perrett v Collins* (above) and *Watson v British Boxing Board of Control* (below) were distinguished because, in those cases, the defendants had had complete control of the danger in question—in *Perrett*, for example, the inspector had had the power to ground the aircraft if he thought it was not safe to fly. Here, by contrast, the defendants had had no control whatsoever over whether and how water was supplied in Bangladesh.

---

193 [1996] A.C. 211 at 237.
194 [1998] 2 Lloyd's Rep 255.
195 [2006] UKHL 33; [2006] 4 All E.R. 490. Comment: D. Howarth, "Poisoned wells: 'proximity' and 'assumption of responsibility' in negligence" [2005] C.L.J. 23.

Sports regulators

2–058

In *Watson v British Boxing Board of Control*,[196] the Court of Appeal was prepared to hold that the BBBC, a private organisation formed for the regulation of boxing, owed a duty of care to ensure an adequate standard of ringside medical treatment for an injured boxer. The case was novel because the claimant's allegation was that the defendant had been negligent in failing to formulate satisfactory rules for the conduct of the sport. Watson had been examined by a doctor at the ringside, and subsequently taken to hospital where he was given resuscitation treatment, but by this time he had already suffered permanent brain damage leading to disability. Watson claimed that immediate resuscitation treatment should have been available at the ringside, and that the BBBC was in breach of its duty of care by not providing for this in its rules.

Lord Phillips MR, giving the judgment of the court, dismissed the BBBC's argument that Watson, knowing of the rules, had been the author of his own misfortune by consenting to box in accordance with them. His Lordship also regarded the fact that the BBBC was a non-profit-making organisation, without insurance, as irrelevant to its liability. Finding that there was a sufficient degree of proximity between Watson and the BBBC, his Lordship pointed out that Watson was one of only a limited class of individuals affected by the rules, so there could be no question of indeterminate liability.[197] Moreover, the BBBC had exclusive control over the provision of ringside medical assistance. Accordingly, it was fair just and reasonable for Watson to rely on the BBBC to look after his safety.

In *Vowles v Evans*,[198] the issue was not whether the rules of the game were adequate to protect the claimant, but whether they had been properly applied by the referee. The claimant was injured during an amateur game of rugby when the referee decided to allow the game to continue with "contestable scrummages" (in which the players are allowed to push against one another to gain possession of the ball) even though the substitution of an inexperienced player by one of the teams meant that this could not be done safely. The Court of Appeal saw no reason why the referee should not owe a duty of care. Even though the referee was acting in an amateur capacity, the second defendants (Welsh Rugby Union Ltd) who had appointed him could be expected to take out insurance against the negligence of their referees. The fact that serious injuries of this kind were comparatively rare meant that this would not create an unfair financial burden nor discourage amateurs from volunteering to act as referees.

---

196 [2000] EWCA Civ 2116; [2001] Q.B. 1134.

197 The High Court of Australia found this a bar to liability in *Agar v Hyde* [2000] HCA 41, where the allegation was that inadequate rules governing rugby scrums had exposed the claimants to injury.

198 [2003] EWCA Civ 318; [2003] 1 W.L.R. 1607. See also *Bartlett v English Cricket Board Association of Cricket Officials* unreported 27 August 2015 CC Wolverhampton: cricket umpire at amateur match owes duty of care to cricket teams but on facts no breach. See N. Partington (2016) 32 P.N. 77.

(4) The legal profession

2–059

Generally, judges[199] and arbitrators[200] cannot be sued in respect of their activities during a case. Prior to the decision of the House of Lords in *Hall v Simons*,[201] barristers and solicitor advocates enjoyed a similar immunity—they could not be sued for negligently conducting a case in court, or for matters intimately connected with the conduct of the case in court.[202] In *Hall v Simons*, however, their Lordships abolished advocates' immunity, stating that the traditional arguments used to support it could no longer be sustained. By analogy, the Supreme Court later removed the immunity of expert witnesses instructed by parties to litigation in 2011.[203]

Although the immunity has been abolished, it remains difficult for a claimant who feels he or she has been the victim of incompetent advocacy to succeed in negligence against an advocate. For reasons we explore below, this is especially true in criminal cases where the claimant has been convicted. In all cases, of course, the claimant must show that the advocate is in breach of the duty of care, and that his or her negligence caused the loss suffered.[204] As we shall see in Chs 5 and 6, this can be difficult to establish.

The old law

2–060

Under the old law, the immunity enjoyed by barristers and solicitor advocates[205] applied only in the context of litigation. Where non-litigious work was concerned, a duty of care was owed. The immunity granted to lawyers was nevertheless questioned by academics and practitioners alike.[206] Moreover, the distinction between "litigious" and "non-litigious" work proved very difficult to draw in practice and led to a lack of clarity in the law. In order to appreciate the modern law, it is convenient to set out briefly the arguments that were formerly used to

---

199 *Sirros v Moore* [1975] Q.B. 118.
200 *Arenson v Arenson* [1977] A.C. 405 (provided they are acting in an arbitral capacity. The immunity does not extend to mutual valuers.)
201 [2002] 1 A.C. 615. *Hall v Simons* has been held to apply retrospectively: *Awoyomi v Radford* [2007] EWHC 1671 (QB); [2008] Q.B. 793. Note, however, that other common law countries such as Australia still maintain a defence of advocates' immunity: see *Giannarelli v Wraith* (1988) 165 C.L.R. 543; *Attwells v Jackson Lalic Lawyers Pty Ltd* (2016) 259 C.L.R. 1, discussed in D. Capper, "Advocates' immunity and the jagged edge" (2016) 32 P.N. 212. The Australian immunity is now confined to conduct of the advocate which contributes to a judicial determination.
202 *Saif Ali v Sydney Mitchell & Co (a Firm)* [1980] A.C. 198.
203 *Jones v Kaney* [2011] UKSC 13; [2011] 2 A.C. 398. For a critical appraisal, see D. Capper, "Professional liability in the trial process" (2013) 29 P.N. 7.
204 See *Moy v Pettman Smith (A Firm)* [2005] UKHL 7; [2005] 1 W.L.R. 581 HL. Comment: C. McIvor, "Advocates' liability for professional negligence" (2005) 21 P.N. 131.
205 See Courts and Legal Services Act 1990 s.62(1).
206 See J. Hill, "Litigation and negligence: a comparative study" (1986) 6 O.J.L.S. 183 and D. Pannick, *Advocates* (OUP, 1992).

support advocates' immunity[207] and to explore how each was addressed by their Lordships in *Hall v Simons*.

Arguments for advocates' immunity

(1) Divided loyalty. This argument rests on the fact that the integrity of our legal system relies on advocates adhering to their overriding duty to the court whilst representing their clients' interests e.g. not to mislead the court, cast aspersions on the other party or its witnesses for which there is insufficient evidence, or withhold authorities or documents relevant to the case. The immunity, it was argued, helped to ensure that advocates did not succumb, through fear of being sued, to pressure from their clients to breach their duties as officers of the court. In *Hall v Simons*, their Lordships dismissed this "divided loyalty" argument.[208] Lord Steyn pointed out that it was difficult to see how the argument could justify the immunity of advocates when doctors, for example, enjoyed no such immunity, even though they too could be faced with questions of "divided loyalty", as where a patient with AIDS asks his doctor not to disclose this fact to his wife. Moreover, their Lordships noted that there was no evidence to suggest that in jurisdictions where advocates had no immunity (Canada, for example) their overriding duty to the court was compromised.

2–061

(2) The "cab-rank" rule. Barristers (but not solicitor advocates) are obliged to act for any client who requests their services, provided that the client's claim is within their field of expertise and a proper fee is offered. This is known as the "cab-rank" rule. It was traditionally thought that the operation of this rule justified advocates' immunity because, if a barrister could not stop representing a client, even when that client threatened to sue the barrister for refusing to behave unethically, it was only fair that the barrister should be immune from suit. It was argued that were matters otherwise, barristers might be beset with unmeritorious negligence claims from "vexatious" clients whose cases they had no choice but to take. This argument, too, was dismissed in *Hall v Simons*. Lord Hope said of the cab-rank rule that "its significance in daily practice is not great".[209] Lord Steyn went so far, perhaps, as to hint that the rule is more often honoured in its breach than its observance when he noted that "in real life" barristers' clerks were free, within limits, to raise the fees for unwanted briefs (i.e. so as to discourage clients from briefing the barrister of their choice).[210] In any event, the Civil Procedure Rules, which allow for "summary disposal" of claims where "the claimant has no real prospect of succeeding"[211] would ensure that barristers were not subject to a flood of unmeritorious claims following the abolition of advocates' immunity.

2–062

---

207 The leading case was *Rondel v Worsley* [1969] 1 A.C. 191, in which the relevant arguments were set out by Lord Reid.
208 A minority of judges believed, however, that it still had force in relation to criminal cases.
209 [2002] 1 A.C. 615 at 714.
210 [2002] 1 A.C. 615 at 678.
211 Civil Procedure Rules r.24.2.

2-063

(3) The collateral challenge rule. To sue successfully for compensation resulting from an advocate's negligence, the claimant must show that the advocate's negligence has caused him or her to lose the case. To assess whether the unfavourable outcome of the trial was in fact the consequence of the advocate's negligence (or whether the client would have lost in any event), a court would effectively have to re-hear the case, evaluating the effect of the advocate's contribution to its outcome in the light of all the evidence.

In fact, the "no re-trial" objective had already been met in the law by different means. The House of Lords' decision in *Hunter v Chief Constable of the West Midlands Police*[212] confirmed that, at least in criminal cases, a collateral attack on the correctness of the final decision of a court would be struck out as an abuse of process where the claimant had had the opportunity of appealing against that decision. *Hunter* was a case in which six convicted IRA terrorists (the "Birmingham Six") had alleged at their trial that the police had beaten them to extract confessions. The trial judge had found that this had not been the case, and they were convicted. They applied for leave to appeal (on other grounds) and this was refused. Whilst in prison, they brought proceedings for assault against the police, alleging the same beatings that had been alleged at the criminal trial. The House of Lords struck out their claim as an abuse of process, because the men were attempting to relitigate issues which had already been decided at their trial.

The rule in *Hunter* reflects considerations of public policy, namely the importance of finality in administering justice, the affront to a coherent system of justice which would arise if there subsisted two inconsistent decisions of the courts, and the virtual impossibility of fairly re-trying, at a later date, issues of fact a court had decided on an earlier occasion.[213] Their Lordships in *Hall v Simons* stressed the importance of maintaining the prohibition on collateral attacks on judicial decisions in criminal cases, but felt that this concern was relatively unimportant in relation to civil cases.

2-064

(4) Other grounds: the length of trials and witness immunity. It was also argued that advocates' immunity ensured that trials were not unnecessarily prolonged by defensive conduct by the advocate, such as over-cautious questioning and that the immunity was consistent with the general immunity from civil liability that attaches to all persons participating in court proceedings, such as the judge, court officials, witnesses and parties. Both of these arguments were rejected in *Hall v Simons*. Lord Hoffmann noted that lengthy submissions by advocates were a problem even with the immunity in place. The disapproval of the court, together with the possibility of the judge making a wasted costs order against the advocate in question, would be sufficient to contain the length of trials in the absence of advocates' immunity. Equally, the rationale for witness immunity was that, without it, witnesses might be less willing to assist the court. The same could not be said for advocates.

---

212 [1982] A.C. 529. For an explanation of the *Hunter* principle, see *R. v Belmarsh Magistrates' Court Ex p. Watts* [1999] 2 Cr. App. R. 188.

213 *Smith v Linskills* [1996] 1 W.L.R. 763.

The decision in *Hall v Simons*

2–065

In *Hall v Simons*, the seven-member House of Lords ruled unanimously that the immunity could no longer stand in civil cases, dismissing the traditional arguments, for the reasons we have examined above. By a majority, their Lordships also held that the immunity should be abolished in criminal cases, although a minority of three[214] thought that it should be preserved in such cases, because the conduct of criminal trials made advocates particularly vulnerable to unmeritorious complaints and the risk of "divided loyalties".

The majority thought that the rule against collateral attack, established in *Hunter*, would be sufficient to prevent the administration of justice being brought into disrepute by negligence claims against advocates. They noted that the rule in *Hunter* will operate differently in relation to criminal and civil cases. In relation to civil cases, it will seldom be possible to say that an action for negligence against a legal representative will bring the administration of justice into disrepute. This is because the correctness of the decision in a civil trial is a matter of concern only to the parties. Unlike a decision in a criminal court, it serves no wider purpose. Therefore, according to Lord Hoffmann, the rule in *Hunter* is unlikely to be used in a civil context, except in rare cases where allowing an action to proceed against an advocate would be unfair to a third party, for example, where a defence of truth[215] has been rejected in a defamation action.

In relation to criminal cases, a distinction was to be drawn between, on the one hand, cases where the accused has been convicted—either after a trial or a guilty plea—and, on the other hand, cases where the accused has had the conviction set aside after a successful appeal. Where the accused still stands convicted of the offence, any attempt to challenge the competence of his or her advocate will generally fall foul of *Hunter* and will be struck out as a collateral attack on the correctness of the conviction. The appropriate way for the accused to challenge a conviction is by an appeal rather than a negligence action against an advocate. On the other hand, if the accused has had his or her conviction set aside on appeal, there can be no such objection to a negligence action.

Duty of care: conclusion

2–066

The Supreme Court in *Robinson* has clarified *when* a duty of care will arise in the tort of negligence and, in particular, the importance of looking to precedents to determine whether a duty of care exists. The aim is to give greater certainty to the law and limit the number of so-called novel cases when the court must determine whether it would be "fair, just and reasonable" to impose a duty of care. It has also made clear in cases such as *Michael* and *Van Colle/Smith* that the duty of care question is distinct from that of the application of the Human Rights Act 1998. Whether you think this latter position is a lost opportunity—the view of the late Lord Bingham—

---

214   Lords Hope, Hutton and Hobhouse.
215   See Ch.14.

or a logical recognition of the different roles of tort and human rights law depends on the degree to which you think negligence law should change and respond to new influences in the law. Recent case-law indicates that the Supreme Court favours a more traditional approach and that change based on public policy concerns has to be justified rather than accepted as part of the judicial role.

To conclude, the (denial of a) duty of care remains one of the most important mechanisms available to the courts in determining the scope of the modern tort of negligence. We have seen that the question of whether a duty should exist in a given situation is answered by reference to a number of considerations, in particular the ideas of ensuring that liability remains proportionate to the defendant's fault, yet consistent with the structure and general objectives of the law. In the chapters which follow, we shall explore the way the courts have incorporated these considerations into their decisions in cases of economic loss and psychiatric illness.

3

Negligence: Economic Loss

Introduction

3–001

Chapter 2 has highlighted that it is generally much more difficult to establish a duty of care in respect of "economic loss" than in respect of damage to property or personal injury. This chapter examines the reasons why this is so. We shall see that, broadly speaking, no duty of care is owed to avoid causing pure economic loss by careless activities, but that very different rules apply to careless statements, making it easier for a claimant to recover. The division between the two situations is largely a matter of historical accident in the way the law has developed, but it also has to do with the fact that, in the "activity" cases, the courts have been more heavily influenced by public policy arguments, in particular the need to limit the liability of local authorities. Different rules again apply to intentionally inflicted economic loss, which will be examined separately in Ch.12.

Definition of "pure economic loss"

3–002

Tort lawyers will often use the term "economic loss" as shorthand for "pure economic loss", but it should be recognised that this is a specific legal term. "Pure economic loss" may be defined as *loss that is purely financial, in the sense that it does not result from damage to the claimant's property or injury to the claimant's person.*

Pure economic loss will result where, for example, a person buys a product which is defective. The person is said to have suffered "pure economic loss" because the only loss in question is the cost of repairing or replacing the product.

"Pure" and "consequential" economic loss

3–003

The courts draw a distinction between "pure" economic loss and "consequential" economic loss. The term "consequential economic loss" simply means financial loss that is *consequent upon damage to the claimant's person or property*. Examples include loss of earnings suffered by a claimant who has been seriously injured, and loss of profits resulting from damage to commercial machinery. Where financial loss is consequential on injury to the person or property, the ordinary test for duty of care (stated in Ch.2) applies. The UK Supreme Court in *Dryden v Johnson Matthey Plc*[1] adopted a generous approach in relation to financial losses suffered by employees who had been negligently exposed to platinum salts in a chemical plant and were unable as a result to work in future in any industry where further exposure might take place. Such losses were regarded as consequential on personal injury. Although the claimants were not otherwise ill and could indeed avoid illness by not working with platinum salts, the court found that there had been a physical change which made them appreciably worse off in their health and capacity to enjoy life. In the words of Lady Black, "The physiological changes to the claimants' bodies may not be as obviously harmful as, say, the loss of a limb, or asthma or dermatitis, but harmful they undoubtedly are."[2]

An illustration: *Spartan Steel*

3–004

The distinctions between "(pure) economic loss", "consequential economic loss" and "damage to property" are neatly illustrated by the decision in *Spartan Steel & Alloys Ltd v Martin & Co (Contractors) Ltd*.[3] The defendants, who were construction workers, negligently cut through a cable which supplied power to the plaintiffs' factory, causing a power cut which lasted for 14½ hours. Without electricity, the plaintiffs' furnace could not operate and they had to close their factory. The metal that was in the furnace at the time the power went off (the "melt") began to solidify, and to save damaging the furnace the plaintiffs had to throw it away. The plaintiffs brought an action for three types of loss:

- damage to the melt that was in the furnace at the time of the power cut (physical damage to property);

- loss of the profit which would have been made on the sale of that melt (consequential economic loss resulting from property damage);

---

1 [2018] UKSC 18; [2019] A.C. 403. For a critical commentary, see J. Morgan (2018) 77 C.L.J. 461.
2 [2018] UKSC 18 at [40]. Contrast *Rothwell v Chemical & Insulating Co Ltd* [2007] UKHL 39; [2008] A.C. 281 where the development of pleural plaques following exposure to asbestos was merely a marker of exposure and being symptomless and not giving rise to any condition would not be treated as personal injury.
3 [1973] Q.B. 27.

■ loss of profits on four further melts which would have been processed during the 14½ hours the factory was closed because of the power cut (pure economic loss).

A majority of the Court of Appeal held that the first two claims were recoverable, but the third claim was not. The defendants owed the plaintiffs a duty not to damage their property, and therefore had to pay for the damaged metal and the loss of profit resulting directly from that damage, but they did not owe a duty of care in respect of the further lost profits, because these did not result from the fact that the plaintiffs' property had been damaged.

Lord Denning MR was unsure whether to approach the question from the point of view of duty of care or remoteness of damage. His Lordship observed:

> **"At bottom I think the question of recovering economic loss is one of policy. Whenever the courts draw a line to mark out the bounds of duty, they do it as matter of policy so as to limit the responsibility of the defendant. Whenever the courts set bounds to the damages recoverable—saying that they are, or are not, too remote—they do it as matter of policy so as to limit the liability of the defendant."[4]**

His Lordship then referred to the policy considerations which precluded liability for the further loss of profits. Observing that power cuts are a fact of life and that they can often cause economic loss, his Lordship stated that people should bear that loss themselves, either by taking out insurance or by installing emergency generators, concluding: ". . . the risk of economic loss should be suffered by the whole community . . . rather than be placed on one pair of shoulders". His Lordship also noted that if claims for pure economic loss due to power cuts were allowed, it would be very easy to make inflated claims—claimants could assert that they had intended to use their machinery for the duration of a power cut, but it would be impossible to prove whether, in fact, they really would have done so. If the courts simply took the claimants' word for it, exaggerated damages awards would result.

Much, then, depends on how the loss is classified. This question arose again in the more recent case of *Network Rail Infrastructure Ltd v Conarken Group Ltd*.[5] Here the defendants had damaged Network Rail's track which had led to interruption in rail services. Following privatisation, the actual train services were run by train operating companies (TOCs), which had track access agreements with Network Rail. These agreements provided for Network Rail to pay compensation to the TOCs when access to the track was interrupted and compensation was calculated on the basis of the potential losses suffered by the TOCs resulting from a public loss of confidence in the service together with penalties they would have to pay for delays. In a test case, Network Rail sought to recover compensation from the defendants for damage to

3–005

---

4   [1973] Q.B. 27 at 36.

5   [2011] EWCA Civ 644; [2012] 1 All E.R. (Comm) 692. Comment: J. O'Sullivan, "Negligence, remoteness and economic loss—Staying on track" [2011] C.L.J. 496, who notes that in many cases the costs of repair will be dwarfed by the compensation payments to the TOCs involving, in one case, over £1 million.

the track (property damage), but also for compensation paid out to the various TOCs during the period the lines were closed as *consequential economic loss*. The Court of Appeal was prepared to allow Network Rail's claim on the basis they *had* suffered property loss and the issue of recovery of compensation payments was one of scope of duty and remoteness of damage. It rejected the argument that the Court should take into account that if the TOCs had brought a claim in their own right for this loss it would have been classified as pure economic loss and so irrecoverable. The contractual agreements between Network Rail and the TOCs permitted them to circumvent this rule.

Policy considerations

3–006

The reasoning of the majority in *Spartan Steel* reflects the three overlapping policy considerations that have traditionally made pure economic loss non-recoverable in tort:

(1) Tort law should not impose "crushing liability" on defendants for financial losses

3–007

Whilst a single negligent act is likely to cause personal injury or property damage only to a limited number of people, the same act may cause an enormous number of people to suffer pure economic loss. The classic illustration of the point is that of a defendant who crashes his car, blocking a busy tunnel. This may cause a plumber on his way to work to be late and lose pay. In turn, the plumber's lateness may cause financial loss to others—a builder, for example, who is waiting for the plumber to complete his tasks before starting his own—and then to a property developer who misses a market opportunity by waiting for the completion of the building works. People's financial interests are so closely interrelated that causing economic loss to one person usually produces a "domino effect". The law's way of dealing with this phenomenon is to allow people, through the mechanism of contract law, to fix the extent of their economic liabilities to others—they will only be liable to others with whom they have contracted. This also prevents one defendant from being liable for an indeterminate amount of loss to multiple claimants (also known as the "floodgates" argument).

(2) Tort law should not undermine the contractual allocation of risk

3–008

Parties by contract, then, are able to allocate the risk of financial losses. Allowing the parties, through contracts, to determine where liability will fall if things go wrong is, it can be argued, economically efficient in that freedom of contract exists precisely to allow the parties to trade off quality against price. If tort law begins to impose obligations to supply goods of a certain quality, it interferes with this process of bargaining, rendering the rules of contract law redundant. If, therefore, the argument runs, the courts awarded damages for pure economic loss, it would interfere with the contractual allocation of risk between the parties and discourage parties from taking out contractual protection via guarantees or insurance policies. This was, indeed, the view of Lord Denning in *Spartan Steel* discussed above. As O'Sullivan has commented, "the courts do not permit claimants to use tort in order to evade a fundamental rule of the law of contract that goes to its essence as a voluntary, objective, commercial institution, or, to 'get round' the contractual structure or terms of the parties' particular transaction."[6]

(3) Financial loss is not considered as important as physical harm

While it might be questioned why a defendant who has caused foreseeable loss is allowed to escape liability, we saw in Ch.2 that there may be countervailing considerations which indicate that a defendant should not be liable in tort without having accepted responsibility for the welfare of others. People are generally more willing to assume a duty to look after the physical safety and property of others than to look after the financial wellbeing of others. In denying recovery for pure economic loss, then, it may be argued that tort law simply reflects the feelings of society.

This argument does, however, raise the question of why financial loss resulting from damage to the claimant's *own* property ("consequential economic loss") is recoverable. In *Spartan Steel*, Edmund-Davies LJ, dissenting, objected to this distinction which he described as "arbitrary". We can see this by a simple example—in the case, the factory-owners did not own the cable that had been cut. They could only recover for financial losses resulting from damage to their property—here the melt in the furnace. If, however, the defendants had owned the cable then, subject to the rules of remoteness, they could have claimed for financial losses resulting from the damage to *their* cable. In his Lordship's view, the law would be clearer if it stated that all foreseeable economic loss was recoverable. His Lordship could not see why the recovery of economic loss should depend on the purely fortuitous circumstance of who happened to own the piece of property that was damaged.[7] Edmund-Davies LJ's view has not, however, found favour with the courts.

With the law's policy objectives in mind, it is now appropriate to examine the relevant case law in more detail. We shall begin with the cases where the pure economic loss has been caused by negligent activities. Here recovery is generally denied. Later in the chapter we consider cases where the courts have been more generous where the pure economic loss has been caused by a negligent misstatement or the negligent provision of services.

---

6   J. O'Sullivan, "Suing in tort where no contractual claim will lie—a bird's eye view" (2007) 23 P.N. 165, 192. See also *Wellesley Partners LLP v Withers LLP* [2015] EWCA Civ 1146; [2016] 2 W.L.R. 1351: where there is concurrent tortious and contractual liability, the contractual rules on remoteness of damages for economic loss apply and, more recently, M. Isaacs, "Understanding the relationship between duties in contract and the tort of negligence" (2019) 35 P.N. 155.

7   [1973] Q.B. 27 at 41.

Pure Economic Loss Caused by Negligent Activities

The traditional approach

3–010

A convenient place to start is *Cattle v Stockton Waterworks*.[8] Here, the defendants, who had laid a pipe under land belonging to Mr Knight, were under a statutory duty to keep the pipe in good repair. Mr Knight contracted with the plaintiff, Mr Cattle, to do some building work. Mr Cattle agreed to do this for a fixed price, but after he had started work, he noticed that the land was becoming hard to excavate because it was waterlogged. He realised that the defendants' pipe was leaking and contacted them about this, but they negligently failed to repair it. The result of this negligence was that Mr Cattle lost profit on his contract, so he sought to recover this from the defendants.

Blackburn J held that Mr Cattle could not sue in his own name for damage that had been done to land belonging to Mr Knight. In other words, he was not owed a duty of care because he had no proprietary interest in the damaged land. In modern terms, we should say that Mr Cattle's loss was purely economic. Blackburn J justified his decision with reference to the "crushing liability" argument: here liability would place the defendants under a financial liability disproportionate to their fault. This policy of avoiding wide and disproportionate liability was subsequently confirmed in *Spartan Steel*, which we have already examined.

The *Stockton Waterworks* case, then, established that a claimant could not recover economic loss resulting from damage to property in which he or she had only a contractual interest. This is sometimes called "relational loss"—the loss relates to the property of another.[9] This is not recoverable. The case, however, indicates more broadly that allowing recovery for pure economic loss is problematic, notably in relation to the risk of crushing liability.

A brief period of expansion: *Anns* and *Junior Books*

3–011

The same reasoning has led the courts to deny the existence of a duty of care where the defendant's negligent activities have created a defect in property owned by the claimant. By defective, we mean a fault affecting the quality of property, such as cracks, such that the claimant will have to spend money fixing it. Defective property is seen as a classic example of pure

---

8 (1875) L.R. 10 Q.B. 453. See also *Weller & Co v Foot and Mouth Disease Research Institute* [1966] 1 Q.B. 569 and *Leigh and Sillivan Ltd v Aliakmon Shipping Co Ltd (The Aliakmon)* [1986] A.C. 785 (no recovery where coils damaged at sea were not yet property of plaintiffs who had contracted to buy them). .

9 Contrast the position in Canada in relation to relational loss: *The Norsk (Canadian National Railway Co v Norsk Pacific Steamship Co)* (1992) 91 D.L.R. (4th) 289; *Bow Valley Husky (Bermuda) v Saint John Shipbuilding Ltd* (1998) 153 D.L.R. (4th) 385.

economic loss. Any defect in quality is seen not as property damage but as the financial cost of repairing the property and so not normally recoverable in tort.

In the late 1970s and early 1980s, however, the House of Lords chose to depart from this long-standing rule in two important cases: *Anns v Merton LBC*[10] (which has now been overruled) and *Junior Books v Veitchi*[11] (which is nowadays unlikely to be followed). These cases were part of the general expansion of negligence liability during that period, discussed in Ch.2.

The decision in *Anns*

Anns involved a claim against a local authority which, it was alleged, had failed properly to supervise the construction of a building, so that cracks appeared in its walls. Lord Wilberforce took the unusual step of categorising these cracks as "damage to property",[12] apparently ignoring (or intending to displace) the traditional position that the loss caused by a defective building is the cost of repair (that is, pure economic loss). Lord Wilberforce, however, appeared to use the word "damaged" in a much looser sense (i.e. in the sense that a lay person might complain that he or she has been supplied with "damaged goods"). On that basis, he found a duty of care was owed. As we shall see, in *Murphy v Brentwood DC*,[13] the House of Lords rejected this broad analysis, stating that the loss in *Anns* had been wrongly categorised, and restored the traditional distinction between defects in quality and "damage to property".

3–012

The decision in *Junior Books*

Anns influenced, however, the later decision of *Junior Books v Veitchi*.[14] This case marked the high point of the expansion of the duty to avoid causing pure economic loss by supplying a defective product. The plaintiffs had entered into a contract with a firm of contractors ("the main contractors") for the construction of a factory. The factory needed a special floor to support heavy machinery, so the plaintiffs instructed the main contractors to sub-contract the flooring work to the defendants, who were flooring specialists. There was, therefore, a contract between the plaintiffs and the main contractors, and a contract between the main contractors and the defendants, but there was no direct contractual relationship between the plaintiffs and the defendants. The floor turned out to be defective and had to be rebuilt, necessitating a temporary closure of the plaintiffs' factory. For reasons which are unknown, the plaintiffs did not pursue their contractual remedy against the main contractors (who were perhaps insolvent),

3–013

---

10   [1978] A.C. 728.
11   [1983] 1 A.C. 520.
12   *Anns v Merton LBC* [1978] A.C. 728 at 759.
13   [1991] 1 A.C. 398.
14   [1983] 1 A.C. 520.

but instead brought a claim against the defendant sub-contractors, claiming the cost of re-laying the floor and lost profits while this was done.

In the House of Lords, it was observed (apparently without noticing any inconsistency with the way the loss had been categorised in *Anns*) that the claim in *Junior Books* was a claim for pure economic loss caused by the supply of a defective product. It was not a "damage to property" claim. Nor, indeed, was there any suggestion that the floor presented a danger to other property or a risk of personal injury (which might have made the plaintiffs' task a little easier). Regarding the case squarely as one of pure economic loss, their Lordships recognised that the question for the House was whether to extend the scope of the duty of care beyond a duty to prevent harm being done by faulty work, to a duty to avoid defects *being present in the work itself*. Normally, such a duty would only be owed in contract. By a 4:1 majority, the House of Lords held that the special circumstances of the case meant that the defendants owed such a duty in tort. Their Lordships gave a number of reasons why this should be so. The gist of their Lordships' argument was that Veitchi had "assumed responsibility" towards the plaintiffs for the quality of the floor, that the plaintiffs had "reasonably relied" on Veitchi's special skill, and that, because Veitchi were nominated sub-contractors, the relationship between the parties was "almost as close a commercial relationship . . . as it is possible to envisage short of privity of contract".[15]

Lord Roskill gave eight specific reasons why the plaintiffs should succeed:

"(1) The appellants were nominated sub-contractors. (2) The appellants were specialists in flooring. (3) The appellants knew what products were required by the respondents and their main contractors and specialised in the production of those products. (4) The appellants alone were responsible for the composition and construction of the flooring. (5) The respondents relied upon the appellants' skill and experience. (6) The appellants as nominated sub-contractors must have known that the respondents relied upon their skill and experience. (7) The relationship between the parties was as close as it could be short of actual privity of contract. (8) The appellants must be taken to have known that if they did the work negligently . . . the respondents would suffer financial or economic loss."[16]

Lord Brandon dissented, arguing that the majority's decision created, between parties who were not in a contractual relationship, the sort of liability that should only arise in the law of contract. It has proved very difficult to extract the *ratio* of *Junior Books*, and the case has met with considerable judicial criticism. In *D & F Estates Ltd v Church Commissioners*,[17] for example,

---

15   per Lord Roskill in *Junior Books v Veitchi* [1983] 1 A.C. 520 at 542.
16   [1983] 1 A.C. 520 at 546.
17   [1989] A.C. 177.

Lord Bridge gave his support to Lord Brandon's dissenting view, stating that his Lordship had enunciated principles of "fundamental importance" and that the decision in *Junior Books* could not be regarded as laying down any principle of general application.[18] Although *Junior Books* has never been overruled, it is nowadays regarded as having turned on its own special facts, and is unlikely to be followed.

The liberal approach to economic loss, then, exemplified by *Junior Books* and *Anns*, was short-lived. The courts quickly came to see that those decisions threatened to undermine the principles of contract law. Moreover, they were concerned that the prospect of widespread local authority liability raised by *Anns* might lead to an unacceptable drain on the public purse. These matters are considered below.

The retreat from *Junior Books*

Decisions such as *Muirhead v Industrial Tank Specialities*[19] in 1986 reflected a policy shift towards reaffirming the sharp distinction between contractual and tortious obligations—only contract law would provide a remedy for "defective product economic loss". Here, a fish-monger contracted with a company (which went into liquation) to build him a tank to store lobsters. The pumps for the tank were supplied by a third party, but failed as they were not suitable for use in the UK, causing the death of the lobsters. Muirhead's claim against the manufacturer of the defective pumps was unsuccessful except for the claim for property damage (loss of lobsters) and loss of consequential profit. Muirhead could not recover for the cost of the pumps nor for the expenditure wasted in trying to fix them. *Junior Books* was distinguished on the basis that it was not possible to say that Muirhead had relied on the manufacturer of the pumps in the same way that Junior Books had relied on Veitchi—he had not nominated the manufacturer to supply the pumps nor knew their identity. *Junior Books* was confined to its own facts.

Muirhead was followed by the Court of Appeal in *Greater Nottingham Co-operative Society v Cementation Piling Ltd*.[20] Here, the plaintiffs had employed contractors to build an extension to one of their buildings and the defendants were nominated sub-contractors, responsible for pile driving. They did this negligently so that completion of the building was delayed, causing the plaintiffs economic loss. Although there was a collateral contract between the plaintiffs and the defendants, the Court of Appeal was not prepared to find liability under *Junior Books*. Woolf LJ stated:

> "Where, as here, the sub-contractor has entered into a direct contract and expressly undertaken a direct but limited contractual responsibility to the building owner, I regard the direct contract as

3–014

---

18 [1989] A.C. 177 at 202.
19 [1986] Q.B. 507.
20 [1989] Q.B. 71.

> **being inconsistent with any assumption of responsibility beyond that which has been expressly undertaken."[21]**

The contract, in setting out which materials were to be used and the design of the piles, therefore set out the sum total of the obligations which the defendants intended to assume towards the plaintiffs. Similar restrictive approaches were adopted by the Court of Appeal in *Simaan v Pilkington Glass Ltd (No.2)*[22] and *Pacific Associates v Baxter*.[23] In both these cases, the courts held that in view of the way in which the parties had structured their contractual relationships, liability in tort would be inappropriate. Dillon LJ, dismissing the argument that the principles of *Junior Books* should apply in *Simaan* to allow the plaintiffs to sue a sub-contractor for supplying a defective product, held that: "I find it difficult to see that future citation from the *Junior Books* case can ever serve any useful purpose".[24]

All of these decisions, then, show that under the modern law the courts are unwilling to allow pure economic loss claims where to do so would interfere with expressed contractual intentions.[25]

Junior Books and the Contract (Rights of Third Parties) Act 1999

3–015 Before examining the current approach to pure economic loss claims in activity cases, it is worth noting briefly the impact of the Contracts (Rights of Third Parties) Act 1999 on future *Junior Books* situations. The Act reforms the law of privity of contract which states that only those who are party to a contract can sue or be sued. Where, as in *Junior Books, the claim* is against a non-contracting party, the Act provides that where a third party is *expressly identified* in a contract (either by name or as a member of a class) and that contract either:

- expressly states that its terms are enforceable by the third party; *or*

- purports to confer a benefit on the third party, and, on a proper construction of the contract, it appears that the parties intend the contract to be enforceable by the third party,

the third party may sue on the contract as if he had been a party to it.[26]

---

21 [1989] Q.B. 71 at 106.
22 [1988] 2 W.L.R. 761.
23 [1990] 1 Q.B. 993.
24 *Simaan v Pilkington Glass Ltd (No.2)* [1988] 2 W.L.R. 761 at 778.
25 This is also now the position adopted in Canada: see *Design Services Ltd v Canada* [2008] 1 S.C.R. 737; 2008 S.C.C. 22.
26 Contracts (Rights of Third Parties) Act 1999 s.1.

It seems probable that Junior Books would have been identified in the contract between the main contractor and Veitchi (the flooring company). It is uncertain, however, whether on a proper construction of that contract, a court would feel able to say that the parties to the contract intended that it should be enforceable by Junior Books. It is important to note that the provisions of the Act place the emphasis firmly on the intentions of the contracting parties. The Act does not allow the courts to *impose* obligations on contracting parties in spite of their intentions. Arguably, this was what happened in *Junior Books*. It seems the Act, therefore, will not assist future *Junior Books* claimants.

The "Activity" Cases: the modern rule against recovery

The courts now adopt a more restrictive approach towards claims for pure economic loss. Put simply, "defective building/product economic loss" is not generally recoverable. As we saw above in *Muirhead* the cost of replacing the pumps was not recoverable in tort. This was a claim for "defective product economic loss"—whilst the pumps had caused damage to *other property* (the lobsters), they were not themselves "damaged" in the tort lawyers' sense of the word; they were simply defective. It is, however, in relation to defective buildings where the most significant claims have arisen. We have seen that in the 1970s, the House of Lords was prepared to allow such a claim in *Anns*. In subsequent cases, however, their Lordships were reluctant to apply the principles in *Anns* with a broad brush, eventually overruling their decision in that case. The House of Lords decision in *D & F Estates Ltd v Church Commissioners*[27] encapsulated the courts' concerns. Here a claim was made against sub-contractors for negligent plastering of the walls of a flat where the plaintiffs sought compensation for the cost of renewing the plaster and for the consequent disruption and loss of rent while the work took place. This was clearly a claim for pure economic loss and was rejected by the House of Lords on this basis. The cost of remedying a defect—even where this is necessary in order to avoid an immediate threat of personal injury or damage to other property—was regarded by the Court as non-recoverable pure economic loss.[28] A clear difference was found between, on the one hand, situations where a latent (undiscovered) defect materialised, causing damage to other property or personal injury, and, on the other hand, situations where a dangerous defect is discovered by the building owner *before* any such damage has occurred. Dealing with *Anns*, Lord Oliver commented that the "underlying logical basis" of the case was "not entirely clear".[29]

3–016

---

27   [1989] A.C. 177.

28   This observation, although obiter to the decision in *D & F Estates*, did much to settle previous debate about whether a duty of care could be owed in respect of defects that posed an imminent danger, but had not yet caused any damage.

29   [1989] A.C. 177 at 216.

3–017

In *Murphy v Brentwood DC*,[30] the House of Lords finally overturned *Anns* and sought to bring greater clarity to the law. Here, Brentwood Council, relying on the negligent advice of its consulting engineers, had approved the building plans for a house. There were certain errors in the design of the foundations which made them defective. Mr Murphy subsequently bought the house, and, while he was in occupation, the foundations cracked, causing extensive damage. The gas, water and sewage pipes underneath the house began to rupture, posing a danger to Mr Murphy and his family and forcing them to move out. Instead of repairing the house, Mr Murphy sold it to a builder for considerably less than he had paid for it. He then sued the council for his financial loss.

The claim failed. The House of Lords held that Mr Murphy could not recover his pure economic loss. On the question of whether the law would allow claims for damage to "other property" caused by a defective building, their Lordships held that, whilst a local authority (or a builder) might be liable in tort if a *latent* (undiscovered) defect suddenly materialised, causing personal injury, or damage to property other than the building itself, no duty of care was owed in respect of damage caused by a defect that had become *apparent*. "Apparent", in this context, meant that the defect had already been discovered by the claimant, or that he or she ought reasonably to have discovered it. The cost of replacing "other property" damaged by an apparent defect was, like the defect itself, to be regarded as pure economic loss. *Murphy* then marks the end of the brief period of expansion and affirms the general rule that claims for pure economic loss for negligence causing a building or product to be defective are *not* recoverable. There can be no liability in tort for damage caused by a defect in a building once that defect has been discovered.

Exceptions to the rule against recovery

3–018

Murphy gives us what economists would call a "bright line" rule—no recovery for pure economic loss resulting from negligent activities. There are, however, four exceptions where the courts or Parliament have allowed recovery. All are limited in scope. In particular, the complex structure exception (ii) is merely a theory which has not been explored by the courts. *Murphy* therefore will generally apply to defective premises, although the Defective Premises Act 1972 (exception iii) amounts to an important exception to the rule against liability.

> **(i) A claimant may recover where the defect is a potential source of liability to neighbouring landowners to neighbouring landowners**

3–019

In *Murphy*, Lord Bridge suggested that:

> "... if a building stands so close to the boundary of the building owner's land that after discovery of the dangerous defect it remains

---

30 [1991] 1 A.C. 398.

> **a potential source of injury to persons or property on neighbouring land or on the highway, the building owner ought, in principle, to be entitled to recover in tort from the negligent builder the cost of obviating the danger . . . so far as that cost is necessarily incurred in order to protect himself from potential liability to third parties."[31]**

His Lordship did not explain the reasoning behind this exception to the general rule, but it has been suggested that it might be explained on the basis that such a building would also constitute a nuisance, entitling the neighbouring land-owner to an injunction ordering that it be demolished or made safe.[32] It is possible, of course, that his Lordship's intention was to create a general exception, going beyond the case of neighbouring land-owners, to the effect that any expenditure in repairing a defective building might be recoverable where it was necessary to avoid liability to a third party. This is unlikely, however, because the implications of such a rule would be, for example, that Mr Murphy could have recovered the cost of repairing his house by arguing that this was necessary to protect himself from a lawsuit by his family or his visitors.

(ii) The "complex structure theory"

In *D & F Estates*, Lords Bridge and Oliver, seeking to distinguish *Anns*, appeared to suggest that the decision might be explained on the basis of the "complex structure theory". According to this theory, it might be possible to regard the constituent parts of a building as *separate items of property*, instead of regarding the whole building as a distinct and indivisible entity. On this basis, their Lordships in *D & F Estates* thought it might be possible to say that the defective foundations in *Anns* were separate from the rest of the building, and that they had caused damage to "other property", namely the walls. It followed that there would be no objection to liability for the cost of repairing the walls, and, of course, to repair the cracked walls properly it would be necessary to rebuild the building, replacing the defective foundations themselves.

3–020

In *Murphy*, however, the House of Lords rejected the "complex structure theory" as an explanation for *Anns*—it was wholly unrealistic to view a building as distinct from its foundations. Lords Keith, Bridge and Jauncey did not, however, rule out the application of a limited version of the theory in appropriate cases. Thus, in a case where a defective central heating boiler (unexpectedly) exploded and damaged a house, or where a defective electrical installation set a house on fire, Lord Bridge thought that the owner of the house could recover damages against a builder on the basis that damage had been caused by one piece of property (for example, the boiler) to "other property" (the house).[33] Lord Jauncey, whilst agreeing that the theory could apply to the examples given by Lord Bridge, went further, stating that the theory might operate where:

---

31 *Murphy v Brentwood DC* [1991] 1 A.C. 398 at 475.
32 W.E. Peel and J. Goudkamp, *Winfield & Jolowicz on Tort*, 19th edn (Sweet and Maxwell, 2014), para.10–052.
33 *Murphy v Brentwood DC* [1991] 1 A.C. 398 at 478.

> ". . . one integral component of the structure was built by a separate contractor and where a defect in such a component had caused damage to other parts of the structure, e.g. a steel frame erected by a specialist contractor which failed to give adequate support to floors and walls."[34]

In Lord Jauncey's example, then, the presence of a separate contractor is the crucial feature which brings the theory into play. The limits of the theory, however, remain unexplored.[35]

(iii) The Defective Premises Act 1972

3–021

At the same time that the judges had been considering liability for defective premises at common law, the matter was being considered by the Law Commission, whose conclusions led to the passing of the 1972 Act. The Act provides for the liability of builders and other professionals involved in the construction of a dwelling-house[36] (it does not cover commercial buildings). The extent of their liability, however, is much more restricted than that which had been envisaged in *Anns*. For a time, the decision in *Anns* had the effect of making the Act something of a dead letter, but the decision in *Murphy* restored its importance.

Under the Act, persons who undertake work for, or in connection with, the provision of a dwelling house have a statutory duty to see that the work is done in a workmanlike or professional manner and with proper materials so that, as regards that work, the dwelling will be fit for habitation when completed.[37] The duty is imposed not only on the builders of dwellings, but also, for example, on the architects, surveyors, engineers and sub-contractors involved.[38] Moreover, the duty is owed not only to a person commissioning the work, but also to every person who later acquires an interest (whether legal or equitable) in the dwelling.

The Act then provides a remedy for mere defects in quality (provided they make the house

---

34 *Murphy* [1991] 1 A.C. 398 at 497.

35 In *Aswan Engineering Establishment Co v Lupdine Ltd* [1987] 1 All E.R. 135, defective containers had caused damage to the proofing compound they contained. Lloyd LJ was of the "provisional view" that the proofing compound was "other property", even though it had been bought in the containers from the same supplier. However, see now *Bacardi-Martini Beverages Ltd v Thomas Hardy Packaging Ltd* [2002] EWCA Civ 549, and the judgment of Mance LJ who, at [18], pointed out that this was a pre-*Murphy* case and so of limited authority.

36 For meaning of "the provision of a dwelling'", see *Jenson v Faux* [2011] EWCA Civ 423; [2011] 1 W.L.R. 3038.

37 Defective Premises Act 1972 s.1. See also *Bole v Huntsbuild Ltd* [2009] EWCA Civ 1146 (comment: J. Murdoch, "How fit is your house?" [2011] E.G. 1125) and *Rendlesham Estates Plc v Barr Ltd* [2014] EWHC 3968 (TCC); [2015] 1 W.L.R. 3663 on the meaning of "dwelling", "in connection with the provision of a dwelling" and "fit for habitation".

38 But not a building inspector who had provided services to ensure compliance with building regulations: see *Lessees & Management Co of Herons Court v Heronslea Ltd* [2019] EWCA Civ 1423; [2019] 1 W.L.R. 5849. As the Court of Appeal identified, inclusion would have been contrary to the natural and ordinary meaning of s.1 and would conflict with the reasoning in *Murphy v Brentwood* which indicated that no duty was owed under s.1 by a local authority inspector.

unfit for habitation) without the claimant having to show an imminent danger of personal injury or damage to other property. There is, however, a further restriction under s.1(5) of the Act which sets a limitation period of six years for claims *from the time the dwelling is completed.* With older properties, this renders the Act of little use. In contrast, under *Anns*, the claimant could have taken advantage of a limitation period that started to run only when symptoms of the defect became reasonably discoverable.[39]

> ### (iv) A landlord may owe a common law duty of care to his tenant for for personal injury caused by an apparent defect

In *Targett v Torfaen BC*,[40] a council tenant was injured when he fell down some steps that had been poorly designed and were not adequately lit. When he sued the council, the defence was raised that because the defect in the steps was apparent, it was a matter of pure economic loss—the tenancy was simply less valuable than it might have been. The Court of Appeal rejected the council's argument, holding that *Murphy* did not lay down any absolute rule to the effect that a claimant who suffered personal injury because of a defect was automatically barred from recovery because of his or her knowledge of the defect.[41] In the case of many tenants, it would be quite unrealistic to expect them to vacate their homes for fear of being injured by a relatively small defect. Therefore, liability should be decided by reference to whether, in the circumstances, it was reasonable to expect the tenant to remain in the building. This rule does appear, however, to be confined to its particular context of landlord and tenant.

Different rules apply, however, when the pure economic loss is a result of a negligent statement or negligent provision of a service. These cases will be examined next.

3-022

Pure Economic Loss Caused by Negligent Statements and Services

The law on negligent misstatement has developed differently from the law relating to negligent activities. This divergence in the law produces a somewhat uneasy result. For example, a surveyor who negligently advises on the purchase of a defective house may, as we shall

3-023

---

39 The Latent Damage Act 1986 made the claimant's position more favourable in building cases by providing a limitation period of three years running from the date damage was reasonably discoverable. The Act is now a dead letter in this regard, however, because, under *Murphy*, claimants have no cause of action in the first place.

40 [1992] 3 All E.R. 27.

41 Such a proposition would have been inconsistent with the Court of Appeal's decision in *Rimmer v Liverpool City Council* [1985] Q.B. 1, which had not been referred to in *Murphy*.

see, be liable for pure economic loss caused as a result of his advice, whilst a builder who causes pure economic loss by constructing a house negligently may escape liability.[42] It must be admitted that it is almost impossible to reconcile the two branches of the law, more especially because, as we point out in the conclusion to this chapter, the distinction between "activity" and "statement" cases is often extremely fine. The lack of clarity in the law is compounded by the fact that, as we shall see, the courts have been prepared to extend the principle developed in negligent misstatement cases to cases involving the negligent provision of services.

The old law

3-024

In 1951, the Court of Appeal decided *Candler v Crane Christmas & Co*.[43] Here, the defendants, a firm of accountants, had prepared the accounts of a company knowing that the figures they produced would be relied on by the plaintiff in deciding whether to invest in the company. The accounts were prepared negligently, causing the plaintiff financial loss. The majority of the Court of Appeal reaffirmed existing precedent, holding that liability for a careless (as opposed to fraudulent) statement could only arise where the maker of the statement had a contractual or fiduciary relationship with the plaintiff. Denning LJ dissented. In his Lordship's view, existing precedent was inapplicable, because it was based on the idea that the existence of a contractual relationship would prevent a duty of care from being owed to third parties—and this was a myth that had been exploded by the decision in *Donoghue v Stevenson*. Denning LJ's dissenting view, then, paved the way for the change in the law that was to take place in *Hedley Byrne & Co v Heller & Partners*.[44]

The *"Hedley Byrne principle"*

3-025

The facts of Hedley Byrne were set out in Ch.2. The claim was in respect of a negligently given banking reference (accompanied by a disclaimer) on which the plaintiffs relied, suffering financial loss. The House of Lords held that, in view of the disclaimer, the defendants had not accepted any legal responsibility towards the plaintiffs, so the claim failed. What is important, however, is that their Lordships went on to consider what the position would have been in the absence of the disclaimer, holding that there was no reason in principle why a duty of care should not be owed in respect of careless statements. Their Lordships held that the

---

42 For further discussion of this anomaly, see J. Stapleton, "Duty of care and economic loss: a wider agenda" (1991) 107 L.Q.R. 249 and B.S. Markesinis and S. Deakin, "The random element of their Lordships' infallible judgment" (1992) 55 M.L.R. 619.

43 [1951] 2 K.B. 164.

44 [1964] A.C. 465.

majority in Candler had wrongly decided that case, and that the view of Denning LJ was to be preferred.

The decision in *Hedley Byrne* represented a radical change in the law, because it was the first time that the duty of care had been extended to cover pure economic loss.[45] The House of Lords was not, however, prepared to decide the case simply by extending the principle of *Donoghue v Stevenson*. Their Lordships noted that because statements may be repeated, and then relied on by an unlimited number of people, the effects of negligent statements have a much greater propensity to spread throughout society than do the effects of negligently manufactured products. In the case of statements, therefore, the law had to impose tighter controls on the scope of liability. Accordingly, their Lordships laid down two requirements which a claimant will need to satisfy to establish a duty of care in respect of a statement. These may be summarised as follows:

- the existence of a "special relationship" between the claimant and the defendant, involving an "assumption of responsibility" by the defendant; and

- "reasonable reliance" by the claimant.

Taken together, these factors may be referred to as the *"Hedley Byrne* principle". We have seen that the factors in question were used to establish liability in *Junior Books*. We have also seen that in *Muirhead*, and in subsequent "careless activity" cases, the courts were critical of the way they had been applied in *Junior Books*, pointing out that where contracts exist, setting out the nature of the relationships between parties, it is inappropriate to talk about "special relationships" existing independently of those contracts. In negligent misstatement cases, however, the *"Hedley Byrne* principle" has continued to be regarded as important, although it is noteworthy that it has not escaped academic criticism. In particular, Tony Weir has pointed out that in *Hedley Byrne*, the plaintiffs, in effect, were given the benefit of a contractual warranty for which they had not paid—there was nothing to stop the plaintiffs from protecting themselves in law by entering into a contract with the defendant bank for the supply of the advice, but instead they sought to "freeload" on the bank's advice, and then to impose a contractual type of liability when the advice proved wrong.[46] Below, we explore each element of the *"Hedley Byrne* principle" in turn.

---

45 This is acknowledged in K. Barker, R. Grantham and W. Swain (eds), *The Law of Misstatements: 50 years on from Hedley Byrne v Heller* (Hart, 2015).

46 See, e.g. J.A. Weir, "Liability for syntax" [1963] C.L.J. 216. See also P.S. Atiyah, "Negligence and economic loss" (1969) 83 L.Q.R. 248.

(1) "Special relationship" and "assumption of responsibility"

3–026 The ideas of "special relationship" and "assumption of responsibility" cannot really be examined in isolation from one another, because both phrases are ways of saying the same thing, namely that there is a sufficient degree of "proximity" between the claimant and the defendant. This is a rather complex area of the law, but it can be broken down into a number of discrete issues, which are considered below.

> ### When will a "special relationship" or "assumption of responsibility" normally arise?

3–027 In *Hedley Byrne*, Lord Reid thought that a "special relationship" would arise where:

> **"it is plain that the party seeking information or advice was trusting the other to exercise such a degree of care as the circumstances required, where it was reasonable for him to do that, and where the other gave the information or advice when he knew or ought to have known that the inquirer was relying on him."[47]**

His Lordship went on to say that a reasonable man, when asked for advice, and realising that his skill and judgment might be relied on, would have three options open to him: he could keep silent; he could give an answer with a clear qualification that he accepted no responsibility for it (a disclaimer); or he could simply answer without any such qualification. A person who chose the last option would be held to have assumed responsibility for his or her answer being given carefully, and therefore would owe a duty of care to the recipient of the advice.

Whether a special relationship exists in any given circumstance is essentially decided by an evaluation of the particular facts of a case. Thus, for example, in *Patchett v Swimming Pool & Allied Trades Association Ltd*,[48] where a trade association had made a statement on its web site, the Court of Appeal decided that it could not fairly be said that the association had "assumed responsibility" for the accuracy of that statement, given that the web site itself urged browsers to make further enquiries. In contrast, in *Sebry v Companies House*,[49] the Registrar of Companies was found to have assumed responsibility to a company, when

---

47 [1964] A.C. 465 at 486.
48 [2009] EWCA Civ 717; [2010] 2 All E.R. (Comm) 138.
49 [2015] EWHC 115 (QB); [2016] 1 W.L.R. 2499. Comment: J. Hartshorne (2016) 32 P.N. 164. See also *Chief Land Registrar v Caffrey & Co* [2016] EWHC 161 (Ch); [2016] P.N.L.R. 23 (solicitors assumed a duty to the Chief Land Registrar to take reasonable care to ensure that the representations he had made, to the effect that the mortgagee consented to the discharge, were true). Contrast, however, *Seddon v DVLC* [2019] EWCA Civ 14; [2019] 1 W.L.R. 4593 (no duty owed by DVLC to purchaser of purported classic car).

entering a winding-up order on the companies register, to take reasonable care to ensure that the order was not registered against the wrong company. More recently in *Playboy Club London Ltd v Banca Nazionale del Lavoro SpA*,[50] a bank was found not to owe a duty of care to a casino despite the fact that it had provided a negligent bank reference which the casino had relied upon in accepting the gambler's cheques (later proved to be counterfeit). The facts resemble those of Hedley Byrne but with a critical difference. Here, to protect the gambler's privacy, the casino had acted through an agent (Burlington) and this had not been disclosed to the bank. The bank then thought it was providing a reference for Burlington. The Supreme Court distinguished *Hedley Byrne* on the facts. Liability would only arise when the person making the statement knew or should have known that it would be likely to be communicated to the defendant herself. Here, the bank had provided a reference having no idea that it was dealing with an agent for a casino, nor indeed the purpose for the reference. It was clear therefore that in such circumstances the bank had not voluntarily assumed any responsibility to the club.

Caparo v Dickman,[51] examined in Ch.2 as setting the general test for the duty of care in negligence in novel cases, was in fact a claim for pure economic loss for negligent misstatement. Here, the plaintiffs had taken over a company called Fidelity and had relied on figures contained in an audit which had been prepared by the defendants, a firm of accountants. The plaintiffs alleged that the audit had been prepared negligently, causing them financial loss. The House of Lords held that the accountants owed them no duty of care. Lord Bridge made it clear that in deciding whether a sufficient relationship of proximity existed between the plaintiffs and the defendants, it was important to consider the *size of the class* to which the plaintiffs belonged. Here, although the plaintiffs were existing shareholders, for the purposes of the decision, they should be regarded as being in the same position as any other person who might wish to buy shares in Fidelity. In other words, they belonged to a class of persons the size of which could not be ascertained and which was potentially very large.[52] We might also suspect fears influencing the courts that liability would give rise to a dramatic rise in accountants' insurance premums which might lead to a rise in the cost of accounting.[53]

3–028

The Court in *Caparo* also found it to be important that, whilst the audit had been prepared for *one purpose*, it had been relied on by the plaintiffs for *another purpose*. Where the primary purpose in making a statement is to advise the "advisee", it may be easy to conclude that he or she is owed a duty of care. However, in cases where a statement is made primarily for a *different*

3–029

---

50 [2018] UKSC 43; [2018] 1 W.L.R. 4041.
51 [1990] 2 A.C. 605.
52 Contrast *Law Society v KPMG Peat Marwick* [2000] 1 W.L.R. 1921 where the Court of Appeal upheld a preliminary ruling that accountants, in auditing solicitors' firms, owed a duty of care to the Law Society in respect of compensation payments made by the Society because the accountants had failed to detect fraud. Here, the scope of potential liability was limited and could arise only during the year for which the audit had been prepared.
53 Hoffmann J, in *Morgan Crucible Co v Hill Samuel & Co* [1991] 2 W.L.R. 655 at 662, remarked that ". . . if the decision in Caparo's case had gone the other way, firms of accountants below a certain size may have been deterred by insurance costs from competing for the audit work of public limited companies potentially liable to take-over bids. This would have driven such companies into the hands of the largest firms".

purpose, it becomes necessary to look carefully at the purpose for which the statement was *communicated* to the advisee and the purpose for which it was *used*. Thus, in *Caparo*, it was important that, whilst the accounts had been prepared for the purpose of fulfilling certain statutory duties placed on auditors for the benefit of shareholders (including the plaintiffs), the plaintiffs had relied on the accounts as a general guide to the performance of investments—a purpose for which they had not been designed. It followed that in the circumstances the plaintiffs' reliance on the accounts had been unreasonable.

In the words of Lord Bridge, there should not be liability where, as in *Caparo*:

> **". . . a statement is put into more or less general circulation and may foreseeably be relied on by strangers to the maker of the statement for any one of a variety of different purposes which the maker of the statement has no specific reason to anticipate."[54]**

3–030

In *James McNaughton Paper Group v Hicks, Anderson & Co*,[55] Neill LJ, in the Court of Appeal summed up the law as follows: it was possible to identify certain matters that, in most cases, were likely to be of importance in deciding whether to impose a duty of care[56]:

(i) What was the purpose of the statement? What was the purpose for which it was communicated?

(ii) In three party situations, what is the relationship between the defendant and any relevant third party?

(iii) What is the size of any class to which the claimant belongs?

(iv) What was the state of knowledge of the defendant at the time?

(v) Did the claimant rely on the defendant?

Can a "special relationship" arise in a purely social context?

3–031

Lord Reid, in *Hedley Byrne*, made it clear that a "special relationship" could only arise where the statement was made in a "business connection". There would be no liability for statements made on purely social occasions. This was because, as his Lordship observed:

> **"Quite careful people often express definite opinions on social or informal occasions even when they see that others are likely to be influenced by them; and they often do that without taking that care**

---

54 [1990] 2 A.C. 605 at 621.
55 [1991] 2 Q.B. 113.
56 [1991] 2 Q.B. 113 at 125–126.

> **which they would take if asked for their opinion professionally or in a business connection."[57]**

However, the Court of Appeal departed from this fundamental principle in *Chaudhry v Prabhakar*.[58] Here, a family friend had agreed to help the plaintiff find a second-hand car, telling her that she could rely on him and that she need not have the car inspected by a mechanic. The defendant, through his negligence, advised the plaintiff to buy a car which, it turned out, was unroadworthy and practically worthless. Before the trial, the defendant conceded that he owed a duty of care to the plaintiff. A majority of the court held that this concession had been rightly made, and that the plaintiff was able to recover her financial loss. May LJ, however, dissented. His Lordship doubted that any duty of care was owed. In May LJ's view, to impose liability in such a situation was undesirable, because it would make social relations between friends unnecessarily hazardous.

What makes the decision in *Chaudhry v Prabhakar* unusual is that there was no suggestion that the defendant, Mr Prabhakar, was securing any benefit to himself by offering the free advice—he offered his services on a purely gratuitous basis. Thus, the situation is to be contrasted with *Hedley Byrne*, where the bank, although not of course paid for the advice, nevertheless supplied it to further their general business interests. As Lord Devlin observed, in *Hedley Byrne*:

> **"It may often be material to consider whether the adviser is acting purely out of good nature or whether he is getting his reward in some indirect form. The service that a bank performs in giving a reference is not done simply out of a desire to assist commerce. It would discourage the customers of the bank if their deals fell through because the bank had refused to testify to their credit when it was good."[59]**

More recently, in *Burgess v Lejonvarn*[60] the Court of Appeal found that an architect who had supplied her professional services to friends free of charge in relation to a landscaping project for their garden owed them a duty of care. Here, her self-interest was self-evident —while not under contract, she possessed a special skill and had assumed responsibility towards her friends with a view to receiving a fee for phase two of the project. In light of the decision in *Burgess*, the finding of a duty of care in *Chaudhry v Prabhakar* seems generous to say the least.[61]

---

57   [1964] A.C. 465 at 482.
58   [1989] 1 W.L.R. 29.
59   [1964] A.C. 465 at 529.
60   [2017] EWCA Civ 254; [2017] P.N.L.R. 25. However, no breach was found on the facts in a later decision: [2018] EWHC 3166 (TCC).
61   In *Hurst v Hone* [2010] EWHC 1159 (QB) at [320], Keith J noted that all three members of the Court of Appeal in *Chaudhry* had been concerned about the concession made by counsel for the plaintiff's friend that a duty of care had arisen.

Must the defendant be "in the business of giving advice"?

3-032

The Privy Council, in *Mutual Life and Citizens' Assurance Co v Evatt*,[62] took a somewhat narrow view of the circumstances in which a "special relationship" could arise. Here, the plaintiff had sought advice from his insurance company about the wisdom of investing in a company with which it was associated. He was given certain information that turned out to be false, and sought to recover the money he lost on his investment. The majority held that the *Hedley Byrne* principle should be confined to cases involving defendants whose profession includes the giving of advice, such as accountants, surveyors and lawyers. Since the defendants were in the business of providing insurance cover, not investment advice, they could not be liable. Lords Reid and Morris, however, dissented, holding that it was sufficient for the *Hedley Byrne* principle to apply if the advice was sought from a business person in the course of business. It is this minority view in *Mutual Life* which has found favour with the courts. Thus, in *Esso v Mardon*[63] (discussed below), Ormrod LJ remarked that if the majority opinion were accepted, "the effect of *Hedley Byrne* would be so radically curtailed as to be virtually eliminated",[64] and in *Howard Marine and Dredging Co Ltd v Ogden & Sons Ltd*,[65] both Lord Denning MR and Shaw LJ made it clear that they preferred the minority view.

In *Esso v Mardon*, the plaintiff leased a filling station on the strength of Esso's advice that he could expect to sell at least 200,000 gallons of petrol a year. This forecast had been based on an assumption that the petrol pumps would be located at the front of the filling station on the main road. It then transpired that the local planning authority in fact required the pumps to be at the back of the filling station, where they would attract much less passing trade. Esso failed to revise its forecast in the light of that fact. The plaintiff sold only 78,000 gallons in 15 months, and sued Esso for his financial loss. Here, clearly Esso were not in the business of giving advice. Nevertheless, in allowing the claim, the Court of Appeal held that Esso had assumed responsibility for the accuracy of its forecast and that it had been reasonable for Mr Mardon to rely on Esso's skill in predicting likely petrol sales.

Assumption of responsibility: an objective test

3-033

Whilst the question of "assumption of responsibility" is decided by reference to things said or done by the defendant, it is clear that the term does *not* imply that the defendant has *expressly indicated* acceptance of legal responsibility. Liability is imposed on the basis of an objective test, to which the expressed intentions of the defendant are only partly relevant. It follows that although a disclaimer will normally work to absolve the defendant from liability (as in *Hedley Byrne*), there may be exceptional circumstances in which liability will be imposed in spite of an

---

62 [1971] A.C. 793.
63 [1976] Q.B. 801.
64 [1976] Q.B. 801 at 827.
65 [1978] Q.B. 574.

assertion that the defendant accepts no legal responsibility for the advice in question. Such was the case in *Smith v Eric Bush.*[66]

Here, the House of Lords decided two appeals in which the plaintiffs had suffered pure economic loss as a result of negligent surveys. In the first appeal (which serves to illustrate the decision), the plaintiff, Mrs Smith, wished to buy a house, and approached a building society for a mortgage. The building society instructed the defendants, a firm of surveyors, to carry out a visual inspection of the house in order to confirm that it was worth at least the money which they were proposing to lend. The defendants' valuer noticed that two chimney breasts had been removed, but he failed to check whether the chimneys had been left adequately supported. His report stated that no essential repairs were necessary.

The mortgage application form and the valuation report contained a disclaimer of liability. Mrs Smith was also informed that the report was not a structural survey and she was advised to obtain independent professional advice. The building society, pursuant to an agreement with Mrs Smith, who had paid an inspection fee, supplied her with a copy of the report. She, like many purchasers of modest houses, relied on it and purchased the house without any further survey. The chimneys were not adequately supported and one of them subsequently collapsed.

When Mrs Smith sought to recover her financial loss, the defendants argued that the disclaimer exempted them from liability. The House of Lords, however, held that the disclaimer was invalid under the Unfair Contract Terms Act 1977 (UCTA) s.2. (At this time, the UCTA applied to all contracts, both consumer and business. Business to consumer contracts are now covered by the Consumer Rights Act 2015[67]). It did not satisfy the requirement of reasonableness set out in s.11(3) of that Act. Since the valuer was a professional, whose services were paid for (albeit indirectly) by Mrs Smith, and since he was aware that Mrs Smith would probably purchase the house in reliance on his valuation without an independent survey, it would not be reasonable to allow the valuer to rely on the disclaimer. Accordingly, the valuer had at law assumed responsibility to Mrs Smith and was liable in negligence. Lord Griffiths observed:

> "... the phrase 'assumption of responsibility' can only have any real meaning if it is understood as referring to the circumstances in which the law will *deem* the maker of the statement to have assumed responsibility ..."[68]

Faced with the familiar "floodgates" argument that indeterminate liability would be created, their Lordships chose to confine the *ratio* of their decision to situations where a private

---

66 [1990] 1 A.C. 831.

67 Changes to the legislative framework regulating exclusion clauses will be examined in Ch.16.

68 [1990] 1 A.C. 831 at 862. See also Lord Slynn, in *Phelps v Hillingdon LBC* [2001] 2 A.C. 619 at 654: "The phrase simply means that the law recognises that there is a duty of care. It is not so much that responsibility is assumed as that it is recognised or imposed by the law".

purchaser was buying a modest house. Commercial purchasers, or purchasers of more expensive houses, could be expected to instruct their own independent surveyors. As Lord Neuberger MR later commented in *Scullion v Bank of Scotland*, "commercial purchasers of low to middle value residential properties, such as those buying to let, can properly be regarded as less deserving of protection by the common law against the risk of negligence than those buying to occupy as their residence".[69] In this way, the decision would not expose surveyors to liability for very large losses, and would have only a small effect on their insurance premiums and the cost of surveys.

3–034   The decision in *Smith v Eric Bush* was subsequently applied in *Merrett v Babb*.[70] Here, the claimant applied to a building society for a mortgage, and the building society commissioned a survey from a firm of which the defendant was an employee. By the time the claimant discovered that the survey had been conducted negligently, causing her economic loss, the firm had gone into liquidation. However, by a majority, the Court of Appeal held that the negligent surveyor, by signing the mortgage valuation report for the building society, had assumed a *personal* responsibility to the claimant for its accuracy. A majority of the court was prepared to hold that the claimant had reasonably relied on the surveyor's professional skill, even though the claimant was unaware of who had conducted the survey. This decision seemed to produce a rather harsh result for the surveyor, and should be contrasted with the decision of the House of Lords in *Williams and Reid v Natural Life Health Foods Ltd and Mistlin*.[71] Here, the plaintiffs had obtained a franchise from a company (the first defendant) to run a health food shop. They had relied on representations made in the company's literature about the likelihood of their shop being successful. In the event, the turnover of the shop proved to be substantially less than the company had predicted—in fact it traded at a loss for 18 months. The plaintiffs sought to recover their financial losses from the company, but the company went into liquidation, so they pursued their action against its managing director, Mr Mistlin. The plaintiffs argued that he had assumed personal responsibility towards them, because the company literature had made it plain that the predictions about profit were based on Mr Mistlin's personal expertise and experience in the health food trade. The House of Lords held, however, that nothing that had been said or done by Mr Mistlin showed that he had assumed responsibility towards the plaintiffs in a personal capacity. The representations on which they had relied had been made by the *company*. It was particularly important, in the context of small businesses, that the court should not be too ready to "lift the corporate veil" and undermine the protection of limited liability conferred by establishing a company.

---

69   *Scullion v Bank of Scotland* [2011] EWCA Civ 693; [2011] 1 W.L.R. 3212 at [49]: purchase of a buy-to-let property was essentially commercial in nature and no inherent likelihood that a purchaser, buying property as an investment, would rely on a valuation provided to the mortgagee rather than obtaining his own valuation.

70   [2001] EWCA Civ 214; [2001] Q.B. 1174.

71   [1998] 1 W.L.R. 830.

(2) "Reasonable reliance"

Hedley Byrne v Heller requires that the claimant prove that he or she did in fact rely on the statement, as opposed to acting on his or her own judgement. Such reliance must also be reasonable in the circumstances.

3–035

There are two issues to consider here:

- Was reliance reasonable in the circumstances?

- Did reliance actually take place?

Reliance must be reasonable

The question of whether a claimant's reliance on advice is "reasonable" is an objective one, which will be decided on the facts of each case. It is not, however, always a straightforward issue and has led to judicial disagreement, as seen in the Court of Appeal decision of *Howard Marine and Dredging Co Ltd v Ogden & Sons Ltd*.[72] In this case, Ogdens had put in a tender relying on the defendants' advice, but the Court was divided whether it was reasonable for Ogdens to rely on the quotation without clearly indicating to the defendants how important this information was to them. In *Reeman v Department of Transport*,[73] the court was asked to determine whether it had been reasonable for the purchaser of a boat to rely on an annual certificate of seaworthiness from the Department of Transport. The boat had been covered by a certificate, but was later discovered to be unseaworthy and worthless. When Mr Reeman sued for his financial loss, the Court of Appeal held that it had not been reasonable for him to rely on the certificate as a means of establishing the boat's commercial value. The certificate had not been provided for this purpose. It had been issued to promote safety at sea.

3–036

The Supreme Court re-examined the requirement of reasonable reliance recently in *Steel v NRAM Ltd*.[74] Here a solicitor had carelessly misrepresented to her client's lender that the whole of the loan had been paid off. Relying on this, the lender discharged its security, suffering a loss of almost £370,000 when this was found to be incorrect. The Supreme Court held that knowledge of the loan had been wholly within the knowledge of the lender. It was therefore not reasonable for the lender to rely on the statement of the borrower's solicitor rather than checking its own records. Equally, the solicitor in such circumstances would not reasonably foresee that the lender would so rely. A commercial lender about to implement

---

72   [1978] Q.B. 574.
73   [1997] 2 Lloyd's Rep. 648. Consider also the purpose of the "statements" in, e.g. *Customs & Excise Commissioners v Barclays Bank* [2006] UKHL 28, and *West Bromwich Albion FC v El-Safty* [2006] EWCA Civ 1299; [2007] P.I.Q.R. P7.
74   [2018] UKSC 13; [2018] 1 W.L.R. 1190.

an agreement with its borrower referable to its security does not therefore act reasonably if he or she simply proceeds upon a description of the terms put forward on behalf of the borrower.

> ## Reliance must, in fact, take place

3–037 Generally, a successful claimant must show that he or she has, in fact, relied on the defendant's advice or services (rather than acting in reliance on his or her own views or the views of another)—otherwise the advice or services cannot be said to be the cause of the claimant's loss.[75] The decision in *Abbott v Strong*[76] illustrates the idea that a claimant cannot be said to have placed reliance on a defendant unless the claimant knows (or acts reasonably in assuming) that the statement in question has been made *by the defendant*.[77] Here, the plaintiffs had been encouraged to invest in a company by a circular that had been sent to them by the company's directors. The circular contained inaccurate profit forecasts, and the company subsequently went into receivership. When the plaintiffs sued the accountants who had prepared the profit forecasts, it was held that the plaintiffs had not relied on the accountants, because, at the time they had acted on the information in the circular, they had thought that it had come solely from the directors of the company.

The question of reliance was also addressed by the House of Lords in *Customs & Excise Commissioners v Barclays Bank*. Lord Bingham noted that the Customs officials could not "in any meaningful sense" be said to have relied on the bank. This was because, as his Lordship put it, the concept of "reliance" in law "is usually taken to mean that if A had not relied on B he would have acted differently".[78] Here, nothing done (or not done) by the bank had had any effect on the commissioners' actions.

Provision of services (the "extended *Hedley Byrne* principle") [79]

3–038 In *Spring v Guardian Assurance Plc*, Lord Goff, with whom Lord Lowry agreed, stated that, in appropriate cases, the *Hedley Byrne* principle should not be limited to the provision of advice,

---

75   *Bristol & West Building Society v Mothew* [1998] Ch. 1.

76   [1998] B.C.L.C. 420.

77   Note, however, that the claimant need not necessarily know the precise identity of the defendant. It may suffice if, as in *Merrett v Babb* [2001] EWCA Civ 214; [2001] Q.B. 1174 (discussed above), the claimant reasonably assumes that the statement must have been prepared by a defendant of a particular type.

78   *Customs & Excise Commissioners v Barclays Bank* [2006] UKHL 28 at [14]. See also the remarks of Lord Mance at [112].

79   This expression was used by Lord Steyn in *Williams and Reid v Natural Life Health Foods Ltd and Mistlin* [1998] 1 W.L.R. 830 at 835.

but could be applied more generally to situations involving the provision of services. The proper interpretation of *Hedley Byrne*, according to Lord Goff, was that:

> "where the plaintiff entrusts the defendant with the conduct of his affairs, in general or in particular, the defendant may be held to have assumed responsibility to the plaintiff . . ."[80]

His Lordship approved Lord Morris's assertion in *Hedley Byrne* that: "The fact that the service is to be given by means of or by the instrumentality of words can make no difference".[81] This is an important development in that it indicates that where the defendant has undertaken the performance of some task or service for the claimant and expressly or impliedly undertakes that reasonable care will be taken, then a duty of care can arise. As Lord Reed commented in *GN v Poole Plc*,[82] what is significant here is that the courts are prepared to imply such an undertaking, usually by reason of the foreseeability of reliance by the claimant on the exercise of such care.

The leading case of *Henderson v Merrett Syndicates Ltd*[83] involved five appeals and arose in the following way: in the early 1990s, there were a number of unusually large claims made against the Lloyds insurance organisation. These losses had to be borne by people known as "Names", who invest in Lloyds by underwriting their insurance policies. The Names are grouped into syndicates. The plaintiffs alleged that the agents who had organised their syndicates had been negligent in handling their affairs. Without having to refer to a specific statement or piece of advice, the House of Lords was able to say that a duty of care was owed because the agents had assumed responsibility for the financial welfare of the Names. Their Lordships also confirmed that the existence of a contractual relationship between the claimant and the defendant does not preclude the existence of a "special relationship", giving rise to liability in tort. Many of the Names had contracts with the defendant agents but sought to sue in tort because the limitation period for actions in contract had expired. Their Lordships held that they were entitled to take advantage of a longer limitation period which (for reasons that do not concern us here) was applicable in tort.

Employment references

The decision in *Spring v Guardian Assurance Plc*[84] itself concerned the question whether a "special relationship" would exist between an employer and an employee who asks for a job

3–039

---

80   *Spring v Guardian Assurance Plc* [1995] 2 A.C. 296 at 318.
81   [1964] A.C. 465 at 503.
82   [2019] UKSC 25, at [88].
83   [1995] 2 A.C. 145. See also *Welton v North Cornwall DC* [1997] 1 W.L.R. 570. The defendants' environmental health officer had imposed excessive hygiene requirements on a guest house. The claim was held to be well within the *Hedley Byrne* principle, even though it could not be described as a case involving negligent "advice".
84   [1995] 2 A.C. 296.

reference. Here, the plaintiff, Mr Spring, had been employed by the defendants but subsequently dismissed. He sought work with one of the defendants' competitors, but received such a bad reference that he failed to get the job. The statements in the reference, although made honestly, had given a misleading impression of the circumstances surrounding Mr Spring's dismissal, and had been made without a proper investigation of the facts. The House of Lords held that the defendants owed a duty of care in preparing the reference and, accordingly, were liable. It made no difference that if Mr Spring had sued in defamation, the defendants would have had the defence of qualified privilege.[85] The existence of this defence did not prevent liability in negligence. Nor, apparently, did it matter that this was a case where, exceptionally, the plaintiff was seeking to recover in respect of a statement that had not been made to *him* but to someone else. The key element was, as Lord Reed explained in *GN v Poole BC*,[86] that the defendant had undertaken the performance of the task for the claimant with an undertaking (express or implied) that reasonable care would be taken.

Will Drafting

3–040 The question, then, is how far liability can extend for those providing services to the public. The will drafting cases involve a solicitor negligently preparing a will for a testator with the result that the intended beneficiaries of the will suffer financial loss. In *Ross v Caunters*,[87] the defendant solicitor had failed to tell a testator that if his will was witnessed by the spouse of a beneficiary, any gift to that beneficiary would be void. The plaintiff, whose husband had witnessed the will, sued the solicitor for the loss of her gift under the will. The court held that the solicitor did owe the plaintiff a duty of care and was liable. Sir Robert Megarry VC was prepared to say that liability in *Ross v Caunters* should follow, either by an extension of the "*Hedley Byrne* principle" or by a direct application of the principle of *Donoghue v Stevenson*.[88] After the decision in *Ross v Caunters*, a number of cases seemed to cast doubt on whether it had been correctly decided. In *White v Jones*, however, the House of Lords (employing different reasoning) upheld the decision in *Ross v Caunters*.

3–041 In *White v Jones*,[89] a testator had quarrelled with his two daughters and had made a will cutting them out of their inheritance. Subsequently, he became reconciled with them, so he instructed the defendants to prepare a new will under which they were to be left £9,000 each. The defendants failed to act promptly on these instructions. The solicitor dealing with the matter arranged to meet the testator three times but failed to keep the appointments. He then went on holiday. When he returned, he made a further appointment to see the testator, but unfortunately the testator, who was 78, died three days before the meeting. The estate was

---

85   See Ch.14.
86   [2019] UKSC 25 at at [68].
87   [1980] Ch.297.
88   [1932] A.C. 562.
89   [1995] 2 A.C. 207.

distributed according to the old will, depriving the daughters of their intended legacies. They brought an action against the defendants, claiming £9,000 each in damages.

By a bare majority, the House of Lords upheld the daughters' claims. Lord Goff was content to decide the case by a very broad application of the principle laid down in *Hedley Byrne v Heller & Partners*, but declined to follow the reasoning in *Ross v Caunters*, stating that that case had raised a number of conceptual difficulties. Lords Browne-Wilkinson and Nolan held that the defendants had assumed responsibility for the task of preparing the new will and that, as a matter of law, this meant that they had *assumed responsibility to the plaintiffs*. Lord Nolan also thought that the plaintiffs could be said to have *relied* on the defendants, who were acting as family solicitors. Lords Keith and Mustill dissented. Lord Keith stated that to allow the claim would, in effect, be to give the plaintiffs the benefit of a contract (between the testator and the defendants) to which they were not parties.

The overriding factor that seemed to influence the decisions in *Ross v Caunters* and *White v Jones* was the need to do practical justice in the circumstances. In such cases, the courts are faced with an exceptional situation where the only people who suffer loss (the intended beneficiaries) would, on traditional principles, be denied a remedy, but the only person who has a traditional remedy (the testator's estate) suffers no loss. This situation leaves, as Lord Goff put it in *White v Jones*, "a lacuna in the law which needs to be filled".[90] It is interesting to note, however, that the decisions in these cases produce, arguably, injustice of a different kind. This is because those legally entitled to the deceased's estate receive a windfall, in the sense that they retain the money which, on the facts, the deceased did not intend to go to them, while those to whom the money *should* have gone recover from the negligent solicitor. It may be argued that a truly coherent legal system should find a way of giving effect to the testator's intentions without causing this enrichment of the estate—after all (as we can see from the early behaviour of the testator in *White v Jones*) an intention to deprive may sometimes be just as important as an intention to bequeath!

Subsequent cases have made it clear that liability will be limited in a number of respects. First, it is unlikely that *White* will have any application to gifts made between living persons.[91] Thus, in *Hemmens v Wilson Browne*,[92] a certain Mr Panter, who was having an affair with the plaintiff, instructed his solicitors to draft a document that would entitle her to call upon him for the sum of £110,000 at any time in the future. The solicitors drafted a document which had no legal effect—it was not a deed (because it was not under seal) and it was not a contract (because there was no consideration). When the plaintiff asked Mr Panter to fulfil his promise, he refused to pay, having gone back to his wife. Unable to enforce the terms of the document, the plaintiff sued the solicitors, arguing that their negligent drafting had caused her to lose her

3–042

---

90 [1995] 2 A.C. 207 at 260. See also *Sebry v Companies House* [2015] EWHC 115 (QB); [2016] 1 W.L.R. 2499 at [91] per Edis J.

91 Although both Sir Donald Nicholls VC in the Court of Appeal in *White v Jones* [1995] 2 A.C. 207 (at 227) and Sir Robert Megarry VC in *Ross v Caunters* [1980] Ch.297 (at 322) thought that the principle could be applied to inter vivos gifts.

92 [1993] 4 All E.R. 826.

gift. It was held that the special policy considerations which had dictated the outcomes in *Ross v Caunters* and *White v Jones*[93] did not apply here—Mr Panter, being still alive, would be able to rectify the situation, if he so wished, by instructing a solicitor to re-draft the document properly.

Secondly, it has been suggested that a duty of care can only be invoked in situations where the claimant has exhausted his or her other remedies. Thus, in *Walker v Geo H Medlicott & Son*,[94] the claimant sued solicitors who had been instructed to include a gift to him in a client's will, but had negligently failed to do so. The circumstances were such that the claimant was entitled to have the will rectified under the Administration of Justice Act 1982 s.20. The Court of Appeal held that he could not bring an alternative claim in negligence.[95]

> ## Pensions advice

3-043

In *Gorham v British Telecommunications Plc*,[96] the Court of Appeal was prepared to hold that the *Hedley Byrne* principle could, in appropriate cases, make providers of financial services liable to the dependants of a deceased person who had been wrongly advised about how to make provision for them. Mr Gorham had opted out of his employer's pension scheme and had sought the advice of the Standard Life Assurance Co, making it clear that his first priority was to make provision for his wife and children in the event of his death. The company negligently failed to advise him that his employer's pension scheme might provide superior cover, and instead sold him one of its personal pension plans. Some months later, the company admitted its mistake and correctly advised Mr Gorham that his employer's scheme was better. Unfortunately, however, Mr Gorham did not re-join his employer's scheme, mistakenly believing that he was already a member. This meant that his dependants were not provided for when he died. The court upheld an action by the wife and children for loss of the pension rights to which they would have been entitled had Mr Gorham been correctly advised in the first place and remained a member of his employer's scheme. Their Lordships took the view that the situation was directly analogous to that in *White v Jones* (discussed above) and that, just as a solicitor owed a duty to see that a testator's intentions were given effect so as to provide for beneficiaries, a company selling a pension plan had a duty not to give negligent advice to a customer which adversely affected the interests of his dependants as he intended them to be.

---

93 *White v Jones* [1995] 2 A.C. 207 was a Court of Appeal decision at the time.
94 [1999] 1 W.L.R. 727.
95 Compare *Horsefall v Haywards* [1999] 1 F.L.R. 1182: there can be no objection to a negligence action where there is little likelihood that rectification will succeed.
96 [2000] 1 W.L.R. 2129. See also *Weldon v GRE Linked Life Assurance Ltd* [2000] 2 All E.R. (Comm) 914 (life insurance company liable for presenting a direct debit mandate to the wrong branch of a bank, so that premiums were not collected and the policy lapsed.)

> **Do you have to prove reliance in relation to the provision of services?**

3–044

Lord Goff in *Henderson v Merrett Syndicates Ltd*[97] explained that in the case of the provision of information and advice, reliance must be proved—without reliance on the statement, the claimant will be unable to prove that the defendant's negligence caused him or her any loss. However, in relation to services, where the claimant has requested performance and entrusted the defendant with the conduct of his or her affairs, the court will find that the claimant has relied on that defendant to exercise due skill and care in performance. On this basis, in relation to the provision of services, the courts do not seek to identify a specific act of reasonable reliance by the claimant, but will assume that, in requesting the service in question, the claimant is relying on the defendant to take reasonable care. This does, however, become more difficult in relation to the "will drafting" cases examined above. These render a negligent solicitor liable to a disappointed beneficiary for failing to take reasonable care in performing services requested by the testator. Liability may arise even where the beneficiary is not aware, at the time the negligence occurs, that but for the negligence he or she would be entitled to a legacy. In these circumstances, it is hard to say that the disappointed beneficiary is "relying" on the skill of the solicitor, except in the very general sense that all members of society, some of whom may unknowingly be intended beneficiaries, rely on solicitors to get things right. The anomaly produced by the "will drafting" cases, however, may be explained on the basis that these cases fall into a special category where the aim of the testator is to benefit others and, for policy reasons, reliance is not regarded as important.

Should the assumption of responsibility test be the only test for recovery?

3–045

As seen above, the courts have used the concept of "assumption of responsibility" to justify imposing a duty of care on the defendant to protect the claimant from pure economic loss caused by negligent statements and services. This concept lies at the heart of the decisions in *Henderson* and *Spring* (discussed above). Yet the concept has not escaped criticism. Academics have suggested that the concept is flawed in that, as an objective test, it often rests on a fiction used to justify a conclusion that a duty of care existed, as seen by its use in *White v Jones* and *Smith v Eric Bush* (discussed above).[98] In *Smith v Eric Bush*, Lord Griffiths indeed agreed that the idea was "unlikely to be a helpful or realistic test in most cases"[99] and in *Caparo v Dickman*, Lord Roskill expressed a similar view.[100] It is difficult to deny that while it makes sense in many

---

97 [1995] 2 A.C. 145 at 180.
98 See K. Barker, "Unreliable assumptions in the modern law of negligence" (1993) 109 L.Q.R. 461; B. Hepple, "Negligence: the search for coherence" (1997) 50 C. L. P. 69 at 88, and P. Cane, *Tort Law and Economic Interests*, 2nd edn (Clarendon Press, 1996), pp.177 and 200.
99 [1990] 1 A.C. 831 at 864–865.
100 [1990] 2 A.C. 605 at 628.

two-party situations, the further the test is removed from the actual intentions of the defendant, the more artificial it seems.

Lord Steyn in *Williams and Reid v Natural Life Health Foods Ltd and Mistlin*[101] defended the concept of assumption of responsibility. Delivering the opinion of the House of Lords, his Lordship argued that:

> "In my view the general criticism is overstated. Coherence must sometimes yield to practical justice. In these circumstances there was, and is, no better rationalisation for the relevant head of tort liability than assumption of responsibility."[102]

3–046

In *Customs & Excise Commissioners v Barclays Bank*,[103] the House of Lords dealt with doubts relating to the assumption of responsibility test (notably the difficulty of determining precisely *when* a defendant can be said to have "assumed responsibility") by adopting a three-fold approach: applying this test *and* the three-fold *Caparo* test of foreseeability, proximity and fair, just and reasonableness *and* the incremental test. If, in a novel case, all three indicated the existence of a duty of care, then the court could be sure that it should exist. Here, Customs officials, who were seeking to recover outstanding tax payments from two companies, had obtained "freezing orders" on those companies' bank accounts. This meant that the defendant bank was prohibited by law from allowing any money in the accounts to be paid out. Through inadvertence, however, the bank allowed funds to be withdrawn from the accounts. The Customs officials sought to recover these funds from the bank, arguing that, on receipt of the freezing order, the bank had "assumed responsibility" to them for financial losses arising from the funds being withdrawn. It was also argued that it would be fair, just and reasonable to impose liability.

In denying the claim, their Lordships stressed that, in deciding a novel case, it was important to appreciate that there is no single common denominator by which liability can be determined. While the concept of "assumption of responsibility", like the concepts of "proximity" and "fair, just and reasonable" to which it is inextricably linked, is useful, such concepts are inherently imprecise and can only provide limited assistance. An important cross-check may also be gained from considering whether it would be appropriate to go beyond existing case-law ("the incremental approach").[104] Here, the bank could not in any meaningful sense be said to have *assumed* responsibility—it had no choice about complying with the freezing order. It was equally not fair, just and reasonable to impose liability in tort where the bank would only have been found in contempt of court if it had knowingly failed to freeze its customer's account and such a duty would conflict with the bank's duties to its customers. Equally imposing a duty of care was not analogous or incremental to any previous decision.

---

101   [1998] 1 W.L.R. 830.
102   [1998] 1 W.L.R. 830 at 837.
103   [2006] UKHL 28; [2007] 1 A.C. 181.
104   See Lord Mance [2006] UKHL 28 at [93].

In novel cases, therefore, the courts will determine liability by reference to all three tests, as explained by Longmore LJ in the *Playboy Club* case in the Court of Appeal:

> "The law about duty of care has not, of course, stood still since *Hedley Byrne*; it is now recognised that there is no single test for determining when a duty arises but since *Caparo* it has become customary to inquire: (1) whether the defendant assumed responsibility to the claimant; (2) whether (to adopt what has been called the threefold test—(a) loss was a foreseeable consequence of the defendant's actions or inactions, (b) the relationship of the parties was sufficiently proximate and (c) it is fair just and reasonable to impose a duty of care on the defendant towards the claimant; and (3) whether the addition to existing categories of duty is incremental rather than indefinable. These inquiries will usually lead to the same answer and can be used as cross-checks on one another."[105]

Economic loss: conclusion

3-047

We have seen that, over the years, the courts have vacillated on the question of pure economic loss. This has resulted in a body of law that lacks coherence.[106] It is convenient, for the purpose of learning the law, to distinguish, as we have done in this chapter, between the "activity" cases and the "statements and services" cases. However, the courts' extension of the "*Hedley Byrne* principle" into the realm of services—in cases like *Spring v Guardian Assurance* and *Henderson v Merrett*—makes this distinction rather artificial. It should be remembered, therefore, that the outcomes of pure economic loss claims depend, not on their classification within an appropriate pigeon-hole, but on the different weight the courts accord to various issues in the unique factual matrix of each case. Detailed consideration of these issues leads the courts to form an overview or "impression" of whether or not, in the particular circumstances, there can sensibly be said to have been an "assumption of responsibility" (with sufficient "proximity" and "reliance") so that a duty of care can arise.

It is noteworthy that in Commonwealth jurisdictions, particularly in Australia, New Zealand and Canada, the UK's restrictive approach to economic loss has not been whole-heartedly embraced. Commonwealth courts have, for example, been more willing to allow recovery where the claimant has only a contractual interest in damaged property, and have taken a

---

105 [2016] EWCA Civ 457 at [17]. See also *BCCI v Price Waterhouse (No 2)* [1998] P.N.L.R. 564, 586–587; *CGL Group Ltd v Royal Bank of Scotland* [2017] EWCA Civ 1073; [2018] 1 W.L.R. 2137 at [59]–[61] per Beatson LJ.

106 A notable critic is Professor K. Stanton. See, e.g. K. Stanton, "Hedley Byrne and Heller: The relationship factor" (2007) 23 P.N. 94, who argues that more than 40 years after the decision in *Hedley Byrne* the law remains vague, giving rise to undesirable uncertainty in this area of law.

more liberal approach to the liability of builders and local authorities for defective premises.[107] Whilst (as we saw in Ch.2) the UK courts have rejected Lord Wilberforce's broad "two-stage test" for finding the duty of care, Commonwealth courts, in pure economic loss cases, have often chosen to apply it, in conjunction with a close examination of the economic and political relationships between the parties.[108] Academic commentators have pointed out that this approach makes much more sense, and that the incoherence of UK law has resulted from the courts' analysis of pure economic loss questions "not on the basis of common policy concerns but in pockets according to how the loss [has] been caused".[109] The reasoning of the House of Lords in *Customs & Excise v Barclays Bank*[110] (in which this commentary was specifically referred to[111]) indicates, perhaps, a new-found willingness to adopt a more flexible approach which brings together alternative tests when deciding economic loss claims. However, it might still be questioned how far this approach has succeeded in its goal to provide clarity and consistency to this complex area of tort law.

---

107 See *Kamloops (City) v Nielsen* (1984) 10 D.L.R. 641 (Supreme Court of Canada); *Bryan v Maloney* (1994–5) 182 C.L.R. 609 (High Court of Australia); *Invercargill v Hamlin* [1994] 3 N.Z.L.R. 513 (New Zealand Court of Appeal, affirmed by Privy Council: [1996] A.C. 624). See R. Tobin, "Local authority liability in tort to owners of defective buildings: the New Zealand position" (2013) 42 C.L.W.R. 151 and G. Yihan, "A Conscious Effort to Develop a 'Different' Common Law of Obligations: A Possible Endeavour?" in A. Robertson and M. Tilbury (eds), *The Common Law of Obligations: Divergence and Unity* (Hart, 2016).

108 In Canada, e.g. the *Anns* test is still applied, although it has been "revisited". See *Cooper v Hobart* (2002) 206 D.L.R. (4th) 193 and *Edwards v Law Society of Upper Canada* (2002) 206 D.L.R. (4th) 211, but contrast the more flexible approach adopted by the High Court of Australia in *Perre v Apand Pty Ltd* (1999) 198 C.L.R. 180 and *Barclay v Penberthy* (2012) 86 A.L.J.R. 1206.

109 See J. Stapleton, "Duty of care and economic loss: a wider agenda" (1991) 107 L.Q.R. 249, 294, and "Comparative Economic Loss: Lessons from Case-Law-Focused 'Middle Theory'" (2002) 50 UCLA L. Rev. 531.

110 [2006] UKHL 28. Comment: J. Morgan, "The rise and fall of the general duty of care" (2006) 22 P.N. 206.

111 [2006] UKHL 28 per Lord Walker at [69].

4

Negligence: Psychiatric Illness

Introduction

This chapter will examine the circumstances in which a defendant owes a claimant a duty of care to avoid causing him or her psychiatric illness. In *White v Chief Constable of South Yorkshire*,[1] Lord Steyn noted that the law in this area is "a patchwork quilt of distinctions which are difficult to justify".[2] This case, in common with the leading case of *Alcock v Chief Constable of South Yorkshire*,[3] arose from events which happened at the Hillsborough football stadium in April 1989, when police negligence caused the overcrowding of spectator stands. As a result, 96 people were crushed to death and hundreds more injured.

The claims in these cases were brought by people who, though not physically injured, suffered psychiatric illness as a result of the tragedy. In *Alcock*, claims were brought by relatives who had witnessed or heard about the death or injury of their loved ones. In *White*, claims were brought by police officers who had assisted in the aftermath of the disaster. In deciding that no duty of care was owed to any of these claimants, the House of Lords developed and applied a set of rules that are hard to justify in terms of logic and morality. The area has been the subject of a report by the Law Commission, whose recommendations are considered at the end of this chapter.

Definition of "psychiatric illness"

It is important to understand that the courts draw a distinction between claims in respect of *medically recognised psychiatric illness*[4] and claims for mere grief, sorrow and distress. The

---

1 [1999] 2 A.C. 455.
2 [1999] 2 A.C. 455 at 500.
3 [1992] 1 A.C. 310.
4 For comprehensive discussion of the types of psychiatric illness that can found an action, see Law Com.249 Pt

latter, being unfortunate but commonplace symptoms of the human condition, are generally afforded no remedy at law.[5] In psychiatric illness cases, successful claimants must establish that they are suffering from medical conditions such as "post-traumatic stress disorder (PTSD)",[6] "organic depression and a change of personality",[7] or "pathological grief disorder".[8] The law recognises that these conditions can be just as serious and debilitating as physical injuries. As we shall see, however, for policy reasons it limits the circumstances in which they can give rise to claims for compensation.

Until very recently, claims for psychiatric illness were described as claims for "nervous shock". This rather quaint terminology served to emphasise the idea that the law would only entertain such claims in cases where psychiatric illness resulted from the "sudden shock" of witnessing or participating in a *specific single event*. Although, in the modern law, this requirement has received criticism,[9] it is generally thought that an element of "sudden shock" remains an ingredient of the cause of action. Thus, a person whose psychiatric illness is brought on by the cumulative effect of prolonged exposure to distressing circumstances (by caring for a brain-damaged accident victim, for example) will normally have no cause of action.[10]

Once the claimant has established that he or she is suffering from a psychiatric condition which the law will recognise as actionable, there are a number of additional hurdles that must be overcome in order to succeed. As in cases of pure economic loss, the law uses the concept of the duty of care as the mechanism to control the scope of liability. The nature of the hurdles which a particular claimant will have to overcome depends on the *type of situation* that has

---

III (paras 3.1–3.33). For criticism that this requirement is too harsh, see R. Mulheron, "Rewriting the requirement for a 'recognized psychiatric injury' in negligence claims" (2012) 32 O.J.L.S. 77. Note, however, that in cases where the shock has led to a heart attack or miscarriage, there is no need to show a recognised psychiatric illness.

5 Lord Denning MR in *Hinz v Berry* [1970] 2 Q.B. 40 made it clear that "in English law no damages are awarded for grief or sorrow caused by a person's death". Subsequent to that decision, however, a modest sum has become payable for bereavement, in limited circumstances, under the Fatal Accidents Act 1976 s.1A (inserted by Administration of Justice Act 1982 s.3), discussed in Ch.17.

6 As in *White v Chief Constable of South York*shire [1999] 2 A.C. 455. Note that in *Ward v Leeds Teaching Hospitals NHS Trust* [2004] EWHC 2106 (QB); [2004] Lloyd's Rep. Med. 530 it was noted that the diagnostic criteria for PTSD required a shocking event of a particularly horrific nature (the death of loved one in hospital would not normally meet this description.) This issue overlaps with the "sudden shock" requirement in *Alcock*, discussed later in this chapter.

7 As in *McLoughlin v O'Brian* [1983] 1 A.C. 410 (per Lord Wilberforce at 417).

8 As in *Vernon v Bosley (No.1)* [1997] 1 All E.R. 577.

9 See the observations of Lord Slynn in *W v Essex CC* [2001] 2 A.C. 592 at 600. See also *Vernon v Bosley (No.1)* [1997] 1 All E.R. 577 (where the claimant's condition results from a combination of grief and "sudden shock", the court will not attempt to draw a fine distinction between the two).

10 See *Alcock v Chief Constable of South Yorkshire* [1992] 1 A.C. 310 at 396, 401 and 416. Note, however, that the position may be different where the defendant has a contractual relationship which requires him or her to exercise reasonable care in respect of the claimant's health: see *Walker v Northumberland CC* [1995] I.C.R. 702.

given rise to the psychiatric illness. The law divides claimants into a number of categories, with very different rules applying to each category.

Types of claimant

4–003

Broadly speaking, and in the light of the decision in *White v Chief Constable of South Yorkshire*, it can be said that there are nowadays three categories of claimant in psychiatric illness cases[11]:

- claimants who suffer psychiatric illness as a result of having been physically injured by the defendant's negligence;

- claimants who are put in physical danger, but who in fact suffer only psychiatric illness (these claimants are known as "primary victims"[12]); and

- claimants who, though not in any physical danger themselves, suffer psychiatric illness as a result of *witnessing the death, injury or imperilment of another person* (known as the "immediate victim") with whom they have a close relationship of love and affection (these claimants are known as "secondary victims").

Arguably, there remains an additional category, namely claimants who suffer psychiatric illness as a result of witnessing the destruction of their property. Such a claim succeeded in *Attia v British Gas Plc*,[13] which is discussed later in this chapter. It should be remembered, however, that this decision was taken in the 1980s, at a time when the courts were in the last throes of expanding the duty of care in negligence, and before the modern rules relating to psychiatric illness had been clearly defined. It is therefore uncertain whether it would nowadays be followed.

---

11 In addition to the three categories listed here, there are other situations where psychiatric illness may be recoverable in negligence. These include situations where psychiatric illness is induced by stress at work (discussed in Ch.7) and a group of situations which the Law Commission classified as "miscellaneous" (see Law Com.249 para.2.51). These include: where a patient suffers psychiatric illness at the hands of a negligent psychiatrist; and where a prisoner suffers psychiatric illness as a result of ill-treatment in prison. Such cases, however, fall outside the traditional focus of psychiatric illness liability and are beyond the scope of this chapter.

12 We use the term "primary victims" here in its "narrow" post-*White* sense. Contrast this with the sense in which it was used by Lord Oliver in *Alcock v Chief Constable of South Yorkshire* [1992] 1 A.C. 310 at 407.

13 [1988] Q.B. 304.

Historical Development

The old law

4–004

Unsurprisingly, perhaps, the law was slow to recognise claims for psychiatric illness. The approach of the courts in the nineteenth century is exemplified by the decision of the Privy Council in *Victorian Railway Commissioners v Coultas*.[14] Here, the defendants' gate-keeper had carelessly allowed the plaintiffs to drive over a level crossing when a train was about to pass. Although no physical injury occurred, the plaintiff, who was being driven by her husband and feared for her life, suffered severe shock. The Privy Council denied that there could be liability for psychiatric illness in the absence of physical injury. As Lord Hoffmann pointed out in *White*,[15] the main reason their Lordships gave for this restrictive approach was the evidential difficulty of deciding on the causes of psychiatric illness at a time when so little was known about the workings of the mind. The Privy Council thought that opening the doors to psychiatric illness liability might have led to a large number of "imaginary claims".[16]

The "impact theory"

4–005

In 1901, however, the courts adopted a more liberal approach in deciding *Dulieu v White & Sons*.[17] Here, the plaintiff, a pregnant barmaid, was behind the bar in a pub when a negligently driven carriage came off the road and crashed into the pub, entering the room where she was standing. She suffered shock and a subsequent miscarriage. Kennedy J upheld her claim. Dealing with *Victorian Railway Commissioners v Coultas*, Kennedy J thought that the problem of exaggerated or fraudulent claims was not a good enough reason for simply denying the existence of a duty of care in respect of psychiatric harm, observing:

> **"Such a course involves the denial of redress in meritorious cases, and it necessarily implies a certain degree of distrust, which I do not share, in the capacity of legal tribunals to get at the truth in this class of claim."[18]**

In allowing liability for psychiatric illness in negligence, Kennedy J was influenced by the case of *Wilkinson v Downton*,[19] which had been decided four years earlier. Here, the defendant, in the exercise of what he regarded as a practical joke, had arrived at the plaintiff's front door

---

14 (1888) 13 App. Cas. 222.
15 *White v Chief Constable of South Yorkshire* [1999] 2 A.C. 455 at 501.
16 (1888) 13 App. Cas. 222 at 226.
17 [1901] 2 K.B. 669.
18 [1901] 2 K.B. 669 at 681.
19 [1897] 2 Q.B. 57.

and announced that her husband had been involved in a serious accident and had broken both his legs. When the plaintiff suffered shock, accompanied by vomiting and other physical symptoms, the defendant was held liable for the effect of his statement, on the basis that he had perpetrated an intentional act of wrongdoing. (Liability under the "rule in *Wilkinson v Downton*", as it is known, is discussed more fully in Ch.11. It should not be confused with liability in negligence.)

In *Dulieu v White & Sons*, then, and in a number of similar cases, the courts sought to control the scope of liability by using what became known as the "impact theory", according to which a plaintiff would be allowed to recover for psychiatric illness provided that this was caused by reasonable fear of being physically injured by the defendant's negligence.

The law expands: *Hambrook v Stokes*

In later cases, the courts abandoned the "impact theory", extending the law to cover claimants who had not been in danger, but had suffered psychiatric illness as a result of witnessing a loved one being injured or placed in peril by a defendant's negligence. (We now call such claimants "secondary victims".)

4–006

Such was the case in *Hambrook v Stokes*.[20] Here, a pregnant mother had accompanied her three children part of the way on their journey to school and then, as usual, had left them to walk a short way by themselves along the bend of a road. The children had passed out of sight when, owing to the defendants' negligence, an out-of-control lorry came down a hill at speed and went round the bend. The mother was afraid that her children would be killed by the lorry (in fact, however, two of them were unharmed, whilst the third was taken to hospital with injuries). She suffered shock which led to a miscarriage with medical complications, causing her death. A majority of the Court of Appeal held the defendants liable. But in extending the law to cover this situation, Bankes LJ was careful to point out that the ratio of the decision was to be confined to situations where the plaintiff suffered psychiatric illness because of fear for the safety of her children. The decision was not intended to overturn previous authority to the effect that a plaintiff could not recover in respect of psychiatric illness caused by witnessing physical injury to a person with whom the plaintiff had no relationship of love and affection.[21]

No further expansion: *Bourhill v Young*

Nearly 20 years later, in *Bourhill v Young*,[22] the question of psychiatric illness liability came before the House of Lords for the first time. The facts of this case were noted in Ch.2. It will be

4–007

---

20 [1925] 1 K.B. 141.
21 e.g. *Smith v Johnson & Co* (unreported, but considered in *Wilkinson v Downton* [1897] 2 Q.B. 57 and *Dulieu v White* [1901] 2 K.B. 669).
22 [1943] A.C. 92.

recalled that it concerned a pregnant woman who, while descending from a tram, heard a road accident occur some distance away. She later attended the scene of the accident, saw blood on the road, and subsequently suffered a miscarriage produced by shock. As was noted in Ch.2, the House of Lords held, in effect, that the woman was not a "foreseeable claimant". In other words, she could not base her action on a wrong done to someone else.

In arriving at this conclusion, their Lordships considered a number of points. First, there was the question of whether the woman might be regarded as being peculiarly susceptible to psychiatric illness because of her pregnant condition (Lord Wright appeared to think this was likely). If so, then she could only recover if it could be said that, in the circumstances, psychiatric illness was reasonably foreseeable *in a person of ordinary fortitude*. On the facts, their Lordships did not think this was the case—ordinary people could be expected to withstand the rigours of witnessing injury to a stranger on the roads without suffering psychiatric illness. Secondly, there was the question of whether it mattered that the plaintiff had not feared for her own physical safety. A majority of their Lordships appeared to answer this question by resurrecting the "impact theory" and holding that she could not recover because she was outside the area of foreseeable physical impact. Their Lordships held that *Hambrook v Stokes* was to be regarded as a special case and was of limited application.

Initially, then, the courts took a narrow view of the decision in *Hambrook v Stokes*. In *King v Phillips*,[23] for example, the Court of Appeal denied recovery to a mother who suffered psychiatric illness when, from an upstairs window some 70 yards away, she saw her son's tricycle disappear under a reversing taxi and heard the boy scream. The decision in *Hambrook v Stokes* was distinguished on the basis that the mother in *King v Phillips* was too far away from the scene of the accident—like the plaintiff in *Bourhill v Young*, she was not, in effect, a "foreseeable claimant".

In the 1960s, however, the courts began to take a more liberal approach, holding in *Boardman v Sanderson*[24] that a plaintiff who suffered psychiatric illness when his son was involved in an accident could recover even though he had not seen the accident but had only heard it from some distance away, and had come to the scene of the accident shortly after its occurrence. This approach was developed a stage further by the House of Lords in 1982, when it decided the landmark case of *McLoughlin v O'Brian*.

The emergence of the modern law: *McLoughlin v O'Brian*

4–008

In *McLoughlin v O'Brian*,[25] the plaintiff's husband and three of her children were involved in a serious road accident, caused by the defendants' negligence. The plaintiff did not witness the accident, being, at the time, at home about two miles away. About an hour after the accident, it was reported to her by a family friend that her 17-year-old son, George (who had been driving the car), was dying. The friend then drove her to a local hospital where she was told that

---

23   [1953] 1 Q.B. 429.
24   [1964] 1 W.L.R. 1317.
25   [1983] 1 A.C. 410.

her three-year-old daughter had died. She could hear George shouting and screaming in an adjoining room. She saw her husband and seven year-old daughter, who were in a distressed state, covered with oil and mud. She was then taken to see George, who appeared to recognise her before lapsing into unconsciousness. These events caused her to suffer psychiatric illness.

In holding the defendants liable, the House of Lords extended the law to cover a situation where the plaintiff had not seen or heard the accident itself, but had come upon its "immediate aftermath", although this case was seen as on the margins of what previous authority would allow. While the House of Lords declined to say, in precise terms, what could constitute the "immediate aftermath" of an accident, it was clearly significant that the plaintiff in *McLoughlin v O'Brian* had seen her family within a fairly short time of the accident, and that, when she saw them, they had not been "cleaned up" and remained in more or less the same condition they had been in immediately after the accident. She had therefore witnessed scenes which went to "make up the accident as an entire event".[26] Lord Wilberforce stressed that in terms of proximity of the victim to the accident, there must be closeness in time and space, finding that the High Court of Australia's decision in *Chester v Waverly Municipal Council*,[27] where a child's body was found floating in a trench after a prolonged search, might "perhaps be placed on the other side of a recognisable line".[28] As we shall see, the question of what can constitute the "immediate aftermath" remains unclear, even after being considered again in the leading case of *Alcock v Chief Constable of South Yorkshire*.[29]

The speech of Lord Wilberforce, then, laid the foundation for the modern approach of the courts in psychiatric illness cases. Whilst his Lordship thought that extending previous authority to assist the plaintiff was a "logical progression", he noted that, because psychiatric illness was capable of affecting such a large number of potential plaintiffs, there was "a real need for the law to place some limitation on the extent of admissible claims".[30]

▶ Lord Wilberforce's "control mechanisms"

In *McLoughlin v O'Brian*, Lord Wilberforce identified three factors that would need to be considered in relation to what we now call secondary victims:

4–009

- ■ the class of persons whose claims should be recognised;

- ■ the proximity of such persons to the accident; and

- ■ the means by which the psychiatric illness was caused.

---

26   [1983] 1 A.C. 410 at 422 (as in *Benson v Lee* [1972] V.R. 879, to which Lord Wilberforce referred).
27   (1939) 62 C.L.R. 1. Compare *Vernon v Bosley (No.1)* [1997] 1 All E.R. 577.
28   [1983] A.C. 410 at 422.
29   A point confirmed by Lord Slynn in *W v Essex CC* [2001] 2 A.C. 592.
30   [1983] 1 A.C. 410 at 422.

These three "control mechanisms" suggested by Lord Wilberforce were subsequently reformulated and applied by a unanimous House of Lords in *Alcock*.

In relation to the class of persons who might claim, Lord Wilberforce recognised that "the possible range is between the closest of family ties, of parent and child, or husband and wife, and the ordinary bystander". He noted that the law, as in *Bourhill v Young*, had always denied recovery to mere "bystanders" who suffered psychiatric illness as a result of witnessing accidents. According to Lord Wilberforce, the law's justification for this approach was either that "such persons must be assumed to be possessed of fortitude sufficient to enable them to endure the calamities of modern life", or that "defendants cannot be expected to compensate the world at large".[31] His Lordship thought that cases brought by plaintiffs who did not have a very close family relationship with the "immediate victim" of the accident would have to be "very carefully scrutinised".

As regards proximity to the accident, this had to be "close in both time and space", but it would be impractical and unjust to insist that plaintiffs must be present at the scene of the accident. As regards the means by which the psychiatric illness was caused, his Lordship noted that there had thus far been no negligence case in which the law had compensated psychiatric illness brought about by mere communication to the plaintiff of distressing news. There was no justification for departing from this position. It followed that the psychiatric illness must arise through direct perception of the accident, or its immediate aftermath, by sight or hearing. Lord Wilberforce left open the question of whether "some equivalent of sight or hearing, e.g. through simultaneous television", would suffice. (This point, as we shall see, was subsequently considered by the House of Lords in *Alcock*.)

Although, as has been said, the "control mechanisms" suggested by Lord Wilberforce in *McLoughlin v O'Brian* were subsequently endorsed in *Alcock*, it was initially unclear whether they formed part of the ratio of the case. This was because other members of the House of Lords did not view them in the same way. Whilst Lord Wilberforce (with whom Lord Edmund-Davies agreed) appeared to think that the "control mechanisms" should be satisfied in addition to a test of reasonable foreseeability, Lords Bridge and Scarman appeared to think that liability for psychiatric illness should be decided by applying a broad test of foreseeability, and that, although the factors suggested by Lord Wilberforce were to be considered in applying that test, they did not exclusively define the circumstances in which psychiatric illness could be recoverable. (Lord Russell's opinion on the point was not clear.) This is why the plaintiffs in *Alcock* felt able to pursue their claims.

The House of Lords in *Alcock*, however, unanimously adopted Lord Wilberforce's approach. After *Alcock* came the important decision in *Page v Smith*,[32] a case involving a "primary victim" of psychiatric illness. Next came the case of *White v Chief Constable of South Yorkshire*.[33] The reasoning of the House of Lords in these three cases forms the core of the modern law which is considered below.

---

31   [1983] 1 A.C. 410 at 422.
32   [1996] A.C. 155.
33   [1999] 2 A.C. 455.

Modern Law: preliminary issues

In this section, we examine certain preliminary issues which will help us understand the modern law. We begin by dealing with the position of claimants who suffer psychiatric illness as a result of suffering physical injury, or through witnessing damage to their property. The position of such claimants can be shortly stated and should not be the focus of too much of our attention. Next, we examine the more important issue of the role of policy in psychiatric illness cases. Then, we consider the courts' use of "reasonable foreseeability" in establishing the duty of care.

4-010

Psychiatric illness resulting from personal injury

Where a claimant has suffered bodily injury as a result of the defendant's negligence, the courts have no difficulty in allowing recovery in respect of psychiatric illness resulting from the injury. It will be treated as an ordinary personal injury claim. While such claimants are sometimes referred to as "primary victims", their position is conceptually distinct from that of the plaintiff in *Page v Smith*—discussed later—who did not suffer physical injury, though he had been placed in physical danger. The ability of such claimants to recover for psychiatric illness follows from the fact that the law has traditionally allowed them to recover damages for pain and suffering consequent upon their injuries. Such damages were awarded, for example, in *Kralj v McGrath*,[34] where the negligence of a defendant obstetrician resulted in the plaintiff suffering psychiatric trauma and losing her baby shortly after its birth. Damages for pain and suffering, including psychiatric injury, consequential on personal injury will be examined in Ch.17.

4-011

Psychiatric illness resulting from property damage

In *Attia v British Gas Plc*,[35] the Court of Appeal was asked to decide, as a preliminary issue, whether a duty of care could arise where the plaintiff had witnessed the destruction of her home, as opposed to injury to a loved one. Their Lordships held that it could. The defendants, by negligently installing a central heating system, had caused a fire which destroyed the plaintiff's house. The plaintiff suffered psychiatric illness when she returned home one day to witness the blaze. Bingham LJ, holding that a duty of care could exist in such a situation, cited other possible examples, such as where "a scholar's life's work of research or composition were destroyed before his eyes as a result of a defendant's careless conduct".[36] The decision in *Attia*, however, is not considered in any of the three modern leading cases on psychiatric illness.[37]

4-012

---

34   [1986] 1 All E.R. 54.
35   [1988] Q.B. 304.
36   [1988] Q.B. 304 at 320.
37   The decision is not mentioned in *Alcock* or *White*, although in *Page v Smith* [1996] A.C. 155 at 179 it is referred to in passing by Lord Jauncey (dissenting) as an illustration of foreseeable damage. It was also considered in

Therefore, as has already been noted, its status remains uncertain. It has been suggested, however, that it might still be possible to justify the decision in *Attia v British Gas* on the basis that a contractual relationship between the defendant and the claimant gave rise to an "assumption of responsibility"' for the claimant's psychiatric well-being.[38]

Policy considerations

4–013

In *White v Chief Constable of South Yorkshire*, Lord Steyn provided a useful summary of the main policy considerations that dictate that claims for psychiatric illness should be treated differently from claims for physical injury.[39] His Lordship identified four such considerations. First, there is the difficulty of drawing the line between acute grief and psychiatric illness.[40] It is difficult to draw this line because the symptoms of both conditions are often the same, but it is necessary to differentiate between them because, as we have noted, the law provides no compensation for the former. Lord Steyn pointed out that establishing psychiatric illness by expert evidence was a costly and time-consuming exercise, so that if claims for psychiatric illness were to be treated as generally on a par with physical injury cases there would be adverse economic implications for the administration of justice. He conceded, however, that this factor had limited weight on its own.

Secondly, Lord Steyn thought it was important to consider the effect on people who had witnessed gruesome events of increasing the availability of compensation. His Lordship did not have in mind fraudulent or bogus claims, saying that it ought to be possible for the courts to expose such claims (although the fear of fraud has clearly affected courts in the past).[41] Rather, he thought that the prospect of compensation might sometimes be an *unconscious disincentive to rehabilitation*. His Lordship noted that in cases where there was generally no prospect of compensation for psychiatric illness, such as where injury had been sustained while playing sport, reports of psychiatric illness were uncommon. On the other hand, in industrial accident cases, where there was often a prospect of compensation, psychiatric illness was repeatedly encountered.

The third policy consideration was that relaxing the special rules governing compensation for psychiatric harm would greatly increase the class of persons who could recover damages in tort. (In other words, it would open the "floodgates of litigation".) Fourthly, his Lordship thought that expanding liability for psychiatric harm might result in liability which was disproportionate

---

Yapp v Foreign and Commonwealth Office [2014] EWCA Civ 1512; [2015] I.R.L.R. 112 (although in relation to the question of the foreseeability of psychiatric illness in claims brought in tort).

38   See M. Lunney, D. Nolan and K. Oliphant, *Tort Law: Text and Materials*, 6th edn (2017), p.372.

39   *White v Chief Constable of South Yorkshire* [1999] 2 A.C. 455 at 493. For further discussion of relevant policy considerations, see Law Com.249 paras 6.5–6.8.

40   See S. Hedley, "Nervous Shock: Wider Still and Wider?" [1997] C.L.J. 254, to which his Lordship refers.

41   See, e.g. Lord Wilberforce in *McLoughlin v O'Brian* [1983] 1 A.C. 410 at 421.

to the tortious conduct involved—perhaps only a momentary lapse of concentration, for example in a road traffic accident. (In other words, it would result in "crushing liability".)

Bearing these policy considerations in mind, we can now examine the various rules that the courts apply in order to limit the scope of the duty of care. The first of these, as may be expected, is the requirement that some harm (either physical or psychiatric, depending on the type of claim) must be reasonably foreseeable.

Foreseeability of psychiatric illness

As in all negligence actions, reasonable foreseeability of damage is an essential ingredient of the duty of care in psychiatric illness cases. In this area of the law, however, the question of foreseeability can sometimes be a source of confusion. This is because different rules apply in relation to "primary victims" and "secondary victims". In both cases, foreseeability is integrated into the duty of care test.

For "primary victims", the leading case of *Page v Smith*,[42] states that provided either physical or psychiatric harm is reasonably foreseeable, a duty of care can arise. This, as discussed below, is an extremely generous test and means that, as in the case itself, liability for psychiatric injury can arise where only physical injury, on the facts, was foreseeable.

For "secondary victims", the test is stricter—the claimant must show that *psychiatric illness* is reasonably foreseeable. This involves showing that a person of ordinary fortitude or "customary phlegm"[43] might reasonably have suffered psychiatric illness in the circumstances.

In both cases, no duty of care will be owed to avoid causing psychiatric harm to people who are "peculiarly susceptible" to such harm because they have a nervous or emotional disposition. (This is one of the reasons the plaintiff in *Bourhill v Young* did not succeed.) For example, in *Grieves v FT Everard & Sons Ltd.*[44] Grieves had developed a psychiatric illness as a result of finding out that he had pleural plaques (changes in his lung tissue) resulting from the fact that, in the past, he had been exposed to asbestos by his employer. The pleural plaques were completely harmless, and could not, therefore, found an action in negligence for personal injury (the claimant having suffered no injury).[45] However, the presence of the plaques indicated past exposure to asbestos, and Grieves had developed psychiatric symptoms through fear that this exposure might cause him to develop a serious lung disease in the future. Relying on *Page v Smith*, he argued that, given that the employer had exposed him to the risk of such disease

4-014

4-015

---

42   [1996] A.C. 155. On the application of the principle in *Page v Smith*, see *Simmons v British Steel Plc* [2004] UKHL 20; [2004] I.C.R. 585.

43   This colourful phrase was coined by Lord Porter in *Bourhill v Young* [1943] A.C. 92 at 117.

44   [2007] UKHL 39; [2008] 1 A. C. 281.

45   Note that this part of the decision has not been followed in Scotland which introduced the Damages (Asbestos-related Conditions) (Scotland) Act 2009 which treats asymptomatic pleural plaques as actionable harm for the purpose of personal injury claims.

(albeit that, fortuitously, that risk of physical harm had not materialised) the employer should be liable for the psychiatric harm that *had* materialised. The House of Lords rejected the claim, holding that the principle in *Page v Smith* could not assist a claimant where the psychiatric illness had been caused by a fear of the *possibility* of an event which had not actually occurred. On this basis, the claim failed in that it was not reasonably foreseeable that a person of reasonable fortitude would suffer psychiatric illness as a result of his employer creating a risk of a possibility of future injury.

But once the reasonable foreseeability test is satisfied, and has been breached, the defendant will be liable for all of the psychiatric illness that results, even though the precise nature and the seriousness of the claimant's particular illness may not have been foreseen. This means that a defendant who could reasonably foresee that his or her negligence might cause a person of ordinary fortitude to suffer from post-traumatic stress disorder, and require, say, two years off work to recuperate, cannot argue that his liability is limited to the cost of that period of recuperation when the claimant, because of his or her special susceptibility to psychiatric illness, will take ten years to recover. Thus, in *Brice v Brown*,[46] where it was reasonably foreseeable that a mother of "customary phlegm" might suffer some psychiatric illness on witnessing injuries to her daughter, the plaintiff was able to recover for the full extent of her psychiatric illness even though the illness was made more severe by the fact that she had an underlying personality disorder.

We have already noted that the courts draw a distinction between "primary" and "secondary" victims of psychiatric illness. In the next two sections, we consider in more detail how this distinction is drawn and explore the law relating to recovery by each type of claimant.

Primary Victims

What is the test for primary victims?

4–016

To qualify as a "primary victim", the claimant must establish that he or she has been placed in immediate physical danger by the defendant's negligence (or at least has been put in reasonable fear for his or her physical safety). The position of "primary victims" is governed by the decision in *Page v Smith*.[47] In this case, Mr Page was involved in a relatively minor car accident, but was not physically injured. Prior to the accident, he had for about 20 years suffered from a condition variously described as myalgic encephalomyelitis (ME), chronic fatigue syndrome, or post-viral fatigue syndrome. This had manifested itself from time to time with different degrees of severity. The illness had been in remission at the time of the accident and Page was

---

46 [1984] 1 W.L.R. 997.
47 [1996] A.C. 155.

expecting to return to work after a period of convalescence, but the crash triggered a recurrence of the disease, which became chronic and permanent, so that it was unlikely he would be able to take up full-time employment again.

In the Court of Appeal, it was held that the defendant driver was not liable, because he could not reasonably have foreseen that his negligence would cause psychiatric illness. A majority of the House of Lords, however, overturned this decision and held that reasonable foreseeability of psychiatric illness need not be established when physical injury was reasonably foreseeable. As Lord Lloyd put it:

> **"Since the defendant was admittedly under a duty of care not to cause the plaintiff foreseeable physical injury, it was unnecessary to ask whether he was under a separate duty of care not to cause foreseeable psychiatric injury."[48]**

Lord Lloyd reasoned that if a plaintiff could recover for psychiatric illness in a case where he or she had *actually suffered* physical harm, it should follow that where the plaintiff had, by good luck, escaped reasonably foreseeable physical harm, he should not be deprived of compensation by the existence of this purely fortuitous fact.

The reasoning in *Page v Smith* is quite difficult to understand.[49] In essence, however, their Lordships held that, where there is a danger of physical injury, the law should regard physical and psychiatric injury as the same kind of harm (personal injury). Then, applying the so-called "eggshell skull rule" (discussed in Ch.6), their Lordships reasoned that, because it was foreseeable that some (minor) harm of a relevant kind would be caused (being "shaken up" by the car crash), the defendant was liable for the full extent of the harm that was actually suffered. The "eggshell skull" rule provides that where it is reasonably foreseeable that an injured claimant will suffer personal injury, the defendant will be liable for *all* the consequences of that injury, even though they could not all have been reasonably foreseen.

Lords Keith and Jauncey dissented in *Page v Smith* on the basis that the defendant could not reasonably have foreseen that a person of ordinary fortitude would suffer *psychiatric* illness as a result of a minor car accident. Lord Jauncey appeared to think the "eggshell skull" rule was not relevant where what was in issue was the existence of a duty of care to avoid causing a particular kind of damage—it was only relevant to the *extent* of the damage which occurred, once an established duty of care had been breached.[50] Similar criticism of the approach of the majority in *Page v Smith* was articulated by Lord Goff in his dissenting judgment in *White v Chief*

---

48   [1996] A.C. 155 at 187.

49   For stringent criticism of its reasoning, see S. Bailey and D. Nolan, "The *Page v Smith* saga: A tale of inauspicious origins and unintended consequences" [2010] C.L.J. 495.

50   [1996] A.C. 155 at 176. Lord Ackner, whilst approving Lord Lloyd's analysis, was content to decide the appeal on the basis that psychiatric illness (as opposed to physical injury) was reasonably foreseeable in the circumstances, and suggested (at 170) that consideration of the eggshell skull rule was "nothing to the point". In the light of Lord Ackner's position, then, it is unclear whether the extended application of the rule forms part of the true ratio of *Page v Smith*.

Constable of South Yorkshire.[51] The Court in *Grieves v FT Everard & Sons Ltd.*[52] also noted that the reasoning in *Page v Smith* was controversial and has attracted much criticism, but declined to say that the case had been wrongly decided. Instead, they expressed the view that the *Page v Smith* principle should be confined to situations where (as Lord Rodger put it) claimants had been exposed to, but had escaped, "instant physical harm".[53]

Page v Smith tells us therefore that a claimant who is a primary victim may recover for *psychiatric* harm, even though only the occurrence of *physical* harm was foreseeable. What is key is that *some form of personal injury to the claimant is reasonably foreseeable.*

4–017   The High Court recently clarified in *YAH v Medway NHS Foundation Trust*[54] that, in contrast to secondary victims, primary victims do not have to prove that the psychiatric illness had been triggered by a sudden shocking event. In *Page v Smith*, liability had arisen in the context of a low-impact collision in which no-one had been hurt. While, then, shock remains a requirement to establish a duty of care towards secondary victims (see below), Whipple J. confirmed that this rule did not apply to primary victims and, on that basis, they would be able to recover for psychiatric injuries which accumulated over a period of time.[55]

What do we mean by "fear for your own safety"?

4–018   Physical imperilment is a precondition of qualifying as a "primary victim". Given the generosity of the *Page v Smith* test, the question arose when could a claimant be said to be in immediate physical danger or have reasonable grounds to fear for his or her physical safety? Guidance was given in *White v Chief Constable of South Yorkshire*[56] which indicated that it is not necessary to show that fear of physical harm is the *cause* of the primary victim's psychiatric illness. (Thus, where the primary victim is a "rescuer", although the element of physical danger—or reasonable fear thereof—must be present, the cause of the psychiatric illness may be witnessing the imperilment of those being rescued.) The decision in *White* is important because, before that decision, it had been unclear whether the category of "primary victims" could be said to encompass a miscellaneous group of claimants, namely employees, rescuers and other "participants" in the circumstances of an accident who, *although placed in no physical danger*, were able to take advantage of liberal rules in recovering for psychiatric illness. *White* seems to make it clear that such claimants are not to be regarded as "primary victims".[57] This aspect of the decision is

---

51   [1999] 2 A.C. 455 at 470.
52   [2007] UKHL 39; [2008] 1 A. C. 281.
53   [2007] UKHL 39; [2008] 1 A.C. 281 per Lord Rodger at [95]. Comment: J. Steele, "Pleural plaques in the House of Lords: the implications for *Page v Smith*" [2008] C.L.J. 28. On the correctness of *Page v Smith*, see also the comments of Lord Neuberger in *Corr v IBC Vehicles* [2008] UKHL 13; [2008] 1 A.C. 884 at [54].
54   [2018] EWHC 2964 (QB); [2019] 1 W.L.R. 1413. The claimant was anonymised in proceedings as YAH.
55   [2018] EWHC 2964 (QB); [2019] 1 W.L.R. 1413 at [34].
56   [1999] 2 A.C. 455.
57   Although this effect of *White* does not seem to have been wholly accepted by the courts. See, e.g. negligent

controversial, and its effects on the position of this group of claimants are discussed later. Here, however, two further points should be noted.

There may be a requirement of "actual danger"

In most cases, of course, a claimant's reasonable grounds for fearing for his or her safety will derive from the fact that he or she is in actual danger. Nevertheless, it is possible to imagine a case where a claimant reasonably thinks that he or she is in danger when, as a matter of fact, no such danger exists. The position of such claimants is unclear because the two leading opinions in *White* do not deal with the point in the same way. Lord Steyn thought that an additional requirement of actual danger was not necessary, saying that it would be sufficient if a claimant had "objectively exposed himself to danger or reasonably believed that he was doing so".[58] According to Lord Hoffmann, however, claimants have to be "within the range of foreseeable physical injury"[59] to qualify as primary victims—it is unclear whether his Lordship meant by this that they must be in actual danger. The point therefore remains unresolved.[60]

The claimant's fear for his or her own safety must be reasonable

Whether or not there is a requirement of "actual danger", the decision of the Court of Appeal, in *McFarlane v EE Caledonia*,[61] makes it clear that claimants who seek to qualify as "primary victims" because they have been put in fear for their physical safety must have some reasonable basis for that fear. Here, the plaintiff alleged psychiatric illness brought on by his involvement in the Piper Alpha oil rig disaster—the rig exploded, causing the death of many workers on board. His claim as a "primary victim" failed, however, because at the time of the disaster he had been working in a support boat about 50 yards away from the rig and it was obvious that the boat had never been in any danger. It followed that his fear for his safety was unreasonable. (The plaintiff could not recover as a "secondary victim", for reasons which are considered below.)

---

misinformation cases such as *Farrell v Avon Health Authority* [2001] Lloyd's Rep. Med. 458 where a claimant was called a "primary victim" by the court.

58   *White v Chief Constable of South Yorkshire* [1999] 2 A.C. 455 at 499.
59   [1999] 2 A.C. 455 at 504, 505 and 509.
60   Note that the Law Commission suggested that it should be a precondition of recovery by secondary victims that the immediate victim be in actual danger. See Law Com.249 para.6.18 (discussed below).
61   [1994] 2 All E.R. 1.

Secondary Victims

What is the test for secondary victims?

4-021

The position of "secondary victims" is governed by the decision in *Alcock v Chief Constable of South Yorkshire*,[62] which must now be examined in detail. The claims in *Alcock* (and in *White*) arose from the tragic events that took place during the 1989 FA Cup semi-final between Liverpool and Nottingham Forest. Tickets to the Hillsborough football stadium were sold out, and the match was being shown on live television. After six minutes of play, however, it had to be stopped because, owing to negligent crowd control, too many spectators had been allowed on to the terraces. It became apparent that some were being crushed against the high fences erected between the terraces and the pitch.

South Yorkshire police admitted that the death of 96 spectators, and injuries to hundreds of others, were caused by their negligence in allowing too many people into the stadium. Claims for physical injury and death were settled by the police, as were certain psychiatric illness claims by police officers who had dragged bodies from the scene of the danger, risking physical injury to themselves. Psychiatric illness claims were then brought by two groups of people who had not been in physical danger: relatives (and a fiancée) who had in various ways witnessed or heard about the death or injury of their loved ones (the plaintiffs in *Alcock*) and police officers who had assisted in the aftermath of the tragedy (the plaintiffs in *White*).

The question for the House of Lords in *Alcock* was whether the plaintiffs were owed a duty of care on the basis that their psychiatric illness was reasonably foreseeable, applying the reasoning of Lords Bridge and Scarman in *McLoughlin v O'Brian*, or whether, *in addition*, their claims should be governed by the "control mechanisms" which had been suggested by Lord Wilberforce in that case. *Alcock* was a test case in which the specific plaintiffs had been chosen because their situations—in terms of closeness of relationship to the dead and injured and proximity to the disaster in time and space—were similar to those of about 150 other people who also wished to claim for psychiatric illness. Their Lordships held that none of the plaintiffs could succeed. Each of the plaintiffs, in one way or another, failed to satisfy the stringent criteria that their Lordships laid down for recovery by "secondary victims".

The Alcock "Control Mechanisms"

4-022

Following *Alcock*, which adopted the approach of Lord Wilberforce in *McLoughlin v O'Brian*, it is clear that "secondary victims" of psychiatric illness have to show not only that their injuries were reasonably foreseeable, but four additional "control mechanisms", designed to restrict the scope of liability, as follows:

---

62   [1992] 1 A.C. 310.

- proximity of relationship with the "immediate victim";

- proximity in "time and space" to the events causing the psychiatric illness;

- the claimant must have directly perceived the incident rather than, for example, hearing about it from a third person; and

- the claimant's illness must be induced by a sudden shocking event.

It should be noted that some elements of the second and third control mechanisms are sometimes called "proximity of perception". Each is considered in turn below.

(1) Proximity of relationship

The plaintiffs in *Alcock* were parents, brothers, sisters, a brother-in-law, a grandparent and a fiancée of the immediate victims. Their Lordships refused to define rigid categories of relationship into which secondary victims of psychiatric illness must fall. Instead, they held that there must generally be a *close relationship of love and affection* between the "secondary victim" and the "immediate victim" of the accident. According to their Lordships, such a relationship could be *presumed* to exist in the case of spouses, parents and children. This presumption could, however, be rebutted by evidence in an appropriate case, such as where the parties were estranged. Lord Keith thought that the presumption relating to spouses should also extend to fiancé(e)s, or, at least, that it should be extended to the plaintiff in *Alcock* who had lost her fiancé, whom she had known for four years.[63] Siblings and other relatives (such as grandparents,[64] uncles and aunts) would *not* normally be regarded as having the requisite closeness of relationship, unless they could show that, because of special factors, such a relationship did in fact exist. (For example, because they had brought up the immediate victim as their own child.) Dealing with the position of the plaintiff who had lost his brother in the disaster, Lord Ackner pointed out: "The quality of brotherly love is well known to differ widely".[65] It followed that this plaintiff did not satisfy the "close tie of love and affection" test in the absence of evidence that his relationship with his brother had been particularly close.

Whilst holding that closeness of relationship was an important factor to consider, their Lordships declined to hold that it was an absolute prerequisite of recovery in every case, leaving open the possibility that a mere "bystander" who witnessed a catastrophe which was *exceptionally horrifying* might be able to recover for psychiatric illness without showing any relationship at

4–023

---

63 *Alcock v Chief Constable of South Yorkshire* [1992] 1 A.C. 310 at 398.

64 But not impossible, see *RE (A Child) v Calderdale and Huddersfield NHS Foundation Trust* [2017] EWHC 824 (QB) where the child's grandmother who had been present at her birth and witnessed the aftermath could recover as a secondary victim.

65 [1992] 1 A.C. 310 at 406.

all with the immediate victim of the catastrophe. Lord Ackner gave the example of a bystander witnessing a petrol tanker careering out of control into a school in session and bursting into flames. Subsequent to the decision in *Alcock*, however, this point was tested in the Court of Appeal in *McFarlane v EE Caledonia Ltd*.[66] When his claim as a "primary victim" failed, the plaintiff, who had been in the support boat when the Piper Alpha oil rig had exploded, claimed to be a "secondary victim", on the basis that he had witnessed the death of fellow workers in exceptionally horrific circumstances. His claim failed. In holding that it was not reasonably foreseeable that a mere "bystander" would suffer psychiatric illness in such circumstances, Stuart-Smith LJ noted that people's reactions to horrific events were "entirely subjective".[67] This meant that there were serious practical and policy objections to allowing recovery by mere bystanders. The reasoning in *McFarlane*, then, has probably excluded the possibility of such claims in the future.

(2) Proximity in time and space

4–024

The various plaintiffs in *Alcock* had witnessed the injury or death of their loved ones in different ways. Some had been in other stands inside the ground and had seen the disaster happen, others had only seen the events on television, or heard about them on the radio. After the disaster had occurred, some of the plaintiffs had gone to the ground to search for their relatives, or had identified their bodies in a mortuary.

Their Lordships held that, to succeed as a secondary victim, a plaintiff had to show a high degree of proximity to the accident in time and space. Thus, the plaintiff must normally witness the accident as it actually occurs, or must come upon its "immediate aftermath" within a very short space of time. Whilst conceding that subsequent identification of the body of an accident victim might, in some circumstances, be regarded as part of the "immediate aftermath", Lord Ackner thought that Mr Alcock, who had identified his brother-in-law in a bad condition in a mortuary some eight hours after the disaster, could not be described as having come upon its immediate aftermath.[68] The decision in *Alcock*, then, took the law on the meaning of "immediate aftermath" little further than it had been taken in *McLoughlin v O'Brian*.

However, in *Galli-Atkinson v Seghal*[69] the Court of Appeal was prepared, on the facts, to take a more generous view of the circumstances in which a subsequent visit to a mortuary could constitute the "immediate aftermath" of an accident. Here, the claimant was a mother whose daughter had been involved in a road accident. The claimant arrived at the scene just over one hour later and was told by a police officer that her daughter had been killed. She then attended the mortuary just over an hour later (that is, 2 hours 10 minutes after the accident)

---

66 [1994] 2 All E.R. 1.
67 [1994] 2 All E.R. 1 at 14.
68 *Alcock v Chief Constable of South Yorkshire* [1992] 1 A.C. 310 at 405. Compare the view of Lord Keith, at 397, who appears to endorse the view of Deane J in *Jaensch v Coffey* (1984) 155 C.L.R. 549, viz. that the "immediate aftermath" will continue for as long as the victim remains in the state caused by the accident.
69 [2003] EWCA Civ 697; [2003] Lloyd's Rep. Med. 285.

and saw her daughter's body which, although it had been cleaned-up, had been badly disfigured by the accident. The trial judge had not been prepared to accept that the visit to the mortuary had formed part of the aftermath and had disallowed the mother's claim because her psychiatric illness had resulted from what she had been told, rather than from witnessing the accident. In allowing her appeal, however, Latham LJ thought that the visit to the mortuary was not, as it had been in *Alcock*, a separate event, taking place after the horror of the accident had unfolded. Rather, it was the last in a sequence of uninterrupted events which went to make up the entirety of the claimant's perception of the tragedy. His Lordship pointed out that the mortuary visit had been made not merely to identify the body, but to "complete the story so far as the appellant was concerned, who clearly at that stage did not want—and one can understand this—to believe that her child was dead".[70]

The Court of Appeal in the more recent case of *Taylor v A Novo (UK) Ltd*[71] indicated, however, that *Galli-Atkinson* should not be considered to give a green light for further substantial extension of the immediate aftermath test by the courts. In this case, the claimant's mother had been injured at work due to her employer's negligence. Three weeks later, she collapsed and died due to injuries sustained in the accident. Her daughter, Crystal, witnessed her death and suffered significant post traumatic stress disorder (PTSD) as a result. The question was straightforward: did the immediate aftermath test apply to the accident at work (which Crystal did not witness) or the death (which Crystal did witness and for which she would satisfy all the relevant *Alcock* criteria)? The Court of Appeal unanimously held that the secondary victim must be in proximity with the actual accident. If not, she might have been able to recover even if her mother had died many years after the accident had taken place, which would stretch the "immediate aftermath" test too far. Lord Dyson MR repeated the words of Lord Steyn in *White*—"the only sensible strategy for the courts is to say thus far and no further"[72]—and indicated that any extension to the scope of liability for secondary victims should be undertaken by Parliament, not the courts.[73]

(3) The means by which the psychiatric illness is caused

In *Alcock*, Lord Jauncey observed:

4-025

> "The means by which the shock is caused constitutes a third control, although in these appeals I find it difficult to separate this from proximity."[74]

---

70 [2003] Lloyd's Rep. Med. 285 at [26].
71 [2013] EWCA Civ 194; [2014] Q.B. 150.
72 [1999] A.C. 455 at 500.
73 [2013] EWCA Civ 194 at [31].
74 [1992] 1 A.C. 310 at 420.

Despite their conceptual similarity to the requirements of "proximity in time and space" considered above, their Lordships chose to consider a number of additional points under this third heading.

No liability where the claimant is merely informed about the accident

4–026

In *Alcock*, their Lordships affirmed that a defendant who causes harm or imperilment to an "immediate victim" will not be liable to a claimant who is merely informed about this by a third party.[75] This rule, of course, may produce some bizarre results. Consider a claimant who, very shortly after an accident, is informed by a friend that his or her loved-one is dying in hospital. If the claimant suffers psychiatric illness there and then and faints on the spot, he or she will have no claim. But if the friend has the legal acumen to revive the claimant and take him or her to the hospital, the claimant may be compensated under the "immediate aftermath" doctrine, as was the plaintiff in *McLoughlin v O'Brian*. We shall see that the Law Commission has suggested that this restrictive rule, like many others, should be abolished.

4–027

It is important to understand that this rule does not mean that there can never be liability where a claimant suffers psychiatric illness as the result of hearing distressing news. The person who *communicates* the news (as opposed to the person who caused the harm the news is about) *may* be liable if the news is broken in a negligently insensitive manner. In *AB v Tameside and Glossop Health Authority*,[76] for example, the defendants sent out letters warning former patients that they were at risk of having contracted HIV, because a health worker who had treated them had tested positive for the disease. The plaintiffs alleged they had suffered psychiatric illness as a result of hearing the news in this way, and argued that they should have been told face-to-face. The Court of Appeal held that the defendants had not been negligent in choosing to communicate the information by letter, but their Lordships made no comment on the fact that counsel in the case had conceded that a duty of care was owed.[77] While such reasoning can be explained on the basis that the person who communicates the news assumes responsibility to the individual concerned, it is not clear why no account is taken of the fact that psychiatric injury, as opposed to physical injury or even pure economic loss, has been caused.

---

75 Their Lordships doubted the correctness of *Hevican v Ruane* [1991] 3 All E.R. 65 and *Ravenscroft v Rederi AB Transatlantic* [1991] 3 All E.R. 73, which had appeared to decide that receiving news of a son's death could be an effective cause of psychiatric illness (latter decision subsequently reversed by the Court of Appeal: [1992] 2 All E.R. 470.)

76 [1997] 8 Med. L.R. 91.

77 See also the reasoning of Morland J in *CJD Group B Plaintiffs v Medical Research Council* [2000] Lloyd's Rep. Med. 161. Comment: N. J. Mullany, "Liability for careless communication of traumatic information" (1998) 114 L.Q.R. 380.

No liability when informed about the accident by live television coverage

This is an extension of the last point. In *Alcock*, the question was raised whether the plaintiffs could claim if their shock had been triggered by viewing a simultaneous live broadcast of the disaster on the BBC. In *McLoughlin v O'Brian*, Lord Wilberforce had left open the question of whether live television could sometimes be treated as the equivalent of being present at the scene of a disaster. Their Lordships held that, in the circumstances of the *Alcock* case, it could not. This was for two reasons. First, broadcasters had not shown the suffering of recognisable individuals—this was prohibited by their professional code of ethics. (If they had done this, then the broadcasters, rather than the police, might have been regarded as the legal cause of the plaintiffs' psychiatric illness.) Secondly, the pictures transmitted from Hillsborough had been taken by cameras from many different viewpoints. They, therefore, showed a combination of scenes which no one individual present at the ground would have been likely to see. On this basis, it could not be said that the plaintiffs could have viewed the disaster "as if" with their own unaided senses. Lord Atkin commented: "Although the television pictures certainly gave rise to feelings of the deepest anxiety and distress, in the circumstances of this case the simultaneous television broadcasts of what occurred cannot be equated with the 'sight or hearing of the event or its immediate aftermath'."[78] Their Lordships were, however, reluctant to lay down an inflexible rule on this point, holding that there might be very exceptional circumstances where a simultaneous broadcast of a disaster would equate with direct perception.

Alcock was decided in November 1991 and technology has moved on. 24 hour news channels, social media, mobile phones and the internet mean that we perceive events as they happen often with limited editorial control, as if we were there. It remains an interesting question to what extent the courts can continue to justify a distinction between the "unaided senses" of the secondary victim and the dispersal of live images through modern technology such as CCTV and Instagram.

Psychiatric illness caused by a defendant harming or imperilling himself or herself

One further point was considered, obiter, in *Alcock*, but was left undecided. This was whether the law would allow a claim in circumstances where a defendant had caused psychiatric illness to a secondary victim by negligently placing himself or herself in danger or causing self-inflicted harm. To take the example given by Lord Oliver, would a mother be able to bring a claim against her son for psychiatric illness caused by witnessing his imperilment when he negligently walked in front of an oncoming car? His Lordship thought that if such a claim were

---

78   [1992] 1 A.C. 310 at 405.

denied, the denial had to be based on policy rather than logic, because it would be difficult to imagine a case in which the elements of foreseeability of psychiatric harm and proximity were more clearly established. Whilst declining expressly to decide the point, Lord Oliver suspected that liability in such a situation would be barred as a matter of policy, noting that this view had been expressed by Deane J in the Australian case of *Jaensch v Coffey*.[79]

The issue subsequently arose for consideration in the extraordinary case of *Greatorex v Greatorex*.[80] Here, the defendant, John Greatorex, had been out drinking with his friend and had then crashed his friend's car while driving on the wrong side of the road. He was trapped in the car, injured and unconscious, when the fire brigade arrived. By co-incidence, the leading fire-officer at the scene was Christopher Greatorex, the defendant's father. Christopher Greatorex suffered psychiatric illness as a result of witnessing his son's injuries, and so brought an action against his son. In denying the father's claim, Cazalet J reasoned that, since the defendant's injuries were self-inflicted, to make him liable to those who witnessed the injuries would be contrary to public policy. The policy consideration in question was that making a person liable in such a situation would restrict his or her right to self-determination—i.e. a person ought to be free to choose to incur personal risks, without exposing himself or herself to liability to others. (This point is considered further in the context of the Law Commission's proposals.) The issue was complicated by the fact that the claimant and defendant were father and son. On this point, Cazalet J thought that if such litigation were allowed, contrived and ill-founded claims might be used to prolong and aggravate family conflicts which might otherwise resolve themselves, causing needless family strife. Therefore, the law should only provide a remedy for psychiatric illness caused when a loved one is harmed by a defendant who is not a family member.

(4) The "sudden shock" requirement

4–030

Lord Ackner reaffirmed in *Alcock* that "'shock', in the context of this cause of action, involves the sudden appreciation by sight or sound of a horrifying event, which violently agitates the mind". It does not, his Lordship concluded, include psychiatric illness caused by the accumulation over a period of time of more gradual assault on the nervous system.[81] It is therefore the sudden psychological impact of witnessing a single event or its immediate aftermath which triggers the action, not trauma caused by subsequent reflection on an event,[82] or prolonged exposure to distressing circumstances. This requirement acts as a barrier to claims or, if you prefer, ensures that the floodgates are not opened to a multitude of claims.

---

79   (1984) 155 C.L.R. 549.
80   [2000] 1 W.L.R. 1970.
81   *Alcock v Chief Constable of South Yorkshire* [1992] 1 A.C. 310 at 401. Contrast with the position for primary victims described above.
82   Note, however, that in *W v Essex CC* [2001] 2 A.C. 592 (discussed later in this chapter) the House of Lords refused to say that a claim in such circumstances would be unarguable.

The application of the "sudden shock" requirement may be seen in *Sion v Hampstead Health Authority*.[83] The claimant, a father whose son had been injured in a motorcycle accident, had stayed by his son's bedside for 14 days, watching his son deteriorate, go into a coma and die. The Court of Appeal denied the father's claim, because his psychiatric illness had not resulted from the sudden appreciation of a horrifying event. (By the time the son died, his death was expected.) The decision of the Court of Appeal in *Walters v North Glamorgan NHS Trust* [84] seemed to indicate, however, a more generous approach to this requirement. Here, the claimant was a mother whose baby, following negligent treatment at a hospital, had suffered an epileptic fit leading to a coma and, some 36 hours later, his death in his mother's arms. The Court of Appeal was prepared to hold that the 36 hours during which the claimant had been subjected to trauma could be regarded as a single event for the purpose of satisfying the sudden shock requirement.

However, more recently, the Court of Appeal decision in *Liverpool Women's Hospital NHS Foundation Trust v Ronayne*[85] has indicated that *Walters* is the exception, with the "unusual feature" that the mother had witnessed at first hand the child's fit in circumstances in which she had not been prepared for this due to further incorrect medical advice. In *Ronayne*, a husband suffered psychiatric injury as a result of seeing his wife in a terrible state on two occasions following the hospital's negligence in performing a hysterectomy operation on his wife which led to emergency exploratory surgery. He had observed her connected to various machines such as drips and monitors and later, post-operation, unconscious and swollen in intensive care. The Court of Appeal took a strict view. The hospital had explained to the husband the nature of his wife's condition and what he saw was unpleasant but not "sudden". Neither was it horrifying, using an objective (not subjective) test which examines the reaction of a person of "ordinary robustness".[86] Patients in this condition would ordinarily have this appearance in the circumstances: "A visitor to a hospital is necessarily to a certain degree conditioned as to what to expect, and in the ordinary way it is also likely that due warning will be given by medical staff of an impending encounter likely to prove more than ordinarily distressing".[87] While this seems harsh, it does indicate that, despite criticism, the sudden shock requirement is here to stay. It also signifies that, in clinical negligence cases at least, it will now be difficult to succeed as a secondary victim.[88]

---

83 [1994] 5 Med. L.R. 170. See also *Wild v Southend University Hospital NHS Foundation Trust* [2014] EWHC 4053 (QB); [2016] P.I.Q.R. P3.

84 [2002] EWCA Civ 1792; [2003] P.I.Q.R. P16.

85 [2015] EWCA Civ 588; [2015] P.I.Q.R. P20. Followed in *Owers v Medway NHS Foundation Trust* [2015] EWHC 2363 (QB) and *Wells v University Hospital Southampton NHS Foundation Trust* [2015] EWHC 2376 (QB).

86 See also *Shorter v Surrey and Sussex HC NHS Trust* [2015] EWHC 614 (QB).

87 [2015] EWCA Civ 588 at [17] per Tomlinson LJ.

88 S. McKinley, "The difficulty of bringing claims for secondary victims in clinical negligence cases" [2018] JPI Law 105. She also notes that, in such cases, there will often be a delay between the negligent treatment and the damage caused to the primary victim rendering it difficult for secondary victims to meet the time and space requirement also.

The Impact of *White*

4-031

The limits of the decision in *Alcock* were also explored in *White v Chief Constable of South Yorkshire*. Here, as has been said, the plaintiffs were police officers who had suffered psychiatric illness as a result of their professional involvement in the Hillsborough disaster. Subsequent to the full height of the disaster, five of the six plaintiffs had assisted the injured and had worked to ensure that there was no further danger to those leaving the stadium. The sixth plaintiff had been on duty at a temporary mortuary which had been set up near the ground. None of the plaintiffs had been in physical danger. A majority of the Court of Appeal held that the five plaintiffs present at the stadium could recover in respect of their psychiatric illness.[89] This decision provoked outrage from the relatives of those killed and injured at Hillsborough, who had recently been refused compensation by the decision in *Alcock*. It was subsequently overturned by the House of Lords, which openly acknowledged the argument that the public would think it unacceptable to compensate police officers at the ground for psychiatric illness sustained simply in the course of doing their jobs, when compensation had been denied to the relatives in *Alcock*.

In the Court of Appeal, it was said that the police officers might be regarded as "primary victims" of the Chief Constable's negligence. This was because previous authority had suggested that the category of "primary victims" included plaintiffs who, though not in any physical danger, had *participated* in the events giving rise to their psychiatric illness. In *Alcock*, their Lordships had been content to divide psychiatric illness claimants into two broad categories—on the one hand, claimants who were *directly involved* in the accident ("primary victims") and, on the other hand, claimants who were only "passive and unwilling" witnesses of injury to others ("secondary victims"). By the time the Court of Appeal came to decide *White*, however, the House of Lords, in *Page v Smith*, appeared to have suggested that only claimants who had been in physical danger could be regarded as "primary victims". This, as Henry LJ recognised in the Court of Appeal, cast doubt on whether the police officers could be regarded as "primary victims".

The Court of Appeal thought, however, that even if there was doubt about their classification as "primary victims", special rules applied where a psychiatric illness claimant was a "rescuer" or an employee, holding that the officers in question were both. However, the House of Lords in *White* took a very different approach, holding that no special rules applied to "rescuers" or employees. The police officers did not qualify as "primary victims"—this classification was to be reserved for people who had been placed in physical danger (or who reasonably believed themselves to be in danger). All other psychiatric illness claimants were "secondary victims" and had to bring themselves within the *Alcock* criteria in order to succeed. On the facts, these criteria had obviously not been met, not least because none of the officers at the scene had a close relationship of love and affection with the dead and injured.

---

89   See *Frost v Chief Constable of South Yorkshire* [1998] Q.B. 254 (from which the appeal to the House of Lords in *White* was made).

Clearly, the decision in *White* has implications for the general law relating to employers' liability. It also appears to be contrary to the general attitude of the courts that rescuers should be treated generously. The decision in *White* also leaves unresolved the law relating to so-called "unwitting agents"—that is to say, claimants who, because of the defendant's negligence, are placed in a position where they themselves bring about the death, injury, or imperilment of the "immediate victim". Below, then, we consider the implications of *White* for three types of claimant:

- employees;

- unwitting agents; and

- rescuers.

The general law of employers' liability is considered in Ch.7, so discussion of it here is omitted. The general law on rescuers, however, is considered here in some detail.

(1) Employees

In *Dooley v Cammell Laird & Co Ltd*[90] (a case decided before *Alcock* and *White*), a crane driver was operating a crane at the docks where he worked when, through the fault of his employers, the sling connecting the load to the crane-hooks snapped, causing the load to fall into the hold of a ship where men were working. The crane driver suffered psychiatric illness, resulting from his fear that the falling load would injure or kill some of his fellow workmen. Donovan J, whilst drawing the inference that the men in the ship were friends of the plaintiff, was prepared to decide liability without requiring the plaintiff to establish any closer degree of relationship with the imperilled workers—the plaintiff's relationship of employment with the defendant created the necessary degree of "proximity" for his negligence action to succeed. Before the decision in *White*, it was thought that this case, and a number of similar decisions,[91] might have established that an employee had a right to recover for psychiatric illness caused by witnessing or fearing injury to fellow workers as a result of an employer's negligence.

In *White*, however, their Lordships held that no such independent right existed. An employer's duty to safeguard employees from psychiatric harm was no different from the general duty of care owed by all people to others whom their conduct might affect. It followed that in cases where an employee suffered psychiatric illness through witnessing the death, injury or imperilment of others, the ordinary rules of tort applied, namely those laid down in *Alcock*. Therefore, there was no advantage to be gained by the police officers framing their action as a case of

4-032

---

90   [1951] 1 Lloyd's Rep. 271.
91   See *Galt v British Railways Board* (1983) 133 N.L.J. 870; *Wigg v British Railways Board, The Times* 4 February 1986; *Mount Isa Mines Ltd v Pusey* (1970) 125 C.L.R 383.

employers' liability. Their Lordships found little assistance in *Dooley v Cammell Laird & Co Ltd* and similar decisions. Dealing with these cases, Lord Hoffmann said:

> "I think that, on a fair reading, they were each regarded by the judges who decided them as raising one question of fact, namely whether psychiatric illness to the plaintiff was a foreseeable consequence of the defendant's negligent conduct. This was in accordance with the law as it was thought to be at the time. There was no reference to the control mechanisms, which had not yet been invented."[92]

(2) "Unwitting agents"

4–033

Although *White* makes it clear that employees are not to be regarded as a special group of psychiatric illness claimants, what remains unclear is whether cases like *Dooley v Cammell Laird & Co Ltd*[93] are still good authority for a different proposition, namely that special treatment should be given to claimants who, because of a defendant's negligence, are placed in circumstances where they accidentally cause the death, injury or imperilment of another through no fault of their own (or reasonably think that they have done so). In *White*, Lord Hoffmann acknowledged that "there may be grounds for treating such a rare category of case as exceptional and exempt from the *Alcock* control mechanisms".[94]

In this context, the decision of the House of Lords in *W v Essex CC*[95] should be noted. Here, an action for psychiatric illness was brought by foster parents against a local authority. The foster parents, who had four young children of their own, had made it clear to the authority that they would not be willing to foster a child who had a history of carrying out sexual abuse. Nevertheless, the authority placed such a child in their care. It was alleged that the child had perpetrated acts of indecency against the claimants' children. The substance of the foster parents' claim was that their psychiatric illness had been caused, not just by discovering the abuse, but also by feelings of guilt that they, by being parties to a decision to bring their children into contact with a child abuser, had unwittingly *caused* harm to their children.

The local authority applied to have the claim struck out as disclosing no cause of action, but the House of Lords refused to do this. Lord Slynn, delivering the unanimous opinion of the House, thought that although the claimants might have difficulty in succeeding, their claim could not be said to be unarguable. His Lordship observed: ". . . the categorisation of those claiming to be included as primary or secondary victims is not as I read the cases finally closed".[96]

---

92 *White v Chief Constable of South Yorkshire* [1999] 2 A.C. 455 at 507.
93 [1951] 1 Lloyd's Rep. 271.
94 [1999] 2 A.C. 455 at 508.
95 [2000] 2 All E.R. 237.
96 [2001] 2 A.C. 592 at 601. See also *Monk v PC Harrington Ltd* [2008] EWHC 1879 (QB), where it was accepted in

(3) Rescuers

First, in this section, it is necessary to consider at some length the approach of the courts towards "rescuers" who suffer physical injury. This provides an understanding of the legal background against which the decision in *White* may seem controversial. We then go on to consider the implications of *White* for "rescuers" who suffer only psychiatric harm.

4-034

Rescuers who suffer physical injury

We have seen in Ch.2 that in English law there is generally no duty to go to the rescue of a person in peril. Here, we are considering a different point: if a person does go to the rescue of another, and suffers physical harm in attempting the rescue, can that person (the "rescuer") claim compensation from the defendant who negligently endangered the person being rescued?

4-035

In 1934, the courts answered this question in the affirmative, and they have done so ever since. The relevant case is *Haynes v Harwood*.[97] In Ch.2, we considered this case in the context of liability for creating a "source of danger" that is "sparked off" by the actions of a third party. Here, we consider it in a different context. The plaintiff was a police constable who was on duty inside a police station in a street where there were a large number of people, including children. The defendants had left their horses unattended in the street. A boy threw a stone at the horses and caused them to bolt ("sparking off" the danger). Seeing the defendants' horses coming down the street, the plaintiff rushed out of the police station and eventually stopped them, sustaining injuries in the process. The question for the Court of Appeal was whether, in the circumstances, physical harm to the plaintiff was reasonably foreseeable by the defendants. The court rejected arguments that rescuers were not, in effect, "foreseeable claimants", holding that a person who can reasonably foresee that his act or omission may imperil another will also be taken to foresee that it may imperil a rescuer. This idea is encapsulated by the well-known words of the US judge, Cardozo J, who, in *Wagner v International Railway Co*,[98] said: "Danger invites rescue. The cry of distress is a summons to relief".

Cardozo J's words were cited and approved by the Court of Appeal in *Baker v TE Hopkins and Son Ltd*,[99] a case which clearly illustrates the approach of the courts in this area. The defendant company was engaged to clean a well and used a petrol-driven pump to clear out the water. The defendant's managing director realised that this would create carbon monoxide fumes inside the well, which could be a danger to his employees. He therefore instructed them not to go down the well until the next day, by which time, he assumed, the fumes would

---

principle that providing assistance, in circumstances where the claimant reasonably believed he had caused the accident, could establish sufficient proximity in the absence of physical danger.

97   [1935] 1 K.B. 146.
98   232 N.Y. Rep. 176 at 180 (1921).
99   [1959] 1 W.L.R. 966.

have dispersed. In fact, when the employees went down the well the next morning, the danger had not passed. They were overcome by the fumes and eventually died. The plaintiff, who was a doctor, was summoned to the scene by concerned farm workers. People who had gathered at the top of the well urged him not to go down, and to wait for the arrival of the fire brigade, but he insisted, saying, "There are two men down there. I must see what I can do for them". Having tied a rope around his waist and asked the people at the top of the well to hold one end of it, and pull him up if he felt ill, he descended the well. He was heard to call up that there was nothing he could do for the men. He had started to climb up again when he was overcome by the fumes and collapsed. The people at the top tried to haul him up, but the rope became caught in a pipe or cross-member of the well and they were unable to raise him. Soon afterwards, the fire brigade arrived and the doctor was brought to the surface. He was unconscious and died before reaching hospital.

The doctor's estate succeeded in its claim. The Court of Appeal (as it had done in *Haynes v Harwood*) rejected the suggestion that a rescuer, by intervening, should be regarded as having caused his or her own loss, or as having voluntarily accepted the risk of injury. Willmer LJ made it clear that, provided the rescue attempt was not foolhardy or "wanton", the presence of a rescuer at the scene of an accident should be regarded as reasonably foreseeable. His Lordship cited with approval some additional words of Cardozo J in *Wagner v International Railway Co*:

> **"The risk of rescue, if only it be not wanton, is born of the occasion. The emergency begets the man. The wrongdoer may not have foreseen the coming of a deliverer. He is accountable as if he had."**

The courts, then, have taken the view that, as a matter of policy, rescue attempts should be encouraged and rewarded. This has led them to hold that a duty may be owed to a rescuer even in circumstances where no duty is owed to the person being rescued. Such was the case in *Videan v British Transport Commission*.[100] Here, a two-year-old boy, who, being the son of a village stationmaster, lived in a house adjoining the platform, strayed on to the railway track. The stationmaster saw his son standing on the track and at the same time saw a power-driven trolley approaching on the track at considerable speed. He signalled to the driver of the trolley to stop, but the driver did not understand the signals and did not see the child until it was too late to pull up. In a desperate effort to rescue his son, the stationmaster leapt from the platform on to the track in front of the trolley, and in so doing was killed. (The child, though saved by this act, suffered severe injuries.)

4–036

In an action by the stationmaster's widow in respect of the death of her husband and on behalf her injured son, the court found that the trolley driver had been careless. He had driven too fast in wet conditions and had failed to keep a proper look-out. The claim in respect of the child's

---

100 [1963] 2 Q.B. 650.

injuries failed, because, at the time the case was decided, only very limited duties were owed to trespassers. This, however, did not prevent a successful claim in respect of the *stationmaster's* death. Harman and Pearson LJJ based their decision on the fact that, because the stationmaster had a duty to rescue trespassers on the line (even though he was off duty at the time), his presence on the track dealing with an emergency was reasonably foreseeable by the trolley driver. Lord Denning MR went a stage further, however, holding that the position would have been the same if the rescuer had been a mere passer-by and not the stationmaster rescuing his son—a person who negligently created a situation of peril should answer for it to anyone who attempted a rescue, whether or not the *victim rescued* had a cause of action.

A number of additional points should be noted about rescuers. First, where a defendant negligently imperils *himself or herself*, as opposed to a third party, a rescuer who suffers *physical injury* will have a cause of action against the defendant,[101] although *Greatorex* suggests that this will not be the case where the rescuer suffers only psychiatric illness.[102] Secondly, it is clear that rescuers have a cause of action where what has been put in peril is not a person, but property. Thus, in *Haynes v Harwood*, it was accepted that the objects of the rescue were not only the people in the street who were endangered by the runaway horses, but the horses themselves. Similarly, in *Ogwo v Taylor*,[103] a fireman succeeded when he was injured trying to save the defendant's property from a fire. Where property is the object of the rescue, however, the question of whether it is reasonable for the rescuer to intervene and risk his own safety will have to be very carefully considered[104] (whereas, in the case of people, rescue attempts are normally regarded as reasonable, provided they are not reckless or "wanton"). Thirdly, the decision in *Ogwo v Taylor* confirmed that in English law there is no equivalent of the "firemen's rule" which applies in some parts of the US. This rule provides that, because members of the emergency services are employed to act as rescuers, defendants cannot be liable to them in respect of the very dangers they are paid to incur. In English law, however, (subject to the qualification that defendants are entitled to expect professional rescuers to use professional skill) professional rescuers are treated in the same way as public-spirited lay rescuers.

Rescuers who suffer only psychiatric harm

4-037

Prior to *White*, by way of an extension of their general approach to rescuers, the courts appeared to have developed a special approach to cases where rescuers suffered only psychiatric harm. The leading case here was *Chadwick v British Transport Commission*.[105] The case arose from the events of a serious train crash which occurred in December 1957 in Lewisham, South London.

---

101 *Harrison v British Railways Board* [1981] 3 All E.R. 679.
102 See *Greatorex v Greatorex* [2000] 1 W.L.R. 1970; the observations of Lord Oliver in *Alcock v Chief Constable of South Yorkshire* [1992] 1 A.C. 310 at 418 (discussed above); and Law Com.249 para.6.18 (discussed below).
103 [1998] A.C. 431.
104 See *Hyett v Great Western Railway* [1948] 1 K.B. 345.
105 [1967] 1 W.L.R. 912.

Mr Chadwick, who lived about 200 yards from the scene of the accident, went to the scene to do what he could to help, and worked all through the night giving assistance to the injured and dying. The key witness at the trial—a woman trapped in the wreckage who had been given an injection by Mr Chadwick at the request of a doctor, who was himself too large to enter the wrecked carriage—described the horrors of the tragedy to which Mr Chadwick had been exposed: there had been a "sea of bodies" and people had been screaming in pain and fear. Before the incident, Mr Chadwick had been a cheerful and active member of the local community and had run a successful window-cleaning business, but as a result of his involvement in the tragedy, he developed severe anxiety and neurosis. Waller J held that the defendants (who admitted the train collision was caused by their negligence) were liable for Mr Chadwick's psychiatric illness.

Before *White*, it was widely thought that the decision in *Chadwick* meant that rescuers were to be given special treatment for the purposes of psychiatric illness claims. In particular, they did not need to establish that they had been in physical danger to qualify as "primary victims". Certainly, this was the view taken by the Law Commission in March 1998, who expressed concern about aspects of the Court of Appeal's reasoning in *McFarlane v EE Caledonia* that might have suggested otherwise.[106] The majority of the Court of Appeal in *White* held that the police officers at the scene were entitled to recover for psychiatric illness as rescuers, even though they had not been in physical danger. By a bare 3:2 majority, however, the House of Lords disagreed. Whilst Lords Goff and Griffiths (dissenting) thought that rescuers were entitled to special treatment, the majority held that rescuers must either satisfy the "narrow" definition of "primary victims" (i.e. by being in physical danger) or must bring their claims as "secondary victims" and satisfy the *Alcock* criteria.

Lord Hoffmann gave two reasons why the law should not give special treatment to rescuers unless they had been placed in physical danger. The first was that, if the control mechanism of physical danger were removed, it would become difficult to define the concept of a "rescuer"—would the term then apply to a bystander who had rendered only some trivial assistance? The second (and in his Lordship's view more important) reason was that removing the control mechanism of physical danger would produce a result in *White* that would be "unacceptable", in the sense that it would offend against the ordinary person's notions of distributive justice. His Lordship said that the ordinary person:

> "... would think it wrong that policemen, even as part of a general class of persons who rendered assistance, should have the right to compensation for psychiatric injury out of public funds while the bereaved relatives are sent away with nothing."[107]

In *White*, then, the majority of the House of Lords distinguished *Chadwick* on its facts, saying that the situation of Mr Chadwick differed from the situation of the police officers at Hillsborough because Mr Chadwick, by entering wrecked train carriages, had been "within the range of fore-

---

106 See Law Com.249 para.7.3.
107 *White v Chief Constable of South Yorkshire* [1999] 2 A.C. 455 at 500.

seeable personal injury". This made him a "primary victim" (in the narrow *Page v Smith* sense). Lords Goff and Griffiths, however, disagreed with the majority about the ratio of *Chadwick*. Lord Goff pointed out that although Mr Chadwick had been exposed to some physical danger, "the trial judge [Waller J] treated that as irrelevant".[108] Lord Steyn, on the other hand (speaking with the majority), thought that the fact that Mr Chadwick had been exposed to personal danger had influenced Waller J's decision, albeit that his Lordship had not held that fear of personal injury was the *cause* of Mr Chadwick's psychiatric illness.[109] Lord Hoffmann was also prepared to take a restricted view of *Chadwick*, stating that the case could be subjected to an "ex post facto rationalisation"[110] and should be regarded as one turning on the presence of physical danger.

In his powerful dissenting speech, Lord Goff clearly stated that he regarded the reasoning of the majority as contrary to the existing authority of *Chadwick*, and noted that introducing what his Lordship saw as a new requirement that rescuers had to be in physical danger could produce very unjust results. His Lordship put forward an extreme example to illustrate the point[111]:

4-038

> "Suppose that there was a terrible train crash and that there were two Chadwick brothers living nearby, both of them small and agile window cleaners distinguished by their courage and humanity. Mr. A. Chadwick worked on the front half of the train, and Mr. B. Chadwick on the rear half. It so happened that, although there was some physical danger present in the front half of the train, there was none in the rear. Both worked for 12 hours or so bringing aid and comfort to the victims. Both suffered P.T.S.D. in consequence of the general horror of the situation. On the new control mechanism now proposed, Mr. A. would recover but Mr. B. would not. To make things worse, the same conclusion must follow even if Mr. A. was unaware of the existence of the physical danger present in his half of the train. This is surely unacceptable."

Despite Lord Goff's objection, the decision of the majority of the House of Lords in *White* has effectively closed the door on future claims by rescuers who have not been placed in physical peril.[112] It remains to be seen, however, whether, in line with their general approach to rescue cases, the courts will adopt a liberal interpretation of this requirement in order to do justice in meritorious cases. In this context, it is interesting to note the (possible) combined effect of

---

108 [1999] 2 A.C. 455 at 484.
109 [1999] 2 A.C. 455 at 499.
110 [1999] 2 A.C. 455 at 509.
111 [1999] 2 A.C. 455 at 487.
112 Thus, the fireman father in *Greatorex v Greatorex* [2000] 1 W.L.R. 1970, although a rescuer, could not succeed as a primary victim because he was not in physical danger.

the decisions in *White* and *Page v Smith*. This is that if rescuers in physical peril are now to be regarded as "primary victims" (in the narrow *Page v Smith* sense), they may be able to take advantage of the "eggshell skull" reasoning in *Page v Smith* to establish a duty of care. Thus (arguably) in a case like *Chadwick*, provided it could be shown that some very minor personal injury to the claimant was reasonably foreseeable, the law would then proceed to regard personal injury and psychiatric injury as the same kind of damage. *Page v Smith* reasoning would then apply, so that the claimant could recover even if he or she were "peculiarly susceptible" to psychiatric illness. This consequence of their Lordship's interpretation of *Chadwick* has the effect of *widening* the scope of liability to rescuers for psychiatric illness—a point that does not appear to have been specifically addressed in *White*.[113]

Psychiatric Illness Law: Proposals for Reform

4-039 In March 1998, the Law Commission published a report which recommended some important changes to the law.[114] In summary, the report concluded that, in relation to secondary victims, whilst the "control mechanism" of "close ties of love and affection" should remain, all of the other *Alcock* "control mechanisms" should be abolished. The Law Commission expressed the view that, with the decision in *Alcock*, the common law had in some respects "taken a wrong turn".[115] The Commission did not think it appropriate, however, to codify *all* of the common law on psychiatric illness—this was not a sensible option, because the flexibility of the common law would allow new areas of liability to develop incrementally, as experts learned more about psychiatric illness, and society further recognised its debilitating consequences. Therefore, the Commission proposed a strategy of minimal legislative intervention to modify and clarify the common law. A draft Bill forms part of the Law Commission's report. With the help of consultants from the insurance industry, the Commission was able to estimate (very roughly and in relation to motor vehicle insurance only) that its proposals to expand the scope of liability might lead to an increase in insurance premiums of between 2 and 5%.[116]

The most radical proposal, then, is that three of the *Alcock* "control mechanisms" should be abolished. Thus, it would no longer be necessary for secondary victims to show proximity to the accident in time and space,[117] or that they had perceived the accident or its aftermath

---

113 Although it is alluded to by Lord Goff at 479–480.

114 "Liability for Psychiatric Illness" Law Com.249 (available from *https://www.lawcom.gov.uk/project/liability-for-psychiatric-illness/* [Accessed 1 August 2020]. Compare the more recent report of the Scottish Law Commission No.196, "Damages for Psychiatric Injury" (2004) (discussed by D. Nolan (2005) 68 M.L.R. 983, who argues that the flexibility it envisages is a recipe for uncertainty.)

115 "Liability for Psychiatric Illness" Law Com.249 para.4.2.

116 "Liability for Psychiatric Illness" Law Com.249 para.1.13.

117 "Liability for Psychiatric Illness" Law Com.249 para.6.12, the report cites *Taylor v Somerset Health Authority*

by their "own unaided senses". This would mean that, provided they could show closeness of relationship with the "immediate victim" (see below), people in the position of the plaintiffs in *Alcock* would be able to succeed, as would claimants whose psychiatric illness resulted from merely being *told* about the accident. The requirement that the claimant's psychiatric illness must be produced by a "sudden shock" would also be abolished. This would allow recovery, for example, by a long-term carer who developed psychiatric illness because of the emotional strain of looking after the victim of the defendant's negligence.

"Close ties of love and affection": the "fixed list"

In deciding to retain the requirement of "close ties of love and affection" between a secondary victim and the immediate victim, the Commission noted that policy considerations dictated limits to recovery by secondary victims and felt that the requirement operated as an appropriate control mechanism. It thought, however, that in *Alcock* the requirement had been too narrowly drawn. Under its proposals, therefore, the *rebuttable* common law presumptions governing spouses, parents and children would be replaced with *conclusive* statutory presumptions in respect of a wider class of relationships. Thus, there would be a statutory "fixed list" of relationships in which close ties of love and affection would be deemed to exist.[118] These relationships would be: parent, child, sibling, spouse, and cohabitant (whether heterosexual or homosexual) for a period of two or more years. (Thus, the list is wider than the categories of presumed close relationships in *Alcock*, because it includes siblings and cohabitants.) Persons outside the "fixed list" would remain in the hands of the common law. Thus, they would not be barred from making a claim, but would be required to establish the necessary ties of love and affection by evidence. (In this context, the Commission thought that the class of potential claimants might extend to non-relatives who could establish a "relationship of care"—such as might exist between a schoolteacher and a pupil.) The Commission saw no need for legislation relating to mere "bystanders", leaving their position to the common law (so the reasoning in *McFarlane v E.E. Caledonia* would probably prevent them recovering).

The Commission also recommended that legislation should provide that the requirement of a close relationship could be satisfied by the existence of such a relationship either at the time of the accident, *or* at the onset of the claimant's psychiatric illness. This provision would be necessary to accommodate, for example, the case of a carer who, whilst having no ties of love and affection with the victim at the time of the accident, subsequently developed such ties in the course of looking after the victim, and suffered psychiatric illness as a result of this task.

(1993) 4 Med. L.R. 34 and *Taylorson v Shieldness Produce Ltd* [1994] P.I.Q.R. P329 as examples where the requirement has produced unjust results.

118   Note, however, as the report points out (at para.6.25), it would still be open to the court to hold that the absence of a de facto close relationship meant that psychiatric illness to the claimant was not reasonably foreseeable, as, e.g. where a mother, who had abandoned her son at birth, suffered psychiatric illness on reading about his death in a newspaper many years later.

The "just and reasonable" proviso

4-041

The report points out that the duty of care owed by a defendant to a secondary victim is an independent duty—its existence does not depend on a duty of care being owed to the immediate victim. (For example, where the immediate "victim" is placed in danger but not actually injured, there may be no tort committed against him or her.) The Law Commission recognised, however, that in certain circumstances it might be undesirable to impose liability on a defendant towards a secondary victim if the defendant would not be liable to the immediate victim (for example because the immediate victim had consented to the risk of injury). To accommodate such circumstances, the Commission proposed a legislative provision stating that defendants should not be liable to secondary victims in cases where the court considers that such liability would not be "just and reasonable".

Such a provision would also cover situations where the immediate victim was the defendant—in other words, where the defendant had injured or imperilled himself or herself, causing a secondary victim psychiatric illness. We have seen that, in *Alcock*, Lord Oliver thought that policy considerations would probably preclude the liability of such a defendant, and that in *Greatorex v Greatorex* such considerations formed part of the reasoning in denying liability. The Law Commission, however, thought that there was no good reason why, generally speaking, a defendant who injured or imperilled himself or herself should not owe a duty of care to others. The Commission was conscious, however, that the imposition of such a duty in all circumstances might severely restrict a person's right to self-determination. For example, it would mean that a person could not, without exposing himself or herself to potential liability, choose to engage in a dangerous sport, or refuse medical treatment for religious reasons. The Commission noted:

> **"there is a difficult balance to be arrived at between respecting self-determination and requiring proper concern to be shown for the consequences for others of choosing to harm or incur the risk of harm to oneself."[119]**

Regarding this as a matter for the courts, it proposed that, whilst the absolute bar to liability in such cases (if it existed) should be removed, the imposition of a duty should be qualified by a requirement that it must be "just and reasonable" in the circumstances.

The "actual danger" proviso

4-042

The Law Commission noted that whilst it was not in doubt that, under existing law, a secondary victim who satisfied the *Alcock* criteria would be able to recover where the immediate victim had been *placed in danger* but had not actually been *injured*, some doubt existed as to

---

119   Law Com.249 para.5.42.

whether a secondary victim could recover in a situation where he or she *reasonably believed* that the "victim" was in danger, whereas, as a matter of fact, he or she was not. The Commission thought that, if liability were allowed in such a situation, "the policy against opening the floodgates of litigation would be undermined".[120] It therefore proposed that "legislation should draw the line at where the loved one has in fact been killed, injured or imperilled by the defendant". Thus, to take the Law Commission's example,[121] there would be no liability in a situation where a wife suffers psychiatric illness after watching evening news reports of a train crash, believing that her husband is on the train, when, in fact, he has been delayed at work and taken a later train, arriving home safely that night.

Defences

Finally, it should be noted that the Law Commission's proposals would preserve certain defences.[122] Thus, there would be no liability to a secondary victim who had voluntarily assumed the risk of suffering psychiatric illness, or in relation to whom a defendant had excluded his or her duty not to cause psychiatric illness (for example by a contract term[123]), or in situations where it would be unjust to allow the secondary victim to recover because he or she was involved in conduct that was illegal or contrary to public policy.

4-043

Liability for psychiatric illness: conclusion

Clearly, the law on psychiatric illness, like the law on pure economic loss, suffers from a lack of coherence. It is an emotionally charged area of liability which raises acute moral problems. The rules developed in *Alcock* and *White* seem to deny liability to many genuinely deserving claimants. Moreover, the application of those rules compounds the moral dilemma. As Lord Hoffmann noted in *Alcock* (echoing the views of the Law Commission)[124]:

4-044

> ". . . the spectacle of a plaintiff who has, ex hypothesi, suffered psychiatric illness in consequence of his brother's death or injury, being cross-examined on the closeness of their ties of love and affection and then perhaps contradicted by the evidence of a private investigator, might not be to everyone's taste."[125]

---

120 Law Com.249 para.6.18.
121 Law Com.249 para.6.69.
122 Law Com.249 para.6.42.
123 Unfair Contract Terms Act 1977 s.2(1) prohibits the valid exclusion of negligence liability for personal injury and death where the liability in question is "business liability". For consumers, see the Consumer Rights Act 2015, s. 65.
124 Law Com.249 para.6.24.
125 *Alcock v Chief Constable of South Yorkshire* [1992] 1 A.C. 310 at 503. See also J. Stapleton, "In Restraint of Tort" in *The Frontiers of Liability* (1994) Vol.2 p.84, who says that a mother who suffers psychiatric illness after finding

It is the prospect of such an undignified spectacle, of course, which led the Law Commission to recommend replacing the rebuttable common law presumptions of close ties of love and affection with conclusive presumptions in statutory form.

In conclusion, we can do little more than endorse the sentiments of Lord Oliver, who stated in *Alcock*: ". . . I cannot, for my part, regard the present state of the law as either entirely satisfactory or as logically defensible". After acknowledging that the answers in this area of the law were to be found "not in logic but in policy", his Lordship concluded that the relevant policy considerations would be "much better accommodated if the rights of persons injured in this way were to be enshrined in and limited by legislation".[126] Unfortunately, however, it seems unlikely that this will happen in the near future. A Government consultation paper was issued in May 2007, in the response to the Law Commission's report.[127] The response to this consultation, published in July 2009, concluded:

> "On balance the Government continues to take the view that it is preferable for the courts to have the flexibility to continue to develop the law rather than attempt to impose a statutory solution."[128]

Such a view may be contrasted, however, with that of the Court of Appeal in the 2013 case of *Taylor v A Novo (UK) Ltd*.[129] The court argued that it was not for the courts to make any substantial development of the principles relating to primary and secondary victims and that this should be left to Parliament subject to modest development by the courts.[130] It would seem, therefore, that despite the concerns of the government and the courts, neither party is currently prepared to undertake the major reforms needed in this area of law. The best we can expect is 'modest' development by the courts.

---

her child's mangled body in a mortuary "might wonder why the law rules her child's blood too dry to found an action".

126 *Alcock v Chief Constable of South Yorkshire* [1992] 1 A.C. 310 at 418 and 419.

127 Government Consultation Paper, The Law of Damages, CP 09/07 (May 2007), Ch.3 para.97.

128 Ministry of Justice, *The Law of Damages: Response to Consultation* CP9 (R) 9/7, 1 July 2009. An attempt was made in October 2015 to introduce a Private Member's bill (the Negligence and Damages Bill 2015–2016) of which the first part sought to amend the law based on the draft provisions prepared by the Law Commission. The Bill aimed to both lower the threshold required to claim compensation successfully for psychological harm and widen the categories of people who could bring such a claim. It ran, however, out of Parliamentary time after the first reading.

129 [2013] EWCA Civ 194; [2013] P.I.Q.R. P15.

130 [2013] EWCA Civ 194 at [24] per Lord Dyson MR.

5

Negligence: Breach of Duty

Introduction

5–001

Once it has been established that the defendant owes the claimant a duty of care, it must next be established that the defendant has breached that duty. In practical terms, breach of duty is the most important element of the tort of negligence, because in everyday cases the existence of a duty of care and questions of causation and remoteness are rarely in issue.

Establishing breach of duty involves showing that the defendant's conduct has fallen below the *standard of care* required in all the circumstances. The standard set by the law is one of "reasonableness". The flexibility inherent in the concept of "reasonableness" is necessary to accommodate the infinite variety of cases that may arise. Thus, for example, the law says that motorists must drive with "reasonable care in all the circumstances" because it cannot possibly prescribe the precise speed at which motorists must drive in each and every possible set of road conditions. In the case of driving, of course, the law makes some attempt to reduce the requirement of "reasonableness" into a set of concrete "rules"—in the form of speed limits and the rules of the Highway Code—but generally speaking the courts have resisted attempts to boil down the requirement of "reasonableness" into a series of precise and definite obligations. Decisions in individual cases as to what amounts to "reasonable conduct" are regarded only as useful guides. To treat them otherwise would introduce a rigidity into the law that might produce injustice.

In this chapter, then, we are not concerned with learning a multiplicity of specific "rules" about what defendants must or must not do in various sets of circumstances. Although it is possible to enumerate a great number of fairly definite "rules" about what the law considers "reasonable" in specific situations (for example, when driving, looking after another's property, or carrying passengers on a ship), it is not usual to consider all of these rules in a book of this kind. The only specific obligations we do consider are those owed by an employer to an employee (see Ch.7) and by an occupier to persons on his or her premises (see Ch.8). This chapter deals with the *general principles* the courts employ in setting the standard of care.

It begins by exploring these principles. It then discusses the extent to which the law expects special standards of care from special categories of defendant (for example from children, or professionals). Finally, it considers the problem of *proving* breach of duty.

The "reasonable person"

5–002

The law's starting point in deciding breach of duty is to judge the defendant's conduct by the standard of the hypothetical "reasonable person" (in older cases referred to as the "reasonable man").[1] The most famous example of the "reasonable person" being used to define the standard of care comes from the judgment of Alderson B in *Blyth v Birmingham Waterworks Co.*[2] His Lordship said:

> **"Negligence is the omission to do something which a reasonable man, guided upon those considerations which ordinarily regulate the conduct of human affairs, would do, or doing something which a prudent and reasonable man would not do."**

Two important points must be noted about the standard of the "reasonable person":

- The standard is objective.

- The standard does not always reflect "average" behaviour.

The standard of care is objective

5–003

The first point to note, then, is that the decision whether the defendant has behaved like a "reasonable person" is an objective one. That is to say, the question for the court is not: "What could we have expected *this particular defendant* to do in the circumstances?" Rather, the question is: "What could we expect a "reasonable person' to do?" Thus, a defendant who is unusually clumsy or absent-minded cannot succeed by arguing that his or her conduct amounts to an "incompetent best". The defendant will be judged according to the best efforts of the hypothetical "reasonable person".

---

1 The focus on the "reasonable man" has received criticism from feminist critics, who argue that it embodies a male point of view or, more generally, permits an unrepresentative judiciary to set standards and that more is needed to achieve a truly objective standard: see, e.g. M. Mayo, *Rethinking the Reasonable Person* (OUP, 2003) and J. Miola, "The Standard of Care in Medical Negligence—Still Reasonably Troublesome?" in J. Richardson and E. Rackley, *Feminist Perspectives on Tort Law* (Routledge, 2012). See also J. Gardner, "The many faces of the reasonable person" (2015) 131 L.Q.R. 563.
2 (1856) 11 Ex. 781 at 784.

The objective nature of the "reasonable person" test was explained by Lord Macmillan in *Glasgow Corp v Muir*.[3] Here, the manageress of the defendants' tea-room, to which access was obtained by way of a small shop, gave a picnic party permission to use the tea-room when rain prevented them from eating their food outside. She allowed two members of the party to carry a tea urn through the shop. Despite taking all due care, one of the carriers let go of the urn, so that tea was spilt, severely scalding several children who were buying sweets at the counter of the shop. The plaintiffs argued that the manageress had been negligent in giving permission for the tea urn to be brought in without first clearing the children out of the shop. On the facts, the defendants were not liable, because the risk of injury was not so high that a reasonable person would have done this in the circumstances. Dealing with the "reasonable person" standard, Lord Macmillan said:

> **"The standard of foresight of the reasonable man is in one sense an impersonal test. It eliminates the personal equation and is independent of the idiosyncrasies of the particular person whose conduct is in question. Some persons are by nature unduly timorous and imagine every path beset with lions; others, of more robust temperament, fail to foresee or nonchalantly disregard even the most obvious dangers. The reasonable man is presumed to be free both from over-apprehension and from over-confidence."[4]**

His Lordship conceded, however, that the test for breach of duty does contain a certain subjective element. This is because the question for the court is: what would the reasonable person have done in the defendant's circumstances? However, although the defendant's conduct must be judged in the light of "all the circumstances of the case", it is important to distinguish between, on the one hand, external circumstances (for example, the defendant was acting in an emergency) and, on the other hand, "circumstances" which are personal characteristics of the particular defendant (for example, the defendant's "circumstances" were that he or she happened to be a novice). Whilst the law will adapt the standard of care to take account of external circumstances, it will not, generally speaking, take account of the defendant's personal characteristics.

The case of *Nettleship v Weston*[5] provides perhaps the most famous illustration of the objective standard of care. The defendant was a learner driver. The plaintiff, a family friend, had agreed to give her driving lessons. On her third lesson, when the car was moving very slowly,

---

3   [1943] 2 A.C. 448.

4   [1943] 2 A.C. 448 at 457. See *Dunnage v Randall* [2015] EWCA Civ 673; [2016] Q.B. 639: objective test applied regardless of physical or mental health problems. Only defendants whose medical incapacity had the effect of entirely eliminating any fault or responsibility could be excused. As Arden LJ commented at [153], "The objective standard of care reflects the policy of the law. It is not a question of the law discriminating unfairly against people with physical or mental illness. The law takes the view as a matter of policy that everyone should owe the same duty of care for the protection of innocent victims".

5   [1971] 2 Q.B. 691.

with the plaintiff moving the gear lever and the defendant steering, the defendant panicked. The car mounted the pavement and struck a lamp-post, causing the plaintiff to suffer a broken knee cap. He sued the defendant for personal injury.

The Court of Appeal held the defendant liable. The majority of the court held that her conduct was not to be judged, as she argued, by the standard of a learner driver, but by the standard of a reasonably competent and experienced one. Lord Denning MR stated that, although the defendant was not *morally* at fault, she should be regarded as *legally* at fault. Since she was legally required to be insured, it made sense that she should bear the risk of her driving. Megaw LJ pointed out that, once the law accepted the principle that the standard of care could be varied according to the experience of the particular defendant, it would be logically impossible to confine application of the principle to cases of driving. This would mean that in every negligence case, the court would be obliged to hear evidence about the level of competence to be expected of a reasonable person with the same level of experience as the defendant. Such an exercise would be costly and time-consuming and would undoubtedly produce unpredictability and uncertainty in the law. His Lordship concluded, therefore, that "the certainty of a general standard is preferable to the vagaries of a fluctuating standard".[6]

The standard of care is a "hypothetical", not an "average" standard

5–004

Although the "reasonable person" is sometimes personified as the "man on the Clapham omnibus",[7] or the "man on the Underground",[8] it is important to appreciate that the standard of care the law requires is sometimes a poor reflection of the standard such a man would probably, in fact, exercise. Whilst evidence of the fact that most people behave in a certain way may, in appropriate cases, be relevant in setting the legal standard of care, the law will not always regard such evidence as conclusive. This is because there are situations where, as a matter of policy, high standards of care are imposed for the purpose of shifting losses on to defendants, with little regard for fault. In such cases, the idea of fault is subordinated to the objectives of compensation and loss distribution, discussed in Ch.1. Below, we discuss how this is achieved in the context of road traffic accidents, but the reader should also consider the issue in the context of the high standards of care required of employers, discussed in Ch.7.

Because the "reasonable person" is a mythical judicial creation, then, he or she may sometimes be credited with a level of skill and prudence that is seldom attainable in the real world. The Pearson Commission, which in 1978 reported on civil liability for personal injury, noted:

"Even good drivers make mistakes. A study by the World Health Organisation in 1962 found that a good driver makes a mistake every

6   [1971] 2 Q.B. 691 at 707.
7   per Greer LJ in *Hall v Brooklands Auto Racing Club* [1933] 1 K.B. 205 at 224.
8   per Lord Steyn in *White v Chief Constable of South Yorkshire* [1999] 2 A.C. 455 at 495.

> **two miles; and an American study in 1964 suggested that on average a good driver makes nine mistakes every five minutes."**[9]

Yet, many of the "mistakes" good drivers make are regarded by the law as conduct falling below the standard expected of a "reasonable driver". This means, in effect, that the standard of care in relation to driving is so high that in certain situations there is almost strict liability (liability without fault) for driving. The reason why this is so has partly to do with historical accident (the rules on driving were developed when many fewer cars were on the roads), but it also has to do with particular policy considerations which apply in road traffic cases. The most important goal of tort law in the context of driving accidents is to provide compensation for victims. The issue of fault, therefore, is subordinated to achieving this goal. As was noted in Ch.1, the law is assisted in this regard by the availability of third party insurance, which is compulsory for motorists.

It should be noted, however, that whilst the standard of care in relation to driving is very high, the courts have stopped short of holding that liability for driving is entirely divorced from fault. In *Mansfield v Weetabix Ltd*,[10] the Court of Appeal held that a driver who becomes unable to control a vehicle will not be liable for damage caused by his or her loss of control if the driver is unaware (and should not reasonably have been aware) of a disabling condition from which he or she is suffering, which suddenly manifests itself, causing the loss of control. Prior to this decision, Neill J had held, in *Roberts v Ramsbottom*,[11] that a driver who suffered a stroke at the wheel remained liable and suggested that this would be so even if the driver had been unaware that he had a medical condition likely to lead to a loss of control. In *Mansfield v Weetabix Ltd*, however, the Court of Appeal held that *Roberts v Ramsbottom* was wrongly decided on this point, although the decision could be supported on the alternative ground that the defendant had carried on driving when he felt strange and ought to have known that he was probably unfit to drive. In *Dunnage v Randall*,[12] Arden LJ drew a distinction between the situation in *Mansfield* where a driver had got into his car or lorry cab mentally and physically fit for the journey, but then experienced an unforeseen episode during the journey which caused him to lose control of the vehicle, and the situation where a mentally ill person acted irrationally injuring another where the objective standard of care would apply. In *Dunnage*, the defendant was suffering from florid paranoid schizophrenia when he set himself on fire with petrol. The claimant (his nephew) suffered serious burns to his face and body in trying to put out the fire. The court held that only defendants whose medical incapacity has the effect of entirely eliminating any fault or responsibility for the injury can be excused.[13] The actions of a defendant, who is merely

---

9   Report of the Royal Commission on Civil Liability and Compensation for Personal Injury, Vol.1 Ch.18 para.983.

10   [1998] 1 W.L.R. 1263. Compare *C (A Child) v Burcome* [2003] C.L.Y. 3030 (liability imposed where a 70-year-old driver with a heart condition had been advised not to engage in strenuous activity, but continued to drive after pulling in to change a wheel).

11   [1980] 1 All E.R. 7.

12   [2015] EWCA Civ 673; [2016] Q.B. 639.

13   e.g. actions done in a state of automatism or while sleepwalking.

impaired by medical problems, whether physical or mental, cannot escape liability if he causes injury by failing to exercise reasonable care.[14] Here, it was not enough that the defendant was acting irrationally, he was still aware of the nature and quality of his actions and his disease did not excuse him from needing to take the care of a reasonable man.

Now that we are familiar with the standard of the "reasonable person", it is appropriate to explore the various factors which the courts take into account in deciding whether this standard has been met.

Factors Relevant to the Standard of Care

5–005

The relevant factors can be stated as follows:

- foreseeability of harm;

- magnitude of the risk;

- burden of taking precautions;

- utility of the defendant's conduct; and

- common practice.

Below, we consider each of these in turn. We then look at how some of them may be considered together in a quasi-mathematical way, using what is known as the "Learned Hand test".

Foreseeability of harm

5–006

If the particular harm the claimant suffers is not foreseeable, the defendant will not be liable. This is because, rather obviously, the "reasonable person" cannot be expected to take any precautions against unforeseeable risks. The point is illustrated by the decision of the Court of Appeal in *Roe v Ministry of Health*.[15] In 1947, the plaintiff went into hospital for a minor operation. He suffered permanent paralysis as a result of being given a spinal anaesthetic which was contaminated with phenol. The contamination had occurred when glass ampoules containing the anaesthetic had been stored in the phenol, which was used as a disinfectant,

---

14   [2015] EWCA Civ 673 at [131] per Vos LJ.
15   [1954] 2 Q.B. 66.

and the phenol had seeped through invisible cracks in the glass. At the time, it was not known that contamination could occur in this way. The action came to trial in 1954, by which time the dangers had become known. The defendants were not liable. Denning LJ made the point that, although in 1954 it would be regarded as negligent to store anaesthetic in phenol, the court "must not look at the 1947 accident with 1954 spectacles".[16]

Whilst the defendant will escape liability where the risk is unforeseeable, it does not follow that he or she will automatically be liable for all risks that are foreseeable. The law insists that a risk must be *reasonably* foreseeable before making a defendant liable. This point is explored below.

The magnitude of the risk

The "reasonable person" does not take precautions against risks that are very small. Assessing the "magnitude" of any risk involves consideration of two factors. First, there is the likelihood that harm will occur. Secondly, there is the question of how serious the consequences will be if harm *does* occur.

5–007

(1) The likelihood of harm

In *Bolton v Stone*,[17] the plaintiff, who was standing outside her house on a quiet street, was hit by a cricket ball which came from a nearby cricket ground. It was clear that the defendant cricketers could have foreseen that a ball might be hit out of the ground, because this had happened before, but it was a very rare occurrence. The evidence established that cricket balls had been hit out of the ground on about six occasions in the previous 30 years. There was a fence around the ground, which was seven feet high and, due to the slope of the ground, the top of the fence was some 17 feet above the level of the pitch. The fence was some 80 yards away from where the batsman stood. The House of Lords held that, in these circumstances, the chance of an injury occurring to someone who was standing in the position of the plaintiff was so slight that the defendants were not negligent in continuing to play cricket without taking additional precautions. Lord Oaksey said that:

5–008

> ". . . an ordinarily careful man does not take precautions against every foreseeable risk. He can, of course, foresee the possibility of many risks, but life would be almost impossible if he were to attempt to take precautions against every risk which he can foresee."[18]

---

16   [1954] 2 Q.B. 66 at 84.
17   [1951] A.C. 850.
18   [1951] A.C. 850 at 863. See also *Whippey v Jones* [2009] EWCA Civ 452 per Aikens LJ at [16] (standard of care of dog owner).

Similarly, Lord Radcliffe thought that a reasonable person, taking account of the chances against such an accident occurring, "would have done what the appellants did: in other words, he would have done nothing".[19]

It is useful to compare *Bolton v Stone* with the decision of Ashworth J in *Hilder v Associated Portland Cement Manufacturers Ltd*.[20] Here, the defendants were the occupiers of some grassland on which they permitted some small boys to play football. One of the boys kicked the ball over a low wall into the adjoining road where it caused the plaintiff, a passing motorcyclist, to fall off his motorbike and suffer fatal injuries. The defendants were held liable. Because the risk of injury to a road user was much greater than the risk in *Bolton v Stone*—the land was only some 15 yards from the road—it was not a risk that the reasonable person would have disregarded.

In *Haley v London Electricity Board*,[21] the House of Lords was presented with detailed statistical evidence about the likelihood of harm occurring. The plaintiff, who was blind, fell into a hole in the pavement that had been dug by the defendants. As a result of the fall he became deaf. The precautions taken to guard the hole were sufficient for sighted people but were insufficient for the blind. Their Lordships considered evidence relating to the number of blind people who lived in the same London borough as the plaintiff and concluded that the likelihood of a blind person falling into the hole was not so small that the defendants could ignore it. The case is authority for the proposition that the reasonable person must tailor his conduct in the light of the characteristics of the people whom he knows it might affect. Thus (as we shall see in Ch.7), a defendant employer has been held liable for causing psychiatric illness to an employee whom he ought to have known was likely to suffer a nervous breakdown,[22] but in other cases, where the risk of psychiatric illness to the particular employee could not reasonably have been known, employers have escaped liability.

(2) The seriousness of the consequences

5-009

The decision in *Bolton v Stone* does not mean that a reasonable person is always justified in ignoring a very small risk. The risk of harm materialising must be weighed against other factors, including the seriousness of the consequences if the harm does materialise. The more serious the consequences, the greater the obligations of the defendant. This point is neatly illustrated by the decision in *Paris v Stepney BC*.[23] The plaintiff, who was blind in one eye, was employed by the defendants in a garage. One day he was called upon to dismantle the chassis

---

19 [1951] A.C. 850 at 869.
20 [1961] 1 W.L.R. 1434. *Bolton v Stone* was applied, e.g. in *Zucchi v Waitrose Ltd* 2000 WL 345171 (30 March 2000) where the risk of customers being injured by a collapsing stack of plastic bottles was so small that the store had acted reasonably in disregarding it.
21 [1965] A.C. 778.
22 *Walker v Northumberland CC* [1995] 1 All E.R. 737.
23 [1951] A.C. 367.

of a large vehicle and had to use a hammer to knock out a rusty bolt. A fragment of metal came off the bolt and hit him in his good eye, causing him to become totally blind. The risk of such an injury occurring was extremely small and did not justify the use of goggles by ordinary workers. Nevertheless, a majority of the House of Lords held that the defendants were liable for failing to provide this particular worker with goggles, knowing that he might suffer such serious consequences if the small risk materialised.

The burden of taking precautions

The court will take account of the cost and practicality of taking precautions against a risk. If the burden of taking steps to eliminate a risk is far greater than the benefit obtained by its elimination, then failure to take those steps will not generally amount to negligence. Thus, one factor which influenced the House of Lords in deciding *Bolton v Stone* was that the only practical way the defendant cricketers could have prevented balls from going out of the ground would have been to erect an extremely high fence—wind conditions made this very difficult, if not impossible. Alternatively, they could simply have stopped playing cricket. In either case, taking precautions against the risk would have placed a burden on the defendants that was out of all proportion to the risk the precautions would avoid.

5–010

The case most often cited in this context is *Latimer v AEC Ltd.*[24] Here, the floor of the defendants' factory was flooded by an exceptionally heavy rainstorm. As a result, an oily cooling mixture, which was normally contained in a channel in the floor, mixed with the flood waters. When the flood subsided, the floor was left in a slippery state. The defendants spread sawdust on the floor, but did not have enough sawdust to go around, so some areas were left untreated. The plaintiff, who was working in an area which had not been treated with sawdust, was attempting to load a heavy barrel on to a trolley when he slipped and injured his ankle. The House of Lords held that the defendants had not been negligent. They had done all that reasonable employers could be expected to do for the safety of their workers. The only way the defendants could have eliminated the risk entirely would have been to close the factory, and this would have been a precaution out of all proportion to the risk in question.

It is useful to compare *Bolton* and *Latimer* with the decision of the Privy Council in *The Wagon Mound (No.2).*[25] Here, the defendants negligently discharged a quantity of furnace oil into the sea. The evidence in the case established that there was an extremely small risk that the oil might ignite in very unusual circumstances. (These circumstances are explained in Ch.6, because the incident also gave rise to another case—*The Wagon Mound (No.1)*—which is the leading authority on remoteness of damage.) The oil ignited, causing damage to the plaintiffs' ships. The defendants argued that, because the risk of damage was very small, they were justified in disregarding it. The Privy Council was unimpressed by this argument. The burden of eliminating the risk in this case was minimal—all the defendants had to do was ensure that

---

24   [1953] A.C. 643.
25   *Overseas Tankship (UK) v Miller Steamship Co Pty Ltd, The Wagon Mound (No.2)* [1967] 1 A.C. 617.

the oil did not discharge into the harbour by keeping a tap turned off. Their Lordships pointed out that a reasonable person would not ignore even a very small risk "if action to eliminate it presented no difficulty, involved no disadvantage and required no expense".[26] In *The Wagon Mound (No.2)*, it was also relevant to a finding of liability that the defendants, in discharging the oil, were not doing anything worthwhile—they were committing an act of pollution. In other words, their act had no "utility". This issue is considered at para.5–012.

The defendant's financial circumstances

5–011
A difficult issue is whether the financial resources available to the defendant should be taken into account in deciding whether the defendant should take precautions against a risk. Where the defendant can be said to have a choice about whether or not to engage in the activity which creates the risk, he or she cannot argue lack of resources as a reason for failing to meet the standard of care. The Australian case of *PQ v Australian Red Cross Society*[27] serves as a vivid illustration. Here, the Australian court firmly rejected the argument that the standard to be expected of the Red Cross in testing blood donations for the AIDS virus should be determined in the light of the financial constraints of the charity. The charity had a choice. If it lacked adequate financial resources to collect blood donations properly, it should choose not to provide that service.

By contrast, there are situations where the defendant's lack of choice in pursuing a certain course of action justifies taking financial constraints into account. Such is the case where an occupier comes under an affirmative duty of care to prevent others being harmed by a natural hazard arising on his land.[28] Acting in an emergency may be regarded as another "no choice" situation in which the actor can only be expected to make use of the financial resources immediately available.

The utility of the defendant's conduct

5–012
The greater the social utility of the defendant's conduct, the less likely it is that the defendant will be held to be negligent. The classic case which illustrates this is *Daborn v Bath Tramways Motor Co Ltd*.[29] The relevant issue was whether, in wartime, the driver of a left-hand drive ambulance had been negligent in turning into a road without giving a hand signal. The Court of Appeal held that she was not liable. During wartime, it was necessary for many highly important operations to be carried out by means of vehicles with left-hand drives, and it was impossible for the drivers of such vehicles to give the warning signals which drivers might normally

---

26 [1967] 1 A.C. 617 at 642.
27 [1992] 1 V.R. 19.
28 See *Goldman v Hargrave* [1967] 1 A.C. 645 and *Leakey v National Trust* [1980] Q.B. 485, discussed in Ch.10.
29 [1946] 2 All E.R. 333.

have been expected to give. Asquith LJ noted that the utility of the defendant's act had to be weighed against the risks it created, saying:

> "... if all the trains in this country were restricted to a speed of five miles an hour, there would be fewer accidents, but our national life would be intolerably slowed down. The purpose to be served, if sufficiently important, justified the assumption of abnormal risk."[30]

His Lordship concluded that, because ambulance drivers were performing a valuable service in a time of national emergency, it would be demanding too high a standard of care from them to say: "Either you must give signals which the structure of your vehicle renders impossible or you must not drive at all".

Similar reasoning was adopted in *Watt v Hertfordshire CC*.[31] Here, the plaintiff was a fireman, who was injured when travelling to rescue a woman reported to have been trapped under a heavy lorry. In the haste of the rescue, the plaintiff's colleagues picked up a jack, which was needed to save the woman's life, and put it into the lorry in which they were travelling. The lorry was not equipped for carrying the jack and the plaintiff was injured when the driver of the lorry braked suddenly and the jack fell on him. It was held that the defendant employers were not negligent because the need to act speedily in an attempt to save the woman's life outweighed the risk to the plaintiff. It should be noted, however, that this decision does not mean that the emergency services will always escape liability for accidents occurring in the haste of a rescue. The court will have regard to all of the circumstances of the particular case. Thus, for example, in *Ward v London CC*[32] the driver of a fire engine was held to have been negligent in driving through a red traffic light.

The Compensation Act 2006 and Social Action, Responsibility and Heroism Act 2015: the deterrent effect of potential liability

5–013

Compensation Act 2006 s.1 is designed to promote the idea that people and organisations wishing to undertake socially worthwhile activities should not be deterred from doing so by an unrealistic fear of negligence liability. As Jackson LJ commented in *Scout Association v Barnes*,[33] "[i]t is the function of the law of tort to deter negligent conduct and to compensate those who are the victims of such conduct. It is not the function of the law of tort to eliminate

---

30   [1946] 2 All E.R. 333 at 336. See also *Humphrey v Aegis Defence Services Ltd* [2016] EWCA Civ 11; [2017] 2 All E.R. 235 (judge entitled to take into account the scarcity of Iraqis willing to act as interpreters, the importance of their role and the need for them to work as part of a team with the security contractors when determining the nature and scope of any duty of care owed to its employees).

31   [1954] 1 W.L.R. 835.

32   [1938] 2 All E.R. 341. See also *Nelson v Chief Constable of Cumbria* [2000] C.L.Y. 4217.

33   [2010] EWCA Civ 1476 at [34].

every iota of risk or to stamp out socially desirable activities". Section 1 was passed following a number of government reports which had examined the question of whether there might be a growing "compensation culture" in the UK (i.e. whether society was becoming more litigious, with citizens believing they had a right to sue someone whenever they suffered a misfortune).[34] These reports had found that, as a matter of fact, this was not the case—the statistical evidence showed that people nowadays were not much more likely to sue than in former times. However, the reports identified that, despite the statistical reality, there was nevertheless a *perception* held by many organisations that they were at risk of being unfairly sued. This fear was leading to unduly cautious practices that were not in the public interest.

The sort of unduly cautious behaviour that Parliament had in mind was exemplified by the attitude adopted by the defendant local authority in *Tomlinson v Congleton BC*[35]—an important House of Lords case on occupiers' liability, considered in Ch.8. The local authority owned and managed a lake for the benefit of the public. Most visitors used the site responsibly, enjoying the sandy beaches and respecting the signs prohibiting them from swimming in the lake. A number of visitors, however, persistently disobeyed these signs. The local authority became concerned that it might be sued if one of these swimmers were to meet with an accident in the water. They therefore resolved to discolour and destroy the beaches by dumping ballast on them and planting vegetation—although this, of course, would have spoiled the enjoyment of the people who used the beaches responsibly.

The authority had not yet carried out this work when the claimant, a young man, severely injured himself by diving into the lake and hitting his head on the bottom. In denying his claim, the House of Lords reasoned that it would be extremely unjust to place the authority under a duty to people who disobeyed the signs and swam. There could be no duty to protect people from their own irresponsible behaviour, especially where this would mean destroying a socially desirable public amenity. Their Lordships expressed concern that, in setting the standard of care, the courts should not allow the fear of liability to deter local authorities and other organisations from engaging in or encouraging socially desirable activity. This sentiment is put on a statutory footing by s.1 of the Act:

> **"s.1. Deterrent effect of potential liability** A court considering a claim in negligence or breach of statutory duty[36] may, in determining whether the defendant should have taken particular steps to meet a standard of care (whether by taking precautions against a

---

34 See Report of the Better Regulation Task Force (2004) and report of the Constitutional Affairs Committee (2006). For comment on the Compensation Act 2006, see R. Herbert, "The Compensation Act 2006" [2006] 4 J.P.I. Law 337; K. Williams, "Politics, the media and refining the notion of fault: Section 1 of the Compensation Act 2006" [2006] 4 J.P.I. Law 347.

35 [2003] UKHL 47; [2004] 1 A.C. 46.

36 The reference in the Act to "breach of statutory duty" was thought necessary to cover claims under the Occupiers' Liability Acts (see Ch.8). However, the Act affects only statutory duties which involve a standard of care. It has no application where liability for breach is strict (see Ch.7).

> risk or otherwise), have regard to whether a requirement to take those steps might—
> (a) prevent a desirable activity from being undertaken at all, to a particular extent or in a particular way, or
> (b) discourage persons from undertaking functions in connection with a desirable activity."

In 2015, the UK Government further introduced the Social Action, Responsibility and Heroism Act 2015 (commonly known as SARAH).[37] Again, the aim was to dampen the "compensation culture". This Act applies when a court, in considering a claim that a person was negligent or in breach of statutory duty, is determining the steps that the person was required to take to meet a standard of care. Sections 2–4 of the Act highlight that the court *must* have regard to:

■ whether the alleged negligence or breach of statutory duty occurred when the person was acting for the benefit of society or any of its members (s.2);

■ whether the person, in carrying out the activity giving rise to the claim, demonstrated a "predominantly responsible approach"[38] towards protecting the safety or other interests of others (s.3); and

■ whether the alleged negligence or breach of statutory duty occurred when the person was acting heroically[39] by intervening in an emergency to assist an individual in danger (s.4).

These provisions seek to provide reassurance, for example, to volunteer groups which organise outdoor pursuits, and schools wishing to take pupils on excursions. It may be noted that the words "steps" to which the court "*may* . . . have regard" in the 2006 Act have been replaced by matters to which a court *must* have regard in SARAH 2015—in other words, the courts now have no choice in the matter. While these Acts do not extend the common law, the aim is to make the law clearer and thereby discourage unmeritorious claims against bodies which organise desirable activities and encourage rescuers who may be fearful of being sued if the rescue goes wrong. Academic commentary to date has, however, been sceptical whether these laudable aims have been fulfilled.[40]

---

37 Note that this Act only extends to England and Wales: s.5(1).
38 This key phrase is not defined.
39 The phrase "acting heroically" is also not defined. It will be for the courts to determine the scope of this concept.
40 See R. Mulheron, "Legislating dangerously: Bad Samaritans, good society and the Heroism Act 2015" (2017) 80 M.L.R. 88 and S. Peyer and R. Heywood, "Walking on thin ice: the perception of tortious liability rules and the effect on altruistic behaviour" (2019) 39 L.S. 266.

Common practice

5-014 Failure to conform to a common practice of taking safety precautions is strong evidence of negligence because it suggests that the defendant did not do what others in the community regard as reasonable. It must be remembered, however, that such a failure is not conclusive evidence of negligence. In *Brown v Rolls Royce Ltd*,[41] for example, the plaintiff contracted dermatitis from contact with grease during the course of her work. She claimed that this was caused by the negligence of her employers, who had not supplied a barrier cream which was commonly supplied by other employers to people doing the same type of work. However, whilst it was the common practice to use this cream, there was conflicting evidence about its efficacy. In such circumstances, the House of Lords held that while good sense indicated that the defendant might be in breach in not adopting commonly used precautions, it is still for the court to determine whether, on the balance of probabilities, it signified a failure to take reasonable care. Here, given that the defendants had relied on the opinion of their own medical officer who, exercising reasonable care, had advised against the cream, they were not in breach.

Conversely, where it can be shown that the defendant *has* complied with a common practice in relation to safety precautions, this is very good evidence that the defendant has not been negligent.[42] Again, however, such evidence cannot be regarded as conclusive. This is because a particular course of conduct may be negligent despite its being common practice. As Lord Tomlin succinctly put it in *Bank of Montreal v Dominion Gresham*: "Neglect of duty does not cease by repetition to be neglect of duty".[43] The question of common practice assumes enormous significance in cases involving professional negligence and is discussed more fully in that context later in this chapter.

The "Learned Hand" test

5-015 It is clear that in deciding breach of duty, the courts "balance" all of the factors we have considered above. In *United States v Carroll Towing Co*,[44] a US case, Learned Hand J provided a useful insight into the way the courts may perform this "balancing act" in some cases. He suggested that some of the factors relevant to breach of duty might be given a notional statistical value, so that the problem could be approached in a quasi-mathematical way. Taking B as the "burden of taking precautions", P as the "probability that the risk will materialise", and L as

---

41 [1960] 1 W.L.R. 210.
42 This is often raised in the context of employers' liability (discussed in Ch.7): see *Stokes v Guest, Keen and Nettlefold (Bolts and Nuts) Ltd* [1968] 1 W.L.R. 1776 where the judge (at 1783) commented that "where there is a recognised and general practice which has been followed for a substantial period in similar circumstances without mishap, [the employer] is entitled to follow it, unless in the light of common sense or newer knowledge it is clearly bad; but, where there is developing knowledge, he must keep reasonably abreast of it and not be too slow to apply it". See also *Baker v Quantum Clothing Group Ltd* [2011] UKSC 17; [2011] 1 W.L.R. 1003.
43 [1930] A.C. 659 at 666.
44 159 F. 2d 169 (1947).

the "loss which will occur if the risk does materialise", one can express the courts' approach in terms of two "equations":

$$B < P \times L = \text{Liability}$$
$$B > P \times L = \text{No Liability}$$

Expressed in words, these "equations" mean that, where the "burden" on the defendant (in terms of taking precautions) *is less than* the notional value achieved by multiplying the "probability" and the "loss", the court will be likely to find the defendant liable. Conversely, where the "burden" on the defendant *is greater than* the product of the "probability" and the "loss", a finding of no liability is likely.

We can see how these "equations" might work by analysing two cases—*Bolton v Stone* and *The Wagon Mound (No.2)*. In *Bolton*, a finding of no liability resulted from the fact that a low value could be given to the probability of the risk materialising (six times in 30 years) and a relatively low value could be given to the loss in question (at worst, injury of one individual). The burden on the defendants (giving up cricket) could be given a high value. By contrast, in *The Wagon Mound (No.2)*, whilst the probability of the risk materialising could also be given a low value, the loss in question (at worst, the complete destruction of Sydney Harbour) would have to be given a relatively high value, whilst the slight burden on the defendants (retaining the oil onboard ship) would obviously be given a very low value. Thus, a finding of liability resulted.

Special Standards of Care

There are certain types of defendant to whom additional special rules apply in determining the standard of care required of them. These are:

5–016

■ children;

■ defendants acting in an emergency;

■ defendants engaged in sport; and

■ defendants claiming to have special or professional skill.

In this section, we consider the standard of care required of the first three of these special types of defendant. The standard of care required of professionals warrants more lengthy discussion and is dealt with in a later section.

Children

5–017

The conduct of a child defendant is judged by reference to the standard of conduct that can be expected of a reasonable child of the defendant's own age. For many years, there was no English authority on the point, but it was assumed that the courts would adopt the reasoning of Kitto J in the Australian case of *McHale v Watson*.[45] Here, the defendant was a 12-year-old boy. He threw a sharp rod which ricocheted off a post and hit a nine-year-old girl. The High Court of Australia declined to apply the standard of the "reasonable person" to cases involving children and applied a lower standard which was appropriate to the defendant's age. Applying that standard, it was held that the boy was not negligent. It should be noted, however, that the standard of care applied to children remains an objective one. As Kitto J remarked:

> **"It is no answer for [a child], any more than it is for an adult to say that the harm he caused was due to his being abnormally slow--witted, quick tempered, absent minded or inexperienced."[46]**

In England, the same approach was adopted by the Court of Appeal in *Mullin v Richards*.[47] Here, the defendant and the plaintiff were 15-year-old schoolgirls. They were fencing with plastic rulers during a lesson, when one of the rulers snapped and a piece of plastic flew into the plaintiff's eye, causing blindness. It was held that the proper test to apply was whether an ordinarily careful and reasonable 15-year-old would have foreseen that the game carried a risk of injury. On the facts, the injury was held to be not reasonably foreseeable by such a child—the game was common and the girls had never been warned that it could be dangerous.

Defendants acting in an emergency

5–018

Where the defendant is forced to act quickly "in the heat of the moment", the standard of care is relaxed to take account of the exigencies of the situation. This was established long ago in the case of *Jones v Boyce*[48] (a case concerned with contributory negligence). Here, the issue was whether a passenger on a coach had acted reasonably when, thinking that the coach was about to overturn, he jumped off in order to save himself, breaking his leg. The jury found in the man's favour, Lord Ellenborough CJ having directed them that the man was not guilty of negligence just because he had selected the more perilous of two alternatives with which he was confronted in an emergency. It made no difference that, with the benefit of hindsight, it was

---

45 (1966) 115 C.L.R. 119.
46 (1966) 115 C.L.R. 119 at 213.
47 [1998] 1 W.L.R. 1304. *Mullin v Richards* was applied in *Etheridge v K* [1999] Ed. C.R. 550 where a teacher was injured by a basketball thrown by a 13-year-old boy. See also *Blake v Galloway* [2004] EWCA Civ 814; [2004] 1 W.L.R. 2844 and *Orchard v Lee* [2009] EWCA Civ 295; [2009] P.I.Q.R. P16 (comment: P. Giliker (2009) 25 P.N. 91–95).
48 (1816) 1 Stark. 493; 171 E.R. 540.

obvious the man had made the wrong decision. This position has been re-iterated in the Social Action, Responsibility and Heroism Act 2015 (SARAH), discussed at para.5–013.

A more modern example of the principle is the case of *Ng Chun Pui v Lee Chuen Tat*.[49] Here, the defendant was driving a coach on a dual carriageway when another vehicle cut in front of him without warning, forcing him to brake suddenly. The coach swerved and skidded across the central reservation, where it collided with a bus travelling in the opposite direction, injuring the plaintiffs, who were passengers on the bus. The Privy Council held that the driver's actions had been reasonable, given the emergency with which he was faced.

It appears from the decision in *Marshall v Osmond*[50] that where the police are chasing a suspected criminal, this may count as an emergency situation. Here, the plaintiff, a suspect, was injured when a police car drew up alongside the car from which he was attempting to run away. It was held that in these circumstances the actions of the police could not be judged by the same standard of care that would apply had there been time for reflection. This decision, however, should be compared with *Rigby v Chief Constable of Northamptonshire*.[51] Here, the police were held liable for fire damage to the plaintiff's shop when they fired a canister of CS gas into the shop to flush out a dangerous psychopath. The nature of the situation did not justify the police's failure to ensure that fire-fighting equipment was at hand.

Participants in sport

It is clear that those engaged in sport owe a duty of care both to other competitors in the sporting event and to spectators. The courts have recognised, however, that a participant in sporting activity is in a similar position to a person faced with an emergency, in the sense that he or she may have to take a decision in the heat of the moment. The required standard of care takes account of this. As summarised by Sir John Donaldson MR in *Condon v Basi*:

5–019

> **"You are under a duty to take all reasonable care taking account of the circumstances in which you are placed, which, in a game of football, are quite different from those which affect you when you are going for a walk in the countryside."[52]**

In the well-known case of *Wooldridge v Sumner*,[53] the Court of Appeal laid down a test for the sporting standard of care that meant that a participant in sport would only be liable

---

49 [1988] R.T.R. 298.
50 [1983] Q.B. 1034. Compare *Nelson v Chief Constable of Cumbria* [2000] C.L.Y. 4217 (police driver causing a crash to be judged by the same standard as an ordinary driver unless in a situation of pursuit at speed) and see also *Henry v Chief Constable of Thames Valley* [2010] EWCA Civ 5; [2010] R.T.R. 14.
51 [1985] 1 W.L.R. 1242.
52 [1985] 1 W.L.R. 866 at 868.
53 [1963] 2 Q.B. 43.

to spectators if he or she had "acted in reckless disregard of the spectators' safety". This test, however, was subjected to severe academic criticism on the basis that the need to show "recklessness" seemed too favourable to the defendant. The courts appear to have responded to this criticism. Thus, in *Wilks v Cheltenham Cycle Club*,[54] the Court of Appeal applied the test suggested by Professor Goodhart in his commentary on *Wooldridge*, namely that there was negligence if injury was caused "by an error of judgment that a reasonable competitor, being the reasonable man of the sporting world, would not have made".[55] Applying this test, it was held that the defendant, a participant in a motorcycle scramble, was not negligent when his bike left the course and hit a spectator. The standard of care would be adjusted to take account of the fact that a competitor could reasonably be expected to "go all out to win", even if this meant exposing others to some risk. This did not mean, however, that it was acceptable for a competitor to expose others to danger by conduct that was "foolhardy".[56]

It is clear that the mere fact that a competitor has broken the rules of a game will not, of itself, provide a conclusive indication of negligence. This point is illustrated by the decision of the Court of Appeal in *Caldwell v Maguire*.[57] The claimant, a professional jockey, was injured when the defendants, two other jockeys, rode in such a way as to cause an accident. The defendants' conduct was investigated by the Jockey Club and found to amount to "careless riding" in breach of its rules. However, the Court of Appeal drew a distinction between a finding of carelessness by a regulatory body and a finding of negligence by a court of law. In the circumstances, it was not possible to characterise the defendants' momentary carelessness as negligence. Nevertheless, we can say that where the sportsman has acted recklessly and broken the rules of the game, the court is more likely to find him to be negligent.

Where referees put competitors at risk by failing to enforce the rules of the game, they may be liable where this causes injury to the competitors. Thus, in *Vowles v Evans*[58] a rugby referee was held liable when a player was injured by a scrummage collapsing in circumstances where the referee should not have allowed the game to continue with contestable scrummages after the substitution of an untrained player. The court was careful to point out, however, that the threshold of referee liability should be a high one, and that the standard of care expected of referees depended on all the circumstances of the case. One of those circumstances was the nature of the game. Thus, in a fast-moving game, a referee could not be expected to avoid some oversight and error of judgment when supervising the game.

54　[1971] 1 W.L.R. 668.

55　A. L. Goodhart, "The sportsman's charter" (1962) 78 L.Q.R. 490, 496.

56　per Lord Denning MR at 670. Compare the behaviour of the defendant in *Condon v Basi* [1985] 1 W.L.R 866 who was liable for a rugby tackle made in a "reckless and dangerous manner".

57　[2001] EWCA Civ 1054; [2002] P.I.Q.R. P6. The approach in *Caldwell v Maguire* was followed in the context of children's horseplay in *Blake v Galloway* [2004] 1 W.L.R. 2844. Comment: P. Charlish, "A reckless approach to negligence" [2004] 4 J.P.I. Law 291.

58　[2003] EWCA Civ 318; [2003] 1 W.L.R. 1607. See also *Smolden v Whitworth* [1997] P.I.Q.R. P 133.

The Professional Standard of Care

In this section, we consider the standard of care demanded of people who, by following a particular trade or profession, hold themselves out as having special skills. In relation to such people, the question of breach of duty is decided by applying the so-called "*Bolam* test".

5–020

The *Bolam* test

The case of *Bolam v Friern Hospital Management Committee*[59] (the facts of which we shall discuss later) confirmed the application of two important principles, which can be summarised as follows:

5–021

- Where the defendant purports to have a special skill, the defendant's conduct is judged according to the standard of a reasonable person having the skill the defendant claims to possess. It is not judged by the standard of the reasonable lay person.

- The law will not regard a professional defendant as having fallen below the required standard of care if it is shown that the defendant's conduct is regarded as proper by one responsible body of professional opinion. This is the case even if some other members of the defendant's profession may think the conduct is negligent.

It is convenient to explore each principle in turn.

The standard of the "reasonable skilled person"

This first element of the "*Bolam* test" is straightforward. The obvious point here is that the law expects a member of a trade or profession to live up to the standard of an ordinary skilled member of the trade or profession in question. As McNair J put it in *Bolam*:

5–022

"Where you get a situation which involves the use of some special skill or competence, then the test as to whether there has been negligence or not is not the test of the man on the top of the Clapham omnibus, because he has not got this special skill. The test is the standard of the ordinary skilled man exercising and professing to have that special skill."[60]

---

59 [1957] 1 W.L.R. 582.
60 [1957] 1 W.L.R. 582 at 586.

Accordingly, the law will not judge a surgeon performing an operation by the standard of a reasonable lay person performing that operation (to do so would be absurd) but by the standard of the "reasonable surgeon". Although most cases of interest in this area concern allegations of medical negligence, it should be remembered that the relevant principles apply equally in other contexts. Thus, a lawyer is judged by the standard of a "reasonable lawyer", an accountant by the standard of a "reasonable accountant", and so on. Similarly, in *Gates v McKenna*,[61] Paul McKenna, the well-known stage hypnotist, was judged by the standard of a "reasonably careful exponent of stage hypnotism".

It is important to note that the relevant issue is not whether the defendant is in fact a member of a trade or profession, but whether, in all the circumstances, by undertaking a particular task, the defendant has held himself or herself out as possessing a trade or professional skill. There are cases, however, where the fact that the defendant is *not* a member of a relevant trade or profession has been seen as important in determining whether the defendant has held himself or herself out as possessing a particular level of skill. In *Philips v William Whiteley Ltd*,[62] for example, it was held that the plaintiff, who had had her ears pierced by the defendants, who were jewellers, could not expect them to exercise the same degree of care and skill that would be exercised by a qualified surgeon. Similarly, in *Wells v Cooper*,[63] where the plaintiff suffered injury when a door handle came off in his hand, it was held that, although householders who decide to carry out work on their property involving carpentry skills must achieve the standards of a reasonably competent amateur carpenter, the safety of their work was not to be judged by reference to the contractual obligations that might be owed by a professional carpenter working for reward, since this would be too high a standard.[64]

In *Wilsher v Essex AHA*[65] it was confirmed that the standard of care to be expected from a professionally qualified defendant is to be determined by considering the nature of his or her "post" and the tasks which it involves. The professional standard of care is objective in the sense that the same standard of care will be required of all professionals holding the same "post". In *Wilsher*, therefore, where a number of medical professionals professed expertise in the care of premature babies, the Court of Appeal held that each of them could be expected to exercise a degree of care and skill appropriate to the tasks usually undertaken by a person holding his or her post. The defendant's "post" was to be distinguished from the defendant's "rank" or "status". This meant that, where a junior doctor was filling a "post" involving the performance of tasks more usually undertaken by someone more senior, the junior doctor would be judged by exactly the same standards as a senior doctor. Dealing with the argument that this placed too great a burden on young doctors, Mustill LJ commented:

61 [1998] Lloyd's Rep. Med. 405. See also *Bhamra v Dubb (t/a Lucky Caterers)* [2010] EWCA Civ 13: standard of care of caterers at a Sikh wedding.

62 [1938] 1 All E.R. 566.

63 [1958] 2 Q.B. 265.

64 [1958] 2 Q.B. 265 per Jenkins LJ at 271. On the standard of care owed by a jobbing labourer, see *James v Butler* [2005] EWCA Civ 1014.

65 [1987] Q.B. 730. The facts of *Wilsher* are considered in Ch.6. The case eventually went to the House of Lords and is important in the context of causation.

"To my mind, it would be a false step to subordinate the legitimate expectation of the patient that he will receive from each person concerned with his care a degree of skill appropriate to the task which he undertakes, to an understandable wish to minimise the psychological and financial pressures on hard-pressed young doctors."[66]

The apparent harshness of this rule, however, is mitigated to some extent by the Court of Appeal's assertion in *Wilsher* that where an inexperienced doctor is called upon to perform a task in which he or she lacks expertise, it is sufficient for the doctor to discharge the duty of care to the patient if he or she seeks and acts on the advice of a more senior colleague.

In this context, it should also be noted that a doctor or other professional may, in certain circumstances, discharge the duty of care by simply refusing to act. In certain professions, the position is straightforward. Barristers, for example, have a professional duty to decline cases that are beyond their competence. In the context of the medical profession, however, the position is more complicated. Junior doctors on duty in casualty departments, for example, cannot, without breaching their duty of care, decline to treat patients whose conditions call for expertise they do not possess. On the other hand, it is clear that a general practitioner, unskilled in open heart surgery, can and should decline to perform that task.

The relevance of common practice and professional opinion

5–023

The second element of the *"Bolam* test"—namely that a professional will escape liability if his or her conduct accords with one view of responsible common practice—has proved controversial. Before considering the nature of this controversy, it is useful to explore the facts of *Bolam*, which neatly illustrate the problem which this part of the test was designed to solve.

Mr Bolam was a mental patient suffering from acute depression. One of the accepted forms of treatment for this condition was (and still is today) to administer electro-convulsive therapy (ECT). The treatment involves the patient being given a brief but severe electric shock. An unfortunate side effect, however, is that the shock causes muscle spasms. These can sometimes be of such magnitude as to break the patient's bones. Mr Bolam suffered a fractured pelvis during a bout of ECT treatment. He contended that the doctor who administered the treatment had been negligent in a number of respects. First, he argued that he should have been given relaxant drugs prior to the treatment. Secondly, he argued that a restraining sheet should have been used to hold him down whilst the shock was being given. His third argument related not to the way in which the treatment was administered, but to the doctor's failure to warn him of the danger of broken bones so that he could decide for himself whether or not to undergo the treatment. (The issue of whether doctors have a duty to disclose the risks of treatment is considered in more detail later.)

---

66 [1987] Q.B. 730 at 751.

At the trial, the expert evidence given showed a marked difference of opinion within the medical profession as to the correct procedure for administering ECT. It became clear that some doctors favoured relaxant drugs, whilst others preferred not to use them because they could depress the respiratory system, causing the patient to stop breathing. Whilst some doctors favoured restraining sheets, others preferred to leave the limbs free during the treatment (as the doctor in this case had done), arguing that if bones were trapped under a sheet, they were, in fact, more likely to break.

In summing up the case for the jury (the case was decided when juries were used in negligence trials), McNair J pointed out that ECT was a "progressive science", on which responsible medical opinion differed. His Lordship stated that, according to the law, a doctor will not be liable in negligence if, "he has acted in accordance with a practice accepted as proper by a responsible body of medical men skilled in that particular art". He went on to say that a professional person would not be liable "merely because there is a body of opinion which would take a contrary view".[67] Unsurprisingly, in the light of this direction, the jury in *Bolam* returned a verdict in favour of the defendant doctor.

The controversial aspect of the approach taken in *Bolam*, which has been followed in subsequent cases, is that, to a great extent, it allows the professions to be "self-regulating"—if the conduct required of a doctor is to be determined, not by a judge, but by evidence of what some other doctors do, then it can be argued that doctors are not truly answerable to their patients through the courts, because they are allowed to set their own standards of care.[68] We shall see, however, that there are limits to the extent to which doctors and other professionals can place themselves "above the law" in this way. These limits were re-affirmed by the House of Lords in the important case of *Bolitho v City and Hackney Health Authority* discussed below.[69]

It is important to recognise that the "*Bolam* test" means that a judge is not normally permitted to substitute his or her own views for the views of the defendant's responsible expert witnesses. In other words, even though a judge, as a lay person in medical (or other professional) terms, may strongly prefer a form of practice advocated by the claimant's expert witnesses, and may instinctively feel that the defendant's way of doing things was wrong, he or she must resist the temptation to choose between two competing "responsible" schools of professional thought.

This point is clearly illustrated by *Maynard v West Midlands Health Authority*.[70] Here, the defendants carried out a diagnostic procedure, in the nature of a biopsy, on the plaintiff's throat. The procedure was performed with all due care and skill, but it carried a small risk of damage to the vocal chords. This risk materialised, and the plaintiff brought a negligence action alleging that the biopsy had been unnecessary. The defendants contended that they

---

67   *Bolam v Friern Hospital Management Committee* [1957] 1 W.L.R. 582 at 587–588.
68   See A. Grubb, "Contraceptive advice and doctors—A law unto themselves?" [1988] C.L.J. 12.
69   [1998] A.C. 232.
70   [1984] 1 W.L.R. 634. It is important to distinguish this type of case from a case such as *Penney v East Kent Health Authority* [2000] Lloyd's Rep. Med. 41 where the expert witnesses agree that the defendant's conduct was wrong but give conflicting opinions about whether it is "excusable".

had acted properly in deciding to perform the procedure, because it was required in order to exclude the possibility (albeit remote) that the plaintiff was suffering from Hodgkin's Disease. The trial judge preferred the view of the plaintiff's experts—who would have waited for the results of blood tests to come through instead of carrying out a biopsy—and held the defendants liable. His Lordship's judgment, however, was overruled by the Court of Appeal and the House of Lords. Lord Scarman said:

> "a judge's 'preference' for one body of distinguished professional opinion to another also professionally distinguished is not sufficient to establish negligence in a practitioner."

The practical result of Lord Scarman's approach, then, is that it is extremely difficult for a claimant to prove professional negligence—he or she must effectively show that no responsible body of professional opinion would have supported what the defendant did. Whilst showing this may be difficult, however, it is not always impossible. This is because the cases have repeatedly made it clear that a judge is only obliged to accept the views of the defendant's experts if those views are "responsible".

The limits of the "Bolam principle"

5–024

As we have already noted, the fact that the defendant has conformed with common practice cannot be regarded as *conclusive* evidence that he or she has met the standard of care, because the common practice in question may itself be negligent. Thus, in *Edward Wong Finance Co Ltd v Johnson, Stokes & Master*,[71] the Privy Council held that a conveyancing practice which involved a risk to the client was negligent, despite its widespread adoption by the legal profession in Hong Kong. The courts clearly have a part to play in setting standards of professional conduct. Were it otherwise, certain professionals might persist with outdated or clearly indefensible practices, and escape justice by saying that are only doing what some other professionals do. This would amount to an abuse of their position in society.

In *Bolam* itself, McNair J made it clear that "mere personal belief that a particular technique is best is no defence unless that belief is based on reasonable grounds".[72] His Lordship went on to explain that it had long been the law, for example, that a doctor who obstinately refused to use anaesthetics or antiseptics could not escape liability simply by calling as witnesses colleagues who took a similarly stubborn and irrational view. More recently, in *Bolitho v City and Hackney Health Authority*,[73] Lord Browne-Wilkinson, delivering the opinion of a unani-

---

71   [1984] A.C. 296.
72   *Bolam v Friern Hospital Management Committee* [1957] 1 W.L.R 582 at 587.
73   [1998] A.C. 232. Comment: R. Heywood (2006) 22 P.N. 225. For a more detailed examination of the impact of *Bolitho* on the *Bolam* test, see R. Mulheron, "Trumping *Bolam*: A critical legal analysis of *Bolitho*'s 'gloss'" [2010] C.L.J. 609.

mous House of Lords, took the opportunity to clarify the circumstances in which a court was entitled to reject the professional opinions of the defendant's experts.

Bolitho is a rather complicated case, because it involves issues of causation as well as issues of breach of duty. It is further considered in Ch.6. For present purposes, it is sufficient to note that the case concerned a two-year-old boy who was admitted to hospital suffering from breathing difficulties. In the events which happened, the boy suffered cardiac arrest leading to brain damage, and his mother brought a negligence action on his behalf. One of the questions for the court was whether the doctor in charge should have intubated the child (put a tube down his throat to assist his breathing) or whether, given the boy's symptoms, she would have been justified in taking no such action. At the trial, the judge heard evidence from eight different experts. Five of them (called for the plaintiff) said that, in the circumstances, any competent doctor should have intubated the boy. Three of them (called for the defendant doctor) said that intubation would not have been appropriate and referred to the fact that intubation carried a very small risk of injuring the child's throat. The trial judge held that the doctor was not liable. Although, having listened to the experts, as a lay person he felt persuaded that intubation would have been the right course of action, he felt bound to hold that the defendant escaped liability because her failure to intubate was endorsed by *one* responsible body of medical opinion. To hold otherwise would amount to substituting his own views for the views of the defendant's expert witnesses, and the *"Bolam* test" did not allow him to do this.

The House of Lords confirmed the judge's approach as correct. What is important to note, however, is that Lord Browne-Wilkinson made it clear that in some circumstances a judge *would* be entitled to reject the opinions of professional experts, if he or she felt that their opinions had no *logical basis*. Thus, where (as in this case) the expert evidence was concerned with the question of weighing up the risks presented by different forms of treatment, the experts, in order to have their evidence accepted, had to show that they had directed their minds to this question and had reached a conclusion that was logically defensible. The Court of Appeal reiterated recently, however, that, in all ordinary circumstances, it would not be appropriate for a judge to hold that a particular clinical decision had no logical basis or was unreasonable *without* the support of expert evidence.[74]

On one view, it can be argued that Lord Browne-Wilkinson's approach entails a slight modification of the *"Bolam* test". That is to say, whilst McNair J had made it clear in *Bolam* that expert evidence could be rejected *if the person giving it* was not "responsible", *Bolitho* now makes it clear that expert evidence, even when given by a responsible and respected expert, can be rejected *if the evidence itself* is not "responsible", in the sense that it does not withstand logical analysis. The distinction between the credibility of the evidence and the credibility of the person giving it is, of course, an extremely fine one. This point did not escape Lord Browne-Wilkinson, who thought that, in most cases, the fact that an opinion was held by a responsible medical expert would, in itself, demonstrate that the opinion was a reasonable one. His Lordship was careful to point out that, this being the case, it would be only in

---

74   *Williams v Cwm Taf Local Health Board* [2018] EWCA Civ 1745 at [14].

very rare cases that a judge would be justified in rejecting professional expert opinion as unreasonable.[75]

Lord Browne-Wilkinson went on to conclude that the case before him was not, in fact, one of these rare cases. On the facts of *Bolitho*, the trial judge had been right in accepting the defendant's expert evidence, because the experts had given a logical justification for their opinion that intubating the child was not appropriate—namely that intubation involved a small risk of injury. Accordingly, because the defendant doctor's failure to intubate had been endorsed by one body of reasonable medical thought, she escaped liability.

It is clear from *Bolitho*, then, that a doctor cannot escape liability for his or her conduct unless that conduct has a rational justification.[76] In particular, one thorny problem remains to be directly addressed by the courts: suppose the defendant's experts say that he or she was justified in withholding a very expensive drug from a patient, on the basis that it is common medical practice to have regard to budgetary constraints in administering treatment. Would a judge be entitled to reject this view because, in the words of Lord Browne-Wilkinson, it "does not withstand logical analysis"?[77]

Disclosure of the risks of treatment

5-025

Here, we consider the extent to which the standard of care expected of doctors requires them to disclose to a patient the risks of treatment, so that the patient can make an informed choice about whether to consent to that treatment. (It will be recalled that this was one of the issues in *Bolam*.) Where the treatment in question involves physical contact (as opposed to taking a drug orally, for example), absence of consent on the part of the patient may render the doctor liable in the tort of battery. This issue is discussed in Ch.11. Here, we are concerned with liability in negligence.

Until recently, the leading case was *Sidaway v Bethlem Royal Hospital Governors*.[78] Here, the plaintiff had not been warned by her surgeon that there was a very small risk (around 1%) of damage being done to her spine during an operation on her back. The plaintiff consented to the operation and it was performed with all due care and skill, but the risk of injury materialised, leaving the plaintiff disabled. She claimed that if she known about the risk, she would not have agreed to the operation.

The House of Lords (Lord Scarman dissenting) held that the surgeon was not liable in negligence for failing to tell her about the risk. The majority were of the view that the *Bolam* test applied in this context. If, therefore, the surgeon had conformed with a responsible body of medical opin-

---

75   Although Mulheron in her survey of the law notes that the *Bolitho* test has changed the outcome of medical negligence cases more often than the label 'rare' would suggest: [2010] C.L.J. 609 at 618.

76   Consider, e.g. *Hucks v Cole (1968)* (1993) 4 Med. L.R. 393: relatively low cost of administering penicillin to prevent septicaemia was a relevant reason for rejecting the defendant's evidence that it was reasonable not to administer the drug.

77   See *Garcia v St Mary's NHS Trust* [2006] EWHC 2314 (QB); [2011] Med. L.R. 348: practice of having no specialist registrar on site overnight to deal with emergencies was reasonable in the circumstances.

78   [1985] A.C. 871.

ion which would not have disclosed the risk, he escaped liability. Only if disclosure of a particular risk was so obviously necessary that no reasonably prudent medical man would fail to make it would liability arise. In *Sidaway*, then, the majority declined to adopt a strict doctrine of "informed consent" and adopted a paternalistic approach to risk disclosure. In the words of Lord Bridge:

> "The doctor cannot set out to educate the patient to his own standard of medical knowledge of all the relevant factors involved. He may take the view, certainly with some patients, that the very fact of his volunteering, without being asked, information of some remote risk involved in the treatment proposed, even though he describes it as remote, may lead to that risk assuming an undue significance in the patient's calculations."[79]

Lord Scarman, however, took a different view. His Lordship thought that the question of disclosure should be decided by the courts, using an objective test whereby doctors should be placed under a duty to disclose all "material" risks to the patient.

5–026   In *Sidaway* Mrs Sidaway had not specifically asked the surgeon about the risks of the operation. Lord Bridge suggested, however, that in a case where a doctor was questioned specifically by the patient, the doctor would be obliged to answer "both truthfully and as fully as the questioner requires".[80] This principle was applied in *Chester v Afshar*.[81] The claimant, who was considering an operation on her spine, specifically asked her consultant about the risks inherent in the operation. The defendant was held to be in breach of duty when, instead of explaining that the operation carried a small but inherent risk, he merely gave the light-hearted reply: "Well, I have never crippled anybody yet". Full risk disclosure thus required a very assertive patient, prepared, when ill, to demand full disclosure from his or her doctor.

The issue of risk disclosure was re-examined in 2015 by the Supreme Court in *Montgomery v Lanarkshire Health Board*.[82] In this important decision, a consultant obstetrician had failed to advise the pregnant Mrs Montgomery of a 9–10% risk of injury to her baby if she chose a natural birth instead of a caesarean section. The baby sadly was born with severe disabilities as a result of this injury occurring. A unanimous seven member Supreme Court accepted that the *Sidaway* approach, relying on *Bolam*, could no longer be considered satisfactory. An adult person of sound mind was entitled to decide which, if any, of the available forms of treatment

---

79   *Sidaway v Bethlem Royal Hospital Governors* [1985] A.C. 871 at 899.

80   [1985] A.C. 871 at 898.

81   [2004] UKHL 41; [2005] 1 A.C. 134. This case is important in the context of causation and is further considered in Ch.6. The court was not required in this case to rule on the appropriate standard of risk disclosure.

82   [2015] UKSC 11; [2015] A.C. 1430. Comment: R. Bagshaw (2016) 132 L.Q.R. 182. Applied in *Webster v Burton Hospitals NHS Foundation Trust* [2017] EWCA Civ 62 and, in the context of financial investment advice, in *O'Hare v Coutts* [2016] EWHC 2224 (QB), but see now *Barker v Baxendale Walker Solicitors* [2017] EWCA Civ 2056; [2018] 1 W.L.R. 1905 at [63]–[64]. Ooi argues that there there is no real basis for extending the reasoning in *Montgomery* outside the context of medical negligence: (2018) 34 P.N. 171.

to undergo, and her consent had to be obtained before treatment interfering with her bodily integrity was undertaken. Doctors were under a duty to take reasonable care to ensure that patients were aware of any *material* risks involved in any recommended treatment, and of any reasonable alternative or variant treatments.[83] Material risks are those to which, in the circumstances of the particular case, a reasonable person in the patient's position would be likely to attach significance <u>OR</u> those to which the doctor is or should reasonably be aware that this *particular patient* would be likely to attach significance.[84] This is not simply a question of percentages, but a matter of assessing the options open to the patient and the likely impact of the risk manifesting itself. On this basis, the doctor had been negligent in failing to tell Mrs Montgomery of the risk of injury and to discuss the alternative of delivery by caesarean section. In a later case, the court confirmed that *Montgomery* applies to post-treatment discussions. It is the patient's right to be informed of the outcome of the treatment, the prognosis, and what the follow-up care and treatment options are.[85]

Montgomery marks a firm step, therefore, from the ideology of "doctor knows best" to that of respecting the autonomy of the patient (as seen earlier in *Chester*). As the Supreme Court noted, this places the UK court in line with other major Commonwealth jurisdictions. The court thus supported an "informed choice" model to disclosure of risks which treats patients as persons holding rights rather than as passive recipients of care by the medical profession. The new rule is, however, subject to two exceptions which are likely to be interpreted narrowly[86]:

■ The therapeutic exception: where the doctor reasonably believes that the disclosure of information would be seriously detrimental to the patient's health; and

■ The necessity exception: where the treatment must be provided before there is any practical possibility of disclosure e.g. the patient is unconscious.

Policy issues in medical negligence cases

It is possible to discern a number of policy considerations underlying the decisions we have examined in this section. The courts have traditionally been concerned that their decisions should not encourage the practice of "defensive medicine", i.e. medical care which involves a "belt and braces" approach to treating patients, motivated by the desire to avoid negligence liability.[87] There is some concern in the US that doctors are adopting this sort of approach,

5–027

---

83   See, in particular, [87]–[89] of *Montgomery v Lanarkshire Health Board* [2015] UKSC 11; [2015] A.C. 1430.

84   See *Duce v Worcestershire Acute Hospitals NHS Trust* [2018] EWCA Civ 1307; [2018] P.I.Q.R. P18 (clinician was not required to warn of a risk of which he could not reasonably be taken to be aware).

85   *Gallardo v Imperial College Healthcare NHS Trust* [2017] EWHC 3147 (QB) (patient only learnt of the true nature of his condition nine years after an operation for the removal of a tumour which had been found to be malignant).

86   See [91] of *Montgomery v Lanarkshire Health Board* [2015] UKSC 11; [2015] A.C. 1430.

87   See J. B. Fanning, "Uneasy lies the neck that wears a stethoscope: Some observations on defensive medicine" (2008) 24 P.N. 93.

which is not always in the best interests of the patient, subjecting them, for example, to unnecessary tests and procedures. In *Whitehouse v Jordan*,[88] Lord Denning MR, in the Court of Appeal, warned of the dangers of following the US example. The case involved an allegation of negligence against a senior registrar who, it was argued, had wrongly persisted in delivering a baby by forceps when a Caesarean section was called for. In holding the defendant not liable, Lord Denning MR expressed the view that if too high a standard of care were demanded of doctors, experienced practitioners might refuse to treat certain patients, and young people might be deterred from entering the medical profession because of the high insurance premiums that would be required to meet professional negligence claims.

The practice of "defensive medicine" would therefore be expensive, because it requires the administration of "precautionary" tests and treatments to exclude remote risks. The courts' attempts to contain the scope of liability for medical negligence may reflect concern about the proper allocation of scarce NHS resources. The courts seem at times anxious also not to encourage a "culture of litigation" in medical cases, because of the harm that unjustified allegations of negligence can do to a defendant's reputation.[89]

It is noticeable, however, that the Supreme Court in *Montgomery* adopted a very different approach. Patients were described, perhaps controversially, as "consumers exercising choices"[90] with every right to be informed of the risks associated with that choice. Rather than giving rise to defensive practices, the Supreme Court argued that encouraging patients to take responsibility for their choices might be *less* likely to encourage recriminations and litigation in the event of an adverse outcome.[91] It took the view that:

> "... a departure from the *Bolam* test will reduce the predictability of the outcome of litigation, given the difficulty of overcoming that test in contested proceedings. It appears to us however that a degree of unpredictability can be tolerated as the consequence of protecting patients from exposure to risks of injury which they would otherwise have chosen to avoid. The more fundamental response to such points, however, is that respect for the dignity of patients requires no less."[92]

It remains to be seen whether this approach, which deals with negligence through the perspective of patient's rights, is applied more generally in medical negligence cases.[93]

---

88 [1980] 1 All E.R. 650 CA. The decision was subsequently upheld by the House of Lords at [1981] 1 W.L.R. 246.

89 See, e.g. *Ashcroft v Mersey Regional Health Authority* [1983] 2 All E.R. 245, affirmed on appeal [1985] 2 All E.R. 96.

90 *Montgomery v Lanarkshire Health Board* [2015] UKSC 11 at [75].

91 Reid regards this view as "optimistic", arguing that it might equally be anticipated that dissatisfied patients will claim that any discussion negligently failed to meet the *Montgomery* test: E. Reid (2015) 19 Edin. L. Rev. 360, 364.

92 *Montgomery v Lanarkshire Health Board* [2015] UKSC 11 at [93].

93 See J. Laing, "Delivering Informed consent post-*Montgomery*: Implications for professional practice and professionalism" (2017) 33 P.N. 128.

Proof of Breach

Although the claimant bears the burden of proving breach of duty, there are certain circumstances in which special rules will assist in discharging this burden.

Civil Evidence Act 1968

Civil Evidence Act 1968 s.11(1) provides that, in a civil trial, proof that a person has been convicted of a criminal offence shall be taken as proof that he or she committed the offence, unless the contrary is proved.[94] What this means in the context of a negligence trial is that, if the claimant shows that the defendant has been convicted of an offence arising out of the same facts as those in issue at the trial, the burden of proof is reversed, so that the defendant will have to disprove negligence. Thus, in *Wauchope v Mordecai*,[95] the plaintiff was injured by being knocked off his bicycle when the defendant suddenly opened the door of a parked car. The defendant had been convicted of an offence arising out of the incident. The Court of Appeal held that the effect of s.11 of the 1968 Act was to shift the burden of proof to the defendant. Since the defendant had failed to prove that he had *not* been negligent, the trial judge had been wrong to dismiss the plaintiff's case on a finding that the plaintiff had not proved negligence.

Res ipsa loquitur

The maxim res ipsa loquitur means "the thing speaks for itself". Where the maxim applies, the court is prepared to draw an inference that the defendant has been negligent without requiring the claimant to bring evidence about the precise way in which the negligence occurred. As Toulson LJ commented recently, it is a "rule of evidence based on fairness and common sense".[96] This idea originates from the judgment of Erle CJ in *Scott v London and St Katherine Docks Co*,[97] a case which provides a good example of when the maxim will apply.

The plaintiff was passing the defendants' warehouse when six bags of sugar, which were being hoisted by the defendant's crane, fell on him. The plaintiff could not prove *how* and *why* this happened—the only thing he could prove was that the bags fell and caused him injury. It was held, however, that these facts were sufficient to give rise to an inference of negligence. Bags of sugar do not usually fall from a crane unless someone *has* been negligent, so the fact

---

94 See M. Dyson and J. Randall, "Criminal convictions and the civil courts" [2015] C.L.J. 78.
95 [1970] 1 W.L.R. 317.
96 *Smith v Fordyce* [2013] EWCA Civ 320 at [61].
97 (1865) 3 Hurl. & C. 596; 159 E.R. 665. For a modern example of the application of the doctrine, see *George v Eagle Services Ltd* [2009] UKPC 21. Comment: K. Williams, "*Res ipsa loquitur* still speaks" (2009) 125 L.Q.R. 567.

of negligence "spoke for itself". Since the defendants had failed to provide an innocent explanation of how the incident had occurred, they were held liable.

When does the maxim apply?

5-031

There are three conditions which must be satisfied before res ipsa loquitur can apply:

(1) The occurrence must be one that will not normally happen

5-032

This requirement was clearly met on the facts of *Scott v London and St Katherine Docks*—there was no obvious alternative explanation why the bags fell off the crane. Similarly, in *Byrne v Boodle*[98] the maxim was held to apply when a barrel of flour fell on the plaintiff as he was passing underneath the defendant's window. The cases in which the requirement has been met are many and varied. In *Chaproniere v Mason*,[99] for example, the court was prepared to infer negligence when a stone was found in a bun, and in *Ward v Tesco Stores Ltd*,[100] negligence was inferred when the plaintiff slipped on a spillage of yoghurt on a supermarket floor, which the defendants had failed to clean up.

As the reliability of machines has improved, the courts have become increasingly willing to conclude that accidents involving machines are more probably due to the negligence of their operators than to mechanical failure. Thus, the courts have been willing to invoke the maxim in road traffic cases where cars skid,[101] or veer on to the pavement[102] or into the opposite carriageway.[103] In a medical context, res ipsa loquitur has been applied, for example, to a case where a surgeon left a swab inside a patient's body.[104] It has also been applied in the context of failed treatment. Thus, in *Cassidy v Ministry of Health*,[105] as Denning LJ put it, the plaintiff was entitled to say:

> **"I went into hospital to be cured of two stiff fingers. I have come out with four stiff fingers and my hand is useless. That should not happen if due care had been used. Explain it if you can."**

98 (1863) 2 Hurl. & C. 722.
99 (1905) 21 T.L.R. 633.
100 [1976] 1 W.L.R. 810. Applied in *Dobson v Asda Stores* [2002] C.L.Y. 4551 and *Hall v Holker Estate Co Ltd* [2008] EWCA Civ 1422.
101 *Richley v Faull* [1965] 1 W.L.R. 1454 but contrast *Smith v Fordyce* [2013] EWCA Civ 320.
102 *Ellor v Selfridge & Co Ltd* (1930) 46 T.L.R. 236.
103 *Ng Chun Pui v Lee Chuen Tat* [1988] R.T.R. 298.
104 *Mahon v Osborne* [1939] 2 K.B. 14.
105 [1951] 2 K.B. 343 at 365.

(2) The defendant must have control of the thing which causes him harm

This requirement can be illustrated by comparing two cases involving railway accidents. In *Gee v Metropolitan Railway*,[106] the plaintiff was injured when he fell out of an underground train, having leaned against a door. Because the train had only just left the station, it could be inferred that the defendants, who clearly had a duty to see that the door was closed before the train departed, had been in control of the door at the time it flew open. By contrast, in *Easson v London and North Eastern Ry Co*,[107] where a four-year-old boy fell through an unsecured train door, it was held that *res ipsa loquitur* did not apply. At the time of the accident, the train was seven miles beyond its last stopping place. In these circumstances, although the accident might have been due to the defendants' negligence, it was not appropriate to infer that it was, because the door might have been opened by a passenger, rather than by one of the defendants' employees.

(3) The cause of the occurrence must be unknown to the claimant

This requirement is not of any great practical significance. All it means is that, where the facts are sufficiently known, there is no need to invoke the maxim because the claimant can prove what actually happened. Thus, in *Bolton v Stone*,[108] the maxim was held to have no application, because it was obvious that the cricket ball must have been hit over the fence by the batsman. In *Barkway v South Wales Transport Co Ltd*,[109] where a burst tyre on a bus caused an accident, it was held that the maxim should not be applied. There was some evidence that the bus company might have prevented the accident if it had told its drivers to report incidents involving blown tyres, and it had failed to do so. Accordingly, the plaintiff was required to investigate this issue, rather than rely on *res ipsa loquitur*.

What is the effect of the maxim?

There has been some debate about whether the effect of res ipsa loquitur is to reverse the legal burden of proof, or whether it places only an *evidential* burden on the defendant to rebut the inference of negligence.[110] In most cases, the point is of little practical importance, but in one circumstance it may be significant. Suppose that, after hearing the defendant's explanation, the judge finds that the balance of probabilities is *equal* as between a negligent and an

---

106 (1873) L.R. 8 Q.B. 161.
107 [1944] 2 K.B. 421.
108 [1951] A.C. 850.
109 [1950] A.C. 185.
110 See, e.g. P. S. Atiyah, "*Res ipsa loquitur* in England and Australia" (1972) 35 M.L.R. 337.

innocent explanation of the occurrence in question. Who should win the case? If the effect of the maxim is to reverse the legal burden of proof, the claimant should win, because the defendant has not proved, on the balance of probabilities, that he or she has *not* been negligent. On the other hand, if the burden of proof stays with the claimant, the defendant should win, unless the claimant can adduce further evidence to tip the scales in his or her favour.

In *Colvilles Ltd v Devine*,[111] Lord Donovan in the House of Lords said that the maxim had no effect on the legal burden of proof. However, a year later, the House of Lords appeared to take a different approach in the case of *Henderson v Henry E Jenkins & Sons*.[112] Here, the plaintiff's husband was killed when the brakes of the defendants' lorry failed. The failure was caused by corrosion of a brake fluid pipe. In answer to the plaintiff's claim of res ipsa loquitur, the defendants gave evidence that they had maintained the lorry in accordance with common practice. They had had the lorry regularly inspected, but the pipe in question could only be fully inspected by removing it from the lorry, and this was not recommended by the manufacturers until the lorry had done a certain mileage. In spite of this, the House of Lords held that the defendants had failed to rebut the inference of negligence—they should have gone on to show that there was nothing in the history of the lorry that would have caused abnormal corrosion and required a special inspection. Thus, although the point was not entirely clear, their Lordships appeared to say that it was for the *defendants* to prove that they were *not* negligent. As Lord Pearson put it, the defendants lost the case because "their answer was incomplete".[113]

More recently, however, in *Ng Chun Pui v Lee Chuen Tat*,[114] the Privy Council has reasserted that in res ipsa loquitur cases the burden of proof does not switch to the defendant. Here, a coach veered across a central reservation into the opposite carriageway, where it collided with oncoming traffic. This fact alone would have justified a finding of negligence, so the plaintiff called no evidence. The defendants, however, explained that a car had suddenly cut across the driver's path, causing him to brake suddenly and skid. In the light of this explanation, the Privy Council held that there could be no inference of negligence, because the driver's actions in such an emergency had not been negligent. What is important is that, rather than saying that the defendants *had discharged the burden of proof*, their Lordships said, in effect, that the explanation had tilted the balance of probabilities against the plaintiff. The burden of proof remained with the plaintiff, who was entitled to bring further evidence to show that the defendants had been negligent. But since he could not do so, he lost the case. Lord Griffiths, delivering the opinion of the Privy Council, said that it was misleading to talk of the burden of proof shifting to the defendant in a res ipsa loquitur situation. The burden of proving negligence rests throughout the case on the plaintiff. Although *Ng Chun Pui v Lee Chuen Tat* is a Privy Council decision, and therefore not technically binding, it is probable that this approach will be followed in future cases.[115]

---

111 [1969] 1 W.L.R. 475.
112 [1970] A.C. 282. A similar approach was taken by the Court of Appeal in *Ward v Tesco Stores Ltd* [1976] 1 W.L.R. 810.
113 [1970] A.C. 282 at 303.
114 [1988] R.T.R. 298.
115 See, e.g. the approach taken by the Court of Appeal in *O'Connor v Pennine Acute Hospitals NHS Trust* [2015]

Breach of duty: conclusion

We have seen that breach of duty is in most respects a relatively straightforward element of the tort of negligence, but one where policy nevertheless plays an important part in the courts' decisions. In Chs 7 and 8, we shall explore breach of duty again in the specific contexts of employers' liability and occupiers' liability. First, however, it is appropriate to examine two further elements of the tort of negligence, namely causation and remoteness.

EWCA Civ 1244; [2016] Med. L.R. 11 at [60]: "the so-called res ipsa loquitur cases are merely cases in which, on the totality of the evidence, the court was able to make a finding of negligence".

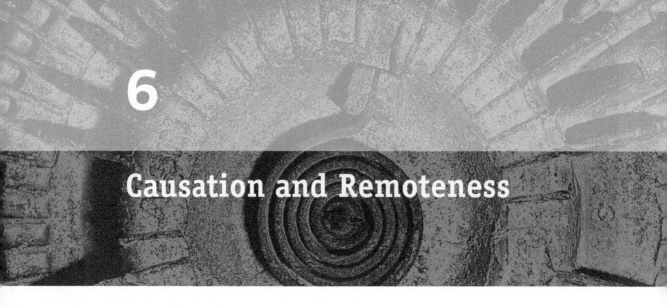

6

Causation and Remoteness

Introduction

6–001 This chapter deals with the question whether the defendant's actions can be said to be the legal cause of a claimant's loss. Essentially, in answering this question, two separate issues need to be considered. First, there is the issue of whether what the defendant did was the factual cause of the defendant's loss (or whether the loss was caused by something else). Secondly, there is the issue of whether, in certain cases, although the claimant's loss is the factual result of the defendant's actions, the law should nevertheless say that the defendant is not liable because that loss is too "remote"—in the sense that it is too unusual or "far removed" a consequence of the defendant's actions. We explore each of these issues in turn.

Factual Causation

6–002 Factual causation is a difficult subject. It divides into a number of separate issues, but there is a considerable degree of conceptual overlap between these issues. Often, when a court focuses on one particular issue, it is merely selecting one particular approach from a number of alternatives. In some cases, a number of approaches are adopted concurrently, and it may be difficult to classify a given case as turning on one issue rather than another.[1] The root of all the

---

1   For more detailed discussion of causation, see H. L. A. Hart and T. Honoré, *Causation in the Law*, 2nd edn (Clarendon Press, 1985), S. Green, *Causation in Negligence* (Hart, 2015), S. Steel, *Proof of Causation in Tort* (CUP, 2015) and G. Turton, *Evidential Uncertainty in Causation in Negligence* (Hart, 2016).

confusion is the difficult nature of causation as a philosophical problem. We begin by examining this problem and noting, in general terms, the law's response to it.

The pragmatic approach

The relationship between "cause" and "effect" is complex. Philosophically speaking, every "effect" is produced by the coming together of many different "causes". Moreover, all of these "causes" will, in truth, themselves be "effects" produced by other "causes". Take an example: I light a cigarette and carelessly discard my lighted match in your wastepaper basket, which results in a fire burning down your house. Who is to blame? Legally speaking, the answer is pretty obvious—it is my carelessness that has caused the fire. But philosophically speaking, the fire has many causes. A philosopher might say that there are many "conditions" without which the fire might not have happened. It might not have happened had you not allowed the wastepaper basket to become so full with paper. It certainly would not have happened without your inviting me to your house in the first place and allowing me to smoke there. Do these factors mean that you are the cause of your own loss? Alternatively, we might say that there would have been no fire if I were not an addicted smoker. Therefore, can we not blame the person who offered me my first cigarette? Ultimately, if I had not been born, your house would not have burned down. Does this mean we can blame my parents? How about fixing the blame on my distant ancestors? Clearly, the law cannot take a philosophical approach to causation. If it did, nobody could ever be said to have caused *anything*. Defendants could always "pass the buck", or, as a lawyer might say, fix responsibility on a person or an event further back in the "chain of causation". Therefore, the law takes a pragmatic, or "common sense" view of causation. As Lord Wright put it in *Yorkshire Dale Steamship Co Ltd v Minister of War Transport*, "Causation is to be understood as the man in the street, and not as either the scientist or the metaphysician, would understand it".[2] Yet this approach can leave us in a position where the reasoning in the cases defies analysis in terms of logical principle. Another unfortunate consequence of the "common sense" approach is that, in causation cases, legal language is particularly apt to produce confusion. For example, judges and writers may say that a defendant is not liable unless he has "caused" the damage; on the other hand, they may say that a defendant is not liable for all of the damage that he has "caused". Qualifying the word "cause" with adjectives such as "legal", "proximate" or "remote" does little to unravel the mysteries of the topic.[3]

In most cases, the application of the "man in the street" approach reveals that there is only one activity or event that can be sensibly regarded as the cause of the claimant's loss, so the issue is straightforward. In a small minority of cases, however, the law must somehow choose between two or more competing causes of the claimant's loss. These problematic cases are the

6–003

---

2   [1942] A.C. 691 at 706.

3   See D. Howarth, M. Matthews, J. Morgan, J. O'Sullivan and S. Tofaris, *Hepple and Matthews' Tort Law: Cases and Materials*, 7th edn (Bloomsbury, 2015), p.345.

focus of this chapter. We shall consider them once we have examined in more detail the test the courts apply in straightforward cases.

The "but for" test

6–004
The law's starting point in determining causation is to apply the "but for" test.[4] In other words, to ask the question, "Can it be said that 'but for' the defendant's conduct, the claimant's loss would not have occurred?" Another way of putting this is to ask, "Would the claimant's loss have occurred *in any event*, even without the defendant's conduct?" If the answer to this question is "yes", then the defendant will not have caused the claimant's loss. The classic illustration of the application of the "but for" test is the case of *Barnett v Chelsea and Kensington Hospital Management Committee*.[5] Here, a man went to a casualty department feeling unwell after having drunk some tea. The doctor in charge sent him away without treatment, telling him to see his own doctor. He subsequently died from arsenic poisoning. It was held that the doctor was in breach of his duty of care in failing to examine the man, but expert evidence indicated that, having drunk the arsenic, the man was beyond help when he arrived at the hospital and would have died in any event. Therefore, the doctor's breach of duty had not caused the man's death.

In applying the "but for" test, the courts take into account not only *existing* causes that might have produced the claimant's loss (for example, the arsenic in *Barnett*), but also *hypothetical* causes that might have produced the loss. For example, in *McWilliams v Sir William Arrol Ltd*,[6] a steel erector fell to his death at work. The defendants were in breach of their statutory duty in failing to provide him with a safety harness, but the evidence was that he had rarely used such a harness in the past. In the House of Lords, the defendants successfully argued that this meant he would not have worn a harness even if one had been provided. This being the case, it followed that the defendants were not liable because the man would probably have died in any event.

Bolitho v City and Hackney Health Authority[7] (considered in Ch.5) was another case in which the House of Lords had to consider the causal effect of a hypothetical omission. Here, a two-year-old boy was admitted to hospital suffering from breathing difficulties and was kept under observation. His condition deteriorated and on two occasions a nurse contacted the doctor in charge, asking her to attend, but she failed to do so. The child subsequently suffered cardiac arrest leading to brain damage. The doctor had clearly been negligent in failing to attend, but the doctor argued that her non-attendance had not caused the child's death. She maintained

---

4   *Cork v Kirby MacLean Ltd* [1952] 2 All E.R. 402. Stapleton argues, however, that a more generous test is needed, see J. Stapleton, "Unnecessary causes" (2013) 129 L.Q.R. 39 and "An 'extended but-for' test for the causal relation in the law of obligations" (2015) 35 O.J.L.S. 697.

5   [1969] 1 Q.B. 428.

6   [1962] 1 All E.R. 623.

7   [1998] A.C. 232. Comment: P. Giliker (1998–99) 9 K.C.L.J. 109 and N. Glover (1999) 15 P.N. 42.

that, given the child's symptoms, even if she had attended and examined the child, she would not have taken any action, but would have left the child for a further period of observation. The plaintiff countered this argument by saying that such a course of action would have been negligent—given the symptoms, a competent doctor should have "intubated" (inserted a tube) to assist the child's breathing.

As was noted in Ch.5, the House of Lords held that the doctor's failure to intubate would not have been negligent, because her reasons for not doing so were supported by a body of responsible medical opinion. What is relevant here, however, is to note that in deciding the question of causation, the House of Lords was prepared to ask not simply, "Would the doctor have intubated if she had attended?", but "*Should* the doctor have intubated in such circumstances?" As Lord Browne-Wilkinson put it:

> **"A defendant [who is in breach of duty] cannot escape liability by saying that the damage would have occurred in any event because he would have committed some other breach of duty thereafter."[8]**

Problems with the "but for" test

The "but for" test works well enough in the majority of cases, but in cases where there are "multiple causes" it runs into problems. The celebrated example is that of two fires—Fire A and Fire B—both started negligently on different pieces of neighbouring land, which each are capable of burning down the claimant's house.[9] The fires converge and destroy the house. If the claimant sues the creator of Fire A, the creator of Fire A can argue that the loss would have happened in any event, because of the existence of Fire B. If the creator of Fire B is sued, he can employ a similar argument. Thus, applying the "but for" test, neither defendant is liable. It is doubtful that the courts would countenance such an unjust result. They would (probably) treat the case as one involving "cumulative causes" (discussed below), making both defendants jointly liable for the full extent of the damage.[10]

In the sections below, we consider the courts' approach to different types of cases involving multiple causes. It is traditional to classify such cases under a number of headings. But this classification, and the traditional accompanying analysis of the various "rules" governing each class of case, can give the misleading impression that causation is a rather "technical" or

6–005

---

8   *Bolitho v City and Hackney Health Authority* [1998] A.C. 232 at 240.
9   See P. Cane and J. Goudkamp, *Atiyah's Accidents, Compensation and the Law*, 9th edn (2018), para.5.2.4 on multiple causal factors.
10 Alternatively, the courts might apportion liability equally between the two defendants. Consider also the alternative NESS test of Richard Wright (Necessary Element of a Sufficient Set), who argues that as long as the factor was necessary for the sufficiency of one of the sets of conditions that actually occurred on the particular occasion then it was a cause: R. Wright, "The NESS Account of Natural Causation: A Response to Criticisms" in Goldberg (ed.), *Perspectives on Causation* (Hart, 2011) p.293.

"evidential" branch of the law, in which policy plays only a minor role. It should not be forgotten that, as in other areas of tort law, the rules are flexible. We shall see that they have often been stretched to accommodate policy concerns. Indeed, they have sometimes been stretched so far that they cease to withstand clear analysis.

Concurrent Causes

6–006

Certain cases are traditionally described as involving "concurrent causes", by which is meant simply that the causes in question occur more or less simultaneously, as opposed to one after another. As a means of classification, the expression is rather inadequate, because, as we shall see, it might equally be applied to certain cases traditionally described as involving "consecutive causes", in which the causes occur at different times but their *effects* operate at the same time. Nevertheless, it is traditional to consider the so-called "concurrent cause" cases separately.

"Concurrent cause" cases can be divided into two groups, as follows:

- "Indeterminate cause": In these cases, there is more than one defendant, but there is only one "operative cause" of the claimant's loss, it being unclear which of the defendants' acts produced this cause. Such is the case, for example, where a claimant has *one* bullet in his leg, but several defendants have been negligent in shooting their guns in the claimant's direction. (As in *Cook v Lewis* and *Summers v Tice*, considered below.)

- "Cumulative cause": In these cases, there is more than one "operative cause" of the claimant's loss, each produced by the act of a different defendant, but the problem is, these causes have combined inextricably to produce the same damage. Such is the case, for example, where a claimant has *two* bullets in his leg, each fired by a different defendant, and as a result of this predicament has to have his leg amputated.

We consider each type of case in turn.

"Indeterminate cause"

6–007

The relevant principles here can be understood by considering the Canadian case of *Cook v Lewis*[11] and the US case of *Summers v Tice*.[12] Both cases involved hunting accidents in which the plaintiff had been shot by *one* bullet, fired by one of two defendants, each of whom had been careless in aiming his gun in the plaintiff's direction. The evidence could not establish from whose gun the shot had been fired. The courts adopted the pragmatic approach of reversing

---

11   [1951] S.C.R. 830.
12   119 P.2d 1 (1948).

the burden of proof. Thus, in the absence of evidence from either defendant that he had *not* been responsible for the bullet, both defendants were held liable as joint tortfeasors.[13] Joint tortfeasors are each potentially liable for the whole of the claimant's loss. Each defendant can then seek a contribution from the other, but that is a separate question relating to damages rather than to liability (see Ch.17).

In *Sindell v Abbott Laboratories*,[14] another US case, the court adopted a more radical solution. The case concerned the liability of manufacturers for a defective pregnancy drug which caused cancer in the female children of mothers who had taken it. The problem did not become apparent until the children had reached puberty and it was then impossible to show which of several hundred manufacturers had produced the particular drug taken by the plaintiffs' mothers. It was known, however, that the drug was inherently defective, so that any one of the manufacturers could have been responsible. The court rejected the solution of imposing joint liability, as in *Summers v Tice*, because only a few of those potentially responsible were defendants before the court and it was unfair to make them responsible to the full extent. Instead, the court held each defendant liable according to the degree of its share of the market for the drug at the relevant time, on the basis that this was the best approximation that could be made of each defendant's likely responsibility.

In the cases discussed above, the courts had to decide which of two human actions produced the claimant's loss. The solutions adopted in these cases, however, have not been favoured by the English courts in cases where the fault of one defendant is competing with one or more "innocent" or "natural" explanations for the claimant's loss. The leading authorities here are *Wilsher v Essex AHA*,[15] *Hotson v East Berkshire AHA*[16] and *Gregg v Scott*.[17] In these cases, the courts have not been prepared to make a defendant liable unless the claimant can show that, on the balance of probabilities, his or her loss was caused by the defendant's fault rather than by a natural occurrence. In such cases, the standard of proof required of the claimant assumes enormous significance. For this reason, these cases are worthy of separate consideration and are discussed in a later section of this chapter, under the heading "proof of causation".

"Cumulative cause"

6–008

We have already considered a good example of a "cumulative cause" situation—that of two negligently started fires, each capable of burning down the claimant's house, which

---

13 In the mesothelioma litigation discussed later in the chapter, the House of Lords attempted to impose several (rather than joint) liability in this type of situation (see *Barker v Corus UK Ltd* [2006] UKHL 20; [2006] 2 A.C. 572), only to be reversed by the Compensation Act 2006.

14 607 P.2d 924 (1980).

15 [1988] A.C. 1074.

16 [1987] A.C. 750.

17 [2005] UKHL 2; [2005] 2 A.C. 176.

converge and destroy the house. We have noted that in such situations, applying the "but for" test would result in neither defendant being liable. Therefore, the usual approach of the courts is to say that, because either negligent act would have produced the same damage, each defendant is liable for the whole of the damage.[18] This is what happened in *The Koursk*,[19] where two ships collided because both were simultaneously subject to negligent navigation.

In the example above, we have made the assumption that the act of one defendant alone would have given rise to the whole of the damage. If we cast aside this assumption, however, we are left with a slightly different and more complex type of "cumulative cause" case. This is the sort of case where one defendant (the "first defendant") commits a tortious act, and then, very shortly afterwards, and before the force of that act is spent, a second defendant commits an act which *combines* with it, producing a single result that might not have occurred without the operation of the second act. In such cases, both the first and the second defendant may be liable for the result produced. Take an example: negligent driver A causes his vehicle to obstruct the highway, and subsequently negligent driver B crashes into it, causing injury to a bystander, C. Here, driver A may be held to have caused C's injuries, and may be jointly liable with driver B.[20] This is so, even though it cannot be said that driver A's negligence alone would have caused the accident.

One of the best-known examples of this type of "cumulative cause" case is *Fitzgerald v Lane*.[21] Here, the plaintiff was crossing a pelican crossing when the lights showed green for cars, but red for pedestrians. He was hit by a car driven negligently by the first defendant. The force of the collision threw him up on the bonnet and propelled him into the middle of the road. He was then hit by a car driven negligently by the second defendant. He suffered severe injuries to his spine resulting in tetraplegia. At the trial, the evidence could not establish whether his tetraplegia resulted from impact with the first car or from impact with the second car. Moreover, it was impossible to say whether the tetraplegia had only one (indeterminate) cause, or whether it was the result of the combined effect of being hit by both cars. It was clear, however, that the plaintiff had himself been careless in crossing when the lights were against him. The judge held that all three parties involved had been negligent and that, since it was impossible to say that one of the parties was more or less to blame than the other, the responsibility should be borne equally by all three. Therefore, both defendants were held liable and the plaintiff was held contributorily negligent.

---

18 Note, however, that where the evidence shows that one defendant is more responsible than another, the court will apportion liability between them in proportion to their fault: see *Holtby v Brigham & Cowan (Hull) Ltd* [2000] 3 All E.R. 421 and *Allen v British Rail Engineering Ltd* [2001] EWCA Civ 242; [2001] I.C.R. 942.

19 [1924] P. 140.

20 See *Rouse v Squires* [1973] Q.B. 889 per Cairns LJ at 898, but see also *Wright v Lodge* [1993] 4 All E.R. 299 (discussed below) for a restriction on the application of this principle, namely that subsequent "reckless" conduct by the second driver will exculpate the first driver.

21 [1987] Q.B. 781 CA. There was an appeal to the House of Lords, but only on the question of apportionment of damages, which is discussed in Ch.17.

Successive Causes

In so-called "successive cause" cases, the key issue is whether, where one act succeeds another, there are circumstances where the effect of the first act can be said to have become "over-taken" or "obliterated" by the effect of the second act, in such a way that the first act ceases to be a cause of the claimant's loss. The classic illustration of this sort of situation is this: Imagine that a man is about to set out on a journey across the desert. He has a lethal dose of poison put into his water bottle by one of his enemies. Later, the bottle is emptied by a second enemy. Ignorant of these events, he sets out on his journey during the course of which he dies of thirst.

Now, in theory we might absolve the second enemy by pointing to the fact that, if the water bottle had not been emptied, the man would have died in any event from poison. But we could also absolve the poisoner by pointing out that, if the water had not been poisoned, the man would still have died of thirst. Thus, applying the "but for" test makes nobody liable. This sort of situation, however, is different from the example of the converging fires, where the law, unable to determine which action caused the loss, may make both actors liable. Here, the factual cause of the traveller's death is clear—he died of thirst and not of poison. In cases of this sort, then, we might say that the effect of the poisoner's act was "overtaken" or "obliterated" by the act of the second enemy. In other words, in the light of what the second enemy did, the act of the poisoner had no effect.

Situations like that in the example above, however, must be distinguished from cases where the effect of the first wrongful act is said to continue, in spite of the effect of the second.[22] Such was the case in *Performance Cars v Abraham*.[23] The plaintiff's Rolls-Royce was involved in two collisions in the space of a fortnight. After the first collision, the car was in need of a respray. It was then hit by a second driver (the defendant), sustaining the sort of damage that would also necessitate a respray. In an action against the second driver, the Court of Appeal rejected the owner's claim for the cost of a respray on the grounds that the loss did not flow from the defendant's wrongdoing—at the time of the second collision, the vehicle was already in need of a respray. Here, then, rather than saying that effect of the first tort was obliterated by the second, the court applied exactly the opposite sort of reasoning: the second tort had no effect, given the continuing effect of the first.

Broadly similar reasoning was applied by the House of Lords in *Baker v Willoughby*.[24] The plaintiff was run down by the defendant's negligent driving, suffering a stiff leg which caused him loss of mobility and a consequent reduction in his earning capacity. Before the action came to trial, the plaintiff was shot in the same leg by armed robbers, after which the

---

22 Also known as multiple sufficient causes cases (see M. Lunney, D. Nolan and K. Oliphant, *Tort Law: Text and Materials*, 6th edn (Oxford, OUP)).

23 [1962] 1 Q.B. 33. Applied in the context of medical negligence in *Reaney v University Hospital of North Staffordshire NHS Trust* [2015] EWCA Civ 1119; [2016] P.I.Q.R. Q3: did negligent treatment of patient with pre-existing condition merely add to her existing needs (a quantitative difference) or cause an injury which was qualitatively difference from her pre-existing needs? Here it was the former, so hospital only liable to the extent to which the existing condition has been worsened by negligence.

24 [1970] A.C. 467.

leg had to be amputated. The defendant driver argued that his liability should be limited to the loss caused by the original injury up to the date of the robbery—any loss of mobility and reduction in earning capacity thereafter had been caused, not by him, but by the amputation of the leg. In other words, it was argued that the effect of the original injury had been submerged or obliterated by the second. The defendant also argued that, because, in assessing the amount of damages, it is the courts' practice to discount the award to take account of the hypothetical "vicissitudes of life" that a claimant may suffer in the future (that is, unexpected changes to his or her fortunes which would have happened in any event), it followed that where these "vicissitudes" had become actual, the damages should be reduced accordingly.

The House of Lords rejected these arguments. Lord Reid, speaking for the majority, held the defendant liable for *all* of the consequences of the first injury, just as if the second injury had not occurred. In essence, his Lordship was treating the case as one where the plaintiff's continuing loss of amenity had *cumulative* causes—the car accident and the shooting. Did, for example, the injury from the motor accident lead Baker to take the menial job in a scrapyard where he was shot or prevent him from escaping from the robbers? Such speculation disguises the fact that the Court was seeking in reality to avoid "manifest injustice" and took the view that this could only be achieved by taking a "comprehensive and unitary view of the damage caused by the original accident".[25] In other words, as Lord Reid put it:

> **"A man is not compensated for the physical injury: he is compensated for the loss which he suffers as a result of that injury. His loss is not in having a stiff leg: it is in his inability to lead a full life . . . and his inability to earn as much as he used to earn or could have earned if there had been no accident. In this case, the second injury did not diminish any of these [losses]. So why should it be regarded as having obliterated or superseded them?"[26]**

It seems likely, therefore, that their Lordships were influenced by the need to do practical justice. The thieves who had shot the plaintiff could not be found, and even if they could be found and sued in tort, it would be unlikely that they would be able to pay compensation. Moreover, if the thieves were sued in tort, they would be entitled to "take their victim as they found him". This meant that they could not be liable for the whole of the plaintiff's loss of amenity, but only for the extent to which they had made his condition worse. In this light, it would be very unfair to say that the first tortfeasor could not be fully liable either, because this would leave the plaintiff under-compensated. He would "fall between two defendants". Policy therefore dictated that a first tortfeasor should remain liable for the continuing effects of his or her tort, even where a second tort produced the same (or worse) effects.

25   See Lord Pearson at [1970] A.C. 467 at 496.
26   [1970] A.C. 467 at 492.

The decision in *Baker v Willoughby* should be contrasted with that in *Jobling v Associated Dairies Ltd*.[27] In *Jobling*, the defendant employers had been responsible for injuring the plaintiff's back, causing him loss of mobility and reduced earning capacity. Before the action came to trial, the plaintiff succumbed to a crippling back disease, completely unrelated to his accident, which rendered him totally unfit for work. As in *Baker*, the House of Lords had to decide whether, in the light of a successive event giving rise to the same loss, the defendants could remain liable for the plaintiff's reduced earning capacity in the future. Here, however, the subsequent event in question was a disease rather than a tort. Their Lordships reached the opposite conclusion from that in *Baker*. Taking account of the aim of an award of damages, their Lordships held that the plaintiff would be over-compensated if he were able to recover from the defendants. It was held, therefore, that the defendants' liability ceased at the time of the onset of the disease.

In *Jobling*, Lord Bridge felt unable to accept the approach that had been adopted in *Baker*. His Lordship pointed out that the decision in *Baker* appeared to ignore the fundamental principle that the aim of a damages award in tort is to put the claimant in the same position he or she would have been in had the tort not occurred. On Lord Bridge's analysis of *Baker*, it could be said that, had the first tort not occurred, the plaintiff would have suffered the same sort of loss *in any event* when he was shot by the thieves. Thus, the outcome of the decision was one which actually put him in a *better* position than he would have been in had the first tort never occurred.[28]

Lord Edmund-Davies, acknowledging academic criticism of the decision in *Baker*,[29] pointed out that the decision had appeared to overlook the fact that the plaintiff could be compensated under the Criminal Injuries Compensation Scheme in respect of the actions of the thieves. This meant that the "injustice" the decision sought to avoid "did not, at least in its full dimensions, exist".[30] Both Lord Edmund-Davies and Lord Wilberforce thought that the decision in *Baker* could not be properly analysed in terms of legal principle and that the case had been decided on policy grounds. Lord Edmund-Davies concluded:

> **"I can formulate no convincing juristic or logical principles supportive of the decision of this House in *Baker v Willoughby*, and none were there propounded."[31]**

Although, in *Jobling*, their Lordships criticised the decision in *Baker*, they were not prepared to overrule it and accepted that the case might have been correctly decided on its facts. Lords Keith and Russell drew a distinction between a supervening illness, which would obliterate the effect of a previous tortious act, and a supervening tort, which might not.[32] This distinction is

---

27 [1982] A.C. 794.
28 [1982] A.C. 794 at 820.
29 e.g. P.S. Atiyah (1969) 85 L.Q.R. 475.
30 *Jobling v Associated Dairies* [1982] A.C. 794 at 807.
31 [1982] A.C. 794 at 808–809.
32 In *Heil v Rankin* [2001] P.I.Q.R. Q3 the Court of Appeal affirmed that there was no absolute rule that the effect of a supervening tort would obliterate the effect of a previous tort.

hard to justify. At bottom, it must be admitted that the decisions in *Baker* and in *Jobling* cannot be satisfactorily reconciled. The decisions show us that the answers to causation questions are heavily dependent on a pragmatic, policy-driven approach.

What might be discerned, however, is a tendency in the modern law to prefer the *Jobling* approach in this type of case. Thus, in *Gray v Thames Trains Ltd*[33] one of the issues which arose was whether a claim for continuing loss of earnings could be made after the claimant had been sentenced for a crime. Although the loss of earnings was initially caused by the injury resulting from the defendant's negligence, the House of Lords held that the principle in *Jobling* prevented such a claim—after the claimant had been sentenced, the effective cause of his continuing lost earnings was to be regarded as his incarceration, rather than the defendant's tort.

Proof of Causation

6–011   In this section we are concerned with the difficult question of how, in cases where the defendant's conduct competes with other possible explanations of the claimant's loss, the courts approach the question of requiring the claimant to prove that the defendant's breach is the cause of his or her loss. The nature of the approach the courts will take depends on the type of case with which they are concerned, and here, again, we can see that the courts' decisions seem heavily influenced by policy considerations. A number of different approaches can be discerned, which may be described as:

- the "all or nothing" approach;

- the "material contribution to injury" approach;

- the "vindication of rights" approach; and

- the "material increase in risk" approach.

It is difficult to reconcile these approaches with one another on the basis of coherent principle. Each is simply a pragmatic response to what the courts perceive as the broad demands of justice in particular circumstances. Indeed, the "vindication of rights" and "material increase in risk" approaches might be better described as exceptions to the "but for" test whose scope is fiercely contested.[34]

---

33   [2009] UKHL 33; [2009] 1 A.C. 1339.

34   Steel argues that acceptance of exceptions does not undermine the general rule: S. Steel, "Justifying exceptions to proof of causation in tort law" (2015) 78 M.L.R. 729.

(i) The "all or nothing" approach

6-012

The "all or nothing" approach is the approach that will be applied in most cases. Applying the "but for" test, it takes as its starting point the proposition that the claimant, who bears the burden of proof in a civil trial, must discharge that burden by meeting the normal civil standard of proof. Thus, the claimant must show that, on the balance of probabilities, it was the defendant's breach (rather than some other event) that caused the loss. This is known as an "all or nothing" approach because, where a claimant succeeds in showing that it is probable (at least 51% likely) that the breach caused the loss, the law will treat this probability as a certainty, so the claimant will win the case and be compensated for all of the loss. If, on the other hand, a claimant can only show, say, a 25% likelihood that the breach caused the loss, the claimant will lose the case and leave court with nothing.

The "all or nothing" approach was adopted by the House of Lords in *Wilsher v Essex AHA*.[35] In *Wilsher*, the plaintiff was a premature baby who suffered from oxygen deficiency. In monitoring the levels of oxygen in his blood, one of the doctors employed by the defendants negligently failed to notice that a catheter had been wrongly placed into a vein instead of an artery. This meant that the monitoring equipment gave a misleading reading, resulting in the plaintiff being given too much oxygen. The plaintiff developed retrolental fibroplasia (RLF)—a condition permanently affecting his retina—which left him almost totally blind. The expert evidence suggested that excess oxygen was a *possible* cause of RLF, but that RLF was a condition that occurred even in premature babies who did not receive oxygen. There was therefore evidence of a causal link between RLF and at least five conditions that were very common in premature babies.

The trial judge and the Court of Appeal (relying on the House of Lords' decision in *McGhee v National Coal Board*—discussed below) had held the defendants liable on the basis that, by supplying excess oxygen, they had "materially increased the risk" that the plaintiff would succumb to RLF. The House of Lords, however, rejected this liberal approach to causation and substituted the "all or nothing" approach, holding that the plaintiff had failed to establish, on the balance of probabilities, that his RLF had been produced by the excess oxygen, rather than by one of the five other possible common causes of RLF. Lord Bridge, who delivered the unanimous opinion of the House of Lords, acknowledged that the application of the "all or nothing" approach had produced a harsh result for the plaintiff. His Lordship said:

> **"Many may feel that [ordering a retrial] serves only to highlight the shortcomings of a system in which the victim of some grievous misfortune will recover substantial compensation or none at all according to the unpredictable hazards of the forensic process. But, whether we like it or not, the law, which only Parliament can change, requires proof of fault causing damage as the basis of liability in tort.**

---

35 [1988] A.C. 1074.

> We should do society nothing but disservice if we made the forensic process still more unpredictable and hazardous by distorting the law to accommodate the exigencies of what may seem hard cases."[36]

6-013

The harshness that can result from this approach may be seen in the so-called "loss of chance" cases. Here the claimant is suing on the basis that his or her chance of recovery was diminished due to the defendant's negligence. In *Hotson v East Berkshire AHA*,[37] the plaintiff, when aged 13, fell while climbing a tree and sustained injury to his hip. He was taken to hospital, but his injury was not correctly diagnosed or treated for five days. In the event, he suffered avascular necrosis—a condition that left him with severe and permanent disability by the time he was 20. Had the hospital treated him promptly when he was first admitted, the plaintiff would have had a 25% chance of making a full recovery, but the effect of the delay in treatment was that the plaintiff lost that 25% chance.

The trial judge (Simon Brown J) awarded the plaintiff a sum in damages which reflected 25% of the damages which might have been awarded had the hospital's negligence been the only possible cause of his disability. This decision was affirmed by the Court of Appeal, but was reversed by the House of Lords. The key finding of the House of Lords was that the plaintiff had failed to prove his case on the balance of probabilities. Simon Brown J, assessing the medical evidence, had found, of course, that there had been a 75% chance that avascular necrosis would have resulted *in any event*, even if the plaintiff had been treated promptly. This meant, in their Lordships' view, that on the balance of probabilities the plaintiff's disability had been caused when he fell out of the tree. In these circumstances, Simon Brown J had been wrong to embark on a "quantification" of the loss caused by the defendant—the issue of quantifying the loss could only arise once the hurdle of causation had been overcome, and this the plaintiff had failed to do.

On the evidence, the reason for the plaintiff's disability was clear—when he fell from the tree, he was, on the balance of probabilities, disabled; the law would treat this probability as a factual certainty, which meant that, by the time the plaintiff arrived at the hospital he was *as a matter of decided fact* already disabled. Thus, in effect, at this point in time the plaintiff had had no chance to lose.[38]

The strict approach to causation exemplified in *Hotson* was subsequently followed by a majority of the House of Lords in *Gregg v Scott*.[39] Here, the defendant, a GP, had negligently failed to refer the claimant to hospital to be tested for cancer, so that there was a delay of nine months before his condition was diagnosed. According to the accepted statistical evidence,

---

36 [1988] A.C. 1074 at 1092.

37 [1987] A.C. 750.

38 For further consideration of all these issues, see J. Stapleton, "The gist of negligence Part 2: the relationship between 'damage' and causation" (1988) 104 L.Q.R. 389 and H. Reece, "Losses of chances in the law" (1996) 59 M.L.R. 189.

39 [2005] UKHL 2; [2005] 2 A.C. 176. Contrast *Oliver v Williams* [2013] EWHC 600 (QB): delayed diagnosis by 5.5 months, but not established that this made any material or measurable difference to patient's life expectancy.

when the claimant had originally gone to see his GP, he had had a 42% chance of making a full recovery with prompt treatment (and, of course, a 58% chance of *not* doing so). The effect of the negligent delay was to reduce the claimant's chance of recovery to 25%.

The claimant felt able to bring his case because, in their decision in *Fairchild v Glenhaven Funeral Services Ltd*[40] (discussed below) the House of Lords had recently ruled that the "all or nothing" approach could be modified in certain circumstances, where the demands of justice made it right to do so. In *Gregg v Scott*, however, their Lordships declined to extend the reasoning in *Fairchild* (which had involved a risk of industrial disease) to cover the claimant's case. By a 3:2 majority, their Lordships held that the traditional rules of causation should apply. Thus, the claimant lost his case because the "but for" test was not satisfied—he could not show, on the balance of probabilities, that the fact that he had failed to make a full recovery was due to the GP's negligence. The probability (58%) was that he would have failed to make a full recovery *in any event*.

The reasoning in *Gregg v Scott* reveals a stark division of opinion between the Law Lords about the correct approach to be taken in medical negligence cases involving loss of a chance of recovery. The key issue is whether justice demands that the tort of negligence should abandon its strict causation rules in this type of case, and, instead, compensate claimants for lost chances that (even though less than 50%) were of real and substantial value to them. Lord Nicholls, in a powerful dissenting judgment, said that if the law failed to do this, it would be "irrational and indefensible".[41] His Lordship went on to say:

6-014

> **"The law should be extremely slow to disregard medical reality . . . In these cases a doctor's duty to act in the best interests of his patient involves maximising the patient's recovery prospects, and doing so whether the patient's prospects are good or not so good. In the event of a breach of this duty the law must fashion a matching and meaningful remedy . . . It cannot be right to adopt a procedure having the effect that, in law, a patient's prospects of recovery are treated as non-existent whenever they exist but fall short of 50%. If the law were to proceed in this way it would deserve to be likened to the proverbial ass."[42]**

Baroness Hale, however, speaking in the majority, explained the difficulty the courts would face if they recognised claims for loss of a (less than 50%) chance of recovery. Such recognition would, as her Ladyship put it, require "that personal injury law should transform itself".[43] If a claimant who had lost, say, a 40% chance of recovery, were entitled to a "proportionate"

---

40   [2002] UKHL 22; [2003] 1 A.C. 32.

41   *Gregg v Scott* [2005] 2 A.C. 176 per Lord Nicholls at [6].

42   [2005] 2 A.C. 176 per Lord Nicholls at [42] and [43].

43   [2005] 2 A.C. 176 per Baroness Hale at [222].

sum representing that loss, where would be the justice in allowing a claimant who had lost a 51% chance of recovery (thereby satisfying the standard of proof) to leave court with 100% of the damages? Surely the idea of proportionate compensation would cut both ways, allowing defendants, if it suited them, to reformulate the gist of the action against them as "loss of a chance". This would lead to the strange proposition (to borrow her Ladyship's example) that, where it is shown that there is a 90% chance that my negligence broke your leg, I am entitled to require the court to reduce your damages by 10%, to reflect the chance that your leg might have become broken in any event. This proposition would create an unwelcome complication in the great majority of personal injury cases and would make recovery of compensation much less predictable for defendants and for the insurance market. For these reasons, then, it was not desirable that the court should view Mr Gregg's loss in a case like *Gregg v Scott* as a "lost chance".[44] Rather, it should be viewed as an *outcome* (i.e. after the negligent treatment, he was unlikely to get better)—and on this basis, of course, the *outcome* of the defendant's negligence had placed the claimant in *no different a position* from the position he had been in before the negligence had occurred, meaning, in effect, that he had suffered no actionable loss.

(ii) The "material contribution to injury" approach

6–015

Despite continued assertions by the judiciary that the rules of causation should not be displaced to accommodate "hard cases", there has been some evidence of flexibility. Where, for example, the claimant suffers from a disease which has been caused by exposure to a particular agent and there has been both innocent (non-negligent) and guilty (negligent) exposure, the courts will find causation to be established where the guilty exposure makes a material contribution to the injury suffered. It remains a source of contention whether this is simply a more fluid interpretation of the "but for" test or a distinct test in its own right.[45] It does differ, however, from the *Wilsher* situation (discussed above) where the disease could have been caused by one or more of a number of disparate factors.

The classic case is that of *Bonnington Castings Ltd v Wardlaw*[46] where the plaintiff had

---

44 Compare the approach of the courts in cases where the lost chance is one of financial gain. See, e.g. *Allied Maples Group Ltd v Simmons and Simmons* [1995] 1 W.L.R. 1602. It is difficult to distinguish such cases from *Gregg v Scott*, save (as Baroness Hale did in *Gregg* at [220]) on the basis that the claimant's loss is different in quality: "There is not much difference between the money one expected to have and the money one expected to have a chance of having: it is all money. There is a difference between the leg one ought to have and the chance of keeping a leg one ought to have". Nevertheless, this distinction was affirmed by Lord Neuberger MR in *Wright (A Child) v Cambridge Medical Group (A Partnership)* [2011] EWCA Civ 669; [2013] Q.B. 312 at [84], arguing that it was not appropriate for the Court of Appeal to expand the loss of chance doctrine into the realm of clinical negligence, while adding that "the question would be appropriate for reconsideration by the Supreme Court".

45 See S. Bailey, "Causation in negligence: What is a material contribution?" (2010) 32 L.S. 396. Lord Phillips in *Sienkiewicz v Greif* [2011] UKSC 10; [2011] 2 A.C. 229 described it at [17] as "an important exception to the 'but for' test".

46 [1956] A.C. 613.

complained that his employer had exposed him to silicone dust while working in his work-shop which had led to pneumoconiosis. The evidence indicated that the dust was created by two sources: the operation of a pneumatic hammer (which was not due to negligence) and the swing grinders (which was). Lord Reid held that it was for the claimant to prove that the defendants' fault on the balance of probabilities caused, or materially contributed to, his injury.[47] Where, as here, the disease had been caused by the cumulative effect of the inhalation of dust from both sources, the real question was whether the dust from the swing grinders materially contributed to his disease: What is "material" will be a question of degree on the facts of each case. Lord Reid held that:

> "A contribution which comes within the exception *de minimis non curat lex* is not material, but I think that any contribution which does not fall within that exception must be material. I do not see how there can be something too large to come within the *de minimis* principle but yet too small to be material."[48]

On the facts, it was shown that the swing grinders contributed a quota of silica dust which was more than negligible to the claimant's lungs and so helped to produce the disease.

The application of this test has inevitably in view of *Wilsher* (above) proven controversial in medical negligence cases. In *Bailey v Ministry of Defence*,[49] for example, it was unclear whether the claimant's condition had been caused by her medical condition (pancreatitis) or by the negligent post-operative care she had received. Treating the case as one of "cumulative causes" which produce indivisible harm, the Court held that where medical science cannot establish the evidence needed to apply the "but for" test, it would suffice to show that the defendants' negligence materially contributed to the injury, that is, made a contribution which is more than negligible.[50] Here, the negligence was found to have materially contributed to the claimant's weakness which led to her choking. The Privy Council in *Williams v Bermuda Hospitals Board*[51] addressed the application of this test again in a medical negligence context: here there had been a negligent delay in treatment and sepsis[52] from a ruptured appendix had damaged the claimant's heart and lungs. The injury to the heart and lungs had been caused by a single known agent (as in *Bonnington*): the sepsis from the ruptured appendix.[53] The negligence had

---

47 [1956] A.C. 613 at 620.

48 [1956] AC 613 at 621.

49 [2008] EWCA Civ 883; [2009] 1 W.L.R. 1052. For criticism, see M. Stauch [2009] C.L.J. 27.

50 *Wilsher v Essex AHA* [1988] A.C. 1074 (discussed above) was distinguished on the basis that it involved "distinct causes" which operated in different ways, and the claimant could not establish which cause had either "caused or contributed" to his injury.

51 [2016] UKPC 4; [2016] A.C. 888 at [47].

52 Sepsis is a potentially life-threatening complication of an infection, which can trigger inflammatory responses throughout the body. This inflammation can trigger a cascade of changes that can damage multiple organ systems, causing them to fail.

53 In *Bailey* [2008] EWCA Civ 883; [2009] 1 W.L.R. 1052, the "single agent" was the patient's overall weakness. It

been to delay the operation and this had extended the period of exposure to sepsis. On the facts, it was held that, on the balance of probabilities, the negligence had materially contributed to the injury to the heart and lungs. The Privy Council maintained that when there are cumulative causes, it did not matter whether they were concurrent (as in *Bonnington*) or successive (as here, the sepsis due to the hospital's negligence developing after the non-negligent sepsis had already begun to develop). The Privy Council (obiter) did, however, throw doubts on *Bailey*, arguing that a departure from the "but for" test had not been necessary in that case. It shared the view of the first instance judge that the totality of the claimant's weakened condition had caused the harm and so "but for" causation had been established. The fact that her vulnerability had been heightened by her pancreatitis was subject to the rule that the tortfeasor must take the victim as he finds him (see para.6–033: The "eggshell skull" rule).[54] Commentators, such as Sarah Green, have been critical of the use of the material contribution test in medical negligence cases such as *Bailey* and *Williams*, however. Green argues that both cases should have failed when the claimant was unable to show that it was more likely than not that the defendant's breach made a difference to the claimant's outcome and warns that they are likely to have significant cost implications for the NHS.[55] Stephen Bailey has argued recently that *Bailey* and *Williams* have confused the material contribution test to such an extent that review by the Supreme Court is urgently needed.[56]

Where the injury caused is in fact divisible (i.e. attributable to a particular source), then the defendant will only be held liable for the part of harm he has been proved to have caused. This is what happened in *Holtby v Brigham & Cowan (Hull) Ltd*.[57] Here, the claimant contracted asbestosis. Asbestosis is a disease that can get progressively worse the more a person is exposed to asbestos. The claimant had been exposed to asbestos for most of his working life, but had only been employed by the defendants for about half that time. The medical evidence stated that if the claimant's exposure to asbestos had been limited to that caused by the defendants, his condition would not be so bad. The Court of Appeal therefore reduced the claimant's damages, holding that the defendants could only be liable to the extent that their fault had made a causal contribution to the claimant's condition. Where, however, the claimant suffers an indivisible single injury (i.e. the sources combine to produce one illness),

---

has been argued, however, that the material contribution approach applies to both single agency and multiple factor cases: *John v Central Manchester and Manchester Children's University Hospitals NHS Foundation Trust* [2016] EWHC 407 (QB); [2016] 4 W.L.R. 54 at [97] per Picken J.

54 For criticism of this view for muddying the waters between factual and remoteness, see J. Stapleton and S. Steel, "Causes and contribution" (2016) 132 L.Q.R. 363, 366–368.

55 See S. Green, *Causation in Negligence* (Hart, 2015), Ch.5 and (2016) 32 P.N. 169. Alternatively, Plunkett argues that they represent a limited extension to the material contribution test where the defendant's negligence has contributed to a condition or state of affairs that *does* cause the damage complained of: J. Plunkett (2016) 32 P.N. 158, 162.

56 S.H. Bailey, "Material contribution after *Williams v The Bermuda Hospitals Board*" (2018) 38 L.S. 411.

57 [2000] 3 All E.R. 421. See also *Allen v British Rail Engineering Ltd* [2001] EWCA Civ 242; [2001] I.C.R. 942, *Bonnington Castings Ltd v Wardlaw* [1956] A.C. 613 and, recently, *Carder v University of Exeter* [2016] EWCA Civ 790.

the claimant will recover in full from the defendant—liability being joint and several. As Lord Phillips clarified in *Sienkiewicz v Greif (UK) Ltd*:

> "Where the disease is indivisible, such as lung cancer, a defendant who has tortiously contributed to the cause of the disease will be liable in full. Where the disease is divisible, such as asbestosis, the tortfeasor will be liable in respect of the share of the disease for which he is responsible."[58]

(iii) The "vindication of rights" approach: Chester v Afshar

6-016

Chester v Afshar[59] adopts a different approach to causation from those examined above. It is a 3:2 majority decision, taken by a House of Lords that was differently constituted from the House that decided *Gregg v Scott* (also a 3:2 majority decision). Here, the claimant, who was suffering from chronic back pain, went to see the defendant, an eminent neurosurgeon. He advised her to have surgery, but failed, in response to her questioning, to warn her that there was a very small risk (1 or 2%) of complications with the surgery. Ignorant of this risk, the claimant consented to the surgery. Unfortunately, the risk materialised, leaving her with pain and disability, for which she sued the defendant in negligence.

It was clear that the defendant had been in breach of duty by failing to warn the claimant of the risk (see Ch.5). The difficulty, however, was that the claimant was unable honestly to say that, if she had known about the risk, she would not have consented to the surgery—the most she could say was that she would not have had the operation immediately, but would have taken time for reflection, and perhaps sought a second opinion, before, perhaps, having the operation (with the same associated risk) at a later date. She could not prove, therefore, that "but for" the negligent failure to warn, her disability would never have arisen.[60] Despite this difficulty, the Court of Appeal upheld her claim, as did the House of Lords (but for different reasons).

The Court of Appeal, taking a robust and pragmatic approach, held that the claimant could succeed by applying conventional causation principles. Thus, it could be said that the claimant's disability had resulted from having a particular operation at a particular time. If the defendant had warned her about the risks, she would not have had that particular operation—she would have had an operation (with the same risks) at a later date. If she had had this later operation, in all probability, the very small risk of disability would not have materialised. On

---

58   [2011] UKSC 10; [2011] 2 A.C. 229 at [90].

59   [2005] 1 A.C. 134. Comment: C. Miller, "Negligent failure to warn: why is it so difficult?" (2012) 28 P.N. 266.

60   Contrast the view of J. Stapleton, who argues that the success of the claimant did not require any departure from orthodoxy: (2006) 122 L.Q.R. 426.

this basis, it could be said that the defendant's failure to warn had resulted in the claimant's disability.

The House of Lords did not find this approach attractive. As Lord Hoffmann put it, the approach of the Court of Appeal was:

> **". . . about as logical as saying that if one had been told, on entering a casino, that the odds on the number 7 coming up were only 1 in 37, one would have gone away and come back next week or gone to a different casino. The question is whether one would have taken the opportunity to avoid or reduce the risk, not whether one would have changed the scenario in some irrelevant detail."[61]**

In the House of Lords, both the majority and the minority rejected the reasoning of the Court of Appeal and held that the claimant could not succeed in proving causation on conventional principles. For the minority (Lords Hoffmann and Bingham), this was sufficient to dispose of the case. However, the majority went on to state that, for policy reasons, the traditional rules of causation ought to be relaxed to allow the claimant to succeed. Central to their Lordship's reasoning was the need to give effect to the right of a patient to make an informed choice about whether and when to undergo medical treatment. In law, this right was underpinned by a doctor's duty to warn the patient about any material risks involved in the treatment. It would therefore be unjust if a breach of this duty did not give rise to a remedy. If the doctor were not made liable for such a breach, the duty to inform the patient about significant risks would, as Lord Hope put it, be a "hollow one". His Lordship said:

> **"The function of the law is to enable rights to be vindicated and to provide remedies when duties have been breached. Unless this is done the duty is a hollow one, stripped of all practical force and devoid of all content. It will have lost its ability to protect the patient and thus to fulfil the only purpose which brought it into existence. On policy grounds therefore I would hold that the test of causation is satisfied in this case."[62]**

The effect of the decision in *Chester v Afshar*, then, is that, for policy reasons, the law requires that a doctor who negligently fails to warn a patient about a complication from treatment must compensate the patient for the consequences of that complication occurring. Lord Steyn thought that such a proposition was sound because it reflected "the reasonable expectations of the public in contemporary society".[63] The approach in *Chester*, however, is very dif-

---

61 [2005] 1 A.C. 134 per Lord Hoffmann at [31].
62 [2005] 1 A.C. 134 per Lord Hope at [87].
63 [2005] 1 A.C. 134 per Lord Steyn at [25]. In *Montgomery v Lanarkshire Health Board* [2015] UKSC 11; [2015] A.C. 1430, the "vindication of rights" approach was approved in the context of the duty of the doctor to disclose

ficult to reconcile with the approach taken in *Gregg* (above). If the claimant in *Chester* is said to have a "right" (to self-determination) that must be "vindicated" by a modification of causation principles, what about Mr Gregg's "right" to be promptly advised about treatment that would maximise his chances of surviving cancer? It is difficult to draw a distinction between the two, because, in both cases, what is in issue is the dignity of the patient, which is supported by a doctor's duty to act in the patient's best interests.[64]

More recently, in *Duce v Worcestershire Acute Hospitals NHS Trust*,[65] the Court of Appeal reviewed *Chester* and effectively restricted its application. Reading the majority judgments "in their factual context", the Court determined *Chester* did not establish a free-standing test for causation, but rather represented a modification of the normal "but for" test, that is, it treated something that did not satisfy the "but for" test as a sufficient cause in law in the unusual circumstances of the case. This meant that, at the very least, the claimant must establish that but for the failure to inform, the operation would not have taken place when it did.[66] In *Chester*, the evidence was that Ms Chester would not have consented to the operation taking place on the stipulated date and sought a second and possibly third opinion, delaying the operation. In *Duce*, however, the causation argument failed in the face of abundant evidence to show that even had Duce been warned, she would have proceeded with the operation as she did.

(iv) The "material increase in risk" approach: Fairchild

This is the true exception to the "all or nothing" version of the "but for" test outlined above. It can be traced back to *McGhee v National Coal Board*,[67] where the plaintiff had contracted the skin disease dermatitis from the presence of abrasive brick dust on his skin. Some exposure to brick dust was an inevitable part of his job—he worked in brick kilns. It was accepted that the defendants were not negligent in exposing him to brick dust during his working day. The plaintiff's argument, however, was that because no washing facilities were provided at his place of work, throughout his working life he had had to cycle home each day with his skin coated with the dust. He argued that, without this additional and unnecessary exposure to the dust, he would not have contracted dermatitis. The defendants admitted that they had been negligent in failing to provide washing facilities, but they argued that their negligence was not the cause of the plaintiff's disease. The medical evidence established that exposure to brick dust caused

6–017

---

material risks to the patient, but the Court found it "unnecessary" to rule on the more controversial issue of the *Chester v Afshar* causation test: [105].

64 On the issue of the "mixed messages" sent by the HL in *Gregg* and *Chester*, see S. Maskrey QC and W. Edis (who were opposing counsel in *Gregg*) [2005] 3 J.P.I. Law 205.

65 [2018] EWCA Civ 1307; [2018] P.I.Q.R. P18, at [66] per Hamblen L.J. The decision has led some commentators to speculate whether *Chester* would now survive a challenge in the Supreme Court: C. Foster (2018) 168(7808) N.L.J. 1.

66 See also *Correia v University Hospital of North Staffordshire NHS Trust* [2017] EWCA Civ 356 at [28].

67 [1973] 1 W.L.R. 1. For a detailed account of the case, see Lord Hope of Craighead, "James McGhee—a second Mrs Donoghue?" [2003] C.L.J. 587 (who had been junior counsel for the respondents in that case).

dermatitis, but the experts were unable to say that, on the balance of probabilities, the *additional* negligent exposure to brick dust had been the cause of plaintiff's condition—it might have occurred in any event, given that he was daily exposed to the "innocent" dust.

The House of Lords held the defendants liable, finding that it was sufficient that, by failing to provide washing facilities, the defendants had "materially increased the risk" of the plaintiff contracting the disease. Their Lordships justified this conclusion in different ways meaning that there was no clear ratio. According to one judge, Lord Wilberforce, the outcome was dictated by policy. The defendants, by their negligence, had created a risk of a particular kind of damage, and when damage of that very kind materialised, they should not be allowed to escape liability because of the claimant's "evidential difficulties" in proving causation. In appropriate cases, where such difficulties became apparent they should, as a matter of policy and justice, be borne by the person who created the risk. As his Lordship put it:

> **". . . it is a sound principle that where a person has, by breach of a duty of care, created a risk, and injury occurs within the area of that risk, the loss should be borne by him unless he shows that it had some other cause."[68]**

The logical objection to Lord Wilberforce's approach, of course, was that it appeared to ignore the fundamental principle that the claimant must prove his case. There was really no evidence to suggest that the plaintiff's damage materialised "within the area of risk" created by the defendants' negligence. (It might have materialised within the area of risk created by his doing his job, for which it was accepted that the defendants could not be liable.) Clearly, Lord Wilberforce's attempt to elide what were, in fact, two distinct "areas of risk" owed much to the broad policy consideration that, as a matter of justice, large employers should be made to compensate their employees for all injuries and diseases occurring in the workplace.

When the House of Lords came to decide *Wilsher*, Lord Bridge, no doubt mindful of this logical objection, sought to explain the decision in *McGhee* by saying that the case had "laid down no new principle of law whatever"—on a proper interpretation, it was simply a case where their Lordships had, in the light of the evidence, felt able to draw a "legitimate inference of fact",[69] namely that the absence of washing facilities had *actually been one of the causes* contributing to the plaintiff's dermatitis. In *Fairchild v Glenhaven Funeral Services Ltd*,[70] however, the House of Lords rejected this explanation of *McGhee*,[71] stating that there had been no evidence in the case from which their Lordships could have legitimately inferred that the defendant's conduct was an *actual cause* of the dermatitis—all the defendants had done was to create an *increased risk* of dermatitis. Accordingly, the decision in *McGhee* should indeed be

---

68   [1973] 1 W.L.R. 1 at 6.
69   [1988] 1 A.C. 1074 at 1090.
70   [2002] UKHL 22; [2003] 1 A.C. 32.
71   *Fairchild v Glenhaven Funeral Services Ltd* [2002] UKHL 22; [2003] 1 A.C. 32 at [22] per Lord Bingham.

seen as having laid down a new principle of law, namely that, in appropriate cases, a claimant will succeed by merely establishing a "material increase in risk".

The approach in *McGhee* was followed in *Fairchild v Glenhaven Funeral Services Ltd*. This was a case concerning a number of claimants who had contracted mesothelioma (a lung tumour) as a result of exposure to asbestos, having worked for a number of different employers during their working life. All the employers admitted they were in breach of their duty of care to protect the claimants against exposure to asbestos. The problem for the claimants, however, was that they could not establish which of their different employers had exposed them to the particular asbestos that had caused their disease. The medical evidence was that the disease did not necessarily build up gradually with continued exposure to asbestos, but could be triggered suddenly at any time, perhaps by one single fibre causing a cell to become malignant. It followed that, while all the employers could be said to have increased the *risk* of mesothelioma, it was not possible to say that all of them had been responsible for *cumulatively causing* the disease. And, of course, it was not possible to say which of them had been responsible for the particular fibre(s) that had suddenly triggered the disease.

The solution adopted by the House of Lords was to make all of the employers liable, on the basis that each had increased the risk of mesothelioma, without requiring the claimants to prove which of the employers had been responsible for causing it. Their Lordships affirmed the principle laid down in *McGhee* that, in appropriate cases, merely establishing a "material increase in risk" would be sufficient to discharge the claimant's burden of proving causation.

Contribution between defendants: The Compensation Act 2006

The House of Lords in *Fairchild* gave no guidance as to how that liability should be shared between the defendants. This omission gave rise to academic criticism[72] and left lawyers to presume that the effect of *Fairchild* was to impose "joint liability". Where this sort of liability is imposed, each defendant is potentially liable for the *whole amount* of the loss—the defendants are then left to argue amongst themselves as to who should contribute how much to the claimant's compensation award, but, at the end of the day, the award must be paid in full by one or more of them. This sort of liability has a clear advantage for the claimant—should one or more of the defendants be insolvent or untraceable, the claimant is entitled to look to the remaining defendant(s) to satisfy judgment.

Almost four years after *Fairchild*, however, the House of Lords again faced a case involving appeals concerning mesothelioma. In *Barker v Corus UK Ltd*,[73] their Lordships held that the sort of liability that should be imposed on employers in cases like *Fairchild* was "several liability", and not "joint liability". This meant that liability to pay compensation was to be apportioned among the various defendants according to their relative degree of contribution to the risk of the

6–018

---

72   See, e.g. J. Stapleton,'Lords a' Leaping Evidentiary Gaps" (2002) 10 Torts L.J. 276.
73   [2006] UKHL 20; [2006] 2 A.C. 572.

claimant contracting the disease. Although their Lordships declined to be specific on the point, it was clear that these contributions would normally be worked out by reference to the length of time each defendant had exposed the claimant to asbestos, the intensity of that exposure, and (where quantifiable) the potency of the type of asbestos in question. This approach was thought necessary in order to be fair to the defendants in these cases. As Lord Hoffmann put it, apportionment of liability would "smooth out the roughness" of the justice created by joint liability.[74] His Lordship took the view that apportionment was appropriate because the fault of each defendant lay in *creating a percentage risk* of mesothelioma. It could not be said that any of the defendants had *actually caused* the mesothelioma.[75] (Indeed, the whole point of the *Fairchild* principle was that it applied where the cause could not be determined.)

The result of the decision in *Barker*, therefore, was that the risk that one or more defendants would be insolvent or untraceable fell on the claimants. In many cases, this meant that claimants' compensation would be substantially reduced, because much of their exposure to asbestos had occurred long ago, and the companies that had employed them were no longer in existence. Moreover, in practice, claimants would have to trace all relevant defendants, so far as possible, before apportionment could be carried out and any compensation could be paid. The practical implication of this was that claims would take much longer to conclude, so claimants and their families, who were already under considerable stress, would have a lengthy wait before receiving any compensation.[76]

When these implications of *Barker* became apparent, there was a public and parliamentary outcry. The government moved swiftly to pass legislation reversing the effect of the decision. The effect of *Barker* was therefore reversed by the Compensation Act 2006 s.3. This provides that, where a defendant, through negligence or breach of statutory duty, has exposed a claimant to asbestos, and that claimant contracts mesothelioma, the defendant is liable "for the whole of the damage caused to the victim by the disease". Liability is declared to exist "jointly and severally" with any other persons responsible for asbestos exposure. It should be noted, however, that s.3 is expressly limited to claimants contracting mesothelioma. Logically, this signifies that *Barker* has not been overturned in relation to claimants able to rely on the *Fairchild* principle, but not suffering from this specific disease. This restrictive view of s.3 was confirmed recently by the Supreme Court in *International Energy Group Ltd v Zurich Insurance plc UK*.[77] Here the claimant had brought his claim in Guernsey where the Compensation Act 2006 had not been enacted. The court held that on this basis, the *Barker* rule of proportionate recovery would apply. Section 3 of the Act did not change the common law, but only overrode it to the extent that the section itself provides.[78]

---

74   [2006] 2 A.C. 572 at [43].

75   The other members of the House of Lords did not go as far as Lord Hoffmann on this point. Baroness Hale, although with the majority on apportionment, agreed (at [120]) with Lord Rodger (who dissented) that the "gist" of the harm was the mesothelioma itself, not the risk of causing it.

76   See Compensation Act 2006, Explanatory Notes para.14.

77   [2015] UKSC 33; [2016] A.C. 509. See S. Green, "Between a rock of uncertainty and a hard case" (2016) 132 L.Q.R. 25.

78   [2015] UKSC 33 at [100] and [201].

When will the "material increase in risk approach" apply?

First, it must be remembered that the *Fairchild* principle will have no application in cases where evidence can be produced to show that particular defendants are responsible for making *distinct and quantifiable causal contributions* to the claimant's loss. In such cases, the courts will apportion liability to each defendant in accordance with his or her degree of fault. The *Fairchild* principle is reserved for the sort of exceptional circumstance that occurred in the case itself, namely where all the defendants are shown to be in breach of duty and it is established that the whole of the damage results *from a single agent* (e.g. exposure to an asbestos fibre) at a specific time in the past, yet the limits of scientific knowledge mean that it is impossible to say which agent, out of a number of identical agents (or agents acting in the same causative way),[79] has actually caused the damage. The Court of Appeal in *Heneghan v Manchester Dry Docks*[80] saw no reason why it would not apply to diseases other than mesothelioma (here lung cancer) where all the material factors which triggered the *Fairchild* principle were present. Such claims would not, however, be able to benefit from the Compensation Act 2006 s.3 and Mr Heneghan's estate therefore would only receive a proportionate amount of liability from the defendants still able to meet his claim.[81]

In cases where the *Fairchild* principle applies, it sits rather uncomfortably alongside the approach adopted by the House of Lords in *Wilsher*. If the claimants in *Fairchild* could succeed simply by showing that exposure to asbestos had *increased the risk* of mesothelioma, why was it that the plaintiff in *Wilsher* could not succeed by showing that exposure to excess oxygen had increased the risk that he would contract RLF? Their Lordships in *Fairchild* were content to say that *Wilsher* had been correctly decided, the majority basing this assertion on the factual differences between that case and cases like *McGhee* and *Fairchild*. The key difference is that, in the *Fairchild* type of case, there is only one "causal agent" of the claimant's injury (brick dust in *McGhee* and asbestos in *Fairchild*) whereas, in a case like *Wilsher*, there are many competing "causal agents" (oxygen and the other possible natural causes of RLF).

It is clear from the decision of the Supreme Court in *Sienkiewicz v Greif*[82] that the *Fairchild* principle will also apply in mesothelioma cases where only a single defendant has negligently exposed the claimant to asbestos. In contrast to the situation in *Fairchild* and *Barker*, where a number of defendants had negligently exposed the victim to asbestos and thereby materially increased the risk of the employee developing mesothelioma, in *Sienkiewicz*, there was only

---

79   *Sienkiewicz v Greif* [2011] UKSC 10; [2011] 2 A.C. 229 at [104] per Lord Phillips.

80   [2016] EWCA Civ 86; [2016] 1 W.L.R. 2036. For criticism, see S. Green (2017) 133 L.Q.R. 25 who argues that this is an illegitimate extension of *Fairchild* to a case where the illness had been found on a particular occasion to be caused by a single agent. In reality lung cancer is not an illness triggered by a single agent like mesothelioma in that it can be triggered by smoking.

81   The defendants were responsible for 35.2% of the whole exposure. It has been argued that such claims give rise to a compelling case to extend the Compensation Act 2006 s.3 to lung cancer victims: D. Allan QC, "The extension of *Fairchild* to lung cancer" [2016] J.P.I. Law 61.

82   [2011] UKSC 10; [2011] 2 A.C. 229. Comment: S. Steel and D. Ibbetson [2011] C.L.J. 451.

one defendant, and evidence that the victim had been at risk in any event of developing the disease from low-level exposure to asbestos in the general atmosphere. Seven Justices of the Supreme Court unanimously provided that the *Fairchild* approach would also apply where a single defendant had negligently exposed the victim to asbestos. Although the claimant could only establish an increased risk of 18% arising from the defendant's negligence, such a risk was material: a risk would only be regarded as immaterial if the negligent exposure had been too insignificant to be taken into account, having regard to the overall exposure. This was a matter for the judge on the facts of the particular case. The Supreme Court did warn, however, that the rule in *Fairchild* and *Barker* had been adopted to cater for an evidential gap that had existed at the time of those decisions about the causes of mesothelioma.[83] This did not preclude the courts from reverting to the conventional approach of balance of probabilities should advances in medical science in relation to the disease make such a step appropriate.[84]

6–020
We might question whether these rather technical distinctions, based on the number of "causal agents" or "distinct causes" present in a case, provide a satisfying or coherent justification for adopting different approaches to causation.[85] They may be justified, however, on policy grounds. Certainly, the distinctions can prevent the *Fairchild* principle from creating widespread negligence liability where the causes of damage are indeterminate. We have seen also that in *Gregg v Scott* the House of Lords declined to adopt a broad interpretation of the *Fairchild* principle in the context of medical negligence, and so refused to apply a "material increase in risk" approach to the fact of Mr Gregg's untimely diagnosis and treatment. Further, the Court of Appeal in *Williams v University of Birmingham*[86] refused to allow the more generous approach to causation in *Fairchild* to influence the ordinary breach of duty test, set out in Ch.5. In contrast, the Supreme Court in *Durham v BAI (Run off) Ltd*[87] was determined to avoid a situation where the insurers of the employers liable under the *Fairchild* principle could avoid paying out under their insurance policies on the basis that it could not be said that the employers "caused" the injury (a requirement of the insurance policies in question), but merely materially increased the risk of injury. Lord Mance, giving the leading judgment, argued that, under *Fairchild*, causation was "deemed" to be proved. This was based on a weak or broad view of the causal link in this particular context. He concluded that the intention under the insurance policies must be taken to have been that they would respond to whatever liability the insured employers might be held to incur within the scope of the risks for which they were insured.[88]

---

83 See Lord Phillips [2011] UKSC 10 at [18]: "The special rule of causation applied to mesothelioma was devised because of ignorance about the biological cause of the disease. It was accepted in *Fairchild* and *Barker* that this rendered it impossible for a claimant to prove causation according to the conventional "but for" test and this caused injustice to the claimants".

84 See Lord Rodger [2011] UKSC 10 at [142].

85 But see S. Steel, "Justifying exceptions to proof of causation in tort law" (2015) 78 M.L.R. 729.

86 [2011] EWCA Civ 1242; [2012] P.I.Q.R. P4. Comment: J. Stapleton [2012] C.L.J. 32.

87 [2012] UKSC 14; [2012] 1 W.L.R. 867 (Lord Phillips dissenting on the causation issue). Comment: N. McBride and S. Steel (2012) 28 P.N. 285.

88 [2012] UKSC 14 at [69].

To decide otherwise would undermine the protective purpose of legislation which requires employers to take out compulsory insurance against liability for injuries suffered by employees in the workplace.[89]

It is clear that this is an area of law where the courts are prepared to sacrifice conceptual clarity to avoid unjust results, but *not* in every case. This means that the limits to the application of the *Fairchild* principle remain a matter of considerable importance. It should also be noted that the *Fairchild* exception has not been recognised in other common law jurisdictions such as Australia.[90] Lord Hoffmann has since expressed his regret at the *Fairchild* decision:

> **"*Fairchild* was wrong because it introduced an arbitrary distinction into what had been a clear principle . . . in *Fairchild* we assumed we alone could do something to put right an injustice to mesothelioma victims. We did not consider that Parliament might intervene."[91]**

In other words, the House of Lords engaged in unwarranted judicial law-making. It remains a matter for debate whether the court in *Fairchild* should have "left well alone", as Lord Hoffmann now advises, or whether the House was correct in reaching the difficult decision that the demands of justice required the courts to develop the law, albeit creating a limited exception to the "but for" test. The Court of Appeal recently resolved that[92]:

> **". . . once the courts can be confident that the objective of ensuring victim protection has been achieved, it is desirable that the anomalies should be corrected and that the law should return to the fundamental principles of the common law. Put shortly, once unorthdodoxy has served its purpose, we should revert to orthodoxy."**

Novus Actus Interveniens

6–021

In certain circumstances, where one act follows another, the law will say that the second act (the "new intervening act") is to be regarded as the true cause of the damage, because it has "broken the chain of causation" and has extinguished the effect of the first act. The rationale of the rule is fairness; it is not fair to hold the defendant liable, however gross his breach of duty,

---

89 The Employers' Liability (Compulsory Insurance) Act 1969 s.1 (discussed in Ch.7).
90 *Amaca Pty Ltd v Ellis* (2010) 240 C.L.R. 111.
91 Lord Hoffmann, "Constitutionalism and private law" (2014–15) 6 UKSCY 177 at 181–182.
92 *Equitas Insurance Ltd v Municipal Mutual Insurance Ltd* [2019] EWCA Civ 718 at [91] per Males L.J.

when some independent supervening cause is the actual cause of the claimant's injury.[93] This idea, known as the doctrine of *novus actus interveniens*, is explored here. It should be noted that the essence of the doctrine overlaps not only with the reasoning in "successive cause" cases, which we have already examined, but with other areas of the law—in particular, the question of whether a person owes a duty to prevent a third party from causing damage (considered in Ch.2) and the defences of Act of God, *volenti non fit injuria* and act of stranger, which are considered in later chapters. Each area of the law simply represents a different way of determining liability. The fact that some cases are decided using the concepts of "duty" or "defence", rather than causation, is sometimes the result of historical accident in the way the law has developed, and sometimes the product of a judicial search for clarity.

It should also be noted that many writers and judges treat the idea of *novus actus interveniens* as part of the test for "remoteness of damage".[94] This is mainly because, as we shall see later, the test for "remoteness" is whether the kind of damage in question is reasonably foreseeable, and the same issue arises when considering whether a defendant is liable in spite of an intervening act. Some writers, on the other hand (myself included), reserve the phrase "remoteness of damage" for a slightly different problem, namely, where, on any sensible view, there is only one true cause of the claimant's loss, but where the loss caused seems too far removed to be recoverable. This problem is explored in a later section.

It is convenient to place the relevant cases into two groups—intervening act of a third party and intervening act of the claimant. It should be noted that, rarely, acts of nature, such as a storm, may also act to break the chain of causation. In such cases, the chain of causation will be broken when it is the act of nature which is the effective cause on the claimant's loss and eclipses the defendant's wrongdoing.[95]

Intervening act of a third party

6–022   It is useful to draw a distinction between three different ways in which a third party may interfere with a course of events—natural (or "instinctive") intervention; negligent intervention; and intervention in the form of intentional wrongdoing. We consider each type of intervention in turn.

Natural or "instinctive" intervention

6–023   The classic example of "instinctive" human conduct failing to amount to a *novus actus interveniens* is the very old case of *Scott v Shepherd*.[96] Here, the defendant threw a lighted firework

---

93   Lord Bingham in *Corr v IBC Vehicles Ltd* [2008] UKHL 13; [2008] 1 A.C. 884 at [15].
94   See, e.g. the terminology used by the Court of Appeal in *Lamb v Camden LBC* [1981] Q.B. 625.
95   *Carslogie Steamship Co v Royal Norwegian Government* [1952] A.C. 292.
96   (1773) 2 Wm. Bl. 892.

into a market place. It landed on a stall belonging to a third party, A, who threw it on so that it landed on the stall of a fourth party, B, who reacted in a similar way. The firework ultimately hit the plaintiff and injured him. It was held that neither the intervening act of A or B broke the causal connection between the defendant's act and the subsequent damage. Both A and B had acted in an instinctive and natural way to avoid damage to themselves and their property.

It is clear from *Scott v Shepherd*, then, that a third party's intervention will not break the chain of causation where it is an involuntary reaction in the "heat of the moment". However, the same sort of reasoning appears to apply in cases where the third party has some opportunity to reflect before taking action. Consider, for example, *The Oropesa*.[97] Here, because of the defendants' negligence, a ship of that name collided with a ship called the Manchester Regiment. The captain of the Manchester Regiment set out in a life boat to consult the captain of The Oropesa about how best to save his crew. The life boat capsized, causing the death of many of those aboard. The captain's intervention did not break the chain of causation.

Negligent intervention

6-024

It is impossible to state with absolute clarity the circumstances in which the negligent conduct of a third party will break the chain of causation. Where A commits a tort, and B commits a subsequent tort, the key question is whether the nature of B's tort is so powerful that it ought to be regarded as rendering A's tort merely part of the surrounding historical circumstances—the backdrop against which B's tort occurred. Thus, negligent conduct will not always break the chain of causation. For example, in *Roberts v Bettany*,[98] the defendant negligently started an underground fire, and was ordered by the council to extinguish it. He failed to comply with this order, so the council intervened to extinguish the fire. Unfortunately, owing to the council's negligence in so doing, subsidence occurred under the claimant's house. The Court of Appeal held that the council's negligence did not break the chain of causation, so the defendant was liable for the subsidence. The defendant, having started the fire, could not be said to be merely part of the "surrounding circumstances" of the council's negligence—it being the direct cause of the council's foreseeable and necessary intervention.

Some flavour of the courts' approach can be gained by considering a number of cases involving negligent driving. In *Knightley v Johns*,[99] for example, the defendant negligently overturned his car in a tunnel. A police inspector then arrived at the scene to take charge of the situation, and negligently ordered a police motorcyclist to secure the closure of the tunnel by riding against the traffic towards its entrance. The motorcyclist collided with the plaintiff's oncoming car. In holding the defendant not liable for this accident, the Court of Appeal stated that the relevant question to ask was whether the whole sequence of events was a natural and

---

97   [1943] P. 32.
98   [2001] EWCA Civ 109; [2001] N.P.C. 45.
99   [1982] 1 W.L.R. 349.

probable consequence of the defendant's negligence, so that it should have been reasonably foreseen by the defendant, or whether the events were foreseeable only as a mere possibility. In answering this question, it was helpful to consider whether the third party's negligent intervention had involved a deliberate choice to do a positive act, as opposed to an error of judgment in the course of performing an act in which the third party was already engaged. Here, the conduct of the police had taken the form of a deliberate positive act and was not reasonably foreseeable by the defendant.

It is useful to compare *Knightley v Johns* with the decision in *Rouse v Squires*.[100] Here, the defendant lorry driver negligently caused an accident which blocked two lanes of a motorway. The plaintiff, who was assisting at the scene, was killed when a second lorry driver negligently drove into the obstruction. The Court of Appeal held that the defendant was 25% to blame. The negligent driving of the second lorry driver did not break the chain of causation between the original accident and the plaintiff's death—a driver who caused an obstruction could be taken reasonably to foresee that a further accident might be caused by other drivers negligently colliding with the obstruction. The matter therefore became a question of cumulative causation.

Whilst an act of *negligent* driving may not break the chain of causation, then, *reckless* driving may amount to a *novus actus interveniens*, because such driving is not normally foreseeable. Such was the case in *Wright v Lodge*.[101] Here, the second defendant was driving her Mini at night along a dual carriageway. It was foggy and the road was unlit. The Mini broke down and came to a stop in the near side lane. A few minutes later, as she was trying to restart her car, it was hit from behind by an articulated lorry being driven at 60 mph by the first defendant. After hitting the Mini, the lorry careered across the central reservation. It ended up on its side, blocking the opposite carriageway, and four oncoming vehicles collided with it. One driver died of his injuries and another was seriously injured. The Court of Appeal accepted that the Mini driver had been negligent in failing to push her car off the road before trying to restart it—which she could easily have done with the help of her passengers—but held that the lorry driver's dangerous driving was to be regarded as the true cause of the plaintiffs' injuries.

A particularly difficult question is whether, when a claimant is injured by a defendant's negligence and subsequently undergoes negligent medical treatment, the latter can be regarded as a *novus actus interveniens*. This should not be confused with the more straightforward question of whether a defendant remains liable when non-negligent medical treatment makes a claimant's position worse because of the claimant's pre-disposition to respond adversely to treatment. This point is discussed in a later section.

The circumstances in which negligent treatment will break the chain of causation cannot be stated with certainty. Assistance, however, may be found from the decision of the House of Lords in *Hogan v Bentinck West Hartley Collieries (Owners) Ltd*.[102] The case concerned a miner

---

100 [1973] Q.B. 889.
101 [1993] 4 All E.R. 299.
102 [1949] 1 All E.R. 588. The case decided a claim under the Workmen's Compensation Act 1925. It is only of persuasive authority in the tort of negligence.

who injured his thumb at work. He was taken to hospital, where, initial treatment having failed to relieve his pain, doctors negligently decided to amputate part of his thumb. This reduced his earning capacity, because it left him able to do only light work. The question before the House of Lords was whether the man's incapacity resulted from the original injury or the operation. The case was complicated by the fact that the man had a congenital abnormality (an additional top joint to his thumb) for which amputation in the event of pain was considered a reasonable form of treatment. By a 3:2 majority, their Lordships held that the amputation amounted to a *novus actus interveniens*, absolving the defendant employers from liability. Lord Reid, however, in a powerful dissenting speech, thought that subsequent medical treatment should only break the chain of causation where there was a "grave lack of skill and care" on the part of the doctors. It should not do so in this case, because it was not abundantly clear that an alternative form of treatment would have cured the plaintiff of his condition. It has been suggested that, nowadays, only where the treatment in question is "so grossly negligent as to be a completely inappropriate response to the injury inflicted by the defendant" should it operate to break the chain of causation.[103]

Intentional acts of wrongdoing

6–025

Where a third party's intervention takes the form of a deliberate act of wrongdoing, the courts are very reluctant to hold a defendant liable and will usually say that the third party's act has broken the chain of causation. However, much will depend on the particular circumstances of the case. In *Att-Gen of the British Virgin Islands v Hartwell*,[104] an emotionally disturbed police officer in the British Virgin Islands, whom the defendant police authority had given access to a gun, deserted his post and travelled to a bar where he shot and injured a British tourist. The Privy Council, whilst conceding that the case was a "closely balanced" one, held that this action did not break the chain of causation. The defendant authority was liable for the tourist's injuries. The standard of diligence expected of the authority in supervising the use of firearms was a high one, in view of the grave risks involved. Moreover, given that the authority knew about the officer's disturbed emotional state, his actions were sufficiently foreseeable.

The case of *Home Office v Dorset Yacht Co Ltd*[105] (discussed in Ch.2) is a further example of a situation where criminal intervention did not break the chain of causation. In the case, because of the carelessness of the guards, a number of prisoners had escaped from detention on an island and caused damage to some yachts moored in the harbour. Such an event was extremely foreseeable by the defendants—there was a close relationship between the

---

103 *Clerk & Lindsell on Torts*, 23rd edn (2020), para.2–121. See also *Webb v Barclays Bank Plc* [2001] EWCA Civ 1141; [2002] P.I.Q.R. P8 and *Wright (A Child) v Cambridge Medical Group (A Partnership)* [2011] EWCA Civ 669; [2013] Q.B. 312 where the judges affirmed that in cases of successive negligent acts, intervening medical negligence would not ordinarily break the chain of causation unless it were gross or egregious.
104 [2004] UKPC 12; [2004] 1 W.L.R. 1273.
105 [1970] A.C. 1004.

negligent guards and the prisoners, and their actions were the "very kind of thing" that was likely to happen if the guards allowed them to escape.

The "foreseeability-based" approach to liability for the criminal acts of third parties caused some difficulty for the Court of Appeal, however, in *Lamb v Camden LBC*.[106] Here, a burst water main, for which the defendant council was responsible, had caused the plaintiff's house to become flooded. The plaintiff, who was living abroad at the time, moved her furniture out of the house and made arrangements for repairing the damage. Whilst the house was left unoccupied, squatters moved in and caused extensive damage to the house. The plaintiff's action in respect of this damage failed. The council was not liable for the squatters' antisocial and criminal behaviour. This was so even though (according to the majority) in modern times the actions of the squatters could be regarded as highly foreseeable.

In *Lamb*, their Lordships arrived at their decision by slightly different routes. Lord Denning MR thought that, as a matter of policy, the responsibility for keeping the squatters out lay with the plaintiff and not the council and that the loss they had caused should be borne by the plaintiff's insurers. (We can see at work here the economic and political consideration that loss should not be transferred from a private insurance arrangement to a publicly funded authority, discussed in Ch.3.) His Lordship thought that, in *Home Office v Dorset Yacht*, Lord Reid had been wrong to decide the question of *novus actus interveniens* using a test of foreseeability, and that it was not helpful to attempt to distinguish between different degrees of foreseeability. To illustrate the point, Lord Denning MR put forward an example: Suppose a prisoner escapes and steals a car. He then drives many miles, abandons the car, breaks into a house to steal a change of clothes, gets a lift in a lorry and continues with his criminal activities. On Lord Reid's test of "very likely to happen", none of the prisoner's intervening acts would break the chain of causation, so that the Home Office would be liable for all of the damage caused by escaped convicts. As a matter of policy, this was unacceptable.

Oliver LJ, on the other hand, was content to say that the squatters' intervention was not reasonably foreseeable (although it was foreseeable as a mere possibility). Watkins LJ thought that, in addition to foreseeability, the court should consider a number of other factors, including:

> **"the nature of the event or act, the time it occurred, the place where it occurred, the identity of the perpetrator and his intentions and responsibility, if any, for taking measures to avoid the occurrence and matters of public policy."[107]**

The authorities suggest that the nature of the relationship between the defendant and the third party is an important consideration for the courts. In *Lamb*, the third parties were strangers to the defendant, whereas in *Dorset Yacht* there was a relationship of supervision and care. The relationship between the defendant and the claimant may also be important. Thus, in *Stansbie*

---

106 [1981] Q.B. 625. Compare *Clark Fixing Ltd v Dudley MBC* [2001] EWCA Civ 1898 (discussed in Ch.2).
107 [1981] Q.B. 625 at 647.

v Troman[108] (considered in Ch.2), the decorator, who had impliedly agreed to look after the plaintiff's house, was liable for the actions of the thief who broke in—the thief's action did not amount to a *novus actus interveniens*. Applying both of these "relationship" considerations, we can explain why, for example, in *Topp v London Country Bus (South West) Ltd*[109] the defendants were not liable when a bus driver, for whose actions the defendants were responsible, left his bus unattended with the keys in the ignition and it was stolen by a third party whose careless driving caused injury to the plaintiff.

In the final analysis, it seems that both "relationship" and "degree of foreseeability" play a part in the courts' reasoning in these cases. Much seems to rest on the judiciary's perception of the scope of the duty of care owed by the defendant. The law reflects, therefore, the view taken more generally in negligence (as seen in Ch.2) that defendants should only rarely be held responsible for the deliberate tortious actions of independent third parties.[110]

Intervening act of the claimant

6–026

In appropriate circumstances, the actions of the claimant can break the chain of causation, so that he or she, rather than the defendant, is to be regarded as the operative cause of his or her own loss. Here, the question is whether the conduct of the claimant is so wholly unreasonable that it eclipses the tort of the defendant and amounts to the effective cause of the injury. Such cases are rare. The courts tend to be more willing to consider whether the claimant's conduct can be characterised as contributory negligence which is a defence (discussed in Ch.16) or even amounts to acceptance of the risk of injury (the defence of *volenti non fit injuria*, also considered in Ch.16). In a sense, it is regarded as unfair to deny a claimant, who has surmounted the hurdles for proving that the defendant has committed a tort, any remedy at all, whereas contributory negligence simply reduces the claimant's damages to the extent that their fault contributed to the harm suffered. In *Scott v Gavigan*,[111] therefore, the court indicated that even recklessly running across the road into the path of traffic was more likely to give rise to an award of damages heavily reduced for contributory negligence, rather than a finding that such conduct amounted to a novus actus interveniens.

As a side note, it should be noted that the "all or nothing" approach to causation, which depends on the balance of probabilities, sits somewhat uneasily alongside the fact that a claimant may be regarded by the law as so contributorily negligent that his or her damages are reduced by an amount greater than 50%. Where this is so, why does the law not regard the claimant, rather than the defendant as the true cause of the loss? There is no clear answer to this question, save to say that the law places the question of contributory negligence in a

---

108 [1948] 2 K.B. 48.
109 [1993] 1 W.L.R. 976.
110 See Lord Goff's analysis of the problem in *Smith v Littlewoods* [1987] A.C. 241, considered in Ch.2.
111 [2016] EWCA Civ 544 at [34] per Christopher Clarke LJ (drunk pedestrian crossing road in front of oncoming traffic).

separate "conceptual compartment" from factual causation, and sees it as a matter relating to the quantification of damages, rather than as a matter relating to the determination of liability in the first place.[112]

The courts' general approach to deciding whether a claimant's own act breaks the chain of causation can be illustrated by comparing two cases: *McKew v Holland and Hannens and Cubitts (Scotland) Ltd*[113] and *Wieland v Cyril Lord Carpets Ltd*.[114]

In *McKew*, the plaintiff suffered a slight injury to his leg as a result of the defendant's negligence, so that it had a tendency to give way when he was walking. Shortly afterwards, he went with his family to look at a flat. He descended a steep staircase with no handrail, ahead of his family, and holding a child by the hand. His injured leg gave way and he fell, fracturing his ankle. The House of Lords held that the plaintiff's unreasonable behaviour was a *novus actus interveniens*. He, not the defendant, had caused his injury by descending the staircase without waiting for the assistance of his wife or brother-in-law, knowing that his leg might give way at any moment.

A claimant's act will only break the chain of causation when it is unreasonable. Thus, in *Wieland v Cyril Lord Carpets Ltd*, although the facts were similar to those in *McKew*, the court reached a different conclusion. The plaintiff suffered an injury to her neck, caused by the defendant's negligence. Shortly after this, the plaintiff, who wore bi-focal spectacles, returned to the hospital where she had originally been taken and was fitted with a surgical collar. The position of her neck in the collar deprived her of her usual ability to use her bi-focals—she could not easily adjust the position of her head. After leaving the hospital, the plaintiff was in a nervous state because of the trauma of the visit, and this, together with the problem with her bi-focals, made her unsteady on her feet. She went to her son's office to ask him to take her home. He accompanied her down the stairs of the office building, but when she neared the bottom she fell and injured her ankles. Eveleigh J held that these injuries were caused by the defendant's negligence, which had impaired her ability to negotiate the stairs. Her actions in descending the stairs had been reasonable and could not be regarded as a *novus actus interveniens*.

More recently, the same principle was applied in *Spencer v Wincanton Holdings Ltd*.[115] Here, the claimant had had his leg amputated as a result of the defendant's negligence. He had been fitted with a prosthesis, but pending further adaptations to his car, this could not be worn whilst he was driving. He pulled into a filling station, and, without the aid of his prosthesis or walking sticks, got out of his car and filled it with petrol, using the car for support. As he was returning to the driver's door, he tripped and fell, sustaining a further injury which confined him to a wheelchair. The Court of Appeal upheld the trial judge's finding that the claimant's actions were not so unreasonable as to break the chain of causation. He had made a misjudgement in

---

112   See, e.g. *Stapley v Gypsum Mines* [1953] A.C. 663 where the damages were reduced by 80% because of contributory negligence. See also P. S. Atiyah, "Causation, Contributory Negligence and Volenti Non Fit Injuria" (1965) 43 Can. Bar. Rev. 609.

113   [1969] 3 All E.R. 1621.

114   [1969] 3 All E.R. 1006.

115   [2009] EWCA Civ 1404; [2010] P.I.Q.R. P8. Comment: K. Hughes [2010] C.L.J. 228.

running a risk by not using his prosthesis or sticks, but this was properly reflected in a finding of contributory negligence.

In a number of cases, the question has arisen whether a claimant's taking his or her own life will break the chain of causation. The courts' approach has been to hold that where the defendant's negligence creates a risk of psychiatric illness leading to suicide, the suicide does not constitute a *novus actus interveniens*. Thus, in *Corr v IBC Vehicles Ltd*,[116] the claimant suffered a head injury at work as a result of his employer's negligence. He succumbed to severe depression and eventually killed himself. In an action by his widow, it was held that his suicide did not break the chain of causation.

A similar conclusion was reached by the House of Lords in *Reeves v Metropolitan Police Commissioner*.[117] Here, the deceased was in police custody. Taking advantage of the police officers' inadvertence in leaving the flap of his cell door open, he hanged himself by tying his shirt through the spy hole on the outside of the door. It had been noted in police records that the deceased was a suicide risk, having made two previous attempts to kill himself whilst in custody. The doctor who had examined him on his arrival at the police station, whilst finding no evidence of psychiatric illness, had noted that he should be kept under frequent observation in the light of his previous suicide attempts. By a 3:2 majority, the House of Lords held that the suicide, although a deliberate and informed act, could not be regarded as having broken the chain of causation, given that the police were under a specific legal duty to guard against the commission of that very act.

Remoteness of Damage

Here, we are not concerned with whether the claimant's loss may have an alternative cause. Rather, the question is whether the law will deny recovery on the basis that the loss in question is a very unusual result of the defendant's conduct.

6–027

The old law

Before 1961, the law was dominated by the decision of the Court of Appeal in *Re Polemis and Furness, Withy & Co*,[118] in 1921. Here, a ship had been loaded with a quantity of petrol, which, unbeknown to any of the parties, had leaked, causing the hold of the ship to fill with vapour. A dock worker employed by the defendants negligently allowed a wooden plank to drop into

6–028

---

116   [2008] UKHL 13; [2008] 1 A.C. 884.
117   [2000] 1 A.C. 360.
118   [1921] 3 K.B. 560.

the hold, where it somehow caused a spark that ignited the petrol vapour, causing the ship to be lost by fire. The Court of Appeal held the defendants liable. Whilst the worker could not have foreseen that the falling plank would cause a fire, he could have foreseen that it might cause some damage to the ship (such as a scratch on the paint work). Given that this was so, the defendants were liable for all of the damage that was a direct factual consequence of the worker's negligence.

The exact ratio of *Re Polemis* is a matter of some confusion. It is often argued that there are two possible interpretations of the decision. On the first interpretation, their Lordships appear to have held that because *some* damage *of the relevant kind* was reasonably foreseeable, the defendants were liable for all damage *of that kind*. In other words, they were liable for the fire because "damage to a ship", whether by fire or by a scratch in the paintwork, was the same kind of damage—damage to property. According to this interpretation, then, all that their Lordships did in *Re Polemis* was to draw a distinction between "damage to property" on the one hand, and other "kinds" of damage (economic loss and personal injury) on the other. The second, wider, interpretation of the case, however, is that so long as *some* damage (of whatever "kind") was the foreseeable result of the defendant's conduct, he or she would be liable for any damage that was a "direct" consequence of his or her conduct (including damage of a different "kind", and even damage to an "unforeseeable claimant").

In the subsequent case of *The Wagon Mound (No.1)*, which is now the leading authority on remoteness of damage, the Privy Council appeared to treat *Re Polemis* as authority for this second, wider, proposition. Their Lordships held that the "rule" in the case—that a defendant was to be liable for all the direct consequences of his or her actions—was wrong, because, if it were right, it would mean that a defendant could be liable even for damage that could not be reasonably foreseen.[119] Such a proposition could not be reconciled with important cases that had been decided after *Re Polemis*, not least of which was *Donoghue v Stevenson*.

The modern law: *The Wagon Mound (No.1)*

6–029

The decision in *Overseas Tankship (UK) Ltd v Morts Dock & Engineering Co Ltd*[120] is known as *The Wagon Mound (No.1)* because it is the first of two cases involving a ship of that name. It will be recalled that the second of these cases—*The Wagon Mound (No.2)*—has already been considered in Ch.5 as a case involving breach of duty. It is important not to confuse the two cases. The difference between them lies in the fact that, whereas in *The Wagon Mound (No.2)* the evidence before the court showed there was a foreseeable risk (albeit a small one) that the oil would ignite, in *The Wagon Mound (No.1)*—the case we are now concerned with—the evidence was that the oil catching fire was unforeseeable. This rather surprising difference is explained by the fact that, at the time *The Wagon Mound (No.1)* was brought to trial in New South Wales,

---

119 *The Wagon Mound (No.1)* [1961] A.C. 388 at 398. See also R.W.M. Dias, "Remoteness of Liability and Legal Policy" [1962] C.L.J. 178.
120 [1961] A.C. 388.

contributory negligence was a complete defence. This meant that the plaintiffs in *The Wagon Mound (No.1)* did not dare allege that it was reasonably foreseeable that the oil might catch fire, for fear that they might be held contributorily negligent in continuing with their welding operations.

It will be recalled that in the *Wagon Mound* litigation the defendants negligently allowed some furnace oil to spill on to the sea while their ship was in Sydney Harbour. In *The Wagon Mound (No.1)*, the plaintiffs were ship repairers. The oil was washed by the tide so that it fouled the plaintiffs' slipways, causing them to stop work. However, having been assured that there was no chance of the oil igniting, the plaintiffs resumed their welding operations. It was not clear what happened next, but it was assumed that some cotton waste, which was floating on the water, was ignited by a fragment of molten metal from the welding operations. The cotton waste, acting as a sort of wick, allowed the oil to ignite, and the plaintiffs' wharf and equipment were extensively damaged in the ensuing blaze. As has been said, the important finding of fact, on which the Privy Council based its decision, was that the occurrence of the fire was not reasonably foreseeable. But it *was* reasonably foreseeable, of course, that the oil might cause *some* damage to the plaintiffs' wharf by fouling it.

The Privy Council held that the defendants were not liable. Declaring *Re Polemis* to have been wrongly decided, their Lordships held that the proper test for remoteness of damage was whether the defendant could have reasonably foreseen the *kind of damage* for which the plaintiffs were suing. Their Lordships thought that "damage by fire" should be regarded as a different "kind" of damage from "damage by fouling", and since the former could not have been foreseen, the defendants were not answerable for it. Viscount Simonds explained the basis for the decision, saying:

> **"It does not seem consonant with current ideas of justice or morality that for an act of negligence, however slight or venial, which results in some trivial foreseeable damage the actor should be liable for all consequences however unforeseeable and however grave."[121]**

It may be argued, of course, that his Lordship's explanation is not wholly satisfactory. It views the matter exclusively from the defendant's point of view, and imports into tort law the criminal law idea that the "punishment" should fit the wrong, ignoring the idea that the traditional role of tort is to compensate the victim. Why should not the defendant, who (unlike the claimant) has been to blame at least in some degree, be made to shoulder all the loss caused by his or her fault? Such considerations have doubtless influenced the courts in their interpretation of the decision in *The Wagon Mound (No.1)*, especially in the context of personal injury cases. This will be explored below.

The principle in The *Wagon Mound (No.1)* contains a number of elements, which (as in the following sections) are traditionally considered in turn. It should be noted, however, that the

---

121   [1961] A.C. 388 at 422.

elements overlap considerably. We shall see that this area of the law is beset with uncertainty and contains many decisions that are quite hard to reconcile.

Foreseeability of the "kind of damage"

6-030

In *Hughes v Lord Advocate*,[122] the Post Office, in breach of its duty, left a manhole open in the street during the course of its work on some telephone cables. The manhole was covered with a tent and, in the evening, left unguarded but surrounded by warning paraffin lamps. The plaintiff was an eight-year-old boy who had picked up one of the lamps and clambered down the manhole. Because of a very unusual set of scientific circumstances, an explosion occurred, causing him severe burns. The House of Lords held that the Post Office was liable, even though it could not reasonably have foreseen that anyone might be burned by an explosion in the manhole. It was sufficient to found liability that there was a reasonably foreseeable risk of the boy being burned by the paraffin lamp. In other words, "damage by burning" was the "kind" of damage in question, there being no distinction between burning caused by the flame of the lamp and burning caused by an unforeseeable explosion.

Similar reasoning was applied in *Bradford Corp v Robinson Rentals Ltd*.[123] Here, the plaintiff suffered frostbite when he was sent on a journey by his employer in a van without a heater. It was held that, although frostbite was a rather unusual consequence in the circumstances (it was practically unheard of in Britain), it was nevertheless "of the type and kind of injury which was reasonably foreseeable".[124]

Both of these cases, then, suggest that the courts are happy to view personal injury as a single and indivisible "kind" of damage. Whilst the decision in *The Wagon Mound (No.1)* shows us that the courts will subdivide "damage to property" into different "kinds" of damage—such as "damage by fire" and "damage by fouling"—the courts appear not to apply the same sort of reasoning in personal injury cases. The difference in approach can be explained in terms of policy. First, the law has always been more anxious to protect physical wellbeing than to protect property. Secondly, if "damage to property" were regarded as a single, indivisible "kind" of damage, defendants might be exposed to "crushing liability" for very large amounts of loss. By contrast, in personal injury cases, losses are generally likely to be less expensive to compensate.

There is one well-known case, however, that appears to conflict with a general proposition that personal injury is an indivisible "kind" of damage. In *Tremain v Pike*,[125] the plaintiff was a herdsman employed by the defendants, who were farmers. The farm became infested with rats and the plaintiff contracted Weil's disease—a rare disease that is caught by coming into contact with rats' urine. Payne J held that, even on the assumption that the defendants had been

---

122 [1963] A.C. 837.
123 [1967] 1 W.L.R. 337.
124 [1967] 1 W.L.R. 337 per Rees J at 344.
125 [1969] 1 W.L.R. 1556.

negligent in failing to control the rat population, the plaintiff could not succeed. His Lordship thought that Weil's disease was both unforeseeable and "entirely different in kind" from the foreseeable consequences of contact with rats, such as food poisoning or the effects of a rat-bite. The status of *Tremain v Pike* is uncertain, especially in the light of *Parsons v Uttley Ingham* (discussed later), where the Court of Appeal implicitly rejected its reasoning.

So far as property damage is concerned, whilst it is clear that *The Wagon Mound (No.1)* allows the courts to subdivide property damage into different "kinds" of damage, the limitations (if any) on their ability to do so remain unclear. Analysis of the issue is difficult for a number of reasons. First, the answer to the question: "what is the kind of damage in question?" is inextricably bound up with the problems (considered below) of whether the *extent* of the damage, and the *way it is caused*, have to be foreseeable. Secondly, the issue is often difficult to separate from the issue of the *measure of damages* necessary to compensate a foreseeable kind of loss. It is well established that if a defendant injures a person with a high earning capacity, or damages a valuable piece of property, he or she cannot object to paying damages on the basis that the cost of compensation is greater than it might have been if the person had had a low income, or if the property had been less valuable.[126] But, suppose that (for some reasonable purpose) you leave a priceless Ming vase on your coffee table and I negligently break it. In such bizarre circumstances, can I not argue that, whilst "damage to a household ornament" might have been a foreseeable consequence of my negligence, "damage to a priceless antique" is an unforeseeable "kind" of damage? Or will the court say that "damage to a vase" was the foreseeable "kind" of damage, and that it matters not that the cost of replacing the vase is much greater than I could have expected?

To make matters worse, all of these issues are difficult to separate from the questions of whether, and how, the "eggshell skull" rule applies in the context of property damage (considered in a later section). In the final analysis, one is left with the suspicion that the courts are reluctant to rule authoritatively on the subdivision of property damage into different "kinds", so as to preserve the flexibility necessary to do justice whilst containing the scope of liability in appropriate cases.

Foreseeability of the "way the damage is caused"

6-031

In *Hughes v Lord Advocate* it was held that the precise manner in which the damage was caused did not have to be reasonably foreseen. So long as the defendant could reasonably foresee damage of the relevant "kind", the damage would not be too remote. In *Hughes*, therefore, the Post Office was liable even though it could not have foreseen the scientific circumstances which led to an underground explosion injuring the plaintiff. The same approach was adopted in *The Trecarrell*.[127] Here, the defendants were held liable when one of their employees, whilst working in a shipyard, carelessly dropped a drum of inflammable lacquer. The drum fell on a

---

126 *Smith v London & South Western Railway Co* (1870) L.R. 6. C.P. 14.
127 [1973] 1 Lloyd's Rep. 402.

temporary electricity cable and severed it, causing a short circuit which ignited the lacquer. The plaintiffs' ship was damaged in the resulting blaze.

There are, however, two cases where precisely the opposite reasoning has been applied—the defendants were not liable because they could not have foreseen harm caused in such an unusual way. In *Doughty v Turner Manufacturing Ltd*,[128] workmen employed by the defendants had allowed an asbestos cover to drop into a vat of very hot liquid. The cover slid in at an angle and did not cause a splash. A few minutes later, however, chemical changes in the asbestos brought about by the high temperature caused an eruption of the liquid, which splashed out of the vat, burning the plaintiff. The possibility of an eruption occurring in this way was unknown at the time. The Court of Appeal, following *The Wagon Mound (No.1)*,[129] held that the defendants were not liable. *Hughes* was distinguished on the basis that, in *Doughty*, the risk which materialised was very substantially different from any that could be foreseen.

This narrow view of risk was also adopted by the Divisional Court in *Crossley v Rawlinson*.[130] Here, the defendant had stopped his lorry when, as a result of his negligence, a tarpaulin covering the body of the lorry had caught fire. The plaintiff, an AA patrolman, who was on duty at a nearby AA service centre, saw the fire and ran out to assist. Whilst running towards the lorry on a rough path, he caught his foot in a concealed hole and fell. His claim for personal injury was dismissed on the basis that his being injured in this way was not reasonably foreseeable. The court drew a fine distinction between injury occurring during the course of tackling the fire (which was foreseeable) and injury occurring on the way to tackle the fire (which was not). Bearing in mind that the plaintiff was a rescuer, and that rescuers usually receive more sympathetic treatment from the courts, this seems a particularly harsh decision which has received considerable criticism.[131]

The validity of such reasoning must now be questioned in the light of the House of Lords' decision in *Jolley v Sutton LBC*.[132] Here, a 14-year-old boy had been severely injured when a boat, abandoned on council land, had fallen upon him, breaking his back. He and his friend had been attempting to repair the boat to take it to Cornwall to sail it. Although the council, as occupier, owed him a duty of care, the Court of Appeal had rejected his claim on the basis that whilst it was foreseeable that children playing on the boat might suffer some minor injuries, it was *not* foreseeable that a teenager would attempt to reconstruct the boat. The House of Lords disagreed. *Hughes* required the court to judge foresight according to the nature of the risk which ought to have been foreseen. Here, in view of the known ingenuity of children in finding unexpected ways of doing mischief to themselves, and the fact that the council had conceded that it was under a duty to remove the boat to avoid the risk of minor injuries—which

---

128 [1964] 1 Q.B. 518.

129 [1961] A.C. 388.

130 [1982] 1 W.L.R. 369.

131 e.g. M. Jones, *Textbook on Torts*, 8th edn (OUP, 2002), p.269 finds the decision "arbitrary and inconsistent with *Hughes*".

132 [2000] 1 W.L.R. 1082. This decision concerns occupiers' liability and will be considered further in Ch.8. The principles of causation and remoteness are the same, however, for common law negligence and under the occupiers' liability statutes.

would have cost it no more than removing it to avoid the injuries that actually occurred[133]— their Lordships adopted a broad view of risk: was it foreseeable that children would meddle with the boat causing some physical injury? On this basis, the council was found liable for the claimant's injuries.

Their Lordships in *Jolley*, then, adopted a far more generous interpretation of risk than that seen in *Doughty* and *Crossley* above, although they did stress that much would depend on the individual facts of each case. Nevertheless, Lord Nicholls, delivering the opinion of the Privy Council in *Att-Gen of the British Virgin Islands v Hartwell*,[134] doubted whether the reasoning in *Doughty* would find favour with modern courts, and suggested that courts now take a more liberal approach in determining whether the way in which the damage is caused is foreseeable.

Foreseeability of the "extent" of the damage

6-032

In *Hughes v Lord Advocate*, Lord Reid made it clear that a defendant can be liable even when the damage caused is greater in extent than was reasonably foreseeable. Only where the damage is different in "kind" can the defendant escape liability.[135] This approach was followed in *Vacwell Engineering Co Ltd v BDH Chemicals Ltd*.[136] The defendants manufactured and supplied a chemical that was liable to explode in contact with water, but they gave no warning of this hazard to the plaintiffs. The plaintiffs bought a quantity of the chemical and a scientist who worked for them put the ampoules containing the chemical in the sink. A violent explosion resulted, causing extensive damage to the plaintiffs' premises. Rees J, whilst holding that an explosion of the magnitude which occurred was not reasonably foreseeable, thought that, given that a *small* explosion was foreseeable, the damage was not too remote. The damage was of a foreseeable kind, and it did not matter that it was greater in extent than could have been foreseen.

Similarly, in *Parsons v Uttley Ingham & Co Ltd*,[137] the defendants installed a feed hopper for the plaintiffs' pigs, but negligently failed to leave open the ventilator, so that the nuts stored inside became mouldy. On eating the nuts, the pigs contracted a rare disease and a number of them died. The Court of Appeal held that, provided *some* damage of the relevant kind was reasonably foreseeable (in the form of mild illness of the pigs), the plaintiffs could recover for the more serious and unforeseeable consequence resulting from the defendants' negligence.

---

133   See Lord Hoffmann [2000] 1 W.L.R. 1082 at 1093.
134   [2004] 1 W.L.R. 1273.
135   *Hughes v Lord Advocate* [1963] A.C. 837 at 845.
136   [1971] 1 Q.B. 88.
137   [1978] Q.B. 791. The action was for breach of contract but was decided on the basis that the rules of remoteness being considered were equally applicable in tort.

The "Eggshell Skull" Rule

6-033

Before the decision in *The Wagon Mound (No.1)*, it was established law that where an injured claimant suffered from some peculiar hypersensitivity which exacerbated his or her loss, then, provided the defendant could reasonably foresee *some* injury to a *normal* claimant,[138] the defendant would be liable for the full extent of the loss. Thus, in *Dulieu v White & Sons*,[139] Kennedy J stated:

> **"If a man is negligently run over or otherwise negligently injured in his body, it is no answer to the sufferer's claim for damages that he would have suffered less injury, or no injury at all, if he had not had an unusually thin skull or an unusually weak heart."[140]**

The "eggshell skull" rule is sometimes also referred to as the maxim that "the defendant must take his victim as he finds him".

For a short time, it was uncertain whether the reasoning in *The Wagon Mound (No.1)* had displaced the rule. The matter was quickly settled, however, by the decision in *Smith v Leech Brain & Co Ltd*.[141] The plaintiff's husband was burned on the lip at work by a splash of molten metal. At the time of the accident, it was not known that he had a form of pre-malignant cancer. The burn triggered the onset of the cancer, from which he died three years later. Lord Parker CJ stated that, in *The Wagon Mound*, whilst the Privy Council had held that a defendant must foresee the kind of damage in suit, their Lordships had not meant to hold that the extent of the damage had to be foreseeable. It followed that the "eggshell skull" rule had not been displaced. Thus, apparently regarding "damage by burning" and "damage by cancer" as the same "kind" of damage (personal injury caused by an accident at work), his Lordship held the defendants liable.

6-034

It is clear that the rule will apply in cases where the particular characteristics of the claimant act in combination with surrounding circumstances (including the reasonable action of a third party) to exacerbate the claimant's loss. Thus, in *Robinson v Post Office*,[142] owing to the defendant's negligence, the plaintiff slipped and wounded his leg at work. He was subsequently given

---

138　It should be remembered that the rule does not come into play unless the claimant first establishes that a duty of care was owed and breached. Thus, in *Bourhill v Young* [1943] A.C. 92 Lord Wright, at 109, correctly stated: "One who suffers from the terrible tendency to bleed on slight contact, which is denoted by the term 'a bleeder', cannot complain if he mixes with the crowd and suffers severely, perhaps fatally, from being merely brushed against. There is no wrong done there". In the context of psychiatric illness, however, consider Lord Lloyd's reasoning in *Page v Smith* [1996] A.C. 155 (explored in Ch.4).

139　[1901] 2 K.B. 669.

140　[1901] 2 K.B. 669 at 679. Note, however, that his Lordship's reference to "no injury at all" seems inconsistent with the modern approach to the rule.

141　[1962] 2 Q.B. 405.

142　[1974] 1 W.L.R. 1176.

an anti-tetanus injection and developed encephalitis because of an unforeseeable reaction to the serum. The defendants were held liable for this consequence.

What is less clear is whether the "eggshell skull" rule applies to claims in respect of damage to "hypersensitive" property as well as to hypersensitive people. It has been convincingly suggested that it should. Thus, for example, where a defendant drops a lighted cigarette on an unexpectedly "hypersensitive" carpet, which catches fire and is destroyed, he or she should be liable for the full extent of the damage, even though the reasonably foreseeable damage is no more than a small hole. It has been suggested that to hold otherwise would present the impossible difficulty of determining the extent of the "foreseeable" damage in circumstances where that damage has been "swallowed up" by events—if the carpet is completely destroyed, how can a court quantify the damage which would have been caused by a mere hole? Damages would have to be awarded by guesswork, rather than to compensate losses proved to have been suffered by the claimant.[143]

Until 2003, however, the courts refused to apply the "eggshell skull" rule to losses which were caused by the claimant's own lack of funds. In *Liesbosch Dredger v SS Edison*,[144] the House of Lords had restricted the plaintiffs' claim for losses caused by the sinking of their dredger due to the defendants' negligence, to exclude the additional costs incurred by hiring a replacement dredger at an exorbitant rate to fulfil an existing contract. Their Lordships awarded the lesser cost of buying a comparable dredger, and refused to recognise that, due to the plaintiffs' impecuniosity, such a purchase had been a financial impossibility. The additional costs incurred in hiring a replacement vessel had an "extraneous cause",[145] namely the plaintiffs' financial circumstances, and were therefore too remote.

This decision received considerable academic criticism,[146] and subsequent courts sought to distinguish it. For example, in *Dodd Properties (Kent) Ltd v Canterbury CC*,[147] it was held that *The Liesbosch* did not govern a situation where the claimant, because of "commercial prudence" rather than impecuniosity, made a decision not to undertake prompt repairs to damaged property. In view of such criticism, the House of Lords in *Lagden v O'Connor*[148] in 2003 finally accepted that *The Liesbosch* should no longer be viewed as good law. In the words of Lord Hope:

> **". . . the law has moved on, and . . . the correct test of remoteness today is whether the loss was reasonably foreseeable. The wrongdoer must take his victim as he finds him . . . This rule applies to the economic state of the victim in the same way as it applies to his physical and mental vulnerability."[149]**

143 *Clerk & Lindsell on Torts*, 23rd edn (Sweet & Maxwell, 2020), para.2–173.

144 (*The Liesbosch*) [1933] A.C. 449.

145 [1933] A.C. 449 per Lord Wright at 460.

146 See, e.g. B. Coote, "Damages, The Liesbosch, and impecuniosity" [2001] C.L.J. 511.

147 [1980] 1 W.L.R. 433. See also *Mattocks v Mann* [1993] R.T.R. 13.

148 [2004] 1 A.C. 1067. Comment: B. Coote (2004) 120 L.Q.R. 382.

149 [2004] 1 A.C. 1067 at [61]. For a recent application, see *Hussain v EUI Ltd* [2019] EWHC 2647 (QB): ability to

Causation and remoteness: conclusion

6–035   In concluding, it is important to note that although the law we have examined in this chapter has developed as part of the tort of negligence (and most of the cases we have discussed are negligence cases), the rules relating to factual causation are applicable to <u>all</u> torts (although it should be noted that for torts actionable per se, no damage need be proved). Equally, the rules relating to remoteness are applicable to all torts, although some torts, for example the tort of deceit, still favour a test based on loss directly resulting from the fraudulent statement in question.[150]

We have seen that causation and remoteness are difficult areas of law, where the courts, in a sense, are faced with the tricky problem of "what to do when the rules run out". The apparent absence of logical rules leaves one with the impression that in many cases the judges adopt a practice of "reasoning backwards". In other words, they decide what would be a fair and just outcome for the case at hand, and then select an appropriate set of rules to justify that decision.

claim for hired replacement vehicles when the vehicles of self-employed drivers were off the road pending repair or replacement.

150   See *Doyle v Olby (Ironmongers) Ltd* [1969] 2 Q.B. 158; *Shelley v Paddock* [1980] Q.B. 348. Uncertainty about the application of *The Wagon Mound (No.1)* to the rule in *Rylands v Fletcher* has been removed by the decision of the House of Lords in *Cambridge Water Co Ltd v Eastern Counties Leather Plc* [1994] 2 A.C. 264 (considered in Ch.10).

7

Employers' Liability

Introduction

Injury in the workplace is a significant problem. The Health and Safety Executive reported that, in 2018–19, 147 people in Great Britain lost their lives at work.[1] The legal response to such injury takes a number of forms. For many injured employees, the simplest option is to turn to social security, which provides specific benefits for industrial injuries. Since 1948,[2] such compensation has been part of the welfare state. Therefore, victims who suffer personal injury due to an industrial accident[3] are entitled to claim benefits from the Department for Work and Pensions. Such benefits are inevitably not as high as any tort award and are subject to restrictions, but, for many victims, they provide a simpler and cheaper way of gaining compensation. Readers are advised to consult textbooks on labour law generally for employers' liability outside tort law[4] and in particular should consider the impact of criminal liability under the Health and Safety at Work etc. Act 1974, which applies to all persons at work in Great Britain, and regulations such as the Management of Health and Safety at Work Regulations 1999[5] and the Provision and Use of Work Equipment Regulations 1998.[6]

---

1   Health and Safety Executive, *HSE Statistics* (*https://www.hse.gov.uk/statistics/* [Accessed 1 August 2020]). In 2017–18, there were over 0.6 million non-fatal injuries reported and an estimated 1.4 million people suffered from ill health which they believed had been caused or made worse by current or past work. 2,523 people died from mesothelioma in 2017 and thousands more from other occupational cancers and diseases such as chronic obstructive pulmonary disease (COPD).
2   Industrial benefits first appeared in 1897 (see Workmen's Compensation Acts 1897, 1925 and 1943), but the changes in 1948 led to industrial benefits being integrated into the welfare state.
3   This includes certain industrial diseases. For its relationship with tort law, see R. Lewis, "Industrial Injuries Compensation: Tort and social security compared" (2017) 46 I.L.J. 445.
4   See, e.g. G. Pitt, *Employment law*, 11th edn (Sweet & Maxwell, 2020).
5   SI 1999/3242, which replaced the Management of Health and Safety at Work Regulations 1992. These are part of significant EU developments to improve workplace conditions.
6   SI 1998/2306, as amended.

This chapter will concentrate on employers' liability in tort. This can take three forms:

- *personal* liability to employees in negligence;

- liability for breach of statutory duty; and

- *vicarious* liability (that is, where the employer is held at law strictly liable for the torts committed by its employees in the course of their employment).

Employers are popular targets for tort claims. As insurance is compulsory,[7] claimants know that if they succeed, the employer is likely to be able to meet their claim and may, for the sake of labour relations or to avoid adverse publicity, be willing to settle. Although this chapter will examine all three forms of liability below, it will spend more time discussing vicarious liability, which plays a significant role in distributing loss and ensuring that claimants receive adequate compensation.

First of all, this chapter will examine the historical development of employers' liability. In seeking to understand the current law, it is particularly important to understand its historical background and why the rules have developed in their present form. For example, it may be questioned why there are three forms of liability and not simply one head of employers' liability. The answer lies in the historical development of the law, which is outlined below.

The development of employers' liability

7–002

The law on employers' liability reflects the economic and political trends of the last 200 years. Courts have always been aware, even if this has not been admitted openly, that their decisions affect the relationship between employers and employees and, more bluntly, the amount of money employers will have to spend on employee protection. It is perhaps unsurprising that in the early nineteenth century, at a time of increasing industrialisation, and with the insurance industry still embryonic, the courts were not prepared to impose a heavy burden of liability on employers and strove instead to urge employees to take responsibility for their own safety. In *Priestley v Fowler*,[8] the Court of Exchequer introduced what became known as the doctrine of common employment. This prevented an employee from suing his or her employer for injury negligently caused by a fellow employee. The courts held that it was implied in the employee's contract of employment that he or she would assume the risk of injury caused by the negligence

---

7   Employers' Liability (Compulsory Insurance) Act 1969. Employers' Liability (Compulsory Insurance) Regulations 1998 (SI 1998/2573) (as amended) reg.3 raises the sum to be insured to not less than £5 million.

8   (1837) 3 M. & W. 1; 150 E.R. 1030. B.A. Hepple and M. Matthews, *Tort: Cases and Materials*, 4th edn (Butterworths, 1991), p.566, report that in addition to losing his case, Priestley spent some years in a debtors' prison because he could not pay the costs of his unsuccessful action.

of fellow employees, provided they had been selected with due care by the employer.[9] Liability was further restricted by the fact that contributory negligence at that time was an absolute bar to any claim in negligence[10]—however minimal the negligence of the claimant—and the fact that the courts were willing to apply the defence of voluntary assumption of risk to tasks undertaken in the workplace.[11] The result of this "unholy trinity" was very limited liability on the employer.

However, as the nineteenth century progressed (and insurance began to develop by which employers could protect themselves against legal claims), attitudes changed. The judiciary and legislature began to take note of the hardship suffered by employees injured by new machinery and the introduction of the railways. New concepts were developed to circumvent the obstacles to recovery. The doctrine of vicarious liability continued to expand,[12] but this could not overcome the obstacle of the doctrine of common employment. The courts therefore developed the idea of a personal duty on the employer towards his employees which was non-delegable, i.e. responsibility could not be displaced onto another party. Personal liability allowed claimants to sue the employer for damages, even if the injury had been caused by another employee and provided a means of circumventing the barriers to liability. *Groves v Lord Wimborne*[13] also established that the doctrine of common employment did not apply to the tort of breach of statutory duty, and therefore boosted the use of this tort to permit an injured employee to sue for an award of damages.

Unsurprisingly, in the twentieth century, the three barriers to employers' liability came under attack. The doctrine of common employment was abolished under the Law Reform (Personal Injuries) Act 1948, and the Law Reform (Contributory Negligence) Act 1945 permitted the courts to apportion liability where the claimant had been contributorily negligent.[14] In *Smith v Charles Baker & Sons*,[15] the House of Lords had already expressed its reluctance to apply the defence of voluntary assumption of risk to employees, and so by 1948, all three obstacles had either been abolished or tightly confined.

Despite these changes, the distinction between personal and vicarious liability remains.[16] Nevertheless, from the perspective of modern law, the employers' personal liability to its employees and for breach of statutory duty are less important than in the past. As we will see, it is the doctrine of vicarious liability which is of particular importance in 21st century tort law.

---

9 See *Bartonshill Coal Co v Reid* (1858) 3 Macq. 266; *Johnson v Lindsay & Co* [1891] A.C. 371.

10 See *Senior v Ward* (1859) 1 El. & El. 385; 120 E.R. 954.

11 This is discussed more fully in Ch.16.

12 See D. Ibbetson, *A Historical Introduction to the Law of Obligations* (OUP, 1999), pp.181–184.

13 [1898] 2 Q.B. 402.

14 See Ch.16.

15 [1891] A.C. 325 HL, unless the job of necessity involved risk. For full discussion, see Ch.16.

16 See *Staveley Iron & Chemical Co v Jones* [1956] A.C. 627. This has nevertheless been the subject of extensive academic debate—see G. Williams, "Vicarious Liability: Tort of the Master or of the Servant" (1957) 72 L.Q.R. 522, F. H. Newark, "*Twine v Bean's Express Ltd*" (1954) 17 M.L.R. 102, R. Stevens, "Vicarious liability or vicarious action?" (2007) 123 L.Q.R. 30—and the distinction is not always clearly expressed by the judiciary—see, e.g. Lord Hobhouse in *Lister v Hesley Hall Ltd* [2001] UKHL 22; [2002] 1 A.C. 215.

Personal Liability

7–003

To understand the nature of the employer's personal liability, it is necessary to remember that it was developed to circumvent the doctrine of common employment. As a result of this doctrine—which prevented employees claiming against the employer in respect of a fellow employee's negligence—where an employee (X) brought an action against his employer (Y) for negligent injury in the workplace, X ran the risk that Y could simply claim that he was not liable because:

- the injury was caused by the action of a fellow employee; and

- Y had taken reasonable care in choosing the employee in question.

The victim would be left with an action against a fellow employee, which would be difficult to establish and, in all probability, worthless.

The leading case of *Wilson and Clyde Coal Co v English*[17] resolved this difficulty by making the duty on the employer non-delegable. "Non-delegable" here does not mean that the employer cannot delegate its health and safety tasks (this would simply be impracticable in modern employment conditions), but that it cannot delegate *responsibility* at law. It is no excuse that the employer has taken care to ensure a competent fellow employee deals with safety: if the employee is injured due to lack of care, the employer is liable.

The facts of *Wilson and Clyde Coal Co v English*[18] illustrate this point. A miner had been crushed in a mining accident, and had sued the mine-owners, on the basis that a safe system of work had not been adopted. The defendants argued that they had delegated pit safety to a qualified manager, as required by statute, and should not be held liable. Lord Wright, in the House of Lords, held that it was not enough for an employer to entrust the fulfilment of its duty of care to its employees, even when they had been selected with due care and skill.[19] The employer retained responsibility to provide a competent staff, adequate plant and equipment and effective supervision. If these were not provided with reasonable care and skill, the employer would be liable. Here, the system of working had not been reasonably safe and so the employers were liable.

The nature of the duty

7–004

This section will examine the nature of the non-delegable duty placed on the employer. An employer's personal duty is a duty to see that reasonable care is taken.[20] This will also apply

---

17 [1938] A.C. 57. See G. Williams, "Liability for Independent Contractors" [1956] C.L.J. 180, 190–192.
18 [1938] A.C. 57
19 [1938] A.C. 57 at 78. See also Lord Herschell in *Smith v Baker* [1891] A.C. 325 at 362.
20 As stated in Ch.5, readers should note the distinction between the employer's duty of care and breach of

to analogous relationships, for example the relationship between the Chief Constable of Police and police officers, although the courts do consider the demands of public policy in this context.[21] To comply with this duty, case law indicates that the employers should take care in the provision of:

- competent staff;

- adequate plant and equipment;

- a safe place of work; and

- a safe system of work.

Each of these matters will be examined in more detail below.

(1) Provision of competent staff

7–005

This was obviously important when the doctrine of common employment barred the employer's liability for the negligence of fellow employees. It meant that the employer would be personally responsible for providing such incompetent staff. It still has some modern relevance, however. A good example is *Hudson v Ridge Manufacturing Co.*[22] An employee had for nearly four years persistently engaged in practical jokes, such as tripping up fellow employees, and had been reprimanded many times. His employers were found to be personally liable when he tripped up the plaintiff and caused him injury. They had failed to exercise reasonable care to put an end to such conduct, which was a potential danger to other employees.[23] Equally an employer may find itself liable for failing to prevent a campaign of sustained bullying when it was in its power to do so.[24]

---

that duty. The duty is to see that reasonable care is taken. Breach of duty can be shown by evidence that the employer had failed to take reasonable steps to provide competent staff or a safe system of work.

21 See *Waters v Commissioner of Police for the Metropolis* [2000] 1 W.L.R. 1607 and *Mullaney v Chief Constable of West Midlands Police* (CA) [2001] EWCA Civ 700.

22 [1957] 2 Q.B. 348. See also *Smith v Crossley Brothers Ltd* (1951) 95 Sol. Jo. 655 and Sir Nicolas Browne-Wilkinson VC in *Wilsher v Essex AHA* [1987] Q.B. 730 CA at 778: "In my judgment, a health authority which so conducts its hospital that it fails to provide doctors of sufficient skill and experience to give the treatment offered at the hospital may be directly liable in negligence to the patient".

23 The employer here is unlikely to be vicariously liable for the "playful" activities of such an employee as it is doubtful whether a court would find such conduct to be in the course of his or her employment: see *Graham v Commercial Bodyworks Ltd* [2015] EWCA Civ 47.

24 See *Waters v Commissioner of Police for the Metropolis* [2000] 1 W.L.R. 1607 (breach of duty found to be arguable).

> ## (2) Provision of adequate plant and equipment and a safe place to work

7–006

The employer should take reasonable care to ensure that the employee's place of work is safe, which extends to access to the premises.[25] This includes a duty to take reasonable care to prevent exposure of its employees, and members of their families, from inhaling asbestos that might cause mesothelioma.[26] In addition, the employer must take reasonable care to provide all necessary equipment and to maintain it in a reasonable condition. An interesting point was raised by *Davie v New Merton Board Mills*.[27] In this case, the plaintiff lost the sight in his left eye when a particle of metal chipped off a tool he was using, due to a fault in its manufacture. The tool had been provided by his employers, who had bought it from a reputable supplier, and the defect could not be detected by reasonable inspection. The House of Lords held that his employers were not liable. Although they had a duty to take reasonable care to provide a reasonably safe tool, this had been discharged[28]—they had bought the tool from a reputable source and they had no means of discovering that it contained a latent defect. The court held that if liability was imposed in such circumstances, any employer "employing another and supplying him with tools for his job acts at his peril".[29]

This decision, which obviously favoured employers, was reversed by the Employer's Liability (Defective Equipment) Act 1969. Section 1 provides that where an employee is injured in the course of his or her employment in consequence of a defect in equipment provided by the employer for the purposes of the employer's business, and the defect is due (wholly or partly) to the fault of a third party, then the injury will be attributed to the fault of the employer. This applies regardless of whether the third party is identified or not and extends to plant, machinery, vehicles, aircraft and even clothing.[30] This provision is obviously intended to make it easier for an employee to sue. He or she is no longer required to pursue a manufacturer[31] who may be overseas, but can sue his or her employer. The employee must nevertheless show that:

- a defect in equipment caused the accident; and

- the defect, on the balance of probabilities, was due to some fault in its manufacture.

---

25   See *Ashdown v Samuel Williams & Sons Ltd* [1957] 1 Q.B. 409 CA.
26   This is unusual in extending the duty to the families of workers but the risk of secondary exposure to asbestos has been known since October 1965: see *Carey v Vauxhall Motors Ltd* [2019] EWHC 238 (QB). The exposure must, however, be more than de minimis.
27   [1959] A.C. 604.
28   The court held that the employer could not be found to have delegated its duty of care to the manufacturer.
29   Viscount Simonds [1959] A.C. 604 at 618. Comment: C. J. Hamson [1959] C.L.J. 157.
30   *Coltman v Bibby Tankers Ltd (The Derbyshire)* [1988] A.C. 276 even extended the Act to a ship which had sunk off the coast of Japan with the loss of all hands. See also *Knowles v Liverpool City Council* [1993] 1 W.L.R. 1428 (not restricted to tools and plant and could include flagstone which broke injuring workman laying the pavement).
31   The employee still has a right to sue the manufacturer. Liability of manufacturers in tort will be discussed in Ch.9.

These matters are not always easy to prove. The Act also provides that the rules relating to contributory negligence still apply.

(3) Provision of a safe system of work

This is difficult to define, but essentially refers to decisions adopted by the employer on the method of working.[32] Employers are required to take reasonable steps to organise and supervise the work of their employees, and to give proper instructions and guidance to employees and check that it is adhered to. Employers must take account of the fact that employees are often heedless of their own safety and so the system of work adopted should, so far as possible, minimise the danger of the employee's own foreseeable carelessness. For example, in *General Cleaning Contractors v Christmas*,[33] there was an obvious danger that if window cleaners stood on the sill to clean the outside of the window, they might suffer injury if the window closed. By failing to instruct the window cleaners to take precautions, their employers had failed to provide a safe system of work. Particular care must be taken if the work is complex or involves a large number of personnel.

The modern scope of personal liability

It can be seen that the personal liability of an employer in negligence to his employees differs from the ordinary duty of care examined earlier in this book. Rather than being a duty to take care, it is perhaps more accurately described as a duty to see that reasonable care is taken. This duty extends not only to the actual work of employees, but to all such acts as are normally and reasonably incidental to a day's work, such as making a cup of tea or going to the toilet.[34] Yet, apart from this, the ordinary rules of negligence apply. The employee must show that the duty of care has been breached and that breach caused the loss suffered. The duty is owed to the individual employee. As seen in Ch.5, the particular characteristics of an employee may require extra care to be taken. In *Paris v Stepney BC*,[35] the court held that the employer was required to undertake extra safety precautions in respect of a one-eyed employee. The defendants were therefore liable for not providing safety goggles, even though they were not required to provide them to two-eyed employees.

Case law suggests that the courts are prepared to adopt a very generous approach towards the personal liability of employers, although this seems to be confined to personal injury rather

---

32   Consider *McGhee v National Coal Board* [1973] 1 W.L.R. 1 discussed in Ch.6 (failure to provide adequate washing facilities).

33   [1953] A.C. 180, see in particular Lord Oaksey at 189–190. See, more recently, *Ammah v Kuehne & Nagel Logistics Ltd* [2009] EWCA Civ 11.

34   *Davidson v Handley Page Ltd* [1945] 1 All E.R. 235.

35   [1951] A.C. 367.

than economic or reputational harm.[36] In *McDermid v Nash Dredging and Reclamation Co Ltd*,[37] the plaintiff was an employee of the defendants, which were a wholly-owned subsidiary of a Dutch company, Stevin. The function of the defendants was to provide and pay the staff engaged in Stevin's operation in Sweden. The plaintiff had been injured whilst working on the deck of a tug owned by Stevin, due to the negligence of one of Stevin's employees. The question was whether the defendants (the subsidiary company) could be liable in such circumstances. The House of Lords held that the defendants could not effectively delegate the task of providing a safe system of work to the Dutch company and its employees and therefore retained personal responsibility for any lack of care which injured the plaintiff.

This decision stretches personal liability very far, but may be explained by the close connection between the Dutch company and the defendants. It should also be noted that the House of Lords was quite happy to base a failure to provide a safe system of work on a negligent failure to devise such a system or negligence in its operation.[38] It has been observed that this represented an extension of existing legal principles.[39]

Stress in the workplace

7–009

A similarly generous approach was adopted in the context of psychiatric illness in *Walker v Northumberland CC*.[40] In this case, Colman J held that there was no logical reason for excluding the risk of psychiatric damage from the scope of an employer's duty to provide a safe system of work. Here, the plaintiff, the defendants' area social services manager, suffered a second nervous breakdown due to stress and pressure at work. The plaintiff had suffered an earlier breakdown due to stress at work and it was therefore reasonably foreseeable that a failure to lessen his workload might lead to a second breakdown.

Colman J in *Walker* applied the ordinary principles of employers' liability. No mention was made of the House of Lords' decision in *Alcock v Chief Constable of South Yorkshire*[41] (discussed in Ch.4) which stipulated that a restrictive approach should be taken towards psychiatric

---

36   The Supreme Court recently refused to hold that an employer owed its employees a duty of care to conduct litigation against itself in a manner which protected them from economic or reputational harm: *James-Bowen v Commissioner of Police of the Metropolis* [2018] UKSC 40; [2018] 1 W.L.R. 4021. See, generally, *Reid v Rush & Tompkins Group Plc* [1990] 1 W.L.R. 212 CA and *Crossley v Faithful & Gould Holdings Ltd* [2004] EWCA Civ 293; [2004] 4 All E.R. 447 (refusal to imply a general term into every contract of employment that an employer should take reasonable care of an employee's economic well being).

37   [1987] A.C. 906. For a commentary on the case, see J. G. Fleming [1988] C.L.J. 11.

38   See also *Mullaney v Chief Constable of West Midlands Police* [2001] EWCA Civ 700 (failure to operate a safe system of work where distress calls from a police officer had not been monitored as instructed with the result that the officer received severe head injuries from an assailant).

39   See E. McKendrick, "Vicarious liability and independent contractors—a re-examination" (1990) 53 M.L.R. 770, 773–774 who remarks that the effect of the decision is as if vicarious liability had been imposed.

40   [1995] I.C.R. 702; [1995] 1 All E.R. 737. Comment: D. Nolan (1995) 24 I.L.J. 280.

41   [1992] 1 A.C. 310.

damage. This led some to question the status of *Walker*, particularly in the light of the subsequent case of *White v Chief Constable of South Yorkshire*,[42] where the House of Lords held that police attending the victims of the Hillsborough disaster could not claim against their employers for psychiatric illness suffered as a result.[43] Although the majority of the House of Lords expressed no clear view on *Walker*, some comments were made. Lord Hoffmann suggested that a distinction may be drawn between claims arising from the work itself and claims due to witnessing injury to others in the course of work.[44] Lord Steyn, however, did seem to advocate that the ordinary rules of tort, which restrict recovery for psychiatric damage, should apply to all employee claims.

Subsequent case law has confirmed the status of *Walker* and attempted to clarify exactly when employers will find themselves liable for psychiatric injury arising from stress or harassment in the workplace. The leading decision is that of *Sutherland v Hatton*.[45] In this case, the Court of Appeal, dealing with four conjoined appeals, sought to give employers guidance. It distinguished:

a   cases where the harm suffered was the reasonably foreseeable product of specific breaches of a contractual duty of care between the defendant and a known primary victim (e.g. the employee in *Walker*);

b   cases where the relationship was only in tort (e.g. *Page v Smith*,[46] *Alcock v Chief Constable of South Yorkshire Police*[47]) and

c   cases where the secondary victim has a contractual relationship with the defendant (e.g. the police officer witnessing the Hillsborough disaster in *White v Chief Constable of South Yorkshire*).

The control mechanisms of *White* and *Alcock* would only apply under (b) and (c), and not where the employee was a primary victim under (a). This seems a rather fine distinction and is clearly introduced to maintain the *Walker* line of authority for potential claimants. Nevertheless, *Hatton* has been welcomed by employers primarily due to its acceptance that an employer is entitled, unless he knows otherwise, to assume that the employee can cope. This is obviously in the employer's favour.[48] Only if the employer knows, or should know, of some particular problem or vulnerability will the employer be liable. This will require the court to look at a number

---

42   [1999] 2 A.C. 455.
43   By a majority of 4 to 1, Lord Goff dissenting. Nevertheless, the Law Commission (Law Commission Report No.249 *Liability for Psychiatric Illness* (1998), para.7.22) had found that *Walker* represented "a just development in the law".
44   See Lord Hoffmann [1999] 2 A.C. 455, 506.
45   [2002] EWCA Civ 76; [2002] 2 All E.R. 1. Hale LJ at [20] cited *Walker* and Lord Hoffmann's judgment in *White* above with approval.
46   [1996] A.C. 155.
47   [1992] 1 A.C. 310.
48   See N. J. Mullany, "Containing claims for workplace mental illness" (2002) 118 L.Q.R. 373.

of relevant factors, including the nature and amount of work undertaken by the employee (is the employee overworked or placed under unreasonable pressure?) and signs of stress in the employee. The indications that a person is about to suffer harm from stress at work must be plain enough for any reasonable employer to realise something should be done about it. *Yapp v Foreign and Commonwealth Office* held that it would require exceptional circumstances for an employer to foresee that an apparently robust employee, with no history of any psychiatric ill-health, would develop a depressive illness as a result even of a very serious setback at work.[49] Even if the risk of harm is foreseeable, the court must in every case examine what the employer could and should have done, bearing in mind the size and scope of the operation, its resources, whether it is in the public or private sector, and other demands placed upon it.[50] The "threshold question" is whether this kind of harm to this particular employee was reasonably foreseeable.[51]

7–010

In the case of *Hatton*, Mrs Hatton had suffered a stress-related psychiatric illness whilst teaching at a comprehensive school. However, like many people, she had struggled to cope and did not complain to her superiors or ask for help. Yet, the fact that she had struggled on without complaint led the court to conclude that there was no clear indication that she was likely to suffer from psychiatric injury and that the school should not be liable.[52] In contrast, in the conjoined case of *Barber v Somerset CC*,[53] another school teacher, Mr Barber, had been forced to take three weeks off school, which had been certified by his GP as due to depression and stress, and could point to several meetings in which he had expressed concern as to his workload and its effect on his health. Although these meetings had taken place before the summer vacation ("usually a source of relaxation and recuperation for hard-pressed teachers") and his actual breakdown had taken place the following November, the House of Lords (on appeal) overturned the view of the Court of Appeal that "it is expecting far too much to expect school authorities to pick up the fact that the problems were continuing without some such indication."[54]

Although the Court of Appeal guidelines in *Hatton* were not appealed,[55] Lord Walker, giving the leading judgment in *Barber*, appeared to favour a more "employee-friendly" approach. His Lordship found that although the *Hatton* guidelines provided practical assistance, the overall test remains "the conduct of the reasonable and prudent employer, taking positive thought for the safety of his workers in the light of what he knows or ought to know."[56]

---

49 [2014] EWCA Civ 1512; [2015] I.R.L.R. 112 per Underhill LJ at [125].

50 Note that this is a more subjective test than that used in ordinary negligence claims (discussed in Ch.5).

51 See Hale LJ in *Hatton* [2002] EWCA Civ 76; [2002] 2 All E.R. 1 at [23]. Her Ladyship lists 16 practical propositions at [43] which aim to provide clear guidance for employers in future.

52 See also *Pratley v Surrey CC* [2003] EWCA Civ 1067; [2004] I.C.R. 159 (foresight of risk of illness arising from continuing overwork in the future not sufficient).

53 [2004] UKHL 13; [2004] 1 W.L.R. 1089 HL ([2002] 2 All E.R. 1 CA).

54 [2004] UKHL 13 at [59].

55 Lord Walker, giving the leading judgment, describes them at [63] and [65] as "a valuable contribution to the development of the law" and "useful practical guidance, but . . . not . . . having anything like statutory force".

56 Quoting Swanwick J in *Stokes v Guest, Keen and Nettlefold (Bolts and Nuts) Ltd* [1968] 1 W.L.R. 1776 at 1783. His

On this basis, although this case was close to the borderline, the school had been negligent in failing to make ongoing inquiries as to Mr Barber's health and in not taking any measures to ease the problem.

The more recent Court of Appeal decision in *Hartman v South Essex Mental Health and Community Care NHS Trust*,[57] involving six conjoined appeals, sought to quash any fears of inconsistency between *Hatton* and *Barber*. Scott-Baker LJ, giving judgment for the court, found that Lord Walker was not disagreeing with the *Hatton* guidelines, but simply sounding a word of caution that no two cases were alike and that the test must be applied to each new set of facts.[58] The decisions reached in *Hartman* indicate that the courts will continue generally to require some specific signs to be evident to the reasonable employer that a problem exists.[59] In *Hartman* itself, the claim of a hard-working nursing auxiliary dealing with children with learning difficulties failed. The Court of Appeal rejected the argument that such a job required a higher degree of alertness from employers. Equally, knowledge of an earlier nervous breakdown disclosed in confidence to the Occupational Health Department would not be attributed to the employer. This decision may be contrasted with the sixth appeal, *Melville v Home Office*. Here, the Home Office had conceded that the job of health care officer in a prison, which included the recovery of the bodies of prisoners who had committed suicide, might cause injury to health and had undertaken to provide support following any such incident. Mr Melville unfortunately had been unable to access this support. The Court of Appeal distinguished ordinary claims for stress in the workplace from a situation where the employer foresaw that a specific task might lead to mental injury and devised a system to deal with this. In such circumstances, a negligent failure to implement this system would lead to liability.[60] It nevertheless cautioned that the mere fact that an employer offered an occupational health service should not lead to the conclusion that the employer had foreseen the risk of injury due to stress at work.

As may be seen, complaints to one's employer will often form the basis for any claim for liability. Yet, few employees in such circumstances will wish to alert their superiors to the fact that they are not doing their job properly. The Court of Appeal in *Hatton* recognised this, but insisted that it is difficult in such circumstances to blame the employer for failing to act. Any stricter regime would be better implemented by way of regulations imposing specific statutory duties.[61]

---

judgment was heavily criticised by Lord Scott dissenting for setting an unrealistically high standard of care on the school.

57 [2005] EWCA Civ 6; [2005] I.C.R. 782. Comment: C. McIvor (2005) 21 P.N. 123.

58 [2005] EWCA Civ 6; [2005] I.C.R. 782 at [10].

59 e.g. in *Garrod v North Devon NHS Primary Care Trust* [2006] EWHC 850; [2007] P.I.Q.R. Q1, a health visitor had already had a breakdown due to pressure of work. Nevertheless, on her return, she was repeatedly put under pressure to the detriment of her health.

60 "It is illogical to argue that when an employer has foreseen a risk of psychiatric injury to employees exposed to certain traumatic incidents, such injury is not foreseeable": Scott-Baker LJ in *Hartman v South Essex Mental Health and Community Care NHS Trust* [2005] I.C.R. 782 at [134].

61 Hale LJ [2002] 2 All E.R. 1 at 9–10. The Court of Appeal further indicated that should the employer set up a confidential advice service, with referral to appropriate counselling or treatment services, it would be

Breach of Statutory Duty

7-011 This is a tort in its own right.[62] Although, as will be seen below, breach of statutory duty is not confined to the employment context, traditionally its main application has been in the employment field, particularly in relation to matters of industrial safety.[63] It therefore forms a part of the potential liability of employers in tort and it is appropriate to deal with it in this chapter. It should be noted, however, that government reforms in 2013 have diminished the role of breach of statutory duty in the employment context. Previously, the Health and Safety at Work etc Act 1974 s.47(2) had provided that breach of a duty imposed by health and safety regulations would, so far as it caused damage, give rise to civil liability. This presumption has now been reversed. From 1 October 2013,[64] s.47(2) now provides that health and safety regulations introduced under the 1974 Act shall *not* be civilly actionable except to the extent that the individual regulations specifically provide.[65] This means that regulations which do not expressly provide for civil liability (and few do) will no longer support an action for breach of statutory duty and, in such circumstances, employees will have to rely on the employer's duty of care in negligence, discussed above.[66] Nevertheless, the tort of breach of statutory duty is still relevant in giving a remedy for breach of statutory duties where the legislature did intend that, in addition to any criminal or administrative penalties, the injured party should have a right to sue in tort. The House of Lords, in *Lonrho Ltd v Shell Petroleum Co Ltd (No.2)*,[67] declined to accept the broader notion that liability could arise whenever damage results from a contravention of a statutory duty. The question, therefore, is when does Parliament intend such a right to exist? Unfortunately, very few statutes expressly deal with this issue.[68] In the absence of an express right to sue[69] (or an

---

unlikely to be found liable, but see now *Daw v Intel Corp (UK) Ltd* [2007] EWCA Civ 70; [2007] 2 All E.R. 126 (counselling services were not a panacea by which employers could discharge their duty of care in all cases. It was a question of fact).

62 Although there are arguments to the contrary, most notably the argument of statutory negligence forwarded by E.R. Thayer, "Public wrong and private action" (1914) 27 Harv. L.R. 317. It should be noted that the tort of breach of statutory duty is distinct from statutes which place liability in negligence in statutory form such as the Occupiers' Liability Acts which are discussed in Ch.8. See, generally, K.M. Stanton, *Statutory Torts* (Sweet and Maxwell, 2003), R.A. Buckley, "Liability in tort for breach of statutory duty" (1984) 100 L.Q.R. 204 and K.M. Stanton, "New forms of the tort of breach of statutory duty" (2004) 120 L.Q.R. 324.

63 See G. Williams, "The Effect of Penal Legislation in the Law of Tort" (1960) 23 M.L.R. 233.

64 Enterprise and Regulatory Reform Act 2013 (Commencement No.3, Transitional Provisions and Savings) Order 2013 (SI 2013/2227) art.2(f).

65 As amended by Enterprise and Regulatory Reform Act 2013 s.69. Section 47(2A) of the 1974 Act confirms that the provisions apply to statutory provisions existing prior to the 2013 Act.

66 See A. Roy, "Without a safety net: Litigating employers' liability claims after the Enterprise Act" [2015] J.P.I. Law 15.

67 [1982] A.C. 173 at 187, rejecting the majority judgment in *Ex p. Island Records Ltd* [1978] Ch.122.

68 Despite the plea by Lord du Parcq in *Cutler v Wandsworth Stadium Ltd* [1949] A.C. 398 at 410 that Parliament should state explicitly whether it intended that there should be a civil remedy or not. See also *McCall v Abelesz* [1976] Q.B. 585.

69 e.g. see Consumer Protection Act 1987 s.41.

express exclusion from suing),[70] the courts are left to construe the statute, and to infer whether Parliament intended to provide a right to damages in tort. This gives the courts a considerable amount of discretion, in the exercise of which they will consider the purpose of the statute and whether, in all the circumstances, individuals such as the claimant could have been intended to have a civil remedy.

The first question in dealing with breach of statutory duty is therefore to look at the wording of the particular statutory provision which has been breached: construing it according to the guidelines established by the courts, does it give a remedy in tort to individuals who suffer harm as a result of its breach? If this is established, there are four further matters to consider:

- Is the duty owed to this particular claimant?

- Has the defendant breached his or her statutory duty?

- Did the breach cause the damage in question?

- Was the injury of the kind which the statute intended to prevent?

Only if all five questions are answered in the affirmative will an action lie for breach of statutory duty. It must be stated that much turns on the interpretative powers of the courts and whether or not they are willing to accept that a regulatory statute was intended to place an additional burden on defendants to pay civil damages. Generally, the courts have shown themselves willing to adopt such a construction in relation to employee safety, but have adopted a more restrictive view in other contexts. In considering the employment cases, it should be borne in mind that until 1948, breach of statutory duty formed one of the ways of circumventing the doctrine of common employment. Policy considerations have therefore been influential in deciding when to allow a remedy for breach of statutory duty—arguably this is inevitable when the courts are given a broad interpretative discretion. The Law Commission, in 1969,[71] attempted to limit this discretion by recommending the enactment of a general statute that would have created a presumption that a civil remedy was intended unless the contrary was stated. This did not become law. Such a provision would have greatly increased the role of this tort, in a way which does not reflect the current restrictive view taken.

Although the courts exercise discretion in such cases, this discretion is not without limits. The courts have developed guidelines which they use in deciding whether a civil remedy was intended. These are examined below.

---

70   e.g. Health and Safety at Work etc Act 1974 s.47(1)(a) which provides that the general duties under the Act do not give rise to civil liability. See also Guard Dogs Act 1975 s.5 and Railways Act 2005 s.44.

71   See Law Commission Report No.21, *The Interpretation of Statutes* (1969) para.38. This proposal did form part of the Interpretation of Legislation Bill 1980, but this was subsequently withdrawn. R.A. Buckley (1984) 100 L.Q.R. 204, 231–232 argues that this provision would not, in any event, have resolved all the problems involved in construing statutes.

Construing Parliamentary intention

7-012

The courts have identified a number of factors which indicate whether Parliament intended a remedy to lie for breach of statutory duty. The leading case of *Lonrho Ltd v Shell Petroleum Co Ltd (No.2)*[72] highlights the most significant factors. The case concerned the supply of oil in breach of certain sanctions following the unilateral declaration of independence (UDI) by Southern Rhodesia in 1965. Lonrho brought an action for breach of statutory duty, alleging that it had suffered heavy losses when (unlike its competitors) it had complied with the sanctions. Lord Diplock, giving the leading judgment, held that the action failed. Whilst confirming that the overall test was one of identifying whether the purpose of the Act was to give the claimant a civil remedy, his Lordship identified a number of factors which assisted the courts in construing statutory provisions. His Lordship held that the courts should generally take a restrictive view where the Act provided its own penalties, but that there were two main exceptions to this rule. The first exception was where the claimant could show that the statute had been enacted for the benefit or protection of a particular class of individuals. The second exception was where the statute conferred a public right and a particular member of the public suffered special damage.[73] Neither exception was applicable in *Lonrho*. The sanctions had been imposed, as a matter of state policy, to destroy the illegal UDI regime and were not intended either to benefit a particular class of individuals, nor to establish a public right. Lonrho therefore had no valid claim for breach of statutory duty.

Whilst the considerations which influence the courts in construing Parliamentary intention are elusive, and difficult to examine in isolation, it is possible to identify and discuss a number of relevant points:

- whether the statute protects a specific "class" of individuals;

- the nature of the legislation;

- whether alternative remedies exist at law.

Each of these points will be examined below.

(1) Protection of a class

7-013

There is clear authority that if the statute is passed for the protection of a limited class of the public, rather than for the benefit of the public as a whole, a court will be more inclined to find

---

72 [1982] A.C. 173 at 185.

73 His Lordship's second exception is contentious and it is fair to say that it has not been taken up by the courts. The best example of liability in such circumstances is that of public nuisance (discussed in Ch.10) which is clearly not statutory.

that a civil remedy was intended.[74] Thus, in *Atkinson v Newcastle Waterworks Co*,[75] the Court of Appeal rejected the claim of a householder whose premises had burnt down. The defendants had been in breach of their statutory duty to maintain water pressure in their pipes. As a result, when the fire broke out, there was insufficient water to extinguish it. Lord Cairns LC held that it would be a startling proposition to place an additional burden on a company supplying a town with water by making it liable to householders whose properties were damaged by fire.[76] The statutory scheme was for the benefit of the public as a whole and not individual householders, otherwise the company would be practically insuring householders against damage by fire.[77]

However, the fact that a particular provision refers to a certain class of individuals will not of itself give rise to an action in tort. As Lord Browne-Wilkinson stated in *X v Bedfordshire CC*:

> **"a private law cause of action will arise if it can be shown, as a matter of construction of a statute, that the statutory duty was imposed for the protection of a limited class of the public *and* that Parliament intended to confer on members of that class a private right of action."[78]**

The *purpose* of the statute remains important. For example, in *Cutler v Wandsworth Stadium Ltd*,[79] the Betting and Lotteries Act 1934 s.11(2) required the owner of a dog-racing track to provide space for bookmakers. The House of Lords held that although bookmakers were indeed an identifiable class, they could not sue for damages when excluded from the track. The purpose of the statute was to regulate the conduct of racetracks, and not to protect the livelihood of bookmakers, who might benefit incidentally from such regulation.

Similarly, in the more recent case of *R. v Deputy Governor of Parkhurst Prison Ex p. Hague*,[80] the House of Lords held that the Prison Rules 1964 were intended to regulate the

---

74   See *X v Bedfordshire CC* [1995] 2 A.C. 633 at 731 and *O'Rourke v Camden LBC* [1998] A.C. 188 at 193. But note criticism of this approach by Atkin LJ in *Phillips v Britannia Hygienic Laundry Co* [1923] 2 K.B. 832 at 841.

75   (1877) 2 Ex.D. 441. This marked a change from the more liberal approach first adopted by the courts, see *Couch v Steel* (1854) 3 E. & B. 402; 118 E.R. 1193.

76   (1877) 2 Ex. D. 441 at 445–446.

77   See also *Thames Trains Ltd v Health and Safety Executive* [2003] EWCA Civ 720; (2003) 147 S.J.L.B. 661 CA (duty owed by Health and Safety Executive to anyone affected by the railway being unsafe did not give rise to individual rights for passengers and train operators).

78   [1995] 2 A.C. 633 at 731 (emphasis added).

79   [1949] A.C. 398.

80   [1992] 1 A.C. 58. The House of Lords held that prisoners' rights were adequately protected by alternative claims in public law and in the torts of misfeasance in public office, trespass to the person and negligence. For the significance of alternative remedies, see below. A restrictive approach was also taken in *Morrison Sports Ltd v Scottish Power Plc* [2010] UKSC 37; [2010] 1 W.L.R. 1934 (legislative scheme pointed against individuals having private right of action) and in *St John Poulton's Trustee in Bankruptcy v Ministry of Justice* [2010] EWCA Civ 392; [2011] Ch 1 (Insolvency Rules 1986 r 6.13, which requires court service to give notice of bankruptcy petition to land registry, not intended to benefit simply creditors as limited class of the public, but all parties intending to deal with relevant property).

-administration of prisons and the management and control of prisoners. They did not give rise to any private rights for prisoners if they were breached.

(2) The nature of the legislation

7-014

This also seems to be significant in recent years. Where a statute has a "social welfare" goal, the courts have resisted imposing the burden of civil liability on usually a public authority defendant. In *X v Bedfordshire CC*[81] (discussed in Ch.2) the plaintiffs brought actions against local authorities concerning the negligent performance of their statutory duties relating to education and child welfare. Actions were also brought for breach of statutory duty. The plaintiffs were unsuccessful in their claims in negligence and, unsurprisingly, their Lordships were also reluctant to impose liability for breach of statutory duty. Lord Browne-Wilkinson held that although the legislation was designed to protect children at risk and ensure adequate educational provision, it was nevertheless not Parliament's intention to allow individual children or their families to sue for damages. The plaintiffs were told to pursue their claims in administrative law, rather than the law of torts. In the later case of *Phelps v Hillingdon LBC*,[82] Lord Slynn reiterated that, despite the existence of a valid claim for negligence, no remedy would lie for breach of statutory duty where the purpose of the legislation was one of social welfare:

> **"The general nature of the duties imposed on local authorities in the context of a national system of education and the remedies available by way of appeal and judicial review indicate that Parliament did not intend to create a statutory remedy by way of damages."[83]**

A similar position was taken in *O'Rourke v Camden LBC*[84] in relation to the local authority's statutory duty to house homeless persons. Lord Hoffmann in *O'Rourke* set out the reasoning of the court:

> **". . . the Act is a scheme of social welfare, intended to confer benefits at the public expense on grounds of public policy. Public money is spent on housing the homeless not merely for the private benefit of people who find themselves homeless but on grounds of general public interest: because, for example, proper housing means that people will be less likely to suffer illness, turn to crime or require the attention of other social services. The expenditure interacts with**

---

81   [1995] 2 A.C. 633.
82   [2001] 2 A.C. 619.
83   [2001] 2 A.C. 619 at 652. See also *Carty v Croydon LBC* [2005] EWCA Civ 19; [2005] 1 W.L.R. 2312 at [19].
84   [1998] A.C. 188. Comment: R. Carnwath [1998] P.L. 407.

> expenditure on other public services such as education, the National Health Service and even the police. It is not simply a private matter between the claimant and the housing authority."[85]

On this basis, the statutes in both cases were passed for the benefit of society in general, and not for the benefit of individuals. This indicator is therefore perhaps better analysed as a particular example of (1) above: the courts rejecting liability where the statute is not for the benefit of a specific class of the public, but for the public at large. The courts are also very conscious of the wide discretion exercised by public authorities in such cases and are reluctant to regulate this discretion through the tort of breach of statutory duty. As Lord Hoffmann commented in *O'Rourke*:

> "the existence of all these discretions makes it unlikely that Parliament intended errors of judgment to give rise to an obligation to make financial reparation. Control by public law remedies would appear much more appropriate."[86]

(3) Alternative remedies

7–015

This overlaps with (2) in that the courts are influenced by the fact that public authorities are accountable in administrative law.[87] Moreover, where the statute sets up a system of fines, the court will be reluctant to assume that Parliament intended the additional burden of civil liability, unless, as stated by Lord Diplock in *Lonrho*,[88] it is apparent that the duty was imposed for the benefit or protection of a particular class.[89] In contrast, if there is no stated remedy for breach and there is an intention to protect a limited class, the court is more likely to hold that the statute gives rise to a civil action.[90]

---

85 [1998] A.C. 188 at 193.
86 [1998] A.C. 188 at 194.
87 See *X v Bedfordshire C.C.* [1995] 2 A.C. 633 and *Phelps v Hillingdon LBC* [2001] 2 A.C. 619.
88 *Lonrho Ltd v Shell Petroleum Co Ltd (No.2)* [1982] A.C. 173 at 185.
89 This may be unclear on the facts. Compare, e.g. the Court of Appeal decisions of *Todd v Adams (The Maragetha Maria)* [2002] EWCA Civ 509; [2002] 2 Lloyd's Rep 293 and *Ziemniak v ETPM Deep Sea Ltd* [2003] EWCA Civ 636; [2003] 2 Lloyd's Rep 214, which both concerned breach of safety rules pursuant to the Merchant Shipping Act 1995. In *Todd*, the court somewhat reluctantly found that breach of rules made under the Act concerning the safety of fishing vessels did not give a right of action following a tragic fishing accident with the loss of all crew. The rules had specifically provided criminal sanctions and penalties and established a certification scheme which rendered civil liability inappropriate. However, in *Ziemniak* breach of rules in a different part of the Act did provide a civil remedy for a claimant seriously injured during a lifeboat test in harbour. Here, the claim was treated as one of safety in the workplace, thereby meriting the more generous treatment given to such claims. The rules did contain criminal sanctions, although they did not cover the accident in question. *Todd* was doubted, but nevertheless distinguished.
90 See *Cutler v Wandsworth Stadium Ltd* [1949] A.C. 398 and *Kirvek Management & Consulting Services Ltd v*

Similarly, if adequate remedies are provided by the common law, or by other statutory provisions, this will indicate that no additional civil action exists. This, however, begs the question as to what is meant by "adequate". In *McCall v Abelesz*,[91] adequate remedies were said to exist against the harassment of tenants, which justified the refusal of liability, but it may be questioned whether this was in fact the case. The court in *Issa v Hackney LBC*[92] held that the adequacy of alternative remedies should be assessed at the date of enactment of the statute in question, and in that case refused to take account of the fact that the protection of tenants had diminished since the enactment of the Public Health Act 1936.

The common law position can impact in a further way. As well as suggesting that no liability should exist where there is an alternative remedy at law, it also indicates that no liability should exist where it is for a type of damage irrecoverable at common law. The case of *Pickering v Liverpool Daily Post*[93] illustrates this point. Here, the plaintiff (a convicted murderer and sex offender) wished to prevent a newspaper from publishing information about his application to a mental health review tribunal to be discharged from a mental hospital. The House of Lords held that any breach of the Mental Health Review Tribunal Rules did not grant him a right to a civil remedy. There is no general tort of breaching privacy in English law,[94] and, at that time the court held that the defendants' actions were not capable of causing the plaintiff loss of a kind for which the law affords a remedy.[95] The courts also, in line with the common law position, seem far more willing to award damages for personal injury than for economic loss.[96]

The considerations discussed above are subject to the underlying policy decisions of the courts. As stated earlier, the courts have shown a notable leniency in finding civil liability for breaches of statutes involving industrial safety.[97] The questionable case of *Monk v Warbey*[98] is also a good example of the influence of policy on the courts. Despite clear authority that road-users did not form an identifiable class,[99] the court held that civil liability would be imposed on the owner of a vehicle who had allowed an uninsured driver to use it, contrary to the Road

---

Attorney General of Trinidad and Tobago [2002] UKPC 43; [2002] 1 W.L.R. 2792 PC. However, this did not assist the plaintiff in *R. v Deputy Governor of Parkhurst Prison Ex p. Hague* [1992] 1 A.C. 58.

91   [1976] Q.B. 585 (the case concerned the Rent Act 1965 s.30(2) which is no longer applicable) See also *Cullen v Chief Constable of the Royal Ulster Constabulary* [2003] UKHL 39; [2003] 1 W.L.R. 1763 HL(NI): adequate public law remedies justified denying the claimant a private law claim when refused a reason for denial of access to solicitor in custody (note the strong dissent of Lords Bingham and Steyn concerning adequacy).

92   [1997] 1 W.L.R. 956.

93   [1991] 2 A.C. 370.

94   *Wainwright v Home Office* [2003] UKHL 53; [2004] 2 A.C. 406, but see now Ch.15.

95   "[T]hough [publication] may in one sense be adverse to the patient's interest" per Lord Bridge at 420. This is applied very narrowly in *Cullen v Chief Constable of the Royal Ulster Constabulary* [2003] UKHL 39; [2003] 1 W.L.R. 1763 HL(NI). Privacy law has since developed following the implementation of the Human Rights Act 1998: see *Campbell v Mirror Group Newspapers Ltd* [2004] UKHL 22; [2004] 2 A.C. 457.

96   See *Richardson v Pitt-Stanley* [1995] Q.B. 123 at 130 and 132.

97   See, e.g. *Groves v Lord Wimborne* [1898] 2 Q.B. 402 and *Black v Fife Coal Co Ltd* [1912] A.C. 149.

98   [1935] 1 K.B. 75 CA.

99   See *Phillips v Britannia Hygienic Laundry Co* [1923] 2 K.B. 832.

Traffic Act 1930 s.35(1).[100] This was obviously an attempt to ensure that the victim received compensation. Nowadays such a problem is dealt with by the Motor Insurers' Bureau (see Ch.1), although *Monk* remains good law.[101]

A contrasting approach was taken by the Court of Appeal, however, in the more recent case of *Richardson v Pitt-Stanley*.[102] In this case, the plaintiff, who had been injured at work, had successfully sued his employers only to find that the company which employed him was in liquidation and unable to pay, and had failed to comply with its obligation under the Employers' Liability (Compulsory Insurance) Act 1969 to obtain insurance against liability. He therefore brought an action against the directors of the company for breach of statutory duty. The majority of the Court of Appeal rejected his claim. *Monk* was distinguished on a number of technical grounds.[103] There was no express provision in the 1969 Act which created a civil liability on the part of an employer for the failure to insure and the Court held that the Act was intended to be a statute within the confines of the criminal law and not to create civil liability on the part of an employer or its directors and officers. The majority of the Supreme Court in *Campbell v Gordon*,[104] in a similar case involving an injured workman suing the sole director of a company which had gone into liquidation and had failed in its obligation to obtain full insurance under the Act, also adopted a formalistic construction of the Act. In the words of Lord Carnwath (speaking for the majority), the case depended "not on general questions of fairness, but on the interpretation of a particular statutory scheme in its context".[105] The majority found that the language of the 1969 Act had been deliberately chosen by Parliament and was specifically directed at criminal, not civil, liability. Where Parliament had used such a well-established formula, it was, in its view, particularly difficult to infer an intention to impose by implication a more general liability of which there was no hint in its actual language. *Monk* was again distinguished—the majority noting that while the Road Traffic Act 1930 imposed direct responsibility on both the user of the vehicle and the person who permits this use, the 1969 Act solely imposes direct responsibility upon the employer company, not its directors. Such a construction undoubtedly masked a policy decision not to render company directors liable in tort for failing to comply with the insurance provisions of the Act. The dissenting Justices, Lord Toulson and Lady Hale (and indeed Sir

---

100 Now the Road Traffic Act 1988 s.143. See also *Roe v Sheffield City Council* [2003] EWCA Civ 1; [2004] Q.B. 653. The duty, however, is limited to third party insurance against liability for death or bodily injury or damage to property and liability will not arise in relation to claims for pure economic loss: see *Bretton v Hancock* [2005] EWCA Civ 404; [2006] P.I.Q.R. P1 (rejecting a claim by joint tortfeasor that, due to the failure to insure, he was unable to recover a contribution to damages payable).

101 See *Norman v Ali (Limitation Period)* [2000] R.T.R. 107 where the MIB required, pursuant to the Uninsured Drivers' Agreement 1988 s.5(1)(d), that the claimant should bring the car-owner (Aziz) into the action, on a *Monk v Warbey* type action, for permitting Ali to drive the car when uninsured against third party risks. The limitation period for such actions is that of personal injury claims, namely, three years.

102 [1995] Q.B. 123 (Sir John Megaw dissenting).

103 Which have been described as "less than compelling": see J. O'Sullivan [1995] C.L.J. 241, 242.

104 [2016] UKSC 38; [2016] A.C 1513 (Lord Toulson and Lady Hale dissenting).

105 [2016] UKSC 38 at [18].

John Megaw in *Richardson*), were critical of an approach which ignored the purpose of the Act (in their view to protect vulnerable employees) in favour of a formal construction of its provisions.

It is therefore impossible to divorce the decisions of the courts from the influence of policy. In fact, the whole task of finding whether Parliament intended civil liability has been dismissed by many writers as a fiction.[106] It is unlikely in many cases that parliamentary drafters actually considered whether a remedy should exist in tort and it might be suspected that, even if the issue was considered, it would have been avoided as politically contentious. This leaves a considerable amount of discretion with the courts. While this may be thought undesirable, the courts have little option until parliamentary drafters deal with the question of civil liability for breach of statutory obligations on a more regular basis. The law at present is unpredictable and reflects the policy choices of the court. It is important, however, not to over-exaggerate these problems. In practice (and particularly in the light of government reforms to the Health and Safety at Work etc Act 1974), the number of claims made for breach of statutory duty is small and the significance of such problems is minimal.

Further considerations

7–017

If the statute is one for which the courts are prepared to find civil liability, then this is not the end of the matter. The claimant has to satisfy four further hurdles:

- Is the duty owed to this particular claimant?

- Has the defendant breached his or her statutory duty?

- Did the breach cause the damage concerned?

- Was the damage of the kind which the statute intended to prevent?

These will be examined below.

(1) Is the duty owed to this particular claimant?

7–018

The claimant must show that he or she is within the class of persons intended to benefit under the statute. This goes back to the construction of the statute. In *Knapp v Railway Executive*,[107] for example, a breach of regulations in maintaining a level crossing, which led to a gate swinging back to injure the driver of an oncoming train, was held not to be actionable. Although the

---

106 G. Williams (1960) 23 M.L.R. 233, 244 describes it as "this process of looking for what is not there".
107 [1949] 2 All E.R. 508 CA.

statutory provisions did give a remedy at common law, they were only for the benefit of road-users and did not benefit persons travelling on the train.

> ## (2) Has the defendant breached his or her duty to the claimant?

The defendant must have acted in breach of his or her duty as set out in the statute. Again, it is important to turn back to the wording of the statute and examine just what the defendant was required to do or not to do. Is the duty one of reasonable care or does the statute impose strict liability? The courts will examine the exact wording of the statute and, again, in the industrial context, have interpreted legislation in a pro-employee manner. For example, the provision that the employer must act "so far as is reasonably practicable" has been interpreted to place the legal burden on the employer to establish that it was not reasonably practicable to take the precautions in question.[108] However, the courts do respect the strict wording of the statute. In *Chipchase v British Titan Products Co Ltd*,[109] a regulation required every working platform from which a person could fall more than six feet six inches to be at least 34 inches wide. The plaintiff fell from a platform that was nine inches wide, but only six feet from the ground. On this basis, no claim could arise under statute and the plaintiff was left to pursue a claim in ordinary negligence.

> ## (3) Did the breach cause the damage concerned?

Causation must be proved, and a similar approach is taken to that adopted for the tort of negligence, as discussed in Ch.6.[110] One particular problem which has arisen is where the statutory duty is placed on both the employer and the employee, and although the employer has taken all reasonable steps, the conduct of the employee has caused the accident. In such cases, the courts are reluctant to find the employer liable for the employee's own breach of statutory duty. In *Boyle v Kodak Ltd*,[111] the plaintiff had been injured when he fell off a ladder which was required by law to be secured. Previous authority demonstrated that civil liability arose from breach, but the House of Lords held that it was not prepared to find the employer liable if only the plaintiff had been at fault. Lord Reid stated that:

---

108 *Nimmo v Alexander Cowan & Sons Ltd* [1968] A.C. 107 HL (admittedly by a slim majority of 3 to 2). Applied in *McDonald v Department for Communities and Local Government* [2013] EWCA Civ 1346; [2014] P.I.Q.R. P 7.

109 [1956] 1 Q.B 545 CA.

110 See, in particular, *McWilliams v Sir William Arrol Ltd* [1962] 1 All E.R. 623 which concerns breach of statutory duty.

111 [1969] 1 W.L.R. 661. See also *Ginty v Belmont Building Supplies Ltd* [1959] 1 All E.R. 414 at 423–424 and *Anderson v Newham College of Further Education* [2002] EWCA Civ 505; [2003] I.C.R. 212. It was also applied in *Brumder v Motornet Services and Repairs Ltd* [2013] EWCA Civ 195; [2013] 1 W.L.R. 2783 where the claimant was actually the sole director and shareholder of the defendant company and it was his own acts and omissions which constituted the defendant company's breach.

> "it would be absurd if, notwithstanding the employer having done all he could reasonably be expected to do to ensure compliance, a workman, who deliberately disobeyed his employer's orders and thereby put the employer in breach of a regulation, could claim damages for injury caused to him solely by his own wrongdoing."[112]

On the facts, however, the court found that the employers had failed to show that the accident was solely due to the fault of the plaintiff and so liability would be divided 50:50, due to the contributory negligence of the plaintiff. The limitations of *Boyle* should be noted. Only if the duty is placed both on the employer and employee and the employee is the only person at fault will the courts refuse liability.

(4) Is the damage of the kind which the statute intended to prevent?

7-021 This, again, is a question of construction. The courts will examine the statute, and if the claimant has suffered an injury different from that mentioned in the statute, then the claimant will not be able to recover. It will therefore depend on how the court interprets "damage". In *Gorris v Scott*,[113] the Court of Exchequer adopted a strict line. Here, the Act in question required that animals be transported in pens to prevent the spread of contagious diseases. In violation of the Act, the plaintiff's sheep had been transported without pens and had been washed overboard in bad weather. The court held that such damage was "something totally apart from the object of the Act of Parliament"[114] and rejected the plaintiff's claim. Nowadays it is unlikely that a court would take such a strict approach. The courts (in line with the approach taken in *The Wagon Mound*) will simply examine whether the damage suffered is of the kind that the statute was designed to prevent.[115]

Defences

7-022 These will be discussed in more detail in Ch.16. It is worth noting at this stage that there is some indecision as to whether the defence of voluntary assumption of risk (or *volenti non fit injuria*) applies to breach of statutory duty. The House of Lords in *ICI v Shatwell*[116] held that the defence

---

112 [1969] 1 W.L.R. 661 at 665–666.
113 (1874) L.R.9 Exch.125.
114 (1874) L.R.9 Exch.125 at 129–130 per Kelly CB. See also *Fytche v Wincanton Logistics Plc* [2004] UKHL 31; [2004] 4 All E.R. 221 (boots provided under Regulations were to protect against impact injury, not frostbite due to leak in boots).
115 *Donaghey v Boulton & Paul Ltd* [1968] A.C. 1 at 26 per Lord Reid HL (who draws a clear comparison with the position in negligence under *The Wagon Mound* [1961] A.C. 388 discussed in Ch.6).
116 [1965] A.C. 656.

would apply where the employer was not at fault and was only liable vicariously for the acts of its employees. Lords Reid and Pearce stressed that the defence should not apply if the employer is in some way at fault in failing to comply with the duty.[117]

Although the principle of contributory negligence clearly applies to the tort of breach of statutory duty,[118] there is some authority that it will be applied leniently towards employees injured in the course of their employment. In *Caswell v Powell Duffryn Associated Collieries*,[119] it was held that the courts should take account of any continual noise, strain and risk to which employees were exposed which might lead to their failure to take reasonable care. This seems to be another example of the preferential treatment given to industrial injury claims.

Breach of statutory duty and EU law

Following the decision of the European Court of Justice in *Francovich v Italy*,[120] prior to Brexit claimants were able to bring a claim against the State (which was interpreted broadly)[121] for breaching EU law, for example, by failing to implement a directive within the stipulated time period. In *Garden Cottage Foods Ltd v Milk Marketing Board*,[122] the House of Lords indicated that remedies would arise under the tort of breach of statutory duty (the statute here being the European Communities Act 1972 s.2(1), which provided that the State has an obligation to ensure that national law shall be consistent with EU law). The ground-breaking decisions of *Francovich v Italy*[123] and *Brasserie du Pêcheur v Germany; R. v Secretary of State for Transport Ex p. Factortame (No.4)*[124] extended liability beyond directly effective Treaty provisions to include breaches of EU law more generally. In the leading case of *Brasserie du Pêcheur v Germany; R. v*

7–023

---

117 Lord Pearce, [1965] A.C. 656 at 687, extends this to where the employer is vicariously in breach of statutory duty through the neglect of some person who is of superior rank to the claimant and whose commands the claimant was bound to obey.

118 See Law Reform (Contributory Negligence) Act 1945 s.4.

119 [1940] A.C. 152 at 166. It should be noted that this case was decided before the Law Reform (Contributory Negligence) Act 1945 when contributory negligence was an absolute defence to the employee's claim which may have encouraged a more generous approach.

120 (C6/90) [1991] E.C.R. I-5357.

121 See *Foster v British Gas Plc* (C-188/89) [1990] E.C.R. I-3133 at [18]: the State will include "organizations or bodies which were subject to the authority or control of the State or had special powers beyond those which result from the normal rules applicable to relations between individuals". It will also include the courts themselves: *Köbler v Austria* (C-224/01) [2004] Q.B. 848 and *Traghetti del Mediterraneo SpA (In Liquidation) v Italy* (C-173/03) [2006] All E.R. (EC) 983; [2006] 3 C.M.L.R. 19.

122 [1984] A.C. 130. See also Lords Nicholls, Walker and Mance in *Sempra Metals Ltd v Inland Revenue Comrs* [2007] UKHL 34; [2008] 1 A.C. 561 at [69], [162] and [225] respectively and *R. v Secretary of State for Transport Ex p. Factortame (No.6)* [2001] 1 W.L.R. 942 QBD (T & CC), Judge Toulmin QC.

123 (C6/90) [1991] E.C.R. I-5357; [1993] 2 C.M.L.R. 66.

124 (C46/93 and C48/93) [1996] Q.B. 404; [1996] 1 C.M.L.R. 889. See P. P. Craig, "Once More Unto the Breach: The Community, The State and Damages Liability" (1997) 113 L.Q.R. 67.

Secretary of State for Transport, Ex p. Factortame (No.4),[125] the European Court of Justice indicated the scope of this new right to sue for damages for breach of EU law:

> **"Community law confers a right to reparation where three conditions are met: the rule of law infringed must be intended to confer rights on individuals; the breach must be sufficiently serious; and there must be a direct causal link between the breach of the obligation resting on the state and the damage sustained by the injured parties."[126]**

7–024

While *Francovich* liability does resemble the traditional tort of breach of statutory duty, there are differences.[127] The first and third conditions of *Brasserie du Pêcheur* are very similar to those of the common law tort, although it should be noted that the English courts have construed the conferral of rights test narrowly.[128] However, the second condition does differ from that of breach of statutory duty. It is not a test of fault, but whether the State has shown a manifest and grave disregard to the limits of its discretion, rendering the breach inexcusable.[129] An obvious example would be acting contrary to a judgment of the Court of Justice of the European Union which had indicated that the conduct in question was a clear infringement of EU law. Other factors which may be taken into account include the clarity and precision of the rule breached, the measure of discretion left by the rule to the national or EU authorities, whether the infringement and the damage caused was intentional or involuntary, whether any error of law was excusable or inexcusable, the fact that the position taken by a EU institution may have contributed towards the omission, and the adoption or retention of national measures or practices contrary to EU law.[130] Where the conditions are met, States must provide remedies which are no less favourable than rules applying to similar claims based on national law.[131] Subject to these principles of equality and effectiveness, it remains for the national court to find the facts, decide whether the rule of law infringed was intended

---

125 [1996] Q.B. 404.

126 [1996] Q.B. 404 at para.51. For recent case-law, see *Energy Solutions EU Ltd v Nuclear Decommissioning Authority* [2017] UKSC 34; [2017] 1 W.L.R. 1373 which highlights the differences between *Francovich* liability and traditional breach of statutory duty claims.

127 The courts have quite rightly rejected the argument that such claims could be classified as misfeasance in public office in that it fails to meet the criteria for this tort: *Three Rivers DC v Bank of England (No.3)* [2003] 2 A.C. 1.

128 See *Poole v HM Treasury* [2007] EWCA Civ 1021; [2008] 1 All E.R. (Comm) 1132: Council Directive 73/239 did not intend to grant rights to Lloyds underwriting names. See also *Three Rivers DC v Bank of England (No. 3)* [2000] UKHL 33; [2003] A.C. 1.

129 See *Brasserie du Pêcheur v Germany; R. v Secretary of State for Transport Ex p. Factortame (No.4)* [1996] Q.B. 404 at para.45.

130 *Brasserie du Pêcheur* [1996] Q.B. 404 at para.56. See also *Haim v Kassenzahnaertzliche Vereinigung Nordrhein (424/97)* [2000] E.C.R. I-5123 at para.43.

131 [1996] Q.B. 404 at 504 para.90.

to confer rights on individuals, the breach of EU law was sufficiently serious[132] and determine whether there was a direct causal link between the breach and the damage suffered. There is no precondition that the claimant should have exhausted all domestic remedies before relying on this cause of action.[133]

Francovich liability was, then, a hybrid form of breach of statutory duty—part European, part UK law. As such, it will not survive the UK leaving the EU. To the end, there was debate whether it could really be regarded as a form of breach of statutory duty given the differences identified above.[134] Nevertheless, the history of *Francovich* liability provides an interesting insight into common law legal development and its ability to deal with external sources of law.

Vicarious Liability

This is a different concept from the two forms of liability examined above. It is not a tort in its own right, but a rule of responsibility which renders the defendant strictly liable for the torts committed by another.[135] The commonest example is that of an employer for its employees and this chapter will therefore focus on the employer/employee relationship. Other examples of vicarious liability include the liability of a firm for the torts of its partners.[136]

7–025

Vicarious liability is essentially a rule of convenience. It does not mean that the tortfeasor (X) is not personally liable for his negligence, but that the claimant has the choice to sue X or his employer (Y) and generally, the claimant will sue Y because Y has more money, or as the courts put it "the deeper pocket". As a matter of strict law, the employer may seek to recover

---

132 In *R. v Secretary of State for Transport Ex p. Factortame (No.5)* [2000] 1 A.C. 524, e.g. the House of Lords found that the Government's breach of EU law in enacting the Merchant Shipping Act 1988 which prevented foreign nationals from fishing in British waters was "sufficiently serious".

133 *Spencer v Secretary of State for Work and Pensions* [2008] EWCA Civ 750; [2009] Q.B. 358.

134 See P. Giliker, "English tort law and the challenge of *Francovich* liability: 20 years on" (2012) 128 L.Q.R. 541 and K. Stanton, "New forms of the tort of breach of statutory duty" (2004) 120 L.Q.R. 324 at 329–330: "The Eurotort [should] simply . . . be classified as a tort in domestic proceedings and the repeated references to breach of statutory duty are a redundancy".

135 See, generally, P S. Atiyah, *Vicarious Liability in the Law of Torts* (Butterworths, 1967) and P. Giliker, *Vicarious Liability in Tort: A Comparative Perspective* (CUP, 2010).

136 Partnership Act 1890 s.10. See *Dubai Aluminium Co Ltd v Salaam* [2002] UKHL 48; [2003] 2 A.C. 366 HL: firm of solicitors liable for partner's dishonest participation in a fraud. Section 10 covers both common law and equitable wrongs. Vicarious liability has also been linked with the concept of agency. For an attempt to use agency to extend the liability of an (insured) car owner, see *Morgans v Launchbury* [1973] A.C. 127 HL. In exceptional circumstances, where the owner of the vehicle retains control and has an interest in the purpose for which the vehicle is being used, the courts have been prepared to find the owner of the vehicle liable for the torts of the driver: see *Ormrod v Crosville Motor Services Ltd* [1953] 1 W.L.R. 1120 CA, confirming the judgment of Devlin J [1953] 1 W.L.R. 409.

damages from the employee who committed the tort.[137] This is known as the employer's indemnity. This may occur either for breach of an implied term in the contract of employment to use reasonable care and skill, or, because vicarious liability is treated as joint and several liability under the Civil Liability (Contribution) Act 1978. The 1978 Act entitles the employer to seek a contribution from the employee with respect to his or her responsibility for the damage caused.[138] However, in practice, this rarely happens. Employers' liability insurers have entered into a "gentlemen's agreement" not to pursue actions against employees except where there has been evidence of collusion or wilful misconduct.[139] This, of course, contradicts completely the idea of corrective justice, discussed in Ch.1, that only those at fault should pay compensation in tort.

There are limits, however, to vicarious liability. It is confined first to "employees" (a category, which we will see, has expanded recently), and secondly to acts committed in the course of employment. An employer is not responsible if the employee's wrongful act does not relate to his or her position, for example, where the employee (X) negligently crashes his car into the claimant whilst driving home from work. This has led to subtle distinctions, which will be discussed below.

To establish vicarious liability against an employer, the claimant must show three things. First prove that X has committed a tort. Once this is shown, the Supreme Court in the leading case of *Various Claimants v Catholic Child Welfare Society* (*CCWS*)[140] indicated two further elements:

■ A relationship between X and Y capable of giving rise to vicarious liability; *and*

■ A close connection that links the relationship between X and Y and the act or omission of X

The Supreme Court noted that these elements may overlap in that what is critical at the second stage is the connection that links *the relationship between X and Y* and the act or omission of X. In 2016, 2017 and 2020, the Supreme Court in five important decisions gave further guidance how to apply the relationship test (in *Cox v Ministry of Justice*,[141] *Armes v Nottinghamshire CC*[142] and *Barclays Bank v Various Claimants*[143]) and the connection test (in *Mohamud v WM Morrison Supermarkets Plc*[144] and *WM Morrison Supermarkets Plc v Various Claimants*[145]).

These requirements are examined below.

---

137 *Lister v Romford Ice and Cold Storage Co Ltd* [1957] A.C. 555.
138 The 1978 Act is discussed in more detail in Ch.17.
139 For commentary, see G. Gardiner (1959) 22 M.L.R. 652 and R. Lewis (1985) 48 M.L.R. 275, 281–282.
140 [2012] UKSC 56; [2013] 2 A.C. 1 at [35].
141 [2016] UKSC 10; [2016] A.C. 660.
142 [2017] UKSC 60; [2018] A.C. 355.
143 [2020] UKSC 13; [2020] 2 W.L.R. 960.
144 [2016] UKSC 11; [2016] A.C. 677.
145 [2020] UKSC 12; [2020] 2 W.L.R. 941.

(1) The employee committed a tort

This may be considered obvious but is worth noting. If the claimant is unable to prove that a tort has been committed against him or her, vicarious liability cannot arise. If, therefore, suing an employer for vicarious liability on behalf of its employees, the claimant must first prove that the employee's conduct satisfies all the requirements of the tort in question.[146]

(2) The relationship between the tortfeasor and the employer

The primary relationship giving rise to vicarious liability remains that of *employer/employee*. The courts draw a distinction between, on the one hand, a contract *of* service[147] or employment—where the person employed is an "employee", and, on the other hand, a contract *for* services—where the person employed is an "independent contractor". An employer will not be vicariously liable for the actions of independent contractors. There is now a third category: workers who are "akin" to employees. These are staff who are not technically working under contracts of service but perform the function of employees and therefore satisfy the relationship test. This category (added recently) will be examined in more detail below.

The key distinction, then, is between employees and independent contractors. If I employ a workman to fix the reception on my television, for example, I have not employed him under a contract of service—he is just visiting to fix my reception—but rather I have entered a contract for services with an independent contractor and I would not be vicariously liable for his torts. Unfortunately, this distinction is not always so easy to draw. In recent times, the nature of employment has changed, with workers far more insecure than they have been in the past. Workers may be employed on a casual basis, or via an employment agency, or on a government scheme, and it is difficult to ascertain their exact status.[148] This difficulty is compounded by the various arrangements undertaken by workers to limit their tax liability, frequently by labelling themselves as independent contractors for this purpose. The courts, therefore, face a real challenge in distinguishing between contracts of employment and contracts for services and this is one of the reasons which led the courts to develop a third category of "quasi-employees" hired in circumstances akin to employment. A number of factors can be identified as important to the courts in deciding this question, but it is fair to state that the courts generally adopt a "broad brush" approach, dependent on the facts of each particular case.[149]

---

146 See *Credit Lyonnais NV v Export Credits Guarantee Department* [2000] 1 A.C. 486 HL.
147 Readers will find reference to "masters and servants" in older case law, but we now speak of "employers and employees".
148 See, for example, the question of the status of the plumber in *Pimlico Plumbers Ltd v Smith* [2018] UKSC 29; [2018] I.C.R. 1511.
149 The question of the existence of a contract of employment will, in most cases, be considered a mixed question of law and fact for the trial judge, and an appeal court will be reluctant to intervene in the absence of an error of law or perversity: see Lord Hoffmann in *Carmichael v National Power Plc* [1999] 1 W.L.R. 2042.

> **Factors identifying "employees"**[150]

THE TERMS OF THE CONTRACT

7–028
The courts have clearly stated that they will not be governed by the wording of the contract but will examine the substance of the contract. In *Ferguson v Dawson*,[151] for example, it had been agreed between the parties that workers employed on a building site would be "self-employed labour only sub-contractors". By this means, the workers avoided the deduction of income tax and national insurance contributions from their weekly payments. The plaintiff, who worked on the defendants' building site, argued when injured that he was an employee and therefore able to sue for breach of statutory duty. The court held that in reality the relationship was indeed one of employer and employee. The defendants could dismiss the workmen, move them between sites, tell them what work to do and had provided them with tools. These factors indicated that they were employees and not independent contractors.

However, the courts have experienced some disquiet in allowing a worker, who deliberately chooses to be employed as an independent contractor to avoid tax, to turn to the courts when he or she wishes to obtain the benefit of employee protection legislation.[152] The Court of Appeal in *Young and Woods v West*[153] was sympathetic to such concerns, but maintained that the court should look to the realities of the situation in the belief that "the Inland Revenue would [not] fail to discharge their statutory duty".[154]

CONTROL

7–029
In the past, the control test was the primary indicator used by the courts.[155] An employer/employee relationship was held to exist when an employer could tell an employee what work to undertake and how it should be done. While this test is still used, it is clearly outdated in relation to modern work practices.[156] In an advanced technological age, employees are frequently expected to be able to exercise discretion and initiative in their performance. Professionals with skill and experience do not expect to be told what to do and how to act during each working day. A good example is that of a doctor in the Accident and Emergency department of a hospital.[157] It is clearly impossible for any employer to tell the doctor how to perform his or her duties. The

---

150 Chief Constables will be vicariously liable for the torts of police officers even though they are not strictly employees: see Police Act 1996 s.88(1). See *Weir v Bettison* [2003] EWCA Civ 111; [2003] I.C.R. 708.

151 [1976] 1 W.L.R. 1213. See also *Mersey Docks and Harbour Board v Coggins and Griffith (Liverpool) Ltd* [1947] A.C. 1.

152 Lawton LJ dissenting in *Ferguson v Dawson* [1976] 1 W.L.R. 1213 at 1227 held that it was contrary to public policy to allow a worker to change his or her status in such a manner and that the worker should be held to the initial bargain. See also comments in *Massey v Crown Life Assurance* [1978] 1 W.L.R. 676 CA.

153 [1980] I.R.L.R. 201.

154 [1980] I.R.L.R. 201 at 207 per Stephenson LJ.

155 Originating in the judgment of Bramwell LJ in *Yewens v Noakes* (1880) 6 Q.B.D. 530.

156 See O. Kahn-Freund, "Servants and Independent Contractors" (1951) 14 M.L.R. 504 who criticised the control test as old-fashioned in 1951. Note, however, that some commentators continue to regard control as important: P. Morgan, "Recasting vicarious liability" [2012] C.L.J. 615.

157 See *Cassidy v Ministry of Health* [1951] 2 K.B. 343 CA.

doctor will be expected to exercise a large amount of discretion in deciding how to deal with patients. As Cooke J commented in *Market Investigations v Minister of Social Security*[158]:

> **"the most that can be said is that control will no doubt always have to be considered, although it can no longer be regarded as the sole determining factor."**

THE RELATIONSHIP AS A WHOLE

7-030

This is the modern approach, which encompasses the two earlier points. The cases reveal a number of factors which the courts will consider in deciding whether an employer/employee relationship exists.[159] These include, in addition to the terms of the contract and the control test:

- the payment of wages and National Insurance contributions etc, on a regular basis;

- an indefinite term of employment;

- a fixed place and time of performance;

- the provision of equipment or materials by the employer;

- the degree of financial risk and investment taken by the worker;

- whether the worker can profit from his or her performance;

- whether the worker must hire his or her own assistants or replacements; and

- whether the work is integrated into the business or accessory to it (the business integration test).[160]

On this basis, in *Market Investigations v Minister of Social Security*,[161] part-time interviewers working under short-term contracts for a market research company were held to be

---

158 [1969] 2 Q.B. 173 at 185. See also Lord Reed in *Cox v Ministry of Justice* [2016] UKSC 10 at [21]: "it is a factor which is unlikely to be of independent significance in most cases".

159 See, notably, Cooke J in *Market Investigations Ltd v Minister of Social Security* [1969] 2 Q.B. 173 at 184–185 ("the matter had never been better put than by Cooke J": Lord Griffiths in *Lee Ting Sang v Chung Chi-Keung* [1990] 2 A.C. 374 at 382 PC).

160 See Denning LJ in *Stevenson, Jordan and Harrison Ltd v Macdonald and Evans* [1952] 1 T.L.R. 101 at 111. It is questionable whether this does any more than restate the question. Nevertheless, the relevance of this factor has been stressed in recent case law, e.g. in the *Catholic Child Welfare Society* case, discussed below.

161 [1969] 2 Q.B. 173.

employees. Their employers exercised extensive control over their work and Cooke J held that the limited discretion given to employees to decide when they would work, and the ability to work for others during the relevant period, were not inconsistent with the existence of a series of contracts of employment. In contrast, in *Ready Mixed Concrete (South East) Ltd v Minister of Pensions and National Insurance*,[162] McKenna J held that arrangements to deliver ready-mixed concrete by "owner-drivers", paid at fixed mileage rates, were not contracts of employment. This difficult case illustrates the problem often facing the court where there are indications both ways. Against a contract of employment was the fact that the drivers had to buy their own vehicles, which were maintained at their own expense, and the fact that the drivers were described in the contracts as independent contractors. Yet in favour of a contract of employment was the high level of control exercised by the company. Vehicles were bought on hire purchase from a company associated with the defendants and had to be painted in the company's colours. The drivers were obliged to wear the company uniform and comply with the company's rules, including a prohibition on using the vehicles for any other business. Nevertheless, McKenna J felt that ownership of the vehicles, and the fact that the drivers took the chance of profit and bore the risk of loss, indicated that the drivers were in reality independent contractors.[163]

RELATIONSHIPS "AKIN" TO EMPLOYMENT[164]

7–031

In the leading Supreme Court decision of *Various Claimants v Catholic Child Welfare Society*,[165] Lord Phillips confirmed that while the vast majority of cases would relate to employer/employee relationships under a contract of employment, English law now recognised that there were relationships "akin" to employment where it would be fair and just to impose vicarious liability.

In so doing, the Supreme Court confirmed the correctness of the Court of Appeal decision in *JGE (or E) v English Province of Our Lady of Charity*[166] which had held that the Catholic Church could be held vicariously liable for the acts of abuse of a priest, despite the fact that he was an "office-holder" and not strictly an employee. In that case, the majority of the court had held that in circumstances where the bishop had exercised some control over the priest (who could be dismissed for gross breach of his duties under canon law) and where, under canon law itself, priests were bound to show reverence and obedience to the bishop, the relationship between bishop and priest was sufficiently close (or "akin") to that of employer and employee for it to be fair and just to impose vicarious liability. The priest had been fully integrated into the

---

162 [1968] 2 Q.B. 497.

163 See also *Todd v Adams (The Maragetha Maria)* [2002] EWCA Civ 509; [2002] 2 Lloyd's Rep 293 where the Court of Appeal held that an arrangement whereby remuneration of the crew of a fishing vessel depended solely on a share of the profits (or losses) of each trip should be characterised as a joint venture rather than a contract of service.

164 The development of this new category of claims was influenced by the articles of McKendrick and Kidner: see E. McKendrick, "Vicarious liability and independent contractors—a re-examination" (1990) 53 M.L.R. 770 and R. Kidner, "Vicarious liability: for whom should the 'employer' be liable?" (1995) 15 L.S. 47.

165 [2012] UKSC 56; [2013] 2 A.C. 1 at [35].

166 [2012] EWCA Civ 938; [2013] Q.B. 722 (Tomlinson LJ dissenting). Comment: P. Giliker (2012) 28 P.N. 291.

Church's mission of spreading the word of God and, on balance, the relationship bore a closer resemblance to that of employer/employee rather than employer/independent contractor.

The same issue arose in the *Catholic Child Welfare Society* case. Here, 170 men had alleged that they had been sexually abused by teachers at a residential school. The headmaster and a number of other teachers at the school had been supplied by a religious organisation (the Institute of the Brothers of the Christian Schools), which consisted of lay Catholic brothers whose mission was to teach and who handed their teaching salaries to the Institute.[167] The Supreme Court held that the Institute would be vicariously liable for their actions, regardless of the absence of any contract of employment linking it to the teachers. The "business" of the Institute was to provide teaching for boys and the lay brothers had been acting in the furtherance of this mission and were expected to abide by the Institute's rules in conducting themselves as teachers. On this basis, the relationship between the Institute and the brothers was sufficiently akin to that of employer/employee and the absence of a contractual link (or indeed any form of payment) was regarded as immaterial.

The Supreme Court in *Cox v Ministry of Justice*[168] and *Armes v Nottinghamshire CC*[169] recently approved this line of reasoning and expanded it to two new contexts: prisoners working in a prison kitchen and foster parents looking after children in care. In *Cox*, a prison catering manager had been injured due to the negligence of one of the prisoners working in the prison kitchen. While the prisoner was clearly not employed by the prison—he was serving a prison sentence—he was paid a nominal sum to work in the kitchen as part of the rehabilitation process. Lord Reed held that prisoners working in the kitchens, under the direction of prison staff, were integrated into the operation of the prison and carried out an integral part of its activities for its benefit: feeding prisoners. They could thus be described as "akin to employees". Similarly, in *Armes*, foster parents, caring for children in local authority care, were deemed to be acting for the benefit of the local authority in enabling it to fulfil its statutory duties to children in care. They had received training, were paid expenses and were subject to inspection and supervision without any parallel to ordinary family life. As such, they provided care as an integral part of the local authority's organisation of its childcare services and could not, in the view of the court, be seen as carrying out an independent business of their own. There is, however, a line to be drawn. Most recently the Supreme Court in *Barclays Bank v Various Claimants*[170] emphasised that the court needed to focus on the details of the parties' relationship—was the person carrying out his or her own independent business or sufficiently analogous to employment to justify the imposition of vicarious liability? In the case, an independent doctor providing health checks for the bank (which was a minor part of his practice) was deemed to be an independent contractor. He worked for a number of different bodies, he was not on retainer and could refuse work at any time.

---

167 The school itself had previously been found vicariously liable but was seeking to establish that the Institute was jointly liable.

168 [2016] UKSC 10.

169 [2017] UKSC 60.

170 [2020] UKSC 13, overturning the Court of Appeal: [2018] EWCA Civ 1670.

LENDING AN EMPLOYEE

7–032

The *Catholic Child Welfare Society* case also casts light on the previously difficult issue of whether more than one defendant could be vicariously liable for the torts of the employee. This arises typically when the errant employee has been hired out to work for a different company at the time of commission of the tort (here the Institute sending the brothers to teach in a school managed by another body). Who will be responsible for the employee's torts? Previously, authority had indicated that only one party could be liable. This would generally be the original employer and only in exceptional circumstances would the hirer be liable. In *Mersey Docks and Harbour Board v Coggins and Griffith (Liverpool) Ltd*,[171] for example, the harbour board had employed Newall as a crane driver and had hired the crane, together with Newall, to a firm of stevedores. The harbour board was held liable when Newall negligently injured one of the hiring firm's employees while loading a ship. At the time of the accident, although the firm had instructed Newall in what work to do, they had no control as to how Newall operated the crane. Looking at all the circumstances of the case, the facts that the harbour board retained authority to control how the crane was driven and paid the wages of Newall were deemed to indicate that it was still his employer. Lord Porter indicated that in future cases, courts should consider a number of factors, including who pays the worker's wages, who has power of dismissal, how long the alternative work lasts and the complexity of the machinery used.[172] The more complex the machinery, the more unlikely it was that the employee would be deemed to work for the company hiring his or her services. In contrast, where the employee is unskilled and loaned out on a labour-only contract, then the stronger the possibility that the hirer may be found vicariously liable for his or her torts.[173]

In 2005, however, the Court of Appeal in *Viasystems (Tyneside) Ltd v Thermal Transfer (Northern) Ltd*[174] rejected the previously held assumption that the court must choose between employers and found that the general and temporary employer could be jointly liable. In this case, both employers had exercised some form of control over the employee, Strang, who had negligently caused a flood in a factory in which he was working. Strang and his immediate boss (a fitter) had been supplied to the subcontractors on a labour-only basis, but at the time of the accident, while acting on the instructions of the fitter, he had also been under the supervision of the subcontractors' employee, Horsley. Unable to choose between defendants, the Court of Appeal found dual liability. The court was split, however, on the appropriate test: May LJ favouring a test based on control[175] and Rix LJ favouring a test based on business

---

171 [1947] A.C. 1.
172 [1947] A.C. 1 at 17.
173 See *Hawley v Luminar Leisure Ltd* [2006] EWCA Civ 18; [2006] P.I.Q.R. P17: nightclub found to be vicariously liable for a doorman hired under a contract for the provision of security services where the doorman could be shown to be acting under the orders of the nightclub manager.
174 [2005] EWCA Civ 1151; [2006] Q.B. 510. Comment: R. Stevens, "A servant of two masters" (2006) 122 L.Q.R. 201.
175 This is the more conservative test; May LJ assuming that in most cases the courts will continue to find the general employer solely liable for the acts of the lent employee: [2005] EWCA Civ 1151 at [46]. It was followed

integration.[176] The *Catholic Child Welfare Society* case resolved that the Rix business integration test was the correct test to apply.[177] This marks a change from the restrictive approach of the past and dual (or multiple) vicarious liability is likely to be easier to establish in future, providing further protection for claimants who may find one of the defendants insolvent or no longer in business. The test can, therefore, now be stated as follows: vicarious liability will be shared where the employee in question is so much a part of the work, business or organisation of both employers that it is just to make both employers answer for his tort.[178]

(3) A connection that links the relationship between the tortfeasor and employer and the commission of the tort—Acting in the course of employment

The employer will be liable for torts committed by the employee "when acting in the course of employment". This phrase has caused considerable problems in interpretation. It has been established that the employer cannot simply argue that the employee was not employed to commit torts and was therefore acting outside the course of his or her employment when committing a tort. This would effectively undermine the whole concept of vicarious liability. A broader test is therefore applied. Traditionally, the test has been that the employee is acting in the course of employment if his or her conduct was authorised by the employer, or was considered to be an unauthorised means of performing the job for which he or she is employed.[179] While it is obvious that an employer will be liable for actions it has authorised,[180] the second category has proven more difficult to explain. It has now been interpreted as covering actions *closely connected* to the job for which the tortfeasor is employed.[181] The "course" or "scope" of employment will depend on the facts of each particular case, but a selection of case law will be discussed below which indicates the approach which the courts have adopted. Again, as will be seen, the recent cases of *Various Claimants v Catholic Child Welfare Society*,[182] *Mohamud v WM Morrison Supermarkets Plc*[183] and *WM Morrison Supermarkets Plc v Various Claimants*[184] make an important contribution to our understanding of this area of law.

7–033

---

initially: see Stanley Burnton LJ in *Biffa Waste Services Ltd v Maschinenfabrik Ernst Hesse GmbH* [2008] EWCA Civ 1257; [2009] Q.B. 725 (subsequently criticised in the *Catholic Child Welfare Society* case at [46]).

176 [2005] EWCA Civ 1151 at [80].

177 [2012] UKSC 56 at [45].

178 [2005] EWCA Civ 1151 at [79].

179 R.E.V. Heuston and R.A. Buckley, *Salmond and Heuston on the Law of Torts*, 21st edn (Sweet & Maxwell, 1996), p.443 (the so-called Salmond test).

180 Although arguably the employer is primarily liable for such actions: see Lord Millett in *Lister v Hesley Hall Ltd* [2001] UKHL 22; [2002] 1 A.C. 215.

181 See *Lister v Hesley Hall Ltd* [2001] UKHL 22; [2002] 1 A.C. 215.

182 [2012] UKSC 56; [2013] 2 A.C. 1.

183 [2016] UKSC 11; [2016] A.C. 677.

184 [2020] UKSC 12; [2020] 2 W.L.R. 941.

Generally, the courts have taken a generous approach to this question. For example, in *Century Insurance v NI Road Transport Board*,[185] a driver of a petrol lorry was held to be acting in the course of his employment when he discarded a lighted match, which he had used to light a cigarette, while delivering petrol. This led to an explosion which damaged the tanker, a car, and several nearby houses. Lighting a cigarette was held to be an act of comfort and convenience which would not be treated as outside the scope of employment.[186]

An equally broad approach was taken by the House of Lords in *Smith v Stages*.[187] This case raised the problem whether employees driving to and from work were acting within the scope of their employment. The court held that generally this will not be the case unless special circumstances exist, for example the employee is required under the contract of employment to use the employer's transport to work.[188] Equally, if the employee's job requires travel, for example because he or she is a sales rep or a gas-fitter, then such travel will be deemed to be within the course of his or her employment. However, a deviation or interruption from a journey taken in the course of employment will, unless incidental, take the employee out of the course of employment for the time being. This last point is illustrated by two cases involving tortfeasors employed to drive a horse and cart for their employers. In *Whatman v Pearson*,[189] the employee had, against strict instructions, chosen to travel home for dinner by horse and cart. His employers were held liable for the damage caused when the horse escaped due to the employee's negligence. Byles J held that the employee was clearly acting within the general scope of his authority in dealing with the horse and cart during the day. In contrast, in *Storey v Ashton*,[190] the court held that an employee who, after business hours, had driven to a friend's house, was not in the course of employment. The trip had nothing to do with his employment and his employer was thus not held liable for the injuries suffered by the plaintiff due to the employee's negligent driving. It may be seen from these cases that the question is therefore one of degree.

The facts of *Smith v Stages* raised a different issue. Here, two employees who normally worked in Staffordshire had been sent to South Wales to undertake certain emergency works. They had been paid their ordinary salary to travel to and from Wales, together with their travel expenses. The employees decided to work non-stop and so return to Staffordshire earlier than anticipated. They drove back immediately on completion of the job without any sleep. A crash occurred in which both men were seriously injured. As the driver (Stages) was uninsured, his passenger sued their employer, claiming that the employer was vicariously liable for Stages' negligent driving.

---

185 [1942] A.C. 509. See also *Bayley v Manchester, Sheffield and Lincolnshire Ry Co* (1873) L.R. 8 C.P. 148: railway porter mistakenly pulling passenger from what he believed to be the wrong train just after the train had started to leave the station found to be in the course of his employment.

186 Would a court take the same view in 2020 when smoking is less common?

187 [1989] A.C. 928.

188 See Lord Goff [1989] A.C. 928 at 936–937 and Lord Lowry [1989] A.C. 928 at 955–956. This is subject, of course, to any express arrangements between employer and employee.

189 (1868) L.R. 3 C.P. 422.

190 (1869) L.R. 4 Q.B. 476.

The court held that the employer was vicariously liable. The employer had paid the men their wages and not merely a travel allowance for the time taken on the journey. This meant that the men were still acting in the course of their employment. This was despite the fact that the employer did not provide the car and left the mode of transport to the discretion of the men. This seems to be a policy decision ensuring that, in the absence of insurance, and in circumstances where the Motor Insurers' Bureau would not provide cover,[191] the victim is fully compensated.

The line distinguishing conduct within and outside the scope of employment can be extremely fine. A good illustration is *Staton v NCB*.[192] Here, an employee at a colliery was held to be within the course of his employment while cycling across his employer's premises at the end of the working day to collect his wages from the pay office. Finnemore J held that it was an act incidental to his employment and, if performed negligently, his employer would be vicariously liable.

Prohibited and criminal conduct by employees

7-035

Even if the conduct in question has been expressly prohibited by the employer, this does not mean that the employee has acted outside the scope of his or her employment. Whilst this may seem unfair to employers, as stated earlier, it would be wrong if the employer could escape liability by simply prohibiting the commission of torts in the course of employment. The test is therefore whether the prohibition limits the scope of employment (as opposed to simply directing how the employee does his or her job). This is not particularly clear, but the courts' decisions provide some assistance.

If the prohibited conduct can be found to benefit the employer in some way, then there is authority that the courts will be willing to find the employer vicariously liable. For example, in *Limpus v London General Omnibus Co*,[193] the company's instructions not to race with, or obstruct, other buses had been disobeyed by one of its drivers who had obstructed a rival bus. This led to a collision with the plaintiff's bus, which overturned. The court found the company vicariously liable for the driver's negligent actions, on the basis that the employee's actions were simply an improper and unauthorised mode of doing an act which he was authorised to do, namely promoting the company's bus service.

More difficult are the cases where the driver of a company vehicle, contrary to express instructions, gives a lift to an unauthorised passenger. Will the employer be vicariously liable for any injury to the passenger in such circumstances? The majority of the Court of Appeal in

---

191 Lord Lowry [1989] A.C. 928 at 939 comments that the case arose because the driver was uninsured and the time limits under the Motor Insurers' Bureau agreement had not been complied with.
192 [1957] 1 W.L.R. 893.
193 (1862) 1 Hurl. & C. 526; 158 E.R. 993. See also *Ilkiw v Samuels* [1963] 1 W.L.R. 991 and *Kay v ITW Ltd* [1968] 1 Q.B. 140, but contrast *Beard v London General Omnibus Co* [1900] 2 Q.B. 530 (bus conductor not in the course of employment when driving bus).

Rose v Plenty[194] found the employer liable for the negligent driving of its milkman, despite the fact he had been warned by his employer not to allow children to assist him, nor to allow passengers on his float. In breach of these instructions, he had engaged the plaintiff, aged 13, to help him and the plaintiff had been injured due to the milkman's negligent driving. The majority held that if the purpose of the prohibited act was to further the employer's business, the act was in the course of employment. The decision may seem generous. There is also authority that an act is not required to benefit an employer to be in the course of employment,[195] but the judgment of Denning LJ, which referred to the introduction of compulsory insurance in 1972 to cover motor vehicle accidents, indicates the influence of policy and the desire to ensure that the injured boy obtained compensation.

7-036   The role of policy may further be seen in relation to vicarious liability for criminal acts by employees. Whilst vicarious liability in tort may seem surprising in this context, it should be remembered that crimes such as assault, theft and fraud are also torts, and employers have been found liable in such circumstances. In *Poland v John Parr and Sons*,[196] for example, the defendants were found liable for their employee assaulting a boy whom he believed had stolen a bag of sugar from his employer's wagon. The court held that the employee had implied authority to make reasonable efforts to protect his employer's property, and that the violence was not so excessive as to take the act outside the scope of his employment. Equally, in *Lloyd v Grace, Smith & Co*,[197] a firm of solicitors was found vicariously liable for the fraudulent activities of its managing clerk, who had defrauded a widow of her property. However, the courts have stressed that for fraudulent misrepresentation, employers will only be liable if they have given the employee actual or ostensible authority to make the statements and this authority is relied upon by the claimant.[198] There is also authority that an employer may be vicariously liable for the theft by an employee of goods entrusted to his or her care.[199]

---

194 [1976] 1 W.L.R. 141. Comment: J. Finch (1976) 39 M.L.R. 575. Contrast, however, the earlier case of *Twine v Bean's Express Ltd* (1946) 62 T.L.R. 458: giving a lift to a hitchhiker was not an act which the driver was employed to perform (Lord Greene MR arguably influenced by the fact that trespassers were owed a minimal duty of care in 1946 (see Ch.8)).

195 See *Lloyd v Grace, Smith & Co* [1912] A.C. 716 overturning *Barwick v English Joint Stock Bank* (1867) L.R. 2 Ex. 259 on this point.

196 [1927] 1 K.B. 236. See also *Dyer v Munday* [1895] 1 Q.B. 742 and F.D. Rose, "Liability for an Employee's Assaults" (1977) 40 M.L.R. 420 who argued for a more liberal approach. The fact that the boy in *Poland* had fallen and had his leg amputated as a result of the injury might have encouraged a more generous approach.

197 [1912] A.C. 716. See also *Uxbridge Permanent Benefit Building Society v Pickard* [1939] 2 K.B. 248 and *Noel v Poland* [2001] 2 B.C.L.C. 645.

198 See *Armagas Ltd v Mundogas SA (The Ocean Frost)* [1986] A.C. 717 HL and *Kooragang Investments Pty v Richardson & Wrench* [1982] A.C. 462 PC but see *Dubai Aluminium Co Ltd v Salaam* [2002] UKHL 48; [2003] 2 A.C. 366. The principle was affirmed recently by the Court of Appeal in *Winter v Hockley Mint Ltd* [2018] EWCA Civ 2480; [2019] 1 W.L.R. 1617.

199 Although the Court of Appeal in *Morris v Martin* [1966] 1 Q.B. 716 found an employer liable for the employee's theft on the basis of the principles of bailment for reward, it has been suggested that this case could simply have been decided on the basis that the act was in the course of the thief's employment: see Lord Steyn in *Lister*

The decisive case, however, is that of the House of Lords in *Lister v Hesley Hall Ltd*.[200] This case reviewed the application of vicarious liability in the context of serious criminal conduct amounting to an intentional tort. Here, the warden of a home for boys with emotional and behavioural difficulties had been found guilty of systematic sexual abuse of some of the boys under his care. In the earlier case of *Trotman v North Yorkshire County Council*,[201] the Court of Appeal had refused to accept that similar misconduct—the antithesis of what a carer was employed to do—could be deemed to be "in the course of his employment". The House of Lords took a different view. Where the intentional tort was closely connected to the work the perpetrator was employed to do, it would be fair and just to find his employer vicariously liable.[202] The warden in *Lister* had been employed to provide a home for the boys and supervise them day-to-day in circumstances where he and his disabled wife were often the only members of staff on the premises. Such close contact was sufficient to satisfy the court that there was a close connection between what he had been employed to do and the acts of abuse committed. If, however, the acts of abuse had been committed by a groundsman, there would have been no close connection between his job and the torts in question.

To establish this connection, then, the court will examine the nature and purpose of the job and the circumstances and context in which the acts took place. Their Lordships maintained, however, that this would not affect existing authority that private acts of passion, resentment or spite were outside the scope of employment. The application of the *Lister* test in subsequent case law was considered in the *Catholic Child Welfare Society* case and, more recently, in *Mohamud v Morrison Supermarkets* and *Morrison Supermarkets v Various Claimants*.

> ## The application of the *Lister* "close connection" test

7–037

In *Various Claimants v Catholic Child Welfare Society*,[203] the question arose whether the acts of abuse had been in the course of employment of the Catholic brother teachers. The Supreme Court examined a number of cases since *Lister* where employers had been held vicariously liable for serious criminal misconduct by employees. For example, in a commercial context, the House of Lords in *Dubai Aluminium Co Ltd v Salaam*[204] had found that work undertaken by a

---

v Hesley Hall Ltd [2001] UKHL 22; [2002] 1 A.C. 215 at [19]. See also *Brink's Global Services Inc v Igrox Ltd* [2010] EWCA Civ 1207; [2011] I.R.L.R. 343.

200   [2001] UKHL 22; [2002] 1 A.C. 215. Comment: P. Giliker (2002) 65 M.L.R. 269 and C.A. Hopkins [2001] C.L.J. 458.

201   [1999] L.G.R. 584.

202   The House noted that a test of "close connection" had been used by the Supreme Court of Canada in *Bazley v Curry* (1999) 174 D.L.R. (4th) 45 and *Jacobi v Griffiths* (1999) 174 D.L.R. (4th) 71, noted by P. Cane (2000) 116 L.Q.R. 21.

203   [2012] UKSC 56; [2013] 2 A.C. 1 at [35].

204   [2002] UKHL 48; [2003] 2 A.C. 366. Contrast *JJ Coughlan Ltd v Ruparelia* [2003] EWCA Civ 1057; [2004] P.N.L.R. 4 CA (no close connection between promotion of "preposterous" fraudulent scheme promising risk-free investment with return of 6,000% per annum and ordinary course of solicitor's business).

solicitor for a client which assisted a fraud was closely connected to his work. Lord Nicholls, in a helpful judgment, set out a general test for identifying the connection needed:

> **"Perhaps the best general answer is that the wrongful conduct must be so closely connected with acts the partner or employee was authorised to do that, for the purpose of the liability of the firm or the employer to third parties, the wrongful conduct *may fairly and properly be regarded* as done by the partner while acting in the ordinary course of the firm's business or the employee's employment."[205]**

This formulation was supported in subsequent decisions. A particularly generous application may be found in *Mattis v Pollock*.[206] Here, the Court of Appeal held a nightclub owner vicariously liable when one of its guests had been rendered paraplegic when stabbed by the bouncer outside the club. Although the act had been one of revenge for injuries and humiliation inflicted on the bouncer some time earlier in the club by the victim's group of friends, the court held that since the employee had been encouraged by his employer to keep order by violent behaviour, the employer would be vicariously liable for an assault linked to the incident in the club.[207] Here, much would seem to turn on the court's condemnation of the employer's behaviour. He had known of and encouraged the violent tendencies of the bouncer and so the court was able to find a close connection between the attack and what the bouncer had actually been employed to do.[208]

Lord Nicholls in *Dubai*, however, did question whether the close connection test provides sufficient guidance in itself to determine when vicarious liability should be found.[209] Judge LJ in *Mattis* described it as "a deceptively simple question".[210] Put simply, just how closely connected does the tort have to be to the employee's job for the employee to be "fairly" and "properly" said to be acting in the course of employment?

In response to such concerns, we now look to three decisions of the Supreme Court in the *Catholic Child Welfare Society* case (*CCWS*), *Mohamud v Morrison Supermarkets (Mohamud)* and, most recently, *Morrison Supermarkets v Various Claimants (Morrisons)* for guidance.

In *CCWS*, the Supreme Court found a common theme in physical and sexual abuse cases.[211] Vicarious liability is imposed where the tortfeasor is employed to work for the defendant in circumstances where the nature of the job created or significantly enhanced the risk of harm to the victim.[212] The creation of the risk thus provided a justification for liability. In the case itself,

---

205 [2002] UKHL 48; [2003] 2 A.C. 366 at [23] (his Lordship's emphasis).

206 [2003] EWCA Civ 887; [2003] 1 W.L.R. 2158 (leave to appeal to HL refused: [2003] 1 W.L.R. 2838).

207 Even where the employee in question had been chased out of the club by the group of friends, gone to his nearby home to fetch a knife and then had returned to the club to wreak revenge.

208 The court was even, in such circumstances, prepared to find the employer primarily liable for the attack.

209 [2003] 2 A.C. 366 at 377–378.

210 [2003] EWCA Civ 887; [2003] 1 W.L.R. 2158 at [19].

211 [2012] UKSC 56 at [87].

212 [2012] UKSC 56 at [86]. See also Lord Millett in *Lister v Hesley Hall Ltd* [2001] UKHL 22 at [65] and Lord Reed

the boys who were abused had lived in the residential school as virtual prisoners and were vulnerable and needing care. The Supreme Court found a very close connection between the brother teachers' employment in the school and the sexual abuse they committed.

In *Mohamud*, the Supreme Court sought to provide a simplied version of the close connection test, looking at: *(1) what functions or "field of activities" had been entrusted by the employer to the employee and (2) whether there was a sufficient connection between the job and the wrongful conduct such as to make it right for the employer to be held vicariously liable?*[213] In the case itself, Mohamud had been seriously assaulted by a Morrison employee when he had made an enquiry at its petrol kiosk concerning the availability of printing facilities. The employee had threatened and then assaulted Mr Mohammed, despite instructions from his supervisor to stop. Lord Toulson found that the employee's job was to attend to customers and respond to their enquiries. This was a foul mouthed and inexcusably bad way of doing this. While a gross abuse of his position, it was sufficiently connected with the business in which he was employed to serve customers. For the court, "the risk of an employee misusing his position is one of life's unavoidable facts"[214] and social justice required that the employer be held vicariously liable.

This new formulation gave rise to fears that claimants need only show a causal link between the tort and the employee's job to establish vicarious liability. This was based on the fact that the decision seemed to replace the "close" connection test with one based on showing merely a "sufficient" connection. In April 2020, in a significant decision, the Supreme Court unanimously stated in *Morrisons* that this was not the case. Any such view[215] was based on a misunderstanding of *Mohamud*. Here the facts were unusual. An internal IT auditor held a grudge against his employers, Morrisons. In revenge, he had posted confidential payroll data for the company's entire workforce on the internet using his home computer. The employees, whose data had been disclosed, sued Morrisons, claiming they were vicariously liable for this misuse of private information. Overturning the view of the Court of Appeal that there was "an unbroken thread that linked [the employee's] work to the disclosure",[216] the Supreme Court held that the employee's wrongful disclosure of data was *not* so closely connected with the tasks he was authorised to do that it could be fairly and properly be regarded as made in the ordinary course of employment. An employer should not normally be liable for an employee, as here, who was not furthering his employer's business, but rather pursuing a personal vendetta. Two points arise here. First, the Supreme Court reasserted the "close" connection test. The test in *Mohamud* was explained as a "simplication" of the close connection test stated in *Dubai*

---

in *Morrisons* [2020] UKSC 12 at [23] who notes the importance of the employer conferring authority on the employee to deal with the victims in such cases.

213 [2016] UKSC 11 at [44]–[45]. The Court of Appeal in *Bellman v Northampton Recruitment Ltd* [2018] EWCA Civ 2214; [2019] I.C.R. 459 described *Mohamud* as "the most recent and authoritative distillation of the relevant legal principles to be applied in this area of the law": [12]. Despite its concerns with the reasoning in *Mohamud*, the Supreme Court in *Morrisons* held that *Bellman* had been correctly decided in that it could not be regarded as a personal vendetta case: [2020] UKSC 12 at [46].

214 [2016] UKSC 11 at [40] per Lord Toulson.

215 Apparently held by the Court of Appeal in this case: [2018] EWCA Civ 2339.

216 [2018] EWCA Civ 2339 at [184].

Aluminium, rather than one intended to make any change in the law.[217] Secondly, the formulation used by the Court is taken from Lord Nicholls in *Dubai Aluminium* (set out above) and not *Mohamud*. In so doing, the Supreme Court avoided the extraordinary finding of the Court of Appeal that an employee seeking revenge on his employers could render his employers vicariously liable for his wrongs and thereby cause the employers further harm.[218]

Summary

7–038

Lord Phillips in the leading case of *Various Claimants v Catholic Child Welfare Society* commented that: "The law of vicarious liability is on the move".[219] Lord Reed added in *Cox v Ministry of Justice* that "it has not yet come to a stop".[220] In recent years, the doctrine of vicarious liability has expanded to include relationships akin to employment and, following *Mohamud*, potentially a very broad notion of the meaning of "course of employment". The Supreme Court in April 2020, however, in *Barclays Bank* and *Morrisons* reminded the lower courts that vicarious liability was not unlimited and that two important limits should be recognised:

(1) It is necessary to maintain a distinction between employees/those akin to employees and independent contractors for whom vicarious liability did not apply. The "akin to employee" category should be interpreted on a case by case basis with a focus on the details of the relationship.

(2) The test of close connection should be applied with reference to previous case-law, recognising that it was a test of principle rather than pure policy. The tort must be so closely connected with the tasks the employee was authorised to do that it could be fairly and properly be regarded as made in the ordinary course of employment.

It is important also not to forget that, in the majority of cases, the employer/employee relationship will be obvious—cases such as *Cox* and *Armes* are the exception. It seems likely, however, that the lower courts will continue to struggle to resolve how broadly they should interpret the close connection test in the light of *Mohamud* and *Morrisons*. *Morrisons* does emphasise, however, that courts should feel free to find employees, particularly those with personal vendettas, to be acting "on a frolic of their own".[221]

Morrisons also reminds us that vicarious liability does not apply to independent contractors,

---

217 [2020] UKSC 12 at [17]. Note the High Court of Australia in *Prince Alfred College Incorporated v ADC* [2016] HCA 37 had rejected the simplified test in *Mohamud* as unprincipled (at [83]), preferring a test whether the employment provides "the occasion for the commission of the wrongful act".

218 The scandal had already cost Morrisons more than £2m, primarily in improving its security following this incident.

219 [2012] UKSC 56; [2013] 2 A.C. 1 at [19].

220 [2016] UKSC 10; [2016] A.C. 660 at [1].

221 See Parke B in *Joel v Morrison* (1834) 6 C. & P. 501; 172 E.R. 1338.

that is, those workers whose relationship with the employer is not that of employee or even akin to employment. However, an employer may find itself *personally* liable for the torts of an independent contractor where the independent contractor has been taken on to perform a task for which the employer is directly responsible and cannot delegate responsibility. The extent of such liability will be examined below.

Liability for the torts of independent contractors

Lord Bridge in *D&F Estates Ltd v Church Commissioners for England*[222] held that it was trite law that the employer of an independent contractor is, in general, not liable for the negligence or other torts committed by the contractor in the course of the execution of the work. Whilst an employer cannot be vicariously liable for the torts of independent contractors, an employer may nevertheless find itself liable where it owes a *non-delegable duty* to the victim,[223] or it has authorised the independent contractor to commit a tort.[224] A non-delegable duty, as discussed at para.7–003, imposes a direct duty on the employer to ensure that reasonable care is taken in relation to the victim. While the employer may hire someone (e.g. an independent contractor) to fulfil its duties to the victim, the employer cannot delegate responsibility at law if the independent contractor fails to take reasonable care. Examples of such non-delegable duties include the employer's duty of care to its employees (discussed from para.7–003), liability under the rule in *Rylands v Fletcher* (discussed in Ch.10), and liability for works conducted on or over the highway, such as occurred in the odd case of *Tarry v Ashton*,[225] where a householder was found strictly liable when a lamp attached to his house, which was adjacent to the highway, fell on a person walking past.[226] An employer will therefore be liable to an employee for breach of its

7–039

---

222 [1989] A.C. 177, 208. See also Widgery LJ in *Salsbury v Woodland* [1970] 1 Q.B. 324, 336. This rule can be traced back to *Quarman v Burnett* (1840) 6 M. & W. 499; 151 E.R. 509.

223 See, generally, G. Williams, "Liability for Independent Contractors" [1956] C.L.J. 180, who is critical of the whole notion of a non-delegable duty of care. Lord Sumption in the now leading case of *Woodland v Essex CC* [2013] UKSC 66 acknowledged at [22] that non-delegable duties are inconsistent with the fault-based principles on which the tort of negligence is based and should therefore be regarded as exceptional.

224 *Ellis v Sheffield Gas Consumers Co* (1853) 2 E. & B. 767; 118 E.R. 955.

225 (1876) 1 Q.B.D. 314. Contrast the two Court of Appeal decisions in *Salsbury v Woodland* [1970] 1 Q.B. 324 and *Rowe v Herman* [1997] 1 W.L.R. 1390, which adopt a narrow interpretation of this category.

226 Other examples include withdrawal of support from neighbouring land: *Bower v Peate* (1876) 1 Q.B.D. 321 and cases involving extra-hazardous acts: *Honeywill & Stein v Larkin Bros* [1934] 1 K.B. 191. Although *Honeywill* is still good law, it is more often distinguished than applied and it has been questioned whether the House of Lords would continue to accept an authority resting on the subtle distinction between what is or is not "extra-hazardous": see Brooke LJ in *Bottomley v Todmorden Cricket Club* [2003] EWCA Civ 1575; [2004] P.I.Q.R. P18. Stanley Burnton LJ in *Biffa Waste Services Ltd v Maschinenfabrik Ernst Hesse GmbH* [2008] EWCA Civ 1257 remarked at [78] that the *Honeywill* case "is so unsatisfactory that its application should be kept as narrow as possible. It should be applied only to activities that are exceptionally dangerous whatever precautions are taken". The Supreme Court in *Woodland* below found it unnecessary to deal with this point, but recognised that *Honeywill* was "ripe for re-examination" at [6].

non-delegable duty of care if reasonable care is not taken in providing a safe place of work, even though the problem has been created by the negligence of an independent contractor.

The Supreme Court recently reconsidered the role of non-delegable duties in protecting victims injured by independent contractors. In *Woodland v Essex CC*,[227] a ten-year-old schoolgirl had suffered severe brain damage after falling into difficulties during a school swimming lesson. The school had contracted out the lessons to a commercial organisation (that is, an independent contractor) and it was alleged that those supervising the lesson had been negligent. The court held unanimously that the school had assumed a duty to ensure that the claimant's swimming lessons were carefully conducted and supervised by whoever it had engaged to perform those functions. The swimming lessons were an integral part of the school's curriculum and had taken place during school hours when the pupil had been entrusted into the school's care and control. The alleged negligence had therefore occurred in the course of the very functions which the school had assumed an obligation to perform. If (and this remained to be determined)[228] the independent contractors had been negligent, the school would have been in breach of its non-delegable duty to the pupil.

Lord Sumption set out a set of five criteria which will help identify the existence of non-delegable duties in future[229]:

- The claimant is a patient or a child, or for some other reason especially vulnerable or dependent on the protection of the defendant against the risk of injury.

- There is a pre-existing relationship between the claimant and the defendant, independent of the negligent act or omission itself, which (i) placed the claimant in the actual custody, charge or care of the defendant, and (ii) from which it was possible to impute to the defendant the assumption of a *positive* duty to protect the claimant from harm, not just a duty to refrain from conduct which would foreseeably damage the claimant. It was characteristic of such relationships that they involved an element of control.

- The claimant had no control over how the defendant chose to perform the relevant obligations (whether personally or through employees or third parties).

- The defendant had delegated to a third party some function which was an integral part of the positive duty which he had assumed towards the claimant; and the third party was exercising, for the purpose of the function thus delegated to him, the defendant's custody or care of the claimant and the element of control that went with it.

- The third party had been negligent in the performance of the very function assumed by the defendant and delegated by the defendant to him.

---

227 [2013] UKSC 66; [2014] A.C. 537.
228 Liability was determined in *Woodland v Maxwell* [2015] EWHC 273 (QB).
229 [2013] UKSC 66 at [23].

The *Woodland* case has the potential to increase the use of the non-delegable duty mechanism and respond to "out sourcing" of duties to independent contractors which might previously have been undertaken by the defendant's employees (and, for whom as Lady Hale pointed out, the school would have been vicariously liable).[230] It will not, however, extend to the defaults of independent contractors providing extra-curricular activities outside school hours, e.g. organising a school trip during the school vacation, or for individuals to whom the duty to care for the pupils has not been delegated e.g. a bus-driver taking the pupils and teachers on a trip to the zoo.[231] The court suggested that other examples of non-delegable duties might include prisoners and residents in care homes.[232] *Woodland* indicates that the more generous approach to vicarious liability identified in this chapter is now extending to the doctrine of non-delegable duties.

It should be noted, however, that the courts are not prepared to find the employer liable, even when a non-delegable duty is owed, for collateral or casual negligence by the independent contractor which is unconnected with the job the independent contractor was engaged to perform.[233] The leading example is that of *Padbury v Holliday and Greenwood Ltd*.[234] Here, a sub-contractor, engaged to place casements in windows on a building site, had negligently placed an iron tool on a window sill. The tool fell and injured a passer-by. The Court of Appeal held that placing the tool on the sill was not an action taken in the ordinary course of doing the work he was employed to do, but was an act of collateral negligence for which the defendants were not liable. The case therefore limits the scope of the employer's duty to guard against risks which are not created by the work itself.

Can vicarious liability be justified?

So far this chapter has discussed the various criteria used by the courts to impose vicarious liability. This section addresses a different issue: should we have a rule of vicarious liability in English law at all? It is plainly inconsistent with any idea that the person at fault should pay the claimant damages, and with the concept of corrective justice (see Ch.1). It also diminishes the deterrent effect of tort law. Why should I take care at work if any harm I cause will be

`7–040`

---

230 Lady Hale commented at [29]: "[T]he public might well be perplexed if one pupil could sue her school for injuries sustained during a negligently conducted swimming lesson but another could not".

231 [2013] UKSC 66 at [25]. See P. Giliker, "Vicarious liability, non-delegable duties and teachers: Can you outsource liability for lessons?" (2015) 31 P.N. 259.

232 [2013] UKSC 66 at [23]. The *Woodland* non-delegable duty was successfully argued in *GB v Home Office* [2015] EWHC 819 (QB) (Home Office owed a non-delegable duty of care to an immigration detainee receiving medical care at immigration removal centre). Contrast, however, *Armes v Nottinghamshire CC* [2017] UKSC 60; [2018] A.C. 355 (non-delegable duty would be inconsistent with statutory regime dealing with responsibilities of local authorities to children in care).

233 But note the criticisms of this rule by Sach LJ in *Salsbury v Woodland* [1970] 1 Q.B. 324 at 348.

234 (1912) 28 T.L.R. 494. See also comments of Denning LJ in *Cassidy v Ministry of Health* [1951] 2 K.B. 343 at 365. But contrast *Holliday v National Telephone Co* [1899] 2 Q.B. 392.

compensated for by my employer?[235] The courts themselves have in the past shown no particular willingness to pin down the rationale behind vicarious liability. Scarman LJ famously in *Rose v Plenty* commented that "It [is] important to realise that the principle of vicarious liability is one of public policy. It is not a principle which derives from a critical or refined consideration of other concepts in the common law".[236] Professor Glanville Williams agreed: "However distasteful the theory may be, we have to admit that vicarious liability owes its explanation, if not its justification, to the search for a solvent defendant".[237]

A number of arguments have nevertheless been put forward to justify vicarious liability.[238] It has been suggested that the employer has, in effect, caused the accident by setting the whole incident in motion by negligently employing a careless employee. Alternatively, the employer takes on the employee in the pursuit of profit, and one of the "costs" of employing the employee is his or her potential to cause harm (the enterprise liability argument).[239] Alternatively, vicarious liability will encourage employers to take greater measures to prevent such accidents occurring in the first place to the benefit of society as a whole. It cannot also be denied that vicarious liability provides an efficient means of compensating claimants in a way that losses are spread efficiently via the network of compulsory employer insurance. Employers are free to spread the cost of insurance either through the price of their goods or by controlling other fixed costs, such as the level of wages. However, little credit is given now to early ideas that vicarious liability rested on the fact that the employee's acts were impliedly authorised, or that the employee should have been controlled by the employer.

Lord Phillips in the leading Supreme Court decision of *Various Claimants v Catholic Child Welfare Society*[240] argued that there was no difficulty in identifying a number of policy reasons that usually make it fair, just and reasonable to impose vicarious liability on the employer:

(i)   the employer is more likely to have the means to compensate the victim than the employee and can be expected to have insured against that liability (the deeper pockets argument);

(ii) the tort will have been committed as a result of activity being taken by the employee on behalf of the employer (delegation of task argument);

(iii) the employee's activity is likely to be part of the business activity of the employer (enterprise risk argument);

---

235 Apart from the fact that failing to take care is unlikely to boost my employment prospects!
236 [1976] 1 W.L.R. 141 at 147. See also Lord Pearce in *ICI v Shatwell* [1965] A.C. 656 at 685: "The doctrine of vicarious responsibility has not grown from any very clear, logical or legal principle, but from social convenience and rough justice".
237 G. Williams, "Vicarious liability and the master's indemnity" (1957) 20 M.L.R. 220 at 232. See also H. J. Laski, "The Basis of Vicarious Liability" (1916) 26 Yale L.J. 105.
238 See P. S. Atiyah, *Vicarious Liability in the Law of Torts* (Butterworths, 1967), Ch.2.
239 See Lord Nicholls in *Dubai Aluminium* [2002] UKHL 48; [2003] 2 A.C. 366 at [21].
240 [2012] UKSC 56; [2013] 2 A.C. 1 at [35].

(iv) the employer, by employing the employee to carry on the activity will have created the risk of the tort committed by the employee (creation of risk argument); and

(v) the employee will, to a greater or lesser degree, have been under the control of the employer (control argument).

In *Cox v Ministry of Justice,*[241] Lord Reed approved these five factors, but noted that they are not all equally significant. The first (deeper pockets) and fifth (control) were, in his view, unlikely to be of independent significance in most cases. In contrast, in *Armes v Nottinghamshire CC*[242] his Lordship did find it helpful to look at all five factors and was notably influenced by the fact that the local authority was far more able than the foster parents to provide substantial sums of compensation and the local authority had exercised significant control over both what the foster parents did and how they did it. The Supreme Court more recently in *Barclays Bank v Various Claimants*[243] and *WM Morrison Supermarkets Plc v Various Claimants*[244] reminded the courts, however, of the need for a principled approach, incrementally developing past case law and that vicarious liability should not be determined simply on the basis of broad tests of social justice.[245] The mere presence of all five of the above factors does not therefore guarantee that vicarious liability will be imposed by the court.[246] Lady Hale in *Barclays Bank* commented specifically on the dangers of favouring policy rather than principle in engaging in legal development.[247]

Looking at past case law, however, it is indisputable that risk-based arguments, as stated in (iii) and (iv) above, have proven particularly influential in cases involving physical and sexual abuse. In *Armes*, for example, the Court highlighted that the placement of vulnerable children into foster care, which was an integral part of the local authority's child care services, created a relationship of authority and trust between foster parents and the children in circumstances where children would be particularly vulnerable to abuse. Lord Phillips in *CCWS* held that in such cases, creation of the risk of abuse is always likely to be an important element in the facts that give risk to such liability.[248] Lord Reed in *Morrisons* recognised the distinct nature of these cases.[249]

To sum up, we can conclude that there are a number of justifications for vicarious liability. The courts have not elected one single justification and seem unlikely at present to do so.

---

241 [2016] UKSC 10 at [20]–[21].
242 [2017] UKSC 60; [2018] A.C. 355, [59]–[63].
243 [2020] UKSC 13, overturning the Court of Appeal: [2018] EWCA Civ 1670.
244 [2020] UKSC 12.
245 *Morrisons* [2020] UKSC 12 at [26]. See also [24] per Lord Reed: "The words 'fairly and properly' are not, therefore, intended as an invitation to judges to decide cases according to their personal sense of justice".
246 [2020] UKSC 12 at [31].
247 [2020] UKSC 13 at [16].
248 [2012] UKSC 56 at [87].
249 [2020] UKSC 12 at [23].

Employers' liability: conclusion

7–041 Employers' liability is a large subject. Tort law forms only a part of the potential liability of an employer. Nevertheless, it is important, particularly in the form of vicarious liability which plays a significant role in ensuring that victims are able to recover compensation in the law of torts and where there have been recently a large number of Supreme Court decisions. Although, following the abolition of the doctrine of common employment, the employer's personal liability to employees is no longer as important, it is still a noteworthy part of negligence liability in tort. Breach of statutory duty is a limited remedy, and until statutory drafters undertake to provide some clarity in this area of law, or a clear policy stance is taken by the Government—such as that suggested by the Law Commission in 1969—this will continue to be a confusing area of law.

8

Occupiers' Liability

Introduction

8-001

An occupier of premises may be liable in tort to a claimant who, whilst on those premises, suffers personal injury or property damage because the premises are in a defective or dangerous condition.[1] As in a common law negligence action, the claimant must prove the existence of a duty of care, breach of that duty, causation, and that the loss suffered is not too remote. Occupiers' liability, therefore, may be thought of simply as an aspect of the tort of negligence. The important difference, however, is that in this area of the law the question of whether or not a defendant owes a duty of care, and the question of the standard of care required of him or her are answered by reference to two statutes, namely the Occupiers' Liability Act 1957 and the Occupiers' Liability Act 1984. In summary, the 1957 Act regulates the duties owed by an occupier to "visitors" to his or her premises, whilst the 1984 Act applies to "others" who enter premises. Usually, these "others" will be trespassers.

This chapter examines both of these statutes in detail, beginning with the Occupiers' Liability Act 1957. Before considering this Act, however, it is appropriate to give an outline of the common law which prevailed before it was passed. The old law relating to occupiers' liability was complex and uncertain. It is useful to have some understanding of the problems associated with the old law, in order to appreciate the purpose of the modern legislation. Reference to the old law is also necessary to explain some of the terminology which the modern legislation employs.

---

1   Liability of non-occupiers for defective premises, at common law and under the Defective Premises Act 1972, is discussed in Ch.3.

The old law

8–002

Prior to the Occupiers' Liability Act 1957, the common law had distinguished between four categories of persons who entered premises. Each category of entrant was owed a different standard of care by the occupier. The distinctions between these categories were extremely fine. The basic idea, however, was that the greater the benefit which accrued to the occupier by the person's presence on the premises, the higher would be the standard of care owed to that person. The four categories of entrant recognised by the common law were as follows:

(1) Contractual entrants

8–003

The highest standard of care was owed to persons who entered premises in accordance with the terms of a contract made with the occupier, for example guests staying in a hotel. The occupier had a duty to see that the premises were as safe as reasonable care and skill could make them for the purposes contemplated by the contract.

(2) Invitees

8–004

Invitees at common law were persons who entered premises to pursue some "common interest" with the occupier, for example customers entering the occupier's shop. Here, the occupier was obliged to use reasonable care to protect the invitee from unusual dangers of which he or she knew or ought to have known.[2]

(3) Licensees

8–005

Where the entrant could not be said to be pursuing any "common interest" with the occupier, but the occupier had simply given his or her permission (express or implied) for the entrant to be on the premises, the entrant was classified as a licensee. Friends invited to dinner by an occupier, for example, were classified as licensees at common law. Here, the occupier merely had a duty to warn the licensee about any trap or concealed danger on the premises of which he or she had actual knowledge.

(4) Trespassers

8–006

The lowest standard of care was owed to trespassers (i.e. those entering without the permission of the occupier). Trespassers generally entered premises at their own risk. The only duty

---

2   See *Indermaur v Dames* (1866) L.R. 1 C.P. 274 per Willes J at 288.

which an occupier had was a duty to refrain from any deliberate act intended to cause bodily harm to the trespasser (firing a shotgun, for example) or done with reckless disregard for the presence of the trespasser (setting a man-trap, for example).[3]

The need for reform

The four categories of entrant described above were regarded by the common law as exhaustive, so that all entrants had to be classified as falling into one category or another. The case law, as it developed, presented a very muddled picture. In particular, the courts experienced difficulty in distinguishing between invitees, who had a "common interest" with the occupier, and licensees, who did not. The legalistic distinction between invitees and licensees eventually appeared artificial and unworkable. The need to revise the old rules prompted the government to appoint a Law Reform Committee, whose report was published in 1954.[4] The committee recommended that the fine distinctions under the old law should be abolished, in favour of a uniform standard of care owed to all *lawful* visitors to premises.[5] The tough attitude towards trespassers, however, was maintained, and it was not until the Occupiers' Liability Act 1984 that unlawful entrants were given statutory protection. The committee's recommendations were given legal force in the Occupiers' Liability Act 1957.

8–007

Occupiers' Liability Act 1957

Under the Occupiers' Liability Act 1957,[6] an occupier owes a single duty to all lawful visitors, irrespective of their purpose in entering the premises. Thus, the Occupiers' Liability Act 1957 states s.2(1):

8–008

> **"An occupier of premises owes the same duty, the 'common duty of care', to all his visitors . . ."**

Section 2(2) goes on to define the "common duty of care", and the sections which follow set out various matters which are relevant in deciding whether the common duty of care has been discharged. Before we embark on a detailed analysis of those sections, however, it is appropriate to make a number of general observations.

---

3   *Robert Addie & Sons (Collieries) Ltd v Dumbreck* [1929] A.C. 358.
4   *Occupiers' Liability to Invitees, Licensees and Trespassers*, Cmnd.9305 (1954).
5   *Occupiers' Liability to Invitees, Licensees and Trespassers*, Cmnd.9305 (1954), paras 78(i) and (ii).
6   See, generally, D. Payne, "The Occupiers' Liability Act" (1958) 21 M.L.R. 359.

The scope of the 1957 Act

(1) The Act covers damage to property as well as personal injury

8-009

Like the common law which it replaced, the Act covers both personal injury caused to a visitor and damage to his or her property. The Act also applies in respect of damage to property lawfully on the premises, even where that property does not belong to a visitor.[7] Thus, if a tile falls from the roof and damages a visitor's borrowed car parked on the premises, the owner of the car may sue for that damage. The Act does not, however, apply to property which is outside the boundaries of the premises. Mocatta J, in *AMF International Ltd v Magnet Bowling Ltd*,[8] remarked that, where property was damaged, there was no reason in principle why consequential economic loss should not be recoverable.[9]

(2) Liability under the Act may be limited by an express term of a contract, or by a notice given to visitors

8-010

It should be appreciated at the outset that, to a certain extent, the Act allows an occupier to limit his or her liability to visitors. An occupier can do this by displaying a notice on the premises, or, where visitors enter under a contract, by including a term in that contract which sets the standard of care he or she owes. These matters are considered more fully towards the end of this chapter.

(3) The Act is thought to apply only to the "occupancy duty"

8-011

It is unlikely that every careless act or omission which causes loss to a visitor on an occupier's premises will give rise to a claim under the Act. Thus, if a visitor is walking up the occupier's drive and is injured by a carelessly driven car, he or she will not sue under the Act, but in ordinary common law negligence. This is because the duty of care he or she is owed has nothing to do with the fact that the accident happened on the occupier's premises.

The old common law had distinguished between situations where the claimant suffered loss because he or she fell foul of some defect in, or dangerous object on, the premises (tripping over a loose floorboard, for example, or being electrocuted by a badly wired plug) and situations where the claimant's loss was caused by some *activity* carried out on the premises (the claimant was knocked down by a car, for example). The former situation was governed by the special rules of occupiers' liability, which laid down the "occupancy duty". This duty arose where the claim-

---

7 s.1(3)(b).
8 [1968] 1 W.L.R. 1028.
9 [1968] 1 W.L.R. 1028 at 1049 (on the basis that the Act makes no attempt to quantify or limit the damages recoverable).

ant's loss could be said to result from the *state of the premises*. The latter situation, however, was governed only by the ordinary rules of negligence, which laid down the "activity duty".

It is unclear whether this distinction has survived the 1957 Act. The wording of the Act does not make it clear whether the Act regulates only the "occupancy duty", or whether it also regulates the "activity duty", and the issue has been the subject of academic debate. The problem is that there are two relevant sections of the Act, each of which appears to give a conflicting answer to the question. Section 1(2) of the Act provides that the Act shall ". . . regulate the nature of the duty imposed by law in consequence of a person's occupation or control of premises". This implies that the Act covers only the "occupancy duty". Section 1(1), on the other hand, provides that the Act shall apply ". . . in respect of dangers due to the state of the premises or to things done or omitted to be done on them". This, then, implies that the modern law of occupiers' liability also covers situations where the claimant's loss is caused by a breach of the "activity duty".

Most academic commentary suggests that the 1957 Act applies only to the "occupancy duty".[10] In other words, it covers only those situations where the claimant's loss is due to the defective or dangerous state of the premises. It appears, however, that where an activity on premises gives rise to a continuing source of danger (use of the premises for motor racing, for example), the Act may apply.[11] The true position remains undecided by the courts because, whilst the debate may be of academic interest, the principles applied in a common law negligence action arising from a harmful activity on premises are so similar to those applied under the 1957 Act that nothing turns on the distinction between the "activity duty" and the "occupancy duty" under the modern law.[12]

Having gained some appreciation of the general scope of the Act, then, our next task must be to examine its precise wording. It is this wording that provides the mechanism by which the interest of an occupier, in maintaining the premises as he or she wishes, is to be balanced against the safety of his or her visitors. It has been said that, under the Act, an "occupier" of "premises" owes a "common duty of care" to all his "visitors". These key terms require clarification.

Definition of "occupier"

8–012

Section 1(2) of the Act states that an "occupier" is simply a person "who would at common law be treated as an occupier". We must therefore examine the relevant case law. What emerges is that the courts have taken a broad approach, holding that a person will be an "occupier"

---

10   A view endorsed by the Law Commission in Report No.75 *Report on Liability for Damage or Injury to Trespassers and Related Questions of Occupiers' Liability*, Cmnd.6428 (1976), para.23, cited by Neill LJ in *Revill v Newbery* [1996] 2 W.L.R. 239 at 245. See also Stephen-Brown LJ, obiter, in *Ogwo v Taylor* [1988] A.C. 431 at 438.

11   Law Commission Report No.75 (above).

12   Several common law jurisdictions have, indeed, absorbed the occupiers' liability rules within the general tort of negligence, see *Australian Safeway Stores v Zaluzna* (1987) 162 C.L.R. 479 in Australia; *Toh Siew Kee v Ho Ah Lam Ferrocement (Pte) Ltd* [2013] 3 S.L.R. 284 in Singapore.

if he or she has a *sufficient degree of control over the state of the premises*. A person need not have a legal estate in land to be the "occupier" of that land, nor need he or she have a right to exclusive possession.[13]

The leading case is *Wheat v E Lacon & Co Ltd*.[14] The defendants, a brewery, owned a public house. They allowed the publican and his wife, Mr and Mrs Richardson, to live in accommodation above the pub, not as tenants, but as mere licensees. The brewery had given Mrs Richardson permission to take in paying guests in part of the upstairs accommodation, access to which was gained by an outside staircase. The staircase was dangerous because its handrail did not go all the way to the bottom, and because it was unlit. One evening, the plaintiff's husband, who was a paying guest, fell down the staircase and was fatally injured. The plaintiff sued the brewery under the 1957 Act, and the question arose whether the brewery were "occupiers" of the private part of the building.

The House of Lords held that, in the circumstances, the brewery had retained sufficient control over the upstairs part of the premises to be regarded as occupiers. Although they had granted Mr and Mrs Richardson a licence to occupy the upstairs part of the premises, they had retained the right to access that part themselves. This meant that they could still exercise some control over the state of that part of the premises. Their Lordships found that the publican, his wife and the brewery were all "occupiers" under the Act. The standard of care required of each, however, was defined by the extent to which each had control over the premises. On the facts, neither the Richardsons nor the brewery had fallen below their respective standards of care. The short handrail did not by itself make the staircase unreasonably hazardous, and they were not responsible for a stranger having caused it to become unlit by removing a light bulb.

Two important points, then, emerge from the decision in *Wheat v E Lacon & Co Ltd*:

■ there can be more than one occupier of premises; and

■ where the owner of premises licenses others to occupy those premises, but retains the right to enter the premises, he or she remains an "occupier" for the purposes of the Act. This is to be contrasted with a situation where the owner grants a tenancy conferring on others exclusive possession of the premises. Here, the landlord will normally have given up control of the premises, so that he or she cannot be regarded as an occupier.

In all cases, the key question for the courts is not whether a person is in actual occupation of the premises, but whether he or she exercises control over the premises. This is clear from the decision in *Harris v Birkenhead Corp*.[15] The defendant was a local authority which had made

---

13 *Humphreys v Dreamland (Margate) Ltd* (1930) 144 L.T. 529; *Hartwell v Grayson Rollo and Clover Docks Ltd* [1947] K.B. 901.

14 [1966] A.C. 552. Compare *Bailey v Armes* [1999] E.G.C.S. 21 (no occupation of a flat roof to which children gained access without the defendants' knowledge.)

15 [1976] 1 W.L.R. 279. See also *Vodden v Gayton* [2001] P.I.Q.R. P4 (where a private right of way ran over land, owners of the servient and dominant tenement were both occupiers for the purposes of the 1984 Act).

a compulsory purchase order on a house. It then served on the owner of the house, and on a tenant who occupied it, a notice of entry under the Housing Acts, which entitled it to take possession of the house within 14 days. The local authority did not in fact take possession of the house after that time, and the tenant remained there for many weeks. Eventually the tenant departed, leaving the house uninhabited, but the local authority took no steps to assert its possession of the house. A four and a half year-old child entered the house through an unsecured door and was injured when he fell from a second floor window.

In the Court of Appeal, the local authority argued that before it could be regarded as the "occupier" of the house, there must have been an actual or symbolic taking of possession of the house on its behalf, and that its mere *right* to take possession was insufficient. This argument was rejected. On the facts, the Court of Appeal held that the local authority became the occupier as soon as the premises were vacated. Although it could not be said that in every case a person with an immediate right to take possession of premises would be an "occupier", in these particular circumstances, actual physical possession of the premises was not necessary before the local authority could be regarded as having control of the premises.

Where an independent contractor enters premises to undertake work, whether or not this contractor becomes an occupier of the premises depends on the nature and scale of the work being undertaken. Thus, a contractor undertaking a large building development would become the occupier of the site, whilst a decorator painting a house would not.[16] Later in this chapter we shall see that where a visitor suffers loss because of a contractor's negligent work, an occupier can sometimes escape liability by arguing that he or she had delegated the work to a contractor. It does not follow, however, that entrusting work to a contractor automatically makes that contractor an occupier.

Definition of "premises"

8–013

There is no explicit definition of "premises" in the Act. Section 1(3)(a), however, states that the Act regulates the obligations of persons occupying or having control over "any fixed or moveable structure, including any vessel, vehicle or aircraft". Case law has established that "premises" covers not only land and buildings, but also such structures as lifts, ladders, diving boards, scaffolding and even large digging machines.[17]

Definition of "visitor"

8–014

Section 1(2) of the Act provides that a "visitor", under the Act, is simply someone who would have been either an "invitee" or a "licensee" at common law before the Act was passed. The

---

16   *Page v Read* (1984) 134 N.L.J. 723.
17   See *Haseldine v Daw* [1941] 2 K.B. 343; *Wheeler v Copas* [1981] 3 All E.R. 405; *Ewa Perkowski v Wellington Corp* [1959] A.C. 53; *Bunker v Charles Brand* [1969] 2 Q.B. 480.

position of contractual entrants is governed by s.5 of the Act. To a limited extent, an occupier is free to set his or her own standard of care in relation to contractual entrants, but where he or she does not do so, such entrants are treated in the same way as visitors and are owed the "common duty of care".[18] As has been said, the Act gives no protection to trespassers. It should also be remembered, of course, that the Act has no application to persons who are outside the premises.

Under the Act, the troublesome distinction between invitees and licensees is replaced by a single test: has the occupier given the entrant permission to be on the premises? In cases where the occupier has expressly given permission to enter, the matter is straightforward. In other cases, the law will sometimes say that an occupier has given *implied permission* for a person to be on the premises. In addition, there are certain rules which govern the status of particular types of entrant. The issues which arise may be considered under the following headings:

Persons entering by authority of law

8–015

By s.2(6) of the Act, persons entering premises in the exercise of a right conferred by law, for example firemen attending a fire, or policemen executing a warrant, are treated as if they had been given permission to enter by the occupier. Strictly speaking, such cases are not cases of implied permission, but of *deemed* permission, because these persons are treated as visitors even where the occupier expressly states that he or she does not want them on the premises.

Persons exercising rights of way

8–016

Persons entering land in the exercise of a public[19] or private[20] right of way, or in the exercise of a statutory right to access land for recreational purposes (conferred under the National Parks and Access to the Countryside Act 1949, or the Countryside and Rights of Way Act 2000) are not "visitors" under the Act.[21] Persons exercising private rights of way are owed a duty under the Occupiers' Liability Act 1984, which is discussed later in this chapter. Those exercising a *public* right of way, however, are only owed the limited duty which had been established at common law. Thus, the occupier is not under a duty to maintain the natural features of public rights of way which run over his or her land.[22]

---

18 Occupiers' Liability Act 1957 s.5(1).
19 *Greenhalgh v British Railways Board* [1969] 2 Q.B. 286; *McGeown v Northern Ireland Housing Executive* [1995] 1 A.C. 233. See J. Murphy, "Public Rights of Way and Private Law Wrongs" [1997] Conv. 362.
20 *Holden v White* [1982] 2 Q.B. 679.
21 Occupiers' Liability Act 1957 s.1(4) (as amended by Countryside and Rights of Way Act 2000 s.13).
22 This position is now reflected in the Occupiers' Liability Act 1984 s.1(6A) (inserted by the Countryside and Rights of Way Act 2000). Persons exercising rights of way conferred by the 2000 Act are owed no duty in respect of dangers arising from natural features of the landscape or when passing through walls, fences etc *except when*

Implied permission

It is clear that a person who enters premises in order to communicate with the occupier will be treated as having the occupier's implied permission to be on the premises. Thus, a postman or other individual has implied permission to walk up the occupier's drive to use the letterbox, or to call at the front door, unless he or she knows, or ought to know, that this is expressly forbidden (for example, by a sign posted on the gate).[23]

Much of the case law on implied permission, however, must nowadays be seen in the context of the state of the common law when it developed. As has been noted, the common law was harsh in its treatment of trespassers. Many judges felt that the rules could produce injustice. They therefore sought to avoid the rigours of the common law in hard cases by classifying trespassers as implied licensees. This often entailed a strained interpretation of the facts.

In *Lowery v Walker*,[24] for example, the plaintiff was using a short-cut across a farmer's field when he was attacked by a horse. The farmer knew that the short-cut had been regularly used by the public for the past 35 years, and had protested about this, although he had never brought legal proceedings. Despite these protests, it was held that the farmer had given implied permission for people to use the short-cut. The plaintiff could therefore be classified as an implied licensee and was able to succeed in his claim. Similarly, in *Glasgow Corp v Taylor*,[25] a council's failure to fence off a poisonous plant near a children's playground made it liable in respect of a seven-year-old child who died after eating berries from the plant. The berries looked like cherries or large blackcurrants and were very alluring and tempting to children. Even though the boy had no right to take the berries, or even to approach the bush, and an adult doing so might have been treated as a trespasser, the boy was treated as an implied licensee.

Now that trespassers are afforded greater protection under the Occupiers' Liability Act 1984 than was the case at common law, there is less need for the courts to resort to the idea of implied permission to do justice in hard cases. The earlier authorities, therefore, are unlikely to be followed unless the court feels that, in a particularly meritorious case, even the protection afforded by the Occupiers' Liability Act 1984 would be insufficient.

Limitations on permission

The permission given by an occupier, whether express or implied, may be limited in three ways. First, the occupier may permit a person to be in some parts of the premises but not others. Secondly, the occupier may permit the person to remain on the premises only for a certain period of time. Thirdly, the occupier may permit the person to be on the premises only

8-017

8-018

---

making proper use of gates and stiles. The Marine and Coastal Access Act 2009 inserts s.1(6AA), extending the provisions of s.1(6A) to coastal land.

23 *Robson v Hallett* [1967] 2 Q.B. 939.
24 [1911] A.C. 10.
25 [1922] 1 A.C. 44. Compare *Edwards v Railway Executive* [1952] A.C. 737.

for certain purposes. It is clear that where a person enters premises with permission, but that permission is subsequently expressly revoked, the law will allow a reasonable time to leave the premises, during which he or she will still be treated as a visitor.[26]

Difficulties arise when visitors stray from the permitted area. In *Gould v McAuliffe*,[27] for example, a customer in a pub, looking for an outside lavatory, wandered through an unlocked gate into a private part of the premises where she was attacked by a dog. The argument that she had become a trespasser was rejected. It was held that where an occupier wishes to exclude a visitor from an area into which visitors are likely to wander, he or she must take reasonable steps to inform the visitor that the area is out of bounds. On the facts, because there was no notice informing the plaintiff that the area beyond the gate was private, this had not been done. Whether it is necessary to post a notice excluding visitors from a particular area will, of course, depend on the facts of each case. Such a notice will not be necessary in respect of a part of the premises to which no one would reasonably expect a visitor to go.[28]

In determining whether or not a person is a visitor, it is relevant to consider the purpose for which that person is permitted to be on the premises. As Scrutton LJ put it, in *The Carlgarth*[29]:

> **"When you invite a person into your house to use the staircase, you do not invite him to slide down the banisters."**

Thus, where a person is invited for one purpose (to sleep in a bed) and starts to pursue an activity unrelated to that purpose (jump up and down on the mattress), that person may cease to be a visitor, even though he or she has not strayed from the permitted area. To understand why this is so, it must be remembered that the Act treats as "visitors" people who were, under the old law, licensees or invitees. A licence to be on premises will almost always have implied conditions. When a person breaches one of these conditions, he or she ceases to be a licensee. It therefore follows that he or she ceases to be a "visitor". It should be noted that the permission to use the premises for the purposes in question must be given *by the occupier*.[30] Permission given by someone else is not sufficient.

The "common duty of care"

8–019

Section 2(2) of the Act defines the "common duty of care" as follows:

---

26   *Robson v Hallett* [1967] 2 Q.B. 939; *Kay v Hibbert* [1977] Crim. L.R. 226; *R. (on the application of Fullard) v Woking Magistrates* [2005] EWHC 2922 (Admin).

27   [1941] 2 All E.R. 527 CA.

28   *Mersey Docks and Harbour Board v Procter* [1923] A.C. 253.

29   [1927] P. 93 at 110. For a real life scenario closely analogous to Scrutton LJ's example, see *Geary v JD Wetherspoon Plc* [2011] EWHC 1506 (QB).

30   See Occupiers' Liability Act 1957 s.2(2), discussed below.

> "The common duty of care is a duty to take such care as in all the circumstances of the case is reasonable to see that the visitor will be reasonably safe in using the premises for the purposes for which he or she is invited or permitted by the occupier to be there."

It should be noted that it is the *visitor*, rather than simply the *premises* which must be reasonably safe. It follows that if the occupier invites or permits, say, a blind man to come onto the premises, he or she must take greater care for that visitor's safety than would be the case in relation to a sighted person.[31] In this regard, it should be noted that liability under the Act can arise where an occupier merely *fails to protect* a visitor from a danger on the premises. The occupier does not need to have created that danger in order to be liable. Thus, the Act imposes liability for mere omissions in a way which, as we saw in Ch.2, is unusual in English law. It imposes on an occupier a duty to his or her visitor which is very different from the duty owed at common law by a bystander to a stranger. It will be recalled that Lord Keith, in *Yuen Kun Yeu v Att-Gen of Hong Kong*,[32] made it clear that there is no liability at common law "on the part of one who sees another about to walk over a cliff with his head in the air, and forbears to shout a warning". This is because, although the danger is foreseeable, there is insufficient "proximity" (closeness of relationship) between the claimant and the defendant. In cases of occupiers' liability, however, the position is different. The fact that the occupier has invited or permitted the claimant to be on the premises creates the necessary degree of proximity. Therefore, the occupier must protect the visitor from danger, even though he or she has not caused the danger by any positive act.

Discharging the common duty of care

8–020

In deciding whether or not the occupier is in breach of the common duty of care, the courts will have regard to the same general factors which would be considered in a common law negligence action. These general factors were discussed in Ch.5. They include the likelihood of a risk materialising, the magnitude of the loss if the risk does materialise, and the cost and practicality of taking precautions.[33] In addition, however, the Act expressly refers to a number of more *specific* factors which are to be considered when deciding the question of breach of duty. In particular, the Act contains a provision relating to warnings, and another governing the extent to which an occupier will be liable for dangers created by independent contractors.

---

31 See, e.g. *Atkins v Butlins Skyline Ltd* [2006] 1 C.L. 510 (Taunton County Court): the defendant holiday camp operators were liable to a blind visitor who was trapped by closing lift doors that were safe for sighted visitors.

32 [1988] A.C. 175 at 192 (see Ch.2).

33 Cases therefore tend to turn on their own particular facts. For some modern examples of various factual scenarios, see *Wattleworth v Goodwood Road Racing Co Ltd* [2004] EWHC 140 (QB); [2004] P.I.Q.R. P25; *Lewis v Six Continents Plc* [2005] EWCA Civ 1805; *Cole v Davis-Gilbert* [2007] EWCA Civ 396; *West Sussex CC v Pierce* [2013] EWCA Civ 1230; [2014] P.I.Q.R. P5.

These provisions are discussed later in the chapter. First, we must examine the extent to which an occupier can rely on a visitor to look after his or her own safety on the premises.

Section 2(3) of the Act provides that, in deciding whether the common duty of care is discharged, it is relevant to consider "the degree of care, and of want of care, which would ordinarily be looked for in such a visitor". For good measure, however, that subsection goes on to refer to two specific types of visitor—children and professionals—and makes it clear what degree of vigilance for their own safety an occupier should expect from each type of visitor. It is convenient to deal with each type of visitor in turn.

Children[34]

8–021

Section 2(3)(a) of the Act provides:

> **"an occupier must be prepared for children to be less careful than adults."**

Children often fail to appreciate dangers that are obvious to adults. Their natural curiosity often leads them into dangerous situations. In discharging his or her duty of care, therefore, an occupier must bear in mind that children tend to be attracted to certain objects, unaware that they are dangerous. This, of course, was what happened in *Glasgow Corp v Taylor*[35] (discussed above) where the poisonous berries, which looked like blackcurrants, were said to be an "allurement" to small children. Similarly, in *Jolley v Sutton LBC*,[36] the council was held to be in breach of its duty of care by allowing an old wooden boat, which was an enticing play area for children, to be left abandoned on its land. A 13-year-old boy (Jolley) and his friend had attempted to repair the boat to take it to Cornwall to sail, and Jolley had been injured when the boat, which had been jacked up, fell on him. Overturning the Court of Appeal decision which had held the activities of the boys too remote a consequence of breach,[37] the House of Lords took the view that the courts should not underestimate the ingenuity of children in finding unexpected ways of doing mischief to themselves and others.[38] On this basis, their Lordships restored the view of the trial judge that the type of accident and injury which occurred was reasonably foreseeable in the context of teenage boys attracted to an obviously abandoned boat.

The decision in *Jolley*, then, makes it clear that the courts will apply the rules of occupiers' liability generously towards children, particularly in relation to serious personal injury.[39]

---

34 See R. Kidner, "The Duty of Occupiers towards Children" (1988) 39 N.I.L.Q. 150.
35 [1922] 1 A.C. 44.
36 [2000] 1 W.L.R. 1082 HL; [1998] 1 W.L.R. 1546 CA.
37 On remoteness generally, see Ch.6.
38 Compare, however, the approach of the CA in *Keown v Coventry Healthcare NHS Trust* [2006] 1 W.L.R. 953: where the danger is obvious to a child, the court should not ignore a child's choice to incur that danger just because he is a child.
39 Justin Jolley had suffered serious spinal injuries rendering him paraplegic.

However, an occupier will not be liable for every action of a child on his or her premises. This is especially true in the case of very young children, for whom even the most innocuous objects on premises may present a danger. An occupier cannot be expected to ensure that his or her premises are as safe as a nursery for any visiting toddler. If some provision were not made in law to limit the scope of an occupier's duty to very young visitors, the occupier might be apt to exclude them from the premises for fear of liability. Such a solution would not be socially acceptable. The law therefore provides that an occupier is entitled to assume that the behaviour of very young children will be supervised by a responsible adult. The leading case is *Phipps v Rochester Corp.*[40]

In *Phipps*, the plaintiff was a five-year-old boy. Accompanied by his sister, aged seven, he went out collecting blackberries on a large open space and fell into a deep trench, breaking his leg. The trench, which would have been an obvious danger to an adult, had been dug by the defendants, who were developing the site. Devlin J, after reviewing the relevant authorities, concluded that where children of "tender years" were concerned, an occupier was entitled to consider how a prudent parent or guardian of the child should behave. As Devlin J remarked:

> "it would not be socially desirable if parents were, as a matter of course, able to shift the burden of looking after their children from their own shoulders to those of persons who happen to have accessible bits of land."[41]

Prudent adults would not have allowed two small children to roam over the site unaccompanied. In the circumstances, therefore, the occupiers of the site escaped liability. Their only duty to very young children was to ensure that they were reasonably safe on the site when accompanied by a responsible adult, and on the facts, this duty had been discharged.

Whether or not an occupier is entitled to expect that very young children on his or her premises will be accompanied by an adult depends on the facts of any given case. Essentially, two matters are relevant, namely the age of the child and the nature of the premises. Thus, a prudent parent should realise that whilst only very young children will be at risk in a playground, a building site, such as that in *Phipps*, would present dangers to older children if unaccompanied. It appears from the decision in *Simkiss v Rhondda BC*,[42] however, that an occupier is required to take account of the social habits of the neighbourhood in which his or her premises are situated. Thus, where a piece of land becomes locally recognised as a playground for unaccompanied small children, an occupier must ensure that these children are reasonably safe.

---

40   [1955] 1 Q.B. 450.
41   [1955] 1 Q.B. 450 at 472.
42   (1983) 81 L.G.R. 460. See also *Bourne Leisure Ltd (t/a British Holidays) v Marsden* [2009] EWCA Civ 671: owner of a holiday site under no obligation to draw parents' attention to precise location of a pond that was an obvious danger to small children. Giving the parents a plan showing the pond was sufficient.

Professional visitors

8-022

Section 2(3)(b) of the Act provides:

> "an occupier may expect that a person, in the exercise of his calling, will appreciate and guard against any special risks ordinarily incident to it, so far as the occupier leaves him free to do so."

This subsection gives statutory force to the position which had been established at common law.[43] An occupier may expect that a skilled visitor, employed to undertake work on the premises, will take appropriate precautions against risks ordinarily associated with his or her work. The subsection does not, of course, cover risks not normally associated with the job. Thus, in *Eden v West & Co*[44] the defendants were liable where a carpenter removed a window and the brickwork above it collapsed on him—the risk of this happening in a modern property was extraordinary and the defendants ought therefore to have warned him that the brickwork was not properly supported.

The leading case is *Roles v Nathan*.[45] (This is also an important case on warnings, discussed below.) Two chimney sweeps had been engaged to clean the flue of a boiler and to seal up some vent holes in the flue so that it would operate more efficiently. The defendant's heating engineer had repeatedly warned the sweeps about the dangers of being overcome by carbon monoxide fumes if they worked on the flue while the boiler was lit. He gave evidence, however, that the sweeps had been inclined to dismiss his warnings, taking the view that *they* were the experts and could look after themselves. The sweeps completed most of their work, telling the man in charge of the boiler room that they would return to finish the job the following day. In fact, the sweeps returned later that evening, by which time the boiler had been lit, and were overcome by fumes while working in the flue.

A majority of the Court of Appeal held that the occupiers were not liable for the death of the sweeps. As Lord Denning MR put it:

> "When a householder calls in a specialist to deal with a defective installation on his premises, he can reasonably expect the specialist to appreciate and guard against the dangers arising from the defect. The householder is not bound to watch over him to see that he comes to no harm."[46]

This view accords with common sense—an occupier would not receive a warm reception if he or she began to tell a specialist contractor all about the usual risks involved in his or her job.

---

43   See *Christmas v General Cleaning Contractors* [1952] 1 K.B. 141, affirmed [1953] A.C. 180, and *Bates v Parker* [1953] 2 Q.B. 231.
44   [2002] EWCA Civ 991; [2003] P.I.Q.R. Q2.
45   [1963] 1 W.L.R. 1117.
46   [1963] 1 W.L.R. 1117 at 1123.

Therefore, since it would be inappropriate for the occupier to give a warning of those risks, the occupier should not be liable if the risks materialise. Both Harman LJ and Pearson LJ agreed with Lord Denning's statement of principle, although Pearson LJ, who dissented, took a different view of the facts. On his Lordship's view, the risk of the boiler being lit was not a risk which was "ordinarily incident" to the sweeps' calling. Rather, it was a special and unusual risk. This was shown by the fact that the defendants had felt it necessary to give repeated warnings about its occurrence.

Sometimes, professional visitors will suffer injury as a result of a danger on the premises, even though they have exercised all due care and skill in taking care of their own safety. In such cases, the courts have held that the mere fact that the visitor is possessed of special skill will not, by itself, entitle the occupier to escape liability. The essential point to grasp is this: the fact that the visitor has special skill does not mean that he or she has *voluntarily assumed the risks* associated with the task, it simply means that he or she is expected to take greater care than would be taken by a lay person in relation to those risks. Thus, in *Ogwo v Taylor*,[47] a fireman injured whilst fighting a fire in a confined space was able to recover from an occupier who had negligently started the fire on the premises. The House of Lords held that whilst an occupier was entitled to expect that the fireman would use his professional skill in tackling a fire, if, despite exercising all due skill, the fireman suffered injury, the occupier would be liable. (It should be noted that *Ogwo v Taylor* was decided on the basis of common law negligence principles. The key finding was that the occupier had put the fireman at risk by negligently *creating* a danger on his premises.)

Giving a warning of the danger

Section 2(4)(a) of the Act provides that in deciding whether or not an occupier has discharged the common duty of care, the fact that he or she has warned visitors of the danger is a relevant consideration. The subsection goes on to state, however, that:

> **"the warning is not to be treated without more as absolving the occupier from liability, unless in all the circumstances it was enough to enable the visitor to be reasonably safe."**

Thus, a distinction must be drawn between a mere warning of the danger, which offers no assistance as to how to avoid the danger, and a warning which *enables the visitor to be reasonably safe*. Under the Act, only the latter type of warning will completely discharge the common duty of care. Again, the leading authority is *Roles v Nathan*,[48] in which Lord Denning MR explained the position as follows:

8–023

---

47 [1988] A.C. 431 HL, approving *Salmon v Seafarer Restaurants Ltd* [1983] 1 W.L.R. 1264.
48 [1963] 1 W.L.R. 1117 at 1124.

> "Supposing, for instance, that there was only one way of getting into and out of premises, and it was by a footbridge over a stream which was rotten and dangerous. According to [the old law] the occupier could escape all liability to any visitor by putting up a notice: 'This bridge is dangerous', even though there was no other way by which the visitor could get in or out, and he had no option but to go over the bridge. In such a case, s.2(4) makes it clear that the occupier would nowadays be liable. But if there were two footbridges, one of which was rotten, and the other safe a hundred yards away, the occupier could still escape liability, even today, by putting up a notice: 'Do not use this footbridge. It is dangerous. There is a safe one further upstream'. Such a warning is sufficient because it does enable the visitor to be reasonably safe."

The chimney sweeps in *Roles v Nathan* had been given clear warnings of the danger by the defendant's heating engineer. According to Lord Denning MR, with whom Harman LJ agreed, these warnings enabled the sweeps to be reasonably safe, by making it clear that the danger could be avoided if they desisted from working in the flue when the boiler was alight. Pearson LJ, however, took a different view, holding that the warnings were of little value to the sweeps, given that the defendant's agents had themselves ignored the advice of the heating engineer and had lit the boiler before the sweeps had completed their work.

Not only must the warning tell the visitor what to do in order to avoid the danger, it must be given in terms which are comprehensible to the visitor. It is recognised that children do not always give warnings the attention they deserve, so that an occupier may be required to take other steps, such as the erection of a barrier, to discharge the common duty of care.

A number of other points should be noted about s.2(4)(a). First, the courts have made it clear that there is no duty to warn irresponsible visitors against dangers which are perfectly obvious. Lord Hoffmann in *Tomlinson v Congleton BC* argued that:

> "A duty to protect against obvious risks or self-inflicted harm exists only in cases in which there is no genuine and informed choice . . . or some lack of capacity, such as the inability of children to recognise danger."[49]

In *English Heritage v Taylor*,[50] therefore, the key issue for the court was whether allowing visitors to a castle to use an informal path down a steep slope where there was a risk of falling from a height into the moat was an obvious danger or not. The court held that it was not an obvious danger and that there had been no warning sign. On that basis, English Heritage were

---

49   [2003] UKHL 47; [2004] 1 A.C. 46 at [46].
50   [2016] EWCA Civ 448; [2016] P.I.Q.R. P14.

found liable.[51] In contrast, in *Darby v National Trust*[52] where the claimant had drowned in a pond of deep murky water, the court found that there were no hidden dangers in the pond. The risk of drowning in deep murky water was one which would have been obvious to any adult who went into the pond. The defendants were therefore not found to be under a duty to place notices around the pond warning of this risk. Similarly, in *Edwards v Sutton LBC*,[53] the Court of Appeal held that an unfenced ornamental bridge with low parapets presented an obvious danger and provision of side barriers or a warning would not have been appropriate.

Secondly, s.2(4)(a) refers to a warning given *by the occupier*.[54] Strictly speaking, it must follow that a warning given by someone other than the occupier is prima facie insufficient to discharge the occupier's duty of care, even if it enables the visitor to be reasonably safe. This being said, a warning given to a visitor by a third party will, of course, form part of "all the circumstances of the case" and as such (according to s.2(2) of the Act) will be a relevant consideration. Thirdly, it should be noted that the words "without more" raise the possibility that a warning which does not by itself enable the visitor to be reasonably safe might be regarded as sufficient to discharge the common duty of care when taken together with some other factor in the case (the presence of a guard rail, for example).

Finally, it should be noted that a sign stating that "visitors enter at their own risk" is *not* a warning at all, but an attempt to invoke the defence of voluntary assumption of risk. Similarly, a sign declaring that "no responsibility is accepted for any loss or damage on the premises" is *not* a warning, but an attempt to exclude liability. These matters are discussed towards the end of this chapter.

Entrusting work to independent contractors

This chapter has set out the extent to which independent contractors, who are possessed of special skill, can be expected to look after their own safety while they are on the premises. Here, we look at a different situation, namely where a visitor (other than the independent contractor) suffers loss because of the independent contractor's negligence in carrying out work for the occupier. The visitor's loss may result from the manner in which the contractors conduct themselves whilst on the premises (the visitor trips over a toolbox left in a corridor), or it may result from a defect in the premises left by poor workmanship (the visitor falls down a staircase negligently erected by the contractors). Under the doctrine of vicarious liability (discussed in Ch.7) an employer is not normally responsible for the negligent actions of independent contractors.

8–024

---

51   Subject to a defence of contributory negligence in that the visitor had taken a risk of falling down the slope in using an informal path.

52   [2001] EWCA Civ 189. See also *Poppleton v Trustees of the Portsmouth Youth Activities Committee* [2008] EWCA Civ 646; [2009] P.I.Q.R. P1 and *Evans v Kosmar Villa Holiday Plc* [2007] EWCA Civ 1003; [2008] 1 W.L.R. 297.

53   [2016] EWCA Civ 1005; [2017] P.I.Q.R. P2. See also *Singh v Cardiff CC* [2017] EWHC 1499 (QB) (no liability for unfenced open land adjacent to footpath leading down to stream into which claimant fell).

54   In *Roles v Nathan* [1963] 1 W.L.R. 1117, this requirement was satisfied because the heating engineer who gave the warnings was the defendant's agent.

Can an occupier therefore escape all blame for dangers created by independent contractors on the premises? The House of Lords decision in *Thomson v Cremin*,[55] in 1941, had suggested that an occupier would usually remain personally responsible for the shortcomings of contractors employed on the premises, but this decision was criticised by the Law Reform Committee in 1954. The committee's recommendations were given statutory force in s.2(4)(b) of the Act.

In summary, s.2(4)(b) provides that where a visitor suffers damage due to "the faulty execution of any work of construction, maintenance or repair"[56] by an independent contractor, the occupier is not normally liable if, in all the circumstances of the case:

- it was reasonable to entrust the work to an independent contractor;

- the occupier took reasonable steps to satisfy himself or herself that the contractor was competent; and

- the occupier took reasonable steps to satisfy himself or herself that the work had been properly done.

The first of these requirements has posed few problems for the courts, which appear to have taken the view that it will be reasonable to entrust work to a contractor whenever that work is of a type which is normally undertaken by contractors. As to the second requirement, a contractor will usually be taken to be competent unless the occupier is aware of facts which suggest incompetence (faulty work carried out in the past, for example). In some circumstances, however, it may be appropriate for an occupier to check a contractor's competence by seeing that he or she is a member of a relevant trade association, holds relevant qualifications, is suitably experienced and is insured. Such circumstances arose in *Bottomley v Todmorden Cricket Club*,[57] where the defendants were held liable for the activities of independent contractors providing a fireworks display—the hazardous nature of the activity placed the defendants under a duty to take positive steps to check the competence of the contractors, and, in particular, to check whether they were insured. In *Gwilliam v West Hertfordshire NHS Trust*,[58] the defendant hospital had engaged a contractor to operate a "splat-wall" at a fund-raising event. (A "splat-wall" is an amusement whereby participants stick themselves to a wall with Velcro by bouncing off a trampoline.) The hospital had selected the contractor's name from the phone book and had

---

55   Reported at [1953] 2 All E.R. 1185.
56   The courts have interpreted these words broadly. It was held in *Ferguson v Welsh* [1987] 1 W.L.R. 1553, e.g. that the section is applicable to demolition work, even though this is, of course, the complete antithesis of "construction, maintenance and repair".
57   [2003] EWCA Civ 1575, [2004] P.I.Q.R. P18.
58   [2002] EWCA Civ 1041; [2003] Q.B. 443. But see *Naylor v Payling* [2004] EWCA Civ 560; [2004] P.I.Q.R. P36 (the duty to ensure that contractors carry public liability insurance is not a general "free-standing" duty. It only arises in special circumstances such as those in *Bottomley* and *Gwilliam*, where the defendant is organising a one-off event and enquiries about the contractor's insurance position are a reasonable means of assessing whether the contractor is likely to be competent).

paid him an extra £100 to operate the amusement, so as to benefit from his public liability insurance. The claimant was injured by the contractor's negligence, and it turned out that his public liability insurance had expired four days before the event. In an action against the hospital, a majority of the Court of Appeal held that, whilst the hospital had been under a duty to inquire into the contractor's insurance position, it would have been unreasonable to expect them to actually check his insurance certificate. Therefore, by accepting the contractor's assurances that he was insured, the hospital had discharged its duty of care to the claimant.[59]

Some difficulty has arisen in deciding whether and when it will be reasonable for an occupier to inspect a contractor's work personally, to see that it has been properly done. Two matters are relevant, namely the nature of the work undertaken and the character of the occupier. Thus, the more complex and technical the work, the less reasonable it is for the occupier to inspect it in person. Where, however, the occupier is a specialist company or a local authority, a more detailed inspection may be called for than would be required of a lay person. Two cases, both decided prior to the 1957 Act, illustrate the principles which the courts will apply.

8–025

In *Woodward v Mayor of Hastings*,[60] a pupil was injured when he slipped on a snow-covered step at school. The local authority was not able to escape liability by claiming that it had delegated the task of cleaning the step to the school cleaner who, it was argued, was an independent contractor.[61] The cleaning of the step was not a specialist task, and the danger was self-evident. The occupiers therefore had a duty to inspect the cleaner's work to see that it had been properly done. This seems a particularly harsh decision, but perhaps may be explained due to the risk of danger to children on an icy day requiring the school to check that such work was properly done, and the courts' sympathy towards child visitors.

In *Haseldine v Daw*,[62] on the other hand, the plaintiff was fatally injured when a lift in a block of flats fell to the bottom of its shaft, due to the negligence of independent contractors employed to repair the lift. It was held that the occupier had discharged his duty to visitors by engaging an apparently competent firm of engineers to maintain the lift. Because the work carried out on the lift was of a technical nature, the occupier could not be expected to ensure that it had been properly done. It was reasonable for him to leave the maintenance of the lift to an expert. Scott LJ observed that, if the occupier were made liable in such circumstances, this would effectively make him the insurer of the contractor's negligence.[63] Such a decision would be inconsistent with the principle discussed in Ch.1 that the law of tort operates most efficiently when it places liability on the party who is able to avoid the risk at least cost.

---

59   Sedley LJ, whilst agreeing with the majority as to the result of the case, thought that there should be no duty on the part of an occupier to check the insurance position of contractors.
60   [1945] 1 K.B. 174.
61   The court in fact found that the cleaner was the agent of the local authority rather than an independent contractor.
62   [1941] 2 K.B. 343.
63   [1941] 2 K.B. 343 at 356.

A few words must be said about the limits of the decision in *Haseldine v Daw*. Clearly, it is authority for the proposition that where the work in question involves complex or technical tasks, the occupier cannot be expected personally to see whether these tasks have been properly performed. It is far from certain, however, that the decision will allow an occupier to wash his or her hands of all responsibility simply by arguing that the work requiring special skill has been delegated to a contractor. Whatever may have been the position when the case was decided, it must be remembered that the 1957 Act requires an occupier to take reasonable steps to check the work. Thus, if contractors were to remove a lift (a specialist task) but were to leave the entrance to the shaft unguarded, it would be difficult for the occupier to escape liability, because the danger would be noticeable, even to a lay person. Where the occupier is a commercial concern, and the work in question is especially complex (such as the construction of a large building or ship), the occupier's duty to check each part of the work, as it is completed, may be onerous. In some cases, he or she may even have to engage independent experts to supervise the contractor's work.[64]

It is to be noted that s.2(4)(b) employs the past tense. It requires an occupier to "satisfy himself . . . that the work *had* been properly done". It follows from this that the section does not require an occupier to supervise a contractor's working practices on a day-to-day basis. However, an occupier may be held in breach of his or her duty to supervise the contractor's activities, not by virtue of s.2(4)(b), but because of a general breach of the "common duty of care", which requires an occupier to do what is reasonable "in all the circumstances of the case". Thus, an ordinary householder will not be expected to supervise the technical aspects of a contractor's day-to-day activities,[65] but may be under a duty to safeguard visitors against clear dangers created by those activities.

It is clear from the House of Lords decision in *Ferguson v Welsh*[66] that an occupier has no general duty to supervise the system of work used by a contractor so as to protect the contractor's employees from harm. Their Lordships stated that in very exceptional cases, an occupier who becomes aware that the contractor's employees are evidently in danger might be under a duty to ensure that dangerous working practices are stopped. Lord Goff, however, doubted whether an ordinary householder could really be expected to challenge the working practices of, for example, an electrician sent to work on his premises, even if he or she knew that those working practices were dangerous.[67]

Exclusion of liability

8–026

It was noted at the beginning of this chapter that an occupier may limit or exclude his or her liability under the Act. This is clear from the wording of s.2(1) of the Act, which imposes the

---

64 *AMF International Ltd v Magnet Bowling Ltd* [1968] 1 W.L.R. 1028. Compare *Gray v Fire Alarm Fabrication Services Ltd* [2006] EWCA Civ 1496; [2007] I.C.R. 247.
65 *Ferguson v Welsh* [1987] 1 W.L.R. 1553 per Lord Goff at 1564; *Green v Fibreglass Ltd* [1958] 2 Q.B. 245.
66 [1987] 1 W.L.R. 1553.
67 [1987] 1 W.L.R. 1553 at 1564.

"common duty of care" on an occupier "except in so far as he is free to and does extend, restrict, modify or exclude his duty . . . by agreement or otherwise". An occupier may exclude or limit his or her liability either by displaying a notice on the premises, or by an express term of a contract governing a visitor's entry. Both of these methods, however, are subject to the restrictions on exclusion of liability contained in the Unfair Contract Terms Act 1977 and Consumer Rights Act 2015. Before considering these Acts, it is convenient to deal with each method of exclusion in turn.

(1) Displaying a notice on the premises

8–027

It has been noted that exclusion notices are conceptually distinct from warning notices. Although it is not uncommon to see notices which combine exclusion of liability with an element of warning, in such cases, each element of the notice should be treated separately.

The fact that the 1957 Act permits an occupier to exclude liability by a notice is a reflection of the position which had been established under the common law. In *Ashdown v Samuel Williams & Sons Ltd*,[68] a licensee was injured while using a short-cut over the defendants' land on her way to work. The defendants were not liable because they had posted notices on the land stating that no person on the land would have any claim against the defendants for any injury whatsoever (a classic exclusion clause). The Court of Appeal held that, provided occupiers took reasonable steps to bring the exclusion of liability to the attention of persons on the premises, they were free to dictate their own terms of entry. The decision reflected the idea that "an Englishman's home is his castle"—it was based on the assumption that if the law allowed an occupier to exclude a person altogether from his or her premises, it followed that the occupier would be entitled to attach whatever conditions he or she liked to a person's permission to enter.

In *Ashdown*, the conflict between the freedom of an occupier to exclude liability and the right of a visitor to claim compensation for injury was resolved in favour of the occupier. Under modern law, however, this conflict is often resolved in favour of the visitor. Thus, if the case were decided today, the defendant would be unable to rely on the notice to exclude liability for personal injury, because the notice would be void under the Unfair Contract Terms Act 1977 s.2(1). The relevant provisions of this Act are considered more fully below.

(2) An express term of a contract

8–028

Where a visitor enters premises in accordance with a contract governing his or her entry, occupiers may include in that contract an express term which specifies the standard of care owed to their visitor. This standard may be lower (or higher) than the "common duty of care".

---

68   [1957] 1 Q.B. 409.

Where the contract in question contains no express term providing for a standard of care (or where it contains an express term which is void under the Unfair Contract Terms Act 1977 or Consumer Rights Act 2015, discussed below), s.5(1) of the Act operates to imply into the contract the "common duty of care". Thus, an occupier cannot argue that there is an implied term in the contract to the effect that the standard of care he or she owes is lower than the standard in the 1957 Act. Conversely, in the absence of an express term, the visitor cannot argue for the existence of an *implied* term to the effect that he or she is owed a *higher* contractual standard of care than the standard in the Act. Thus, in *Maguire v Sefton MBC*[69] the claimant contracted to use a leisure centre run by the defendants and was injured when one of the exercise machines malfunctioned. The Court of Appeal held that, since that contract was silent on the standard of care owed, the trial judge had been wrong to imply into the contract a strict term amounting to a warranty that the machine would be safe to use—in the absence of an express term, the only standard of care that could be implied was the standard demanded by the 1957 Act.

THE CONTRACT'S EFFECT ON THIRD PARTIES

8–029

It is important to note the effect of s.3 of the 1957 Act. The wording of this section is rather complex, but its effect is simple. The section deals with a situation where: (1) an occupier enters into a contract with A, under which the occupier permits A to use his or her premises, *and* (2) the contract contains an express term setting a standard of care in relation to A, *and* (3) the occupier agrees, by the terms of the contract, to let B enter the premises (even though the occupier has no contract with B). This situation may arise, for example, where a landlord occupier lets a room to A on terms which allow B to visit him.

In such cases, s.3 provides that if the relevant term of the contract sets a standard of care *lower* than the standard set in the 1957 Act, then that term does not apply to B. This is a straightforward application of privity of contract. Instead, B is owed the "common duty of care" under the Act. The section also provides, however, that if the term in question sets a *higher* standard of care than the Act demands, B is entitled to the benefit of the term, unless the contract expressly provides to the contrary. Thus, if a person, while visiting a tenant, suffers loss because of some defect in a part of the building over which the landlord retains occupational control (the stairway, for example), he or she can sue the landlord irrespective of any exclusion clause in the lease, but will also be able to sue if he or she suffers injury because the landlord has not provided security lighting as promised in the lease.

The Unfair Contract Terms Act 1977

8–030

Despite its title, the Unfair Contract Terms Act (UCTA) does not apply just to exclusion clauses in contracts, it also applies where the defendant attempts to restrict his or her liability in tort by displaying a notice when liability arises from the occupation of premises used for *business*

---

69   [2006] EWCA Civ 316; [2006] 1 W.L.R. 2550.

purposes by the occupier. Unfair Contract Terms Act 1977 s.1(1)(c) expressly states that the Act applies to notices excluding or limiting the common duty of care under the 1957 Act. Unfair Contract Terms Act 1977 s.2 provides that where the liability in question is "business liability", notices or contract terms which attempt to exclude liability for personal injury or death are void.[70] Notices or contract terms which attempt to exclude liability for other matters (damage to property, for example) are valid only if they are "reasonable".[71]

The main difficulty, here, is working out *when* UCTA applies. First, it must be shown that the occupier is attempting to exclude "business liability". Section 1(3) of the Act defines "business liability" as liability for the breach of an obligation arising from "things done . . . in the course of a business[72] . . . or . . . from the occupation of premises used for business purposes of the occupier". Clearly, then, an ordinary householder, unless he or she is using their house for business purposes, will not be affected by the 1977 Act. Secondly, UCTA s.2(4) makes it clear that the 1977 Act does not apply to "consumer notices", that is, notices which seek to exclude or restrict a trader's liability to a consumer,[73] which are regulated by the Consumer Rights Act 2015. This means that even if the defendant is occupying premises for business purposes, if the entrant is a "consumer" then the 1977 Act will not apply. It is important, therefore, not only to identify whether the defendant is a business, but whether the claimant is a consumer or non-consumer.

The rather vague definition of "business liability" in the 1977 Act has given rise to uncertainty in cases where the occupier used his or her land for a business purpose (farming or forestry, for example) but allowed people to access that land for a purpose unrelated to the business (to view an ancient monument, for example). This uncertainty was resolved by the Occupiers' Liability Act 1984 s.2. That section amended the definition of "business liability" to make it clear that in such cases the 1977 Act does not generally apply. According to the amended definition, liability to persons accessing premises for "recreational or educational purposes" is not "business liability" unless those persons are also accessing the premises for the business purposes of the occupier. Thus, a farmer can exclude liability to persons viewing an ancient monument on his land (unless he or she charges them a fee). It should be noted, however, that in such cases the occupier is only free to exclude liability resulting from the dangerous or defective state of the premises (i.e. liability for breach of the "occupancy duty"). The occupier cannot exclude liability for breach of the "activity" duty. Thus, if the visitor were hit by a negligently driven tractor, the 1977 Act would apply to prohibit exclusion of liability.

It remains unclear how far the words "recreational . . . purposes" can cover a situation where the occupier allows his or her premises to be used for charity fund-raising events. It is noteworthy that the word "charitable" is omitted from the description of purposes for which exclusion of liability is permitted. It is also noteworthy that the definition of "business" in s.14 of

---

70   s.2(1).
71   s.2(2). For the test of reasonableness, see s.11 and Sch.2.
72   "Business" includes the activities of professionals, government departments and local authorities: s.14.
73   See Consumer Rights Act 2015 s.61(4).

the 1977 Act includes activities which would not normally be thought of as "business", namely the activities of government departments and local authorities. This suggests that the courts would have little difficulty in extending the definition of "business" to cover charitable activities. "Professional fund raising", where only a proportion of the proceeds are donated to charity, is clearly a business activity, so the 1977 Act's prohibitions on excluding liability will apply. But do these prohibitions also apply even in cases where the use of the premises is wholly for a charitable purpose? The point is undecided, although some assistance may be derived from the pre-1977 decision in *White v Blackmore*.[74] Here, the plaintiff was killed because of defective barrier ropes at a charity motor-racing event. A majority of the Court of Appeal held that the organisers had effectively excluded liability by posting a notice outside the premises. The fact that the premises were being used for a charitable purpose, however, forms no part of the ratio of the case. Only Lord Denning MR (dissenting) refers to the point. In his view, the court should not be "over-anxious" about imposing liability on a charity where that liability is covered by insurance.

The Consumer Rights Act 2015

8–031

From October 2015, the Consumer Rights Act 2015 (CRA) alone now deals with exclusion clauses in consumer contracts and notices. The Act applies to notices seeking to exclude or restrict liability to the extent that it (a) relates to rights or obligations as between a trader and a consumer, or (b) purports to exclude or restrict a trader's liability to a consumer.[75] A "consumer" is a person acting for purposes that are wholly or mainly outside that person's trade, business, craft or profession. In contrast, a "trader" is a person or company acting for purposes relating to its trade, business, craft or profession.[76] So if my family and I visit a funfair and see a notice excluding liability put up by the business running the funfair, the validity of that notice would be governed by the 2015 Act, not the 1977 Act.

The CRA 2015 does have an equivalent provision to UCTA 1977 s.2(1). Section 65 provides:

> "(1) A trader cannot by a term of a consumer contract or by a consumer notice exclude or restrict liability for death or personal injury resulting from negligence.
>
> (4) In this section *"negligence"* means the breach of—
>   (a) any obligation to take reasonable care or exercise reasonable skill in the performance of a contract where the obligation arises from an express or implied term of the contract,

---

74 [1972] 2 Q.B. 651.
75 s.61(4).
76 Both definitions are found in s.2 of the 2015 Act.

> **(b) a common law duty to take reasonable care or exercise reasonable skill,**
> **(c) the common duty of care imposed by the Occupiers' Liability Act 1957."**

For notices or contract terms which attempt to exclude liability for other matters (damage to property, for example), the test is not reasonableness (as under UCTA 1977 s.2(2)), but fairness. A notice is unfair if, contrary to the requirement of good faith, it causes a significant imbalance in the parties' rights and obligations to the detriment of the consumer.[77] No mention is made in the 2015 Act of the Occupiers' Liability Act 1984. This seems to be an oversight, but is unfortunate nevertheless.

A MINIMUM NON-EXCLUDABLE STANDARD OF CARE?

8–032

In cases where the Unfair Contract Terms Act 1977 and Consumer Rights Act 2015 do not prohibit exclusion of liability, it is unclear whether the occupier is entitled to exclude liability altogether, or whether he or she will always owe his or her visitors some minimum standard of care, such as the lesser duty owed to trespassers, discussed below. Certainly, the 1957 Act does not entitle an occupier to exclude liability where he or she would not have been allowed to do so under the pre-Act common law. Thus, it has been suggested that there can be no exclusion of the common duty of care in relation to persons who enter premises under authority of law.[78] It might also be argued that a court should not allow an occupier ever to exclude the duty of "common humanity"[79] because, as a matter of policy, this represents a minimum standard of care owed to all, and should therefore be non-excludable. There is, however, no authority to support this argument and, unlike the 1957 Act, the 1984 Act does not mention whether an occupier is able to modify or restrict the duty of care. The point remains undecided therefore and, in the absence of case-law to the contrary, we must conclude that no such minimum non-excludable standard of care exists.[80]

---

77 CRA 2015 s.62(6). See also s.62(7): Whether a notice is fair is to be determined— (a)taking into account the nature of the subject matter of the notice, and (b) by reference to all the circumstances existing when the rights or obligations to which it relates arose and to the terms of any contract on which it depends.

78 W. E. Peel and J. Goudkamp, *Winfield & Jolowicz on Tort*, 19th edn (Sweet and Maxwell, 2014), 10–26.

79 See the House of Lords in *British Railways Board v Herrington* [1972] A.C. 877.

80 For further discussion, see L. C. B. Gower, "A Tortfeasor's Charter?" (1956) 19 M.L.R. 532, M. A. Jones, "The Occupiers' Liability Act 1984" (1984) 47 M.L.R. 713 and R. A. Buckley, "The Occupiers' Liability Act 1984. Has *Herrington* Survived?" [1984] Conv. 413.

Liability to Non-Visitors

8-033 We have seen that the 1957 Act applies only to "visitors", but that certain persons who enter premises are not "visitors", either because they were not invitees or licensees at common law, or because the Act specifically excludes them from its scope. All of these persons, however, with the exception of individuals exercising a public right of way,[81] are owed a duty under the Occupiers' Liability Act 1984.

The 1984 Act, then, applies to people who are on the premises without the occupier's permission. Usually, such people are trespassers, although it should be noted that a person who, for example, falls on to premises from other premises, is not, technically, a trespasser, because the tort of trespass requires that a defendant must intend to be on the land. It should also be noted that, especially in the case of children, it is not true to say that all trespassers are committing a moral wrong. People can become trespassers by accident if they wander on to an occupier's land not realising they need permission to be there.

Sometimes, a person enters premises as a visitor, but becomes a trespasser when he or she breaches some express or implied condition of his or her licence to be there. Thus, a visitor who strays from the permitted area, outstays his welcome, or begins to pursue some purpose unauthorised by the occupier will lose his protection under the 1957 Act and will be protected only by the 1984 Act.

The old law

8-034 In order to appreciate the scope of the 1984 Act, it is necessary to refer to the position at common law before it was passed. This is useful not only by way of background, but because the reasoning of Lord Diplock in *British Railways Board v Herrington*,[82] the leading pre-Act case, has influenced the courts when interpreting the Act's provisions.

The law as it stood in 1929 was shortly stated by Lord Hailsham in *Robert Addie & Sons (Collieries) Ltd v Dumbreck*[83]:

> **"The trespasser comes on to the premises at his own risk. An occupier . . . is liable only where the injury is due to some wilful act involving something more than the absence of reasonable care. There must be some act done with the deliberate intention of doing harm to the trespasser, or at least some act done with reckless disregard of the presence of the trespasser."**

---

81 *McGeown v Northern Ireland Housing Executive* [1995] 1 A.C. 233. As to persons exercising the "right to roam" under the Countryside and Rights of Way Act 2000, see Occupiers' Liability Act 1984 s.1A. See M. Stevens-Hoare and R. Higgins, "Roam free?" (2004) 154 N.L.J. 1846.
82 [1972] A.C. 877.
83 [1929] A.C. 358 at 365.

This approach reflected the idea that, as a matter of policy, an occupier should not be bound to protect a wrongdoer who violated his or her property rights by entering without permission. Yet, the rule could produce some harsh results. In *Addie* itself, for example, a child trespasser, playing in a field owned by the colliery, got caught in the machinery and died. The boy could not, as in *Glasgow Corp v Taylor*,[84] be classified as an implied licensee, because he had been repeatedly warned not to go into the field. The colliery therefore escaped liability.

In 1954, the Law Reform Committee, whose proposals formed the basis of the 1957 Act, stated that although it felt that the existing law relating to trespassers could be harsh when applied to children, it could find no adequate way of providing for child trespassers without imposing too great a burden on occupiers.[85] Trespassers were therefore omitted from the 1957 Act. In 1972, however, the law underwent a fundamental change with the decision in *British Railways Board v Herrington*.[86]

In *Herrington*, a six-year-old boy climbed through a gap in a fence beside an electrified railway line and was severely injured when he came into contact with the live rail. The defendants knew that children had been using the gap in the fence as a short-cut, but had taken no steps to deter them. The House of Lords held that the defendants were liable, observing that the policy considerations which had formed the basis of the old law on trespassers were no longer persuasive. Society's attitude towards trespassers had changed, so *Addie* was no longer good law. Their Lordships held that occupiers owed a duty of "common humanity" to trespassers. This was more than a duty to refrain from causing deliberate harm, but lower than the duty imposed by the 1957 Act. The precise scope of the duty, however, was unclear, because each of the Law Lords appeared to regard the matter slightly differently. In 1976, the Law Commission reported that it could not extract from the decision any single clear principle, and that legislation was required.[87] Eventually, this came in the form of the Occupiers' Liability Act 1984.

Occupiers' Liability Act 1984

8–035

It is convenient to speak of the 1984 Act applying to "trespassers", because this covers the majority of cases, although, as explained above, technically it can apply to other people as well. In summary, where the Act provides that an occupier owes a duty to a trespasser, the duty is to take reasonable care to see that a trespasser does not suffer personal injury on his or her

---

84   [1922] 1 A.C. 44.
85   *Occupiers' Liability to Invitees, Licensees and Trespassers*, Cmnd.9305 (1954), para.80.
86   [1972] A.C. 877.
87   Law Commission Report No.75, Cmnd.6428 (1976).

premises.[88] No duty is owed in respect of a trespasser's property.[89] According to s.1(3)(a)–(c), the duty in respect of personal injury is owed if:

- the occupier is aware of the danger, or has reasonable grounds to believe it exists;

- the occupier knows or has reasonable grounds to believe that a trespasser is in the vicinity of the danger, or may come into that vicinity; and

- the risk of personal injury is one against which, in all the circumstances of the case, the occupier may be expected to offer the trespasser some protection.

Section 1(4) provides that where an occupier does owe a duty of care to a trespasser in respect of a risk, the duty is to take such care as is reasonable in all the circumstances of the case to see that the claimant does not suffer injury on the premises due to this danger. An occupier may discharge his or her duty to trespassers either by giving a warning of the danger, or by taking other reasonable steps to discourage trespassers from encountering the danger,[90] for example by securing the premises behind a locked gate. Note that, in contrast to the 1957 Act, there is no requirement under s.1(5) that the warning must enable the entrant to be reasonably safe. Thus, the duty can be discharged by a notice posted on the premises which gives a simple warning of the danger (for example "Danger–Rotten Footbridge"). The notice need not inform trespassers how to use the premises safely.

In applying these provisions, the courts have been anxious not to impose too onerous an obligation on occupiers. They have often held that there is no liability, either because no duty is owed under the Act, or because the duty has been discharged, or because the claimant voluntarily assumed the risk and is the author of his or her own misfortune. All three of these factors found favour with the House of Lords in *Tomlinson v Congleton BC*[91] to produce a finding of no liability. It was noted in Ch.5 that the reasoning in this case gave rise to, and is reflected in, the Compensation Act 2006 s.1. This provides that, in considering whether a defendant is in breach of a duty of care, courts should have regard to whether imposing liability might deter potential defendants from carrying out desirable activities.

Tomlinson v Congleton BC

8–036

In *Tomlinson*, the defendant council was in charge of a piece of recreational land on the site of a disused quarry. A lake had formed in part of the old quarry, which attracted many visitors in

---

88 s.1(4).
89 s.1(8), but see *Tutton v Walter* [1986] Q.B. 61.
90 s.1(5).
91 [2003] UKHL 47; [2004] 1 A.C. 46. See also *Donoghue v Folkestone Properties* [2003] EWCA Civ 231; [2003] Q.B. 1008 and *Rhind v Astbury Water Park Ltd* [2004] EWCA Civ 756.

hot weather. The defendant council had placed notices around the lake, reading: "Dangerous water: no swimming", and had employed rangers to warn visitors of the dangers of swimming in the lake. However, visitors would frequently swim in the lake, ignoring the notices, and were often rude to the rangers when asked to get out of the water. Following a number of serious incidents in which visitors nearly drowned, the council had resolved to make the beaches of the lake less attractive by dumping ballast on the shore to discolour the sand, and by planting vegetation at the lakeside, but, owing to financial constraints, this had not been done at the time of the claimant's accident. The claimant was an 18-year-old man, who entered the water, and, from a standing position in the shallows, executed a dive.[92] He hit his head on the sandy bottom, suffering severe injury which rendered him tetraplegic.

The House of Lords held that the risk of the claimant suffering injury had not arisen from the "state of the premises, or things done or omitted to be done on them" within the meaning of the 1984 Act. Rather, it had arisen from the claimant's own mis-judgment in attempting to dive into shallow water. It followed that the risk was not one against which the Act obliged the council to offer him any protection. According to Lord Hoffmann,[93] there was "an important question of freedom at stake" in the case. The Court of Appeal had held that the council, having been aware of the number of accidents suffered by irresponsible visitors swimming in the lake, was under a duty to safeguard those visitors by implementing its resolution to destroy the beaches. Lord Hoffmann pointed out, however, that the majority of people at the lakeside were behaving quite properly, enjoying themselves in a way which posed no risk to themselves or to others, and continued:

"It is unjust that the harmless recreation of responsible parents and children with buckets and spades on the beaches should be prohibited in order to comply with what is thought to be a legal duty to safeguard irresponsible visitors against dangers which are perfectly obvious."[94]

Accordingly, the "social cost" involved in denying responsible visitors access to recreational facilities should have been taken into account in deciding whether it was reasonable for the council to have destroyed the beaches in order to discourage irresponsible visitors from harming themselves. In their Lordships' view, this "social cost" could not be justified.

The approach in *Tomlinson* was followed in *Simonds v Isle of Wight Council*.[95] Here, the claimant, a five-year-old child, broke his arm when he fell from a swing near to a playing field being used for a school sports day. It had been argued that the school was under a duty to

92   There was some indecision as to whether he had become a trespasser by so doing—it was "swimming" that was prohibited by the notices, not entering the water.
93   *Tomlinson v Congleton BC* [2004] 1 A.C. 46 at 85.
94   [2004] 1 A.C. 46 at 85.
95   [2003] EWHC 2303 (QB); [2004] E.L.R. 59. See also *Poppleton v Trustees of the Portsmouth Youth Activities Committee* [2008] EWCA Civ 646.

immobilise the swings, or at least to place a cordon around them to discourage children from using them. In denying that the school was under such a duty, Gross J, referring to *Tomlinson*, pointed out that the result of a finding of liability might be that pleasurable sporting events such as the one in question would cease to be held, because of the high cost of liability insurance.

Applying the 1984 Act

8-037

The general principles the courts adopt in applying the Act are adequately illustrated by the reasoning in *Tomlinson*. There are few other noteworthy cases on the 1984 Act. This is largely because, as Lord Steyn observed in *Jolley v Sutton LBC*,[96] cases on occupiers' liability are "invariably very fact-sensitive". In other words, because the statutes (particularly the 1984 Act) are framed in such broad terms, the question of whether or not they produce liability in any given situation will depend heavily on the particular factual circumstances of each case. One interesting point of law, however, has arisen in respect of the words "has reasonable grounds to believe" under s.1(3). The decision in *White v St Albans City and DC*[97] made it clear that where an occupier erected a fence around the premises, this did not necessarily mean that he or she had "reasonable grounds" to expect trespassers in the vicinity, but uncertainty remained about how the words should be interpreted.

In *Herrington*, Lord Diplock had expressed the view that no duty to trespassers could arise unless an occupier had actual knowledge of facts as to the condition of his or her land, and actual knowledge of facts which suggested the likely presence of trespassers. An occupier was under no duty to make inquiry as to the state of the premises for the benefit of trespassers.[98] Under the 1984 Act, it was unclear whether this remained the position, or whether the words "reasonable grounds to believe" meant, for example, that an occupier who had no actual knowledge of a dangerous object on the premises could be liable in circumstances where a reasonable occupier *ought* to have known about its presence. However, in *Swain v Natui Ram Puri*[99] and *Ratcliff v McConnell*,[100] the Court of Appeal expressly endorsed Lord Diplock's views, suggesting that, on a proper construction of the Act, an occupier must actually know the primary facts (from which a reasonable occupier would conclude that there was a danger, or a likelihood of trespassers) before he or she can be liable. The judgment in *Ratcliff* also endorsed Lord Diplock's view that the financial resources of the particular occupier are relevant in deciding what level of protection he or she can reasonably be expected to offer to trespassers.

In *Swain*, a child trespasser had been seriously injured when, having scaled a seven foot

---

96   [2000] 1 W.L.R. 1082 at 1089.
97   *The Times* 12 March 1990. On the application of s.1(3) generally, see *Donoghue v Folkestone Properties* [2003] EWCA Civ 231; [2003] Q.B. 1008 and *Maloney v Torfaen CBC* [2005] EWCA Civ 1762; [2006] P.I.Q.R. P21.
98   [1972] A.C. 877 at 941.
99   [1996] P.I.Q.R. P442 CA.
100 [1999] 1 W.L.R. 670.

fence and wall covered with barbed wire to reach a roof, he fell through a skylight. It was argued that although the occupier did not know of trespassers in the vicinity, he should have known that a large unoccupied factory, adjacent to an inner-city council estate where many children lived, would be bound to attract child trespassers. The Court of Appeal rejected this view. A duty would only arise under the 1984 Act when the occupier had actual knowledge[101] of the relevant facts (here, that children would climb on the roof) or had known facts which gave reasonable grounds for this belief (e.g. had known about gaps in the barbed wire over the perimeter fence). Constructive knowledge would not suffice.

This view is supported by the later case of *Higgs v WH Foster (t/a Avalon Coaches)*.[102] Here, a policeman, investigating a theft at night, had fallen into a pit on the defendant's land used for inspecting the undersides of his coaches and which was usually covered. He was found to be a trespasser and the Court held that, under s.1(3)(b), it was not enough that it was easy to access the defendant's land. There was nothing to attract someone to the area nor which indicated an obvious short-cut for a trespasser from one place to another. The mere risk that someone might steal the defendant's coaches did not suffice. On this basis, there was no duty of care owed to the claimant—there were no reasonable grounds to suggest that the claimant might come into the vicinity of the uncovered pit late at night.

Equally in *Donoghue v Folkestone Properties*,[103] the Court found no liability towards a trespasser who had decided in late December to dive from a slipway into the harbour after midnight and had suffered serious injuries after hitting a grid pile some two feet below the surface of the water. Applying s.1(3)(b), the harbour owners had no reasonable grounds to believe trespassers would seek to dive from the slipway into Folkestone Harbour after midnight in mid-winter.

It should be noted that although the 1984 Act refers to liability for "things done or omitted to be done" on premises,[104] the decision in *Revill v Newbery*[105] makes it clear that the Act applies only to liability for the state of premises. It does not regulate the "activity duty". Thus, in considering whether the defendant was liable for accidentally injuring a trespasser, when firing a shotgun towards him intending to frighten him off, the Court of Appeal held that the provisions of the 1984 Act were not, strictly speaking, relevant, although they assisted greatly in determining the nature of the duty owed at common law, which was virtually identical to that owed under the Act.

Finally, it is worth remembering that, because the 1984 Act imposes liability for "the state of the premises",[106] there can be no liability in a situation where non-dangerous premises cause injury simply because of the unorthodox way the trespasser has chosen to use them.

---

101 This would extend to "shut eye" knowledge, that is, facts which are obvious but which the occupier chooses to ignore.
102 [2004] EWCA Civ 843.
103 [2003] EWCA Civ 231; [2003] Q.B. 1008.
104 s.1(1)(a).
105 [1996] 2 W.L.R. 239.
106 Occupiers' Liability Act 1984 s.1(1)(a).

(This, of course, was what happened in *Tomlinson*—the lake was not dangerous per se.) The point is illustrated by *Keown v Coventry Healthcare NHS Trust*.[107] Here, an 11-year-old boy fell while, in effect, using the underside of a fire escape as climbing frame. The defendant hospital escaped liability. In the circumstances, the boy had been aware of the danger, and in any event, the risk arose not from the state of the fire escape (which was just as one would expect it to be) but from the fact that the boy had chosen to trespass on it in such an unusual way.

Defences

8–038

The defences of voluntary assumption of risk and contributory negligence will arise under the Occupiers' Liability Act 1957 and the Occupiers' Liability Act 1984. It is not a defence that the claimant was trespassing illegally on the defendant's land as this would undermine the whole purpose of the 1984 Act. There is no explicit reference to the Law Reform (Contributory Negligence) Act 1945 in either the 1957 or the 1984 Act, which is surprising, in that the matter was expressly mentioned in the Law Reform Committee's recommendations which led to the passing of the 1957 Act.[108] Nevertheless, the courts have regularly applied the principle of contributory negligence in deciding cases under both Acts.[109] In contrast, the defence of voluntary assumption of risk is expressly preserved in both Acts[110] and plays a significant role in occupiers' liability cases such as *Ratcliff v McConnell*.[111] In *Ratcliff*, the occupiers of a college swimming pool were not liable when a student trespasser broke into the pool and dived head first into the water, suffering severe injuries. The Court of Appeal held that the student had voluntarily assumed the risk of his activities. He knew that the pool was closed for the winter and had been partially drained, and ought to have realised that it was dangerous to dive into shallow water.

These defences, together with other defences, are discussed further in Ch.16.

---

107 [2006] EWCA Civ 39; [2006] 1 W.L.R. 953. See also *Siddorn v Patel* [2007] EWHC 1248 (QB) (no liability where the claimant danced on a flat roof and fell through a skylight) and *Kolasa v Ealing Hospital NHS Trust* [2015] EWHC 289 (QB) (no liability when drunken man taken to the A & E department of a hospital climbed over a well-lit wall when the 30 foot drop was obvious).

108 *Occupiers' Liability to Invitees, Licensees and Trespassers*, Cmnd.9305 (1954) at para.78(ix).

109 See, e.g. *Stone v Taffe* [1974] 1 W.L.R. 1575, *Bunker v Charles Brand* [1969] 2 Q.B. 480 and *English Heritage v Taylor* [2016] EWCA Civ 448 where damages were reduced by 50%. In *Taylor*, the court justified its apportionment on the basis the defendant's fault had been of long standing, while the claimant's fault in taking a steep informal path had been momentary.

110 Occupiers' Liability Act 1957 s.2(5) and Occupiers' Liability Act 1984 s.1(6).

111 [1999] 1 W.L.R. 670.

9

Strict Liability Statutes

9–001

This chapter will examine two forms of strict liability imposed by statute: for defective products under the Consumer Protection Act 1987 and for damage caused by animals under the Animals Act 1971. In both cases, these forms of liability are in addition to the existing common law. The first part of this chapter will deal with the important provisions relating to defective products. This will be followed by a brief discussion of the Animals Act 1971.

Consumer Protection Act 1987

Introduction

9–002

In this section, we will examine liability for defective products in the law of torts, that is, products which are faulty and cause damage to individual victims. At common law, this is simply part of the tort of negligence, with which we should now be familiar. It should not be forgotten that *Donoghue v Stevenson*[1] involved an allegation that Mrs Donoghue's ginger beer bottle contained a snail, or, in other words, that Mrs Donoghue had been the victim of a defective product. The case is therefore not only the classic example of the duty of care in negligence, but also the classic example of liability for a defective product. However, the common law has now been supplemented by the enactment of the Consumer Protection Act 1987 Pt 1, which was introduced to comply with EC Directive 85/374[2] on liability for defective products. The

---

1 [1932] A.C. 562.
2 Directive 85/374 on the approximation of the laws, regulations and administrative provisions of the Member States concerning liability for defective products [1985] OJ L210/29.

aim of Pt 1 of the Act is to assist consumers in their claims against manufacturers of defective products by rendering the manufacturer (and associated parties) strictly liable, that is, liable without the need to prove fault. Despite Brexit, the UK government has indicated its firm intention to retain Pt 1 of the Act subject to minor amendments.[3]

We shall proceed by considering, first of all, the position at common law. This is of interest in highlighting why reform of this area of law was necessary and, more significantly, in understanding the position in law when the provisions of the 1987 Act do not apply. It is important to remember that the 1987 Act supplements the common law—it does not replace it. Secondly, we shall examine the provisions of the 1987 Act and the extent to which it imposes strict liability on manufacturers of products and on associated parties.

The Common Law Position

9-003

Prior to *Donoghue v Stevenson*, tort law provided little assistance to persons injured by a defective product. Most claimants were forced to rely on contract law, provided, of course, that they could establish the necessary contractual relationship. There are a number of benefits in bringing a contractual claim. First, the claimant is not required to show the fault of the seller, but simply that the seller is in breach of a term of the contract. The seller is therefore strictly liable for his or her breach. Secondly, contract law has no problem in awarding compensation for personal injury and property damage caused by the supply of a defective product[4] and will also award compensation for the cost of replacing the defective product itself. The buyer's position is further improved by the existence of implied terms. For example, under the Consumer Rights Act 2015, it is implied that, where the trader contracts to supply goods to a consumer, the goods must be of satisfactory quality[5] and be fit for their purpose.[6] On this basis, the consumer can sue for breach of contract if the goods fail to satisfy these terms.

There are, however, a number of disadvantages in bringing a claim in contract law. First, there must be a term (express or implied) in the contract which provides that the product should not be defective. Secondly, subject to the provisions of the Contract (Rights of Third Parties) Act 1999,[7] the rules of privity of contract only allow the parties to the contract to take

---

3 The Product Safety and Metrology etc. (Amendment etc.) (EU Exit) Regulations 2019 (SI 2019/696) reg.6

4 Subject of course to the rules of remoteness stated in *Hadley v Baxendale* (1854) 9 Ex 341. See *Grant v Australian Knitting Mills Ltd* [1936] A.C. 85 where the plaintiff sued the retailer under the contract of sale for the skin disease he suffered as a result of the defective state of the product sold.

5 Consumer Rights Act 2015 s.9.

6 Consumer Rights Act 2015 s.10.

7 s.1(1) provides that a third party may be able to enforce a term of a contract in his or her own right if either (a) the contract expressly provides for this or (b) the parties intend by a term of the contract to confer a benefit on him or her. The third party must be expressly identified in the contract by name, as a member of a class or as

the benefit of such terms.[8] Thirdly, the seller may exclude or limit liability for breach, although this will be subject to the provisions of the Consumer Rights Act 2015 and (for non-consumers) the Unfair Contract Terms Act 1977. Fourthly, although the chain of contracts between the manufacturer and the buyer will ultimately pass liability back up the chain to the manufacturer, this chain is easily broken, for example, by exclusion clauses or the insolvency of one of the parties. Liability may therefore fall arbitrarily on one party in the chain, regardless of the fact that the fault is solely that of the manufacturer.

As stated earlier, prior to 1932, tort law had a very limited application to defective products. A manufacturer would only be liable in tort if the product was classified as "dangerous" (for example, dynamite) or was actually known to the manufacturer to be dangerous, in which case he or she would then be obliged to warn the product's recipient of the danger. The distinction between "dangerous" and "non-dangerous" products was not particularly helpful and indeed made little sense. As Scrutton LJ famously commented:

> "Personally, I do not understand the difference between a thing dangerous in itself, as poison, and a thing not dangerous as a class, but by negligent construction dangerous as a particular thing. The latter, if anything, seems the more dangerous of the two; it is a wolf in sheep's clothing instead of an obvious wolf."[9]

The courts' reluctance to adopt a general principle of negligence liability and their adherence to the "privity of contract fallacy" (by which the contract between the manufacturer and the retailer was deemed to obstruct any other form of liability in favour of third parties)[10] prevented the emergence of a general defective product action in tort.

In *Donoghue v Stevenson*,[11] the majority of the House of Lords overturned the questionable distinction between dangerous and non-dangerous chattels and discarded the "privity of contract fallacy". The court saw no reason why the same set of facts should not give one person a right in contract and another a concurrent right to sue in tort.[12] It will be recalled that the case concerned the decomposed remains of snail, alleged to have been found in an opaque bottle of ginger beer that had been bought by Mrs Donoghue's friend. The existing rules of tort law seemed to preclude Mrs Donoghue's claim. A ginger beer bottle is not dangerous in itself and it was not known to contain a noxious substance. Mrs Donoghue had no contractual relationship

---

answering a particular description: s.1(3). These requirements will limit the number of possible claims under the Act.

8 Unless, of course, the purchaser sues for his or her own loss, which includes that arising from the injury of a third party. e.g. in *Frost v Aylesbury Dairy* [1905] 1 K.B. 608, the purchaser sued to recover the expenses to which he had been put by the illness and death of his wife due to typhoid fever caught from the milk supplied by the defendants.

9 *Hodge & Sons v Anglo-American Oil Co* (1922) 12 Lloyd's Rep. 183 at 187.

10 See *Winterbottom v Wright* (1842) 10 M. & W. 109; 152 E.R. 402, discussed in Ch.2.

11 [1932] A.C. 562.

12 [1932] A.C. 562 per Lord Macmillan at 610.

with any of the parties and so could not rely on any implied terms as to quality. Nevertheless, the majority of the House of Lords held that where a manufacturer sells goods in such a manner that he intends them to reach the ultimate consumer in the form in which they have left him, with no reasonable possibility of intermediate examination, then the manufacturer will be liable for the absence of reasonable care in manufacturing the products.[13]

Three points may be noted about the decision in *Donoghue v Stevenson*. First, no distinction is drawn between different types of products. Logically, however, in assessing breach of duty (i.e. whether the manufacturer has exercised reasonable care), greater care would be required in the manufacture of explosives than in the manufacture of ginger beer. Indeed, the standard of care required for particularly dangerous products may be so high as practically to amount to a guarantee of safety.[14] Secondly, it should be noted that the manufacturer must intend the goods to reach the consumer intact. A reasonable possibility of intermediate examination would appear to exclude liability. Thirdly, the case deals with the manufacture of products and not with design. Design defects in products are of particular concern. Whereas a problem with manufacture may be limited to a particular batch, a design defect will affect many more products, thereby increasing the possibility of harm. We shall have to consider how *Donoghue v Stevenson*[15] applies to defects in design and what protection it gives to potential claimants.

The scope of *Donoghue v Stevenson*

9–004

The burden will be on the claimant to satisfy the ordinary rules of negligence, i.e. to establish a duty of care, breach, causation and remoteness. Their application to defective product claims will be discussed below.

The duty of care

9–005

This is the ordinary common law duty of care, discussed in Ch.2. It is not confined to the relationship between manufacturers and ultimate consumers. Makers of component parts, repairers, fitters, erectors, assemblers and even distributors may find themselves liable to the consumer for their failure to exercise reasonable care in dealing with a product. Equally, the range of claimants has extended beyond the ultimate consumer to parties coming into contact with the product. In *Stennett v Hancock and Peters*,[16] for example, a decision which followed shortly after *Donoghue*, the plaintiff suffered injury when part of a wheel from a passing lorry flew off and struck her on the leg. The lorry had recently been repaired by the second defend-

---

13   [1932] A.C. 562 per Lord Atkin at 599. Contrast Lord Buckmaster's strong dissenting judgment at 577–8.
14   [1932] A.C. 562 per Lord Macmillan at 612.
15   [1932] A.C. 562.
16   [1939] 2 All E.R. 578. See also *Haseldine v Daw* [1941] 2 K.B. 343 where a visitor using a lift in a block of flats was allowed to sue the repairers of the lift when the lift fell to the bottom of its shaft.

ants, who were found to have re-attached the wheel negligently. The court rejected the claim against the owners of the lorry, but the claim against the second defendants succeeded. *Donoghue v Stevenson* was held to extend to repairers where a bystander had suffered injury on the road as a result of their negligence. Moreover, it is clear that the duty may extend beyond the product itself to include its container, packaging, and directions or instructions for use.[17]

Breach

9–006

Whether the defendant has exercised reasonable care will obviously depend on the particular facts of each case, to which the general principles relating to breach stated in Ch.5 will be applied. Obviously, once the manufacturer knows of the defect, he or she will be negligent if production and marketing of the unsafe product continues.[18] It has been held that even when using component parts, a manufacturer should exercise care in purchasing suitable parts and should not simply assume that the component part is sound.[19] It is a more difficult question whether the manufacturer's duty extends to taking steps to recall products found to be defective after the products have gone into circulation. The best view, perhaps, is that the manufacturer may find himself or herself liable for failing to recall products already in circulation, particularly if the products have just entered the market, and should recall the product line in question as soon as practicable. As Sir Michael Ogden QC commented in *E. Hobbs v Baxenden Chemical Co*[20]:

> ". . . a manufacturer's duty of care does not end when the goods are sold. A manufacturer, who realises that omitting to warn past customers about something might result in injury to them, must take reasonable steps to attempt to warn them, however lacking in negligence he may have been at the time the goods were sold."

Where, however, the customer becomes aware of the defect and voluntarily chooses to use the product regardless, the Court of Appeal in *Howmet Ltd v Economy Devices Ltd*[21] held that the customer will use the product at his or her own risk—the manufacturer's liability to the end user would be limited in circumstances where the manufacturer has no control over who would use it or how. The true cause of the accident in *Howmet* was deemed to be not the defective product, but the failure of the factory-owner to put in place a reasonable system to deal with the malfunctioning product.

---

17   *Watson v Buckley, Osborne, Garrett & Co* [1940] 1 All E.R. 174.
18   *Wright v Dunlop Rubber Co Ltd* (1972) 13 K.I.R. 255 at 272.
19   *Winward v TVR Engineering* [1986] B.T.L.C. 366.
20   [1992] 1 Lloyd's Rep. 54 at 65. See also *Hamble Fisheries Ltd v L Gardner & Sons Ltd* [1999] 2 Lloyd's Rep. 1 at 9 per Mummery LJ; *Hollis v Dow Corning* (1996) 129 D.L.R. (4th) 609; *Carroll v Fearon* [1998] P.I.Q.R. P416.
21   [2016] EWCA Civ 847; 168 Con. L.R. 27.

Breach will generally not cause the claimant particular problems.[22] Although there is some authority that the *res ipsa loquitur* rule (see Ch.5) does not apply to defective products,[23] the courts have shown themselves willing to infer the absence of reasonable care from the fact a defect exists. For example, in *Grant v Australian Knitting Mills Ltd*,[24] Dr Grant claimed that he had suffered a skin disease from wearing underpants manufactured by the defendants, because they contained an excess of sulphites. The fact that the manufacturers had specifically adopted precautions against excess sulphite did not assist them. Lord Wright inferred that, in such circumstances, the chemicals could only be present in the garment if someone had been at fault. The plaintiff was not required to identify the exact person responsible for the breach, or to specify what he or she did wrong. The burden was therefore on the manufacturer to rebut the inference of negligence with sufficient evidence. This sort of approach lightens the claimant's burden considerably. It would, for example, have been very difficult for Mrs Donoghue to specify exactly what was so wrong with the manufacturing process that a snail could have entered a ginger beer bottle. Equally, in *Mason v Williams & Williams Ltd*,[25] the court was prepared to infer negligence where a plaintiff had been injured using a chisel which was too hard for its purpose. The chisel had come straight from the manufacturers and the court was prepared to find that the undue hardness must have been produced by carelessness in the course of manufacture, rather than by anything that had happened at the plaintiff's place of work. Finnemore J stated that showing that the chisel was defective was "as far as any plaintiff can be expected to take his case".[26] It should be noted, however, that his Lordship was careful to distinguish this approach from the doctrine of res ipsa loquitur. It should also be noted that the approach has only been applied in relation to manufacturing defects and appears to have little application to design defects.

Causation and remoteness

9–007 The ordinary rules of negligence apply and reference should be made to the principles outlined in Ch.6. The ordinary "but for" test will apply. Note, however, that particularly in medical cases, it may be difficult to differentiate between different possible causes of the injury.

---

22 The particular situation of defective equipment in the workplace should be noted. While at common law, employers will not be found negligent for supplying defective tools if they have taken reasonable care to purchase the tools from a reputable supplier (*Davie v New Merton Board Mills Ltd* [1959] A.C. 604), the Employer's Liability (Defective Equipment) Act 1969 imposes strict liability on employers providing defective equipment for the purposes of their business. See, further, Ch.7.

23 Lord Macmillan in *Donoghue v Stevenson* [1932] A.C. 562 at 622: "There is no presumption of negligence in such a case at present, nor is there any justification for applying the maxim *res ipsa loquitur*".

24 [1936] A.C. 85 at 101. See also *Carroll v Fearon* [1998] P.I.Q.R. P416.

25 [1955] 1 W.L.R. 549. See also *Hill v Crowe* [1978] 1 All E.R. 812.

26 [1955] 1 W.L.R. 549 at 552.

The type of loss recoverable

In defective product cases, the type of loss recoverable is limited by the same rules that apply in other negligence cases. A claimant, therefore, may recover foreseeable personal injury and property damage, but will not succeed in recovering pure economic loss. In *Murphy v Brentwood DC*,[27] the House of Lords emphasised that the cost of replacing a defective product will be classified as pure economic loss and is therefore non-recoverable. It was noted in Ch.3 that a claim for loss of profits is unlikely to succeed unless that loss of profits is consequential on property damage caused by the defective product supplied.[28] Whilst the "complex structure theory" was discussed in Ch.3 in relation to defective buildings,[29] its relevance to defective products generally must be considered here.[30] Component parts installed at the time of manufacture will be considered part of the product supplied.[31] In contrast, it appears that replacement parts, such as a replacement wheel, will be regarded as a separate product.[32] The decision of the Court of Appeal in *M/S Aswan Engineering Establishment Co v Lupdine Ltd*[33] highlights the difficulties of applying the complex structure idea to products. The plaintiffs in this case had shipped a consignment of a waterproofing compound (Lupguard) to Kuwait in plastic pails. The pails, which had been selected by the sellers of the compound, had collapsed in the high temperatures of Kuwait with the result that the entire consignment had been lost. As the seller of the compound was in liquidation, Aswan brought an action against the manufacturers of the pails for the loss suffered. The Court of Appeal dismissed the claim on the basis that the loss was not reasonably foreseeable, but Lloyd LJ expressed the provisional view that there was damage to "other property", namely the Lupguard, which would be recoverable even though the compound had been purchased in the pails.[34] Whilst finding such reasoning logical, Nicholls LJ expressed reservations as to a rule which would impose liability on the maker of a container—such as a bag, carton or bucket—for loss of its contents.[35] The authority of this case has, however, since been questioned.[36]

---

27 [1991] 1 A.C. 398; [1990] 2 All E.R. 908.
28 *Spartan Steel & Alloys Ltd v Martin & Co (Contractors) Ltd* [1973] Q.B. 27 CA.
29 See *D & F Estates v Church Commissioners* [1989] A.C. 177.
30 See A. Tettenborn, "Components and product liability: damage to 'other property'" [2000] L.M.C.L.Q. 338.
31 See, e.g. *The Rebecca Elaine (Hamble Fisheries Ltd v L Gardner & Sons Ltd)* [1999] 2 Lloyd's Rep. 1 (defective pistons in an engine where the manufacturer of the engine was sued) cf. *Nitrigin Eireann Teoranta v Inco Alloys* [1992] 1 W.L.R. 498, May J.
32 See *M/S Aswan Engineering Establishment Co v Lupdine Ltd* [1987] 1 W.L.R. 1 at 21.
33 [1987] 1 W.L.R. 1.
34 Fox LJ in agreement.
35 [1987] 1 W.L.R. 1 at 29.
36 See Mance LJ in *Bacardi-Martini Beverages Ltd v Thomas Hardy Packaging Ltd* [2002] EWCA Civ 549; [2002] 2 Lloyd's Rep 379 at [18], who doubted the authority of this case in that it preceded *Murphy v Brentwood DC* and "occurred when the star of *Junior Books Ltd v Veitchi Co Ltd* [1983] 1 A.C. 520 was still high in the sky".

Particular problems relating to defective products

▶ (1) What is a product?

9–009

In *Donoghue v Stevenson*, Lord Atkin restricted himself to consideration of articles of common household use, where everyone, including the manufacturer, would know that the articles would be used by persons other than the actual ultimate purchaser.[37] The courts have subsequently been prepared to interpret "product" quite broadly to include tombstones,[38] hair dye,[39] industrial chemicals,[40] lifts[41] and motor cars.[42]

▶ (2) Has there been intermediate examination or interference?

9–010

This is, in a sense, a question of causation. To find the defendant liable, the court must be satisfied that he or she caused the defect, and that it was not due to the fault of another party in the supply chain (or even the claimant). In *Grant v Australian Knitting Mills Ltd*,[43] it was argued that the mere possibility that the goods might be tampered with after they had left the factory should enable the manufacturer to escape liability. The defendants claimed that because the garments had been wrapped in paper packets to allow shopkeepers to sell each garment separately, there was a possibility of interference with the goods, and this meant the defendants should not be liable. The Privy Council dismissed this argument. Interference was a question of fact, and here it was beyond question that the garment had reached Dr Grant subject to the same defect as when it left the manufacturer.

Where, however, there is a reasonable possibility or probability[44] of interference, the court will take a different line. In *Evans v Triplex Safety Glass Co Ltd*,[45] Mr Evans had bought a car which had been fitted with a "Triplex Toughened Safety Glass" windscreen. One year later, the windscreen shattered whilst Mr Evans was driving the vehicle, injuring himself, his wife and his son. In an action against the manufacturers of the safety glass, Porter J held that Mr Evans had not given sufficient evidence to satisfy the court that the manufacturers were at fault. His Lordship suspected that the real fault lay with the fitting of the windscreen into its frame. In

---

37 [1932] A.C. 562 at 583.
38 *Brown v Cotterill* (1934) 51 T.L.R. 21.
39 *Watson v Buckley, Osborne, Garrett & Co* [1940] 1 All E.R. 174.
40 *Vacwell Engineering Co v BDH Chemicals* [1971] 1 Q.B. 88.
41 *Haseldine v Daw* [1941] 2 K.B. 343.
42 *Andrews v Hopkinson* [1957] 1 Q.B. 229 at 237.
43 [1936] A.C. 85.
44 Goddard LJ in *Haseldine v Daw* [1941] 2 K.B. 343 at 376 suggested that the word "probability" is more accurate. In that case, the engineers repairing the lift could not have reasonably contemplated any immediate inspection and so owed a duty to any person who, in the ordinary course of events, would be expected to make use of the thing repaired.
45 [1936] 1 All E.R. 283.

addition, Mr Evans had owned the car for a year before the accident and either he or his supplier might reasonably have inspected the windscreen prior to the accident.

The question of inspection or examination may be a difficult one, particularly where one party in the contractual chain, other than the manufacturer, has had the opportunity to examine the product but chooses not to do so. There is no general obligation at law on such parties to subject all goods to exhaustive examination. The manufacturer will therefore remain liable where he or she has no reason to contemplate that the defect will be discovered before the product reaches the consumer. There may be circumstances, however, when the manufacturer may reasonably expect a third party to examine the product and, if such examination would have revealed the defect, assert that it is the third party's failure to examine the product adequately (rather than defective manufacture) which has caused the injury. In such circumstances, it will be the third party and not the manufacturer who is liable to the claimant.

This question did not arise in *Donoghue*. The ginger beer bottle was opaque and had been sealed, so no-one could have examined its contents prior to consumption. In *Andrews v Hopkinson*,[46] however, a second-hand car dealer, who did have the opportunity to check cars for defects, was held liable for failing to inspect his cars for obvious defects. In this case, which involved a hire purchase agreement for a second-hand car, the plaintiff brought an action against the dealer for injuries resulting from an accident due to the defective steering mechanism of the car. The car was around 18 years old and had been in the dealer's possession for a week. The court heard evidence that the steering mechanism was a particular danger in an old car, which could have been discovered on inspection. In such circumstances, McNair J was in no doubt that the defendant was liable for failing to examine the vehicle, or at least for failing to warn the claimant that no examination had been carried out. Similarly, in *Vacwell Engineering Co v BDH Chemicals*,[47] a party supplying chemicals was expected to inform himself about the potential hazards and warn the recipient accordingly.

The real question is whether the defendant can reasonably expect a third party or the consumer to undertake an inspection in the circumstances. For example, in *Griffiths v Arch Engineering Co Ltd*,[48] a sub-contractor, who had hired a portable grinding tool which was in a dangerous condition, was not liable to an injured workman for failing to examine the tool. It was clear that the tool had been hired for immediate use, and because the plant hire company had no reason to suppose that an examination would be carried out, they would be liable. The defendant can secure his or her position by attaching a warning to the product that it must be examined prior to use. This places a duty on the third party to examine the product and, of course, renders intermediate examination reasonably probable. By this means, the seller of a dangerously defective car in *Hurley v Dyke*,[49] who had warned that the car was sold "as seen

---

46 [1957] 1 Q.B. 229 at 237. See also *White v Warwick* [1953] 1 W.L.R. 1285; *Griffiths v Arch Engineering Co Ltd* [1968] 3 All E.R. 217.
47 [1971] 1 Q.B. 88.
48 [1968] 3 All E.R. 217.
49 [1979] R.T.R. 265 HL. See also *Kubach v Hollands* [1937] 3 All E.R. 907.

and with all its faults", avoided liability to a claimant, who had been injured in a subsequent accident caused by the car's defective condition.

▶ (3) The manufacture/design distinction

9–011

The cases discussed so far have been concerned with manufacturing defects where, due to a problem at the manufacturing stage, the product contains a particular defect which has injured the claimant. This is distinct from a design defect, which arises from the very nature of the product itself. The latter is obviously more potentially damaging. Whilst a bad batch of goods will affect a number of consumers, a design defect will affect every consumer of the product and may be impossible to discover on inspection or examination. In considering liability for defective goods, therefore, design defects must be given particular attention.

The case law, however, is primarily concerned with manufacturing defects. There are a number of reasons for this. First, *Donoghue*, the main precedent in this area of law, concerns a manufacturing defect. Secondly, and more fundamentally, it is more difficult to show breach of duty and causation for design defects. This presents particular problems for litigants. As shown above, the courts are prepared to infer breach in respect of manufacturing defects and this places the burden on the defendant to rebut this inference by giving evidence that the defect has been caused by the fault of another party, or that its manufacturing system operates in a reasonable manner. The burden on the defendant has been held to be close to strict liability. In contrast, the same reasoning does not apply to design defects. If a person develops cancer after taking drug X, the claimant must establish not only fault by the manufacturer in designing drug X, but that his cancer has been caused by drug X and not other factors, for example, the claimant's genetic makeup, or environmental pollution. This is a far from easy task and is rendered more difficult if the person is taking other drugs or undertaking other medical treatment. The claimant will only be able to obtain disclosure of the relevant design documentation after he or she has commenced the claim and incurred considerable costs. Without an admission of fault by the manufacturer, or inside information, it will be difficult to bring a claim in the first place. In contrast where a person bites into a bar of chocolate and finds a lump of metal in it, the court will infer that the metal can only be present due to the fault of someone in the manufacturing process and, in the absence of evidence of interference, or a duty to inspect, will turn to the manufacturer to meet this claim.

The problems arising from design defects were only too apparent in the thalidomide scandal of the 1960s and 1970s.[50] Thalidomide was a drug used by mothers to counter morning sickness, but which was subsequently found to have appalling side-effects, in that between 1959 and 1962 an estimated 10,000 children were born with physical deformities. This was a classic example of a design defect. Yet, when the parents brought claims in negligence, they experienced difficulty in showing that the manufacturers had failed to

---

50   Discussed by Teff and Munro in H. Teff and C. Munro, *Thalidomide: the legal aftermath* (Saxon House, 1976).

take reasonable care in producing the drug. The manufacturer's conduct is, as discussed in Ch.5, judged by reference to what was reasonable at the time the product was put into circulation.[51] The manufacturer will not be judged with hindsight if the dreadful consequences were not foreseeable by the reasonable manufacturer at the time the product was put in circulation.[52]

The need for change?

Whilst the common law had reached a fairly satisfactory position in relation to manufacturing defects—with the courts willing to infer negligence and adopt a flexible approach towards liability–the thalidomide tragedy focused attention on the problems litigants might experience in relation to design defects. This led to demands for a change in the law. At this time (the 1970s), the concept of strict liability as a means of ensuring loss distribution and compensation was particularly fashionable (see the Report of the Pearson Commission in 1978, discussed in Ch.1). It was suggested that manufacturers should be strictly liable for defects in their products for the following reasons:

9–012

- the manufacturer created the product and therefore the hazard. Since this risk was created in the pursuit of profit, it was reasonable to expect the manufacturer to accept liability for the hazards caused;

- the manufacturer was best placed to insure against the risk, and the price of insurance could be distributed via the price of the product; and

- liability would give the manufacturer a greater incentive to take safety precautions.

Such arguments are not without problems. For example, where individuals have contents insurance for their personal property, forcing manufacturers to take out insurance against product liability would lead to double cover, which is economically inefficient. The Law Commission in its 1977 Report, *Liability for Defective Products*,[53] suggested that this could be dealt with by limiting strict liability to claims for personal injury and death, but this has not been implemented. A manufacturer is also likely to disagree fundamentally with the first argument which arguably penalises the manufacturer's initiative in placing a product on the market which may have enormous social benefits and responds to consumer choice.

Nevertheless, growing pressure for reform, combined with European initiatives to harmonise the rules on defective products in Member States, resulted in a change in the law: the EC

---

51   See *Roe v Ministry of Health* [1954] 2 Q.B. 66 at 84: "We must not look at the 1947 accident with 1954 spectacles".
52   The legal issues were never decided as the thalidomide litigation was settled.
53   Report No.82, Cmnd.6831.

Directive 85/374 of 25 July 1985 (the Product Liability Directive).[54] This required Member States to bring into force, within three years, changes in their national laws to comply with the Directive.[55] The UK, on 1 March 1988, brought into force the Consumer Protection Act 1987 Pt 1. Section1(1) stated that:

> **"This Part shall have effect for the purpose of making such provision as is necessary in order to comply with the product liability Directive and shall be construed accordingly."**

This meant that, if the wording of the Act appeared to conflict with the Directive, this conflict should be resolved in favour of the Directive and any dispute would be settled by the Court of Justice of the European Union (CJEU). Post-Brexit, an amended s.1(1) will read in the past tense: "This Part was enacted . . .".[56] It should be remembered, however, that leaving the EU does not mean that future case-law of the CJEU will not be considered as persuasive authority, simply that it will not be binding on the UK courts. It remains to be seen how far UK courts will continue to consider EU case-law when applying this Part of the Act.

Consumer Protection Act 1987

9–013

The Product Liability Directive, in its preamble, states:

> **". . . liability without fault on the part of the producer is the sole means of adequately solving the problem, peculiar to our age of increasing technicality, of a fair apportionment of the risks inherent in modern technological production."**

Consumer Protection Act 1987 Pt 1 (the Act) therefore seeks to make the manufacturer of a product (and others dealing with it) liable without proof of fault for personal injury and property damage caused wholly or partly by a defect in a product. The provisions of the Act and the way in which they operate are set out below. It should be noted, however, that by granting the manufacturer certain defences and failing to give a precise definition of "defect", the Act has led many to question how "strict" the liability imposed by the Act actually is.[57]

---

54 Directive 85/374 on the approximation of the laws, regulations and administrative provisions of the Member States concerning liability for defective products [1985] OJ L210/29.
55 Directive 85/374 art.19.
56 The Product Safety and Metrology etc. (Amendment etc.) (EU Exit) Regulations 2019 (SI 2019/696) reg.6.
57 See, e.g. J. Stapleton, "Products liability reform—real or illusory?" (1986) 6 OJLS 392 and *Product Liability*

Who can sue?

This obvious question is not dealt with expressly by the Act. However, reading ss.2(1) and 5(1), it clearly allows litigants to sue if they suffer damage as a result of a defective product.

Who is liable?

Reference should be made here to s.1(2) and s.2 generally. The Act includes not only manufacturers (or "producers") but extends to own-branders and, until Brexit, parties importing goods into the EU. Suppliers are not generally liable, except under the special provisions of s.2(3). However, the Act does not, of course, prevent a supplier from being sued for breach of contract.

(1) Producer—ss.1(2) and 2(2)(a)

Section 1(2) gives three different meanings for a "producer". The first and simplest is that of a manufacturer of a product.[58] It should be noted that a manufacturer of a component part of the product is equally classified as a producer, so that if the product fails due to a malfunction of a component part, both the manufacturer of the final product and the manufacturer of the component part will be liable.[59]

The second and third meanings relate to goods which have not been manufactured. If the defendant has "won or abstracted" the product[60] (for example, mined coal), or has carried out an industrial or other process on the goods to which the essential characteristics of the goods are attributable[61] (as in the case of canned peas or frozen fish, for example), he or she will be classified as a producer. This last category is not particularly clear and leaves a number of important questions (such as what are the "essential characteristics" of the goods) to the discretion of the court. Those involved in packaging will not be affected unless the packaging alters the essential characteristics of the product.

(2) Own-brander—s.2(2)(b)

Section 2(2)(b) states that liability may attach to:

(Butterworths, 1994) and C. Newdick, "The future of negligence in product liability" (1987) 103 L.Q.R. 288. For general reference, see D. Fairgrieve and R.S. Goldberg, *Product Liability*, 3rd edn (OUP, 2020).

58   Consumer Protection Act 1987 s.1(2)(a).
59   Consumer Protection Act 1987 s.2(5). Liability is "joint and several". This is discussed in Ch.17.
60   Consumer Protection Act 1987 s.1(2)(b).
61   Consumer Protection Act 1987 s.1(2)(c).

> "any person, who, by putting his name on the product or using a trade mark or other distinguishing mark in relation to the product, has held himself out to be the producer of the product."

The important question here is whether the person has held himself out as the producer. This will not be so in the case of a product in a supermarket marked, for example, "made for Sainsburys". It is a more difficult question if the product is marketed as "Sainsburys baked beans"—is Sainsburys claiming to be the producer of the product or simply selling it at a negotiated reduced price under its own label? The general view is that unless a supermarket can be said to be holding itself out as having produced the product, it will not satisfy this category.[62] This will obviously make it more difficult for the consumer to identify who the actual manufacturer of the goods really is, but s.2(3) below may assist.

(3) Importer into EU (pre-Brexit); importer into the UK (post-Brexit)—s.2(2)(c)

9–018   This provision seeks to save claimants the time and expense of pursuing defendants outside the EU. Pre-Brexit, the subsection provides that:

> "any person who has imported the product into a member State from a place outside the member States in order, in the course of any business of his, to supply it to another"

will be liable. This provision is confined to imports into the EU. It does not affect those who import from one EU country to another, where liability will remain with the first importer.

Post-Brexit, it will be amended to cover "any person who has imported the product into the United Kingdom in order, in the course of any business of his, to supply it to another".[63]

The product must be imported for supply "in the course of any business of his" and so if person X imports a car from Japan privately for his own use, he will not be liable under the Act to any person who is injured when it explodes due to a defect in its manufacture.

(4) Supplier—s.2(3)

9–019   The supplier is not generally liable under the Act. However, s.2(3) deals with the situation where the consumer has bought defective goods which do not indicate the identity of the pro-

---

62   For a contrary view, see F. Dias Simões, "Private labels and products liability: hypermarkets as apparent producers" [2013] Jur. Rev. 469.

63   The Product Safety and Metrology etc. (Amendment etc.) (EU Exit) Regulations 2019 (SI 2019/696) reg.6.

ducer. Where damage has been caused wholly or partly by a defect in a product, the supplier will be liable if:

- the claimant has requested the supplier to identify the producer/own-brander or importer of the product;

- the request is made within a reasonable period after the damage has occurred and at a time when it is not reasonably practicable for the person making the request to identify those persons; and

- the supplier fails within a reasonable period after receiving the request either to comply with the request or to identify the person who supplied the product to him.

The consumer can therefore trace the producer through the chain of supply. The supplier will be able to pass on liability, provided, of course, he or she has maintained proper records of his or her dealings. It should be noted that the mere supply of the end product does not mean that the supplier is deemed to have supplied all the component parts.[64] This means that the supplier will not be liable for failing to identify the producers of all the component parts.

Liability under the Act therefore extends beyond the manufacturer, but it should be noted that it is nevertheless not as wide as the common law, which extends to repairers, fitters, erectors and assemblers.

What is a product?

This is defined by s.1(2) to include any goods[65] or electricity and includes a product which is comprised in another product, whether by virtue of being a component part or raw material or otherwise. From 4 December 2000, "product" includes all primary agricultural products (that is, food sold in its raw state such as meat or vegetables) and game. Although these products were previously excluded from the Act,[66] it became desirable in the wake of the BSE crisis to include these products and "help restore consumer confidence in the safety of agricultural products".[67] Accordingly, following Directive 1999/34, the Act was modified.[68]

`9–020`

---

64   Consumer Protection Act 1987 s.1(3).

65   Consumer Protection Act 1987 s.45(1) defines "goods" to include substances, growing crops and things comprised in land by virtue of being attached to it and any ship, aircraft or vehicle. It does not seem to include the land itself.

66   Article 15(1)(a) of the 1985 Directive rendered it optional to include primary agricultural produce and game within the definition of "product". Solely Greece, France, Luxembourg, Finland, Sweden and Austria (with respect to GMOs) chose to include such products.

67   Recital 5 to Directive 1999/34 on the approximation of the laws, regulations and administrative provisions of the Member States concerning liability for defective products [1999] OJ L141/20. The BSE crisis related to a disease found in cattle (commonly known as "mad cow" disease) which led to fears that victims suffering from the brain disease vCJD had been infected by eating meat from BSE infected cattle.

68   See Consumer Protection Act 1987 (Product Liability) (Modification) Order 2000 (SI 2000/2771). Unfortunately,

Buildings are not covered by the Act, although individual goods from which they are built (for example, bricks and beams) are. The Act is additionally not intended to extend to pure information, except in the case of printed instructions or warnings for a product, which will render the producer (not the printer) liable for errors or omissions in the instructions or warnings which make the product unsafe. The Government guidance on the Act[69] indicates that in relation to computer software supplied as an intrinsic part of a product, liability will rest on the producer of the product and not on the consultant who designed the package.

What is a defect?

9–021

This is the key concept in the Act.[70] The defendant is liable for damage caused wholly or in part by a "defect" in a product. Section 3 defines a defect as existing when "the safety[71] of the product is not such as persons generally are entitled to expect". A product may be unsafe because it is positively dangerous (e.g. a badly wired electric fire likely to explode when it reaches a certain temperature) or is less effective than expected (e.g. a pacemaker which does not detect all heart problems). The standard is set at what "persons generally are entitled to expect". This ambiguous phrase has led to some difficulty. It would appear to include the expectations not only of consumers, but also of the manufacturing community. Manufacturers, however, are likely to have lower expectations than those of consumers, who may view themselves as entitled to a product perfect in every way, despite its low market price. The manufacturers' view will inevitably reflect a cost/benefit analysis, whereby the product is only "defective" if the costs in terms of harm to consumers outweigh the utility of the product. It is not clear from the section which form of reasoning a court should utilise in deciding whether a product is "defective" under the Act. Subsequent case law has, by reference to the wording of the Directive and its preamble, specified that the standard is "the safety which the public at large is entitled to expect".[72]

This leads to a related question: *what* safety is the public at large entitled to expect? For example, a knife, due to its very nature, has an obvious risk of danger, but it nevertheless provides a useful tool. Equally, a drug may have side-effects, but may provide the sole means of curing a serious illness. It would clearly be unrealistic if the public could legitimately expect to

---

no corresponding alteration has been made to the definition of "producer" in s.1(2), although agriculture will no doubt often involve some form of "industrial process".

69   *Guide to the Consumer Protection Act 1987* (HMSO, 2001), p.5.

70   See A. Stoppa, "The concept of defectiveness in the Consumer Protection Act 1987: a critical analysis" (1992) 12 L.S. 210.

71   "Safety" is defined to include safety with respect to products comprised in that product and safety in the context of risks of damage to property, as well as in the context of risks of death and personal injury: s.3(1).

72   See *Abouzaid v Mothercare (UK) Ltd* [2000] All E.R. (D) 2436 *The Times* 20 February 2001, where Pill LJ relied on Recital 6 to the Directive, and *A v National Blood Authority* [2001] 3 All E.R. 289 at 334: "the court will act as . . . the appointed representative of the public at large".

be protected from any harm at all. Certain practical limits are therefore necessary in applying the "public expectation" test.

This application of this test will ultimately be determined by the court. Section 3(2), does, however, provide that in assessing whether a defect exists, the court should take all the circumstances into account, including:

"(a)   (i)   the manner in which and purposes for which the product has been marketed;

(ii)   the get-up (or packaging) of the product;

(iii)   the use of any mark (for example the 'kite mark') in relation to the product;

(iv)   any instructions for, or warnings with respect to doing or refraining from doing anything with or in relation to the product;

(b)   what might reasonably be expected to be done with or in relation to the product; and

(c)   the time when the product was supplied by its producer to another. It is irrelevant that products supplied after that time are generally safer than the product supplied to the claimant."

Nevertheless, for many years, due to the absence of reported cases, it was difficult to identify how this test would be applied in practice. This position has improved since 1999 and a number of reported cases now give valuable assistance in assessing the meaning of "defect" under the Act. Initially, the courts had adopted an approach similar to that used in negligence (discussed in Ch.5). In *Richardson v LRC Products*,[73] for example, Mrs Richardson brought an unsuccessful action under the Act when she became pregnant when a condom used by her husband failed. In the absence of any convincing explanation for its failure, the judge examined the care taken by the manufacturer in producing the goods and noted that its standards exceeded the relevant British Standard. It is difficult to reconcile such concerns with a regime of strict liability. A better approach would be to recognise that the public do not expect condoms to be 100% effective and that, on this basis, the product could not be said to be defective.

The Court of Appeal in *Abouzaid v Mothercare (UK) Ltd*,[74] in its first full judgment on the Act, was critical of such fault-based reasoning. In this case, a child of 12 had been injured when attempting to fasten a sleeping bag manufactured by the defendants to the back of a pushchair. The buckle on the elastic fastenings had sprung back, hitting him in the eye. As a

---

73   [2000] Lloyd's Rep. Med. 280. See also *Worsley v Tambrands Ltd* [2000] P.I.Q.R. P95 (toxic shock syndrome resulting from use of tampon), the highly questionable decision of *Foster v Biosil* (2001) 59 B.M.L.R. 178 (CC (Central London)) (ruptured breast implant) and *Sam B v McDonald's Restaurants Ltd* [2002] EWHC 490 (QBD) (spillage of hot drinks). See R. Freeman [2001] J.P.I.L. 26.

74   [2000] All E.R. (D) 2436 *The Times* 20 February 2001 CA, also known as the "Cosytoes" case.

result, the child suffered a significant loss of vision in his left eye. The Court of Appeal adopted a strict interpretation of "defect". In examining the safety which the public at large is entitled to expect, Pill LJ found that, although this was a borderline case, the severe consequences of injury indicated that the product was defective.[75] It was irrelevant whether this defect should have reasonably come to the manufacturer's attention. The fact that the court found that the defendants would not have been liable in negligence highlighted the distinction between fault-based liability and liability under the Act.

This distinction is further reinforced by the judgment of Burton J in the leading case of *A v National Blood Authority*.[76] This was a class action brought by over 100 claimants who had been infected with the virus Hepatitis C through blood transfusions which had used blood or blood products obtained from infected donors. It was alleged that, although the risk of the virus had been known since at least the 1970s, it was, at the time of infection, impossible to detect. Screening for the virus was available only from September 1991. On that basis, the defendants argued that the most that the public could have legitimately expected up to that date was that all reasonable precautions would be carried out, not that the blood would be 100% clean. In the view of the judge, this was a blatant attempt to re-introduce fault-based ideas which were contrary to the purpose of the Directive. Section 3 would be confined to *relevant* circumstances,[77] and the steps taken by the manufacturer to avoid the risk would not be relevant in a strict liability regime. On this basis, "avoidability" of the harmful characteristic would be ignored,[78] as would the impracticality, cost or difficulty of taking precautionary measures. Burton J equally refused to take account of the fact that the defendants were obliged to supply blood to hospitals and patients as a service to society. There was no necessary reason why a public body should receive preferential treatment where a product was unsafe.[79] The public at large were entitled to expect that the blood transfusion would be free from infection. There was no publicity or information to make them consider otherwise.[80]

9–022

It is no longer clear, however, that the courts will continue to follow the strict *A* approach to the defect test, at least in relation to design defects. The Court of Appeal in *Tesco Stores Ltd v Pollard*[81] was prepared to accept that dishwasher powder with a child resistant closure cap (CRC), which was less safe than that specified in the British Standard certificate, was not

---

75 "Members of the public were entitled to expect better from the appellants": at [27].

76 [2001] 3 All E.R. 289. Comment: C. Hodges, "Compensating patients" (2001) 117 L.Q.R. 528; G. Howells and M. Mildred, "Infected blood: defect and discoverability. A first exposition of the EC Product Liability Directive" (2002) 65 M.L.R. 95.

77 This is not obvious from the wording of s.3(2), which states that "all the circumstances shall be taken into account": see C. Hodges (2001) 117 L.Q.R. 528, 530.

78 "Indeed . . . had it been intended that it would be included as a derogation from, or at any rate a palliation of [the purpose of the Directive] then it would certainly have been mentioned": [2001] 3 All E.R. 289 at 336.

79 [2001] 3 All E.R. 289 at 318.

80 Burton J questioned at 338 whether, in any event, even express warnings would have been sufficient or whether they would have been ruled out as an attempt to exclude or limit liability which, under s.7, is not permitted.

81 [2006] EWCA Civ 393; (2006) 150 S.J.L.B. 537.

defective.[82] In the view of Laws LJ, the public were only entitled to expect that the bottle would be more difficult to open than if it had an ordinary screw-top.[83] The Court of Appeal expressly rejected the argument that the Act effectively provides a warranty of the safety of products by the producer.[84] In *Wilkes v DePuy International Ltd*,[85] Hickinbottom J supported a move away from the *A* approach, finding that safety should be regarded as a relative concept. No medicinal product, he argued, can be absolutely safe. While the test was still what persons generally were entitled to expect, the question should not be over-analysed. On this basis:

> . . . however consumer expectations are defined and gauged, there cannot be a sensible expectation that any medicine or medicinal product is entirely risk-free. As I have described, the potential benefits (including potential utility) of such a product have to be balanced against its risks. . . Therefore, in considering whether a product suffered from a defect, the court must assess the appropriate level of safety, exercising its judgment, and taking into account the information and the circumstances before it, whether or not an actual or notional patient or patients, or indeed other members of the public, would in fact have considered each of those factors and all of that information. [86]

The case concerned a metal artificial hip which had fractured three years after surgery and caused damage to the patient's hip joint. The patient sued the manufacturer, alleging a design defect. Given the very low failure rate of the product, the difficulty of avoiding fractures and the fact that it had complied with all mandatory standards and regulatory requirements, no such defect could be found.

This is a markedly different approach to *A*—notably in accepting the validity of a risk/benefit analysis and comparing the manufacturer's conduct with that of regulatory requirements rather than demanding a higher standard.[87] Further the judge stated that the question of *avoidability*, that is, whether and how easily a risk might be avoided, may, in appropriate cases be relevant (contrast with *A* above).[88] It does reflect, however, the approach seen in *Pollard*.[89] There is at present a conflict of approach between that stated in *Wilkes* and *A* and it remains to

---

82   For criticism, see M. Mildred [2006] J.P.I. Law C130, who argues that there may be good common sense grounds for tying the public expectation test to that of the British Standard. Contrast *Palmer v Palmer* [2006] EWHC 1284 (QBD (Admin)): "Klunk Klip" device, which introduced slack into seat-belts to make them more comfortable, was defective.

83   [2006] EWCA Civ 393 at [18].

84   [2006] EWCA Civ 393 at [17] per Laws LJ.

85   [2016] EWHC 3096 (QB); [2018] Q.B. 627.

86   [2016] EWHC 3096(QB) at [65] and [72].

87   Nolan, however, has sought to reconcile the two approaches: (2018) 134 L.Q.R. 176.

88   [2016] EWHC 3096(QB) at [85] (obiter).

89   Cited with approval in [54]. The judge, however, had "substantial difficulties" with some of the reasoning in *A*.

be seen which will be followed (both are High Court decisions).[90] It does seem clear that while the *A* approach is harsh to manufacturers, it is also more straightfoward and predictable for consumers. In aiming for flexibility, the *Wilkes* approach is likely to be more fact-specific involving broader consideration of factors; many of which will be unknown to consumers. If the *Wilkes* approach is followed, it is also likely to take English law further away from the strict approach of the European Court.[91]

9–023

It is uncontroversial, however, that the factors expressly mentioned in s.3(2) will be of assistance. For example, the use of warnings may provide a means to avoid liability. In *Worsley v Tambrands Ltd*,[92] the fact that the risk of toxic shock syndrome had been mentioned on the packaging of the product, and in detail in a leaflet which accompanied the product which the purchaser was advised to read and keep, led to a finding of no liability. It will be a question for the court whether the warning is sufficient. In *Worsley*, for example, the claimant suffered a near-fatal illness, but the risk of such an event was very small. The courts are likely to be particularly demanding in relation to products aimed at children or other vulnerable parties.

Further, s.3(2)(c) ensures that defendants are not discouraged from making improvements in product safety. This subsection prevents the claimant from arguing that the very act of improving the product amounts to an admission that it was defective in the past. The product is judged at the time that it is supplied by the producer, not when it is received by the claimant. On this basis, the producer will not be liable for ordinary wear and tear to goods which may have lingered on the shelves for months or even years. It will not protect the producer, however, where safety expectations and the product design have not changed in the intervening years.[93]

---

90 *Gee v DePuy International Ltd* [2018] EWHC 1208 (QB) preferred the *Wilkes* approach. Eisler, in contrast, argues that "*Wilkes* deconstructs the most well-established framework while advancing no helpful alternative": [2017] C.L.J. 233, 234.

91 See *Boston Scientific Medizintechnik GmbH v AOK Sachsen-Anhalt* (C-503/13 & C-504/13) [2015] 3 C.M.L.R. 6: in relation to medical care (including the insertion of medical devices such as pacemakers), due to the particularly vulnerable situation of patients, the safety requirements which such patients were entitled to expect were particularly high. More controversially where such products belonging to the same group or forming part of the same production series had a potential defect, it was possible to classify as defective all the products in that group or series without the need to show that the specific product in question was defective. See D. Fairgrieve and M. Pilgerstorfer (2017) 28 E.B.L. Rev 879.

92 [2000] P.I.Q.R. P95. See also *Buckley v Henkel Ltd* unreported 25 November 2013 Liverpool CC,) where the claimant suffered an allergic reaction to hair dye: no liability where clear from the instructions that there was a risk of an allergic reaction, and a number of warnings and precautions were highlighted. The court also found that in the case of hair dyes generally there will arguably be a greater awareness of risk given that the very nature of hair dye involves a chemical process.

93 See *Abouzaid v Mothercare (UK) Ltd* [2000] All E.R. (D) 2436 *The Times* 20 February 2001.

What damage?

9–024

Section 5(1) provides that death and personal injury[94] are covered by the Act. The Act is more restrictive, however, in relation to property damage,[95] and does not include pure economic loss. This is consistent with the common law position, which excludes liability for pure economic loss resulting from a defective product (set out in Ch.3). Section 5(2) excludes loss or damage to the product itself and loss or damage to the whole or any part of the final product which has been supplied with the product as a component. On this basis, if the windscreen of a vehicle shatters due to a defect and causes the vehicle to crash, the claimant cannot sue for the cost of the windscreen or the vehicle itself. If, however, the driver had purchased a replacement tyre for the vehicle, which burst due to a defect and caused the car to crash, the driver would be able to recover for damage to the car. The tyre was not supplied with the vehicle when purchased, and so recovery is not excluded by s.5(2).

Property claims are further excluded if the loss or damage suffered, excluding interest, does not exceed £275 (s.5(4)). By this means, the courts avoid having to consider very small claims. Claims are also excluded if the property at the time it is lost or damaged is not of a description ordinarily intended for private use, occupation or consumption, and not intended to be so used (s.5(3)).[96] The Act therefore gives primary protection to the consumer. Again, there will be definitional problems. For example, if a lecturer buys a computer for use in his research, but also for his family to use recreationally, can it be viewed as property ordinarily intended for private use and intended to be so used?

The UK Government chose not to implement an option in the Directive to set a maximum level of damages for which a defendant could be liable. Article 16(1) of the Directive states that the producer's total liability for damage resulting from death or personal injury caused by the product and identical items with the same defect may be limited to an amount not less than €70 million. This has only been implemented in a few countries such as Germany, Spain and Portugal.

Defences

9–025

Section 4, or more specifically s.4(1)(e), of the Act has caused the most controversy and has even led to a reference to the European Court of Justice challenging the UK's

---

94 Consumer Protection Act 1987 s.45(1) defines "personal injury" to include any disease and any other impairment of a person's physical or mental condition.

95 Which includes damage to land: Consumer Protection Act 1987 s.5(1).

96 See *Renfrew Golf Club v Motocaddy Ltd* [2016] CSIH 57; 2016 S.L.T. 781: no recovery for fire to golf clubhouse caused by electric golf trolley going on fire. The clubhouse, although owned by members of the club, was not property ordinarily intended for private use or occupation. It was materially a commercial concern used by its 700 members and other members of the public.

implementation of the Product Liability Directive. Section 4 gives the defendant six possible defences. It is important to recognise that the mere existence of defences does not mean that the Act does not impose strict liability on the defendant. The aim of strict liability is simply to remove from the claimant the burden of proving that the defendant has been at fault.

Let us examine the defences in turn.

(a) The defect is attributable to compliance with a requirement imposed by law

9–026 This is obviously necessary, because otherwise the defendant would be torn between complying with two conflicting legal provisions. However, compliance with a legal requirement will only absolve a producer from liability if the defect was an inevitable result of compliance.[97]

(b) The defendants did not at any time supply the product to another

9–027 This protects the defendants if they have not put the product in circulation, for example, the product is stolen or a counterfeit copy, and found to be defective. It should be noted, however, that "supply" is defined quite generously under the Act.[98]

(c) Supply by the defendants was not in course of their business

9–028 Defendants can take advantage of this defence if the only supply of the product was not in the course of their business and either:

- section 2(2) does not apply (i.e. they are only suppliers), or

- they are within s.2(2) (i.e. they are producers, own-branders or importers), but are not acting at the time with a view to profit.

This is somewhat confusing and is best illustrated by examples. If I make a cake and sell it at the local craft fair, I am not acting in the course of business, but I am a producer and acting

---

97 *Guide to the Consumer Protection Act 1987* (HMSO, 2001).

98 "Supply" is defined in Consumer Protection Act 1987 s.46 to include selling, hiring out or lending goods, entering into a hire-purchase agreement to furnish the goods, the performance of any contract for work and materials to furnish the goods or even giving the goods as a prize or otherwise making a gift of the goods.

with a view to profit.[99] I cannot therefore use the defence. If, however, I wish to get rid of my old car and sell it to my neighbour for £300, I am not acting in the course of business and I am not a producer, own-brander or importer and so can rely on the defence if the car proves to be defective. It is irrelevant whether I have profited from the transaction or not.

(d) The defect did not exist in the product at the relevant time, i.e. when it was put into circulation[100]

9–029

This makes the simple point that if the defect is due to wear and tear resulting from use of the product after the product has been put into circulation, the defendant will not be liable. As a defence, the burden will be on the defendant to establish this. The defence was raised in *Piper v JRI (Manufacturing) Ltd*.[101] Here, the claimant had undergone a total hip replacement operation. Unfortunately, after an apparently successful operation, the prosthesis implanted into his right hip sheared in two. Piper alleged that the prosthesis was defective. However, the manufacturer alleged that the defect had not existed when the product had been supplied to the hospital. The Court of Appeal found that, on the evidence, the manufacturer had discharged the burden of proving the defence by showing that any defect would have been picked up by their inspection system.

(e) The development risk defence

9–030

This defence is optional to Member States (see art.15(1)(b)), although it has generally been implemented within the EU.[102] Its implementation in English law has, however, proved controversial.[103] Section 4(1)(e) provides a defence where:

> "... the state of scientific and technical knowledge at the relevant time was not such that a producer of products of the same descrip-

---

99   Query the situation if I sold it at the school fête for charity.
100 Consumer Protection Act 1987 s.4(2) defines the "relevant time" to signify (a) if the defendant is within s.2(2), the time when he supplied the product to another, or (b) if the defendant is not within s.2(2) (for example, a supplier), the time when the product was last supplied by a person to whom s.2(2) does apply.
101 [2006] EWCA Civ 1344; (2006) 92 B.M.L.R. 141.
102 Except in Finland and Luxembourg. Spain excludes the defence for food and medicinal products and France excludes the defence for products derived from the human body. Germany has permitted liability for development risks in the area of pharmaceutical products since 1978.
103 The UK's implementation of the defence may be contrasted with the view of the Law Commission, in their 1977 report, *Liability for Defective Products* No.82, Cmnd.6831 para.105, that if the product was found to be defective, in the light of the thalidomide case, the injured person should be compensated by the producer however careful the producer had been. The report of the *Royal Commission on Civil Liability and Compensation for Personal Injury*, Cmnd.7054 (1978), Vol.1 para.1259 also recommended that the defence should not be allowed.

> tion as the product in question might be expected to have discovered the defect if it had existed in his products while they were under his control."

This may be contrasted with the wording of art.7(e) of the Directive, which the Act seeks to transpose into English law:

> ". . . the state of scientific and technical knowledge at the time when [the producer] put the product into circulation was not such as to enable the existence of the defect to be discovered."

At first sight, there appears to be a substantive difference between the two provisions. Whilst the Directive suggests that the producer must establish, objectively, that the knowledge available at the time of circulation would not have alerted the defendant to the particular risk, s.4(1)(e) appears more generous. Its wording suggests that the producer need only show that a "reasonable producer", i.e. another producer in the same market, would not have known of the risks in question. Such a test is reminiscent of the *Bolam* test for breach of duty, discussed in Ch.5, and is hardly indicative of strict liability on the producer. Indeed, it seems to suggest simply that the defendant will not be liable if he or she can demonstrate that he or she has exercised the care of a "reasonable producer" in the market in assessing the risks associated with the product.[104]

The possible conflict between these two provisions was examined by the European Court of Justice in *European Commission v United Kingdom*.[105] The European Commission had initiated infringement proceedings against the UK in April 1989, alleging that the Act did not properly transpose the Directive into English law, as required by art.19 of the Directive. It was argued that s.4(1)(e) was broader than the defence in art.7(e). The European Court of Justice rejected this claim. It held that art.7(e) imposed an objective test on the producer as to the state of scientific and technical knowledge at the time the product was put in circulation, which would include the most advanced level of knowledge in the relevant field. The producer would be presumed to possess such knowledge, and it was not a question of the producer's subjective state of knowledge or the particular practices and safety standards of the producer's industrial sector. However, the court was not prepared to go so far as to presume that the producer would be acquainted with *all* relevant scientific knowledge at the time the product was put into circulation. It approved the view of Advocate General Tesauro that the knowledge in question must be accessible. It would thus be unfair to expect the producer to be familiar with research carried out by an academic in Manchuria who published in a local scientific journal in Chinese, which was not circulated outside the boundaries of the region. If the relevant scientific research

---

104 This provoked a considerable academic debate: see, e.g. J. Stapleton, *Product Liability* (Butterworths, 1994) and C. Newdick, "The development risk defence of the Consumer Protection Act 1987" [1988] C.L.J. 455.
105 [1997] All E.R. (EC) 481; [1997] 3 C.M.L.R. 923. Comment: C. Hodges, "Development risks: unanswered questions" (1998) 61 M.L.R. 560.

is accessible, however, it will not be a valid excuse to argue that it represents an isolated opinion: the producer is expected to keep note of, and consider, all relevant research.

In the view of the court, there was no clear indication that s.4(1)(e) was inconsistent with a proper interpretation of the Directive. Whilst the section could be interpreted in a broader sense, the court held that its wording did not suggest that the availability of the defence depended on the subjective knowledge of the producer. There was, in any event, no English decision which indicated that the English courts would interpret s.4(1)(e) in a way which would conflict with their duty, stated in s.1(1) of the Act, to construe the Act in accordance with the Directive. The Advocate General suggested that, in this light, the Commission's application had been "overhasty, to say the least".

9–031

One might consider that, due to the absence of case law, English law had a fortunate escape, but the legacy of this case is that, in future, s.4(1)(e) will be interpreted in a manner consistent with the comments of the European Court of Justice in this case. Indeed, in the leading case of *A v National Blood Authority*,[106] Burton J referred not to the sections of the Act, but to the Directive itself, in considering this defence. It is clear from this decision that the courts will, in future, adopt a strict approach to this defence and reject any approach based on fault.

As stated above, *A v National Blood Authority* concerned a class action by over 100 claimants who had been infected with Hepatitis C through blood transfusions. At the time of infection, the relevant defendants had been aware of the risk of the disease but did not possess the requisite technology to identify infected blood until a later date. They therefore sought to rely on the "development risk" defence on the basis that the state of scientific and technical knowledge was such that the existence of the defect in the product itself was undetectable. Burton J adopted a firm line. The defendants did know of the possible existence of a defect in blood generally. Their absence of knowledge related to the ability to devise a test to identify which blood was infected. In such circumstances, it would be inconsistent with the purpose of the Directive if the producer, knowing of a risk, continued to supply the product without liability simply because he or she could not identify in which of his products the defect would occur:

> "If there is a known risk, i.e. the existence of the defect is known or should have been known in the light of . . . accessible information, then the producer continues to produce and supply at his own risk. It would, in my judgment, be inconsistent with the purpose of the directive if a producer, in the case of a known risk, continues to supply products simply because, and despite the fact that, he is unable to identify in which if any of his products that defect will occur or recur."[107]

---

106 [2001] 3 All E.R. 289. Comment: C. Hodges (2001) 117 L.Q.R. 528; G. Howells and M. Mildred (2002) 65 M.L.R. 95.
107 [2001] 3 All E.R. 289 at 340.

This firm line was also adopted by the Court of Appeal in *Abouzaid v Mothercare (UK) Ltd*.[108] It had been argued that since the defendants had been unaware of the potential problems with the buckle fastening, and no record of any comparable incident had been recorded by the Department of Trade and Industry accident database, the state of scientific and technical knowledge did not indicate a problem at the relevant time. The Court of Appeal gave this argument short shrift. The defence was present to deal with technical advances, not to deal with problems which no-one had thought about. A simple practical test would have identified how a buckle would spring back if extended. Equally, Pill LJ doubted whether a DTI database fell within the category of "scientific and technical knowledge".[109]

The strict line taken in these cases would seem finally to allay fears that s.4(1)(e) has re-introduced negligence into the Act with a reversed burden of proof on the manufacturer.

> **(f) The defect was a defect in a finished product (X) in which the product in question had been comprised AND was wholly attributable the design of X or to compliance with the producer of X's instructions**

9–032

This protects the defendant who has supplied a component part of a product, and risks being found to be jointly and severally liable, under s.2(5), when a defect is found in the finished product. It is essentially a denial of causation: my product has no causal link with the injury caused to the claimant. The defence is somewhat complicated and best illustrated by an example. A instructs B to supply tyres which are suitable for a family car, which A decides would be ideal in constructing his new racing car. A is wrong, and the tyres burst at 100 mph, causing A to crash. B will be able to rely on this defence to deny liability. If, however, B was aware of the purpose for which A was purchasing the tyres (for which they were clearly deficient), it is likely that B would be liable in negligence for failing to warn A that they were not suitable for racing cars. Equally, if the tyres burst not because they were used for the wrong purpose, but because they were defectively manufactured, the defence would not apply. The defect must be wholly attributable to A's conduct and the burden will be on the component producer to prove this to the court.

Contributory negligence

9–033

Section 6(4) ensures that the principle of contributory negligence is also available to the defendant.[110] This may appear somewhat odd. The defendant is liable without proof of fault, but the claimant's damages may be reduced if the claimant's fault has increased the damage

---

108 [2000] All E.R. (D) 2436 *The Times* 20 February 2001.
109 [2000] All E.R. (D) 2436 *The Times* 20 February 2001 at [29].
110 Consumer Protection Act 1987 s.6 also renders the Fatal Accidents Act 1976 and the Congenital Disabilities (Civil Liability) Act 1976 applicable.

suffered by him or her. Law Reform (Contributory Negligence) Act 1945 s.1(1) states that the defence applies "where any person suffers damage as the result partly of his own fault and partly of the fault of any other person", but "fault" is interpreted broadly by s.4 of that Act to include any "act or omission which gives rise to a liability in tort". The defendant, if liable, is therefore presumed to be at "fault", and the claimant's actual fault is balanced against the responsibility of the defendant. This again gives rise to concern as to the intrusion of fault into a strict liability statute. It should also be noted that the claimant's contributory negligence, for example in using a product in an unreasonable way, may indicate that the product is not defective, in any event, under the criteria set under s.3(2) (see, in particular, s.3(2)(b)).

Exclusion clauses

In view of the aim of the Act to protect claimants from injury due to defective products, s.7 provides that such claims "shall not be limited or excluded by any contract term, by any notice or by any other provision". This avoids the technicalities of the Unfair Contract Terms Act 1977 and Consumer Rights Act 2015 Pt 2 and sends a clear message to defendants that exclusion clauses are not an adequate response to potential liability.

`9-034`

Limitation periods: s.11A of the Limitation Act 1980

The limitation period indicates the time period within which a claimant must bring a claim. If a claim is brought after this period, however good the claim, the courts will refuse to allow the claim to proceed. By this means, the courts avoid dealing with stale claims and claimants are encouraged to act promptly when the evidence is fresh. Section 11A of the Limitation Act 1980 sets a specific limitation period for defective product actions. In relation to claims for personal injury or property loss, the claim must be brought within three years from the date on which the cause of action accrued.[111] The cause of action will accrue either when the damage is caused or, if later, when the damage is reasonably discoverable[112] by the claimant.

`9-035`

Section 11A(3) provides that an action under Pt 1 of the 1987 Act shall not be brought after the expiration of the period of ten years from the time the product was put into circulation.[113] This long-stop provision will serve to protect defendants from claims in respect of design defects which come to light long after products have been in circulation.

A series of cases (the *O'Byrne* litigation) have highlighted tensions between the application of the Limitation Act and the application of the long-stop provision which derives from the

---

111   Consumer Protection Act 1987 s.11A(4).
112   The date of knowledge is defined in Limitation Act 1980 s.14.
113   There is no provision to extend this, in contrast to negligently caused death and personal injury: Limitation Act 1980 s.33(1A). Section 11A(3) also applies regardless of the provisions for extension of time due to fraud, concealment or mistake (see s.32(4A)) or disability (see s.28(7)(a)) in the Limitation Act 1980.

Directive. Declan O'Byrne had been vaccinated in 1992 and subsequently suffered severe brain damage. It was alleged that the vaccine was defective. An action had mistakenly been brought against the defendant's English subsidiary. Realising the mistake, the claimant applied to substitute as defendant the parent company and manufacturer of the vaccine (Limitation Act 1980 s.35, granting a discretion to the court to substitute a new party). However, the s.11A(3) ten year long-stop period had expired by this stage. The English High Court, at the request of both parties, made a preliminary reference to the European Court of Justice (ECJ) asking how to deal with this. In *O'Byrne v Sanofi Pasteur MSD Ltd*,[114] the ECJ made two rulings. First, it found that in determining the ten year period after the product was put into circulation, time would start for the purposes of s.11A(3) "when [the product] leaves the production process operated by the producer and enters a marketing process in the form in which it is offered to the public in order to be used or consumed".[115] Secondly, and perhaps most importantly, the question of the substitution of parties after the ten year long-stop was left to the national court to decide, but with a proviso:

> "it is as a rule for national law to determine the conditions in accordance with which one party may be substituted for another in the context of such an action. A national court . . . must, however, ensure that due regard is had to the personal scope of Directive 85/374, as established by articles 1 and 3 thereof."[116]

The matter was then referred back to the English court.

This less than straightforward statement resulted in a second reference to the European Court of Justice in 2008.[117] The ECJ was asked, bluntly, did the Directive permit the substitution of one defendant for another after the expiry of the ten year long-stop period? The Grand Chamber in 2009[118] held that where national legislation allowed for substitution of parties, it should *not* be applied in a way which permitted the producer to be sued after the expiry of the limitation period even though the action had been begun within time, albeit against the wrong defendant. It did accept, however, that where the proceedings had been issued within time against a wholly-owned subsidiary of the producer, the Product Liability Directive did not prevent the national court from substituting the producer for the subsidiary if it found that the putting into circulation of the product had been determined by the producer.

Applying this ruling, the Supreme Court in *O'Byrne v Aventis Pasteur MSD Ltd*[119] held in 2010 that a new party could not be substituted in this case, despite the fact that the manufacturer

---

114   (C127/04) [2006] 1 W.L.R. 1606 ECJ.
115   (C127/04) [2006] 1 W.L.R. 1606 ECJ at [27]–[29]. The term "put into circulation" was not defined in the Directive as it was considered self-explanatory. As this rather unclear definition indicates, this is far from the case.
116   (C127/04) [2006] 1 W.L.R. 1606 ECJ at [39].
117   *OB v Aventis Pasteur* [2008] UKHL 34; [2008] 3 C.M.L.R. 10.
118   (C-358/08) *O'Byrne v Aventis Pasteur SA* [2010] 1 W.L.R. 1375.
119   [2010] UKSC 23; [2010] 1 W.L.R. 1412, reversing Court of Appeal in [2007] EWCA Civ 966.

wholly-owned its English subsidiary. The ECJ's core ruling had been that a national rule allowing substitution should not be invoked against a producer after expiry of the ten year period. The exception for wholly-owned subsidiaries was interpreted narrowly to indicate a situation where, as a matter of fact, a distribution subsidiary was so closely involved with the parent producer that they could, in effect, also be regarded as a producer. This was not the case here. O'Byrne, therefore, finally lost his battle for compensation some 18 years after the vaccination had taken place. Applying s.11A(3) is not, therefore, always a straightforward exercise!

Causation and remoteness

There are no specific rules in the Act and so the ordinary rules described in Ch.6 of this book will apply. The Act gives the claimant no further assistance in what, as stated earlier, may be a difficult task, particularly in cases of illness and disease.[120] This was illustrated in *X v Schering Health Care Ltd*[121] in relation to the third generation oral contraceptive pill. In a trial lasting three months and hearing the conflicting evidence of ten experts, Mackay J concluded, in a judgment of 200 pages, that there was insufficient evidential basis to establish that an increased risk of cardio-vascular injury was caused by the product. On this basis, there was therefore no need to examine the law under the Act.[122]

9–036

Assessment of the Impact of the Act

Continuing practical problems

Whilst it took almost 12 years from the introduction of the Act for a claimant to bring a successful claim,[123] the two important cases of *Abouzaid* and *A* have done much to allay fears that the

9–037

---

120 There is, however, evidence of some willingness by the courts to infer causation by a process of eliminating non-causes as in *Ide v ATB Sales Ltd* [2008] EWCA Civ 424 where two alternative explanations for the cause of Mr Ide's accident had been put before the court. The court indicated that the question was whether, having eliminated all of the causes of the loss but one, the remaining cause had on the balance of probabilities caused the damage sustained.

121 [2002] EWHC 1420 (QB); (2003) 70 B.M.L.R. 88. Comment: M. Mildred [2002] J.P.I.L. 428 and A. McAdams (2002) 146 S.J. 900.

122 Recent guidance from the European Court states that national courts have to ensure that the evidence adduced is sufficiently serious, specific and consistent to warrant the conclusion that a defect in the product appeared to be the most plausible explanation for the occurrence of the damage: *W v Sanofi Pasteur MSD* (C-621/15) [2018] 1 C.M.L.R. 16.

123 The first edn of this book in 2000 noted only one reported case which was directly in point: *European*

Act provided little addition to the common law.[124] The ruling of the European Court of Justice in *European Commission v United Kingdom*[125] has proved a significant milestone in affirming the objectives of the Directive and its goal in providing consumer protection. Nevertheless, as seen in the cases discussed above, litigation will often prove an expensive and lengthy process, particularly if complex medical evidence is involved. Further, the claimant receives no assistance in proving causation, which may be an onerous task. The claimant's position is moreover weakened by the strict time limits on his or her action. It is entirely probable that it would take more than 10 years for certain injuries resulting from design defects to become apparent, and yet the long-stop provision bars the litigant's claim absolutely. Miller and Goldberg further question whether the Thalidomide victims would, in fact, have recovered if an action had been possible under Pt 1 of the 1987 Act in view of the development risk defence and suggest that the victims would have had to identify accessible information that it was necessary to test the drug on pregnant animals.[126]

Standard and non-standard products

9–038

In *A*, Burton J drew a distinction between two categories of product—standard and non-standard. "Standard" products are those which perform as the producer intends. Any defect will thus show up in every product produced. A "non-standard" product, in contrast, is a rogue product, which differs from the normal product manufactured for use by the public, for example, a chocolate bar containing a piece of metal. Where a product is "non-standard", Burton J noted that it will be easier to establish that it is defective unless it can be shown that the public have accepted its non-standard nature (for example, due to warnings, its presentation or publicity). In the judge's view, infected blood fell into the "non-standard" category.[127] It differed from the norm intended for use by the public. Further, the public (unlike the medical profession) had not been aware of the risk of Hepatitis C and could not be said to have accepted its non-standard nature. In contrast, a standard product will raise more complex issues. The courts will be forced to consider, and take expert evidence on, the relevant factors under s.3(2) and the nature of comparable products in the market (and their price) to ascertain the product's safety for foreseeable use.

This distinction, however, has not really caught on and reference is still made to manufacturing and design defects. Academics have questioned its merits and what it positively

---

Commission v United Kingdom [1997] 3 C.M.L.R. 923.

124 See E. Deards and C. Twigg-Flesner, "The Consumer Protection Act 1987: proof at last that it is protecting consumers?" (2001) 10 Nott L.J. 1.

125 [1997] All E.R. (EC) 481; [1997] 3 C.M.L.R. 923, discussed above.

126 C. J. Miller and R. S. Goldberg, *Product Liability*, 2nd edn (Oxford, 2004), p.520. See also C. Johnston [2012] J.P.I. Law 1, 15–16.

127 Burton J in [2001] 3 All E.R. 289 at 337 rejected the view that blood with a risk of virus could be treated as a "standard" product as too "philosophical".

contributes to our understanding of this area of law,[128] although it has been defended recently as "fundamental to the analysis of the defectiveness issue in strict product liability regimes".[129] In *Wilkes v DePuy International Ltd*,[130] the Court described the distinction as "unnecessary and undesirable", having no basis in the Directive nor the Act. In the judge's view, it acts as a distraction from the real exercise facing the court: consideration of the appropriate level of safety taking into account all relevant circumstances. It remains to be seen whether this strikes the death knell of the distinction—as indicated above, *A* and *Wilkes* are both first instance decision so neither overrules the other.

Use of settlements

It is likely to remain the case that most litigation under the 1987 Act will be settled out of court. There are still a limited number of reported cases to be found and a 2018 survey identified that most European product liability claims between 2000 and 2016 were actually settled out of Court.[131] 46% of cases were settled in direct negotiation, 32% in Court, 15% through alternative dispute settlement mechanisms, and 7% were resolved through other means such as through the insurer of the responsible party. It is difficult, however, to obtain reliable data, particularly as settlements will frequently require the parties not to publicise the terms of the agreement.

In contrast, in the US, the Consumer Product Safety Act s.37 (codified at 15 USC ss.2051–2089) obliges producers to announce cases involving defective products and notify the Consumer Product Safety Commission (CPSC).[132] If the product which has allegedly caused death or grievous bodily injury is the subject of at least three civil cases in a two-year period, producers (and importers as well) have to notify the Commission of the circumstances of the case as soon as the cases have been settled, either by a ruling in favour of the claimant, or as the result of an out of court agreement.[133] There is no equivalent provision in the UK. Arguably, it would be in the public interest for greater information to be available on such settlements, which would enable a clearer assessment to be made of the impact of the Act on UK law. Certainly, it would assist the European Commission in its review of the operation of the Product Liability Directive within the EU. Such measures, however, are likely to be opposed by manufacturers, who are far from willing to allow their competitors access to such information.

9–039

---

128   See G. Howells and M. Mildred (2002) 65 M.L.R. 95, 101. For a more positive view, see J. Eisler [2017] C.L.J. 233.

129   D. Nolan, "Strict product liability for design defects" (2018) 134 L.Q.R. 176.

130   [2016] EWHC 3096 (QB); [2018] Q.B. 627, paras.90–96.

131   Commission Staff Working Document, Evaluation of Council Directive 85/374/EEC (SWD(2018)157). The percentages listed in the text are based on the responses to the open public consultation and are averages across 28 Member States.

132   This is an independent federal regulatory agency created in 1972 to "protect the public against unreasonable risks of injuries and deaths associated with consumer products". It covers about 15,000 types of consumer products used in home, schools and recreation, but does not regulate on-road motor vehicles, boats, aircraft, cosmetics, pesticides, alcohol, tobacco, firearms and medical devices. See *www.cpsc.gov/* [1 August 2020].

133   See 15 USC s.2084, "Information reporting".

Breach of Statutory Duty

9–040 Consumer Protection Act 1987 Pt II provides for the Secretary of State to make safety regulations prescribing rules as to design, manufacture and packaging of certain classes of goods. This replaced earlier legislation in the Consumer Safety Act 1978. Although breach of such regulations generally incurs only criminal liability, s.41 expressly provides that an individual injured by a defect in a product resulting from breach of safety regulations has an action for breach of statutory duty. This provides a further option for litigants, although it should be noted that the regulations only cover a limited class of goods.[134]

Reform of the Product Liability Directive[135]

9–041 Leaving the EU does not signify that it is not of interest to consider what lessons might be learnt from the implementation of the Product Liability Directive in other European States. The European Commission is required to undertake a review of the Product Liability Directive every five years.[136] In July 1999, it published a Green Paper on Liability for Defective Products,[137] in which it outlined the Commission's proposals to consult interested parties to assess the impact of the Directive on victims and on the sectors of the economy concerned, and to reflect on the need for reform. In particular, it sought views on:

- the burden of proof imposed on victims;

- the operation of the "development risks" defence;

- the existence of minimum and maximum values for claims and their justification;

- the ten-year longstop and the effects of a possible modification of this;

- assessment of the insurability of risks deriving from defective production;

---

134 See Consumer Protection Act 1987 s.11(7).

135 Details of European Commission documents on defective products may be found at *http://ec.europa.eu/growth/single-market/goods/free-movement-sectors/liability-defective-products_en* [Accessed 1 August 2020].

136 The Commission has to report regularly to the Community institutions on the state of the application of the Directive. Article 21 of the Directive stipulates that it must report every five years on the general application of the Directive. Articles 15(3) and 16(2) stipulate that it must report every 10 years after notification of the Directive on development risks and financial limits.

137 COM (1999) 396, final.

- improved information on the settlement of cases concerning defective products;

- the supplier's liability; and

- the type of goods and damage covered.

In its report of January 2001,[138] the Commission resolved that in view of the belated transposition of the Directive in certain countries,[139] the possibility given to the Member States to apply their own national law, and the lack of available data, it would not recommend any change to the Directive.[140] Nevertheless, the Commission resolved actively to seek further information for future reforms. This included setting up a study to analyse and compare the practical effects of the different systems applicable in EU Member States regarding the procedural aspects of claims for defective products,[141] and launching a study into the economic impact of the development risk defence.[142] In 2006 and 2011, further reviews took place.[143] The latest review took place in 2018.[144] Here the Commission recognised the challenges to product liability that arise due to the greater technological sophistication of products (digitisation, the Internet of Things, artificial intelligence and cybersecurity) and by specific products such as pharmaceuticals. While concluding that the Directive continues to be an adequate tool, the Commission identified the need to provide greater clarification for key concepts such as "product", "producer", "defect", "damage" and of the burden of proof. The aim is to draw up comprehensive guidance on how to apply the Directive today.[145]

All the reports have noted the tension which exists between the expectations of consumer groups, producers and insurers, whose viewpoints naturally conflict. In general, consumers would like more protection at a lower cost. Producers and insurers, however, continue to

---

138 COM (2000) 893, final.

139 e.g. France only implemented the Directive on 23 May 1998 (see Act Nos 389–98 of 19 May 1998). Its legislation was successfully challenged twice by the European Commission for failing to implement the Directive correctly: see *EC Commission v France* (C-52/00) [2002] E.C.R. I-3827 and *EC Commission v France* (C-177/04) [2006] E.C.R. I-2461. The final amended provisions now constitute the French Civil Code arts 1245 to 1245–17. See P. Shears, "The EU Product Liability Directive—twenty years on" [2007] J.B.L. 884.

140 This is the second report of the Commission. In its first report of December 1995 (COM (1995) 617, final), the Commission concluded that, on the basis of the limited information available as to the operation of the Directive, it was not appropriate to submit any proposals for amendments.

141 Lovells, *Product liability in the European Union* (2003).

142 F. Rosselli, *Analysis of the economic impact of the development risk clause as provided by Directive 85/374/EEC on liability for defective products* (2004).

143 *Third Report and Fourth Report on the application of Council Directive 85/374*, COM (2006) 496 final and COM (2011) 547 final. For a critical assessment of the Third Report, see D. Fairgrieve and G. Howells (2007) 70 M.L.R. 962.

144 Fifth Report on the application of Council Directive 85/374 COM (2018) 246 final (see *https://eur-lex.europa.eu/legal-content/en/TXT/?uri=CELEX%3A52018DC0246* [Accessed 1 August 2020]). The Commission did not receive any complaints or launch any infringement proceedings during the 2011–2017 reporting period.

145 For comment, see D. Fairgrieve [2019] J.P.I. Law 33.

express concern that over-zealous product liability will slow down innovation and discourage the development of new products, whilst making insurance premiums unduly high.

It is clear that product liability will continue to be provoke debates, both inside and outside the EU. It is also evident that interpreting the meaning of key concepts such as "defect" is a problem not only in the UK but throughout the whole of Europe. The 2018 European Commission report also highlights the likelihood that the meaning of "product" is likely to arise in future case-law. We know it includes blood, surgical implants, vaccines, even dishwasher powder containers from the cases above, but new technology brings new challenges in how we assess the "defectiveness" of smart fridges and what exactly is the "product" in question?

Animals Act 1971

9–042

The last part of this chapter will look briefly at the liability imposed by the Animals Act 1971. This was brought in to replace the rather complicated existing common law provisions which imposed strict liability on those responsible for wild and domestic animals.[146] The Act imposes strict liability for damage caused by animals under the care of another. It should be noted that the Act applies in addition to ordinary common law principles. Therefore, an owner of a dog may still find himself or herself liable under occupiers' liability for injuries caused (see Ch.8),[147] liable in nuisance (for example, for the smell caused by his or her pigs: see Ch.10)[148] or liable in trespass (for example, for allowing hounds to stray onto another's land: see Ch.11).[149] Owners may equally find themselves liable under the ordinary rules of negligence where they have failed to exercise reasonable care to prevent their pet causing foreseeable harm to another.[150]

The main provisions of the 1971 Act are set out below. It will not deal with liability for

---

146   Note the 1967 Report of the Law Commission, *Civil Liability for Animals* (Law Com No.13) on which the Act is based and the classic work of P. M. North, *The Modern Law of Animals* (Butterworths, 1972). For modern law, see P. North, *Civil Liability for Animals* (OUP, 2012). For the background to the Act, see R. Bagshaw, "The Animals Act 1971" in T. T. Arvind and J. Steele (eds), *Tort Law and the Legislature* (Hart, 2012).

147   See *Gould v McAuliffe* [1941] 1 All E.R. 515.

148   See *Wheeler v JJ Saunders Ltd* [1996] Ch.19. Note also *Leeman v Montague* [1936] 2 All E.R. 1677.

149   See *League against Cruel Sports v Scott* [1986] Q.B. 240 (owner responsible for the damage caused if he or she intended animals to enter the claimant's land or, knowing that there was a real risk that they would enter, failed to take reasonable care to prevent their entry.)

150   See *Fardon v Harcourt-Rivington* (1932) 146 L.T. 391 HL, *Draper v Hodder* [1971] 2 Q.B. 556 and *Whippey v Jones* [2009] EWCA Civ 452. A further action may lie for a compensatory award from the Criminal Injuries Compensation Authority if the victim can establish that a criminal offence has taken place: see *Re C [CICA: Liability: 2002]* 3 December 2002; [2003] 7 C.L.10 (horses straying onto the highway amounting to a criminal offence under the Highways Act 1980 s.155).

injuries committed by dogs to livestock (s.3),[151] liability for damage caused by straying livestock (s.4),[152] or liability for damage caused by horses to land when on any land in England without lawful authority (s.4A),[153] which are not generally considered in tort courses.

Dangerous/non-dangerous species

The fundamental distinction in the Act is between wild animals (or dangerous species) and domestic animals (non-dangerous species). For example, a tiger will be classified as the former, a cat the latter. Different provisions apply according to the classification of the animal in question. Liability will be imposed on the "keeper" of the animal in both cases. "Keeper" is defined in s.6(3) as the owner of the animal, someone who has it in his possession, or the head of a household where a minor under 16 owns or possesses the animal.[154]

9–043

Dangerous species

These are defined in s.6(2) of the Act.

9–044

> "A dangerous species[155] is a species—
> (a) which is not commonly domesticated in the British Islands; and
> (b) whose fully grown animals normally have such characteristics that they are likely, unless restrained, to cause severe damage or that any damage they may cause is likely to be severe."

This will therefore include animals such as tigers, elephants[156] and lions. As noted in the leading case of *Mirvahedy v Henley*,[157] cases will generally arise in the context of escapes from circuses

---

151   See also Animals Act 1971 ss.5(4) and 9.

152   See also Animals Act 1971 ss.5(5), 5(6), 7 and 8.

153   See also Animals Act 1971 ss.5(5A), 5(6) and 7A- 7C.

154   It should be noted that there may be more than one keeper: see *Flack v Hudson* [2001] Q.B. 698 where an action was brought on behalf of the person with possession of the horse against its owner. The Court of Appeal held that there was nothing in the Act to prevent one keeper suing another. See also Animals Act 1971 s.6(4): "Where an animal is taken into and kept in possession for the purpose of preventing it from causing damage or of restoring it to its owner, a person is not a keeper of it by virtue only of that possession".

155   "Species" includes sub-species and variety: Animals Act 1971 s.11.

156   See *Behrens v Bertram Mills Circus Ltd* [1957] 2 Q.B. 1 (Devlin J) in which it was held to be irrelevant that the elephant in question was a trained circus animal rather than a wild animal. See also *Filburn v People's Palace and Aquarium Co* (1890) L.R. 25 Q.B.D. 258.

157   [2003] UKHL 16; [2003] 2 A.C. 491 at [13] per Lord Walker.

or zoos. Section 2(1) provides that the keeper of the dangerous animal will be strictly liable for any damage caused by such an animal, subject to the defences outlined below. Liability will be regardless of fault and irrespective of any awareness of the animal's dangerous propensities. This appears to be entirely sensible. It is no excuse that your pet tiger escaped despite your reasonable efforts to fence it in. The risk of injury lies firmly on the keeper of any such animal.

Non-dangerous species

9–045

This is rather more complicated. It concerns domesticated animals, e.g. dogs, horses and cattle, and here liability is limited to circumstances where the keeper knows of the danger and that severe injury is likely to arise due to the particular characteristics of the animal. Section 2(2) sets three conditions for liability which must all be satisfied:

> **"(a) the damage is of a kind which the animal, unless restrained, was likely to cause or which, if caused by the animal, was likely to be severe; and**
>
> **(b) the likelihood of the damage or of its being severe was due to characteristics of the animal which are not normally found in animals of the same species or are not normally so found except at particular times or in particular circumstances; and**
>
> **(c) those characteristics were known to that keeper or were at any time known to a person who at that time had charge of the animal as that keeper's servant or, where that keeper is the head of a household, were known to another keeper of the animal who is a member of that household and under the age of sixteen."**

The courts will generally consider each matter in turn. The first two conditions set an objective test. First of all, was the type of damage foreseeable? This has two limbs: either there is a likelihood of damage if the animal is not restrained *or*, if the animal causes any damage, it is likely that the damage will be severe. "Likely" has been interpreted as "to be reasonably expected".[158] It does not require probability, but equally a mere possibility will not suffice. Secondly, did the relevant characteristic of the animal cause the harm suffered? The third condition is subjective: did the keeper know of this characteristic? This requires actual knowledge of the potential danger by the keeper.[159] It does not, however, require the keeper to have actual knowledge of

---

158 Lord Scott in *Mirvahedy v Henley* at [95]; *Freeman v Higher Park Farm* [2008] EWCA Civ 1185; [2009] P.I.Q.R. P6 at [33]. See also Neill LJ in *Smith v Ainger The Times* 5 June 1990: "such as might happen" and "such as might well happen".

159 It is not enough that the keeper ought to have known of the danger: see *Hunt v Wallis* [1994] P.I.Q.R. P128.

the particular circumstances in which the injury arose. It is enough that the keeper knows that animals of the relevant species would behave in that way in those circumstances.[160]

The application of these conditions has caused problems in practice, largely due to their wording, which has been described as giving rise to "several difficulties",[161] "remarkably opaque",[162] "somewhat tortuous",[163] "grotesque"[164] and "inept".[165] The real difficulty arises in interpreting s.2(2)(b). The first limb is fairly straightforward: you will be liable if your animal has characteristics which other animals of the same species do not possess, for example, it is more vicious than usual. These have been called "permanent characteristics".[166]

The second limb deals with "temporary characteristics" and has been described by the House of Lords itself as "ambiguous" and "opaque". It contains a double negative: characteristics not normally found except at particular times or in particular circumstances. Does this mean:

- Normal characteristics which arise at particular times or in particular circumstances?

- Abnormal characteristics which only manifest themselves at particular times?

The House of Lords in the leading case of *Mirvahedy v Henley*[167] by a bare majority (3:2) chose the first explanation. On this basis, normal characteristics which only manifest themselves at particular times or on particular occasions might give rise to liability if the other two conditions are met. As Lord Nicholls indicated, as a matter of social policy, the choice is between placing the burden of liability on those who care for the animals and undertake any associated risks or forcing the public in general to accept that animals inevitably bring with them a risk of injury.[168] In adopting a broad interpretation of s.2(2)(b), the majority ensured that it would be easier in future to bring a claim under the 1971 Act without the necessity to show that the animal at that time was acting abnormally.

The case itself concerned a car accident caused by an alarmed horse bolting onto a busy dual carriageway. Mirvahedy suffered serious personal injuries and his car was badly damaged. The

9–046

---

160 See *Welsh v Stokes* [2007] EWCA Civ 796; [2008] 1 W.L.R. 1224 at [71] per Dyson LJ. Contrast *McKenny v Foster (t/a Foster Partnership)* [2008] EWCA Civ 173 (escape by "extraordinarily agitated" cow in a manner which was not a normal characteristic of breed and was not known to defendant).

161 Lord Denning MR in *Cummings v Grainger* [1977] Q.B. 397 at 404.

162 Ormrod LJ in *Cummings v Grainger* [1977] Q.B. 397 at 407.

163 Slade LJ in *Curtis v Betts* [1990] 1 W.L.R. 459 at 462.

164 Maurice Kay LJ in *Turnbull v Warrener* [2012] EWCA Civ 412; [2012] P.I.Q.R. P16 at [4].

165 Nourse LJ in *Curtis v Betts* [1990] 1 W.L.R. 459 at 468.

166 See Stuart-Smith LJ in *Curtis v Betts* [1990] 1 W.L.R. 459 at 469.

167 [2003] 2 A.C. 491. Comment: K. Amirthalingam (2003) 119 L.Q.R. 563.

168 [2003] 2 A.C. 491 at [6], although his Lordship indicated that where the law in question was governed by statute, such policy decisions must be deemed to have been dealt with by Parliament and it was not for the courts to intervene.

owners of the horse had taken reasonable care to fence in the horse and were not found to be liable on the basis of common law negligence. The case rested on the interpretation of s.2(2) of the Act. It was accepted that there was nothing abnormal in a horse bolting when frightened. It was entirely normal.[169] However, a horse would only bolt in particular circumstances, here where it had been terrified by some unknown event into escaping. The owners of the horse would therefore be strictly liable for the damage caused.

In reaching its decision, the majority affirmed the approach taken in two earlier Court of Appeal decisions in *Cummings v Grainger*[170] and *Curtis v Betts*.[171] In *Cummings*, the plaintiff was attacked and seriously injured by an untrained Alsatian guard dog let loose in the defendant's scrap yard. But for certain defences discussed below, the plaintiff would have succeeded in her claim under the second limb of s.2(2)(b). This was not a ferocious dog possessed of characteristics not normally possessed by Alsatians, but just a typical guard dog which would be likely to attack any intruder into its territory. This was enough to establish the second limb.

Equally, in *Curtis v Betts*,[172] a bull mastiff named Max attacked a ten-year-old child in the street while being transferred from the defendants' house to a Land Rover to be taken to the local park for exercise. The judge found that bull mastiffs[173] have a tendency to react fiercely at particular times and in particular circumstances, namely when defending the boundaries of what they regard as their own territory. Slade LJ remarked that:

> **"The mere fact that a particular animal shared its potentially dangerous characteristics with other animals of the same species will not preclude the satisfaction of requirement (b) if on the particular facts the likelihood of damage was attributable to characteristics normally found in animals of the same species at times or in circumstances corresponding with those in which the damage actually occurred."[174]**

On this basis where an animal is only aggressive in particular circumstances, for example, a dog guarding its territory or, if a bitch, when it has a litter of pups,[175] the keeper may be found liable under s.2(2). Equally, in *Welsh v Stokes*,[176] a "sensible" horse with no history of misbehaviour

---

169 "Normal" is defined in the later case of *Welsh v Stokes* [2007] EWCA Civ 796; [2008] 1 W.L.R. 1224 as "conforming to type", that is, behaving in the same manner as any other type of animal of the species. Dyson LJ advised at [46] that the best evidence of such a characteristic is that it is usually found in such animals.

170 [1977] Q.B. 397.

171 [1990] 1 W.L.R. 459.

172 [1990] 1 W.L.R. 459.

173 The species here is treated as that of a "bull mastiff" rather than dogs in general. See also *Hunt v Wallis* [1994] P.I.Q.R. P128 (comparison with other border collies). From the case law, this only seems to apply to breeds of dogs (except mongrels: *Smith v Ainger The Times* 5 June 1990). Other animals are treated generally, e.g. horses.

174 [1990] 1 W.L.R. 459 at 464.

175 See *Barnes v Lucille Ltd* [1907] L.T.R. 680.

176 [2007] EWCA Civ 796. See also *Collings v Home Office* [2006] 12 C.L. 22 (the fact that the dog, which bit its handler, was in pain, was a circumstance within s.2(2)(b)) and more recently *Williams v Hawkes* [2017] EWCA

which reared up and threw its rider could be regarded as displaying a normal characteristic (rearing as a reaction to fear) in the particular circumstances of the case. However, the mere fact that a horse is heavy and capable of inflicting serious damage to a vehicle is not a characteristic giving rise to liability under s.2(2)(b).[177] As Sedley LJ indicated in *Clark v Bowlt*,[178] the Act does not aim to render the keepers of domesticated animals routinely liable for damage. Some particular characteristic must be relied upon.

Defences

As we saw in relation to the Consumer Protection Act 1987, strict liability does not prevent defences arising. Indeed, Ormrod LJ suggested in *Cummings v Grainger* that in a strict liability situation, defences provide an important means of ensuring fair treatment on both parties and, on this basis, they should not be whittled away.[179] These are listed primarily in s.5 of the Act, although s.10 does provide a defence of contributory negligence.

9–047

(i) Fault of the victim

Section 5(1) provides that the keeper will not be liable where the damage suffered is due wholly to the fault of the person suffering it, for example the claimant is bitten by a dog he has just kicked.

9–048

(ii) Voluntary acceptance of risk

Section 5(2) provides that the keeper will not be liable under s.2 where the victim has voluntarily accepted the risk of injury or damage,[180] that is, the victim has fully appreciated the risk and nevertheless exposed himself to it.[181] There is some possible overlap with s.5(1). For example, a person who tries to escape despite being warned that a police dog will be released may be

9–049

Civ 1846 (escaping steer running onto the road in a panic had acted in accordance with Charolais cattle's propensity to behave unpredictably to averse stimuli) .

177 *Clark v Bowlt* [2006] EWCA Civ 978; [2007] P.I.Q.R. P12: no liability when Chance, a 600 lb horse, moved and hit the front nearside of Clark's car. See also Lord Nicholls in *Mirvahedy v Henley* [2003] 2 A.C. 491 at [46].

178 [2006] EWCA Civ 978; [2007] P.I.Q.R. P12 at [24].

179 [1977] Q.B. 397 at 407.

180 Note also Animals Act 1971 s.6(5): "Where a person employed as a servant by a keeper of an animal incurs a risk incidental to his employment he shall not be treated as accepting it voluntarily".

181 *Cummings v Grainger* [1977] Q.B. 397 at 410; *Freeman v Higher Park Farm* [2008] EWCA Civ 1185; [2009] P.I.Q.R. P6 at [48].

found to be at fault and to have voluntarily accepted the risk of being bitten.[182] Commentators have noted that recent cases have focused on the extent to which defendants can rely on this defence to counteract the strict liability provisions of the Act.[183] In *Turnbull v Warrener*,[184] an experienced horsewoman had fallen off her horse when it had reacted badly to a "bitless" bridle used for the first time. The court found that she knew of, and had accepted, that there was a small chance of an adverse reaction by the horse. On this basis, a s.5(2) defence was made out. *Goldsmith v Patchcott*[185] also involved an experienced horsewoman falling from her horse, but this time she argued that while it was foreseeable that a horse might buck or rear when startled or alarmed, here the horse had bucked and reared far more aggressively than she had anticipated. The Court of Appeal nevertheless found the s.5(2) defence made out. Having known and accepted the risk of such a reaction, the fact the horse reacted more violently than expected was irrelevant. It was not a requirement of s.5(2) that the claimant should foresee the precise degree of energy with which the horse engage in the "characteristic" behaviour complained about under s.2(2) of the Act.

(iii) The victim is a trespasser

9–050

Section 5(3) is divided into two limbs. Under the first limb, the keeper will not be liable for any damage caused by an animal kept on the premises to a trespasser if it is proved that the animal was not kept there for the protection of persons or property. If it is kept there for protection, the keeper will not be liable if it is kept for a purpose which is not unreasonable.

The operation of these defences is illustrated in *Cummings v Granger*.[186] Here, the plaintiff had been bitten when entering a scrap yard at night as a trespasser. Here, the Court of Appeal found s.2(2) to be satisfied, but that the defendant had good defences under s.5(2) and 5(3). Section 5(1) was not satisfied as the incident had not solely been due to the plaintiff's fault. However, she had known that there was a fierce guard dog in the yard and could be taken to have knowingly accepted the risk of injury, satisfying s.5(2). Further it was held that a defence existed under s.5(3) as well:

> **"Old scrap and bits of spares for motor cars are fair game in most parts of the country to anybody who is minded to steal that kind of thing. I do not think that it was in the least unreasonable to keep a guard dog in the yard."[187]**

---

182 See *Dhesi v Chief Constable of West Midlands The Times* 9 May 2000.
183 See B. Compton and J. Hand, "The Animals Act 1971—the statutory defences to strict liability" [2012] J.P.I. Law 18.
184 [2012] EWCA Civ 412; [2012] P.I.Q.R. P16.
185 [2012] EWCA Civ 183; [2012] P.I.Q.R. P11. See also *Bodey v Hall* [2011] EWHC 2162 (QB).
186 [1977] Q.B. 397.
187 Ormrod LJ at [1977] Q.B. 397 at 408. This is now subject to the Guard Dogs Act 1975 s.1, which regulates the use of guard dogs.

Conclusion

As a result of *Mirvahedy*, it will be easier to establish liability under the 1971 Act. The judges in the 2012 Court of Appeal decision in *Turnbull v Warrener* expressed concern at this result: "I cannot help but express my concern about the way that the law has developed".[188] Maurice Kay LJ in that case also mentioned with approval the consultation process launched by Department for Environment, Food and Rural Affairs in March 2009 which sought to amend s.2(2) of the Act, while noting that it had not borne "statutory fruit".[189] Commentators remain pessimistic on the likelihood of immediate change, suggesting that reform at this stage is only likely to come via a Private Member's Bill.[190] The clear message, therefore, is that owning a pet is not only a privilege, but a potential basis for liability.

9–051

---

188 Lewison LJ at [2012] EWCA Civ 412 at [43] with whom Stanley Burnton LJ agreed.
189 [2012] EWCA Civ 412 at [24]. For ongoing criticism of s.2, see Davis L.J. in *Williams v Hawkes* [2017] EWCA Civ 1846 at [4].
190 P. North, *Civil Liability for Animals* (OUP, 2012), p.60.

10

Nuisance and the Rule in *Rylands v Fletcher*

Introduction

10–001

So far, this book has primarily focused on torts which seek to protect the individual from the negligent infliction of harm. The only exception has been liability under certain statutes which, as discussed in Ch.9, impose a form of strict liability on the producer of a defective product or the keeper of an animal. This chapter will consider the torts of nuisance and the rule in *Rylands v Fletcher*.[1] These torts have a different role from that discussed in earlier chapters. Private nuisance, for example, seeks to protect the claimant's ability to use and enjoy his or her land freely without undue interference by the defendant. Here, fault plays only a limited role. The main concern of the courts is to protect the claimant's rights in land. This chapter will examine the rules governing the different types of nuisance recognised at law, the tensions between them, and their relationship with the rule in *Rylands v Fletcher*—which deals only with isolated cases of interference with the claimant's land. It will also consider the impact of the House of Lords' judgments in *Hunter v Canary Wharf Ltd*[2] and *Transco Plc v Stockport MBC*,[3] which have had a dramatic effect on the law of private nuisance and the rule in *Rylands v Fletcher*. This is a developing area of law, impacting on the lives of ordinary individuals and the protection of the environment as a whole.[4] The ongoing role of these torts,

---

1 (1865) 3 H. & C. 774 (Court of Exchequer); (1866) 1 L.R. 1 Ex. 265 (Court of Exchequer Chamber); (1868) L.R. 3 H.L. 330 (House of Lords).
2 [1997] A.C. 655.
3 [2003] UKHL 61; [2004] 2 A.C. 1. See also *Cambridge Water Co v Eastern Counties Leather Plc* [1994] 2 A.C. 264.
4 There is, of course, a limit to what the private action of nuisance or *Rylands v Fletcher* liability can do to protect the environment and such protection is perhaps more efficiently dealt with on a national or international level by legislation in favour of the public at large.

and their difficult relationship with negligence, will be discussed in this chapter. The chapter begins by considering the role of nuisance in the law of torts, before considering liability under the rule in *Rylands v Fletcher*.

Nuisance

There are three main types of nuisance, which should be distinguished:

- Private nuisance.

- Public nuisance.

- Statutory nuisance.

Private nuisance is generally defined as an "unlawful interference with a person's use or enjoyment of land, or some right over, or in connection with it".[5] Consideration of this tort will form the main body of this chapter. Public nuisance, in contrast, is both a crime and a tort. An individual can bring an action where he or she has suffered particular harm from a nuisance which has materially affected the reasonable comfort and convenience of life of a sufficiently large number of citizens who come within the sphere or neighbourhood of its operation. Although the courts frequently draw comparisons between private and public nuisance, they are in reality, very different torts, which seek to protect different interests. Whilst private nuisance seeks to protect private rights, public nuisance is primarily a crime, and acts as a general measure of public protection. Whilst the claimant may seek in his or her Statement of Case to allege that both torts have been committed,[6] it is important to recognise that in character, they have little in common bar their name.

Both private and public nuisance are distinct from statutory nuisances, which are nuisances which operate by virtue of particular statutes. The best example perhaps is that of the Environmental Protection Act 1990 Pt III, which is primarily concerned with matters of public health. As statutory nuisances are unlikely even to provide a claim for breach of statutory duty,[7] they are not dealt with in this book. Readers are advised to consult specialist texts.[8]

---

5 W.E. Peel and J. Goudkamp, *Winfield & Jolowicz on Torts*, 19th edn (Sweet and Maxwell, 2014), para.15–08. P. H. Winfield, "Nuisance as a tort" (1930–32) 4 C.L.J. 189, 190.

6 See, e.g. *Halsey v Esso Petroleum* [1961] 1 W.L.R. 683.

7 *Issa v Hackney LBC* [1997] 1 W.L.R. 956.

8 See, e.g. S. Bell et al, *Environmental Law*, 9th edn (OUP, 2017).

Private Nuisance

10–003

There are three main forms of private nuisance:

- Physical injury to land (for example, by flooding or noxious fumes).

- Substantial interference with the enjoyment of land (for example smells, dust and noise).

- Encroachment on a neighbour's land (for example, by spreading roots or overhanging branches).[9] This is of minor significance but will be considered further in the section on remedies.

While these are merely examples of private nuisance, they do cover most cases. All three forms seek to protect the claimant's use and enjoyment of land from an activity or state of affairs for which the defendant is responsible. A fourth form of nuisance exists which is generally discussed in works on land law, namely where the defendant has interfered with a particular proprietary right the claimant possesses over the land, for example a right of way. Such interference is generally treated by analogy to trespass, in that provided a substantial degree of interference can be shown, the tort will be actionable per se (without proof of damage).[10] By this means, the claimant's rights over land are vindicated, although where the right in question is simply a right to support, damage must be shown.[11]

The main distinction drawn by the courts is between physical damage to property and interference with one's enjoyment of land or personal comfort. Put simply, the courts are more willing to find a nuisance where physical damage to property has been caused. Mere personal discomfort will be treated with latitude unless the interference is such that it is "materially interfering with the ordinary comfort physically of human existence, not merely according to elegant or dainty modes and habits of living".[12] On this basis, loss of a view from one's property is a loss of "elegant" living and not such as to interfere with the ordinary comfort of human existence.[13] So, while the courts are willing to protect the claimant's personal comfort, they are more willing to protect the claimant's property. Thus, there is clear House of Lords authority that matters such as the nature of the locality will not be relevant where there has been material injury to property.[14]

---

9   See *Lemmon v Webb* [1895] A.C. 1, *Delaware Mansions Ltd v Westminster City Council* [2001] UKHL 55; [2002] 1 A.C. 321 and *LE Jones (Insurance Brokers) Ltd v Portsmouth CC* [2002] EWCA Civ 1723; [2003] 1 W.L.R. 427. The rules of causation are the same as for negligence: did the tree roots materially contribute to the damage? (*Loftus-Brigham v Ealing LBC* [2003] EWCA Civ 1490; 103 Con. L.R. 102).

10   *Nicholls v Ely Beet Sugar Factory Ltd* [1936] 1 Ch.343.

11   *Midland Bank v Bardgrove Property Services* [1992] 37 E.G. 126.

12   Sir Knight-Bruce VC in *Walter v Selfe* (1851) 20 L.J. Ch. 433 at 435.

13   *Aldred's Case* (1610) 9 Co. Rep. 57b.

14   *St Helen's Smelting Co v Tipping* (1865) 11 H.L.C. 642 at 651.

What amounts to a private nuisance?

It must be self-evident that not every interference with the claimant's use and enjoyment of land can amount to a private nuisance. For example, I enjoy playing the piano, but of necessity must practise. Can my neighbour complain (a) because I play at all; or (b) because he or she enjoys fine music and the sound of my bad playing is unbearable? If either of the above were actionable, I would be severely limited in my ability to play the piano. My neighbour would be given the power to veto my choice of activity. However, if in a fit of enthusiasm, I decide to practice my scales between 2.00am and 4.00am every morning, my neighbour would appear to have legitimate grounds for complaint.[15] The tort of nuisance must balance my rights against those of my neighbour. Whilst it may be easy to say that noxious fumes which destroy every plant in my garden should be actionable, it is far more difficult to weigh up the complaints of a resident in an industrial area that lorries travelling to a factory cause noise and dust which affect his or her property. The test is one of "reasonable user", balancing the interest of the defendant to use his or her land as is legally permitted against the conflicting interest of the claimant to have quiet enjoyment of his or her land. The ordinary use of your home will not amount to a nuisance, even if it discomforts your neighbour due to poor soundproofing or insulation.[16] As Lord Wright stated in the leading case of *Sedleigh-Denfield v O'Callaghan*[17]:

> **"A balance has to be maintained between the right of the occupier to do what he likes with his own, and the right of his neighbour not to be interfered with."**

"Reasonable user"

The first point to stress is that this is not a standard of reasonable care as in negligence. The rule is one of give and take. I do not expect my neighbours to be perfect or to exist in hermit-like silence and isolation, but neither do I expect my neighbours to use their property in such a way as to render my existence unbearable: I therefore expect them to use it reasonably. However, as in negligence, what is "unreasonable" is difficult to define. It does not require that the defendant's actions must be deliberate. Equally, it is clearly established that, in nuisance,

---

15   The neighbour might in practice prefer to rely on the procedures under the Environmental Protection Act 1990 Pt III, ss.79–80 (duty on the local authority to abate a statutory nuisance where, inter alia, noise is prejudicial to health or a nuisance) and, if available, under the Noise Act 1996 (duty on local authorities to investigate complaints of excessive levels of noise from a dwelling house at night). See, further, texts on environmental law and F. McManus "Noise nuisance in the United Kingdom—a very British solution" (2000) 20 L.S. 264.

16   *Southwark LBC v Mills; Baxter v Camden LBC (No.2)* [2001] 1 A.C. 1; approving Court of Appeal in *Baxter v Camden LBC (No.2)* [1999] 1 All E.R. 237. See J. O'Sullivan, "Nuisance, local authorities and neighbours from hell" [2000] C.L.J. 11.

17   [1940] A.C. 880 at 903.

the defendant's use of land can be "unreasonable" even though he or she has taken all reasonable care to prevent the nuisance occurring.[18] The courts' approach is therefore results-based: is the result of the defendant's conduct such that it is likely to cause unreasonable interference with the claimant's use or enjoyment of land? It is not a question of blaming the defendant, but of protecting the claimant's interest. The question is simply what, objectively, a normal person would find it reasonable to have to put up with.[19] There is, predictably, no set formula for determining what results are unreasonable. It is possible to list a number of circumstances which are clearly relevant to the courts' decisions in particular cases, the answer will vary according to the circumstances of each case.

Factors determining reasonable user

10–006

The following factors are considered in turn below:

- The nature of the locality.

- The duration and frequency of the defendant's conduct.

- The utility of the defendant's conduct.

- Abnormal sensitivity of the claimant.

- Malice on the part of the defendant.

▶ (1) The nature of the locality

10–007

As stated above, this is not relevant where material physical damage has been suffered by the claimant. Where the claimant has suffered personal discomfort and inconvenience, however, it is relevant. The classic quotation is that of Thesiger LJ in *Sturges v Bridgman*: "What would be a nuisance in Belgrave Square would not necessarily be so in Bermondsey".[20] Therefore, in considering whether noise from a local factory causes a nuisance to local residents, the courts will examine the nature of the locality, and if it is an industrial area, will be less likely to find an actionable nuisance.

---

18   *Rapier v London Tramways Co* [1893] 2 Ch.588.
19   *Barr v Biffa Waste Services Ltd* [2012] EWCA Civ 312; [2013] Q.B. 455 at [72] per Carnwath LJ. Note also his Lordship's comments in *Coventry v Lawrence* [2014] UKSC 13; [2014] A.C. 822 at [179]–[180].
20   (1879) 11 Ch.D. 852 at 865. See also Veale J in *Halsey v Esso Petroleum* [1961] 1 W.L.R. 683 and *Miller v Jackson* [1977] Q.B. 966 at 986. For a discussion of the justifications for the locality principle, see S. Steel, "The locality principle in private nuisance" (2017) 76 C.L.J. 145.

The nature of the locality may change over time from industrial to residential, and therefore the courts must have regard to the locality as it is today. Change may happen naturally, or may be due to deliberate development of the locality, as seen with the development of the London Docklands, which was classified as an urban development area. Indeed, in *Gillingham BC v Medway (Chatham) Dock Co Ltd*,[21] Buckley J held that planning permission to develop a disused naval dockyard as a 24-hour commercial dock had changed the character of the neighbourhood. Local residents therefore could not complain about the serious disruption caused to them by its operation. More recently, the Supreme Court in *Coventry v Lawrence*[22] reviewed the extent to which planning permission might change the character of the neighbourhood where the defendants had long-standing planning permission to build a speedway racing stadium and later permission for a motocross track. Lawrence, who had moved into the area in 2006, alleged that there was a noise nuisance. The Supreme Court overturned the decision of the Court of Appeal that the grant of planning permission had by itself changed the nature of the locality. It would be wrong in principle if, through the grant of planning permission, a planning authority would be able to deprive a property-owner of a right to object to what would otherwise be a nuisance, without providing her with compensation. While planning permission could be relevant in, for example, indicating acceptable levels of noise in the neighbourhood and (see para.10–065) in determining the appropriate remedy, the decision whether the activity causes a nuisance or not is for the court, not the planning authority. Giving the leading judgment, Lord Neuberger found that in relation to claims for loss of amenity in nuisance, "the mere fact that the activity which is said to give rise to the nuisance has the benefit of planning permission is normally of no assistance to the defendant in a claim".[23] It should be remembered, therefore, that planning permission is not a defence to nuisance. Where planning permission was given to expand a pig farm adjacent to holiday accommodation, this did not change the nature of the locality, and so did not excuse the nuisance caused to the plaintiffs by the smell of the pigs.[24] Equally, planning permission granted to a landfill site did not prevent local residents from successfully claiming for the amenity loss caused by an odour nuisance.[25]

(2) Duration and frequency

It is a matter of common sense that the claimant will have to endure *some* inconvenience in his or her enjoyment of land. What is unreasonable is when it occurs frequently and for long

10–008

---

21   [1993] Q.B. 343.
22   [2014] UKSC 13; [2014] A.C. 822.
23   [2014] UKSC 13 at [94]. On this basis, Lord Neuberger stated that any argument to the contrary in *Gillingham* [1993] Q.B. 343 could not stand: [99]. His Lordship did accept, however, that there may be an exceptional case in which planning permission will be a consideration in assessing liability: [138].
24   *Wheeler v JJ Saunders Ltd* [1996] Ch.19.
25   *Barr v Biffa Waste Services Ltd* [2012] EWCA Civ 312; [2013] Q.B. 455 (overturning Coulson J at first instance who had argued that acting within statutory permits in the absence of negligence was evidence of reasonable user). Comment: M. Lee, "Nuisance and regulation in the Court of Appeal" [2013] J.P.E.L. 277.

periods of time.[26] Therefore, my neighbour undertaking DIY on Sunday morning must be endured, but my neighbour drilling for 24 hours, or every day between midnight and 2.00am, is unreasonable.

Again, the courts will use a largely common-sense approach to this factor. In *De Keyser's Royal Hotel Ltd v Spicer Bros Ltd*,[27] the court was willing to grant an injunction for a temporary interference when it consisted of pile-driving in the middle of the night, but confined the injunction to forbidding work between 10.00pm and 6.30am. An action for physical damage to property is likely to succeed even where the nuisance is temporary, but in such a case the court will only award damages rather than an injunction. In *Crown River Cruises Ltd v Kimbolton Fireworks Ltd*,[28] the plaintiffs' vessels had suffered substantial fire damage caused by falling debris from a fireworks display to celebrate the fiftieth anniversary of the Battle of Britain. The display had only lasted about 20 minutes, but it was found to be inevitable that debris, some of it hot and burning, would fall on nearby property of a potentially flammable nature. The plaintiffs were therefore awarded damages.

Much ink has been spilt analysing whether an isolated escape can amount to an actionable nuisance. It is true that it is easier to obtain an injunction where the interference is continuous or recurrent, but this does not necessarily exclude an isolated escape of sufficient gravity. The court in *SCM (United Kingdom) Ltd v WJ Whittal & Son Ltd*[29] accepted that such liability could arise where the plaintiff was affected by the state of the defendant's land or activities upon it, but excluded liability for a single negligent act, which it held would only found an action in negligence. Isolated escapes may, of course, be actionable in any event under the rule in *Rylands v Fletcher*, which will be considered later in this chapter, provided the damage suffered is reasonably foreseeable. It is a question, then, of the degree of interference—where an isolated act causes physical damage to property, the courts will generally look for negligence.[30]

▶ (3) Utility of the defendant's conduct

10–009

This is not generally an important consideration. Private nuisance is concerned with the results of the defendant's conduct on the claimant and not on the community as a whole. It has been argued, however, that it should influence the court in exercising its equitable jurisdiction whether to grant an injunction, and will therefore be considered further in the section on remedies.[31]

---

26   See *Andreae v Selfridge* [1938] Ch.1 at 5–6 per Lord Greene MR.
27   (1914) 30 T.L.R. 257.
28   [1996] 2 Lloyd's Rep. 533.
29   [1970] 1 W.L.R. 1017 at 1031—point not considered on appeal [1971] 1 Q.B. 337. See also *British Celanese v Hunt* [1969] 1 W.L.R. 959 at 969 (liability for the way in which metal foil was stored on land) and *Colour Quest Ltd v Total Downstream UK Plc* [2009] EWHC 540 (Comm); [2009] 2 Lloyd's Rep. 1 at [421].
30   *Northumbrian Water Ltd v Sir Robert McAlpine* [2014] EWCA Civ 685.
31   See, further, M. Lee, "The public interest in private nuisance: Collectives and communities in tort" [2015] C.L.J. 329.

(4) Abnormal sensitivity

The result of the defendant's conduct must be such as to unreasonably affect the ordinary citizen. Discomfort resulting from personal sensitivity to noise or heat which would not affect the ordinary citizen will not found an action in nuisance. The leading case is *Robinson v Kilvert*,[32] where the defendant operated a business in the lower part of a building, which required hot and dry air. As a result, the temperature of the floor of the plaintiff's premises above rose to 80°F, which diminished the value of the brown paper stored there. The heat was not such as to affect ordinary paper or to cause discomfort to the plaintiff's workforce. The Court of Appeal refused the plaintiff damages. He had undertaken an exceptionally delicate trade and had not shown an actionable nuisance. This must be correct. It cannot be just to impose a burden on the defendant to compensate all claimants for interference, no matter how sensitive they are. This would unduly interfere with the defendant's own freedom to enjoy his or her property. It should be noted, however, that once an actionable nuisance is shown, the claimant may recover the full extent of his or her losses, even where they result from interference with an exceptionally delicate use of the land.[33]

Yet it may be difficult to determine what we would now regard as "unduly sensitive". It is clear that a person who cannot stand any noise or odours is more sensitive than normal. Does this extend, however, to interference with TV reception or wifi? Unfortunately, there are dicta suggesting exactly that. The root of the problem lies with the decision of Buckley J in *Bridlington Relay v Yorkshire Electricity Board*.[34] The court in that case was unimpressed with the claim of a company, which relayed sound and television broadcasts, that its business would be interfered with by the erection of two pylons within 250 feet of its mast. Buckley J refused an injunction because the defendants had given an assurance that the interference could be remedied, but his Lordship went further and doubted whether interference with a primarily recreational activity could ever found an actionable nuisance. This decision has been dismissed as out-of-date,[35] and Buckley J expressly stated that he was not laying down an absolute rule. Nevertheless, the House of Lords in *Hunter v Canary Wharf Ltd*[36] gave no clear indication as to whether the case would be decided differently today.

More recently, in *Network Rail Infrastructure Ltd v Morris (t/a Soundstar Studio)*,[37] however, the Court of Appeal adopted a more considered approach. Here the claimant was complaining about electromagnetic interference from a section of Railtrack's signalling system to the music created by electric guitars in his recording studio. The court recognised that, although this might have been dismissed as "extra-sensitive" in the past, the use of

---

32 (1889) 41 Ch.D. 88. See also *Heath v Mayor of Brighton* (1908) 98 L.T. 718.
33 *McKinnon Industries Ltd v Walker* (1951) 3 D.L.R. 577 at 581 PC
34 [1965] Ch.436.
35 See *Nor-Video Services v Ontario Hydro* (1978) 84 D.L.R. (3d) 221.
36 [1997] A.C. 655.
37 [2004] EWCA Civ 172; [2004] Env. L.R. 41.

electric and electronic equipment was now a feature of modern life. It thus focused on what was reasonable in the circumstances of the case. Buxton LJ also went further to question the continued utility of *Robinson v Kilvert* when loss, in any event, must be reasonably foreseeable to be actionable in nuisance (see Remoteness below). It is submitted that the concept of abnormal sensitivity is still helpful in indicating when an actionable nuisance will arise, but that the courts should refer to contemporary standards when judging what is an extra-sensitive use of land.

(5) Malice

10–012

In assessing whether the defendant's use of his or her land is reasonable, regard will be had to his or her frame of mind. This can be criticised for judging the defendant's conduct, which is not the role of nuisance, but there seems good authority for the fact that malice will encourage the courts to find an unreasonable user. The case of *Christie v Davey*[38] is the leading authority. The plaintiff was a music teacher who gave lessons at her home. The defendant, her neighbour, found the noise irritating and chose to express his displeasure by knocking on the party wall, beating trays, whistling and shrieking. The plaintiff succeeded in her claim for an injunction. North J held that:

> "... what was done by the defendant was done only for the purpose of annoyance and in my opinion, it was not a legitimate use of the defendant's house."[39]

Christie was followed in *Hollywood Silver Fox Farm Ltd v Emmett*,[40] where Macnaghten J granted an injunction against a defendant who had deliberately fired guns on his own land near its boundary with the plaintiffs' land. The plaintiffs carried on the business of breeding silver foxes on their land, and evidence was given that the discharge of guns during breeding time would frighten the vixens leading them to refuse to breed, miscarry, or kill their young. Although the use of land for breeding foxes was obviously sensitive, the presence of malice was sufficient to overcome this objection.

Such authority should be contrasted with that of the House of Lords in *Bradford Corp v Pickles*.[41] The defendant had deliberately drained his own land, with the intention of diminishing the water supply leading into the plaintiffs' land, and thereby forcing them to purchase his land. The House of Lords did not, however, grant an injunction, and refused to take note of the alleged malice of the defendant. This decision can nevertheless be distinguished from *Christie* in a number of ways. First, the plaintiffs in *Bradford* had no right

---

38   [1893] 1 Ch.316.
39   [1893] 1 Ch.316 at 327.
40   [1936] 2 K.B. 468.
41   [1895] A.C. 587.

to receive the water, and therefore no right had been interfered with on which to found the nuisance. Secondly, at least from the laissez-faire perspective of the nineteenth century, the defendant had done no more than exercise his right to appropriate or divert underground water to obtain a better deal from the plaintiffs. Could this really be regarded as malicious?

Malice will therefore be considered relevant by the courts in applying the test of "reasonable user". Caution should be adopted, however, towards comments in the leading case of *Hunter v Canary Wharf Ltd* (see below)[42] by Lord Cooke, who suggested that malicious erection of a structure for the purpose of interfering with television reception should be actionable in nuisance. These comments were based on Lord Cooke's minority belief that the interference caused by building the Canary Wharf tower was actionable, but could be justified on the ordinary principles of give and take. On this basis, malice (as in *Christie*) would be capable of converting a reasonable user into an unreasonable user. This was not, however, the majority view. On the majority view, as seen above, the claimant has no right to complain in such circumstances. The appropriate analogy would therefore be that of *Bradford Corp v Pickles*: the defendant had a right to build the tower; the claimant had no right which had been interfered with, and so malice would be irrelevant.

Who can sue?

The aim of private nuisance is to protect the claimant's use and enjoyment of land. It is therefore logical that the claimant must have some land which has been unreasonably interfered with. The more difficult question is: what link must the claimant have with the land? Does the law of tort demand an interest in land, as defined by property law, or simply some substantial link with the land? The traditional view was that an interest in land had to be shown. In *Malone v Laskey*,[43] the Court of Appeal refused the plaintiff's action for damages for personal injury when vibrations emitted from the defendant's premises caused an iron bracket supporting a cistern to fall upon her. She was a mere licensee without any interest in land, and so had no cause of action.

This position was challenged, however, by Dillon LJ in *Khorasandjian v Bush*.[44] In this case, Miss Khorasandjian had been subjected to a campaign of harassment by a former boyfriend, for which he had spent some time in prison. She sought an injunction to prevent him "harassing, pestering or communicating" with her, particularly by means of persistent and unwanted telephone calls to her mother's home where she lived. Miss Khorasandjian, in common with Mrs Malone, had no proprietary interest in the home, but Dillon LJ held that "the court has at times to reconsider earlier decisions in the light of changed social conditions" and therefore supported her claim in private nuisance.

10–013

---

42   [1997] A.C. 677.
43   [1907] 2 K.B. 141. See also *Read v Lyons* [1947] A.C. 156 at 183.
44   [1993] Q.B. 727 at 735, relying on the Canadian case of *Motherwell v Motherwell* (1976) 73 D.L.R. (3d) 62.

Khorasandjian was in turn rejected by the majority of the House of Lords in the leading case of *Hunter v Canary Wharf Ltd*.[45] In this case, a number of local residents, who included home-owners, their families and other licensees, had complained about the Canary Wharf tower, which forms part of the Docklands development in London. The tower is nearly 250 metres in height and over 50 metres square, with a metallic surface, and, when erected, was found to interfere with the television reception of neighbouring homes. Two preliminary questions arose:

■ *Did an actionable nuisance exist?*

The House of Lords held that the interference with television reception by the erection of a building did not amount to an actionable nuisance. It was held, by analogy to cases which refused liability for blocking a view,[46] that the defendants were free to build what they wanted on their land, subject to planning controls and proprietary restrictions, such as easements, over the land. Complaints could thus only be made at the planning stage and not by means of the tort of private nuisance.[47] The Court of Appeal recently approved this view, rejecting the argument that erecting a viewing platform which allowed visitors to the Tate Gallery to look into glass-fronted flats nearby could amount to a private nuisance.[48]

■ *If an actionable nuisance existed, who could sue?*

Their Lordships reasserted the traditional view stated in *Malone v Laskey*[49] and held that **only claimants with an interest in land or exclusive possession could bring an action for nuisance**. In the words of Lord Goff: ". . . on the authorities as they stand, an action in private nuisance will only lie at the suit of a person who has a right to the land".[50] This represented a return to the historical roots of private nuisance as a tort to land. It also meant that it would be easier for anyone creating a nuisance to ascertain who to deal with if trying to settle any potential claim. In so doing, the majority of the House of Lords (Lord Cooke dissenting) rejected the opportunity given in *Khorasandjian* to develop the tort to protect the personal interests of anyone occupying the land.

---

45   [1997] A.C. 677.

46   See *Dalton v Angus* (1881) 6 App Cas 740.

47   However, in *Hunter* [1997] A.C. 655, due to the fact that the Secretary of State for the Environment had designated the area an enterprise zone, planning permission was deemed to have been granted for any form of development and no application for permission had to be made.

48   *Fearn v Board of Trustees of the Tate Gallery* [2020] EWCA Civ 104: "the planning system is, I think, a far more appropriate form of control, from the point of view of both the developer and the public" per Sir Terence Etherton MR at [82].

49   [1907] 2 K.B. 141.

50   [1997] A.C. 677 at 692, relying heavily on the classic article of Professor Newark, "The Boundaries of Nuisance" (1949) 65 L.Q.R. 480.

Rights in the land

These were defined by the House of Lords in *Hunter* as consisting of interests in land or exclusive possession. On this basis, if you are a landowner, tenant, grantee of an easement or profit à prendre, or simply have a right to exclusive possession of the land, you may sue, but any lesser right will not suffice. This division was justified by Lord Hoffmann in *Hunter*:

> **"Exclusive possession distinguishes an occupier who may in due course acquire title under the Limitation Act 1980 from a mere trespasser. It distinguishes a tenant holding a leasehold estate from a mere licensee. Exclusive possession de jure or de facto, now or in the future, is the bedrock of English land law."[51]**

The importance of exclusive possession may be seen in the Court of Appeal decision in *Pemberton v Southwark LBC*.[52] In this case, a "tolerated trespasser", that is a former secure tenant, against whom an order for possession had been obtained but suspended whilst she continued to occupy the property and pay rent,[53] was allowed to sue for nuisance when her flat became infested with cockroaches. As stated by Roch LJ:

> **"Possession or occupation by the tolerated trespasser may be precarious, but it is not wrongful and it is exclusive ... In those circumstances, in my judgment, the tolerated trespasser does have a sufficient interest in the premises to sustain an action in nuisance."[54]**

You will not be able to claim, however, if you are simply a member of the landowner's family, a guest, lodger or employee. This does not, of course, stop you seeking alternative remedies in negligence, occupiers' liability, or resorting to the Protection from Harassment Act 1997 (which will be discussed further in Ch.11) providing you can satisfy the necessary requirements to establish liability.

Losses incurred prior to acquisition of a right to land

It should be noted that, provided the nuisance is continuing, there is authority that the claimant may sue for his or her losses even if they began prior to acquisition of the premises. In *Masters v Brent LBC*,[55] Talbot J held that the plaintiff was able to recover the losses incurred by him in

---

51 [1997] A.C. 655 at 703.
52 [2000] 1 W.L.R. 1672 (leave to appeal denied by the House of Lords: [2001] 1 W.L.R. 538).
53 The term comes from *Burrows v Brent LBC* [1996] 1 W.L.R. 1448.
54 [2000] 1 W.L.R. 1672 at 1682.
55 [1978] Q.B. 841, although the close connection between the former owner (the plaintiff's father) and the plaintiff had placed doubt on the scope of this decision.

remedying damage caused by encroaching tree roots, which caused subsidence to the house he had recently acquired. He could show a continuing actionable nuisance and so could recover the total cost of the works necessary to remedy the damage caused by the tree roots to the property. In *Delaware Mansions Ltd v Westminster City Council*,[56] the House of Lords approved this approach. Here, the roots of a tree on council land had caused damage to an adjoining building. Although most of the damage had occurred prior to the claimant's purchase of the property, their Lordships found that where there was a continuing nuisance of which the defendant knew or should have known, the purchaser would be able to recover reasonable remedial expenditure. The claimant was thus able to recover the cost of underpinning works which amounted to over £570,000. It should be noted that in both *Masters* and *Delaware*, there was no possibility of double recovery. Where, for example, the previous owner has incurred some remedial expenditure, a court would apportion the damages awarded between the two parties.

Landlords

10–016

A landlord whose property is leased retains only a "reversionary interest" in the premises, namely his or her right to possession at the end of the term of the lease. The landlord can only sue where the nuisance has harmed this interest in a permanent way, i.e. the value of the property will be diminished when the landlord comes back into possession.[57] Examples include vibrations which affect the structure of the property, and nuisances where there is a risk of the perpetrator gaining a legal right to commit the nuisance by prescription (see below). In contrast, the landlord cannot sue if the interference is of a temporary nature, such as noise or smoke which is unlikely to have any permanent effect on the land. In these circumstances, the action can only be brought by the tenant. The landlord can do nothing if the tenant decides instead to leave, or demands a decrease in rent.

The Human Rights Act 1998

10–017

It has been questioned whether the test in *Hunter v Canary Wharf* confining the right to sue to those with rights to land is compatible with the Human Rights Act 1998. For example, Professor Wright in the first edition of her book, *Tort Law and Human Rights*, suggested that:

> **"it is time for English law to move beyond the straitjacket of the forms of action, so that the boundaries of private nuisance are determined by the link with one's home."**[58]

---

56 [2001] UKHL 55; [2002] 1 A.C. 321. Comment: B. Parker [2002] C.L.J. 260.
57 See *Jones v Llanrwst UDC* [1911] 1 Ch.393 at 404.
58 J. Wright, *Tort Law and Human Rights* (Hart, 2001), p.194. For latest edition see: J. Wright, *Tort Law and Human Rights*, 2nd edn (Hart, 2017).

As explained in Ch.1, HRA 1998 s.6 provides that it is unlawful for a public authority to act in a way which is incompatible with a Convention right and the term "public authority" includes the courts themselves. On this basis, the courts must also take account of the rights established in the Convention and the case law of the Strasbourg court when relevant.[59] The issue here is the European Convention on Human Rights art.8(1). This states that "Everyone has the right to respect for his private and family life, his home and his correspondence".[60] This has been interpreted by the European Court of Human Rights in a broad sense, permitting parties without rights in the home to sue.[61] For example, in *Khatun v United Kingdom*[62]—an appeal from part of the *Hunter* litigation in which the applicants had complained of dust arising from construction of the Limehouse Link Road—the European Commission of Human Rights found that:

> **"in domestic proceedings, a distinction was made between those applicants with a proprietary interest in the land and those without such an interest. For the purposes of Article 8 (art.8) of the Convention, there is no such distinction. 'Home' is an autonomous concept which does not depend on classification under domestic law. Whether or not a particular habitation constitutes a 'home' . . . will depend on the factual circumstances, namely, the existence of sufficient and continuous links."[63]**

This suggests that in a suitable case, a court would be able to challenge the limitation in *Hunter* in favour of a test based on a sufficient link with the land. In *McKenna v British Aluminium Ltd*,[64] for example, Neuberger J in a striking-out decision was prepared to contemplate such a move. Here, over 30 children from a number of households had brought actions for private nuisance and under the rule in *Rylands v Fletcher*, alleging that emissions and noise from the defendants' neighbouring factory had caused them mental distress, physical harm and an invasion of privacy. The judge rejected the defendants' argument that their claims should be struck out unless they could point to a proprietary right.

> **"There is obviously a powerful case for saying that effect has not been properly given to Article 8.1 if a person with no interest in the home, but who has lived in the house for some time and had his enjoyment**

---

59   See HRA 1998 s.2.
60   See HRA 1998 Sch.1 Pt 1.
61   See, e.g. H. Fenwick and R. Edwards, *Fenwick on Civil Liberties & Human Rights*, 5th edn (Routledge-Cavendish, 2016).
62   (38387/97) (1998) 26 E.H.R.R. CD 212. The applicants complained that the work disrupted their rights under art.8 (home and family life) and art.14 (discrimination on the grounds of poverty in that due to the low value of their homes, any diminution of the market value was minimal).
63   (1998) 26 E.H.R.R. CD 212 at 215.
64   [2002] Env LR 30, Birmingham District Registry.

> of the home interfered with, is at the mercy of the person who owns the home, as the only person who can bring proceedings."[65]

Over 15 years later, however, the rule in *Hunter* remains. The evident intention of the House of Lords in *Hunter* was to provide a straightforward rule which sets out the boundaries of the tort and facilitates negotiated settlements of claims. It should also be noted that art.8 is a qualified right and interference may, under art.8.2, be justified on the basis that it is:

> "necessary in a democratic society in the interests of national security, public safety or the economic well-being of the country, for the prevention of disorder or crime, for the protection of health or morals, or for the protection of the rights and freedoms of others."

On the facts of *Khatun*, the Commission ruled that the defendants' activities could be justified as pursuing a legitimate and important aim, given the importance of the public interest in developing the Docklands area of London and the limited interference to the applicants' homes.[66] The proposed change would have altered the fundamental character of the tort.

Despite the implementation of the Human Rights Act 1998, *Hunter* remains good law. The Court of Appeal in the recent case of *Fearn v Board of Trustees of the Tate Gallery*[67] confirmed that "overlaying the common law tort of private nuisance with art.8 would significantly distort the tort in some important respects."[68] Private nuisance being a property tort, mere licensees, said the Court, should have no cause of action despite the fact that art.8 is not limited in this way. It seems that the death knell for *McKenna* has finally been struck.

Who can be sued?

10–018

The most obvious defendant is the person who *created* the nuisance. This is not contentious, but it is important to recognise that the liability of the creator of the nuisance is not dependent on occupation of the land. Even if the defendant no longer occupies the land, and cannot therefore abate (or "stop") any nuisance, he or she may still be liable.[69] However, if the creator cannot be traced or it is not financially viable to sue the creator, a number of other defendants exist:

---

65   Neuberger J left open the question whether the common law should be extended by reference to the law of nuisance, the rule in *Rylands v Fletcher*, negligence or a common law tort analogous to nuisance.

66   The Commission additionally rejected the claim under art.14, on the basis that there were no other persons in "relevantly" similar situations to the applicants.

67   [2020] EWCA Civ 104.

68   [2020] EWCA Civ 104 at [91].

69   See *Thompson v Gibson* (1841) 7 M. & W. 456; 151 E.R. 845.

- the *occupier* of the land; and

- the *landlord*.

We deal with each of these potential defendants in turn.

(1) The occupier of the land

The occupier may find himself or herself liable for nuisances occurring during the period of occupancy even where he or she is not the creator. This will occur in four particular instances.

(I) THE OCCUPIER EXERCISES CONTROL OVER THE CREATOR

The occupier will be liable for a nuisance created by its employees in the course of their employment (under the principles discussed in Ch.7), which will extend to independent contractors where the duty not to create a nuisance is non-delegable. Liability for independent contractors has caused some problems, and the concept of a non-delegable duty has been interpreted broadly. In *Matania v National Provincial Bank*,[70] the occupier of two floors of a building brought an action for nuisance against the occupier of the first floor in respect of the dust and noise caused by the work of his independent contractors. The Court of Appeal held that the employer in such circumstances is liable for the damage occasioned by its independent contractors when their operations, by their very nature, involve a risk of damage to the claimant.

(II) THE OCCUPIER HAS ADOPTED OR CONTINUED A NUISANCE CREATED BY A TRESPASSER

Here, the defendant is rendered liable for his or her omissions in failing to deal with a nuisance created by a trespasser. Liability is, however, far from strict. The defendant is only liable if he or she (i) adopts the nuisance, i.e. uses the state of affairs for his or her purposes or (ii) continues the nuisance, i.e. with actual or presumed knowledge of the nuisance, fails to take reasonably prompt and efficient steps to abate it. The same rule applies to private and public nuisance.[71] The leading case is the House of Lords decision of *Sedleigh-Denfield v O'Callaghan*.[72] A local

10-019

10-020

10-021

---

70 [1936] 2 All E.R. 633. See also *Bower v Peate* (1876) 1 Q.B.D. 321 and *Spicer v Smee* [1946] 1 All E.R. 489.

71 See *Att-Gen v Tod Heatley* [1897] 1 Ch.560, *R. v Shorrock* [1994] Q.B. 279 (liability for rave held on defendant's field) and *Wandsworth LBC v Railtrack Plc* [2001] EWCA Civ 1236; [2002] Q.B. 756 (Railtrack liable for failing to abate public nuisance caused by pigeons roosting under its railway bridge). It is not clear, however, whether the measured duty of care (see below) applies to public nuisance. *Wandsworth* states the law in objective terms and states that nothing in the later authorities should throw doubt on the law as stated in *Tod Heatley* in 1897. However, it also found that Railtrack had the means to abate the nuisance and, in view of its small cost of £9,000, liability would have been found in any event.

72 [1940] A.C. 880.

authority, without the defendant's permission (and therefore as a trespasser), had placed a drainage pipe in a ditch on the defendant's land, with a grating designed to keep out leaves. The grating had not been fixed in the correct position, with the result that during a heavy rainstorm the pipe became choked with leaves and water overflowed onto the plaintiff's land. The House of Lords held the defendant liable. He had adopted the nuisance by using the drain for his own purposes to drain water from his land. He had also continued the nuisance because his manager should have realised the risk of flooding created by the obstruction and taken steps to abate it.

The rule can be justified as one of good sense and convenience. The occupier is best placed to deal with the nuisance, and the House of Lords rejected the idea that it was enough to give the claimant the right to enter on to the land to abate the nuisance. The Court of Appeal has more recently decided that there is no relevant distinction between a nuisance caused by the state of the property and one caused by the activities of trespassers upon it. Therefore, in *Page Motors Ltd v Epsom and Ewell BC*,[73] the local authority was found liable for failing to take reasonable steps to evict travellers whose activities had been harming the plaintiffs' businesses.

(III) THE OCCUPIER HAS ADOPTED OR CONTINUED A NUISANCE CREATED BY AN ACT OF NATURE

10–022

Until *Goldman v Hargrave*,[74] the courts had drawn a distinction between nuisances created by third parties and those resulting from acts of nature. Occupiers were under no duty to abate the latter, although they would have to allow their neighbours reasonable access to abate the nuisance. The Privy Council in *Goldman* refused to maintain this distinction, and held that the House of Lords decision in *Sedleigh-Denfield* should be applied equally to situations where the nuisance had been created by an act of nature. In *Goldman*, a 100 feet high redgum tree, growing in the centre of the defendant's land, was struck by lightning and caught fire. The defendant quite properly cut down the tree, but left it to burn itself out when he could have simply eliminated any risk of fire by dousing the smouldering sections of the tree with water. The wind later picked up and rekindled the fire, which spread, causing damage to the plaintiff's land. In a significant judgment, Lord Wilberforce held that the defendant was liable for not acting against the foreseeable risk of fire.

The Court of Appeal approved Lord Wilberforce's judgment in *Leakey v National Trust*.[75] In this case, it was found that there was no valid distinction between an act of nature affecting something on the land and one deriving from the state of the land itself. In 1976, an exceptionally dry summer, followed by a very wet autumn, had led to subsidence of a hill above the plaintiffs' properties, causing damage to the properties. There was evidence that the defendants had been aware of this potential problem, indeed they had been warned by the plaintiffs,

---

73 (1982) 80 L.G.R. 337. See also *Cocking v Eacott* [2016] EWCA Civ 140; [2016] Q.B. 1080.
74 [1967] 1 A.C. 645.
75 [1980] Q.B. 485. For a recent application, see *Network Rail Infrastructure Ltd v Williams* [2018] EWCA Civ 1514; [2019] Q.B. 601 (infestation by Japanese knotweed diminishing amenity value of neighbouring land).

but had refused to act. The Court of Appeal held that they were liable. Megaw LJ found that it would be a "grievous blot on the law"[76] if the law did not impose liability on the defendants in such circumstances.

THE MEASURED DUTY OF CARE

In finding liability in *Goldman*, Lord Wilberforce, however, made it clear that the defendant's conduct should be judged in the light of his or her resources and ability to act in the circumstances:

10–023

> "The law must take account of the fact that the occupier on whom the duty is cast has, ex hypothesi, had this hazard thrust upon him through no seeking or fault of his own. His interest, and his resources, whether physical or material, may be of a very modest character either in relation to the magnitude of the hazard, or as compared with those of his threatened neighbour. A rule which required of him in such unsought circumstances in his neighbour's interest a physical effort of which he is not capable, or an excessive expenditure of money, would be unenforceable or unjust . . . In such situations the standard ought to be to require of the occupier what it is reasonable to expect of him in his individual circumstances."[77]

Where, therefore, the defendant is poor, and abatement will require vast expense, the defendant will not be considered liable.[78] Equally, less will be expected of the infirm than of the able-bodied. This subjective approach would seem to extend to situations where the occupier is liable for the act of a trespasser or for a failure to support his or her neighbour's land. In *Page Motors Ltd v Epsom and Ewell BC*,[79] for example, the Court of Appeal applied and extended the test to include consideration of the particular character of the defendant. In that case, the defendant was a local authority. The court, in deciding whether it had failed to take reasonable steps, therefore considered the responsibilities of the local authority to the public at large, for example, for the problems likely to be produced by moving the travellers to another site in the borough. Whilst this would justify it acting more slowly than a private individual, permitting the nuisance to continue for five years was clearly excessive. Equally, in

---

76 [1980] Q.B. 485 at 524. See also *Bybrook Barn Garden Centre Ltd v Kent County Council* [2001] Env L.R. 30 CA and *Green v Lord Somerleyton* [2003] EWCA Civ 198; [2004] 1 P. & C.R. 33 (applied to naturally flowing water). The House of Lords in *Marcic v Thames Water Utilities Ltd* [2003] UKHL 66; [2004] 2 A.C. 42, however, distinguished an ordinary occupier of land from statutory occupiers where the law of nuisance must be careful not to impose obligations inconsistent with the statutory scheme under which they operate.

77 [1967] 1 A.C. 645 at 663.

78 Although contrast *Abbahall Ltd v Smee* [2002] EWCA Civ 1831; [2003] 1 W.L.R. 1472, (no allowance made for elderly flat-owner reliant on state benefits), although this may be distinguished on its facts—common sense and justice indicated that cost of repairs to communal roof should be shared equally amongst flat-owners.

79 (1982) 80 L.G.R. 337.

Holbeck Hall Hotel Ltd v Scarborough BC (No.2),[80] the Court of Appeal applied the test to a local authority sued for loss of support. Here, a massive landslip in 1993 had led to the collapse of part of the four star Holbeck Hall Hotel, which was situated at the top of a cliff overlooking the North Sea. As a result, the hotel had to be demolished. The hoteliers sued the local council, which owned the land forming the undercliff between the hotel and the sea, for loss of support, claiming that they should have taken measures to prevent the damage caused. The council had been aware of the danger of landslips due to marine erosion, and had undertaken works in the past, but had not foreseen a landslip of this magnitude. The Court of Appeal rejected the claim. The Wilberforce test would apply to claims for loss of support,[81] but the council could not be found liable for failing to undertake measures which only a geological expert could have identified as necessary. The defendant would thus not be liable where he or she was unable to foresee the extent of the loss suffered. In any event, even if the loss had been foreseeable, in view of the extensive and expensive nature of the works necessary:

> **"the scope of the duty may be limited to warning neighbours of such risk as they were aware of or ought to have foreseen and sharing such information as they had acquired relating to it."[82]**

This subjective test may be contrasted with the objective standard of care adopted in negligence (discussed in Ch.5). We may also note the more restrictive test of remoteness employed in *Holbeck Hall* which requires foreseability of the *extent* of the loss suffered in comparison to the more generous *Wagon Mound* test discussed in Ch.6. The test is confined, however, to circumstances in which the defendant has not created the nuisance.

One final point of comparison may be drawn between *Sedleigh-Denfield* liability, and the duty of care imposed on landowners in negligence for omissions discussed in Ch.2. It will be recalled that in *Smith v Littlewoods*,[83] the occupier was held not to be liable to adjoining occupiers for the acts of vandals who had set fire to a derelict cinema on its land. The court held

---

80   [2000] Q.B. 836. Comment: M.P. Thompson, "Coastal erosion and collapsing hotels" [2001] Conv 177 and C.A. Hopkins, "Slipping into uncertainty" [2000] C.L.J. 438. Applied to loss of support when wall between adjoining properties collapsed in *Ward v Coope* [2015] EWCA Civ 30; [2015] 1 W.L.R. 4081 (measured duties of care on both sides).

81   Thereby overturning previous authority which indicated that there was no positive duty in such circumstances to provide support: *Sack v Jones* [1925] Ch. 235; *Macpherson v London Passenger Transport Board* (1946) 175 L.T. 279. *Holbeck Hall* was applied in *Rees v Skerrett* [2001] EWCA Civ 760; [2001] 1 W.L.R. 1541 where the owner of a terraced house had, when demolishing the house, failed to take reasonable steps to protect the party wall where it was reasonably foreseeable that, if not properly weatherproofed, the wall would suffer damage.

82   See Stuart-Smith LJ [2000] Q.B. 836 at 863. See also *Lambert v Barratt Homes Ltd* [2010] EWCA Civ 681; [2010] 33 E.G. 72 where the court expressly recognised that most local authorities operate under a degree of financial pressure and held that the measured duty of care involved, here, only a duty to co-operate in a solution which involved the construction of suitable drainage.

83   [1987] A.C. 241. See B. S. Markesinis, "Negligence, nuisance and affirmative duties of action" (1989) 105 L.Q.R. 104.

that the occupier would not be responsible where it was no more than a merely foreseeable possibility that trespassers would gain access to land and cause damage to the property of neighbouring owners.[84]

(IV) THE CREATOR IS THE OCCUPIER'S PREDECESSOR IN TITLE

Liability in this context is limited. It can only arise where the nuisance was created by a predecessor in title to the occupier and the occupier knew or ought reasonably to know of the existence of the nuisance.[85] In this sense, it strongly resembles the *Sedleigh-Denfield* principle. Although there is no authority that the subjective standard of care applies, it would be illogical not to apply it in such a case.

10-024

(2) The landlord

On the grant of a lease, the tenant will be in possession and will be liable for any nuisance he or she creates. However, there may be circumstances where an alternative action lies against the landlord. There are three main situations where this may occur.

10-025

(I) WHERE THE LANDLORD PARTICIPATES DIRECTLY IN THE COMMISSION OF OR AUTHORISES THE NUISANCE[86]

The Supreme Court in *Coventry v Lawrence (No.2)* confirmed that the landlord will be liable for nuisance if he/she has actively and directly participated in the commission of the nuisance, or let the property in circumstances where there was a very high degree of probability that the letting would result in the nuisance.[87] The fact that a landlord had done nothing to stop or discourage the nuisance would not be considered to amount to participation. In so doing, it approved the view of Lord Millett in *Southwark LBC v Mills*:

10-026

> "It is not enough for [landlords] to be aware of the nuisance and take no steps to prevent it. They must either participate directly in the commission of the nuisance or they must be taken to have authorised it by letting the property."[88]

Much, therefore, will turn on the facts. The courts will examine, in particular, the purpose for which the premises are let. In *Tetley v Chitty*,[89] for example, the local authority had let

---

84 See Lord Griffiths [1987] A.C. 241 at 251.
85 *St Anne's Well Brewery Co v Roberts* (1928) 140 L.T. 1; *Wilkins v Leighton* [1932] 2 Ch.106.
86 See *Harris v James* (1876) 45 L.J.Q.B. 545.
87 [2014] UKSC 46; [2015] A.C. 106.
88 [2001] 1 A.C. 1 at 22 per Lord Millett, relying on *Malzy v Eichholz* [1916] 2 K.B. 308 (for criticism, see I. Loveland [2005] J.P.L. 405).
89 [1986] 1 All E.R. 663.

a parcel of its land in a residential area to a go-kart club, in the full knowledge that the club intended to use and develop the land for go-karting. The local residents complained, however, at the noise which came from the track. The court found the local authority liable for the nuisance. The noise was the natural and necessary consequence of that activity, and by granting a lease for this purpose, the authority had given express or at least implied consent to the nuisance. In contrast, in *Coventry (No.2)*, the court found no question of the landlords having authorised the nuisance in this case (noise from a speedway racing stadium and motocross track). The nuisance could not be said to be inevitable, or nearly certain, consequence of the letting to the tenants of the premises, the stadium and the track.

Landlord liability equally did not lie in *Smith v Scott*[90] and *Mowan v Wandsworth LBC*.[91] In *Smith*, a dwelling house had been let to a family known by the landlord to be likely to cause a nuisance. The tenants proceeded to cause damage to the neighbouring property of an elderly couple and caused such a nuisance that the couple were obliged to leave their home and seek other accommodation. The landlord had inserted in the tenancy agreement a clause expressly prohibiting the committing of a nuisance. The insertion of this covenant was found to counter any arguments of implied authorisation. It could not be said on the facts that the nuisance was a necessary consequence of the letting. Lord Neuberger warned in *Coventry (No.2)*, however, that if, at the time the lease was granted, a nuisance was inevitable, or close to inevitable, a landlord could not escape liability by simply including a covenant against nuisance in the lease.[92]

In *Mowan v Wandsworth LBC*,[93] the Court of Appeal also struck out a claim against the council on the basis that it could not be said to have authorised the conduct of a tenant suffering from a mental disorder, who lived above the home of the claimant. Reasonable foresight of the nuisance was not sufficient to impose liability on the landlord.

This would seem to let the landlord off fairly easily.[94] In *Smith v Scott*, for example, it was obvious that the tenants would not respect this clause, but foresight was not enough to establish liability. In reality, the courts are being asked to deal with difficult social problems through the imperfect medium of the tort of private nuisance. Issues such as anti-social behaviour and care in the community cannot realistically be dealt with by the courts alone. This provides little consolation, however, to those suffering as a result of these problems.[95]

10–027　The law differs, however, where the person creating the nuisance is not a tenant, but a *licensee*, i.e. not paying rent, but on land with the permission of the "licensor". In *Lippiatt v South*

90　[1973] Ch.314.
91　(2001) 33 H.L.R. 56.
92　[2014] UKSC 46 at [17].
93　(2001) 33 H.L.R. 56.
94　See M. Davey, "Neighbours in law" [2001] Conv 31 and J. Morgan, "Nuisance and the unruly tenant" [2001] C.L.J. 382.
95　See S. Bright and C. Bakalis, "Anti-social behaviour: Local authority responsibility and the voice of the victim" [2003] C.L.J. 305.

Gloucestershire CC,[96] the Court of Appeal was prepared to find a licensor liable for the acts of licensees on its property. In this case, travellers allowed onto the council's land had undertaken a number of acts which harmed the land of neighbouring farmers. Such activities included frequent acts of trespass, stealing timber, gates and fences, dumping rubbish and damaging crops. The local authority was found liable for failing to exercise its powers to evict travellers from its land at an earlier stage. More recently, in *Cocking v Eacott*,[97] the Court of Appeal rejected the argument that licensors should be treated in the same way as landlords where, as here, it was a question of a mother allowing her daughter to stay in residential property on a bare licence. Licensors would be treated in law in the same way as occupiers (see paras 10–020–10–024 above). On this basis, the mother would be liable in nuisance if found to have adopted or continued the nuisance.

Lippiatt and Cocking highlight that the key distinguishing factor between the liability of landlords and licensors is that of possession and control. The licensor, unlike the landlord, has a right to immediate possession and licensees may be evicted more easily than tenants. The licensor is also in a position in law and in fact to control the property. It is deemed irrelevant that the licensor's control is over land and not over the licensee him or herself.

One may question whether such a distinction is fair and always clear, particularly in relation to residential property.[98] It will in practice be far more difficult to bring a claim against a landlord than a licensor. The justification that the claimant may sue the tenant directly, whilst he or she may have difficulties pursuing a licensee, ignores the potential difficulties in obtaining a remedy against a particular tenant (for example, in *Mowan*, the court was not convinced that an injunction would be awarded against a person suffering from a mental disorder).[99] It might be argued that the underlying issue—to what extent can private nuisance deal with the issues arising from problem tenants/occupants?—is equally applicable whether the nuisance is created under a lease or licence. This is not, however, the position of the law.

(II) THE LANDLORD KNEW OR OUGHT TO HAVE KNOWN OF THE NUISANCE BEFORE LETTING

10–028

There is authority that where the nuisance consists of lack of repair, the landlord cannot avoid liability by simply inserting into the lease a covenant that the tenant must undertake the repairs. As Sachs LJ commented in *Brew Bros Ltd v Snax (Ross) Ltd*[100]:

---

96   [2000] Q.B. 51.

97   [2016] EWCA Civ 140; [2016] Q.B. 1080. See R. Hickey, "Possession, control and a licensor's liability for nuisance" [2016] Conv. 296.

98   The distinction is blurred, for example, in cases such as *Chartered Trust Plc v Davies* (1998) 76 P. & C.R. 396, where a landlord was found liable for continuing the nuisance where it had retained control over the common parts in which the nuisance created by its tenant had taken place. For the lease/licence divide, see *Street v Mountford* [1985] A.C. 809; *Bruton v London & Quadrant Housing Trust* [2000] 1 A.C. 406.

99   See *Wookey v Wookey* [1991] Fam 121.

100   [1970] 1 Q.B. 612 at 638–9. Contrast, however, the principle of caveat lessee whereby the tenant cannot sue the landlord for nuisance on the basis that, on taking a lease of the property, he or she takes the property as he or she finds it: *Baxter v Camden LBC (No.2)* [2001] Q.B. 1.

> "As regards nuisance of which [the landlord] knew at the date of the lease, the duty similarly arises by reason of his control before that date. Once the liability attaches I can find no rational reason why it should as regards third parties be shuffled off merely by signing a document which as between owner and tenant casts on the latter the burden of executing remedial work. The duty of the owner is to ensure that the nuisance causes no injury, not merely to get some-one else's promise to take the requisite steps to abate it."

(III) THE LANDLORD COVENANTED TO REPAIR, OR HAS A RIGHT TO ENTER TO REPAIR

10–029

This may be express or implied.[101] Liability is based on the fact that the landlord has retained a degree of control over the condition of the premises. One particular example of implied retention of control is through the Landlord and Tenant Act 1985 ss.11 and 12. If a dwelling house is let for a term of less than seven years, there is an implied and non-excludable covenant to keep in repair the structure and exterior of the house and certain installations for the supply of water, gas, sanitation and electricity. This is supplemented by negligence liability under the Defective Premises Act 1972 s.4. Section 4(1) provides that:

> "Where premises are let under a tenancy which puts on the land-lord an obligation to the tenant for the maintenance or repair of the premises, the landlord owes to all persons who might reasonably be expected to be affected by defects in the state of the premises a duty to take such care as is reasonable in all the circumstances to see that they are reasonably safe from personal injury or from damage to their property caused by the relevant defect."[102]

This duty is owed only if the landlord knows of the defect (whether as the result of being notified by the tenant or otherwise) or ought in all the circumstances to have known of the relevant defect.[103] A defect cannot be a "relevant defect" unless it also amounts to a failure to repair. As the courts have clarified, it is a duty to repair, not a statutory warranty that the premises are reasonably safe.[104]

---

101   See *Mint v Good* [1951] 1 K.B. 517.

102   "Relevant defect" is defined in Defective Premises Act 1972 s.4(3). See *Dodd v Raebarn Estates Ltd* [2017] EWCA Civ 439; [2017] H.L.R. 34. For a recent application of s.4, see *Rogerson v Bolsover* DC [2019] EWCA Civ 226; [2019] 2 W.L.R. 1199.

103   Defective Premises Act 1972 s.4(2). See also s.4(4), which extends the duty to situations where the landlord has reserved the right to enter the premises to carry out any description of maintenance or repair of the premises.

104   *Alker v Collingwood Housing Assoc* [2007] EWCA Civ 343; [2007] 1 W.L.R. 2230.

Must the nuisance emanate from the defendant's land?

Lord Goff commented in *Hunter v Canary Wharf Ltd* that the nuisance would generally arise from something emanating from the defendant's land.[105] He did, however, recognise that there were exceptions to this rule. Injunctions have been granted against brothels and "sex centres", where the complaint has been about the presence of prostitutes and clients visiting the premises, rather than an "emanation" from the land.[106] Some confusion has been caused, however, by the case of *Hussain v Lancaster CC*.[107] Here, the claimants were shopkeepers in a council housing estate, who had been subjected to racial harassment and vandalism by other council tenants. Some individuals were prosecuted, but a total of 106 people had been involved in these actions. The Court of Appeal rejected a claim for nuisance on the basis that while the actions of the tenants unquestionably interfered with the claimants' enjoyment of their land, they did not involve the use of the defendants' land and so fell outside the scope of the tort. As explained in the subsequent decision of *Lippiatt v South Gloucestershire CC*,[108] *Hussain* concerned individual acts by perpetrators who just happened to live in council property. Their conduct was in no sense linked to, nor did it emanate from, their homes. In contrast, in *Lippiatt*, the court held that the land on which the travellers resided had been used as a "launching pad" for repeated acts of damage, and so the council would be liable. Whilst Evans LJ suggested that there had thus been an "emanation" in *Lippiatt*—namely the travellers themselves—Staughton LJ was less convinced:

> "It seems to me that there is not a great difference in such a case whether the offending act of the defendant takes place on his land, or on the public road outside his gate. But we need not rule on that today."[109]

Despite *Hussain*, we can conclude that a nuisance will *generally* emanate from the defendant's land, but there is no real authority to render it an absolute requirement.

Relevant defences

There are a number of defences which apply to an action for nuisance. The general defences of voluntary assumption of risk and contributory negligence apply but will be discussed in more detail in Ch.16. It should be noted that although the Law Reform (Contributory Negligence) Act

---

105 [1997] A.C. 655 at 685–686.
106 *Laws v Florinplace* [1981] 1 All E.R. 659, *Thompson-Schwab v Costaki* [1956] 1 All E.R. 652 and *Church of Jesus Christ of the Latter-Day Saints v Price* [2004] EWHC 3245 (QB).
107 [2000] Q.B. 1.
108 [2000] Q.B. 51.
109 [2000] Q.B. 51 at 65.

1945 does not expressly mention nuisance, its provisions are generally accepted to apply. We confine our examination here to defences which are peculiar to nuisance. These are:

- Statutory authority.

- 20 years' prescription.

- Inevitable accident.

- Act of a stranger.

The most significant defence is that of statutory authority.

(1) Statutory authority

10-032   Many nuisances are caused by activities undertaken by local authorities or other bodies acting under statutory powers. If their actions are within the scope of the statute (or intra vires), they are authorised by Act of Parliament and cannot be challenged by the courts. Parliament is presumed to have considered the competing interests, and to have determined which is to prevail in the public interest and whether or not compensation is to be paid to those adversely affected. It is important to distinguish this defence from planning permission, by which the applicant is given permission to construct a particular building.[110] This does not mean that his or her actions have been authorised by Parliament. Planning permission is, at most, a matter to be considered in identifying the nature of the locality of the nuisance. The question here is very different: does the defendant have statutory authority to commit the nuisance?

The vital question, then, is whether the operations causing the alleged nuisance are within the authority given by statute. Generally, this will be the case if the statute expressly or by necessary implication authorises the nuisance, or the nuisance is the inevitable consequence of the performance of the authorised operations. The leading case on statutory authority is *Allen v Gulf Oil Refining Ltd*.[111] Gulf Oil had obtained its own private Act of Parliament to authorise its expansion in Milford Haven, South Wales. The Act provided specifically for the acquisition of all necessary land and the construction of a refinery, but no express provision was made for the use and operation of the refinery once it had been built. Local residents complained about the noise and vibrations emitted by the refinery and *Allen* was brought as a test case. The House of Lords took the question to be one essentially of statutory construction. Was the nuisance authorised, expressly or implicitly, by the relevant statute? If so, the defendant would not be liable. The burden was, however, on the defendant to satisfy the court that this was in fact so.

---

110   As emphasised by the Court of Appeal in *Barr v Biffa Waste Services Ltd* [2012] EWCA Civ 312; [2013] Q.B. 455.
111   [1981] A.C. 1001.

The court held, by a majority of four to one, that the operation of the refinery was implicitly authorised by the Act, the nuisances were inevitable, and so Gulf Oil had a good defence to the plaintiffs' action. The plaintiffs would only have a remedy to the extent to which any nuisance exceeded the statutory immunity.

The nuisance will not be inevitable if it has been caused by the negligence of the defendant. "Negligence" here is used in a special sense to mean a failure by the undertaker to carry out the work and conduct the operation with all reasonable regard and care for the interests of other persons.[112] It should be noted that an inevitable nuisance, even when committed without negligence, is unlikely to be considered authorised if the statute contains a "nuisance clause" providing that nothing in the Act shall exonerate the undertaker from liability for the nuisance.[113] Equally, if the defendant has a choice how to exercise a statutory power, and chooses an option which creates a nuisance when there are other options which would not have raised such problems, it is unlikely to be found to be authorised.[114]

The Human Rights Act 1998 may, additionally, have some impact on this defence. Section 3(1) of the Act provides that:

> "So far as it is possible to do so, primary legislation and subordinate legislation must be read and given effect in a way which is compatible with the convention rights."

It is possible that conduct authorised by statute may conflict with an individual's rights, for example, in relation to art.8 (right to private and family life). The House of Lords' decision in *Ghaidan v Godin-Mendoza*[115] indicates that the courts do possess broad interpretative powers to avoid all such conflicts without resorting to a declaration of incompatibility under s.4 of the Act.

(2) 20 years' prescription

10–033

Prescription provides a means by which the defendant obtains a legal right to act in a certain way, which would ordinarily be contrary to the law, due to the passage of time. In this context, it will be a valid defence for the defendant to show that the nuisance complained of had interfered with the claimant's interest in land for more than 20 years. The defendant must, however, be able to show at least 20 years' uninterrupted enjoyment *as of right*, that is, not by force,

---

112 See *Wildtree Hotels Ltd v Harrow LBC* [2001] 2 A.C. 1 at 13 per Lord Hoffmann.
113 See *Department of Transport v NW Water Authority* [1983] 3 W.L.R. 105 at 109, approved [1984] A.C. 336 at 359. This only applies to statutory powers and will not apply to statutory duties.
114 *Metropolitan Asylum District v Hill* (1881) 6 App. Cas. 193.
115 [2004] UKHL 30; [2004] 2 A.C. 557 (Millett dissenting): interpretation of the Rent Act 1977 Sch.1 para.2 to comply with arts 8 and 14. See also *R. v A (No.2)* [2001] UKHL 25; [2002] 1 A.C. 45 (interpretation of Youth Justice and Criminal Evidence Act 1999 s.41(3) to comply with art.6), and A. Kavanagh, "The role of parliamentary intention in adjudication under the Human Rights Act 1998" (2006) 26 O.J.L.S. 179.

stealth or with the permission of the owner. If objections are made but the activity carries on regardless, prescription cannot be established.[116]

It should be noted, however, that this applies only to private nuisance. It does not apply to public nuisance, on the basis that length of time should not legitimise a crime. The period is judged carefully, because the law does not easily diminish property rights. Time will only run when the nuisance is known by the claimant to affect his or her interests and can be objected to. The difficulties faced in successfully relying on this defence were shown in *Sturges v Bridgman*.[117] In this case, a confectioner had used large pestles and mortars at the back of his premises for more than 20 years. His premises were adjacent to the garden of a doctor, who made no complaint until he decided to build a consulting room at the end of his garden. Then, for the first time, he became aware that the noise and vibration materially interfered with the pursuit of his practice. The court granted the doctor an injunction, despite the fact that the noise and vibrations had existed for over 20 years and that he had chosen to build in his garden in the full knowledge of the defendant's operations (it was no defence that the plaintiff came to the nuisance—see below). Here, the nuisance only became actionable when the doctor had built and started to use his new consulting room. On this basis, the nuisance in *Sturges* had not been actionable for more than 20 years so prescription was not a defence.

(3) Inevitable accident

10–034   The defence of inevitable accident is based on the fact that the damage suffered by the claimant occurred despite the exercise of all reasonable care by the defendant. On this basis, this defence can only be relevant to torts where the exercise of reasonable care is necessary for liability and is essentially an argument that the defendant was not in breach. It therefore plays a minimal role in the tort of nuisance and is only relevant where liability is dependent upon proof of negligence.

(4) Act of a stranger

10–035   This defence is subject to the principle in *Sedleigh-Denfield v O'Callaghan*.[118] Reference should therefore be made to the earlier part of this chapter.

---

116   *Coventry v Lawrence* [2014] UKSC 13 at [31], *Peires v Bickerton's Aerodromes Ltd* [2016] EWHC 560 (Ch); [2016] Env. L.R. 27 at [87].
117   (1879) 11 Ch.D. 852.
118   [1940] A.C. 880.

Ineffective defences

The following are defences which have been rejected by the courts:

- The claimant came to the nuisance.

- The defendant's conduct has social utility.

- *Jus tertii.*

- The nuisance is due to many.

(1) Coming to the nuisance

It is a well-established rule that the claimant may sue even though the nuisance was, to his or her knowledge, in existence before he or she arrived at the premises. By upholding such a rule, the courts clearly favour the right of the claimant to enjoy his or her land freely. The claimant is able to attack the status quo on the basis of his or her own personal interests, despite the fact it may result in the closing down of established businesses or put an end to activities which benefit the community as a whole. The classic case is that of *Bliss v Hall*,[119] in which the defendant's business of manufacturing candles gave off offensive smells. It was no defence to the plaintiff's action that the business had already been in existence for three years before the plaintiff moved in nearby. In more recent times, the rule has been criticised as being unduly favourable to the claimant. In *Miller v Jackson*,[120] the defendants had used a cricket ground for over 70 years. In 1972, the land to the north of the cricket ground was sold to developers, who built a line of semi-detached houses there. The plaintiffs bought one of these properties and complained that despite the fence around the ground (which was increased in height in 1975) cricket balls had been struck into their garden or against their house on a number of occasions. The Court of Appeal was sympathetic to the club. If the plaintiffs were granted an injunction, the club would be closed down at the instigation of parties who had chosen to move to a property adjoining a cricket club. Nevertheless, the majority held that *Sturges v Bridgman*[121] was still good law, and they were bound to hold that it was not a good defence that the plaintiffs had come to the nuisance. As Geoffrey Lane LJ explained, ". . . it is not for this court as I see it to alter a rule which has stood for so long".[122] This did not prevent the majority ruling that it would not be equitable to award an injunction in such circumstances, thereby confining the plaintiffs' remedy to an award of damages. The Supreme Court in *Coventry*

---

119 (1838) 4 Bing. N.C. 183 at 185; 132 E.R. 758 at 759.
120 [1977] Q.B. 966.
121 (1879) 11 Ch.D. 852.
122 [1977] Q.B. 966 at 987.

v Lawrence[123] did, however, suggest that in cases where the complaint relates to discomfort, it may be necessary to review this position where it is only because the claimant has changed the use of, or built on, her land that the defendant's pre-existing activity is claimed to have become a nuisance. This, it argued, was consistent with the principle of "give and take" between neighbours. This case will be discussed further in the section on remedies below.

(2) Utility

10–038

The courts will not accept a defence that the nuisance caused by the defendant has a benefit to the public at large. This is a further example of the law's support for the property rights of the individual, as is clearly seen in the case of *Adams v Ursell*.[124] The defendant ran a fried fish shop in a residential part of a street. The court granted an injunction restraining the defendant from carrying on his fried fish business on the premises, and rejected the argument that the closure of the shop would cause great hardship to the defendant and to his customers, for whom it was a cheap source of nourishment.

(3) Jus Tertii

10–039

This rests on the allegation that a third party has a better title to the affected land than the claimant, and that the third party should therefore be bringing the action. It has been rejected in a number of cases.[125] It seems correct that where the claimant must show an interest in land or right to exclusive possession, this should be sufficient to found his or her claim.

(4) Due to many

10–040

It is no excuse that the defendant was simply one of many causing the nuisance in question. This will be so even if his or her actions in isolation would not amount to a nuisance. In *Lambton v Mellish*,[126] the plaintiff sought an injunction against two rival businessmen who operated merry-go-rounds accompanied by music on their premises. The combined noise was found to be "maddening". Chitty J was not prepared to excuse one of the defendants on the basis that his contribution to the noise was slight:

> "if the acts of two persons, each being aware of what the other is doing, amount in the aggregate to what is an actionable wrong,

---

123 [2014] UKSC 13 at [58] (although this point was obiter).
124 [1913] 1 Ch.269.
125 See, e.g. *Nicholls v Ely Beet Sugar Factory* Ltd [1936] 1 Ch.343.
126 [1894] 3 Ch.163.

> each is amenable to the remedy against the aggregate cause of complaint."[127]

Again, this seems to be a rule of convenience in favour of the claimant, although it may be justified on the basis that the defendant's conduct should be considered in the light of all the surrounding circumstances, including the conduct of others. Therefore, an act which would have been reasonable in isolation may, in the light of all the circumstances, amount to an unreasonable interference with the claimant's use and enjoyment of land.

Relationship between Private Nuisance and Other Torts

It is important to distinguish private nuisance from other torts, such as negligence and trespass, which are commonly claimed in the same action. The relationship between private and public nuisance has already been dealt with above (see para.10–002).

`10–041`

The relationship between private nuisance and negligence[128]

This has caused the most controversy over the years, primarily due to a number of cases which focus on negligence in determining whether the defendant has committed an actionable nuisance. The clearest example of this is the group of cases on continuing or adopting a nuisance. In *Goldman v Hargrave*,[129] Lord Wilberforce remarked that:

`10–042`

> "The present case is one where liability, if it exists, rests upon negligence and nothing else; whether it falls within or overlaps the boundaries of nuisance is a question of classification which need not here be resolved."

---

127 [1894] 3 Ch.163 at 166.
128 See C. Gearty, "The place of private nuisance in a modern law of torts" (1989) 48 C.L.J. 211; M. Lee, "What is private nuisance?" (2003) 119 L.Q.R. 298; A. Beever, *The Law of Private Nuisance* (Hart, 2013), Chs 7 and 8.
129 [1967] 1 A.C. 645 at 657. Consider, also, defences such as act of stranger (paras 10–035 and 10–060).

However, Megaw LJ in *Leakey v National Trust*[130] described the claim as one in nuisance, and, as stated earlier, such cases are distinct from ordinary claims in negligence in that (a) they impose liability for an omission, and (b) they impose a subjective standard of care.

The accepted position is that the two torts are conceptually distinct, and this was emphasised by the House of Lords in *Hunter v Canary Wharf Ltd*[131] and *Cambridge Water Co v Eastern Counties Leather Plc*.[132] The central concept of private nuisance is that of "reasonable user". This is distinct from negligence. There is clear authority that the defendant may be liable in spite of exercising reasonable care and skill.[133] As stated above, the concept of reasonable user is results-based: is the result of the defendant's conduct such that the claimant suffers unreasonable interference with the use and enjoyment of his or her property? This is a very different approach from that in negligence. For example, the classic case of negligence is that of a road traffic accident caused by the negligent driving of a motorist. The court does not consider the degree of injury suffered by the particular claimant, and weigh this against the right of the particular motorist to drive his or her car without restriction. Rather, it draws on case law which has established that the motorist owes a duty of care to pedestrians and other road-users, and ascertains whether he or she has driven below the standard of the ordinary reasonable driver, thereby causing the accident.

A further distinction is that while negligence primarily protects against personal injury, private nuisance seeks to protect interests in land. This is forcefully stated by the majority of the House of Lords in *Hunter*. The role of private nuisance is to remedy undue interference with rights in land—therefore the only parties who can sue are those with an interest in land or exclusive possession which has been interfered with. Their Lordships, in *Hunter* and *Transco*, went further, suggesting that only negligence was capable of protecting against personal injury, as this is not the concern of private nuisance. The implications of this will be considered further in para.10–068.

It is clear, therefore, that while the torts overlap, and the fact that the defendant's actions were committed negligently may encourage a court to find liability, the torts are distinct. This is not to deny that the growth of negligence in the twentieth century has influenced the development of the older tort of private nuisance. This influence may be seen in relation to the rules relating to the continuation or adoption of a nuisance (see above) where an occupier may be found liable for failing to take reasonable steps to abate the nuisance on land. Equally, the rules of remoteness set out in *The Wagon Mound (No.1)*[134] are common to negligence, private and public nuisance.[135] This does not signify, however, that the courts will not continue to distinguish between the two different torts.

---

130 [1980] Q.B. 485.
131 [1997] A.C. 655.
132 [1994] 2 A.C. 264.
133 *Rapier v London Tramways Co* [1893] 2 Ch. 588.
134 [1961] A.C. 388.
135 See *The Wagon Mound (No.2)* [1967] 1 A.C. 617. See below.

The relationship between private nuisance and trespass to land

10–043

Both torts have the common aim of protecting those with an interest in or exclusive possession of land. Trespass to land will be discussed in more detail in our next chapter: Ch.11. For the moment, it should be noted that trespass involves an intentional and direct act which interferes with the land. It is actionable without proof of damage. In contrast, nuisance involves an indirect act which is only actionable on proof of damage. The distinction is historical, and results from the old rigid forms of action, which required that a claim had to be made in a certain form or not at all. Although the forms of action were abolished in the nineteenth century, the distinction between direct and indirect forms of interference with land persists. The distinction may be illustrated by the following classic example: I throw a log onto your land—this is a direct interference and therefore I am liable in trespass even if it does not cause you injury or property damage. (Obviously more compensation will be recovered if it crashes through your greenhouse!) Alternatively, I pile up some logs on my land and one of them rolls off the pile and onto your land. Here, the interference is indirect and it will only be actionable in nuisance if you can show that it has caused some injury to your rights in the land.

Public Nuisance[136]

10–044

It is important, before examining the rule in *Rylands v Fletcher*, to give an overview of the tort of public nuisance. Public nuisance has a minor role to play in the law of torts – its role has been largely overtaken by statute—and so the aim of this section will be to give the reader a general idea of its impact rather than a detailed discussion of its application. The classic definition may be found in Romer LJ's judgment in *Att-Gen v PYA Quarries Ltd*[137]:

> **"any nuisance is 'public' which materially affects the reasonable comfort and convenience of life of a class of Her Majesty's subjects. The sphere of the nuisance may be described generally as 'the neighbourhood'; but the question whether the local community within that sphere comprises a sufficient number of persons to constitute a class of the public is a question of fact in every case."**

---

136 See J. Spencer, "Public nuisance—A critical examination" [1989] C.L.J. 55, who, at 59, describes it as "a ragbag of odds and ends".

137 [1957] 2 Q.B. 169 at 184. See also Denning LJ at 190–191.

It is not necessary to show that every member of the class has been affected, but the nuisance must be shown to injure a representative cross-section of the class.

More recently, the House of Lords in *R. v Rimmington; Goldstein*[138] examined the application of public nuisance in modern law. In *Rimmington*, the defendant had sent over 500 racially abusive letters and packages to different individuals all over the country. In *Goldstein*, the defendant, as a joke, had sent an envelope containing salt to a friend, which backfired completely when it leaked out in the postal sorting office and triggered an anthrax scare. Neither defendant was found guilty of public nuisance. In the first case, their Lordships emphasised that a section of the community must be affected.[139] It was not enough to inconvenience selected individuals. Mr Goldstein was equally not guilty of a public nuisance where it could not be shown that he knew or reasonably should have known that a public nuisance would occur as a consequence of his actions.[140]

As Lord Denning remarked in *Southport Corp v Esso Petroleum Co Ltd*,[141] "the term 'public nuisance' covers a multitude of sins, great and small". The tort has indeed been used to deal with a variety of situations including pollution from oil and silt, pigeon droppings, bogus bomb alerts, pirate radio broadcasting and raves. Its most common use, however, is in relation to claims for unreasonable interference with the claimant's use of the highway. Obviously, in such cases, it will be difficult to bring a claim in private nuisance unless the interference affects the use and enjoyment of the claimant's land, and here the complaint will generally relate to the claimant's right to pass along the highway.

Obstructions on the highway

10–045

While complaints as to the condition of the highway itself will now largely be covered by the Highways Act 1980, the claimant may wish to bring an action relating to unreasonable obstructions on the highway. As noted in *Dymond v Pearce*,[142] some obstructions are inevitable. It is generally acceptable for vehicles to stop on the highway to deliver goods or to park in a lay-by, but a prima facie nuisance would be created where a vehicle is left for a considerable period without any valid justification. Equally, whilst it is reasonable for a person to put up scaffolding for works on his or her house which obstructs the highway on a temporary basis, a nuisance would be created if the erection of the scaffolding was unreasonable in size or duration.[143] It is a matter of degree. It is still unclear whether fault is necessary to

---

138 [2005] UKHL 63; [2006] 1 A.C. 459. Although these are criminal cases, Lord Bingham expressly stated that the ingredients of public nuisance as a crime or a tort were the same: at [7].

139 "A core element of the crime of public nuisance is that the defendant's act should affect the community, a section of the public, rather than simply individuals": Lord Rodger [2005] UKHL 63; [2006] 1 A.C. 459 at [47]. See also *DPP v Fearon* [2010] EWHC 340 (Admin): single act of soliciting not a public nuisance.

140 Following *R. v Shorrock* [1994] Q.B. 279.

141 [1954] 2 Q.B. 182 at 196.

142 [1972] 1 All E.R. 1142.

143 *Harper v Haden* [1933] Ch.298.

establish that the obstruction is unreasonable. Certainly, the majority in *Dymond* were prepared to contemplate liability where an action for negligence would fail, despite statements to the contrary in *The Wagon Mound (No.2)*.[144] Lord Denning MR attempted a compromise in *Southport Corp v Esso Petroleum Co Ltd*[145] by suggesting that for public nuisance, unlike negligence, once the nuisance was proved, the legal burden would fall on the defendant who caused it to justify or excuse himself or herself. This would serve to keep the torts logically distinct, but as the House of Lords on appeal did not deal with this matter, the view of Lord Denning MR is not authoritative. The courts still experience difficulty in separating the question whether there is a nuisance (i.e. an unreasonable obstruction of the highway) from the question of fault.

Projections over the highway

There is further confusion whether fault is relevant when the claimant's injuries are caused by an object projecting onto the highway from the defendant's land. In *Tarry v Ashton*,[146] an occupier had been found liable when a heavy lamp, attached to the front of his building on the Strand, fell on a passer-by. The occupier was held to owe a positive, continuing and non-delegable duty to keep the premises in repair so as not to prejudice the public. In *Noble v Harrison*,[147] however, the court held that the defendant could only be liable if he or she knew, or should have known, of the circumstances which caused the injury. Here, a branch of a beech tree growing on the defendant's land, which overhung the highway, had suddenly broken and damaged the plaintiff's vehicle. The fracture had been due to a latent defect which could not have been detected by reasonable and careful inspection. Rowlatt J held that the defendant was not liable and distinguished the earlier decision of *Tarry v Ashton*[148] on the basis that it applied to artificial rather than natural objects.

The Court of Appeal in *Wringe v Cohen*[149] continued to follow *Tarry* as imposing a rule of strict liability in respect of artificial structures projecting onto the highway:

> "... if, owing to want of repair, premises on a highway become dangerous and, therefore, a nuisance and a passer-by or an adjoining owner suffers damage by their collapse, the occupier, or owner if he has undertaken the duty of repair, is answerable whether he knew or ought to have known of the danger or not."

10–046

---

144 *Overseas Tankship (UK) Ltd v Miller Steamship Co Pty* [1967] 1 A.C. 617.
145 [1954] 2 Q.B. 182 at 197.
146 (1876) 1 Q.B.D. 314.
147 [1926] 2 K.B. 332.
148 (1876) 1 Q.B.D. 314.
149 [1940] 1 K.B. 229 at 233.

This line of authority was followed by the Court of Appeal in *Mint v Good*.[150] As a result of these decisions, the courts apply different rules depending on whether the projection onto the highway is artificial or natural. This distinction is difficult to justify on principle, but, as may be seen above, owes more to the court's willingness in *Noble* to distinguish a line of authority it preferred not to follow.

However, in practice, the distinction between the different rules is not great. The court in *Wringe v Cohen* recognised two defences which had been mentioned by Blackburn J in *Tarry*: (i) where the danger had been caused by the unseen act of a trespasser, and (ii) where the damage is due to a "secret and unobservable operation of nature" (a latent defect) of which the occupier does not know or ought not to have known. Such defences largely undermine the idea of strict liability for projections on the highway and clearly inject an element of fault. Here, once again, we can observe the influence of negligence on the development of the tort of nuisance. It should also be noted that the Court of Appeal in *Salsbury v Woodland*[151] refused to extend *Tarry* to work undertaken near the highway in circumstances where, if care was not taken, injury to passers-by might be caused. The court held that no such category of strict liability existed, and that the ordinary rules of negligence would apply. The occupier would, however, have been strictly liable for the actions of his independent contractors if the work had been inherently dangerous (see our earlier discussion of this point under Private Nuisance, at para.10–20).

Particular damage

10–047

It is not enough for the claimant to show that he or she is a member of the class whose reasonable comfort and convenience has been materially affected by the defendant. To bring an action in tort, the claimant must show that he or she has suffered "special" or "particular" damage in excess of that suffered by the public at large.[152] This is largely a measure to limit the number of claims and avoid the defendant being deluged with claims from every member of the class affected. Such special damage must be direct and substantial and includes personal injury, property damage, loss of custom or business and, it is claimed, delay and inconvenience. The latter category is contentious, and it has been suggested that the claimant must also show pecuniary loss due to the delay.[153] If the individual cannot prove special damage, the only other basis on which an action may be brought in tort is in the name of the Attorney-General by means of a relator action (for example, see *PYA Quarries* above). This is seldom used. Alternatively, the local authority may be persuaded to exercise its power under the Local Government Act 1972 s.222 to bring proceedings for an injunction when it considers it "expedient for the promotion or protection of the interests of the inhabitants of their area".[154]

---

150 [1951] 1 K.B. 517.
151 [1970] 1 Q.B. 324 at 345, CA.
152 See G. Kodilinye, "Public nuisance and particular damage in the modern law" (1986) 2 L.S. 182.
153 See *Winterbottom v Lord Derby* (1867) L.R. 2 Ex. 316 at 321–322.
154 See, e.g. *Stoke-on-Trent City Council v B & Q (Retail) Ltd* [1984] A.C. 754. In *Wandsworth LBC v Railtrack Plc*

The Rule in *Rylands v Fletcher*

10–048

So far, we have considered the way in which nuisance protects the claimant's ability to exercise his or her rights over land without undue interference by the defendant. In this section, we consider a particular cause of action which protects an occupier against interference *due to an isolated escape* from his or her neighbour's land. The particular rules relating to this cause of action, and its relationship with nuisance, will be considered below. First, let us examine the case which provides both the principle and the name for this cause of action: *Rylands v Fletcher*.[155]

The defendant was a millowner, who had employed independent contractors to build a reservoir on his land to provide water for his mill. During the course of building, the independent contractors discovered some old shafts and passages of an abandoned coalmine on the defendant's land, which appeared to be blocked. When the reservoir was filled, the water burst through the old shafts, which were subsequently found to connect with the plaintiff's mine. As a result, the plaintiff's mine was flooded and he sought compensation.

Although the independent contractors had clearly been negligent in failing to ensure that the mine shafts were blocked off securely, the plaintiff's action was against the millowner. The millowner had not been shown to be negligent. The plaintiff also faced the added obstacle that the courts had severe doubts whether an isolated escape, as opposed to a continuous state of affairs, could found an action in nuisance. This did not prevent his action succeeding. The case was finally resolved at House of Lords level, but the classic statement of principle was given by Blackburn J in the Court of Exchequer Chamber:

> **"We think that the true rule of law is that the person who for his own purposes brings on his lands and collects and keeps there anything likely to do mischief if it escapes, must keep it in at his peril, and, if he does not do so, is prima facie answerable for all the damage which is the natural consequence of its escape."**

This was approved by the House of Lords, although Lord Cairns added the term "non-natural user" in explaining the principle.

[2001] EWCA Civ 1236; [2002] Q.B. 756, the local authority was able to complain about the damage caused by pigeons roosting under the defendant's railway bridge under Local Government Act 1972 s.222 and, because the nuisance affected those using the highway when passing under the bridge, by virtue of the Highways Act 1980 s.130. There is no obstacle to the local authority bringing an action under both provisions in highway cases: *Nottingham City Council v Zain* [2001] EWCA Civ 1248; [2002] 1 W.L.R. 607.

155   (1865) 3 H. & C. 774 (Court of Exchequer); (1866) 1 L.R. 1 Ex. 265 (Court of Exchequer Chamber); (1868) L.R. 3 H.L. 330 (House of Lords).

What is the significance of *Rylands v Fletcher?*

10–049

This has caused some controversy. Blackburn J reasoned by analogy to existing examples of liability, such as cattle trespass and nuisance, and clearly did not believe himself to be laying down any new principle of law. Liability under the rule is therefore closely related to these torts. However, in the first part of the twentieth century, *Rylands v Fletcher* liability developed as a separate "rule" with its own requirements, which will be outlined below. It has been suggested that the rule can be explained as a decision to impose strict liability on persons conducting ultra-hazardous activities. Certainly, this idea has received support in the US. The US Restatement (3d) on Torts—Liability for Physical and Emotional Harm imposes strict liability for abnormally dangerous activities,[156] when:

> **"(1) the activity creates a foreseeable and highly significant risk of physical harm even when reasonable care is exercised by all actors; and (2) the activity is not one of common usage."[157]**

This idea was not, however, accepted in England. The Law Commission, in its 1970 Report, *Civil Liability for Dangerous Things and Activities*,[158] expressed doubts as to its usefulness, finding that any benefits provided by its relative simplicity and flexibility would be outweighed by difficulties in application. The House of Lords sounded the death-knell for strict liability for ultra-hazardous activities in *Read v Lyons*,[159] where their Lordships clearly rejected this as an explanation of *Rylands v Fletcher* liability. (This case is discussed below). Lord Goff in *Cambridge Water Co v Eastern Counties Leather Plc* took the view that, as a general rule, strict liability for operations of high risk would be more appropriately imposed by statute than the courts and that, in any event, *Read v Lyons* served to preclude any such development.[160]

A further suggestion has been that the rule should be absorbed into the law of negligence. Whilst this may seem an odd suggestion, the High Court of Australia in *Burnie Port Authority v General Jones*[161] decided exactly that in 1984. The court held, by a majority of five to two, that

---

156 § 20(b) (2010), replacing para.519 of the Second Restatement. See, generally, K. N. Hylton, "The Theory of Tort Doctrine and the Restatement (Third) of Torts" (2001) 54 *Vanderbilt Law Review* 1413 and K. W. Simons, "The Restatement Third of Torts and Traditional Strict Liability: Robust Rationales, Slender Doctrines" (2009) 44 *Wake Forest Law Review* 1355.

157 This is a modification of para.520 of the Second Restatement.

158 Law Commission Report No.32 (1970), Pt III. However, the idea did receive some support in the report of the Pearson Commission in 1978 (*Report of the Royal Commission on Civil Liability and Compensation for Personal Injury*, Cmnd.7054 (1978), Vol.1 Ch.31 para.1651) which recommended a statutory scheme making the controller of any listed dangerous thing or activity strictly liable for death or personal injury resulting from its malfunction. As discussed in Ch.1, the broad views of the Pearson Commission on liability have never been adopted in this country.

159 [1947] A.C. 156 at 167, 181, 186 (liability rejected in respect of a high explosive shell which exploded and injured a munitions inspector).

160 [1994] 2 A.C. 264 at 305.

161 (1994) 120 A.L.R. 42. For a discussion of the case, see R.F.V. Heuston and R.A. Buckley, "The return of *Rylands v Fletcher*" (1994) 110 L.Q.R. 506.

the occupier was liable for fire damage caused by the negligence of his independent contractors under the ordinary rules of negligence. The reasoning in this case, which relied heavily on the concept of non-delegable duties of care, is somewhat strained and, despite the growing influence of negligence in the twentieth century, has received little support in England.

The English courts have questioned, however, the relationship between the rule in *Rylands v Fletcher* and private nuisance. Lord Goff in *Cambridge Water*,[162] relying on historical analysis,[163] commented that:

> "it would . . . lead to a more coherent body of common law principles if the rule were to be regarded as essentially an extension of the law of nuisance to isolated escapes from land."

Transco and the role of *Rylands* in modern society

10–050

The 2003 House of Lords ruling in *Transco Plc v Stockport MBC*[164] confirmed that the rule should be treated as a sub-species of private nuisance.[165] In this case, their Lordships took the opportunity to review the scope and application in modern conditions of the rule in *Rylands v Fletcher*. It therefore provides helpful guidance as to the future application of this tort. In particular, the court:

- rejected the suggestion that it should be absorbed into the tort of negligence or fault-based principles, as in Australia and Scotland[166];

- rejected the suggestion of a more generous application of the rule. Their Lordships favoured a more restrictive approach, confining the rule to exceptional circumstances where the occupier has brought some dangerous thing onto his land which poses an exceptionally high risk to neighbouring property should it escape, and which amounts to an extraordinary and unusual use of land; and

- clarified that only those with rights to land could sue.

This decision ends a long period of speculation as to the relationship between this tort and private nuisance. It serves also to emphasise the residuary role of the rule in modern society where

---

162 [1994] 2 A.C. 264 at 306.

163 Particularly, the article of F. H. Newark, "The Boundaries of Nuisance" (1949) 65 L.Q.R. 480.

164 [2003] UKHL 61; [2004] 2 A.C. 1.

165 For criticism, see D. Nolan, "The distinctiveness of *Rylands v Fletcher*" (2005) 121 L.Q.R. 421 (who favours abolition of the rule) and J. Murphy, "The merits of *Rylands v Fletcher*" (2004) 24 O.J.L.S. 643 (who defends the rule (at 669) as "a useful residual mechanism for securing environmental protection by individuals affected by harmful escapes from polluting heavyweight industrialists").

166 See *RHM Bakeries (Scotland) Ltd v Strathclyde Regional Council* 1985 S.L.T. 214.

statutes and regulations largely cover the area of dangerous escapes which the rule once covered e.g. the discharge of water is now regulated by the Water Industry Act 1991 s.209.[167] The Court of Appeal in *Stannard v Gore*[168] also clarified that the *Transco* restrictive approach would apply to cases involving fire, which would no longer be regarded as a particular category of the tort.[169] On this basis, liability would be very rare in that it would only arise if the defendant had brought fire onto his land and it had escaped. This was not the case when an electrical fault led to a fire which had ignited a large number of tyres stored on the defendants' premises and which had subsequently spread to and destroyed Gore's property. Tyres were not an exceptionally dangerous thing to bring onto land. Nor was their storage a non-natural use of land. Indeed, it had been the fire, not the tyres which had escaped. On this basis, it could not be said that the defendant had brought the fire onto the land. While occupiers might find themselves liable for collecting combustible material on their land where they had failed to take reasonable precautions to prevent it catching fire or to prevent any fire spreading, this was a question for fault-based liability and not liability under the rule in *Rylands v Fletcher*.[170] Commentators have noted that *Stannard* provides a further restriction to an already narrow rule.[171] It remains to be seen, following such a review, how useful such a limited claim will now be. Lord Hoffmann commented in *Transco* that he was not surprised "that counsel could not find a reported case since the second world war in which anyone had succeeded in a claim under the rule".[172]

Liability under the rule in *Rylands v Fletcher*

10–051

There are four requirements which must be established for the claimant to sue under the rule. The first two derive from Blackburn J's statement of principle. The third derives from Lord Cairns in the House of Lords. The fourth requirement, namely foreseeability of the kind of damage suffered, is of more recent origin and comes from the leading judgment of Lord Goff in *Cambridge Water Co v Eastern Counties Leather Plc*.[173]

---

167   See also Environmental Protection Act 1990 s.73(6) (pollution by escape of waste) and Nuclear Installations Act 1965 s.7 (radio-active matter).
168   [2012] EWCA Civ 1248; [2014] Q.B. 1.
169   The Court of Appeal thus resolved ongoing doubt whether liability for the escape of a fire was covered by the rule in *Rylands v Fletcher* or under a parallel rule of the common law: see *Musgrove v Pandelis* [1919] 2 K.B. 43 and *H&N Emanuel v Greater London Council* [1971] 2 All E.R. 835 at 839 per Lord Denning MR For a historical overview, see A. Ogus, "Vagaries in liability for the escape of fire" (1969) 28 C.L.J. 104. *Musgrove v Pandelis* was distinguished as a fact-sensitive case which would be resolved differently today.
170   Consider, e.g. *Goldman v Hargrave* [1967] 1 A.C. 645 (failure to take reasonable steps to extinguish fire). Negligence had not been found on the facts of the case.
171   S. Tofaris, "*Rylands v Fletcher* restricted further" [2013] C.L.J. 11.
172   [2003] UKHL 61; [2004] 2 A.C. 1 at [39].
173   [1994] 2 A.C. 264.

(1) The defendant brings on his lands for his own purposes something likely to do mischief

This requires a voluntary act of bringing something on the land.[174] What is "likely to do mischief" is an interesting question. In *Rylands* itself, water was held to be within this category, and other case law has referred to electricity, oil, noxious fumes and even a flagpole or a fairground ride.

This requirement seems to have been toughened up since *Transco*. Lord Bingham remarked that:

> **"I do not think the mischief or danger test should be at all easily satisfied. It must be shown that the defendant has done something which he recognised, or judged by the standards appropriate at the relevant place and time, he ought reasonably to have recognised, as giving rise to an *exceptionally high risk of danger* or mischief if there should be an escape, however unlikely an escape may have been thought to be."[175]**

This again will serve to restrict the application of the rule.

10–052

(2) If it escapes

Proof of an actual escape of the thing brought onto land is vital.[176] Ward LJ in *Stannard v Gore* remarked that at the very heart of the rule is the desire to protect against the exceptional danger or mischief that will be caused if there is an escape from the defendant's land.[177] The classic case is that of the House of Lords in *Read v Lyons*,[178] where their Lordships took the opportunity to review the law and establish clear rules of liability. In the case itself, an inspector of munitions had been injured by an explosion of a shell whilst inspecting the defendants' munitions factory. Their Lordships held that there had not been an "escape" within the rule. An escape would only occur when the object moved from the defendant's premises to a place which was outside his occupation or control.

10–053

---

174   The rule does not apply, therefore, to the escape of stythe gas as a naturally occurring phenomenon of mining: *Willis v Derwentside DC* [2013] EWHC 738 (Ch); [2013] Env. L.R. 31 at [45].

175   [2003] UKHL 61; [2004] 2 A.C. 1 at [10] (emphasis added).

176   See *Stannard v Gore* [2012] EWCA Civ 1248. On this basis logically a complaint about vibrations should be brought in private nuisance, not *Rylands v Fletcher*, because vibrations are not the thing brought onto the site even though they could be said to "escape": see *Lindsay v Berkeley Homes (Capital) Plc* [2018] EWHC 2042 (TCC).

177   [2012] EWCA Civ 1248 at [61].

178   [1947] A.C. 156.

There is some debate whether an intentional release of an object is capable of being regarded as an "escape". Taylor J in *Rigby v Chief Constable of Northamptonshire*[179] held that trespass would seem to be the correct action for the intentional and direct infliction of harm. However, this was questioned by Potter J in *Crown River Cruises Ltd v Kimbolton Fireworks Ltd*,[180] at least where the intentional release was not deliberately aimed in the direction of the claimant, or with the intention of impinging on his or her property. With respect, Taylor J's view is probably more consistent with the traditional division between nuisance and trespass, and with Lord Goff's return to the traditional view of these torts in *Cambridge Water* and *Hunter v Canary Wharf*.

(3) Non-natural user

10–054

Blackburn J in *Rylands v Fletcher* referred to the defendant bringing onto the property something "which was not naturally there", which Lord Cairns in the House of Lords interpreted as a "non-natural use". On this basis, thistledown, blowing from the defendant's land onto the plaintiff's land, has been held not to found an action.[181] Over time, however, the "non-natural" use requirement came to be interpreted as "non-ordinary" use, so as to limit the application of the rule in *Rylands v Fletcher*. In *Rickards v Lothian*,[182] Lord Moulton defined "non-natural" as "some special use bringing with it increased dangers to others". This would exclude, in his view, uses which were for the general benefit of the community. On this basis, uses such as domestic water, electricity and gas supplies could be regarded as a "natural" use of land. "Natural user" has even controversially been extended to the manufacture of explosives during war-time,[183] although this was doubted in *Transco*.[184] This has not, however, made the test easier to interpret; Viscount Simon commenting in *Read v Lyons*,

> "I confess to finding this test of 'non-natural' user (or of bringing on the land what was not 'naturally there', which is not the same test) difficult to apply."[185]

179 [1985] 2 All E.R. 985 at 996.
180 [1996] 2 Lloyd's Rep. 533.
181 *Giles v Walker* (1890) 24 Q.B.D. 656.
182 [1913] A.C. 263 at 280.
183 *Read v Lyons* [1947] A.C. 156 at 174, 176. In contrast, keeping a car was "non-natural" in 1919: *Musgrove v Pandelis* [1919] 2 K.B. 43.
184 See Lords Bingham [2003] UKHL 61; [2004] 2 A.C. 1 at [11] and Walker at [105]. Note also criticism of this decision by Lord Goff in *Cambridge Water Co v Eastern Counties Leather Plc* [1994] 2 A.C. 264 at 308 and contrast *Rainham Chemical Works v Belvedere Fish Guano Co* [1921] 2 A.C. 465 where the manufacture of explosives during the First World War was regarded as "non-natural".
185 [1947] A.C. 156 at 166. See also F. H. Newark, "Non-natural user and *Rylands v Fletcher*" (1961) 24 M.L.R. 557, 571: "the result as applied in the modern cases is, we believe, one which would have surprised Lord Cairns and astounded Blackburn."

The meaning of "non-natural user" must now be viewed in the light of Lord Goff's comments in *Cambridge Water Co v Eastern Counties Leather Plc*[186] and the House of Lords ruling in *Transco Plc v Stockport MBC*.[187] Lord Goff remarked in *Cambridge Water* that "the storage of substantial quantities of chemicals on industrial premises should be regarded as an almost classic case of non-natural use".[188] His Lordship held that this was regardless of any benefit the factory may give to the public by means of increased employment (thereby criticising the "general benefit of the community" section of Lord Moulton's test). Equally, his Lordship refused to accept that storing chemicals in industrial premises might be regarded as an "ordinary" use of such premises.

The House of Lords in *Transco* approved Lord Goff's judgment, while restating the test again. The rule should, in the words of Lord Bingham, be confined to cases where the defendant's use of the land is shown to be extraordinary and unusual.[189] On this basis, his Lordship believed that the term "ordinary use" might be clearer than "natural use".[190] The case itself was concerned with whether the storage of water in pipes was a "non-natural" use of the land. Stockport MBC were the owners of a block of flats and an adjacent disused railway embankment. A water pipe serving the flats had leaked and the water had percolated to the surface and onward into the embankment through a crack in the ground. There was no evidence that this was due to negligence. The embankment collapsed as a result of having become saturated with water, and the void left by the collapse exposed a high pressure gas main owned by British Gas (now Transco). The claimants wisely acted promptly to prevent a potential fracture of the pipe, incurring costs of around £94,000.

The House of Lords agreed with the Court of Appeal that the provision of a water supply to a block of flats by means of a connecting pipe was a natural/ordinary use of land. This is consistent with prior authority and indeed it would have been odd to regard having a water supply as raising any special hazard. All five judges argued that *Rylands v Fletcher* would only apply to some use which was *extraordinary and unusual according to contemporary standards*.[191] This clearly did not exist on the facts. Lord Hoffmann suggested that:

> **"A useful guide in deciding whether the risk has been created by a 'non-natural' user of land is therefore to ask whether the damage which eventuated was something against which the occupier could reasonably be expected to have insured himself."**[192]

---

186 [1994] 2 A.C. 264.

187 [2003] UKHL 61; [2004] 2 A.C. 1.

188 [1994] 2 A.C. 264 at 309.

189 [2003] UKHL 61 at [11]. His Lordship warned, however, against a too inflexible approach. A use might be extraordinary and unusual at one time or place, but not so at another.

190 Lord Hoffmann, however, remained concerned that the term "ordinary" was too vague, preferring risk-based analysis: [2003] UKHL 61 at [37].

191 Lord Walker [2003] UKHL 61 at [103] remarked that "It is the extraordinary risk to neighbouring property, if an escape occurs, which makes the land use 'special' for the purposes of the principle in Rylands v Fletcher."

192 [2003] UKHL 61 at [46].

While this can only be a rule of thumb,[193] it offers at least some assistance in determining this aspect of the test.

(4) Foreseeability of damage of the relevant type

10–055 This requirement comes from the review undertaken by the House of Lords of liability under the rule in *Cambridge Water Co v Eastern Counties Leather Plc*.[194] In this case, the defendants had used a chemical called perchloroethene (PCE) for degreasing pelts at their tannery. There were regular spillages, which gradually seeped into and built up under the land. The chemical seepage was such that it contaminated the plaintiffs' water supply 1.3 miles away, forcing them to find another source at a cost of nearly £1 million. The plaintiffs sued in negligence, nuisance and under the rule in *Rylands v Fletcher*. By the time the case reached the House of Lords, only liability under the latter head was in issue.

The House of Lords held that the defendants were not liable. It was not foreseeable to the skilled person that quantities of chemical would cause damage to the plaintiffs' water, and foreseeability of damage was a requirement of liability under the rule in *Rylands v Fletcher*.[195] Lord Goff justified his conclusion by analogy to nuisance, and by reference to Blackburn J's statement of principle in *Rylands* itself, namely that the rule referred to "anything likely to do mischief if it escapes".

There has been some discussion as to how far this test of foreseeability goes. Must the escape also be foreseeable? Although Lord Goff's judgment is not entirely clear, the best view is that the escape need not be foreseeable. As Lord Goff commented:

> **"the principle is one of strict liability in the sense that the defendant may be held liable notwithstanding that he has exercised all due care to prevent the escape from occurring."[196]**

Lord Hoffmann in *Transco* confirmed that *Rylands v Fletcher* established that, in a case to which the rule applies, the defendant will be liable even if he could not reasonably have foreseen the escape.[197]

---

193 Lord Hobhouse in his speech highlighted that insurance against risks is not always cheap and accessible and its availablity is dependant on the insurance market: [2003] UKHL 61 at [60].

194 [1994] 2 A.C. 264.

195 See also *Savage v Fairclough* [2000] Env L.R. 183 CA where pollution of a private water supply, which had arisen due to nitrate contamination from a neighbour's farm, was not considered foreseeable by a "hypothetical good farmer" running a farm such as the one in question. Note also *Hamilton v Papakura DC* [2002] UKPC 9, where the Privy Council held that damage caused to crops due to the presence of a herbicide in the town water supply (which remained fit for human consumption) did not lead to foreseeable loss.

196 [1994] 2 A.C. 264 at 302.

197 [2003] UKHL 61 at [33].

Lord Goff also considered the position in relation to the continuing contamination by PCE. The problem had been identified. Could the defendants be liable for such ongoing damage now it was clearly foreseeable? His Lordship found this argument to be ill-founded. The chemical was now beyond the control of the defendants, and to impose liability would be to adopt a stricter position than that adopted in nuisance or negligence.

Who can sue?

Before the House of Lords' decision in *Transco*, it had been unclear in light of *Cambridge Water* and *Hunter* whether it was necessary to have an interest in land or exclusive possession to sue, as required for private nuisance. Non-occupiers had in the past recovered damages under this head[198]; although this line of authority had been criticised in the leading case of *Read v Lyons*.[199] Yet, in view of Lord Goff's comment in *Cambridge Water* that the focus of both torts is the same—namely the protection of rights to land—logically, only claimants with a right to land should be able to sue.[200] *Transco* confirms the force of Lord Goff's logic: only parties with rights over land may bring an action under the rule in *Rylands v Fletcher*.

10–056

Who can be sued?

The occupier of land will be liable if he or she satisfies the requirements for establishing the tort. Therefore, if you have accumulated the mischief which has escaped etc, you may be liable. There is clear authority that licensees may be sued.[201] Indeed, in *Rylands* itself, although the millowner was treated as the owner of the land, on the facts of the case, the millowner had built the reservoir to serve his mill on land belonging to a certain Lord Wilton (with his Lordship's permission) and was therefore strictly only a licensee.

10–057

Defences

There are a number of relevant defences:

10–058

---

198   See, e.g. dicta in *Shiffman v Order of the Hospital of St John of Jerusalem* [1936] 1 All E.R. 557 (although decided on negligence) and *Perry v Kendricks Transport Ltd* [1956] 1 W.L.R. 85 at 92.

199   [1947] A.C. 156 at 173 (per Lord Macmillan) and at 186 (per Lord Uthwatt). See also Widgery J in *Weller & Co v Foot and Mouth Disease Research Institute* [1966] 1 Q.B. 569 at 588.

200   Such reasoning convinced Neuberger J in *McKenna v British Aluminium Ltd* [2002] Env. L.R. 30.

201   See *Rainham Chemical Works v Belvedere Fish Guano Co* [1921] 2 A.C. 465 at 479 per Lord Sumner, who cited *Eastern and South African Telegraph Co v Cape Town Tramways Cos Ltd* [1902] A.C. 381 at 392; *Midwood v Manchester Corp* [1905] 2 K. B. 597; *Charing Cross Electricity Supply Co v Hydraulic Power Company* [1914] 3 K. B. 772.

- Claimant's default.

- Unforeseeable act of a stranger.

- Act of God.

- Statutory authority.

- Consent.

The first three derive from the judgment of Blackburn J in *Rylands*.

(1) Claimant's default

10–059
It is a valid defence that the escape was due wholly or partially to the claimant's fault. In *Ponting v Noakes*,[202] the plaintiff's horse had died when it had reached over the fence and eaten leaves from a poisonous tree on the defendant's land. The defendant was not found to be liable when the harm suffered was due to the horse's own conduct. (There had equally been no "escape"). Reference should also be made to the Law Reform (Contributory Negligence) Act 1945 s.1.

(2) Unforeseeable act of stranger

10–060
This is a well-established defence. In *Box v Jubb*,[203] the court again faced the consequences of a reservoir overflowing onto the plaintiff's land, but this time the defendant was not liable. The overflow had been due to the actions of another neighbouring reservoir owner, over which the defendant had no control, and of which he had no knowledge. In such circumstances, the defendant was not held liable for the flooding.

This approach was followed in *Rickards v Lothian*.[204] Here, the plaintiff's premises had been flooded due to a continuous overflow of water from a sink on the top floor of the building. The overflow had been caused by a water tap being turned on full, and the wastepipe plugged, by the deliberate act of a third party. The defendant escaped liability as he could not reasonably have known of the act so as to prevent it.

The act of the third party must be unforeseeable. If the defendant should have foreseen the intervention, the defence will not be established. For example, in *North Western Utilities Ltd v London Guarantee Co*,[205] it was held to be foreseeable that works undertaken by a third party

---

202 [1894] 2 Q.B. 281.
203 (1879) 4 Ex. D. 76.
204 [1913] A.C. 263. See also *Perry v Kendricks Transport Ltd* [1956] 1 W.L.R. 85.
205 [1936] A.C. 108.

near the defendants' gas mains might damage their mains and require remedial work. It was therefore no defence to claim that the gas leak, which caused the fire destroying the plaintiff's hotel, was due to damage to the mains by the acts of a third party. The defendants had left the matter to chance, and this was not sufficient to excuse them from liability.

Three points of contention remain. First, and simplest, there has been some debate as to who is a "stranger". It obviously includes trespassers, but it has been suggested that it should also include licensees over whom the defendant does not exercise control, in order to keep liability within reasonable bounds. This view received support in *Ribee v Norrie*.[206] Here, Miss Ribee, described as a sprightly 70-year-old lady, suffered property damage and personal injury when her home caught fire.[207] The fire had started in an adjoining property which had been divided into bedsit accommodation. It was suspected that the fire had been caused by one of the occupants leaving a smouldering cigarette on the settee in the common area. The Court of Appeal held the landlord of the hostel liable. On the facts, his plea of act of stranger was rejected. He could have exercised some control over the persons occupying the hostel, for example, by putting up notices prohibiting smoking, and could have foreseen such an accident occurring. It could not be said that the fire was due to the unforeseeable act of a stranger.

Secondly, it is unclear whether the defence applies to the *negligent* act of a third party. It would seem that, as a matter of logic, the defence should not be defeated on proof that the third party did not act intentionally. The real emphasis should be on whether the defendant should have been able to foresee, and therefore react to, the actions of the third party. This takes us to our third problem. The formulation of this defence is sounding more and more like an action for negligence. Defendants will not be liable if they can show that they did not foresee, or should not have foreseen, the actions of the third party. *Street on Torts*[208] has gone so far as to say that the cases are more in line with the principles of negligence, rather than *Rylands*, liability and should be regarded as authority for the question whether there has been a negligent failure to control the unforeseeable harmful acts of a third party. This, perhaps, is to take conceptual neatness a step too far. Undoubtedly, negligence principles have influenced the development of the rule as much as they have influenced nuisance, but it is still conceptually distinct.

(3) Act of God

10–061

This defence is, due to the advances in modern technology and science, largely defunct. The defendant will not be liable where the escape is due solely to natural causes, in circumstances where no human foresight or prudence could reasonably recognise the possibility of such an occurrence and provide against it. So far, there has been only one successful English case,

---

206 [2001] P.I.Q.R. P8.
207 She was saved, we are told, by her heroic spaniel, which jumped on her bed and whimpered until she awoke!
208 C. Witting, *Street on Torts*, 15th edn (OUP, 2018) pp.466–467.

which was decided in 1876. In *Nichols v Marsland*,[209] the defendant had some ornamental pools on his land, which contained large quantities of water. These pools had been formed by damming up with artificial banks a natural stream which flowed through his property. Due to extraordinary rainfall, the banks broke down, and the rush of escaping water carried away four bridges. The Court of Appeal held that the defendant should not be held liable for an extraordinary act of nature which could not have been reasonably anticipated.

A stricter view was taken in *Greenock Corp v Caledonian Ry*,[210] in which the court was critical of the approach taken by the court in *Nichols*. In this case, a concrete paddling pool for children had been constructed by the local authority in the bed of a stream, requiring the course of the stream to be altered. Again, there was an extraordinary level of rainfall, which caused the stream to overflow at the pool. Due to the construction of the pool, water which would have otherwise flowed down stream flowed down a public street. The House of Lords held that such an event did not qualify as an act of God.

In view of *Greenock*, it is most unlikely that the defence would succeed today. However, it is possible that a situation may exist where modern precautions against exceptional natural conditions were defeated (for example, an earthquake in a London suburb) and the defence might come into play, but such circumstances would be very rare indeed.

(4) Statutory authority

10–062   Again, this defence is important, and the approach is the same as that taken in nuisance (see above). It will therefore be a question of construction in each case. The courts will examine whether the breach of the rule in *Rylands v Fletcher* was authorised by the statute in question. In *Green v Chelsea Waterworks Co*,[211] the defendants, who were under a statutory duty to maintain a continuous supply of water, were not liable when, in the absence of negligence, the water main burst, damaging the plaintiff's premises, horse and stock. However, the defendants were liable for a burst water main in *Charing Cross Electricity Supply Co v Hydraulic Power Co*.[212] Here, the defendants were operating under a statutory power to supply water for industrial purposes. These powers were subject to a "nuisance clause", which provided that nothing in the Act should exonerate the undertakers from liability for nuisance. On this basis, the defendants remained liable even in the absence of negligence.

The Court of Appeal in *Dunne v North Western Gas Board*[213] sought to clarify the different treatment of statutory duties and powers. In this case, there was a series of 46 explosions of coal gas in Liverpool, which resulted when a water main had leaked and water had washed away the soil supporting a gas main. The plaintiffs sued both the Gas Board and the

---

209 (1876) 2 Ex. D. 1.
210 [1917] A.C. 556.
211 (1894) 70 L.T. 547.
212 [1914] 3 K.B. 772.
213 [1964] 2 Q.B. 806 at 833–837.

Corporation which was responsible for the water main. The Gas Board had a statutory duty to supply gas and it had, in the absence of negligence, a good defence of statutory authority. The Corporation, in contrast, only acted under a statutory power. Here, unlike *Charing Cross*, the Act did not contain a nuisance clause, and so the Corporation would not be liable in the absence of negligence.

The House of Lords in *Transco* emphasised the significance of this defence in limiting the application of the rule by excluding claims for high risk activities arising from work conducted under statutory authority.[214]

(5) Consent

This may be express or implied. Consent will be implied where the escape results from something maintained for the common benefit, for example, in a block of flats, from the guttering, or from common utilities such as water, gas or electricity. The tenant in such circumstances is assumed to forego any rights against the landlord, due to the benefit he or she gains, provided the escape occurs without negligence.[215]

10–063

Remedies

There are three main remedies:

10–064

- Injunctions.

- Abatement.

- Damages.

The main remedy for nuisance is the injunction. Where liability lies under the rule in *Rylands v Fletcher*, the escape has usually occurred, and the damage has already been caused, so the claimant will be seeking damages. Remedies will be discussed generally in Ch.17, but this section will examine their particular application in relation to nuisance and the rule in *Rylands v Fletcher*. It will also consider the possibility of a claimant recovering under the Human Rights Act 1998.

---

214 See Lord Hoffmann [2003] UKHL 61; [2004] 2 A.C. 1 at [31].
215 *Kiddle v City Business Properties Ltd* [1942] 1 K.B. 269 at 274. See also *Carstairs v Taylor* (1871) L.R. 6 Ex. 217. See L. Kadirgamar [1973] Conv. 179.

▶ (1) Injunctions

10–065

As will be discussed further in Ch.17, an injunction is an equitable and therefore a discretionary remedy. As a remedy, it is well suited to nuisance, because it can be adapted to meet the balance of competing interests. The courts are generally willing to grant an injunction, unless there are exceptional circumstances which mean that damages are seen as the most appropriate remedy. In such circumstances, damages are said to be given "in lieu of" (instead of) an injunction. Whilst the Senior Courts Act 1981 s.50 is the section governing this matter, the leading case is that of *Shelfer v City of London Electric Lighting Co.*[216] In this case, A.L. Smith LJ laid down the four conditions which would lead a court to grant damages in lieu of an injunction:

- where the injury to the claimant's legal rights is small;

- where the injury is capable of being estimated in money;

- where the injury can be adequately compensated by a small money payment; *and*

- where it would be oppressive to the defendant to grant an injunction.

In the case itself, the court granted an injunction against vibrations and noise caused by the defendant's machinery, even though the result would deprive many of its customers of electricity. The courts are unwilling to allow a defendant essentially to buy the right to commit the nuisance by paying damages to the claimant.[217]

The exercise of the discretion to award an injunction was discussed by the Court of Appeal in *Miller v Jackson*[218] and *Kennaway v Thompson*.[219] In the former case, the majority of the court held that an injunction was inappropriate, on the basis that the public interest in cricket should prevail (Lord Denning MR) and that the plaintiffs had knowingly bought the property in the knowledge that a nuisance would be likely to occur (Cumming-Bruce LJ). Damages were therefore awarded.[220] In *Kennaway*, Lawton LJ held that the relevant authority remained that of *Shelfer*, which did not support either proposition. Accordingly, the plaintiff would be awarded an injunction against power boat racing on a nearby lake, regardless of any public interest in power boat racing, and regardless of the fact that she had chosen to build a house near the lake

---

216 [1895] 1 Ch.287.
217 See Lindley LJ [1895] 1 Ch.287 at 315–316.
218 [1977] Q.B. 966.
219 [1981] Q.B. 88. See R. A. Buckley, "Injunctions and the public interest" (1981) 44 M.L.R. 212. On the need for flexibility in applying remedies in nuisance, see M. Lee, "Tort law and regulation" [2011] J.P.L. 986.
220 See also *Dennis v Ministry of Defence* [2003] EWHC 793 (QB); [2003] Env L.R.34: damages appropriate when contrary to public interest to prevent RAF flying Harrier jets from its base. This was justified as consistent with developing human rights case law.

in the knowledge that some racing took place.[221] Nevertheless, the injunction was awarded on terms. The court used its discretion to stipulate a strict timetable for international, national and club events, thereby allowing the racing to continue in a limited form. By such means, and also by using their power to suspend the injunction to give the defendant the opportunity to remedy the nuisance, the courts recognise and balance the competing rights of the litigants.[222]

The Supreme Court recently in *Coventry v Lawrence*[223] reviewed the application of the *Shelfer* test and argued that it should not be applied mechanically. It found that the time had come to signal a move away from the strict criteria derived from *Shelfer*, particularly where an injunction would have serious consequences for third parties, such as employees of the defendant's business, or, in the case itself, members of the public using or enjoying a speedway racing stadium. While the court accepted that claimants would still be prima facie entitled to an injunction to restrain the defendant from committing a nuisance in the future, it held that it was important not to fetter the discretion of judges. The court was, in particular, critical of recent decisions where judges had been too ready to grant injunctions without considering whether to award damages instead.[224] On this basis, the existence of planning permission would be a relevant consideration at the remedy stage: the fact that an activity benefitted the community might be a factor in favour of refusing an injunction and compensating the claimant in damages.[225] This suggests that a more flexible approach towards the award of damages and/or an injunction will now be adopted.

(2) Abatement

This is a form of self-help, by which claimants intervene themselves to stop the nuisance. Generally, the courts are reluctant to encourage such actions. Claimants who wish to take the law into their own hands must do so at their peril and run the risk of countervailing claims for trespass and conversion. Generally, however, it is an acceptable response towards encroaching roots and branches, where it would make little sense to go to court.[226] For example, in *Delaware Mansions Ltd v Westminster City Council*,[227] discussed at para.10–015, the House of Lords accepted that the claimant company was entitled to recover the costs which had been incurred in remedying a continuing nuisance caused to its property by tree roots when the defendant council had refused its request that the tree be removed. Even in the face of such obvious nuisances, however, claimants proceed at their own risk and their actions must be no more than necessary to abate the nuisance. Lord Cooke also warned against imposing

10–066

221 Although it had increased in volume and noise beyond tolerable levels in subsequent years.
222 See S. Tromans, "Nuisance—Prevention or Payment" (1982) 41 C.L.J. 87, 93–95, who argues for greater use of damages awards.
223 [2014] UKSC 13; [2014] A.C. 822.
224 e.g. in *Watson v Croft Promo-Sport Ltd* [2009] EWCA Civ 15; [2009] 3 All E.R. 249.
225 [2014] UKSC 13 at [125].
226 See *Lemmon v Webb* [1895] A.C. 1.
227 [2001] UKHL 55; [2002] 1 A.C. 321.

unreasonable burdens on local authorities to pay for remedial works and advised that "as a general proposition, I think that the defendant is entitled to notice and a reasonable opportunity of abatement before liability for remedial expenditure can arise".[228] The claimant should therefore take care not to enter his or her neighbour's land, and give notice if entry is necessary, except in an emergency. Any branches or roots which have been lopped off remain the neighbour's property and if they are kept, the claimant may be held liable for conversion (civil theft). Abatement, therefore, is a remedy of limited utility.

(3) Damages

10–067

All of the three heads of liability discussed in this chapter become actionable only on proof of damage.[229] In the recent case of *Network Rail Infrastructure Ltd v Williams*,[230] the Court of Appeal indicated that, for private nuisance, this can take the form of physical or tangible damage to property or simply interference with the utility and amenity value of the claimant's property. In this case, an infestation of Japanese knotweed had spread from the defendants' land to that of the claimants. This particularly invasive weed carries with it the risk of future physical damage to buildings and is costly to remove. The Court held that it was a "natural hazard", affecting the owner's ability fully to use and enjoy the land, and therefore a classic example of an interference with the amenity value of the land.[231] Special damage must of course be proved for an individual to claim a remedy for public nuisance.

Personal injury

10–068

Public nuisance, as discussed above, protects the individual who, as a member of the public, has suffered particular damage due to the defendant's actions. Any damages award will therefore cover personal injury, damage to property, loss of custom, and perhaps even particular inconvenience caused to the individual. Private nuisance and the rule in *Rylands v Fletcher*, in contrast, are aimed specifically at protecting the interests of claimants with rights to land. They therefore award damages for the diminution in the value of the land, or lesser enjoyment of the use of land or its fixtures. On this basis, this would seem to exclude damages for personal injury. Professor Newark, in an article cited by Lord Goff in *Cambridge Water* and *Hunter*, explained that the land merely provided the setting for the injury, and therefore there was no

---

228 [2001] UKHL 55; [2002] 1 A.C. 321 at [34]. But see *Kirk v Brent LBC* [2005] EWCA Civ 1701; [2006] Env. L.R. D7 where the Court of Appeal questioned whether this was an absolute rule and refused to strike out a claim where no notice had been given for substantial works until four years after the event and it could be argued that the local authority were put on notice by the fact that similar damage had been caused to other nearby property.

229 Although the courts are sometimes generous in finding damage for certain types of private nuisance, e.g. interference with certain easements.

230 [2018] EWCA Civ 1514; [2019] Q.B. 601. Comment: S. Steel, "The gist of private nuisance" (2019) 135 L.Q.R. 192.

231 [2018] EWCA Civ 1514 at [55].

special reason for distinguishing personal injury caused by a nuisance from other cases of personal injury to which the ordinary rules of negligence apply.[232]

This view has been followed by the leading authorities on private nuisance and the rule in *Rylands v Fletcher*, namely *Hunter v Canary Wharf Ltd*[233] and *Transco Plc v Stockport MBC*,[234] although the issue was not strictly in point in either case. The majority in *Hunter* held that only those with an interest in land or exclusive possession could sue in private nuisance, and Lords Lloyd and Hoffmann expressly stated that compensation should not be awarded for personal injury, as it represents harm to the person, not the land. This view was also taken by the House of Lords in *Transco*, despite mixed authority in the past where damages for personal injury had been awarded under the rule in *Rylands v Fletcher*,[235] although not without challenge.[236] Lord Bingham affirmed that "the claim cannot include a claim for death or personal injury, since such a claim does not relate to any right in or enjoyment of land."[237] This position was confirmed by Dyson LJ in *Corby Group Litigation Claimants v Corby BC*[238] who distinguished public from private nuisance. Only public nuisance—a tort seeking to protect against unlawful acts or omissions which endanger the life, safety, health, property or comfort of the public (and which says nothing about enjoyment of land)—will permit damages for personal injury to be recovered. The torts are distinct, and the rights created by them different.[239]

As a result of *Hunter v Canary Wharf* and *Transco*, therefore, damages for private nuisance are awarded for the injury to the land, not the person. Personal injury will be protected by the torts of negligence, public nuisance and by claims under the Protection from Harassment Act 1997.[240] It is important not to confuse claims for personal injury, however, with the private nuisance concept of "personal discomfort", which is related to the diminished utility of the land. *Bone v Seale*[241] illustrates this distinction. Here, damages were awarded to compensate for the personal discomfort caused by smells from an adjacent pig farm. The award represented the diminished utility value of the land "suffering" from the smells. Such an award could be made

---

232 (1949) 65 L.Q.R. 480 at 489.

233 [1997] A.C. 655. Followed by *Vukelic v Hammersmith and Fulham LBC* [2003] EWHC 188 (QB (TCC)).

234 [2003] UKHL 61; [2004] 2 A.C. 1.

235 *Hale v Jennings* [1938] 1 All E.R. 579; *Shiffman v Order of the Hospital of St John of Jerusalem* [1936] 1 All E.R. 557 (although decided on negligence) and *Perry v Kendricks Transport Ltd* [1956] 1 W.L.R. 85 at 92.

236 See *Read v Lyons* [1947] A.C. 156.

237 [2004] 2 A.C. 1 at [9]. See also Lord Hoffmann at [35].

238 [2008] EWCA Civ 463; [2009] Q.B. 335. Comment: M. Lee, "Personal injury, public nuisance, and environmental regulation" (2009) 20 K.L.J. 129.

239 [2008] EWCA Civ 463 at [27]–[30]. There is, however, no reason why claimants cannot raise both torts in litigation; they are not mutually exclusive.

240 See e.g. *Jones v Ruth* [2011] EWCA Civ 804; [2012] 1 W.L.R. 1495 where, in a private nuisance claim, the claimant succeeded in her claim for personal injury damages under the 1997 Act.

241 [1975] 1 All E.R. 787. See also *Raymond v Young* [2015] EWCA Civ 456; [2015] H.L.R. 41: no separate award of damages for inconvenience and distress caused by the nuisance when substantial damages already awarded for diminution in value as such sum was likely to include loss of amenity. Courts should seek to avoid double recovery in this context.

even in the absence of evidence that the value of land had diminished, and irrespective of the number of people affected and any injury the smell may have caused them.

It may be questioned, however, whether this distinction is entirely convincing. It is hard to persuade the average "man or woman in the street" that damages are awarded not for their twitching nostrils, but for the "suffering" of the land on which they are standing. Equally, if such "suffering" cannot always be converted into market loss (i.e. diminution of value of the land), it is difficult to say on what basis such damages are awarded, if not on a personal basis. Lords Lloyd and Hoffmann suggested that the loss is one of "loss of amenity". This was recognised by the House of Lords in the contract law case of *Ruxley Electronics and Construction Ltd v Forsyth*.[242] In this case, Mr Forsyth had contracted for a swimming pool of a certain depth, and this had not been provided, although this did not diminish the actual value of the pool. The House of Lords in *Ruxley* approved the trial judge's award of damages for loss of amenity in such a case. It is not clear, however, that this case in reality establishes a principle under which damages can be assessed independently of the personality of the occupants of land. Lord Mustill clearly supported the award of amenity damages on the basis that the consumer's subjective preference, expressed in the contract, had not been satisfied. Indeed, the exact status of the case in contract law remains uncertain. Doubts may also be expressed in relation to the treatment of this issue by the Court of Appeal in *Dobson v Thames Water Utilities Ltd*.[243] Here the court ruled that in the case of a transitory nuisance caused by odours and mosquitoes from a sewage treatment works, which did not affect the market value of the land, damages should be assessed by taking account of the actual experiences of the people in occupation of the property. On this basis, an unoccupied house awaiting renovation would receive only nominal damages, while damages for a family home would be assessed on the experiences of the family members. This, the court insisted, was entirely consistent with awarding damages for injury to land; it simply represented a means of placing a value on this loss. This ruling is difficult to reconcile with the statement of Lord Hoffmann in *Hunter* that "damages cannot be increased by the fact that the interests in the land are divided; still less according to the number of persons residing on the premises".[244] It also suggests that a family of four will recover more damages than the old widowed lady next door, who suffers exactly the same interference with land. Further, it might be questioned why actual occupation is necessary to assess amenity loss when the courts use hypotheticals to assess loss on a regular basis. *Dobson* highlights the difficulties of conceiving of "personal discomfort" as an injury to land and, in so doing, raises questions as to the degree to which the "personal" element can be removed from the equation.

Economic loss

10–069

In *Hunter*, Lord Hoffmann recognised that loss of profits was recoverable as consequential loss when it resulted from the claimant's inability to use the land for the purposes of his or her

---

242 [1996] A.C. 344.
243 [2009] EWCA Civ 28; [2009] 3 All E.R. 319. Comment: S. Tofaris [2009] C.L.J. 273.
244 [1997] A.C. 655 at 707.

business.[245] Recovery of such losses has been accepted in a number of cases. For example, in *Andreae v Selfridge & Co Ltd*[246] the owner of a hotel was allowed to recover damages for the loss of custom suffered by her business due to noise and dust caused by the defendants' construction work. Equally, in *Jan de Nul (UK) Ltd v AXA Royale Belge SA (Formerly NV Royale Belge)*,[247] the Court of Appeal permitted the Hampshire Wildlife Trust to recover over £100,000 for an investigation into silting of feeding grounds at the head of an estuary. Although the report had indicated no long-term damage would occur, the court found that it had acted reasonably in commissioning such a report and the cost of the survey was consequential on physical interference with its property rights.

Damage to chattels

10–070

By chattels, we mean personal property which happens to be on the land. One would expect that if the courts are reluctant to award damages for personal injuries, they would be equally reluctant to award damages for loss of chattels. If you cannot recover for your own broken leg, it would seem incongruous if you could recover for the broken leg of your poodle. Certainly, this is the view of Professor Newark in his much-cited article.[248] Unfortunately, this point is not dealt with in *Hunter*, except by Lord Hoffmann, who supports a continuing right to sue for damage to chattels and livestock in nuisance as consequential loss. There is clear authority in support of this position. In *Halsey v Esso Petroleum Co Ltd*,[249] damage to laundry hanging in the garden was deemed actionable in private nuisance and under the rule in *Rylands v Fletcher*. Equally, damage to the paintwork of the plaintiff's car on the highway was held to be actionable in public nuisance and under the rule in *Rylands v Fletcher*.

Whilst the position seems difficult to justify, it may, perhaps, be explained if we consider the practical impact of not allowing recovery for damage to chattels. For example, a farmer complains that the defendant emits noxious fumes over his land. These fumes have ruined his crops and trees, and harmed the health of his livestock. If only damage to land is recoverable, the farmer will only be awarded damages for his crops and the trees.[250] Yet, these are simply alternative means of farming one's land, and why should the law draw an arbitrary distinction between the different modes of farming?

---

245 [1997] A.C. 655 at 706.
246 [1938] Ch.1. See, also, Lawton J in *British Celanese v Hunt* [1969] 1 W.L.R. 959.
247 [2002] EWCA Civ 209; [2002] 1 Lloyd's Rep. 583.
248 (1949) 65 L.Q.R. 480 at 490.
249 [1961] 2 All E.R. 145.
250 Crops and trees are, of course, treated as part of the land in question.

> ## Remoteness

10–071

Damages under private nuisance, public nuisance and the rule in *Rylands v Fletcher* are all subject to the test set out in *The Wagon Mound (No.1)*,[251] namely that the defendant is only liable for damages of a type which can be reasonably foreseen. Reference should be made here to Ch.6. Lord Reid, in *The Wagon Mound (No.2)*, held foreseeability to be an essential element in determining liability in both public and private nuisance: "It would not be right to discriminate between different cases of nuisance".[252] In *Cambridge Water*, Lord Goff clarified that the *Wagon Mound* test would apply to the rule in *Rylands v Fletcher*. The reader should therefore ignore Blackburn J's statement, in the case itself, that the defendant will be liable for all the natural consequences of the escape.

The Human Rights Act 1998

10–072

The case of *Marcic v Thames Water Utilities Ltd*[253] provides a useful illustration of the potential for the Act to supplement and change the law of nuisance, but also of the reluctance of the courts to overwhelm public bodies with excessive liability. Peter Marcic brought a claim against his statutory water and sewage undertaker, Thames Water Utilities Ltd (TWUL), complaining of its failure since 1992 to prevent persistent external flooding and back flow of foul water from its sewer system into his home at times of heavy rain. Although it was reasonably practicable for TWUL to prevent the flooding, it had refused to do so. Under its then scheme of priorities, there was no prospect of such works being undertaken in the foreseeable future. After nine years, Marcic turned to law and brought this action for damage to his property in nuisance and under the 1998 Act.

Although his claim in private nuisance was rejected at first instance as contrary to existing authority, Judge Havery QC had approved the claim under the Human Rights Act 1998 founded on infringement of the claimant's rights to private and family life (under art.8) and peaceful enjoyment of his possessions (art.1 of Protocol 1).[254] TWUL was a public authority under s.6 of the Act, and the case law of the European Court of Human Rights supported use of art.8 and art.1 of Protocol 1 in this context.[255] Although both art.8 and art.1 of Protocol 1 are qualified rights—the court must consider "the protection of the rights and freedoms of

---

251 *Overseas Tankship (UK) Ltd v Morts Dock and Engineering Co Ltd* [1961] A.C. 388 at 427.
252 *The Wagon Mound (No.2) (Overseas Tankship (UK) Ltd v Miller Steamship Co Pty)* [1967] 1 A.C. 617 at 640.
253 [2003] UKHL 66; [2004] 2 A.C. 42.
254 Where there is a demonstrable and significant fall in the value of the property, without proper compensation, this amounts to a partial expropriation: see *S v France* (1990) 65 D. & R. 250 at 261. See D. Anderson, "Compensation for interference with property" [1999] E.H.R.L.R. 543.
255 The court relying on *Baggs v UK* (1987) 9 E.H.R.R. 235, (a case of nuisance by noise from Heathrow airport affecting the applicant's enjoyment of his home); *S v France* (1990) 65 D. & R. 250 (effect of nuclear power station near home); *Guerra v Italy* (1998) 26 E.H.R.R. 357 (toxic emissions from factory); *Lopez Ostra v Spain* (1994) 20 E.H.R.R. 277 (fumes and smells from waste treatment plant).

others"[256] and "the public interest"[257]—in view of the frequent flooding of Marcic's property and TWUL's unsatisfactory system of prioritisation, the judge supported Marcic's claim under the Act.

The Court of Appeal, in supporting Marcic's claim in private nuisance, rendered any claim under the Act unnecessary. Section 8(3) of the Act provides that:

> **"No award of damages is to be made unless, taking account of all the circumstances of the case, including–(a) any other relief or remedy granted, or order made, in relation to the act in question (by that or any other court) . . . the court is satisfied that the award is necessary to afford just satisfaction to the person in whose favour it is made."**

Nevertheless, the Court of Appeal supported the reasoning of the first instance judge. The court suggested that even if the court had decided that a fair balance had been struck between the competing interests of Marcic and TWUL's other customers, the defendant might, in any event, be required to pay compensation to ensure that one person did not bear an unreasonable burden.[258]

The Court of Appeal ruling in *Marcic* was applied by Buckley J in *Dennis v Ministry of Defence*.[259] This case involved a claim for compensation by Mr and Mrs Dennis whose property was adjacent to an RAF base and who had suffered deafening noise due to the flying of Harrier jets over their land. Although the court again found a nuisance at common law, it held that the noise and the resultant reduction in the value of the estate did amount to a breach of the Dennis's rights under art.8 and art.1 of Protocol 1, although any breach would be balanced by the state's interest in national security and the cost and inconvenience of uprooting a military base. Nevertheless, the court saw no reason why the Dennis's should bear the cost of this disturbance alone and that damages of £950,000 would have been payable under the Act to cover the period until 2012 when Harrier training was expected to be phased out. This sum was thus awarded for common law nuisance.

When *Marcic* reached the House of Lords, the award in *Dennis* of £950,000 and the potential liability of Thames Water for £1 billion if it compensated every customer in Marcic's position[260] did not go unnoticed. Their Lordships rejected liability either at common law or under

---

256 Article 8 para.2: "except such as is in accordance with the law and is necessary in a democratic society in the interests of national security, public safety or the economic well-being of the country, for the prevention of disorder or crime, for the protection of health or morals, or for the protection of the rights and freedoms of others".

257 Article 1 Protocol 1.

258 [2002] Q.B. 929 CA. See *S v France* (1990) 65 D. & R. 250 at 263 and *James v United Kingdom* (A/98) (1986) 8 E.H.R.R. 123 at [54]: "under the legal systems of the contracting states, the taking of property in the public interest without payment of compensation is treated as justifiable only in exceptional circumstances".

259 [2003] EWHC 793 (QB); [2003] Env L.R.34. Followed by *Andrews v Reading BC (No.2)* [2005] EWHC 256 (QB); [2006] R.V.R. 56 (£2,000 for noise arising from new traffic scheme).

260 In the financial year 1999–2000, the profits of the whole group (of which TWUL formed only a part) amounted to only £344 million after tax.

the Act. Parliament, under the Water Industry Act 1991, had established a comprehensive statutory scheme of regulation in which an independent regulator would seek to balance the competing interests of the parties involved. Where a statute contains its own compensation scheme, it is a matter of construction for the court to determine whether Parliament intended a common law claim to exist alongside the statutory remedy.[261] The House held that, in this case, liability in nuisance would be inconsistent with the statutory scheme. Further, given the need to balance competing interests and the availability of judicial review, the scheme was in any event compatible with art.8 and art.1 of Protocol 1 of the Convention. Following the European Court of Human Rights decision in *Hatton v United Kingdom*,[262] which confirmed the margin of appreciation given to States in matters of general policy, the House found that the scheme did strike a reasonable balance: "Parliament acted well within its bounds as policy maker."[263]

The reluctance of the House in *Marcic* to intervene on the basis of the Human Rights Act 1998 is particularly notable in view of its criticism of TWUL's treatment of Mr Marcic. Such concerns, however, did not persuade the House of Lords to support his claim.[264] The subsequent Court of Appeal decision in *Dobson v Thames Water Utilities Ltd*[265] offers a further indication of the reluctance of the English courts to award damages under the HRA 1998 in addition to those awarded in private nuisance. In this case (discussed above at para.10–068), the court took the view that the claims of residents with rights over land would most probably be satisfied by the award of damages in private nuisance without any need for additional damages under the Act.[266] For a claimant with no right over land (for example, a child living with her parents who could only sue for breach of her art.8 rights), the court suggested that the claim would be satisfied by a declaration that her rights had been violated under the Act. Her loss would be covered by the damages award to the property owner in private nuisance which would reflect the impact of the nuisance on the entire household. It seems an understatement to remark that following *Marcic* and *Dobson*, the HRA 1998 has not had the impact on nuisance claims which had been anticipated by some commentators at the time the Act came into force.

---

261 See, recently, *Southern Gas Networks Plc v Thames Water Utilities Ltd* [2018] EWCA Civ 33; [2018] 1 W.L.R. 5977 (common law negligence claim permitted where nothing within the statutory scheme suggested Parliament did not intend there to be two different schemes in play).

262 (36022/97) (2003) 37 E.H.R.R. 28.

263 [2003] UKHL 66; [2004] 2 A.C. 42 HL at [43]. See also *Arscott v Coal Authority* [2004] EWCA Civ 892; [2005] Env. L.R. 6 (common enemy defence to flooding reached a fair balance between interests of person affected and general public and was Convention-compliant). This defence permits the occupier of land to use or develop it so as to prevent floodwaters coming on to the land without being liable if flood water which would have entered the land consequently damages that of another. Contrast *Giacomelli v Italy* (59909/00) (2007) 45 E.H.R.R. 38; *Fadeyeva v Russia* (55723/00) (2007) 45 E.H.R.R. 10.

264 Although Lord Hoffmann noted that Thames Water had agreed with the Regulator in 2002 to free 250 properties (including that of Marcic) from the risk of external flooding.

265 [2009] EWCA Civ 28; [2009] 3 All E.R. 319.

266 Relying on the HRA 1998 s.8(3).

Conclusion

The House of Lords' decisions in *Hunter v Canary Wharf Ltd*,[267] *Cambridge Water Co v Eastern Counties Leather Plc*[268] and *Transco Plc v Stockport MBC*[269] have shed new light on the nature of the torts of private nuisance and *Rylands v Fletcher* liability. In so doing, the House of Lords clearly distinguished these torts from the tort of negligence, examined earlier in this book, although in practice the dividing line is not so clear. Nevertheless, these decisions are highly significant in indicating the future development of these torts, and their importance should not be underestimated. In contrast, public nuisance plays a limited role in tort law, and should be noted primarily in connection with obstruction of the highway, although it is the only tort in this chapter which protects against personal injury.

The next chapter will examine the tort of trespass in its many forms: trespass to the person, goods and land. In considering trespass to land, readers should note the discussion in this chapter of its relationship with private nuisance.

---

267 [1997] A.C. 655.
268 [1994] 2 A.C. 264.
269 [2003] UKHL 61; [2004] 2 A.C. 1.

11

Trespass

Introduction

The tort of trespass is one of the oldest torts in English law. In modern law, it takes three forms—trespass to the person, to land and to goods. All three torts have the same characteristics: they must be committed intentionally, cause direct and immediate harm and are actionable per se, i.e. without proof of damage. Although these three criteria have not always been followed—for example in the past, the courts have been willing to impose liability for trespass to the person where the tort has been committed negligently[1]—they are generally followed today. They serve to distinguish trespass from other actions, such as negligence and nuisance, which were traditionally called "actions on the case" and deal with indirect harm.

It is important to recognise that the tort of trespass operates in a different manner from torts such as nuisance and negligence. These torts, which we have already looked at, compensate the claimant for damage incurred unintentionally or indirectly, and act as a form of loss-spreading. The aim of trespass, however, is to vindicate the claimant's right to be free from interference either to his or her person, property or goods. On this basis, the torts are actionable per se. Damage is not the trigger for compensation. It is the wrongful actions of the defendant in interfering with a recognised legal interest possessed by the claimant which trigger compensation. Of course, in awarding damages the courts will examine whether any loss or damage has been suffered. They will generally only award nominal damages in trespass to land or goods if no damage exists, but the existence of aggravated and exemplary/punitive damages[2] in these fields highlights the willingness of the courts to acknowledge the importance of protecting these interests in modern society.

The tort of trespass does, however, have a close connection with other areas of law. Trespass to the person, in dealing with interference with the person in terms of personal integ-

---

1   See *Weaver v Ward* (1617) Hob. 134; 80 E.R. 284 and *Scott v Shepherd* (1773) 2 Wm. Bl. 892; 96 E.R. 525.
2   See Ch.17.

rity and freedom of movement, bears a close relationship with criminal law and the offences found in the Offences against the Person Act 1861.[3] Trespass to land, in contrast, deals with interference with the claimant's possession of land and therefore bears a close relationship with the tort of private nuisance, discussed in the previous chapter. Trespass to goods is also very closely connected to the tort of conversion (civil theft). The significance of this will be discussed below.

This chapter will concentrate on trespass to the person and trespass to land which are the topics most likely to be covered in a tort unit. Trespass to goods will be dealt with briefly at the end of the chapter.

Trespass to the Person

As stated above, trespass to the person protects the claimant against interference with his or her person. This may be attempted by means of assault, battery or false imprisonment. These torts possess the classic "trespass" characteristics in that they must be committed intentionally, by direct and immediate actions and are actionable without proof of damage.[4] To the reader, these torts are perhaps better recognised as criminal offences and indeed, the defendant will normally face criminal, rather than civil, charges for such actions. There are a number of reasons for this. First of all, the police will usually be called in, which makes criminal proceedings more likely. Secondly, the claimant may not wish the pressure of further civil proceedings brought at his or her own instigation (and cost) when the defendant may not have the means to satisfy judgment. Thirdly, the criminal courts now possess at least some means of awarding compensation to a victim of crime,[5] and victims may also recover under the Criminal Injuries Compensation Scheme[6] which is a national fund, granting compensation for personal injury caused by crimes of violence. The Scheme will award compensation to any person who has sustained personal injury directly attributable to a crime of violence or to the apprehension of an offender or the prevention of an offence. Such compensation is unlikely to be as high as that awarded in a successful tort action, but is undoubtedly an easier option for the victim.

A tort action will generally be motivated by more than just a desire for compensation. It may be pursued to highlight a refusal of the Director of Public Prosecutions to bring a criminal prosecution[7] or in the face of an unsuccessful prosecution. As the burden of proof is lower in

11–002

---

3   See, e.g. M. Dyson (ed), *Unravelling Tort and Crime* (CUP, 2014).

4   See F. A. Trindade, "Intentional Torts: Some Thoughts on Assault and Battery" (1982) 2 O.J.L.S. 211.

5   See Powers of the Criminal Courts (Sentencing) Act 2000 ss.130–134 (as amended).

6   See generally the Criminal Injuries Compensation Act 1995 and the government website at *https://www.gov.uk/government/organisations/criminal-injuries-compensation-authority* [Accessed 1 August 2020].

7   See, e.g. *Halford v Brookes* [1991] 1 W.L.R. 428.

the civil courts, the claimant may succeed in proving his or her case on the balance of probabilities where the prosecutor has failed to prove the allegations in a criminal court beyond reasonable doubt. In the US case concerning O.J. Simpson, for example, the defendant, an ex-football star and celebrity, was found not guilty of the murder of his ex-wife and her lover, but was nevertheless subsequently found liable to pay damages by a civil court.[8] A tort action may also be brought to highlight abuse of power by public bodies such as the police, and a successful claimant may have his or her point reinforced by an award of exemplary damages.[9] In seeking to gain compensation where criminal proceedings have failed, litigants should note the limitations in the Offences against the Person Act 1861 ss.44 and 45.[10] These sections relate to assault and battery charges heard in the magistrates' courts.[11] Section 45 provides that where a summary hearing brought by or on behalf of the party aggrieved has been held and has ended, after a hearing on the merits, either with a certificate of dismissal,[12] or with the accused being convicted and fined or imprisoned, civil proceedings for the same cause will be barred.[13] As most criminal offences, save the most serious, are tried in the magistrates' court, this in practice limits the situations in which the victim can sue for compensation in tort.

Most cases are therefore decided by the criminal courts and for this reason, the civil courts will often reason by analogy to criminal cases. Criminal cases will be used, where appropriate, to illustrate the likely treatment of a tort claim. Criminal law authorities, however, should be treated with caution. They are not authority in the law of tort and can therefore only be treated as guidance. Proper regard must be had to the differing concerns of criminal law (which are largely punitive) and trespass to the person (which protects the personal integrity and right to self-determination of the claimant). This section of the chapter will examine battery, assault and false imprisonment in turn.

Battery

11-003

This has a number of components. Force must be applied intentionally by immediate and direct means to another individual. This can vary from the most minor contact with the claimant, such

---

8 See the controversial publication: O.J. Simpson and R. Goldman, *If I did it: Confession of the killer* (Gibson Square Books, 2007). A more recent example is that of *Ashley v Chief Constable of Sussex Police* [2008] UKHL 25; [2008] 1 A.C. 962 (civil claim following death of unarmed man, shot by police, when officer responsible had been acquitted of murder).

9 See, e.g. the guidelines given by Lord Woolf in *Thompson v Commissioner of Police of Metropolis* [1998] Q.B. 498.

10 The Law Commission Report No.218, *Criminal law: Legislating the criminal code: Offences against the person and general principles* (1993) recommended the repeal of these sections. This has not occurred.

11 Note that common assault and battery are summary offences by virtue of the Criminal Justice Act 1988 s.39.

12 This cannot be given when the defendant has pleaded guilty: *Ellis v Burton* [1975] 1 W.L.R. 386.

13 See *Wong v Parkside Health NHS Trust* [2001] EWCA Civ 1721; [2003] 3 All E.R. 932 at 937. The question focuses on the conduct in question, e.g. an assault. The courts will not allow the claimant to circumvent s.45 by framing the claim under a different cause of action e.g. under the rule in *Wilkinson v Downton*. See also *Masper v Brown* (1876) 1 C.P.D. 97.

as an unwanted peck on the cheek, to a violent blow in the chest. Because the tort is actionable without proof of damage, both types of battery render the defendant liable to pay damages. The requirements of battery are examined below.

(1) It must be intentional

This means that the act of force must be voluntary. For example, Y has not committed a battery if X grasps his arm and pulls it to strike Z. Intention relates only to the action of the defendant. It is not necessary that the defendant intends the consequences of his or her actions. On this basis, the defendant will be liable for all the consequences flowing from the tort, whether or not they are foreseeable.[14] Equally, if I intend to hit A and instead hit B, I commit a battery against B.[15] This rule, which is essentially one of convenience, has been explained as the concept of "transferred intent".

The tort may be committed even if the original action was unintentional, if the defendant at some point intends to apply force. For example, in *Fagan v Metropolitan Police Commissioner*,[16] the defendant unintentionally stopped his car on a policeman's foot. At this stage, no tort had been committed. However, by deliberately failing to move until the police officer had shouted "Get off my foot" several times, he committed a battery. It seems likely that, as in criminal law, recklessness in the use of force is sufficient to establish intent in battery.[17]

(2) It must be direct

It is a basic requirement of any trespass that the injury must be direct. If the injury is indirect, the claimant must find another basis for recovery. However, this requirement has been interpreted flexibly. In the eighteenth century case of *Scott v Shepherd*,[18] for example, the defendant was found liable for battery when he had thrown a lighted squib into a market place. This was despite the fact that the squib had been thrown on by two stallholders, to protect themselves and their wares, before it had exploded in the face of Scott. The majority of the court found the battery to be sufficiently direct. Equally, in *DPP v K*,[19] the force was considered sufficiently

---

14   See *Williams v Humphrey The Times* 20 February 1975 where the defendant was liable for deliberately pushing a guest in his swimming pool, although he clearly did not intend to cripple the plaintiff, who broke his ankle and foot.

15   *James v Campbell* (1832) 5 C. & P. 372; 172 E.R. 1015, and *Bici v Ministry of Defence* [2004] EWHC 786 (QB) *The Times* 11 June 2004. For criticism, see A. Beever, "Transferred malice in tort law?" (2009) 29 L.S. 400.

16   [1969] 1 Q.B. 439.

17   *R. v Venna* [1976] Q.B. 421. Subjective recklessness will suffice: see *R. v Savage* [1992] 1 A.C. 699 HL and *Bici v MOD* [2004] EWHC 786 (QB) at [67]: "it must be a subjective recklessness that they appreciated the potential harm to the claimants and were indifferent to it".

18   (1773) 2 W. Bl. 892; 96 E.R. 525.

19   [1990] 1 W.L.R. 1067. See also *Haystead v Chief Constable of Derbyshire* [2000] 3 All E.R. 890 QBD.

immediate and direct where a schoolboy had poured some concentrated sulphuric acid, stolen from a chemistry lesson, into a hand-dryer which was later used by another pupil with horrific results. The court held that the boy had known full well that he had created a dangerous situation, but had nevertheless taken the risk of injury to another. It was no excuse that he had panicked and had intended to remove the acid as soon as he was able.

(3) Immediate force

11–006

The tort of battery applies to any form of bodily contact. This causes a potential problem. If applied literally, it would cover all forms of contact. For example, A would commit a battery by tapping B on the shoulder to get his attention. It would clearly be a nonsense if an actionable battery was committed in such circumstances, and the law would, in effect, provide a charter for vexatious litigants to sue. Whilst this is common sense, the courts have experienced difficulties in finding a theoretical basis on which to draw a line between actionable batteries and ordinary social contact. Lord Holt CJ's comments in *Cole v Turner*[20] have been cited, where his Lordship held that "the least touching of another in anger is a battery". On this basis, the Court of Appeal in *Wilson v Pringle*[21] held that battery must be committed with "hostile" intent. On the facts of the case, a boy had suffered serious injury due to the antics of a fellow pupil. The defence alleged that the defendant had merely pulled the schoolbag off the schoolboy's shoulder, which had led him to fall on the ground and injure himself. The court held that liability depended on whether the pupil's actions had been "hostile" and not simply a schoolboy prank. It can be questioned whether this is helpful. What is hostile to one person may seem quite the opposite to another. For example, should an over-enthusiastic slap on the back or a surgeon's mistaken amputation of a leg be regarded as non-hostile and therefore not a battery? Even if an objective interpretation is adopted, it simply seems to mean that the reasonable person would view the action as contrary to the ordinary rules of social conduct. If this is so, then the view of Robert Goff LJ in *Collins v Wilcock*[22] is preferable. His Lordship took the entirely sensible view that instead of adopting complicated legal rules based on implied consent to the battery, or hostile intent, the law should just exclude liability for conduct generally acceptable in the ordinary conduct of daily life—a view which he reiterated in *Re F*[23]:

> "... a broader exception has been created to allow for the exigencies of everyday life: jostling in a street or some other crowded place, social contact at parties and such like. This exception has been said to be founded on implied consent, since those who go about in public places, or go to parties, may be taken to have impliedly con-

---

20 (1704) 6 Mod. Rep. 149; 90 E.R. 958.
21 [1987] Q.B. 237. Followed by *Flint v Tittensor* [2015] EWHC 466 (QB); [2015] 1 W.L.R. 4370 at [32].
22 [1984] 1 W.L.R. 1172. See also Lord Goff in *Re F* [1990] 2 A.C. 1.
23 [1990] 2 A.C. 1 at 72–73.

sented to bodily contact of this kind. Today this rationalization can be regarded as artificial: and, in particular, it is difficult to impute consent to those who, by reason of their youth or mental disorder, are unable to give their consent. For this reason I consider it more appropriate to regard such cases as falling within a general exception embracing all physical contact which is generally acceptable in the ordinary conduct of everyday life."

Assault

This tort protects the claimant *in fear of* battery. Where the defendant's actions cause the claimant reasonably to apprehend the direct and immediate infliction of force on him or her, the tort is committed. It is important to stress first of all that this is distinct from the popular meaning of "assault", which in tort equates with the tort of battery. So, if I point a gun at you, I have only committed an assault. It is irrelevant that the gun is unloaded—you do not know that, and have every reason to apprehend a battery.[24] Only when I shoot the gun and hit you have I committed a battery. If my aim is poor and I miss, only an assault has been committed.

The requirements of assault are as follows:

(1) Reasonable apprehension of harm

The key to assault is the reasonable apprehension of harm. If I creep up and strike you from behind without your knowledge, I have only committed a battery. It is only assault if you are aware of my approach. Equally, if you are lucky enough to be saved from physical harm by the intervention of a third party, or if I change my mind, I have only committed an assault. In *Stephens v Myers*,[25] for example, the plaintiff was threatened with violence whilst attempting to expel the defendant from a parish meeting. The defendant had approached the plaintiff threatening violence, but, due to the intervention of the churchwarden, was liable only for assault. Passive obstruction, however, such as that seen in *Innes v Wylie*,[26] where a policeman stopped the plaintiff from entering a room, will not amount to assault. If the human obstruction is passive, like a door or a wall preventing entry, the claimant has no reason to anticipate the direct and immediate infliction of force, so the defendant cannot be liable. The test of reasonable apprehension is an objective one. It is irrelevant whether the particular claimant was actually in fear, or could have defended himself or herself successfully.

11–007

11–008

---

24 *R. v St George* (1840) 9 C. & P. 483 at 493; 173 E.R. 921 at 926. See also *Logdon v DPP* [1976] Crim. L.R. 121.
25 (1830) 4 C. & P. 349; 172 E.R. 735.
26 (1844) 1 C. & K. 257 at 263; 174 E.R. 800. Contrast *Chief Constable of Thames Valley Police v Hepburn* [2002] EWCA Civ 1841 *The Times* 19 December 2002 CA.

(2) It must be intentional

11–009

This is a basic requirement of the tort and here signifies that the defendant intended the claimant to apprehend reasonable force would be used or was reckless as to the consequences of his or her actions.[27]

(3) It must be immediate and direct

11–010

This is really part of the test of reasonable apprehension. If the claimant can see that the defendant is not in a position to inflict immediate and direct harm on the claimant, then the claimant has nothing to fear and so the defendant is not liable for assault. Therefore, if I threaten you with violence as I am passing you in a train, I have not committed assault. More controversially, in *Thomas v National Union of Mineworkers (South Wales Area)*,[28] striking miners, who hurled insults at working miners who had been transported into work in vehicles, were not held liable for assault, because the vehicles had been protected by a police cordon.

CAN WORDS AMOUNT TO AN ASSAULT?

11–011

There is old authority that words by themselves cannot amount to an assault.[29] This may now be challenged in the light of the House of Lords case of *R. v Ireland*.[30] Here, three women had been harassed by Ireland. He was alleged to have made repeated telephone calls to them, generally at night, during which he remained silent. The women suffered psychiatric illness as a result. The House of Lords rejected the proposition that an assault could never be committed by words as unrealistic and indefensible. Liability would in fact depend on whether the claimant, in the circumstances before the court, reasonably believed that the oral threat could be carried out in the sufficiently near future to qualify as an immediate threat of personal violence. On the facts, the court was prepared to accept that silence would be capable of giving rise to such fears. This seems sensible and it is to be hoped that although the decision was made in criminal law, it will be applied by analogy to tort law. Whilst the old saying goes that "sticks and stones may break my bones, but words will never hurt me", this seems to require an unduly high level of courage from the reasonable person. Few amongst us would not experience fear if telephoned by a stalker. As recognised by the court in *R. v Ireland*, whilst the recipient of the call may have no knowledge of the stalker's whereabouts, the fear lies with the knowledge that the stalker, in contrast, may know exactly where the recipient is at the time of the call.

---

27 *R. v Venna* [1976] Q.B. 421; *Bici v MOD* [2004] EWHC 786 (QB) (subjective recklessness).
28 [1986] Ch.20 at 65. More recently, the Court of Appeal rejected a claim by the President of Equatorial Guinea that the advance group participating in an attempted coup (which failed) had the means to carry out the threat alleged: *Mbasogo v Logo Ltd (No.1)* [2006] EWCA Civ 1370; [2007] Q.B. 846.
29 See *Meade's & Belt's Case* (1823) 1 Lew. C.C. 184; 168 E.R. 1006: "no words or singing are equivalent to an assault".
30 [1998] A.C. 147.

Conversely, it has long been accepted that words may negative an assault. In the classic case of *Tuberville v Savage*,[31] the defendant placed his hand on his sword and stated that "If it were not assize time, I would not take such language from you". It was assize time and so, in reality, the defendant was stating that he did not intend to strike the plaintiff. This must be distinguished from a conditional threat, where the claimant is merely given an option to avoid violence. It was no excuse for the highwayman to claim that his victims had a viable alternative option when he stated "stand and deliver, your money or your life!" On this basis, in *Read v Coker*,[32] the defendant was liable for assault when he and his servants threatened to break the plaintiff's neck unless he left the defendant's workshop.

False imprisonment

This tort is concerned with the claimant's right to freedom of movement. A complete restriction of this freedom, unless it is expressly or impliedly authorised by the law, will render the defendant liable. It is necessary to exclude conduct expressly or impliedly authorised by the law from this tort in view of the custodial powers of the state and the powers of the police force, provided, of course, these bodies act within the powers given them by law. It is no excuse that the defendant had wrongfully assumed in good faith that he had a legal right to detain the claimant.[33] In this sense, false imprisonment is a strict liability tort. It is not the conduct of the defendant which is judged, but the injury to the claimant. "False" simply means wrongful. Equally, "imprisonment" does not require the defendant to put the claimant in prison, but will extend to any actions which deprive the claimant of his or her freedom of movement. It should be noted that it need not be shown that force has been used.

One question which has arisen is this: where A has given orders to B to restrain C, is A or B liable for false imprisonment? Generally, the actor (here B) will be liable, unless B exercises no discretion in the matter and is forced to obey the instructions of A. An example of this may be found in *Austin v Dowling*.[34] Here, a police inspector had refused to take the responsibility for arresting the plaintiff on a charge made by the defendant's wife, but finally did arrest the plaintiff when the defendant signed the charge sheet. It was held that the defendant was liable for false imprisonment. In modern times, however, the courts have taken the view that the police, as professionals, are expected to exercise their own judgment and not simply follow the instructions of others. This view formed part of the reasoning of the Court of Appeal in

11–012

---

31 (1669) 1 Mod. Rep. 3; 86 E.R. 684.

32 (1853) 13 C.B. 850; 138 E.R. 1437.

33 See *R. v Governor of Brockhill Prison Ex p. Evans (No.2)* [2001] 2 A.C. 19 (prison governor liable for unauthorised detention of prisoner when his sentence, calculated by him on the law as then understood, was subsequently found to be incorrect). Equally a breach of the principles of public law may render detention unlawful even if the claimant could have been detained if the correct procedures had been followed, although it is likely to lead to no more than nominal damages: *R. (on the application of Lumba) v Secretary of State for the Home Department* [2011] UKSC 12; [2012] 1 A.C. 245.

34 (1870) L.R. 5 C.P. 534.

Davidson v Chief Constable of North Wales,[35] where a store detective had given evidence to the police which led to the arrest of Davidson for shoplifting. Davidson and a friend were detained by the police for two hours before it became clear that the store detective's suspicions were unfounded. Davidson sued the store detective for false imprisonment. The Court of Appeal held that no action lay against the store detective where she had merely given information to the police, who could act as they saw fit. Only if the detective had been the instigator, promoter and active inciter of the action would the detective be liable.

The requirements of false imprisonment are examined below:

(1) A complete restriction of the claimant's freedom of movement

11–013

This requirement refers to any actions which restrict the claimant's freedom of movement in every direction. In *Walker v Commissioner of Police of the Metropolis*,[36] the Court of Appeal made it clear that confining an individual in a doorway for however short a time (here a few seconds) without lawful authority would amount to a false imprisonment. As Tomlinson LJ commented, "a fundamental constitutional principle is at stake. The detention was indeed trivial, but that can and should be reflected in the measure of damages and does not render lawful that which was unlawful".[37]

The requirement is not satisfied, however, if the claimant is able to move in one direction. For example, in *Bird v Jones*,[38] the plaintiff had insisted on passing along the public footway on Hammersmith Bridge in London, which the defendants had partially enclosed without due permission. The plaintiff had climbed over a fence erected by the defendants to close off the footway on one side of the bridge, but was prevented from moving along the footway by the defendants. He was told that he might go back and use the public footway on the other side of the bridge, but the plaintiff would not do so. The court held that the defendants were not liable for false imprisonment. They had not imposed a complete restriction on the plaintiff's freedom of movement.

The Supreme Court most recently held that:

> "[t]he essence of imprisonment is being made to stay in a particular place by another person. The methods which might be used to keep a person there are many and various."[39]

---

35 [1994] 2 All E.R. 597 CA. Comment: J. R. Spencer [1994] C.L.J. 433. See also *Ali v Heart of England NHS Foundation Trust* [2018] EWHC 591 (Ch): witness passing information to police is not liable even if information was incorrect.

36 [2014] EWCA Civ 897; [2015] 1 W.L.R. 312.

37 [2014] EWCA Civ 897 at [46]. Here nominal damages of £5 were awarded.

38 (1845) 7 Q.B. 742; 115 E.R. 668.

39 *R. (Jalloh (formerly Jollah) v Secretary of State for the Home Department* [2020] UKSC 4; [2020] 2 W.L.R. 418 at [24] per Lady Hale.

They include physical barriers, guards or threats of force or of legal process. In *Jalloh*, the Home Office had imposed a curfew condition requiring him to remain at home every night, backed by an electronic tag and the threat of criminal prosecution if the curfew was breached. Unfortunately, the Home Office had no legal authority to do this and Jalloh successfully sued for false imprisonment. The Court held that the idea that the claimant was a free agent, able to come and go as he pleased, was "completely unreal."[40] It was irrelevant that Jalloh had not been put in prison and, indeed, could have physically left his home, given the threat of serious legal consequences if he did so.[41]

Such a restriction will generally involve a positive act. Trespass is concerned with intentional, immediate and direct actions, not omissions. On this basis, an omission or refusal to release the claimant from confinement will not amount to false imprisonment, unless the claimant has a legal right to be released and the defendant is under a positive obligation to release the claimant. The majority of the Court of Appeal in *Iqbal v Prison Officers Assoc*[42] thus held that the claimant, who was confined to his cell as a result of a prison officers' strike, could not sue for false imprisonment. Their omission to act—in refusing to let him out of his cell—did not entail liability. The claimant was legally detained and the officers were under no duty to the prisoner to release him (their duty was to their employer).[43] Lord Neuberger MR did suggest, however, that a deliberate and dishonest refusal to unlock the cells might give rise to a claim for misfeasance in public office.[44]

The issue of confinement remains a question of fact. If the claimant is able to return in the same direction in which he or she came, or is given reasonable means of escape, the defendant will not be liable. The means of escape must be reasonable—a rope left by the window of a seven storey building will clearly not suffice. This question did, however, divide the House of Lords in *R. v Bournewood Community and Mental Health NHS Trust Ex p. L*.[45] The majority found that a mentally disordered patient who had been placed voluntarily in an unlocked ward and showed no desire to leave had not been detained, despite the fact that the hospital gave evidence that he had been sedated and would have been detained compulsorily had he sought to leave. Lord Steyn, however, dissented, remarking that, "The suggestion that L was free to go is a fairy tale".[46] The European Court of Human Rights in 2005[47] found unanimously that the applicant had been deprived of his liberty, contrary to art.5.1 of the Convention. The Strasbourg Court noted, however, that the House of Lords had considered the question solely on the basis of false imprisonment,[48] rather than in terms of art.5.1, and the criteria for assessing domes-

---

40 [2020] UKSC 4 at [27].
41 Breaking the curfew could lead to a £5,000 fine or imprisonment for up to six months or both.
42 [2009] EWCA Civ 1312; [2010] Q.B. 732 (Sullivan LJ dissenting on the issue of liability).
43 The court also found that the direct and immediate cause of the prisoner's confinement was the order of the Governor that, because of the strike, prisoners should remain in their cells throughout the day.
44 [2009] EWCA Civ 1312 at [40]–[42], discussed at para.11–033.
45 [1999] 1 A.C. 458.
46 [1999] 1 A.C. at 495. Lord Nolan also dissented on this point.
47 *HL v United Kingdom (45508/99)* (2005) 40 E.H.R.R. 32.
48 The decision of the House of Lords pre-dated the coming into force of the Human Rights Act 1998.

tic and Convention issues were different.[49] Lady Hale in *Jalloh* suggested, however, that the broader view of imprisonment used in that case made the decision of the narrow majority in *Bournewood* difficult to justify.[50]

11–014

It is a matter of contention whether a reasonable means of escape exists when the defendant imposes conditions on the manner in which visitors leave his or her premises. There is authority that, provided the conditions are reasonable, the defendant is not liable if he or she refuses to allow the claimant to leave until these conditions are satisfied. In *Robinson v Balmain Ferry Co Ltd*,[51] for example, the plaintiff had contracted to enter the defendants' wharf to catch a ferry boat to cross the river. For reasons of efficiency, the fee of one penny was paid on one side of the river, on entering and exiting the wharf. Having a 20 minute wait for the next boat, the plaintiff changed his mind and tried to exit the wharf. He refused to pay the stipulated charge of one penny to leave the wharf, as required by a notice above the turnstile. The defendants refused to let him leave until the charge was paid. In an action for false imprisonment, the Privy Council held that a penny charge was a reasonable condition for leaving by a route different from the one stipulated in the contract:

> **"There is no law requiring the defendants to make the exit from their premises gratuitous to people who come there upon a definite contract which involves their leaving the wharf by another way."[52]**

This approach was taken a step further by the House of Lords' decision five years later in *Herd v Weardale Steel, Coal and Coke Co Ltd*.[53] Here, a miner had refused to do certain work, on the basis that it was dangerous, and had demanded to be taken to the surface before the end of his shift. His employer refused. Their Lordships held that the employer was not liable for false imprisonment. The miner had voluntarily entered the mine under a contract of employment and was deemed to have impliedly consented that he would not be brought to the surface until the end of the shift.

These cases involve a worrying invasion of the civil liberties of those involved.[54] However, there is clearly a line to be drawn. As Viscount Haldane pointed out in *Herd*, a claimant cannot expect to be able to stop an express train because he or she now wishes to get off the train. The traveller consents to a restriction on his or her freedom of movement for the duration of the journey. If this consent is withdrawn, logically he or she should be permitted to alight at the

---

49 *HL v United Kingdom (45508/99)* (2005) 40 E.H.R.R. 32 at [90].
50 *R. (Jalloh (formerly Jollah) v Secretary of State for the Home Department* [2020] UKSC 4 at [23]: "So far as is known, this is the only example of a deprivation of liberty which did not amount to imprisonment at common law: generally speaking, one may well be imprisoned without being deprived of one's liberty, but the other way round is harder to envisage."
51 [1910] A.C. 295 PC.
52 [1910] A.C. 295 PC at 299.
53 [1915] A.C. 67.
54 See generally K.F. Tan, "A misconceived issue in the tort of false imprisonment" (1981) 44 M.L.R. 166.

first reasonable opportunity, which will usually be the next designated stop. It does not entail a right to stop the train immediately. On this basis, the miner in *Herd* quite rightly limited his claim for false imprisonment to the period during which the lift was available to take him out of the mine. It is when the defendant refuses to allow the claimant to leave in such circumstances that a claim for false imprisonment should lie.

Robinson may, however, be defended on the basis that the plaintiff's restraint was not complete, as he could have crossed the river (subject to a query as to whether this is reasonable). *Herd* is more difficult to defend. It is difficult to see the decision as anything but a harsh ruling in favour of an employer's rights over his employees. It is scarcely legitimate to suggest imprisonment as a reasonable response to the employee's breach of contract. A better explanation of *Herd* (and certainly one more palatable to modern industrial relations) is to view it as an omission case; an interpretation supported by the Court of Appeal in *Iqbal* (above).

It is unnecessary to show the claimant knew of the imprisonment

11–015

Here the point is simply that the tort protects the claimant's freedom of movement, because it is a recognised interest the legal system wishes to protect. Proof of damage is not required, and so it is not necessary that the claimant has suffered from the knowledge of his or her false imprisonment. *Grainger v Hill*[55] established that the tort exists even if the claimant is too ill to move, and in *Meering's* case,[56] the Court of Appeal held that the tort can be committed even where the claimant does not know that he or she is being detained. In this case, the plaintiff had been suspected of stealing from his employer, the defendants, and so he had been asked to accompany two of his employer's private police force to the company's office. He had agreed and waited as instructed in the waiting room. Unknown to the plaintiff, the two policemen remained nearby and had been instructed not to let him leave the waiting room until the Metropolitan Police arrived. He later sued for false imprisonment. The court held that the tort had been committed as soon as the defendant was under the control of the defendants' police. Atkin LJ stated the legal position:

> **"It appears to me that a person could be imprisoned without his knowing it. I think a person can be imprisoned while he is asleep, while he is in a state of drunkenness, while he is unconscious, and while he is a lunatic . . . Of course the damages might be diminished and would be affected by the question whether he was conscious of it or not."**[57]

---

55 (1838) 4 Bing. N.C. 212; 132 E.R. 769.
56 *Meering v Grahame-White Aviation Co Ltd* (1920) 122 L.T. 44.
57 (1920) 122 L.T. 44 at 53.

This is a strong statement, indicating the courts' disapproval of any unjustified and complete restriction on the claimant's freedom of movement.[58] As Lord Griffiths commented in *Murray v Ministry of Defence*[59]:

> "... the law attaches supreme importance to the liberty of the individual and if he suffers a wrongful interference with that liberty it should remain actionable even without proof of special damage."

(2) Without legal authorisation

11–016

The burden of proof lies on the defendant to justify the lawfulness of the arrest and the claimant is only required to show that he or she has been denied freedom of movement. On this basis, this requirement should be treated as a defence to be established by the defendant and will be so treated in a later section, below. Again, we can see that the rule seeks to protect the civil liberties of the claimant.

The Rule in *Wilkinson v Downton*

11–017

In all three torts above, the three characteristics of a trespass action are apparent: intentional acts, which directly harm the claimant, and which are actionable without proof of harm. This does not include intentional harm which has been *indirectly* caused. This gap is filled by the so-called rule in *Wilkinson v Downton*. Like the rule in *Rylands v Fletcher* seen in the previous chapter, the rule is named after its leading case, where the relevant legal principles were set out. In *Wilkinson v Downton*[60] the defendant falsely told the plaintiff that her husband had been involved in an accident in which he had been seriously injured. The defendant later claimed that it had been a practical joke, but the shock suffered by the plaintiff as a result led her to suffer weeks of illness. She sued the defendant for damages. His actions had been

---

58 There is authority to the contrary in *Herring v Boyle* (1834) 1 Cr. M. & R. 377; 149 E.R. 1126 which was not cited in *Meering*. This was criticised, however, by Lord Griffiths in *Murray v Ministry of Defence* [1988] 1 W.L.R. 692 at 701.

59 [1988] 1 W.L.R. 692 at 703 (although the comment was obiter). See also Sedley LJ in *Chief Constable of Thames Valley Police v Hepburn* [2002] EWCA Civ 1841 *The Times* 19 December 2002 at [14]. This comment was approved by the majority of the Supreme Court in *R. (on the application of Lumba) v Secretary of State for the Home Department* [2011] UKSC 12; [2012] 1 A.C. 245 (see, e.g. Lord Dyson at [64]).

60 [1897] 2 Q.B. 57.

intentional, but the harm had been indirect. Nevertheless, Wright J held that where the defendant had wilfully undertaken an act calculated to cause physical harm to the plaintiff, there was a good cause of action. It is clear, however, that, unlike trespass, harm must be proved.

The case was applied by the Court of Appeal in *Janvier v Sweeney*.[61] In this case, a private detective had pretended to be a police officer, and, in order to obtain access to her employer's correspondence, had threatened the plaintiff that she was in danger of arrest for association with a German spy (her fiancé was German). The plaintiff suffered psychiatric illness as a result, and was allowed to recover damages under the rule in *Wilkinson v Downton*.

However, despite such a rapid start, and the potential breadth of the rule, it has not been much relied upon by the courts, due to the increasing role of the tort of negligence in recent times. It was resurrected by the Court of Appeal in the 1993 case of *Khorasandjian v Bush*[62] to deal with the problem of harassment. In the absence of a tort of harassment,[63] the court resorted to existing tortious actions (private nuisance and the rule in *Wilkinson v Downton*) to protect a young woman who had been suffering from a campaign of harassment undertaken by a former boyfriend. The rule was relied upon by the court to support the grant of an injunction against the defendant for wilful actions calculated to cause physical harm to the plaintiff. But one problem existed. In both *Wilkinson* and *Janvier*, the plaintiffs had suffered physical or psychiatric injury. In contrast, in *Khorasandjian*, the plaintiff had merely suffered from stress. Nevertheless, Dillon LJ took a broad approach. His Lordship held that there was "an obvious risk that the cumulative effect of continued and unrestrained further harassment such as she has undergone would cause [psychiatric] illness",[64] which would suffice for a quia timet injunction (an injunction given to prevent an apprehended tort).

The courts have subsequently disapproved of such a broad approach. Harassment is now dealt with specifically by means of the Protection from Harassment Act 1997 (see below). In *Hunter v Canary Wharf*,[65] the House of Lords found that, in view of the Act, the decision in *Khorasandjian* granting the plaintiff a remedy in private nuisance should be overruled. Whilst their Lordships did not overturn the alternative ground for the decision based on the rule in *Wilkinson v Downton*, Lord Hoffmann in the later decision of *Wainwright v Home Office*[66] favoured a narrower interpretation of the law. Whilst expressly questioning the continued need for this tort, he was reluctant to see it extended beyond claims for indirectly inflicted physical and recognised psychiatric injury. The view of the court was clearly that, in view of the

---

61   [1919] 2 K.B. 316.
62   [1993] Q.B. 727.
63   *Patel v Patel* [1988] 2 F.L.R. 179.
64   [1993] Q.B. 727 at 736.
65   [1997] A.C. 655.
66   [2003] UKHL 53 [2004] 2 A.C. 406. See also *Wong v Parkside Health NHS Trust* [2001] EWCA Civ 1721; [2003] 3 All E.R. 932 CA.

expansion of the tort of negligence to cover claims for psychiatric illness since 1901,[67] this tort was effectively defunct.[68]

This view must now be re-examined in the light of the Supreme Court decision in *OPO v Rhodes*.[69] In this case, the court unanimously rejected the argument that the rule would support a claim made on behalf of the 12 year old autistic son of James Rhodes to restrain the publication of his father's semi-autobiographical book. The book described Rhodes' traumatic upbringing and it was argued that publication would constitute wilful conduct likely to cause the son psychiatric harm if he read it. In so doing, the court clarified the nature of the rule in *Wilkinson v Downton* and confirmed that it was still alive and well. To succeed, a claimant must establish three elements:

- the conduct element (words or conduct directed towards the claimant for which there is no justification or reasonable excuse);

- the mental element (wilful); and

- the consequence element (physical harm or recognised psychiatric illness).

There was no arguable case on the facts that the claimant could establish either the conduct or the mental element in this case. Recklessness would not satisfy the mental element: "to hold that the necessary mental element is intention to cause physical harm or severe mental or emotional distress strikes a just balance".[70]

Rhodes was applied in *C v WH*.[71] Here, a former Vice Principal of a special educational needs school was found liable under the rule in *Wilkinson v Downton* for the grooming and sexual abuse of a 16-year-old female student including the exchange of explicit texts. While the mental element of the action required that the claimant establish that the defendant intended to cause severe mental or emotional distress to the girl, the obvious consequences of the actions of the defendant in grooming a vulnerable pupil in a special school some 39 years younger than himself signified that the perpetrator could not realistically say that those consequences were unintended. It was obvious that the relationship would, in the end, cause C harm, which it in fact did.

---

67 *Dulieu v White & Sons* [1901] 2 K.B. 669.
68 Field J in *C v D* [2006] EWHC 166 (QBD) approved Lord Hoffmann's view, although he found that the sexually abused claimant had succeeded in part in his claim under the rule.
69 [2015] UKSC 32; [2016] A.C. 219. See C. D. L. Hunt, "*Wilkinson v Downton* revisited" [2015] C.L.J. 392.
70 [2015] UKSC 32 at [87] per Baroness Hale and Lord Toulson. The book was later published and became a best-seller, see J. Rhodes, *Instrumental* (Canongate Books, 2015).
71 [2015] EWHC 2687 (QB); [2016] P.I.Q.R. Q2.

Trespass to the Person: Defences

Defences generally are dealt with in Ch.16. This section will highlight the defences which are of particular importance in actions for trespass to the person.

11-018

(1) Consent

This is an obvious defence. If I expressly consent to contact or implicitly lead the defendant to believe that I am consenting, I cannot later sue the defendant. It would be highly inconvenient if no such rule existed. On this basis, hospitals can ensure that they commit no torts against patients whilst operating by asking them to sign consent forms. Equally, a patient who presents his or her arm for an injection is clearly consenting to the infliction of immediate and direct force on their person. Team sports similarly rely on the ability of the individual to consent to the rough and tumble which may ensue (but not, of course, to a violent blow by an opposing team member contrary to the rules of the game). In this way, the self-determination of the individual is protected.

11-019

The consent must, of course, be real and not induced by fraud, misrepresentation or duress. So, in *R. v Williams*,[72] the defendant, a singing tutor, was liable in battery for sexually assaulting a naive plaintiff who had been falsely informed that this would improve her voice. The traditional rule is that the fraud must go to the very nature and quality of the act or to the identity of the assailant, and that fraud as to the effect and consequences of the act is not deemed sufficient to nullify consent.[73] It is submitted that this may lead to unduly harsh results in practice. The criminal court in *R. v Dica*[74] held that this distinction would not apply to the offence of unlawful infliction of grievous bodily harm under the Offences Against the Person Act 1861 s.20. Here, Dica had had unprotected sexual intercourse with the complainants without informing them that he knew himself to be HIV positive. They were later found to be infected with the HIV virus. The Court of Appeal held that although there was consent to the act of intercourse, his conduct amounted to an offence under s.20.[75] It remains unclear whether what is essentially a claim for fraud as to the risk of infection would give rise to civil liability.

It is not necessary in English law for the claimant to be aware of *all* the relevant facts in giving his or her consent. Nevertheless, the recent Supreme Court decision in *Montgomery v Lanarkshire Health Board*[76] held that doctors are under a duty to take reasonable care to ensure that patients are aware of any *material* risks involved in any recommended treatment, and of

---

72 [1923] 1 K.B. 340.

73 *Hegarty v Shine* (1878) 14 Cox C.C. 124; *R. v Clarence* (1888) 22 Q.B.D. 23; *R. v Linekar* [1995] Q.B. 250 CA. Query its application in *R. v Tabassum (Naveed)* [2000] 2 Cr. App. R. 328.

74 [2004] EWCA Crim 1103; [2004] Q.B. 1257.

75 Offences Against the Person Act 1861 s.20 does not require proof of assault or battery.

76 [2015] UKSC 11; [2015] A.C. 1430. Comment: R. Bagshaw (2016) 132 L.Q.R. 182. See also *Chester v Afshar* [2004]

any reasonable alternative or variant treatments. This decision indicates that the courts are looking for "informed consent", at least in the context of negligence claims. Material risks are those to which, in the circumstances of the particular case, a reasonable person in the patient's position would be likely to attach significance OR those to which the doctor is or should reasonably be aware that this particular patient would be likely to attach significance. This does not, however, signify that doctors have to disclose every possible alternative treatment, regardless of its feasibility.[77] Provided, therefore, the patient is informed in broad terms of the nature of the procedure to be undertaken and of any material risks which would affect the judgment of a reasonable patient,[78] real consent is given. If the claimant believes the information given is deficient, the remedy lies in the tort of negligence, not trespass to the person.[79]

One peculiar aspect of consent is that for trespass to the person, but not, it should be noted, for trespass to land, the burden is on the claimant to prove absence of consent. Generally, the burden is on the defendant to establish any defences. This suggests that in trespass to the person, consent is not a defence at all. Rather, absence of consent is part of the cause of action to be proved on the balance of probabilities by the claimant. At first instance, in *Freeman v Home Office (No.2)*,[80] McCowan J held that the burden of proof was on the claimant, because the tort consists of a trespass against the will of the party. In practice, however, the issue of consent will usually be raised by the defendant and is therefore generally treated as a defence.

Refusal of consent

11-020

It seems logical that if I have a right to consent to a trespass to my person, I have a corresponding right to refuse consent to such actions. But whilst it is clearly desirable that I have the right to refuse consent to your violent actions, it is more contentious when I wish to refuse to consent to life-saving medical treatment. The idea of self-determination implies that the doctor should not be allowed to overrule my express wishes, even with my best interests at heart. Therefore, if a Jehovah's Witness clearly states that, because of her religious beliefs, she is not prepared to authorise a blood transfusion, the doctor will commit a battery if he administers blood against her will.[81]

It has been held that an adult of sound mind and full understanding should be able to

---

UKHL 41; [2005] 1 A.C. 134. Applied recently in *Diamond v Royal Devon and Exeter NHS Foundation Trust* [2019] EWCA Civ 585; [2019] P.I.Q.R. P12.

77 R. Heywood, "Medical disclosure of alternative treatments" [2009] C.L.J. 30 at 31.

78 See also *Pearce v United Bristol Healthcare* [1999] P.I.Q.R. P53 CA.

79 See *Chatterton v Gerson* [1981] Q.B. 432 at 443 per Bristow J. Note that if the patient has consented to one procedure, it does not mean that the patient has consented to any further invasion unless the doctor has ensured that the terms of consent authorise such further treatment as the doctor considers necessary or desirable.

80 [1984] 1 Q.B. 524. Contrast majority view of the Supreme Court of Canada in *Non-Marine Underwriters v Scalera* (2000) 185 D.L.R. (4th) 1.

81 *Malette v Shulman* (1990) 67 D.L.R. (4th) 321.

decide to refuse treatment, even if the treatment is necessary to save his or her life or even, controversially, that of her unborn child.[82] Capacity will be presumed unless shown otherwise.[83] Only where there is doubt as to the patient's free will and capacity will no trespass take place. For example, in *Re T (Adult: Refusal of Treatment)*,[84] a patient had refused a blood transfusion, following a road traffic accident and subsequent Caesarian section to deliver her premature baby. She was not a Jehovah's Witness, but had been brought up by her mother, who was a devout Witness, to believe that blood transfusions were wrong. Her refusal followed time alone with her mother. It was held that in the light of her illness, the incomplete information she had been given, and the perceived influence of her mother, the doctors had acted lawfully in the circumstances in giving her a transfusion. This case shows how narrow the line between autonomy and lack of capacity may sometimes be.

This does not mean that a patient suffering from some mental disability cannot refuse consent. The question remains one of capacity. In *Re JT (Adult: refusal of medical treatment)*,[85] the patient had a learning disability which in the past had been associated with extremely severe behavioural disturbance. She was being detained under the Mental Health Act 1983. Wall J held that, nevertheless, she was capable of comprehending and retaining the information given, believing it, and making a choice in the light of it.[86] She was therefore competent to refuse the renal dialysis necessary to keep her alive. These cases will never be easy to decide, but the courts are reluctant to deny the right of the individual to retain self-determination over his or her body.

Difficult problems arise in determining the extent to which a child may be able to refuse to give consent to medical treatment.[87] In relation to consent, the Family Law Reform Act 1969 s.8(1) permits children of 16 and over to consent to surgical, medical or dental treatment without the consent of a parent or guardian. In relation to children below 16, the House of Lords in *Gillick v West Norfolk AHA*[88] held by a majority that a child below 16 is capable of giving valid consent, provided that the child is of sufficient intelligence and understanding to appreciate

---

82 *St George's Healthcare NHS Trust v S* [1999] Fam. 26. Scott highlights the difficulties in determining the nature of moral and legal duties in such situations: R. Scott, "The Pregnant Woman and the Good Samaritan: Can a Woman have a Duty to Undergo a Caesarean Section?" (2000) 20 O.J.L.S. 407. See also *Re AK (Adult patient) (Medical Treatment: Consent)* [2001] 1 F.L.R. 129 (victim suffering from motor neurone disease but, although severely disabled, intellect unimpaired). Note also the guidance set out in *Re B v NHS Hospital Trust* [2002] EWHC 429 (Fam); [2002] 2 All E.R. 449 at 473–474 by Dame Elizabeth Butler-Sloss.

83 *Re MB* [1997] 2 F.C.R. 541 at 553 per Butler-Sloss LJ.

84 [1993] Fam. 95.

85 [1998] 1 F.L.R. 48.

86 Applying the test stated in *Re C (Refusal of medical treatment)* [1994] 1 F.L.R. 31. See also *Re MB* [1997] 2 F.C.R. 541 (fear of needles rendered patient temporarily incompetent) and *Re W* [2002] EWHC 901 (Fam) *Independent* 17 June 2002 (psychopathic disorder, but sufficient mental capacity to weigh the information required to reach a decision as to treatment).

87 S. Gilmore and J. Herring, "'No' is the hardest word: Consent and children's autonomy" (2011) 23 C.F.L.Q. 3.

88 [1986] A.C. 112. See, for example, *JA (A Minor) (Medical Treatment: Child Diagnosed with HIV)* [2014] EWHC 1135 (Fam); [2015] 2 F.L.R. 1030 (not *Gillick* competent to refuse to take anti-retroviral therapy medication).

what is proposed. This is regardless of the feelings of his or her parents. However, this is not the same as giving the child a right to refuse consent. In *Re W*,[89] W was a girl of 16 who was suffering from anorexia nervosa. She opposed the local authority's decision to move her to a unit specialising in the treatment of eating disorders. The Court of Appeal held that even if the child is 16 or over, or "*Gillick* competent", a parent or guardian may nevertheless consent on the minor's behalf. The court warned doctors to listen to the objections of minors, whose views would increase in importance according to the age and maturity of the minor, but held that such objections would not be an absolute bar to treatment. In any event, the court has an inherent jurisdiction to intervene to protect minors irrespective of their wishes. This allows the court to intervene and overrule a minor's objection to treatment.

In the case of younger children, parental consent will suffice for general medical treatment. Even where the parents refuse consent, the court's inherent power may be invoked to ensure the child receives the appropriate treatment.[90] In the case of *Re C*,[91] Wilson J overruled parental objections to HIV testing of their baby girl. The mother was HIV positive and the child had a 20 to 25% chance of infection. Whilst the court was prepared to accord great importance to the wishes of her parents, the arguments in favour of testing the baby were overwhelming. This view was approved by the Court of Appeal,[92] in which Butler-Sloss LJ emphasised that the welfare of the child was the paramount concern of the court.

Limits to consent

11–021

Criminal law has refused to accept the defence of consent where the defendant has inflicted bodily harm on the claimant: ". . . it is not in the public interest that people should try to cause, or should cause, each other actual bodily harm for no good reason".[93] The House of Lords decision in *R. v Brown*,[94] which found a group of sado-masochists liable for acts of violence in which they had willingly and enthusiastically participated, was challenged in the European Court of

---

89　[1993] Fam. 64. See also *Re M (A child) (Medical treatment)* [1999] 2 F.L.R. 1097. See M. R. Brazier and C. Bridge, "Coercion or caring: analysing adolescent autonomy" (1996) 16 L.S. 84, although A. Morris in 2005 argued that the increasingly rights-based approach in this area may lead to greater autonomy for adolescents: "*Gillick*, 20 years on: arrested development or growing pains?" (2005) 21 P.N. 158.

90　The judgment of the European Court of Human Rights in *Glass v United Kingdom* (61827/00) (2004) 39 E.H.R.R. 15 stressed the role of the court in protecting the personal integrity of the child under art.8, even where emergency procedures are involved if sufficient time exists.

91　[2000] Fam. 48. See also *Re C (a child) (Immunisation: Parental rights)* [2003] EWCA Civ 1148; [2003] Fam Law 731 (immunisation ordered despite mothers' objections) and the more drastic *Re A (Children) (Conjoined Twins)* [2001] Fam. 147 CA (parents' objections to separation of conjoined twins overruled, although the inevitable result was that one of the girls would die).

92　[1999] 2 F.L.R. 1004 CA.

93　*Att-Gen's Reference (No.6 of 1980)* [1981] Q.B. 715 at 719 per Lord Lane CJ. Infliction of harm is permissible, however, in the course of properly conducted games and sports or the lawful chastisement or correction of children.

94　[1994] 1 A.C. 212. See also *R. v Emmett The Times* 15 October 1999 and *R. v BM* [2018] EWCA Crim 560; [2019]

Human Rights. The Strasbourg court held that the decision was not contrary to the European Convention on Human Rights art.8, which grants everyone a right to respect for their private and family life.[95] The UK Government was permitted under art.8.2 to take measures necessary to protect its citizens from personal injury and its response had not been disproportionate to the need in question. The same approach has been adopted towards terminally ill patients who, unable to act due to their disability, wish to seek the assistance of another to commit suicide. In *Pretty v United Kingdom*,[96] Diane Pretty had sought an undertaking from the Director of Public Prosecutions that her husband would not be prosecuted under the Suicide Act 1961 for helping her to commit suicide. She was suffering from motor neurone disease and wished to avoid the extremely distressing and undignified final stages of the disease. The DPP refused her request. The European Court of Human Rights found that this refusal did not conflict with Mrs Pretty's human rights. Limiting her right to self-determination might interfere with her rights under art.8, but this could be justified as "necessary in a democratic society"[97] due to the need to safeguard life and protect the weak and vulnerable in society, who might be exploited by permitting assisted suicide. Whilst there was no evidence to suggest that Mrs Pretty fell into this category, this broader social goal was found to justify the DPP's position.[98]

It remains an open question whether such policy arguments will extend to tort. Much no doubt will depend on the nature of the injury inflicted: is the claimant consenting to a tattoo, ear-piercing, or serious physical injury? Lord Denning MR, in *Murphy v Culhane*,[99] suggested that a defence of voluntary assumption of risk (or *volenti non fit injuria*, see Ch.16) might still apply, for example where a burglar had taken upon himself the risk that the householder might defend his or her property, but there is little real authority on this point, and a court is unlikely to wish to be seen to condone disproportionate physical injury.

(2) Necessity

This is a limited defence. It allows the defendant to intervene to prevent greater harm to the public,[100] a third party, the defendant or the claimant. The courts are careful to keep

`11–022`

Q.B. 1 (body modification), but contrast *R. v Wilson* [1997] Q.B. 47 CA (wife able to consent to branding buttocks with hot knife on the basis that it was analogous to tattooing!)

95   *Laskey, Jaggard and Brown v UK* (1997) 24 E.H.R.R. 39.
96   (2346/02) (2002) 35 E.H.R.R.1.
97   ECHR art.8.2.
98   The Strasbourg court also found no violation of art.2 (right to life) and art.3 (right not to be subjected to degrading treatment). See also *R. (on the application of Nicklinson) v Ministry of Justice* [2014] UKSC 38; [2015] A.C. 657 (Suicide Act 1961 s.2 did not impose what would be regarded under the ECHR as a "blanket ban" on assisted suicide, which would take it outside the margin of appreciation afforded to Convention states on that issue).
99   [1977] Q.B. 94. See also Lord Mustill in *Airedale NHS v Bland* [1993] A.C. 789.
100 See, e.g. *Austin v Commissioner of Police for the Metropolis* [2007] EWCA Civ 989; [2008] 1 All E.R. 564 (police preventing crowd from leaving public place where unauthorised demonstration was taking place amounted to

this defence within strict bounds and generally the defendant must act reasonably in all the circumstances. This defence solves a particular practical problem experienced by the emergency services. If a patient is brought into the accident and emergency section of a hospital unconscious, or is mentally ill and incapable of consenting, when can the medical practitioners involved be certain that their intervention is legal? It would be absurd and discriminatory if they were permitted to refuse to treat such patients in the absence of express evidence of consent. This problem was addressed by the House of Lords in *Re F; F v West Berkshire Health Authority*.[101] Lord Goff held that the doctors may intervene in the best interests of the patient where: (a) it is necessary to act in circumstances where it is not practicable to communicate with the patient; and (b) the action taken is such as a reasonable person would in all the circumstances take. On this basis, where a patient is unconscious but otherwise competent and not known to object to the treatment, treatment may be legally justified. Where the incapacity is temporary, the doctor should do no more than is reasonably required in the best interests of the patient before he or she recovers consciousness.

The situation where the incapacity is permanent, for example where the patient is in a permanent coma or permanently mentally ill, is more difficult. In *Re F* itself, an application was made to the court to authorise a sterilisation operation on a woman of 36, with a mental age between five and six years old, who was clearly incapable of consenting to the operation. The House of Lords held that treatment would be justified if it would be in the patient's best interests and would be endorsed by a reasonable body of medical opinion. Where a number of reasonably suitable treatments were available, treatment should, however, be determined according to the best interests of the patient, taking into account broader ethical, social, moral and welfare considerations.[102] On this basis, hospitals would be permitted to undertake treatment necessary to preserve the life, health and wellbeing of the patient and this might extend beyond surgical operations or substantial treatment to include routine medical and dental treatment, provided it was in the best interests of the patient. Their Lordships held in *Re F* (Lord Griffiths dissenting) that the law should not require judicial approval to be sought on each occasion treatment was given, although they felt it would be "highly desirable" to seek judicial approval for operations such as sterilisations.

The Mental Capacity Act 2005 now deals with situations involving individuals of 16 or over who are unable to make decisions for themselves.[103] For the first time, there is a statutory

---

false imprisonment, but was justified by necessity due to threat of imminent breach of the peace). The appeal to the House of Lords on the basis of breach of ECHR art.5(1) was rejected: crowd control measures resorted to for public order and public safety reasons did not amount to a deprivation of liberty provided that they were not arbitrary, were proportionate and were enforced for no longer than was reasonably necessary [2009] UKHL 5; [2009] 1 A.C. 564. For criticism, see D. Feldman, "Containment, deprivation of liberty and breach of the peace" [2009] C.L.J. 243.

101 [1990] 2 A.C. 1.

102 *Re S (Adult Patient: Sterilisation: Patient's Best Interests)* [2001] Fam 15 CA. See also *Re A (Mental Patient: Sterilisation)* [2000] 1 F.L.R. 549 CA, *Simms v Simms* [2002] EWHC 2734 (Fam); [2003] Fam. 83 and *Portsmouth NHS Trust v Wyatt* [2005] EWCA Civ 1181; [2005] 1 W.L.R. 3995.

103 Previously, statutory provision had been limited e.g. provision was made under the Mental Health Act 1983 for psychiatric treatment of persons formally detained in a mental hospital. For the correct approach to be taken

definition of capacity (ss.1–3). Section 1(2) provides for a presumption of capacity: a person is assumed to have capacity unless it is established otherwise. Sections 4 to 6 provide for care or treatment (within limits) of a person without capacity provided, before doing the act, reasonable steps are taken to establish the patient lacks capacity in relation to the matter in question and it is reasonably believed that the patient lacks capacity and the act is in the patient's best interests.[104] These sections are said to codify existing common law rules and so the pre-existing law set out in *Re F* remains relevant. One leading commentator has commented that:

> "it is likely that in substance the outcomes of decisions about medical treatment made in the 'best interests' of incompetent adults will differ little from the common law approach that the courts have developed over the last 20 years or so."[105]

A good example of the dilemmas involved in such decisions is found in the well-known case of *Airedale NHS v Bland*.[106] This involved another victim of the tragic Hillsborough disaster discussed in Ch.4. Tony Bland had been in a persistent vegetative state (PVS) for three and a half years following injuries suffered by him at the match, which had caused him to suffer irreversible brain damage. He continued to breathe unaided and his digestion continued to function, but he could not see, hear, taste, smell or communicate in any way. He was given no prospect of recovery. The doctors, with the support of his parents, applied to the court to withhold all life-sustaining treatment. Lord Goff, in the House of Lords, applied the principles stated in *Re F*. His Lordship held that there was no absolute rule that a patient's life had to be prolonged by treatment or care regardless of all the circumstances and the quality of the patient's life. Treatment could be withdrawn if the patient had no hope of recovery and a reasonable medical practitioner would hold that it was not in the patient's best interests to prolong the patient's life. If an adult of full understanding has the right to withhold consent to medical treatment due to his right to self-determination, his Lordship held that it would be inconsistent if there was no corresponding rule to deal with the refusal of consent where the patient is incapable of indicating his wishes.

One might criticise the court's distinction between a doctor actively taking life (i.e. euthanasia, which is prohibited) and one in which the doctor discontinues life-saving treatment (which is allowed provided that the court's approval is sought). In the latter case, the

---

under the 2005 Act when making decisions on whether to give or withdraw life-sustaining treatment to persons lacking capacity to make such decisions themselves, see *Aintree University Hospitals NHS Foundation Trust v James* [2013] UKSC 67; [2014] A.C. 591; *An NHS Trust v Y* [2018] UKSC 46; [2019] A.C. 978.

104 The Court of Appeal has resolved that proper consideration may be given to issues arising under ECHR art.8 (right to private and family life) in the context of the s.4 appraisal of the person's best interests: *K v A Local Authority* [2012] EWCA Civ 79; [2012] 1 F.C.R. 441.

105 M. A. Jones (2007) 23 P.N. 238, 248. For a more detailed discussion of the statutory provisions, see P. Bartlett and R. Sandland, *Mental Health Law: Policy and Practice*, 4th edn (OUP, 2013) and E. Jackson, *Medical Law: Text, Cases and Materials*, 5th edn (OUP, 2019).

106 [1993] A.C. 789.

patient is allowed to die of his or her pre-existing condition, which the court classifies as an omission for which the doctors will not be judged responsible. Yet, in both cases the doctor may be acting in the best interests of the patient to relieve the patient's condition, and indeed, the latter option will generally result in the patient starving to death or dying from infection, which is a far from dignified end. In *NHS Trust A v M*,[107] the court was asked to consider whether discontinuance of treatment did, in fact, violate art.2 (right to life) and art.3 (right not to suffer degrading treatment) of the European Convention on Human Rights. The court held that, generally, art.2 would require a deliberate act, not an omission, by someone acting on behalf of the state, which results in death. Where treatment has been discontinued in the best interests of a patient, in accordance with the views of a respectable body of medical opinion, the state's positive obligations under art.2 were discharged. Equally, there was no violation of art.3. It could not in any event be invoked where the patient was unable to experience pain and was unaware of the nature of the treatment. The court thus approved Lord Goff's distinction in *Re F* as convention-compatible. Such rulings may be seen as a compromise: the judiciary avoids ruling on the controversial question of euthanasia but provides patients and their families with a limited remedy in extremely distressing circumstances.

(3) Self-defence

11–023

As a defence, the burden of proof lies on the defendant.[108] There is a clear analogy with criminal law where the Criminal Law Act 1967 s.3 provides that a person has the right to use "such force as is reasonable in the circumstances in the prevention of crime".[109] There are two limbs to the test. The defendant's force must be reasonable and not out of proportion to force exerted against him or her. It must also be based on an honest and, in contrast to criminal law, reasonable belief that the claimant will be attacked by the defendant.[110] In judging what is reasonable, the court will consider all the circumstances of the case, including the fact that the action may have had to be taken in the heat of the moment.[111]

---

107 [2001] Fam. 348 (Fam Div).

108 *Ashley v Chief Constable of Sussex* [2008] UKHL 25; [2008] 1 A.C. 962 (was policeman who fatally shot unarmed and naked suspect in the dark acting in self-defence?) Comment: N. J. McBride (2008) 67 C.L.J. 461.

109 See also Criminal Justice and Immigration Act 2008 s.76 (Reasonable force for purposes of self-defence etc).

110 See *Ashley v Chief Constable of Sussex* [2008] UKHL 25; [2008] 1 A.C. 962, and *Bici v MOD* [2004] EWHC 786 (QB) where both courts distinguished the position in criminal law where an honest belief of attack will suffice. Lord Scott in *Ashley* [2008] UKHL 25 at [17] and [18] justified this distinction on the basis of the different functions of criminal and civil law. In *Bici*, the soldiers, who had shot and injured a group of men travelling together in a car in Kosovo, failed to satisfy the court that there were reasonable grounds for them to believe that they were being threatened with being shot by the men.

111 See *Ashley v Chief Constable of Sussex* [2006] EWCA Civ 1085; [2007] 1 W.L.R. 398 at [82] per Sir Anthony Clarke MR.

This will be a question of fact. In *Lane v Holloway*,[112] where an elderly plaintiff had struck the young defendant on the shoulder during an argument, and the defendant had responded with an extremely severe blow to the plaintiff's eye, the defendant was held liable. The blow in the circumstances was out of proportion to the plaintiff's actions. This may be contrasted with *Cross v Kirkby*.[113] Here a farmer, who had been struck by a hunt saboteur with a baseball bat, wrestled the bat from him and struck a single blow to the head which, unfortunately, caused him serious injuries. In finding self-defence, the Court of Appeal took into account the anguish of the moment in assessing whether this was an excessive and disproportionate response to the threat posed, and held that the law did not require the defendant to measure the violence to be deployed with mathematical precision. It should be noted that the right to defend oneself in self-defence extends to defence of one's spouse, and, if the analogy with s.3 of the Criminal Law Act 1967 is correct, to defence of others.

(4) Provocation

The general view, stated in *Lane v Holloway*,[114] is that provocation is not a valid defence. It may reduce or extinguish the claimant's entitlement to exemplary damages, but will not reduce ordinary compensatory damages. This was followed by May LJ in *Barnes v Nayer*[115] where the court held that prolonged abuse and threats from a neighbouring family were insufficient provocation to justify the defendant attacking the mother with a machete. Lord Denning, in *Murphy v Culhane*,[116] modified his view in *Lane*, holding that it could reduce the compensatory measure where the victim is at least partly responsible for the damage suffered. This seems questionable and is really an argument for reducing the damages for contributory negligence (see below). It is submitted that the view in *Lane* is to be preferred.

11-024

(5) Contributory negligence

In *Murphy v Culhane*,[117] Lord Denning had suggested that the principles of contributory negligence would also apply to battery. In that case, Murphy was alleged to have been part of a gang which had set out to attack Culhane. Murphy had been killed when Culhane struck him on the head with a plank. Lord Denning saw no reason why the deceased's fault should not result in a reduction in his widow's damages under the Law Reform (Contributory) Negligence Act 1945 ss.1(1) and 4.

11-025

---

112 [1968] 1 Q.B. 379.
113 *The Times* 5 April 2000.
114 [1968] 1 Q.B. 379.
115 *The Times* 19 December 1986.
116 [1977] Q.B. 94.
117 [1977] Q.B. 94.

Lord Rodger in *Standard Chartered Bank v Pakistan National Shipping Corp (No.2)*,[118] however, raised doubts whether this line of authority, in fact, reflected the common law position. The Court of Appeal in *Co-operative Group Ltd v Pritchard*[119] confirmed that contributory negligence would not be a defence to battery. "Fault", as defined by s.4 of the 1945 Act, signifies:

> "negligence, breach of statutory duty or other act or omission which gives rise to a liability in tort or would, apart from this Act, give rise to the defence of contributory negligence."

The first part of this definition applies to the defendant, i.e. it must be a claim giving rise to liability in tort (here battery). The second half relates to the claimant's position prior to the Act and whether at common law there would have been a defence of "contributory negligence" in these circumstances. Evidence showed that there had been no case before 1945 which had applied such a defence in the case of an "intentional tort" such as battery. On this basis, in common with the tort of fraud/deceit,[120] contributory negligence is not a defence to the tort of trespass to the person. Smith LJ, however, in *Co-operative Group Ltd v Pritchard* did express regret at this result. While accepting that it was correct at law, his Lordship argued that it would be in the interests of justice to require that apportionment should be available in cases of battery where the claimant had been at fault and this had been one of the causes of his injury. A change to that effect would, however, require the intervention of Parliament.

(6) Lawful authority

11–026

This defence is generally applied in relation to false imprisonment where the defendants have specific statutory authority to deprive the claimant of his or her complete freedom of movement. It should be noted that even the European Convention on Human Rights art.5, which gives a right to liberty and security and which, under the Human Rights 1998, can now be enforced against public authorities such as the police, recognises that this will be limited in accordance with procedures prescribed by law.[121] This is obviously an important defence—without it our criminal justice system would fall apart. Prison Act 1952 s.12(1) authorises the imprisonment of persons sentenced to imprisonment or committed to prison on remand pending trial.

Equally, a lawful arrest will not render a police officer or citizen liable for false imprison-

---

118   [2002] UKHL 43; [2003] 1 A.C. 959 at [45], although his Lordship reserved his opinion on this point.
119   [2011] EWCA Civ 329; [2012] Q.B. 320.
120   See *Alliance and Leicester BS v Edgestop Ltd* [1994] 2 All E.R. 38 and *Standard Chartered Bank v Pakistan National Shipping Corp (Nos 2 and 4)* [2002] UKHL 43; [2003] 1 A.C. 959.
121   Article 5.1 lists six cases where an individual may legitimately be deprived of his liberty and these include detention after conviction by a competent court and lawful arrest for the purpose of bringing a person before a competent legal authority on reasonable suspicion of having committed an offence.

ment.[122] Reference should be made here to the provisions of the Police and Criminal Evidence Act 1984, particularly ss.24, 24A and 28. Readers are advised to consult specialist texts for detailed study of the requirements of a lawful arrest.[123] Basically, a police officer may legally arrest a person under a warrant. Section 24[124] makes provision for a police officer to arrest an individual without a warrant if the individual is about to commit an offence, is in the act of committing an offence, or if he or she has reasonable grounds for suspecting the individual to be about to commit an offence or in the act of committing such an offence. These powers of summary arrest are, however, subject to s.24(5): the constable must have reasonable grounds for believing that for one of the listed specific reasons, e.g. to prevent physical injury or damage to property, it is necessary to arrest the person in question.

A different regime applies to private individuals undertaking a "citizen's arrest". Section 24A(1)[125] states that a person, other than a constable, may arrest without a warrant a person in the act of, or whom he has reasonable grounds for suspecting to be in the act of, committing an indictable offence (that is, an offence which may be put before a judge and jury, not before a magistrate).[126] If the indictable offence has already been committed, s.24A(2) extends the power of arrest to anyone guilty of the offence or whom he or she has reasonable grounds for suspecting guilty of it. However, for s.24A(2), unlike s.24A(1), an offence must actually be committed.[127] As was the case prior to the introduction of s.24A, private individuals will not be protected from civil liability if they arrest someone under the mistaken belief that an offence has been committed.[128] There are also two further conditions to avoid a claim in tort for false imprisonment or battery.[129] First, the person making the arrest must have reasonable grounds for believing that one of the four conditions listed in s.24A(4) render it necessary to arrest the person in question. Secondly, it must appear to the person making the arrest that it is not reasonably practicable for a constable to make the arrest instead. The four conditions are as follows:

■ to prevent the person causing physical injury to himself or others;

■ to prevent the person suffering physical injury;

---

122 Note also Criminal Justice Act 2003 s.329: civil proceedings by convicted offender for trespass to the person in circumstances where the act is alleged to be committed on the same occasion as the imprisonable offence for which the claimant has been convicted. An action may only be brought with permission of the court (see ss.329(2) and (3)) and it is a defence if the defendant can prove both that the condition in subs.(5) is met, and that, in all the circumstances, his act was not grossly disproportionate.

123 e.g. see P. Ozin and H. Norton, *PACE: A practical guide to the Police and Criminal Evidence Act 1984*, 5th edn (OUP, 2019).

124 As amended by the Serious Organised Crime and Police Act 2005.

125 As inserted by the Serious Organised Crime and Police Act 2005 s.110(1) and (4).

126 Police and Criminal Evidence Act 1984 s.24A(1).

127 See *Sowande v Crown Prosecution Service* [2017] EWHC 1234 (Admin).

128 See *R. v Self* [1992] 3 All E.R. 476 at 480.

129 Police and Criminal Evidence Act 1984 s.24A(3).

- to prevent the person causing loss or damage to property; or

- to prevent the person making off before a constable can assume responsibility for him.

As one commentator has stated,[130] this is likely to deter all but the foolhardy from exercising their citizen's right of arrest. Few citizens will be aware which offences are indictable and s.24A limits the situations generally when such a right may be exercised. These provisions are much narrower than those applicable to police constables and there is a clear risk that the unwary will find themselves liable in tort.

Finally, reference should also be made to the Criminal Law Act 1967 s.3 (and Criminal Justice and Immigration Act 2008 s.76), which allows a person to use such force as is reasonable in the circumstances to prevent crime or in effecting or assisting in the lawful arrest of offenders, suspected offenders or persons unlawfully at large. There are also common law powers to intervene and take reasonable steps to prevent breaches of the peace.[131]

Can Trespass to the Person be Committed Negligently?

11-027

As stated in the introduction, early authority does seem to indicate the existence of a tort of negligent trespass to the person. It is doubtful, however, whether this tort has survived the growth and dominance of the tort of negligence outlined in earlier chapters of this book. Nevertheless, Diplock J in *Fowler v Lanning*[132] did not rule out the existence of such a tort. In this case, his Lordship held that a pleading which simply stated that "the defendant shot the plaintiff" disclosed no cause of action. The plaintiff should have pleaded either intention or negligence on the part of the defendant and if negligence was alleged, the burden of proof generally lay on the plaintiff. Diplock J therefore left open the question whether the plaintiff could have brought an action for negligent trespass to the person.

Lord Denning, in *Letang v Cooper*,[133] was perhaps predictably more forthright. Here, the plaintiff had suffered injuries when the defendant had driven over her legs whilst she was

---

130 See R. C. Austin, "The new powers of arrest: plus ça change: more of the same or major change?" [2007] Crim. L.R. 459.

131 See *Albert v Lavin* [1982] A.C. 546 at 565 and *R. (on the application of Laporte) v Chief Constable of Gloucestershire* [2006] UKHL 55; [2007] 2 A.C. 105. See also police powers to enforce public order, primarily under the Public Order Act 1986 and the Criminal Justice and Public Order Act 1994.

132 [1959] 1 Q.B. 426 at 433.

133 [1965] 1 Q.B. 232.

sunbathing outside a hotel on a piece of grass which was used as a car park. Her obvious course of action would have been to sue in negligence, but due to the three-year limitation period for personal injuries, she was out of time. She therefore tried to claim within the six-year limitation period allocated for trespass, by framing her case as one of unintentional trespass to the person. The Court of Appeal rejected her claim, drawing a distinction between intentional and unintentional trespass to the person. Although Diplock LJ was more cautious, suggesting that it was irrelevant whether the tort was described as unintentional trespass or negligence, Denning LJ refused to accept the existence of a tort of unintentional trespass:

> "... when the injury is not inflicted intentionally but negligently, I would say the only cause of action is negligence and not trespass."[134]

If this is correct, then any claims for injury to the person which are not intentional must be brought in negligence. This does not seem to involve a dramatic step. It is difficult to see, in any event, why negligent conduct should be actionable without proof of damage. The courts then will not allow a claimant to plead negligent trespass to gain an advantage over a straightforward negligence claim. Lord Denning's view also consolidates the position of trespass in the law of torts as a tort seeking to compensate for intentional conduct which unduly interferes with the personal integrity and autonomy of the individual.

Before moving on to consider trespass to land, there are two further related torts which should be considered. Harassment has been discussed above, and the next section will outline the provisions of the Protection from Harassment Act 1997, which are likely to be relevant to litigants considering an action for intentional injury by another. Equally, malicious prosecution, although not a form of trespass and only actionable on proof of damage, is frequently pleaded in common with false imprisonment and it is therefore convenient to consider its operation in this chapter.

Protection from Harassment Act 1997

11–028

At common law, harassment was not a recognised tort[135] and litigants were forced to frame their claims in trespass or nuisance.[136] However, the Protection from Harassment Act 1997 s.3 creates a statutory tort of harassment. Yet, despite the importance of this provision, it has been

---

134 [1965] 1 Q.B. 232 at 240. Approved in *Wilson v Pringle* [1987] Q.B. 237. See also *Bici v Ministry of Defence* [2004] EWHC 786 (QB). In *A v Hoare* [2008] UKHL 6; [2008] 1 A.C. 844, the House of Lords ruled that this did not prevent the Limitation Act 1980 s.11 including both claims in negligence and in trespass to the person due to its broad wording and legislative history.

135 *Patel v Patel* [1988] 2 F.L.R. 179 CA.

136 See *Khorasandjian v Bush* [1993] Q.B. 727.

the criminal provisions of the Act which have received the most attention due to a rise in the number of reported incidents of harassment, notably through social media.[137]

What is "harassment"?

11–029 "Harassment" is described in s.1(1) as a course of conduct which amounts to harassment of another, and which the defendant knows or ought to know amounts to harassment of the other. Section 1(1A), added under the Serious Organised Crime and Police Act 2005 to counteract animal rights extremists, now also provides that

> "A person must not pursue a course of conduct—
> (a) which involves harassment of two or more persons, and
> (b) which he knows or ought to know involves harassment of those persons, and
> (c) by which he intends to persuade any person (whether or not one of those mentioned above)–
>   (i) not to do something that he is entitled or required to do, or
>   (ii) to do something that he is not under any obligation to do."

This seeks to prohibit intimidating conduct which prevents people going about their lawful business.

Section 1(2) further provides that the defendant ought to know that his or her conduct amounts to or involves harassment if a reasonable person in possession of the same information would think the course of conduct amounted to or involved harassment of the other. This is an objective test. The court will not take account of any mental disorder from which the defendant is suffering, or any other characteristics, as this would substantially lessen the protection given to victims by the Act.[138]

The description of "harassment" in s.1(1) is somewhat circular. It has been deliberately defined broadly and clearly goes beyond mere stalking which was the principal target of the Act. The general feeling stated in *Thomas v News Group Newspapers Ltd* is that "'Harassment' is . . . a word which has a meaning that is generally understood".[139] Section 7 provides some

---

137 Protection from Harassment Act 1997 ss.2 (offence of harassment), 2A (offence of stalking), 2B (right of entry in relation to stalking) and 4 (putting people in fear of violence). The police recorded crime statistics for 2018–2019 report 458,881 recorded offences of stalking and harassment: see *https://www.ons.gov.uk/peoplepopulationandcommunity/crimeandjustice/bulletins/crimeinenglandandwales/yearendingjune2019* [Accessed 1 August 2020].

138 *R. v C (Sean Peter)* [2001] EWCA Crim. 1251; [2001] 2 F.L.R. 757 CA (Crim).

139 *Thomas v News Group Newspapers Ltd* [2001] EWCA Civ 1233; [2002] E.M.L.R. 4 at [30] per Lord Phillips MR.

assistance. "Harassment" is defined as conduct which includes "alarming the person or causing the person distress".[140] "Course of conduct" is stated to involve conduct on at least two
occasions,[141] and may include speech.[142] Although the cases now give some guidance,[143]
Baroness Hale noted in *Majrowski v Guy's and St Thomas's NHS Trust* that:

> "A great deal is left to the wisdom of the courts to draw sensible
> lines between the ordinary banter and badinage of life and genu-
> inely offensive and unacceptable behaviour."[144]

As Lord Nicholls explained in that case, there is a boundary between conduct which is unat-
tractive, even unreasonable, and conduct which is oppressive and unacceptable[145]; the court
keeping in mind whether the conduct is of such gravity as to justify the sanctions of criminal
law.[146] A good example of oppressive and unacceptable conduct may be found in *Ferguson v
British Gas Trading Ltd*[147] where the persistent sending of unjustified bills and threatening letters to a former customer of British Gas was found to be of sufficient gravity to constitute harassment. The Court of Appeal was unimpressed by British Gas' argument that it could not be
held responsible for its own computerised debt recovery system or that the threats were diminished by the fact that Mrs Ferguson knew them to be unjustified. In the words of Jacob LJ:

> "a victim of harassment will almost always know that it is unjustified.
> The Act is there to protect people against unjustified harassment."[148]

The ability to bring a harassment claim is not restricted to the individual targeted by the course

---

140 Protection from Harassment Act 1997 s.7(2).
141 Protection from Harassment Act 1997 s.7(3)(a) in relation to a single person. In the case of conduct in relation
to two or more persons (see s.1(1A)), conduct is required on at least one occasion in relation to each of those
persons.: s.7(3)(b). See also s.7(3A). See *Lau v DPP* [2000] 1 F.L.R. 799 (the fewer the number of incidents and
the wider the time lapse, the less likely a finding of "course of conduct").
142 Protection from Harassment Act 1997 s.7(4). It may even on rare occasions extend to press articles which
provoke reader hostility to a particular individual, although the courts are very conscious of the risk of violating
art.10 of the Convention (freedom of expression): *Thomas v News Group Newspapers Ltd* [2001] EWCA Civ 1233;
[2002] E.M.L.R. 4. More recently, see *Howlett v Holding* [2006] EWHC 41 (QB) *The Times*
8 February 2006 (flying banners from aircraft referring to Mrs Howlett in abusive and derogatory
terms).
143 See *Banks v Ablex Ltd* [2005] EWCA Civ 173; [2005] I.C.R. 819 (failure to show misconduct amounting to
harassment on 2 occasions), *Conn v Sunderland City Council* [2007] EWCA Civ 1492; [2008] I.R.L.R. 324
(foreman shouting at employee and threatening to smash a window did not amount to oppressive conduct).
144 [2006] UKHL 34; [2007] 1 A.C. 224 at [66].
145 [2006] UKHL 34; [2007] 1 A.C. 224 at [30].
146 *Veakins v Kier Islington Ltd* [2009] EWCA Civ 1288; [2010] I.R.L.R. 132.
147 [2009] EWCA Civ 46; [2010] 1 W.L.R. 785. See also *Roberts v Bank of Scotland Plc* [2013] EWCA Civ 882
(hundreds of calls from bank call centre amounted to harassment). Contrast *Calland v Financial Conduct
Authority* [2015] EWCA Civ 192, notably comments of Lewison LJ at [31].
148 [2009] EWCA Civ 46; [2010] 1 W.L.R. 785 at [20].

of conduct complained of, but extends to other persons who are foreseeably and directly harmed by the course of conduct.[149]

Claims will be restricted in a number of ways. First, a "course of conduct" must be proved. Secondly, s.1(3) provides that a valid defence exists when the conduct was pursued for the purpose of detecting crime,[150] under any legal requirement, or was reasonable in the circumstances. Thirdly, it has been held that remedies will not be granted in favour of limited companies as opposed to individuals.[151] Despite the fact that the Act has been used to curb the activities of activists, for example animal rights protesters, the courts have indicated that the Act should not be used to restrict the citizen's right to protest in the public interest.[152]

Remedies

11–030

If harassment is shown, s.3 allows the claimant to sue for damages and/or an injunction.[153] Damages here may include a sum for anxiety and any financial loss resulting from the harassment.[154] In *Jones v Ruth*,[155] the Court of Appeal noted that the Act does not state a test of remoteness and chose to apply the test for intentional torts: the defendant is liable for all losses which directly flow from the harassment. There was nothing in the language of the Act to suggest that the *Wagon Mound* test of reasonable foreseeability would apply. In the case itself, Ms Jones' alternative claim for personal injury damages in negligence had failed, but she was able to recover substantial damages under the Act in circumstances where her (unforeseeable) psychiatric injury had been caused by aggressive and intimidatory conduct by the

---

149 *Levi v Bates* [2015] EWCA Civ 206; [2016] Q.B. 91.
150 *KD v Chief Constable of Hampshire* [2005] EWHC 2550 (QB); [2005] Po. L.R. 253 stated that s.1(3)(a) (course of conduct pursued for the purpose of preventing or detecting crime) should be interpreted subject to the defences of necessity and proportionality in the light of ECHR art.8.1. This defence is, however, only available if the purpose behind the actions had a rational basis and was not, for example, based on a personal vendetta: *Hayes v Willoughby* [2013] UKSC 17; [2013] 1 W.L.R. 935.
151 *DPP v Dziurzynski* [2002] EWHC 1380 (Admin); (2002) 166 J.P. 545 and *Daiichi Pharmaceuticals UK Ltd v Stop Huntingdon Animal Cruelty* [2003] EWHC 2337 (QB); [2004] 1 W.L.R. 1503, although this does not prevent the managing director of the company in question bringing a claim on his own behalf and on behalf of the employees of the company in a representative capacity (see *Bayer Plc v Shook* [2004] EWHC 332 (QB)). See J. Seymour, "Who can be harassed? Claims against animal rights protestors under section 3 of the Protection from Harassment Act 1997" (2005) 64 C.L.J. 57. Note that s.1(1A) can be relied upon by a corporate claimant: *Merlin Entertainments Plc v Cave* [2014] EWHC 3036 (QB); [2015] E.M.L.R. 3.
152 See *Huntingdon Life Sciences Ltd v Curtin The Times* 11 December 1997, but also *DPP v Moseley The Times* 23 June 1999.
153 The civil standard of proof is applied to proceedings under s.3: *Hipgrave v Jones* [2004] EWHC 2901 (QB); [2005] 2 F.L.R. 174.
154 Protection from Harassment Act 1997 s.3(2).
155 [2011] EWCA Civ 804; [2012] 1 W.L.R. 1495.

Ruths. In *Majrowski v Guy's and St Thomas's NHS Trust*[156] the House of Lords recognised that the doctrine of vicarious liability would apply to harassment by employees in the course of their employment. An injunction may be granted for actual or apprehended acts of harassment. If the defendant breaches the injunction, s.3(3) controversially permits a civil court to issue a warrant for the arrest of the defendant.[157] Section 3A provides for injunctions (but not damages) to protect persons from harassment within s.1(1A).[158]

Malicious Prosecution

11-031

This tort has much in common with the tort of false imprisonment. Both torts focus on loss of liberty. Whilst, in false imprisonment, the defendant exercises direct restraint over the movements of the claimant, malicious prosecution may be seen as indirect restraint by means of setting the prosecution in motion. This tort is not, however, actionable per se and damage must be proved. The classic definition of damage was given by Holt CJ in *Savile v Roberts*,[159] namely damage to a man's fame (or reputation), person or property. It is clear that an unwarranted prosecution may damage a person's reputation. Harm to the person has been interpreted broadly to include both the threat of imprisonment and actual imprisonment. Harm to property signifies the costs incurred by the claimant in defending the charges.

The tort has four requirements:

■ the defendant has prosecuted the claimant;

■ maliciously (i.e. with some wrongful or improper motive);

■ without reasonable and probable cause; and

■ the prosecution ended in the claimant's favour. (This may be by acquittal, discontinuance by the prosecution, conviction quashed on appeal or on technical grounds.)

---

156 [2006] UKHL 34; [2007] 1 A.C. 224.
157 The court in *Silverton v Gravett* unreported 19 October 2001 QBD) held that this did not breach art.10 (freedom of expression) nor art.11 (freedom of association) of the ECHR as such restrictions could be justified as being "for the prevention of disorder or crime" or "for the protection of the reputation or rights of others": see arts 10.2 and 11.2.
158 Added by the Serious Organised Crime and Police Act 2005 s.125(5). See, e.g. *Monarch Airlines Ltd v Yaqab* [2016] EWHC 1003 (QB); *CSC Computer Sciences Ltd v Price* [2018] EWHC 3990 (QB).
159 (1698) 1 Ld. Raym. 374; 91 E.R. 1147. See, more recently, Roch LJ in *Clark v Chief Constable of Cleveland* [2000] C.P. Rep. 22.

Actions for malicious prosecution will generally be against the police.[160] Actions may be brought against private individuals, however, if they can be shown to have falsely and maliciously given information to the police, in circumstances where the police had no effective discretion whether to prosecute. This will not be established simply on the basis that the defendant has given information to the police, or prepared a report for the police. The leading case is that of *Martin v Watson*,[161] where the defendant maliciously made a groundless accusation of indecent exposure against the plaintiff, who was subsequently prosecuted. Lord Keith, in his leading judgment, held that:

> **"Where an individual falsely and maliciously gives a police officer information indicating that some person is guilty of a criminal offence and states that he is willing to give evidence in court of the matters in question, it is properly to be inferred that he desires and intends that the person he names should be prosecuted. Where the circumstances are such that the facts relating to the alleged offence can be within the knowledge only of the complainant, as was the position here, then it becomes virtually impossible for the police officer to exercise any independent discretion or judgement, and if a prosecution is instituted by the police officer the proper view of the matter is that the prosecution has been procured by the complainant."[162]**

11–032

This is not an easy tort to establish and the courts are careful not to allow the tort to be used to discourage the prosecution of suspected criminals.[163] The most difficult obstacle for a claimant is to prove that the defendant had no reasonable and probable cause for the prosecution. This involves proving a negative, which is always problematic. The claimant must establish on the balance of probabilities that the defendant did not have an honest belief in the guilt of the accused founded on objective facts which gave reasonable grounds for the existence of this belief.[164] The test thus has objective and subjective elements. Malice alone will not suffice.

---

160 See, for example, the recent case of *Rees v Commissioner of Police of the Metropolis* [2018] EWCA Civ 1587 where a senior police officer had encouraged an unreliable witness to implicate the claimants in a murder even though the CPS had brought the actual prosecution. It was inconceivable that the CPS would have advised that murder charges be brought without the intervention of the officer.

161 [1996] 1 A.C. 74 at 86–87. Note further guidance given by Brooke LJ in *Mahon v Rahn (No.2)* [2000] 1 W.L.R. 2150 at 2205–2206. *Martin* was applied in *Sallows v Griffiths* [2001] F.S.R. 15, and, more recently, in *Copeland v Commissioner of Police of the Metropolis* [2014] EWCA Civ 1014; [2015] 3 All E.R. 391.

162 But contrast *H v B* [2009] EWCA Civ 1092 (complainant in prosecution for rape not prosecutor when no more than key witness and had done nothing improper to influence CPS's decision to prosecute).

163 In Canada, malicious prosecution is now being supplanted by the more straightforward tort of negligent investigation: *Hill v Hamilton-Wentworth Regional Police Services Board* 2007 S.C.C. 41; (2007) 285 D.L.R. (4th) 620 (comment: E. Chamberlain (2008) 124 L.Q.R. 205). However, such an approach has been rejected by the English courts for policy reasons: see Ch.2 and *Van Colle v Chief Constable of Hertfordshire* [2008] UKHL 50; [2009] 1 A.C. 225.

164 See *Herniman v Smith* [1938] A.C. 305 and, more recently, *Isaac v Chief Constable of the West Midlands Police*

This is particularly difficult to establish if, for example, the defendant has taken legal advice (provided of course the legal adviser was given all the relevant facts). A defendant may have a reasonable and probable cause for the prosecution even when he does not believe that the proceedings will succeed. It is enough that, on the material on which he acted, there was a proper case to lay before the court.[165] In *Rees*,[166] however, the court was not prepared to find an honest belief that there was a proper case to lay before the court where the senior investigating officer had persuaded an individual to make a false statement implicating the claimants in a murder. Malicious prosecution is usually heard by a judge and jury[167] and while it is for the judge to determine whether the prosecutor had reasonable and probable cause, it remains nevertheless for the jury to determine any disputed facts relevant to that question. It is for the jury to decide whether the defendant honestly believed the guilt of the accused.[168]

The jury will also determine whether the defendant was malicious.[169] Lord Toulson in *Willers v Joyce*[170] explained that this means that the claimant must prove that the defendant deliberately misused the process of the court. The critical issue is whether the proceedings instituted by the defendant were a bona fide use of the court's process. His Lordship argued that the most obvious case is where the claimant can prove that the defendant brought the proceedings in the knowledge that they were without foundation, but that it would extend to cases where a person was indifferent whether the allegation was supportable but still brought the proceedings, not for the bona fide purpose of trying that issue, but to secure some extraneous benefit to which he had no right. The court emphasised in *Rees* that a sincere belief that the claimants were guilty of the crime cannot prevent the prosecution having been malicious.[171]

In the past, it was unclear whether the tort of malicious prosecution was confined to prosecutions, i.e. criminal charges or would extend to the malicious institution of civil proceedings.[172] In a variety of cases, liability had been imposed at or close to the outset of civil proceedings, for

---

[2001] EWCA Civ 1405, *Quaquah v Group 4 Falck Global Solutions Ltd (Malicious Prosecution)* [2003] EWHC 1504 (QB); [2004] Prison L.R. 1 and *Moulton v Chief Constable of West Midlands* [2010] EWCA Civ 524.

165   *Glinski v McIver* [1962] A.C. 726 at 758–759 per Lord Denning.

166   *Rees v Commissioner of Police of the Metropolis* [2018] EWCA Civ 1587.

167   In common with false imprisonment.

168   *Glinski v McIver* [1962] A.C. 726.

169   On guidance for juries in awarding damages for malicious prosecution, see *Manley v Commissioner of Police of the Metropolis* [2006] EWCA Civ 879; [2006] Po. L.R. 117. Note that in addition to the civil action, a defendant who maliciously induces the authorities to bring unwarranted charges may face prosecution for wasting police time, for perverting or attempting to pervert the course of justice, or (if he or she gives evidence) for perjury.

170   [2016] UKSC 43; [2018] A.C. 779 at [55]. See also Lord Toulson in *Juman v Att-Gen of Trinidad and Tobago* [2017] UKPC 3 at [17]: malice is not constituted by mere recklessness nor sloppiness. See, generally, J. Murphy, "Malice as an ingredient of tort liability" (2019) 78 C.L.J. 355.

171   [2018] EWCA Civ 1587 at [89]: "[The officer] knowingly put before the decision-maker a case which he knew was significantly tainted by his own wrongdoing and which he knew could not be properly presented in that form to a court. To find that the element of malice was not satisfied in this case, to my mind, would be, quite simply, a negation of the rule of law" per McCombe L.J.

172   This was doubted in *Metall und Rohstoff v Donaldson, Lufkin & Jenrette Inc* [1990] 1 Q.B. 391.

example, for the malicious procurement of a search-warrant[173] and malicious presentation of a winding up order or petition for bankruptcy[174] without reasonable or probable cause. There is also a tort of abuse of process, which deals with circumstances where civil proceedings have been initiated or conducted for an improper (or collateral) purpose other than that for which they were designed.[175] Lord Steyn in the House of Lords decision of *Gregory v Portsmouth CC*[176] indicated, however, that the law, by providing adequate alternative remedies in defamation, malicious falsehood, conspiracy and misfeasance in public office, made it unnecessary and undesirable to extend this tort to civil proceedings generally. A majority of 3:2 in the later Privy Council decision of *Crawford Adjusters v Sagicor General Insurance (Cayman) Ltd*[177] disagreed, arguing that claimants should be able to recover damages for foreseeable economic loss caused by the malicious institution of civil proceedings (in this case, the claim was for Cayman $1.335 million). Lords Sumption and Neuberger in the minority, however, disagreed strongly and expressed the fear that this new tort would be both uncertain and potentially very wide and would offer litigants an occasion for prolonging disputes by way of secondary litigation.

In July 2016, the Supreme Court (by a majority of 5:4) in *Willers v Joyce*[178] took the view that it would be unjust *not* to extend the tort to the malicious prosecution of civil proceedings. On this basis, the malicious prosecution of civil proceedings, like malicious prosecution of criminal proceedings, is a tort. In the case itself, Willers had alleged that the defendant had caused the company (of which he was a former director) to sue him for breach of contractual and fiduciary duties knowing that the claim was brought without reasonable cause. The claim brought against Willers was found to have all the necessary ingredients for a claim for malicious prosecution of civil proceedings provided such an action was sustainable in English law. Lord Toulson (giving judgment for the majority) dismissed the counter-arguments against the tort extending to such civil proceedings[179]:

---

173   *Reynolds v Commissioner of Police of the Metropolis* [1985] Q.B. 881; *Gibbs v Rea* [1998] A.C. 786 PC; *Kennedy v Chief Constable of Merseyside* [2004] Po. L.R. 226. See also *Keegan v Chief Constable of Merseyside* [2003] EWCA Civ 936; [2003] 1 W.L.R. 2187 where the Court of Appeal found, on the facts, no improper motive, but noted that had the Human Rights Act 1998 been in force, art.8 might have made a difference.

174   *Johnson v Emerson* (1870–71) L.R. 6 Ex 329; *Quartz Hill Gold Mining Co v Eyre* (1883) 11 Q.B.D. 674. See, more recently, *Tibbs v Islington LBC* [2002] EWCA Civ 1682; [2003] B.P.I.R. 743.

175   The origin of this tort is *Grainger v Hill* (1838) 4 Bing (NC) 212; 132 E.R. 769. See also *Land Securities Plc v Fladgate Fielder (A Firm)* [2009] EWCA Civ 1402; [2010] 2 W.L.R. 1265, where the Court of Appeal refused to extend this tort to applications for judicial review for which the court had given permission and where only general economic losses had been suffered.

176   [2000] 1 A.C. 419, which held that the tort does not apply to internal disciplinary proceedings. For comment, see P. Cane (2000) 116 L.Q.R. 346.

177   [2013] UKPC 17; [2014] A.C. 366 (appeal from Cayman Islands Court of Appeal). Comment: T.K.C. Ng (2014) 130 L.Q.R. 43.

178   [2016] UKSC 43; [2018] A.C. 779. Lords Neuberger and Sumption again dissented, together with Lords Mance and Reed.

179   See, in particular, the criticisms of Lord Mance at *Willers v Joyce* [2016] UKSC 43; [2018] A.C. 779 at [131]–[136] who found the majority view to be "unjustified and unwise". The minority also indicated that the new tort could create real problems both in identifying what constitutes malice and in deciding

- Despite the limited number of actions for malicious prosecution in relation to criminal proceedings, the tort is not defunct and is not a thing of the past.

- It was "intrinsically unlikely" that the action would deter people from bringing civil claims for fear of a vindictive action for malicious prosecution.

- An action for malicious prosecution did not amount to a collateral attack on the outcome of the first proceedings.

- A fear of a flood of unmeritorious claims was also unwarranted. Indeed, it was argued that *Willers* and *Crawford* both highlighted the fact that Lord Steyn's view in *Gregory* that any manifest injustices were already covered by tort law.

- Liability would not be inconsistent with witness immunity from civil liability (see para.14–012).

> "The combination of requirements that the claimant must prove not only the absence of reasonable and probable cause, but also that the defendant did not have a bona fide reason to bring the proceedings, means that the claimant has a heavy burden to discharge."[180]

Lord Kerr in the majority in *Crawford* was of the same view, commenting that establishing the tort of malicious prosecution is no easy task and demonstrating together these two requirements would present a formidable hurdle for anyone contemplating the launch of a claim for malicious prosecution.[181]

Misfeasance in public office

11–033

Lord Sumption dissenting in *Crawford Adjusters v Sagicor* took the view that malicious prosecution had much in common with another malice-based tort—misfeasance in public office—in that they both dealt with the wrongful exercise of a public function.[182] Misfeasance in public office is

---

what types of loss and damage should be recoverable in connection with claims based on the proposed tort.
180 [2016] UKSC 43 at [56].
181 [2013] UKPC 17 at [109]–[110].
182 [2013] UKPC 17 at [145]. On this basis, he argued that it made no sense to extend malicious prosecution to civil proceedings where the claimant was not exercising a public function. This view has, however, not been followed.

indeed unusual in being essentially a public law tort and requiring malice as a condition for liability.[183] Its continued vitality was recognised by the House of Lords in *Three Rivers DC v Bank of England (No.3)*.[184] The rationale of this tort is that executive or administrative power should only be exercised for the public good and not for ulterior and improper purposes.[185] In *Three Rivers*, the House of Lords found that liability in the tort of misfeasance in public office arose where the actions of a public officer[186] were carried out in the knowledge of, or with reckless indifference to the probability of,[187] injury being caused to a claimant, or a class[188] of persons of which the claimant was a member. Two forms of liability for misfeasance in public office exist at common law:

- exercise of public power for improper or ulterior motives ("targeted malice"); and

- where a public officer knowingly acts beyond his or her powers and in the knowledge that such actions would probably result in injury to the claimant ("untargeted malice"). Reckless indifference is sufficient to establish liability, but not mere negligence.[189]

Both forms impose liability for an abuse of power by a public official activated by subjective bad faith.[190] The claimant must show special damage.[191] Although this will generally be economic loss, it will include personal injury.[192] Mere distress or normal emotion will not suffice.[193]

---

183 See J. Murphy, "Misfeasance in a public office: a tort law misfit?" (2012) 32 O.J.L.S. 51 who argues that this tort serves a discrete and vital role in holding public officers to account and, more recently, M. Aronson, "Misfeasance in public office: Some unfinished business" (2016) 132 L.Q.R. 427 and D. Nolan, "Tort and public law: Overlapping categories?" (2019) 135 L.Q.R. 272.

184 [2001] UKHL 16; [2003] 2 A.C. 1. The tort itself can be traced back to the 17th century (see *Turner v Sterling* (1671) 2 Vent. 25) and was described as "well established" by the Privy Council in *Dunlop v Woollahra Municipal Council* [1982] A.C. 158 at 172 per Lord Diplock.

185 See Nourse LJ in *Jones v Swansea City Council* [1990] 1 W.L.R. 54 at 85.

186 This is a broad concept: *Calveley v Chief Constable of the Merseyside Police* [1989] A.C. 1228. In the case, the Bank of England was held to satisfy this requirement.

187 *Akenzua v Secretary of State for the Home Department* [2002] EWCA Civ 1470; [2003] 1 W.L.R. 741. Comment: J. R. Spencer [2003] C.L.J. 543.

188 This is defined loosely: see *Akenzua v Secretary of State for the Home Department* [2002] EWCA Civ 1470; [2003] 1 W.L.R. 741 (victim did not need to be known prior to the expected harm occurring).

189 *Muuse v Secretary of State for the Home Department* [2010] EWCA Civ 453. See also *Mouncher v Chief Constable of South Wales* [2016] EWHC 1367 (QB).

190 *Southwark LBC v Dennett* [2007] EWCA Civ 1091; [2008] H.L.R. 23 at [21]–[22].

191 *Watkins v Secretary of State for the Home Department* [2006] UKHL 17; [2006] 2 A.C. 395 (special damage required even where a public officer has infringed a constitutional right—here, that of a prisoner to receive unopened correspondence from his legal advisers or the court). Loss of liberty will, however, by analogy with false imprisonment be regarded as special damage: *Karagozlu v Commissioner of Police of the Metropolis* [2006] EWCA Civ 1691; [2007] 1 W.L.R. 1881.

192 *Akenzua v Secretary of State for the Home Department* [2002] EWCA Civ 1470.

193 *Hussain v Chief Constable of West Mercia* [2008] EWCA Civ 1205.

Trespass to Land

Trespass to land is clearly a different type of tort from those examined above. Its rationale is not to protect the integrity or reputation of the claimant, but to protect the claimant against direct and unjustifiable interference with his or her possession of land. There is an obvious similarity here with the tort of private nuisance which equally deals with an unjustifiable interference with the claimant's use and enjoyment of land. However, there is a notable distinction. Trespass to land, in common with all forms of trespass, must be direct and immediate and is actionable without proof of damage. In contrast, nuisance, as discussed in Ch.10, involves an indirect act which is only actionable on proof of damage. The distinction, which derives from the old rigid forms of action, survives despite the abolition of the forms of actions over 100 years ago. On this basis, if I throw a brick and destroy your prize flowers, I have committed an actionable trespass. If, however, I build a fire in my garden and noxious fumes blow over and harm your prize flowers, I have only committed a nuisance.

Unlike trespass to the person, trespass to land does not generally lead to criminal liability, although there are a number of statutory exceptions.[194] It is actionable per se, which may seem surprising. Tort law in the twenty-first century is generally more concerned with protecting personal interests, such as those discussed above, than with protecting interests in land, but historical concerns that trespass would lead to a breach of the peace led the courts to find liability without proof of harm.[195] Nevertheless, a claimant is likely to receive only nominal damages without proof of loss. Trespass also serves a useful function in determining boundaries to land (although claimants may alternatively seek a declaratory judgment) and in dealing with persistent trespassers by means of injunctive relief.

In common with trespass to the person, it is an intentional tort, but it is the act of entry which must be intentional and not the act of trespass. On this basis, provided your actions are voluntary, you are a trespasser whether you know you are trespassing or not.[196] It is therefore no excuse that you are utterly lost, although the courts will not impose liability where you were forcibly thrown or pushed onto the land.[197] Where animals stray onto another's land, Park J in *League against Cruel Sports v Scott*[198] indicated that the owner will be responsible for the damage they cause if he or she intended them to enter the claimant's land or, knowing that there was a real risk that they would enter, failed to take reasonable care to prevent their entry. On this basis, the master of a hunt was liable when his hounds entered land belonging to the League against Cruel Sports, who were, unsurprisingly, not prepared to tolerate such a trespass. This case raises the question whether, in spite of *Letang v Cooper*,[199] a defendant

---

194 e.g. "aggravated trespass" under the Criminal Justice and Public Order Act 1994 s.68 (as amended), where persons have trespassed on the land to disrupt a lawful activity taking place on the land (e.g. hunt saboteurs).

195 See *Clerk & Lindsell on Torts*, 23rd edn (Sweet and Maxwell, 2020), para.19–09.

196 *Conway v George Wimpey & Co Ltd* [1951] 2 K.B. 266 at 273–274.

197 *Smith v Stone* (1647) Style 65; 82 E.R. 533.

198 [1986] Q.B. 240.

199 [1965] 1 Q.B. 232 (which of course only deals with trespass to the person).

may commit a trespass to land negligently. It is submitted that a consistent approach should be adopted to trespass, which should be confined to intentional voluntary acts. It is contrary to the general development of the law for a tort actionable per se to be committed negligently.

To establish trespass, the claimant must also show a direct and unjustifiable interference with the claimant's possession of land. The nature of these two requirements will be examined below.

(1) Direct and unjustifiable interference

11–035

This can occur in a number of ways. The obvious examples are walking on my lawn or entering my house without my permission, but it will also include such diverse examples as throwing a CS gas canister on my land[200] or allowing sheep to stray onto my land.[201] Trespass may be committed by interference with the subsoil[202] and even airspace if it is within the height necessary for the ordinary use and enjoyment of the land and structures on it.[203] On this basis, the defendants in *Bernstein v Skyviews & General Ltd*[204] were not liable for taking aerial photographs of the landowner's home at a height of many hundreds of metres above the ground. This is re-affirmed by the Civil Aviation Act 1982 s.76(1), which provides that civil aircraft flying at a reasonable height do not commit a trespass. A reasonable height will be determined by the court with regard to the wind, weather and all the circumstances of the case. A claimant may recover damages, however, from the owner of the aircraft for property damage or personal injury caused by something falling from an aircraft while in flight, taking off or landing. The claimant need not prove negligence or intention, or establish any other cause of action, provided that the loss or damage was not caused or contributed to by the negligence of the claimant.[205]

It should also be noted that the public have a right to use the public highway for any reasonable purpose, which will extend to peaceful assembly, provided their acts do not amount

---

200 *Rigby v Chief Constable of Northamptonshire* [1985] 1 W.L.R. 1242.

201 This has been found to extend to the discharge of water into a canal without permission: *British Waterways Board v Severn Trent Water Ltd* [2001] EWCA Civ 276; [2002] Ch. 25.

202 See *Bocardo SA v Star Energy UK Onshore Ltd* [2010] UKSC 35; [2011] 1 A.C. 380 (owner of surface land was also owner of strata beneath it, including minerals found there unless alienated by conveyance, the common law or statute to someone else). Lord Hope acknowledged, however, at [27] that there must be some stopping point where the concept of strata belonging to anybody would be so absurd to be not worth arguing.

203 See *Kelsen v Imperial Tobacco Co Ltd* [1957] 2 Q.B. 334 and, more recently, *Anchor Brewhouse Developments Ltd v Berkley House (Docklands Developments) Ltd* (1987) 38 B.L.R. 82 (injunction awarded to stop a developer's cranes oversailing the plaintiff's land, even though they were high enough not to affect the normal use of that land). See also *Laiqat v Majid* [2005] EWHC 1305 (QB); [2005] 26 E.G. 130 (CS) (an overhanging that occurred four metres above ground level would be regarded as an interference with airspace and would amount to trespass).

204 [1978] Q.B. 479.

205 Civil Aviation Act 1982 s.76(2).

to a public or private nuisance and do not obstruct the highway by unreasonably impeding the public's primary right to pass and repass.[206]

(2) Possession of land

This is the interest protected by the tort of trespass. Only those with possession of the land can sue for trespass. It is not enough to be physically on the land or to have control over the land. A mere licensee, such as a lodger or guest in a hotel, cannot sue for trespass. The claimant must have an interest in land in possession or at least exclusive possession to maintain an action for trespass.[207] An interest in land without possession will not suffice. For example, when a landlord has leased his property, the tenant is the party in possession. The landlord will only be able to sue if the trespasser injures the interest he or she has in possession, namely the reversionary interest in land, i.e. the landlord's right to possession at the end of the term of the lease.[208] Ordinarily, it will be the tenant who sues for trespass. The similarities with the right to sue in private nuisance, discussed in Ch.10, should be noted. The claimant will be able to sue regardless of the fact that he or she was out of the premises at the time the trespass took place or had only just acquired the right to possession. The concept of "trespass by relation" allows the claimant to sue for trespass even if the trespass took place between the time when the right to possession was obtained and actual entry into possession.[209]

11-036

Trespass to Land: Defences

The defences bear a clear resemblance to the defences discussed above for trespass to the person, namely consent, necessity and lawful authority. Similarly to nuisance, there is generally no defence of *jus tertii* to trespass. *Jus tertii* alleges that the claimant cannot succeed because a third party has a better title to the land than the claimant and should therefore be bringing the action instead of the claimant. It has been rejected in a number of cases.[210]

11-037

---

206 *DPP v Jones* [1999] 2 A.C. 240 HL (peaceful assembly on highway did not amount to trespass necessary to invoke police powers against trespassory assembly under the Public Order Act 1986).

207 *Nicholls v Ely Beet Sugar Factory* [1931] 2 Ch.84.

208 See *Jones v Llanrwst Urban DC* [1911] 1 Ch.393 at 404.

209 See *Clerk & Lindsell on Torts*, 23rd edn (Sweet and Maxwell, 2020), para.19–027.

210 *Nicholls v Ely Beet Sugar Factory* [1931] 2 Ch. 84; *Chambers v Donaldson* (1809) 11 East. 65; 103 E.R. 929. It may, however, be used in relation to actions for the recovery of land: see below.

(1) Licence

11–038 The defendant will not be liable for trespass where he or she has permission to act, be it express or implied, from the party in possession. A licence should be distinguished from interests in property, such as easements or profits à prendre which give the grantee a proprietary right to enter the land. These are dealt with in the standard works on land law.[211] Although a licence to act is a good defence, it has two notable limitations. It may be restricted by express or implied terms and if they are exceeded, the defendant has committed a trespass. As noted in Ch.8, "When you invite a person into your house to use the staircase, you do not invite him to slide down the banisters".[212] Equally, permission can be withdrawn, thereby rendering the defendant a trespasser if he or she fails to leave within a reasonable period of time.

Express or implied limits on permission to enter have been discussed in Ch.8. However, the ability to withdraw or revoke a licence is more complicated. Where the claimant has also been granted a property interest such as a profit à prendre,[213] or has a licence coupled with an equity,[214] the licence cannot simply be revoked. In other circumstances, it will depend on whether the claimant has been given permission to enter under a bare licence (i.e. in the absence of consideration), or under a contractual licence (i.e. in return for consideration, for example by purchasing a ticket to watch a football match). A bare licence may be revoked at any time,[215] although public law may impose some limits on the power of a public body to revoke its licence.[216] A contractual licence may be revoked (although this may result in a claim for breach of contract) unless (a) there is an express or implied term in the contract limiting the power to revoke the licence for a defined or reasonable time, and (b) the court would be prepared to grant an injunction to prevent breach of contract.[217] The existence of any implied term will be a question of construction on the facts of the case. For example, if I buy a ticket for the cinema, it is implied that (provided I behave myself) I can stay in the cinema until the end of the film.[218] If the licence is revocable, the defendant must be given reasonable time to leave and remove his or her goods.

---

211 Note also that such rights may be acquired by prescription (see Ch.10).

212 See Scrutton LJ in *The Carlgarth* [1927] P. 93 at 110.

213 A right to take goods from the land—see *Thomas v Sorrell* (1673) Vaugh. 330; 124 E.R. 1098.

214 See *National Provincial Bank Ltd v Hastings Car Mart Ltd* [1964] Ch. 665 and M. Dixon, *Modern Land Law*, 11th edn (Routledge, 2018), 9.3.

215 See *CIN Properties Ltd v Rawlins* [1995] 2 E.G.L.R. 130 which applied this rule even to quasi-public places such as a shopping centre and survived a challenge to the European Commission on Human Rights (*Anderson v United Kingdom* [1998] E.H.R.L.R. 218). This was applied in *Porter v Commissioner of Police for the Metropolis* unreported 20 October 1999), despite the highly critical academic response of K. Gray and S. F. Gray, "Civil Rights, Civil Wrongs and Quasi-Public Space" [1999] E.H.R.L.R. 46.

216 See *Wandsworth v A* [2000] 1 W.L.R. 1246 CA (attempt to deny parent access to a primary school).

217 *Winter Garden Theatre (London) Ltd v Millennium Productions Ltd* [1948] A.C. 173.

218 Compare *Hurst v Picture Theatres Ltd* [1915] 1 K.B. 1. There is also authority that if the court is prepared to award an order for specific performance, the licence cannot be revoked even where the licensee has yet to enter into possession of the premises: *Verrall v Great Yarmouth BC* [1981] Q.B. 202.

(2) Necessity

Necessity is also a valid defence to trespass to land. The necessity may be public or private, but in both cases, there must be an actual or reasonably perceived danger in relation to which reasonable steps are taken. For example, if there is a fire and the defendant enters another's land or destroys another's property to stop the spread of the fire, the defence will be one of public necessity if the actions are in the public interest. If the defendant has intervened to save his or her own person or property from imminent danger, the defence will be one of private necessity.[219] In *Rigby v Chief Constable of Northamptonshire*,[220] a young psychopath broke into a gun shop and armed himself. To end the siege, the police fired a canister of CS gas into the shop to smoke out the intruder. Unfortunately, it set the shop alight. The shopkeeper sued the police for damages. Taylor J held that the police could rely on the defence of necessity provided they could show that they had not been negligent in creating or contributing to the necessity. On the facts, the intruder had been a clear threat to the public and the police had clearly not caused or contributed to the problem at hand. They were therefore not liable in trespass.[221]

In recent years, the Court of Appeal has expressed concern as to the operation of this defence and advocated that it should be confined to very limited circumstances. Lord Denning MR in *Southwark LBC v Williams*[222] highlighted the concern that it could be used to justify public unrest. Here, a group of individuals in dire need of accommodation had relied on necessity to justify taking over a number of empty houses belonging to the local authority which were due for development. Lord Denning MR held that such behaviour was not acceptable in society and that the defence should only apply to urgent situations of immediate peril:

> "If homelessness were once admitted as a defence to trespass, no-one's house could be safe. Necessity would open a door which no man could shut. It would not only be those in extreme need who would enter. There would be others who would imagine that they were in need or would invent a need, so as to gain entry . . . So, the courts must for the sake of law and order take a firm stand. They must refuse to admit the plea of necessity to the hungry and the homeless, and trust that their distress will be relieved by the charitable and the good."[223]

This approach was approved by the Court of Appeal in *Monsanto Plc v Tilly*.[224] Here, campaign-

---

219   Although it has been held that it is no excuse to an action in trespass that you entered due to threats to your life: *Gilbert v Stone* (1647) Style 72; 82 E.R. 539.
220   [1985] 1 W.L.R. 1242.
221   They were, however, found to be negligent in firing the canister when no fire-fighting equipment had been present, as discussed at para.2–045.
222   [1971] 1 Ch.734.
223   [1971] 1 Ch.734 at 744.
224   [2000] Env. L.R. 313 *The Times* 30 November 1999.

ers against genetically modified (GM) crops had entered onto land and destroyed some of the GM crops growing there. Monsanto, a company licensed by the Department of the Environment to carry out trials on GM crops, sought injunctions against the defendants prohibiting them from trespassing on the land. The defendants claimed that they had a valid defence of necessity, but this was dismissed by the Court of Appeal. The court held that the real purpose of the campaign was to attract publicity for their cause, and their actions did not fit within the very narrow defence of necessity. The defence would only apply where the defendants faced an emergency where it was necessary for the defendants to act in the face of immediate and serious danger to life or property, and where their actions were reasonable. In any event, there was a public authority responsible for the public interest in relation to GM crops, namely the Department of Environment. Again, the Court of Appeal stressed that the defence of necessity should not be used to justify "all sorts of wrongdoing".

(3) Justification by law

11-040 It is a valid defence that the defendant was legally authorised to enter onto the claimant's land. The most obvious example is that of a police officer entering premises under warrant. Reference should be made again to the Police and Criminal Evidence Act 1984 (ss.16 to 18, as amended) and the Criminal Justice and Public Order Act 1994.[225] One particular problem, which has now been resolved by statute, is the difficulty experienced by householders who needed access to neighbouring land to undertake repairs to their property. Their neighbours at common law were quite entitled to refuse, or charge a premium. The Access to Neighbouring Land Act 1992 now provides that the court may make an order allowing access to land for the purpose of carrying out works which are reasonably necessary for the preservation of adjoining or adjacent land and which cannot be carried out, or would be substantially more difficult to carry out, without entry upon the land. The scope of the Act is limited, however, by the fact that the court cannot make such an order if it would cause unreasonable interference with the neighbour's enjoyment of the land or unreasonable hardship. Equally, it is confined to work to "preserve" the land, although it will extend to improvement work incidental to such works: s.1(5).[226]

Abuse of such legal authority is treated severely. Where the defendant has entered the property with legal authority, but subsequently abuses that authority, the trespass is deemed to have taken place from the moment of entry (the so-called doctrine of trespass ab initio).[227] This only applies, however, to positive acts of abuse and does not apply to omissions. It also does not seem to apply to cases of partial abuse. In *Elias v Pasmore*,[228] the police had lawfully entered the plaintiff's premises to arrest a man, and had seized a number of documents, some of them unlawfully. Horridge J held that the original entry was not a trespass to land. The only

---

225 See also Countryside and Rights of Way Act 2000 s.2.
226 See also Party Wall etc. Act 1996.
227 See the *Six Carpenters' Case* (1610) 8 Co Rep. 146a; 77 E.R. 695.
228 [1934] 2 K.B. 164.

action was for trespass to the goods unlawfully seized. It is submitted that, despite criticism of trespass ab initio,[229] the doctrine is sound and should be preserved. It is important in a democratic society that any abuse of legal authority which interferes with the claimant's right to possession should not be tolerated.

Trespass to Land: Remedies

The ordinary remedies of damages and/or an injunction may be obtained for trespass. The trespass may consist of a single act or be continuous. If the trespass is continuous, the claimant will have a right to sue for as long as it lasts. On this basis, the claimant may bring a second action for damages if the trespass persists.[230] The assessment of damages will be discussed in more detail in Ch.17. Here, therefore, we confine our study to remedies which are particularly relevant to the tort of trespass. Further details may be found in texts on land law.

11–041

(1) Self-help

This is mentioned to stress its limits.[231] A party in possession may use reasonable force to resist wrongful entry or attempted entry by a trespasser. Such people are therefore perfectly within their rights to erect fences or put up barbed wire fences. The force must be reasonable and any force in excess of what is reasonably necessary will render the person liable for trespass to the person.

A guard dog is equally permissible, provided that it is reasonable to keep the dog on the premises for that purpose: the Animals Act 1971 s.5(3). Guard Dogs Act 1975 s.1 further provides, however, that a guard dog should not be used unless the dog is secured, or his handler is on the premises and the dog is under the control of the handler at all times. In any event, a notice containing a warning that a guard dog is present should be clearly exhibited at each entrance to the premises.[232]

11–042

---

229 The doctrine has been criticised as antiquated and for failing to recognise that a lawful act should not be rendered unlawful by subsequent events: see the Court of Appeal obiter in *Chic Fashions (West Wales) Ltd v Jones* [1968] 2 Q.B. 299 at 313, 317, 320. Lord Denning was critical of the doctrine in *Chic Fashions* when it is used against the police, but nevertheless used it against taxi-drivers in *Cinnamond v British Airports Authority* [1980] 1 W.L.R. 582 at 588 who had abused their right to set down passengers at London airport by touting for business.

230 *Holmes v Wilson* (1839) 10 Ad. & E. 503; 113 E.R. 190.

231 As emphasised by the Court of Appeal in *Macnab v Richardson* [2008] EWCA Civ 1631; [2009] 35 E.G. 108, notably where it is not a clear and simple case of trespass, nor an emergency.

232 See *Hobson v Gledhill* [1978] 1 W.L.R. 215.

Although anyone in possession of land has a right to re-enter at all times,[233] this is limited by the Criminal Law Act 1977.[234] Section 6 renders it an offence for anyone without lawful authority (other than a displaced residential occupier[235]) to use or threaten violence for the purposes of securing entry to any premises occupied by another. Readers should also note the restrictions on entry contained in the Protection from Eviction Act 1977, which renders it an offence to unlawfully evict or harass any person with a right to remain in occupation of the premises.

(2) Order for possession of land

11–043 This is an action for the recovery of land (formerly called "Ejectment"), by which the person entitled to possess the land seeks a court order to recover the land. This is usually achieved by the claimant proving his or her own title to land.[236] There is now a special summary procedure the claimant can use against persons entering or remaining on their premises without the claimant's licence or consent, whether or not the claimant is able to identify them.[237] This permits the claimant to take action against squatters within a short period of time. This is essentially a proprietary action, but is mentioned because it has evolved from the tort of trespass.

(3) Mesne[238] profits

11–044 These will usually be claimed in addition to the action for recovery of possession of land. They are a form of consequential damages, given to the claimant for the time he or she has been kept out of possession of his or her land and allow the owner to make a fair and reasonable charge for the use of the land. By this means, the claimant can seek a reasonable rent for the defendant's possession of the property. The remedy is usually used against a tenant who has refused to leave at the end of the lease. It is irrelevant that the claimant cannot show that the property could have been let during this period or that the defendant did not profit from the property. The damages are for the lost use of the property. Therefore, in *Inverugie Investments Ltd v Hackett*,[239] the Privy Council held that the plaintiff could recover a reasonable rent for every apartment in a hotel block, in spite of the defendants' objections that they had never

---

233 Note *Ropaigealach v Barclays Bank Plc* [2000] Q.B. 263 CA (mortgagee permitted to exercise right to take possession without court order).

234 As amended by the Criminal Justice and Public Order Act 1994 and Serious Organised Crime and Police Act 2005.

235 This is defined by s.12(3) as any person who was occupying the premises as a residence immediately before being excluded from occupation by a trespasser.

236 On this basis, there is authority that the defence of *jus tertii* applies to an action for recovery of land.

237 See the Civil Procedure Rules Pt 55.

238 Pronounced "mean".

239 [1995] 1 W.L.R. 713.

been fully booked and indeed had an average occupancy of 35 to 40%. Lord Lloyd held that it was not a question of the actual loss suffered, or whether the defendants had derived any actual benefit from the use of the premises, but of assessing a reasonable rate for the 15½ years the plaintiff had been out of possession:

> **"If a man hires a concrete mixer, he must pay the daily hire, even though he may not in the event have been able to use the mixer because of rain. So also must a trespasser who takes the mixer without the owner's consent. He must pay the going rate, even though in the event he had derived no benefit from the use of the mixer."**[240]

On this basis, it was acceptable to calculate the sum due on the wholesale rate paid by tour operators, which took into account seasonal variations in the booking fee. It is important to remember, however, that care must be taken if the claimant also makes a claim for damages which includes loss of profit arising from the inability to use the property. The courts will endeavour to ensure that claimants do not receive double recovery for the same loss.[241]

Trespass to Goods[242]

11–045

Finally, we shall briefly examine the tort of trespass to goods. This tort is now largely covered by the Torts (Interference with Goods) Act 1977, which brings together torts dealing with wrongful interference with goods, such as trespass and conversion, although s.2(1) abolishes the old tort of detinue. Conversion is essentially theft in civil law and is defined as wilfully dealing with the claimant's property in a way which amounts to a denial of the claimant's rights over it, whereby the claimant is deprived of the use and possession of the property.[243] Reference should be made to other texts for a full understanding of wrongful interference with goods.[244] Here, we confine ourselves to a general discussion of trespass to goods.

This form of trespass deals with intentional and direct interference with the possession of

---

240 [1995] 1 W.L.R. 713 at 718. See also *Horsford v Bird* [2006] UKPC 3; [2006] 1 E.G.L.R. 75 (mesne profits awarded up to date that judge awarded damages in lieu of an injunction for trespassory encroachment of boundary wall on Horsford's land).

241 See *Ramzan v Brookwide Ltd* [2011] EWCA Civ 985; [2012] 1 All E.R. 903. Both may, however, be awarded where the damages claim relates to future use and account needs to be taken of past trespass.

242 See, generally, S. Green, "Understanding the wrongful interference actions" [2010] Conv. 15.

243 Consider S. Green, "Theft and conversion—tangibly different?" (2012) 128 L.Q.R. 564, who argues that the civil action should be reformed so that its scope is similar to that of theft.

244 See, e.g. D. Sheehan, *The Principles of Personal Property Law* 2nd edn (Hart, 2017) and M.G. Bridge, *Personal Property Law*, 4th edn (OUP, 2015).

goods. This includes removing or damaging goods—in fact, any act interfering with the claimant's possession of the goods. It is unnecessary to show the defendant has removed the goods to establish this tort. Scraping your keys on the side of a vehicle would amount to trespass to goods.[245] In contrast to the other forms of trespass discussed above, the requirements of this tort are not particularly clear. They will be examined below.

The requirements of trespass to goods

▶ (1) It must be intentional

11–046

Generally, it would seem that the act of interference with the goods must be intentional. It is, however, irrelevant whether the defendant realised that he or she was committing a trespass. For example, in *Wilson v Lombank Ltd*,[246] a car had been sent to a garage for repair. The defendant, believing wrongly that the car was his, removed it from the garage. It was held that the defendant was liable in trespass. He had intentionally removed the vehicle and it was irrelevant that it was due to a mistake.

However, a number of cases have suggested negligence to be a sufficient condition of liability. In *National Coal Board v JE Evans & Co (Cardiff) Ltd*,[247] for example, the court excused the conduct of the defendants who, in digging a trench, had damaged an underground cable belonging to the plaintiffs. The court found that the defendants had not been negligent—there was no way they could have known of the presence of the cable, which had been laid by the plaintiffs or by the plaintiffs' predecessors in title without informing the landowner. The cable was not visible and had not been marked on the plan given to the defendants by the landowners. On this basis, where the claimant cannot reasonably know of the existence of the goods, but nevertheless harms them, a court will not find liability for trespass. There are also a number of road accident cases where the courts again look for negligence even when the action is brought in trespass.[248] This raises the *"Fowler v Lanning*[249] question" of whether there is a parallel claim for unintentional trespass to goods. It must be doubted whether such a claim is necessary and it may be preferable simply to treat such claims as negligence. Nevertheless, there is still some support for a tort of unintentional trespass to goods. For example, Torts (Interference with Goods) Act 1977 s.11(1) refers to "intentional trespass to goods", which suggests that it should be distinguished from "unintentional" trespass to goods.

---

245 See the example given by Alderson B obiter in *Fouldes v Willoughby* (1841) 8 M. & W. 540 at 549; 151 E.R. 1153 at 1157: "Scratching the panels of a carriage would be a trespass".
246 [1963] 1 W.L.R. 1294.
247 [1951] 2 K.B. 861.
248 *Holmes v Mather* (1875) 133 L.T. 361.
249 [1959] 1 Q.B. 426.

(2) It must be direct

The interference must be direct and immediate.[250] This raises all the questions we have seen considered above in relation to the other forms of trespass. For example, if I put out poison for my neighbour's dog, is this direct enough to amount to trespass to goods? It may be argued that it is no more indirect than the acid put in the hand-dryer in *DPP v K*,[251] discussed above. Nevertheless, the general view is that it is probably not direct enough.[252]

11–047

(3) Actionable per se?

This tort is generally regarded as actionable without proof of damage. Thus, it covers activities such as the unauthorised touching of museum exhibits, which would not otherwise be protected in tort. There is some authority in favour of proof of damage, but these cases can generally be explained as highway cases based on negligence.[253]

11–048

(4) Possession

The key to this tort is interference with the possession, not the ownership, of goods. In *Wilson v Lombank Ltd*,[254] for example, the plaintiff was found not to be the true owner of the car, having purchased the vehicle from a person who had no right to sell the car. Nevertheless, he was found to be in possession at the time of the trespass, and was therefore able to bring an action for trespass to goods. The question is therefore whether the claimant was in possession at the time the interference took place. Bailees,[255] trustees, executors, administrators of estates and owners of franchises will all satisfy this requirement.

11–049

Defences

The defences are similar to those mentioned for other forms of trespass. It is a valid defence that the claimant has consented to the interference. Equally, if the trespass in question was necessary for the preservation and protection of the goods and reasonable steps were taken,[256]

11–050

---

250 For a recent example, see *White v Withers LLP* [2009] EWCA Civ 1122; [2010] 1 F.L.R. 859 (estranged wife intercepting husband's post).
251 [1990] 1 W.L.R. 1067.
252 See *Clerk & Lindsell on Torts*, 23rd edn (Sweet and Maxwell, 2020), para.15–09.
253 *Everitt v Martin* [1953] N.Z.L.R. 298 and *Slater v Swann* (1730) 2 Str. 872; 93 E.R. 906.
254 [1963] 1 W.L.R. 1294.
255 See *Owen and Smith (trading as Nuagin Car Service) v Reo Motors (Britain) Ltd* (1934) 151 L.T. 274 CA.
256 See *Kirk v Gregory* (1876) 1 Ex. D. 55 where the defence failed because, although the defendant had acted bona

the defendant has a good defence. Readers should note that under the Police and Criminal Evidence Act 1984,[257] the police are given specific powers to search for and seize property without liability. Section 11(1) of the 1977 Act states that contributory negligence is no defence to proceedings based on "intentional" trespass to goods. Again, this begs the question whether contributory negligence could be a defence should unintentional trespass to goods be recognised, but as this is essentially a claim for negligence, the answer is obviously yes. Section 8 of the 1977 Act also provides a further defence:

> **"The defendant in an action for wrongful interference shall be entitled to show, in accordance with rules of court, that a third party has a better right than the plaintiff in respect of all or any part of the interest claimed by the plaintiff, or in right of which he sues."**

Under this provision, the defendant may protect himself or herself against double liability by identifying who had the interest protected by the tort at the relevant time. Rules of court now provide that the claimant should give particulars of title and identify any other person who, to his or her knowledge, has or claims to possess an interest in the goods.[258] Readers should also note that the 1977 Act gives the claimant a wider range of remedies than the common law remedies of damages and/or injunction, which include a final order for special delivery, or for delivery or damages, if the defendant is in possession or control of the goods.[259]

Trespass to goods is therefore a means by which the claimant's possession of goods can be protected from unwarranted interference by others. It is limited in scope, but presents an example of one of the many varied interests protected by the law of torts.

---

fide, it was not proved that the interference was reasonably necessary.
257 See Police and Criminal Evidence Act 1984 ss.8–22.
258 CPR r.19.5A.
259 See Torts (Interference with Goods) Act 1977 s.3.

12

The Economic Torts

Introduction

This chapter will examine a number of different torts which protect a claimant (usually a business[1]) from infliction of pure economic loss by intentional acts.[2] These are the so-called "economic torts". It is important to distinguish these torts from the tort of negligence, in which pure economic loss may be caused by careless, rather than intentional, misconduct. Until quite recently, there was much confusion about the nature and scope of the economic torts. This is because they were often invoked in rather complex commercial circumstances, and, as the courts wrestled with the appropriate principles to apply in such circumstances, a number of different and overlapping causes of action emerged.

Until 2007, it was usual to think in terms of there being at least four different economic torts. These included torts called "conspiracy", "intimidation", "inducing a breach of contract" and "interference with contractual relations". However, some of the case law dealing with the last two of these torts had blurred the distinction between them. In some cases, it had been suggested that both these torts might be dealt with according to a single set of rules (the so-called "unified theory"). To make matters worse, in other cases, it had been suggested that some of the economic torts were in fact just ways of committing a wider "generic" tort called "causing loss by unlawful means".

Thankfully, however, the 2007 decision of the House of Lords in *OBG v Allan*[3] has provided

---

1 Claims are occasionally made outside of a commercial context. See, e.g. *Falconer v ASLEF* [1986] I.R.L.R. 331 (a claim for hotel expenses by a traveller who could not use his train ticket because of unlawful industrial action).

2 See, generally, H. Carty, *An Analysis of the Economic Torts*, 2nd edn (OUP, 2010) and H. Carty, "The modern functions of the economic torts: reviewing the English, Canadian, Australian and New Zealand positions" [2015] C.L.J. 261.

3 [2007] UKHL 21; [2008] 1 A.C. 1. See also H. Carty, "The economic torts in the 21st century" (2008) 124 L.Q.R 641; J. O'Sullivan, "Intentional economic torts, commercial transactions and professional liability" (2008) 24 P.N. 164.

much-needed clarity. In the light of this decision, we can say that there are nowadays three "economic torts", as follows:

- Inducing or procuring a breach of contract.

- Causing loss by unlawful means.

- Conspiracy.

The important thing to note is that, in *OBG v Allan*, their Lordships confirmed that the second of these torts is indeed a generic tort. As such, it encompasses a number of torts that formerly went by different names. Although, no doubt, these old names will continue to be used to describe different factual scenarios in which the generic tort is committed, the rules governing these scenarios are now the same.

In earlier times, the economic torts were often invoked to provide a remedy where trade unions caused loss to commercial parties by organising industrial disputes. Nowadays, however, the right to take or incite industrial action without being exposed to tortious liability is enshrined in legislation. Thus, although the economic torts continue to play a small role in regulating trade union activity (claims may be brought where economic loss is caused by "unofficial" action taken in breach of the statutory rules), their main purpose in modern times is to regulate competition between commercial parties.[4] Essentially, they do this by making some forms of unreasonable business practice unlawful.[5] Bearing in mind this purpose, it will be useful, before exploring the rules of each tort, if we consider in general terms the extent to which the courts have felt able to interfere with commercial competition. An understanding of the problem the courts face will help us to understand why the specific rules of the torts are framed as they are.

Regulating competition: the scope of the economic torts

12–002

In developing the economic torts, the courts have had to strike a delicate balance between the need to protect traders from unreasonable behaviour and the desirability of allowing vigorous competition, which is necessary for a thriving economy. The general approach of the courts was established in *Mogul Steamship Co Ltd v McGregor, Gow & Co*,[6] an important decision of the House of Lords taken at the end of the nineteenth century.

---

4 Although note the distinction between tortious liability arising from breach of UK competition law and the economic torts, see C. A. Banfi, "Defining the competition torts as intentional wrongs" [2011] C.L.J. 83.

5 Note that this is also the function of a related tort called "passing off", consideration of which is beyond the scope of this book. Interested readers should consult specialist texts on intellectual property, e.g. T. Aplin and J. Davis, *Intellectual Property Law: Text, Cases and Materials*, 3rd edn (OUP, 2017), Ch.5.

6 [1892] A.C. 25. See also *Allen v Flood* [1898] A.C. 1 (no liability for simply causing loss, even if intentional, if the defendant's actions are lawful).

The defendants were various shipowners involved in the highly lucrative trade of importing tea from China. They sought to obtain a monopoly in this trade by driving the plaintiff, a rival shipping company, out of business. To achieve this, the defendants formed an association and began to ship tea at heavily discounted prices, so that the plaintiff company could not compete and lost all its business. The plaintiff company brought an action against the defendants to recover its financial loss, arguing that the defendants' actions should be declared unlawful.

The House of Lords held that the plaintiff company had no cause of action. The defendants had engaged in vigorous, cut-throat competition, but what they had done could not be called unlawful. The effect of this decision was to establish the ground rules for the subsequent development of the economic torts: the courts would be wary of interfering with market competition, even where this had the effect of driving a trader out of business.

What this means, in a modern context, is that where, for example, a new "superstore" opens, selling goods at bargain prices, small local traders whose businesses suffer have no remedy in law—the law does not prohibit simple competition, even though it might be regarded by some as unfair (or, perhaps, as contrary to the wider social interest in preserving the traditional identities of communities). As the Supreme Court stated in the recent case of *JSC BTA Bank v Ablyazov*,[7] the elements of the established economic torts are carefully defined so as to avoid trespassing on legitimate business activities and should not impose any wider liability than can be justified in principle. Tort law will therefore only provide a remedy for unfair trading practices in certain very limited circumstances. It is to these that we now turn.

Inducing a Breach of Contract

12–003

This tort is committed where A, knowing of a contract between B and C, and intending that it should be breached, persuades B to breach that contract, and as a result B does breach the contract, causing loss to C. Actual breach of contract is obviously an essential requirement of this tort and the claim will fail if the contract in question was void or voidable.[8]

Liability for inducing a breach of contract was established in the famous case of *Lumley v Gye*.[9] The defendant, Mr Gye, was the proprietor of a theatre. He wished to secure the services of a certain opera singer by the name of Miss Wagner, who was, at the time, under a contract to sing for the plaintiff, Mr Lumley. Mr Gye offered Miss Wagner a large sum of money to break this contract. When she did so and performed in Mr Gye's theatre, the plaintiff brought an action claiming that Mr Gye had unlawfully induced Miss Wagner to breach her contract,

---

7   [2018] UKSC 19; [2018] 2 W.L.R. 1125 at [6].

8   *Proform Sports Management Ltd v Proactive Sports Management* Ltd [2006] EWHC 2903 (Ch); [2007] 1 All E.R. 542.

9   (1853) 2 El. & Bl. 216; 118 E.R. 749.

thereby causing him financial loss. The court upheld this claim, holding that a person who procures another to commit an actionable wrong[10] (in this case a breach of contract) is liable *as an accessory*.

Note that the essence of the *Lumley v Gye* tort is that the defendant, by approaching and persuading, *joins with the contract-breaker* in committing a wrong against the claimant—the breach thereby has the flavour of a joint enterprise. This is what justifies the imposition of accessory liability. Liability cannot be established simply on the basis that the defendant has factually caused non-performance of the contract (say, by making available to the contract-breaker, without persuasion, a more attractive deal). It will also help with our understanding at this stage if we remember that there is no tort of inducing lawful termination of a contract.[11] On this basis where a representative of an energy company knocks at your door and persuades you to "switch" service providers, the tort is not committed, because their intention is that you should *lawfully* terminate your contract with your existing provider.

For the *Lumley v Gye* tort to be established, the defendant must:

- know of the existence of the contract;

- know that his or her behaviour will (if acted on) induce a *breach*; and

- intend to induce that breach.

It is worth considering each point in turn:

The defendant must know of the existence of the contract

12-004

This requirement is fairly straightforward. The simple point is that there can be no liability where A does something which causes the breach of a contract between B and C unless A knows that there *is* such a contract. The point is illustrated by the decision in *Smith v Morrison*.[12] Here, the first defendant (a farmer) accepted a deposit from the plaintiff in respect of the sale of his farm. In the particular circumstances of the case, he did not believe that this constituted a binding contract to sell the farm. He subsequently sold the farm to the second defendant (a company) which shared his belief that the previous dealings did not amount to a contract. In the action, the plaintiff claimed, amongst other things, that the second defendant had induced

---

10   For the sake of simplicity, it is convenient to refer to the tort as "inducing a breach of contract". Strictly speaking, however, the principles of the tort apply equally to a (limited) number of other situations where the defendant procures a third party to commit an actionable wrong against the claimant. Such situations include procuring a breach of a company director's fiduciary duty, or a breach of an agent's duty to account to a principal. For some modern examples, see *Kallang Shipping SA Panama v AXA Assurances Senegal* [2008] EWHC 2761 (Comm); [2009] 1 Lloyd's Rep. 124 and *Colliers CRE plc v Pandya* [2009] EWHC 211 (QB).

11   *DC Thomson & Co Ltd v Deakin* [1952] Ch. 646 at 679.

12   [1974] 1 W.L.R. 659.

a breach of contract by dealing with the first defendant. However, Plowman J accepted the company's evidence that it had honest and genuine doubts about the existence of any valid previous contract to sell the farm. In these circumstances, there could be no liability for inducing a breach of contract.

The requirement of knowledge of the existence of a contract is, of course, necessary to fulfil the requirement that interference with the contract must be *intentional*. As Lord Nicholls put it in *OBG v Allan*[13]: "Intentional interference presupposes knowledge of the contract". In many situations, however, A may know that B and C have a contractual relationship, but may not fully appreciate its terms. A may therefore not realise (and so not intend) that persuading B to act in a certain way will result in a *breach*. (A may think, for example, that B's conduct will result in terminating the contract lawfully.) In these circumstances, A cannot normally be liable.

The defendant must know that the induced conduct will amount to a breach

12–005

As has been said, the defendant must normally know that his or her inducement will (if acted on) result in a breach of contract. In order for this to be so, two things are necessary:

- the defendant (A) must have knowledge of any relevant contractual terms that might be broken if B acts in response to the inducement; and

- the defendant (A) must *realise* that the *legal effect* of B taking the induced course of conduct vis-à-vis C will be to put B in breach of those terms.

Knowledge of the contractual terms

12–006

The defendant (A) must normally have knowledge of the contractual term(s) between B and C that might be broken as a result of dealing with B. Such knowledge can sometimes be inferred from the fact that the defendant is familiar with the usual terms incorporated into contracts of the relevant kind.[14] Yet, where this is not the case, the law will not fix A with constructive knowledge of the contractual term(s) just because A has dealings with B but carelessly fails to make appropriate inquiries about the extent of B's contractual obligations to C.[15] The position is dif-

---

13 *OBG v Allan* [2007] UKHL 21 per Lord Nicholls at [192].

14 *Middlebrook Mushrooms Ltd v Transport and General Workers' Union* [1993] I.C.R. 612 per Neil LJ at 621.

15 See *British Industrial Plastics Ltd v Ferguson* [1940] 1 All E.R. 479. per Lord Hoffmann in *OBG v Allan* [2007] UKHL 21 at [41]: "Mr Ferguson did not deliberately abstain from enquiry . . . He negligently made the wrong inquiry, but that is an altogether different state of mind". See also *Swiss Bank Corp v Lloyds Bank Ltd* [1979] Ch.548 (constructive knowledge of the contractual terms will not suffice, per Browne-Wilkinson J at 572).

ferent, however, where A's failure to acquire the relevant knowledge results from deliberately "turning a blind eye" (i.e. where A deliberately refrains from making inquiries because of a suspicion that they would reveal something to A's disadvantage.)

Thus, in *Emerald Construction Co Ltd v Lowthian*,[16] union officers (A) took unlawful industrial action against a building contractor (B) with the purpose of inducing it to terminate its arrangements with the plaintiff (C) for the supply of labour. One of the issues in the case was whether the union officers *knew* that, if B terminated these arrangements with C, it would amount to a breach of contract. The union officers had had sight of the contract between B and C, but had not investigated its terms. Lord Denning MR said:

> **"Even if they did not know of the actual terms of the contract, but had the means of knowledge—which they deliberately disregarded—that would be enough. Like the man who turns a blind eye. So here, if the officers deliberately sought to get this contract terminated, heedless of its terms, regardless of whether it was terminated by breach or not, they would do wrong."[17]**

Similarly, in the recent case of *One Money Mail Ltd v Ria Financial Services*,[18] the Court of Appeal held that the defendants had known of the exclusivity provision in Mr Wasilewski's contract with the claimants which prevented him from working for competing firms. This was despite the fact that Mr Wasilewski had told them that he "thought" that there was no such restriction (it did not help that Mr Wasilewski had a limited command of English when he signed his contract with the claimants and so could not be relied upon to have read and understood all the provisions in a closely printed ten page contract). Even if true "knowledge" could only be obtaining by reading the contract itself, evidence indicated that the defendants knew that all agents working for the claimants operated on an exclusive basis and so it could not rely on turning a blind eye. In the circumstances, Ria were found to have known of (or at least been reckless as to) the existence of the exclusivity clause.

Knowledge of the legal effect of the induced conduct

12–007

In some situations, the defendant (A) may know about the relevant contractual terms between B and C, but not realise that, as a matter of law, B will be in breach these terms by responding to the inducement. Addressing this sort of situation, Lord Hoffmann, in *OBG v Allan*, said:

> **"To be liable for inducing a breach of contract, you must know that you are inducing a breach of contract. It is not enough that you know**

---

16   [1966] 1 W.L.R. 691 at 700. Recently affirmed by *TCP Europe Ltd v Perry* [2012] EWCA Civ 1940 (QB) at [32].
17   *Emerald Construction Co Ltd v Lowthian* [1966] 1 W.L.R. 691 per Lord Denning MR at 700.
18   [2015] EWCA Civ 1084.

> that you are procuring an act which, as a matter of law or construction of the contract, is a breach. You much actually realize that it will have this effect."[19]

There can therefore be no liability in a case where the defendant (A) is honestly mistaken about the legal effect of B's actions on B's contract with C. Such was the case in *British Industrial Plastics Ltd v Ferguson*.[20] Here, a former employee (B) of the plaintiff company (C) offered the defendant (A) information about one of the company's secret processes which he (B) had invented while working for the company. The defendant knew that the employee had a continuing contractual obligation to the company not to reveal trade secrets. However, he dealt with the employee in the honest (but mistaken) belief that this obligation did not, in law, extend to patentable processes, so that dealing with the employee would not give rise to a breach of contract.

In the Court of Appeal, McKinnon LJ observed that, in accepting this evidence, the trial judge had "vindicated [the defendant's] honesty . . . at the expense of his intelligence".[21] The House of Lords agreed, however, that the defendant's lack of intelligence about the law was nothing to the point—he could not be liable unless he had actually known that the legal effect of the employee's conduct would be a breach of contract.

The defendant must "intend" to induce the breach

The *Lumley v Gye* tort is a tort of intention. It is not sufficient for liability that a defendant's dealings cause a breach of contract if that is not what was intended. As Lord Nicholls put it in *OBG v Allan*:

12–008

> "Causative participation is not enough. A stranger to the contract may know nothing of the contract. Quite unknowingly and unintentionally he may procure a breach of the contract by offering an inconsistent deal to a contracting party which persuades the latter to default on his contractual obligations. The stranger is not liable in such a case. Nor is he liable if he acts carelessly. He owes no duty of care to the victim of the breach. Negligent interference is not actionable."[22]

---

19 *OBG v Allan* [2007] UKHL 21 per Lord Hoffmann at [39].
20 [1940] 1 All E.R. 479. Contrast *Wolff v Trinity Logistics USA Inc* [2018] EWCA Civ 2765; [2019] 1 W.L.R. 3997 at [46]–[47].
21 *British Industrial Plastics Ltd v Ferguson* [1938] 4 All E.R. 504 CA per McKinnon LJ at 513 (noted by Lord Hoffmann in *OBG v Allan* [2007] UKHL 21 at [39]).
22 *OBG v Allan* [2007] UKHL 21 per Lord Nicholls at [191].

What counts as "intending"?

12–009

The difficult question, of course, is to what extent a defendant can be said to "intend" a breach of contract where that is not what he or she necessarily desires, but is nevertheless the foreseeable, probable or inevitable consequence of taking a particular course of action. Before the decision in *OBG v Allan*, the law on this point was extremely confused. The leading case, *Millar v Bassey*,[23] was a Court of Appeal decision concerning the well-known singer, Shirley Bassey. She breached a recording contract, knowing that this would result in her record company having to breach its contracts with the plaintiffs—a record producer and a group of musicians who had already been engaged to make the record. A majority of the Court of Appeal declined to strike out the plaintiffs' action. Beldam LJ thought that Miss Bassey might be said to have "intended" those breaches, even though she had not "desired" them.[24]

This approach, however, was disapproved of by the House of Lords in *OBG v Allan*. Explaining the correct approach to be taken, Lord Hoffmann said that it was necessary to distinguish between "ends, means and consequences". In the first two cases, there would be liability, but not in the third. Thus, in the first case, it is conceivable (though it would be unusual) that a defendant might desire the breach purely as an end in itself, to serve some spiteful purpose. Here, there would be the required degree of intention. Equally, in the second (usual type of) case, the necessary intention will be present. Here, the defendant does not desire the breach as an end in itself, but only as the *means* of achieving a different end (usually his or her own enrichment or advantage). As Lord Hoffmann put it:

> **"If someone knowingly causes a breach of contract, it does not normally matter that it is the means by which he intends to achieve some further end or even that he would rather have been able to achieve that end without causing a breach. Mr Gye would very likely have preferred to be able to obtain Miss Wagner's services without her having to break her contract. But that did not matter."[25]**

In the third type of case, however, the defendant neither desires the breach as an end in itself nor as a means of achieving a further end. This was the situation in *Millar v Bassey*. The breaches of the contracts with the producer and musicians were not a means by which Miss Bassey sought to achieve her desired end (freedom from her own recording obligations), nor, of course, were they a desired end in themselves. Their Lordships in *OBG v Allan* thought that, this being so, Miss Bassey could not be said to have "intended" those breaches in the necessary sense. The Court of Appeal had therefore been wrong to allow the action to proceed.

---

23   [1994] E.M.L.R. 44.
24   Peter Gibson LJ dissented, expressing a diametrically opposed view.
25   *OBG v Allan* [2007] UKHL 21 per Lord Hoffmann at [42].

12-010

> ▶ **Must the defendant intend to cause loss?**

It will suffice if the defendant intends to cause a breach of contract. There is no further require-ment that the defendant must intend to cause loss to the claimant.[26] Thus, for example, in *South Wales Miners' Federation v Glamorgan Coal Co Ltd*,[27] the defendant, a miners' union, was held liable for inducing breaches of contracts between miners and their employers when it instructed the miners to stop work for a time. The union's purpose was to restrict the supply of coal, in order to keep the price of coal high (thereby maintaining the level of miners' wages, which were paid by reference to that price). Maintaining the price of coal, of course, would also be of benefit to the employers. It was clear, therefore, that the union did not intend to cause the employers any loss as a result of their members' actions. However, when, in the event, some loss was suffered, the union was liable—it was sufficient that it had intended to cause breaches of contract, and its conduct could not be excused on the basis that it had not intended to cause any loss. (Note, however, that the tort of "causing loss by unlawful means"—discussed below—does require an intention to cause the claimant loss.)

What counts as "inducing"?

12-011

To be liable for the *Lumley v Gye* tort of "inducing" (or "procuring")[28] a breach of contract, there must be a sufficient causal connection between the behaviour of the defendant (A) and the actions of the third party (B) in breaching his or her contract with C. Since liability under the tort is "accessory" liability, the applicable principles are to be found in other cases dealing with the question of when a defendant can be liable as an accessory to a civil wrong committed by anoth-er.[29] In the leading case of *Fish & Fish Ltd v Sea Shephard UK*,[30] for example, Lord Toulson indi-cated that to establish accessory liability in tort, "it is not enough to show that D did acts which facilitated P's commission of the tort. D will be jointly liable with P if they combined to do or secure the doing of acts which constituted a tort". In essence, these cases hold that the defend-ant must "join with" the other person to commit the wrong, in furtherance of some shared pur-pose. We can see that this was true in *Lumley v Gye*, since both Mr Gye and Miss Wagner sought to achieve the same purpose—namely that she would sing for Mr Gye instead of the plaintiff.

By contrast, no such common purpose existed in *CBS Songs v Amstrad Consumer Electronics Plc*.[31] This case concerned (amongst other things) an allegation of procuring (or "inducing")

---

26   Although the claimant must suffer some loss. The tort is not actionable per se. See *Sefton v Tophams Ltd* [1965] Ch. 1140 (CA) (overruled by HL on different grounds at [1967] 1 A.C. 50.)

27   [1905] A.C. 239 (cited by Lord Hoffmann in *OBG v Allan* [2007] UKHL 21 at [62]).

28   The terms are used inter-changeably.

29   *OBG v Allan* [2007] UKHL 21 per Lord Hoffmann at [36].

30   [2015] UKSC 10; [2015] A.C. 1229 at [21].

31   [1988] A.C. 1013. See also *Unilever v Chefaro* [1994] F.S.R. 135. Contrast, however, *Football Dataco Ltd v Sportradar GmbH* [2013] EWCA Civ 27; [2013] F.S.R. 30.

copyright infringement. The defendants manufactured and marketed a hi-fi music centre featuring an integrated record-player, radio, and twin cassette-deck with high-speed dubbing. This equipment could be used by members of the public to copy commercial broadcasts, records and tapes. Lord Templeman, giving the leading speech in the House of Lords, held that the defendants' conduct could not be regarded as analogous to the situation in *Lumley v Gye*—merely making available the means of committing a wrong was not the same as jointly committing that wrong. It could not be said that the defendants' *purpose* in selling such equipment was to infringe copyrights (though this might, of course, be the purpose of people who bought the machines).

Defences to inducing a breach of contract

12–012

The Trade Union and Labour Relations (Consolidation) Act 1992[32] sets out a number of defences to the economic torts, including the *Lumley v Gye* tort. Detailed consideration of the circumstances in which these defences operate is beyond the scope of this book. For present purposes it will suffice to note that, because most forms of industrial action involve breach of a contract of employment, in the absence of such statutory protection it would be impossible for a trade union to encourage its members to take industrial action without exposing itself to a claim by the employer for inducing a breach of contract.

In addition to the statutory defences, there is the common law defence of "justification". This can operate in a number of different circumstances, as follows:

Where the defendant has an equal or superior right to the third party's performance

12–013

This form of justification will arise where the third party (the contract-breaker) has, under a previous contract, assumed obligations towards the defendant which are inconsistent with performing the contract with the claimant. In such a case, it can be said that the defendant has an equal or superior legal right to the third party's services which justifies inducing the third party to breach.[33]

---

32 s.219. See also B. Simpson, "Trade Disputes Legislation and the Economic Torts" in T.T. Arvind and J. Steele (eds), *Tort Law and the Legislature* (Hart, 2012).

33 *Smithies v National Association of Operative Plasterers* [1909] 1 K.B. 310; *Edwin Hill & Partners v First National Finance Corp Plc* [1989] 1 W.L.R. 225; *Royal Bank of Scotland Plc v McCarthy* [2015] EWHC 3626 (QB).

Where the defendant has statutory authority to interfere with the contract

In *Stott v Gamble*,[34] for example, a licensing authority, constituted under the Cinematograph Act 1909, had a statutory power to prevent films they considered "objectionable or indecent" from being shown in theatres. The plaintiffs, distributors of a film called "Five Nights", had a contract with a theatre-owner under which a fee was to be paid when the film was shown. As a result of the licensing authority's decision to ban the film, the theatre-owner did not show the film or pay the fee. The plaintiffs' action against the licensing authority failed. Horridge J held that the licensing authority had not sought to cause the breach "for their own ends" (as required by *Lumley v Gye*) but had done so to serve a statutory purpose.

12-014

Where the defendant has a moral or social duty to interfere with the contract

In *Brimelow v Casson*[35] the defence of justification succeeded when the defendant (a trade union official) induced a number of women employed as actresses to breach their contracts of employment. The defendant argued that he was morally justified in taking this action because the women's wages were so low that they were compelled to supplement their income by prostitution.

12-015

This form of the defence, however, is of quite limited scope. It will not cover a situation where trade union officials merely seek to improve workers' wages or conditions,[36] and is probably confined to extreme circumstances such as those in *Brimelow v Casson* where (as Goff LJ subsequently put it) "the conduct of the party whose contracts were interfered with was utterly disgraceful and the circumstances produced were in the nature of a public scandal".[37]

Causing Loss by Unlawful Means

The key elements of this tort were examined by Lord Hoffmann in *OBG v Allan*. His Lordship said:

12-016

> "The essence of the tort . . . appears to be (a) a wrongful interference with the actions of a third party in which the claimant has an

---

34 [1916] 2 K.B. 504.
35 [1924] 1 Ch. 302.
36 See *South Wales Miners' Federation v Glamorgan Coal Co Ltd* [1905] A.C. 239.
37 *Pritchard v Briggs* [1980] Ch.338 per Goff LJ at 416.

> economic interest and (b) an intention thereby to cause loss to the claimant."[38]

This general formulation can be taken to encompass the types of wrongdoing that were formerly regarded as the commission of the separate economic torts known as "interference with contractual relations" and "intimidation".[39]

The "unlawful means tort" differs from the "*Lumley v Gye* tort" in that the defendant does not "join with" the third party in committing a wrong against the claimant. Rather, the defendant acts independently to bring about the claimant's loss by doing something unlawful vis-à-vis the third party, which affects the third party's ability to deal with the claimant. Liability for commission of the unlawful means tort is therefore primary or "stand alone" liability, rather than accessory liability.

In summary, to establish the unlawful means tort, the following three things must be shown:

- the defendant must take some action in relation to the third party which is "unlawful" in the relevant sense;

- the action in question must affect the third party's freedom to deal with the claimant; and

- the defendant must intend to cause the claimant loss.

We consider each proposition in turn:

The defendant's actions must be "unlawful" in the relevant sense

12–017 A memorable example of "unlawful" conduct towards third parties giving rise to liability is to be found in the early case of *Tarleton v McGawley*.[40] Here, the plaintiff, wishing to trade with the native inhabitants of Cameroon, had anchored his ship near the shore, loaded with trading goods. As the inhabitants approached the ship in their canoes, the defendant, the master of a rival trading ship, thought to secure their trade exclusively for himself. He therefore fired a cannon at them, intending to frighten them off and deter them from trading with the plaintiff. This unlawful act produced the desired effect, and the plaintiff suffered economic loss when

---

38   *OBG v Allan* [2007] UKHL 21 per Lord Hoffmann at [47].
39   It should be noted that only 3 party intimidation fits under the "unlawful means" tort. Lord Hoffmann acknowledged in *OBG* [2007] UKHL at [61] that two party intimidation—where a claimant is compelled by unlawful intimidation to act to his own detriment—raised different issues.
40   (1794) 1 Peake 270; 170 E.R. 153.

the inhabitants refused to trade with him. The court held that the plaintiff could recover this loss from the defendant.

Under the modern law (somewhat confusingly perhaps), not every form of conduct that is against the law will count as "unlawful" for the purpose of establishing the tort of "causing loss by unlawful means".[41] As Lord Walker observed in *OBG v Allan*, in deciding what sort of actions should count as "unlawful" for this purpose, it is necessary for the law to identify a suitable control mechanism "to stop the notion of unlawful means getting out of hand". Otherwise (to use his Lordship's example) there might be liability in tort where, say, a pizza delivery business obtains more custom, to the detriment of its competitors, because its drivers regularly exceed the speed limit or jump red lights.[42]

The majority[43] in *OBG v Allan* agreed that a suitable way of confining the scope of the unlawful means tort was to insist that actions by the defendant will only count as "unlawful" if they are *independently actionable at the suit of the third party against which they are directed*. Examples would include breach of contract and torts such as trespass to the person. Lord Hoffmann added one qualification—this would extend to unlawful means even if they were not technically actionable because the third party had suffered no loss.[44] On this basis, the "intimidation" scenario (see below) would be included, even if, despite the threat, the third party suffers no loss by submitting to the threat and the only loss suffered falls on the claimant. It is nevertheless unlawful means.

Taking this approach rules out liability in Lord Walker's pizza delivery example, because the conduct in question, though it involves the commission of criminal offences, is not actionable at the suit of the third parties affected by it (the customers who buy pizzas with a faster delivery time, to the detriment of the claimant). Moreover, there can be no liability in such a case because the conduct in question does not affect the freedom of the third parties to deal with the claimant (see below)—the customers can still order a slower, lawfully-delivered pizza if they want to.

By contrast, such an approach would allow for liability in a case where (to extend Lord Walker's example) a pizza business prevented customers from contracting to buy pizzas from a rival by, say, unlawfully detaining the rival's customers or threatening them with violence.[45]

---

41 What makes matters more confusing is that what counts as "unlawful" for the purpose of this tort is different from what counts as "unlawful" for the purpose of establishing the tort of "unlawful means conspiracy" (discussed in later section).

42 *OBG v Allan* [2007] UKHL 21 per Lord Walker at [266].

43 Lords Hoffmann, Brown and Baroness Hale. Lord Nicholls took an alternative line, based on the idea that the defendant must be said to cause the claimant's loss through the "instrumentality" of the third party, which would have cast the net wider. Lord Walker declined to prefer either approach.

44 [2007] UKHL 21 at [49], giving the example of *National Phonograph Co Ltd v Edison-Bell Consolidated Phonograph Co Ltd* [1908] 1 Ch. 335.

45 What would be the position if a pizza business unlawfully interfered with customers' phone calls, so as to prevent them ordering pizzas from a rival? This would (probably) not give rise to a cause of action at the suit of the customer, but it would prevent the customer from dealing with the claimant. Such an example shows us how, in some circumstances, the wider "instrumentality" test suggested by Lord Nicholls might be useful.

This sort of unlawful conduct gives rise to a cause of action at the suit of the third parties (trespass to the person), and affects their freedom to deal with the claimant.

The defendant's actions must affect the third party's freedom to deal with the claimant

12-018

This requirement explains why the courts have refused to impose liability in the so-called "bootlegging" cases. In *RCA Corp v Pollard*,[46] for example, the plaintiff company had the exclusive right to exploit records made by Elvis Presley. The defendant sold bootleg records that had been made without consent at Elvis concerts before his death. The plaintiff company claimed that this activity amounted to an unlawful interference with the contractual relationship between it and the Presley estate, and had the potential to cause the company loss, in the form of lost sales of authorised Elvis records. The Court of Appeal declined to hold the bootlegger liable for causing loss by unlawful means. Although bootleg recording was a criminal offence, it did not interfere with the Presley estate's freedom to deal with the company—it made no difference to the estate's ability to honour its contractual obligation to the company, because that obligation was merely an undertaking not to *consent* to the exploitation of Elvis recordings by persons other than the plaintiff. In other words, there could be no liability because, in spite of the bootlegger's activity, the third party (the estate) was still free to deal with the plaintiff on the same terms as it always had done.

More recently, in *Secretary of State for Health v Servier Laboratories Ltd*,[47] Servier had obtained a European patent for a drug from the European Patent Office (EPO) and obtained an injunction from an English court to stop another company selling a generic version in the UK. Following further court proceedings, the patent was declared invalid in the UK and was later revoked by the EPO. Servier were sued by the claimants for causing them loss by unlawful means—namely that by obtaining the patent/injunction with fraudulent misrepresentations, they had used unlawful means in a way which caused the NHS loss (it had been unable to buy generic drugs which were cheaper generally to purchase than patented drugs). The Court of Appeal struck the case out. Following *OBG*, interference by the defendant with the liberty of a third party to deal with the claimant was an essential element of the tort. The claimants could not show that the liberty of either the EPO or the English court to deal with the claimants had been affected.

The defendant must intend to cause the claimant loss

12-019

Without an intention to cause the claimant loss, there can be no liability, even if the loss is the inevitable result of the defendant's actions. Mere causative participation in the circumstances

---

46 [1983] Ch. 135. See also Ex *p. Island Records* [1978] Ch. 122; *Issac Oren v Red Box Toy Factory Ltd* [1999] F.S.R. 785.
47 [2019] EWCA Civ 1160; [2019] 3 W.L.R. 938. For commentary, see Jacob and Strath (2019) 14 JIPL & P 922.

producing the loss will not suffice. Thus, for example, if you always drive to the supermarket on Saturday afternoons, but one Saturday I crash into your car—inevitably resulting in loss of custom for the supermarket—I will not, without more, be liable to the supermarket. This is because the essence of the unlawful means tort is that I must intend to "strike at" the supermarket through you—it will not be sufficient if I simply could not care less whether you get to the supermarket or not.

As with the *Lumley v Gye* tort, it is necessary here to distinguish between "ends, means and consequences". Intention will be established in the first two cases, but not in the third. In some cases, therefore, it will be sufficient if the defendant's principal desire (the "end") is personal enrichment, and injuring the claimant through the third party is only a means of achieving this end. Thus, as Lord Hoffmann explains in *OBG v Allan*, the ship's master who fired the cannon in *Tarleton v McGawley*:

> **". . . may have had nothing against the other trader. If he had gone off to make his fortune in other waters, he would have wished him well. He simply wanted a monopoly of the local trade for himself. But he nevertheless intended to cause him loss."[48]**

By contrast, there will be no "intention" in cases where the loss is only a foreseeable consequence. For example, in *Barretts & Baird (Wholesale) Ltd v Institution of Professional Civil Servants*[49] the defendant trade union called a strike by civil servants in the Ministry of Agriculture in support of a pay claim. As a result, the plaintiffs, an abattoir, were unable to obtain certificates necessary for exporting meat and claiming subsidies. The defendants could not be liable, however, because causing economic loss to the abattoir was neither the purpose of the strike nor was it desired as a means of achieving that purpose.

Ways of committing the unlawful means tort

It will be instructive here to consider a number of scenarios in which, under the old law before *OBG v Allan*, the courts used to say that defendants were liable for committing the economic torts of "interference with contractual relations" and "intimidation". Considering these scenarios will show us how these old economic torts were really just different ways of committing the modern tort of causing loss by unlawful means.

12–020

---

48   *OBG v Allan* [2007] UKHL 21 at [63].
49   [1987] I.R.L.R. 3. Approved by Lord Hoffmann in *OBG v Allan* [2007] UKHL 21 at [64]. See also *Emerald Supplies Ltd v British Airways plc (Nos 1 and 2)* [2015] EWCA Civ 1024; [2016] Bus L.R. 145 at [169]: no intention to injure when it was not known whether anyone from the alleged class would in fact suffer at all.

The "interference with contractual relations" scenarios

12–021

Before *OBG v Allan*, it used to be said that there could be two additional "indirect" ways of committing the *Lumley v Gye* tort.[50] Thus, under the old law, the *Lumley v Gye* tort could actually be committed in three ways:

(1) The "classic" or "direct" form of the tort (the only form that now survives) was committed where the defendant made a direct approach to the third party and persuaded or procured ("induced") the third party to breach a contract with the claimant (as in *Lumley v Gye* itself).

(2) One of the (old) "indirect" forms was committed where the defendant brought about the breach by doing something else (other than "inducing") in relation to one of the contracting parties (e.g. taking away a party's tools so they could not perform the contract).[51]

(3) Another of the (old) "indirect" forms was committed where the defendant (a trade union) induced a breach of "Contract A" (e.g. between workers and employer), so as to prevent performance of "Contract B" (e.g. between employer and customer), intending to cause loss to the customer as a means of putting pressure on the employer.[52]

The courts had held that the "indirect" forms of the *Lumley v Gye* tort (scenarios 2 and 3) amounted to the commission of a tort called "interference with contractual relations". They had also held that it was a requirement in such cases that the defendant must have used "unlawful means" to interfere with the contract—e.g. trespass to goods in scenario 2, or the "direct" form of the *Lumley v Gye* tort (which would suffice as "unlawful means") in scenario 3.

However, in *OBG v Allan*, Lord Hoffmann (with whom the majority agreed) stated:

> "... the distinction between direct and indirect interference is unsatisfactory and it is time for the unnatural union between the *Lumley* v *Gye* tort and the tort of causing loss by unlawful means to be dissolved."[53]

---

50 See, e.g. *DC Thomson & Co Ltd v Deakin* [1952] Ch.646, where the CA adopted the "unified theory" of liability under *Lumley v Gye*.

51 This example is given by Jenkins LJ in *Thomson & Co Ltd v Deakin* [1952] Ch.646 at 696. See also *GWK Ltd v Dunlop Rubber Co Ltd* (1926) 42 T.L.R. 376.

52 See, e.g. *JT Stratford & Son Ltd v Lindley* [1965] A.C. 269. Note that an intention to injure the customer was here inferred from the fact that this was an inevitable result of the defendant's conduct. In the new language of *OBG v Allan*, it would have to be said that injuring the customer was a "means" of achieving the union's "end" (putting pressure on the employer) as opposed to a mere by-product of achieving that end.

53 *OBG v Allan* [2007] UKHL 21 per Lord Hoffmann at [38].

Nowadays, therefore, we can say, much more simply, that scenarios 2 and 3 are just examples of the tort of "causing loss by unlawful means". The wrongs in question are actionable because they meet the requirements of this tort, as set out in *OBG v Allan*, not because they represent "extensions" of the *Lumley v Gye* principle.

The "intimidation" scenario

12–022

The classic example of the old tort of "intimidation" is *Rookes v Barnard*.[54] The plaintiff was employed by BOAC. The three defendants were union officials. There was an informal agreement between the union and BOAC that all employees would belong to the union. When the plaintiff resigned from the union, the defendants threatened BOAC with an unlawful strike unless they dismissed him. BOAC gave in to this threat, and lawfully brought the plaintiff's contract to an end. The plaintiff had no remedy against BOAC for breach of contract because he had been dismissed lawfully. He therefore brought an action against the defendants. The House of Lords held that the defendants had committed the tort of intimidation against the plaintiff. This tort would be established where a defendant threatened to use unlawful means against a third party to compel that third party to act in such a way as to cause economic loss to the claimant.

If we re-examine *Rookes v Barnard*, using the language of *OBG v Allan*, we can see that its facts will fit within the rules for establishing the modern unlawful means tort. First, the threat of a strike would clearly count as "unlawful" because it was potentially actionable as a breach of contract by the third party (BOAC). Secondly, the threat clearly affected BOAC's ability to deal with the plaintiff (they could no longer employ him). Lastly, the defendants intended to cause loss to the plaintiff (have him dismissed), albeit that causing this loss was only a means of securing their primary objective of maintaining a union-only workforce.

The modern torts applied: the *OBG v Allan* appeals

12–023

In *OBG v Allan* the House of Lords decided three appeals. It will be convenient here to note how the modern torts were applied in the factual context of each case.

---

54   [1964] A.C. 1129. For a critical appraisal of the new approach to intimidation as stated by Lord Hoffmann in *OBG v Allan*, see J. Murphy, "Understanding intimidation" (2014) 77 M.L.R. 33.

Mainstream Properties Ltd v Young

12-024

Here, two employees of the claimant property company, in breach of their contracts of employment, diverted a development opportunity to another company which they ran. The defendant, who provided financial assistance for this transaction, knew that the employees worked under contracts with the claimant company, but accepted the employees' assurances that their involvement in the transaction would not put them in breach of those contracts. Their Lordships dismissed the claimant company's contention that the defendant's actions should amount to inducing a breach of contract. On the facts, whilst the defendant had known about the existence of the contracts, he had not known (or turned a blind eye to) their terms. Therefore, it could not be said that he had intended to cause the breaches.

OBG v Allan

12-025

In this case, the defendants were official receivers, who, it turned out, had been wrongly appointed. Acting in good faith, however, the receivers took control of the claimants' company and so caused them loss that would not have resulted if the company had continued to trade normally. The claimants argued that the receivers' actions amounted not only to trespass to their land and conversion of their goods,[55] but to the commission of an economic tort involving interference with contractual relations. Their Lordships held that, under the rules of the modern unlawful means tort, such a claim could not succeed. The receivers had not done anything unlawful (in the relevant sense) when dealing with the company's assets. Moreover, since they had acted in good faith, the receivers had not intended to cause loss to the claimants.

Douglas v Hello!

12-026

This appeal concerned the publication of wedding photographs of the film-stars Michael Douglas and Catherine Zeta-Jones. The magazine "OK!" had contracted with the Douglases for the exclusive right to publish photos of the wedding. The defendants—a rival magazine called "Hello!"—published photographs that it knew had been taken secretly at the wedding by an unauthorised photographer pretending to be a waiter. This, of course, deprived "OK!" of their "scoop" and caused them loss, in the form of lost magazine sales. "OK!" claimed that "Hello!" were liable for misuse of confidential information,[56] and also for the tort of causing loss by unlawful means. Their Lordships held that the unlawful means claim could not

---

55 The claimants also sought to extend the tort of conversion to cover choses in action (i.e. their outstanding contractual claims at the time the receivers were appointed). However, the majority (Lord Nicholls and Baroness Hale dissenting) declined to extend the scope of this tort.

56 The majority (Lords Nicholls and Walker dissenting) held that this should succeed. This aspect of the case is discussed in Ch.15.

succeed. The defendants' actions in publishing the secret pictures had not interfered with the third parties' ability to deal with the claimant (the Douglases were not actually prevented from honouring their agreement to supply "OK!" with wedding pictures). This meant that one of the essential ingredients for establishing the modern tort was missing.

Conspiracy

The tort of conspiracy[57] has two forms:

12-027

- unlawful means conspiracy; and

- lawful means conspiracy (also known as "conspiracy to injure" or "simple conspiracy").

Both forms share the requirement that two or more defendants must "combine" with a common purpose so as to cause the claimant loss. Usually, this means that the defendants will *agree* to pursue a common course of action, but there is no need for an express agreement between them.[58]

Unlawful means conspiracy

This tort is committed where two or more defendants act together with a shared intention of using "unlawful means" to cause loss to the claimant. The elements of unlawful means conspiracy are, then, as follows: (i) an agreement between one or more people to act unlawfully or to use unlawful means; (ii) these people act with the intention of causing damage to the claimant; and (iii) the claimant must suffer damage.[59] Until quite recently, the rules of this tort were rather uncertain. Much ink had been spilt by judges and academics alike in discussing two things:

12-028

---

57 Conspiracy as a tort is not to be confused with criminal conspiracy, which has different rules. See *Meretz Investments v ACP Ltd* [2007] EWCA Civ 1303; [2008] Ch 244 at [174] per Toulson LJ. For an argument that a separate tort of conspiracy in either of its forms is no longer needed post-*OBG*, see P.S. Davies and P. Sales, "Intentional harm, accessories and conspiracies" (2018) 134 L.Q.R. 69.

58 *Belmont Finance Corp v Williams Furniture Ltd (No.2)* [1980] 1 All E.R. 393.

59 See, e.g. *Tullett Prebon Plc v BGC Brokers LP* [2011] EWCA Civ 131; [2011] I.R.L.R. 420 and *Bank of Tokyo-Mitsubishi UFJ Ltd v Baskan Gida Sanayi Ve Pazarlama AS* [2009] EWHC 1276 (Ch). Loss must be proved: *Stevenson v Singh* [2012] EWHC 2880 (QB). So long as each individual conspirator knows the central facts and entertains the same object, it is not necessary that all conspirators join the agreement at the same time: *QBE Management Services (UK) Ltd v Dymoke* [2012] EWHC 80 (QB) at [198].

■ What degree of "intention" should be required?

■ What should count as "unlawful means"?

It will be helpful to examine these two issues in the light of a number of recent decisions that have clarified the law.

What must the conspirators intend?

12–029 A distinction must first be drawn between the different degrees of intention required for the two different forms of conspiracy. To establish "lawful means conspiracy" (discussed below) the conspirators must intend to injure the claimant in the sense that this is their predominant purpose. (This effectively limits the application of "lawful means conspiracy" to very rare situations where the defendants act purely out of malice.) However, to establish "unlawful means conspiracy" it is sufficient if the conspirators "intend" to injure the claimant in the wider *OBG v Allan* sense that they intend to do so only as a means of achieving an end (usually their own enrichment).[60] It is not, therefore, a problem that their predominant motive was their own self interest. It is clear from the decision of the Court of Appeal in *Meretz Investments v ACP Ltd*[61] that what is said in *OBG v Allan* about intention in the context of the "causing loss by unlawful means" tort applies equally in the context of "unlawful means conspiracy". Thus, the conspirators must intend not simply that unlawful means will be used—they must also intend to cause the claimant loss.

Although the conspirators must share the relevant degree of intention or "common design",[62] they do not all have to share the same degree of participation in the use of the unlawful means. Indeed, the whole purpose of invoking the tort of conspiracy is to attribute to all conspirators responsibility for actions committed by other members of the conspiracy. Thus, for example, where A and B conspire to ruin C's business by shooting all his customers, but B acts alone in firing the gun, A may be liable to C in conspiracy, even though A has not committed the unlawful act.[63] In this example, of course, one of the conspirators (B) has also committed the tort of "causing loss by unlawful means". Invoking the tort of conspiracy here simply has the effect of creating secondary liability for that tort, and so widening the class of potential defendants.

In the recent past, it was sometimes said that "unlawful means conspiracy" was a tort of

---

60   *Lonrho Plc v Fayed* [1992] 1 A.C. 448; *Kuwait Oil Tanker Co SAK v Al Bader* [2000] 2 All ER (Comm) 271 at [107] per Nourse LJ.

61   [2007] EWCA Civ 1303; [2008] Ch. 244 at [146] per Arden LJ.

62   Arguably, a conspirator who has played some part in the proceedings but lacks the required degree of intention might be liable on the basis that other conspirators have that intention. This is doubtful, however, because it would involve the proposition that persons can be liable for being in a combination without a true meeting of their minds.

63   Responsibility may be attributed on the basis of the "common enterprise" principle. See *Brook v Bool* [1928] 2 K.B. 578.

rather limited usefulness, because its only function seemed to be to impose secondary liability for committing the tort of "causing loss by unlawful means". In other words, whenever the tort was invoked, it was merely an "added extra", because one or more of the conspirators would turn out to be liable anyway for "causing loss by unlawful means".[64] However, the recent House of Lords decision in *Total Network SL v Revenue and Customs Commissioners*[65] shows us that the tort is, in fact, much more useful than this. First, it can be used in situations where it is extremely unlikely that a single defendant acting alone would have been able to cause the loss in question. Secondly, because of the extended meaning given to the phrase "unlawful means", it can be used in situations where none of the conspirators has actually committed the unlawful means tort.

> ### What counts as "unlawful means" for the purpose of establishing this tort?

In *Total Network SL v Revenue and Customs Commissioners* the defendants had perpetrated a complex VAT fraud—known as a "carousel fraud"—with the intention of obtaining tax rebates from the Revenue to which they were not entitled. For technical reasons, the Revenue were unable to use statutory procedures to reclaim the money they had wrongly paid out. They therefore sought to recover the money in an action for "unlawful means conspiracy". The Court of Appeal thought that, in principle, such an action ought to succeed. The problem, however, was that what the defendants had done, although a criminal offence, was not actionable in civil law as a tort. This meant that, according to existing authority,[66] it could not qualify as "unlawful means" for the purpose of establishing the tort. The relevant cases had held (as in *OBG v Allan*) that not every illegal act would count as "unlawful means"—an act would only count as "unlawful" if it was unlawful in the special sense of being actionable in civil law. The Court of Appeal therefore felt constrained to decide the issue in the defendants' favour, but gave leave to the Revenue to appeal to the House of Lords.

In the House of Lords, Lord Walker observed that the development of the economic torts had been "a long and difficult process" that had resulted in some confusion. A particular difficulty, he said, was that:

> "... it has been generally assumed, throughout the 20th-century cases, that "unlawful means" should have the same meaning in the intentional harm tort and in the tort of conspiracy."[67]

12–030

64   See, e.g. per Lord Devlin in *Rookes v Barnard* [1964] A.C. 1129 at 1204: "... the element of conspiracy is usually only of secondary importance since the unlawful means are actionable by themselves".
65   [2008] UKHL 19; [2008] 1 A.C. 1174. Comment: J. O'Sullivan [2008] C.L.J. 459.
66   *Powell v Boladz* [1998] Lloyd's Med. Rep. 116.
67   *Total Network SL v Revenue and Customs Commissioners* [2008] UKHL 19 per Lord Walker at [89]. His Lordship

His Lordship went on to explain, however, that this assumption was unnecessary—there was no reason why "unlawful means" could not mean different things for the purposes of the two different torts.

Following this reasoning, the House of Lords concluded that, in the context of the tort of "unlawful means conspiracy", the phrase "unlawful means" can have a wider meaning than it does in the context of the tort of "causing loss by unlawful means". For the latter tort, following *OBG v Allan*, the defendant's actions must be "unlawful" in the special sense that they are actionable in civil law by the party against whom they are directed, and affect that party's ability to deal with the claimant. However, this restrictive meaning of "unlawful" does not apply in the context of "unlawful means conspiracy". It is sufficient to establish this tort if the conspirators have merely done something unlawful in the wider sense, for example, criminal conduct (at common law or statute). On this basis, the defendants in the case could be held liable. The commission of a criminal offence could be a sufficient unlawful means for the purpose of the law of conspiracy, provided it was objectively directed against the claimant.

The Supreme Court reviewed this position in *JSC BTA Bank v Ablyazov*.[68] Here the Court was asked whether contempt of court, specifically dealing with assets subject to a freezing order against the bank's former Chairman (C), amounted to "unlawful means" for the purposes of the tort of conspiracy. The bank had brought a claim against the son-in-law of C on the basis that he had conspired with C (who had since disappeared) to breach the freezing order by helping him conceal his assets. Contempt of court is not a tort but a criminal offence punishable in civil proceedings, but the Supreme Court nevertheless found it to amount to unlawful means.[69] The defendants had intended to damage the claimant's interests and while damage to the bank was not the predominant purpose of the concealment, the damage was more than incidental—it had prevented the claimant from enforcing its order against C. In the words of Lords Sumption and Lord Lloyd-Jones:

> **Conspiracy being a tort of primary liability, the question what constitute unlawful means cannot depend on whether their use would give rise to a different cause of action independent of conspiracy. The real test is whether there is a just cause or excuse for combining to use unlawful means. That depends on (i) the nature of the unlawfulness, and (ii) its relationship with the resultant damage of the claimant.[70]**

12–031   The problem with the approach in *Total Network SL and JSC BTA Bank*, of course, is that it raises the prospect of widespread liability for unlawful means conspiracy. The Court openly

---

uses the phrase "intentional harm tort" to mean what we (and their Lordships in *OBG v Allan*) refer to as the tort of "causing loss by unlawful means".

68   Also known as *JSC BTA Bank v Khrapunov* [2018] UKSC 19; [2018] 2 W.L.R. 1125.

69   The Court also rejected the argument that there was a principle of public policy that persons in contempt of court should not be exposed to anything other than criminal penalities at the discretion of the court.

70   [2018] UKSC 19; [2018] 2 W.L.R. 1125 at [11].

recognised in *JSC BTA Bank* that the reasoning in *Total Network* leaves open the question how far it should apply to non-criminal acts, such as breaches of statutory duty, contract or fiduciary duties—this will need to be resolved in future cases. It will be recalled that, in *OBG v Allan*, Lord Walker noted that a restricted definition of "unlawful means" was needed in order to stop liability for "causing loss by unlawful means" from getting out of hand. Thus, where a pizza delivery business employs motorcyclists who exceed the speed limit and jump red lights (criminal offences), intending to take custom away from a rival, no action will lie, because the "unlawful means" in question are not actionable in civil law. But what if (as seems not unlikely) the owners, managers, chefs and motorcycle-riders involved in the defendant pizza business are all acting in combination, with a common intention to enrich themselves at the claimant's expense by breaking the law? Surely then we have an "unlawful means conspiracy" in the terms allowed by *Total Network SL*? Leading academic, Hazel Carty, has expressed real concern that lawyers will try to rely on the wider definition of "unlawful means conspiracy" to circumvent the limits of the tort of causing loss by unlawful means, arguing that it will not be too difficult to prove the conspiracy element when the claimant can place the intentional economic harm in a corporate context.[71] Her view is that the economic torts should remain a modest common law contribution to policing excessive competitive behaviour and no more.

There are potentially two ways in which this problem of expansive liability might be avoided. The first is to confine the application of the new, wider, meaning of "unlawful means" to situations where the criminal offences committed are breaches of criminal laws *designed specifically for the protection of the claimant's interests*. On this basis, it would, as in *Total Network SL*, be a conspiracy where defendants combine to defraud the Revenue by committing the offence of common law "cheat" (specifically preserved in revenue cases by Theft Act 1968 s.32(1)(a)) because the very reason that offence exists is to protect the Revenue from loss of money. Equally it can be argued that the crime of dealing with assets subject to a freezing order in contempt of court protects not only the authority and dignity of the court, but also the claimant's interest in the defendant's assets. On the other hand, it would not be a conspiracy to combine to exceed the speed limit or jump red lights with an intention to injure the claimant's business, because the criminal offences in question are not designed to protect the claimant from economic loss, but to serve very different purposes.

The second is to limit the application of the tort in its wider form to situations where the unlawful conduct was directed against the claimant and the injury was not incidental. In the pizza example, the injury to third parties (customers, or other road users) is indirect and any damage incidental to the defendants' purpose of "striking at" the claimant's business through the third parties. This seems to find favour in *JSC BTA Bank*,[72] although its lack of precision is self-evident.

The reasoning of their Lordships in *Total Network SL and JSC BTA Bank* suggest that either

---

71   H. Carty, "The modern functions of the economic torts: reviewing the English, Canadian, Australian and New Zealand positions" [2015] C.L.J. 261, 280–281.

72   See also *Palmer Birch (A Partnership) v Lloyd* [2018] EWHC 2316 (TCC); [2018] 4 W.L.R. 164 at [189].

or both of these approaches might serve as a suitable control mechanism to confine the scope of liability in future cases.

Lawful means conspiracy

12–032

The anomalous[73] tort of "lawful means conspiracy" is committed where two or more persons in combination intentionally cause loss to the claimant by acts that would be perfectly lawful if done by one person alone. Essentially, the tort makes defendants liable for "ganging up" on the claimant for no good reason and exercising their (lawful) rights in such a way as to cause the claimant loss. The tort's distinguishing feature is that, to establish liability, it must be shown that causing the claimant loss is the defendants' *predominant purpose*—if it can be shown that their predominant purpose was to achieve some other objective (e.g. their own enrichment) there will be no liability.[74] (In the language of *OBG v Allan*, it will not be sufficient if the defendants intend to injure the claimant only as a means of achieving an end—they must intend to injure the claimant as an end in itself.) Thus, the tort could not apply in a case like *Mogul Steamship Co Ltd v McGregor, Gow & Co*—which we considered at the beginning of this chapter—because the predominant purpose of the defendants in that case was to further their own interests by gaining a monopoly in the tea trade—intentionally driving the plaintiff out of business was just the means of achieving that goal.

Of course, this restrictive "predominant purpose" requirement makes the tort very difficult to establish. It was, however, said to have been established by the House of Lords in the 1901 case of *Quinn v Leathem*,[75] where a number of butchers (at the behest of their trade union) agreed to inflict economic loss on the plaintiff (who was employing non-union workers) by exercising their lawful entitlement not to handle the plaintiff's meat. Subsequent attempts to establish the tort have not been so successful. For example, in *Crofter Hand Woven Harris Tweed Co Ltd v Veitch*,[76] dock workers lawfully refused to handle the plaintiffs' machine-spun imported yarn. Their hope was that preventing mill-owners from obtaining such yarn would advance the pay claims of workers in traditional mills (using hand-spun, home-produced yarn) who were members of the dock workers' union. It was held that the plaintiffs had no cause of action against the dock workers, whose "predominant purpose" had not been to injure the plaintiffs but to further the interests of their fellow union members.[77]

It may seem strange that liability should ever attach to lawful acts simply because they are

---

73   *Lonrho Ltd v Shell Petroleum Co Ltd (No.2)* [1982] A.C. 173 at 188 per Lord Diplock: "as a civil tort, however, conspiracy is a highly anomalous cause of action". See S. Daly, "The aberrant tort of lawful means conspiracy?" (2020) 31 K.L.J. 145, who argues that it is no longer required as an independent tort as it is superceded by statute.

74   See *Lonrho Plc v Fayed* [1992] 1 A.C. 448.

75   [1901] A.C. 495.

76   [1942] A.C. 435.

77   Compare *Huntley v Thornton* [1957] 1 W.L.R. 321 where union officials were held liable when they sought to prevent the plaintiff from getting a job, after losing their argument with the union that he should be expelled.

done in concert with others. The traditional rationale for such liability, as expressed by Bowen LJ in *Mogul Steamship Co Ltd v McGregor, Gow & Co* (when that case was before the Court of Appeal) is that:

> "... a combination may make oppressive or dangerous that which if it proceeded only from a single person would be otherwise."[78]

In *Lonrho v Shell*,[79] however, Lord Diplock pointed out that such a proposition is really quite absurd when seen in the context of the modern business world. His Lordship said:

> "... to suggest today that acts done by one street-corner grocer in concert with a second are more oppressive and dangerous to a competitor than the same acts done by a string of supermarkets under a single ownership or that a multinational conglomerate such as Lonrho or oil company such as Shell or BP does not exercise greater economic power than any combination of small businesses, is to shut one's eyes to what has been happening in the business and industrial world since the turn of the century."

His Lordship concluded, however, by saying:

> "The civil tort of conspiracy to injure ... must I think be accepted by this House as too well-established to be discarded however anomalous it may seem today."

The application of the tort is not extensively considered in either *OBG v Allan* or *Total Network SL*. On the other hand, its continued existence was not doubted by their Lordships. Conceivably, therefore, it remains applicable in very special circumstances.

The economic torts: conclusion

12–033

We have seen that the economic torts, though complex, have gained a good deal of coherence from recent House of Lords decisions. Thanks to modern industrial-relations legislation, these torts no longer serve so directly one of the main purposes for which they were developed—the regulation of trade union activity. However, it is clear that they still have an important function in setting the boundaries of acceptable commercial conduct.

Harman J (at 340) found that the officials had not acted to further the union's interest, but to uphold "their own ruffled dignity", and this did not qualify as a legitimate ulterior purpose.

78 *Mogul Steamship Co Ltd v McGregor, Gow & Co* (1889) 23 Q.B.D. 598 CA per Bowen LJ at 616.

79 [1982] A.C. 173.

13

Defamation

Introduction

13–001

Defamation is a different type of tort from those examined in earlier chapters. It does not protect the personal safety of the individual or even the right to self-determination of the claimant. It protects something far more indistinct: the reputation of the claimant. On this basis, while abuse of the claimant in private can only give rise to liability for harassment or possibly assault, unjustified criticism of the claimant to another, which has caused or is likely to cause serious harm to the claimant's reputation, gives rise to the tort of defamation. It is the claimant's *reputation*, not injured feelings, which the tort aims to protect.

The tort raises a number of difficult problems. For example, a basic democratic right stated in the European Convention on Human Rights art.10 is the right to freedom of expression, which includes the right to "hold opinions and to receive and impart information and ideas without interference by public authority". Article 10 is now incorporated into English law by the Human Rights Act 1998 and s.6 of the Act provides that it is unlawful for a public authority (which includes courts) to act in a way which is incompatible with a Convention right.[1] Freedom of expression includes the right to criticise, and is particularly important in relation to politicians and officials who occupy positions of power. This is further supported by s.12 of the 1998 Act which provides that when a court is considering whether to grant any relief which, if granted, might affect the exercise of freedom of expression, it must have particular regard to the importance of this right and, inter alia, the public interest in the publishing of such material by the press.[2]

On the other hand, the reader will be fully aware of the frequent complaints of press intrusion and irresponsible reporting where journalists, anxious for a "scoop" in a very competitive media market, publish without fully checking their facts. Such complaints were highlighted

---

1 The Act came into force on 2 October 2000.
2 See Human Rights Act 1998 s.12(1) and (4).

by the Leveson Inquiry into the Culture, Practices and Ethics of the Press, whose report was published in November 2012.[3] A person mistakenly named as a serial rapist is unlikely to fight the corner of freedom of expression. Article 10.2 of the Convention recognises that the right to freedom of expression cannot go unchallenged. Such a right:

> **"carries with it duties and responsibilities [and so] may be subject to such formalities, conditions, restrictions or penalties as are prescribed by law and are necessary in a democratic society . . . for the protection of the reputation or rights of others."**

The tort of defamation must therefore attempt to balance the competing rights of freedom of expression and protection of one's reputation. As Laws LJ has commented, the focus of the tort "is not on reputation as akin to a right of property. It is on the balance to be struck between public interest and individual right: between free speech and private claims".[4] This is a far from easy task and, unfortunately for the reader, has led to a complex and frequently confusing area of law. This will be examined below.

It should be noted, however, that the UK Government has recognised the need for change and the Defamation Act 2013 introduces a number of key reforms into this area of law.[5] The Government argued that the previous law on defamation was old-fashioned, costly and unfair, and had resulted in a chilling effect on freedom of expression and the stifling of legitimate debate. The new Act, it stated, would take defamation into the twenty-first century and create a more balanced and fair law.[6] This chapter (and the next) will examine the nature of these reforms and the extent to which these ambitious goals have been met.

Chapters 13 and 14 will approach defamation in four logical stages. This aids clarity and helps to minimise the difficulties outlined above. Four main questions must be addressed:

- Is the statement defamatory?

- Does it refer to the claimant?

- Has it been published?

- Do any of the defences apply?

---

3   See *https://www.gov.uk/government/publications/leveson-inquiry-report-into-the-culture-practices-and-ethics-of-the-press* [Accessed 1 August 2020].

4   *Rothschild v Associated Newspapers* Ltd [2013] EWCA Civ 197; [2013] E.M.L.R. 18 at [25].

5   It should be noted that most of the Act's provisions only apply to England and Wales (although certain provisions such as s.6 on peer-reviewed statements in scientific or academic journals also extend to Scotland). The Act came into force on 1 January 2014: Defamation Act 2013 (Commencement) (England and Wales) Order 2013 (SI 2013/3027) art.2.

6   Government Press Release, 25 April 2013.

This chapter will focus on the first three stages, establishing when a claimant can bring an action for defamation and who can sue and be sued. Chapter 14 will set out the defences available to defendants, particularly in the light of the Defamation Acts of 1996 and 2013 and the important House of Lords judgment in *Reynolds v Times Newspapers Ltd*.[7] It will also consider alternatives to defamation law (for example the tort of malicious falsehood).[8]

The first step must, however, be to examine the long-standing division of defamation into two parts: libel and slander. Both are examples of defamation, but for historical reasons are treated separately. It would make life easier for all if this distinction were abolished (unless the reader has a particular desire to maintain a distinction logical in Tudor times, but sadly not our own). Abolition has been suggested from 1843 without success.[9] The Defamation Act 2013, as will be seen below, has merely amended some of the rules relating to slander.

Libel and Slander

13-002 These torts are generally distinguished on the basis that libel takes permanent form, for example, an article or a photograph published in a daily newspaper,[10] while slander is temporary, for example words shouted across a classroom or gestures made to a crowd.[11] The permanency of libel is deemed to make it more serious—more people will possibly see it and it will not be forgotten. In the past damage was presumed,[12] making libel actionable *per se* (i.e. without proof of damage). This position has changed following the Defamation Act 2013 s.1 (discussed at para.13–011) in that the claimant must now show that serious reputational harm has been caused by, or is likely to result in future from, the publication complained of.[13] Slander requires proof of special damage, that is, damage that can be proved by evidence of financial loss or any other material loss capable of estimation in financial terms. Being shunned by friends is not sufficient. However, being shunned by clients will suffice, due to the financial impact on your business.[14] The damage must, as always, not be too remote. In defamation cases, the test for remoteness, as stated by *Lynch v Knight*,[15] is that the loss is such as might fairly and reasonably

---

7   [2001] 2 A.C. 127.

8   A claimant may also wish to consider an action in negligence or misuse of private information. See Chs 2 and 15.

9   See, in particular, Ch.2 of the report of the Faulks Committee in 1975 (Report of the Committee on Defamation, Cmnd.5909).

10   Or even a waxwork: *Monson v Tussauds Ltd* [1894] 1 Q.B. 671 CA.

11   It is generally suggested that sign language would be treated as slander.

12   See, e.g. *Jameel v Dow Jones & Co Inc* [2005] EWCA Civ 75; [2005] Q.B. 946.

13   *Lachaux v Independent Print Ltd* [2019] UKSC 27; [2020] A.C. 612.

14   See *Storey v Challands* (1837) 8 Car. & P. 234; 173 E.R. 475 and *McManus v Beckham* [2002] EWCA Civ 939; [2002] 1 W.L.R. 2982.

15   (1861) 9 H.L Cas. 577 at 600; 11 E.R. 854 (Lord Wensleydale).

on the facts of the case have been anticipated and feared to result. Libel, unlike slander, is also a crime, although few prosecutions are brought.

Unfortunately, the distinction between libel and slander is far from watertight. A spoken insult in the presence of your peers may do more harm to your reputation than insults in a disreputable newspaper. The distinction may also be quite complicated. For example, I dictate a letter to my secretary who then posts it. It contains defamatory material. On the current case law, the letter once sent amounts to libel for which I am responsible, but my dictation to the secretary is merely slander.[16] Further problems arise if you consider what happens if the spoken words are recorded on tape: do they now amount to libel? What about insulting words in a long-running play—can they really be considered slander when repeated every night? In the latter case, Parliament has helpfully intervened and stated that performances of a play (except when given on a domestic occasion in a private dwelling) shall be treated as publication in permanent form and therefore libel.[17] Equally, broadcasts on television or on radio are treated as libel.[18] *Youssoupoff v MGM Pictures Ltd*[19] deals somewhat confusingly with our first problem. Here, a Russian Princess complained about words used in the film soundtrack to "Rasputin, the Mad Monk", which she claimed had falsely suggested that she had been raped or seduced by Rasputin. The court took the view that speech which was synchronised with the film took a permanent form and should be treated as libel. Logically, therefore, if the film broke down but the words continued it would be slander. Yet, this ignores the fact that although the words are merely heard, they are permanently recorded which, it is submitted, suggests that they should be considered to be libel. Further examples of unresolved problems include whether writing in chalk on a wall[20] or sky-writing by aeroplanes[21] amounts to libel or slander. Such uncertainty, it is submitted, is as good a reason as any for abolishing the distinction between libel and slander.

Types of slander actionable per se

In the past, there were four occasions where slander was actionable without proof of damage. These represented occasions where the court felt safe in presuming damage, because of the nature of the allegations made. As will be seen, the Defamation Act 2013 s.14 abolishes the third and fourth examples, but leaves the first two occasions intact. They will, however, be subject to the s.1 threshold of the Defamation Act 2013.

13–003

---

16   *Osborn v Thomas Boulter & Son* [1930] 2 K.B. 226.

17   Theatres Act 1968 s.4(1).

18   Broadcasting Act 1990 s.166.

19   (1934) 50 T.L.R. 581.

20   See *Monson v Tussauds Ltd* (1894) 1 Q.B. 671 at 692 which suggests it should be treated as libel.

21   The Faulks Committee at para.76 suggested that it would be libel due to the fact that the vapour takes some time to disperse.

(1) Imputation of a criminal offence punishable by imprisonment

13–004

There must be an imputation that a criminal offence has been committed. For example, in *Webb v Beavan*,[22] it was stated that "I will look you up in Gloucester gaol next week. I know enough to put you there". This was held to imply that a criminal offence had been committed and so was actionable per se. An allegation that an individual is suspected of a criminal offence will not suffice.[23]

(2) Imputation of professional unfitness or incompetence

13–005

This is the most important exception. A statement criticising a person's professional competence or fitness for office may affect his or her reputation and will be difficult to brush off. The only question which has arisen here relates to the scope of the exception. At common law, it was held that the accusation had to relate directly to the person's professional competence. The exception therefore did not apply where the accusation was unrelated to the post, for example where a headmaster was accused of committing adultery with one of the school's cleaners.[24] The exception was broadened by the Defamation Act 1952 s.2 to include all words likely to disparage the claimant's official, professional or business reputation, whether or not the words relate to the claimant's office, profession, calling, trade or business.

(3) Imputation of unchastity or adultery by a female (abolished by the Defamation Act 2013 s.14(1))

13–006

This was stated to be actionable per se under the Slander of Women Act 1891 s.1. The Ministry of Justice in its consultation for the Defamation Bill found it to be outdated and potentially discriminatory[25] and the 1891 Act has now been repealed.

(4) Imputation of a contagious disease (now requires special damage: Defamation Act 2013 s.14(2))

13–007

This was originally used in relation to allegations that the claimant had a contagious disease such as venereal disease, leprosy or plague. The last reported case under this head was in

---

22 (1883) 11 Q.B.D. 609.
23 *Simmons v Mitchell* (1880) 6 App. Cas. 156 PC.
24 *Jones v Jones* [1916] 2 A.C. 481. Applied in *Hopwood v Muirson* [1945] K.B. 313 (solicitor criticised whilst acting as referee for friend).
25 See *Draft Defamation Bill Consultation* (Consultation Paper CP3/11), 9.

1844,[26] but it had been suggested that it might still be relevant to diseases such as AIDS. Again, the Ministry of Justice found it to be outdated and s.14(2) now provides that:

> "the publication of a statement that conveys the imputation that a person has a contagious or infectious disease does not give rise to a cause of action for slander unless the publication causes the person special damage."

As may be seen, the distinction between libel and slander still has a basis at law and the Defamation Act 2013 makes no effort to change this. It has been justified on the basis that the requirement of special damage excludes minor claims for slander where the claimant has suffered little harm, but in reality, the cost of bringing a defamation claim, and procedural rules against vexatious litigants, are likely to deter such claimants in any event.

The General Requirements of Defamation

As stated above, the best way of approaching defamation is by logically answering the following four questions:

13–008

- Is the statement defamatory?

- Does it refer to the claimant?

- Has it been published to a third party?

- Can the defendant rely on any of the defences?

Judge and jury?

An action for defamation, unlike one for negligence, has traditionally been heard by a judge and jury. This presumption could be rebutted, however, where the court was of the opinion that the trial required a prolonged examination of documents or accounts, or any scientific or local investigation which could not conveniently be made with a jury.[27] In practice, this occurred in a large number of cases. Defamation Act 2013 s.11 now changes this presumption. It provides

13–009

---

26   *Bloodworth v Gray* (1844) 7 Man & G 334; 135 E.R. 140 (venereal disease).

27   Senior Courts Act 1981 s.69.

that the defamation trial should be *without a jury* unless the court orders otherwise.[28] By removing the presumption in favour of jury trial in defamation cases, the Government hoped to reduce the cost and length of defamation cases.

In *Yeo v Times Newspapers Ltd*,[29] the operation of s.11 was immediately tested. The case concerned a libel claim brought by an MP (Tim Yeo) who had chaired a Parliamentary select committee and related to the publication of articles alleging that he had been prepared to abuse his position by acting as a paid Parliamentary advocate. *The Times* newspaper applied for an order that the case be tried with a jury. The court held, however, that there was no reason to rebut the presumption in s.11 against a jury trial. Section 11 meant that trial by jury for libel and slander *would be the exception rather than the rule*. The defendant had not identified any skills, knowledge, aptitudes or other attributes likely to be possessed by a jury which would make it better equipped than a judge to grapple with the issues that needed to be tried. Indeed, the judge added that where the subject-matter of a libel case was political, it was especially desirable that the court's judgment explained what conclusions it had reached and why. Yeo's prominent status and powerful position did not mean that there would be any suspicion of bias if a judge returned a verdict in his favour so as rebut the presumption against jury trial. Moreover, trial by jury invariably took longer and was more expensive than a trial without a jury. On this basis, the court concluded that "Parliament no longer regards jury trial as a right of 'the highest importance' in defamation cases. It is no longer a right at all".[30]

If the court does order a jury trial, the role of judge and jury are as follows. The judge will determine, as a matter of law, whether the words are capable of being defamatory, that is, could a reasonable jury come to the conclusion that the statement was capable of bearing a defamatory meaning?[31] The jury will determine whether, as a matter of fact, the words in the case are defamatory. The jury will also determine the level of damages and may, if appropriate, award aggravated or punitive damages.

The first three questions listed above will be examined in this chapter. Defences will be examined in Ch.14.

(1) Is the statement defamatory?

13–010

The test of what is defamatory is now partly statutory and partly common law, by virtue of the Defamation Act 2013 s.1. We can say then: a statement is defamatory if it has caused or is likely to cause serious harm to a person's reputation.

It is important, first of all, to identify whether the claimant's reputation has been harmed.

---

28   Amending the Senior Courts Act 1981 s.69(1) to exclude libel and slander from its list.
29   [2014] EWHC 2853 (QB); [2015] 1 W.L.R. 971.
30   [2014] EWHC 2853 (QB); [2015] 1 W.L.R. 971 at [47] per Warby J.
31   *Capital and Counties Bank Ltd v Henty* (1882) 7 App. Cas. 741, although the application of the test in this case is less than satisfactory. See also *Mark v Associated Newspapers Ltd* [2002] EWCA Civ 772; [2002] E.M.L.R. 38.

The classic definition is found in *Sim v Stretch*,[32] where statements were held to be defamatory and therefore to harm a person's reputation when they "tend to lower the plaintiff in the estimation of right-thinking members of society generally".[33] This has been extended by *Youssoupoff v MGM Pictures Ltd*[34] to circumstances where the claimant is "shunned or avoided" as a result of the statements. The question is therefore whether your reputation has been harmed in the eyes of "right-thinking members of society". Essentially, this is the standard of the "reasonable person", who is, of course, a fiction, but this sets at least an objective standard to be applied by the courts. The reasonable person, we are told, is fair-minded, neither unduly suspicious nor unduly naive, nor avid for scandal, nor bound to select one defamatory meaning when non-defamatory meanings are available.[35] (If there is a jury trial, it will be determined partly by the judge, who decides whether the statement in question is capable of being defamatory before it can be put before a jury). This can raise questions as to the ability of the courts to relate to the standards of society in general. For example, in *Byrne v Deane*,[36] a verse had been placed on the notice-board of a golf club which stated: "But he who gave the game away, may he byrnne [*sic*] in hell and rue the day". Mr Byrne, who was a member of the club, alleged that it implied that he had informed the police of certain illegal gambling machines which had been on the premises and which had been removed as a result. The Court of Appeal held that the verse was not defamatory. An allegation that he had reported a crime to the police could not be regarded as lowering the reputation of Mr Byrne, certainly not in the eyes of a "good and worthy subject of the King". The resulting distress and perhaps isolation suffered by Mr Byrne as a result of the verse were regarded as irrelevant. There is therefore a distinct danger that the standard of "right-thinking people" may rise far above the general standards of society, and fail to protect the claimant's reputation adequately by assuming that right-thinking people could not possibly conclude that a particular statement is defamatory.

Further difficulties may be seen when this test is applied to allegations of adultery and homosexuality. Whilst clearly defamatory in the past, it might be suggested that in more liberal times, they would no longer affect a person's reputation. The court must choose between a liberal approach and an appreciation that such a view may not be shared by every member of society. Who, then, is the right-thinking member of society? In *R. v Bishop*,[37] the court

---

32 [1936] 2 All E.R. 1237.

33 [1936] 2 All E.R. 1237 at 1240 HL per Lord Atkin. This presumes that the claimant's reputation can be lowered: see *Williams v MGN Ltd* [2009] EWHC 3150 (QB) claimant in a libel action with a background of serious criminal convictions had no reputation capable of protection.

34 (1934) 50 T.L.R. 581. See L. Treiger-Bar-Am, "Defamation law in a changing society" (2000) 20 L.S. 291.

35 See *Lewis v Daily Telegraph* [1964] A.C. 234 at 259–260 per Lord Reid and *Jeynes v News Magazines Ltd* [2008] EWCA Civ 130 at [14] per Sir Anthony Clarke MR. Society would appear to signify society as a whole and not simply a section of the community: *Tolley v Fry* [1930] 1 K.B. 467 at 479. It has been suggested that, in view of the more diverse nature of society today and the fact that the reputation of a person within his or her own racial or religious community may be damaged by a statement which would not be regarded as damaging by society at large, this may need to be re-addressed in future: *Arab News Network v Al-Khazen* [2001] EWCA Civ 118.

36 [1937] 1 K.B. 818 at 833.

37 [1975] Q.B. 274 at 281. The case itself concerned the admissibility of character evidence.

recognised that the legalisation of homosexuality in the Sexual Offences Act 1967 did not necessarily change the views of society, and that, in 1975, many still regarded homosexuality as immoral. It is an open question whether this is still the case today. Arguably, the situation is different for adultery. In a society where one in three marriages fail, one might expect a more tolerant view of adultery and sex outside marriage. On this basis, a statement that X is an adulterer should not be regarded as defamatory, unless it suggests that X is a hypocrite, for example, he is a clergyman or the Minister for the Family.[38]

13–011

In recent years, the courts have added the requirement that, to be defamatory, a statement must surmount what has been called "a threshold requirement of seriousness". By this means the courts have sought to exclude trivial claims, taking the view that the hypothetical reasonable claimant should not be unduly sensitive to criticism which does little harm to his or her reputation. In *Thornton v Telegraph Media Group*,[39] Tugendhat J argued that imposing liability for defamation where the claimant had suffered no or minimal damage to his or her reputation would constitute an interference with freedom of expression which could not be justified under ECHR art.10.2.[40]

Defamation Act 2013 s.1 now imposes a test of "serious harm" to the reputation. This provides that:

> **"(1) A statement is not defamatory unless its publication has caused or is likely to cause serious harm to the reputation of the claimant.**
> **(2) For the purposes of this section, harm to the reputation of a body that trades for profit is not 'serious harm' unless it has caused or is likely to cause the body serious financial loss."**

This means, therefore, that to be defamatory, the claimant musts show, on the balance of probabilities, that the statement has caused (or is likely to cause) "serious harm" to the claimant's reputation. "Serious harm" is not defined, however, and so we must look to cases for guidance. In the first case on this topic—*Cooke v MGN Ltd*[41]—the court held that s.1 raised the bar for claimants. It is not enough simply to show injury to feelings, even if grave. The court will have regard to all the relevant circumstances, including evidence of what happened after publication. A prompt and prominent apology which minimised any unfavourable impression of the claimant would, therefore, be taken into account in assessing harm to reputation, particularly

---

38   See also *Gatley on Libel and Slander*, 12th edn (Sweet and Maxwell, 2013), para.4.17, which suggests that an imputation against a judge of inattentiveness or falling asleep on the bench would qualify as defamatory but not, today, one of adultery.

39   [2010] EWHC 1414 (QB); [2011] 1 W.L.R. 1985.

40   [2010] EWHC 1414 (QB); [2011] 1 W.L.R. 1985 at [90].

41   [2014] EWHC 2831 (QB); [2015] 1 W.L.R. 895. For criticism of the requirement of serious harm, see E. Descheemaeker, "Three errors in the Defamation Act 2013" (2015) 6 J.E.T.L. 1.

if the apology remained available online and was more accessible than the original article. The court also suggested that evidence of serious harm could be presumed where the statements in question were obviously likely to cause serious harm to a person's reputation, such as where a national newspaper wrongly accuses someone of being a paedophile or a terrorist.

The question of serious harm was re-examined by the Supreme Court in 2019. In *Lachaux v Independent Print Ltd*,[42] a number of newspaper articles had alleged that Lachaux had mistreated his ex-wife. Faced with a defamation action, the newspapers claimed that the articles were not defamatory because they had neither caused nor were likely to cause Lachaux serious harm to his reputation under s.1(1). The Supreme Court emphasised that s.1(1) had altered the previous law and this meant that it would no longer suffice that the statement had an inherent tendency to cause some harm to the reputation (the "meaning" test). The Court had to address the actual impact of the words used on those to whom they were communicated. In looking at the consequences of publication, the Court would still consider the meaning of the words, but in combination with consideration of their impact on others.

> "Mr Lachaux must demonstrate as a fact that the harm caused by the publications complained of was serious . . . [A] finding of serious harm [could be based] on (i) the scale of the publications; (ii) the fact that the statements complained of had come to the attention of at least one identifiable person in the United Kingdom who knew Mr Lachaux and (iii) that they were likely to have come to the attention of others who either knew him or would come to know him in future; and (iv) the gravity of the statements themselves . . . There is no reason why inferences of fact as to the seriousness of the harm done to Mr Lachaux's reputation should not be drawn from considerations of this kind."[43]

The emphasis of the Court is that s.1 has changed the common law in the interests of protecting free speech. The claimant can show serious harm by relying on extrinsic evidence e.g. statements from witnesses, or inferences of fact.

For companies (i.e. a body that trades for profit),[44] more is required—serious <u>financial</u> loss. For companies, therefore, it is not enough to show that the defamatory statement is likely to cause serious harm to their reputation, the claimant must show that actual financial loss is likely to result. While the Government admitted that this raised a little the hurdle for claimants in defamation, it took the view that it would not bar any claimant who had serious problems as a result of a publication.[45] The clear aim is to prevent trivial and unfounded actions going to

---

42 [2019] UKSC 27; [2020] A.C. 612.

43 [2019] UKSC 27 at [21] per Lord Sumption.

44 See D. J. Acheson, "The Defamation Act 2013: What exactly is 'a body that trades for profit'?" (2015) 20 Comms L. 113.

45 Lord Chancellor and Secretary of State for Justice, *Hansard* HC 12 June 2012: col.181 (Second Reading of Defamation Bill).

trial.[46] In *Brett Wilson LLP v Person(s) Unknown*,[47] for example, the solicitors' firm was able to show serious financial loss where unknown persons had been operating a website which had accused the firm of misconduct. It was able to point to a prospective client who had withdrawn instructions on the basis of the website and, as a firm that attracted a considerable amount of its work from the internet, it was inevitable that it would impact on prospective clients in general.

13–012

It should also be noted that it is no excuse that the defendant did not intend the words to be defamatory.[48] The law protects reputation and it cannot be said that the statement does not affect the claimant's reputation just because the insult was unintentional. The test is objective, and it is irrelevant that the defendant did not intend to defame the claimant, or even whether the people to whom the statement was communicated actually believed the statement to be true.[49] The defendant may, however, be able to claim that the words should not be treated as defamatory because the statement was mere abuse uttered in rage ("You idiot!") and was not intended to be taken seriously. This is a very fine line. While the courts may be prepared to disregard words spoken in the heat of the moment, which the hearer must have understood to be mere abuse, they are unlikely to dismiss written words on this basis. A number of claims have arisen from postings on social media and the courts have made clear that outrageous statements on Twitter can give rise to successful claims for defamation.[50] In terms of articles in newspapers, the general view is that the writer will have had the opportunity to cool down and repent, so that if the words are published nevertheless, they cannot be dismissed as mere abuse. In *Berkoff v Burchill*,[51] the majority of the Court of Appeal held that a published description of the actor, director and writer Steven Berkoff as "hideously ugly" was capable of being defamatory and could not be dismissed as mere abuse. He was a person in the public eye and it was held that such a description would expose him to ridicule as it suggested that he had a repulsive appearance. Such cases must now be read, however, in the light of the s.1(1) serious harm test.

---

46   It should also be noted that trivial claims may be struck out under the doctrine of abuse of process: *Jameel v Dow Jones & Co Inc* [2005] EWCA Civ 75; [2005] Q.B. 946 (needs to be a real and substantial tort).

47   [2015] EWHC 2628 (QB); [2016] 4 W.L.R. 69. Contrast *Undre v Harrow LBC* [2016] EWHC 931 (QB); [2017] E.M.L.R. 3 where the judge advised that a good starting point would be to ask whether the company has proved that its financial position had worsened after the publication complained of, compared with its previous position.

48   The intention of the defendant may, however, be relevant in relation to possible defences (see Ch.14) or at least diminish the award of damages.

49   See *Morgan v Odhams Press* [1971] 1 W.L.R. 1239 at 1246 and 1252.

50   *Monroe v Hopkins* [2017] EWHC 433 (QB); [2017] 4 W.L.R. 68 (journalist Katie Hopkins was ordered to pay damages of £24,000 to Jack Monroe, a food blogger with left-wing views whom she had defamed on Twitter.)

51   [1996] 4 All E.R. 1008. But contrast *Norman v Future Publishing Ltd* [1999] E.M.L.R. 325 CA.

Innuendo

Defamation is not confined to direct attacks on the claimant's reputation. If this were so, a defendant could easily resort to indirect attacks, safe in the knowledge that the audience would be well aware of what was actually being alleged, and yet the claimant could do nothing. To protect the claimant's reputation, defamation must also include implied or veiled attacks, which are generally known as "innuendo". An innuendo consists of an implied attack on a person's reputation. The test is objective: what view would a reasonable person take of the statement? It is no defence that the defendant had not (or could not have) reasonably foreseen that the statement contained an innuendo.[52] There are two types of innuendo: true (or legal) and false (or popular). A true innuendo is one where the attack is truly hidden in the absence of special facts and circumstances, which the claimant must show are known by some of the people to whom the statement is published. The court will obviously have to be informed in the Statement of Case what special meanings are alleged and what facts support this meaning.[53] A false or popular innuendo is one which a reasonable person guided by general knowledge would infer from the natural and ordinary meaning of the words.[54] The court does not have to be informed of any specific facts to draw this inference. This is a complicated distinction, and an example will help the reader to understand the distinction between true and false innuendo. Suppose that A publishes a statement that B works for "the family business". By itself, this is not defamatory unless:

- B's father has been arrested for involvement with the Mafia. With this extra knowledge, we now know that A is implying that B works for the Mafia and is involved in organised crime. This is defamatory as a true innuendo.

- B can show that the term "family business" is known to be a slang term for the Mafia. This is unlikely here, but if B were successful, he would be relying on a false or popular innuendo.

A true innuendo was relied upon in *Tolley v JS Fry & Sons Ltd*,[55] where a famous amateur golfer alleged that a caricature of him had appeared without his knowledge or consent in an advertisement for Frys Chocolate. This, in itself, was not defamatory. However, Tolley claimed that for people who knew of his amateur status it would imply that, contrary to acceptable amateur conduct, he had accepted money. The House of Lords held the advertisement to be capable of bearing the meaning alleged in the innuendo. People knowing of Tolley's amateur status might think less of him and therefore his reputation would be diminished.[56] Equally, in *Cassidy*

---

52 *Baturina v Times Newspapers Ltd* [2011] EWCA Civ 308; [2011] 1 W.L.R. 1526. This position was held to be consistent with ECHR art.10.
53 See Practice Direction–Defamation Claims Pt 53B r.4.2.
54 See, generally, *Lewis v Daily Telegraph Ltd* [1964] A.C. 234 at 271–272 per Lord Hodson.
55 [1931] A.C. 333.
56 Evidence was given that he would have been called on to resign the membership of any reputable golf club.

v Daily Mirror Newspapers Ltd,[57] there was nothing defamatory in publishing a photograph depicting Cassidy and a young woman announcing that they were engaged. However, the fact that Mr Cassidy was still married led the majority of the Court of Appeal to recognise that the words were defamatory of the existing Mrs Cassidy, on the basis that a reasonable person knowing of their relationship might assume that she had cohabited with Cassidy outside marriage. This, in 1928, would be regarded in a negative light. It was no excuse that the newspaper did not know that Cassidy was already married, and had in fact been told by Cassidy that he was engaged to the woman with whom he had been photographed.

Lewis v Daily Telegraph Ltd[58] is a good illustration of how courts deal with a false innuendo. Here, the defendants had published a paragraph in their newspaper which indicated that the Fraud Squad was investigating the affairs of a company and its chairman, Mr Lewis. This was in fact true, and so the claim for defamation on the literal meaning of the words failed. However, it was also claimed that the paragraph contained an innuendo—it indicated that the company was being operated in a fraudulent and dishonest way. The majority of the House of Lords held that the words were not capable of bearing that meaning. The test was an objective one: what would an ordinary and reasonable person infer as the natural and ordinary meaning of these words? The court held that a reasonable person might infer from the paragraph that the company and Lewis were *suspected* of fraud, but held that a reasonable person would not assume that a police investigation indicated that Lewis and the company were *guilty* of such conduct. This has to be correct, otherwise newspapers would be unable to report investigations prior to their final result. The court also recommended that, for clarity, claimants should set out the meaning of the false innuendo on which they wish to rely if it does not speak for itself.[59] This will enable the defendant to be fully aware of the case against him or her and will clarify issues prior to trial.

13–014

The general test is therefore: would the reasonable person view the statement as defamatory on the particular facts of the case? The courts do look at the statements in context. It is not enough to point to a particular sentence or isolated paragraph. The court will look at the article as a whole. This is illustrated by the approach of the House of Lords in *Charleston v News Group Newspapers Ltd*.[60] The *News of the World* had run a story about a computer game, which featured near-naked bodies of models in pornographic poses, on which the heads of two characters from the Australian soap "Neighbours" (Madge and Harold Bishop) had been

---

57 [1929] 2 K.B. 331.
58 [1964] A.C. 234 at 258. See also *Mapp v News Group Newspapers Ltd* [1998] Q.B. 520. Contrast *Hayward v Thompson* [1982] Q.B. 47, where the words "connected with" a murder plot were held to be plainly capable of conveying to ordinary persons the imputation of Hayward's guilt.
59 [1964] A.C. 234 at 281 and 273. Note Lord Denning MR in *Allsop v Church of England Newspaper Ltd* [1972] 2 Q.B. 161 at 167 who stated that, in most cases, it is not only desirable but necessary for the claimant to set out in the Case Statement the meaning which he or she says the words bear unless there is only one ordinary meaning which is clear and explicit. See now CPR Pt 53.
60 [1995] 2 A.C. 65. See also *Butt v Secretary of State for the Home Department* [2019] EWCA Civ 933 (cannot read one paragraph of a government press release in isolation—this is something an ordinary reader would not do).

superimposed. The headline read "Strewth! What's Harold up to with our Madge?" and was accompanied by photographs of the characters as depicted in the game. The actors complained that the photographs suggested that they had participated in some way in the making of the game. Although the accompanying article made it clear that the actors had not participated in any way, it was argued that a significant proportion of readers skimming through the newspaper would only read the headlines and look at the photographs, and would come to the wrong conclusions. The court refused to approach the case in this way. "Defamatory" was judged by the standard of the ordinary reasonable person, who would have taken the trouble to discover what the article was about. It was therefore irrelevant that the *News of the World* might have had some readers who only read the headlines.[61] Lord Nicholls did warn newspapers, however, that they were "playing with fire", and that if the explanatory text were tucked away further down the article or on a continuation page, the court would be likely to take a different view.[62]

More recently, the question has arisen to what extent the context of social media should be taken into account, given that people tend to engage with it more casually, in the nature of a conversation rather than a written text. In *Stocker v Stocker*,[63] the Supreme Court advised that a judge tasked with deciding how a reasonable social media user would interpret a statement made on social media, such as a Facebook post or a tweet on Twitter, had to keep in mind the way in which such postings and tweets were made and read, i.e. quickly whilst scrolling through messages. Here "tried to strangle" was taken more generally than its dictionary definition of attempted murder to signify an allegation that the claimant had grasped the defendant by the throat (for which she could establish a defence of truth).

Once the claimant has shown that the words used were defamatory, he or she must move on to the second requirement and show that the words in fact referred to him or her.

(2) Does the statement refer to the claimant?

This is obviously not a problem if the claimant is mentioned by name, but otherwise the question is: would the reasonable person, having knowledge of the special circumstances, understand the words to refer to the claimant?[64] This was considered by the House of Lords in *Morgan v Odhams Press Ltd*.[65] A newspaper article in *The Sun* newspaper had reported that a girl had been kidnapped by a dog-doping gang. This was incorrect and the girl had been staying at Mr Morgan's flat at the relevant time. Morgan produced a small number of witnesses who had seen the two together and who claimed that, having read the article, they assumed it to suggest that Morgan was part of the dog-doping gang. The majority of the House held that

13–015

---

61 [1995] 2 A.C. 65 at 73 per Lord Bridge.
62 [1995] 2 A.C. 65 at 74.
63 [2019] UKSC 17; [2019] 2 W.L.R. 1033.
64 *Morgan v Odhams Press Ltd* [1971] 1 W.L.R. 1239.
65 [1971] 1 W.L.R. 1239 at 1245 and 1269–1270.

on the facts there was sufficient material for a jury to find that the statement referred to him. It was not necessary to find a specific "pointer" in the article, or a "peg" on which to hang such a reference. Although a careful study of the article would have suggested that it could not refer to Morgan, it was held that the ordinary, reasonable reader did not have the forensic skills of a lawyer. The majority of the House held that, taking account of the sensationalist nature of the article, and the fact that the average reader was likely to read the story casually, gaining a general impression of it, the ordinary reasonable person would, on the facts, have drawn the inference that the article referred to Morgan.[66] A new trial was ordered nevertheless, due to the judge's misdirection to the jury on the assessment of damages.

It is generally the rule that the meaning of any statement must be judged at the time of publication. Liability will not arise where an innocent statement is later rendered defamatory by subsequent events.[67] However, the courts will not allow this rule to be used to "cover up" defamatory statements where the defendant has made a defamatory statement, but only identified the claimant in a later article. Therefore, in *Hayward v Thompson*,[68] the Court of Appeal admitted in evidence a later article identifying the plaintiff where the first article had merely referred to "a wealthy benefactor of the Liberal party". On this basis, both articles were found to be defamatory of the defendant.[69] The key, as the Privy Council explained recently, is that there must be created a sufficient nexus, connection or association between the statements in the mind of the reasonable reader to enable the reader to identify the claimant as the subject of the defamatory accusation.[70] Further, the Privy Council warned, even where this exists, there is the possibility that the later article identifying the claimant may take away the defamatory sting of the first.

13–016

As stated above, it is irrelevant whether the defendant intended the words to be defamatory. It is equally irrelevant whether the defendant intended to refer to the claimant. Provided reasonable persons would find the statement defamatory, and to refer to the claimant, the defendant who publishes the statement will be liable. *Hulton & Co v Jones*[71] is the classic example. The defendant newspaper had published a humorous account of a motor festival in Dieppe, featuring the antics of a fictional churchwarden from Peckham called Artemus Jones. Unfortunately for the newspaper, this was also the name of a barrister, who sued for libel. The real Mr Jones was not a churchwarden, had not gone to the Dieppe festival and did not live in Peckham, but friends of his swore that they believed the article to refer to him. The House of Lords held that there was evidence upon which the jury could conclude that reasonable people would believe

---

66 Note the contrast with the approach taken by the House of Lords in the more recent case of *Charleston v News Group Newspapers Ltd* [1995] 2 A.C. 65, discussed above.
67 *Grappelli v Derek Block (Holdings) Ltd* [1981] 1 W.L.R. 822.
68 [1982] Q.B. 47.
69 In any event, there was evidence that a number of people had identified Mr Hayward from the context of the first article, including his family, other members of the Liberal party and innumerable journalists.
70 *Simon v Lyder* [2019] UKPC 38; [2020] A.C. 650 at [21] per Lord Briggs.
71 [1910] A.C. 20. The Faulks Committee recommended no change in the rule of *Hulton v Jones* (para.123).

Mr Jones was referred to and it was irrelevant that the defendants had no intention to defame him.[72]

It is of no assistance to the defendant that the words were true of another individual. In *Newstead v London Express Newspaper Ltd*,[73] a report of the conviction for bigamy of a Harold Newstead, aged 30, of Camberwell, London provoked an action for defamation from another Harold Newstead who also lived in Camberwell and who was about the same age. The Court of Appeal upheld his claim against the newspaper. *Newstead* is perhaps a more meritorious case than *Hulton*. Such a coincidence was obviously prejudicial to the reputation of the innocent Mr Newstead, and the newspaper should therefore have made greater efforts to identify the real culprit. The decision does impose a considerable burden on newspapers, however, which cannot possibly check every story to ascertain whether there is any chance of confusion as to the identity of the person involved. This was recognised by the court, but it was held that it was not unreasonable to place a burden on the party who puts the statements into circulation to identify the person so closely that little or no risk of confusion arises.[74]

The question arises, however, whether it is reasonable to expect newspapers to bear the risk of a person being mistaken for another individual in a photograph in the paper. This problem arose in *O'Shea v MGN Ltd*,[75] where the *Sunday Mirror* had published an advertisement for an adult internet service featuring a "glamour" model, who resembled the claimant. Ms O'Shea complained that ordinary sensible readers, who were aware of her resemblance to the model, would have concluded that she had consented to appear on a highly pornographic website. Whilst concluding that, as a matter of law, the image was defamatory,[76] Morland J held that liability would be contrary to the European Convention on Human Rights art.10. Protection of Ms O'Shea's reputation could not be said to meet a "pressing social need"[77] and to be necessary in a democratic society for the protection of the reputation of others.[78] The judge distinguished *Hulton* and *Newstead* on the basis that the existence of the claimants could have been discovered in those cases, whereas it would have been impossible in *O'Shea*. Liability would impose an "impossible burden" on the publisher, which could not be justified.[79]

It may be questioned whether such a distinction is valid. Ms O'Shea had been accidentally defamed, as had Mr Jones, and it may be challenged whether the form the statement takes should be of such crucial importance. If the true objection is to liability for unintentional

---

72 W.E. Peel and J. Goudkamp, *Winfield & Jolowicz on Torts*, 19th edn (Sweet and Maxwell, 2014), 13–08, note that Jones had once worked for the newspaper. This might have influenced the jury, even though his counsel accepted that the newspaper staff had forgotten about him.

73 [1940] 1 K.B. 377.

74 [1940] 1 K.B. 377 at 388 per Greene MR.

75 [2001] E.M.L.R. 40 (QBD).

76 See *Dwek v Macmillan Publishers Ltd* [2000] E.M.L.R. 284 CA (photograph described as Dodi Fayed with a prostitute was, in fact, of the claimant).

77 See Lord Keith in *Derbyshire CC v Times Newspapers* [1993] A.C. 534 at 550.

78 See ECHR art.10.2.

79 *O'Shea v MGN Ltd* [2001] E.M.L.R. 40 (QBD) at [43]. Morland J was additionally concerned that liability would inhibit investigative journalism into drug dealing, corruption, child abuse and prostitution.

defamation, can the art.10 right to freedom of expression be confined to photographs? At present, *O'Shea* appears to be treated as an isolated exception[80] and the general rule remains. It remains to be seen whether the case can in future found a basis to challenge this form of liability.

If confusion as to identity does arise, the defendant has only two options:

- To argue that there is not enough evidence for a reasonable person to identify the claimant; or.

- To adopt a defence of unintentional defamation. This will be discussed in the next chapter, but generally involves an apology and offer to pay some compensation.

Group defamation

13-017

If the statement in question relates to a group of individuals, it will be difficult for the claimant to establish that the words refer to him or her directly. Unless the group in question has legal identity, for example is a company, and can therefore sue for loss of the group's reputation, no action will stand unless:

- the class is so small that the claimant can establish that the statement must apply to every member of the class; or

- the claimant can show that the statement refers to him or her directly.

The leading case on group defamation is the House of Lords case of *Knuppfer v London Express Newspaper Ltd*.[81] In this case, an article had been published which criticised the Young Russian political party, Mlado Russ. The party consisted of several thousand members, but they were mainly overseas and the British branch consisted of only 24 members. Knuppfer was one of these members. To establish that the libel referred directly to him, he alleged that because he was the head of the British branch, British readers would assume the remarks referred to him. This argument was rejected by the House of Lords. It was held that the article was not capable of referring to Knuppfer. There had been no mention of the activities of the party in the UK and their Lordships found no evidence to infer that the article referred to Knuppfer. Lord Porter advised that in deciding whether the article was capable of referring to the claimant, the court should examine the size of the class, the generality of the charge and the extravagance of the

---

80 The Court of Appeal in *Baturina v Times Newspapers Ltd* [2011] EWCA Civ 308; [2011] 1 W.L.R. 1526 (at [29]) argued that it might be better explained as a small extension of the *Reynolds* qualified privilege defence, discussed in Ch.14.

81 [1944] A.C. 116. For a more recent example on similar facts, see *Tilbrook v Parr* [2012] EWHC 1946 (QB): unsuccessful claim of chairman of English Democrats party.

accusation.[82] The true test was whether a reasonable man could find that the article was capable of referring to the claimant.

As a general rule, therefore, a statement aimed at a group will not be considered to refer to its individual members. On this basis, a politician could not sue a newspaper which printed "All politicians are liars" unless he or she could show something which referred specifically to him or her.[83] It will depend on the facts of the case. Obviously, the smaller the group and more specific the charge, the easier it will be to show that the article refers to the claimant. For example, a statement that the local five-a-side team are utterly incompetent obviously refers to five particular individuals.[84]

(3) Has the statement been published to a third party?

This third requirement is vital.[85] It is not enough, for example, that the defendant sends a letter to the claimant making lurid accusations against him or her. This will not harm his or her reputation, although he or she may be distressed by it. It is only when the letter is seen by a third party (or "published") that the claimant's reputation will be harmed.[86] It can be seen that "publication" has nothing to do with printing presses, but signifies that the libel or slander has come to the knowledge of a third party. The claimant's reputation will only suffer harm when the offending words are communicated to someone other than the claimant and the defendant. Insulting words spoken to the claimant in private by the defendant are not defamatory, although they may of course give rise to claims for harassment or assault. Although readers may see the term "malicious publication" used, this should not be taken literally. Malice is not required. I therefore use the simple term "publication".

The requirement of publication is obviously met by printing an article in a newspaper or book, or by shouting a remark in a lecture theatre, and will not generally be a problem. It is really a matter of common sense. For example, if I make defamatory statements in my lecture and the students (a) cannot understand me because I am speaking in old Norse,[87] or (b) cannot hear me because my microphone is not working, I have not published my statements. Publication requires that the words must be intelligible and reach the third party.

Problems have arisen when the defendant alleges that he or she did not intend to publish the words. For example, A sends a letter defamatory of B to B. B alleges in court that it was opened by his wife, Mrs B, and it has therefore been published to a third party enabling him to sue for defamation. A states that he did not intend the letter to be published and therefore he

13–018

---

82 [1944] A.C. 116 at 124.
83 Although political parties cannot sue for defamation, politicians can sue in their own right. This is discussed below under "Who can sue?".
84 See also *Aspro Travel v Owners Abroad Group Plc* [1996] 1 W.L.R. 132, where directors of a limited family company were allowed to sue for defamation in their own right.
85 The Defamation Act 2013 does not seek to change the common law meaning for publication: s.15.
86 This is not the case, however, for criminal libel, where publication to the prosecutor alone will suffice.
87 Unless I am very unlucky and one of my audience understands old Norse!

should not be liable. The courts deal with this by having a test of reasonable foresight: if it is reasonably foreseeable that a third party would see the statement, then the defendant will be liable. On that basis, in *Theaker v Richardson*,[88] the defendant was liable for sending a defamatory letter to a married woman, which had been opened by her husband. The letter, which had been addressed to the wife, had been sealed in a brown envelope which looked like an election circular. The court upheld the view of the jury that it was foreseeable that the husband would open the letter. In contrast, in *Huth v Huth*,[89] it was found that it was not foreseeable that a butler would open his employer's mail. Defendants wishing to avoid publication should ensure that the document is in a sealed envelope marked "private and confidential". Making defamatory remarks on a postcard is obviously unwise and the court will presume, in the absence of evidence to the contrary, that someone will have read the remarks along the way.[90] Similarly, a careless defendant who leaves documents open on his or her desk runs the risk of publication to visitors or perhaps cleaners, but not, it would seem, to a burglar who steals the document from a locked drawer.[91]

A few odd rules remain. It is still the rule (despite the fact that the law no longer regards husband and wife as one person) that a husband does not publish words by telling his wife (or vice versa).[92] A modern explanation for this rule may be a concern for "marital harmony" whereby the courts are reluctant, save in exceptional circumstances, to see spouses give evidence against one another. It also seems to be the rule that while an author who dictates a document to a typist is liable for publication,[93] a typist or printer who hands back to the author a document containing defamatory statements made by the author is deemed not to be liable for publication. This is easier to explain. The typist can hardly publish the document to the author of the document itself.[94] The typist and printer are effectively acting as the author's agents, and an agent repeating back the statements of the principal cannot be treated as publication to a third party. However, if the documents are shown to anyone else, the typist or printer (as well as the author) may be liable for publication of the statements.

In this regard, it should be noted that it is no defence that the defendant is merely repeating the defamatory statements of another.[95] Repetition will increase the harm to the claimant's reputation, for which the defendant will be obliged to pay compensation. The fact that the

---

88   [1962] 1 W.L.R. 151.
89   [1915] 3 K.B. 323.
90   See, e.g. *Sim v Stretch* [1936] 2 All E.R. 1237.
91   *Pullman v Hill* [1891] 1 Q.B. 524 at 527 per Lord Esher MR.
92   *Wennhak v Morgan* (1888) 20 Q.B.D. 635.
93   *Osborn v Thomas Boulter & Son* [1930] 2 K.B. 226.
94   See *Eglantine Inn Ltd v Smith* [1948] N.I. 29 at 33 and *Osborn v Thomas Boulter & Son* [1930] 2 K.B. 226 at 237 per Slesser LJ.
95   *Weld-Blundell v Stephens* [1920] A.C. 956. See also *Stern v Piper* [1997] Q.B. 123 and *Shah v Standard Chartered Bank* [1999] Q.B. 241. This rule was strongly affirmed in *Mark v Associated Newspapers Ltd* [2002] EWCA Civ 772; [2002] E.M.L.R. 38, where it was held to be consistent with the European Convention on Human Rights art.10.

person repeating the libel or slander expresses a doubt or disbelief as to the truth of the statement is irrelevant—repetition is sufficient to incur liability.[96] This has particular impact in relation to social media, e.g. it would be unwise to retweet a serious accusation of criminal behaviour to followers of a popular Twitter account.[97]

There are a limited number of situations, however, where the original defamer will remain liable, namely:

- where the original defamer has authorised or requested publication[98];

- where he or she intended that the statement should be repeated or republished;

- where he or she has informed a person who is under a moral duty to repeat or republish the statement[99]; or, generally,

- where the re-publication is, on the facts, the natural and probable result of the original publication.

This last point was argued in *Slipper v BBC*.[100] Slipper, a former detective superintendent, had complained about a film made and broadcast by the BBC which dealt with his abortive efforts to bring back one of the Great Train Robbers, Ronnie Biggs, from Brazil. Slipper claimed that a press review of the film portrayed him in a defamatory light, and that the BBC were responsible for the repetition of the libel in the newspaper reviews of the film. The Court of Appeal treated the matter as one of causation and remoteness, rather than turning on any particular rule relating to defamation: did the reviews amount to a *novus actus interveniens* breaking the chain of causation? Therefore, if repetition of the libel was the natural and probable consequence of the original publication, the original publisher would remain liable. On the facts, the court held that this was a question for the jury and refused to strike out this part of Slipper's case.

The application of this test was discussed more recently in *McManus v Beckham*.[101] Here, McManus had complained that Victoria Beckham, wife of footballer David Beckham, had entered his memorabilia shop and had advised customers that a signed photograph of her husband for sale in the shop was a forgery. The incident received extensive press coverage, and McManus brought a claim based on subsequent damage to his business. The question

13–019

---

96   *Slipper v BBC* [1991] 1 Q.B. 283.
97   Consider *Lord McAlpine v Bercow* [2013] EWHC 1342 (QB) where Bercow had merely tweeted "why is Lord McAlpine trending? * innocent face* "to her more than 56,000 followers. Mrs Bercow settled the case and advised other Twitter users to behave more responsibly in how they use this platform: Statement in Court, 21 October 2013.
98   e.g. by requesting journalists present to note allegations made during a parish meeting: see *Parkes v Prescott* (1869) L.R. 4 Ex. 169 at 179.
99   *Slipper v BBC* [1991] 1 Q.B. 283 at 301 per Slade LJ.
100 [1991] 1 Q.B. 283.
101 [2002] EWCA Civ 939; [2002] 1 W.L.R. 2982.

remained whether it was a natural and probable consequence of her outburst that it would receive media attention. The Court of Appeal rejected a simple test of reasonable foresight, which had been suggested in *Slipper*. This would impose an unfair burden on the defendant. A just and reasonable result would be achieved by imposing liability:

- where the defendant is actually aware that what she says or does is likely to be reported, and, that if she slanders someone that slander is likely to be repeated in whole or in part; or

- where she should have appreciated that there was a significant risk that what she said would be repeated in whole or in part in the press and that that would increase the damage caused by the slander.[102]

In other words, she will be liable where it was foreseeable to a reasonable person in the position of the defendant that there was a significant risk of repetition, either in whole or in part, and that, in consequence, increased harm to the claimant would ensue.[103] On the facts of the case, it could not be said that it was impossible for the claimants to satisfy this test.[104]

One last question is whether it is possible to publish by omission. For example, in *Byrne v Deane*,[105] discussed earlier, the question arose whether the club could be liable for failing to remove the notice in question. The court held that those responsible for the club would be liable if they failed to remove defamatory matter attached to the club notice-board within a reasonable time.[106] However, if the defamatory matter was not readily removable (for example, carved deep into stonework) and could only be removed at great inconvenience and expense, its non-removal would not amount to publication. Equally, the host of a phone-in show might find himself or herself liable for failing to take reasonable care to prevent controversial guests making defamatory statements. It is therefore a question of control. In this last case, however, the host may now have a defence of innocent dissemination under the Defamation Act 1996 s.1 (see Ch.14).

---

102   [2002] 1 W.L.R. 2982 at 2998 per Waller LJ.

103   [2002] 1 W.L.R. 2982 at 3001 per Laws LJ.

104   The case was ultimately settled, Mrs Beckham paying the claimants £55,000 for the hurt and damage suffered together with a set of official merchandise signed by her husband: Statement in Open Court, 11 March 2003 (QBD, Gray J).

105   [1937] 1 K.B. 818.

106   More recently this has been applied by analogy to a web service which provided a platform for blogs: see *Tamiz v Google Inc* [2013] EWCA Civ 68; [2013] 1 W.L.R. 2151 (arguable that Google had associated itself with publication when notified of defamatory material on blog and could have readily removed or blocked access to any notice which did not comply with its own terms and conditions).

Who can sue?

▶ (1) Any living human being

We have seen numerous examples of this already, such as Princess Youssoupoff and Artemus Jones. It should be noted, however, that the action does not survive death,[107] so the estate of a person who has been defamed has no cause of action.

▶ (2) Companies

This is more controversial. A company is a corporate entity, not a real person, and is incapable of having its "personal feelings" injured by the defendant's statements. Yet, as stated at the start of this chapter, the tort of defamation is concerned with reputation, not personal feelings. A company does have a business reputation to protect. Despite arguments that this interest is sufficiently protected by other torts, such as malicious falsehood and deceit, it is clear that companies can sue for defamation. The classic authority is *South Hetton Coal Co v North-Eastern News Assoc Ltd*,[108] where the Court of Appeal held that the company was entitled to sue a newspaper which had alleged that properties in which the company housed its employees were highly insanitary. A libel calculated to injure the company's trading reputation was held to be actionable. A more modern example is the long-running "McLibel" trial[109] in which the fast-food chain McDonalds brought a case against two environmental campaigners for allegedly defamatory statements about the company.

The reasoning of the Court of Appeal in *South Hetton* was approved by the House of Lords in *Jameel v Wall Street Journal Europe SPRL (No.3)*.[110] In this case, a trading company, incorporated in Saudi Arabia, had brought an action for libel in response to a newspaper article which suggested that its bank accounts were being monitored to prevent their use for channelling funds to terrorist organisations. The company was found to have a trading reputation in the UK, despite the fact that it conducted no business in the jurisdiction. It was argued that to allow such a company to bring a claim in libel which at the time required no proof of damage amounted to an undue restriction of freedom of speech, contrary to art.10. The majority of the House of Lords disagreed.[111] In the words of Lord Bingham:

---

107   Law Reform (Miscellaneous Provisions) Act 1934 s.1(1).
108   [1894] 1 Q.B. 133.
109   *McDonald's Corp v Steel (No.4)* [1995] 3 All E.R. 615. The trial itself lasted 313 days (the longest trial in English history). See J. Vidal, *McLibel–Burger culture on trial* (Pan, 1997).
110   [2006] UKHL 44; [2007] 1 A.C. 359.
111   Lord Hoffmann and Baroness Hale dissenting. Lord Hoffmann at [91] distinguished an individual's reputation (part of his or her personality) from that of a company (really no more than a commercial asset) and questioned why defamation should differ from other torts, such as malicious falsehood, where a company is required to show proof of damage to bring an action to protect its commercial assets from tortious harm.

> "the good name of a company, as that of an individual, is a thing of value. A damaging libel may lower its standing in the eyes of the public and even its own staff, make people less ready to deal with it, less willing or less proud to work for it . . . I find nothing repugnant in the notion that this is a value which the law should protect."[112]

In view of the margin of appreciation given to national courts in their interpretation of art.10,[113] his Lordship was not prepared to alter the well-established rule in *South Hetton* and require a company to show special damage. He added, however, that where the trading corporation had suffered no financial loss, damages should be kept strictly within modest bounds.[114]

This position had been criticised by Faulks Committee in 1975, which had recommended that companies should not be able to sue unless they had suffered financial loss or the words were likely to cause the company financial damage.[115] As seen in para.13–011, the Defamation Act 2013 s.1(2) finally brings reform to this area and provides that a company (i.e. "a body that trades for profit") cannot sue for defamation unless the statement caused or is likely to cause the body serious financial loss. The aim is to exclude trivial claims. It is also likely to serve, to a limited extent, as a means to prevent possible abuses of power by companies which use the threat of litigation to discourage defendants from criticising their activities.

Who cannot sue?

(1) Governmental bodies

13–022

The House of Lords in *Derbyshire CC v Times Newspapers Ltd*[116] held that institutions of central or local government, such as local authorities, could not sue for defamation. This is an important decision. The plaintiff, a local authority, had brought an action for damages for libel against *The Times* in respect of two newspaper articles which had questioned the propriety of its financial dealings. On a preliminary issue, as to whether the plaintiff had a cause of action against the defendants, the House of Lords upheld the view of the Court of Appeal that a local authority could not bring an action for libel. Lord Keith, giving the leading judgment, commented that:

---

112 [2006] UKHL 44; [2007] 1 A.C. 359 at [26]. Concern was also raised that if special damage was required, a company would not be able to avert irreparable damage to its reputation by a prompt issue of proceedings: see Lord Bingham at [26] and Lord Hope at [102].

113 See *Steel and Morris v United Kingdom (68416/01)* (2005) 41 E.H.R.R. 22.

114 [2006] UKHL 44; [2007] 1 A.C. 359 at [27]. See also his remark at [19].

115 Report of the Committee on Defamation, Cmnd.5909 para.342.

116 [1993] A.C. 534. Comment: B. Bix and A. Tomkins (1993) 56 M.L.R. 738; S. Palmer [1993] C.L.J. 363, and E. Grant and J. G. Small (1994) 14 O.J.L.S. 287.

> "It is of the highest public importance that a democratically elected governmental body, or indeed any governmental body, should be open to uninhibited public criticism. The threat of a civil action for defamation must inevitably have an inhibiting effect on freedom of speech."[117]

The decision is therefore significant in recognising that it is in the public interest that individuals are free to question and criticise central and local government. It would be contrary to the democratic process and freedom of expression for such bodies to have a right to sue in defamation, and would "place an undesirable fetter on freedom of speech".[118] In reaching this conclusion, the House of Lords, unlike the Court of Appeal,[119] did not rely on the European Convention on Human Rights, but relied on English and US case law.[120] However, with the incorporation of the Convention into English law by the Human Rights Act 1998, art.10 is now the main focus of any discussion of freedom of expression. The decision marks welcome recognition that open government is a valuable part of modern democratic society and that any restrictions of freedom of expression in this context should be examined very carefully.

(2) Political parties

13-023

The logic of (1), namely the requirement that the public should be able to question the executive, applies equally to political parties. Buckley J in *Goldsmith v Bhoyrul*[121] applied *Derbyshire* to exclude a claim for defamation by the Referendum Party.[122] Despite the fact that the party had yet to be elected, Buckley J held that defamation actions, or the threat of such actions, would restrict free speech, which would be contrary to the public interest. The public should be free to discuss and criticise political parties putting themselves forward for election.

It is important, however, to note the limited effect of these two decisions. These decisions do not prevent individual politicians from suing, and indeed a number of politicians have sued in recent years (for example, former Conservative MPs Rupert Allason and Neil Hamilton) with mixed success.[123] There is an obvious argument that politicians, involved in

---

117 [1993] A.C. 534 at 547.
118 [1993] A.C. 534 at 549 per Lord Keith.
119 [1992] Q.B. 770.
120 Lord Keith commented ([1993] A.C. 534 at 541): "My Lords, I have reached my conclusion upon the common law of England without finding any need to rely upon the European Convention . . . I can only add that I find it satisfactory to be able to conclude that the common law of England is consistent with the obligations assumed by the Crown under the Treaty in this particular field".
121 [1998] Q.B. 459 at 463.
122 The Referendum party had been founded by Sir James Goldsmith (father of former MP and now life peer Zac Goldsmith) and sought to secure a referendum on Britain's future in Europe. It put up 547 candidates in the 1997 election.
123 As re-iterated by Tugendhat J in *McLaughlin v Lambeth LBC* [2010] EWHC 2726 (QB); [2011] E.M.L.R. 8: the

the democratic process, should also be prevented from suing for defamation for the reasons stated in *Derbyshire*, at least when the statements relate to their performance as Members of Parliament.[124] This is not the legal position at present. There is no English equivalent to the US restrictions on the ability of public figures to sue for defamation, stated by the US Supreme Court in *New York Times v Sullivan*.[125] In that case, the Supreme Court held that in the light of the protection of free speech in the First Amendment to the US Constitution, public figures may only sue if they can present clear and convincing evidence of actual malice by the publisher. Actual malice is shown by proving that the defendant published the piece with knowledge that the defamatory statement was false or at least with reckless disregard as to its falsity. The rule in *Derbyshire* is further undermined by the fact that governmental bodies still have the right to sue for malicious falsehood (see Ch.14) and to prosecute for criminal libel. The impact of the decision must therefore be questionable when the restriction can so easily be circumvented in this way.[126] In *Derbyshire* itself, the council leader, Bookbinder, was able to sue in his own right for damages. Mr Bookbinder's earlier action against Norman Tebbit, former Chairman of the Conservative party, will be discussed in the next chapter.

Conclusion

13–024

This chapter has examined the elements that the claimant must establish to bring an action for defamation. The next chapter will concentrate on the defences available to the defendant. As will be seen, it is with the defences that the real tensions between the right to freedom of expression and the need to protect the claimant's reputation show themselves. The Defamation Act 2013 seeks to address these tensions by placing key defences in a statutory form. The defences available in defamation are somewhat complicated and therefore warrant a chapter of their own.

---

right to sue of any individual who carried on the day to day management of the affairs of a governmental body was subject to no limitation other than the requirement that the words complained of should refer to, and be defamatory of, that individual.

124 See E. Barendt, "Libel and freedom of speech in English law" [1993] P.L. 449.

125 376 U.S. 254 (1964). See also *Lingens v Austria* (1986) 8 E.H.R.R. 407 in which the European Court of Human Rights adopted an approach towards public figures similar to that adopted in the US. For a comparison, see D. Elder, "Freedom of expression and the law of defamation: the American approach to problems raised by the *Lingens* case" (1986) 35 I.C.L.Q. 891. See, generally, A.T. Kenyon (ed), *Comparative Defamation and Privacy Law* (CUP, 2016).

126 See B. Bix and A. Tomkins, "Local authorities and libel again" (1993) 56 M.L.R. 738.

14

Defences to Defamation

Introduction

Chapter 13 examined the basic requirements of a defamation action. The burden is on the claimant to establish (a) that the statement is defamatory, (b) that it refers to the claimant and (c) that it has been published to a third party. This chapter will examine the defences open to the defendant once the claimant has established these three requirements. The Human Rights Act 1998 has made an inevitable impact on this area of law. As seen in Ch.13, it places particular importance on freedom of expression (ECHR art.10) and requires the courts to balance the protection of a party's reputation against the public interest in allowing individuals to "hold opinions and to receive and impart information and ideas without interference" by the courts. Section 12(4) of the Act further provides that the courts "must have particular regard to the importance of the Convention right to freedom of expression." Although the law of defamation has always recognised these two conflicting interests, it cannot be denied that the 1998 Act has brought this debate to the fore.

The most significant development in recent years is, however, the Defamation Act 2013 which came into force on 1 January 2014.[1] This introduces new defences (notably for operators of websites and for authors of peer-reviewed scientific or academic articles) and places the main defamation defences in a statutory form. The aim is to simplify and clarify the law, whilst ensuring protection of the right to freedom of expression in the public interest. The common law defence, therefore, of justification becomes the s.2 defence of truth; that of fair comment, the s.3 defence of honest opinion with the new s.4 defence of "publication on matter of public

14–001

---

1 Defamation Act 2013 (Commencement) (England and Wales) Order 2013 (SI 2013/3027) art.2. See A. Mullis and A. Scott, "Tilting at windmills: the Defamation Act 2013" (2014) 77 M.L.R. 87 for an overview of the potential impact of the Act. For a critical review of the defences post-Act, see E. Descheemaeker, "Mapping defamation defences" (2015) 78 M.L.R. 641 and "Three errors in the Defamation Act 2013" (2015) 6 J.E.T.L. 1.

interest" replacing the common law defence established in *Reynolds v Times Newspapers*.[2] It should also be noted that although these are the most important defences, other defences exist. It is a defence, for example, if the claimant has expressly or impliedly consented to the publication of the defamatory matter,[3] and under the Defamation Act 1996[4] a number of further options arise: unintentional defamation and innocent dissemination. Consent will be discussed generally in Ch.16, but the other defences will be examined below. If all the defences fail, the defendant has one final option. This is to mitigate the level of damages by raising arguments in his or her favour, for example that an apology was made or that the defamatory material was not shown to a large number of people. Such arguments will not amount to a defence, but may at least lead the court to award a lesser amount of damages against the defendant.

Each defence will be discussed in turn.

Truth[5]

14-002

It is a valid defence to show that the defamatory statements were in fact true. Two points should be noted here. First, defamatory statements are presumed to be untrue.[6] The claimant does not have to show that the statements were false. The burden therefore will be on the defendant to show that the statements were true and so justified. Secondly, the claimant has no right to complain about true statements which lower his or her reputation. Logically, such statements merely bring the individual's reputation down to its appropriate level.[7] It is also irrelevant whether the statements are published out of malice or to let others know the truth. The only exception to this is contained in the Rehabilitation of Offenders Act 1974 s.8. Section 8(5)[8] provides that where the claimant complains that the defendant has published information concerning his or her spent convictions, the defendant cannot rely on the defence of truth

---

2   [2001] 2 A.C. 127.

3   *Cookson v Harewood* [1932] 2 K.B. 478n; *Chapman v Lord Ellesmere* [1932] 2 K.B. 431 at 463–465 per Slesser LJ.

4   See K. Williams, "Reforming Defamation Law in the UK" (1997) 5 Tort L. Rev. 206.

5   Formerly also known as justification. The term "truth" was favoured by the Faulks Committee (Report of the Committee on Defamation, 1975, Cmnd.5090) para.129, which believed that it would save confusion.

6   This was challenged in the Court of Appeal in *Jameel v Wall Street Journal Europe SPRL (No.3)* [2005] EWCA Civ 74; [2005] Q.B. 904 at [55]–[57] for infringing the ECHR arts 6 and 10 (not raised on appeal to HL). Although the point was dismissed as having been raised too late in proceedings, the court gave it little support, stressing that it would require a major change of the law of defamation. The point does, however, remain open and there is some indication in *Steel and Morris v United Kingdom (68416/01)* (2005) 41 E.H.R.R. 22 that it may, in exceptional circumstances, give rise to a breach of art.10.

7   *M'Pherson v Daniels* (1829) 10 B. & C. 263 at 272; 109 E.R. 448 at 451. It is irrelevant that the defendant did not know the statements to be true at the time they were made, provided they are of course in fact true.

8   As amended by Defamation Act 2013 s.16(3).

if the publication is proved to have been made with malice. The burden will be on the claimant to show the presence of malice.[9]

The key provision is now Defamation Act 2013 s.2, which abolishes the common law defence of justification.[10] Section 2(1) provides that "it is a defence to an action for defamation for the defendant to show that the imputation conveyed by the statement complained of is substantially true". This reflects the pre-existing common law position. The defendant is expected to prove, on the balance of probabilities, that the words used are substantially true. This includes their express meaning, but also extends to any innuendoes deriving from the statement. In *Wakley v Cooke*,[11] for example, the defendant had called the plaintiff a "libellous journalist". He was able to show that a judgment had once been obtained against the plaintiff for libel. However, because the words, by innuendo, were capable of meaning that the plaintiff was in the habit of libelling people, the comment could not be justified by referring to only one previous incident of libel. The defendant's claim of justification therefore failed. The operation of the "substantially true" test may be seen in *Alexander v North Eastern Railway Co.*[12] Here, the defendants had stated that the plaintiff had been convicted of an offence of dishonesty and sentenced to three weeks' imprisonment in default of payment of a fine. In fact, they could only prove the conviction and a sentence of two weeks' imprisonment. Nevertheless, the court found the statement to be substantially true and the defendants therefore succeeded in their defence of justification. It is clear that existing case law will be helpful in applying this test. The defendant can also, when appropriate, rely on the Civil Evidence Act 1968 s.13 (as amended by the Defamation Act 1996 s.12(1)). This provides that if the defendant has alleged that the claimant has committed an offence, this can be proved to be true simply by giving evidence of the conviction. It is not necessary to prove that the claimant was rightly convicted.

Sections 2(2)–2(4) deal with a different issue: where the claimant alleges that the statement in question conveys more than one defamatory allegation. Section 2(3) provides that:

14-003

> **"If one or more of the imputations is not shown to be substantially true, the defence under this section does not fail if, having regard to the imputations which are shown to be substantially true, the**

---

9   Eady J in *Silkman v Heard* unreported 28 February 2001 QBD raised the question whether this is compatible with the right to freedom of expression in ECHR art.10 in that the information is in the public domain and this section has been relied on so rarely in defamation actions. He nevertheless added in *KJO v XIM* [2011] EWHC 1768 (QB) that it could be argued that such restrictions are necessary and proportionate for the legitimate objective of rehabilitation: [13].

10   Defamation Act 2013 s.2(4).

11   (1849) 4 Exch. 511; 154 E.R. 1316.

12   (1865) 6 B. & S. 340; 122 E.R. 1221. Note also the comments of Eady J in *Turcu v News Group Newspapers Ltd* [2005] EWHC 799 (QB) at [109]: "English law is generally able to accommodate the policy factors underlying the Article 10 jurisprudence by means of established common law principles; for example that a defamatory allegation need only be proved, on a balance of probabilities, to be *substantially* true".

> imputations which are not shown to be substantially true do not seriously harm the claimant's reputation."

Defamation Act 1952 s.5 had previously dealt with this issue and is now repealed by the Act.[13] On this basis, where the defendant has made two or more defamatory allegations (or imputations), the defence of truth is not lost if the most serious allegations are substantially true and those which are not do not seriously harm the claimant's reputation. The Explanatory Notes to the Act indicate that these provisions have the same effect as s.5, but seek to use more "user-friendly" modern terminology.[14]

This situation should be distinguished from that where the defendant argues that a number of different defamatory allegations have a "common (or general) sting" which he or she is able to show is substantially true. For example, in *Williams v Reason*,[15] a Welsh amateur rugby player sued in respect of an article which accused him of writing a book for profit, contrary to his amateur status. The defendants claimed justification and were permitted to allege in support of the article that the player had previously taken money for wearing a particular brand of boots. The sting of the defamatory words was that Williams had compromised his amateur status (so-called "shamateurism") and the evidence of the boots money went to justify that charge. However, the "common sting" argument will not work where the allegation against the claimant is specific. In such cases, the court will focus on each individual allegation and the defendant will not be permitted to raise matters with a "common sting".[16] On this basis, the Court of Appeal in *Bookbinder v Tebbit*[17] struck out part of the defence put forward by Norman Tebbit, the former chairman of the Conservative party, which referred to general examples of irresponsible spending by Derbyshire City Council. The court found that Tebbit had made a specific allegation against Bookbinder that the council, under his leadership, had squandered public money by overprinting stationery with a political message. He would therefore have to justify that particular allegation.

The difficulties in proving that a particular allegation is true should not be underestimated despite current reforms. The burden is on the defendant to justify the substantial truth or "sting" of the allegations. If the defendant cannot show that the statements were substantially true, the defence fails. Evidence that the statement is partially true will not constitute a defence, although it may serve to reduce the level of damages awarded. In contrast, an unsuccessful attempt to justify the defamatory statement may be deemed to aggravate the injury to the claimant by giving the statement extra publicity at trial, and so merit a higher award of damages.[18] It is therefore a calculated risk whether to raise this defence.

---

13   Defamation Act 2013 s.2(4).
14   Explanatory Note to Defamation Act 2013 para.17.
15   [1988] 1 W.L.R. 96 at 103 per Stephenson LJ. See also *Rothschild v Associated Newspapers Ltd* [2013] EWCA Civ 197; [2013] E.M.L.R. 18, notably at [24].
16   *Polly Peck (Holdings) Plc v Trelford* [1986] Q.B. 1000. See also *Cruise v Express Newspapers Plc* [1999] Q.B. 931 CA.
17   [1989] 1 W.L.R. 640.
18   See Lord Diplock in *Broome v Cassell & Co Ltd* [1972] A.C. 1027 at 1125.

Where the defendant raises a defence of truth or honest opinion, the defendant must specify the defamatory meanings he or she seeks to justify[19] or defend as honest opinion and give details of the matters on which he or she relies in support of the allegation.[20]

Honest Opinion

14-004

This defence, previously known as fair comment and, from 2010, honest comment,[21] is under the Defamation Act 2013 s.3 now entitled "honest opinion".[22] Section 3(8) abolishes the common law defence of fair comment. It should be distinguished from that of truth (discussed above). Here, the defendant does not have to show that his or her words are true, but that he or she has exercised the right to criticise the claimant. It is therefore closely linked to the right to freedom of expression. The question for the courts is to what extent the defendant's right to freedom of expression should be kept within bounds. The aim of the 2013 Act is to simplify and clarify the operation of this defence, but it also, by removing the common law requirement that the opinion must be on a matter of public interest,[23] extends its scope. There are now three conditions for the application of this defence: (a) it must be a statement of opinion; (b) the statement must indicate, in general or specific terms, the basis for this opinion; and (c) it must be honest. These conditions are discussed below.

Condition one: statement of opinion

14-005

Section 3(2) provides that the statement complained of must be a statement of opinion. This reflects the pre-existing common law position and the Explanatory Note to the Act expressly states that the Act wishes to embrace the requirement established in *Cheng v Tse Wai Chun*[24] that the statement must be recognisable as comment and not a statement of fact. Cases such

---

19   *Lucas-Box v News Group Newspapers Ltd* [1986] 1 W.L.R. 147.

20   See Practice Direction to Pt 53B paras 4.3 and 4.4 to the Civil Procedures Rules.

21   The change of name was introduced by Lord Phillips in *Spiller v Joseph* [2010] UKSC 53; [2011] 1 A.C. 852 at [117].

22   See H. Brown, "Fair comment to honest opinion—what's new?" (2013) 24 Ent. L.R. 236 and J. Bosland, A.T. Kenyon and S. Walker, "Protecting inferences of fact in defamation law: Fair comment and honest opinion" [2015] C.L.J. 234.

23   See *Seymour v Butterworth* (1862) 3 F.&F. 372; 176 E.R. 166; *South Hetton Coal Co v North-Eastern News Assoc Ltd* [1894] 1 Q.B. 133; *London Artists v Littler* [1969] 2 Q.B. 375. Lord Phillips in the leading case of *Spiller v Joseph* had suggested that there was a case for widening the scope of the defence by removing the requirement that it must be in the public interest: [2010] UKSC 53 at [113].

24   Also known as *Tse Wai Chun Paul v Albert* [2001] E.M.L.R. 31; 10 B.H.R.C. 525 CFA (HK).

as *British Chiropractic Association v Singh*[25] indicated that the distinction between fact and opinion might not always be straightforward, but the Act now adopts a definition based on what an ordinary person would understand it to be.[26] In *Singh*, the issue was whether a criticism of lack of scientific evidence to support a particular treatment amounted to an opinion or was a statement of fact. The Act supports the Court of Appeal's view that an inference from facts may be a form of opinion, particularly where it is clear that the defendant is not in a position to know whether this represents the true position. The recent case of *Butt v Secretary of State for the Home Department*[27] affirmed that a statement based on an assessment or evaluation of evidence would be regarded as a statement of opinion, not fact. In the case itself, a statement in a government press release concerning tackling extremism referred to Butt (the editor of a website) as expressing views "contrary to British values". This was regarded as a statement of opinion. The ordinary reasonable reader would appreciate that this was an assessment reached by looking at the claimant's public pronouncements and how they conformed to certain values. Case law has indicated, however, that an allegation of dishonesty, fraud or attempted fraud, attacking the claimant's integrity, would usually fall on the side of fact rather than opinion.[28]

Condition two: the statement must indicate, in general or specific terms, the basis for this opinion

14–006

It is well established that, for this defence, the defendant must show that the words in question consist of a comment on a true set of facts. (The defendant will obviously not be able to invent facts and then "comment" on them.) It is, however, sometimes a difficult question whether the defendant has sufficiently stated or indicated the facts on which the comment is made. Failure to do so may make the court treat the statement as one of fact to which this defence would not apply. In *Kemsley v Foot*,[29] for example, Lord Kemsley (a well-known newspaper proprietor at the time) had complained about an article entitled "Lower than Kemsley", which criticised the quality of a newspaper unconnected with him. The article contained no other reference to Kemsley, but the inference was obviously that Kemsley produced low quality newspapers. It was questioned whether the defendants could rely on the defence of what was then called "fair comment" when there were no facts in the article to "comment" upon. The House of Lords took a very broad view of the headline and held that where a "substratum of fact" could be inferred from the words used, the defence of fair comment could be put to the jury. Here, the defendants

25 [2010] EWCA Civ 350; [2011] 1 W.L.R. 133. See also *Waterson v Lloyd* [2013] EWCA Civ 136; [2013] E.M.L.R. 17: "scandalous expenses claim" a statement of fact or opinion?
26 Explanatory Note to the Defamation Act 2013 para.21.
27 [2019] EWCA Civ 933.
28 *Wasserman v Freilich* [2016] EWHC 312 (QB).
29 [1952] A.C. 345. Described by Lord Phillips in *Spiller v Joseph* [2010] UKSC 53 at [91] as "an absurd libel action. It was not about vindicating the reputation of Viscount Kemsley but about *amour propre*".

had clearly referred to Lord Kemsley, who was well known to the public generally. A stricter line was taken, however, by the House of Lords in the later case of *Telnikoff v Matusevitch*.[30] In this case, a letter was published in the *Daily Telegraph* which criticised an article by the plaintiff, published in the same newspaper, concerning recruitment to the BBC Russian service. The letter suggested that the plaintiff was racist. The plaintiff brought an action against the letter writer for libel. The question arose whether, in considering the letter writer's defence of fair comment, the letter should be considered in the context of the article it criticised. The majority of the House of Lords held that in considering whether the letter amounted to "comment", the court should not look at the article, since many readers of the letter would not have read the article or, if they had read it, would not have had its terms fully in mind. If, in isolation, remarks in the letter were adjudged to be statements of fact rather than comment, then the defence of fair comment would not lie, and the defendant would have to resort to the alternative defence of justification (now truth). Lord Keith denied that this would require future letter writers to include the entire text of the article in the letter. The onus would simply be on the letter writer to make it clear that he or she was writing comment and not making statements of fact. His Lordship thought that newspaper editors would not have any difficulty in observing whether this had in fact been achieved.[31]

In 2010, the Supreme Court in *Spiller v Joseph*[32] reviewed these two cases and suggested that the test should be whether the comment has explicitly or implicitly indicated, at least in general terms, the facts on which it is based. It was not, however, necessary to identify the facts with such particularity that the reader could judge for himself whether it was well founded. In the words of Lord Phillips, the key issue is that:

> "... the reader can understand what the comment is about and the commentator can, if challenged, explain by giving particulars of the subject matter of his comment why he expressed the views that he did. A fair balance must be struck between allowing a critic the freedom to express himself as he will and requiring him to identify to his readers why it is that he is making the criticism."[33]

Defamation Act 2013 s.3(3) now provides that "the second condition is that the statement complained of indicated, whether in general or specific terms, the basis of the opinion". This seeks to reflect the *Spiller* test and avoid the complexity of earlier cases such as *Kemsley v Foot*[34] and *Telnikoff v Matusevitch*[35] in which the case law struggled to articulate with clarity the extent to which reference to the facts on which the opinion was based was needed.

---

30 [1992] 2 A.C. 343.
31 Note, however, Lord Ackner's vigorous dissenting judgment in favour of freedom of speech.
32 [2010] UKSC 53; [2011] 1 A.C. 852.
33 [2010] UKSC 53 at [104].
34 [1952] A.C. 345.
35 [1992] 2 A.C. 343.

Condition three: honest

14–007

The common law found this final condition difficult to define. It is not a question whether the words used are true or not, but merely whether the opinion, however exaggerated, obstinate or prejudiced, was honestly held by the person expressing it.[36] The fact that the comment was expressed strongly, provided it does not descend into mere abuse, did not make a difference.[37] It was also the case that the defence would be defeated by malice, although, confusingly, Lord Nicholls in *Cheng v Tse Wai Chun*[38] determined that this had a different meaning to that used to defeat the defence of qualified privilege (discussed below). His Lordship held that the touchstone of the defence was honesty. Regardless of motive, if the defendant honestly believed the truth of his comment, then a court would not find malice. Spite, animosity, intention to injure or other motivation would only be relevant as evidence that the defendant did not genuinely believe the view expressed.

Section 3(4) now provides that:

> "[t]he third condition is that an honest person could have held the opinion on the basis of—(a) any fact which existed at the time the statement complained of was published; (b) anything asserted to be a fact in a privileged statement published before the statement complained of."

It thus sets an objective test with two elements: (a) could an honest person have held that opinion on the basis of "any" fact which existed at the time; or (b) on the basis of a fact in a privileged statement?[39] The defence will be lost, however, if the defendant did not actually hold the opinion in question: s.3(5). This is a subjective test, although it should be noted that the term "malice" is no longer used. Section 3(6) also deals with a situation where the publisher of the opinion is not the actual author of the piece, for example, where an action is brought against a newspaper editor for a comment in his or her newspapers. The editor will not be affected by the s.3(5) defence unless he or she knew or ought to have known that the author did not hold the opinion in question.

The Act also abolishes the Defamation Act 1952 s.6 on the basis that the problem it dealt with—defamatory statements which consist partly of allegations of fact and partly of expressions of opinion where the truth of every allegation of fact cannot be proved—is now covered by

---

36   See *Reynolds v Times Newspapers Ltd* [2001] 2 A.C. 127 at 193 per Lord Nicholls; *Slim v Daily Telegraph* [1968] 2 Q.B. 157 at 170; *Merivale v Carson* (1887) 20 Q.B.D. 275 at 281; *Turner v Metro-Goldwyn-Mayer Pictures* Ltd [1950] 1 All E.R. 449 at 461; *Silkin v Beaverbrook Newspapers Ltd* [1958] 1 W.L.R. 743 at 747.

37   *Merivale v Carson* (1887) 20 Q.B.D. 275.

38   Also known as *Tse Wai Chun Paul v Albert* [2001] E.M.L.R. 31; 10 B.H.R.C. 525 CFA (HK). Comment F.A. Trindade (2001) 117 L.Q.R. 169. See also *Associated Newspapers Ltd v Burstein* [2007] EWCA Civ 600; [2007] 4 All E.R. 319.

39   A privileged statement is defined in Defamation Act 2013 s.3(7). Note that there is no requirement that the fact in question was one known to the defendant at the time.

the new approach set out in s.3(4).[40] Section 3(4)(a) achieves this by providing that "any fact" can provide a sufficient factual basis for the opinion in question.[41] So, for example, where A has published an article in which she states that schoolteacher B had failed his examinations at university, was always late for class and is therefore incompetent to teach at the local school in circumstances where A can prove that B failed his examinations, but not that he is always late, A will be able to rely on s.3 despite the fact she cannot show the truth of all the allegations of fact.

Privilege

This is the third main defence and has been subject to significant changes under the Defamation Act 2013 ss.4, 6 and 7. Here, while the defendant is unable to prove that the allegations made are substantially true, the public interest in freedom of expression is nevertheless such that it overrides any concerns as to the effect of this freedom on the claimant's reputation. There are two types of privilege in English law. Absolute privilege is the stronger form of privilege and applies on occasions where the need to protect freedom of speech is so important as to create an absolute defence to any action for defamation, irrespective of the motives or words of the author. Qualified privilege is the weaker form of privilege. It applies in situations where it is desirable that freedom of speech should be protected, but only where the author is acting without malice. If the claimant can show that the defendant has acted maliciously, the qualified privilege is lost. If there is a jury trial, the judge will decide whether the occasion is a privileged one, and whether a reasonable jury could find that the author's dominant motive was malice. The jury will decide whether any allegation of malice has been proved.

Decisions determining the occasions that merit absolute or qualified privilege have been taken over the last 500 years and represent the policy choices of Parliament and the judiciary at particular moments in history. Privilege has also been subject to statutory intervention, most recently in the Defamation Acts of 1996 and 2013. Defamation Act 2013 s.4 is particularly important in that it places the defence set out in the leading House of Lords case of *Reynolds v Times Newspapers*[42] in statutory form. Absolute and qualified privilege are discussed below.

---

40   Defamation Act 2013 s.3(8).

41   This is confirmed by the Explanatory Note to the Act which states that a defendant should be able to satisfy the three conditions set out in Defamation Act 2013 s.3 without needing to prove the truth of every single allegation of fact relevant to the statement complained of: para.28.

42   [2001] 2 A.C. 127.

Absolute privilege

14-009 Absolute privilege applies to statements made in Parliament, in court and by certain officers of state. There are five main occasions when the defence will apply.

(1) Statements in Parliament

14-010 Bill of Rights 1688 art.9 provides that:

> **"the freedom of speech and debates or proceedings in Parliament ought not to be impeached or questioned in any court or place out of Parliament."**

This preserves parliamentary autonomy and allows Members of Parliament freely to criticise individuals as they feel appropriate. It also prevents the courts from inquiring into the conduct of parliamentary business.[43] The defence is confined, however, to statements made in Parliament.[44] As the Privy Council commented in *Buchanan v Jennings*:

> **"A degree of circumspection is accordingly called for when a Member of Parliament is moved or pressed to repeat out of Parliament a potentially defamatory statement previously made in Parliament."[45]**

In *Church of Scientology of California v Johnson-Smith*,[46] the plaintiff was not permitted to rely upon statements made by an MP in Parliament as evidence of malice, even though the action was based on comments made by the MP outside Parliament. The rule can be a mixed blessing for MPs. When the former Conservative MP, Neil Hamilton, sued *The Guardian* for libel, the action was stayed by May J, on the basis that the defendants would be unable to mount an effective defence because of parliamentary privilege.[47] This left Hamilton unable to clear his own name and pressure mounted for a change in the law. In an attempt to avoid any unfair-

---

43 The defence has been found to be consistent with the European Convention on Human Rights in that it does not impose a disproportionate restriction on the individual's right of access to the court: *A v United Kingdom (35373/97)* (2003) 36 E.H.R.R. 51.

44 *Buchanan v Jennings* [2004] UKPC 36; [2005] 1 A.C. 115 (absolute privilege does not extend to repetition of statements outside Parliament for the MP's own purposes even where the MP merely adopts and confirms a previous statement made in Parliament). There may, however, by exceptional cases where it is in the public interest to extend the protection of art.9 to extra-Parliamentary speech: *Makudi v Baron Triesman* [2014] EWCA Civ 179; [2014] Q.B. 839 at [25].

45 Lord Bingham in *Buchanan v Jennings* [2004] UKPC 36; [2005] 1 A.C. 115 at [20].

46 [1972] Q.B. 522.

47 *Hamilton v Guardian Newspapers The Times* 22 July 1995, following the Privy Council decision in *Prebble v Television New Zealand* [1995] 1 A.C. 321 (see A. Sharland and I. Loveland, "The Defamation Act 1996

ness, Parliament passed the Defamation Act 1996 s.13, which provided that an MP may waive privilege for the purpose of defamation proceedings.[48] This section was, however, criticised for unduly favouring MPs over their opponents and was repealed in 2015.[49]

> ## (2) Reports, papers, votes and proceedings ordered to be published by either House of Parliament

14–011

Statements in these documents are absolutely privileged by virtue of the Parliamentary Papers Act 1840 s.1. Absolute privilege does not extend, however, to extracts from, or abstracts of, parliamentary papers, or to reports of parliamentary proceedings, but all of these are covered by qualified privilege, which will be discussed below.

> ## (3) Judicial proceedings

14–012

It is important that the court should hear all relevant and admissible evidence, and it would be contrary to public policy if witnesses were reluctant to give evidence for fear that they may subsequently be sued for defamation. To ensure a fair trial, absolute privilege is therefore given to all oral and written statements made in the course of judicial proceedings. "Judicial proceedings" are defined broadly, and cover all tribunals exercising functions equivalent to a court of justice.[50] The privilege extends to statements made by the judge, jury, advocates, the parties and witnesses.[51] This freedom to comment may be abused, but it is for the judge to regulate the conduct of the case in court. The defence also applies to statements made on occasions that can be regarded as a step in judicial proceedings, for example witness statements.[52]

---

and Political Libels" [1997] P.L. 113). For a recent example of parliamentary privilege, see *Foreign and Commonwealth Office v Warsama* [2020] EWCA Civ 142.

48 See *Hamilton v Al Fayed (No.1)* [2001] 1 A.C. 395, where the House of Lords applied s.13 in Hamilton's favour—a short lived victory for Mr Hamilton whose claim ultimately failed. Comment: A.W. Bradley [2000] P.L. 556.

49 Deregulation Act 2015 Sch.23 para.44.

50 See *O'Connor v Waldron* [1935] A.C. 76 and *Trapp v Mackie* [1979] 1 W.L.R. 377 HL. It also applies to statements made to regulatory bodies responsible for disciplinary proceedings, as long as those bodies are recognised by law and are operating in the public interest e.g. General Medical Council's Fitness to Practise Directorate (*White v Southampton University Hospitals NHS Trust* [2011] EWHC 825 (QB)).

51 *Royal Aquarium and Summer and Winter Garden Society v Parkinson* [1892] 1 Q.B. 431 at 451 per Lopes LJ. Note, however, that both advocates and expert witnesses may now find themselves liable for negligence in court regardless of the defence of absolute privilege: see *Arthur J Hall & Co v Simons* [2000] UKHL 38; [2002] 1 A.C. 615 (advocates) and *Jones v Kaney* [2011] UKSC 13; [2011] 2 A.C. 398 (friendly experts).

52 *Watson v McEwan* [1905] A.C. 480 at 487; *Buckley v Dalziel* [2007] EWHC 1025 (QB); [2007] 1 W.L.R. 2933. This avoids the potential difficulty of individuals being reluctant to make witness statements due to their fear of being sued for defamation. However, the rule has boundaries and the statements in question must have reference to the subject-matter of proceedings: *Iqbal v Mansoor* [2013] EWCA Civ 149. It is also confined to the statement itself and would not extend, for example, to the fabrication of documentary evidence: *Darker v Chief*

Whilst the defence applies to the solicitor/client relationship in connection with litigation, it is not clear whether it applies to communications between a solicitor and client which are not related to judicial proceedings. Logically, perhaps, it should not. In *More v Weaver*,[53] however, the Court of Appeal held that all relevant communications between solicitor and client were absolutely privileged. The question was left open by the House of Lords in *Minter v Priest*,[54] and it is more likely that such communications are covered by qualified privilege (discussed below).

(4) Reports of UK court proceedings

14–013

Defamation Act 1996 s.14 (as amended by the Defamation Act 2013 s.7(1))[55] provides that absolute privilege is accorded to all fair and accurate contemporaneous reports of public proceedings in any court in the UK, any court established under the law of a country or territory outside the UK and in any international court or tribunal established by the Security Council of the United Nations or by an international agreement. This will include the Court of Justice of the European Union and the European Court of Human Rights. Thus, a newspaper can give an account of national and international court proceedings without fearing actions for defamation. "Contemporaneous" is the main limiting factor. This seems to mean as soon as practicable.[56] In a jury trial, it will be for the jury to decide whether the report is a fair and accurate one.

(5) Communications between certain officers of state

14–014

The argument here is that officers of state will perform their duties better if they are not acting under fear of litigation. This is essentially the familiar public policy argument that is used in the tort of negligence to justify not imposing liability on the police and other public bodies

---

Constable of the West Midlands [2001] 1 A.C. 435 and *Singh v Reading BC* [2013] EWCA Civ 909; [2013] 1 W.L.R. 3052.

53 [1928] 2 K.B. 520 CA.

54 [1930] A.C. 558 (see Lord Buckmaster at 570, Viscount Dunedin at 575 and Lord Atkin at 586). Note also the judgments of Brooke LJ (with whom Nourse LJ and Sir Brian Neill agreed) in *Waple v Surrey CC* [1998] 1 W.L.R. 860 and Gray J in *Clarke v Davey* [2002] EWHC 2342 (QB), who found a realistic prospect that Ms Clarke would be able to establish at trial that *More v Weaver* could no longer stand in the light of subsequent authority.

55 This replaces the very similar Law of Libel Amendment Act 1888 s.3 (as amended) which was confined to television, newspapers and the radio. The amendments, however, only apply to England and Wales.

56 Defamation Act 1996 s.14(2). *Alsaifi v Amunwa* [2017] EWHC 1443 (QB); [2017] 4 W.L.R. 172 suggests that it should be as nearly at the same time as the proceedings as is reasonably possible. The privilege extends to the reporting of previous court hearings, insofar as it was reasonably necessary to give context to a contemporaneous report of a court hearing: *Crossley v Newsquest (Midlands South) Ltd* [2008] EWHC 3054 (QB).

(see Ch.2). The leading case on this category of absolute privilege is *Chatterton v Secretary of State for India*.[57] Here, the Court of Appeal held that an action for libel based on a letter written by the Secretary of State for India to his parliamentary under-secretary, to enable the latter to answer questions in Parliament concerning the plaintiff, was rightly dismissed by the trial judge. To allow any judicial inquiry into such matters would tend to deprive officers of state of their freedom of action. The scope of this immunity is a matter of some debate, and it has been narrowly construed in more recent times. The immunity does not, for example, extend to communications between civil servants. Henn-Collins J in *Szalatnay-Stacho v Fink*[58] suggested that it does not extend to officials below the rank of Minister, and in *Merricks v Nott-Bower*[59] the Court of Appeal refused to strike out a claim simply because the report was written by high-ranking police officers.

Qualified privilege

This is the more limited form of privilege and takes two forms: common law qualified privilege and statutory qualified privilege. As stated above, unlike absolute privilege, this defence is defeated by proof of malice, that is, the claimant can show either that the statement was made maliciously (for example, the defendant abused the privilege by using it for some purpose other than that for which the privilege was given) or that the defendant has exceeded the privilege (for example by publishing the statements more widely than necessary). In *Horrocks v Lowe*,[60] Lord Diplock considered the meaning of "malice" and held that the defendant is entitled to be protected by the privilege unless a "dominant and improper" motive is proved. His Lordship emphasised, however, that judges (and juries when relevant) should be slow to find a defendant malicious on the sole ground that the publication of the defamatory words (even though he believed them to be true) was prompted by the dominant motive of injuring the claimant. Generally, an extra element was required. The defence of qualified privilege would be lost only if it could be shown that the defendant did not honestly believe that what he or she said was true or was reckless as to its truth or falsity.[61]

Common law and statutory qualified privilege will be examined below. The Defamation Act 1996 put on a statutory basis a number of miscellaneous occasions on which qualified privilege had previously arisen at common law. The 1996 Act has been subject to amendment by the Defamation Act 2013 which adds two new statutory categories of qualified privilege: publication on matter of public interest (s.4) and peer-reviewed statements in scientific or academic journals (s.6). We will start, however, with the common law doctrine of qualified privilege.

14–015

---

57 [1895] 2 Q.B. 189.
58 [1946] 1 All E.R. 303 at 305; not considered by Court of Appeal [1947] K.B. 1.
59 [1965] 1 Q.B. 57.
60 [1975] A.C. 135 at 149–150.
61 Except where the person is under a duty to pass on, without endorsing, defamatory reports made by some other person.

Traditional common law qualified privilege: the duty/interest test

14–016   Here, we are concerned with qualified privilege which arises in situations where there is a "reciprocal duty and interest" between the defamer and the person to whom the statement is published. Unfortunately, as we shall see, it has proved difficult to define precisely when such situations will arise. The defence has a number of forms, but in its basic form has two requirements:

- X has a duty or interest in communicating with Y (this duty may be legal, moral or social); and

- Y has a corresponding interest or duty in receiving the information in question.[62]

The element of reciprocity is essential. On this basis, if X writes a letter to Y which contains false defamatory statements about Z, but (a) X has a duty to inform Y, and (b) Y has an interest in receiving this information, X has a good defence of qualified privilege provided he is not malicious.

Qualified privilege will also extend to situations where X publishes a statement to Y who shares a "common interest" with X, for example in the business in which they both work.[63] Further, it will include the situation where X has published the statement to defend his or her own interests and it is in the interest of Y to receive and consider the statement. For example, in *Osborn v Boulter*[64] the plaintiff had claimed that he had been supplied with poor quality beer. The defendant's response—that the plaintiff watered down his beer—was sent to meet this accusation and was therefore privileged. The courts have found that the law will generally attach privilege more readily to communications within an existing relationship than to communications between strangers.[65]

The privilege will not be lost by dictating a letter to a secretary or delivering a circular to a printer.[66] These are reasonable and ordinary means of communication in business and are therefore privileged. It is not clear, however, whether they are covered by an ancillary form of privilege, which is dependent on the defendant establishing qualified privilege between the defendant and the intended recipient of the letter, or whether they form their own head of qualified privilege because of the common interest between the author and the typist in getting the letter written. Divergent views were expressed in *Bryanston Finance Ltd v de Vries*,[67] and the point therefore remains open.

---

62   See *Adam v Ward* [1917] A.C. 309 at 334 per Lord Atkinson.
63   See, e.g. *Bryanston Finance Ltd v de Vries* [1975] Q.B. 703.
64   [1930] 2 K.B. 226 at 233–234.
65   See *Kearns v General Council of the Bar* [2003] EWCA Civ 331; [2003] 1 W.L.R. 1357.
66   *Osborn v Boulter* [1930] 2 K.B. 226 at 234.
67   [1975] Q.B. 703—Lord Denning MR arguing for original privilege at 719 and Lawton LJ arguing for ancillary privilege at 736–738.

WHAT IS A LEGAL, MORAL OR SOCIAL DUTY?

The observations of Lindley LJ, in *Stuart v Bell*,[68] make it clear that the law simply leaves this question to be answered at the discretion of the judge:

> "The question of moral or social duty being for the judge, each judge must decide it as best as he can for himself. I take moral or social duty to mean a duty recognised by English people of ordinary intelligence and moral principle, but at the same time not a duty enforceable by legal proceedings, whether civil or criminal."

This provides little assistance. At best, we can say that the law applies an objective test, having regard to the moral and social duties prevalent in society. This inevitably raises a question as to the ability of the courts to ascertain the views of modern society. In practice, it will be a matter of looking at past case law and ascertaining what situations in recent times have given rise to such duties.

WHAT IS AN INTEREST?

Generally, this is easier to define. The courts will interpret "interest" broadly to include, for example, financial and business interests such as an interest in the financial stability of an individual or company. Again, an objective test will be applied, and the question will be decided by the judge, who will ascertain whether the interest is legitimate and should be protected for the common convenience and welfare of society.

EXAMPLES

The rationale for this head of qualified privilege is said to be the "common convenience and welfare of society".[69] In other words, it is necessary at times for people to be free to communicate without fear of litigation, in order to protect their own interests or because they are under a duty to communicate. The law will respect this freedom as being in the public interest provided it is not abused (i.e. exercised with malice).[70] A few examples will assist. On applying for a job, your new employer will generally require a reference from your former employer. Your former employer is under no legal duty to provide the reference, but is under a social duty to do so. It is very much in the interest of your new employer to see your reference. Therefore, the reference will be protected by qualified privilege: *Spring v Guardian Assurance*.[71] The same reasoning will apply in respect of complaints made or information given to the police or appropriate authorities regarding suspected crimes.

14–017

14–018

14–019

---

68 [1891] 2 Q.B. 341 at 350.
69 *Toogood v Spyring* (1834) 1 Cr.M. & R. 181 at 193 per Parke B; 149 E.R. 1044 at 1049–1050; *Davies v Snead* (1870) LR 5 QB 608 at 611 per Blackburn J.
70 See Lord Nicholls in *Reynolds v Times Newspapers* [2001] 2 A.C. 127 at 194.
71 [1995] 2 A.C. 296. In this case, the plaintiff relied on negligence and breach of contract following a finding that none of the persons involved in the giving of the reference had acted maliciously.

Another example may be seen in the case of *Watt v Longsdon*.[72] In this case, the plaintiff was managing director of a company overseas. The defendant was also a director of the company. The defendant had been informed by a manager (B) of various allegations of misconduct relating to the plaintiff. The defendant wrote back to B, adding his own suspicions, and asking B to obtain sworn statements to support the allegations. Without waiting to verify the complaints, the defendant wrote to the chairman of the board of directors, and to the plaintiff's wife (who was an old friend of his), informing them of the allegations. The allegations proved to be false and the plaintiff sued the defendant for libel. The question arose whether publication of the allegations to the chairman of the board and to the plaintiff's wife were covered by qualified privilege. The Court of Appeal held that the defendant's letter to the chairman of the board of directors was covered by qualified privilege. Employees of a company would have a common interest in the affairs of the company, which entitled them to discuss the behaviour and conduct of another employee. Additionally, there was a possibility that the chairman might be asked to provide a reference for the plaintiff at a future date. The qualified privilege did not extend, however, to the defendant's letter to the plaintiff's wife. Here, the defendant was held to have no duty to pass this information to the wife, particularly when it had not been verified. Yet, this is not clear-cut. Arguably, a wife has an interest in hearing about the misconduct of her husband, and there may sometimes be a "moral" or "social" duty to inform her of his misconduct. The court held that it would depend on the circumstances of each case. If the defendant had known the information to be genuine, it may have been found that the defendant had a moral duty to pass the information to the wife.[73] This case illustrates the problems which can arise in dealing with the vague concepts of "duty" and "interest".

Common law qualified privilege and the media: the *Reynolds* test

14–020

The important case of *Reynolds v Times Newspapers Ltd*[74] called into question the relationship between qualified privilege and the press. *Reynolds* was heard in 1999; a year before the Human Rights Act 1998 came into force. Although the Act did not apply in this case, the House of Lords expressly acknowledged that, in a democracy, the press plays a vital role in ensuring that the public are informed and are aware of the laws and regulations which affect their daily lives. This view is also reflected in s.12(4) of the 1998 Act which provides that the courts should have a particular regard to the importance of freedom of expression and, in deciding cases which concern journalistic, literary or artistic material, should examine: (i) the extent to which the material has, or is about to, become available to the public; (ii) the extent to which it is, or would be, in the public interest for the material to be published; and (iii) any relevant privacy code.[75]

---

72   [1930] 1 K.B. 130.
73   See Scrutton LJ [1930] 1 K.B. 130 at 149–150.
74   [2001] 2 A.C. 127 HL; [1998] 3 W.L.R. 862 CA. Comment: F.A. Trindade (2000) 116 L.Q.R. 185; I. Loveland [2000] P.L. 351.
75   Human Rights Act 1998 s.12(1) provides that: "This section applies if a court is considering whether to

In view of such advocacy of press freedom, the argument was raised that the defence of qualified privilege should be extended to *all* statements published in the public interest. Society has a clear interest in such stories, and the press may regard itself as under a duty to publish such material. Such an extension would ensure that the press, provided it acted without malice, would have the freedom to discuss important issues without the "chill" of a potential libel claim. This argument is particularly strong in relation to political discussion. Political matters are of direct concern to the electorate. Therefore, it can be argued that the electorate has a "right to know". Nevertheless, in *Reynolds v Times Newspapers*, the House of Lords reiterated that the media did not possess its own head of qualified privilege, even when dealing with matters of political information. However, a more liberal stance was suggested. This decision, and its implications, will be examined below.

In *Reynolds*, the former Prime Minister of the Republic of Ireland, Albert Reynolds, brought an action against *The Times* over an article which he claimed implied that he had deliberately misled the Irish Parliament and his cabinet colleagues during a political crisis in Ireland in 1994. He succeeded at first instance, but the jury awarded him one penny in damages. He appealed. *The Times* also appealed, claiming that it was protected by qualified privilege. The Court of Appeal set aside the jury's verdict and ordered a retrial, but held that the article was not covered by qualified privilege. *The Times* appealed to the House of Lords, but the majority of the House rejected its appeal. It was held that there was no special head of qualified privilege for the media based on the public interest in political information and discussion. However, their Lordships were of the view that the "duty/interest" test was flexible enough to include consideration of diverse factors such as the nature, status and source of the material published and the circumstances of publication. Applying this test, the majority agreed with the Court of Appeal that the article did not contain information which the public had a right to know.[76] Their Lordships particularly focused on the fact that the article had failed to mention Mr Reynolds' own explanation of his conduct to the Irish Parliament. The case nevertheless marked a clear recognition by the House of Lords of the importance of the European Convention on Human Rights art.10, and of the need to balance the countervailing interests of reputation and freedom of speech. Lord Nicholls advised future courts to consider a number of factors (which are not exhaustive) in deciding whether a duty to publish political discussion could be established, namely:

14-021

- the seriousness of the allegation—the more serious the charge, the more the public is misinformed and the individual harmed if the allegation is not true;

- the nature of the information—whether it is a matter of public concern;

grant any relief which, if granted, might affect the exercise of the Convention right to freedom of expression". Section 12(5) adds that "relief" includes any remedy or order (other than in criminal proceedings).

76   The minority felt that the issue of qualified privilege should be reconsidered at the re-trial in the light of their Lordships' judgments.

- its source;

- what steps had been taken to verify the information;

- the status of the information, i.e. the reliability of the report;

- the urgency of the matter (news being a perishable commodity);

- whether comment is sought from the claimant;

- whether the gist of the claimant's side of the story has been told;

- the tone of the article; and

- the general circumstances and timing of the publication.

This flexible approach left the courts free to weigh up the competing interests of freedom of expression and reputation on the facts of each case, but also brought uncertainty. While Lord Nicholls asserted that courts should be slow to find that publication is not in the public interest, particularly in relation to political discussion,[77] it remained for the courts to determine how his Lordship's ten guidelines would be applied. It should be noted, however, that these ten factors incorporate both the test for privilege and the question of malice.

THE APPLICATION OF REYNOLDS

14-022

The courts in a number of subsequent decisions sought to clarify the operation of the *Reynolds* test for qualified privilege, notably in the *Loutchansky* litigation[78] and in *Bonnick v Morris*,[79] which stressed that the *Reynolds* test was one of responsible journalism. If the newspaper could satisfy the *Reynolds* criteria and demonstrate that it had acted responsibly, the defence of qualified privilege would apply.

Despite such guidance, the House of Lords in *Jameel v Wall Street Journal Europe SPRL (No.3)*[80] in 2006 noted that the lower courts had been interpreting the *Reynolds* defence in an unduly restrictive manner. It was necessary, therefore, to restate the principles of *Reynolds* qualified privilege.[81] The Court of Appeal in this case had rejected the defence of qualified privilege due to the failure of the newspaper to delay publication to allow the claimant to comment. Whilst this is one of Lord Nicholls' relevant factors, the House of Lords stressed that the

---

77 Lord Nicholls [2001] 2 A.C. 127 at 205.
78 See, in particular, *Loutchansky v Times Newspapers Ltd (Nos 2–5)* [2001] EWCA Civ 1805; [2002] Q.B. 783.
79 [2002] UKPC 31; [2003] 1 A.C. 300.
80 [2006] UKHL 44; [2007] 1 A.C. 359 (also discussed in Ch.13 in the context of a company's right to sue in defamation).
81 [2006] UKHL 44 at [38] per Lord Hoffmann.

ten factors were not hurdles, but merely pointers towards the correct approach to adopt.[82] Their Lordships identified two questions to be addressed in cases of media qualified privilege:

■ that the subject-matter of the article, taken in context and as a whole, was in the public interest; and

■ that the publication met the objective standard of responsible journalism.

On the facts of the case, their Lordships were in no doubt that, despite the failure to contact Mr Jameel,[83] the article as a whole, dealing with the thorny issue of the funding of international terrorism in the wake of the 9/11 attacks, raised a matter of public interest and that the *Wall Street Journal* (described as a respected, influential and non-sensational newspaper)[84] had acted responsibly in taking reasonable steps to verify the facts relied upon. The House of Lords stressed the need to apply the *Reynolds* test more generously and with greater flexibility.[85] Lord Hoffmann also commented that allowance should be made for editorial judgement and the fact that the judge, with the benefit of hindsight, might have made a different editorial decision should not destroy the defence.[86]

In 2012, the Supreme Court felt it necessary to reiterate its guidance in *Flood v Times Newspapers Ltd*.[87] Again the argument was that the Court of Appeal had been too harsh in judging an article which had named Flood as a detective accused of corruption. The court ruled that a story relating to police corruption was of high public interest and that in circumstances where there had been a strong circumstantial case against Flood, it would suffice that the journalist had believed in the truth of the allegations, that this was based on a reasonable investigation and that it was a reasonable belief for him to hold. Lord Mance argued that the courts should take a "broad and practical" approach to the standard of responsible journalism,[88] and that while the courts must have the last word in setting the boundaries of this test, within those boundaries the judgment of responsible journalists and editors would merit respect.[89] Lord Phillips also approved the view expressed by the Privy Council in *Seaga v Harper*[90] that *Reynolds*

---

82   [2006] UKHL 44 at [33] per Lord Bingham and at [56] per Lord Hoffmann.
83   Scepticism was expressed whether any useful response could in any event have been obtained.
84   Lord Bingham [2006] UKHL 44 at [2]. Query to what extent the "quality" of the newspaper should be relevant.
85   The House was divided, however, whether the *Reynolds* defence should be seen as a development of the common law duty/interest test (Lords Bingham, Scott and Hope) or whether it is, in reality, a distinct public interest defence (Lord Hoffmann and Baroness Hale). This did not appear, however, to have any impact on the actual content of the defence and their Lordships were in agreement as to its application to the facts of the case.
86   [2006] UKHL 44 at [51].
87   [2012] UKSC 11; [2012] 2 A.C. 273, reversing the Court of Appeal [2010] EWCA Civ 804. Comment: D. Tan (2013) 129 L.Q.R. 27.
88   *Flood v Times Newspapers Ltd* [2012] UKSC 11; [2012] 2 A.C. 273 at [127].
89   *Flood v Times Newspapers Ltd* [2012] UKSC 11; [2012] 2 A.C. 273 at [137].
90   [2008] UKPC 9; [2008] 1 All E.R. 965. See also Lord Hoffmann in *Jameel* [2006] UKHL 44; [2007] 1 A.C. 359 at [54].

privilege was not simply reserved for the media (although this was the most likely context in which it would be raised) and that it could extend to any publication made by a person who publishes material of public interest in any medium, so long as the "responsible journalism" test is satisfied.[91] On this basis, *Reynolds* privilege could be extended to quasi-media defendants, such as bloggers, and other bodies acting in the public interest such as NGOs.

NEED FOR REFORM?

14–023

The *Reynolds* test, as interpreted in *Jameel* and *Flood*, represented a liberalisation of traditional rules, but the repeated intervention of the highest court suggested that it was being applied inconsistently. The English position may be compared with that of New Zealand, where the New Zealand Court of Appeal rejected *Reynolds* as too uncertain and restrictive and favoured a press-specific head of privilege.[92] In so doing, the court commented that this could be justified on the basis that New Zealand newspapers were more responsible than their English counterparts.[93] The *Reynolds* test may also be contrasted with the position in the US where, following *New York Times v Sullivan*,[94] public figures may only recover damages for defamation if they are able to show by clear and convincing evidence that the defendant published with malice. The UK Government sought in the Defamation Act 2013 to give greater certainty and ensure that freedom of expression received sufficient protection by codifying the *Reynolds* defence based on the Supreme Court's ruling in *Flood*. By giving the defence statutory form both the lower courts and litigants would, in its view, have a clearer picture how the defence should operate. Section 4(6) of the 2013 Act therefore abolishes the *Reynolds* common law defence of qualified privilege in favour of a new defence. The Government has noted, however, that the case law discussed above will provide a helpful (albeit not binding) guide to interpreting how the new statutory defence should be applied.[95]

Qualified privilege under the Defamation Act 2013

SECTION 4: PUBLICATION ON MATTER OF PUBLIC INTEREST

14–024

In contrast to earlier drafts of this section which sought to incorporate the Lord Nicholls' *Reynolds* criteria, s.4 provides that:

> **"(1) It is a defence to an action for defamation for the defendant to show that—**

---

91 [2012] UKSC 11 at [44].
92 See *Lange v Atkinson* [2000] 3 N.Z.L.R. 385 (where a genuine political discussion is involved). Consider also the different Australian test set out in *Lange v Australian Broadcasting Co* (1997) 189 C.L.R. 520 based on a test of reasonableness. For a comparison with Canada, see R. Mullender, "Defamation and responsible communications" (2010) 126 L.Q.R. 368.
93 [2000] 3 N.Z.L.R. 385 at 398.
94 66 376 U.S. 254 (1964).
95 Explanatory Note to Defamation Act 2013 at para.35.

> **(a) the statement complained of was, or formed part of,[96] a statement on a matter of public interest; and**
> **(b) the defendant reasonably believed that publishing the statement complained of was in the public interest."**

The defence is clearly not confined to the media and applies to any statement on a matter of public interest. The two-stage test remains but with a difference: (1) public interest (not defined in the Act but it will have its common law meaning) and (2) instead of "responsible journalism", the test that the defendant reasonably believed that publishing the statement was in the public interest. Again, no express reference is made to malice. The stage (2) test is, as stated in *Flood*, both a subjective and objective test: the defendant must believe publication was in the public interest at the time of publication and the court must find that the belief was a reasonable one to hold in all the circumstances. What is a "reasonable belief" is not defined. In determining whether the belief was a reasonable one, although it is not specified, the courts take into account the *Reynolds* criteria discussed above. Section 4(2) further directs the court to consider all the circumstances of the case, but notes, at s.4(4), that the court should make such allowance for editorial judgement as it considers appropriate.[97] Section 4(5) adds that for the avoidance of doubt, the defence may be relied upon irrespective of whether the statement complained of is a statement of fact or a statement of opinion.

We now have some cases to help us interpret s.4. In *Economou v de Freitas*,[98] a grieving father, whose daughter had killed herself while awaiting trial on charges of fabricating a rape allegation against the claimant, had been sued for making statements to the press that the CPS had been wrong to prosecute his daughter. The Court of Appeal held that although s.4 replaces the common law *Reynolds* defence, the factors identified by Lord Nicholls in that case would be relevant in determining whether the defendant reasonably believed that publication was in the public interest. The criteria should be applied flexibly, however, taking account of the circumstances of the case which would include the role of the defendant. Here, the fact that the statements concerned a matter of public interest[99] which the father actually believed should be published in the public interest was not appealed. The question was whether Mr de Freitas had *reasonably* held that view. The Court noted that while not all of the *Reynolds* criteria were satisfied e.g. he had not sought a comment from the claimant, Mr de Freitas had made some efforts to investigate the merits of the case against his daughter. Acknowledging his status as a

---

96   The Explanatory Note to Defamation Act 2013 at para.30 explains that this phrase serves to indicate that either the words complained of may be on a matter of public interest or that a holistic view may be taken of the statement in the wider context of the document in which it is contained.

97   Defamation Act 2013 s.4(4): "In determining whether it was reasonable for the defendant to believe that publishing the statement complained of was in the public interest, the court must make such allowance for editorial judgement as it considers appropriate".

98   [2018] EWCA Civ 2591; [2019] E.M.L.R. 7.

99   Namely whether the CPS as a public body had been wrong to prosecute Ms de Freitas, a vulnerable rape complainant.

contributor to various articles, the Court held that the test was satisfied. Contributors to media publications and "citizen journalists"/bloggers should not be subject to the same standards as professional journalists.

Economou should not be taken to give a green light to non-journalists. The community blogger in *Doyle v Smith*[100] who falsely alleged that a property developer had admitted to fraud was not allowed to rely on s.4 as a defence. He knew that a major component of the factual account which he presented to readers was untrue. That was fatal. Even if he subjectively believed that it was in the public interest to present false information to the public, such a belief would not be regarded as reasonable. Equally, it should not be seen to justify a harsher approach to journalists. The Supreme Court in *Serafin v Malkiewicz*[101] criticised the Court of Appeal below for rejecting the defence on the basis that not all the Reynolds criteria had been satisfied. The Court firmly stated that while the Reynolds criteria could help guide the application of s.4, they were not to be treated as a mandatory checklist for journalists. Section 4 is a statutory defence in its own right and should be construed as such. On this basis, a failure to invite comment from the claimant prior to publication would no doubt be the subject of some consideration under s.4(1)(b), but doing so was not a requirement to establish the defence.

Section 4(3) retains the controversial defence of "reportage".[102] This was described in *Flood* as "a special, and relatively rare, form of *Reynolds* privilege [which] arises where it is not the content of the reported allegation that is of public interest, but the fact that the allegation has been made".[103] The key issue here is that the article in question involves the neutral reporting of allegations made by one named party against another without adopting, embellishing or endorsing the allegations.[104] If the defendant can show that he or she has not adopted the statement, the defendant is not required to verify the truth of the allegation but simply to check that the allegation has been made. There have only been two successful cases to date.[105] In *Galloway v Telegraph Group Ltd*,[106] the court rejected the defence of reportage in circumstances where the *Daily Telegraph* was found to have gone a long way to adopt and embellish the allegations contained in documents found by its reporter and had done so with relish. Section 4(3) now provides that:

> **"If the statement complained of was, or formed part of, an accurate and impartial account of a dispute to which the claimant was a**

---

100 [2018] EWHC 2935 (QB); [2019] E.M.L.R. 15.

101 [2020] UKSC 23; [2020] 1 W.L.R. 2455.

102 Described by Ward LJ as a "fancy word": *Roberts v Gable* [2007] EWCA Civ 721; [2008] Q.B. 502 at [34].

103 [2012] UKSC 11 at [77] per Lord Phillips.

104 See *Al-Fagih v HH Saudi Research & Marketing (UK) Ltd* [2001] EWCA Civ 1634; [2002] E.M.L.R. 13 (Mantell LJ dissenting) and *Roberts v Gable* [2007] EWCA Civ 721; [2007] E.M.L.R. 16.

105 Namely *Al-Fagih v HH Saudi Research & Marketing (UK) Ltd* [2001] EWCA Civ 1634 and *Roberts v Gable* [2007] EWCA Civ 721.

106 [2006] EWCA Civ 17; [2006] E.M.L.R. 11. The defence also failed in *Charman v Orion Publishing Group Ltd* [2007] EWCA Civ 972; [2008] 1 All E.R. 750.

> party, the court must in determining whether it was reasonable for the defendant to believe that publishing the statement was in the public interest disregard any omission of the defendant to take steps to verify the truth of the imputation conveyed by it."

Section 4 marks a significant step in the history of qualified privilege. *Reynolds* privilege is now replaced by express recognition of a distinct public interest defence. The aim is clearly that s.4 will provide statutory recognition of the value played in a democracy of publication of matters of public interest, subject, of course, to the test stated in s.4(1)(b).

SECTION 6: PEER-REVIEWED STATEMENTS IN SCIENTIFIC OR ACADEMIC JOURNALS ETC

14-025

The introduction of s.6 is perhaps less momentous than s.4, but nevertheless it also represents a reaction to criticism that the defamation defences did not provide sufficient protection for freedom of expression. Section 6 responds to concerns that the threat of defamation proceedings might discourage research in science (which includes medicine and engineering), or academic research more generally, which was critical of the views of others. This problem was brought to the public's attention by the case of *British Chiropractic Association v Singh*,[107] discussed above in the section on honest opinion. Section 6 now provides that the publication of a statement in a scientific or academic journal (whether published electronically or not) is privileged if two conditions are met:

- the statement relates to a scientific or academic matter; and

- before the statement was published in the journal an independent review of the statement's scientific or academic merit was carried out by—(a) the editor of the journal,[108] and (b) one or more persons with expertise in the scientific or academic matter concerned.[109]

Section 6(4) extends the defence to any assessment of the statement's scientific or academic merit in the course of peer review, that is, to cover the reviewers of the article in question. Qualified privilege is lost, however, by malice: s.6(6). It should be noted, however, that it would not have covered the Simon Singh case—a scientist writing an article in a national newspaper which presumably did not undergo any peer review—and for such general scientific debate, the defence of honest opinion will still be relevant.

---

107 [2010] EWCA Civ 350; [2011] 1 W.L.R. 133 (the *Simon Singh* case).

108 In the case of a journal with more than one editor, this signifies the editor or editors who were responsible for deciding to publish the statement concerned: Defamation Act 2013 s.6(8).

109 Where the statement is privileged, this will extend to publication of a fair and accurate copy of, extract from or summary of the statement: Defamation Act 2013 s.6(5).

> ## Qualified privilege under the Defamation Act 1996

14–026

The Defamation Act 1996 provides for numerous occasions on which qualified privilege will arise. This is now subject to amendment by the Defamation Act 2013 s.7 and the amended provisions are listed below. The key section is that of 15(1) which provides that:

> **"The publication of any report[110] or other statement mentioned in Sch.1 to this Act is privileged unless the publication is shown to be made with malice."**

Some of the most important examples in Sch.1 are considered below.

(I) REPORTS OF PARLIAMENTARY PROCEEDINGS

14–027

Absolute privilege only extends to reports, papers, votes and proceedings ordered to be published by either House of Parliament. It does not include fair and accurate reports of parliamentary proceedings, which were covered by common law qualified privilege[111] and are now covered by the Defamation Act 1996. Sch.1 para.1 provides that there is privilege for a fair and accurate report of proceedings in public of a legislature anywhere in the world.[112] Schedule 1 para.7 also provides that a fair and accurate copy of, or extract from, matter published by or on the authority of a government or legislature anywhere in the world is privileged. This expands the previous privilege granted under the Parliamentary Papers Act 1840 s.3.[113] In both cases, publication is covered by qualified privilege "without explanation or contradiction" (the meaning of this phrase is discussed later).

(II) REPORTS OF JUDICIAL PROCEEDINGS

14–028

Defamation Act 1996 s.14 provides that absolute privilege is accorded to fair and accurate contemporaneous reports of court proceedings in public. Fair and accurate non-contemporaneous reports of public judicial proceedings are covered by qualified privilege.[114] The common law is now replaced by the Defamation Act 1996 (Sch.1 para.2) which provides that a fair and accurate report of proceedings in public before a court anywhere in the world is privileged without explanation or contradiction.

---

110 *Henry v BBC (Qualified Privilege)* [2005] EWHC 2787 (QB): broadcast was so heavily laden with editorial comment that it did not qualify as a report protected by Defamation Act 1996 s.15.

111 *Wason v Walter* (1868) L.R. 4 Q.B. 73.

112 For a recent application, see *Curistan v Times Newspapers Ltd* [2008] EWCA Civ 432; [2009] Q.B. 231.

113 As amended by Defamation Act 1952 s.9(1).

114 This did not extend to fair and accurate reports of judicial proceedings in foreign courts: *Webb v Times Publishing Co* [1960] 2 Q.B. 535.

(III) REGISTERS

14–029

Likewise, publication of a fair and accurate copy of or extract from a register required by law to be open to public inspection, for example the register of county court judgments, was privileged under the common law[115] and is now privileged without explanation or contradiction under the Defamation Act 1996 (Sch.1 para.5).

(IV) OTHER MATTERS COVERED BY THE DEFAMATION ACT 1996 S.15 AND SCH.1

14–030

We have already seen the operation of Sch.1 in the examples above. Schedule 1 replaces previous statutory provisions for privilege in the Law of Libel Amendment Act 1888 and the Defamation Act 1952. It also covers some of the common law examples of qualified privilege. It is divided into two sections. Part I deals with reports which are privileged "without explanation or contradiction". Part II deals with reports which are privileged "subject to explanation or contradiction". This distinction is important. Qualified privilege may be lost (for Pt II reports only) if it is proved that the defendant has been requested, by the claimant, to publish in a suitable manner[116] a reasonable letter or statement by way of explanation or contradiction, and has refused or neglected to do so: s.15(2). In other words, the claimant must be given the right of reply with respect to Pt II reports. However, the courts will not permit Sch.1 to be abused. Section 15(3) provides that the privilege will not extend to matters which are not of public interest and the publication of which is not for the public benefit.[117] It will equally not protect the publication of matters prohibited by law.[118]

We shall refrain from repeating the long list of reports and statements given in Sch.1. Readers are advised to look at the Defamation Act 1996. Generally, Pt I covers fair and accurate reports of legislative, court or government body proceedings anywhere in the world, as may be seen from the examples given above. The Pt II list consists of a number of different types of reports, including a fair and accurate copy of, extract from or summary of a document made available by a court anywhere in the world, or by a judge or officer of such a court (para.10)[119]; fair and accurate reports of proceedings at any public meeting held anywhere in the world (para.12)[120]; and fair and accurate reports of proceedings at a general meeting of a listed company, i.e. public companies all over the world (para.13).[121]

---

115 *Searles v Scarlett* [1892] 2 Q.B. 56.
116 That is, in the same manner as the publication complained of or in a manner that is adequate and reasonable in the circumstances: Defamation Act 2013 s.15(2).
117 As amended by Defamation Act 2013 s.7(2).
118 Defamation Act 2013 s.15(4)(a).
119 As substituted by Defamation Act 2013 s.7(4).
120 As amended by Defamation Act 2013 s.7(6).
121 As amended by Defamation Act 2013 s.7(7). The term "listed company" has the same meaning as in the Corporation Tax Act 2009 Pt 12.

Offer of Amends Under the Defamation Act 1996

14–031
This defence applies to unintentional defamation. It may be recalled that the publication of a statement may amount to defamation even though the defendant did not intend to harm the claimant's reputation. For present purposes, there are two senses in which the publication of a defamatory statement might be said to be "unintentional". First, there is the situation where, for example, a newspaper publishes a defamatory statement, knowing that it refers to the claimant, but honestly and reasonably believing that the statement is true (as in *Cassidy v Daily Mirror*, discussed in Ch.13). Secondly, there is the "mistaken identity" situation, where a newspaper publishes a statement which is false and defamatory in relation to the claimant, but intends the statement to refer to someone else, about whom it is true (as in *Newstead v London Express*, also discussed in Ch.13).

Defamation Act 1952 s.4 did provide some mechanism whereby a defendant could, in such circumstances, make an "offer of amends" which, if accepted, would end proceedings, and if not accepted would amount to a defence. But this provision was little used, mainly because of the difficulties defendants had in proving that the statement was published "innocently", as required by s.4(5). A revised version appears in the Defamation Act 1996.[122] Sections 2 to 4 set out the new procedure for making an offer of amends. As May LJ stated in *Milne v Express Newspapers*[123]:

> **"The main purpose of the statutory provisions is plain. It is to encourage the sensible compromise of defamation proceedings without the need for an expensive jury trial."**

Under s.2, the defendant must be prepared:

- To admit that he or she was wrong (or partly wrong);

- To offer in writing to make a suitable correction and apology;

- To publish the correction and apology in a manner that is reasonable and practicable in the circumstances; and

- To pay the claimant such compensation (if any) and such costs as may be agreed or determined to be payable.

The offer may relate to the statement generally, or only to a specific defamatory meaning (known as a "qualified offer"). Timing is important. The offer must be made before service of

---

122 As recommended by the *Neill Committee on Practice and Procedure in Defamation* 1991, Ch.VII.
123 [2004] EWCA Civ 664; [2005] 1 W.L.R. 772 at [14].

a defence.[124] This forces the defendant to decide whether to fight the action or admit that he or she is wrong. If the offer is accepted, the claimant must discontinue the action against the defendant.[125] If the parties cannot agree the amount of compensation to be paid, s.3(5) provides that it will be settled by the court, sitting without a jury, "on the same principles as damages in defamation proceedings".[126] This will involve questions such as mitigation, aggravation and causation of loss. Recent case law has clarified that if an early unqualified offer to make amends is accepted and an agreed apology published, the court is likely to find substantial mitigation, reducing the level of damages awarded.[127]

If the offer is not accepted, the action may continue, but the defendant may use the making of the offer as a defence unless the claimant is able to show that the defendant knew or had reason to believe that the statement referred to the claimant (or was likely to be understood as referring to him) and was both false and defamatory of him. The test is one of bad faith, not negligence.[128] In other words, the burden is on the claimant to show that the defamation was intentional or reckless. Section 4(4) provides that the defendant cannot rely on an offer of amends by way of defence in combination with any other defence. The defence is therefore of limited use, and a defendant would be wise to consider his or her tactical position before relying on an offer or qualified offer of amends as a defence. It should be noted that even if the offer is not accepted, it may be relied upon in mitigation of damages.[129]

On a historical note, the defendant still has a defence under the Libel Act 1843 s.2 (as amended by the Libel Act 1845). This provides that it is a defence, when a libel is published in a newspaper without actual malice or gross negligence, for the defendant to publish a full apology in the newspaper and pay money into court by way of amends. This has not been repealed by the Defamation Act 1996, but has been little used due to substantial procedural disadvantages to the defendant. The Faulks Committee in 1975 recommended its repeal "with a view to simplifying this aspect of the law of defamation",[130] but this sensible suggestion has not been taken up. After the 1996 Act, however, it is only of historical interest.

---

124 Defamation Act 1996 s.2(5).

125 Subject to a residual court discretion to allow a party to resile from an accepted offer in exceptional circumstances: *Warren v Random House Group Ltd* [2008] EWCA Civ 834; [2009] Q.B. 600.

126 See *Abu v MGN Ltd* [2002] EWHC 2345 (QB); [2003] 1 W.L.R. 2201.

127 See *Nail v News Group Newspapers Ltd* [2004] EWCA Civ 1708; [2005] 1 All E.R. 1040 (reduced by 50% but no standard percentage discount and each case would require individual consideration). This is because, due to the early capitulation of the defendant, the claimant's reputation has been vindicated whilst he or she has been spared the anxiety and costs risk of contested proceedings. Where only one defendant (out of several) makes an unqualified offer of amends with published apology, the court will cap his liability when considering joint and several liability with the other defendants: *Veliu v Mazrekaj* [2006] EWHC 1710 (QB); [2007] 1 W.L.R. 495.

128 Defamation Act 1996 s.4(3). "Reason to believe" imports the concept of recklessness, discussed by Lord Diplock in *Horrocks v Lowe* [1975] A.C. 135: see *Milne v Express Newspapers* [2004] EWCA Civ 664; [2005] 1 W.L.R. 772.

129 Defamation Act 1996 s.4(5): "The offer may be relied on in mitigation of damage whether or not it was relied on as a defence".

130 Report of the Committee on Defamation, Cmnd.5909 at para.373.

Innocent Dissemination

14–032 This defence applies to parties involved in the distribution process, who inadvertently become involved in the publication of defamatory material. It therefore has no application to the actual author of the defamatory material, or to the publisher who actively produces the work. An example will help us understand the problem. I write a defamatory article for the Daily Rag. I have published the libel and will be liable, but so at law have the editor, publisher and the distributors of the Daily Rag, including Mr X, the newsagent. Each repetition of the libel is actionable by the claimant. It seems harsh to allow the claimant to sue all of the above parties. Therefore, the defence of innocent dissemination seeks to draw a distinction between those who produce the libel (here myself, my editor and publisher) and those who "disseminate" or distribute it (here the distributors and Mr X). Originally, the defence was part of the common law, as stated in *Vizetelly v Mudie's Select Library Ltd*.[131] The court in this case held that the mechanical distribution of defamatory material by agencies such as newsagents or libraries would be protected against claims for defamation provided they could show that:

- they did not know that the work contained a libel of the claimant;

- it was not by negligence that they did not know of the libel; and

- the defendants did not know, nor ought to have known, that the works were of such a character that they were likely to contain defamatory material.

In the case itself, the defendants were held liable for defamation because they had overlooked a publisher's circular which had requested the return of copies of the book in question, and in fact had no procedure for checking whether the books they lent contained defamatory material.

The common law has now been superseded by the Defamation Act 1996 s.1. It is now a defence to show that:

- the defendant is not the author,[132] editor or commercial publisher (in the sense of issuing material to the public in the course of business)[133] of the statement;

- the defendant took reasonable care in relation to the publication; and

- the defendant did not know, and had no reason to believe, that what he or she did caused or contributed to the publication of a defamatory statement.

---

131   [1900] 2 Q.B. 170, applying *Emmens v Pottle* (1885) 16 Q.B.D. 354.
132   Defamation Act 1996 s.1(2) defines "author" as originator of the statement, but does not include a person who did not intend that his or her statement be published at all.
133   Defamation Act 1996 s.1(2).

In assessing the above criteria, the court will have regard to the extent of the defendant's responsibilities for the content of, or decision to publish, the statement; the nature or circumstances of the publication; and the previous conduct or character of the author, editor or publisher (s.1(5)). For example, if the defendant distributes work by an author renowned for controversy, the defendant will be expected to vet the work carefully for defamatory material. Sections 1(3)(a) to (e) list a number of individuals who do not qualify as "authors", "editors" or "publishers". These provisions are not comprehensive, and do not prevent the courts from reasoning by analogy. Section 1(3)(a) provides that distributors and printers[134] can rely on a s.1 defence. Interestingly, broadcasters of live programmes may also rely on the defence if, in the circumstances, they have no effective control over the maker of the statement, for example in live phone-in programmes.[135] Again, however, if controversial guests are invited, editors would be wise to employ some kind of screening process, and consider devices such as a delay mechanism on the transmission of material, if they wish to show that they have taken reasonable care.

INTERNET DEFAMATION

The internet is provided for, in s.1(3)(c) and (e). Section 1(3)(e) covers the "operator or provider of access to a communications system by means of which the statement is transmitted, or made available, by a person over whom he had no effective control"—essentially an internet service provider or "ISP". This particular provision was considered in the case of *Godfrey v Demon Internet Ltd*.[136] The defendants were an ISP which provided a particular newsgroup, which stored postings for about a fortnight. In January 1997, an unknown person made a posting to the newsgroup which was defamatory of Dr Godfrey. Godfrey contacted the defendants four days later, requesting that the posting be removed from their news server. The defendants failed to do so, and the posting remained on the server for the full two-week period. It was accepted that the defendants could have removed the posting had they chosen to do so. Godfrey sued the defendants for libel. Morland J struck out the defendants' s.1 defence. The defendants had known of the posting's defamatory contents and, by failing to remove the statements, lost the protection of s.1 of the Act. While the defendants were not the author, editor or commercial publisher of the statement, they could not show that they had taken reasonable care in relation to the publication, nor that they did not know that what they did caused or contributed to the publication of a defamatory statement. Morland J also refused to accept that an ISP could not "publish" information.[137] An ISP which transmitted a defamatory posting on a news server would, by analogy to a bookseller, be deemed to publish the

14–033

---

134   Ch.11 of the report of the Faulks Committee in 1975 (Report of the Committee on Defamation, Cmnd.5909) recommended that the defence of innocent dissemination should be extended to printers.
135   Defamation Act 1996 s.1(3)(d).
136   [2001] Q.B. 201.
137   In effect, rejecting the "mere conduit" argument that has gained acceptance in the US. Contrast the position where the information is "cached", that is stored temporarily on the computer system for the purpose of enabling the efficient availability of internet material. Here, *Bunt v Tilley* [2006] EWHC 407 (QB); [2007] 1 W.L.R. 1243 held that the role of the ISP is passive and it would not be liable unless it had been knowingly involved

information contained in the posting.[138] Subsequent case law has indicated that an ISP can only avoid being held accountable for publishing information if its role is purely passive.[139]

Fears were expressed after *Godfrey* that the decision would lead to a restriction of freedom of speech on the internet. Faced with an allegation that a posting is defamatory, most ISPs would simply withdraw the posting to avoid potential litigation and would not bother to check whether the allegation is well founded. Arguably, this would give individuals the opportunity to "veto" any posting which contains information they do not wish to be published and consequently limit free speech. It is notable that the US Supreme Court, when faced with a similar case in *Lunney v Prodigy*,[140] chose to find in favour of the ISP. The introduction of the Electronic Commerce (EC Directive) Regulations 2002 did not remove these fears.[141] These Regulations, implementing EC Directive 2000/31,[142] limit the potential liability of ISPs in relation to a number of legal claims, including defamation, obscenity and copyright. Regulation 19 grants immunity to the ISP which hosts the relevant site, but only if two conditions are met:

■ The ISP does not have actual knowledge of the unlawful activity or information and is not aware of facts or circumstances from which it would have been apparent to the ISP that the activity or information was unlawful; and

■ It acts expeditiously to remove such information on obtaining any such knowledge.

The Law Commission in its 2002 report discussed below concluded that this would act in the same manner as s.1, again leaving the ISP potentially liable where it has been notified of an allegedly defamatory posting.[143]

---

in the process of publication (see also Electronic Commerce (EC Directive) Regulations 2002 (SI 2002/2013) reg.18).

138 Dr Godfrey's claim against Demon was finally settled, with much publicity, with an agreement to pay Godfrey £15,000 in damages plus costs which amounted to almost £250,000: *The Times* 31 March 2000.

139 *Tamiz v Google Inc* [2013] EWCA Civ 68; [2013] 1 W.L.R. 2151: Google provided a platform for blogs and was found to have associated itself with their publication when it was notified of defamatory material on a blog in circumstances in which it could have readily removed or blocked access to any notice which did not comply with its own terms and conditions. Contrast *Metropolitan International Schools Ltd (t/a SkillsTrain and t/a Train2game) v Designtechnica Corp (t/a Digital Trends)* [2009] EWHC 1765 (QB); [2011] 1 W.L.R. 1743 (Google not publisher of allegedly defamatory material appearing on a search return).

140 See 529 US 1098 (2000) *The Times* 3 May 2000, where the US Supreme Court let stand a decision of the New York Court of Appeals (94 N.Y. 2d 242; 701 N.Y.S. 2d 684; 723 N.E. 2d 539) that Prodigy was a "common carrier" who would not be responsible for what appeared on its site.

141 Electronic Commerce (EC Directive) Regulations 2002 (SI 2002/2013) in force from 21 August 2002.

142 Directive 2000/31 on certain legal aspects of information society services, in particular electronic commerce, in the Internal Market [2000] OJ L178/1.

143 *Defamation and the Internet: A preliminary investigation*: para.2.23. Not all commentators agree, however, arguing that the term "unlawful" in reg.19 makes it a more generous defence than s.1. Eady J remarked in *Bunt v Tilley* [2006] EWHC 407 (QB) at [72] that "in order to be able to characterise something as 'unlawful' a person would need to know something of the strength or weakness of available defences", e.g. privilege or honest opinion.

Loutchansky v Times Newspapers Ltd (No.2)[144] highlighted a further risk of liability for internet publishers. Here, the article in question had been posted as part of *The Times* (at that time) publicly accessible online archive. The Court of Appeal held that every hit of the article on this site would amount to publication. This is consistent with *Godfrey*, but the decision in *Duke of Brunswick v Harmer*[145] meant that every publication would give rise to a cause of action and so the claimant would be able to sue every time someone accessed the article. It was argued that such ongoing liability would be contrary to free speech, place an unfair burden on the ISP and totally undermine the one-year limitation period for defamation claims (see below under "Limitation"). The court rejected these arguments. As "stale news", such information had limited public interest value and, in any event, the court concluded that the attachment of an appropriate notice, warning that any suspected article should not be treated as the truth, would remove the sting from the material and that any claims for damages would be modest. The court thus refused to change the law in favour of the US "single publication" rule,[146] whereby an article is published only once when it is first posted on the archive.[147]

The Court of Appeal in *Jameel v Dow Jones & Co Inc*[148] suggested that defendants would find more success in claiming abuse of process. Here, an article had listed a number of alleged donors, including the claimant, to an organisation that was claimed to be a front for Al Qaeda. It had been posted on the internet in the US for the *Wall Street Journal On-Line*, a subscriber service. Evidence suggested that only five[149] subscribers had accessed the article in the UK. It was held that, in such circumstances, the court could strike out the libel action as an abuse of process. Where publication within the jurisdiction was minimal and did not amount to a real and substantial tort harming the claimant's reputation, the claim could be struck out on the basis that the costs of proceeding to trial would be out of all proportion to what would be achieved. The burden is therefore on the claimant to establish that there has been more than minimal access to the material. The courts are not prepared to presume at law that there has been substantial publication, even where the site is open to general access.[150]

REFORM: DEFAMATION ACT 2013 SS.5, 8 AND 10

Despite the possibility of striking out claims for abuse of process, doubts were expressed whether the current state of the law in relation to internet defamation was satisfactory. The

---

144 [2001] EWCA Civ 1805; [2002] Q.B. 783.

145 (1849) 14 Q.B. 185; 117 E.R. 75. Upheld in *Berezovsky v Michaels* [2000] 1 W.L.R. 1004 HL.

146 *Gregoire v GP Putnam's Sons* (1948) 81 NE 2d 45 (applied to a website publication in *Firth v State of New York* (2002) NY Int 88).

147 *The Times*' appeal to the European Court of Human Rights was dismissed: *Times Newspapers Ltd v United Kingdom (3002/03 and 23676/03)* [2009] E.M.L.R. 14. The court did, however, express concern that, on different facts, libel proceedings against a newspaper after a significant lapse of time might, in the absence of exceptional circumstances, give rise to a disproportionate interference with press freedom under ECHR art.10.

148 [2005] EWCA Civ 75; [2005] Q.B. 946.

149 Three of whom were said to be agents or associates of the claimant.

150 *Al Amoudi v Brisard* [2006] EWHC 1062 (QB); [2007] 1 W.L.R. 113.

Law Commission in its report, "Defamation and the Internet: A preliminary investigation",[151] found a "strong case" for changing the law. It had been given evidence that ISPs were receiving over 100 complaints each year, and concluded that, under the present law, the safest course for any ISP in such circumstances would be to remove the material, whether or not the alleged defamatory material was in the public interest or true. This caused a potential conflict with ECHR art.10. Equally, although it agreed with the view that damages arising from online archives would generally be modest, it noted concerns as to the costs and difficulties facing publishers in defending such cases if brought many years after the original publication.

Defamation Act 2013 s.8 finally introduces a single publication rule. It provides that where a person publishes a statement to the public[152] and then subsequently publishes a statement (whether or not to the public) which is substantially the same, any cause of action for the purpose of the one-year limitation period for defamation claims[153] accrues on the date of the first publication: ss.8(1) and (3). The test will be whether the subsequent publication is "materially different" from the manner of the first publication. Relevant factors for the court to consider will be the level of prominence that a statement is given and the extent of the subsequent publication.[154] This removes the multiple publication rule stated above.

Defamation Act 2013 s.5 goes further to provide ISPs with positive protection against defamation claims. It provides for a new defence: the operator of the website on which the statement is posted did not post the statement on the website itself. The defence will be defeated, however, if the claimant can show:

■ it was not possible for the claimant to identify[155] the person who posted the statement;

■ the claimant gave the operator a notice of complaint in relation to the statement; and

■ the operator failed to respond to the notice of complaint in accordance with any provision contained in regulations.[156]

The Defamation (Operators of Websites) Regulations 2013[157] set out what must be included in the notice of complaint, what the operator must do in response to it to retain the defence and the period within which it should act. It should also be noted that the defence is defeated by malice, but that the operator will not lose the defence simply by moderating the statements posted on the site by others.[158] It was hoped that such a defence would prove useful for opera-

---

151 Scoping study No.2, December 2002.
152 "Publication to the public" includes publication to a section of the public: Defamation Act 2013 s.8(2).
153 See below.
154 See Defamation Act 2013 ss.8(4) and (5).
155 It is possible for a claimant to "identify" a person only if the claimant has sufficient information to bring proceedings against the person: Defamation Act 2013 s.5(4).
156 Defamation Act 2013 s.5(3).
157 Defamation (Operators of Websites) Regulations 2013 (SI 2013/3028).
158 Defamation Act 2013 ss.5(11) and (12) respectively.

tors of discussion forums and blog sites, but to date there are no reported cases. It would seem that the take-up of the s.5 procedure has been very low to its complicated and onerous nature, with website operators preferring to rely on other defences if sued.

More generally, the Defamation Act 2013 s.10 provides that:

> "a court does not have jurisdiction to hear and determine an action for defamation brought against a person who was not the author, editor or publisher[159] of the statement complained of unless the court is satisfied that it is not reasonably practicable for an action to be brought against the author, editor or publisher."

The aim of this section is to focus defamation claims on the primary publisher of the allegedly defamatory statement and stop secondary publishers such as booksellers and newsagents being unfairly targeted. One potential difficulty remains, however. Even if the claimant is successful against the primary publisher, the latter may not be in a position to remove the defamatory statement from the website or stop booksellers or newsagents from distributing the material. This is resolved by s.13 of the 2013 Act which provides that where a court gives judgment for the claimant in an action for defamation, the court may order (a) the operator of a website on which the defamatory statement is posted to remove the statement, or (b) any person who was not the author, editor or publisher of the defamatory statement to stop distributing, selling or exhibiting material containing the statement.

Sections 5, 10 and 13 stand alongside the existing Defamation Act 1996 s.1. Agate comments that these sections are to be welcomed for moving the focus away from the web operator and onto the user responsible for the statement, although she expresses some concerns how they will operate in practice.[160]

Limitation

14-036

This is not really a defence, but an assertion that the claimant has run out of time to bring his or her claim for defamation. The Limitation Act 1980 sets out time limits for claimants bring a claim. In defamation the time limit is very short. Defamation Act 1996 ss.5 and 6 amend the Limitation Act 1980 to reduce the time limit from three years to one year. Limitation Act 1980 s.4A now provides that the ordinary six year time limit for claims in tort does not apply. After one year has expired, the claimant cannot normally sue, however bad the injury to his or her reputation. The assumption is that if your reputation has been injured, you should have

---

159 The terms "author", "editor" and "publisher" have the same meaning as in Defamation Act 1996 s.1: s.10(2).
160 See J. Agate, "The Defamation Act 2013—key changes for online" [2013] C.T.L.R. 170.

realised this and be sufficiently incensed to bring the claim within a short period of time.[161] This logic is supported by the introduction of the single publication rule under the Defamation Act 2013 s.8 explained above: the one-year time limit in such cases accrues on the date of first publication. The court does, however, have a largely unfettered discretion to hold that the time limit should not apply under the Limitation Act 1980 s.32A.[162] In so doing, it must balance the interests of the parties with regard to all the circumstances of the case. Section 32A(1) provides that:

> "If it appears to the court that it would be equitable to allow an action to proceed having regard to the degree to which—(a) the operation of s.4A of this Act prejudices the plaintiff . . . and (b) any decision of the court under this subsection would prejudice the defendant . . . the court may direct that that section shall not apply to the action."

The court will consider the length of the delay, why it occurred and, if it is due to lack of knowledge of certain facts, how soon the claimant acted once these facts were known.[163] The court will also examine the extent to which the delay has weakened the evidential basis for the claim.[164] The provisions also apply to malicious falsehood.[165]

Remedies: Damages and Injunctive Relief

14-037   The main remedy for defamation is that of damages, although the claimant may also seek an injunction to stop future publication of the defamatory statements. One particular concern has been the level of damages awarded in libel trials. Commentators have argued that this is due to the use of juries and have contrasted the level of damages awarded for libel with that awarded for personal injury; the latter being strictly controlled by the courts and often considerably less in value. This section will examine attempts by the courts to control the level of damages awards before looking at the impact of the Defamation Act 2013 s.11, which provides for trial without a jury in defamation cases unless the court orders otherwise. It will also consider procedural reforms which seek to reduce the costs of a defamation claim and why

---

161   Although it should be noted that in the case of slander not actionable per se, the one year time limit will only start to run from the date on which the special damage occurs.

162   See *Steedman v BBC* [2001] EWCA Civ 1534; [2002] E.M.L.R. 17 (extension rejected where good claim against solicitor and absence of any contemporary complaint). Defamation Act 2013 s.8(6) clarifies that the single publication rule does not affect the court's discretion under s.32A.

163   See Limitation Act 1980 s.32A(2)(a) and (b).

164   See Limitation Act 1980 s.32A(2)(c).

165   See *Cornwall Gardens PTE Ltd v RO Garrard & Co Ltd* [2001] EWCA Civ 699; *The Times*, 19 June 2001.

it is difficult to obtain an interim injunction for defamation. Damages and injunctions will be examined in more detail in Ch.17.

Damages: controlling the level of damages awarded

Damages traditionally have been assessed by the jury, not the judge. Initially, the Court of Appeal was reluctant to interfere with jury awards, but, by 1990, faced with a series of notoriously high awards, this attitude had to change.[166] Courts and Legal Services Act 1990 s.8 empowered the Court of Appeal to substitute its own figure of damages for that of the jury without the need for a retrial.[167] More fundamentally, the Court of Appeal recognised that the judge must exercise some degree of control over jury awards, by ensuring that they receive appropriate guidance in the summing-up.

14-038

This can be seen in the 1994 case of *Rantzen v Mirror Group Newspapers (1986) Ltd*,[168] where the newspaper had accused the television presenter Esther Rantzen, who had founded the children's charity ChildLine, of knowingly protecting a person guilty of sexual abuse. The jury had awarded £250,000. The Court of Appeal set this aside under the Courts and Legal Services Act 1990 s.8 and substituted the figure of £110,000. Neill LJ held that:

> "We consider therefore that the common law if properly understood requires the courts to subject large awards of damages to a more searching inquiry than has been customary in the past . . . The question becomes: 'Could a reasonable jury have thought that their award was necessary to compensate the plaintiff and to re-establish his reputation?'"[169]

Further guidance was given in *John v Mirror Group Newspapers Ltd*.[170] Despite the ruling in *Rantzen*, the court found that there was still evidence of disproportionate libel awards, and thought further action was necessary. On this basis, the court accepted that juries should be informed, by way of guidance, of the level of damages awarded in personal injury cases. While it was clearly impossible to compare severe brain damage with an attack on a person's reputation, it would give the jury some guidance as to the level of damages necessary in the

---

166 In *Tolstoy Miloslavsky v United Kingdom* (1995) 20 E.H.R.R. 442, the European Court of Human Rights found the law prior to the Courts and Legal Services Act 1990 and *Rantzen v Mirror Group Newspapers (1986) Ltd* [1994] Q.B. 670 to be contrary to the European Convention on Human Rights art.10. The jury's award of £1.5 million in damages at trial (which was three times the size of the highest libel award previously made in England) was therefore a violation of art.10.

167 Note also that in *Grobbelaar v News Group Newspapers Ltd* [2002] UKHL 40; [2002] 1 W.L.R. 3024, the House of Lords exercised its inherent power to alter the award.

168 [1994] Q.B. 670.

169 [1994] Q.B. 670 at 692.

170 [1997] Q.B. 586. Applied in *Kiam v MGN Ltd* [2002] EWCA Civ 43; [2003] Q.B. 281.

circumstances. The judge, and advocates for both sides, would now be permitted to address the jury on what they considered to be the correct level of damages. Such changes, it was hoped, would make the assessment of damages "more rational and so more acceptable to public opinion".[171] The courts would continue to refer to decisions under the 1990 Act (as suggested in *Rantzen*), but nevertheless still refused to allow references to defamation awards which had been made on different sets of facts. The Court of Appeal reduced the jury's award of compensatory damages in this case from £75,000 to £25,000.

AGGRAVATED AND EXEMPLARY DAMAGES

14-039

Aggravated and exemplary damages will be discussed generally in Ch.17, but it is worth highlighting the important role they play in defamation cases. Aggravated damages will be awarded for additional injury to the claimant's feelings.[172] Further, defamation remains one of the few occasions when exemplary or punitive damages may be awarded. The court will award exemplary damages where the defendant, either knowing a statement to be false or careless whether it be true or false, has deliberately published the statement because the profit gained from publication will outweigh any financial penalties.[173] This obviously is particularly apposite to newspapers publishing sensational stories such as the one concerning Elton John in *John*. Nevertheless, such sums are also controlled, and the Court of Appeal reduced the exemplary damages in *John* from £275,000 to £50,000. Sir Thomas Bingham MR warned that:

> "principle requires that an award of exemplary damages should never exceed the minimum sum necessary to meet the public purpose underlying such damages, that of punishing the defendant, showing that tort does not pay and deterring others."[174]

THE IMPACT OF DEFAMATION ACT 2013 S.11

14-040

Prior to the Act, there had been concern that the controls listed above still did not prevent juries from awarding disproportionate sums as damages. In *Kiam v MGN Ltd*,[175] Sedley LJ dissenting complained that the *John* case had failed in its purpose of limiting damages: "the train has left the station again and is now accelerating".[176] The Court of Appeal noted that whatever guidance was given to juries, the sums awarded still remained large. This was exacerbated

---

171   [1997] Q.B. 586 at 616 per Sir Thomas Bingham MR. But note the doubts expressed by Lord Hoffmann in *Gleaner Co Ltd v Abrahams* [2003] UKPC 55; [2004] 1 A.C. 628 as to the comparability of personal injury and defamation awards due to their different purpose and differing impact on society.
172   See, e.g. *Cairns v Modi* [2012] EWCA Civ 1382; [2013] 1 W.L.R. 1015: aggravated damages to former professional cricketer following unsubstantiated match-fixing allegations on Twitter.
173   See *Broome v Cassell* [1972] A.C. 1027.
174   [1997] Q.B. 586 at 619.
175   [2003] Q.B. 281.
176   [2003] Q.B. 281 at 302.

by changes in personal injury law which increased awards for non-pecuniary loss[177]—to which libel juries were asked in *John* to refer. The conclusion had to be that however much the courts refined the guidance given to juries, ultimately the question would arise whether it would be simpler just to abolish the jury in defamation cases, or, less drastically, place assessment of damages in the hands of the judge as in personal injury cases. The Faulks Committee in 1975 had recommended removing the right to trial by jury and permitting only a judicial discretion to allow trial by jury if necessary.[178] Lord Phillips in 2010 again asked whether "the time [had] come to recognise that defamation is no longer a field in which trial by jury is desirable?"[179] This is now the case under s.11. It remains to be seen whether, following the implementation of the Act, complaints continue to arise in this area of law. Warby J in *Barron v Vines* was optimistic, commenting that:

> "Practice in libel actions has developed considerably since 1997, and the Defamation Act 2013 has removed the presumption in favour of trial by jury in defamation cases. As a result, most damages awards in recent years have been made by judges, rather than juries. It is fair to say that a more or less coherent framework of awards has been built up."[180]

Procedural reforms

14–041

Much of the cost of defamation cases comes from the complicated trial process. Defamation Act 1996 s.8 establishes that some cases may be dealt with by a summary non-jury procedure.[181] Under s.8(2), where the claimant has no realistic prospect of success, and there is no reason why the claim should be tried, a judge without a jury may dismiss the claim. Alternatively, where there is no defence which has a realistic prospect of success, and there is no other reason why the claim should be tried,[182] a judge may give judgment for the claimant and grant the claimant summary relief.[183] The remedies open to the claimant are limited, however. Under s.9(1), the court has a range of options which consist of: (i) a declaration that

---

177 See Ch.17; *Heil v Rankin* [2001] Q.B. 272.
178 Report of the Committee on Defamation, Cmnd.5909 at para.516.
179 *Spiller v Joseph* [2010] UKSC 53 at [116].
180 [2016] EWHC 1226 (QB) at [81].
181 The new procedure was brought into force on 28 February 2000.
182 In deciding whether the claim should be tried, the judge will consider, amongst other things, how serious the defamation is and whether it is justifiable in the circumstances to proceed to a full trial: Defamation Act 1996 s.8(4).
183 Defamation Act 1996 s.8(3). See *James Gilbert Ltd v MGN Ltd* [2000] E.M.L.R. 680 and, generally, CPR r.53.2. The test is the same as that under CPR Pt 24, which allows for summary disposal of cases generally. In *Loutchansky v Times Newspapers Ltd (Nos 2–5)* [2001] EWCA Civ 1805; [2002] Q.B. 783, the Court of Appeal

the statement was false and defamatory; (ii) an order that the defendant publish a suitable correction and apology; (iii) an award of damages not exceeding £10,000; and (iv) an injunction restraining publication. It is for the parties to arrange the correction and apology. If they cannot agree on its content, s.9(2) provides that the claimant must be satisfied by a summary of the court's judgment. The advantages to the parties are obvious: a speeded-up procedure which avoids a long-winded and costly trial. The claimant can ensure that the statement is corrected and may obtain a certain amount of damages. The judge is given a discretion under s.8(3) to force the claimant to follow the summary route if it "will adequately compensate him for the wrong he has suffered".

Use of this provision will inevitably be confined to straightforward cases where the claimant is prepared to accept an award not exceeding £10,000. Additionally, in the light of ECHR, which (under art.6) grants the defendant a right to a fair trial, it must be questioned to what extent courts should restrict the defendant's ability to assert his or her right to freedom of expression in a full trial. It is a first step, however, in trying to simplify the complicated and costly procedure involved in defamation cases.

Interim injunctions

14–042
Injunctions will be considered in more detail in Ch.17. It is worth noting, however, in the context of defamation that although the claimant may wish to obtain an injunction to prevent publication of the statement in question, the courts will only rarely grant an injunction prior to a full hearing at the trial. Therefore, even if the claimant is given prior notice of publication of statements which may diminish his or her reputation, it will be difficult to prevent publication. The award of an injunction is at the court's discretion and the court will not ordinarily grant interim relief to restrain a libel where the defendant alleges a defence. In particular, if truth is raised as a defence, interim relief will not be granted unless the claimant can prove that the libel is plainly untrue.[184] In *Holley v Smyth*,[185] the majority of the Court of Appeal upheld this rule as supporting the right to free speech, even where the defendant's motives were questionable.[186] More recently, the Court of Appeal in *Greene v Associated Newspapers Ltd*[187] confirmed that such a rule was consistent with the European Convention on Human Rights and that a lesser test would seriously weaken the effect of art.10.[188]

---

held that there was no reason why the summary procedure should not also be used for disposing of questions of quantum alone once liability had been determined or admitted.

184 See *Bonnard v Perryman* [1891] 2 Ch. 269 CA. See also *William Coulson & Sons v James Coulson and Co* (1887) 3 T.L.R. 846: an interim injunction should only be used in the clearest of cases.

185 [1998] Q.B. 726 (Staughton LJ dissenting).

186 The defendant had used the threat of publication as a means of putting pressure on the claimant to compensate him for an alleged wrong.

187 [2004] EWCA Civ 1462; [2005] Q.B. 972.

188 The Court of Appeal accepted that a different rule would apply for breach of confidence: see Ch.15 and *LNS v Persons Unknown* [2010] EWHC 119 (QB); [2010] E.M.L.R.16.

This chapter will end with an examination of an alternative to suing in defamation: the tort of malicious falsehood. The advantages and disadvantages of this option will be examined below.

Malicious or Injurious Falsehood

Malicious falsehood is generally classified as an economic tort, i.e. a tort which specifically protects the economic interests of the claimant.[189] Here, the claimant is complaining that the defendant has made a false statement to a third party which has damaged his or her business interests. This is distinct from defamation. Defamation protects the business reputation of the claimant. Malicious falsehood protects the financial interests of the claimant. This distinction is illustrated in the following example. The defendant has told X that the claimant's shop does not sell paper. This is untrue. X, as a result, buys his paper from the defendant's shop. Such a statement will not necessarily affect the claimant's trading reputation but will obviously reduce the income of the shop, and affect the claimant's financial position. On this basis, the Court of Appeal in *Ratcliffe v Evans*[190] held that the plaintiff had a valid action when a newspaper published a statement that the plaintiff's firm had gone out of business. It was held that the statement did not reflect on the plaintiff's character, but nevertheless the plaintiff could sue for the general loss of business which resulted from publication.

14-043

To bring a case for malicious falsehood, there are four main requirements:

- the defendant made a false statement concerning the claimant or his or her property;

- maliciously;

- to some person other than the claimant; and

- as a result the claimant suffered economic loss.

The tort is therefore not actionable without proof of damage. Special damage must be proved, such as loss of business.[191] However, the claimant may be assisted by the Defamation Act 1952 s.3(1), which provides that it is sufficient if the words are published in writing and are calculated to cause pecuniary damage to the claimant. This provision covers many of the occasions giving

---

189 For economic torts generally, see Ch.12.
190 [1892] 2 Q.B. 524.
191 *Royal Baking Powder Co v Wright Crossley & Co* (1900) 18 R.P.C. 95 at 99: "The damage is the gist of the action and therefore . . . it must be especially alleged and proved".

rise to the action and makes the tort largely actionable without proof of special damage, provided the words are calculated to cause the claimant financial loss. Moore-Bick LJ in the case of *Tesla Motors Ltd v BBC*[192] explained that the term "calculated" means that the statement complained about must be more likely than not to cause the claimant pecuniary damage. A claimant who is unable to prove actual damage and who relies on s.3 may still recover substantial damages and is not restricted to nominal damages.[193]

The other requirements must, however, be met. The statement must be proved to be false.[194] This, unlike in defamation, will not be presumed. The claimant must also show that the statement was made maliciously, i.e. that the defendant knew that the statement was false, or was reckless as to whether it was true or not,[195] or was actuated by some indirect, dishonest or improper motive.[196] It is always a defence that the statement was made in good faith.[197]

14-044

Damages may extend to distress and injury to feelings consequential on financial loss. In *Khodaparast v Shad*,[198] an Iranian woman had lost her part-time job as a teacher in a religious school and found it difficult to gain employment when a former lover had distributed mock-up advertisements for telephone sex services using her photograph. At trial, he had persisted in claiming that these were genuine advertisements and such behaviour was typical of her loose morals. The trial judge had found in favour of the claimant and awarded additional aggravated damages[199] to reflect the injury to the claimant's feelings from the defendant's conduct prior to and during the trial. The Court of Appeal approved this award. As stated by Stuart-Smith LJ:

> "once the plaintiff is entitled to sue for malicious falsehood, whether on proof of special damage or by reasons of s.3 of the 1952 Act I can see no reason why, in an appropriate case, he or she should not recover aggravated damages for injury to feelings . . . justice requires that it should be so."[200]

---

192 [2013] EWCA Civ 152 at [27]. The claimant in this case experienced difficulties in establishing causation and the claim was ultimately struck out.

193 *Joyce v Sengupta* [1993] 1 W.L.R. 337 at 347.

194 It does not include mere advertising "puffs": *White v Mellin* [1895] A.C. 154.

195 *Shapiro v La Morta* (1923) 40 T.L.R. 201. See also *Cruddas v Calvert* [2015] EWCA Civ 171; [2015] E.M.L.R. 16 at [111]: foreseeability does not constitute malice for the purpose of malicious falsehood.

196 *Balden v Shorter* [1933] Ch. 427. For a recent example, see *Al-Ko Kober Ltd v Sambhi* [2019] EWHC 2409 (QB): rival trader making false statements about the claimant's product in YouTube videos.

197 *Spring v Guardian Assurance* [1995] 2 A.C. 296.

198 [2000] 1 W.L.R. 618.

199 See Ch.17: Damages.

200 [2000] 1 W.L.R. 618 at 630–631, relying heavily on dicta from Nicholls VC and Sir Michael Kerr in *Joyce v Sengupta* [1993] 1 W.L.R. 337 and distinguishing previous negative dicta in *Fielding v Variety Inc* [1967] 2 Q.B. 841.

It should be noted that this is a supplementary claim. The tort does not permit a claimant to obtain damages solely for emotional distress or injury to his or her reputation. Any claim for the latter must be brought under the tort of defamation.

Generally, therefore, defamation will be easier (depending, of course, on the facts) for the claimant to prove, so few actions are brought for malicious falsehood. In the past, claimants have also had the benefit of a jury in defamation, which is not available for malicious falsehood, although this has now changed. There may nevertheless be advantages to suing for malicious falsehood. First, the claimant does not have to show an attack on his or her business *reputation*, and, if a company, serious financial loss under Defamation Act 2013 s.1(2), but simply that the false statement has resulted in the business losing money.[201] Secondly, the tort may prove useful where other causes of action fail. For example, in *Kaye v Robertson*,[202] the court, horrified by the behaviour of the newspaper in question, relied on malicious falsehood to support Kaye's claim. Gorden Kaye, a popular actor, had been seriously injured when a piece of wood smashed through his car windscreen during a bad storm in 1990. He was in a critical condition for many days, and a special notice was placed on his door to keep out visitors. A journalist and photographer from the *Sunday Sport* newspaper nevertheless entered the room, obtained a picture of Mr Kaye using a flash camera, and claimed that Kaye had consented to an "interview". The paper alleged that it had obtained "a great old-fashioned scoop". In fact, Kaye was in intensive care and could not remember the incident 15 minutes after the event. The Court of Appeal took a dim view of such conduct, but struggled to find a basis for liability in tort. Trespass to the person (see Ch.11) did not work. The use of a flash by itself did not amount to battery.[203] The judges were tempted by libel, on the basis that it was defamatory to state falsely that Kaye had consented to give an exclusive interview to the *Sunday Sport*. However, the court adhered to the rule that interim injunctions (i.e. injunctions before the final hearing) should be used sparingly in libel.[204] The court therefore resorted to malicious falsehood: the paper's allegation that the story and photograph had been taken with Kaye's consent was clearly false, and Kaye had lost the right to sell his first interview after the accident for profit.[205] Bingham LJ commented that:

---

201 The courts have also suggested that, unlike defamation, the claimant can allege that the words used do not have a single meaning to the reasonable reader and, on this basis, rely on the false meaning of the words: see *Ajinomoto Sweeteners Europe SAS v Asda Stores Ltd* [2010] EWCA Civ 609; [2011] Q.B. 497.

202 [1991] F.S.R. 62.

203 Although Glidewell LJ suggested at 68 that a bright light deliberately shone into another's eyes which injured his sight or damaged him in some other way might at law be a battery.

204 See para.14–042 above.

205 The Court of Appeal also considered the economic tort of passing off, in which the claimant sues for a misrepresentation made to the claimant's prospective or existing customers which is calculated to injure the business or goodwill of the claimant and which has caused or threatened actual damage to the business or goodwill of the claimant. The claimant must be a "trader". The court held that the possibility of Kaye selling the story of his accident did not make him a "trader".

> "Fortunately, a cause of action in malicious falsehood exists, but ... the present case strengthens my hope that the review [of the need for a tort of privacy] may prove fruitful."[206]

Defamation: conclusion

14–045 As may be seen, defamation is a difficult and complex area of law, but one which is of considerable interest to anyone who is concerned to see how tort law deals with the difficult issue of balancing freedom of expression against the rights of individuals to protect their reputation from attack. The best way to approach this area of law is in stages, following the method indicated above. In this way, the reader can understand the reasoning adopted by the courts and appreciate the problems inherent in this area of law. The Defamation Act 2013 has made significant changes to defamation law, notably in relation to defences protecting freedom of expression. The Government describes the 2013 Act as rebalancing the law on defamation to provide more effective protection for freedom of speech while ensuring that people who have been defamed are able to protect their reputation.[207] Only now are we starting to see cases appearing under the Act. It remains to be seen whether the Government's intention to clarify and simplify the law and provide the correct balance between freedom of expression and protection of reputation will prove to be successful in practice.

---

206 [1991] F.S.R. 62 at 70. This deficiency has now been met by the courts' development of a tort of misuse of private information to protect an individual's right to privacy (see Ch.15).

207 Explanatory Memorandum to the Defamation (Operators of Websites) Regulations 2013 (SI 2013/3028) para.7.1.

15

Privacy (or Misuse of Private Information)

15–001

As stated in Ch.13, defamation protects the reputation of the claimant against untrue statements of fact. The common law has found more difficulty in deciding whether the claimant should be able to obtain a remedy in tort for the publication of *true* facts which the claimant does not wish others to know. Until recently, litigants were forced to resort to torts such as trespass and private nuisance to find some protection. With the advent of the Human Rights Act 1998, the question has arisen whether English law should now accept a new tort based on invasion of privacy.

The existence of such a tort is controversial. Whilst a privacy tort would protect the claimant from invasion of his or her private life, it would be at the expense of the public's right to know and the defendant's freedom of expression, protected by the European Convention on Human Rights (ECHR) art.10. At worst, it would give claimants a means of suppressing true, but damaging, information which it is in the public interest to disclose. Yet, it cannot be denied that publication of details of an individual's private life, even when they are accurate, can be distressing. In particular, advances in modern technology have led to an increasing number of intrusions into the private lives of individuals, be they public or private figures. Many other countries have accepted the need for laws protecting privacy.[1] The 1998 Act, which incorporates ECHR art.8 (right to respect for private and family life), brings to the fore the question of whether, and to what extent, English law should recognise a right to privacy.

---

1   e.g. the United States Restatement (Second) of Torts recognises 4 types of invasion of privacy: intrusion, appropriation of name or likeness, unreasonable publicity and placing a person in a false light (paras 652A–652I) (1977). New Zealand finally confirmed the existence of a tort protecting informational privacy in *Hosking v Runting* [2005] 1 N.Z.L.R. 1 and *C v Holland* [2012] 3 N.Z.L.R. 672. In contrast, France introduced a new provision into its Civil Code: art.9 (by virtue of the Law 70–643 of 17 July 1970), whilst German courts recognised privacy as a right (*Persönlichkeitsrecht*) protected by its Civil Code para.823(1) in the 1950s: see W. van Gerven, J. Lever and P. Larouche, *Tort Law* (Hart, 2000). See, generally, A.T. Kenyon (ed), *Comparative Defamation and Privacy Law* (CUP, 2016),

Protection of privacy by existing torts

15–002 Prior to the Human Rights Act 1998, it seemed clear that there was no general right to privacy in English law. Tort law did, however, offer some protection on an ad hoc basis. Whilst the claimant would have to satisfy the basic requirements for each tort, some protection could thereby be obtained, even if it was merely indirect and the remedy often ill-suited to the protection of privacy. Trespass to land, private nuisance, malicious falsehood and even defamation were therefore relied upon by claimants.

Trespass, notably, provided a means of preventing direct interference with the claimant's possession of land and has long been used to protect the claimant against invasion of privacy.[2] Yet, with the advent of long-range lenses, photographers are no longer required to intrude onto the claimant's land, thereby limiting the effectiveness of this action. For example, in *Bernstein v Skyviews Ltd*,[3] Lord Bernstein failed in his action for trespass against the defendants. The defendants had taken aerial photographs of his country house without his consent, but the court held that the rights of a landowner did not extend to airspace exceeding that necessary for the ordinary use and enjoyment of land.[4] Equally, private nuisance may assist in preventing indirect interference with one's enjoyment of land, although its use is limited by the House of Lords decision in *Hunter v Canary Wharf Ltd*,[5] which confined the right to sue for private nuisance to those with an interest in land or exclusive possession.[6] Defamation can offer only limited protection against the invasion of privacy, although innuendo may assist a claimant in bringing an action. In *Tolley v Fry*,[7] for example, Tolley successfully sued the defendants for an advertisement in which his caricature was pictured promoting the defendants' chocolate bars. However, this case rested on the innuendo that Tolley (an amateur golfer) had violated his amateur status. He would have been unable to sue simply on the basis that he had been caricatured in an advertisement. More fundamentally, the protection provided by defamation is subject to the defence of truth, which permits the defendant to publish any statement provided he or she can show that it is substantially true.[8] Malicious falsehood also came to the assistance of Gorden Kaye in *Kaye v Robertson*[9]

---

2 See *Entick v Carrington* (1765) 2 Wils. K.B. 275; 95 E.R. 807.
3 [1978] 1 Q.B. 479.
4 See Ch.11.
5 [1997] A.C. 655, discussed in Ch.10.
6 Thereby overturning the Court of Appeal's decision in *Khorasandjian v Bush* [1993] Q.B. 727 that the daughter of the house (who was a licensee) could obtain an injunction for private nuisance to stop harassment by a former boyfriend. For a recent attempt to rely on nuisance to protect privacy rights, see *Fearn v Board of Trustees of the Tate Gallery* [2019] EWHC 246 (Ch); [2019] Ch 369 where Mann J argued that peering from the viewing gallery in the Tate Modern into a nearby block of flats could amount to a private nuisance. This was firmly rejected, however, on appeal as contrary to principle: [2020] EWCA Civ 104.
7 [1931] A.C. 333. See also *Charleston v News Group Newspapers* [1995] 2 A.C. 65.
8 Defamation Act 2013 s.2. Note, however, that under the Rehabilitation of Offenders Act 1974 s.8 (as amended) truth is not a defence where the defendant has maliciously published details of a person's distant criminal past. The defences of honest opinion and privilege may also limit the claimant's ability to complain.
9 [1991] F.S.R. 62.

where the court, horrified by the behaviour of the newspaper in question, sought to find some way of supporting his claim. Following an accident, Kaye was in intensive care in hospital. A journalist and photographer from the *Sunday Sport* newspaper nevertheless entered the room, obtained a picture of Mr Kaye using a flash camera, and claimed that Kaye had consented to an "interview", although he was unable to recollect the incident 15 minutes after the event.[10] The Court of Appeal took a dim view of such conduct, but struggled to find a basis of liability in tort,[11] resorting finally to malicious falsehood: the paper's allegation that the story and photograph had been taken with Kaye's consent was clearly false, and Kaye had lost the right to sell his first interview after the accident for profit. Bingham LJ commented that:

> "this case nonetheless highlights, yet again, the failure of both the common law of England and statute to protect in an effective way the personal privacy of individual citizens."[12]

Such provisions are thus limited and, at best, provide only indirect protection of an individual's private life. However, the Human Rights Act 1998 raised the prospect of change. The Act expressly refers to the art.8 right to respect for one's private and family life. The remainder of this chapter will examine the impact of this development. Has the Act, despite Government denials, introduced a right to privacy into English law?

The Impact of the Human Rights Act 1998

15–003

In October 2000, the Human Rights Act 1998 came into force in England and Wales. This Act gives domestic legal effect to the vast majority of the rights contained in the European Convention on Human Rights. Under s.6, the courts (as a public authority) must act in a way which is compatible with the Convention.

Article 8 of the Convention states that:

---

10   The paper alleged that it had obtained "a great old-fashioned scoop".
11   Trespass to the person failed as the use of a flash by itself did not amount to battery. Nor did Kaye have sufficient possessory rights to bring an action for trespass to land. Defamation (that is, the newspaper had falsely stated that Kaye had consented to give an exclusive interview to the *Sunday Sport*) equally failed as the court was not prepared to impose an interim injunction except in the clearest of cases.
12   [1991] F.S.R. 62 at 70. Further protection is provided by copyright law where the claimant owns the copyright of the work or photograph disclosed: see *Williams v Settle* [1960] 1 W.L.R. 1072; Copyright, Designs and Patents Act 1988 s.85. Specific statutes also offer protection: Protection from Harassment Act 1997, Data Protection Act 1998 (which extends the rights of individuals to control the use of personal data stored on computers or manually).

> "(1) Everyone has the right to respect for his private and family life, his home and his correspondence.
>
> (2) There shall be no interference by a public authority with the exercise of this right except such as is in accordance with the law and is necessary in a democratic society in the interests of national security, public safety or the economic well-being of the country, for the prevention of disorder or crime, for the protection of health or morals, or for the protection of the rights and freedoms of others."

This imposes a positive obligation on States to see that such rights are respected.[13] Nevertheless, it is qualified. It must also be considered in the light of art.10, which protects freedom of expression:

> "(1) Everyone has the right to freedom of expression. This right shall include freedom to hold opinions and to receive and impart information and ideas without interference by public authority and regardless of frontiers.
>
> (2) The exercise of these freedoms, since it carries with it duties and responsibilities, may be subject to such formalities, conditions, restrictions or penalties as are prescribed by law and are necessary in a democratic society, in the interests of national security, territorial integrity or public safety, for the prevention of disorder or crime, for the protection of health or morals, for the protection of the reputation or the rights of others, *for preventing the disclosure of information received in confidence*, or for maintaining the authority and impartiality of the judiciary."[14]

The question arises whether such provisions are sufficient to give claimants a "right" to privacy, or require or empower the courts to develop a tort protecting claimants from invasion of their privacy. The Government's response was in the negative. The Lord Chancellor, during the reading of the Human Rights Bill, stated:

> "This Bill does not impose any statutory controls on the press by a back-door privacy law . . . I would not agree with any proposition

---

13 *Von Hannover v Germany (59320/00)* (2005) 40 E.H.R.R. 1.
14 Emphasis added.

> that the courts as public authorities will be obliged to fashion a law on privacy because of the terms of the Bill."[15]

Further, s.12(4) of the 1998 Act provides that:

> "The court must have particular regard to the importance of the Convention right to freedom of expression and, where the proceedings relate to material which the respondent claims, or which appears to the court, to be journalistic, literary or artistic material (or to conduct connected with such material), to—
> (a) the extent to which—
>   (i) the material has, or is about to, become available to the public; or
>   (ii) it is, or would be, in the public interest for the material to be published;
> (b) any relevant privacy code."

This does not prevent, however, the courts choosing to develop the common law in a way which provides greater protection of privacy rights.[16] The subsequent development of the law illustrates two propositions:

- there is still no general tort of invasion of privacy; and

- claimants may nevertheless seek a remedy against the publication of private information relating to their personal lives. The nature of this action will be discussed below.

The Current Legal Position

(1) Rejection of a stand-alone tort of invasion of privacy

The leading case is that of *Wainwright v Home Office*.[17] Here, a mother and son visiting a relative in prison were strip-searched for drugs under humiliating conditions. No drugs were found. The search was conducted in breach of prison rules (and therefore not protected by statutory

15-004

---

15   Lord Irvine of Lairg, *Hansard*, 24 November 1997, cols 784–5.
16   The so-called "indirect" horizontal effect: see M. Hunt, "The 'horizontal effect' of the Human Rights Act" [1998] P.L. 423.
17   [2003] UKHL 53; [2004] 2 A.C. 406. See J. Morgan, "Privacy torts: out with the old, out with the new" (2004)

authority) and both claimants suffered distress as a result; the son, who suffered from physical and learning difficulties, developing post-traumatic stress disorder. It was claimed that such conduct invaded their rights to privacy.[18]

In the House of Lords, Lord Hoffmann rejected the existence of a common law tort of invasion of privacy. Whilst existing torts might provide some protection, this did not indicate that the common law should regard privacy as a principle of law worthy of protection in itself. Any such development could only be undertaken by Parliament, which could provide specific detailed rules to deal with privacy issues.[19] In any event with the coming into force of the Human Rights Act 1998, in future claims against public authorities could be brought under the Act. The creation of a general tort was not, in his Lordship's opinion, necessary to comply with art.8.

The 1998 Act was not applicable on the facts of *Wainwright* which occurred before the Act was in force. Their Lordships accepted that a challenge might subsequently be made to the European Court of Human Rights in Strasbourg. This, indeed, occurred and the Strasbourg Court held unanimously that the prison officers' conduct was a breach of art.8. The requirement to submit to a strip-search would generally amount to an interference with the right to respect for private life under art.8, and it could not be said that the searches were a proportionate response to the legitimate aim of combating the drugs problem within the prison.[20] Each applicant was awarded €3,000 in compensation.

Nevertheless, the basic proposition in *Wainwright* stands: a general tort of privacy has not been accepted by the courts. It should be noted, also, that a *Wainwright* claim under the 1998 Act will only work against a public authority and not against a private citizen.

(2) The "extended" breach of confidence action

15–005 Lord Hoffmann, in rejecting a general tort of privacy in *Wainwright*, noted that the law of breach of confidence had in recent years undergone "judicious development" to provide a remedy for some invasions of privacy.[21] This is somewhat of an understatement. Despite the

---

120 L.Q.R. 393 and A. Johnston, "Putting the Cart Before the Horse? Privacy and the Wainwrights" [2004] C.L.J. 15.

18　It was also argued that the parties could claim under the rule in *Wilkinson v Downton*. This claim, which was rejected, is discussed in Ch.11.

19　[2004] 2 A.C. 406 at [33].

20　*Wainwright v United Kingdom (12350/04)* (2007) 44 E.H.R.R. 40. See also *Peck v United Kingdom (44647/98)* (2003) 36 E.H.R.R. 41 (footage broadcast of Mr Peck's suicide attempt captured on CCTV cameras breached his art.8 rights and no effective remedy existed at the time). Both cases indicate that the law prior to the Human Rights Act 1998 was not fully compatible with art.8, as interpreted by the European Court of Human Rights (contrast the Commission ruling in *Earl Spencer v United Kingdom (28851/95)* (1998) 25 E.H.R.R. CD 105: applicants did not demonstrate that the remedy of breach of confidence was insufficient or ineffective in the circumstances of their case).

21　[2004] 2 A.C. 406 at [18]. The first step was taken by Lord Goff in *Att-Gen v Guardian Newspapers Ltd (No.2)* [1990] A.C. 109 at 281–282.

courts' doubts in relation to a new tort protecting privacy, they have been far less reticent in re-moulding the equitable doctrine of breach of confidence[22] as a means of protecting the private lives of claimants. Traditional breach of confidence exists where (a) information is of a confidential nature; (b) communicated in circumstances importing an obligation of confidence and (c) has been used in an unauthorised way.[23] For example, in *Argyll v Argyll*,[24] an ex-wife was able to obtain an injunction preventing her former husband revealing confidences of their married life. The key to breach of confidence is, however, the existence of a genuine relationship of confidence between the parties and to information said to possess the necessary quality of confidence.[25]

However, the courts have extended breach of confidence to adopt a far more generous interpretation which covers not only confidential information, but *private* information.[26] The inspiration was the Human Rights Act 1998 and art.8 ECHR. As stated in the leading case of *Campbell*:

> **"The time has come to recognise that the values enshrined in articles 8 and 10 are now part of the cause of action for breach of confidence ... The values embodied in articles 8 and 10 are as much applicable in disputes between individuals or between an individual and a non-governmental body such as a newspaper as they are in disputes between individuals and a public authority."[27]**

Under the "extended" breach of confidence action, it was no longer necessary to identify a "relationship of confidence" or "confidential information". It is enough that the information is private. Was this still breach of confidence? For Lord Nicholls in *Campbell*, "[t]he essence of the *tort* is better encapsulated now as misuse of private information".[28] At first, the courts resisted recognising a new cause of action. The Court of Appeal in *Douglas v Hello! Ltd (No.3)*, for example, rejected this description.[29] However, over time, the courts started to refer to the action as a tort,[30] and academics openly criticised the courts for failing to recognise the need for some

---

22 Breach of confidence is an independent equitable principle: see *Att-Gen v Guardian Newspapers Ltd (No.2)* [1990] A.C. 109 at 280–283 per Lord Goff.

23 *Coco v AN Clark (Engineers) Ltd* [1969] R.P.C. 41 at 47–48 per Megarry J.

24 [1967] Ch. 302. See also *Stephens v Avery* [1988] Ch. 449 and the early case of *Prince Albert v Strange* (1849) 1 De G & Sm 652; 1 Mac. & G. 25 (publisher obtaining copies of private etchings made by the Prince Consort of members of the royal family at home from an employee of a printer to whom the Prince had entrusted the plates).

25 *Coco v AN Clark (Engineers) Ltd* [1969] R.P.C. 41 at 47–48 per Megarry J.

26 Note the influential article, G. Phillipson, "Transforming breach of confidence? Towards a common law right of privacy under the Human Rights Act" (2003) 66 M.L.R. 726.

27 *Campbell v Mirror Group Newspapers Ltd* [2004] UKHL 22; [2004] 2 A.C. 457 at [17] per Lord Nicholls.

28 *Campbell v Mirror Group Newspapers Ltd* [2004] UKHL 22; [2004] 2 A.C. 457 at [14]. Emphasis added.

29 *Douglas v Hello! Ltd (No.3)* [2005] EWCA Civ 595; [2006] Q.B. 125.

30 See, e.g. Lord Neuberger MR in *Tchenguiz v Imerman* [2010] EWCA Civ 908; [2011] Fam 116 at [65] who remarked that "following [the] decision in *Campbell*, there is now a tort of misuse of private information". For

form of privacy tort.[31] Finally, in 2015, the Court of Appeal in *Vidal-Hall v Google Inc*[32] accepted the existence of a distinct tort of misuse of private information, at least for the purposes of service of a claim outside jurisdiction. A clear dividing line therefore exists between traditional breach of confidence actions (which still exist, notably in relation to disclosure of trade secrets) and the tort of misuse of private information. The Court of Appeal did note, however, that in creating a new tort, the courts would have to resolve matters such as the correct limitation period and appropriate remedies for the action.[33]

Below we examine the key modern cases in the development of the tort of misuse of private information, namely *Campbell v Mirror Group Newspapers Ltd*[34] and *McKennitt v Ash*.[35] These cases provide a framework for the modern action and illustrate its development from a "modified" form of the breach of confidence action to a cause of action in its own right.

▶ *Campbell v Mirror Group Newspapers Ltd: protecting private information*

15–006

Naomi Campbell is a well-known "supermodel". The *Daily Mirror* published a number of articles which revealed that, contrary to her previous statements, she was a drug addict and attending Narcotics Anonymous meetings to deal with her addiction. Photographs were taken without her knowledge, showing her in a public street leaving a group meeting, and details were given of her treatment. In response to her action for breach of confidence,[36] the *Daily Mirror* alleged that it had acted in the public interest in correcting her previous denials and that the photographs and other details were merely peripheral to this information.

The House of Lords accepted that the *Mirror* was entitled to set the record straight and correct Ms Campbell's previous untrue statements, but their Lordships were divided whether the additional details were peripheral or not. The majority argued in favour of Ms Campbell[37]: details relating to her treatment were akin to the private and confidential information contained

---

the background to this debate, see P. Giliker, "English tort law and the 'tort' of breach of confidence" [2014] J.R. 15.

31 See, e.g. J. Morgan, "Privacy, Confidence and Horizontal Effect: 'Hello' Trouble" [2003] C.L.J. 444, R. Mulheron, "A Potential Framework for Privacy? A Reply to Hello!" (2006) 69 M.L.R. 679.

32 [2015] EWCA Civ 311; [2016] Q.B. 1003, noting that the speech of Lord Nicholls in *Campbell v Mirror Group Newspapers Ltd* [2004] UKHL 22; [2004] 2 A.C. 457 has been highly influential in this process of development (at [22]). Comment: J. Folkard (2016) 132 L.Q.R. 31.

33 *Vidal-Hall v Google Inc* [2015] EWCA Civ 311; [2016] Q.B. 1003 at [51].

34 [2004] UKHL 22; [2004] 2 A.C. 457. Comment: J. Morgan, "Privacy in the House of Lords, again" (2004) 120 L.Q.R. 563 and N. Moreham, "Recognising privacy in England and New Zealand" [2004] C.L.J. 555. Appeal to the European Court of Human Rights for violation of art.10 was rejected by a majority of 6:1: *MGN Ltd v United Kingdom* (39401/04) (2011) 29 B.H.R.C. 686.

35 [2006] EWCA Civ 1714; [2008] Q.B. 73. Comment: N. Moreham, "Privacy and horizontality" (2007) 123 L.Q.R. 373.

36 A claim was also brought under the Data Protection Act 1998, but all parties agreed that this claim would succeed or fail depending on the success of the breach of confidence action.

37 Lords Nicholls and Hoffmann dissenting.

in medical records and their publication might deter Ms Campbell from seeking help for her addiction and thereby harm her health. On balance, her art.8 rights therefore outweighed the newspaper's right to freedom of expression. Ms Campbell was entitled to an award of damages.

A number of points arise from the *Campbell* decision. First, it is clear that although the action is stated to be that of breach of confidence, their Lordships are focussing on issues of private information. Lord Nicholls is perhaps most overt in recognising that what is being applied in *Campbell* is a *new* form of the "breach of confidence" action:

> "The common law or, more precisely, courts of equity have long afforded protection to the wrongful use of private information by means of the cause of action which became known as breach of confidence . . . This cause of action has now firmly shaken off the limiting constraint of the need for an initial confidential relationship. In doing so it has changed its nature . . . Now the law imposes a 'duty of confidence' whenever a person receives information he knows or ought to know is fairly and reasonably to be regarded as confidential . . . the more natural description today is that such information is private."[38]

Secondly, this action does not protect all privacy rights, but is confined to private information. For example, the strip-searches in *Wainwright* would not fit under this action. Future Wainwrights would have to seek a remedy not in tort, but under the Human Rights Act 1998 ss.7 and 8.[39] Thirdly, liability will only arise if the defendant discloses private, not public, information. This is therefore a key issue. When will information be private? Clearly if a public figure discusses her private life in the press, she will run the risk, as with Ms Campbell, that this will be viewed as a matter of public debate. Finally, art.8 rights are not, as stated above, absolute. The courts will in each case balance the claimant's rights to private and family life against the defendant's freedom of expression. It is clear in *Campbell* that, despite the Human Rights Act 1998 s.12, neither right has pre-eminence. Lord Steyn in *Re S (a child)*[40] provided a useful summary of four key propositions to be taken from *Campbell*:

- Neither art.8 nor art.10 has precedence over the other.

- Where the values under the two articles conflict, an intense focus on the comparative importance of the specific rights being claimed in the individual case is necessary.

---

38 [2004] UKHL 22 at [13]–[14]. See also Lord Hoffmann at [50]: "What human rights law has done is to identify private information as something worth protecting as an aspect of human autonomy and dignity".

39 For criticism of limiting privacy protection to private information, see N. Moreham, "Beyond information: Physical privacy in English law" [2014] C.L.J. 350.

40 [2004] UKHL 47; [2005] 1 A.C. 593 at [17] per Lord Steyn.

- The justifications for interfering with or restricting each right must be taken into account.

- The proportionality test must be applied to each (which his Lordship termed "the ultimate balancing test").

The test is therefore whether publication pursues a legitimate aim and whether the benefit of publication is proportionate to the harm done by interference with privacy.[41]

McKennitt v Ash: the two stage test

15–007

Unlike Naomi Campbell, Loreena McKennitt, despite being a well-known Canadian folk musician, had carefully guarded her personal life and was distressed when a former close friend wrote a book that contained personal and private details of her life. She sought an injunction on the basis of breach of privacy or confidence to prevent further publication of certain private material. Her friend, Niema Ash, alleged that this prevented her telling her own story which included her friendship with Ms McKennitt.

The Court of Appeal was, perhaps understandably, unconvinced by Ms Ash's argument. In reality, her book (entitled *Travels with Loreena McKennitt*) was only of interest due to revelations arising from her close and confidential relationship with Ms McKennitt. As Buxton LJ commented:

> **"the matters related in the book were specifically experiences of . . . Ms McKennitt. Ms Ash cannot undermine their confidential nature by the paradox of calling in aid the confidential relationship that gave her access to the information in the first place."[42]**

Yet, *McKennitt* is important not due to its application of the law, which can be argued to satisfy even the traditional conception of the breach of confidence action, but in its guidance as to the nature of the "extended" action. Buxton LJ confirmed that the action lies in the case law of arts 8 and 10 and that, as a result, there are two key questions for the court to resolve[43]:

- Is the information private in the sense that it is in principle protected by art.8? If no, that is the end of the case. If yes, then;

- In all the circumstances, must the interest of the owner of the private information yield to the right of freedom of expression conferred on the publisher by art.10? (the "balancing exercise").

---

41 *Campbell* [2004] UKHL 22 at [113] per Lord Hope.
42 [2006] EWCA Civ 1714; [2008] Q.B. 73 at [32].
43 [2008] Q.B. 73 at [11].

Much then will depend on the facts of the case, although undoubtedly some guidance may be gained from examining previous decisions. Caution must, however, be taken with early cases such as *Douglas v Hello! Ltd (No.1)*[44] and *A v B Plc*,[45] in that more recent decisions indicate that the courts would now be far more willing to protect the privacy rights of the claimants in question.[46]

(3) Application of the two-stage test

(i) Is the information private?

15–008

Whether a particular piece of information qualifies as private will depend on all the circumstances of the case, and the courts proceed case by case. At times this may be obvious. For example, the journals of the Prince of Wales recording his impressions of the handing over of Hong Kong in 1993 were considered to be paradigm examples of private documents.[47] Equally issues relating to sexual behaviour (and sexuality) and physical and mental health are matters protected by art.8 ECHR.[48] Information may also be private even if the individual in question wishes to exploit it commercially, although this is likely to reduce the level of damages awarded.[49] In *Campbell*, Lord Nicholls explained the test as follows: in respect of the disclosed facts, did the person in question have a reasonable expectation of privacy?[50]

Subsequent cases have helped to explain the "reasonable expectation of privacy" test. It is primarily an objective question: what would a reasonable person feel to be private if placed in the claimant's position? The courts therefore will look to the nature of the activity in which the claimant was engaged, the place at which it was happening, the nature and purpose of the

---

44   [2001] Q.B. 967. The later Court of Appeal decision in *Douglas v Hello! Ltd (No.3)* [2005] EWCA Civ 595; [2006] Q.B. 125 stated, obiter, that in the light of the subsequent development of the law, the decision to lift the interlocutory injunction had been wrong (decision in favour of Douglases' claim not appealed to HL: *OBG Ltd v Allan* [2007] UKHL 21; [2008] A.C. 1).

45   [2003] Q.B. 195. The Court in *McKennitt v Ash* [2006] EWCA Civ 1714 commented at [62]: "The width of the rights given to the media by *A v B* cannot be reconciled with *Von Hannover*".

46   Note, in particular, the influence of the subsequent decision of the European Court of Human Rights in *Von Hannover v Germany (59320/00)* (2005) 40 E.H.R.R. 1 (publication of photographs and articles relating to Princess Caroline of Monaco in her daily life without her consent, the sole purpose of which was to satisfy the curiosity of a particular readership regarding the applicant's private life, did not contribute to any debate of general interest—breach of art.8).

47   *HRH Prince of Wales v Associated Newspapers Ltd* [2006] EWCA Civ 1776; [2008] Ch. 57 at [35] per Lord Phillips CJ.

48   See *Mosley v News Group Newspapers Ltd* [2008] EWHC 1777 (QB), *PJS v News Group Newspapers Ltd* [2016] UKSC 26; [2016] A.C. 1081 and most recently *BVC v EWF* [2019] EWHC 2506 (QB).

49   *Douglas v Hello! Ltd (No.3)* [2005] EWCA Civ 595; [2006] Q.B. 125 (wedding photos).

50   [2004] UKHL 22 at [21]. See also Lord Hope: "a duty of confidence will arise whenever the party subject to the duty is in a situation where he knows or ought to know that the other person can reasonably expect his privacy to be protected" [2004] UKHL 22 at [85].

intrusion, absence of consent (known or inferred), the effect on the claimant, and the circumstances in which, and purposes for which, the information came into the hands of the publisher.[51] The attributes of the claimant will also be relevant (although not decisive), for example, is the claimant a publicity-seeking celebrity or a mere child? In *Murray v Express Newspapers Plc*,[52] for example, the Court of Appeal held that it was arguable that a photograph of JK Rowling's infant son taken without his parents' consent in a public street infringed the child's reasonable expectation of privacy. It made no difference on the facts that the photo had been taken in a public place.[53] Further in *Weller v Associated Newspapers*,[54] the children of well-known British musician, Paul Weller, were found to have a reasonable expectation of privacy when on a family outing in the shops and cafés of Los Angeles, California. In a considered judgment, Lord Dyson MR indicated that while a child does not automatically have a reasonable expectation of privacy, it might be easier to establish than for an adult. The courts in such cases should, in applying the objective test set out above, take into account the child's age,[55] parental lack of consent, the effect on the child and any security concerns, although ultimately it would depend on the facts of each individual case. The courts will look, in particular, at whether the parent has placed the child in the lime-light e.g. taking the child to a film première.[56] More recently, a case, brought by veteran entertainer Cliff Richard,[57] questioned to what extent the media could report on the fact that someone was being investigated for a crime, when he had yet to be charged by the police. Accusations, particularly of serious crimes such as abuse, carry obvious stigma, despite the fact that, at law, a person is presumed innocent until proven guilty. As a general rule, then, up to the point of charge, a person will have a reasonable expectation of privacy in a police investigation and should not normally be identified due to the risk of unfair damage to reputation. This is not, however, a universal rule and will remain fact sensitive.[58]

(ii) Balancing art.8 and art.10

15–009

Here, the key is to identify whether it is proportionate to prevent disclosure of private information, having regard to the competing Convention right of freedom of expression. Neither article has precedence over the other. The cases indicate that a number of factors may affect the balancing exercise. A court is far more likely to permit discussion of matters of legitimate

---

51 *Murray v Express Newspapers Plc* [2008] EWCA Civ 446; [2009] Ch 481 per Sir Anthony Clarke MR at [36].
52 [2008] EWCA Civ 446; [2009] Ch. 481. The case was ultimately settled prior to trial.
53 See also *Von Hannover v Germany (59320/00)* (2005) 40 E.H.R.R. 1 (photographs taken of Princess Caroline of Monaco in her daily life).
54 [2015] EWCA Civ 1176; [2016] 1 W.L.R. 1541. Note that one critical factor in this case was that the children's faces were clearly visible (despite assurances that they would be pixelated) and they had been identified by surname.
55 An older child is likely to have a greater perception of his or her own privacy and his or her experience of an interference with it might well be more significant than for a younger child.
56 [2015] EWCA Civ 1176; [2016] 1 W.L.R. 1541, at [29]–[38].
57 *Richard v BBC* [2018] EWHC 1837 (Ch); [2019] Ch 169.
58 For example, where there may be an immediate risk to the public.

public interest, for example information relating to politicians in the exercise of their functions, than tittle-tattle related to parties with no real public function,[59] as exemplified by the European Court of Human Rights judgment in favour of Princess Caroline of Monaco who, despite having no official functions, had been photographed dining, with her children, shopping, playing tennis and bicycling.[60] The court found that:

> "the publication of the photos and articles in question, of which the sole purpose was to satisfy the curiosity of a particular readership regarding the details of the applicant's private life, cannot be deemed to contribute to any debate of general interest to society despite the applicant being known to the public."[61]

In contrast, where the photograph is related to a debate of legitimate interest to society, art.8 will not be breached, For example, in a later case (*Von Hannover (No.2)*), a photograph of Princess Caroline on holiday while her father Prince Rainier of Monaco was ill was found to be part of a discussion how the prince's children reconciled their obligations of family solidarity with the legitimate needs of their private life and did not breach art.8.[62] Certain matters may help tip the balance. Special considerations apply to photographs, which are, by their very nature, more intrusive than words.[63] Equally, the fact that the revelation might harm the claimant's children or step-children may tip the balance in the claimant's favour in that particular weight is accorded to the art.8 rights of any children likely to be affected by the publication.[64] In the *Prince of Wales* case, the fact that the information was disclosed to the newspaper by an employee in Prince Charles' private office, who was under a contractual obligation to keep the contents of the journal confidential, was also said to support Prince Charles's claim.[65] In *Weller*,[66] Lord Dyson MR, guided by *Von Hannover (No.2)*, in addition to examining whether the publication made a contribution to a debate of general interest, considered the circumstances

---

59 See Baroness Hale in *Campbell v Mirror Group Newspapers Ltd* [2004] UKHL 22; [2004] 2 A.C. 457 at [148]–[149].
60 *Von Hannover v Germany (59320/00)* (2005) 40 E.H.R.R. 1.
61 *Von Hannover v Germany (59320/00)* (2005) 40 E.H.R.R. 1 at [65].
62 *Von Hannover v Germany (40660/08 and 60641/08)* (2012) 55 E.H.R.R. 15 (Grand Chamber). See E. Reid, "Rebalancing Privacy and Freedom of Expression" (2012) 16 Edin. L.R. 253. See also *Axel Springer AG v Germany (39954/08)* (2012) 55 E.H.R.R. 6; *Sihler-Jauch v Germany (68273/10)* [2016] E.C.H.R. 456.
63 See *Von Hannover* (2005) 40 E.H.R.R. 1 at [59]; *Campbell* [2004] UKHL 22 at [123] and [155] (Lord Hope and Baroness Hale respectively) and *Douglas v Hello! Ltd (No.3)* [2005] EWCA Civ 595 at [84]–[91]. In *Theakston v MGN Ltd* [2002] EWHC 137 (QB); [2002] E.M.L.R. 22, e.g. Ouseley J was prepared to restrain photographs of the celebrity, but not the information that he had visited a brothel.
64 *K v News Group Newspapers Ltd* [2011] EWCA Civ 439; [2011] 1 W.L.R. 1827 (interest in preserving stability of family and saving claimant's children from ordeal of playground ridicule which would inevitably follow publicity); *Rocknroll v News Group Newspaper Ltd* [2013] EWHC 24 (Ch) (risk of stepchildren being subjected to teasing or ridicule at school).
65 [2006] EWCA Civ 1776 at [71].
66 [2015] EWCA Civ 1176 at [72]–[78].

in which the photographs were taken, the content, form and consequences of the publication, the subject of the report, whether the person concerned was well known and their prior conduct. In this case, the photographs of Weller's children were only of interest because they had a famous father and, in the court's words, were published for "the sole purpose of satisfying public curiosity". On this basis, their art.8 rights outweighed the defendant's art.10 right. In the Cliff Richard case, the question was less straightforward. It was argued that there was a significant public interest in publicising investigations into historic sexual abuse, not least that it encouraged other victims to come forward. Nevertheless, the consequences of disclosure would be great stigma to those investigated,[67] which, in this case, had been severely magnified by the dramatic and sensationalist style of reporting by the BBC, which was rightly condemned by the Court. Cliff Richard was awarded general and aggravated damages of £210,000.

Information in the public domain

15-010
This is a defence for breach of confidence. It is also relevant to the tort of misuse of private information. The basic principle is that information will not be protected against publication if it is already known to the public. However, the Court of Appeal in *Browne v Associated Newspapers Ltd* drew an important distinction between information which is made available to a person's circle of friends or work colleagues, and information which is widely published in a newspaper.[68] Only the latter is in the public domain. This raises difficult questions of degree. For example, in *McKennitt*, despite Ms McKennitt's insistence of her avoidance of publicity, evidence was given that she had discussed the death of her fiancé in a drowning accident and its impact on her in a number of articles. The Court of Appeal refused to accept that limited disclosure of personal details permitted subsequent scrutiny of every detail of her personal life. On the facts, the articles had been part of a campaign by McKennitt to promote water safety and it was regarded as "cruelly insensitive"[69] to suggest that this opened up her entire life to scrutiny as a result.

Remedies

15-011
A claimant, if aware of or suspecting disclosure, will frequently seek an injunction to prevent publication. Bearing in mind the time it takes to go to trial, a claimant will often seek an interlocutory injunction, that is, a court order that the defendant may not publish the information before the matter is resolved at trial. As noted in Ch.14, English courts are particularly aware of the dangers that the award of interlocutory injunctions may pose to the right of freedom of expression. This does not, of course, prevent the claimant bringing an action for damages, but

---

67   It should be noted that Cliff Richard was never arrested nor charged.
68   [2007] EWCA Civ 295; [2008] Q.B. 103 at [61].
69   [2006] EWCA Civ 1714 at [54].

in the past, there was limited incentive to do so when the damages awarded were not large. Further, damages can do little to lessen the claimant's distress once the information is publicly known. As will be seen below, recent court decisions on remedies have brought important changes to this area of law.

▶ (i) Damages

Claims for damages have been made, but until recently, the awards made by the courts have been relatively low. Michael Douglas and Catherine Zeta-Jones, for example, in the *Douglas v Hello! Ltd* litigation were awarded a mere £3,750 each for the distress arising from infringement of their privacy rights when an unauthorised photographer sold photographs of their wedding reception (although this was no doubt reduced by their willingness to grant exclusive rights to their wedding pictures to Hello!'s rival, OK! Ltd).[70] A claim for an account of profits—that is, requiring the defendant to hand over his profits to the claimants—was accepted to be possible, but unavailable on the facts.[71] Ms McKennitt received a mere £5,000.

However, this changed with *Mosley v News Group Newspapers Ltd*,[72] where Eady J awarded Max Mosley £60,000 in view of the scale of distress and indignity he had suffered. The newspaper had published salacious details of the claimant's involvement in sadomasochistic activities, which, it alleged, had a Nazi theme and mocked the way that Holocaust victims had been treated in concentration camps. In addition to being (at the time) President of the FIA (the organisation running Formula 1 motor-racing), Mr Mosley is the son of Sir Oswald Mosley, a noted Fascist leader during the Second World War, rendering such allegations doubly embarrassing. Sexual activity of this nature was, predictably, deemed to give rise to a reasonable expectation of privacy and, in the absence of proof of the Nazi or concentration camp allegations, publication could not be said to be in the public interest. In awarding damages, Eady J highlighted that the court should award an adequate financial remedy, capable of acknowledging the infringement

---

70 They were also awarded £7,000 for the cost and inconvenience of making a hurried selection of photographs for *OK! Magazine*, which represented their commercial interest in exploiting private information about their wedding: see R. Bagshaw, "Unauthorised wedding photographs" (2005) 121 L.Q.R. 550. The House of Lords, on appeal by *OK!* Magazine only, made it clear that the ordinary principles of breach of confidence would apply to claims to protect commercial confidential information, which did not concern privacy rights: see Lord Hoffmann, who adopts a pragmatic commercial approach to such claims: *OBG Ltd v Allan* [2007] UKHL 21; [2008] A.C. 1 at [118].

71 *Douglas v Hello! Ltd (No.3)* [2005] EWCA Civ 595; [2006] Q.B. 125 at [249]. See G. Jones, "Restitution of Benefits Obtained in Breach of Another's Confidence" (1970) 80 L.Q.R. 463; N. Witzleb, "Justifying gain-based remedies for invasion of privacy" (2009) 29 O.J.L.S. 325. The availability of this remedy remains controversial.

72 [2008] EWHC 1777 (QB). Mr Mosley subsequently brought a case to the European Court of Human Rights, arguing for a prior notification rule by which newspapers, intending to publish details of an individual's private life, must notify the individual in advance and thereby give him or her the opportunity to apply for an interlocutory injunction to block publication. The court ruled unanimously, however, that ECHR art.8 does not require a legally binding pre-notification requirement: *Mosley v United Kingdom (48009/08)* (2011) 53 E.H.R.R. 30.

of privacy and compensating for injury to feelings, embarrassment and distress. Exemplary damages would not, however, be awarded.[73] Whilst accepting the sums previously awarded had been modest, in view of the infringement in question, which included video footage of the claimant which was freely accessible on the *News of the World*'s website and persistent reference to the unproven Nazi allegations, Eady J was prepared to be more generous.[74]

This new approach was followed by the Court of Appeal in *Gulati v MGN Ltd*[75] and *Richard v BBC* (discussed above, where the Court awarded general and aggravated damages). In *Gulati*, the voicemails of numerous celebrities had been hacked by journalists in pursuit of information to generate articles about the victims. Such blatant intrusion into their private lives, causing considerable distress and anxiety, led to awards of damages ranging from £72,500 to £260,250. These awards place damages for misuse of private information on a par with those awarded for defamation (discussed in Ch.14). In rejecting the newspaper's appeal, the court recognised that while these were the largest awards ever made for breach of a person's privacy, it was important to compensate not only for the distress caused by misuse of private information, but also for the fact that the defendant had deprived the claimants of their right to control the use of private information relating to them. The court rejected the argument that awards should be limited by reference to the awards given by the European Court of Human Rights: "the conditions of the tort are governed by English law and not the Convention . . . national courts are intrinsically better able to assess the adequacy of an award in their jurisdiction than an international body".[76] Damages might be limited, however, if mitigating circumstances were shown e.g. the repeated misuse of information where there had been some genuine mistake as to its source or the defendant had made a timely apology or where the information would, on the facts, have become public knowledge anyway.

(ii) Interlocutory injunctions

15-013

For many, however, it is the question of obtaining an interlocutory injunction to prevent the information being revealed in the first place which is the most important issue. In *Cream Holdings Ltd v Banerjee*,[77] the House of Lords indicated when a court should make an interim order for what was then called a breach of confidence claim. The question is complicated by the Human Rights Act 1998 s.12(3), which states:

---

73   The availability of exemplary damages was discussed by the Supreme Court in *PJS v News Group Newspapers Ltd* [2016] UKSC 26, but not resolved. Lord Mance commented that it remained open to argument at higher levels whether exemplary damages and an account of profits should be recoverable in misuse of private information actions ([42]) and Lord Toulson doubted whether the view of Eady J in *Mosley* would be the final word on the subject ([92]).

74   Eady J remarked at [2008] EWHC 1777 (QB) at [236] that: "[Mr Mosley] is hardly exaggerating when he says that his life was ruined".

75   [2015] EWCA Civ 1291; [2017] Q.B. 149.

76   *Gulati v MGN Ltd* [2015] EWCA Civ 1291; [2017] Q.B. 149 at [89] per Arden LJ.

77   [2004] UKHL 44; [2005] 1 A.C. 253.

> "No such relief is to be granted so as to restrain publication before trial unless the court is satisfied that the applicant is likely to establish that publication should not be allowed."

This form of wording differs from the traditional test stated in *American Cyanamid Co v Ethicon Ltd*,[78] namely that the court must be satisfied that there is a real prospect of success. Lord Nicholls, with the full agreement of the House, considered the meaning of the word "likely" in s.12(3) and how it differed from the traditional test. Did it, in other words, make it easier or harder for the claimant to obtain an interlocutory injunction for misuse of private information, or did it simply maintain the status quo? In his Lordship's view, the principal purpose of this section was to buttress the protection given to freedom of expression. It thus set a higher threshold for the grant of an interlocutory injunction than existed previously. Although bearing in mind that informational privacy, once breached, is lost forever, his Lordship concluded:

> "There can be no single, rigid standard governing all applications for interim restraint orders. Rather, on its proper construction the effect of section 12(3) is that the court is not to make an interim restraint order unless satisfied the applicant's prospects of success at the trial are sufficiently favourable to justify such an order being made in the particular circumstances of the case. As to what degree of likelihood makes the prospects of success 'sufficiently favourable', *the general approach should be that courts will be exceedingly slow to make interim restraint orders where the applicant has not satisfied the court he will probably ('more likely than not') succeed at the trial.* In general, that should be the threshold an applicant must cross before the court embarks on exercising its discretion, duly taking into account the relevant jurisprudence on article 10 and any countervailing Convention rights."[79]

His Lordship accepted that there will be cases where the courts will be required to depart from this general approach and require a lesser degree of likelihood, for example, where the potential adverse consequences of disclosure are particularly grave or where a short-lived injunction is needed to enable the court to hear and give proper consideration to an application for interim relief pending the trial or any relevant appeal. Generally, however, the test

---

78   [1975] A.C. 396 at 407–408 per Lord Diplock.
79   [2005] 1 A.C. 253 at [22] (emphasis added). For examples, see *Rocknroll v News Group Newspaper Ltd* [2013] EWHC 24 (Ch) (interim injunction granted where R had a substantially better than even chance of establishing a reasonable expectation of privacy in relation to the photographs and their contents and nothing in his conduct gave rise to a matter of public debate) and *Hutcheson v News Group Newspapers Ltd* [2011] EWCA Civ 808 (application dismissed where tenuous claim to privacy and very real likelihood that H would fail at trial). Contrast with the treatment of interlocutory injunctions in defamation: see *LNS v Persons Unknown* [2010] EWHC 119 (QB); [2010] 2 F.L.R. 1306.

enunciated by Lord Nicholls places the burden on the claimant to persuade the judge that his prospects of success at trial are sufficiently favourable.[80] The court will, in most cases, be slow to grant an interim restraint order where the claimant has *not* satisfied the court that, once the relevant balancing exercise between art.8 and art.10 rights has been carried out, he or she would be more likely than not to succeed at the trial.

In *PJS v News Group Newspapers Ltd*,[81] the Supreme Court examined once again the operation of interlocutory injunctions in circumstances where the information in question (which concerned revelations of adultery) had already been revealed in the US, Canada and Scotland and evidence was given that "those interested in a prurient story" could probably find out details by using the internet. In such circumstances, should a court exercise its discretion to continue an injunction to stop the defendant disclosing "private" information which could, in any event, be found on the internet? Human Rights Act 1998 ss.12(4)(a)(i) and (ii) specifically provide that where the proceedings relate to journalistic material, the court must have particular regard to the extent to which the material has, or is about to, become available to the public or it is, or would be, in the public interest for the material to be published. The majority of the Supreme Court found for the claimant (Lord Toulson dissenting). There was no public interest in the revelation of matters of a sexual nature which were clearly private. Further there was a qualitative difference between the intrusiveness and distress likely to be involved between disclosures already made on the internet and unrestricted publication by the English media in hard copy as well as on the internet.[82] Unrestricted publication would undoubtedly give rise to a "media storm" to the great distress of the claimant, his partner and their young children.[83] On this basis, where the claimant was deemed likely to establish at trial that publication should not be allowed (the *Cream Holdings* test) and damages would not be an adequate remedy, the majority of the Court would not be swayed by the fact that the uncontrollable world of the internet and social media might make further inroads into the protection intended by the injunction. Lord Toulson, in contrast, was of the view that "the court needs to be very cautious about granting an injunction preventing publication of what is widely known, if it is not to lose public respect for the law by giving the appearance of being out of touch with reality".[84] Lord Neuberger's response was robust: "if Parliament takes the view that the courts have not adapted the law to fit current realities, then, of course, it can change the law".[85]

---

80   See *Browne v Associated Newspapers Ltd* [2007] EWCA Civ 295; [2008] Q.B. 103.
81   [2016] UKSC 26; [2016] A.C. 1081. Comment: K. Yoshida [2016] E.H.R.L.R. 434. The case was later settled with the claimant and claimant's partner remaining anonymous: [2016] EWHC 2770 (QB).
82   *PJS v News Group Newspapers Ltd* [2016] UKSC 26; [2016] A.C. 1081 at [35] per Lord Mance (with whom Lord Neuberger, Baroness Hale and Lord Reed agreed).
83   Baroness Hale paid particular attention to the interests of the children.
84   *PJS v News Group Newspapers Ltd* [2016] UKSC 26; [2016] A.C. 1081 at [88].
85   *PJS v News Group Newspapers Ltd* [2016] UKSC 26; [2016] A.C. 1081 at [71] (with whom Baroness Hale, Lord Mance and Lord Reed agreed).

Conclusion

This is an area of law that is still developing. We can now draw a clear line between traditional actions for breach of confidence—where confidential information is disclosed without authorisation when the defendant has an express or implied duty of confidence (e.g. an employee giving away trade secrets)—and the action for misuse of private information. At times, the courts will face both claims, for example, in actions such as *McKennitt*[86] and the *Prince of Wales* case discussed above. Nevertheless, the law relating to misuse of private information is becoming clearer even though, as seen in *PJS* above, the world of the internet and social media continue to present challenges for the courts. It is to be hoped that formal recognition of a *tort* of misuse of private information will bring clarity to this area of law and permit the law to develop its own rules and remedies out of the shadow of the action for breach of confidence.

The tort of misuse of private information also provides a novel example where the Human Rights Act 1998 has influenced the development of an action in the law of tort.[87] The unanswered question, however, is to what extent privacy rights not protected by the tort of misuse of private information should be protected by tort law. The tort only protects informational privacy. It has been argued that it should also extend to "intrusion upon seclusion" cases, that is, where the defendant observes the claimant in a private, or even public, place without his or her consent (in a New Zealand case illicitly videoing a woman in the shower).[88] The answer is currently no—the tort requires that information is "misused", that is, distributed to a third party. However, it remains an open question whether the courts could interpret the term "misuse" more broadly to include, for example, the intrusion upon seclusion situation.[89] Mann J recently in *Fearn v Board of Trustees of the Tate Gallery*[90] had an alternative suggestion: that, following the Human Rights Act 1998, the tort of private nuisance might be extended to protect ordinary householders from intrusion from people prying into their homes from a nearby gallery viewing platform. This view, however, was firmly rejected by the Court of Appeal as wrong in principle, distorting the tort of private nuisance.[91] In the view of the Court of Appeal: "This is an area in which the legislature has intervened and is better suited than the courts to weigh up competing interests."[92] Extension of the tort of misuse of private information to protect wider privacy interests remains therefore a matter for ongoing debate.

---

86 Ms Ash was a long-term confidant of Ms McKennitt and had at one stage signed a contract with her containing express obligations of confidence.

87 See Lord Toulson in *Michael v Chief Constable of South Wales Police* [2015] UKSC 2; [2015] A.C. 1732 at [124].

88 See *C v Holland* [2012] 3 N.Z.L.R. 672 (liability found). For a discussion, see J. Hartshorne, "The need for an intrusion upon seclusion privacy tort within English law" (2017) 46 C.L.W.R. 287; N. Moreham, "Beyond information: Physical privacy in English law" (2014) 73 C.L.J. 350.

89 Wragg has argued recently that this is possible in that informational privacy and intrusion occupy the same conceptual space and that the barrier between informational and physical privacy should be broken down: P. Wragg, "Recognising a privacy-invasion tort" (2019) 78 C.L.J. 409.

90 [2019] EWHC 246 (Ch); [2019] Ch 369 at [174]. See J. Morgan (2019) 78 C.L.J 273.

91 [2020] EWCA Civ 104.

92 [2020] EWCA Civ 104 at [84].

16

General Defences and Extinction of Liability

Introduction

16–001 This chapter will examine defences generally and a number of ways in which the defendant's liability can be extinguished. We have already considered a number of defences in this book, for example defences to defamation claims in Ch.14, defences such as act of God or statutory authority in Ch.10 on nuisance, and necessity in Ch.11 on trespass. They will therefore not be considered here. This chapter will examine the remaining general defences in tort and should therefore be used in conjunction with earlier chapters outlining the requirements of the tort in question. Each defence will be examined in turn.[1] It should be noted that, in general, the burden of proof in establishing a defence will rest on the defendant on the balance of probabilities. There is no limit on the number of defences a defendant may allege.

The second part of this chapter deals with ways in which the defendant's liability can be extinguished. The primary method is limitation. The Limitation Act 1980 imposes strict time limits within which the claimant must start his or her action. If these time limits are missed, then, subject to certain statutory discretions, the court will refuse to hear the claimant's action, however strong the claim. This ensures that claimants do not bring stale claims which it would be difficult for the defendant to defend. We shall also consider the effect of death of either party to the action. We begin by examining the main general defences in the law of torts.

---

1   For a theoretical analysis of tort law defences, see J. Goudkamp, *Tort Law Defences* (Hart, 2013).

Defences

(1) Consent

16–002

We saw the defence of "consent" in Ch.11 on trespass to the person where the surgeon, for example, operates on a patient. The surgeon is not committing a trespass if he or she has obtained the patient's consent to the procedure in question. In negligence, the terminology is different, and the courts prefer the term volenti non fit injuria or "voluntary assumption of risk". In relation to property, it is usually termed "leave" or "licence". Although the courts may use the terms interchangeably,[2] the defence is applied differently and we shall therefore divide consent into three categories:

- consent;

- voluntary assumption of risk; and

- leave or licence.

Each category will be examined in context. Therefore, consent will be considered in the context of trespass to the person, voluntary assumption of risk in relation to negligence and leave or licence in relation to property torts.[3]

(i) Consent

16–003

The defendant will not be liable for trespass to the person where the claimant has consented to such actions. Consent may be express or implied. For example, by presenting your arm for an injection, you are impliedly showing that you consent to the physical contact involved. Following *Freeman v Home Office (No.2)*,[4] the burden is on the claimant to show the absence of consent. Although ordinarily the burden is on the defendant to establish a defence, the nature of trespass to the person is such that the claimant must show that the physical contact was incurred without his or her consent. In reality, however, the defendant is more likely to produce evidence showing consent than rely on the hope that the claimant will be unable to establish absence of consent. Practically, therefore, it works as a defence. This topic is discussed fully in Ch.11 and therefore readers are advised to refer further to the section on "Consent" in that chapter.

---

2 See, e.g. *Arthur v Anker* [1997] Q.B. 564 at 572.
3 The term "property torts" indicates torts protecting land such as private nuisance and trespass to land: see D. Nolan, "'A Tort Against Land': Private Nuisance as a Property Tort" in D. Nolan and A. Robertson (eds), *Rights and Private Law* (Hart, 2011).
4 [1984] 2 W.L.R. 130; affirmed [1984] 1 Q.B. 524.

> ## (ii) Voluntary assumption of risk

16–004

In the tort of negligence, consent takes the form of an agreement to run the risk of the defendant's negligence. It may be express or implied and forms an absolute defence. There are traditionally said to be three main requirements for the defence:

- agreement to the risk;

- full knowledge of the nature and extent of the risk; and

- voluntary choice by the claimant.

The three requirements will be examined below.

(A) AGREEMENT

16–005

There is mixed authority as to what is meant by "agreement". Lord Denning in *Nettleship v Weston*[5] took a very formalistic view, holding that "nothing will suffice short of an agreement to waive any claim for negligence".[6] This clearly did not exist on the facts of the case. It may be recalled from earlier chapters that a friend, who had been teaching the defendant to drive, had been injured by the defendant's negligent driving. The court held that the friend had not agreed to take the risk of this happening as he had specifically asked, prior to the lesson, whether he would be protected by the car-owner's insurance policy. It is unclear, however, whether such a stringent test for agreement applies generally. Such a test would rarely be satisfied, and his Lordship's view would severely limit the application of this defence. A more flexible approach was clearly evident in the House of Lords' decision in *ICI v Shatwell*.[7]

In this case, the plaintiff and his brother worked together at the defendant's quarry. With complete disregard to their employer's safety instructions (and certain statutory duties imposed on them) which required them to test detonators from a proper shelter, they decided to test the detonators in the open to save time. There was an explosion in which the plaintiff was seriously injured. He sued his employer as vicariously liable for his brother's negligence. The House of Lords was not prepared to allow him to recover damages. It was held that the plaintiff had voluntarily assumed the risk, having fully appreciated the potential danger which led to the injury. Although it is possible to explain this decision in terms of an implied agreement between the two brothers, little attention was paid by their Lordships to the requirement of agreement.[8] A clearer example of the artificiality of a formal requirement of express or implied agreement may be found in the House of Lords case of *Titchener v British Railways*

---

5   [1971] 2 Q.B. 691.
6   [1971] 2 Q.B. 691 at 701.
7   [1965] A.C. 656, see, in particular, Lord Reid.
8   Although Lord Pearce referred to a genuine full agreement at 687.

Board.[9] In this case, a 15-year-old girl had been struck by a train while crossing a railway line. She was seriously injured. She was a trespasser, having passed through a gap in the boundary fence, and it was held that she clearly knew of the risk of being hit by trains when crossing the line. She had nevertheless taken that risk and, had the train driver been negligent, a defence of voluntary assumption of risk would have applied. In this case, it is difficult to see how any agreement (express or otherwise) could be found between the plaintiff and the train driver. The defence seemed to be based simply on her free acceptance of the risks involved.

"Agreement" should thus be interpreted loosely to mean that the claimant has clearly consented to the risk.[10] Obviously, this will be easier to establish where the claimant has openly agreed with the defendant to undertake the risk, but this is not a necessary requirement. On this basis, "agreement" cannot be considered as a separate requirement. It is simply part of the question whether the defendant has fully consented to the risk, which also involves an examination of the claimant's knowledge and understanding of the risks involved. It is submitted therefore that (a) and (b) should be merged to form a single requirement that the claimant has full knowledge of and has accepted the nature and extent of the risks involved.

(B) FULL KNOWLEDGE AND ACCEPTANCE OF THE NATURE AND EXTENT OF THE RISK

16–006

This is the key issue. To lose the right to sue for negligence, it is not sufficient that the claimant simply consented to the defendant's activities. Such consent will only provide a defence if it is of a particular quality: it is given with a full understanding and acceptance of the nature and extent of the risks involved. For example, if I agree to attend your barbecue, I accept the risk of smoke and perhaps even the risk of undercooked food. However, unless you tell me, I do not accept the risk that you will try to set the barbecue alight with petrol, causing a massive explosion. My agreement to attend the barbecue was not with the full knowledge of the risks involved. This can lead to difficult questions of fact and has given rise to a number of controversial decisions, none more so than the Court of Appeal decision in *Dann v Hamilton*.[11]

In this case, the plaintiff and her mother had accepted a lift from Hamilton to see the coronation decorations. During the evening, Hamilton had consumed a certain amount of alcohol, but the plaintiff nevertheless accepted a lift home. This was despite the warning from a fellow passenger, who refused to travel any further in the car, that she should find an alternative means of transport. Due to Hamilton's negligent driving, the vehicle was involved in an accident in which Hamilton was killed and the plaintiff injured. The question arose whether the plaintiff had voluntarily assumed the risk of negligent driving. When warned by her friend, she had merely responded: "You should be like me. If anything is going to happen, it will happen". Was this statement sufficient to establish the defence?

Perhaps surprisingly, Asquith J held that it was not. He distinguished between knowledge of a risk and consent to the risk. The plaintiff clearly knew that the driver was intoxicated, but

---

9   [1983] 1 W.L.R. 1427.
10   Note, however, A. J. E. Jaffey, 'Volenti non fit injuria' (1985) 44 C.L.J. 87.
11   [1939] 1 K.B. 509. See D. M. Gordon, "Drunken drivers and willing passengers" (1966) 82 L.Q.R. 62 for criticism.

Asquith J held that this did not mean that she had accepted the risk of him driving negligently. However, the judge did concede that if the drunkenness of a driver was so extreme and glaring that to travel with him would be to engage in an intrinsically and obviously dangerous occupation, such as meddling with an unexploded bomb, or walking on the edge of an unfenced cliff, the defence would be established.

This decision draws the defence very narrowly indeed.[12] One explanation is the fact that it is a driving case where, of course, the driver is required to be insured.[13] The insurance cover ensures that the victim is fully compensated whilst the cost is spread throughout the driving community. This explanation is nowadays further supported by the Road Traffic Act 1988 s.149, which excludes the defence of voluntary assumption of risk in all road traffic cases. It provides that when a person uses a motor vehicle which is required by law to be insured:

> **"any antecedent agreement or understanding between them (whether intended to be legally binding or not) shall be of no effect so far as it purports or might be held:**
>   **(a) to negative or restrict any such liability of the user in respect of persons carried in or upon the vehicle as is required . . . to be covered by a policy of insurance, or**
>   **(b) to impose such conditions with respect to the enforcement of any such liability of the user."**

The defence will therefore never work against car passengers, who should be regarded as in a category of their own. This provision does not, however, prevent other defences applying, such as contributory negligence. In *Owens v Brimmell*,[14] for example, the plaintiff had accompanied the defendant to a number of public houses and finally to a club. Both men had drunk about eight to nine pints of beer. Driving home, the defendant lost control of the car, which collided with a lamp-post. The plaintiff suffered severe injuries and brain damage. Watkins J held that where a passenger rides in a car with a driver whom he knows has consumed enough alcohol to impair to a dangerous degree his ability to drive properly and safely, the passenger will be found to be contributorily negligent. This will obviously apply where a passenger, knowing that he is relying on the driver for a lift home, accompanies him on a bout of drinking which diminishes the driver's ability to drive properly and safely. On this basis, although the defence of voluntary assumption of risk was not available, damages were reduced by 20%.

In addition, s.149 does not mean that the defence of voluntary assumption of risk will not work in relation to other types of vehicle. The leading modern case on the nature and extent

---

12   The decision was questioned by the Court of Appeal in *Pitts v Hunt* [1991] 1 Q.B. 24 who suggested that riding pillion on a motorbike after the plaintiff and the driver had been drinking for hours would, but for the Road Traffic Act 1988 s.149, have amounted to voluntary assumption of risk. In any event, the court found a good defence of illegality and the case will be considered fully in that section.
13   The Road Traffic Act 1930 first introduced compulsory third party insurance.
14   [1977] Q.B. 859.

of the risk is now *Morris v Murray*.[15] In this case, the plaintiff chose to fly in a light aircraft piloted by his friend, with whom he had consumed a considerable amount of alcohol prior to the flight.[16] The aircraft crashed shortly after take-off, killing the pilot and badly injuring the plaintiff. The Court of Appeal found in such circumstances that the defence had been established. The plaintiff was well aware of the extreme risk involved in flying with his friend. It was so dangerous that it amounted to an intrinsically dangerous activity, such as that outlined by Asquith J in *Dann v Hamilton*. Such an adventure was wildly irresponsible.[17]

(C) VOLUNTARY CHOICE BY THE CLAIMANT

Even if the claimant has clearly consented, with full knowledge of the risks involved, the defence will not be established if the consent cannot be said to be voluntary. Whilst this may seem obvious, the question of "voluntary choice" has at times been contentious. For example, in the nineteenth century the courts held that the defence applied to employees working under dangerous conditions, and refused to acknowledge that an employee's desire to keep his or her job might force him or her to agree to work under appalling conditions. In such circumstances, the employee, in the absence of statutory rights, was in no position to threaten the employer that unless working conditions improved, he or she would leave. The employer would simply accept the employee's resignation. The House of Lords' decision in *Smith v Charles Baker & Sons*[18] marked welcome recognition of the injustice of this approach. Here, the plaintiff was an employee, who worked on the construction of a railway where a crane would swing heavy stones above his head without warning. The employee was fully aware of the danger of stones falling, but carried on working. He was seriously injured when a stone fell from the crane. The House of Lords (Lord Bramwell dissenting) held the employer liable. Their Lordships refused to accept the argument that by continuing to work, the employee had voluntarily accepted the risk of the stones falling. Nevertheless, it was recognised that a balance had to be struck. If the work was intrinsically dangerous, despite reasonable steps by the employer to minimise risks, the employee would be deemed to accept those risks.[19] Here, this was not the case, and so the employer would be found liable.

No such risk of pressure was found in *ICI v Shatwell*[20] where the brothers, testing the detonators in the quarry, had been clearly instructed to take precautions, but nevertheless chose to accept the risk. The court held that, in the light of *Smith v Baker*, it would apply the rule very carefully to employees and be alert to pressure from employers. However, on the facts of this case, no such pressure had been exerted.

Consent is equally not voluntary if the claimant is so drunk that he or she is incapable of understanding the nature and extent of the risk. Again, this is a fine line. In *Morris v Murray*,

16–007

16–008

---

15   [1991] 2 Q.B. 6. Comment: K. Williams (1991) 54 M.L.R. 745.
16   The pilot was found to have consumed 17 whiskies.
17   See Fox LJ at 17.
18   [1891] A.C. 325 HL.
19   See Lord Herschell [1891] A.C. 325 HL at 360.
20   [1965] A.C. 656.

despite his consumption of alcohol, it seems that the plaintiff was capable of realising the risks of flying with an intoxicated pilot,[21] but if he had drunk even more, the defence might not have been established. It has equally been questioned whether a defendant should be liable where, due to the defendant's negligence, the claimant has been given the opportunity to commit suicide. There is a clear argument that where the claimant has deliberately decided to end his or her life, the defence of voluntary assumption of risk should stand. This issue has been raised in two cases where the suicide took place when the deceased was under the care of the police or custodial authorities. In *Kirkham v Chief Constable of Greater Manchester*,[22] the plaintiff's husband had committed suicide while in a remand centre. The plaintiff had warned the police at time of his arrest of her husband's suicidal tendencies, but the police had negligently failed to pass on this information to the remand authorities. The Court of Appeal held that in the light of her husband's clinical depression, he could not be held to have voluntarily accepted the risk. This must be correct. If you are found to be of unsound mind, then an argument that you weighed up and decided to assume the risks of injury can hardly stand.

However, Lloyd LJ indicated (obiter) that the defence would apply if the deceased had been of sound mind at the time of the suicide.[23] This was not followed by the House of Lords in the later case of *Reeves v Metropolitan Police Commissioner*.[24] In this case, Martin Lynch had committed suicide in police custody by hanging himself from a cell door. Although a doctor had found Lynch to be of sound mind, the police had known that he was a suicide risk and had kept him under frequent observation. Nevertheless, they had failed to take all adequate precautions to prevent the suicide. In an action for negligence under the Fatal Accidents Act 1976, the majority of the House of Lords (Lord Hobhouse dissenting) found the police liable. They had undertaken a specific duty to protect Lynch from the risk of suicide and this they had failed to do. Any defence of voluntary assumption of risk would be inconsistent with such a duty:

> **"If the defence were available in circumstances such as the present where a deceased was known to have suicidal tendencies it would effectively negative the effect of any duty of care in respect of such suicide."[25]**

It made no difference whether the victim was of sound or unsound mind at the time of the suicide.

The limitations of this decision should be noted:

■ The police admitted to owing a specific duty to protect Lynch from the risk of suicide. If it was simply a duty to take reasonable care of him, voluntary assumption of risk could

---

21 He had in fact driven from the public house to the airfield and had helped start the aircraft and fuel it.
22 [1990] 2 Q.B. 283.
23 [1990] 2 Q.B. 283 at 290.
24 [2000] 1 A.C. 360 HL.
25 Lord Jauncey [2000] 1 A.C. 360 HL at 375–376.

still be argued. This duty will only arise where the police knew or ought to have known that the individual was a suicide risk.[26]

■   The House of Lords stressed that such a specific duty of care would be rare.

■   Their Lordships were far from happy in treating Lynch as being of sound mind (the main reason for departing from the view of Lloyd LJ in *Kirkham*). Lord Hoffmann remarked that "I confess to my unease about this finding, based on a seven minute interview with a doctor of unstated qualifications".[27] This highlights the practical difficulties which would arise if liability were held to depend on whether the deceased was of sound or unsound mind.

■   The damages were reduced in any event by 50% for contributory negligence (see below).

A final example of where the courts have considered the "voluntariness" of the assumption of risk is in relation to rescuers. We have considered liability towards rescuers in Ch.4, but one argument against liability would be that, in relation to non-professional rescuers at least, they have chosen to act. They are under no obligation to intervene but have chosen to do so freely and so (arguably) have voluntarily accepted the risk of injury involved. If I choose to go into a burning building to save a baby, I must have appreciated the risk of injury and so (arguably) I have voluntarily accepted the risk and cannot sue. The courts have rejected this argument. In this situation, the rescuer is not regarded as acting voluntarily. The legal, social or moral duty which forces the rescuer to intervene is such that he or she does not act voluntarily in the circumstances. On this basis, the defence of voluntary assumption of risk will not work against rescuers.

A good example is the well-known case of *Haynes v Harwood*.[28] Here, a police officer had been injured whilst stopping runaway horses attached to a van in a crowded street. The defendant had negligently left the horses unattended on the highway and they had bolted when a boy had thrown a stone at them. The Court of Appeal held that the police officer's reaction had been reasonably foreseeable in the circumstances and refused to accept a defence of voluntary assumption of risk.[29] It was also held that the reaction need not be instinctive to be reasonable. This seems sensible. It is surely better to intervene having considered the dangers than to jump in immediately.

---

26   See *Orange v Chief Constable of West Yorkshire Police* [2001] EWCA Civ 611; [2002] Q.B. 347 CA. cf. *Keenan v United Kingdom* (27229/95) (2001) 33 E.H.R.R. 38 (no breach of ECHR art.2).

27   [2000] 1 A.C. 360 at 372. See also Lord Hope at 385.

28   [1935] 1 K.B. 146.

29   [1935] 1 K.B. 146 at 156–157 per Greer LJ. See also *Baker v TE Hopkins* [1959] 1 W.L.R. 966.

> ## Other uses of "consent" in negligence

16–009   The courts have not always approached consent in negligence on a consistent basis. In addition to the defence of voluntary assumption of risk, the claimant's consent has been used by the courts in two further ways. First, the claimant's consent may limit the standard of care owed to the claimant by the defendant. Secondly, the claimant may consent to a clause excluding liability. These will be examined below. In both situations, the courts deny that they are applying the defence of voluntary assumption of risk, but the dividing line, as will be seen, is far from clear.

(A) SETTING THE STANDARD OF CARE IN NEGLIGENCE

16–010   Here, the claimant's acceptance of risk does not go to establish a defence but lowers the standard of care owed by the defendant to the claimant. This is particularly relevant to injuries suffered in the course of sporting activities. Here, in establishing the standard of care, the court will look at all the circumstances of the case, including the fact that a competitive sport, with associated risks to participants, is taking place. This is illustrated by the case of *Wooldridge v Sumner*.[30] In this case, a professional photographer at a horse show had been knocked down by a galloping horse whose rider had taken the corner too fast.[31] The Court of Appeal held that the question in issue was the standard of care expected of a jockey in a race. In setting the standard, regard would be had to the fact that any reasonable spectator would: (a) expect the jockey to concentrate his attention on winning the race, and (b) accept the existence of certain risks, provided the jockey stayed within the rules of the race and was not reckless. On this basis, the jockey was not in breach of his duty of care to the spectator. The Court of Appeal in *Blake v Galloway*[32] extended this approach to informal games which could be said to be played subject to a tacitly agreed understanding or convention—in this case, a group of 15-year-old friends, throwing twigs and pieces of bark chipping at each other. In examining such "horseplay", Dyson LJ found that a breach of duty would only occur where the defendant's conduct amounted to recklessness[33] or a high degree of carelessness, which was not the case here.

The dividing line between "no breach of duty" and the defence of voluntary assumption of risk is unclear. The principle on which they rest is the same: the defendant is not liable where the claimant knows and assents to a particular risk. The courts utilise both approaches, and Fox LJ in *Morris v Murray*[34] held that the gap between the two approaches is not a wide one.

---

30   [1963] 2 Q.B. 43. See also *Condon v Basi* [1985] 1 W.L.R. 866 CA, *Caldwell v Maguire* [2001] EWCA Civ 1054; [2002] P.I.Q.R. P6 and C. Gearty, "Tort: Liability for injuries incurred during sports and pastimes" [1985] C.L.J. 371.

31   Who went on to win!

32   [2004] EWCA Civ 814; [2004] 1 W.L.R. 2844.

33   There is some debate as to whether "reckless disregard" sets too low a standard—compare *Wooldridge v Sumner* with *Caldwell v Maguire* [2001] EWCA Civ 1054. See para.5–019.

34   [1991] 2 Q.B. 6 at 15.

(B) EXCLUSION CLAUSES

There is an obvious similarity between an express agreement to assume the risk of negligence and an exclusion clause, in which the claimant agrees to exclude or limit the defendant's liability. However, they are treated as distinct. *White v Blackmore*[35] is a good example of this distinction in operation. The plaintiff's husband had been killed in an accident at a race meeting for old cars. He had been thrown in the air when the rope behind which he was standing had been pulled away by an accident some distance away. Buckley LJ held that the defendants (who organised the meeting) had successfully excluded liability by notices which absolved them from all liability for accidents howsoever caused. The circumstances did not, however, support the defence of voluntary assumption of risk. By simply standing behind a rope to observe a race, the spectator did not accept the risk of such injury due to the defendants' negligence. Buckley LJ nevertheless admitted the close relationship between the defence and the operation of exclusion clauses.

The distinction between voluntary assumption of risk and exclusion clauses is nevertheless important, particularly in the light of the strict legal requirements applied to exclusion clauses. For example, to be valid an exclusion clause must be incorporated either by writing, custom or reasonable notice. Equally, exclusion clauses are now regulated by statute: the Consumer Rights Act 2015 (CRA 2015) (if you are a "consumer" dealing with a trader) and the Unfair Contract Terms Act 1977 (UCTA 1977) (if not a consumer). Section 2(3) of the 2015 Act specifies that a consumer is an individual who is "acting for purposes that are wholly or mainly outside that individual's trade, business, craft or profession." So, a notice in a sweet shop excluding liability to customers for any injuries caused by the negligence of staff would fall under the 2015, not the 1977, Act. The CRA 2015 regulates contract terms and "consumer notices" which seek to exclude or restrict the liability of a trader[36] to its consumers. Under s.62:

- An unfair consumer notice or term is not binding on the consumer.

- A notice is unfair if, contrary to the requirement of good faith, it causes a significant imbalance in the parties' rights and obligations to the detriment of the consumer.

- Whether a notice is unfair is to be determined—(a) taking into account the nature of the subject matter of the notice, and (b) by reference to all the circumstances existing when the rights or obligations to which it relates arose and to the terms of any contract on which it depends.

Section 65(1) further adds that a trader *cannot* by a consumer notice exclude or restrict liability for death or personal injury resulting from negligence. Where a consumer notice tries to

---

35   [1972] 2 Q.B. 651.

36   Trader is defined, in Consumer Rights Act 2015 s.2(2), as a "person acting for purposes relating to that person's trade, business, craft or profession, whether acting personally or through another person acting in the trader's name or on the trader's behalf".

exclude or restrict a trader's liability for negligence, a person is not to be taken to have voluntarily accepted any risk merely because the person agreed to or knew about the notice: s.65(2). Section 65 mirrors that of UCTA 1977 s.2, discussed below. Where the notice relates to loss or damage to property or other damage caused by negligence, the s.62 test will apply.

For non-consumer situations, the Unfair Contract Terms Act 1977 applies. It regulates the ability of the defendant to rely on exclusion clauses to exclude or limit liability for negligence as follows[37]:

- The Act regulates exclusion clauses dealing with business liability, i.e. where liability arises:

    (a) from things done or to be done by a person in the course of a business (whether his own business or another's); or

    (b) from the occupation of premises used for business purposes of the occupier.[38]

- Negligence is dealt with in s.2. This provides that a person cannot by reference to any contract term or notice exclude or restrict liability for death or personal injury resulting from negligence.[39] If the claim is for property or other damage, s.2(2) provides that a person cannot exclude or restrict liability for negligence except in so far as the term or notice satisfies the requirement of reasonableness.

- The reasonableness test is set out in s.11 and Sch.2. These provide that the term must be reasonable having regard to all the circumstances at the time liability arose, including the relative bargaining positions of the parties, any inducement to agree to the clause and, where liability is limited, the resources available to the defendant to meet such liability and the ability of the defendant to obtain insurance cover.

- Section 2(3) deals specifically with the defence of voluntary assumption of risk and distinguishes the defence from exclusion clauses generally. It states: "Where a contract term or notice purports to exclude or restrict liability for negligence, a person's agreement to or awareness of it is not of itself to be taken as indicating his voluntary acceptance of any risk" (see also CRA 2015 s.65(2) above). Therefore, the defendant cannot necessarily ensure that the defence will apply by means of a notice excluding liability. It will remain a question of fact, although it may be questioned what extra element is required to establish the defence of voluntary assumption of risk where the claimant has by contract agreed to exclude liability.

37　We list here only the main provisions of the Act relevant to this topic. Further reference should be made to works on the law of contract.

38　Unfair Contract Terms Act 1977 s.1(3).

39　Unfair Contract Terms Act 1977 s.2(1).

> ### (iii) Leave or licence

16–012

Consent in relation to claims for property torts such as trespass to land or private nuisance has been mentioned in earlier chapters. As stated earlier, the courts prefer to use the terms "leave" or "licence" in this context. Reference should be made to the relevant chapter.

(2) Illegality

16–013

This defence is also known by its Latin name, *ex turpi causa non oritur actio*, which means that an action cannot be founded on a base cause.[40] As Lord Mansfield classically explained in *Holman v Johnson*: "No Court will lend its aid to a man who founds his cause of action upon an illegal or an immoral act".[41] It is essentially then a matter of public policy and prevents a claimant from obtaining compensation for the consequences of his own criminal act.[42] It is obviously a matter of degree. If you are attacked when your car is parked on a double yellow line, then a court is not going to dismiss your claim for trespass to the person because you were parked illegally. However, if you were involved in a burglary and seriously injured by your fellow burglar negligently handling explosives while trying to blow open the safe, the court would not tolerate your claim.[43] As the Court of Appeal commented in *Joyce v O'Brien*,[44] the doctrine is one of public policy and so must operate flexibly, albeit that there may be on occasion some uncertainty whether the offence is sufficiently serious to attract the ex turpi doctrine.[45] The key question is whether the criminal or immoral act is the basis for the claim or simply background information. This can be a matter of degree. In *Ashton v Turner*,[46] the plaintiff and two other men had been in a car crash which was due to the negligent driving of the defendant. All three men were involved in a burglary, and the crash occurred while driving away from the scene of the crime. The court held that any negligence during the course of the burglary and the

---

40 The defence does not, however, operate to bar a claim based on the European Convention on Human Rights and so is inapplicable to claims under the Human Rights Act 1998: *Al Hassan-Daniel v Revenue and Customs Commissioners* [2010] EWCA Civ 1443; [2011] Q.B. 866, "Human rights are not just for the virtuous" per Sedley LJ at [12].

41 (1775) 1 Cowp. 341 at 343; 98 E.R. 1120.

42 See Lord Hoffmann in *Gray v Thames Trains Ltd* [2009] UKHL 33; [2009] 1 A.C. 1339 at [24].

43 See *National Coal Board v England* [1954] A.C. 403 at 429. Contrast, however, the approach of criminal law which is prepared to find manslaughter due to gross negligence where the victim has participated in the unlawful activity: see *R. v Wacker* [2002] EWCA Crim 1944; [2003] Q.B. 1207, where a lorry driver was convicted for the manslaughter of 58 illegal immigrants who suffocated when he closed the air vent in the back of his lorry.

44 [2013] EWCA Civ 546; [2014] 1 W.L.R. 70.

45 [2013] EWCA Civ 546 at [51] per Elias LJ (defence applied to theft of ladders—an imprisonable offence carrying a seven year maximum sentence). Contrast *Wallett v Vickers* [2018] EWHC 3088 (QB); [2019] P.I.Q.R. P6: racing with another car down a dual carriage way amounted to dangerous driving, but without joint enterprise, it was not sufficiently serious to give rise to the illegality defence, although it clearly amounted to contributory negligence. This was despite the defendant being sentenced to six months' imprisonment for dangerous driving.

46 [1981] Q.B. 137.

subsequent flight in the getaway car would be met by the defence of illegality. The plaintiff's claim was therefore rejected.

16-014   It should be noted, however, that illegal activities will not always obstruct the claimant's action in tort. In *Revill v Newbery*,[47] for example, the plaintiff was a burglar who had been shot whilst attempting to enter the defendant's shed to steal his property. The owner of the shed, who was 76, had been concerned about the spate of burglaries in the area and had resolved to wait in his shed with a shotgun to defend his property. The burglar sued the defendant for negligence and the court rejected the defence of illegality. Parliament, in enacting the Occupiers' Liability Act 1984,[48] had clearly indicated that in future trespassers, including burglars, should not be treated as outlaws by the occupiers of land. The illegal activities of the burglar therefore did not affect his claim. It should be noted that the court did reduce the damages awarded to the burglar by two-thirds, under the principle of contributory negligence.

Establishing the test for illegality

16-015   Attempts to provide a single test for the illegality defence have proved inconclusive. In *Jetivia SA v Bilta (UK) Ltd*,[49] Lord Neuberger noted that there were strongly held differing views as to the proper approach to be adopted to the defence of illegality and that it needed to be addressed by the Supreme Court, with a panel of seven or even nine justices, "as soon as appropriately possible". The tension, he noted, was caused by the need to provide a rule giving clarity and certainty and one which achieved a fair and appropriate result in each case.

Two main tests may be identified: one based on public policy and one examining whether the claim is "founded" on (or "linked to") the illegal act. Beldam LJ in *Pitts v Hunt*[50] (a case involving an underage, uninsured and drunk motorcyclist driving recklessly) favoured a test based on public policy and whether it would be an affront to the public conscience to compensate the claimant (riding pillion on the cycle), although his view was not shared by the rest of the court.[51] In *Tinsley v Milligan*,[52] however, the House of Lords was openly critical of the uncertainty inherent in the public conscience test. The majority in the later Court of Appeal decision of *Vellino v Chief Constable of the Greater Manchester Police*[53] examined whether the

---

47 [1996] Q.B. 567.
48 See Ch.8.
49 Also known as *Bilta (UK) Ltd v Nazir (No.2)* [2015] UKSC 23; [2016] A.C. 1 at [13]–[15].
50 [1991] 1 Q.B. 24.
51 Balcombe LJ argued that due to the nature of the joint illegal activity undertaken by the plaintiff and Hunt, it was impossible for the court to determine the standard of care which is appropriate to this situation (see also *Jackson v Harrison* (1978) 138 C.L.R. 438). Unfortunately, the Balcombe test is by its nature limited in application to the tort of negligence.
52 [1994] 1 A.C. 340. *Tinsley* was overturned by the Supreme Court in *Patel v Mirza* [2016] UKSC 42 (discussed below).
53 [2001] EWCA Civ 1249; [2002] 1 W.L.R. 218. Comment C. A. Hopkins [2002] C.L.J. 257. See also *Sacco v Chief Constable of the South Wales Constabulary* unreported 15 May 1998 CA.

claimant's injuries could be said to be inextricably linked to his criminal conduct. Here, the police had attempted to arrest Vellino at his second floor flat. He had previously evaded arrest by climbing out of a window and lowering himself onto the ground. On this occasion, however, his escape had tragic consequences when he fell badly and was left with severe brain damage and tetraplegia. In response to his claim against the police for negligence in allowing him to escape, it was held that his claim was inextricably linked to his criminal act of escaping lawful custody. Further:

> **"to suggest that the police owe a criminal the duty to prevent the criminal from escaping, and that the criminal who hurts himself while escaping can sue the police for the breach of that duty, seems to me self-evidently absurd."[54]**

16–016

The nature of the test for illegality was considered again by the House of Lords in 2009 in *Gray v Thames Trains Ltd*.[55] Here, Gray, whilst suffering from post-traumatic stress disorder (PTSD), had stabbed to death a drunken pedestrian, who had stepped in front of his car. He was found guilty of manslaughter on the grounds of diminished responsibility and detained in a hospital indefinitely as a result. The PTSD, however, had been caused by the negligence of the defendants (Mr Gray had been involved in the Ladbroke Grove rail crash in which 31 people had been killed) and Gray argued that, despite his conviction for manslaughter, he should be able to recover for ongoing loss of earnings caused by the accident. The defendants argued that any claim for loss of earnings must terminate once he had been imprisoned and that the defence of illegality would bar any claim for financial losses resulting from his conviction for manslaughter.

Their Lordships found in favour of the defendants. Lord Hoffmann in his leading judgment addressed the question of *when* the illegality defence would apply and preferred arguments based on public policy. His Lordship rejected the tests, mentioned in earlier case law, of "an inextricable link"[56] between the claim and the illegality, or the claim arising "directly ex turpi causa"[57] as unhelpful.[58] The defence of illegality applied where it would be *inconsistent with the sentence of the criminal court*. Here a criminal court had held Gray responsible for his crime albeit whilst suffering from diminished responsibility. It would be inconsistent for a civil court to

---

54 See Schiemann LJ [2002] 1 W.L.R. 218, 224.

55 [2009] UKHL 33; [2009] 1 A.C. 1339. There was also some discussion of illegality in *Stone & Rolls Ltd (in liquidation) v Moore Stephens (a firm)* [2009] UKHL 39; [2009] 1 A.C. 1391, but in view of the disparate reasoning of their Lordships, it is difficult to ascertain any clear guidance from this case: for criticism, see P. S. Davies, "'Auditors' liability: No need to detect fraud?" [2009] C.L.J. 505.

56 The "inextricable link" test was suggested by Judge LJ in *Cross v Kirkby The Times* 5 April 2000 and adopted by Sir Murray Stuart-Smith in *Vellino v Chief Constable of the Greater Manchester Police* [2001] EWCA Civ 1249.

57 *Saunders v Edwards* [1987] 1 W.L.R. 1116 at 1134.

58 See *Gray v Thames Trains Ltd* [2009] UKHL 33; [2009] 1 A.C. 1339 at [54]. See also Lord Rodger at [74].

compensate him for an injury or disadvantage resulting from the punishment for the crime.[59] Further, it rejected Gray's claim for an indemnity against any claims brought against him by the victim's family and damages for feelings of guilt and remorse consequent on the killing. These, held Lord Hoffmann, were *caused by Gray's own crime*, not the defendants' negligence.[60]

In so doing, their Lordships approved the earlier Court of Appeal decision of *Clunis v Camden & Islington Health Authority*.[61] In this case, Clunis had been convicted of manslaughter on the grounds of diminished responsibility when he had, for no reason, attacked and killed a man at an underground station. He had a long history of mental illness and seriously violent behaviour, but had been discharged from hospital, with after-care services in the community to be provided by the defendant health authority. The plaintiff claimed that, due to the negligence of the health authority, his condition had not been properly assessed and he was therefore not prevented from committing the attack. The Court of Appeal rejected this claim. The criminal court had found Clunis to be of diminished responsibility, rather than insane, which indicated that he had appreciated what he was doing and that it was wrong. It would be contrary to public policy to support such a claim arising out of commission of a crime.[62]

Much would, however, depend on the facts. Lord Hoffmann acknowledged that in each case the policy reasons must be considered against the facts of the case to reach a fair outcome.[63] His Lordship identified narrow and broad forms of the illegality defence:

- *Narrow policy ground*: you cannot recover for damage which flows from loss of liberty, a fine or other punishment lawfully imposed upon you in consequence of your own unlawful act. The policy here is to avoid inconsistency between criminal and civil law and is used in both *Gray* and *Clunis*. (inconsistency argument)

- *Wide policy ground*: you cannot recover compensation for loss which you have suffered in consequence of your own criminal act. It would be offensive to public notions of the fair distribution of resources to permit compensation in such circumstances. An example of such reasoning may be seen in *Vellino* above. (causation argument).

THE WIDE POLICY GROUND AND JOINT CRIMINAL ENTERPRISE

16–017

Although the facts of *Gray* did not cover joint criminal activities, it has been established that the wide policy ground will apply whether the criminal is acting alone or as part of a joint enterprise.

---

59 Their Lordships rejected the argument that the conviction for manslaughter should be disregarded in assessing damages for loss of earnings. The court would examine the facts as they happened, not a counter-factual scenario. His loss of earnings was thus caused by his conviction for manslaughter.

60 [2009] UKHL 33; [2009] 1 A.C. 1339 at [51].

61 [1998] Q.B. 978.

62 The court refused to follow *Meah v McCreamer* [1985] 1 All E.R. 367 where a convicted rapist had been allowed to recover damages when a head injury in a road accident had led to a dramatic personality change (see also *Gray v Thames Trains Ltd* [2009] UKHL 33 per Lord Rodger at [65]).

63 [2009] UKHL 33 at [30]–[31].

In *Joyce v O'Brien*,[64] the Court of Appeal applied *Gray* to a case of joint criminal enterprise: here the theft of ladders transported in a van driven so recklessly by the defendant that the claimant, holding onto the ladders in the back of the van, fell out suffering serious injuries. On this basis, the defence would apply "where the character of the joint criminal enterprise is such that it is foreseeable that a party or parties may be subject to unusual or increased risks of harm as a consequence of the activities of the parties in pursuance of their criminal objectives".[65] The focus is therefore on the risks associated with the criminal activity in question and whether the injury falls within the scope of these risks: if the risk materialises, then the claimant's injury can be said to be caused by his or her criminal act even if it results from the negligent or intentional act of another party to the illegal enterprise.

Rationalising the illegality defence: the Law Commission and *Patel v Mirza*

16–018

Following *Gray*, the illegality defence was raised in two important Supreme Court decisions—*Allen v Hounga*[66] and *Les Laboratoires Servier v Apotex Inc.*[67] Commentators noted that two differently constituted divisions of the Court had handed down, within four months of each other, leading judgments which embodied radically different (and potentially conflicting) approaches to the defence and that a detailed review of this area of law was badly needed.[68] Two earlier papers of the Law Commission had tried to suggest a way forward but had not been adopted. The Law Commission's 2001 Consultation Paper, *The Illegality Defence in Tort*,[69] had found the law relating to illegality to be at times confusing, lacking a clear rationale. It therefore proposed a structured statutory discretion directing the court to ask itself whether the claim should be allowed in the light of the rationale behind the illegality defence—in general, it stated, to maintain the internal consistency of the law in the interest of promoting the integrity of justice—and taking certain factors into account. In its later 2009 *Consultative Report*, the Law Commission suggested that relevant policy factors would be: (a) furthering the purpose of the rule which the illegal conduct has infringed; (b) consistency; (c) that the claimant should not profit from his or her own wrong; (d) deterrence; and (e) maintaining the integrity of the legal system.[70] It also concluded that whenever the illegality defence is successful, the court should make clear the justification for its application. This Consultation Paper received, however, a mixed reception. There was a fear that a statutory discretion would introduce greater

---

64   [2013] EWCA Civ 546; [2014] 1 W.L.R. 70. Contrast *Delaney v Pickett* [2011] EWCA Civ 1532; [2012] 1 W.L.R. 2149 (joint criminal enterprise of transporting drugs with intent to supply) where the defence failed.

65   [2013] EWCA Civ 546 at [29].

66   [2014] UKSC 47; [2014] 1 W.L.R. 2889 (concerning statutory tort of unlawful discrimination).

67   [2014] UKSC 55; [2015] A.C. 430 (concerning patent law).

68   See, e.g. R. A. Buckley, "Illegality in the Supreme Court" (2015) 131 L.Q.R. 341. See also J. C. Fisher, "The ex turpi causa principle in *Hounga* and *Servier*" (2015) 78 M.L.R. 854.

69   Law Commission Consultation Paper No.160 (2001).

70   Law Commission, *The Illegality Defence*, CP No.189 at para.7.69.

uncertainty to the law. The Law Commission, in its final report of March 2010,[71] concluded that, in the light of recent case law such as *Gray v Thames Trains* which expressly took into account the policy factors which underlie the illegality defence, no proposals for reform would be made. The Government in March 2012 confirmed that no change would be made: "reform of this area of the law cannot be considered a pressing priority for the Government at present".[72]

Finally, in *Patel v Mirza* in 2016,[73] a nine justice Supreme Court intervened. The majority of the court gave its support to the structured discretion approach favoured by the Law Commission. The case itself involved an illegal contract—the claimant paying the defendant £620,000 to bet on the movement of shares using insider information contrary to the Criminal Justice Act 1993 s.52. The information never materialised, and the claimant unsurprisingly wanted his money back. Was he barred due to the illegality? Although all nine justices agreed to the result—Mr Patel should get his money back—they had different views as to the basis for the illegality defence. The majority (Lords Toulson, Kerr, Hale, Wilson and Hodge JJSC) favoured a policy rationale: it would be contrary to the public interest to enforce a claim if to do so would be harmful to the integrity of the legal system.[74] Lord Toulson, giving the lead judgment, found:

> "In assessing whether the public interest would be harmed in that way, it is necessary (a) to consider the underlying purpose of the prohibition which has been transgressed and whether that purpose will be enhanced by denial of the claim, (b) to consider any other relevant public policy on which the denial of the claim may have an impact and (c) to consider whether denial of the claim would be a proportionate response to the illegality, bearing in mind that punishment is a matter for the criminal courts . . . The public interest is best served by a principled and transparent assessment of the considerations identified, rather by than the application of a formal approach capable of producing results which may appear arbitrary, unjust or disproportionate."[75]

This gives the courts discretion to ascertain what the "other relevant public policies" are in each case, although Lord Toulson warned that it would be a mistake to suggest that the court would be free to decide each case in an undisciplined way. Lord Neuberger equally came to the conclusion that, despite initial doubts, a structured discretion was the best test the courts

---

71   Law Commission, *The Illegality Defence*, Law Com. No.320, (2010).

72   *Report on the implementation of Law Commission proposals* HC 1900 (2012) at para.52.

73   [2016] UKSC 42; [2017] A.C. 467. Comment: J. Goudkamp, "The end of an era? Illegality in private law in the Supreme Court" (2017) 133 L.Q.R. 14.

74   Relying on the test stated by McLachlin J in *Hall v Herbert* (1993) 2 S.C.R. 159 at 178 Supreme Court of Canada.

75   [2016] UKSC 42 at [120]. In relation to proportionality, potentially relevant factors include the seriousness of the conduct, its centrality to the contract, whether it was intentional and whether there was marked disparity in the parties' respective culpability: [107].

could offer at this moment in time. In contrast, Lords Sumption, Mance and Clarke (dissenting) were critical of this "range of factors" approach which they predicted would lead to complexity, uncertainty, arbitrariness and a lack of transparency. Lord Sumption argued, in particular, that "We would be doing no service to the coherent development of the law if we simply substituted a new mess for the old one".[76] It remains to be seen whether such predictions are proven to be correct or whether, as the majority argue, the only viable test is one based on a structured discretion which will allow the courts the flexibility they need to reach a just result.

We do, however, have one important tort case. *Patel*, as noted above, was not a tort case, but decided in contract/unjust enrichment. The Court of Appeal in *Henderson v Dorset Healthcare University NHS Foundation Trust*[77] considered its application in a tort situation. Here a mentally ill patient under the care of the NHS Trust had stabbed her mother to death. It was admitted that, but for the NHS Trust's breach of duty, the tragic event would not have happened. Ms Henderson was convicted of manslaughter by reason of diminished responsibility. She sought damages which included claims for compensation for her compulsory detention and loss of her share of her mother's estate.[78] The Court held that *Clunis* was still good law. *Gray* made it clear that, for policy reasons, you could not recover damages in tort where punishment had been imposed by criminal law and nor could you recover for losses which were a consequence of your criminal act. It could not be said that the patient did not know the quality and nature of her act when she did not run an insanity defence. The Court did, however, state that it still felt bound by *Gray*, placing greater emphasis on this case than the more general discussion in *Patel*, arguing that considerable caution must be taken in relying on cases decided in contract and unjust enrichment law rather than the law of tort.[79] Todd argues that the decision in *Henderson* "leaves the potential impact of *Patel* in tort cases generally somewhat up in the air."[80] Students should therefore still pay attention to *Gray* when applying the illegality defence in tort.

(3) Contributory negligence[81]

It is convenient to refer to the principle of contributory negligence as a "defence", although, as will be seen, it can no longer operate as a complete defence to a claimant's action. Contributory negligence is generally raised in cases involving the tort of negligence, although it has a wider

16–019

---

76 [2016] UKSC 42 at [265].
77 [2018] EWCA Civ 1841; [2018] 3 W.L.R. 1651 (on appeal to Supreme Court).
78 Lost under the Forfeiture Act 1982.
79 [2018] EWCA Civ 1841 at [87]. See also *Day v Womble Bond Dickinson (UK) Ltd* [2020] EWCA Civ 447 at [34] (professional negligence case): "There can be no doubt that the rule in *Gray* was not undermined by the decision in *Patel*".
80 S. Todd (2019) 35 P.N. 6 at 31.
81 See N. Gravells, "Three heads of contributory negligence" (1977) 93 L.Q.R. 581. For an empirical study of the operation of the contributory negligence defence, see J. Goudkamp and D. Nolan, "Contributory negligence in the twenty-first century: An empirical study of first instance decisions" (2016) 79 M.L.R. 575.

application, for example in breach of statutory duty.[82] It permits a defendant to argue that the damages awarded in favour of the claimant should be reduced because some of the damage was caused by the fault of the claimant. It has obvious links with causation, examined in earlier chapters. Indeed, it is impossible to have 100% contributory negligence for the very reason that this in fact amounts to a statement that the claimant is the cause of the accident (or the *novus causa interveniens*) and has no right to sue the defendant.[83]

The principle of contributory negligence is now found in the Law Reform (Contributory Negligence) Act 1945 s.1(1). The common law position prior to 1945 was complicated. The rule at common law was that the claimant could recover nothing if he or she was contributorily negligent.[84] The obvious injustice of this rule led the courts to modify this rule to:

- First, the rule of last opportunity. This was where the court found that although both parties were negligent, the defendant had the last chance to avoid the accident.[85] If so, the claimant would recover in full.

- Secondly, the rule of constructive last opportunity. This is where the defendant would have had the last opportunity to avoid the accident, but for his or her own negligence.[86] If proved, the claimant again would recover in full.

Such solutions served only to complicate the law, and of course did not remove the injustice of the former rule. Instead of the claimant's action failing, the claimant recovered full damages. This ignored his or her fault entirely. Neither the old rule nor the courts' modifications were fair to both parties. The law is now stated in the Law Reform (Contributory Negligence) Act 1945 (the Act).

The statutory position

16–020 Section 1(1) of the Act provides:

> **"Where any person suffers damage as the result partly of his own fault and partly of the fault of any other person or persons, a claim**

---

82 Although it cannot be used in deceit (*Alliance and Leicester BS v Edgestop Ltd* [1994] 2 All E.R. 38 and *Standard Chartered Bank v Pakistan National Shipping Corp (Nos 2 and 4)* [2002] UKHL 43; [2003] 1 A.C. 959) nor for intentional torts such as trespass to the person: *Co-operative Group (CSW) Ltd v Pritchard* [2011] EWCA Civ 329; [2012] Q.B. 320. The Torts (Interference with Goods) Act 1977 s.11(1) also provides that it is not a defence to proceedings founded on conversion or intentional trespass to goods.

83 See *Pitts v Hunt* [1991] 1 Q.B. 24 and *Anderson v Newham College of Further Education* [2002] EWCA Civ 505; [2003] I.C.R. 212.

84 See *Butterfield v Forrester* (1809) 11 East 60; 103 E.R. 926.

85 *Davies v Mann* (1842) 10 M. & W. 546; 152 E.R. 588.

86 *British Columbia Electric Ry v Loach* [1916] 1 A.C. 719.

> in respect of that damage shall not be defeated by reason of the fault of the person suffering the damage, but the damages recoverable in respect thereof shall be reduced to such extent as the court thinks just and equitable having regard to the claimant's share in the responsibility for the damage."

This section finally allowed the courts to apportion damages as they deem "just and equitable" and marked a welcome move away from the technicalities of the common law. Damages will be reduced according to the claimant's responsibility for the damage (not the accident). On this basis, damages may be reduced in a car crash when the claimant has failed to wear a seatbelt.[87] This may not have led to the accident, but may have added to the injury suffered.

"Damage" is defined in s.4 to include loss of life and personal injury, and it continues to include property damage. It would also appear to cover claims for pure economic loss.[88] Section 4 also defines "fault" as:

> ". . . negligence,[89] breach of statutory duty or other act or omission that gives rise to liability in tort or would, apart from the Act, give rise to the defence of contributory negligence."

This is not particularly clear. The accepted view is that s.1 refers to "fault" both in relation to the claimant and the defendant. On this basis, the first part of the definition refers to the nature of the claim against the defendant, which can be for negligence, breach of statutory duty or any other act or omission giving rise to liability in tort. The second part of the definition refers to negligence, breach of statutory duty or the acts or omissions of the claimant which would at common law have given the defendant an absolute defence. On this basis, tortious conduct by the claimant that would not at common law have given rise to a defence of contributory negligence—the classic example being deceit/fraud—would not affect the claim.[90]

A very broad interpretation of s.4 was adopted by the majority of the House of Lords in *Reeves v Metropolitan Police Commissioner*,[91] where their Lordships held that it included intentional acts by the claimant. On this basis, the deliberate act of the deceased in committing

---

87 See *Froom v Butcher* [1976] Q.B. 286.
88 See *Platform Home Loans v Oyston Shipways Ltd* [2000] 2 A.C. 190 HL.
89 This has raised problems whether contributory negligence can be a defence when the claimant alleges that the defendant's negligence amounts to breach of contract. The leading case of *Forsikringsaktieselskapet Vesta v Butcher* [1989] A.C. 852 limits the defence to where the defendant's liability in contract is the same as his liability in the tort of negligence independently of the existence of any contract. See also *Barclays Bank Plc v Fairclough Building Ltd* [1995] Q.B. 214 and *Raflatac Ltd v Eade* [1999] 1 Lloyd's Rep. 506.
90 This was confirmed by the House of Lords in *Standard Chartered Bank v Pakistan Shipping Corp (Nos 2 and 4)* [2002] UKHL 43; [2003] 1 A.C. 959. In deceit, it is irrelevant that the claimant may have allowed himself or herself to be influenced by other factors or has failed to verify the statement in question: *Edgington v Fitzmaurice* (1885) L.R. 29 Ch. D. 459 and *Redgrave v Hurd* (1881–82) L.R. 20 Ch.D. 1.
91 [2000] 1 A.C. 360.

suicide in police custody amounted to contributory negligence within the Act. This is a very generous interpretation of "fault"—it can hardly be termed "negligent" to deliberately commit suicide—and it is somewhat artificial to claim that a person's act of suicide "contributed" to the damage, i.e. his death. However, the section is broadly phrased, and in view of the defendant's duty to prevent this very act occurring, the majority held that a "common sense" approach should prevail. Both the deceased's intentional act and the negligence of the police had contributed to his death and so a 50:50 division of responsibility was appropriate.[92]

It should be noted that the aim of this section is not to show that the claimant owes the defendant a duty of care to protect him or her against liability, but to show that the claimant failed to exercise reasonable care and this added to his or her injuries.[93] In applying the test the court will have regard both to the relative blameworthiness of the parties and the causal "potency" of the claimant's acts, that is, the relative importance of his or her acts in causing the damage apart from his or her blameworthiness.[94] It will be a question of fact in each case. There are three main questions the court should address:

- Was the claimant acting negligently?

- Did his or her actions contribute to the damage suffered?

- To what extent should his or her damages be reduced?

These questions will be examined below.

(i) Was the claimant acting negligently?

16–021   As we have seen above, the question is whether the claimant has exercised reasonable care. As Lord Denning stated in *Jones v Livox Quarries*:

> "A person is guilty of contributory negligence if he ought reasonably to have foreseen that, if he did not act as a reasonable, prudent man, he might hurt himself; and in his reckonings, he must take into account the possibility of others being careless."[95]

---

92   But note the divergence in the House of Lords in *Corr v IBC Vehicles Ltd* [2008] UKHL 13; [2008] 1 A.C. 884 as to the correct approach to use when a victim, driven by severe depression caused by the defendant's negligence, takes his own life. Lords Scott, Mance and Neuberger were all prepared to contemplate a reduction for contributory negligence, but argued in favour of a more nuanced approach which would take into account to what extent the deceased's personal autonomy had been overborne by the impairment to his mind attributable to the defendant.

93   *Nance v British Columbia Electric Ry Co Ltd* [1951] 2 All E.R. 448.

94   See Lord Reid in *Stapley v Gypsum Mines Ltd* [1953] A.C. 663 at 682.

95   [1952] 2 Q.B. 608 at 615. Reference will be made to changes in the public perception of risk. On this basis, the reasonable man, warned that there was a substantial risk that smoking would seriously damage his health,

It is clearly an objective test, but the courts will make allowances for children[96] and the aged and infirm. In the recent case of *Ellis v Kelly*,[97] the court clarified that there was no hard and fast rule when a child could be found to be contributory negligence—it would depend on what could reasonably be expected of a child of the same age, intelligence and experience. Here an 8-year-old crossing a road unaccompanied near a pedestrian crossing was not found to be contributory negligent when he had assumed (wrongly) that a speeding car would stop for him. The courts will equally recognise that in an emergency (which is due to the fault of the defendant), some allowance must be made for decisions taken in the heat of the moment. In *Jones v Boyce*,[98] for example, the plaintiff was a passenger on top of the defendant's coach. In realising correctly that the coach was in danger of being overturned due to a defective coupling rein, he decided to jump off and broke his leg. The coach, in fact, did not overturn. The court nevertheless held that it was a question of whether the plaintiff had acted reasonably, and allowances should be made for the actions of parties placed in such a dangerous predicament. However, the reaction must be reasonable and respond to some danger. In *Adams v Lancashire and Yorkshire Ry Co*,[99] for example, it was not deemed reasonable to deal with the inconvenience of a draft from an open train door by leaning out of the moving train to close it. The court held that the plaintiff should simply have moved seats or waited until the next station.[100] He therefore had no right to sue the defendant for negligence when he fell out of the train.

The same approach applies to rescuers. Whilst allowances will be made for the heat of the moment, the rescuer cannot claim for injuries which are due to his or her unreasonable response to the danger. For example, in *Harrison v British Railways Board*,[101] a misguided train guard attempted to assist a passenger who was trying to join a moving train by signalling the driver to stop. Unfortunately, he gave the wrong signal and the driver continued to accelerate. He then tried to pull the passenger into the rapidly accelerating train, but both of them fell out. The guard sued the passenger for negligence. The court held that the passenger did owe the guard a duty of care when, through lack of care for his own safety, he had put himself in a situation of danger in which it was reasonably foreseeable that someone would intervene to help, but that a reasonable guard would have applied the emergency brake. On this basis, the guard's damages were reduced by 20%. Boreham J warned, however, that rescuers should be treated leniently: "One has a feeling of distaste about finding a rescuer guilty of contributory negligence. It can rarely be appropriate to do so".[102]

---

would stop smoking: *Badger v Ministry of Defence* [2005] EWHC 2941 (QB); [2006] 3 All E.R. 173 (contributory negligence to fail to give up smoking when risk to health known).

96 Depending on the age of the child, see *Yachuk v Oliver Blais Co Ltd* [1949] A.C. 386, *Gough v Thorne* [1966] 3 All E.R. 398 and *Probert v Moore* [2012] EWHC 2324 (QB) (decision of 13 year old child to walk along unlit road in the dark without high visibility jacket or torch was ill-advised but not negligent).

97 [2018] EWHC 2031 (QB); [2018] 4 W.L.R. 124.

98 (1816) 1 Stark 493; 171 E.R. 540.

99 (1869) L.R. 4 C.P. 739.

100 The next station was 3 minutes away.

101 [1981] 3 All E.R. 679.

102 [1981] 3 All E.R. 679 at 686.

(ii) Did the claimant's actions contribute to the damage suffered?

16–022

The classic case is that of *Stapley v Gypsum Mines Ltd*.[103] Stapley had been killed in a mining accident when a large piece of the roof where he was working fell upon him. He, and another miner, Dale, had been instructed earlier to make that part of the mine safe by bringing down a section of the roof. The men tried unsuccessfully to bring down the roof and then carried on working. In an action by Stapley's widow, it was argued that Stapley's own negligence had been the substantial cause of his death. The majority of the House of Lords held that Dale had also been responsible for the accident, for whom the employers were vicariously liable, but that damages should be reduced by 80% for contributory negligence. Lord Reid found the question of who had contributed to the damage to be one of common sense, depending on the facts of each particular case. Where a number of people had been at fault, it would be a matter of isolating those parties whose fault had led to the accident and was not too remote. Here, the question was whether the fault of Dale was so mixed up with the accident that, as a matter of common sense, his actions must be regarded as having contributed to his accident. On the facts, there was insufficient separation of time, place or circumstance to find that Dale had not contributed to the accident.

It is also important that the claimant's negligence exposed him or her to the particular type of damage suffered. For example, if I drive without a seatbelt and suffer injuries whilst stationary when a lorry negligently drops its load on my car, it cannot be said that my failure to wear a seatbelt exposed me to that particular risk of damage. Conversely, the damages were reduced in *Jones v Livox Quarries*,[104] where the plaintiff had been injured when, whilst riding on the back of a vehicle to the works canteen, he was struck from behind by the driver of a dumper truck. Riding on the back of the vehicle was contrary to his employers' express instructions and what materialised was precisely the type of danger to be expected from such conduct. However, if a passing sportsman had negligently shot him in the eye, he could hardly be said to be contributorily negligent since this was not a risk to which his negligent actions exposed him.[105]

---

103 [1953] A.C. 663. Note, however, P.S. Atiyah, "'Causation, Contributory Negligence and Volenti Non Fit Injuria" (1965) 43 Can. Bar. Rev. 609, who criticises the court's analysis of causation, and the discussion of this point in Ch.6.

104 [1952] 2 Q.B. 608.

105 Lord Denning's somewhat graphic example [1952] 2 Q.B. 608 at 616. This was, however, cited in *St George v Home Office* [2008] EWCA Civ 1068; [2009] 1 W.L.R. 1670 (drug addict, who suffered brain damage due to the negligence of the prison service when suffering withdrawal symptoms whilst in custody, at fault in becoming addicted to drugs from the age of 16, but such fault was too remote in time, place and circumstances to be sufficiently connected with the negligence of the prison staff and to be regarded as a cause of the injury).

> **(iii) To what extent should the claimant's damages be reduced? What is "just and equitable" in these circumstances?**

This is generally a matter of the court's discretion and therefore will depend on the facts of the case. The wording of the Act gives the courts considerable flexibility, which they utilise to the full.[106] In *Jackson v Murray*, the majority of the Supreme Court admitted that:

> "the apportionment of responsibility is inevitably a somewhat rough and ready exercise (a feature reflected in the judicial preference for round figures) . . . That is consistent with the requirement under s.1(1) to arrive at a result which the court considers 'just and equitable'."[107]

As a result, it is difficult critically to evaluate the court's assessment of contributory negligence, because the courts generally give a bald figure, with little guidance as to the reasoning underlying the sum. The courts have given some indications that they will be influenced by the relative blameworthiness of each party in addition to considering the degree to which their fault contributed towards the damage suffered.[108] Recent case law has also indicated that car-drivers will generally be deemed to have greater "causal potency" than pedestrians because a car can do more damage to a person than a person to a car.[109] However, in certain circumstances, guideline figures have been given to provide some certainty and consistency, and these are generally followed.

(A) FAILURE TO WEAR A SEATBELT

Guidelines were given by the Court of Appeal in *Froom v Butcher*.[110] In this case, despite driving carefully, Mr Froom had been struck head-on by a speeding car overtaking in the opposite direction. He suffered head and chest injuries, which were found to have been caused by his failure to wear a seatbelt. At the time, it was not compulsory to wear a seatbelt, and Froom had argued that he had made a conscious decision not to wear one, having seen a number of accidents where drivers wearing seatbelts had been trapped in the vehicle following an accident. The Court of Appeal held that his failure to wear a seatbelt did amount to contributory

---

106 An appeal court will only overturn a finding of contributory negligence where it finds that the judge had gone wrong in principle, misunderstood the facts or was clearly wrong: see *Kerry v Carter* [1969] 1 W.L.R. 1372 at 1376.

107 [2015] UKSC 5; [2015] 2 All E.R. 805 at [28] per Lord Reed.

108 See *Davies v Swan Motor Co (Swansea) Ltd* [1949] 2 K.B. 291 at 326 per Lord Denning. Hale LJ more recently recognised that the role of the court is to compare the claimant's share in responsibility for the damage with that of the defendant: "to do what is 'just and equitable' . . . includes being fair to the claimant as well as to the defendant. Realistically, therefore, the court has to compare the one with the other": *Eagle v Chambers (No.1)* [2003] EWCA Civ 1107; [2004] R.T.R. 9 at [14].

109 *Jackson v Murray* [2015] UKSC 5; [2015] 2 All E.R. 805 at [26]), *Sabir v Osei-Kwabena* [2015] EWCA Civ 1213; [2016] R.T.R. 9.

110 [1976] Q.B. 286.

negligence. It had added to the injury suffered and it was irrelevant that Froom believed that it would be safer not to wear a seatbelt—the test was of the reasonable person who would, according to the court, wear a seatbelt. Damages were therefore reduced by 20%.

The court gave general guidance as to the appropriate reduction for not wearing a seatbelt:

- 25% if the injury would have been prevented altogether;

- 15% if the injury would have been less severe; and

- 0% if wearing the seatbelt would not have prevented injury.

This will tend to be followed save in exceptional cases; the courts acknowledging the value of having clear guidelines which will encourage parties to reach sensible settlements.[111] The binding nature of these guidelines was recently reaffirmed in *Stanton v Collinson*,[112] where the Court of Appeal acknowledged the powerful public interest in there being no intensive inquiry into fine degrees of contributory negligence so that the vast majority of cases could be settled according to a well-understood formula and that exceptional cases did not get out of control.

It should be noted that seatbelt wearing is now compulsory for front and back seats (where available).[113] Although Lord Denning also suggested in *Froom* that exceptions may be made for pregnant women or "unduly fat" passengers,[114] pregnant women are not exempt, unless their doctor certifies that they should be for medical reasons.[115] A doctor may exempt any party if he or she decides that it is warranted and issue a formal "Certificate of Exemption from Compulsory Seat Belt wearing".[116] This must be produced on request by the police.[117]

(B) FAILURE TO WEAR A CRASH HELMET

16–025

Capps v Miller[118] applied the *Froom* guidelines to crash helmets,[119] although the majority held that a reduction of only 10% would be appropriate where a crash helmet had been worn but not fastened. Road Traffic Act 1988 s.16 provides that it is compulsory to wear protective head

---

111   See Keene LJ in *J (a minor) v Wilkins* [2001] P.I.Q.R. P12.

112   [2010] EWCA Civ 81; [2010] R.T.R. 26.

113   For adults, see Road Traffic Act 1988 s.14 (Seat belts: adults), as amended. Motor Vehicles (Wearing of Seat Belts) Regulations 1993 (SI 1993/176) reg.5 requires adults and children aged 14 and over to wear seat belts where available in the rear of all classes of motor vehicle (as amended by Motor Vehicles (Wearing of Seat Belts) (Amendment) Regulations 2006 (SI 2006/1892)). For children under 14, see Road Traffic Act 1988 s.15 (as amended) and the Motor Vehicles (Wearing of Seat Belts) (Amendment) Regulations 2006 (SI 2006/1892).

114   [1976] Q.B. 286 at 295.

115   See Road Traffic Act 1988 s.14(2)(b)(iii) and Motor Vehicles (Wearing of Seat Belts) Regulations 1993 (SI 1993/176) reg.6 and Sch.1 (exemptions).

116   See Motor Vehicles (Wearing of Seat Belts) Regulations 1993 (SI 1993/176) Sch.1.

117   Road Traffic Act 1988 s.14(4).

118   [1989] 1 W.L.R. 839. See also *O'Connell v Jackson* [1972] 1 Q.B. 270.

119   This is now authority that failure to wear a bicycle helmet, which is recommended by the Highway Code but not legally required, may be treated as contributory negligence: *Smith v Finch* [2009] EWHC 53 (QB) (but not

gear when riding a motor bike. It should be noted that exceptions are made for Sikhs wearing turbans.[120]

Apart from this guidance, the court is free to assess what is just and equitable. It should be remembered that the reduction cannot be 100%, as this is essentially a denial of causation.[121] Croom-Johnson LJ in *Capps v Miller*[122] also advised the courts against making fine distinctions in percentages, although he disapproved of dicta indicating that an award of less than 10% should not be given.[123]

(C) NEGLIGENT VALUATION CASES

16–026

The House of Lords in *Platform Home Loans Ltd v Oyston Shipways Ltd*[124] dealt with the application of the defence of contributory negligence in the wake of the House of Lords' decision in *South Australia Asset Management Corp v York Montague Ltd* (commonly known as *SAAMCO*).[125] This decided that damages for a negligent valuation would not extend to losses due to a fall in market price,[126] but would be capped at the amount of the overvaluation at the time the valuation takes place. Here, the lender was found to be contributorily negligent in making the loan without having obtained from the borrower information required by its own form, and in advancing as much as 70% of the valuation of the property. Due to the negligent valuation of the property and fall in the market, it had lost £611,748 ("the basic loss"). However, under *SAAMCO*, this would be capped at the overvaluation: the property was valued at £1.5 million but actually worth at that time £1 million, therefore £500,000. Controversially, the majority of the House deducted 20% contributory negligence from the whole losses suffered by the claimant (£611,748). In the view of the majority, the damage referred to in s.1(1) was the damage suffered by the claimant as a result of the transaction (the basic loss). Although the claimant's damages would be capped under *SAAMCO*, the majority held that it was not just and equitable to reduce the capped amount by 20%. This left the claimants with damages of £489,398.

Multiple defendants

16–027

One final problem we must address before moving on to the next defence is how to approach a situation where the claimant is suing more than one defendant. For example, the claimant

---

causative of injury on the facts). Fulbrook commented in 2004 that, in practice, a 25% deduction was becoming the standard response in settlements of traffic accidents in any event: [2004] J.P.I. Law 171.

120 Road Traffic Act 1988 s.16(2).

121 See *Pitts v Hunt* [1991] 1 Q.B. 24 at 48 per Beldam LJ and *Anderson v Newham College of Further Education* [2002] EWCA Civ 505; [2003] I.C.R. 212 (breach of statutory duty).

122 [1989] 1 W.L.R. 839 at 849.

123 As suggested by the Court of Appeal in *Johnson v Tennant Bros Ltd* unreported 19 November 1954.

124 [2000] 2 A.C. 190 (Lord Cooke dissenting). For criticism, see J. Stapleton, "Risk taking by commercial lenders" (1999) 115 L.Q.R. 527.

125 [1997] A.C. 191 HL.

126 Such losses are not within the scope of the duty owed to the lender by the valuer.

(C) is suing two defendants (D and T) for negligence. C's contributory negligence is assessed at 20%. How will this sum be deducted from the defendants' liability for damages?

The first point is that the two defendants are treated as jointly and severally liable at law.[127] This means that the claimant is entitled to sue one or both of the defendants for the full sum due. Under the Civil Liability (Contribution) Act 1978 s.1, if only one defendant is sued, he or she is fully liable, but is entitled to claim a contribution from any other person liable in respect of the same damage. The contribution, under s.2, will be assessed by the court as the sum which is "just and equitable having regard to the extent of that person's responsibility for the damage in question". This is therefore a matter for the defendants to sort out and not for the claimant to worry about. Secondly, the contributory negligence of the claimant will be compared with the total responsibility of the defendants. In our example, the 20% contributory negligence of C would be compared with the 80% liability of D and T, and C would be awarded 80% of the damages due. This is irrespective of whether C is suing D, T, or D and T together. It is irrelevant at this stage to what extent D and T are individually responsible. Thirdly, it is for D and T to argue their individual degree of responsibility.

By this means, the claimant is fully compensated, and it is for the defendants to sort out the division of responsibility between them. This is seen in practice in *Fitzgerald v Lane*,[128] a case mentioned in Ch.6. Here, the plaintiff had stepped out into traffic on a busy road when the lights at the pedestrian crossing had been against him. He had been struck by a vehicle driven by the first defendant, which pushed him into the path of the second defendant's car. Both the defendants were negligent, but the plaintiff had also been contributorily negligent in not looking properly before crossing the road. The House of Lords adopted the reasoning outlined above. First of all, to what extent was the plaintiff contributorily negligent in comparison with the fault of both defendants? Here, it was found to be 50%. Secondly, how should the remaining 50% be divided between the two defendants?

Contributory negligence is a popular defence. Under the statute, the courts now have flexibility to allocate damages according to the fault of the parties involved. Unlike the defences of voluntary assumption of risk and illegality, this defence gives the courts the power to reduce damages without removing the claim altogether, and therefore is more readily used than the former, more drastic, defences.

---

127 This is discussed more fully in Ch.17. A more complicated situation is where not all defendants can plead contributory negligence against the claimant (e.g. where one defendant is liable for deceit for which contributory negligence is not a defence): see *Nationwide Building Society v Dunlop Haywards (DHL) Ltd (t/a Dunlop Heywood Lorenz)* [2009] EWHC 254 (Comm); [2010] 1 W.L.R. 258 where Christopher Clarke J applied the contributory negligence deduction to the "relevant damage" before apportioning liability.

128 [1989] A.C. 328.

General defences: conclusion

We can therefore conclude that out of the defences referred to in this chapter, contributory negligence is the most flexible, permitting the courts to limit the claimant's damages, but to not disallow the claim altogether. This is preferred by the courts to more drastic defences which provide a full defence to the claimant's action for damages. As stated earlier, these are not the only defences, and reference should be made to defences which apply to particular torts, discussed in the relevant chapters.

The second part of this chapter will consider other means by which the claimant's right of action can be lost. If a claim is extinguished, for example, there is no further scope for the claim, however strong the claim may be. The main grounds for extinction will be set out below. The primary example is that of limitation, essentially where the claimant has run out of time to bring his or her claim. It should be noted that this is a significant source of negligence claims against solicitors, who are frequently sued by their clients for failing to commence proceedings within the time limits set by law.

`16–028`

Extinction of Liability

(1) Limitation of Actions for personal injury

Limitation is the main reason why claims in tort are extinguished.[129] It should be noted that it is a procedural, not a substantive, bar to the claimant's action. Its rationale is clear: it would cause obvious problems if there were no time limit within which the claimant should bring an action in tort. For example, if the victim of a car accident were able to claim damages in tort 20 years after the accident, a number of problems would arise:

`16–029`

- witnesses would be unlikely to remember the event;

- witnesses may have disappeared or have died;

- documentation would be lost; and

- the defendant, for an indeterminate time, would have to live with the possibility of being sued.

---

129 The term "extinguished" is used for convenience, but generally, limitation only amounts to a statutory bar to the claim.

As Lord Wilson commented in the Supreme Court, there are two main reasons for statutes of limitation: one is to protect defendants from being vexed by stale claims and the other is to require claims to be put before the court at a time when the evidence necessary for their fair adjudication is likely to remain available.[130] In view of these reasons, the law sets a time limit on such claims.[131] The Limitation Act 1980 contains the main provisions. Section 2 of the Act provides that actions founded on a tort[132] should be brought within six years of the date when the cause of action accrued, i.e. when the cause of action arises against a potential defendant. Where the tort is actionable on proof of damage, for example negligence, then the cause of action will only arise when the damage has taken place. Where the tort is actionable per se (i.e. without proof of damage), the cause of action will arise on the date of the defendant's act or omission.

However, not all tort claims are within s.2. This part will focus on the special provisions for personal injury claims.[133]

> ### Limitations Act 1980 ss.11, 14, 12 and 33

SECTION 11 (THE THREE YEAR TIME LIMIT)

16–030

This provides that where, due to negligence, nuisance or breach of duty,[134] the claimant's action for damages consists of or includes damages for personal injury, the claim must be brought within three years from the date on which:

- the action accrued; or

- the date of knowledge (if later) of the injured person.[135]

---

130 *AB v Ministry of Defence* [2012] UKSC 9; [2013] 1 A.C. 78 at [6].

131 It should be noted that limitation periods are purely statutory. Statutes of limitation may be traced back to the Act of Limitation 1540 (actions to recover property) with the first statute of limitations dealing with common law actions in 1623. There were no time limits imposed at common law.

132 "Tort" is defined widely by Toulmin QC in *R. v Secretary of State for Transport Ex p. Factortame (No.7)* [2000] EWHC (Tech) 179; [2001] 1 W.L.R. 942, QBD (T & CC) at 171 to cover: "breach of non-contractual duty which gives a private law right to the party injured to recover compensatory damages at common law from the party causing the injury".

133 For defective products and defamation/malicious falsehood, see Chs 9 and 14 respectively. The limitation period for claims under the Human Rights Act 1998 is one year, although this may be extended if equitable in the circumstances: s.7(5).

134 This can be breach of statutory duty or contractual duty or any other breach of duty. It covers breach of contract, whether the duty is strict or to take reasonable care: *Foster v Zott GmbH & Co* Unreported 24 May 2000 CA.

135 Limitation Act 1980 s.11(4). Section 11(1A) provides that s.11 does not apply to damages under the Protection from Harassment Act 1997 s.3 which will be governed by s.9. Section 9 deals with sums recoverable by statute and sets a 6 year limitation period.

"Personal injury" is defined in s.38 as including any disease or impairment of a person's physical or mental condition and will thus extend to psychiatric injuries, including dyslexia.[136] If the injured person dies before the expiration of either of these periods, then the action will run for the benefit of the estate for three years from: (a) the date of death; or (b) the date of the personal representative's knowledge; whichever is later.[137] It should be noted that s.11 covers claims which *include* damages for personal injury. The time limit will therefore apply to any additional claims, for example for property damage.

SECTION 14 (DATE OF KNOWLEDGE)

Section 14 defines "the date of knowledge".[138] This is deemed to be the date on which the claimant first had knowledge:

16–031

- that the injury in question was significant;

- that the injury was attributable in whole or in part to the act or omission which is alleged to constitute negligence, nuisance or breach of duty[139];

- of the identity of the defendant; and

- if it is alleged that the act or omission was that of a person other than the defendant, of the identity of that person and the additional facts supporting the bringing of an action against the defendant.

It is irrelevant that the claimant is unaware that, as a matter of law, the acts or omissions in question gave her a legal right to sue.[140] The majority of the Supreme Court in *AB v Ministry of Defence*[141] also found it a legal impossibility for a claimant to argue she lacked s.14 knowledge after she had issued proceedings.[142] Section 14(2) provides that the injury is "significant" if the claimant would reasonably have considered it sufficiently serious to justify instituting proceedings for damages against a defendant who did not dispute liability and was able to satisfy

---

136 See *Phelps v Hillingdon LBC* [2001] 2 A.C. 619, *Robinson v St Helens MBC* [2002] EWCA Civ 1099; [2003] P.I.Q.R. P9 and *Adams v Bracknell Forest BC* [2004] UKHL 29; [2005] 1 A.C. 76.
137 Limitation Act 1980 s.11(5).
138 For guidance, see *Spargo v North Essex District Health Authority* [1997] P.I.Q.R. P235 at P242 per Brooke LJ and the majority in *AB v Ministry of Defence* [2012] UKSC 9; [2013] 1 A.C. 78.
139 "Attributable" has been interpreted as directed to a real possibility of a causal link and not a fanciful one: *Haward v Fawcetts* [2006] UKHL 9; [2006] 1 W.L.R. 682 at [11] per Lord Nicholls.
140 Limitation Act 1980 s.14(1).
141 [2012] UKSC 9; [2013] 1 A.C. 78.
142 [2012] UKSC 9; [2013] 1 A.C. 78 at [6] per Lord Wilson: "It is in my view heretical that a claimant can escape the conventional requirement to assert his cause of action for personal injuries within three years of its accrual by establishing that, even after his claim was brought, he remained in a state of ignorance entirely inconsistent with it".

judgment. After some debate,[143] this has been found to set an impersonal standard[144]—in the words of Lord Hoffmann in *A v Hoare*:

> **"you ask what the claimant knew about the injury he had suffered, you add any knowledge about the injury which may be imputed to him under section 14(3) and you then ask whether a reasonable person with that knowledge would have considered the injury sufficiently serious to justify his instituting proceedings for damages against a defendant who did not dispute liability and was able to satisfy a judgment."[145]**

Section 14(3) provides for constructive knowledge, which includes knowledge which the claimant might reasonably be expected to acquire from facts observable or ascertainable by the claimant, or from facts ascertainable with the help of medical or other professional advice it is reasonable to expect the claimant to seek.[146] The majority of the House of Lords in *Adams v Bracknell Forest BC* held that this would be a mainly objective test: what would a reasonable person, placed in the situation in which the claimant was placed, have said or done?[147] This may, however, take account of the effect of the injury on the claimant, for example, if it renders the claimant blind, the court will not assume that the claimant should have acquired knowledge by seeing something, or if it causes celebral palsy, the level of disability of the claimant.[148]

As Lord Hoffmann made clear in *A v Hoare*,[149] more subjective matters, such as the victim's character or intelligence, should not be considered under s.14. They will still be relevant, however, under the s.33 discretion, discussed below.[150]

---

143 See *McCafferty v Receiver for the Metropolitan Police District* [1977] 1 W.L.R. 1073, which is no longer good authority.

144 For a recent application, see *Albonetti v Wirral MBC* [2008] EWCA Civ 783: A person who had been raped must know that he or she had suffered not only a grave wrong but also a significant injury for the purposes of the Limitation Act 1980 s.14.

145 [2008] UKHL 6; [2008] 1 A.C. 844 at [34]. See also *McCoubrey v Ministry of Defence* [2007] EWCA Civ 17; [2007] 1 W.L.R. 1544 in which Neuberger LJ noted at [44] that this means that s.14(2) has a comparatively limited application, having been enacted to extend the limitation period for personal injury victims who were effectively unaware that they had been injured at all or who had suffered an injury originally thought (reasonably) to be minor but which subsequently turned out to be very serious.

146 The claimant will not be fixed with expert knowledge which he or she has failed to obtain despite taking all reasonable steps to consult (and, where appropriate, to act on) expert advice.

147 [2004] UKHL 29; [2005] 1 A.C. 76 (Baroness Hale, in contrast to the majority, favoured a more subjective approach). Constructive knowledge may arise when claimant given reasonable opportunity to acquire information but declines to do so: *Pierce v Doncaster MBC* [2008] EWCA Civ 1416; [2009] 1 F.L.R. 1189. See A. McGee, "Triggering the date of knowledge in personal injury" (2015) 31 P.N. 95.

148 *Whiston v London SHA* [2010] EWCA Civ 195. The court also noted that account should also be taken of the fact that a claimant born with a disability was likely to be less curious about the reasons for his disability than one who had become disabled in adulthood following an adverse incident: at [60]–[63].

149 [2008] UKHL 6; [2008] 1 A.C. 844 at [45].

150 Notably Limitation Act 1980 s.33(3)(a): "In acting under this section the court shall have regard to all the

SECTION 12 (DEPENDANTS)

Section 12 makes special provision for dependants claiming under the Fatal Accidents Act 1976 (which will be discussed in Ch.17).[151] Section 12(1) requires the dependant to show that the deceased had a valid cause of action on death. If the action had been lost, for example due to a time limit or any other reason, the claim under the Fatal Accidents Act is lost. If the deceased did have a valid cause of action on death, then the dependant has three years to bring the action starting from:

- the date of death; or

- the date of knowledge of the person for whose benefit the action is brought; whichever is the later. ("Knowledge" is as defined in s.14, discussed above.)

SECTION 33 (EXTENSION)

It can be seen that, generally, claims for personal injury, or under the Fatal Accidents Act 1976, are subject to the short time limit of three years. This, however, must be considered in the light of the discretion provided under s.33 of the Act.[152] Section 33 permits the court to override the statutory time limits if it appears equitable to the court to allow the case to proceed, having regard to the prejudice of denying the claim to the claimant[153] and the prejudice of allowing the claim to the defendant.[154] Section 33(3) directs the court, in considering whether to exercise its discretion, to have regard to all the circumstances of the case and in particular to:

- the length of, and the reasons for, the delay on the part of the claimant;

- the extent to which, having regard to the delay, the evidence in the case is likely to be less cogent;

- the conduct of the defendant after the cause of action arose, including (when relevant) the response made to any reasonable request by the claimant for information or inspection for the purpose of ascertaining facts which were or might be relevant to the claimant's cause of action against the defendant;

- the duration of any disability[155] of the claimant arising after the date of the accrual of the cause of action;

---

circumstances of the case and in particular to the length of, and the reasons for, the delay on the part of the plaintiff".

151 See also Limitation Act 1980 s.13.
152 In narrowing its interpretation of Limitation Act 1980 s.14, the courts have assumed that there will be a more generous exercise of the s.33 discretion in future: see Lord Hoffmann in *Adams v Bracknell Forest BC* [2004] UKHL 29; [2005] 1 A.C. 76 at [45].
153 Or any person he or she represents.
154 Or any person he or she represents.
155 Limitation Act 1980 s.38(2) provides that "For the purposes of this Act a person shall be treated as under

- the extent to which the claimant acted promptly and reasonably once he or she knew that there was a possible action for damages; and

- the steps, if any, taken by the claimant to obtain medical, legal or other expert advice and the nature of any such advice he or she may have received.

The House of Lords, in *Thompson v Brown*[156] and *Donovan v Gwentoys*[157] indicated at an early stage that s.33 was not confined to exceptional cases and that the courts could adopt a broad approach to its provisions. The judge is therefore given a broad and unfettered discretion to assess the matter generally with reference to the factors highlighted in s.33(3).[158] The burden, however, of showing that it would be equitable to disapply the limitation period lies on the claimant. While the claimant is seeking the indulgence of the court in applying an exception in her favour, the Court of Appeal has reminded courts that the weight of the burden on the claimant will depend on the facts of each particular case.[159]

16–034

One particular issue which has arisen relates to the courts' treatment of so-called "windfall defence" claims where the claimant (having otherwise a good case) issues proceedings out of time due to the negligence of his solicitor. The Court of Appeal in the conjoined road traffic cases of *Cain v Francis; McKay v Hamlani*[160] took the opportunity to lay down guidelines. In both cases, there was no dispute over liability, but in *Cain* proceedings had been issued one day late and in *McKay* just under a year late. The Court of Appeal ruled that in such a case, where the defendant had had early notice of the claim, the accrual of a limitation defence would be regarded as a complete windfall to the defendant and he could not argue that losing this defence would itself amount to prejudice to be considered under s.33.[161] The relevant prejudice was harm to the defendant's ability to defend his claim. Equally, the existence of an alternative claim against the claimant's solicitor for negligence would not necessarily signify that the time limit should not be disapplied. On the facts, the slight delay was deemed to have no prejudicial effect—the defendants had had early notification of a claim and every possible opportunity to

---

a disability while he is an infant, or lacks capacity (within the meaning of the Mental Capacity Act 2005) to conduct legal proceedings".

156 [1981] 1 W.L.R. 744.

157 [1990] 1 W.L.R. 472. See also the Court of Appeal in *Nash v Eli Lilly & Co* [1993] 1 W.L.R. 782 and *Firman v Ellis* [1978] Q.B. 886.

158 See also *Horton v Sadler* [2006] UKHL 27; [2007] 1 A.C. 307. In *Robinson v St Helens MBC* [2002] EWCA Civ 1099; [2003] P.I.Q.R. P9, the Court of Appeal refused to exercise its discretion to support a claim by a 33-year-old claimant that the local authority had negligently failed to treat his dyslexia during his primary and secondary schooling where there was no cogent medical evidence showing serious injury and the long delay would place the defendant in great difficulty in contesting the claim.

159 *Sayers v Hunters* [2012] EWCA Civ 1715; [2013] 1 W.L.R. 1695 at [55]; *Chief Constable of Greater Manchester v Carroll* [2017] EWCA Civ 1992; [2018] 4 W.L.R. 32 at [42].

160 [2008] EWCA Civ 1451; [2009] Q.B. 754, notably at [69]–[74]. Contrast *McDonnell v Walker* [2009] EWCA Civ 1257; [2010] P.I.Q.R. P5 (inexcusable delay causing prejudice to defendant and little if any prejudice to claimant in suing solicitors).

161 At most it was slight prejudice as in the case of *Donovan v Gwentoys Ltd* [1990] 1 W.L.R. 472.

investigate and to collect evidence. Section 33 would therefore be exercised in the claimants' favour.

A second issue which has arisen is that s.33 only applies to claims for personal injury or under the Fatal Accidents Act 1976 under s.11. It has no application to tort claims outside these sections. Until recently, the House of Lords had found that it did not apply to actions for intentional harm (trespass to the person) which were solely governed by s.2.[162] This led to difficulties in relation to claims by adults for child abuse. Even with the provision under s.28 (see below) that time will only run from the age of majority, the trauma of childhood sexual abuse may take many years to manifest itself or to be appreciated by the victim. However, the courts only have the discretion to extend the time limit under s.33 if it is classified as a personal injury claim under s.11. The House of Lords in *A v Hoare* finally overruled its previous decision in *Stubbings v Webb* and accepted that <u>all</u> personal injury claims, caused by negligence or trespass to the person, should fall within s.11.[163] In *A v Hoare* itself, the defendant had been convicted in 1989 of the attempted rape of the claimant and sentenced to life imprisonment. Only when he won £7 million on the lottery, whilst on day release in 2004, did the victim consider it worthwhile pursing a claim for compensation, only to face the argument that she was out of time. Their Lordships confirmed that, having suffered personal injury from the assault, she was entitled to rely on s.11 and ask the court to exercise its discretion in her favour under s.33.[164] This is an important ruling. As Case has commented:

> "[t]he strict construction of section 14 required by *A v Hoare* . . . will mean that most claimants seeking compensation for historic abuse will be reliant on a generous application of the court's discretion under section 33 if they are to defeat the limitation defence."[165]

The claimant will, however, still have to satisfy the criteria of s.33 which will not always be easy.[166]

---

162 See *Stubbings v Webb* [1993] A.C. 498 which held that the ordinary s.2 6-year limit would apply. *Stubbings* was upheld by the European Court of Human Rights in *Stubbings v United Kingdom (22083/93)* (1997) 23 E.H.R.R. 213.

163 [2008] UKHL 6; [2008] 1 A.C. 844.

164 Discretion was ultimately exercised in the claimant's favour on the basis of its exceptional circumstances: [2008] EWHC 1573 (QB); (2008) 152(29) S.J.L.B. 29 per Coulson J.

165 See P. Case, "Limitation periods and sexual abuse" (2009) 25 P.N. 22, 25.

166 The Court of Appeal delivered guidance as to the correct approach to the application of s.33 to historic sexual abuse claims in *B v Nugent Care Society* [2009] EWCA Civ 827; [2010] 1 W.L.R. 516. See F. Burton, "Limitation, vicarious liability and historic actions for abuse: a changing legal landscape" [2013] J.P.I. Law 95. In some cases, however, the delay in bringing the action may mean that the courts will not exercise their discretion to extend the time limit if deemed disproportionately prejudical to the defendant: see, e.g *JL v Bowen* [2017] EWCA Civ 82; [2017] P.I.Q.R. P11.

▶ Limitation problems

(I) DELIBERATE CONCEALMENT

16–035
One obvious problem with limitation periods is where the defendant has concealed the damage. Section 32 deals directly with this problem. If the action is based on fraud or mistake, or where the defendant has deliberately concealed any fact relevant to the cause of action from the claimant, the limitation period will only start when the claimant has discovered the fraud, mistake or concealment or could, with reasonable diligence, have discovered it. An example of concealment may be found in the case of *Kitchen v RAF Assoc*[167] where a claim was made against a firm of solicitors for negligence. It was held that the solicitors' failure to inform Mrs Kitchen of her possible claim against the local electricity board, when her husband had been electrocuted by a defectively installed cooker, did not amount to concealment. It was certainly negligent, but there was no evidence to show deliberate concealment of this fact. However, their failure to inform her of an offer by the electricity board to pay £100 was within the relevant section, as it amounted to deliberate concealment (basically to cover up for their mistake).

This interpretation of s.32 was confirmed by the House of Lords in *Cave v Robinson Jarvis & Rolf*,[168] which overturned the Court of Appeal ruling in *Brocklesby v Armitage & Guest*.[169] In *Brocklesby*, the court had interpreted s.32 very broadly, notably relying on s.32(2) which defines deliberate concealment as the "deliberate commission of a breach of duty in circumstances in which it is unlikely to be discovered for some time". The Court of Appeal held that, in view of s.32(2), deliberate concealment could be proved by showing simply that the defendant's negligence consisted of an intentional act or omission in circumstances where the negligence would not be immediately apparent. It was not necessary to show that the defendant was aware of the breach of duty in question.[170] The House of Lords in *Cave* rightly pointed out that this would disapply the limitation period in every case where a professional had acted on behalf of a client and was subsequently found to be negligent. This would extend dramatically professional liability, and force such defendants to defend every action, however stale. Lord Millett considered such a result to be "neither just, nor consistent with the policy of the Limitation Acts".[171] "Deliberate concealment" should therefore be interpreted as requiring the defendant to be aware of the breach of duty, and to conceal or fail to disclose the wrongdoing in circumstances where it is unlikely to be discovered for some time.[172]

---

167 [1958] 1 W.L.R. 563 (concerning Limitation Act 1939 s.26, the statutory predecessor of s.32).
168 [2002] UKHL 18; [2003] 1 A.C. 384 HL. Comment; T. Dugdale (2002) 18 P.N. 156.
169 [2002] 1 W.L.R. 598.
170 In *Brocklesby*, e.g. the solicitors' negligence in failing to secure the claimant's release from his mortgage obligations had not become apparent until much later. The solicitors had not been aware that they had been negligent, but were nevertheless found to have acted "deliberately" in that they had intended to act for the claimant.
171 [2002] UKHL 18; [2003] 1 A.C. 384 at [15]. The Law Commission in its report, *Limitation of Actions* (2001), was also critical at 3.136: "*Brocklesby* . . . ignores the rationale of s.32, which is that the defendant should not be able to profit from his own behaviour in concealing facts relevant to the claimant's claim".
172 See *Williams v Fanshaw Porter & Hazelhurst* [2004] EWCA Civ 157; [2004] 1 W.L.R. 3185 (if the defendant

The section does also seek to protect innocent third parties. Section 32(3) states that nothing in the section shall extend the limitation period for actions (a) to recover property or recover its value or (b) to enforce a charge against any property or set aside a transaction affecting property, when the action is brought against an innocent third party who purchased the property for valuable consideration after the fraud, mistake or concealment had taken place.

(II) DISABILITY

16–036

A further problem arises where the claimant cannot sue due to a disability. This is dealt with in s.28 which provides that if the person is under a disability on the date on which the action accrues, the limitation period will only start when he or she has ceased to be under a disability or has died (whichever occurs first). By "disability", we mean that a person is under 18 or lacks capacity (within the meaning of the Mental Capacity Act 2005) to conduct legal proceedings.[173] The main problem arises when the disability affects the claimant after the cause of action has arisen. In such cases, there is nothing in s.28 to stop the ordinary limitation period applying.[174]

▶ The burden of proof

16–037

The issue of limitation will generally be raised by the defendant. However (although the law is not clear on this point), it seems that it is the claimant who bears the burden of proof, and who has to establish that the cause of action arose during the limitation period.[175] Claimants should note that it is not always enough to start the action within the limitation period. The court retains the power to dismiss a claim for want of prosecution where there has been prolonged or "inordinate and inexcusable" delay in the prosecution of the action. It should be noted that this is now governed by the Civil Procedure Rules r.3.4(2) and the courts have discouraged judges from seeking guidance from case law prior to the implementation of the Rules.[176] In practice, it would seem that, in keeping with the strict timetables established by the Rules, the courts will be less tolerant of delays in pursuing a claim. Further, a court may find that a failure to proceed promptly amounts to an abuse of process, for example, where the claimant has commenced and continued litigation which he or she has no intention of bringing to a conclusion.[177]

---

appreciated that he or she had committed a serious mistake or had been negligent and made a conscious decision not to disclose that fact, this amounted to deliberate concealment even though the defendant had acted to avoid embarrassment or for some other innocent reason).

173   Limitation Act 1980 s.38(2).

174   See Limitation Act 1980 s.28(1) and (2) and *Purnell v Roche* [1927] 2 Ch. 142. However, disability is expressly mentioned as a ground for extending the time limit for personal injury under s.33 above.

175   See *Crocker v British Coal Corp* (1996) 29 B.M.L.R. 159 and the Law Commission Report No.270 (2001), *Limitation of Actions*, para.5.29, although it is for the defendant in his or her defence to raise the question of limitation: Practice Direction to Civil Procedure Rules Pt 16 para.13.1.

176   See, for example, *Biguzzi v Rank Leisure Inc* [1999] 1 W.L.R. 1926.

177   *Grovit v Doctor* [1997] 1 W.L.R. 640; *Arbuthnot Latham Bank Ltd v Trafalgar Holdings Ltd* [1998] 1 W.L.R. 1426,

> ### Reform?

There has been much criticism of the limitation regime. In *AB v Ministry of Defence*[178] Baroness Hale commented that:

> "[t]he current law of limitation is complicated and incoherent . . . largely because it has been subjected to a wide range of ad hoc reforms, following the recommendations of reform bodies charged with recommending reforms of particular pockets of law."

There have been, however, attempts to improve the current regime. Following a 1998 Consultation Paper,[179] the Law Commission produced a report in 2001 that came to the conclusion that "the present law on limitation suffers from a number of defects: it is incoherent, needlessly complex, outdated, uncertain, unfair and wastes costs".[180] It put forward a simplified regime based on a primary limitation period of three years for the majority of claims in tort (including defamation), extending to contract, unjust enrichment and trust law. This would be subject to a long-stop of 10 years. Its main recommendations are outlined below:

- The primary or "core" limitation period of three years should run from the date on which the claimant knows, or ought reasonably to know: (a) the facts which give rise to the cause of action, (b) the identity of the defendant, and (c) that the injury suffered is significant.

- Personal injury should continue to be treated differently. The Commission backed down on its more radical proposals in the Consultation Paper that personal injury claims should be included within the core regime, subject only to an extended long-stop of 30 years.[181] It proposed instead that the courts should continue to have a discretion to disapply the three-year limitation period and that no long-stop should apply.[182]

---

but contrast *Aktas v Adepta* [2010] EWCA Civ 1170; [2011] Q.B. 894 (something more than a single negligent oversight in timely service of claim form was required).

178   [2012] UKSC 9; [2013] 1 A.C. 78 at [163].
179   Law Commission Consultation Paper No.151 (1998), *Limitation of Actions*.
180   Law Commission Report No.270 (2001), *Limitation of Actions*.
181   This was largely due to evidence which indicated that the long-term effects of sexual abuse and mesothelioma, caused by exposure to asbestos, could manifest themselves over a period greater than 30 years: paras 3.102–3.104.
182   This was subject to a number of exceptions, for example, where an adult claimant is suffering from a disability and under the Consumer Protection Act 1987. Claims under the Fatal Accidents Act 1976 and under the Law Reform (Miscellaneous Provisions) Act 1934 would equally be subject to the statutory discretion to disapply the primary limitation period and will not be subject to a long-stop.

- The long-stop would not apply to deliberate concealment, but only where the concealment is dishonest.

The proposals received considerable criticism, not least the recommendation to reverse the one year limitation period for defamation and malicious falsehood which had recently been introduced. Ultimately no legislation followed, and the House of Lords intervened itself in *A v Hoare*[183] in 2008 (as discussed above) to resolve the limitation problems facing abuse victims suing for trespass to the person. There are currently no proposals for reform despite the concerns raised by Baroness Hale above.

(2) Judgment

Note also that final judgment in a case will extinguish the right of future action. The action effectively merges into the judgment. This is primarily on public policy grounds and prevents the parties to litigation disputing the validity of the decision. The rule only applies where the decision is final, and it does not of course prevent either party appealing that the decision is wrong, in terms of law or fact, up until final judgment.

16–039

(3) Death

At common law, the general rule was that the death of either party extinguished any existing cause of action in tort (*actio personalis moritur cum persona*). It was not until 1934 that the problems arising from this rule forced the legislature to act. The growth of road traffic, and its accompanying accidents, led to complaints that it was unjust that where the defendant's negligent driving had led to an accident in which the defendant had been killed, the claimant would receive nothing from the defendant's estate or insurers. Law Reform (Miscellaneous Provisions) Act 1934 s.1(1) now provides for the general survival of actions in tort. It states that:

16–040

> "... all causes of action subsisting against or vested in [any person on death] shall survive against, or, as the case may be, for the benefit of [the] estate."

This does not provide a cause of action for death itself. It is simply a question of the survival of actions existing at the time of death. This leaves one remaining problem. The claimant is penalised if the defendant dies before the claimant suffers damage due to the defendant's wrongful actions. For example, I negligently bake a cake which is contaminated, but die before you eat it. An action for negligence is dependent on proof of damage and so your action would only arise after my death. Section 1(4) deals with this problem. It provides that where damage

---

183 [2008] UKHL 6.

has been suffered as a result of a wrongful act which would have allowed the claimant to sue the defendant if the wrongdoer had not died before or at the same time as the damage was suffered, an action will nevertheless subsist against him as if he had died after the damage had been suffered.

Section 1(1) does <u>not</u> apply to defamation claims. It was deemed too controversial to allow an action for defamation once the person defamed had died. However, there is no real reason why an action should not continue just because the defendant making the defamatory remarks is deceased. The harm to the reputation may still continue. The Faulks Committee[184] made some proposals for the survival of claims against the estate of the deceased defamer, and for limited recovery when the defendant has defamed a person now dead, but such recommendations have not been implemented.[185]

General defences and extinction of liability: conclusion

16–041

This chapter has examined a number of defences and considered ways in which the claimant can lose his or her claim due to extinction of liability. The courts, as we have seen, have a number of alternatives open to them when considering defences, and will tend to favour those defences which allow them to take a flexible approach to the claim. The Limitation Act 1980 forms a considerable barrier to claims where the claimant has delayed and, as we have shown, provides rules of considerable complexity.

The next chapter considers the matter most important to claimants: what remedies will the law award them for the torts committed against them?

---

184 Cmnd.5909 (1975), Ch.15.
185 The Neill Committee on defamation found the recommendations problematic and resolved that the law should not be changed.

17

Remedies

Introduction

This chapter will examine the remedies available to claimants in actions in tort. It will concentrate on three main remedies: damages, injunctions and self-help. Readers will note that other remedies specific to particular torts have been discussed in earlier chapters. The main subject of this chapter will be damages. The courts have developed a complex framework of rules which govern the assessment of damages, which will be set out below. Readers should not forget, however, that for certain torts, such as nuisance, the equitable remedy of an injunction may prove more effective than damages, for example where the claimant wishes to prevent further interference with his or her enjoyment of land.

17–001

Damages

Damages are the most commonly sought remedy in the law of tort. They provide a means by which the courts can vindicate the rights of the claimant against the defendant by means of a financial award. They can therefore be awarded for torts which are actionable without proof of damage, such as trespass, where they vindicate the claimant's right to be free from interference with his or her person, land and goods. They are equally significant, however, where the claimant has suffered actual damage or loss. Here, the claimant seeks not only to vindicate his or her rights, but a financial award which compensates the claimant for his or her losses (provided they are not too remote). In such circumstances, it can be said that compensatory damages serve a dual purpose in that they both compensate for the loss and vindicate the right that has been infringed, although the courts have not gone so far as to recognise a distinct award of

17–002

vindicatory damages.[1] The claimant may also seek a sum which compensates for any additional distress, and which punishes the defendant for particularly bad misconduct. The rules as to the assessment of such awards are complex and will be set out below, but first we shall outline the different types of damages available to the claimant. Although the claimant will generally seek compensatory damages, these are not the only form of damages available. We will also examine damages awarded under the Human Rights Act 1998.

Types of damages

17–003

The court may award six different kinds of damages:

- compensatory;

- contemptuous;

- nominal;

- aggravated;

- exemplary or punitive; and

- restitutionary.

We shall examine all six types of damages in turn and then damages under the Human Rights Act 1998.

(1) Compensatory

17–004

Tort law seeks to fully compensate the victim. The underlying principle is expressed by the term restitutio in integrum. This is explained by Lord Blackburn in *Livingstone v Rawyards Coal Co*[2] as:

> **"the sum of money which will put the party who has been injured, or who has suffered, in the same position as he would have been in if**

---

1 See *R. (on the application of Lumba) v Secretary of State for the Home Department* [2011] UKSC 12; [2012] 1 A.C. 245 where the majority rejected the option of awarding vindicatory damages on the basis that it would lead to undesirable uncertainty: see Lord Dyson JSC at [101]. See J. Edelman, "Vindicatory damages" in K. Barker et al, *Private Law in the 21st Century* (Hart, 2017).
2 (1880) 5 App. Cas. 25 at 39 per Lord Blackburn.

> he had not sustained the wrong for which he is now getting his com-
> pensation or reparation."

The aim is therefore to award a sum in compensation to the claimant which puts the claim-ant in his or her pre-tort position. Obviously, this is not always possible. If the claimant has suffered personal injury, a court cannot literally return the claimant to his or her pre-tort position. The court therefore seeks to find a financial sum which, as far as possible, will com-pensate the claimant. There is also a duty to mitigate loss in tort. The courts will not allow a claimant to recover losses which he or she could have reasonably avoided. Although the main authorities on mitigation are in contract law (where the same rule applies), it seems clear that a court in tort will not require strenuous attempts by the claimant to reduce the loss suffered.[3] The old rule that losses incurred due to lack of funds were irrecoverable, e.g. expensive hire charges where it would have been more economical to purchase a new vehi-cle[4] has been overturned.[5]

Assessing compensation, particularly for personal injury, is often a far from easy task. While financial losses before trial can be estimated with some exactitude, the claimant may seek damages for future financial loss due to the tort, and again the court is forced to produce an approximate figure which it believes will cover this head of loss. The problems that arise in rela-tion to the assessment of compensation for personal injury and death will be examined in more detail from para.17–019 onwards. For the moment, it is worth noting that courts will generally award damages in one lump sum. This gives a claimant one chance to go to court to obtain damages, and the court will not allow a claimant to go back to court to recover a further award of damages, even if his or her loss has significantly increased, unless:

17–005

- the claimant is suing for breach of a separate and distinct legal right[6];

- the injury continues, such as under a continuing nuisance where a fresh cause of action occurs (see Ch.10);

- a provisional award of damages has been made under the Senior Courts Act 1981 s.32A (see below); or

---

3 See *British Westinghouse Electric & Manufacturing Co Ltd v Underground Electric Railways Co of London Ltd (No.2)* [1912] A.C. 673 HL. The burden of proof rests on the defendant to show that the claimant has unreasonably neglected to mitigate the damages.
4 See *The Liesbosch* [1933] A.C. 449.
5 *Lagden v O'Connor* [2003] UKHL 64; [2004] 1 A.C. 1067. Comment: B. Coote (2004) 120 L.Q.R. 382.
6 See *Brunsden v Humphrey* (1884–85) L.R. 14 Q.B.D. 141 where the plaintiff was able to claim for damage to his vehicle and later for personal injury. However, note the rule in *Henderson v Henderson* (1843) 3 Hare 100; 67 E.R. 313 that it would be an abuse of process if the claimant did not bring forward their whole case in the first action. The court in *Talbot v Berkshire CC* [1994] Q.B. 290 cast doubt on *Brunsden* for not considering *Henderson* in its decision. See also *Johnson v Gore Wood & Co* [2002] 2 A.C. 1.

- the first award was an interim award prior to trial made under the Senior Courts Act 1981 s.32 (see below).

Compensatory damages are often divided in personal injury claims into special and general damages. These are terms used by the parties in their case statements. General damages are damages which cannot be precisely quantified, for example loss of future earnings or pain and suffering. Special damages are claimed for particular forms of pre-trial loss resulting from the tort, which the claimant can quantify, for example medical expenses and loss of earnings prior to trial. These should be set out clearly.

(2) Contemptuous

17–006

This is a derisory award of the lowest coin in the land—now one penny—by which the court indicates that although the claimant has a good cause of action, it is a bare technical victory. Such awards have, for example, been found in the past in libel actions.[7] The court, more drastically, can deny the claimant his or her costs, and this imposes a greater penalty on the claimant. In English law, costs usually follow the event, so the losing defendant will have to pay not only his or her own costs but also those of the claimant. However, under the Senior Courts Act 1981 s.51, the award of costs is at the discretion of the court, and contemptuous damages may lead a court to exercise its discretion to order the claimant to pay his or her own costs. In such circumstances, any victory is wholly illusory.

(3) Nominal

17–007

Nominal damages are a token amount which recognises that the claimant's legal right has been infringed, but that no actual damage has been caused.[8] They therefore generally will apply to torts actionable per se (i.e. without proof of damage) such as trespass to the person or land. An award of nominal damages should not affect the ordinary rule as to costs, as it does not indicate any negative finding.

---

7   For example, the jury award in *Reynolds v Times Newspapers Ltd* [2001] 2 A.C. 127 (see Ch.14).

8   See, e.g. *Constantine v Imperial Hotels Ltd* [1944] K.B. 693, and, more controversially, the false imprisonment case of *R. (on the application of Lumba) v Secretary of State for the Home Department* [2011] UKSC 12; [2012] 1 A.C. 245 (where principles of public law rendered detention unlawful, despite the fact that the claimant could have been detained if the correct procedures had been followed, no more than nominal damages would be awarded). For criticism of *Lumba*, see S. Steel (2011) 127 L.Q.R. 527.

(4) Aggravated

These form a further level of compensatory damages granted by the courts to compensate for additional mental distress inflicted on the claimant due to the malicious, high-handed, insulting or oppressive conduct of the defendant.[9] The manner in which the tort is committed or the motives of the defendant may therefore justify an award of aggravated damages.[10] For example, in libel, if the defendant has published the statement out of malice, or has persisted at trial with an insupportable plea of truth, an additional sum on top of compensatory damages may be awarded to the claimant. Such damages are not available for all torts. The courts will award aggravated damages for torts where the injury to the claimant's feelings and self-esteem are closely connected to the type of damage for which compensation is awarded. On this basis, they are not awarded for negligence,[11] but are commonly awarded for intentional torts such as trespass[12] and for libel.[13] This raises a potential problem of double recovery. The Court of Appeal in *Richardson v Howie*[14] suggested that, in view of their compensatory nature, this should be dealt with by including the award of damages for injury to feelings within the general damages award and only in exceptional cases making a separate award of aggravated damages. Nevertheless, the Court of Appeal in *Rowlands v Chief Constable of Merseyside Police*[15] remained willing to impose an award of aggravated damages where police misconduct in the arrest and prosecution of Mrs Rowlands had induced feelings of humiliation and resentment, which had been exacerbated by the willingness of the police to give false evidence in support of an unjustified prosecution. The court warned, however, that attention should be paid to the dangers of compensating the claimant twice in respect of the same harm.

The sum awarded is at the discretion of the court but is usually moderate. Some guidelines exist. For example, the Court of Appeal in *Thompson v Metropolitan Police Commissioner*[16] indicated the level of awards suitable for damages against the police for false imprisonment and malicious prosecution. Indeed, claims against the police form a major reason for the award of

17–008

---

9   See Law Commission Report No.247, *Aggravated, exemplary and restitutionary damages* (1997) which recommended at para.6.1 that for clarity, these damages should in future be termed "damages for mental distress"

10   See Lord Devlin in *Rookes v Barnard* [1964] A.C. 1129 at 1221 and Lord Diplock in *Cassell v Broome* [1972] A.C. 1027 at 1124.

11   *Kralj v McGrath* [1986] 1 All E.R. 54. See, however, J. Murphy, "The nature and domain of aggravated damages" [2010] C.L.J. 353, who argues that aggravated damages provide compensation for violation of dignitary interests and on that basis should extend to high-handed and malicious breaches of contract and negligence.

12   e.g. *Appleton v Garrett* [1996] P.I.Q.R. P1 where a dentist had deliberately undertaken unnecessary dental work on unsuspecting young patients. The Privy Council in *Horsford v Bird* [2006] UKPC 3 held that "[i]t is well established that trespass to land accompanied by high-handed, insulting or oppressive conduct may warrant an award of aggravated damages": [14].

13   See *John v MGN Ltd* [1997] Q.B. 586 at 607. Pearson LJ gives an excellent summary of the law in *McCarey v Associated Newspapers* Ltd [1965] 2 Q.B. 86 at 104–105.

14   [2004] EWCA Civ 1127; [2005] P.I.Q.R. Q3.

15   [2006] EWCA Civ 1773; [2007] 1 W.L.R. 1065.

16   [1998] Q.B. 498.

aggravated damages. Recent authority indicates also that they will not be awarded in favour of companies which are unable, subjectively, to experience injury to feelings or distress.[17]

(5) Exemplary (or punitive)

17–009

The leading case here is that of *Rookes v Barnard*.[18] In this case, Lord Devlin distinguished punitive damages[19] from aggravated damages and set out when punitive damages would be granted in English law. The concept of punitive damages may seem odd in tort. They are a form of damages which punish the defendant for his or her conduct and attempt to deter the defendant and others from undertaking such conduct in future. Punitive damages are concerned with the conduct of the defendant rather than the damage suffered by the claimant. Although they are sometimes confused with aggravated damages, there is a clear division. Aggravated damages seek to compensate the claimant for any additional injury due to the manner in which the tort was committed. In contrast, punitive damages aim to punish the defendant.

In *Rookes v Barnard*, Lord Devlin restricted punitive damages to three kinds of case. His Lordship doubted the legitimacy of such damages, which, in his view, confused the civil and criminal functions of the law, and brought punishment into civil law without the procedural safeguards of criminal law. However, his Lordship admitted that punitive damages were firmly established in English law and therefore decided not to abolish this head of damages but held that a restrictive approach should be taken in future. Further, juries (if present) should be directed that they should only award punitive damages when ordinary compensatory damages are inadequate to punish the defendant for his or her outrageous conduct, to show that tort does not pay, and to deter others.[20] The means of the parties would be taken into consideration in determining any award. This approach was approved by the House of Lords in the later case of *Cassell v Broome*.[21]

The three kinds of punitive damages

17–010

Lord Devlin recommended that punitive damages should only be awarded in the three following situations:

---

17   *Eaton Mansions (Westminster) Ltd v Stinger Compania de Inversion SA* [2013] EWCA Civ 1308; [2014] 1 P & C.R. 5, overturning *Messenger Newspaper Group v National Graphical Assoc (NGA)* [1984] I.R.L.R. 397.
18   [1964] A.C. 1129. See P. R. Ghandi, "Exemplary Damages in the English Law of Tort" (1990) 10 L.S. 182; J. Goudkamp and E. Katsampouka, "An empirical study of punitive damages" (2018) 38 O.J.L.S. 90 and H. Koziol and V. Wilcox (eds), *Punitive damages: Common law and civil law perspectives (Tort and Insurance Law)* (Springer, 2009).
19   The Law Commission recommended that the term "punitive" should be used in future rather than "exemplary" in their 1997 Report No.247. It will therefore be used in this section.
20   [1964] A.C. 1129 at 1228. Punitive damages cannot be awarded where there is no material damage to be compensated: *Watkins v Secretary of State for the Home Department* [2006] UKHL 17; [2006] 2 A.C. 395.
21   [1972] A.C. 1027.

- oppressive, arbitrary or unconstitutional actions by government servants;

- conduct calculated by the defendant to make a profit, which may well exceed any compensation payable to the claimant; and

- when expressly authorised by statute.

These will be examined below.

(I) OPPRESSIVE, ARBITRARY OR UNCONSTITUTIONAL ACTIONS BY GOVERNMENT SERVANTS

Here, the defendant is penalised for the abuse of executive power. It is therefore no excuse, as in *Huckle v Money*,[22] that the claimant was only wrongfully detained for no more than six hours, had been treated well, and provided with beefsteaks and beer. The court held that "to enter a man's house by virtue of a nameless warrant, in order to procure evidence, is worse than the Spanish Inquisition".[23] However, punitive damages will not be awarded on this basis against private individuals or corporations, however powerful they may be. They will also not be awarded against public bodies such as a nationalised water authority which is not exercising an executive function.[24] However, they may be awarded against the police or local government officials.[25] The court in *Holden v Chief Constable of Lancashire*[26] held that not all false arrests will merit punitive damages and that this will be a matter for the jury.[27] The court did find, however, that the claimant was not required to show oppressive, arbitrary *and* unconstitutional conduct by the official. Punitive damages could therefore be awarded where there was no oppressive behaviour by the arresting officer. Nor, it would seem, is it necessary to prove that the official's conduct was malicious, fraudulent, insolent, cruel, or other similar conduct. It must simply be outrageous and thus require punitive damages to mark disapproval, to deter and to vindicate the strength of the law.[28]

There is no clear reason why punitive damages under this head should be confined to misconduct by the executive. In modern times, where much power lies with private individuals or corporations, the distinction between public and private bodies seems increasingly arbitrary. This, however, is the inevitable result of the approach taken by Lord Devlin in *Rookes v Barnard*, which sought to limit punitive damages to the bare minimum required by existing case law. It would be too much to expect analytical consistency from such an approach.

17–011

---

22   (1763) 2 Wils. K.B. 206; 95 E.R. 768.

23   (1763) 2 Wils. K.B. 206 at 207.

24   *AB v South West Water Services* [1993] Q.B. 507.

25   See *Cassell v Broome* [1972] A.C. 1027.

26   [1987] Q.B. 380.

27   False imprisonment being one of the few torts usually heard by a judge and jury.

28   *Muuse v Secretary of State for the Home Department* [2010] EWCA Civ 453 at [67]–[71] per Thomas LJ.

(II) CONDUCT CALCULATED BY THE DEFENDANT TO MAKE A PROFIT WHICH MAY WELL EXCEED ANY COMPENSATION PAYABLE TO THE CLAIMANT

17-012

The aim here is to teach the defendant that tort does not pay and to deprive the defendant of the fruits of his or her tort. However, it is approached in a rough and ready way, and the court will not require the claimant to set out the profit obtained by the defendant from the tort. The real question is whether the conduct of the defendant was "calculated" to make a profit. To prove this, the claimant must show something calculated and deliberate in the defendant's actions, although it is not necessary that the defendant engaged in any precise balancing of the chances of profit and loss.[29] What matters is that the defendant decided to commit the wrong because they considered the prospective gain would outweigh any potential liability.[30] Examples are frequently found in libel and, more recently, insurance fraud.[31] In *Cassell v Broome*,[32] the House of Lords held that the court should investigate whether the defendant was aware of the fact that what he was planning to do was against the law (or had shown reckless disregard as to whether the proposed conduct was legal or illegal) and had nevertheless decided to carry on because the prospects of material advantage outweighed the prospects of material loss. In *Axa Insurance UK Plc v Financial Claims Solutions Ltd*,[33] punitive damages were awarded where motor accidents had been faked in order to extract large sums of money from an insurance company by making fraudulent claims. Such a cynical and abusive misuse of the court system was regarded as a paradigm case for punitive damages.

(III) EXPRESSLY AUTHORISED BY STATUTE

17-013

This is very rare. It has been argued that the Copyright, Designs and Patents Act 1988 s.97(2)[34] authorises punitive damages by virtue of its reference to "additional damages",[35] although its statutory predecessor did not.[36] The House of Lords in *Redrow Homes Ltd v Bett Brothers Plc*[37] left this question expressly open, although Lord Clyde suggested obiter that they should be regarded as aggravated only.[38] More recently, Pumfrey J in *Nottinghamshire Healthcare*

---

29 See *Cassell v Broome* [1972] A.C. 1027 at 1094 per Lord Morris.
30 *Axa Insurance UK Plc v Financial Claims Solutions Ltd* [2018] EWCA Civ 1330; [2019] R.T.R. 1 at [27].
31 Awards are also frequently made against landlords evicting tenants to obtain a higher level of rent from a new tenant (see *Drane v Evangelou* [1978] 1 W.L.R. 455). For trespass generally, see *Ramzan v Brookwide Ltd* [2011] EWCA Civ 985; [2012] 1 All E.R. 903 (neighbour deliberately expropriating part of his neighbour's property).
32 [1972] A.C. 1027. See also *John v MGN Ltd* [1997] Q.B. 586 at 618 per Bingham MR.
33 [2018] EWCA Civ 1330; [2019] R.T.R.1.
34 "(2) The court may in an action for infringement of copyright having regard to all the circumstances, and in particular to—(a) the flagrancy of the infringement, and (b) any benefit accruing to the defendant by reason of the infringement, award such additional damages as the justice of the case may require."
35 See also Reserve and Auxiliary Forces (Protection of Civil Interests) Act 1951 s.13(2).
36 Copyright Act 1956 s.17(3).
37 [1999] 1 A.C. 197.
38 [1999] 1 A.C. 197 at 207. For a contrary view, see C. Michalos, "Copyright and punishment: the nature of additional damages" (2000) 22 E.I.P.R. 470.

National Health Service Trust v News Group Newspapers Ltd[39] has found that the section permits only aggravated damages, but on a basis far wider than that admitted at common law, and contains an element of restitutionary damages. It may be questioned whether "a wider form of aggravated damages" which expressly addresses the flagrancy of the breach can be viewed as distinct from punitive damages or, more likely, the statute in reality gives a discretion to award damages which include a punitive element.[40]

The "cause of action" test

17–014

The Court of Appeal decision in *AB v South West Water Services*[41] imposed one further restriction on punitive damages: they should only be awarded for torts which had received punitive awards at the time of *Rookes v Barnard* (the "cause of action" test). If no such case had been reported, then no award would be given. This excluded punitive damages awards for torts such as negligence, public nuisance, deceit and for sex and race discrimination. This rule had no basis in principle and was simply a crude method of limiting claims. It predictably received well-deserved criticism in the Law Commission report on *Aggravated, Exemplary and Restitutionary Damages*.[42] The House of Lords in *Kuddus v Chief Constable of Leicestershire Constabulary*[43] finally overturned this "arbitrary and irrational restriction".[44] In future, the court would examine the facts of the case and would not be deflected by the claimant's cause of action. In the case itself, the fact that no-one had received punitive damages for the tort of misfeasance in public office prior to *Rookes v Barnard* did not preclude the claimant from recovering such damages. Subsequent courts have also been ready to grant punitive damages for deceit.[45]

The House in *Kuddus* expressed concern, however, that counsel had not raised the fundamental question of the role of punitive damages in English tort law. Views varied from the critical approach of Lord Scott[46] to the more positive view of Lord Nicholls who considered that punitive damages perform an important function in buttressing civil liberties, for example

---

39 [2002] EWHC 409 (Ch); [2002] E.M.L.R. 33. See also Pumfrey J in *Phonographic Performance Ltd v Reader* [2005] EWHC 416 (Ch); [2005] E.M.L.R. 26.

40 Gray J in *Collins Stewart Ltd v Financial Times Ltd (No.2)* [2005] EWHC 262 (QB); [2006] E.M.L.R. 5 at [33] described them as having more in common with punitive damages than aggravated damages.

41 [1993] Q.B. 507. In any event, the defendants had been convicted for contamination of the water supply and fined (see *Archer v Brown* [1985] Q.B. 401, below). See generally A. S. Burrows, "The Scope of Exemplary Damages" (1993) 109 L.Q.R. 358.

42 Law Commission Report No.247 (1997).

43 [2001] UKHL 29; [2002] 2 A.C. 122.

44 See Lord Nicholls [2001] UKHL 29; [2002] 2 A.C. 122 at [55].

45 See *Axa Insurance UK Plc v Financial Claims Solutions Ltd* [2018] EWCA Civ 1330. Eady J ruled out, however, the award of exemplary damages for invasion of privacy (discussed in Ch.15) in *Mosley v News Group Newspapers Ltd* [2008] EWHC 1777 (QB).

46 [2001] UKHL 29; [2002] 2 A.C. 122 at [119]–[121]. Note also the view of A. Beever, "The structure of aggravated and exemplary damages" (2003) 23 O.J.L.S. 87, who argues that punitive damages are an anomaly which should be expunged from the law.

in relation to claims of false imprisonment and wrongful arrest by the police.[47] It is an ongoing question whether punitive damages should continue to be part of English law. The Law Commission felt that they still played a valuable role and that they should be available for all torts or equitable wrongs (but not for breach of contract) where the defendant, in committing the tort, or by his or her subsequent conduct, has deliberately and outrageously disregarded the claimant's rights.[48] The Law Commission recommended, nevertheless, that punitive damages should remain a last resort remedy, and should not be awarded when other remedies adequately punish the defendant for his or her conduct.

Such suggestions are helpful, although the government at the time decided not to implement the reforms.[49] Although the primary aim of the law of tort is compensation, this does not mean that tort law cannot have other objectives, including deterrence of particularly reprehensible behaviour. Indeed, other Commonwealth countries, such as Canada,[50] Australia[51] and New Zealand[52] have adopted a more generous treatment of punitive damages. A problem arises, however, in relation to vicarious liability. Lord Scott in *Kuddus* maintained that no defendant should pay punitive damages unless he or she had committed punishable behaviour and that, on this basis, an employer should not be vicariously liable for the punitive damages awarded against an errant employee.[53] To allow such damages would be to punish the wrong person and to allow the guilty party to escape punishment. However, the Law Commission has argued that punitive damages may play a positive role in encouraging employers to exercise greater control over their workforce and will assist claimants who are unable to identify which member of the employer's workforce had committed the tort. In *Rowlands v Chief Constable of Merseyside Police*,[54] the Court of Appeal confirmed that an employer could be vicariously liable for punitive damages. Despite arguments to the contrary,

---

47 [2001] UKHL 29; [2002] 2 A.C. 122 at [63].
48 Law Commission Report No.247 (1997) at para.6.3.
49 *Hansard* (HC Debates), 9 November 1999 col.502. The Government suggested that further judicial development of the law in this area might help clarify the issues.
50 *Hill v Church of Scientology of Toronto* (1995) 126 D.L.R. (4th) 129 and *Whiten v Pilot Insurance Co* (2002) 209 D.L.R. (4th) 257. See M. Graham, "Exemplary and punitive damages in contract and tort" [2002] L.M.C.L.Q. 453.
51 *Uren v John Fairfax & Sons Pty Ltd* (1966) 117 C.L.R. 118, High Court of Australia. Note, however, that in some Australian jurisdictions, the circumstances in which punitive damages may be awarded have been drastically limited by legislation, e.g. the Personal Injuries (Liabilities and Damages) Act 2003 (NT) s.19 abolishes them entirely.
52 Note, however, that the Supreme Court of New Zealand in *Couch v Att-Gen (No.2)* [2010] NZSC 27; [2010] 3 N.Z.L.R. 149 overturned the earlier Privy Council decision in *A v Bottrill* [2002] UKPC 44; [2003] 1 A.C. 449 and now requires at least conscious awareness of the risk, or subjective recklessness, to be shown when suing for exemplary damages in negligence claims (Elias CJ dissenting). This issue is particularly contentious in New Zealand in the light of the no-fault compensation scheme, discussed in Ch.1, which serves to exclude any common law claim for personal injury but permits a claim for exemplary damages. Comment: H. Wilberg [2010] P.L. 809.
53 [2001] UKHL 29; [2002] 2 A.C. 122 at [123[–[137]. Such comments were, however, obiter.
54 [2006] EWCA Civ 1773; [2007] 1 W.L.R. 1065. Comment: H. Gow, "A sorry tale" (2007) 157 N.L.J. 164.

it was felt desirable to make such an award which would ensure that the victim received damages of an adequate amount which would be paid by those who bore ultimate responsibility for the tortfeasor's conduct. It is submitted that such an award is contentious. It subverts the punitive element of the damages and places an extra burden on the employer, who is *not* at fault. The Supreme Court of Canada in *Blackwater v Plint*[55] rejected punitive damages in this context, although there is no Commonwealth consensus on this controversial issue.[56]

Further concerns may be raised. Punitive damages are paid, not to the State as is the case with criminal fines, but to the claimant. The victim thus receives a windfall irrespective of his or her actual loss. In addition, there is the potential for double or excessive punishment if the defendant's conduct amounts to a crime for which he or she has been prosecuted. This problem was addressed by the court in *Archer v Brown*,[57] which held that if the defendant had already been prosecuted and sentenced in a criminal court for precisely the conduct which forms the basis of the suit, no punitive award should be made. Peter Pain J stated that a man should not be punished twice for the same offence.[58] The Law Commission, in their 1997 report, proposed that the courts should have a discretion in such circumstances to refuse to consider or make an award of punitive damages where a defendant had already been convicted by a criminal court.[59]

17–015

(6) Restitutionary (or gain-based damages)

For some torts, the claimant will have the option to choose between compensatory and restitutionary damages. Restitutionary damages are assessed not on the loss caused to the claimant, but on the gain obtained by the defendant at the claimant's expense. It should be noted, however, that not all torts allow for restitutionary damages. The courts seem more willing to award restitutionary damages for what they call "proprietary torts", that is torts such as trespass to land or goods which involve the defendant misappropriating the claimant's property rights.[60] However, there remains a lack of clarity here.[61] The Law Commission, in their 1997

17–016

---

55   (2005) 258 D.L.R. (4th) 275. The Court dealt with the point in only one paragraph, commenting that "The trial judge . . . . correctly stated that punitive damages cannot be awarded in the absence of reprehensible conduct specifically referable to the employer": at [91].

56   See the High Court of Australia in *State of New South Wales v Ibbett* [2006] HCA 57; (2007) 231 A.L.R. 485 (punitive damages may be awarded against the police).

57   [1985] Q.B. 401.

58   [1985] Q.B. 401 at 423. Contrast *Borders (UK) Ltd v Commissioner of Police of the Metropolis* [2005] EWCA Civ 197; [2005] Po. L.R. 1 (award of punitive damages did not duplicate criminal penalties).

59   Law Commission Report No.247 paras 5.112–5.115.

60   *Devenish Nutrition Ltd v Sanofi-Aventis SA* [2008] EWCA Civ 1086; [2009] Ch. 390 held that non-proprietary torts are still bound by Court of Appeal authority in *Stoke on Trent City Council v W&J Wass Ltd (No.1)* [1988] 1 W.L.R. 1406 that only compensatory damages could be awarded.

61   e.g. the damages awarded for trespass to land in *Horsford v Bird* [2006] UKPC 3; [2006] 1 E.G.L.R. 75 have been described by some authors as restitutionary (Edelman (2006) 122 L.Q.R. 391), but by others as compensatory:

report, decided that no attempt should be made at present to state comprehensively in legislation the situations in which torts should trigger restitutionary damages, and this should be left to common law development.[62] They nevertheless proposed legislation which would allow the courts to award restitutionary damages as an alternative to punitive damages.[63] The nature and availability of restitutionary damages has been a topic of active debate for scholars and further reference should be made to works on the law of restitution.[64]

▶ (7) Damages under the Human Rights Act 1998[65]

17–017 Section 8(1) of the Act sets out the judicial remedies which arise when a public authority has acted in a way which is incompatible with a Convention right.[66] It states that, in such a case, the court "may grant such relief or remedy, or make such order, within its powers as it considers just and appropriate". This broad discretion, which includes the award of damages, has three main limitations:

- ■ damages can only be awarded where the court has the power to award damages in civil proceedings[67];

- ■ no award of damages can be made unless, taking account of all the circumstances of the case,[68] the court is satisfied that the award is necessary to afford just satisfaction to the claimant; and

---

Severn Trent Water Ltd v Barnes [2004] EWCA Civ 570; [2004] 2 E.G.L.R. 95 and *Eaton Mansions (Westminster) Ltd v Stinger Compania de Inversion SA* [2013] EWCA Civ 1308. See also Lord Scott, "Damages" [2007] L.M.C.L.Q. 465, 467.

62 At para.6.2.

63 At paras 3.48–3.57. See para.3.51: "We therefore recommend that: legislation should provide that restitutionary damages may be awarded where: (a) the defendant has committed: (i) a tort or an equitable wrong, or (ii) a civil wrong (including a tort or an equitable wrong) which arises under an Act, and an award of restitutionary damages would be consistent with the policy of that Act, and (b) his conduct showed a deliberate and outrageous disregard of the plaintiff's rights. (Draft Bill, cl.2(1), 12(3))".

64 See, e.g. G. Virgo, *The Principles of the Law of Restitution*, 3rd edn (OUP, 2015) Chs 16 and 17, S. Watterson, "Gain-Based Remedies for Civil Wrongs in England and Wales" in E. Hondius and A. Janssen (eds), *Disgorgement of Profits* (Springer, 2015), pp.29–69.

65 See, generally, the Law Commission Report No.266 (2000), *Damages under the Human Rights Act 1998*, J. Steele, "Damages in tort and under the Human Rights Act: remedial or functional separation?" [2008] C.L.J. 606 and J. Varuhas, *Damages and Human Rights* (Hart, 2016).

66 The cause of action is set out in s.7(1): "(1) A person who claims that a public authority has acted (or proposes to act) in a way which is made unlawful by section 6(1) may—(a) bring proceedings against the authority under this Act in the appropriate court or tribunal, or (b) rely on the Convention right or rights concerned in any legal proceedings, but only if he is (or would be) a victim of the unlawful act".

67 Human Rights Act 1998 s.8(2).

68 These include: (a) any other relief or remedy granted, or order made, in relation to the act in question (by that

■ in determining whether to award damages or the amount of the award, the court must take into account the principles applied by the European Court of Human Rights.[69]

There is thus no right to damages. The courts will examine all the circumstances of the case and consider whether "just satisfaction" has been achieved, even in the absence of an award of damages under the Act. Damages are thus a residual remedy.

There is some dispute as to how such damages should be assessed. It was argued that damages under the Act should differ from the ordinary compensatory damages discussed above and be lower than those awarded for any comparable tort.[70] Lord Bingham in *R. (on the application of Greenfield) v Secretary of State for the Home Department*[71] agreed, stating that damages would indeed be distinct from those awarded in ordinary tort law:

> "the 1998 Act is not a tort statute. Its objects are different and broader. Even in a case where a finding of violation is not judged to afford the applicant just satisfaction, such a finding will be an important part of his remedy and an important vindication of the right he has asserted . . . Secondly, the purpose of incorporating the Convention in domestic law through the 1998 Act was not to give victims better remedies at home than they could recover in Strasbourg but to give them the same remedies without the delay and expense of resort to Strasbourg."[72]

This is consistent with s.8(4), which instructs the court to take account of the principles applied by the European Court of Human Rights. On this basis, the Supreme Court ruled in *R. (on the application of Sturnham) v Parole Board* that in awarding damages under the Human Rights Act s.8, the courts should primarily be guided (but were not bound) by any clear and consistent practice of the Strasbourg court.[73] In particular, the value (or quantum) of such awards should broadly reflect the level of awards made by that court in comparable cases brought by

---

or any other court), and (b) the consequences of any decision (of that or any other court) in respect of that act: Human Rights Act 1998 s.8(3).

69 Human Rights Act 1998 s.8(4). These are set out under art.41 of the Convention.

70 See Lord Woolf CJ, "The Human Rights Act 1998 and Remedies" in M. Andenas and D. Fairgrieve (eds), *Judicial Review in International Perspective: II* (Kluwer Law International, 2000), pp.429–436.

71 [2005] UKHL 14; [2005] 1 W.L.R. 673 at [19].

72 This has led to relatively modest awards: see *Savage v South Essex Partnership NHS Foundation Trust* [2010] EWHC 865 (QB); [2010] P.I.Q.R. P14 (£10,000 for breach of art.2 in permitting compulsorily detained mental patient to escape and commit suicide) and *R. (on the application of Pennington) v Parole Board* [2010] EWHC 78 (Admin) (£1,750 for breach of art.5(4) due to 3 month delay in informing prisoner that he was to be released on licence, rejecting the argument raised by Varuhas (2009) 72 M.L.R. 750 for a tort-based approach to damages under the Human Rights Act).

73 [2013] UKSC 23; [2013] 2 A.C. 254 at [13] per Lord Reed giving the leading judgment with Lord Carnwath concurring (violation of ECHR art.5(4)). Followed by *R. (on the application of Lee-Hirons) v Secretary of State for Justice* [2016] UKSC 46; [2017] A.C. 52.

applicants from the UK or (note the limitation) other countries with a similar cost of living.[74] In practice, however, it remains a difficulty that the European Court of Human Rights rarely gives guidance as to the principles adopted or even a breakdown of the award in question.[75] This means that the courts can only aim to pitch their awards so far as is possible at the general level of damages awarded by the Strasbourg Court in comparable cases.

17–018

A number of observations may be made. The primary objective (in common with English law) is that the victim[76] should, as far as possible, be placed in the same position as if the violation of his or her rights had not occurred. The European Court of Human Rights is, however, clearly more willing to award damages for distress and disappointment than the English courts, although it has been suggested that such injury must be significant and of sufficient intensity before it could sound in damages.[77] The Strasbourg court is equally willing to consider the character and conduct of the parties and the scale and manner of the violation of rights in deciding on the most appropriate response. The court does not, however, award punitive damages.[78] Ultimately it will be a matter of judgment for the court, reflecting the facts of the individual case and taking into account such guidance as is available from awards made by the Strasbourg court, and, as more claims are brought in the domestic courts, comparable national awards of damages. Lord Reed in the Supreme Court predicted that:

> "[A]s the practice of the European court comes increasingly to be absorbed into our own case law . . . the remedy should become naturalised. While it will remain necessary to ensure that our law does not fall short of Convention standards, we should have confidence in our own case law under section 8 once it has developed sufficiently, and not be perpetually looking to the case law of an international court as our primary source."[79]

---

74 M. Andenas, E. Bjorge and D. Fairgrieve (2014) 130 L.Q.R. 48 comment that Lord Reed thus regarded the economic context of the award as a relevant concern.

75 See Law Commission Report No.266; para.3.4: "Perhaps the most striking feature of the Strasbourg case-law, to lawyers from the UK, is the lack of clear principles as to when damages should be awarded and how they should be measured".

76 HRA 1998 s.7(7) provides that a person is a "victim" of an unlawful act only if he would be a victim under art.34 of the Convention. The definition of victim under the Convention is quite broad. For example, there is clear authority that family members (and not simply the deceased) may bring claims in their own right for breach of ECHR art.2 (right to life): applied, recently, in *Rabone v Pennine Care NHS Foundation Trust* [2012] UKSC 2; [2012] 2 A.C. 72.

77 *R. (on the application KB) v Mental Health Review Tribunal* [2003] EWHC 193 (Admin); [2004] Q.B. 936, relying on *Silver v United Kingdom* (1983) 6 E.H.R.R. 62. The court is equally more willing to award damages for negligently-incurred pure economic loss than in English law: see Ch.3.

78 See Law Commission Report No.266 para.3.47 which examined the case law of the European Court of Human Rights.

79 *R. (on the application of Sturnham) v Parole Board* [2013] UKSC 23 at [29].

In other words, over time, enough English cases will be decided to give the courts clearer guidance as to how to assess damages for breach of s.8. Nevertheless, English judges continue to complain that there is limited guidance to the assessment of the level of awards which appear to be "highly fact sensitive".[80] The recent Supreme Court decision in *DSD v Commissioner of Police of the Metropolis*[81] reminded judges that any award of compensation serves a distinctly different purpose to an award of damages in tort law. In a case where the police had failed to properly investigate a series of rapes due to systemic and operational failures, any award of damages would be geared principally to the upholding of standards concerning the police's failure to conduct proper investigations into criminal conduct leading to a breach of art.3 ECHR (inhuman and degrading treatment). Damages of £22,500 were awarded in favour of D.

One final point should be noted. Proceedings for damages must be brought quickly under the Act, normally within one year of the act complained of.[82]

Actions for Personal Injury

Having discussed the different kinds of damages available to claimants, we now focus on a specific type of action: a claim for compensation for personal injury. As highlighted above, the courts experience particular problems in assessing such awards. It is impossible to put a financial price on the loss of a limb, or the pain and suffering endured during an accident. Further, even financial losses cause difficulties when future financial loss is claimed. The courts are required to predict the future financial position of the claimant if the tort had not taken place. For example, if the claimant wishes to recover future loss of earnings, a court should take account of the fact that he or she may have been dismissed or made redundant, or taken a career break, or even promoted to run the company. Such prospects should be brought into the calculation of any compensatory sum, but achieving this with any degree of accuracy is obviously difficult. As Lord Scarman commented in *Lim v Camden AHA*[83]: "There is really only one certainty: the future will prove the award to be either too high or too low".

The courts have adopted a number of principles which seek to achieve the goal of full compensation, which will be considered below, but a number of matters should be noted. First, the courts assess the claimant's loss on an individual basis. They therefore have no

17–019

---

80   Theis J in *Kent CC v M* [2016] EWFC 28; [2016] 4 W.L.R. 97 at [79] (breach of ECHR arts 6 and 8).
81   [2018] UKSC 11; [2019] A.C. 196 at [64]–[65].
82   See Human Rights Act s.7(5): "Proceedings under subs.7(1)(a) must be brought before the end of—(a) the period of one year beginning with the date on which the act complained of took place; or (b) such longer period as the court or tribunal considers equitable having regard to all the circumstances, but that is subject to any rule imposing a stricter time limit in relation to the procedure in question". Such an extension was granted in *Rabone v Pennine Care NHS Foundation Trust* [2012] UKSC 2.
83   [1980] A.C. 174 at 183.

problem with the fact that claimant X, who is a company director living in a large house in Surrey, will receive far more damages for loss of earnings than claimant Y, a worker in a fast food outlet living in rented accommodation, even though they have received exactly the same injuries due to the tort.[84] X will have suffered greater financial losses than Y and will therefore deserve a larger award. The courts have also traditionally been wary of the use of actuarial evidence in the calculation of awards. Actuarial evidence is used by insurance companies to calculate premiums, and it has been suggested that it may form a more accurate basis for assessing future financial losses in tort. The courts have in the past been reluctant to embrace such evidence, a judge commenting in 1985 that "the predictions of an actuary can be only a little more likely to be accurate (and will almost certainly be less interesting) than those of an astrologer".[85] Nevertheless, in the House of Lords decision in *Wells v Wells*[86] (which will be discussed in more detail below), Lord Lloyd adopted a far more positive view of actuarial evidence, holding that whilst such evidence should not govern personal injury claims, it should certainly be referred to, and used as a starting-point rather than a check.

We shall look first at how the courts assess past and future financial losses (or pecuniary loss). This will be followed by an examination of the most difficult category to assess: non-pecuniary loss.

Pecuniary loss

17–020

If the claimant has suffered severe injuries, the largest part of the claim is likely to be for financial loss, including loss of earnings, cost of care and expenses. As stated above, while financial losses before trial can be assessed with some degree of accuracy, future losses are very difficult to calculate. This is not assisted by the general rule that the courts will award a once-and-for-all lump sum. The court must find a sum which, if properly invested, will cover the claimant for all future losses incurred due to the tort. The best the courts can do is to make a "guesstimate" of future losses. The difficulties in assessing the different types of financial loss suffered by the claimant will be examined below.

(1) Loss of earnings

17–021

While loss of earnings before trial can be assessed with a degree of accuracy, calculation of loss of future earnings is obviously more problematic. The method used by the courts is known as the "multiplier/multiplicand method". Essentially, a figure is reached by the court multiplying the multiplier by the multiplicand.

---

84 See *H West & Son Ltd v Shephard* [1964] A.C. 326.
85 *Auty v National Coal Board* [1985] 1 All E.R. 930 at 939 per Oliver LJ.
86 [1999] 1 A.C. 345.

$$\text{MULTIPLIER} \times \text{MULTIPLICAND} = \text{future loss of earnings}$$

The multiplicand is the claimant's net annual loss.[87] This is his or her gross annual salary, less income tax and National Insurance contributions.

The multiplier is the number of years for which this loss will continue. However, this is not a question of the difference between the claimant's age at the time of the accident and the age he or she resumes work or retires. The courts will take account of the possibilities of unemployment, redundancy and other factors reducing salary (although they will also take account of promotion prospects, etc to increase the figure). They will also note the fact that the claimant is being paid "up front". On this basis, the multiplier will be discounted to take account of accelerated receipt, mortality risks and, in relation to claims for loss of earnings and pension, discounts for contingencies other than mortality. The multiplier will therefore usually be set at a rate far lower than the actual number of years during which the injury will be suffered.

This formula is stated to give a lump sum sufficient, if invested, to produce an income equal to the loss of income suffered by the claimant.[88] Whether in fact this is achieved is highly questionable and in fact most unlikely. It is on this principle, however, that the courts award a lump sum.

Pressure has mounted, however, for the courts to adopt a more scientific approach. The Ogden Tables, which first appeared in 1984,[89] have made a considerable impact in persuading the courts of the merits of actuarial evidence. These are a set of actuarial tables, prepared by a working party of lawyers, insurers, accountants and actuaries for use in personal injury and fatal accident cases, which are published by the Government Actuary's Department. They assist in identifying the most appropriate multiplier, based on the most recent mortality rates produced by the Office for National Statistics. The Ogden Tables are now regularly cited in court, and the Civil Evidence Act 1995 s.10 provides that they are admissible as evidence in court.[90] Any doubts about using the Tables were laid to rest in *Wells v Wells* where Lord Lloyd argued that the tables should be a starting point in assessing damages for future loss.[91] Yet, reference to the Ogden Tables has only added to the criticism of the courts' refusal to take account of inflation when establishing the multiplier.[92] In setting up the multiplier, the courts assume that the interest on the lump sum will cover inflation, and so this can be ignored.[93]

---

87 See *British Transport Commission v Gourley* [1956] A.C. 185 HL.

88 Assuming the claimant will draw on the income and part of the capital from the sum invested so that the lump sum is exhausted at the end of the relevant period.

89 Now in their 7th edn (October 2011), with online supplementary tables (2019). As well as providing tables of multipliers, the publication provides explanatory notes as to how the tables should be used: see *http://www.gad.gov.uk/services/Other%20Services/Compensation_for_injury_and_death.html* [Accessed 1 August 2020].

90 This provision has, however, never been brought into force.

91 [1999] 1 A.C. 345 at 379.

92 In *Lim Poh Choo v Camden and Islington AHA* [1980] A.C. 174 at 193, Lord Scarman held that only in exceptional circumstances would any allowance be made for inflation.

93 This process was affirmed by the Court of Appeal in *Cooke v United Bristol Health Care* [2003] EWCA Civ 1370; [2004] 1 W.L.R. 251.

DISCOUNT RATE

17-022

The discount rate is the rate used by the courts in the UK to calculate the amount by which an award of damages for personal injuries paid by way of a lump sum should be reduced to allow for the accelerated payment of future pecuniary loss. This will be factored into the calculation of the multiplier. The courts had in the past presumed a return on investments of 4 to 5%.[94] It was questioned whether this was a realistic figure, since it assumed that the successful claimant would invest in equities which, in an unstable stock market, could prove a risky investment. With the advent of index-linked government securities (gilts), a safer alternative existed. These are bonds under which the return on capital is fully protected against inflation. On this basis, if inflation increases and so the lump sum is worth less, the claimant will be protected by the bond. However, greater security comes at a price, and the interest on such bonds is less than the general commercial rate. The Law Commission, in its 1994 report *Structured Settlements and Interim and Provisional Damages*,[95] recommended that the courts, in assessing the multiplier, should use the rate for index-linked government securities unless there are special reasons affecting the individual case. While legislation at that time allowed the Lord Chancellor to alter the discount rate,[96] no steps were taken and the House of Lords intervened in 1998 in *Wells v Wells*,[97] holding that it was no longer appropriate to act on the assumption that the claimant will invest his or her damages in equities and to apply a discount rate of 4 to 5%. Rather, the courts should recognise the suitability of index-linked government securities for a prudent investment of a large lump sum of damages, and, in the light of this, their Lordships applied a discount rate of 3%.

This led to a dramatic increase in multipliers, previously capped at 18. In the case of *Thomas v Brighton Health Authority* (which was joined in *Wells*), serious injuries had been suffered by a child at birth, and the court raised the multiplier from 17 to 26.58. The Court of Appeal held in *Warren v Northern General Hospital Trust*[98] that the discount rate should remain at 3% until the Lord Chancellor set a rate under the Damages Act 1996 s.1. This was regardless of the fact that the net yield of index-linked government securities was found to have dropped to 2.5%. In 2001, the Lord Chancellor intervened, and the rate was set at 2.5%.[99] As a result of *these changes*, damages for future pecuniary loss rose considerably. This brought with it a consequential rise in liability insurance premiums.[100]

---

94 Since *Mallett v McMonagle* [1970] A.C. 166 HL.

95 Law Commission Report No.224 paras 2.25–2.28.

96 Damages Act 1996 s.1 (now repealed and replaced by s.A1).

97 [1999] 1 A.C. 345. A case described as "one of the most important decisions in personal injury litigation since the Second World War": D. Kemp (1998) 114 L.Q.R. 570, 571.

98 [2000] 1 W.L.R. 1404.

99 Damages (Personal Injury) Order 2001 (SI 2001/2301) art.2.

100 The Lord Chancellor's Department March 2000 Consultation Paper para.14, reported that insurance industry sources estimated that reducing the guideline rate of return from 4.5% to 3% would increase by £115 million the sum needed to be paid out in damages.

Criticism continued, however, that this rate was still too high.[101] In 2012–2013 the Ministry of Justice undertook a two-part consultation into the methodology used to set the discount rate for personal injury damages and the legal basis on which it is set.[102] The outcome of the government review was published in 2017 and a reduction of the discount rate to minus 0.75% was announced.[103] This reflected the fact that since 2001 the real yields on index-linked gilts investments has fallen, but was regarded by many (notably insurers) as an over-reaction. The Civil Liability Act 2018 added a new section A1 to the Damages Act 1996.[104] This states that in assessing damages for future pecuniary loss, the court must take into account the rate of return set by the Lord Chancellor following the procedure set out in Schedule A1.[105] Different rates of return may be prescribed for different classes of cases e.g. one rate for loss of future earnings and another for the cost of future care.[106] The 2018 Act seeks to provide a new methodology that better reflected the investments actually made by claimants and to provide a rate that is fairer to both claimants and defendants.[107] Notably the rate would be set by reference to "low" rather than "very low risk" investments.

In July 2019, the Lord Chancellor announced that the prescribed discount rate would be increased from minus 0.75% to minus 0.25% with effect from 5 August 2019.[108] The Government justified the change on the basis that the 2017 order had produced a rate that was too favourable to claimants, as compared to defendants. Subsequent reviews of the rate will be undertaken at least every five years. Lump sum payments of damages for future loss can thus be expected to be lower than they would have been had the law remained unchanged.

One final point. Current policy should also be considered in the light of the fact that the courts do not check what the claimant actually does with the sum awarded. It is accepted that, in reality, it is unlikely that a claimant would place the entire award of damages in index-linked government securities. Nevertheless, if the claimant chooses to invest all the lump sum in the stock market or in his or her bank account, this is disregarded and will not affect the court's calculation of damages.[109]

17–023

---

101   C. Daykin, "Fair compensation needs actuaries" [2009] J.P.I. Law 48.

102   See Joint Consultations by the Ministry of Justice, the Scottish Government and the Department of Justice, Northern Ireland, *Damages Act 1996: The Discount Rate—How should it be set?* (Consultation Paper CP 12/2012) and *Damages Act 1996: The Discount Rate—Review of the Legal Framework* (Consultation Paper CP 3/2013).

103   Damages (Personal Injury) Order 2017 (SI 2017/206) art.2. This change became effective on 20 March 2017.

104   Civil Liability Act 2018 s.10 (Assumed rate of return on investment of damages). In force from 1 July 2019, replacing s.1.

105   Schedule A1 introduces a requirement for the Lord Chancellor to review the discount rate on a regular basis according to the procedure set out in the Schedule. The objective of every review is to decide whether the rate should be retained or changed.

106   Damages Act 1996 ss.A1(3) and (4).

107   Explanatory notes to Damages (Personal Injury) Order 2019 (SI 2019/1126) [7].

108   Damages (Personal Injury) Order 2019 (SI 2019/1126) art.2.

109   *Wells v Wells* [1999] 1 A.C. 345 at 365 per Lord Lloyd.

(2) Lost years

17-024

This is a claim for loss of earnings during the period the claimant would have been able to work, but for the fact that his or her life has been shortened by the defendant's tort. In other words, suppose that claimant A was expected to live to 70. Following the tort, A will only live to 40. The claim will be for the loss of earnings from the age of 40. In the past, A could have claimed damages for loss of expectation of life for which the courts awarded a small sum, even though the claimant might be unaware of the loss or had been killed instantaneously.[110] In view of this award, the court in *Oliver v Ashman*[111] held that no additional award for loss of earnings during the "lost years" would be allowed. However, damages for loss of expectation of life were abolished by the Administration of Justice Act 1982 s.1(1)(a). In 1980, the majority of the House of Lords in *Pickett v British Rail Engineering Ltd*[112] finally overturned *Oliver v Ashman* and accepted that a claim for loss of earnings during the "lost years" should stand. Their Lordships were influenced by the predicament of dependants, for whom the victim would have provided financial support during this period. If the victim cannot claim, and the dependants are unable to bring a claim in their own right under the Fatal Accidents Act 1976 (see below),[113] then this head of damage would go uncompensated. This was held to be contrary to logic and justice.[114] In assessing the award, the court will look at the claimant's life expectancy before the accident and deduct the sum the claimant would have spent on supporting him or herself, including a proportion of the household bills.[115] The sum awarded will vary. *Croke v Wiseman* holds that for a very young child any such loss is highly speculative and the court is likely to award nil damages.[116] While this has been criticised as unduly harsh by both the Court of Appeal and more recently the High Court, the general view is that it will take a decision of the Supreme Court to overturn the ruling in *Croke*.[117]

---

110 e.g. £200 in *Benham v Gambling* [1941] A.C. 157.

111 [1962] 2 Q.B. 210.

112 [1980] A.C. 136.

113 A claim by dependants under the Fatal Accidents Act 1976 can only stand when the deceased's claim has not proceeded to judgment or settled.

114 This action does not, however, survive for the benefit of the claimant's estate. Law Reform (Miscellaneous Provisions) Act 1934 s.1(2)(a) (as amended by the Administration of Justice Act 1982 s.4) provides that the estate cannot recover any damages for loss of income in respect of any period after the victim's death. This prevents any possibility of double recovery by the claimant as the executor of the estate and dependant.

115 See *Harris v Empress Motors Ltd* [1984] 1 W.L.R. 212. This is far stricter than the approach under the Fatal Accidents Act 1976 which will be discussed below.

116 *Croke v Wiseman* [1982] 1 W.L.R. 71. Comment: P. J. Davies (1982) 45 M.L.R. 333.

117 *Croke* was followed unenthusiastically by the Court of Appeal in *Iqbal v Whipps Cross University Hospital NHS Trust* [2007] EWCA Civ 1190; [2008] P.I.Q.R. P9 and by the High Court in *Totham v King's College Hospital NHS Foundation Trust* [2015] EWHC 97 (QB) at [42]–[47] where the judge argued that *Croke* is inconsistent with the principle of full compensation and the policy reasoning in *Pickett v British Rail*. See also *JR v Sheffield Teaching Hospitals NHS Foundation Trust* [2017] EWHC 1245 (QB); [2017] 1 W.L.R. 4847 (*Croke* distinguished on questionable ground that although the claimant was injured at birth, claim was brought as an adult making it less speculative: at [33]).

(3) Loss of earning capacity

This is a claim for losses due to the fact that, although the claimant can carry on working, his or her ability to obtain employment is hindered by the continuing effects of the accident. For example, claimants disabled due to the accident may find it more difficult to obtain a new job if their employment ends for some reason, particularly if they were employed in a physically demanding job. This is often difficult to assess[118] and, particularly in relation to children,[119] highly speculative.

(4) Deductions

In assessing the claimant's compensation, the court seeks to compensate the victim fully, but is also careful to avoid over-compensation which may unnecessarily penalise the defendant for his or her tort and be a wasteful use of resources. The problem of over-compensation arises when it is shown that, following the accident, the claimant has received sums of money which also compensate him or her for the loss suffered. Consider, for example, where, due to the tort, the defendant cannot work and seeks compensation from the defendant for her loss of earnings. Prior to trial, the claimant may be forced to rely on government social security payments or, if she is lucky, may be entitled to statutory sick pay or payments due under an insurance policy providing critical illness cover. Should these payments be taken into account in the action against the defendant for loss of earnings, reducing the burden on the defendant? If they are not, the claimant gets too much compensation. If they are, the defendant pays less at the expense of other innocent parties. There are a number of possible options open to the courts:

- Make the defendant liable only for the actual losses suffered by the claimant, deducting social security payments, etc received. This option means that the State, employer or insurance company which has provided financial support is effectively subsidising the defendant who is at fault.

- Ignore other benefits and make the defendant fully liable. Here, it is accepted that the claimant is over-compensated.

- Make the defendant liable only for the actual losses suffered by the claimant but make the defendant liable to repay all those who supported the claimant prior to trial.

The courts confusingly adopt all three approaches. Lord Reid in *Parry v Cleaver* explains the rules as depending on justice, reasonableness and public policy,[120] but this takes us little

---

118   See *Smith v Manchester Corp* (1974) 17 K.I.R. 1 CA. For a classic recent example of such an award, see *Billett v Ministry of Defence* [2015] EWCA Civ 773; [2016] P.I.Q.R. Q1.

119   See, e.g. *Croke v Wiseman* [1982] 1 W.L.R. 71 where the plaintiff was 21-months-old at the time of the accident.

120   [1970] A.C. 1 at 13.

further. This section will therefore set out how these rules work. Essentially, it depends on the *nature of the benefit* received by the claimant. The principles involved are not particularly clear. The general approach seems to be that when the claimant has received a benefit which reduces the actual loss suffered, it should be deducted, but that the claimant should keep all "collateral payments". This distinction is not, however, always clear. The simplest way is to examine each individual benefit in turn.

(I) CHARITY

17–027

The law is reluctant to reduce the damages payable to the claimant due to receipt of charitable payments. There is a no doubt realistic fear that individuals would be reluctant to donate money to charity if the net result was to reduce the defendant's liability for damages at trial. Policy therefore dictates that such sums should not be deducted.[121]

(II) VOLUNTARY PAYMENTS BY THE DEFENDANT

17–028

If the defendant has given any money to the claimant, or provided facilities such as a wheelchair, this will be deducted from the award. This will not include a company pension, as this is distinguishable from compensation for lost wages (see **17–031** below).[122] In *Williams v BOC Gases Ltd*,[123] an ex gratia payment from the defendant employers, given as an advance against any damages awarded, was deducted. The Court of Appeal held that, as a matter of public policy, employers ought to be encouraged to make payments of this kind. This would not be treated as a charitable payment, even if given for benevolent reasons, unless the employer explicitly spelt out that it should be ignored if damages were awarded in future litigation.[124]

(III) INSURANCE

17–029

Again, if the claimant has had the foresight to purchase an insurance policy to cover some of his or her losses, the courts are reluctant to penalise the claimant.[125] It would seem wrong that a claimant who has paid no premiums should obtain a higher damages award. Arguably this could be met by giving the claimant a credit for the premiums paid, but the courts have not chosen this path. In any event, if the insurance policy is one of indemnity (for example property insurance is usually indemnity insurance), the insurer is likely to seek to recover the monies paid by exercising its right of subrogation. The action will then be brought by the insurance company in the claimant's name. However, personal injury insurance is not generally indemnity insurance, and the claimant will be able to recover both the proceeds of the policy and the damages awarded by the court.[126]

---

121   See *Parry v Cleaver* [1970] A.C. 1; *Hussain v New Taplow Paper Mills Ltd* [1988] A.C. 514; and *Gaca v Pirelli General Plc* [2004] EWCA Civ 373; [2004] 1 W.L.R. 2683.

122   See *Parry v Cleaver* [1970] A.C. 1.

123   [2000] I.C.R. 1181.

124   See *Gaca v Pirelli General Plc* [2004] EWCA Civ 373; [2004] 1 W.L.R. 2683, overruling *McCamley v Cammell Laird Shipbuilders Ltd* [1990] 1 W.L.R. 963.

125   See *Bradburn v Great Western Rail Co* (1874) L.R. 10 Ex 1.

126   See, generally, P. Cane and J. Goudkamp, *Atiyah's Accidents, Compensation and the Law*, 9th edn (CUP, 2018), para.15.4.3.

(IV) SICK PAY

This is deductible from damages for loss of earnings, whether or not it is paid by the defendant. It is not treated as insurance against loss of earnings, but as a substitute for wages. This extends to long-term sickness benefit paid by the employer.[127]

(V) PENSION

If, as a result of the injury, the claimant retires from his or her job and receives a pension, this is not deductible from the claim for loss of earnings, because the pension is not deemed to be of the same nature as lost wages, but a form of insurance. In *Parry v Cleaver*, a 35-year-old policeman had been severely injured in a road accident and was discharged from the police force. However, whilst in employment, he had made compulsory contributions to a police pension fund, and he became entitled to a pension for life on being discharged. The question was whether this pension should be taken into account when assessing the policeman's loss of earnings following the accident. The majority of the House of Lords held that it should be ignored. A contributory pension scheme was treated as a form of insurance, rather than sick pay, and should not be taken into account when assessing future loss of earnings. It would, however, be taken into account in assessing the loss suffered on reaching police retirement age, when there would be a diminution in pension entitlement. Lord Reid stressed that it was simply a case of comparing "like with like".[128] The minority favoured deduction. Lord Morris (dissenting) held that where there is no discretionary element, and the arrangements leading to the pension are an essential part of the contract, then the pension payments should be taken as a form of deferred pay, and deducted.[129] The majority view, however, was approved by the House of Lords in *Smoker v London Fire and Civil Defence Authority*.[130] Lord Templeman approved Lord Reid's statement in *Parry* that:

> "a pension is the fruit, through insurance, of all the money which was set aside in the past in respect of [an employee's] past work."[131]

The House of Lords, in *Hussain v New Taplow Paper Mills Ltd*,[132] however, distinguished payments under a permanent health insurance scheme set up by the employer, to which employees were not required to contribute. Lord Bridge, delivering the unanimous opinion of the House, viewed such payments as the very opposite of a pension, and indistinguishable from long-term sick pay. On this basis, such payments were deductible. His Lordship commented:

---

127 *Hussain v New Taplow Paper Mills Ltd* [1988] A.C. 514.
128 [1970] A.C. 1 at 21.
129 [1970] A.C. 1 at 32.
130 [1991] 2 A.C. 502. See also *Longden v British Coal Corp* [1998] A.C. 653 HL: contributory incapacity and disability pensions are non-deductible.
131 [1991] 2 A.C. 502 at 543.
132 [1988] A.C. 514.

> "It positively offends my sense of justice that a plaintiff, who has certainly paid no insurance premiums as such, should receive full wages during a period of incapacity to work from two different sources, his employer and the tortfeasor."[133]

It would therefore seem that, in his Lordship's view at least, the claimant must have contributed to the pension to avoid any deduction of this benefit.

(VI) SOCIAL SECURITY BENEFITS

17–032

For political reasons, deduction of social security benefits is largely governed by statute. When the National Health Service was introduced in the late 1940s, this matter was governed by the Law Reform (Personal Injuries) Act 1948.[134] Section 2 provided for a deduction from damages for loss of earnings of one-half the value of certain benefits, such as sickness benefit and invalidity benefit, receivable by the claimant in the five years following the accident. This did not include all benefits, however, and the common law developed complementary rules deducting these other benefits in full for the period of the disability.[135]

The current legal position modifies the rules to resemble the third option mentioned above.[136] It represents a political decision to ensure that the overstretched welfare state is not subsidising defendants, and that social security payments made to claimants should be recovered whenever possible. Social Security (Recovery of Benefits) Act 1997 s.6 now provides for the defendant to pay to the Department for Work and Pensions an amount equal to the total amount of specified social security benefits[137] payable to the victim in respect of his or her injury during the five years immediately following the accident (or until the making of the compensation payment whichever is earlier[138]). The claimant will get the difference (if any) between the damages awarded and recoverable benefits.[139] Section 4 provides that the defendant should not make any compensation payment in consequence of an accident, injury or disease suffered by the claimant until he or she has applied to the Secretary of State for a certificate of recoverable benefits. These are processed by the Compensation Recovery Unit

---

133 [1988] A.C. 514 at 532.

134 This still applies to torts which occurred before 1 January 1989 and which are not barred by the Limitation Act 1980.

135 See *Hodgson v Trapp* [1989] A.C. 807. These rules still apply for benefits not covered by the 1997 Act, e.g. statutory payments under the Pneumoconiosis etc (Workers' Compensation) Act 1979 or housing benefit (*Clenshaw v Tanner* [2002] EWCA Civ 1848).

136 Namely that the defendant is liable only for the actual losses suffered by the claimant, but the defendant is rendered liable to repay all those who supported the claimant prior to trial.

137 They are listed in Social Security (Recovery of Benefits) Act 1997 Sch.2, col.2 and cover most benefits. There are exemptions, however, such as payments made under the Criminal Injuries Compensation Scheme and charitable trusts: see Sch.1, Pt I. Claims under the Fatal Accidents Act 1976 are also excluded: Social Security (Recovery of Benefits) Regulations 1997 (SI 1997/2205) reg.2(2)(a).

138 Social Security (Recovery of Benefits) Act 1997 s.3. This is inserted to encourage early settlements.

139 Social Security (Recovery of Benefits) Act 1997 s.8(2).

(CRU) of the Department for Work and Pensions.[140] The provisions apply not only to court judgments, but extend to out-of-court settlements.[141]

The 1997 Act is more generous to claimants than the earlier Social Security Act 1989 it replaced.[142] Benefits are now deducted only from certain heads of damages, namely loss of earnings, cost of care and loss of mobility, which are set out in Sch.2. This Schedule helpfully lists the relevant benefits to be deducted from each individual head. On this basis, income support will be deducted from any award for loss of earnings, and attendance allowance from damages for the costs of nursing and care. The State can no longer deduct any sum from damages awarded for pain and suffering and loss of amenity, because there is no equivalent state benefit. The defendant, who remains liable to the Secretary of State for "an amount equal to the total amount of the recoverable benefits",[143] may therefore be in a difficult position. Consider the following example. The claimant suffers injuries in an accident caused by the defendant's negligence. Damages are assessed at £10,000 (£7,000 loss of earnings and £3,000 non-pecuniary losses). The claimant has received £8,000 in income support. Under the 1997 Act, the defendant is liable to pay £8,000 to the State, although the claimant's award will only be reduced by £7,000 as no deduction can be made against non-pecuniary losses. The claimant will in such circumstances receive £3,000 damages (£10,000 minus £7,000). The defendant will be liable to pay £11,000 in total (£8,000 to the State and £3,000 to the claimant).[144]

Summing up, the current law on deductions demonstrates no clear overall policy. Whilst trying to prevent over-compensation, the courts are generous in relation to charitable donations, insurance and pensions, but tough in relation to sick pay. The current distinction between a disablement pension and sick pay also demonstrates the confusion existing in this area of law.[145] The strict line taken in relation to recovery of social security benefits may additionally

---

140 See https://www.gov.uk/government/collections/cru [Accessed 1 August 2020]. The CRU seeks to recover social security benefits paid as a result of an accident, but also costs incurred by NHS hospitals and Ambulance Trusts for treatment from injuries from road traffic accidents and personal injury claims: see Health and Social Care (Community Health and Standards) Act 2003 Pt 3. There is a limit to the amount of NHS charges that can be recovered: see Personal Injuries (NHS Charges) (Amounts) Regulations 2015 (SI 2015/295). Contrast the position of the local authority: *Islington LBC v University College Hospital NHS Trust* [2005] EWCA Civ 596; [2006] P.I.Q.R. P3.

141 See s.1(3) of the 1997 Act.

142 Later incorporated in the Social Security Administration Act 1992. The 1997 Act came into force on 6 October 1997.

143 Social Security (Recovery of Benefits) Act 1997 s.6(1).

144 The Court of Appeal in *Griffiths v British Coal Corp* [2001] EWCA Civ 336; [2001] 1 W.L.R. 1493 modified this result slightly by allowing defendants to offset their liability to the State against any award of interest under each head. Further potential difficulties arise due to the failure of the 1997 Act to make allowances for any reduction in the claimant's damages for contributory negligence.

145 See Law Commission Report No.262, *Damages for Personal Injury: Medical, Nursing and Other Expenses; Collateral Benefits* (1999). The Commission rejected (at paras 11.51–11.52) treating pensions and sick pay alike and deducting both. It felt that there would be practical difficulties in distinguishing between some disablement pensions and some insurance policies.

be criticised. The system involves administration costs and may leave the successful claimant without any damages and the defendant incurring considerable costs in ascertaining his or her liability to the State. In examining the current legal position, the Law Commission concluded that in view of the lack of consensus as to any reform, it could not at present recommend any changes to the law.[146] Nevertheless, the Commission hoped that its report might assist the judiciary, and also the Government, in developing this area of law. The confusion is therefore likely to continue in the immediate future.

(5) Expenses

17–033

The claimant can also recover reasonably incurred expenses, which will include medical expenses, increased living expenses and the cost of transport to and from hospital.[147] These will include past and future expenses incurred due to the injury. It is not unreasonable to choose private medical treatment instead of treatment under the National Health Service. Law Reform (Personal Injuries) Act 1948 s.2(4) provides that the claimant is not obliged to use the NHS to mitigate loss.[148] Equally, provided that there is no risk of double recovery, claimants are entitled to claim cost of future private health care even where a local authority would have a statutory obligation to care and accommodate them.[149] Controversially, the Supreme Court recently found it reasonable, and not contrary to public policy, to seek the cost of commercial surrogacy arrangements overseas (here California), provided the costs were reasonable and there was a reasonable prospect of success.[150] However, any saving the claimant makes due to being wholly or partly maintained at public expense in a hospital, nursing home or other institution will be set off against any loss of income due to the injury.[151] The courts are careful to avoid overcompensation, and therefore will deduct the cost of food, heating, etc from the award.[152]

---

146   Law Commission Report No.262, *Damages for Personal Injury: Medical, Nursing and Other Expenses; Collateral Benefits* (1999), para.11.53.

147   *Cunningham v Harrison* [1973] Q.B. 942.

148   The Government in its Consultation Paper, *The Law on Damages* (CP 09/07, May 2007) queried whether the time had come to repeal this section to prevent litigants claiming the cost of medical care and then using the NHS free of charge, although there seems little empirical evidence to suggest this is widespread in practice.

149   *Peters v East Midland Strategic Health Authority* [2009] EWCA Civ 145; [2010] Q.B. 48. Where the claimant lacks capacity (as in *Peters*) the court held that the Court of Protection could provide against the risk of double recovery e.g. by requiring notification of any future application for public funding of the claimant's care.

150   *Whittington Hospital NHS Trust v XX* [2020] UKSC 14; [2020] 2 W.L.R. 972 at [53] per Lady Hale. This is despite the fact that commercial surrogacy is not permitted in the UK.

151   Administration of Justice Act 1982 s.5. *Lim Poh Choo v Camden and Islington AHA* [1980] A.C. 174 applies the same rule to private care.

152   See *Housecroft v Burnett* [1986] 1 All E.R. 332.

COST OF A CARER

A further expense following a serious accident may be the cost of a carer.[153] The court again will award compensation for the cost of a carer if such expense is reasonably incurred. However, the carer in question may not be a professional carer, but a close relative or partner who wishes to care for their loved one. Such relatives are unlikely to charge a fee, but of course make considerable sacrifice in both financial and emotional terms. The Court of Appeal in *Donnelly v Joyce*[154] recognised that such carers should not go unrewarded.

In *Donnelly v Joyce*, the victim's mother had given up her part-time job to nurse her six-year-old son. The court awarded a sum for her nursing services, but held that the loss was suffered by the victim, namely the need to receive nursing services due to the tort. It was not the loss of the mother which was being compensated. The court held, however, that it was unnecessary to show a contract between the victim and his mother to obtain the award.[155]

Donnelly was taken a step further by the House of Lords in *Hunt v Severs*.[156] In this case, the victim had been injured when riding as a pillion passenger on a motorbike driven by the defendant, who later became her husband. In claiming damages, she requested a sum for her carer, namely her husband. The House of Lords held that although the sum was awarded to the victim, it would be held on trust for the carer.[157] Here, the carer and the defendant were the same person. On this basis, the court held that there was no ground in public policy or otherwise to justify requiring the defendant to pay a sum to the claimant to be held on trust for himself.

On its face, the decision of the House of Lords seems entirely correct. It would be ridiculous to force the defendant to pay a sum to the claimant to be paid back to the defendant, but this ignores the reality of the situation. The husband was insured, and therefore the person paying the money (the real defendant) was not the husband, but his insurance company.[158] On this analysis, there is nothing wrong with an insurance company paying a sum to the wife to compensate her carer, whoever he or she may be. Following *Hunt v Severs*, if the carer is the tortfeasor, in order to obtain full compensation, the victim is forced to contract for a carer or use a different relative, even though the best person to care for the victim may be the tort-

---

153 One decision has suggested that this may extend to the cost of palliative care prior to death, despite the fact that hospices do not charge for care but request a voluntary contribution from relatives: *Drake v Foster Wheeler Ltd* [2010] EWHC 2004 (QB); [2011] 1 All E.R. 63 (criticism: N. Cooksley [2010] J.P.I. Law C203).

154 [1974] Q.B. 454.

155 The Court of Appeal in *Hardwick v Hudson* [1999] 3 All E.R. 426 distinguished this situation from where the victim's wife had provided commercial services for the claimant's business. Different considerations apply in a commercial environment where such services are usually paid for and the victim could only recover if there was evidence of an express or implied contract for the work. This approach is approved by the Law Commission in their Report No.262, *Damages for Personal Injury: Medical, Nursing and Other Expenses; Collateral Benefits* (1999).

156 [1994] 2 A.C. 350. Comment: D. Kemp (1994) 110 L.Q.R. 524.

157 Adopting the view of Lord Denning MR in *Cunningham v Harrison* [1973] Q.B. 942 at 951–952.

158 Lord Bridge held that at common law the fact that the defendant is insured can have no relevance in assessing damages: [1994] 2 A.C. 350 at 363.

feasor. Certain disabilities render the victim very wary of strangers, and it seems a worrying development for the law to penalise a victim financially for choosing to be cared for by a loved one who happened to have caused the accident in question. The Law Commission, in their 1999 report, recommended that there should be a legislative provision reversing the result in *Hunt*, and that the carer should have a legal entitlement to the claimant's damages for past (although not future) care.[159] The Labour Government in its 2007 Consultation Paper, *The Law on Damages*[160] proposed that the claimant should be under a personal obligation to account to the carer for damages awarded for past and future care, but that where services were provided by the defendant, damages could only be awarded for future gratuitous services. These recommendations were, however, never followed.

The cost of a carer is generally assessed at the commercial rate for such services.[161] If a mother gives up a highly paid employment, the loss will be capped at the commercial rate for the services provided.[162] Equally, if, due to the accident, a person cannot undertake the household tasks undertaken prior to injury, the reasonable cost of substitute services should be awarded.[163]

(6) Other damages

17–035   The examples of expenses listed above are not exhaustive, and damages claims will often consist of a large number of claims, depending on the particular facts of the case. For example, a claimant may wish to sue for the loss of pension rights or the inability to continue a profitable hobby. Subject to the rules of remoteness, the claimant may sue for any losses which are due to the defendant's tort.

Non-pecuniary loss

(1) Pain and suffering

17–036   The court will award a sum which represents the pain and suffering experienced by the claimant. The two are generally considered together. The Law Commission in 1995 defined "pain"

---

159   Law Commission Report No.262 (1999) paras 3.76 and 3.62. The High Court of Australia has refused to follow *Hunt* and followed the principle of *Donnelly v Joyce: Kars v Kars* (1996) 141 A.L.R. 37.

160   Government Consultation Paper, *The Law on Damages* (CP 09/07, May 2007), paras 114–120.

161   This is usually subject to a discount to represent non-payment of tax and national insurance and the belief that care provided out of love and care makes commercial considerations less relevant: *Evans v Pontypridd Roofing Ltd* [2001] EWCA Civ 1657; [2002] P.I.Q.R. Q5.

162   *Housecroft v Burnett* [1986] 1 All E.R. 332 at 343 per O'Connor LJ.

163   See *Daly v General Steam Navigation Co Ltd* [1981] 1 W.L.R. 120. In *Lowe v Guise* [2002] EWCA Civ 197; [2002] Q.B. 1369, the Court of Appeal extended recovery to a claimant who, due to the injury, was unable to continue to provide gratuitous care for his disabled brother on which the family depended.

as "the physical hurt or discomfort attributable to the injury itself or consequent on it", whilst "suffering" was defined as "mental or emotional distress which the plaintiff may feel as a consequence of the injury: anxiety, worry, fear, torment, embarrassment and the like".[164] It is a subjective test, and no sum will be awarded if the claimant is unconscious or unable to experience pain or suffering due to his or her condition.[165] The courts will concentrate on the actual condition of the victim and consider past, present and future suffering.

Administration of Justice Act 1982 s.1(1)(b) also permits an award of damages to victims suffering or likely to suffer on the realisation that their expectation of life has been reduced as a result of the injuries.[166] This will form part of the award for pain and suffering. As the award is subjective, the claimant must be aware of his or her condition. Damages will be refused if the victim is rendered permanently unconscious either immediately or within a short time of the injury. In *Hicks v Chief Constable of South Yorkshire*,[167] for example, where medical evidence indicated that the plaintiffs' daughters, crushed in the Hillsborough disaster, would have lost consciousness within a matter of seconds and would have died within five minutes, the court rejected a claim for the distress suffered by the girls in their last moments.

(2) Loss of amenity

17–037

This is distinct from pain and suffering and is a claim for the loss of enjoyment of life experienced after the injury. For example, suppose that due to an injury to her leg, the claimant cannot play tennis or go for long country walks as she could prior to the accident. An objective test is applied, so the fact that the claimant is unable to appreciate this loss is irrelevant. This is clearly seen in *H West & Son Ltd v Shephard*.[168] Here, the plaintiff had been badly injured in a road traffic accident and had sustained severe head injuries, resulting in cerebral atrophy and paralysis of all four limbs. Due to her injuries, her ability to appreciate her condition was severely limited. She was 41 at the time of accident, but had no prospect of improvement, and required full-time hospital nursing for the rest of her life, which was estimated as five years. The majority of the House of Lords held that she had suffered loss of amenity and approved the trial judge's award of £17,500.[169] The court was not prepared to treat such a victim as dead and reduce the damages on this basis.

---

164   Law Commission Consultation Paper No.140, *Damage for Personal Injury: Non-Pecuniary Loss* (1995), para.2.10. The Law Commission Report No.257, *Damages for Personal Injury: Non-Pecuniary Loss* (April 1999) recommended that the present system of assessment by judges should continue and made no proposals for reform.

165   *H West & Son Ltd v Shephard* [1964] A.C. 326; *Lim Poh Choo v Camden and Islington AHA* [1980] A.C. 174 in contrast to loss of amenity which is assessed objectively.

166   Administration of Justice Act 1982 s.1(1)(a) abolished a claim for loss of expectation of life per se.

167   [1992] 2 All E.R. 65. See also *Grieves v FT Everard & Sons Ltd* [2007] UKHL 39; [2008] 1 A.C. 281 (no recovery for anxiety caused by fear of future life-threatening disease).

168   [1964] A.C. 326 at 368–369 per Lord Pearce. See also *Wise v Kaye* [1962] 1 Q.B. 638.

169   The minority (Lords Reid and Devlin) favoured a far smaller award.

This was approved by the House of Lords in *Lim v Camden AHA*.[170] In this case, a 36-year-old senior psychiatric registrar had suffered extensive and irremediable brain damage following a minor operation. As a result, Dr Lim was barely conscious and totally dependent on others. She was awarded £20,000 for pain and suffering and loss of amenity. This was approved by the House of Lords, which held that *West* could only be reversed by a comprehensive Act of Parliament which dealt with all aspects of damages for personal injury. The court was not prepared to overturn a decision which had formed the basis for settlements and damages awards for almost 20 years. A review of the position was undertaken by the Law Commission which, in its April 1999 Report No.257, *Damages for Personal Injury: Non-Pecuniary Loss*, did not recommend changing the rules for damages for non-pecuniary loss in respect of permanently unconscious or conscious but severely brain-damaged claimants.[171]

(3) Injury itself

17–038

This is difficult to assess. The courts have developed a system of tariffs which guide judges. Reference is made to previous case law and to the Judicial College guidelines,[172] with the stated aim of ensuring uniformity whilst keeping the level of such claims within reasonable bounds.

Assessment

17–039

The Law Commission in its 1999 report stated that damages for non-pecuniary loss in cases of serious personal injury were generally too low, and should be increased generally by a factor of at least 50% for awards over £3,000.[173] It was recommended that this should be achieved by guidelines set down by the Court of Appeal or House of Lords, but if this was not achieved within a reasonable period, then legislation should follow. A five judge Court of Appeal responded in March 2000 in *Heil v Rankin*.[174] In dealing with eight conjoined appeals, Lord Woolf MR proposed a more modest increase in awards than that suggested by the Law Commission. His Lordship suggested that in seeking to make compensation awards for non-pecuniary losses which were fair, reasonable and just, the awards should be subject to a tapered increase, from a maximum of one third, to nil when the award was below £10,000. Such increases would take account of the fact that people now live longer, but his Lordship

---

170 [1980] A.C. 174.
171 See paras 2.19 and 2.24.
172 Since 1992, the Judicial Studies Board (now Judicial College) has published *Guidelines for the Assessment of General Damages in Personal Injury Cases* (latest edition: 15th edn, OUP, 2019) and summaries of awards may be found in *Kemp & Kemp: Quantum of Damages* (Sweet and Maxwell).
173 See para.5.8.
174 [2001] Q.B. 272. Comment: R. Lewis (2001) 64 M.L.R. 100 and D. Campbell, "The *Heil v Rankin* approach to law-making: Who needs a legislature?" (2016) 45 C.L.W.R. 340.

also noted the impact of any increase on the level of insurance premiums.[175] This decision gave rise to a considerable increase in the level of awards. However, the threshold of £10,000, rather than the £3,000 suggested by the Law Commission, limited the impact of the decision and excluded a large number of claims for minor injuries. In the case itself, Heil lost his appeal because the award was less than £10,000.

More recently, the Court of Appeal in *Simmons v Castle*[176] announced a further increase of 10% from 1 April 2013 on the level of general damages in all civil claims. This expressly covers damages for pain and suffering, loss of amenity, physical inconvenience and discomfort, social discredit and mental distress.[177] The increase is primarily a reaction to the changes to the funding of civil litigation introduced by the Legal Aid, Sentencing and Punishment of Offenders Act 2012 Pt 2 (discussed in Ch.1). The Act prevents claimants, who fund their claim by relying on a conditional fee agreement (a "no win no fee" agreement) from recovering any success fee charged by their lawyer or the cost of an "after the event" insurance policy from the losing party.[178] From 1 April 2013, these costs will be deducted from the damages awarded to the claimant for general (and past) damages. As the Court of Appeal commented in *Simmons*, the quid pro quo for this change was that the courts would be expected to increase the amount of general damages awarded, which, indeed, the court did in that case. It should be noted, however, the *Simmons* goes far beyond tort claimants suing under conditional fee agreements and applies to all civil litigation.[179]

Interest

Interest will be added to damages depending on the nature of the injury suffered. Unless the claimant is awarded interim damages, he or she will be deprived of the damages award until the case is finally heard in court, which unfortunately may take a considerable amount of time. Senior Courts Act 1981 s.35A provides for interest in actions for personal injuries in which the claimant recovers more than £200, unless the court is satisfied that there are special reasons why interest should not be given.[180] The rates are as follows.

---

175 *The Times* 24 March 2000 reported that the Association of British Insurers believed that, following *Heil v Rankin*, the likely rise in premiums would be less than 10%.

176 [2012] EWCA Civ 1288; [2013] 1 W.L.R. 1239, amending earlier judgment: [2012] EWCA Civ 1039. The increase will not apply to claimants falling under the Legal Aid, Sentencing and Punishment of Offenders Act 2012 s.44(6), that is, claimants under pre-April 2013 CFA agreements who are still able to recover the success fee from the losing party.

177 [2012] EWCA Civ 1288 at [50].

178 LASPO Act 2012 ss.44 and 46, which amended the Courts and Legal Services Act 1990 (see ss.58 58A and 58C) in line with recommendations made by the Jackson Review.

179 Confirmed in *Summers v Bundy* [2016] EWCA Civ 126; [2016] P.I.Q.R. Q6 (no discretion to judges in relation to 10% uplift in award of general damages).

180 County Courts Act 1984 s.69 makes similar provision for actions in the county court. The interest awarded will be simple interest, although the Law Commission has recommended that the court should have a discretion to

▶ (1) Pecuniary loss

17–041

No interest will be awarded for future pecuniary loss, because there has been no delay in receipt. For sums due from the date of the accident up to the date of trial, interest will be awarded at half the current short-term rate during that period to reflect the gradual nature of the loss.[181]

▶ (2) Non-pecuniary loss

17–042

Interest will be awarded at 2% from the date of service of proceedings to the date of trial.[182] The figure is deliberately low, because the only loss suffered is the inability to use the money prior to trial.[183]

Alternatives to lump sum payments

17–043

Damages will usually be awarded, as stated earlier, in the form of a lump sum. This does possess, however, a number of disadvantages. There is a distinct danger that a lump sum may run out due to poor investment, reckless spending, a higher than expected life expectancy, or inflation, leaving the claimant with insufficient funds to meet his or her needs. The lump sum is a "once-and-for-all" payment. This has led to calls for alternative forms of award which more closely reflect the actual needs of the claimant. Although there is already provision for provisional damages and interim awards, there is growing support for the use of periodical payments in certain cases. These will be examined below.

▶ (1) Provisional damages

17–044

Senior Courts Act 1981 s.32A[184] provides for provisional damages where it is proved or admitted that there is a chance that, at some definite or indefinite time in the future, the injured person will develop some serious disease, or suffer some serious deterioration in his or her physical or

---

award compound interest: Law Commission Consultation Paper No.167, *Compound Interest* (2002) and Report No.287, *Pre-judgment Interest on Debts and Damages* (2004).

181   See *Jefford v Gee* [1970] 2 Q.B. 130 at 151. *Cookson v Knowles* [1979] A.C. 556 applies the decision to fatal accident cases; guidelines approved in *A Train & Sons Ltd v Fletcher* [2008] EWCA Civ 413; [2008] 4 All E.R. 699.

182   See *Birkett v Hayes* [1982] 1 W.L.R. 816 and *Wright v British Railways Board* [1983] 2 A.C. 773. Affirmed in *L (a patient) v Chief Constable of Staffordshire* [2000] P.I.Q.R. Q349 CA, which rejected the argument based on Lord Lloyd's reasoning in *Wells v Wells* [1999] 1 A.C. 345 that the rate should also be set at the index-linked government securities rate.

183   Damages for non-pecuniary loss being assessed as at the date of trial.

184   Inserted by Administration of Justice Act 1982 s.6. See also CPR r.41.

mental condition. Damages will be awarded on the basis that the claimant's condition will not deteriorate, but that the claimant can return to court for further damages if this occurs. The claimant is only entitled, however, to apply once for further damages, and these must be for a disease or type of injury specified in the original action.[185]

In *Willson v Ministry of Defence*,[186] the plaintiff sued his employer following an injury to his ankle at work when he slipped on a polished floor. He applied for an award of provisional damages on the basis that there was a possibility that he would develop arthritis, which might require surgery. Scott Baker J refused to award provisional damages. The judge asked three questions:

- Was there a chance of deterioration?

- Would the deterioration be serious?

- Should the court exercise its discretion in the claimant's favour in the circumstances of the case?

Whilst the plaintiff had shown a chance of deterioration which was measurable, rather than fanciful, the judge held that "serious deterioration" required more than the ordinary progression of a disease. A clear and severable risk was required which would trigger entitlement to further compensation. Arthritis following an ankle injury was not such an event. Epilepsy following a head injury would, however, seem to satisfy this test.[187] In practice, therefore, provisional damages will very rarely be awarded.

(2) Interim payments

17-045

The court has also, under the Senior Courts Act 1981 s.32, a discretion to make an interim award prior to trial where the defendant has admitted liability to pay damages, the claimant has obtained judgment against the defendant with damages to be assessed, or where it is satisfied that claimant will obtain substantial damages at trial.[188] The court may order an interim payment to be paid in one sum or by instalments.[189]

---

185 Damages Act 1996 s.3 provides that a provisional award will not stop the victim's dependants from bringing a claim under the Fatal Accidents Act 1976, but any part of the provisional award which was intended to compensate the victim for pecuniary loss during a period that in the event falls after his or her death shall be taken into account in assessing the amount of any loss of support suffered by the dependants under the Act.

186 [1991] 1 All E.R. 638.

187 See *Wan v Fung* [2003] 7 CL 113 (QBD)—1–2% risk sufficient on the facts. See also *Chewings v Williams* [2009] EWHC 2490 (QB); [2010] P.I.Q.R. Q1 (real and not just fanciful chance that claimant would suffer further extremely serious physical damage as a result of chance he would seek surgery with real risk of complications leading to amputation of lower leg).

188 See CPR rr.25.6–25.9.

189 CPR r.25.6(7).

(3) Periodical payments and structured settlements

17–046 The option of a structured settlement has been available to claimants from 1988. Here, the idea is to structure the payment of damages such that the traditional lump sum would be replaced by an annuity (a form of insurance/investment which provides an annual sum of money over a period of time) purchased by the tortfeasor and managed by an assurance company.[190] The concept of the structured settlement received a boost in 1987 when the Inland Revenue indicated that the revenue from such annuities would not be taxed. On this basis, the recipient would receive income free from tax, and, if an index-linked annuity was chosen, protected against inflation. If the claimant's disability continued for a long time, there was also the possibility that the annuity as a whole might exceed any lump sum. It would also benefit the defendant's insurers, who might be able to negotiate a lower settlement to produce the necessary annual income. Lewis noted in 2006 that since 1988, more than 1500 seriously injured people had received part of their compensation via a structured settlement.[191]

Despite this, support subsequently arose for a more radical proposal, namely to give the court the power to award periodical payments instead of/in conjunction with a lump sum award.[192] Originally, the Damages Act 1996 s.2 provided that such awards could only be made with the consent of both parties.[193] As recognised by Lord Steyn, this provision was effectively a dead letter as the consent of both parties was virtually never forthcoming.[194] The majority of the Pearson Commission had recommended that the court should be obliged to award damages for future pecuniary loss caused by death or serious and lasting injury in the form of periodical payments, unless it is satisfied, on the application of the claimant, that a lump sum award would be more appropriate.[195] This proposal was not, however, adopted.

From 2000, however, the Lord Chancellor's Department in two Consultation Papers recommended that the courts should be given the power to order periodical payments for significant future financial loss, which should be reviewable in the light of changing medical or other exceptional circumstances.[196] These proposals formed the basis for the Courts Act 2003

---

190 See R. Lewis, *Structured Settlements: the Law and Practice* (Sweet and Maxwell, 1993) and Law Com. No.224 (1994), *Structured Settlements and Interim and Provisional Damages*. Following the Law Commission Report, structured settlements received legislative support in the Finance Act 1995 and Damages Act 1996.

191 See R. Lewis, "The politics and economics of tort law: Judicially imposed periodical payments of damages" (2006) 69 M.L.R. 418, 420.

192 Periodical payment orders (PPOs) are distinct from structured settlements in that damages do not have to be calculated as a lump sum which is then "structured" to purchase an annuity. Instead, the courts adopt a "bottom up" approach by which the court assesses the periodical payment the claimant will need for the future, regardless of the capital cost.

193 Damages Act 1996 s.2(1): "A court awarding damages in an action for personal injury may, with the consent of the parties, make an order under which the damages are wholly or partly to take the form of periodical payments".

194 Lord Steyn in *Wells v Wells* [1999] 1 A.C. 345 at 384.

195 *Royal Commission on Civil Liability and Compensation for Personal Injury*, Cmnd.7054 (1978), vol.1 para.576.

196 *The discount rate and alternatives to lump sum payments* (March 2000) and *Damages For Future Loss: Giving the Courts the Power to Order Periodical Payments for Future Loss and Care Costs in Personal Injury Cases* (March

ss.100–101, which came into force in April 2005, and replace the Damages Act 1996 ss.2, 4 and 5. The revised Damages Act 1996 s.2 now states that a court, in awarding damages for future pecuniary loss due to personal injury, "(a) may order that the damages are wholly or partly to take the form of periodical payments, and (b) shall consider whether to make that order".[197] With respect to other forms of damages, the rule remains that the consent of the parties is required.[198] In considering whether periodical payments are appropriate for all or part of an award of damages, the courts will look at all the circumstances of the case and in particular the form of award which best meets the claimant's needs.[199]

One particular concern has been the security of these future payments. What will happen, for example, if the defendant (or his or her insurers) becomes insolvent? Section 2(3) of the Act provides that no order should be made unless the court is satisfied that the continuity of payments is reasonably secure.[200]

Indexation

Controversy has arisen over one particular provision. Once the court considers that a periodical payment order is appropriate, the question of indexation, that is, the rate by which the payment should be increased to cover inflation, needs to be resolved. Section 2(8) provides that:

17–047

> **"An order for periodical payments shall be treated as providing for the amount of payments to vary by reference to the retail prices index."**

but is qualified by s.2(9) which allows for an order to include a provision which disapplies or modifies subs.(8). This raises the question as to the extent to which s.2(9) allows claimants to argue for a different index by which their payments should be updated.[201] Despite strong arguments that the RPI should be the ordinary index of choice until Parliament indicated

---

2002). Note also recommendations of the Master of the Rolls' Working Party on Structured Settlements in August 2002.

197 Damages Act 1996 s.2(1). Note, however, that this power only arises when the matter is before the court, that is, the court is giving judgment on damages or required to approve a settlement made on behalf of a minor or a person lacking capacity. It will not arise when the parties settle out of court.

198 Damages Act 1996 s.2(2).

199 CPR r.41.7. This directs the courts to have regard to the factors set out in the Practice Direction 41B(1) which include the scale of the annual payments taking into account any deduction for contributory negligence, and the form of award preferred by the claimant and defendant.

200 See E. Tomlinson and H. Smith, "Periodical payment orders" [2016] J.P.I. Law 243. See also ss.2(4)–(5).

201 Such an argument seems to conflict with the approach taken by the Court of Appeal in *Cooke v United Bristol Health Care* [2003] EWCA Civ 1370; [2004] 1 W.L.R. 251 discussed at 17–021 above. The latter issue was resolved in *Thompstone* (see below) by distinguishing *Cooke* on the basis that lump sums raised distinct investment questions to periodical payments.

otherwise,[202] the Court of Appeal in *Thompstone v Tameside and Glossop Acute Services NHS Trust*[203] sought to provide general guidance for future courts and accepted that in deciding what order would best meet the claimant's needs, the court should consider the RPI in the light of other alternative indexes.[204] In the cases before the court, the claimants had suffered severe injuries at birth as a result of negligence. In such actions, the main claim is likely to be for future care costs and expert evidence suggested that the wages of carers would increase at a faster rate than the RPI. There was thus a danger of the claimant receiving insufficient funds. In such circumstances, the principle of full compensation indicated that use of the ASHE 6115 index (annual earnings survey for care assistants and home carers) would be appropriate, fair and reasonable.

The Court of Appeal in *Thompstone* expressed its wish that the NHS and other defendants would now accept the appropriateness of indexation on the basis of ASHE 6115 in catastrophic injury cases and only seek to reopen the issue on production of significantly different evidence.[205] Its decision has undoubtedly rendered PPOs more popular with future claimants.[206]

Section 2B also provides for variation of orders and settlements. If there is a chance that at some time in the future the claimant will, as a result of the tortious act, develop some serious disease or suffer some serious deterioration or enjoy some significant improvement, the court may provide that the order for periodical payments may be varied.[207] These provisions largely reflect those which apply to provisional damages (see above), except significant improvements will also allow for variation and the defendant, as well as the claimant, may apply. It is anticipated that the use of such orders would be very limited.[208]

The aim of these reforms is to promote the widespread use of periodical payments for awards for future pecuniary loss in personal injury cases. It was described at the time as a "revolutionary change".[209] It is important to recognise, however, that such payments are aimed at

---

202 W. Norris [2005] J.P.I. Law 59.

203 [2008] EWCA Civ 5; [2008] P.I.Q.R. Q2, approving *Flora v Wakom (Heathrow) Ltd (formerly Abela Airline Catering Ltd)* [2006] EWCA Civ 1103; [2007] 1 W.L.R. 482. Comment: R. Lewis, "The indexation of periodical payments of damages in tort: the future assured?" (2010) 30 L.S. 391.

204 Suitability should be tested by the following criteria: (i) Accuracy of match of the particular data series to the loss or expenditure being compensated; (ii) Authority of the collector of the data; (iii) Statistical reliability; (iv) Accessibility; (v) Consistency over time; (vi) Reproducibility in the future; and (vii) Simplicity and consistency in application: [2008] EWCA Civ 5 at [75].

205 [2008] EWCA Civ 5 at [100]. ASHE 6115 was split in 2012 into two new codes: ASHE 6145 (care workers and carers) and ASHE 6146 (senior care workers).

206 See N. Bevan, "Future proof: Part 1" (2008) 158 N.L.J. 283: "This decision will propel the periodical payments regime from the backwaters into the mainstream as a means of delivering compensation for future loss in personal injury claims". See also C. Daykin, "Fair compensation needs actuaries" [2009] J.P.I. Law 48.

207 See Damages (Variation of Periodical Payments) Order 2005 (SI 2005/841) art.2.

208 See DCA Guidance at para.11. It should also be noted that art.7 of the Order provides that: "A party may make only one application to vary a variable order in respect of each specified disease or type of deterioration or improvement".

209 H. McGregor, *McGregor on Damages*, 17th edn (Sweet and Maxwell, 2003).

claimants with long-term or permanent personal injuries where a significant award for future care costs and loss of earnings will be made. They offer few advantages where the level of future loss is low or where the care is only needed for a short time. Most claimants will thus continue to be awarded lump sums. Nevertheless, in a 2013 consultation paper, the Ministry of Justice highlighted the benefits of periodical payments in rendering claimants more secure with a lifetime of payments as opposed to a lump sum whose estimation is often inaccurate,[210] and there is evidence post-*Thompstone* that PPOs are gaining in popularity in relation to most catastrophic injury claims.[211] The former Chair of Personal Injuries Bar Association has commented that PPOs are likely to be ordered for future care (and case management) in the vast majority of high value personal injury claims.[212]

Actions on Death

The death of a victim of a tort gives rise potentially to two different claims: claims from the deceased's estate and from those who were financially dependent on the deceased. Both will be examined below.

`17–048`

(1) Action by the deceased's estate

In Ch.16, we looked at the survival of actions for or against the deceased's estate. Such claims are governed by the provisions of the Law Reform (Miscellaneous Provisions) Act 1934. Section 1(1) of the 1934 Act provides for the general survival of actions in tort:

`17–049`

> ". . . all causes of action subsisting against or vested in [any person on death] shall survive against, or, as the case may be, for the benefit of [the] estate."

It is important to remember that this does not give the estate a cause of action for death itself. It simply means that the estate may pursue actions existing at the time of victim's death.

Damages for pecuniary and non-pecuniary losses up to the date of death may be recovered under the 1934 Act. Any claim for non-pecuniary loss will consist of pain and suffering and loss of amenity during any significant period between injury and death. No sum will be

---

210 *Damages Act 1996: The Discount Rate—Review of the Legal Framework* (Consultation Paper CP 3/2013), para.83.

211 C. Malla, "PPOs in catastrophic injury claims" [2013] J.P.I. Law 169.

212 R. Weir, "Periodical payment orders—where are we now?" [2014] J.P.I. Law 16.

awarded if death is instantaneous or quick.[213] Pecuniary loss may be claimed, but s.1(2)(a) excludes a claim for damages for loss of income in respect of any period after a person's death. Section 1(2)(a) also excludes any award of punitive damages.[214] Any loss or gain to the estate consequent on death will not be taken into account, but a sum in respect of funeral expenses may be claimed.[215] The Law Reform (Contributory Negligence) Act 1945 will also apply to such claims.

(2) Action by the deceased's dependants

17–050

There is a second possible claim arising from the death of the victim. This is a claim not by the deceased's legal representatives, but by those for whom the deceased provided financial support. For example, the death of a victim who is a father is likely to affect his family financially as well as emotionally. At common law, the rule was that the victim's death would not give a cause of action to other persons, even when they were financially dependent on the deceased.[216] However, legislation has intervened, first in the Fatal Accidents Act 1846 (also known as Lord Campbell's Act)[217] and more recently in the form of the Fatal Accidents Act 1976.

Fatal Accidents Act 1976

17–051

This consolidates earlier legislation. Sections 1(1) and (2) provide that:

> "(1) If death is caused by any wrongful act, neglect or default which is such as would (if death had not ensued) have entitled the person injured to maintain an action and recover damages in respect thereof, the person who would have been liable if death had not ensued shall be liable to an action for damages, notwithstanding the death of the person injured.
>
> (2) ... every such action shall be for the benefit of the dependants of the person ('the deceased') whose death has been so caused."

---

213 *Hicks v Chief Constable of South Yorkshire* [1992] 2 All E.R. 65.
214 Law Commission Report No.247, *Aggravated, exemplary and restitutionary damages* (1997), para.6.3 proposed that this should be repealed and the Act amended to allow claims to survive for the benefit of the estate of a deceased victim, but that they should not be available against a wrongdoer's estate.
215 Law Reform (Miscellaneous Provisions) Act 1934 s.1(2)(c).
216 See *Baker v Bolton* (1808) 1 Camp. 493; 170 E.R. 1033 where the plaintiff failed despite the fact that he "was much attached to his deceased wife and that, being a publican, she had been of great use to him in conducting his business". See also *The Amerika (Admiralty Commissioners v SS Amerika)* [1917] A.C. 38 HL.
217 For historical background, see P. Handford, "Lord Campbell and the Fatal Accidents Act" (2013) 129 L.Q.R. 420.

This is not particularly clear, but s.1 essentially provides an action for damages for the deceased's "dependants", i.e. the group of persons, defined in s.1(3), who were financially dependent on the deceased. The statute creates a hybrid action: it is the action of the dependants but relies on the fact that the deceased could have sued the tortfeasor. If the deceased's action would have failed, for example because the defendant had a good defence or could rely on a valid exclusion clause (unlikely in the event of death),[218] the dependants have no claim. Equally, if the deceased had settled the claim[219] or obtained judgment[220] prior to death,[221] then the dependants have no right of action. Under s.5 of the Act, any damages may be reduced due to the contributory negligence of the deceased. If the dependant has also contributed to the accident, the share of that particular dependant will also be reduced, but this will not affect other dependants.[222]

The dependants will not usually sue in their own right. Section 2 provides for the action to be brought by and in the name of the executor or administrator of the deceased. If there is no such person, or no action has been brought within six months after the demise of the deceased, then an action may be brought by and in the name of all or any of the dependants.[223]

The action, as stated above, is brought on behalf of the deceased's dependants. The court must be satisfied that each dependant:

- is a dependant within s.1(3) of the Act; and

- was, as a matter of fact, financially dependent on the deceased.

Only if the court is satisfied on (1) and (2) will any sum be awarded. Each question will be examined in turn.

(1) Is the claimant a dependant within s.1(3) of the Act?

17–052

Section 1(3) (as amended by the Administration of Justice Act 1982 and Civil Partnership Act 2004) gives a statutory list of those parties classified by law as dependants, namely:

---

218 Unfair Contract Terms Act 1977 s.2(1) and Consumer Rights Act 2015 s. 65(1) render invalid notices excluding liability in negligence for personal injury and death in relation to business and consumer liability respectively—see para.16–011.
219 *Read v Great Eastern Ry* (1868) L.R. 3 Q.B. 555.
220 *Murray v Shuter* [1976] Q.B. 972.
221 But not where the deceased's solicitors had negligently discontinued his action *after* his death which does not extinguish the dependants' FAA claim: *Reader v Molesworths Bright Clegg* [2007] EWCA Civ 169; [2007] 1 W.L.R. 1082.
222 *Dodds v Dodds* [1978] Q.B. 543.
223 s.2(2), although not more than one action shall lie for and in respect of the same subject matter of complaint (s.2(3), but note broader interpretation under *Cachia v Faluyi* [2001] EWCA Civ 998; [2001] 1 W.L.R. 1966).

- the spouse or former spouse of the deceased[224];

- the civil partner or former civil partner of the deceased[225];

- a common law spouse, i.e. a person who was living with the deceased in the same household immediately before the date of the death and had been living with the deceased in the same household for at least two years before that date and was living during the whole of that period as the husband or wife or civil partner of the deceased;

- the deceased's parents, ascendants or anyone treated by the deceased as a parent;

- the deceased's children (including any person treated as a child of the family in relation to a marriage/civil partnership to which the deceased was at any time a party) and other descendants; and

- any person who is, or is the issue of, a brother, sister, uncle or aunt of the deceased.

Section 1(5) adds that for the purposes of subs.(3) above:

- any relationship by marriage or civil partnership shall be treated as a relationship of consanguinity (i.e. blood), any relationship of the half blood as a relationship of the whole blood, and the stepchild of any person as his child; and

- an illegitimate person shall be treated as (i) the legitimate child of his mother and reputed father or (ii) in the case of a person who has a female parent by virtue of s.43 of the Human Fertilisation and Embryology Act 2008,[226] the legitimate child of his mother and that female parent.

As can be seen, the above list has been extended to cover stepchildren, adopted and illegitimate children, some cohabitees and, from 2005, civil partners. The provision in relation to cohabitees, brought in under the 1982 amendment, still leaves much to chance,[227] and is further weakened by s.3(4), which states that under s.1(3)(b) [iii above], in assessing damages:

---

224 Including a person whose marriage to the deceased had been annulled or declared void as well as a person whose marriage to the deceased has been dissolved: s.1(4). See also s.1(4A) for former civil partners.

225 s.1(3)(aa), as inserted by the Civil Partnership Act 2004. This includes a person whose civil partnership with the deceased has been annulled as well as a person whose civil partnership with the deceased has been dissolved: s.1(4A).

226 s.1(5)(b)(ii) was added by virtue of the Marriage (Same Sex Couples) Act 2013 (Consequential and Contrary Provisions and Scotland) Order 2014 (SI 2014/560).

227 See, e.g. *Kotke v Saffarini* [2005] EWCA Civ 221; [2005] 2 F.L.R. 517 (claimant unable to obtain compensation for the death of her partner, despite the fact that the relationship had lasted some years and they had a child

> "there shall be taken into account . . . the fact that the dependant had no enforceable right to financial support by the deceased as a result of their living together."[228]

This means that the award for a cohabitee is likely to be lower than for a lawful spouse or civil partner. The Law Commission, in its 1999 report, *Claims for Wrongful Death*, recommended adding a further class of claimant to the s.1(3) list, namely any individual:

> "who was being wholly or partly maintained by the deceased immediately before the death or who would, but for the death, have been so maintained at a time beginning after the death."[229]

This would be a considerable improvement, fitting neatly with the Commission's stated aim of bringing this area of law into line with the values of modern society. The then government, in its 2007 response, supported only the first part of this test: persons wholly or partly maintained by the deceased immediately before death.[230] Subsequent governments have not, however, implemented these changes.[231]

(2) Was the claimant financially dependent on the deceased?

17-053

Even if the individual is within s.1(3), the court will only make an award if it is shown that the individual was financially dependent on the deceased. It is the financial, not emotional, dependency of the claimant on the deceased which is in question.[232] The assessment of damages is dealt with under s.3, which provides that damages should be awarded "as are proportioned to the injury resulting from the death to the dependants respectively". This is far from clear. It seems that the courts will examine whether the individual had a reasonable expectation of pecuniary benefit, as of right or otherwise, from the deceased.[233] This will be assessed at the

---

together due to failure to satisfy s.1(3)(b) test). Section 1(3)(b) has, however, been found to be consistent with ECHR arts 8 and 14: *Swift v Secretary of State for Justice* [2013] EWCA Civ 193; [2014] Q.B. 373.

228 The Government in its 2007 Consultation Paper, *The Law on Damages* had proposed that s.3(4) should be repealed and replaced by a provision to the effect that the prospect of breakdown in the relationship between the deceased and his or her partner should not be taken into account when assessing damages under the FAA.

229 para.3.45; Draft Bill, cl.1. A person is treated as being wholly or partly maintained by another if that person "otherwise than for full valuable consideration, was making a substantial contribution in money or money's worth towards his reasonable needs".

230 *The Law on Damages*, Ch.1 (CP 09/07, May 2007). The second part of the definition was rejected as meeting no significant need, being too open-ended and encouraging loosely framed and speculative claims: at para.8.

231 Ministry of Justice, "Civil Law Reform Bill: Response to Consultation" (2011).

232 See Latham LJ in *Thomas v Kwik Save Stores Ltd* The Times 27 June 2000.

233 See, e.g. *Davies v Taylor* [1974] A.C. 207 where a wife, who had deserted her husband, failed to show some significant prospect, rather than a mere speculative possibility, of a reconciliation with her husband had he

date of death.[234] Public policy will exclude some forms of benefit, for example if the deceased provided for his family by means of armed robberies.[235] It will be a matter of common sense. For example, if the deceased child helped out in the family business, or the deceased spouse cared for the children and the home, the court will award a sum representing the benefit given to the family. However, if the child was employed by the family business and received a wage, then it would be a different matter, since the family has not suffered any financial loss.[236] The court will have to look at the prospects of the deceased (as we saw in personal injury claims), but also this time the prospects of the dependants. For example, if a husband dies and leaves an elderly wife who was financially dependent on him, then the length of the dependency is unlikely to be long. Equally, children are (hopefully) not financially dependent forever, and account must be made for their increasing independence as they grow older.

One point of controversy has been in estimating the likely period of dependency of a widow. If she remarries, then she has a right to be supported by her new husband and would be overcompensated if she could also claim loss of dependency under the Act. However, the only way to prevent this overcompensation was for the court to estimate the widow's likelihood of remarrying and reduce damages accordingly. It is clearly somewhat objectionable for the court to be seen to assess the widow's possible value on the marriage market, and in view of this, the law was changed by the Law Reform (Miscellaneous Provisions) Act 1971. Fatal Accidents Act 1976 s.3(3) now provides that the court should not take into account the remarriage of the widow or her prospects of remarriage. Arguably, this goes too far in ignoring the fact that the widow may have remarried prior to trial, but if this was not included, the inevitable result would be the postponement of such marriages until after the trial.

Again, this problem was addressed by the Law Commission in their 1999 report, *Claims for Wrongful Death* whose proposals were considered by the then government in its 2007 Consultation Paper, *The Law on Damages*. The Commission recommended that s.3(3) should be repealed, and the fact of a marriage or financially supportive cohabitation taken into account when relevant.[237] This removes the problem of overcompensation, but does not mean a return to pre–1971 law. The Commission proposed that unless a person is engaged to be married at the time of trial, the prospect that he or she will marry, remarry, or enter into financially supportive cohabitation with a new partner, should not be taken into account when assessing the claim.[238] Neither should the prospect of divorce or breakdown in the relationship be taken

----

lived. Consider also *Welsh Ambulance Service NHS Trust v Williams* [2008] EWCA Civ 81, family members, who worked for family business but received benefits far exceeding the value of their services due to profits created by deceased, deemed dependants.

234 On this basis, a dependant cannot by his own conduct after death reduce the value of the dependency: *Welsh Ambulance Service NHS Trust v Williams* [2008] EWCA Civ 81, dependency of family members not reduced despite the fact they had successfully taken over the family business.

235 See *Burns v Edman* [1970] 2 Q.B. 541.

236 *Sykes v North Eastern Ry* (1875) 44 L.J.C.P. 191.

237 Note also the compromise position taken by the High Court of Australia in *De Sales v Ingrilli* (2002) 193 A.L.R. 130.

238 para.4.53, Draft Bill, cll.4 and 6(5).

into account, unless the couple were no longer living together at the time of death, or one of the couple had petitioned for divorce, judicial separation or nullity.[239] The then government agreed in part to these proposals. It endorsed the proposals on divorce or breakdown of the relationship and recommended that the fact of a person's remarriage, entry into a civil partnership and, possibly, financially supportive cohabitation of at least two years following death should be taken into account. This seems a valid compromise and would have been a welcome development. Nevertheless, subsequent governments have not proceeded with these reforms.

Assessment

17–054

The courts adopt an approach similar to that used in the assessment of awards for future pecuniary loss in a personal injury claim. Again, the claimant will receive a lump sum, which represents the loss of dependency of that particular claimant (although a court in practice will tend to determine the total liability of the defendant and then apportion damages between the various dependants). The court will use the multiplier/multiplicand method. This time the multiplicand will be the net loss of support, namely the deceased's net income less expenditure on his or her own behalf.[240] This will be multiplied by the multiplier. The multiplier will take account of the possible duration of the support, based on the likelihood of continued provision by the deceased and factors such as the life expectancy of the dependant (for example, if the dependant is a widow) or likely period of dependency (for example, if the dependant is a child). It will also be reduced for accelerated receipt.

The multiplier will be set at the date of trial as is the case in personal injury claims. In *Knauer v Ministry of Justice*, the Supreme Court overturned previous authority suggesting that it should be set at the date of death due to the added uncertainty of what would have happened to the deceased prior to trial.[241] The previous rule, while straightforward, had created a problem of under-compensation for pre-trial losses which, under the multiplier, would be discounted for early receipt which, of course, did not in fact occur.[242] Bearing in mind that the courts now have access to actuarial evidence or tables and more sophisticated methods of calculating damages, the Supreme Court unanimously took the view that it was right to change the law.

---

239 para.4.66, Draft Bill, cl.4.
240 See *Harris v Empress Motors* [1984] 1 W.L.R. 212 at 216–217 per O'Connor LJ.
241 [2016] UKSC 9; [2016] A.C. 908, overturning *Cookson v Knowles* [1979] A.C. 556 and *Graham v Dodds* [1983] 1 W.L.R. 808.
242 For criticism, see Nelson J in *White v ESAB Group (UK) Ltd* [2002] P.I.Q.R. Q6 and the 1999 Law Commission Report, *Claims for Wrongful Death*.

> ### Deductions

17-055

Again, concerns as to overcompensation arise when the deceased's dependants receive money, such as insurance or a widow's pension, from other sources which reduce their financial losses. Here the position is far simpler than for personal injury. Section 4 of the Act provides that:

> **"benefits which have accrued or will or may accrue to any person from his estate or otherwise as a result of his death shall be disregarded."[243]**

In *Arnup v MW White Ltd*,[244] Smith LJ clarified that all benefits received as a result of death were to be disregarded. A defendant providing dependants with ex gratia financial support could only avoid this result and have the payment taken into account when damages are assessed if the payment was made subject to the stipulation that it was a conditional payment on account. This is very generous (and may be contrasted with the position relating to damages for personal injury described above). Whilst it may be welcomed for its simplicity, it will result in some dependants being overcompensated at the expense of the State or insurance company.

Unfortunately, the apparent simplicity of s.4 has been thrown into question by two Court of Appeal decisions which interpret the meaning of "benefit" in that section somewhat differently. In *Stanley v Saddique*,[245] the Court of Appeal was asked whether, in awarding a child damages under the Act following the death of his mother, account should be taken of the fact that his father had remarried soon after his mother's death, and that he received better care from his stepmother. It was argued that this was a benefit which accrued as a result of his mother's death and should be disregarded under s.4. Such a benefit is indirect at best, but the court was prepared to give "benefit" a wide meaning and held that it was not confined to direct payments in money or money's worth. It would include the benefit of absorption into a new family unit of father, stepmother and siblings. On this basis, the child was able to recover damages for the loss of his mother's care, even though he was currently receiving better care from his stepmother. A further implication of *Stanley* is that the benefit of a widow or widower remarrying should be regarded as a "benefit" under s.4 and disregarded. This renders s.3(3) defunct.

17-056

Stanley can be contrasted with the court's decision in *Hayden v Hayden*.[246] Here, the child's mother had been killed in an accident caused by the negligent driving of the defendant, the

---

243 As amended by Administration of Justice Act 1982 s.3(1). Social Security (Recovery of Benefits) Regulations 1997 (SI 1997/2205) reg.2(2)(a) also provides that the recovery provisions for social security benefits do not apply to fatal accidents claims. See *McIntyre v Harland & Wolff Plc* [2006] EWCA Civ 287; [2006] 1 W.L.R. 2577 for a literal interpretation of the section.

244 [2008] EWCA Civ 447; [2008] I.C.R. 1064: refusal to deduct sums paid to dependants from death in service benefit scheme and discretionary trust by defendant employer.

245 [1992] Q.B. 1.

246 [1992] 1 W.L.R. 986.

child's father. As a result, the defendant gave up work and looked after the child himself, who was four years old at the time of the accident. The majority (McCowan LJ dissenting) held that s.4 did not apply in this case, and therefore the care given by the father would be taken into account when assessing loss of care. The majority judges adopted different reasoning, however. Croom-Johnson LJ (who had also given judgment in *Stanley*) held that *Stanley* could be distinguished on the facts. In *Stanley*, death had led to an unstable relationship being replaced by a successful marriage, whereas in *Hayden* the child remained in the family home with her father, who continued to look after her. The continuing care of a father could not be regarded as a benefit accruing as a result of death. Parker LJ, in contrast, chose not to follow *Stanley* in reaching his conclusion,[247] and found that no loss had in fact been suffered when the child enjoyed uninterrupted care.

The law was left far from clear after *Hayden*. The Divisional Court in *R. v Criminal Injuries Compensation Board Ex p. K*[248] reviewed the conflict between the two cases and preferred the decision in *Stanley*. *Hayden* was distinguished on its own particular facts, namely that it concerned a situation where the replacement care was provided by the tortfeasor who was an existing carer, who had been looking after the child prior to her mother's death. *Hayden* was further isolated by the Court of Appeal in the later case of *H v S*.[249] Again, the children had been cared for by their father after the death of their mother, but in this case, the parents had been divorced, and the father had lived separately with his new wife. He had, in fact, offered no financial support to the children prior to their mother's death. The court distinguished *Hayden*. It could not be argued that the father was discharging pre-existing parental obligations where he had not supported his children in the past and had shown no real likelihood of doing so in the future. On such a basis, his care was a "benefit" resulting from death which could be disregarded by the court. The situation would have been different, however, if the parents had been living together before the death, or there had been a financial order[250] or actual/potential support in place before the mother died.[251]

H v S thus supports the general proposition that the tortfeasor should not be allowed to benefit from the generosity of a third party volunteering to care gratuitously for the victim's dependants by a reduction in the damages awarded. The term "benefit" is thus a disguised claim for the cost of care to be held on trust for the carer by the claimant (see *Hunt v Severs*, above). Yet, in this light, it becomes increasingly difficult to understand why an immediate

---

247 Relying on the pre-s.4 case of *Hay v Hughes* [1975] Q.B. 790 CA. This was disapproved by the Divisional Court in *R. v Criminal Injuries Compensation Board Ex p. K* [1999] Q.B. 1131. Parker LJ also added as a postscript that difficulties would arise in any event where the carer was in fact the tortfeasor; a reason which the Divisional Court did support (see below).

248 [1999] Q.B. 1131. It may be noted that the case concerned a claim to the Criminal Injuries Compensation Board. However, the courts use similar criteria to those adopted in ordinary civil claims for damages and so the issue was in point.

249 [2002] EWCA Civ 792; [2003] Q.B. 965.

250 There was a maintenance order in place against the father, but solely for a nominal sum which the court decided to ignore.

251 See also *L v Barry May Haulage* [2002] P.I.Q.R. Q3.

family member (as in *Hayden*) undertaking greater parental duties should be denied the cost of his care whilst an uncle or estranged father will succeed, unless his claim is to be excluded due to the fact he or she is the tortfeasor.[252] It would seem to penalise parents taking their parental responsibilities seriously. Clarification of the status of cost of care claims for dependants, removed from the artificial wording of s.4, would be a welcome addition to the law.

The operation of s.4 was examined by the Law Commission in their report, *Claims for Wrongful Death*. The Commission's proposal was radical. Section 4 should be repealed and the position in fatal accident claims made consistent with that in personal injury claims. On this basis, charity, insurance, survivors' pensions and inheritance would continue to be non-deductible.[253] The Commission also recommended extending the recoupment of social security benefits to claims under the Fatal Accidents Act. Whilst this makes economic sense and would clarify the law, it is unlikely to prove popular with the public, as it would have a significant impact on the level of dependants' claims. It was not adopted by the then government in its 2007 Consultation Paper on damages.

> ### Damages for bereavement

17–057   It should be noted that under s.1A of the Act (as inserted by the Administration of Justice Act 1982 s.3 and amended by the Civil Partnership Act 2004), bereavement damages will be awarded to:

- the spouse or civil partner of the deceased (s.1A(2)(a)); or

- the parents (the mother only if the child is illegitimate) of a minor who was never married or a civil partner (s.1A(2)(b)).[254]

This is a rare example of a third party succeeding in a claim for mental distress, which is generally not recoverable in the law of torts, although it is important to note that the claimant need not prove actual distress.[255] It is in reality a form of consolatory damages. This is shown

---

252 Assuming, of course, the correctness of *Hunt v Severs* [1994] 2 A.C. 350.

253 para.5.39, Draft Bill, cl.5.

254 Parents of an adult deceased may, however, be able to claim damages under the Human Rights Act 1998 against a public authority for breach ECHR art.2: see *Rabone v Pennine Care NHS Foundation Trust* [2012] UKSC 2; [2012] 2 A.C. 72. It may be questioned whether the Supreme Court was correct to see the remedy granted under the HRA 1998 as an alternative action to that in tort or whether the HRA 1998 claim potentially undermines the policy underlying the bereavement provisions of the FAA 1976: see A. Tettenborn, "Wrongful death, human rights, and the Fatal Accidents Act" (2012) 128 L.Q.R. 327.

255 For claims for mental distress in tort generally, see P. Giliker, "A 'new' head of damages: damages for mental distress in the English law of torts" (2000) 20 L.S. 19; E. Descheemaeker, "Rationalising Recovery for Emotional harm in tort law" (2018) 134 L.Q.R. 602.

by the relatively low amount awarded, which is increased periodically: the current figure as at May 2020 is £15,120.[256] The sum will be awarded to the spouse/civil partner or between the parents equally[257] and the claim does not survive for the benefit of the recipient's estate on death.[258]

Section 1A does not, unlike s.1(3), extend to cohabitees. In *Smith v Lancashire Teaching Hospitals NHS Trust*,[259] Ms Smith had lived with the deceased for 11 years prior to his death and claimed that denying her bereavement damages was contrary to Art.14 ECHR (prohibition of discrimination) read in conjunction with art.8 (respect for family life). The Court of Appeal agreed and made a declaration of incompatibility under s.4 Human Rights Act 1998 between s.1A(2)(a) of the FAA 1976 and the ECHR on the basis that it excluded cohabitees of more than two years. Declarations of incompatibility, however, do not change the law—it is up to Parliament whether it wishes to respond and change the law. To date, no such change has been made despite strong calls that, in the light of *Smith*, s.1A is no longer fit for purpose.

Calls for change are not, however, new. In 1999, the Law Commission, in its report, *Claims for Wrongful Death*, proposed a significant reform of bereavement damages. First of all, their availability should be extended to include the child of the deceased (including adoptive children), the parents of the deceased (including adoptive parents), a fiancé(e), a brother or sister of the deceased (including adoptive brothers and sisters) and a cohabitee who lived with the deceased for not less than two years immediately prior to the accident.[260] This latter provision would include same sex relationships. Secondly, the Commission recommended that the sum should be increased and linked to the Retail Prices Index.[261] The award would be reduced if the deceased had been contributorily negligent.

In its 2007 consultation paper, *The Law on Damages*, the then Labour Government announced its intention to increase the award of bereavement damages on a regular basis in line with the Retail Prices Index (rounded to the nearest £100). By increasing the sum every three years in line with inflation, the Government sought to ensure a regular and consistent increase which would assist insurers and the NHS in building the effect of future increases into their reserves and financial plans. Consistent with this intention, the amount has been consistently raised. It also proposed, in the light of the 2005 extension of bereavement damages to civil partners, a more limited extension to that put forward by the Law Commission: to children of the deceased under 18 at the time of death half the full award and the full award to any person living with the deceased as spouse/civil partner for at least two years immediately

---

256 See Damages for Bereavement (Variation of Sum) (England and Wales) Order 2020 (SI 2020/316) art.2 (from 1 May 2020). This is an increase from the previous sum of £12,980: see Damages for Bereavement (Variation of Sum) (England and Wales) Order 2013 (SI 2013/510) art.2.

257 s.1A(4).

258 Law Reform (Miscellaneous Provisions) Act 1934 s.1(1A).

259 [2017] EWCA Civ 1916; [2018] Q.B. 804.

260 para.6.31, Draft Bill, cl.2.

261 Such damages would be capped at £30,000 and, if there are more than three claimants, apportioned accordingly: paras 6.41–6.51, Draft Bill, cl.2.

prior to the accident[262] and to unmarried fathers with parental responsibility.[263] The proposal to extend the category of recipients has not been implemented.

Actions for Loss or Damage to Property

17–058 This will be dealt with briefly. Loss or damage to property is subject to the same compensatory principles outlined above: to put, as far as possible, the claimant in the position as if the tort had not taken place.[264] Where the property has been totally destroyed, the courts will assess the market value of the property at the time and place of its destruction. The market value is the sum of money required to enable the claimant to purchase a replacement in the market at the price prevailing at the date of destruction or as soon thereafter as is reasonable. The claimant will also be able to claim consequential damages, provided they are not too remote. A good example may be found in the case of *Liesbosch Dredger v SS Edison*.[265] Here, the plaintiffs' dredger had been sunk as a result of the defendants' negligence. The court awarded the plaintiffs the market value of a comparable dredger, the cost of adapting the new dredger, insuring it and transporting it to where they were working, and compensation for disturbance and loss in carrying out their contract work from the date of the loss until a substitute dredger could reasonably have been available for use. A claimant will also be able to claim for such things as the reasonable amount of hire of a substitute until a replacement can be bought.[266] The claimant is unlikely to be awarded the cost of restoration of the property, unless there are exceptional circumstances, for example that there is no market for the property destroyed.[267]

If the property is merely damaged, then the court will award a sum for the diminution in value of the property, normally assessed as the cost of repair.[268] The cost of repair will normally be calculated at the time of damage, but there are exceptions to this rule where it would lead to injustice,[269] for example where it is reasonable for the claimant to postpone repairs

---

262 Should the deceased have both a spouse/partner from whom s/he is separated and a cohabiting partner of over 2 years duration, the sum will be divided between the 2: at para.64.
263 Government Consultation Paper, *The Law on Damages* (CP 09/07, May 2007) Ch.2.
264 *Livingstone v Rawyards Coal Co* (1880) 5 App. Cas. 25 at 39 per Lord Blackburn.
265 [1933] A.C. 449. The case is also authority for the rule that losses incurred due to impecuniosity are not recoverable. This rule was overturned by the House of Lords in *Lagden v O'Connor* [2003] UKHL 64; [2004] 1 A.C. 1067 on the basis that the law has moved on and that such a rule would be inconsistent with the general rules of remoteness: see Lord Hope at [61]–[62].
266 See *Moore v DER Ltd* [1971] 1 W.L.R. 1476.
267 *Hall v Barclay* [1937] 3 All E.R. 620.
268 *The London Corp* [1935] P. 70.
269 See Lord Wilberforce in *Miliangos v George Frank (Textiles) Ltd* [1976] A.C. 443 at 468.

to a later date.[270] The cost of repair will only be awarded if reasonable in the circumstances. Consistent with the duty to mitigate, the court will not award such damages if they exceed the market value of the goods, although allowance is made if the goods are unique.[271] If the claimant reasonably intends to sell the property in its damaged state, the court will not award the cost of repair, but a sum representing the diminution in capital value of the property. Consequential damages may be awarded, such as cost of substitute hire[272] and loss of use during the period of repairs.

Joint and Several Liability

17-059

So far, we have looked at damages generally. This section will examine the legal position where two or more defendants are liable for the *same damage*,[273] that is, where two or more defendants have committed concurrent torts which lead to a single indivisible injury.[274] This is distinct from the situation where the claimant has suffered different injuries due to the independent actions of two or more people—here it is for the claimant to bring independent claims against each of them. Our situation is where A has suffered one set of injuries resulting from an incident where both D1 and D2 are at fault, for example A was hit when crossing the road because of a car crash between two cars negligently driven by D1 and D2. Here the defendants are said to be jointly and severally liable. This means that the claimant has the choice to sue one or all of the defendants. In either case, the claimant will receive the full amount of damages. Therefore, if A suffered damages assessed at £300,000, A could sue D1 for this sum. If successful, D1 would then have to bring a claim against D2 for his share of the damages due.

270 *Dodd Properties (Kent) Ltd v Canterbury City* Council [1980] 1 W.L.R. 433 where it made commercial good sense to delay repairs until the time when the action had been heard and liability decided. See also *Alcoa Minerals of Jamaica Inc v Broderick* [2002] 1 A.C. 371 PC.

271 See *O'Grady v Westminster Scaffolding* [1962] 2 Lloyd's Rep. 238: 1938 MG car known as Mademoiselle Hortensia!

272 Although the court will seek proof that the goods were indeed hired and that the price paid was reasonable: *HL Motorworks (Willesden) Ltd v Alwahbi* [1977] R.T.R. 276 CA. On the use of credit hire companies, see the House of Lords in *Dimond v Lovell* [2002] 1 A.C. 384 and *Lagden v O'Connor* [2003] UKHL 64; [2004] 1 A.C. 1067 (cost of credit hire agreement recoverable when claimant could not afford hire of a private car while his car was being repaired, but note the limitations: *Beechwood Birmingham Ltd v Hoyer Group UK Ltd* [2010] EWCA Civ 647; [2011] Q.B. 357 (motor dealer with substantial stock of alternative vehicle denied cost of hire)).

273 "Same damage" is be interpreted according to its natural and ordinary meaning and does not extend to substantially or materially similar damage: *Royal Brompton Hospital NHS Trust v Hammond (No.3)* [2002] UKHL 14; [2002] 1 W.L.R. 1397. For discussion of the application of the principle of joint and several liability to victims of mesothelioma and asbestosis, see Ch.6.

274 *Rahman v Arearose Ltd* [2001] Q.B. 351 CA, although the application of the rule in this case is questionable: comment T. Weir [2001] C.L.J. 237.

Alternatively, A could sue both D1 and D2 for this sum. The aim is that the claimant can sue any of the defendants without worrying whether all the possible defendants are in court and is able to avoid defendants who have no funds or are uninsured. It is of no concern to the claimant that one defendant is paying for liability for which he or she is only partially at fault.

It will, however, be seen differently from the perspective of the defendant who is the only person sued, but in fact only partially at fault. This situation is now governed by the Civil Liability (Contribution) Act 1978.[275] Section 1(1) provides that:

> **"any person liable in respect of any damage suffered by another person may recover a contribution from any other person liable in respect of the same damage."**

Liability includes liability in tort, for breach of contract, breach of trust or otherwise.[276] The defendant (D1) may therefore claim a contribution from any other wrongdoer (D2) responsible for the "same damage" for the amount by which his payment to the claimant exceeds his responsibility for the loss.[277] The contribution must be claimed, however, within the limitation period of two years.[278]

Assessment

17–060

Section 2 deals with assessment of contribution. Section 2(1) provides that:

> **"in any proceedings under s.1 above the amount of the contribution recoverable from any person shall be such as may be found by the court to be just and equitable having regard to the extent of that person's responsibility for the damage in question."**

This is very similar to the wording of the Law Reform (Contributory Negligence) Act 1945 s.1 and the same principles seem to apply.[279] The courts will look at causation, and at times, the

---

275 See generally T. Dugdale, "The Civil Liability (Contribution) Act" (1979) 42 M.L.R. 182 and Law Commission, *Report on Contribution* No.79 (1977).

276 Civil Liability (Contribution) Act 1978 s.6(1).

277 D1 is entitled to recover a contribution "notwithstanding that he has ceased to be liable in respect of the damage in question since the time when the damage occurred, provided that he was liable immediately before he made or was ordered or agreed to make the payment in respect of which the contribution is sought": s.1(2).

278 Limitation Act 1980 s.10. Time runs from the date on which the right to a contribution accrues, which is the date on which the judgment is given, the date of the arbitration award or the date on which the amount of settlement is agreed between the defendant and the person to whom the payment is to be made: ss.10(3), (4) of the 1980 Act.

279 In *Hughes v Williams (deceased)* [2013] EWCA Civ 455; [2013] P.I.Q.R. P17, e.g. the Court of Appeal found that

blameworthiness of the defendants involved.[280] The court has a considerable discretion and may even, if it considers it appropriate, at one extreme, exempt the defendant from any liability to make a contribution or, at the other extreme, direct that the contribution to be recovered from any person shall amount to a complete indemnity.[281] The court will also take into account any defence of contributory negligence, any enforceable exclusion clause[282] and any statutory limits on liability which the other wrongdoer could have used against the original claimant.[283] The Act also does not stop any tortfeasor contracting to indemnify him or herself against liability for contribution.[284]

By this means, the claimant is fully compensated, and it is for the defendants to sort out the division of responsibility between them. A good example is *Fitzgerald v Lane*,[285] discussed in Chs 6 and 16, where the plaintiff had negligently stepped out into traffic on busy road and had been struck by a vehicle driven by the first defendant, which pushed him into the path of the second defendant's car. Both the defendants were negligent, but the plaintiff had also been contributorily negligent in not looking properly before crossing the road. The House of Lords held the plaintiff to be 50% contributorily negligent. It then examined the position of the two defendants and found that they were jointly and severally liable, but that each of them was 25% responsible for the injuries. Thus, if only one defendant had been sued, he would have been liable to the claimant for 50% of the damages due, but could have claimed a contribution from the other driver of 25%. In practice, the parties will attempt to get all other relevant parties before the court, and a defendant may take advantage of the "third party" procedure to add a defendant to the case, even when that person has not been mentioned in the claimant's statement of case.[286]

Settlements

The 1978 Act also makes special provision for settlements. A settlement does not deprive a defendant, who has agreed to make a payment in bona fide settlement or compromise of the claim, from seeking a contribution from any other parties he or she believes liable for the

17–061

---

the trial judge had been correct to apply the guidelines found in the contributory negligence case of *Froom v Butcher* [1976] Q.B. 286 (discussed in Ch.16).

280 See *Madden v Quirk* [1989] 1 W.L.R. 702; *Re-Source America International Ltd v Platt Site Services Ltd* [2004] EWCA Civ 665; [2004] N.P.C. 89 and *Brian Warwicker Partnership Plc v HOK International Ltd* [2005] EWCA Civ 962; [2006] P.N.L.R. 5: causative responsibility is likely to be the most important factor, but the court can consider non-causative fault.

281 Civil Liability (Contribution) Act 1978 s.2(2). Apportionment by the trial judge will only be interfered with on appeal where it is clearly wrong or where there has been an error in principle or a mistake of fact: *Kerry v Carter* [1969] 1 W.L.R. 1372 at 1376.

282 Subject to the statutory controls discussed in Ch.16.

283 Civil Liability (Contribution) Act 1978 s.2(3).

284 Civil Liability (Contribution) Act 1978 s.7(3).

285 [1989] A.C. 328.

286 See now Civil Procedure Rules Pt 19: Parties and group litigation.

same damage.[287] However, a settlement with one defendant which is "full and final and in satisfaction of all causes of action" may prevent the claimant from pursuing other tortfeasors responsible for the same damage,[288] although much depends on the context and the actual words used.[289]

Other Remedies

Self-help

17–062

Reference should be made to earlier chapters which discussed other remedies available for specific torts. Readers should specifically note occasions where the claimant can resort to self-help. In Ch.10, we looked at abatement in nuisance, and in Ch.11 we saw that the claimant may use reasonable force to resist trespass. However, such rights should be exercised with extreme caution. Overstepping the mark can lead to legal action, as the householder found in *Revill v Newbery*[290] when he was found liable to a burglar while seeking to defend his allotment shed with a gun (see Chs 8, 11 and 16). This section will concentrate on the equitable remedy of an injunction.

Injunctions

17–063

Injunctions are an important tool by which the court can order the defendant to stop a continuing or recurring act, or order the defendant to act in a certain way. The courts will only grant an injunction if the claimant has a good cause of action; the most obvious examples being nuisance or trespass.[291] It is an equitable remedy and so lies at the discretion of the court. An injunction cannot be demanded as of right and will not be awarded where damages are an adequate remedy, or where the claimant's conduct is such that it would not be equitable to make such an award. The court also has the option to award damages in addition to or in substitution for an injunction,[292] but the courts have traditionally only awarded damages instead

---

287 Provided the defendant would have been liable assuming that the factual basis of the claim against him could be established: see s.1(4). For the impact of a settlement on potential claims by the victim's dependants, see *Jameson v CECB (No.1)* [2000] 1 A.C. 455.

288 See *Jameson v CECB (No.1)* [2000] 1 A.C. 455 HL.

289 *Heaton v Axa Equity & Law Life Assurance Society Plc* [2002] UKHL 15; [2002] 2 A.C. 329.

290 [1996] Q.B. 567.

291 Injunctive relief is not generally granted for negligence, but see J. Murphy, "Rethinking injunctions in tort law" (2007) 27 O.J.L.S. 509.

292 See now Senior Courts Act 1981 s.50.

of (or "in lieu of") an injunction in exceptional circumstances. In *Shelfer v City of London Electric Lighting Co*,[293] A.L. Smith LJ indicated four conditions which would lead a court to grant damages in lieu of an injunction:

- where the injury to the claimant's legal rights is small;

- where the injury is capable of being estimated in money;

- where it can be adequately compensated by a small money payment; and

- where it would be oppressive to the defendant to grant an injunction.

The court in *Shelfer* was keen to resist greater use of damages in lieu of an injunction, as it would amount to a licence to commit a nuisance. For example, if drilling at night entitled the claimant to an injunction, but the court chose to award damages of £5,000, this would entitle the defendant to drill at a cost of £5,000. The court felt that damages should not be used to legalise a wrongful act by placing a premium on the right to injure the claimant's legal rights.[294] Carnwath LJ in *Barr v Biffa Waste Services Ltd*[295] argued, however, that a more flexible approach might be needed where important public interest issues were at stake. More recently, the Supreme Court (which by then included Lord Carnwath) in *Coventry v Lawrence*[296] argued that the time had come to signal a move away from a strict application of *Shelfer*, particularly where an injunction would have serious consequences for third parties, such as employees of the defendant's business, or, in the case itself, members of the public using or enjoying a speedway racing stadium. While it accepted the claimants would still be prima facie entitled to an injunction to restrain the defendant from committing a nuisance in the future, it held that it was important not to fetter the discretion of judges. Lord Sumption added:

> "In my view, the decision in *Shelfer* is out of date, and it is unfortunate that it has been followed so recently and so slavishly. It was devised for a time in which England was much less crowded, when comparatively few people owned property, when conservation was only beginning to be a public issue, and when there was no general system of statutory development control. The whole jurisprudence in this area will need one day to be reviewed in this court."[297]

---

293 [1895] 1 Ch.287. See also J. A. Jolowicz, "Damages in equity" [1975] C.L.J. 224 and the discussion in Ch.10.
294 But see *Jaggard v Sawyer* [1995] 1 W.L.R. 269.
295 [2012] EWCA Civ 312; [2013] Q.B. 455 at [124].
296 [2014] UKSC 13; [2014] A.C. 822.
297 [2014] UKSC 13 at [161].

It is likely, therefore, that courts will now be more willing to award damages in lieu of an injunction. A court should not feel bound to grant an injunction simply because all four of the *Shelfer* conditions are not satisfied.[298]

Nevertheless, injunctive relief remains important. There are a number of different types of injunction, which will be discussed below.

Prohibitory and mandatory injunctions

17–064 A prohibitory injunction is an injunction which orders the defendant not to act in a certain way. This is the most common injunction granted, and deals with situations where, unless it is granted, the defendant is likely to continue acting in a tortious manner. A mandatory injunction, in contrast, is an injunction ordering the defendant to act in a certain way and is granted more rarely. The courts will look at the facts of the case and decide whether damages would be appropriate. For example, the courts are generally more likely to award damages in lieu of an injunction where the defendant has erected a building in breach of a restrictive covenant, although inevitably much will turn on the facts of each case.[299] The court must also be careful that, in granting an injunction, it ensures that the defendant knows exactly what in fact he or she has to do or not to do.[300]

Interim injunctions[301]

17–065 Prohibitory and mandatory injunctions can be given provisionally prior to the final hearing (interim injunctions), or at the final hearing (perpetual injunctions). The court, faced with an application for an interim injunction, is in a difficult position. The rights of the parties have yet to be determined, and the full facts of the case have yet to be set out. Nevertheless, due to the likely harm of letting the defendant's conduct continue, the court may award an interim injunction but place conditions on its grant. For example, it is common for the court to require the claimant to give an undertaking to pay damages to the defendant for any loss suffered while the injunction is in force, should it prove to be wrongfully issued. This may be expensive. For example, the claimant (C) obtains an interim injunction which prevents the defendant (D) from operating his car plant during the night. At the full hearing of C's claim for nuisance, it is found that the area is classified as an industrial zone and the conduct does not amount to a nuisance. C therefore had no right to an interim injunction and may find himself liable for the loss of profits experienced by D during the period of the injunction. The principles for the grant of an interim injunction are set out in *American Cyanamid Co v Ethicon Ltd*,[302] and reference should

---

298 [2014] UKSC 13 at [123] per Lord Neuberger (who gave the leading judgment in this case).
299 *Jaggard v Sawyer* [1995] 1 W.L.R. 269 at 284.
300 per Lord Upjohn in *Redland Bricks Ltd v Morris* [1970] A.C. 652 at 666.
301 See CPR Pt 25.
302 [1975] A.C. 396.

be made to specific practitioners' texts. It should be noted that, as seen in Ch.14, the courts are very reluctant to impose interim injunctions for claims for libel, despite *American Cyanamid*. If the defendant has pleaded truth, honest opinion or qualified privilege, the court will only grant such an injunction when convinced that the defence will fail. The Court of Appeal in *Greene v Associated Newspapers Ltd*[303] confirmed that such a rule was consistent with the European Convention of Human Rights and that a lesser test would seriously weaken the effect of art.10. It will, however, be marginally easier to obtain an interim injunction for breach of confidence/misuse of private information.[304] In *Cream Holdings Ltd v Banerjee*,[305] the House of Lords found, having regard to the Human Rights Act 1998 s.12(3),[306] that, in most cases, an interim injunction should only be awarded where it is more likely than not that the applicant will succeed at trial, although there could be no single, rigid standard governing all applications in such cases.[307]

Quia timet injunctions

These are injunctions granted to prevent a legal wrong before it occurs. This is obviously an extreme remedy, and the courts will be careful to ensure that the conduct of the defendant is such that substantial damage to the claimant is almost bound to occur, and that damages are not an adequate remedy. As may be expected, the court uses the power to grant such an injunction rarely. The main authority here is Lord Upjohn's judgment in *Redland Bricks Ltd v Morris*,[308] which held that quia timet injunctions are granted in two particular types of case:

17–066

- Where the defendant has, as yet, not harmed the claimant, but is threatening and intending to do so, and if the defendant acts it will cause irreparable harm to the claimant or his or her property; and

- Where the claimant has been compensated for past damage, but alleges that the earlier actions of the defendant may lead to future causes of action.

---

303 [2004] EWCA Civ 1462; [2005] Q.B. 972.
304 The courts accept that there is a difference between the treatment of interlocutory injunctions in defamation and privacy law: see *LNS v Persons Unknown* [2010] EWHC 119 (QB); [2010] 2 F.L.R. 1306 (nub of applicant's true complaint was protection of reputation rather than private life and so defamation rule in *Bonnard v Perryman* would be applied).
305 [2004] UKHL 44; [2005] 1 A.C. 253 (discussed in more detail in Ch.15).
306 Human Rights Act 1998 s.12(3): "No such relief is to be granted so as to restrain publication before trial unless the court is satisfied that the applicant is likely to establish that publication should not be allowed".
307 Lord Nicholls accepted in *Cream Holdings Ltd v Banerjee* [2004] UKHL 44; [2005] 1 A.C. 253 at [22], that there will be cases where the courts will be required to depart from this general approach and require a lesser degree of likelihood, for example, where the potential adverse consequences of disclosure are particularly grave or where a short-lived injunction is needed to enable the court to hear and give proper consideration to an application for interim relief pending the trial or any relevant appeal.
308 [1970] A.C. 652 at 665–666.

Remedies: conclusion

17–067

The courts therefore employ a number of remedies in dealing with claims in tort. Although the primary remedy is that of compensatory damages, the courts will also use injunctions to meet the needs of claimants or rely on damages to punish the misconduct of the defendant or vindicate his or her rights. The claimant may seek to use self-help remedies but should be careful to stay within the remit of the law. In the field of damages for personal injury and death, there have been proposals for reform, notably by the Law Commission, but disappointingly the majority of the proposals for change have not been implemented. It is to be hoped that reform of damages for personal injury and death will return to the government's agenda at a future date. In particular, while the Civil Partnership Act 2004 has led to recognition of the rights of civil partners, cohabitees still remain vulnerable. Given that non-marital relationships are common, legal recognition is a necessary step forward. Equally, as medical science improves and life expectancies increase, compensatory principles must adapt to these new conditions. A system of tort law which is responsive to such needs, and sufficiently flexible to change, is one which will hopefully thrive and continue to develop in the twenty-first century and beyond.

Index